VOX

Pocket

SPANISH

and

ENGLISH

Dictionary

New York Chicago San Francisco Lisbon London Madrid Mexico City
Milan New Delhi San Juan Seoul Singapore Sydney Toronto

The **McGraw·Hill** Companies

2 3 4 5 6 7   CTP/CTP   1 9 8 7 6 5 4 3   (0-07-178086-6)
       6 7   CTP/CTP   1 9 8 7 6 5   (0-07-174290-5)

ISBN 978-0-07-178086-5 (VOX bolsillo)
MHID   0-07-178086-6

Library of Congress Control Number 2011020642

ISBN 978-0-07-174290-0 (VOX pocket)
MHID   0-07-174290-5

Library of Congress Control Number 2009051798

Dirección editorial: Jordi Induráin Pons
Coordinación editorial: Ma José Simón Aragón
Coordinación de la obra: Andrew Hastings
Diseño de cubierta: Francesc Sala

Online Dictionary Access Instructions

To access the free twelve-month subscription to www.diccionarios .com, please follow these instructions:

1. Go to http://www.diccionarios.com.
2. Click on Subscription.
3. Enter your name and e-mail address.
4. Enter the promotional code: VOXMGHPOCKET2011. Please note that the promotional code is case sensitive.

Promotional Code: VOXMGHPOCKET2011
Promotion Terms: The free subscription is valid until July 15, 2012. Users must register by this date to obtain twelve months of free access to the online dictionary. This is an exclusive promotion for buyers of *VOX Pocket Spanish and English Dictionary* and *VOX Diccionario de bolsillo español e inglés.* Only one code per user will be accepted.

Table of contents
Índice

Foreword

This new *VOX Pocket Spanish and English Dictionary* has been compiled by a team of experienced lexicographers, translators, and language teachers. It has been designed specifically to be a modern reference that is useful, practical, and easy to navigate. The clear typography, blue headwords, and simple, logical organization of entries make it easy to look up words in Spanish or English and make it an ideal reference for any student or professional who uses either language at school or at work.

With more than 28,000 entries and 65,000 translations, this dictionary includes all of the basic vocabulary necessary to communicate in and understand Spanish, both European and Latin American varieties. Many of the translations feature examples of usage that clarify and illustrate how the language is used. There are also abundant idiomatic expressions, slang, and vocabulary related to technology and the Internet. A review of Spanish grammar and conjugation tables for key verbs provide important context for the Spanish language.

This dictionary contains all the information required by any beginning or intermediate learner who uses Spanish in his or her studies or at work. This up-to-date reference is an indispensable tool not only in the classroom and the workplace, but also in the home, or in any situation where there is interaction between these two important world languages.

Prólogo

Dada la importancia que ha adquirido el inglés en tantas esferas de la actividad humana en el mundo de hoy, no es de extrañar que tanta gente en tantos países lo usen a diario como primera o segunda lengua para comunicarse con sus congéneres. Entre el grupo creciente de hablantes del inglés se encuentran muchísimos españoles, algunos que acaban de iniciar sus estudios del idioma y otros que llevan ya tiempo estudiándolo y han llegado a tener cierto dominio de sus estructuras y vocabulario; este diccionario ha sido concebido para ellos.

Este nuevo *Diccionario Pocket English-Spanish, Español-Inglés* Vox recoge alrededor de 15.000 entradas por idioma, cifra que supera ampliamente el vocabulario activo medio de una persona culta, y contiene no solamente el léxico básico, sino también frases hechas, expresiones populares, palabras de argot, tecnicismos que han pasado al uso cotidiano, vocabulario de informática e Internet, etcétera. Ha sido diseñado específicamente para que el hispanohablante pueda tener siempre a mano una obra útil, práctica, fácil de manejar, completa y moderna. En este sentido se ha cuidado de forma especial la presentación de los contenidos para que el diccionario sea lo más inteligible posible y, sobre todo, fácil de consultar.

El principiante encontrará en él todas las palabras básicas que necesitará tanto para hacerse entender en inglés como para comprender a los demás, y en el resumen de gramática inglesa obtendrá las respuestas a sus preguntas y dudas sobre la construcción de las frases. Al usuario más avezado le resultará útil no solo para refrescar su memoria en aquellas ocasiones en que no se acuerda de una determinada traducción, sino también para aprender nuevas y más variadas maneras de expresarse en inglés, mejorando así, con cada consulta, su dominio del idioma.

Estamos convencidos de que todos los usuarios hispanohablantes, sean principiantes o de nivel más avanzado, hallarán en sus más de setecientas páginas una información práctica, amplia y actualizada que responde plenamente a las exigencias del siglo XXI.

Abbreviations used in this dictionary
Abreviaturas usadas en el diccionario

abbreviation, acronym	*abbr, abr*	abreviatura, sigla
adjective	*adj*	adjetivo
adverb	*adv*	adverbio
somebody	algn	alguien
architecture	ARCH, ARQ	arquitectura
slang	*arg*	argot
auxiliary	*aux*	auxiliar
commercial	COMM, COM	comercio
computing	COMPUT	informática
conditional	*cond*	conticional
conjunction	*conj*	conjunción
determiner	*det*	determinante
euphemism	*euf, euph*	eufemismo
familiar	*fam*	familiar
figurative	*fig*	uso figurado
finance	FIN	finanzas
formal	*fml*	formal
future	*fut*	futuro
British English	GB	inglés británico
geography	GEOG	geografía
history	HIST	historia
indicative	*ind*	indicativo
computing	INFORM	informática
interjection	*interj*	interjección
invariable	*inv*	invariable
ironic	*iron, irón*	irónico
law	JUR	derecho
mathematics	MATH, MAT	matemáticas
medicine	MED	medicina
music	MUS, MÚS	música
noun	*n*	nombre
feminine noun	*nf*	nombre femenino
masculine noun	*nm*	nombre masculino
masc. and fem. noun	*nm,f*	nombre masc. y fem.
masc. or fem. noun	*nm & f*	género ambiguo
plural noun	*npl*	nombre plural
number	*num*	número
pejorative	*pej, pey*	peyorativo
perfect	*perf*	perfecto
person	*pers*	persona
phrase	*phr*	locución
pluperfect	*pluperf*	pluscuamperfecto
politics	POL	política
past participle	*pp*	participio pasado
preposition	*prep*	preposición
present	*pres*	presente
pronoun	*pron*	pronombre
past	*pt*	pasado
somebody	sb	alguien
singular	*sing*	singular
slang	*sl*	argot
sport	SP	deportes
something	*sth*	algo
American English	US	inglés de América
intransitive verb	*vi*	verbo intransitivo
reflexive verb	*vpr*	verbo pronominal
transitive verb	*vt*	verbo transitivo
vulgar	*vulg*	vulgar
approximate equivalente	≈	equivalente aproximado
see	→	véase
registered trademark	®	marca registrada

GRAMÁTICA INGLESA

Fonética

Todas las entradas inglesas en este diccionario llevan transcripción fonética basada en el sistema de la Asociación Fonética Internacional (AFI). He aquí una relación de los símbolos empleados. El símbolo ' delante de una sílaba indica que es esta la acentuada.

Las consonantes

[p]	pan [pæn], happy ['hæpɪ], slip [slɪp].
[b]	big [bɪg], habit ['hæbɪt], stab [stæb].
[t]	top [tɒp], sitting ['sɪtɪŋ], bit [bɪt].
[d]	drip [drɪp], middle ['mɪdəl], rid [rɪd].
[k]	card [kɑːd], maker ['meɪkəʳ], sock [sɒk].
[g]	god [gɒd], mugger ['mʌgəʳ], dog [dɒg].
[tʃ]	chap [tʃæp], hatchet ['hætʃɪt], beach [biːtʃ].
[dʒ]	jack [dʒæk], digest [daɪ'dʒest], wage [weɪdʒ].
[f]	wish [wɪʃ], coffee ['kɒfɪ], wife [waɪf].
[v]	very ['verɪ], never ['nevəʳ], give [gɪv].
[θ]	thing [θɪŋ], cathode ['kæθəʊd], filth [fɪlθ].
[ð]	they [ðeɪ], father ['fɑːðəʳ], loathe [ləʊð].
[s]	spit [spɪt], stencil ['stensəl], niece [niːs].
[z]	zoo ['zuː], weasel ['wiːzəl], buzz [bʌz].
[ʃ]	show [ʃəʊ], fascist [fæ'ʃɪst], gush [gʌʃ].
[ʒ]	gigolo ['ʒɪgələʊ], pleasure ['pleʒəʳ], massage ['mæsɑːʒ].
[h]	help [help], ahead [ə'hed].
[m]	moon [muːn], common ['kɒmən], came [keɪm].
[n]	nail [neɪl], counter ['kaʊntəʳ], shone [ʃɒn].
[ŋ]	linger ['fɪŋgəʳ], sank [sæŋk], thing [θɪŋ].
[l]	light [laɪt], illness ['ɪlnəs], bull [bʊl].
[r]	rug [rʌg], merry ['merɪ].
[j]	young [jʌŋ], university [juːnɪ'vɛːsɪtɪ], Europe ['jʊərəp].
[w]	want [wɒnt], rewind [riː'waɪnd].
[x]	loch [lɒx].
[']	"linking r": se encuentra a final de palabra. Se pronuncia solo cuando la palabra siguiente empieza por vocal: ***mother and father came*** ['mʌðər ən 'fɑːðə keɪm].

Las vocales y los diptongos

[iː]	sheep [ʃiːp], sea [siː], scene [siːn], field [fiːld].
[ɪ]	ship [ʃɪp], pity ['pɪtɪ], roses ['rəʊzɪz], babies ['beɪbɪz], college ['kɒlɪdʒ].
[e]	shed [ʃed], instead [ɪn'sted], any ['enɪ], bury ['berɪ], friend [frend].
[æ]	fat [fæt], thank [θæŋk], plait [plæt].
[ɑː]	rather ['rɑːðəʳ], car [kɑːʳ], heart [hɑːt], clerk [klɑːk], palm [pɑːm], aunt [ɑːnt].
[ɒ]	lock [lɒk], wash [wɒʃ], trough [trɒf], because [br'kɒz].
[ɔː]	horse [hɔːs], straw [strɔː], fought [fɔːt], cause [kɔːz], fall [fɔːl], boar [bɔːʳ].
[ʊ]	look [lʊk], pull [pʊl], woman ['wʊmən], should [ʃʊd].
[uː]	loop [luːp], do [duː], soup [suːp], elude [i'luːd], true [truː], shoe [ʃuː], few [fjuː].
[ʌ]	cub [kʌb], ton [tʌn], young [jʌŋ], flood [flʌd], does [dʌz].
[ɛː]	third [θɛːd], herd [hɛːd], heard [hɛːd], curl [kɛːl], word [wɛːd], journey ['dʒɛːnɪ].
[ə]	actor ['æktəʳ], honour ['ɒnəʳ], about [ə'baʊt].
[ə]	opcional. En algunos casos se pronuncia y en otros se omite: trifle ['traɪfəl].
[eɪ]	cable ['keɪbəl], way [weɪ], plain [pleɪn], freight [freɪt], prey [preɪ], great [greɪt].

[əʊ]	go [gəʊ], toad [təʊd], toe [təʊ], though [ðəʊ], snow [snəʊ].
[aɪ]	lime [laɪm], thigh [θaɪ], height [haɪt], lie [laɪ], try [traɪ], either ['aɪðəʳ].
[aʊ]	house [haʊs], cow [kaʊ].
[ɔɪ]	toy [tɔɪ], soil [sɔɪl].
[ɪə]	near [nɪəʳ], here [hɪəʳ], sheer [ʃɪəʳ], idea [aɪ'dɪə], museum [mju:'zɪəm], weird [wɪəd].
[eə]	hare [heəʳ], hair [heəʳ], wear [weəʳ].
[ʊə]	pure [pjʊəʳ], during ['djʊərɪŋ], tourist ['tʊərɪst].

Ortografía

1. El sufijo -s/-es según la forma de la raíz.

a) Para formar la tercera persona del singular del presente de indicativo y los plurales de los sustantivos se añade **s** al infinitivo, pero si el infinitivo acaba en **-sh, -ch, -s, -x, -z** y, a veces, **-o**, se añade **es**.

wish	-	*wishes*		*fix*	-	*fixes*
teach	-	*teaches*		*buzz*	-	*buzzes*
kiss	-	*kisses*		*go*	-	*goes*

b) Si la raíz acaba en cualquier consonante + **y**, ésta se convierte en **i** y se añade **-es**. Pero si la **y** va precedida de una vocal no experimenta ningún cambio.

| *fry* | - | *fries* | | pero | *play-* | *plays* |

2. Cambios ortográficos en la raíz al añadir ciertos sufijos.

a) Para formar el gerundio o participio presente se añade **-ing** al infinitivo, pero si el infinitivo acaba en cualquier consonante + **e**, ésta desaparece. Si acaba en **-ie** esta combinación se convierte en **y**.

| *give* | - | *giving* | | *lie* | - | *lying* |

b) Si se trata de una raíz monosílaba que acaba en una sola consonante precedida de una sola vocal, la consonante se duplica en los siguientes casos: al añadir

-**ing** al verbo para formar el gerundio o participio presente
-**ed** al verbo para formar el pasado simple
-**er** al verbo para formar el agente,
-**er** o -**est** al adjetivo para formar el comparativo y superlativo

	stab	-	*stabbing*		*run*	-	*runner*
	swim	-	*swimming*		*clap*	-	*clapped*
	wet	-	*wetter, wettest*		*big*	-	*bigger, biggest*
pero	*look*	-	*looked*		*grasp*	-	*grasped*
	cold	-	*colder, coldest*		*fast*	-	*faster, fastest*

NB Las consonantes **y**, **w** y **x** no se duplican.

c) También se duplica la consonante final de los verbos de más de una sílaba si el acento tónico recae en la última sílaba.

| | *begin* | - | *beginning* | | *admit* | - | *admitted* |
| pero | *offer* | - | *offering* | | *open* | - | *opened* |

Sin embargo, si la consonante final es **l**, ésta se duplica independientemente de donde recaiga el acento tónico. Véase también el apartado 4f.

| *travel* | - | *travelling* | | *model* | - | *modelled* |

d) Si la raíz acaba en cualquier consonante + *y*, al añadir *-ed* a la raíz del verbo o *-er* o *-est* a la del adjetivo, la *y* se convierte en *i*.

carry	- *carried*	*pretty*	- *prettier, prettiest*

e) Si un adjetivo acaba en *-y*, al formar el adverbio añadiendo *-ly* la *y* se convierte en *i*.

happy	- *happily*	*gay*	- *gaily*

3. Las contracciones

En inglés familiar se suelen usar las formas contractas de ciertos verbos con un após-trofo en el lugar de una letra suprimida. He aquí una lista de las más usuales:

's	is, has	*'re*	are
've	have	*'d*	would, had
'm	am	*'ll*	will, shall
-n't	not	*can't*	cannot
won't	will not		

4. Diferencias ortográficas entre el inglés británico y el americano.

Hay varias diferencias entre la ortografía británica y la americana. Aquí se resumen las diferencias regulares, pero todas las formas diferentes constan en el cuerpo del diccio-nario. El punto de referencia es siempre el inglés británico.

a) Algunas palabras que acaban en *-tre* se escriben con *-ter* en inglés americano.

centre	- *center*	*mitre*	- *miter*
theatre	- *theater*		

b) Algunas palabras que acaban en *-our* se escriben con *-or* en inglés americano.

harbour	- *harbor*	*vapour*	- *vapor*
colour	- *color*		

c) Algunas palabras que contienen el dígrafo *ae* en inglés americano se escriben con *e*.

mediaeval	- *medieval*	*gynaecology*	- *gynecology*

d) Algunas palabras que contienen el dígrafo *oe* en el inglés americano se escriben con *e*.

manoeuvre	- *maneuver*	*oestrogen*	- *estrogen*

e) Algunas palabras que acaban en *-ogue* acaban en *-og* en inglés americano.

catalogue	- *catalog*	*dialogue*	- *dialog*

f) Mientras que en el inglés británico una *l* final suele duplicarse independien-temente de donde recaiga el acento tónico (véase el apartado 2c), en el inglés americano esta *l* sólo se duplica si el acento recae en la última sílaba:

travel	- *traveled, traveling*	*rebel*	- *rebelled, rebelling.*

El determinante

El artículo indefinido

El artículo indefinido es *a* y es invariable: *a man, a young woman, a boy a girl, a big dog, a tree, a planet.*

Delante de las palabras que empiecen por vocal, *a* se convierte en *an*: *an apple, an eagle, an easy test, an Indian, an untidy room.*

Sin embargo una palabra puede empezar por una vocal escrita y no empezar por sonido vocálico: esto ocurre con las palabras que empiezan por *eu-* y algunas de las que empiezan por *u-* (véanse las transcripciones fonéticas en el diccionario). En estos casos se usa *a* en vez de *an*: *a European; a union, a university professor.*

Asimismo, si una *h* inicial se pronuncia se empleará *a*, si es muda *an*: *a house, a helpful person,* pero *an hour, an honest man.*

El artículo indefinido solo se pone delante de los sustantivos en singular.

a dog	*un perro*	*dogs*	*unos perros*
an old house	*una casa antigua*	*old houses*	*casas antiguas*

El artículo definido

El artículo definido es *the* y es invariable. Sirve tanto para el singular como para el plural: *the man, the men, the children, the earth, the sea.* Su pronunciación es [ðə], pero delante de las palabras que empiecen por un sonido vocálico se pronuncia [ðɪ].

El sustantivo

Género

En inglés, a diferencia del español, los sustantivos carecen de género gramatical y los artículos y adjetivos son invariables. Sólo algunos nombres referentes a las personas tienen forma femenina y en algunos casos existen palabras diferentes para designar el varón y la hembra:

actor	-	*actress*	*prince*	-	*princess*	*host*	-	*hostess*
king	-	*queen*	*boy*	-	*girl*	*son*	-	*daughter*
cock	-	*hen*	*bull*	-	*cow*	*ram*	-	*ewe*

El genitivo sajón

Para indicar la relación de poseedor/posesión en inglés se usa el llamado genitivo sajón, que consiste en añadir *'s* al poseedor y colocarlo delante de lo poseído. Funciona para las personas y también para los animales:

Lawrence's mother	la madre de Lawrence
the boy's bicycle	la bicicleta del chico
my teacher's glasses	las gafas de mi profesor

Si el poseedor está en plural y acaba en *-s*, en vez de añadir *'s* se añade únicamente el apóstrofo, pero si se trata de un plural irregular que no acaba en *-s*, se añade *'s*:

the boys' bicycles	las bicicletas de los chicos
my parents' car	el coche de mis padres
men's trousers	pantalones de caballero

Si el poseedor acaba en *-s* en el singular se suele añadir *'s*, aunque a algunos nombres extranjeros, antiguos o clásicos, se añade solo el apóstrofo:

Mrs Jones's house	la casa de la Sra. Jones
Cervantes' novels	las novelas de Cervantes

Sustantivos contables e incontables

En inglés los sustantivos son contables o incontables. Los primeros pueden ser contados: *boy, boys; knife, knives; pencil, pencils.* Sin embargo, *electricity* es incontable: la electricidad no se puede contar.

Mientras que los contables pueden tener singular y plural, los incontables sólo tienen forma singular: *furniture, advice, news, information, health, chaos, honesty, peace*. No obstante, algunos pueden contarse con el uso de *a piece of*:

furniture	los muebles	*a piece of furniture*	un mueble
advice	los consejos	*two pieces of advice*	dos consejos
news	las noticias	*three pieces of news*	tres noticias

Plurales irregulares

La mayoría de sustantivos en inglés son regulares y el plural se forma añadiendo *-s* o *-es* al singular. Existen plurales irregulares y formas invariables, los cuales constan en el diccionario.

Los sustantivos que acaban en *-o* pueden formar el plural añadiendo *-s, -es*, o bien cualquiera de las dos. Para comprobar la forma correcta, véase la entrada.

Los sustantivos que acaban en *-f* pueden formar el plural añadiendo *-s*, cambiando la *f* en *v* y añadiendo *-es*, o bien de cualquiera de las dos maneras. Los que acaban en *-ff* siempre forman el plural añadiendo una sola *s*.

Los sustantivos que acaban en *-fe* suelen formar el plural en *-ves*, mientras que *safe* y los acabados en *-ffe* solo añaden una *-s*.

El pronombre

Cuadro de pronombres y adjetivos posesivos

pronombre sujeto	pronombre c. dir./indir.	adjetivo posesivo	pronombre posesivo	pronombre reflexivo
I	me	my	mine	myself
you	you	your	yours	yourself
he	him	his	his	himself
she	her	her	hers	herself
it	it	its	—	itself
we	us	our	ours	ourselves
you	you	your	yours	yourselves
they	them	their	theirs	themselves

Los pronombres sujeto

En inglés el pronombre sujeto debe figurar siempre:

> *I was very pleased to see him there,*

aunque en una misma frase no es preciso repetir el pronombre si el sujeto no varía:

> *She locked the door and then put the key in her pocket.*

Los pronombres de complemento directo/indirecto

El pronombre de complemento directo se coloca detrás del verbo que complementa:

> *She shot him; I washed and dried it.*

El pronombre de complemento indirecto, si acompaña un complemento directo que es un sustantivo, se coloca también detrás del verbo que complementa:

> *She made me a cake; I gave him the keys,*

pero cuando acompaña un complemento directo que es pronombre es más corriente usar las preposiciones *to* o *for*, nótese también el cambio de orden:

She made it for me; I gave them to him.

El pronombre con función de complemento también se usa:

1 - detrás de una preposición: **She goes out with him; Look at them.**
2 - detrás de *than* y *as ... as ...* en los comparativos: **He's taller than her; She's as quick as him.**

3 - en inglés informal detrás del verbo *to be*: **It's me, John; It wasn't me, it was him.**
4 - para respuestas cortas como: **Who's got my pencil? —Me!**

Los adjetivos posesivos

Los adjetivos posesivos no varían según lo poseído sino según el poseedor:

my sister, my sisters; their friend, their friends.

Los pronombres posesivos

Los pronombres posesivos se usan para sustituir la estructura adjetivo posesivo + nombre: **This is my car. Where's yours?** (= your car); **His family is bigger than mine.** (= my family).

Los pronombres reflexivos

Los pronombres reflexivos se usan:

1 - cuando el sujeto y el complemento del verbo son el mismo: **I've hurt myself; Please help yourselves!**
2 - cuando se quiere remarcar que es una persona y no otra quien realiza la acción: **If nobody will do it for me, I'll have to do it myself.**

El pronombre impersonal

Como pronombre impersonal en inglés coloquial se usa *you*, mientras que en inglés formal se usa *one*:

You can't drive if you're under 17.
One must be sure before one makes such serious accusations.

El adjetivo

General

Los adjetivos en inglés son invariables y casi siempre van delante de los sustantivos: **an old man, an old woman; old men, old women.** Pueden ir después de los siguientes verbos: **be, look, seem, appear, feel, taste, smell, sound.**

Si un sustantivo en una expresión numérica se usa como adjetivo, siempre va en singular: **a two-mile walk; an eight-hour day.**

El comparativo y el superlativo

Los comparativos se usan para comparar entidades entre ellas. Los superlativos se usan para comparar una entidad de un grupo con el resto del grupo.

Añaden a la raíz *-er* para el comparativo y *-est* para el superlativo:

— los adjetivos de una sola sílaba: **cold → colder/coldest.**
— los de dos sílabas que acaban en *-y*: **pretty → prettier/prettiest.**

Forman el comparativo con **more** y el superlativo con **most**:

— la mayoría de los demás adjetivos de dos sílabas: **boring** → **more boring/the most boring**.

— los de tres sílabas y más: **beautiful** → **more beautiful/the most beautiful**.

Pueden formar el comparativo y superlativo de las dos maneras los adjetivos de dos sílabas acabados en **-er, -ure, -le** y **-ow** así como **common, quiet, tired, pleasant, handsome, stupid, cruel, wicked** y **polite**, aunque es más corriente la forma con **more** y **most**.

Son irregulares los siguientes: **good (better/best), bad (worse/worst), far (farther** o **further/farther** o **furthest)**.

El adverbio

General

Los adverbios muy a menudo pueden formarse a partir de los adjetivos añadiendo **-ly**: **sad - sadly, quick - quickly, happy - happily, beautiful - beautifully**.

Si el adjetivo acaba en **-ly**, no tiene adverbio: los adjetivos **lovely, friendly, ugly, lonely** y **silly**.

Algunos adverbios tienen la misma forma que el adjetivo correspondiente: **hard, late, early, fast, far, much, little, high, low, near**.

Algunos adverbios cambian de sentido respecto al adjetivo al que corresponden:

hard = duro; duramente	**hardly** = apenas
late = tarde	**lately** = últimamente
near = cercano	**nearly** = casi
high = alto	**highly** = muy; muy favorablemente

Posición

Aunque los adverbios pueden ir al principio de la frase, la posición más frecuente es después del verbo y el complemento. Hay ciertos adverbios que suelen ir delante del verbo (tras el auxiliar si es un tiempo compuesto) y después del verbo **be**: **always, usually, generally, normally, often, sometimes, occasionally, seldom, rarely, never, almost, just, still, already** y **only**.

El comparativo y el superlativo

Los adverbios de dos o más sílabas anteponen siempre **more** para la comparación y **most** para el superlativo y los de una sola sílaba añaden los sufijos **-er** y **-est**:

quickly	*more quickly*	*most quickly*
fast	*faster*	*fastest*
near	*nearer*	*nearest*

pero

early	*earlier*	*earliest*

Son irregulares: **well (better/best), badly (worse/worst), little (less/least), much (more/most), far (farther** o **further/farthest** o **furthest), late (later/last)**.

El verbo

Conjugación

La mayoría de los verbos ingleses son regulares y el pasado simple y participio pasado se forman añadiendo **-ed** a la raíz; solo **-d** si la raíz ya tiene **-e** final. El participio presente se forma añadiendo **-ing** a la raíz. Véase también la sección de ortografía.

Infinitivo	Pasado simple	Participio pasado	Participio presente
sail	*sailed*	*sailed*	*sailing*
grab	*grabbed*	*grabbed*	*grabbing*
kiss	*kissed*	*kissed*	*kissing*
waste	*wasted*	*wasted*	*wasting*

Pronunciación del pasado y participio pasado regulares

El sufijo **-ed** siempre se escribe igual, pero se pronuncia de tres maneras distintas según la pronunciación (fíjese en la transcripción fonética) de la raíz a la que se añade.

Se pronuncia [d] si la raíz acaba en una consonante sonora [b], [g], [dʒ], [v], [ð], [z], [ʒ], [m], [n] y [l] o cualquier vocal: ***stabbed*** [stæbd], ***begged*** [begd], ***opened*** ['əʊpənd], ***filled*** [fɪld], ***vetoed*** ['viːtəʊd].

Se pronuncia [t] si la raíz acaba en una consonante sorda [p], [k], [tʃ], [f], [θ], [s], [ʃ]: ***clapped*** [klæpt], ***licked*** [lɪkt], ***kissed*** [kɪst], ***wished*** [wɪʃt].

Se pronuncia [id] si la raíz acaba en [t] o [d]: ***tasted*** ['teɪstɪd], ***defended*** [dɪ'fendɪd].

Para los verbos irregulares véase la tabla al final de esta sección y las respectivas entradas.

Phrasal verbs

Los *phrasal verbs* o verbos preposicionales son muy numerosos en inglés. Al añadir una partícula adverbial o preposición a un verbo, se modifica o cambia totalmente el significado del verbo original.

    put (poner)   ***put out*** (apagar)   ***turn*** (girar)   ***turn on*** (encender)

En este diccionario los *phrasal verbs* aparecen como entradas aparte a continuación del verbo básico.

La formación de los tiempos verbales

Presente simple

Tiene la misma forma que el infinitivo del verbo en todas las personas excepto en la tercera persona del singular, en la que se añade la terminación **-s** o **-es** (véase el apartado de ortografía):

I sail	*we sail*
you sail	*you sail*
he/she/it sails	*they sail*

Los verbos ***to be*** y ***to have*** son irregulares:

I am	*we are*	*I have*	*we have*
you are	*you are*	*you have*	*you have*
he/she/it is	*they are*	*he/she/it has*	*they have*

Presente continuo

Se forma del presente del verbo ***to be*** + el participio presente: ***I am resting***.

Pretérito perfecto

Se forma del presente del verbo ***to have*** + el participio pasado: ***He has arrived***.

Pretérito perfecto continuo

Se forma del presente del verbo *to have* + *been* + el participio presente: *I have been dreaming*.

Pasado simple

Véase el principio de esta sección y la tabla de verbos irregulares. El verbo *to be* es irregular:

I was	*we were*
you were	*you were*
he/she/it was	*they were*

Pasado continuo

Se forma del pasado simple de to be + el participio presente: *It was raining*.

Pluscuamperfecto

Se forma del pasado simple de *to have* + el participio pasado: *I had lost my slippers*.

Pluscuamperfecto continuo

Se forma del pasado simple de *to have* + *been* + el participio pasado: *He had been repairing his motorbike*.

Futuro

Se forma de *will/shall* + el infinitivo. (Como norma general *will* se usa para todas las personas aunque, en el lenguaje formal, *shall* lo sustituye en la primera persona tanto del singular como del plural): *It will be here next week*.

Futuro continuo

Se forma de *will/shall* + *be* + el participio presente: *They will be lying on the beach*.

Futuro perfecto

Se forma de *will/shall* + *have* + participio pasado: *I will have finished in ten minutes*.

Futuro perfecto continuo

Se forma de *will/shall* + *have* + *been* + participio presente: *We will have been living here for forty years*.

Las oraciones condicionales

Hay tres tipos de oraciones condicionales en inglés: las reales, las irreales y las imposibles. Las dos primeras hacen referencia al presente y futuro mientras que la tercera describe situaciones en el pasado.

1) Condicional real (first conditional)

If + presente simple   *will/shall* + infinitivo
If it snows this week,   *we will go skiing on Saturday*

2) Condicional irreal (second conditional)

If + pasado simple   *would* + infinitivo
If we had a corkscrew,   *we would be able to open the bottle*

3) Condicional imposible (third conditional)

If + pluscuamperfecto   *would have* + participio pasado
If you had run a little faster,   *you would have caught the train.*

La voz pasiva

La voz pasiva es frecuente en inglés. Se forma de la siguiente manera: se invierten el sujeto y el complemento directo, se pone el verbo *be* en el mismo tiempo que el verbo en la frase activa seguido del participio pasado del verbo y se coloca la partícula *by* delante del sujeto:

> *John broke the window*   -   *The window was broken by John.*

A menudo se emplea para dar más énfasis al complemento directo o cuando el sujeto no se conoce o no tiene mucha importancia:

> *The police will tow away your car*   -   *Your car will be towed away (by the police)*
>
> *Someone has stolen my pen*   -   *My pen has been stolen.*

El imperativo

Tanto en singular como en plural, el imperativo se forma con el infinitivo sin *to*: *Give me my umbrella!*

Las oraciones negativas se forman con *do not* (*don't*) + infinitivo: *Don't put your feet on the chair!*

Se usa *let's* (*let us*) + infinitivo (sin *to*) como imperativo para la primera persona del plural o para hacer sugerencias: *Let's watch the other channel.*

La construcción de las frases negativas e interrogativas

Negativas

Los tiempos compuestos forman las frases negativas intercalando *not* después del verbo auxiliar:

> *He has finished*   -   *He has not finished*
> *It is raining*   -   *It is not raining*

En el presente simple la negación se forma empleando el infinitivo del verbo junto con el verbo auxiliar *do* (*does* para la tercera persona singular) seguido de *not*:

> *He works on Saturdays*   -   *He does not work on Saturdays*
> *You make a lot of mistakes*   -   *You do not make a lot of mistakes*

Para el pasado simple el auxiliar *do/does* toma la forma del pasado *did*:

> *He worked last Saturday*   -   *He did not work last Saturday*
> *You made a lot of mistakes*   -   *You did not make a lot of mistakes*

Interrogativas

En los tiempos compuestos las frases interrogativas se forman anteponiendo el verbo auxiliar al sujeto:

> *She is having a shower*   -   *Is she having a shower?*
> *We shall come to help you*   -   *Shall we come to help you?*

El presente simple se forma empleando el infinitivo del verbo junto con el verbo auxiliar *do* (*does* para la tercera persona singular) que se coloca antes del sujeto:

> *He works on Saturdays*   -   *Does he work on Saturdays?*
> *They eat fish*   -   *Do they eat fish?*

Para el pasado simple el auxiliar *do/does* toma la forma del pasado *did*:

> *He worked last Saturday*   -   *Did he work last Saturday?*
> *They ate all of it*   -   *Did they eat all of it?*

Verbos irregulares ingleses

Infinitivo	Pasado simple	Participio pasado
arise	arose	arisen
awake	awoke	awaked/awoken
be	was/were	been
bear	bore	borne/born
beat	beat	beaten
become	became	become
begin	began	begun
behold	beheld	beheld
bend	bent	bent
beseech	besought/beseeched	besought/beseeched
beset	beset	beset
bet	bet/betted	bet/betted
bid	bid/bade	bid/bidden
bide	bode/bided	bided
bind	bound	bound
bite	bit	bitten
bleed	bled	bled
blow	blew	blown
break	broke	broken
breed	bred	bred
bring	brought	brought
broadcast	broadcast	broadcast
build	built	built
burn	burnt/burned	burnt/burned
burst	burst	burst
buy	bought	bought
cast	cast	cast
catch	caught	caught
choose	chose	chosen
cling	clung	clung
clothe	clothed/clad	clothed/clad
come	came	come
cost	cost	cost
creep	crept	crept
crow	crowed/crew	crowed
cut	cut	cut
deal	dealt	dealt
dig	dug	dug
dive	dived, US dove	dived
do	did	done
draw	drew	drawn
dream	dreamed/dreamt	dreamed/dreamt
drink	drank	drunk
drive	drove	driven
dwell	dwelt/dwelled	dwelt/dwelled
eat	ate	eaten
fall	fell	fallen
feed	fed	fed
feel	felt	felt

fight	fought	fought
find	found	found
flee	fled	fled
fling	flung	flung
fly	flew	flown
forbid	forbade/forbad	forbidden
forecast	forecast/forecasted	forecast/forecasted
forego	forewent	foregone
foresee	foresaw	foreseen
foretell	foretold	foretold
forget	forgot	forgotten
forgive	forgave	forgiven
forgo	forwent	forgone
forsake	forsook	forsaken
freeze	froze	frozen
get	got	got, US gotten
give	gave	given
go	went	gone
grind	ground	ground
grow	grew	grown
hang	hung/hanged	hung/hanged
have	had	had
hear	heard	heard
hew	hewed	hewed/hewn
hide	hid	hidden/hid
hit	hit	hit
hold	held	held
hurt	hurt	hurt
input	input	input
keep	kept	kept
kneel	knelt, US kneeled	knelt, US kneeled
knit	knit/knitted	knit/knitted
know	knew	known
lay	laid	laid
lead	led	led
lean	leant/leaned	leant/leaned
leap	leapt/leaped	leapt/leaped
learn	learnt/learned	learnt/learned
leave	left	left
lend	lent	lent
let	let	let
light	lighted/lit	lighted/lit
lose	lost	lost
make	made	made
mean	meant	meant
meet	met	met
mislay	mislaid	mislaid
mislead	misled	misled
mistake	mistook	mistaken
misunderstand	misunderstood	misunderstood
mow	mowed	mowed/mown
offset	offset	offset
outdo	outdid	outdone
outgrow	outgrew	outgrown
outrun	outran	outrun
overcome	overcame	overcome

overdo	overdid	overdone
overhear	overheard	overheard
override	overrode	overridden
overrun	overran	overrun
oversee	oversaw	overseen
oversleep	overslept	overslept
overtake	overtook	overtaken
overthrow	overthrew	overthrown
pay	paid	paid
prove	proved	proved/proven
put	put	put
read	read	read
rebuild	rebuilt	rebuilt
remake	remade	remade
rend	rent	rent
repay	repaid	repaid
rerun	reran	rerun
reset	reset	reset
retell	retold	retold
rewind	rewound	rewound
rewrite	rewrote	rewritten
rid	rid/ridded	rid/ridded
ride	rode	ridden
ring	rang	rung
rise	rose	risen
run	ran	run
saw	sawed	sawed/sawn
say	said	said
see	saw	seen
seek	sought	sought
sell	sold	sold
send	sent	sent
set	set	set
sew	sewed	sewed/sewn
shake	shook	shaken
shear	sheared	sheared/shorn
shed	shed	shed
shine	shone	shone
shoe	shod	shod
shoot	shot	shot
show	showed	shown/showed
shrink	shrank	shrunk
shut	shut	shut
sing	sang	sung
sink	sank	sunk
sit	sat	sat
slay	slew	slain
sleep	slept	slept
slide	slid	slid
sling	slung	slung
slink	slunk	slunk
slit	slit	slit
smell	smelled/smelt	smelled/smelt
sow	sowed	sowed/sown
speak	spoke	spoken
speed	speeded/sped	speeded/sped

spell	spelled/spelt	spelled/spelt
spend	spent	spent
spill	spilled/spilt	spilled/spilt
spin	spun/span	spun
spit	spat	spat
split	split	split
spoil	spoiled/spoilt	spoiled/spoilt
spread	spread	spread
spring	sprang	sprung
stand	stood	stood
steal	stole	stolen
stick	stuck	stuck
sting	stung	stung
stink	stank/stunk	stunk
stride	strode	stridden
strike	struck	struck
string	strung	strung
strive	strove	striven
sublet	sublet	sublet
swear	swore	sworn
sweep	swept	swept
swell	swelled	swollen
swim	swam	swum
swing	swung	swung
take	took	taken
teach	taught	taught
tear	tore	torn
tell	told	told
think	thought	thought
thrive	throve/thrived	thrived/thriven
throw	threw	thrown
thrust	thrust	thrust
tread	trod	trodden/trod
undergo	underwent	undergone
understand	understood	understood
undertake	undertook	undertaken
underwrite	underwrote	underwritten
undo	undid	undone
unwind	unwound	unwound
uphold	upheld	upheld
upset	upset	upset
wake	woke	woken
wear	wore	worn
weave	wove	woven
wed	wedded/wed	wedded/wed
weep	wept	wept
wet	wetted/wet	wetted/wet
win	won	won
wind	wound	wound
withdraw	withdrew	withdrawn
withhold	withheld	withheld
withstand	withstood	withstood
wring	wrung	wrung
write	wrote	written

A

a [eɪ, ə] *det* **1** un, una. **2** por: *three times a week*, tres veces por semana; *£2 a kilo*, dos libras el kilo. **3**: *She's a teacher*, es maestra.

Se usa delante de las palabras que empiezan con sonido no vocálico. Véase también **an**.

A [eɪ] *abbr* **1** sobresaliente *(calificación)*. **2** la *(nota musical)*.

AA[1] ['eɪ'eɪ] *abbr (Alcoholics Anonymous)* Alcohólicos Anónimos, AA.

AA[2] ['eɪ'eɪ] *abbr* GB *(Automobile Association)* automóvil club británico.

AB ['eɪ'biː] *abbr* US *(Bachelor of Arts)* licenciado,-a en letras.

aback [ə'bæk] *adv* .

● **to be taken aback** asombrarse, quedarse atónito.

abandon [ə'bændən] *vt* abandonar.

abattoir ['æbətwɑːˈ] *n* matadero.

abbess ['æbes] *n (pl -es)* abadesa.

abbey ['æbɪ] *n* abadía.

abbot ['æbət] *n* abad.

abbreviate [ə'briːvɪeɪt] *vt* abreviar.

abbreviation [əbriːvɪ'eɪʃən] *n* abreviatura.

ABC ['eɪ'biː'siː] *abbr* **1** abecedario. **2** abecé.

abdicate ['æbdɪkeɪt] *vt - vi* abdicar.

abdication [æbdɪ'keɪʃən] *n* abdicación.

abdomen ['æbdəmən] *n* abdomen.

abdominal [æb'dɒmɪnəl] *adj* abdominal.

abduct [æb'dʌkt] *vt* raptar, secuestrar.

abduction [æb'dʌkʃən] *n* rapto, secuestro.

abductor [æb'dʌktəˈ] *n* secuestrador,-ra.

aberration [æbə'reɪʃən] *n* aberración.

abhor [əb'hɔːˈ] *vt (pt & pp **abhorred**, ger **abhorring**)* aborrecer, detestar.

abhorrent [əb'hɒrənt] *adj* detestable, odioso,-a.

abide [ə'baɪd] *vt* soportar, aguantar: *I can not abide her*, no la aguanto.

to abide by *vt* cumplir con, acatar.

abiding [ə'baɪdɪŋ] *adj* duradero,-a.

ability [ə'bɪlɪtɪ] *n (pl -ies).* **1** capacidad. **2** talento, aptitud.

ablaze [ə'bleɪz] *adj* ardiendo, en llamas.

● **ablaze with light** resplandeciente de luz.

able ['eɪbəl] *adj (comp **abler**, superl **ablest**)* hábil, capaz.

● **to be able to 1** poder: *will you be able to come?*, ¿podrás venir? **2** saber: *he was able to drive when he was sixteen*, sabía conducir a los dieciséis años.

ably ['eɪblɪ] *adv* hábilmente.

abnormal [æb'nɔːməl] *adj* **1** anormal. **2** inusual.

abnormality [æbnɔː'mælɪtɪ] *n (pl -ies)* anormalidad.

aboard [ə'bɔːd] *adv* a bordo: *welcome aboard*, bienvenidos a bordo.

abolish [ə'bɒlɪʃ] *vt* abolir.

abolition [æbə'lɪʃən] *n* abolición.

abominable [ə'bɒmɪnəbəl] *adj* abominable, terrible, horrible.

aborigine [æbə'rɪdʒɪnɪ] *n* aborigen.

abort [ə'bɔːt] *vi* abortar.

abortion [ə'bɔːʃən] *n* aborto *(provocado)*: *to have an abortion*, abortar.

■ **abortion pill** píldora abortiva.

abound [ə'baund] *vi* abundar.

about [ə'baut] *prep* **1** de, sobre, acerca de: *to speak about ...*, hablar de ...; *what is the book about?*, ¿de qué trata el libro?; *what did you do about ...?*, ¿qué hiciste con ...? **2** por, en: *he's somewhere about* *the house*, está por algún rincón de la casa.

▶ *adv* **1** alrededor de: *about £500*, unas quinientas libras; *at about three o'clock*, a eso de las tres. **2** por aquí, por ahí: *there was nobody about*, no había nadie.

● **to be about to ...** estar a punto de ....

● **how about ...?/what about ...?**: *how about a drink?*, ¿te apetece tomar algo?; *how about going to Paris?*, ¿qué te parece ir a París?

above [ə'bʌv] *prep* **1** por encima de: *above our heads*, por encima de nuestras cabezas; *above suspicion*, por encima de toda sospecha; *only the manager is above him*, sólo el gerente está por encima de él. **2** más de, más que: *above 5,000 people*, más de 5.000 personas; *those above the age of 65*, los mayores de 65 años.

▶ *adv* **1** arriba, en lo alto: *the flat above*, el piso de arriba. **2** arriba: *see above*, véase arriba.

● **above all** sobre todo.

above-board [əbʌv'bɔːd] *adj* legal, honrado,-a.

above-mentioned [əbʌv'menʃənd] *adj* mencionado,-a anteriormente.

abreast [ə'brest] *adv* en línea, hombro con hombro: *to walk four abreast*, en columnas de cuatro a cuatro.

● **to keep abreast with** mantenerse al corriente de.

abridged [ə'brɪdʒd] *adj* abreviado,-a.

abroad [ə'brɔːd] *adv* al extranjero: *they went abroad*, fueron al extranjero; *she lives abroad*, vive en el extranjero.

abrupt [ə'brʌpt] *adj* **1** repentino,-a, súbito,-a. **2** brusco,-a, arisco,-a.

abscess ['æbses] *n* (*pl* **-es**) absceso.

abscond [əb'skɒnd] *vi* fugarse.

abseil ['æbseɪl] *vi* hacer rappel.

abseiling ['æbseɪlɪŋ] *n* rappel.

absence ['æbsəns] *n* **1** ausencia. **2** falta, carencia.

absent [(*adj*) 'æbsənt(*vb*) æb'sent] *adj* ausente.

▶ *vt* **to absent oneself** ausentarse.

absentee [æbsən'tiː] *n* ausente.

absenteeism [æbsən'tiːɪzəm] *n* absentismo.

absent-minded [æbsənt'maɪndɪd] *adj* distraído,-a.

absolute ['æbsəluːt] *n* absoluto,-a: *it's absolute rubbish*, es una perfecta tontería.

absolutely [æbsə'luːtlɪ] *adv* totalmente, completamente.

▶ *interj* ¡por supuesto!, ¡desde luego!

absolution [æbsə'luːʃən] *n* absolución.

absolve [əb'zɒlv] *vt* absolver.

absorb [əb'zɔːb] *vt* **1** absorber. **2** *fig* asimilar *(información)*.

● **to be absorbed in** STH estar absorto,-a en algo.

absorbent [əb'zɔːbənt] *adj* absorbente.

absorbing [əb'zɔːbɪŋ] *adj* absorbente, apasionante.

absorption [əb'zɔːpʃən] *n* absorción.

abstain [əb'steɪn] *vi* abstenerse.

abstention [əb'stenʃən] *n* abstención.

abstinence ['æbstɪnəns] *n* abstinencia.

abstract [(*adj-n*) 'æbstrækt(*vb*) æb'strækt] *adj* abstracto,-a.

▶ *n* resumen, sinopsis.

▶ *vt* resumir, sintetizar.

● **in the abstract** en abstracto.

abstraction [æb'strækʃən] *n* **1** abstracción. **2** distracción, ensimismamiento.

absurd [əb'sɜːd] *adj* absurdo,-a: *don't be absurd!*, ¡no seas ridículo!

absurdity [əb'sɜːdɪtɪ] *n* (*pl* **-ies**) irracionalidad.

abundance [ə'bʌndəns] *n* abundancia.

abundant [ə'bʌndənt] *adj* abundante.

abuse [(*n*) ə'bjuːs(*vb*) ə'bjuːz] *n* **1** insultos: *they shouted abuse at us*, nos insultaron. **2** malos tratos. **3** abuso: *an abuse of power*, abuso de poder.

▶ *vt* **1** insultar. **2** maltratar. **3** abusar de: *he abuused his authority*, abusó de su autoridad.

abusive [ə'bjuːsɪv] *adj* **1** injurioso,-a, insultante. **2** abusivo.

abysmal [ə'bɪzməl] *adj fam* malísimo,-a, fatal.

abyss [ə'bɪs] *n* (*pl* **-es**) abismo.

a/c [ə'kaʊnt] *abbr* (*account*) cuenta, cta.

AC ['eɪsiː] *abbr* (*alternating current*) CA.

academic [ækə'demɪk] *adj* académico,-a.

▶ *n* profesor,-ra de universidad.

■ **academic year** curso escolar.

academy [ə'kædəmɪ] *n* (*pl* **-ies**) academia.

accede [æk'siːd] *vi* **1** *fml* acceder. **2** *fml* ascender *(al trono)*.

accelerate [æk'seləreɪt] *vt - vi* acelerar.

acceleration [æksələˈreɪʃən] *n* aceleración.

accelerator [əkˈseləreɪtəʳ] *n* acelerador.

accent [*(n)* ˈæksənt*(vb)* ækˈsent] *n* acento.
▶ *vt* acentuar.

accentuate [ækˈsentʃʊeɪt] *vt* acentuar, poner de relieve.

accept [əkˈsept] *vt* **1** aceptar. **2** admitir, creer.

acceptable [əkˈseptəbəl] *adj* aceptable.

acceptance [əkˈseptəns] *n* **1** aceptación. **2** acogida, aprobación.

access [ˈækses] *n* acceso.
▶ *vt* COMPUT acceder a.
■ **access code** código de acceso.
■ **access provider** proveedor de acceso a Internet.
■ **access road** carretera de acceso.

accessible [ækˈsesɪbəl] *adj* accesible.

accessory [ækˈsesərɪ] *n* (*pl* **-ies**). **1** accesorio. **2** cómplice.

accident [ˈæksɪdənt] *n* accidente: *a car accident*, un accidente de coche; *I'm sorry, it was an accident*, lo siento, lo hice sin querer.
● **by accident** por casualidad.

accidental [æksɪˈdentəl] *adj* fortuito, casual: *an accidental remark*, un comentario fortuito; *it was accidental*, ha sido un accidente.

accident-prone [ˈæksɪdəntprəʊn] *adj* propenso,-a a los accidentes.

acclaim [əˈkleɪm] *n* aclamación, elogio.
▶ *vt* aclamar, elogiar.

acclimatize [əˈklaɪmətaɪz] *vt-vi* aclimatar(se).

accommodate [əˈkɒmədeɪt] *vt* alojar, hospedar.

accommodation [əkɒməˈdeɪʃən] *n* alojamiento.

accompaniment [əˈkʌmpənɪmənt] *n* acompañamiento.

accompany [əˈkʌmpənɪ] *vt* (*pt & pp* **-ied**) acompañar.

accomplice [əˈkɒmplɪs] *n* cómplice.

accomplish [əˈkɒmplɪʃ] *vt* lograr, conseguir.

accomplishment [əˈkɒmplɪʃmənt] *n* **1** realización. **2** logro.
▶ *npl* **accomplishments** aptitudes, dotes, habilidades.

accord [əˈkɔːd] *vt* conceder, otorgar.
▶ *vi* concordar.
● **of one's own accord** por propia voluntad.

● **with one accord** unánimemente.

accordance [əˈkɔːdəns] *n* .
● **in accordance with** de acuerdo con.

according to [əˈkɔːdɪŋtʊ] *prep* **1** según: *according to the paper/my watch*, según el periódico/mi reloj. **2** de acuerdo: *it went according to plan*, salió tal como se había previsto; *we were paid according to our experience*, se nos pagó de acuerdo con nuestra experiencia.

accordingly [əˈkɔːdɪŋlɪ] *adv* **1** como corresponde, en consecuencia: *to act accordingly*, obrar en consecuencia. **2** por consiguiente.

accordion [əˈkɔːdɪən] *n* acordeón.

account [əˈkaʊnt] *n* **1** cuenta: *to open an account*, abrir una cuenta. **2** relato, descripción, versión: *Paul's account of the events is different from yours*, la versión de los hechos que cuenta Paul difiere de la tuya. **3** importancia: *it is of no account*, no tiene importancia.
● **on account** a cuenta.
● **on account of** por, a causa de.
● **on no account** bajo ningún concepto.
● **there's no accounting for tastes** sobre gustos no hay nada escrito.
● **to call SB to account** pedir cuentas a ALGN.
● **to give an account of** describir, narrar.
● **to take into account** tener en cuenta.
● **to turn STH to (good) account** sacar (buen) provecho de algo.

to account for *vi* **1** explicar. **2** representar. **3** acabar con.

accountable [əˈkaʊntəbəl] *adj* responsable.

accountant [əˈkaʊntənt] *n* contable.

accounting [əˈkaʊntɪŋ] *n* contabilidad.

acct. [əˈkaʊnt] *abbr* (*account*) cta.

accumulate [əˈkjuːmjʊleɪt] *vt-vi* acumular(se).

accumulation [əkjuːmjʊˈleɪʃən] *n* acumulación.

accuracy [ˈækjʊrəsɪ] *n* exactitud, precisión.

accurate [ˈækjʊrət] *adj* exacto,-a, preciso,-a.

accusation [ækjuːˈzeɪʃən] *n* acusación: *to bring an accusation against*, presentar una denuncia contra.

accuse [əˈkjuːz] *vt* acusar.

accused [əˈkjuːzd] *n* el acusado, la acusada.

accustom [əˈkʌstəm] *vt* acostumbrar.

accustomed [əˈkʌstəmd] *adj* acostumbrado,-a.

● **to get accustomed to** acostumbrarse a.

ace [eɪs] *n* as.

● **within an ace of** a punto de.

ache [eɪk] *n* dolor.

▶ *vi* doler: *my head aches*, me duele la cabeza, tengo dolor de cabeza.

> Se usa para formar palabras compuestas como **headache** (dolor de cabeza), **toothache** (dolor de muelas), **earache** (dolor de oídos) o **stomach ache** (dolor de estómago).

achieve [əˈtʃiːv] *vt* lograr, conseguir.

achievement [əˈtʃiːvmənt] *n* **1** realización. **2** logro.

aching [ˈeɪkɪŋ] *adj* dolorido,-a.

acid [ˈæsɪd] *n* ácido.

▶ *adj* ácido,-a.

■ **acid rain** lluvia ácida.

acidic [əˈsɪdɪk] *adj* ácido,-a.

acidity [əˈsɪdɪtɪ] *n* acidez.

acknowledge [əkˈnɒlɪdʒ] *vt* **1** reconocer, admitir: *to acknowledge defeat*, admitir la derrota. **2** reconocer: *he is an acknowledged expert*, es un experto reconocido. **3** agradecer.

● **to acknowledge receipt of** acusar recibo de.

acknowledgement [əkˈnɒlɪdʒmənt] *n* **1** reconocimiento. **2** acuse de recibo.

acne [ˈækni] *n* acné.

acorn [ˈeɪkɔːn] *n* bellota.

acoustic [əˈkuːstɪk] *adj* acústico,-a.

acoustics [əˈkuːstɪks] *npl* acústica.

acquaint [əˈkweɪnt] *vt* informar, poner al corriente.

● **to be acquainted with** SB conocer a ALGN, tener trato con ALGN.

● **to be acquainted with** STH conocer algo, tener conocimientos de algo.

acquaintance [əˈkweɪntəns] *n* **1** conocimiento. **2** conocido,-a, persona conocida.

● **to make** SB's **acquaintance** conocer a ALGN.

acquiesce [ækwɪˈes] *vi* consentir.

acquire [əˈkwaɪəʳ] *vt* **1** adquirir *(posesiones)*. **2** obtener, conseguir *(información)*.

● **to acquire a taste for** STH tomarle gusto a algo.

acquisition [ækwɪˈzɪʃən] *n* adquisición.

acquit [əˈkwɪt] *vt* absolver, declarar inocente.

acre [ˈeɪkəʳ] *n* acre.

> Un **acre** son 0,4047 hectáreas.

acrimonious [ækrɪˈməʊnɪəs] *adj* **1** agrio, -a, enconado,-a *(disputa)*. **2** cáustico,-a *(palabras)*.

acrimony [ˈækrɪmənɪ] *n* acritud, acrimonia.

acrobat [ˈækrəbæt] *n* acróbata.

acrobatics [ækrəˈbætɪks] *npl* acrobacias.

acronym [ˈækrənɪm] *n* sigla.

across [əˈkrɒs] *prep* **1** a través de: *to go across the road*, cruzar la carretera; *to swim across a river*, cruzar un río nadando/a nado; *to fly across the Atlantic*, sobrevolar el Atlántico. **2** al otro lado de: *they live across the road*, viven enfrente; *she looked across the room*, miró al otro lado de la habitación.

▶ *adv* de un lado a otro: *it's 4 metres across*, mide 4 metros de lado a lado; *he ran/swam across*, cruzó corriendo/nadando.

> Con verbos como **walk**, **run**, **swim**, etc, se suele traducir por *cruzar* o *atravesar*: *walk across the street*, cruza la calle, atraviesa la calle; *they sailed across the Atlantic*, atravesaron el Atlántico a vela.

act [ækt] *n* **1** acto, hecho, acción: *this is the act of a madman*, esto es la acción de un loco; *an act of terrorism*, una acción terrorista; *an act of war*, un acto de guerra. **2** acto, número: *tonight's first act is a clown*, el primer número de la noche es un payaso. **3** acto: *Hamlet, Act II, Scene 1*, Hamlet Acto II, escena 1. **4** *(Act of Parliament)* ley.

▶ *vi* **1** actuar: *we must act quickly to save her*, hemos de actuar con rapidez para salvarla; *he acted as if nothing had happened*, actuó cono si no hubiese pasado nada. **2** comportarse: *she acted stupidly*, se comportó de manera estúpida. **3** representar: *who is acting for the accused?*, ¿quién representa al acusado? **4** actuar, trabajar: *she's acted in over 50 films*, ha trabajado en más de 50 películas.

● **get your act together** organízate.

- **to catch SB in the act** coger a ALGN en el acto.
- **act of God** fuerza mayor.

acting ['æktɪŋ] n **1** profesión de actor/actriz, interpretación. **2** actuación: *her acting was brilliant*, su actuación fue fantástica.
▶ *adj* en funciones.

action ['ækʃən] n **1** acción. **2** acto. **3** actuación, intervención: *her pompt action saved our lives*, su rápida actuación nos salvó la vida. **4** medidas: *we must take immediate action*, debemos tomar medidas inmediatamente. **5** combate, acción: *the troops are waiting to go into action*, las tropas esperan para entrar en combate.
- **actions speak louder than words** hechos son amores y no buenas razones.
- **killed in action** muerto,-a en combate.
- **out of action** fuera de servicio.
- **to bring an action against SB** entablar una demanda contra ALGN.

activate ['æktɪveɪt] vt activar.

active ['æktɪv] adj **1** activo,-a *(persona)*. **2** en activo *(volcán)*.

activity [æk'tɪvɪtɪ] n *(pl* **-ies)** actividad.

actor ['æktə'] n actor.

actress ['æktrəs] n *(pl* **-es)** actriz.

actual ['æktʃʊəl] adj **1** real: *it's all conjecture, there's no actual evidence*, todo son conjeturas, no hay pruebas reales. **2** exacto,-a: *it's a book about wine, but I don't know the actual title*, es un libro sobre vino, pero no sé el título exacto; *those were her actual words*, esas fueron sus palabras exactas. **3** mismo,-a: *this is the actual gun the murderer used*, esta es la misma arma que utilizó el asesino. **4** en sí, propiamente dicho,-a: *the actual plot was weak, but I liked the film*, el argumento en sí era flojo, pero la película me gustó.
- **in actual fact** en realidad.

Actual no significa lo mismo que *actual* en español.

actually ['æktʃʊəlɪ] adv **1** en realidad, de hecho: *actually, my name isn't John, it's Johnathan*, en realidad no me llamo John, sino Jonathan. **2** de verdad: *have you actually seen a ghost?*, ¿de verdad que has visto un fantasma? **3** bueno: *actually, I don't know*, bueno, no lo sé.

actuate ['æktjʊeɪt] vt mover.

acute [ə'kjuːt] adj **1** agudo,-a, muy fino,-a, perspicaz. **2** agudo,-a, acusado,-a.

acutely [ə'kjuːtlɪ] adv extremadamente.

ad [æd] n fam anuncio.

Es una forma abreviada de **advertisement**.

AD ['eɪ'diː] abbr **(Anno Domini)** después de Cristo, d.J.C.

Adam ['ædəm] n Adán.
- **Adam's apple** nuez.

adamant ['ædəmənt] adj firme, inflexible.

adapt [ə'dæpt] vt-vi adaptar(se).

adaptable [ə'dæptəbəl] adj .
- **to be adaptable** saber adaptarse, adaptarse a todo.

adaptor [ə'dæptə'] n ladrón *(enchufe)*.

add [æd] vt añadir: *add the milk and stir well*, añada la leche y remueva bien; *have you anything to add?*, ¿tienes algo que añadir?
▶ *vt-vi* sumar: *add these figures together*, suma estas cantidades.

to add to vt aumentar, incrementar: *the rain only added to our problems*, la lluvia no hizo más que aumentar nuestros problemas.

to add up vt-vi sumar: *it adds up to a total of 2500 euros*, suma un total de 2500 euros.
▶ *vi fig* cuadrar: *his version doesn't add up*, su versión no cuadra.

adder ['ædə'] n víbora.

addict ['ædɪkt] n adicto,-a.

addicted [ə'dɪktɪd] adj adicto,-a.

addiction [ə'dɪkʃən] n adicción.

addictive [ə'dɪktɪv] adj adictivo,-a.
- **to be addictive** crear adicción.

addition [ə'dɪʃən] n **1** adición. **2** suma.
- **in addition to** además de.

additional [ə'dɪʃənəl] adj adicional.

additive ['ædɪtɪv] n aditivo.

address [ə'dres] n *(pl* **-es).** **1** dirección. **2** discurso. **3** conferencia.
▶ *vt* **1** dirigirse a. **2** tratar a alguien de.
- **address book** agenda.

adenoids ['ædənɔɪdz] npl vegetaciones *(adenoideas)*.

adept [ə'dept] adj experto,-a, hábil.

adequate ['ædɪkwət] adj **1** suficiente. **2** adecuado,-a, satisfactorio,-a.

adhere [əd'hɪə'] vi **1** adherirse. **2** adherirse *(a una creencia).* **3** observar, acatar *(una decisión).*

adhesive [əd'hiːsɪv] *adj* adhesivo,-a.
▶ *n* adhesivo, pegamento.

adjacent [ə'dʒeɪsənt] *adj* adyacente.

adjective ['ædʒɪktɪv] *n* adjetivo.

adjoin [ə'dʒɔɪn] *vt* lindar con.

adjoining [ə'dʒɔɪnɪŋ] *adj* contiguo,-a, colindante.

adjourn [ə'dʒɜːn] *vt* aplazar, posponer.
▶ *vi* levantarse: *the court adjourned*, se levantó la sesión.

adjournment [ə'dʒɜːnmənt] *n* aplazamiento.

adjust [ə'dʒʌst] *vt* ajustar, regular *(temperatura).*
▶ *vi* adaptarse, amoldarse.

adjustable [ə'dʒʌstəbəl] *adj* regulable, graduable.
■ **adjustable spanner** llave inglesa.

adjustment [ə'dʒʌstmənt] *n* **1** ajuste, modificación. **2** adaptación, amoldamiento.

administer [əd'mɪnɪstə'] *vt* **1** administrar, dirigir *(organización).* **2** administrar *(medicamento).* **3** aplicar *(castigo).*

administration [ədmɪnɪs'treɪʃən] *n* administración.

administrator [əd'mɪnɪstreɪtə'] *n* administrador,-ra.

admirable ['ædmɪrəbəl] *adj* admirable.

admiral ['ædmərəl] *n* almirante.

admiration [ædmɪ'reɪʃən] *n* admiración.

admire [əd'maɪə'] *vt* admirar.

admirer [əd'maɪərə'] *n* admirador,-ra.

admissible [əd'mɪsɪbəl] *adj* admisible.

admission [əd'mɪʃən] *n* **1** ingreso *(en hospital, institución).* **2** entrada: *"Admission free"*, "Entrada gratuita". **3** reconocimiento: *an admission of guilt*, un reconocimiento de culpabilidad.

admit [əd'mɪt] *vt (pt & pp* **admitted***, ger* **admitting***).* **1** admitir, dejar entrar: *women are not admitted to this club*, en este club no se admiten mujeres. **2** ingresar *(en hospital).* **3** admitir, confesar, reconocer: *she admitted to the theft*, se confesó culpable del robo.

admittance [əd'mɪtəns] *n* entrada.
● **"No admittance"** "Prohibida la entrada".

admittedly [əd'mɪtɪdlɪ] *adv* lo cierto es que.

admonish [əd'mɒnɪʃ] *vt* amonestar.

ado [ə'duː] *n* .
● **without further ado** sin más preámbulos.
● **much ado about nothing** mucho ruido y pocas nueces.

adolescence [ædə'lesəns] *n* adolescencia.

adolescent [ædə'lesənt] *adj* adolescente.
▶ *n* adolescente.

adopt [ə'dɒpt] *vt* adoptar.

adoption [ə'dɒpʃən] *n* adopción.

adorable [ə'dɔːrəbəl] *adj* adorable.

adore [ə'dɔː'] *vt* adorar.

adorn [ə'dɔːn] *vt* adornar.

adrenalin [ə'drenəlɪn] *n* adrenalina.

Adriatic [eɪdrɪ'ætɪk] *adj* adriático,-a.
■ **the Adriatic Sea** el mar Adriático.

adrift [ə'drɪft] *adj* a la deriva.

adult ['ædʌlt] *adj* adulto,-a.
▶ *n* adulto.

adulterate [ə'dʌltəreɪt] *vt* adulterar.

adultery [ə'dʌltərɪ] *n* adulterio.

advance [əd'vɑːns] *n* **1** avance: *the army's advance*, el avance del ejército. **2** adelanto, progreso: *an advance in science*, un adelanto científico. **3** anticipo, adelanto *(de dinero).*
▶ *npl* **advances** insinuaciones *(amorosas).*
▶ *vt* **1** adelantar, avanzar *(tropas).* **2** ascender *(empleado).* **3** adelantar *(reunión).* **4** anticipar *(dinero).*
▶ *vi* avanzar.
● **in advance** por adelantado, con antelación.

advanced [əd'vɑːnst] *adj* **1** avanzado,-a. **2** superior.
● **of advanced years** entrado en años.

advantage [əd'vɑːntɪdʒ] *n* ventaja.
● **to take advantage of** aprovechar, aprovecharse.

advantageous [ædvən'teɪdʒəs] *adj* ventajoso,-a, provechoso,-a.

adventure [əd'ventʃə'] *n* aventura.
■ **adventure playground** parque infantil.

adventurer [əd'ventʃərə'] *n* aventurero.

adventurous [əd'ventʃərəs] *adj* **1** aventurero,-a. **2** arriesgado,-a.

adverb ['ædvɜːb] *n* adverbio.

adversary ['ædvəsərɪ] *n (pl* **-ies***)* adversario,-a.

adverse ['ædvɜːs] *adj* adverso,-a.

7

adversity [əd'vɜːsɪtɪ] *n* (*pl* -**ies**) adversidad.
advert ['ædvɜːt] *n fam* anuncio.

Es una forma abreviada de **advertisment**.

advertise ['ædvətaɪz] *vt* anunciar.
▶ *vi* hacer publicidad.
advertisement [əd'vɜːtɪsmənt] *n* anuncio.
advertiser ['ædvətaɪzə'] *n* anunciante.
advertising ['ædvətaɪzɪŋ] *n* publicidad,
propaganda: ***advertising campaign***,
campaña publicitaria.
advice [əd'vaɪs] *n* **1** consejos: ***a piece of
advice***, un consejo. **2** asesoramiento.
● **to give advice** aconsejar.
advisable [əd'vaɪzəbəl] *adj* aconsejable.
advise [əd'vaɪz] *vt* **1** aconsejar. **2** recomendar.
● **to advise against** STH desaconsejar
algo.
adviser [əd'vaɪzə'] *n* consejero,-a, asesor,-a.
advocate [(*n*) 'ædvəkət(*vb*) 'ædvəkeɪt] *n*
partidario,-a.
▶ *vt* abogar por, propugnar.
Aegean [iˈdʒiːən] *adj* egeo,-a.
■ **the Aegean Sea** el mar Egeo.
aerial ['eərɪəl] *n* antena.
▶ *adj* aéreo,-a.
aerobics [eəˈrəʊbɪks] *n* aerobic.

Es incontable y el verbo va en singular.

aerodrome ['eərədrəʊm] *n* aeródromo.
aerodynamic [eərəʊdaɪˈnæmɪk] *adj* aerodinámico,-a.
aerodynamics [eərəʊdaɪˈnæmɪks] *n* aerodinámica.
aeronautics [eərəˈnɔːtɪks] *n* aeronáutica.

Es incontable y el verbo va en singular.

aeroplane ['eərəpleɪn] *n* avión.
aerosol ['eərəsɒl] *n* aerosol.
aesthetic [iːsˈθetɪk] *adj* estético,-a.
aesthetics [iːsˈθetɪks] *n* estética.

Es incontable y el verbo va en singular.

affable ['æfəbəl] *adj* afable.
affair [əˈfeə'] *n* **1** asunto. **2** caso: ***the watergate affair***, el caso watergate. **3** lío,
aventura *(amorosa)*.
■ **foreign affairs** asuntos exteriores.
affect [əˈfekt] *vt* **1** afectar, influir en. **2**
conmover, impresionar.
affected [əˈfektɪd] *adj* afectado,-a, falso,-a.
affection [əˈfekʃən] *n* afecto, cariño.
affectionate [əˈfekʃənət] *adj* afectuoso,-a,
cariñoso,-a.
affiliated [əˈfɪlɪeɪtɪd] *adj* afiliado,-a.

affiliation [əfɪlɪˈeɪʃən] *n* afiliación.
affinity [əˈfɪnɪtɪ] *n* (*pl* -**ies**) afinidad.
affirm [əˈfɜːm] *vt* asegurar, afirmar.
affirmative [əˈfɜːmətɪv] *adj* afirmativo,-a.
▶ *n* afirmativo.
afflict [əˈflɪkt] *vt* afligir.
● **to be afflicted with** sufrir de.
affluence ['æfluəns] *n* riqueza, prosperidad.
affluent ['æfluənt] *adj* rico,-a, próspero,-a.
afford [əˈfɔːd] *vt* **1** permitirse, costear: ***I
can't afford to pay £750 for a coat***, no
puedo permitirme pagar 750 libras por
un abrigo; ***how does she afford it?***,
¿cómo se lo costea?; ***can you afford to
reject his offer?***, ¿puedes permitirte el
lujo de rechazar su oferta? **2** *fml* dar, proporcionar.
affordable [əˈfɔːdəbəl] *adj* asequible.
Afghan ['æfgæn] *adj* afgano,-a.
▶ *n* afgano,-a.
Afghanistan [æfgænɪˈstæn] *n* Afganistán.
afield [əˈfiːld] *adv* .
● **far afield** lejos.
● **further a field** más lejos.
afloat [əˈfləʊt] *adj* a flote.
afoot [əˈfʊt] *adv* .
● **something's afoot** se está tramando
algo.
afraid [əˈfreɪd] *adj* temeroso,-a.
● **to be afraid** tener miedo: ***to be afraid
to do*** STH, no atreverse a hacer algo.
● **to be afraid that...** temerse que...: ***I'm
afraid he's not here***, me temo que no
esté aquí.
● **I'm afraid so/not** me temo que sí/no.
afresh [əˈfreʃ] *adv* de nuevo.
Africa ['æfrɪkə] *n* África.
■ **South Africa** Sudáfrica.
African ['æfrɪkən] *adj* africano,-a.
▶ *n* africano,-a.
■ **South African** sudafricano,-a.
after ['ɑːftə'] *prep* **1** después de: ***after
class***, después de la clase. **2** detrás de:
we all went after the thief, todos fuimos
detrás del ladrón; ***the police are after us***,
la policía nos está persiguiendo.
▶ *adv* después: ***the day after***, el día después.
▶ *conj* después de que: ***after he left, I
went to bed***, después de que se marchara, me acosté.
● **after all** al fin y al cabo.

after-effect ['ɑːftərɪfekt] *n* efecto secundario.

afterlife ['ɑːftəlaɪf] *n* vida después de la muerte.

aftermath ['ɑːftəmɑːθ] *n* **1** periodo posterior. **2** repercusiones.

afternoon [ɑːftə'nuːn] *n* tarde: *good afternoon*, buenas tardes; *in the afternoon*, por la tarde.

afters ['ɑːftəz] *npl fam* postre.

after-sales ['ɑːftə'seɪlz] *adj* posventa.

aftershave ['ɑːftəʃeɪv] *n* loción para después del afeitado.

afterwards ['ɑːftəwədz] *adv* después, luego.

again [ə'gen, ə'geɪn] *prep* de nuevo, otra vez.

● **again and again** repetidamente.

● **now and again** de vez en cuando.

against [ə'genst, ə'geɪnst] *prep* **1** contra: *against the wall*, contra la pared. **2** en contra de: *it's against the law*, va en contra de la ley; *I am against the plan*, me opongo al plan.

age [eɪdʒ] *n* edad: *what is your age?*, ¿qué edad tienes?

▶ *vi - vt* envejecer.

● **of age** mayor de edad.

● **under age** menor de edad.

■ **age of consent** edad núbil.

■ **the Middle Ages** la Edad Media.

aged[1] [eɪdʒd] *adj* **1** de ... años: *a boy aged ten*, un niño de diez años. **2** viejo, -a, anciano, -a: *the aged*, los ancianos.

agency ['eɪdʒənsɪ] *n* (*pl* -**ies**). **1** agencia. **2** delegación.

agenda [ə'dʒendə] *n* orden del día.

agent ['eɪdʒənt] *n* agente.

ages ['eɪdʒɪz] *npl* años, siglos: *it's ages since she left*, hace años que se marchó.

aggravate ['ægrəveɪt] *vt* **1** agravar, empeorar. **2** *fam* irritar, molestar.

aggression [ə'greʃən] *n* agresión, agresividad.

aggressive [ə'gresɪv] *adj* agresivo, -a.

aggressor [ə'gresə'] *n* agresor, -ra.

aghast [ə'gɑːst] *adj* horrorizado, -a.

agile ['ædʒaɪl] *adj* ágil.

agility [ə'dʒɪlɪtɪ] *n* agilidad.

agitate ['ædʒɪteɪt] *vt* **1** agitar *(líquido)*. **2** preocupar, inquietar.

● **to agitate for** hacer campaña a favor de.

● **to agitate against** hacer campaña en contra de.

● **to agitate oneself** ponerse nervioso, -a.

agitated ['ædʒɪteɪtɪd] *adj* inquieto, -a: *to get agitated*, inquietarse.

ago [ə'gəʊ] *adv* hace: *two years ago*, hace dos años; *a long time ago*, hace mucho tiempo.

agonize ['ægənaɪz] *vi* atormentarse, angustiarse.

agony ['ægənɪ] *n* (*pl* -**ies**). **1** dolor. **2** angustia.

agree [ə'griː] *vi - vt* **1** estar de acuerdo: *I agree with you*, estoy de acuerdo contigo. **2** ponerse de acuerdo, acordar: *we agreed not to say anything*, nos pusimos de acuerdo en no decir nada. **3** acceder, consentir: *will he agree to our request?*, ¿accederá a nuestra petición? **4** concordar, encajar: *the two men's stories don't agree*, las historias de los dos hombres no encajan. **5** sentar bien: *the prawns didn't agree with me*, las gambas no me sentaron bien. **6** concordar *(gramaticalmente)*.

agreeable [ə'griːəbəl] *adj* **1** agradable. **2** conforme.

agreement [ə'griːmənt] *n* **1** acuerdo, conformidad. **2** acuerdo, convenio. **3** concordancia *(gramatical)*.

● **to be in agreement** estar de acuerdo.

agricultural [ægrɪ'kʌltʃərəl] *adj* agrícola, agrario.

agriculture ['ægrɪkʌltʃə'] *n* agricultura.

ahead [ə'hed] *adv* delante: *there's a police checkpoint ahead*, hay un control de policía aquí delante; *Tom went on ahead to look for water*, Tom se adelantó a por agua; *we are ahead of the others*, llevamos ventaja sobre los otros.

● **ahead of time** antes de la hora prevista.

● **go ahead!** ¡adelante!

● **to plan ahead** planear para el futuro.

● **to think ahead** pensar en el futuro.

aid [eɪd] *n* ayuda, auxilio.

▶ *vt* ayudar, auxiliar.

● **in aid of** en beneficio de.

AIDS [eɪdz] *abbr* SIDA.

ailing ['eɪlɪŋ] *adj* pachucho, -a.

ailment ['eɪlmənt] *n* dolencia, achaque.

aim [eɪm] *n* **1** puntería. **2** meta, objetivo.

- **to take aim** apuntar.
- **to miss one's aim** errar el tiro.

to **aim at** *vt* apuntar a.

to **aim to** *vt* tener la intención de, proponerse.

air [eəʳ] *n* **1** aire. **2** aire, aspecto.
▶ *vt* **1** airear. **2** ventilar.
- **to put on airs** darse aires.
- **to be in the air** estar en el aire.
- **to be on the air** estar en antena.
- **by air 1** *(enviar)* por vía aérea. **2** en avión *(viajar)*.
■ **air conditioning** aire acondicionado.
■ **air force** fuerzas aéreas.
■ **air gun** pistola de aire comprimido.
■ **air hostess** azafata.
■ **air mail** correo aéreo.
■ **air raid** ataque aéreo.

airbag ['eəbæg] *n* airbag.

air-conditioned [eəkən'dɪʃənd] *adj* con aire acondicionado, climatizado,-a.

aircraft ['eəkrɑːft] *n* *(pl* **aircraft**) avión, aparato.
■ **aircraft carrier** portaaviones.

airline ['eəlaɪn] *n* compañía aérea.

airman ['eəmən] *n* *(pl* **airmen**) aviador, piloto.

airplane ['eəpleɪn] *n* US avión.

airport ['eəpɔːt] *n* aeropuerto.

airship ['eəʃɪp] *n* dirigible.

airsick ['eəsɪk] *adj* mareado,-a *(en el avión)*.

airspace ['eəspeɪs] *n* espacio aéreo.

airstrip ['eəstrɪp] *n* pista de aterrizaje.

airtight ['eətaɪt] *adj* hermético,-a.

airway ['eəweɪ] *n* **1** *(of body)* vía respiratoria. **2** *(for planes)* ruta aérea.

airy ['eərɪ] *adj* (-**ier**, -**iest**). **1** bien ventilado,-a. **2** despreocupado,-a.

aisle [aɪl] *n* **1** pasillo. **2** nave lateral.

ajar [ə'dʒɑːʳ] *adj* entreabierto,-a.

aka [eɪkeɪ'eɪ] *abbr (also known as)* alias.

akin [ə'kɪn] *adj* parecido,-a.

alabaster ['æləbɑːstəʳ] *n* alabastro.

alarm [ə'lɑːm] *n* **1** alarma. **2** temor.
▶ *vt* alarmar, asustar.
■ **alarm clock** despertador.

alarming [ə'lɑːmɪŋ] *adj* alarmante.

alas [ə'læs] *interj* ¡ay!, ¡ay de mí!

Albania [æl'beɪnɪə] *n* Albania.

Albanian [æl'beɪnɪən] *adj* albanés,-esa.
▶ *n* **1** albanés,-esa. **2** albanés.

albeit [ɔːl'biːɪt] *conj fml* aunque.

albino [æl'biːnəʊ] *adj - n* albino,-a.

album ['ælbəm] *n* álbum.

alcohol ['ælkəhɒl] *n* alcohol.

alcoholic [ælkə'hɒlɪk] *adj* alcohólico,-a.

ale [eɪl] *n* cerveza.

alert [ə'lɜːt] *adj* alerta, vigilante.
▶ *n* alarma, aviso: **bomb alert**, aviso de bomba.
▶ *vt* alertar, avisar.
- **on the alert** alerta, sobre aviso.

algae ['ældʒiː] *npl* algas.

algebra ['ældʒɪbrə] *n* álgebra.

Algeria [æl'dʒɪərɪə] *n* Argelia.

Algerian [æl'dʒɪərɪən] *adj* argelino,-a.
▶ *n* argelino,-a.

Algiers [æl'dʒɪəz] *n* Argel.

algorithm ['ælgərɪðəm] *n* algoritmo.

alias ['eɪlɪəs] *adv* alias.
▶ *n (pl* **aliases**) alias.

alibi ['ælɪbaɪ] *n* coartada.

alien ['eɪlɪən] *adj* **1** extranjero,-a. **2** extraterrestre. **3** extraño,-a, ajeno,-a: **his ideas are alien to me**, sus ideas me son ajenas.
▶ *n* **1** extranjero,-a: **an illegal alien**, un inmigrante ilegal. **2** extraterrestre.

alienate ['eɪlɪəneɪt] *vt* ganarse la antipatía de.

alight [ə'laɪt] *adj* encendido,-a, ardiendo.
▶ *vi fml* apearse.

to **alight on** *vt* **1** posarse en. **2** darse cuenta de.

align [ə'laɪn] *vt-vi* alinear(se).

alike [ə'laɪk] *adj* igual: **you men are all alike!**, ¡todos los hombres sois iguales!
▶ *adv* igual, de la misma forma, igualmente: **dressed alike**, vestidos,-as iguales; **men and women alike**, tanto hombres como mujeres.
- **to look alike** parecerse.

alimony ['ælɪmənɪ] *n* pensión alimenticia.

alive [ə'laɪv] *adj* vivo,-a.
- **alive to** consciente de.
- **alive with** lleno,-a de.

alkali ['ælkəlaɪ] *n* álcali.

alkaline ['ælkəlaɪn] *adj* alcalino,-a.

all [ɔːl] *adj* todo,-a, todos,-as: **all the money**, todo el dinero; **all the ink**, toda la tinta; **all the books**, todos los libros; **all the chairs**, todas las sillas; **all kinds of** ..., toda clase de ....
▶ *pron* **1** todo, la totalidad: **we did all we could**, hicimos todo lo que pudimos. **2** lo único, sólo: **all you need is a bit of**

luck, lo único que necesitas es un poco de suerte, sólo necesitas un poco de suerte. **3** todos, todo el mundo.
► *adv* **1** completamente, muy: *you're all dirty!*, ¡estás todo sucio! **2** empatados, iguales: *the score was three all*, empataron a tres.
● **after all** después de todo.
● **all but** todos menos.
● **all of a sudden** de pronto, de repente.
● **all over** en todas partes.
● **all right 1** bueno,-a. **2** bien: *are you all right?*, ¿estás bien?
● **all the better** tanto mejor.
● **all the same** igualmente, a pesar de todo.
● **at all** en absoluto: *he didn't like it at all*, no le gustó nada.
● **it's all the same to me** me da lo mismo.
● **not at all 1** en absoluto: *Were you frightened? -Not at all*, ¿Tenías miedo? -En absoluto. **2** no hay de qué, de nada: *Thank you very much. -Not at all*, Muchas gracias. -De nada.

allegation [ælə'geɪʃən] *n* acusación, imputación.

allege [ə'ledʒ] *vt* alegar.

alleged [ə'ledʒd] *adj* presunto,-a, supuesto,-a.

allegiance [ə'li:dʒəns] *n* lealtad.

allegory ['ælɪgərɪ] *n* (*pl* -**ies**) alegoría.

allergic [ə'lɜ:dʒɪk] *adj* alérgico,-a.

allergy ['ælədʒɪ] *n* (*pl* -**ies**) alergia.

alleviate [ə'li:vɪeɪt] *vt* aliviar.

alley ['ælɪ] *n* callejuela, callejón.

alliance [ə'laɪəns] *n* alianza.

allied ['ælaɪd] *adj* **1** aliado,-a. **2** relacionado,-a, afín.

alligator ['ælɪgeɪtə'] *n* caimán.

allocate ['æləkeɪt] *vt* asignar, destinar.

allocation [ælə'keɪʃən] *n* asignación.

allot [ə'lɒt] *vt* (*pt & pp* **allotted**, *ger* **allotting**) asignar.

allotment [ə'lɒtmənt] *n* **1** asignación. **2** huerto, parcela.

allow [ə'laʊ] *vt* **1** permitir, dejar: *to allow* SB *to do* STH, dejar que ALGN haga algo. **2** admitir: *dogs are not allowed in*, no se admiten perros. **3** conceder, dar, asignar: *they allowed us an hour to do the test*, nos dieron una hora para hacer la prueba.
to allow for *vt* tener en cuenta.

allowance [ə'laʊəns] *n* **1** prestación, subsidio, dietas: *disability allowance*, prestación por invalidez. **2** US paga semanal.
● **to make allowances for** tener en cuenta.

alloy ['ælɔɪ] *n* aleación.

allude [ə'lu:d] *vi* aludir.

alluring [ə'ljʊərɪŋ] *adj* seductor,-ra.

allusion [ə'lu:ʒən] *n* alusión.

ally ['ælaɪ] *n* (*pl* -**ies**) aliado,-a.
► *vt-vi* (*pt & pp* -**ied**) aliar(se).

almighty [ɔ:l'maɪtɪ] *adj* **1** todopoderoso,-a. **2** *fam* enorme, tremendo,-a.

almond ['ɑ:mənd] *n* almendra.
■ **almond tree** almendro.

almost ['ɔ:lməʊst] *adv* casi.

alone [ə'ləʊn] *adj* solo,-a.
● **leave me alone!** ¡déjame en paz!

along [ə'lɒŋ] *prep* a lo largo de, por: *they walked along the street*, caminaron por la calle.
► *adv* hacia delante: *their house is a bit further along*, su casa está un poco más adelante; *she was walking along*, iba caminando; *bring some friends along*, tráete algunos amigos.
● **all along** desde el principio.
● **along with** junto con.
● **come along!** ¡ven!, ¡venid!

alongside [əlɒŋ'saɪd] *prep* al lado de.
► *adv* al costado.

aloof [ə'lu:f] *adv* a distancia: *to remain aloof*, mantenerse a distancia.
► *adj* distante.

aloud [ə'laʊd] *adv* en voz alta.

alphabet ['ælfəbet] *n* alfabeto.

alphabetical [ælfə'betɪkəl] *adj* alfabético,-a.

Alps [ælps] *npl* **the Alps** los Alpes.

already [ɔ:l'redɪ] *adv* ya: *they have already left*, ya se han marchado.

also ['ɔ:lsəʊ] *adv* también.

altar ['ɔ:ltə'] *n* altar.

alter ['ɔ:ltə'] *vt* **1** cambiar, modificar. **2** arreglar (*ropa*).
► *vi* cambiarse.

alteration [ɔ:ltə'reɪʃən] *n* **1** cambio, modificación. **2** reforma.

alternate [(*adj*) ɔ:l'tɜ:nət(*vb*) 'ɔ:ltɜ:neɪt] *adj* alterno,-a: *he works alternate weekends*, trabaja fines de semana alternos.
► *vt-vi* alternar(se).

alternating current [ˈɔːltɜːneɪtɪŋˈkʌrənt] *n* corriente alterna.

alternative [ɔːlˈtɜːnətɪv] *adj* alternativo,-a.
► *n* alternativa.

although [ɔːlˈðəʊ] *conj* aunque.

altitude [ˈæltɪtjuːd] *n* altitud, altura.

altogether [ɔːltəˈɡeðəˈ] *adv* **1** del todo, completamente. **2** en conjunto, en total.
● **in the altogether** en cueros.

altruism [ˈæltruɪzəm] *n* altruismo.

altruist [ˈæltruɪst] *n* altruista.

aluminium [æljʊˈmɪnɪəm] *n* GB aluminio.

aluminum [əˈluːmɪnəm] *n* US aluminio.

always [ˈɔːlweɪz] *adv* siempre.

a.m. [ˈeɪˈem] *abbr (ante meridiem)* de la mañana.

AM[1] [ˈeɪˈem] *abbr (amplitude modulation)* AM.

AM[2] [ˈeɪˈem] *abbr* US → MA.

amalgam [əˈmælɡəm] *n* amalgama.

amalgamate [əˈmælɡəmeɪt] *vt* amalgamar, fusionar.
► *vi* fusionarse.

amass [əˈmæs] *vt* acumular, amasar.

amateur [ˈæmətəˈ] *adj* - *n* aficionado,-a.

amaze [əˈmeɪz] *vt* asombrar, pasmar.

amazement [əˈmeɪzmənt] *n* asombro: *to my amazement*, para gran sorpresa mía.

amazing [əˈmeɪzɪŋ] *adj* **1** asombroso,-a, pasmoso,-a. **2** increíble.

Amazon [ˈæməzən] *n* **the Amazon** el Amazonas.

ambassador [æmˈbæsədəˈ] *n* embajador,-a.

amber [ˈæmbəˈ] *adj* ámbar.
► *n* ámbar.

ambience [ˈæmbɪəns] *n* ambiente.

ambiguity [æmbɪˈɡjuːɪtɪ] *n (pl -ies)* ambigüedad.

ambiguous [æmˈbɪɡjʊəs] *adj* ambiguo,-a.

ambition [æmˈbɪʃən] *n* ambición.

ambitious [æmˈbɪʃəs] *adj* ambicioso,-a.

ambivalent [æmˈbɪvələnt] *adj* ambivalente.

ambulance [ˈæmbjʊləns] *n* ambulancia.

ambush [ˈæmbʊʃ] *n (pl -es)* emboscada.
► *vt* tender una emboscada a.

amen [ɑːˈmen] *interj* amén.

amenable [əˈmiːnəbəl] *adj* receptivo,-a: *she's amenable to reason*, atiende a razones.

amend [əˈmend] *vt* **1** enmendar. **2** corregir.

amendment [əˈmendmənt] *n* enmienda.

amends [əˈmendz] *n*: *to make amends to SB for STH*, compensar a ALGN por algo.

amenities [əˈmiːnɪtɪz] *npl* **1** servicios, instalaciones. **2** comodidades.

America [əˈmerɪkə] *n* **1** América. **2** Estados Unidos.
■ **Central America** América Central, Centroamérica.
■ **Latin America** América Latina, Latinoamérica.
■ **North America** América del Norte, Norteamérica.
■ **South America** América del Sur, Sudamérica.

American [əˈmerɪkən] *adj* **1** americano, -a. **2** estadounidense.
► *n* **1** americano,-a. **2** estadounidense.
■ **Latin American** Latinoaméricano,-a.
■ **North American** norteamericano,-a.
■ **South American** sudaméricano,-a.

amiable [ˈeɪmɪəbəl] *adj* amable.

amicable [ˈæmɪkəbəl] *adj* amistoso,-a, amigable.

amid [əˈmɪd] *prep* en medio de, entre.

amidst [əˈmɪdst] *prep* en medio de, entre.

amiss [əˈmɪs] *adj* - *adv* mal.
● **to take amiss** tomar a mal.

ammonia [əˈməʊnɪ] *n* amoníaco.

ammunition [æmjʊˈnɪʃən] *n* municiones.

amnesia [æmˈniːzɪə] *n* amnesia.

amnesty [ˈæmnəstɪ] *n (pl -ies)* amnistía.

amoeba [æˈmiːbə] *n (pl -s o amoebae* [əˈmiːbiː]) ameba.

amok [əˈmɒk] *adv* .
● **to run amok** volverse loco,-a.

among [əˈmʌŋ] *prep* entre: *you're among my friends*, te cuento entre mis amigos.

amongst [əˈmʌŋst] *prep* entre.

amoral [eɪˈmɒrəl] *adj* amoral.

amount [əˈmaʊnt] *n* **1** cantidad, suma *(de dinero)*. **2** cantidad: *she's got an enormous amount of energy*, tiene una gran cantidad de energía.

to amount to *vt* **1** ascender a. **2** *fig* equivaler a: *it amounts to the same thing*, viene a ser lo mismo.

amp [æmp] *n* amperio, ampere.

ampere [ˈæmpeəˈ] *n* amperio, ampere.

amphetamine [æmˈfetəmiːn] *n* anfetamina.

amphibian [æmˈfɪbɪən] *n* anfibio.

amphibious [æmˈfɪbɪəs] *adj* anfibio,-a.

amphitheatre [ˈæmfɪθɪətəʳ] (US **amphitheater**) n anfiteatro.
ample [ˈæmpəl] adj **1** abundante. **2** amplio,-a *(habitación)*.
amplifier [ˈæmplɪfaɪəʳ] n amplificador.
amplify [ˈæmplɪfaɪ] vt (pt & pp -ied) amplificar.
amputate [ˈæmpjʊteɪt] vt amputar.
amputation [æmpjʊˈteɪʃən] n amputación.
amuck [əˈmʌk] adv → amok.
amuse [əˈmjuːz] vt entretener, divertir.
● **to amuse oneself** entretenerse.
amusement [əˈmjuːzmənt] n **1** diversión, entretenimiento. **2** pasatiempo. **3** atracción.
■ **amusement park** parque de atracciones.
amusing [əˈmjuːzɪŋ] adj **1** entretenido,-a, divertido,-a. **2** gracioso,-a.
an [ən, æn] det **1** un,-a: *an orange*, una naranja. **2** por: *50 kilometers an hour*, 50 kilómetros por hora.

Se usa delante de las palabras que empiezan por un sonido vocálico. Véase también **a**.

anaemia [əˈniːmɪə] n GB anemia.
anaemic [əˈniːmɪk] adj GB anémico,-a.
anaesthesia [ænəsˈθiːzɪə] n GB anestesia.
anaesthetic [ænəsˈθetɪk] n GB anestésico.
● **to be under anaesthetic** estar anestesiado.
anaesthetist [əˈniːsθətɪst] n GB anestesista.
anaesthetize [əˈniːsθətaɪz] vt GB anestesiar.
anagram [ˈænəgræm] n anagrama.
anal [ˈeɪnəl] adj anal.
analgesic [ænəlˈdʒiːzɪk] adj analgésico,-a.
► n analgésico.
analog [ˈænəlɒg] adj US analógico,-a.
analogue [ˈænəlɒg] adj GB analógico,-a.
analogy [əˈnælədʒɪ] n (pl -ies) analogía, semejanza.
analyse [ˈænəlaɪz] vt analizar.
analysis [əˈnælɪsɪs] n (pl **analyses** [əˈnælɪsiːz]) análisis.
analyst [ˈænəlɪst] n analista.
anarchism [ˈænəkɪzəm] n anarquismo.
anarchist [ˈænəkɪst] n anarquista.
anarchy [ˈænəkɪ] n (pl -ies) anarquía.
anatomy [əˈnætəmɪ] n anatomía.
ancestor [ˈænsəstəʳ] n **1** antepasado. **2** antecesor.

anchor [ˈæŋkəʳ] n ancla.
► vt - vi anclar.
anchovy [ˈæntʃəvɪ] n (pl -ies) anchoa, boquerón.
ancient [ˈeɪnʃənt] adj **1** antiguo,-a, histórico,-a. **2** fam viejísimo,-a.
and [ænd, ənd] conj y, e: *one and a half*, uno y medio; *try and finish it*, intenta acabarlo.
Andalusia [ændəˈluːzɪə] n Andalucía.
Andalusian [ændəˈluːzɪən] adj andaluz, -za.
► n **1** andaluz,-za. **2** andaluz.
Andes [ˈændiːz] npl **the Andes** los Andes.
Andorra [ænˈdɔːrə] n Andorra.
Andorran [ænˈdɔːrən] adj andorrano,-a.
► n andorrano,-a.
anecdote [ˈænɪkdəʊt] n anécdota.
anemia [əˈniːmɪə] n US anemia.
anemic [əˈniːmɪk] adj US anémico,-a.
anemone [əˈnemənɪ] n anémona.
anesthesia [ænəsˈθiːzɪə] n US anestesia.
anesthetic [ænəsˈθetɪk] n US anestésico.
● **to be under anesthetic** estar anestesiado,-a.
anesthetist [əˈniːsθətɪst] n US anestesista.
anesthetize [əˈniːsθətaɪz] vt US anestesiar.
angel [ˈeɪndʒəl] n ángel.
anger [ˈæŋgəʳ] n cólera, ira.
angle¹ [ˈæŋgəl] n **1** ángulo. **2** ángulo, punto de vista.
angle² [ˈæŋgəl] vi pescar *(con caña)*.
angler [ˈæŋgləʳ] n pescador,-ra *(de caña)*.
■ **angler fish** rape.
Anglican [ˈæŋglɪkən] adj - n anglicano,-a.
angling [ˈæŋglɪŋ] n pesca *con caña*.
Anglo-Saxon [æŋgləʊˈsæksən] adj anglosajón,-ona.
► n **1** anglosajón,-ona. **2** anglosajón.
Angola [æŋˈgəʊlə] n Angola.
Angolan [æŋˈgəʊlən] adj - n angoleño,-a.
angry [ˈæŋgrɪ] adj (-ier, -iest) enfadado, -a, enojado,-a.
● **to get angry** enfadarse, enojarse.
anguish [ˈæŋgwɪʃ] n angustia.
animal [ˈænɪməl] n animal.
animate [(adj) ˈænɪmət(vb) ˈænɪmeɪt] adj animado,-a, vivo,-a.
► vt animar.
animated [ˈænɪmeɪtɪd] adj animado,-a.
ankle [ˈæŋkəl] n tobillo.

annex [*(vb)* ə'neks*(n)* 'aneks] *vt* **1** anexar. **2** adjuntar.
▸ *n* (*pl* **annexes**) US anexo.
annexe ['ænəks] *n* GB anexo.
annihilate [ə'naɪəleɪt] *vt* aniquilar.
annihilation [ənaɪə'leɪʃən] *n* aniquilación.
anniversary [ænɪ'vɜːsərɪ] *n* (*pl* **-ies**) aniversario.
announce [ə'naʊns] *vt* anunciar.
announcement [ə'naʊnsmənt] *n* anuncio.
announcer [ə'naʊnsə'] *n* presentador,-ra, locutor,-a.
annoy [ə'nɔɪ] *vt* molestar, fastidiar.
annoyance [ə'nɔɪəns] *n* molestia, fastidio.
annoyed [ə'nɔɪd] *adj* enfadado,-a.
● **to get annoyed** enfadarse.
annoying [ə'nɔɪɪŋ] *adj* molesto,-a, enojoso,-a.
annual ['ænjʊəl] *adj* anual.
annul [ə'nʌl] *vt* (*pt & pp* **annulled**, *ger* **annulling**) anular.
anomaly [ə'nɒməlɪ] *n* (*pl* **-ies**) anomalía.
anonymous [ə'nɒnɪməs] *adj* anónimo,-a.
anorak ['ænəræk] *n* **1** (*prenda*) anorak. **2** petardo,-a (*persona*).
anorexia [ænə'reksɪə] *n* anorexia.
anorexic [ænə'reksɪk] *adj* anoréxico,-a.
another [ə'nʌðə'] *adj* - *pron* otro,-a: *another one*, otro; *I want another three books*, quiero tres libros más.
answer ['ɑːnsə'] *n* **1** respuesta: *the correct answer*, la respuesta correcta. **2** solución: *there's no answer to this problem*, este problema no tiene solución.
▸ *vt* - *vi* responder, contestar.
● **to answer the door** abrir la puerta.
● **to answer the phone** contestar al teléfono.
to answer back *vt* - *vi* replicar (*con insolencia*).
to answer for *vt* responder por, responder de.
answering machine ['ɑːnsərɪŋməʃiːn] *n* contestador automático.
ant [ænt] *n* hormiga.
■ **ant hill** hormiguero.
antagonize [æn'tægənaɪz] *vt* enfadar, enojar.
Antarctic [ænt'ɑːktɪk] *adj* antártico,-a.
▸ *n* el Antártico.
■ **the Antarctic Ocean** el océano Antártico.
Antarctica [ænt'ɑːktɪkə] *n* Antártida.

antelope ['æntɪləʊp] *n* antílope.
antenna [æn'tenə] *n* (*pl* **-s** o **antennae** [æn'teniː]) antena (*de insecto, radio, etc*).
anthem ['ænθəm] *n* himno.
anthology [æn'θɒlədʒɪ] *n* (*pl* **-ies**) antología.
anthracite ['ænθrəsaɪt] *n* antracita.
anthropologist [ænθrə'pɒlədʒɪst] *n* antropólogo,-a.
anthropology [ænθrə'pɒlədʒɪ] *n* antropología.
anti-aircraft [æntɪ'eəkrɑːft] *adj* antiaéreo,-a.
antibiotic [æntɪbaɪ'ɒtɪk] *n* antibiótico.
▸ *adj* antibiótico,-a.
antibody ['æntɪbɒdɪ] *n* (*pl* **-ies**) anticuerpo.
anticipate [æn'tɪsɪpeɪt] *vt* **1** esperar: *we anticipate problems*, esperamos problemas. **2** prever: *as anticipated*, de acuerdo con lo previsto.
▸ *vi* anticiparse a, adelantarse a.
anticipation [æntɪsɪ'peɪʃən] *n* **1** expectación. **2** previsión.
anticlockwise [æntɪ'klɒkwaɪz] *adj* en el sentido contrario al de las agujas del reloj.
antics ['æntɪks] *npl* **1** payasadas. **2** gracias.
antidote ['æntɪdəʊt] *n* antídoto.
antifreeze ['æntɪfriːz] *n* anticongelante.
antiquated ['æntɪkweɪtɪd] *adj* anticuado,-a.
antique [æn'tiːk] *adj* antiguo,-a.
▸ *n* antigüedad.
■ **antique shop** anticuario, tienda de antigüedades.
antiseptic [æntɪ'septɪk] *adj* antiséptico,-a.
▸ *n* antiséptico.
antithesis [æn'tɪθəsɪs] *n* (*pl* **antitheses**) antítesis.
antivirus [æntɪ'vaɪrəs] *adj* antivirus.
■ **antivirus software** antivirus.
antlers ['æntlə'] *npl* cornamenta.
anus ['eɪnəs] *n* (*pl* **anuses**) ano.
anvil ['ænvɪl] *n* yunque.
anxiety [æŋ'zaɪətɪ] *n* (*pl* **-ies**) ansiedad, preocupación.
anxious ['æŋkʃəs] *adj* **1** ansioso,-a, preocupado,-a. **2** ansioso,-a, deseoso: *I'm anxious to meet him*, estoy deseando conocerlo.
any ['enɪ] *adj* algún,-una, ningún,-una (*con*

el verbo negativo), cualquier,-ra, todo,-a: *have you got any money/gloves?*, ¿tienes dinero/guantes?; *he hasn't bought any milk/biscuits*, no ha comprado leche/galletas; *any fool knows that*, cualquier tonto sabe eso; *without any difficulty*, sin ninguna dificultad; *any old rag will do*, cualquier trapo sirve.
▶ *pron* alguno,-a, ninguno,-a *(con el verbo negativo)*, cualquiera: *those biscuits were delicious, are there any left?*, esas galletas eran deliciosas, ¿queda alguna?; *I asked for some records, but they hadn't got any left*, pedí unos discos pero ya no quedaba ninguno; *esas galletas estaban buenísimas*, ¿queda alguna?; *any of those computers will do*, cualquiera de esos ordenadores puede servir.
▶ *adv*: *I don't work there any more*, ya no trabajo allí; *do you want any more?*, ¿quieres más?; *she can't walk any faster*, no puede caminar más rápido.

anybody ['enɪbɒdɪ] *pron* alguien, alguno, -a, nadie *(con el verbo negativo)*, cualquiera: *is anybody home?*, ¿hay alguien en casa?; *don't tell anybody*, no se lo digas a nadie; *ask anybody*, pregúntale a cualquiera.

anyhow ['enɪhaʊ] *adv* **1** en todo caso. **2** bueno, pues. **3** de cualquier forma.

anyone ['enɪwʌn] *pron* → anybody.

anything ['enɪθɪŋ] *pron* algo, alguna cosa, nada *(con el verbo negativo)*, cualquier cosa, todo cuanto: *do you want anything else?*, ¿quieres algo más?; *she didn't say anything*, no dijo nada; *I'll try anything*, probaré cualquier cosa.

anyway ['enɪweɪ] *adv* → anyhow.

anywhere ['enɪweəʳ] *adv* **1** (en) algún sitio, a algún sitio: *is there anywhere I can buy a film?*, ¿hay algún sitio donde pueda comprar un carrete?; *have you seen my watch anywhere?*, ¿has visto mi reloj en algún sitio? **2** (en) ningún sitio, a ningún sitio *(con el verbo negativo)*: *they haven't got anywhere to sleep*, no tienen dónde dormir; *I'm not going anywhere*, no voy a ningún sitio. **3** donde sea, en cualquier sitio, a donde sea, a cualquier sitio: *I'd go anywhere with you*, iría a cualquier sitio contigo.

aorta [eɪˈɔːtə] *n* aorta.

apart [əˈpɑːt] *adv* separado,-a: *these nails*

are too far apart, estos clavos están demasiado separados.
● **apart from** aparte de, excepto, menos.
● **to take apart** desarmar, desmontar.
● **to fall apart** deshacerse.

apartment [əˈpɑːtmənt] *n* **1** piso. **2** apartamento.

apathetic [æpəˈθetɪk] *adj* apático,-a.

apathy ['æpəθɪ] *n* apatía.

ape [eɪp] *n* simio.
▶ *vt* imitar.

Apennines ['æpənaɪnz] *npl* **the Apennines** los Apeninos.

aperitif [əperɪˈtiːf] *n* (*pl* **aperitifs**) aperitivo.

apex ['eɪpeks] *n* (*pl* **apexes**) ápice, vértice.

APEX ['eɪpeks] *abbr* (*Advance Purchase Excursion*) APEX.

aphrodisiac [æfrəˈdɪzɪæk] *n* afrodisíaco.
▶ *adj* afrodisíaco,-a.

apiece [əˈpiːs] *adv* cada uno,-a.

apologetic [əpɒləˈdʒetɪk] *adj* compungido,-a, arrepentido,-a.

apologetically [əpɒləˈdʒetɪklɪ] *adv* disculpándose.

apologize [əˈpɒlədʒaɪz] *vi* disculparse, pedir perdón.

apology [əˈpɒlədʒɪ] *n* (*pl* **-ies**) disculpa.

apoplexy ['æpəpleksɪ] *n* (*pl* **-ies**) apoplejía.

apostle [əˈpɒsl] *n* apóstol.

apostrophe [əˈpɒstrəfɪ] *n* apóstrofo.

appal [əˈpɔːl] *vt* (*pt & pp* **appalled**, *ger* **appalling**) GB horrorizar.

appall [əˈpɔːl] *vt* (*pt & pp* **appalled**, *ger* **appalling**) US horrorizar.

appalling [əˈpɔːlɪŋ] *adj* horroroso,-a, terrible.

apparatus [æpəˈreɪtəs] *n* equipo, aparatos.

Es incontable y el verbo va en singular.

apparent [əˈpærənt] *adj* **1** evidente. **2** aparente.

apparently [əˈpærəntlɪ] *adv* **1** por lo visto, según parece, al parecer. **2** aparentemente: *an apparently easy victory*, una victoria aparentemente fácil.

appeal [əˈpiːl] *n* **1** llamamiento: *an appeal for peace*, un llamamiento a la paz. **2** petición, súplica. **3** atractivo. **4** apelación *(contra sentencia judicial)*.
▶ *vi* **1** pedir, solicitar, suplicar: *to appeal*

for help, pedir ayuda. **2** atraer: *it doesn't appeal to me*, no me atrae. **3** apelar *(contra sentencia judicial)*.

appealing [ə'pi:lɪŋ] *adj* **1** de súplica. **2** atractivo.

appear [ə'pɪə'] *vi* **1** aparecer. **2** comparecer. **3** actuar, salir, aparecer: *he has appeared in many films*, ha salido en muchas películas. **4** parecer: *this appears to be a mistake*, parece que hay un error.
● **to appear on television** salir en televisión.

appearance [ə'pɪərəns] *n* **1** aparición: *the appearance of cholera in Mexico*, la aparición del cólera en México. **2** comparecencia. **3** actuación. **4** apariencia, aspecto. **5** impresión: *he gave the appearance of being self-confident*, daba la impresión de tener confianza en sí mismo.

appendicitis [əpendɪ'saɪtɪs] *n* apendicitis.

appendix [ə'pendɪks] (Cuando **appendix** se refiere al órgano del cuerpo, el plural es **appendixes**; cuando se refiere al apéndice de un libro es **appendices**) *n* apéndice.

appetite ['æpɪtaɪt] *n* **1** apetito. **2** deseo.

appetizer ['æpɪtaɪzə'] *n* aperitivo.

appetizing ['æpɪtaɪzɪŋ] *adj* apetitoso,-a.

applaud [ə'plɔːd] *vt - vi* aplaudir.
► *vt* alabar.

applause [ə'plɔːz] *n* aplausos.
⎣Es incontable y el verbo va en singular.⎦

apple ['æpəl] *n* manzana.
■ **apple of one's eye** niña del ojo.
■ **apple pie** tarta de manzana.
■ **apple tree** manzano.

appliance [ə'plaɪəns] *n* aparato: *electrical appliance*, electrodoméstico.

applicable ['æplɪkəbəl] *adj* aplicable, pertinente.

applicant ['æplɪkənt] *n* candidato,-a, solicitante.

application [æplɪ'keɪʃən] *n* **1** solicitud. **2** aplicación.
■ **application form** impreso de solicitud.

apply [ə'plaɪ] *vt (pt & pp -ied)* aplicar: *apply the paint evenly*, aplique la pintura uniformemente.
► *vi* **1** aplicarse, ser aplicable. **2** dirigirse, presentarse, solicitar: *to apply for a job*, solicitar un trabajo.

appoint [ə'pɔɪnt] *vt* **1** nombrar. **2** fijar, señalar *(lugar)*.

appointment [ə'pɔɪntmənt] *n* **1** cita, hora: *I've got an appointment with the doctor*, tengo hora con el médico. **2** nombramiento.

appraisal [ə'preɪzəl] *n* valoración, evaluación.

appraise [ə'preɪz] *vt* valorar, evaluar.

appreciate [ə'priːʃɪeɪt] *vt* **1** agradecer. **2** entender. **3** valorar, apreciar.
► *vi* revalorizarse.

appreciation [əpriːʃɪ'eɪʃən] *n* **1** agradecimiento, gratitud. **2** comprensión. **3** evaluación. **4** revalorización, aumento de valor.

apprehend [æprɪ'hend] *vt* **1** detener, capturar. **2** comprender, darse cuenta de.

apprehension [æprɪ'henʃən] *n* **1** detención, captura. **2** aprensión, recelo.

apprehensive [æprɪ'hensɪv] *adj* aprensivo, receloso,-a: *to be aprehensive about STH*, estar enquieto por algo.

apprentice [ə'prentɪs] *n* aprendiz,-za.

apprenticeship [ə'prentɪʃɪp] *n* aprendizaje.

approach [ə'prəʊtʃ] *n (pl -es)*. **1** aproximación, acercamiento. **2** entrada, acceso *(a un lugar)*. **3** enfoque *(de un problema)*.
► *vi* acercarse, aproximarse.
► *vt* **1** acercarse a, aproximarse a: *she is approaching 40*, se acerca a los 40 años. **2** enfocar, abordar, dirigirse *(a un problema)*.
■ **approach road** vía de acceso.

approbation [æprə'beɪʃən] *n* aprobación.

appropriate [*(adj)* ə'prəʊprɪət *(vb)* ə'prəʊprɪeɪt] *adj* apropiado,-a, adecuado,-a.
► *vt* apropiarse de.
● **at the appropriate time** en el momento oportuno.

appropriation [əprəʊprɪ'eɪʃən] *n* **1** asignación. **2** apropiación.

approval [ə'pruːvəl] *n* aprobación, visto bueno.
● **on approval** a prueba.

approve [ə'pruːv] *vt* aprobar, dar el visto bueno a.

to approve of *vt* aprobar.

approx [ə'prɒx] *abbr* **1** *(approximate)* aproximado,-a. **2** *(approximately)* aproximadamente.

approximate [*(adj)* ə'prɒksɪmət*(vb)* ə'prɒksɪmeɪt] *adj* aproximado,-a.
► *vi* aproximarse.

approximately [ə'prɒksɪmətlɪ] *adv* aproximadamente, más o menos.

apricot ['eɪprɪkɒt] *n* albaricoque.
■ **apricot tree** albaricoque, albaricoquero.

April ['eɪprɪl] *n* abril.
■ **April Fool's day** el día de los Inocentes *(celebrado el 1 de abril)*.

apron ['eɪprən] *n* delantal.

apt [æpt] *adj* apropiado,-a, acertado,-a: *to be apt to do STH*, tender a hacer algo.

APT ['eɪ'pi:'ti:] *abbr* GB (*Advanced Passenger Train*) Tren de Alta Velocidad.

aptitude ['æptɪtju:d] *n* aptitud.

aquarium [ə'kweərɪəm] *n* (*pl* -**s** o **aquaria** [ə'kweərɪə]) acuario.

Aquarius [ə'kweərɪəs] *n* Acuario.

aquatic [ə'kwætɪk] *adj* acuático,-a.

aqueduct ['ækwɪdʌkt] *n* acueducto.

Arab ['ærəb] *adj* árabe.
► *n* árabe.

Arabia [ə'reɪbɪə] *n* Arabia.

Arabian [ə'reɪbɪən] *adj* árabe, arábigo,-a.
► *n* árabe.
■ **Arabian Sea** Mar Arábigo.

Arabic ['ærəbɪk] *adj* arábigo,-a, árabe: *Arabic numerals*, números arábigos.
► *n* árabe.

arable ['ærəbəl] *adj* cultivable: *arable land*, tierrra de cultivo.

arbitrary ['ɑːbɪtrərɪ] *adj* arbitrario,-a.

arbitrate ['ɑːbɪtreɪt] *vt* - *vi* arbitrar.

arc [ɑːk] *n* arco.

arcade [ɑː'keɪd] *n* **1** galería comercial. **2** salón recreativo.
■ **arcade game** videojuego.

arch [ɑːtʃ] *n* (*pl* -**es**) arco, bóveda.
► *vt* **1** arquear, enarcar. **2** abovedar.
► *vi* **1** arquearse, combarse. **2** formar bóveda.

archaeological [ɑːkɪə'lɒdʒɪkəl] *adj* arqueológico,-a.

archaeologist [ɑːkɪ'blədʒɪst] *n* arqueólogo,-a.

archaeology [ɑːkɪ'blədʒɪ] *n* arqueología.

archaic [ɑː'keɪɪk] *adj* arcaico,-a.

archbishop [ɑːtʃ'bɪʃəp] *n* arzobispo.

archer ['ɑːtʃəʳ] *n* arquero.

archery ['ɑːtʃərɪ] *n* tiro con arco.

archetypal [ɑːkɪ'taɪpəl] *adj* arquetípico,-a.

archipelago [ɑːkɪ'pelɪgəʊ] *n* (*pl* -**s** o -**es**) archipiélago.

architect ['ɑːkɪtekt] *n* arquitecto,-a.

architecture ['ɑːkɪtektʃəʳ] *n* arquitectura.

archive ['ɑːkaɪv] *npl* archivo.

Arctic ['ɑːktɪk] *adj* ártico,-a.
► *n* el Ártico.
■ **the Arctic Circle** el Círculo Polar Ártico.
■ **the Arctic Ocean** el Océano Ártico.

ardent ['ɑːdənt] *adj* apasionado,-a, fervoroso,-a.

ardour ['ɑːdəʳ] (US **ardor**) *n* ardor.

arduous ['ɑːdjʊəs] *adj* arduo,-a.

are [ɑːʳ, əʳ] *pres* → be.

area ['eərɪə] *n* **1** área, superficie. **2** región, zona. **3** campo *(de conocimientos)*.

arena [ə'riːnə] *n* **1** estadio. **2** ruedo *(de plaza de toros)*. **3** *fig* ámbito.

Argentina [ɑːdʒən'tiːnə] *n* Argentina.

Argentine ['ɑːdʒəntaɪn] *adj-n* argentino,-a.

Argentinian [ɑːdʒən'tɪnɪən] *adj* argentino,-a.
► *n* argentino,-a.

argue ['ɑːgjuː] *vi* **1** discutir. **2** argüir, argumentar.

argument ['ɑːgjʊmənt] *n* **1** discusión, disputa. **2** argumento: *to have an argument with SB*, discutir con ALGN.

argumentative [ɑːgjʊ'mentətɪv] *adj* con ánimo de discutir, que le gusta replicar.

arid ['ærɪd] *adj* árido,-a.

Aries ['eəriːz] *n* Aries.

arise [ə'raɪz] *vi* (*pt* **arose** [ə'rəʊz], *pp* **arisen** [ə'rɪzən]). **1** surgir, provenir de. **2** presentarse.

aristocracy [ærɪs'tɒkrəsɪ] *n* aristocracia.

aristocrat ['ærɪstəkræt] *n* aristócrata.

aristocratic [ærɪstə'krætɪk] *adj* aristocrático,-a.

arithmetic [ə'rɪθmətɪk] *n* aritmética.

ark [ɑːk] *n* arca.
■ **Noah's ark** el arca de Noé.

arm [ɑːm] *n* **1** brazo. **2** manga. **3** arma.
► *vt* armar.
► *vi* armarse.
► *npl* **arms** armas.
● **arm in arm** cogidos,-as del brazo.
● **with open arms** con los brazos abiertos.
● **to keep SB at arm's length** mantener a ALGN a distancia.
■ **arms race** carrera armamentística.

armament ['ɑːməmənts] *n* armamento.

armchair [ɑːm'tʃeəʳ] *n* sillón.

armistice ['ɑːmɪstɪs] *n* armisticio.

armour ['ɑːməʳ] (US **armor**) *n* **1** armadura. **2** blindaje.

armpit ['ɑːmpɪt] *n* sobaco, axila.

army ['ɑːmɪ] *n* (*pl* **-ies**) ejército.

aroma [ə'rəʊmə] *n* aroma.

aromatic [ærə'mætɪk] *adj* aromático,-a.

arose [ə'rəʊz] *pt* → arise.

around [ə'raʊnd] *adv* **1** alrededor: *is there anybody around?*, ¿hay alguien?, ¿hay alguien cerca?; *don't leave your money around, put it away*, no dejes tu dinero por ahí, guárdalo. **2**: *they cycle around together*, van juntos en bicicleta. **3**: *£1 coins have been around for some time*, hace tiempo que circulan las monedas de una libra; *there isn't much fresh fruit around*, hay poca fruta fresca. **4**: *turn around please*, dese la vuelta por favor.
► *prep* **1** alrededor de: *they sat around the table*, estaban sentados alrededor de la mesa. **2** más o menos, sobre, cerca de: *it costs around £5,000*, cuesta unas cinco mil libras. **3**: *there aren't many shops around here*, hay pocas tiendas por aquí. **4**: *there were clothes all around the room*, había ropa por toda la habitación. **5** alrededor de: *he put his arms around her*, la rodeó con sus brazos.
● **around the corner** a la vuelta de la esquina.

arouse [ə'raʊz] *vt* **1** despertar, suscitar. **2** excitar.

arrange [ə'reɪndʒ] *vt* **1** arreglar, colocar, ordenar. **2** planear, organizar, concertar: *to arrange a meeting*, concertar una reunión. **3** acordar, arreglar.
● **to arrange to do** STH quedar en hacer algo.

arrangement [ə'reɪndʒmənt] *n* **1** arreglo *(floral)*. **2** acuerdo, arreglo: *to reach an arrangement*, llegar a un acuerdo. **3** arreglo *(musical)*.
► *npl* **arrangements** planes, preparativos.

arrears [ə'rɪəz] *npl* atrasos.

arrest [ə'rest] *n* arresto, detención.
► *vt* arrestar, detener: *to be under arrest*, estar detenido.

arrival [ə'raɪvəl] *n* llegada.
● **on arrival** al llegar.

arrive [ə'raɪv] *vi* llegar.

arrogance ['ærəgəns] *n* arrogancia.

arrogant ['ærəgənt] *adj* arrogante.

arrow ['ærəʊ] *n* flecha.

arse [ɑːs] *n vulg* culo.

arsenal ['ɑːsənəl] *n* arsenal.

arsenic ['ɑːsənɪk] *n* arsénico.

arson ['ɑːsən] *n* incendio provocado.

art [ɑːt] *n* arte.
► *npl* **arts** letras: *faculty of Arts*, Facultad de Filosofía y Letras.
■ **arts and crafts** artes y oficios.
■ **art gallery** galería de arte.
■ **the arts** las bellas artes.

artery ['ɑːtərɪ] *n* (*pl* **-ies**) arteria.

arthritic [ɑː'θrɪtɪk] *adj* artrítico,-a.

arthritis [ɑː'θraɪtəs] *n* artritis.

artichoke ['ɑːtɪtʃəʊk] *n* alcachofa.

article ['ɑːtɪkəl] *n* artículo.
■ **article of clothing** prenda de vestir.
■ **leading article** editorial.

articulate [(*adj*) ɑː'tɪkjʊlət(*vb*) ɑː'tɪkjʊleɪt] *adj* que se expresa bien, articulado,-a.
► *vt* **1** articular. **2** expresar.

artificial [ɑːtɪ'fɪʃəl] *adj* artificial.
■ **artificial flavouring** aroma artificial.

artillery [ɑː'tɪlərɪ] *n* artillería.

artisan ['ɑːtɪzæn] *n* artesano,-a.

artist ['ɑːtɪst] *n* artista.

artistic [ɑː'tɪstɪk] *adj* artístico,-a.

as [æz, əz] *prep* como: *he works as a clerk*, trabaja de oficinista; *dressed as a monkey*, disfrazado,-a de mono.
► *conj* **1** mientras, cuando: *she sang as she painted*, cantaba mientras pintaba. **2** como, ya que, puesto que: *as the hotel was full, we had to look for another*, como el hotel estaba completo, tuvimos que buscar otro. **3** como: *leave everything as it is*, deja todo tal como está; *as you know*, como sabes.
● **as ... as 1** tan ... como: *as big as an elephant*, tan grande como un elefante. **2** tanto como: *eat as much as you like*, come tanto como quieras; *he works as little as possible*, trabaja lo mínimo posible.
● **as a rule** como regla.
● **as far as** hasta.
● **as far as I know** que yo sepa.
● **as far as I'm concerned** por lo que a mí respecta.
● **as for** en cuanto a.

● **as regards** en cuanto a.

● **as if** como si.

● **as long as** mientras.

● **as of** desde.

● **as soon as** tan pronto como.

● **as soon as possible** cuanto antes.

● **as though** como si.

● **as well as** además de.

● **as yet** hasta ahora.

a.s.a.p. [ˈeɪˈesˈeɪˈpiː] *abbr* (**as soon as possible**) en cuanto sea posible.

asbestos [æsˈbestəs] *n* amianto.

ascend [əˈsend] *vt - vi* ascender, subir.

ascendancy [əˈsendənsɪ] *n* ascendiente.

ascendant [əˈsendənt] *n* ascendiente: **to be in the ascendant**, estar en auge.

ascent [əˈsent] *n* **1** subida, ascenso, escalada. **2** cuesta.

ascertain [æsəˈteɪn] *vt* averiguar.

ASCII [ˈæskiː] *abbr* (**American Standard Code for Information Interchange**) ASCII.

ascribe [əˈskraɪb] *vt* atribuir.

ash¹ [æʃ] *n* (*pl* **-es**) ceniza.

■ **Ash Wednesday** miércoles de ceniza.

ash² [æʃ] *n* (*pl* **-es**) fresno.

ashamed [əˈʃeɪmd] *adj* avergonzado,-a.

● **to be ashamed of** avergonzarse de, tener vergüenza de.

ashore [əˈʃɔːˈ] *adv* en tierra, a tierra.

● **to go ashore** desembarcar.

ashtray [ˈæʃtreɪ] *n* cenicero.

Asia [ˈeɪʃə, ˈeɪʒə] *n* Asia.

Asian [ˈeɪʃən, ˈeɪʒən] *adj* asiático,-a.

▶ *n* asiático,-a.

aside [əˈsaɪd] *adv* al lado, a un lado.

▶ *n* aparte (*en teatro*).

● **to set aside** apartar, reservar.

● **to step aside** apartarse.

● **to take SB aside** separar a ALGN para hablarle aparte.

ask [ɑːsk] *vt* **1** preguntar: **to ask a question**, hacer una pregunta. **2** pedir. **3** invitar, convidar: **they asked me to dinner**, me invitaron a cenar.

to ask after *vt* preguntar por.

to ask back *vt* **1** invitar a casa. **2** volver a invitar.

to ask for *vt* pedir.

to ask out *vt* invitar a salir.

asleep [əˈsliːp] *adj - adv* dormido,-a: **to fall asleep**, dormirse.

asparagus [æsˈpærəgəs] *n* espárragos.

Es incontable y el verbo va en singular: **an asparagus tip**, un espárrago.

aspect [ˈæspekt] *n* **1** aspecto. **2** orientación (*de edificio*).

asphalt [ˈæsfælt] *n* asfalto.

asphyxiate [əsˈfɪksɪeɪt] *vt* asfixiar.

▶ *vi* asfixiarse.

aspiration [æspəˈreɪʃən] *n* aspiración, ambición.

aspire [əˈspaɪəˈ] *vi* aspirar.

aspirin® [ˈæspɪrɪn] *n* aspirina®.

ass¹ [æs] *n* (*pl* **-es**) burro,-a, asno,-a.

ass² [æs] *n* (*pl* **-es**) US *vulg* culo.

assailant [əˈseɪlənt] *n* atacante, agresor,-ra.

assassin [əˈsæsɪn] *n* asesino,-a.

Se emplea sólo cuando la víctima es un personaje importante. **murderer** es de uso más general.

assassinate [əˈsæsɪneɪt] *vt* asesinar.

Se emplea sólo cuando la víctima es un personaje importante. **murder** es de uso más general.

assassination [əsæsɪˈneɪʃən] *n* asesinato.

Se emplea sólo cuando la víctima es un personaje importante. **murder** es de uso más general.

assault [əˈsɔːlt] *n* **1** asalto (*militar*). **2** agresión (*a persona*).

▶ *vt* **1** asaltar (*militar*). **2** agredir (*a persona*).

assemble [əˈsembəl] *vt* **1** reunir. **2** montar, armar.

▶ *vi* reunirse.

assembly [əˈsemblɪ] *n* (*pl* **-ies**). **1** reunión, asamblea. **2** montaje, ensamblaje.

■ **assembly hall** salón de actos.

assent [əˈsent] *n* asentimiento.

▶ *vi* asentir.

assert [əˈsɜːt] *vt* **1** aseverar, afirmar. **2** imponer (*autoridad*).

● **to assert oneself** imponerse.

assertion [əˈsɜːʃən] *n* aseveración (*afirmación*).

assess [əˈses] *vt* **1** tasar, valorar. **2** calcular. **3** *fig* evaluar.

assessment [əˈsesmənt] *n* **1** tasación, valoración. **2** cálculo. **3** *fig* evaluación.

asset [ˈæset] *n* cualidad positiva, ventaja, baza.

▶ *npl* **assets** bienes.

assign [əˈsaɪn] *vt* **1** asignar, encomendar. **2** designar. **3** destinar.

assignment [ə'saɪnmənt] *n* **1** misión. **2** tarea, trabajo.

assimilate [ə'sɪmɪleɪt] *vt-vi* asimilar(se).

assimilation [əsɪmɪ'leɪʃən] *n* asimilación.

assist [ə'sɪst] *vt* ayudar.

assistance [ə'sɪstəns] *n* ayuda.

assistant [ə'sɪstənt] *n* ayudante.

■ **assistant manager** subdirector,-ra.

associate [(*adj-n*) ə'səʊʃiət(*vb*) ə'səʊʃieɪt] *adj* asociado,-a.

► *n* socio,-a.

► *vt-vi* asociar(se).

● **to associate with** SB relacionarse con ALGN.

association [əsəʊsɪ'eɪʃən] *n* asociación.

assorted [ə'sɔːtɪd] *adj* surtido,-a, variado,-a.

assortment [ə'sɔːtmənt] *n* surtido, variedad.

assume [ə'sjuːm] *vt* **1** suponer. **2** tomar, asumir *(responsabilidad)*. **3** adoptar *(actitud)*.

assumption [ə'sʌmpʃən] *n* **1** suposición. **2** toma, asunción *(de poder)*.

assurance [ə'ʃʊərəns] *n* **1** garantía. **2** confianza. **3** certeza. **4** seguro.

assure [ə'ʃʊəʳ] *vt* asegurar, garantizar.

assured [ə'ʃʊəd] *adj* seguro,-a.

asterisk ['æstərɪsk] *n* asterisco.

asthma ['æsmə] *n* asma.

asthmatic [æs'mætɪk] *adj - n* asmático,-a.

astonish [əs'tɒnɪʃ] *vt* asombrar, sorprender.

astonishing [əs'tɒnɪʃɪŋ] *adj* asombroso,-a, sorprendente.

astonishment [əs'tɒnɪʃmənt] *n* asombro, estupefacción.

astound [əs'taʊnd] *vt* pasmar, asombrar.

astray [əs'treɪ] *adj - adv* extraviado,-a.

● **to go astray** descarriarse.

astride [ə'straɪd] *prep* a horcajadas sobre.

astrologer [əs'trɒlədʒəʳ] *n* astrólogo,-a.

astrology [əs'trɒlədʒɪ] *n* astrología.

astronaut ['æstrənɔːt] *n* astronauta.

astronomer [əs'trɒnəməʳ] *n* astrónomo,-a.

astronomical [æstrə'nɒmɪkəl] *n* astronómico,-a.

astronomy [əs'trɒnəmɪ] *n* astronomía.

astute [əs'tjuːt] *adj* astuto,-a, sagaz.

asylum [ə'saɪləm] *n* **1** asilo, refugio. **2** manicomio.

at [æt, ət] *prep* **1** en, a: *at the door*, a la puerta; *at home*, en casa; *at school*, en el colegio; *at work*, en el trabajo. **2** a: *at two o'clock*, a las dos; *at night*, por la noche; *at Christmas*, en Navidad; *at the beginning/end*, al principio/final. **3** a, contra: *to shout at somebody*, gritarle a alguien; *to shoot at*, disparar contra; *to throw a stone at*, lanzar una piedra contra. **4** a: *at 50 miles an hour*, a 50 millas la hora; *at £1000 a ton*, a mil libras la tonelada; *three at a time*, de tres en tres. **5**: *he's good at French*, se le da bien el francés; *he's good at painting*, pinta bien.

● **at first** al principio.

● **at last!** ¡por fin!

● **at least** por lo menos.

● **at once** en seguida.

ate [et, eɪt] *pt* → eat.

atheism ['eɪθɪɪzəm] *n* ateísmo.

atheist ['eɪθɪɪst] *n* ateo,-a.

athlete ['æθliːt] *n* atleta.

athletic [æθ'letɪk] *adj* atlético,-a.

athletics [æθ'letɪks] *n* atletismo.

Es incontable y el verbo va en singular.

Atlantic [ət'læntɪk] *adj* atlántico,-a.

■ **the Atlantic Ocean** el océano Atlántico.

atlas ['ætləs] *n (pl* **atlases***)* atlas.

atmosphere ['ætməsfɪəʳ] *n* **1** atmósfera. **2** ambiente.

atom ['ætəm] *n* átomo.

■ **atom bomb** bomba atómica.

atomic [ə'tɒmɪk] *adj* atómico,-a.

atrocious [ə'trəʊʃəs] *adj* atroz.

atrocity [ə'trɒsɪtɪ] *n (pl* **-ies***)* atrocidad.

attach [ə'tætʃ] *vt* **1** sujetar. **2** atar. **3** pegar. **4** adjuntar: *please see the attached letter*, véase la carta adjunta.

● **to attach importance to** STH considerar importante algo.

● **to be attached to** tener cariño a.

attachment [ə'tætʃmənt] *n* **1** accesorio. **2** archivo adjunto, anexo. **3** cariño, apego.

attack [ə'tæk] *n* **1** ataque. **2** atentado.

► *vt* **1** atacar. **2** combatir.

attain [ə'teɪn] *vt* lograr, alcanzar.

attempt [ə'tempt] *n* intento, tentativa.

► *vt* intentar.

● **to make an attempt on** SB's **life** atentar contra la vida de ALGN.

● **to make an attempt to do** STH intentar hacer algo.

attend [ə'tend] *vt* **1** asistir a: *the course*

was well attended, asistió mucha gente al curso. **2** atender, cuidar, ocuparse de.
▶ *vi* asistir.

to attend to *vt* **1** ocuparse de: *I have an urgent matter to attend to*, tengo que ocuparme de un asunto urgente. **2** despachar.

attendance [əˈtendəns] *n* **1** asistencia. **2** asistentes.

attendant [əˈtendənt] *n* vigilante, encargado,-a.

attention [əˈtenʃən] *n* atención.
● **attention!** ¡firmes!
● **to pay attention** prestar atención.
● **to stand to attention** cuadrarse.

attentive [əˈtentɪv] *adj* atento,-a.

attic [ˈætɪk] *n* desván, buhardilla.

attire [əˈtaɪəʳ] *n* atuendo, atavío.

attitude [ˈætɪtjuːd] *n* **1** actitud. **2** postura.

attn [fɔːrˈaɪəˈtenʃənv] *abbr* **(for the attention of)** a la atención de.

attorney [əˈtɜːnɪ] *n* US abogado,-a.
■ **Attorney General** GB Fiscal General.

attract [əˈtrækt] *vt* atraer.
● **to attract attention** llamar la atención.

attraction [əˈtrækʃən] *n* **1** atracción. **2** atractivo.

attractive [əˈtræktɪv] *adj* atractivo,-a.

attribute [*(n)* ˈætrɪbjuːt*(vb)* əˈtrɪbjuːt] *n* atributo.
▶ *vt* atribuir.

aubergine [ˈəʊbəʒiːn] *n* berenjena.

auction [ˈɔːkʃən] *n* subasta.
▶ *vt* subastar.

audacity [ɔːˈdæsɪtɪ] *n* audacia.

audible [ˈɔːdɪbəl] *adj* audible, perceptible.

audience [ˈɔːdɪəns] *n* **1** público, espectadores. **2** audiencia *(de TV)*.

audio-visual [ɔːdɪəʊˈvɪzjʊəl] *adj* audiovisual.

audit [ˈɔːdɪt] *n* revisión de cuentas, auditoría.
▶ *vt* revisar, auditar.

audition [ɔːˈdɪʃən] *n* prueba, audición.

auditor [ˈɔːdɪtəʳ] *n* revisor,-ra de cuentas, auditor,-a.

auditorium [ɔːdɪˈtɔːrɪəm] *n (pl* **auditoria)** auditorio, sala.

augment [ɔːgˈment] *vt-vi* aumentar.

august [ɔːˈgʌst] *adj* augusto,-a.

August [ˈɔːgəst] *n* agosto.

aunt [ɑːnt] *n* tía.

auntie [ˈɑːntɪ] *n fam* tita.

au pair [əʊˈpeəʳ] *n* au pair.

aura [ˈɔːrə] *n* aura, halo.

auspices [ˈɔːspɪsɪz] *npl* auspicios: *under the auspices of*, bajo los auspicios de.

austere [ɒsˈtɪəʳ] *adj* austero,-a.

austerity [ɒsˈterɪtɪ] *n (pl* **-ies)** austeridad.

Australia [ɒˈstreɪlɪə] *n* Australia.

Australian [ɒˈstreɪlɪən] *adj* australiano,-a.
▶ *n* **1** australiano,-a. **2** australiano.

Austria [ˈɒstrɪə] *n* Austria.

Austrian [ˈɒstrɪən] *adj* austríaco,-a, austriaco,-a.
▶ *n* austríaco,-a, austriaco,-a.

authentic [ɔːˈθentɪk] *adj* auténtico,-a.

authenticity [ɔːθenˈtɪsɪtɪ] *n* autenticidad.

author [ˈɔːθəʳ] *n* autor,-ra, escritor,-ra.

authoritarian [ɔːθɒrɪˈteərɪən] *adj* autoritario,-a.

authoritative [ɔːˈθɒrɪtətɪv] *adj* **1** autorizado,-a, fidedigno,-a *(fuente)*. **2** autoritario,-a *(persona)*.

authority [ɔːˈθɒrɪtɪ] *n (pl* **-ies)** autoridad.
● **on good authority** de buena tinta.

authorization [ɔːθəraɪˈzeɪʃən] *n* autorización.

authorize [ˈɔːθəraɪz] *vt* autorizar.

autobiographical [ɔːtəbaɪəˈgræfɪkəl] *adj* autobiográfico,-a.

autobiography [ɔːtəbaɪˈɒgrəfɪ] *n (pl* **-ies)** autobiografía.

autograph [ˈɔːtəgrɑːf] *n* autógrafo.

automatic [ɔːtəˈmætɪk] *adj* automático,-a.

automaton [ɔːˈtɒmətən] *n* autómata.

automobile [ˈɔːtəməbiːl] *n* automóvil.

autonomous [ɔːˈtɒnəməs] *adj* autónomo,-a.

autonomy [ɔːˈtɒnəmɪ] *n* autonomía.

autopsy [ˈɔːtɒpsɪ] *n (pl* **-ies)** autopsia.

autoteller [ˈɔːtəʊtələʳ] *n* cajero automático.

autumn [ˈɔːtəm] *n* otoño.

auxiliary [ɔːgˈzɪljərɪ] *adj* auxiliar.
■ **auxiliary verb** verbo auxiliar.

avail [əˈveɪl] *n* .
● **to no avail** en vano.
● **to avail oneself of** servirse de.

available [əˈveɪləbəl] *adj* **1** disponible: *it's available in four colours*, lo hay en cuatro colores. **2** libre.

avalanche [ˈævəlɑːnʃ] *n* alud, avalancha.

Ave [ˈævənjuː] *abbr* **(Avenue)** Av., Avda.

avenge [əˈvendʒ] *vt* vengar.

avenue [ˈævənjuː] *n* avenida.

average ['ævərɪdʒ] *n* promedio, media.
► *adj* **1** medio,-a: *average temperature*, temperatura media. **2** corriente, regular, normal.
► *vt* hacer un promedio de: *I average 10 cigarettes a day*, fumo un promedio de medio paquete al día.
● **above average** por encima de la media.
● **below average** por debajo de la media.
● **on average** por término medio.

aversion [əˈvɜːʒən] *n* aversión.

avert [əˈvɜːt] *vt* evitar.
● **to avert one's eyes** apartar la vista.

aviary ['eɪvjəri] *n* (*pl* **-ies**) pajarera.

aviation [eɪvɪˈeɪʃən] *n* aviación.

aviator ['eɪvɪeɪtəʳ] *n* aviador,-ra.

avid ['ævɪd] *adj* ávido,-a.

avocado [ævəˈkɑːdəʊ] (También **avocado pear**) *n* (*pl* **avocados**) aguacate.

avoid [əˈvɔɪd] *vt* **1** evitar *(lugar)*. **2** eludir *(responsabilidad)*. **3** esquivar *(golpe)*.

await [əˈweɪt] *vt fml* aguardar, esperar.

awake [əˈweɪk] *adj* despierto,-a.
► *vt-vi* (*pt* **awoke** [əˈwəʊk], *pp* **awoken** [əˈwəʊkən]) despertar(se).

awaken [əˈweɪkən] *vt - vi* → awake.

award [əˈwɔːd] *n* **1** premio. **2** beca. **3** indemnización.
► *vt* **1** otorgar, conceder. **2** adjudicar.

aware [əˈweəʳ] *adj* consciente.
● **to be aware of** ser consciente de.
● **to become aware of** darse cuenta de.

away [əˈweɪ] *adv* **1** lejos, fuera: *he lives 4 km away*, vive a 4 km de aquí; *the wedding is 6 weeks away*, faltan 6 semanas para la boda. **2**: *they worked away all day*, trabajaron todo el día; *to talk away*, no parar de hablar.
● **to be away** estar fuera, estar ausente.
● **to go away** irse, marcharse.
● **to play away** jugar fuera de casa *(equipo deportivo)*.
● **to run away** irse corriendo.

> **away** también se combina con muchos verbos, por ejemplo: *to give away*, regalar; *to go away*, irse; *to keep away*, no acercarse; *to look away*, apartar la vista.

awe [ɔː] *n* **1** sobrecogimiento. **2** temor.

awful ['ɔːfʊl] *adj* **1** atroz, horrible. **2** tremendo.

awfully ['ɔːfʊli] *adv* **1** *fam* terriblemente. **2** tremendamente.

awkward ['ɔːkwəd] *adj* **1** torpe *(gesto)*. **2** difícil, complicado,-a. **3** embarazoso,-a, delicado,-a *(situación)*. **4** inconveniente, inoportuno,-a. **5** incómodo,-a *(silencio)*.
● **to feel awkward** encontrarse incómodo.

awning ['ɔːnɪŋ] *n* toldo.

awoke [əˈwəʊk] *pt* → awake.

awoken [əˈwəʊkən] *pp* → awake.

ax [æks] *n* (*pl* **axes** ['æksɪz]) US hacha.

axe [æks] *n* (*pl* **axes** ['æksɪz]) GB hacha.

axis ['æksɪs] *n* (*pl* **axes** ['æksiːz]) eje.

axle ['æksəl] *n* eje.

azure ['eɪʒəʳ] *adj-n* azul celeste.

B

b [bɔːn] *abbr (born)* nacido,-a.

B & B [ˈbiːənˈbiː] *abbr (bed and breakfast)* fonda, hotel.

BA [ˈbiːˈeɪ] *abbr (Bachelor of Arts)* licenciado,-a en letras.

baa [bɑː] *vi* balar.

babble [ˈbæbəl] *vt-vi* **1** farfullar. **2** balbucear.
► *vi* parlotear.
► *n* murmullo.

baboon [bəˈbuːn] *n* babuino.

baby [ˈbeɪbɪ] *n (pl -ies)* bebé, niño,-a: *a new born baby*, un recién nacido.

babyish [ˈbeɪbɪ] *adj* de niño pequeño.

baby-sit [ˈbeɪbɪsɪt] *vi (pt & pp **baby-sat**, ger **baby-sitting**)* hacer de canguro, cuidar niños.

baby-sitter [ˈbeɪbɪsɪtə] *n* canguro.

bachelor [ˈbætʃələ] *n* soltero.
■ **Bachelor of Arts** licenciado,-a en Filosofía y Letras.
■ **Bachelor of Science** licenciado,-a en Ciencias.

back [bæk] *adj* trasero,-a, posterior: *the back seat*, el asiento trasero.
► *n* **1** espalda: *lie on your back*, échate de espaldas. **2** lomo *(de animal)*. **3** respaldo *(de silla)*. **4** dorso, revés. **5** fondo, parte de atrás: *can you hear me at the back?*, ¿me escucháis al fondo? **6** defensa *(en deportes)*.
► *adv* **1** atrás, hacia atrás, hace: *several years back*, hace varios años. **2** atrás, hacia atrás: *stand back from the edge*, apártate del filo; *stand back*, ¡atrás! **3** de vuelta: *on the way back home*, en el camino de vuelta a casa.
► *vt* **1** apoyar, respaldar. **2** financiar. **3** apostar por. **4** dar marcha atrás a *(coche)*.
► *vi* **1** retroceder. **2** ir marcha atrás.
● **back to front** al revés.
● **behind SB's back** a espaldas de ALGN.
● **to answer back** contestar, replicar.
● **to be back** estar de vuelta.
● **to come/go back** volver.
● **to hit back** devolver el golpe, contraatacar.
● **to have one's back to the wall** estar entre la espada y la pared.
● **to put/give back** devolver.
● **to phone back** volver a llamar.
● **to turn one's back on** volver la espalda a.
■ **back door** puerta trasera.
■ **back number** número atrasado.
■ **back pay** atrasos.
■ **back seat** asiento de atrás.
■ **back street** callejuela.
■ **back wheel** rueda trasera.

to back away *vi* retroceder.

to back down *vi* claudicar.

to back out *vi* echarse atrás, volverse atrás.

to back up *vt* **1** hacer una copia de seguridad. **2** apoyar.

backache [ˈbækeɪk] *n* dolor de espalda.

backbone [ˈbækbəʊn] *n* **1** columna vertebral. **2** *fig* carácter, empuje.

backdated [bækˈdeɪtɪd] *adj* con efecto retroactivo.

backer [ˈbækə] *n* promotor,-ra.

backfire [bækˈfaɪə] *vt* fallar: *our plan backfired*, nos salió el tiro por la culata.

background [ˈbækɡraʊnd] *n* **1** fondo *(de imagen)*. **2** *fig* origen, formación: *he comes* *from a humble background*, es de origen humilde.

■ **background music** música de fondo.

backhand ['bækhænd] *n* revés.

backing ['bækɪŋ] *n* **1** apoyo, respaldo. **2** acompañamiento *(musical)*.

backlash ['bæklæʃ] *n* (*pl* **-es**) reacción violenta y repentina.

backlog ['bæklɒg] *n* acumulación.

backpack ['bækpæk] *n* mochila.

backside [bæk'saɪd] *n fam* trasero.

backstroke ['bækstrəʊk] *n* espalda *(en natación)*.

● **to do the backstroke** nadar de espaldas.

backup ['bækʌp] *n* apoyo.

■ **backup copy** copia de seguridad.

backward ['bækwəd] *adj* **1** hacia atrás: *he took a backward step*, dio un paso hacia atrás. **2** atrasado,-a, retrasado. **3** subdesarrollado,-a.

▶ *adv* → backwards.

backwards ['bækwədz] *adv* **1** hacia atrás: *he was walking backwards*, caminaba hacia atrás. **2** al revés: *you're doing it backwards*, lo estás haciendo al revés.

● **backwards and forwards** de acá para allá.

bacon ['beɪkən] *n* bacon.

bacterium [bæk'tɪərɪəm] *n* (*pl* **bacteria** [bæk'tɪərɪə]) bacteria.

bad [bæd] *adj* (*comp* **worse**, *superl* **worst**). **1** malo,-a, mal. **2** podrido,-a, malo,-a, pasado,-a. **3** grave, fuerte: *a bad accident*, un accidente grave. **4** nocivo,-a, perjudicial. **5** malo,-a, travieso, -a. **6** fuerte *(dolor de cabeza)*.

▶ *n* lo malo.

● **to be bad at something** darse mal algo, ser malo en algo.

● **to come to a bad end** acabar mal.

● **to go bad, echarse a perder** pudrirse.

● **to go from bad to worse** ir de mal en peor.

baddie ['bædɪ] *n fam* malo,-a de la película.

baddy ['bædɪ] *n* (*pl* **-ies**) *fam* malo,-a de la película.

bade [beɪd] *pt* → bid.

badge [bædʒ] *n* **1** insignia, distintivo. **2** chapa.

badger ['bædʒə'] *n* tejón.

badly ['bædlɪ] *adv* **1** mal: *they behaved badly*, se portaron mal. **2** gravemente. **3** muchísimo,-a, muy: *we badly need the money*, nos hace mucha falta el dinero.

badminton ['bædmɪntən] *n* bádminton.

bad-tempered [bæd'tempəd] *adj* .

● **to be bad-tempered** tener mal carácter, estar de mal humor.

baffle ['bæfəl] *vt* confundir, desconcertar.

BAFTA ['bæftə] *abbr (British Academy of Film and Television Arts)* Academia británica de cine y televisión.

bag [bæg] *n* **1** bolsa, saco. **2** bolso.

● **bags of** montones de.

baggage ['bægɪdʒ] *n* equipaje.

baggy ['bægɪ] *adj* (**-ier**, **-iest**) holgado,-a, ancho,-a.

bagpipes ['bægpaɪps] *npl* gaita.

bail [beɪl] *n* fianza.

to bail out *vt* **1** conseguir la libertad de alguien bajo fianza. **2** *fig* sacar de un apuro. **3** achicar *(barco)*.

bailiff ['beɪlɪf] *n* (*pl* **bailiffs**) alguacil.

bait [beɪt] *n* cebo.

▶ *vt* **1** cebar. **2** atosigar.

bake [beɪk] *vt* cocer al horno, hornear.

▶ *vi* asarse.

■ **baked beans** alubias cocidas con salsa de tomate.

baker ['beɪkə'] *n* panadero,-a.

baker's ['beɪkəz] *n* panadería.

bakery ['beɪkərɪ] *n* (*pl* **-ies**) panadería.

balance ['bæləns] *n* **1** equilibrio: *to lose balance*, perder el equilibrio. **2** balanza. **3** saldo, balance. **4** resto.

▶ *vt* **1** equilibrar, mantener en equilibrio. **2** equilibrar, saldar *(cuentas)*.

▶ *vi* **1** mantenerse en equilibrio. **2** cuadrar *(cuentas)*.

balcony ['bælkənɪ] *n* (*pl* **-ies**). **1** balcón. **2** anfiteatro, galería.

bald [bɔːld] *adj* **1** calvo,-a. **2** escueto,-a.

baldly ['bɔːldlɪ] *adv* francamente.

baldness ['bɔːldnəs] *n* calvicie.

Balearic [bælɪˈærɪk] *adj* balear.

■ **the Balearic Islands** las islas Baleares.

balk [bɔːk] *vt* poner obstáculos a, frustrar.

▶ *vi* negarse.

Balkan ['bɔːlkən] *adj* balcánico,-a.

■ **the Balkans** los Balcanes.

ball [bɔːl] *n* **1** pelota, balón, bola. **2** ovillo. **3** baile, fiesta.

▶ *npl* **balls** *vulg* cojones, huevos.

ballad ['bæləd] *n* balada.

ballerina [bælə'ri:nə] *n* bailarina.
ballet ['bæleɪ] *n* ballet.
■ **ballet dancer** bailarín, bailarina.
ballistics [bə'lɪstɪks] *n* balística.
Es incontable y el verbo va en singular.
balloon [bə'lu:n] *n* globo.
ballot ['bælət] *n* 1 votación. 2 papeleta.
■ **ballot box** urna *(para votar)*.
ballpoint pen ['bɔ:lpɔɪnt pen] *n* bolígrafo.
ballroom ['bɔ:lru:m] *n* sala de baile.
balm [ba:m] *n* bálsamo.
balmy ['ba:mɪ] *adj* (**-ier**, **-iest**) suave, apacible.
balsam ['bɔ:lsəm] *n* → balm.
Baltic ['bɔ:ltɪk] *adj* báltico,-a.
■ **the Baltic Sea** el mar Báltico.
balustrade [bælə'streɪd] *n* balaustrada.
bamboo [bæm'bu:] *n* (*pl* **bamboos**) bambú.
ban [bæn] *n* prohibición.
▶ *vt* (*pt & pp* **banned**, *ger* **banning**) prohibir.
banal [bə'nɑːl] *adj* banal.
banana [bə'nɑːnə] *n* plátano, banana.
band [bænd] *n* 1 banda, conjunto, grupo de música. 2 cinta, tira: *a hair band*, una cinta para el pelo. 3 raya, franja: *a jersey with a red band*, un jersey con una franja roja. 4 pandilla, banda.
● **to band together** unirse.
bandage ['bændɪdʒ] *n* venda, vendaje.
▶ *vt* vendar.
bandit ['bændɪt] *n* bandido,-a.
bandstand ['bændstænd] *n* quiosco de música.
bandwagon ['bændwægən] *n* .
● **to jump on the bandwagon** subirse al tren.
bandy ['bændɪ] *vt* **bandy words with** discutir con.
to bandy about *vt* comentar, barajar.
bandy-legged ['bændɪ'legd] *adj* estevado,-a, de piernas arqueadas.
bang [bæŋ] *n* 1 golpe. 2 porrazo, estampido, estallido, portazo.
▶ *vt* golpear, dar un golpe a.
▶ *vi* golpear, dar golpes: *the window banged shut*, la ventana se cerró de golpe.
▶ *adv fam* justo: *bang in the middle*, justo en medio.
● **to bang the door** dar un portazo.

banger ['bæŋəʳ] *n* 1 petardo. 2 GB *fam* salchicha. 3 *fam* tartana.
bangle ['bæŋgəl] *n* pulsera, brazalete.
banish ['bænɪʃ] *vt* desterrar.
banister ['bænɪstəʳ] *n* barandilla.
banjo ['bændʒəʊ] *n* (*pl* **-s** o **-es**) banjo.
bank¹ [bæŋk] *n* banco, caja.
▶ *vt* ingresar, depositar.
■ **bank account** cuenta bancaria.
■ **bank holiday** GB día festivo.
bank² [bæŋk] *n* 1 banco *(para sentarse)*. 2 ribera, orilla *(de río)*. 3 loma, terraplén.
to bank on *vt* contar con.
banker ['bæŋkəʳ] *n* banquero,-a.
banking ['bæŋkɪŋ] *n* banca.
banknote ['bæŋknəʊt] *n* billete de banco.
bankrupt ['bæŋkrʌpt] *adj* en quiebra, en bancarrota.
● **to go bankrupt** quebrar.
bankruptcy ['bæŋkrʌptsɪ] *n* (*pl* **-ies**) bancarrota, quiebra.
banner ['bænəʳ] *n* 1 estandarte. 2 pancarta.
banquet ['bæŋkwɪt] *n* banquete.
banter ['bæntəʳ] *n* bromas, chanzas.
▶ *vi* bromear.
baptism ['bæptɪzəm] *n* 1 bautismo. 2 bautizo.
baptize [bæp'taɪz] *vt* bautizar.
bar [ba:ʳ] *n* 1 barra, barrote *(en ventana)*. 2 pastilla *(de jabón)*. 3 tableta *(de chocolate)*. 4 obstáculo. 5 barra, mostrador. 6 bar. 7 **the Bar** GB conjunto de los abogados que ejercen en los tribunales superiores.
▶ *vt* (*pt & pp* **barred**, *ger* **barring**). 1 atrancar *(puerta)*. 2 cortar *(el paso)*. 3 prohibir, vedar.
▶ *prep* excepto.
● **behind bars** entre rejas.
barb [ba:b] *n* 1 púa. 2 lengüeta.
barbarian [ba:'beərɪən] *adj-n* bárbaro,-a.
barbaric [ba:'bærɪk] *adj* bárbaro,-a.
barbecue ['ba:bəkju:] *n* barbacoa.
barbed [ba:bd] *adj* armado,-a con púas, punzante.
barber ['ba:bəʳ] *n* barbero.
barber's ['ba:bəʳs] *n* barbería.
barbiturate [ba:'bɪtʃərət] *n* barbitúrico.
bare [beəʳ] *adj* 1 desnudo,-a, descubierto,-a: *in bare feet*, descalzo,-a. 2 vacío, -a: *the shelves were bare*, las estanterías estaban vacías. 3 mero,-a: *a bare 10%*, sólo el 10%. 4 justo: *the bare minimum*,

lo justo; **the bare necessities**, lo estricta-
mente necesario.

▶ *vt* desnudar, descubrir.

● **with my bare hands** sólo con mis
manos, con mis propias manos.

barefaced ['beəfeɪst] *adj* descarado,-a.

barefoot ['beəfʊt] *adj* descalzo,-a.

bareheaded [beə'hedɪd] *adj* con la cabeza descubierta, sin sombrero.

barely ['beəlɪ] *adv* apenas.

bargain ['bɑːgən] *n* **1** trato. **2** ganga.

▶ *vi* **1** negociar. **2** regatear.

to bargain for *vt* contar con.

barge [bɑːdʒ] *n* gabarra.

▶ *vi* irrumpir.

baritone ['bærɪtəʊn] *n* barítono.

bark[1] [bɑːk] *n* ladrido.

▶ *vi* ladrar.

● **to bark up the wrong tree** ir desen-
caminado,-a.

bark[2] [bɑːk] *n* corteza *(de árbol)*.

barley ['bɑːlɪ] *n* cebada.

barmaid ['bɑːmeɪd] *n* camarera.

barman ['bɑːmən] *n* *(pl* **barmen**
['bɑːmen]) camarero, barman.

barmy ['bɑːmɪ] *adj* (**-ier**, **-iest**) *fam* chiflado,-a.

barn [bɑːn] *n* granero.

barnacle ['bɑːnəkəl] *n* bálano.

barometer [bə'rɒmɪtə'] *n* barómetro.

baron ['bærən] *n* barón.

baroness ['bærənəs] *n* (*pl* **-es**) baronesa.

baroque [bə'rɒk] *adj* barroco,-a.

barrack ['bærək] *vt* abuchear.

barracks ['bærəks] *n* cuartel.

Puede considerarse singular o plural:
where is/are the barracks?, ¿dónde
está el cuartel?

barrage ['bærɑːʒ] *n* **1** presa, dique. **2** barrera de fuego *(balas, bombas)*. **3** *fig* bombardeo.

barrel ['bærəl] *n* **1** barril, tonel, cuba. **2** cañón *(de fusil)*.

barren ['bærən] *adj* estéril, árido,-a.

barricade [bærɪ'keɪd] *n* barricada.

▶ *vt* poner barricadas en.

barrier ['bærɪə'] *n* barrera.

barrister ['bærɪstə'] *n* abogado,-a *(capacitado,-a para actuar en tribunales superiores)*.

barrow ['bærəʊ] *n* carretilla.

barter ['bɑːtə'] *n* trueque.

▶ *vt* trocar.

basalt ['bæsɔːlt] *n* basalto.

base[1] [beɪs] *n* **1** base, pie *(de columna)*. **2**
sede, central *(de empresa)*. **3** base *(militar)*.

▶ *vt* basar: **the book is based on fact**, el
libro se basa en hechos reales; **he's based
in Cádiz**, tiene su base en Cádiz; **the
company is based in Paris**, la compañía
tiene su sede en París.

base[2] [beɪs] *adj* bajo,-a, vil.

■ **base metal** metal común.

baseball ['beɪsbɔːl] *n* béisbol.

basement ['beɪsmənt] *n* sótano.

bash [bæʃ] *n* (*pl* **-es**). **1** *fam* golpe, porrazo. **2** *fam* juerga.

▶ *vt* *fam* golpear.

● **to have a bash at** STH probar algo, intentar algo.

bashful ['bæʃfʊl] *adj* vergonzoso,-a, tímido,-a, modesto,-a.

basic ['beɪsɪk] *adj* básico,-a, elemental,
fundamental.

▶ *npl* **the basics** lo esencial.

basically ['beɪsɪklɪ] *adv* básicamente.

basin ['beɪsən] *n* **1** cuenco. **2** lavabo. **3**
cuenca.

basis ['beɪsɪs] *n* (*pl* **bases** ['beɪsiːz]) base,
fundamento.

En ocasiones, **basis** puede traducirse al
español mediante un adverbio: *on a
temporary basis*, temporalmente; *on a
regular basis*, regularmente; *on a weekly basis*, semanalmente.

bask [bɑːsk] *vi* tumbarse al sol.

basket ['bɑːskɪt] *n* cesta, cesto.

basketball ['bɑːskɪtbɔːl] *n* baloncesto.

Basque [bɑːsk] *adj* vasco,-a.

▶ *n* **1** vasco,-a. **2** vasco, euskera.

■ **the Basque Country** el País Vasco,
Euskadi.

bass[1] [bæs] *n* (*pl* **bass**) lubina.

bass[2] [beɪs] *adj* bajo,-a *(cantante, voz)*.

▶ *n* (*pl* **-es**). **1** bajo *(cantante)*. **2** graves
(tono). **3** bajo *(instrumento eléctrico)*. **4** contrabajo *(instrumento)*.

bassoon [bə'suːn] *n* fagot.

bastard ['bɑːstəd] *adj-n* bastardo,-a.

▶ *n* *vulg* cabrón.

baste [beɪst] *vt* bañar, mojar *(carne asada)*.

bat[1] [bæt] *n* murciélago.

bat[2] [bæt] *n* bate, pala.

▶ *vi* (*pt & pp* **batted**, *ger* **batting**) batear.

● **without batting an eyelid** sin inmu-
tarse.

batch [bætʃ] *n* (*pl* **-es**) lote, remesa, hornada.

■ **batch processing** tratamiento por lotes.

bath [bɑ:θ] *n* **1** baño. **2** bañera.
► *vt* bañar.
► *vi* bañarse.
► *npl* **baths** piscina (*pública*).
● **to have a bath** bañarse.

bathe [beɪð] *vi* bañarse.
► *vt* lavar (*herida*).

bather ['beɪðəʳ] *n* bañista.

bathing ['beɪðɪŋ] *n* baño.

■ **bathing costume** traje de baño, bañador.

■ **bathing suit** traje de baño.

bathrobe ['bɑ:θrəʊb] *n* albornoz.

bathroom ['bɑ:θru:m] *n* cuarto de baño.

bathtub ['bɑ:θtʌb] *n* bañera.

baton ['bætən] *n* **1** porra (*de policía*). **2** batuta (*música*). **3** testigo (*carrera de relevos*).

batsman ['bætsmən] *n* (*pl* **batsmen** ['bætsmən]) bateador (*en cricket*).

battalion [bə'tæljən] *n* batallón.

batter[1] ['bætəʳ] *n* rebozado.
► *vt* rebozar.
● **in batter** rebozado,-a.

batter[2] ['bætəʳ] *vt* golpear, apalear.

batter[3] ['bætəʳ] *n* bateador, -ra (*en cricket*).

battery ['bætəri] *n* (*pl* **-ies**). **1** batería, pila (*eléctrica*). **2** batería (*cañones*).

battle ['bætəl] *n* batalla, lucha.
► *vi* luchar (**with/against**, con/contra).

battlefield ['bætəlfi:ld] *n* campo de batalla.

battlements ['bætəlmənts] *npl* almenas.

battleship ['bætəlʃɪp] *n* acorazado.

bauble ['bɔːbəl] *n* baratija.

baulk [bɔːk] *vt* → balk.

bawdy ['bɔːdɪ] *adj* (**-ier**, **-iest**) verde, picante.

bawl [bɔːl] *vi* chillar, gritar.

bay[1] [beɪ] *n* bahía, golfo.

bay[2] [beɪ] *n* laurel.

■ **bay leaf** hoja de laurel.

bay[3] [beɪ] *vi* aullar.
● **to keep at bay** mantener a raya.

bay[4] [beɪ] *n* hueco.

■ **bay window** ventana en saliente.

■ **loading bay** cargadero.

■ **parking bay** plaza de parking.

bayonet ['beɪənət] *n* bayoneta.

bazaar [bə'zɑːʳ] *n* **1** bazar. **2** venta benéfica.

BBC ['biː'siː] *abbr* (**British Broadcasting Corporation**) BBC.

BC ['biː'siː] *abbr* (**before Christ**) antes de Cristo, antes de Jesucristo, a.C., a.de.C.

be [biː] (Presente singular, 1ª **am**, 2ª **are**, 3ª **is**; plural **are**. Pasado, 1ª y 3ª pers sing **was**; 2ª pers sing y pl **were**. Participio pasado, **been**) *vi* **1** ser: *she's clever*, ella es inteligente; *diamonds are hard*, los diamantes son duros; *John's English*, John es inglés; *we are both teachers*, los dos somos profesores; *they are from Manchester*, son de Manchester; *this house is ours*, esta casa es nuestra; *this painting is by Fraser*, este cuadro es de Fraser. **2** estar: *Whitby is on the coast*, Whitby está en la costa; *how are you?*, ¿cómo estás?; *your supper is cold/in the oven*, tu cena está fría/en el horno. **3** tener: *Philip is 17*, Philip tiene 17 años; *I'm cold*, tengo frío; *he's hungry*, tiene hambre; *you are right*, tienes razón. **4** costar, valer: *a single ticket is £7.50*, un billete de ida cuesta £7,50; *prawns are cheap today*, las gambas están bien de precio hoy. **5** hacer: *it's sunny*, hace sol; *it was cold*, hacía frío.
► *aux* **1** **be** + *pres participle* estar: *it is raining*, está lloviendo; *the train is coming*, viene el tren; *I am going tomorrow*, iré mañana. **2** **be** + *past participle* ser: *he was sacked*, fue despedido, lo despidieron; *it has been sold*, ha sido vendido, se ha vendido; *he will be given a medal*, se le dará una medalla. **3** **be** + *infinitive*: *you are not to come here again*, no debes volver aquí; *you are to do as I say*, tienes que hacer lo que yo te diga. **4** **be** + *infinitive*: *the King is to visit Egypt*, el Rey visitará Egipto.
● **there is/are** hay.
● **there was/were** había.
● **there will be** habrá.
● **there would be** habría.

beach [biːtʃ] *n* (*pl* **-es**) playa.
► *vt* varar, embarrancar.

■ **beach umbrella** sombrilla.

beacon ['biːkən] *n* **1** almenara (*hoguera*). **2** baliza (*de señalización*).

bead [biːd] *n* **1** cuenta (*de collar*). **2** gota (*de sudor*).

beak [biːk] *n* pico.

beaker ['biːkə'] *n* **1** taza alta, tazón. **2** vaso de precipitación.

beam [biːm] *n* **1** viga. **2** rayo *(de luz)*. **3** sonrisa radiante.

► *vi* **1** brillar. **2** sonreír.

► *vt* transmitir, emitir.

bean [biːn] *n* **1** alubia, judía, haba. **2** grano *(de café)*.

● **to be full of beans** rebosar vitalidad.

● **to spill the beans** descubrir el pastel.

bear¹ [beə'] *n* oso.

bear² [beə'] *vt* (*pt* **bore** [bɔː'], *pp* **borne** [bɔːn]). **1** llevar *(señal)*. **2** soportar, aguantar, resistir *(dolor)*. **3** soportar, aguantar *(carga)*. **4** producir, dar.

● **to bear in mind** tener presente.

● **to bear a grudge** guardar rencor.

● **to bear a resemblance to** parecerse a.

to bear out *vt* confirmar.

to bear up *vi* mantenerse firme, resistir.

to bear with *vt* tener paciencia con.

bearable ['beərəbəl] *adj* soportable.

beard [bɪəd] *n* barba.

bearded ['bɪədɪd] *adj* barbudo,-a.

bearer ['beərə'] *n* **1** portador,-ra. **2** titular.

bearing ['beərɪŋ] *n* **1** porte. **2** relación. **3** cojinete. **4** orientación, rumbo.

● **to lose one's bearings** desorientarse, perder el norte.

beast [biːst] *n* bestia, animal.

beastly ['biːstlɪ] *adj* (-**ier**, -**iest**) GB horroroso,-a, horrible.

beat [biːt] *vt* (*pt* **beat** [biːt], *pp* **beaten** ['biːtən]). **1** golpear, martillear, azotar. **2** batir *(huevos, alas)*. **3** vencer, derrotar. **4** batir *(récord)*.

► *vi* latir *(corazón)*.

► *n* **1** latido. **2** ritmo.

► *adj fam* agotado,-a.

● **to beat about the bush** andarse por las ramas.

● **to beat time** llevar el compás.

to beat up *vt* dar una paliza a.

beater ['biːtə'] *n* batidora.

beating ['biːtɪŋ] *n* **1** paliza. **2** derrota. **3** latidos.

beautician [bjuːˈtɪʃən] *n* esteticista.

beautiful ['bjuːtɪfʊl] *adj* **1** hermoso,-a, bonito,-a. **2** maravilloso,-a, magnífico, estupendo.

beauty ['bjuːtɪ] *n* (*pl* -**ies**) belleza, hermosura.

■ **beauty parlour** salón de belleza.

■ **beauty spot 1** lunar. **2** lugar pintoresco.

beaver ['biːvə'] *n* castor.

became [bɪˈkeɪm] *pt* → become.

because [bɪˈkɒz] *conj* porque.

► *prep* **because of** a causa de.

beckon ['bekən] *vt* llamar por señas.

► *vi* hacer señas.

become [bɪˈkʌm] *vi* (*pt* **became** [bɪˈkeɪm], *pp* **become** [bɪˈkʌm]). **1** convertirse en, hacerse, llegar a ser: *she became a teacher*, se hizo maestra; *he never became president*, nunca llegó a la presidencia. **2** volverse, ponerse: *to become angry*, enfadarse, enojarse; *to become sad*, entristecerse. **3** favorecer.

● **to become of** ser de: *what has become of Peter?*, ¿qué ha sido de Peter?

becoming [bɪˈkʌmɪŋ] *adj* **1** que sienta bien. **2** apropiado,-a.

bed [bed] *n* **1** cama. **2** macizo *(de flores)*. **3** lecho, cauce *(de río)*, fondo *(del mar)*. **4** capa, yacimiento.

● **to go to bed** acostarse.

● **to go to bed with someone** acostarse con alguien.

● **to make the bed** hacer la cama.

● **to get out of bed on the wrong side** levantarse con el pie izquierdo.

bed and breakfast [bedən'brekfəst] *n* fonda, hotel *(que ofrece alojamiento y desayuno)*.

bedbug ['bedbʌg] *n* chinche.

bedclothes ['bedkləʊðz] *npl* ropa de cama.

bedding ['bedɪŋ] *n* ropa de cama.

bedpan ['bedpæn] *n* cuña.

bedridden ['bedrɪdən] *adj* postrado,-a en la cama.

bedroom ['bedruːm] *n* dormitorio.

bedside ['bedsaɪd] *n* cabecera.

■ **bedside table** mesita de noche.

bedsitter [bed'sɪtə'] *n* habitación amueblada de alquiler.

bedspread ['bedspred] *n* cubrecama, colcha.

bedtime ['bedtaɪm] *n* la hora de acostarse.

bee [biː] *n* abeja.

● **to have a bee in one's bonnet** tener algo entre ceja y ceja.

beech [biːtʃ] *n* (*pl* -**es**) haya.

beef [biːf] *n* carne de vaca.

beefburger ['biːfbɜːgəʳ] n hamburguesa (de vacuno).

beefsteak ['biːfsteɪk] n bistec (de ternera).

beehive ['biːhaɪv] n colmena.

beeline ['biːlaɪn] n.
● **to make a beeline for** ir directamente hacia.

been [biːn, bɪn] pp → be.

beer [bɪəʳ] n cerveza.

beetle ['biːtəl] n escarabajo.

beetroot ['biːtruːt] n remolacha.

before [bɪ'fɔːʳ] prep **1** antes de. **2** delante de, ante: *before God*, ante Dios.
► conj antes de + inf, antes de que + subj: *before you go*, antes de irte, antes de que te vayas.
► adv **1** antes: *I told you before*, te lo he dicho antes. **2** anterior: *the day before*, el día anterior. **3** ya: *I've seen this film before*, ya he visto esta película.
● **the day before yesterday** antes de ayer.

beforehand [bɪ'fɔːhænd] adv **1** antes. **2** de antemano, con antelación.

befriend [bɪ'frend] vt hacerse amigo de.

beg [beg] vi (pt & pp **begged**, ger **begging**) mendigar, pedir limosna.
► vt pedir, suplicar, rogar.
● **I beg your pardon?** ¿cómo ha dicho usted?, ¿qué ha dicho?
● **I beg your pardon!** ¡perdón!, ¡perdone!

began [bɪ'gæn] pt → begin.

beggar ['begəʳ] n mendigo,-a.

begin [bɪ'gɪn] vt-vi (pt **began** [bɪ'gæn], pp **begun** [bɪ'gʌn]) empezar, comenzar.
● **to begin with** para empezar: *I didn't like the film to begin with*, para empezar, no me gustó la película.

beginner [bɪ'gɪnəʳ] n principiante.

beginning [bɪ'gɪnɪŋ] n principio: *at the beginning of the month*, a principios de mes.

beguile [bɪ'gaɪl] vt **1** engañar. **2** seducir, atraer.

begun [bɪ'gʌn] pp → begin.

behalf [bɪ'hɑːf] n.
● **on behalf of** en nombre de, de parte de.

behave [bɪ'heɪv] vi comportarse, portarse.
● **to behave oneself** portarse bien.

behaviour [bɪ'heɪvjəʳ] (US **behavior**) n conducta, comportamiento.
● **to be on your best behaviour** comportarse de la mejor manera posible.

behead [bɪ'hed] vt decapitar.

beheld [bɪ'held] pt-pp → behold.

behind [bɪ'haɪnd] prep detrás de: *he hid behind a car*, se escondió detrás de un coche.
► adv **1** detrás: *the children went on ahead and the grown-ups walked behind*, los niños se adelantaron y los adultos fueron detrás. **2** atrasado,-a: *he's behind with his work*, va atrasado con el trabajo.
► n fam trasero.
● **behind SB's back** a espaldas de ALGN.
● **behind schedule** atrasado,-a.
● **behind the scenes** entre bastidores.
● **to leave STH behind** olvidar algo.

behindhand [bɪ'haɪndhænd] adj atrasado,-a, retrasado,-a.

behold [bɪ'həʊld] vt (pt & pp **beheld** [bɪ'held]) contemplar.

beige [beɪʒ] adj beige.
► n beige.

being ['biːɪŋ] n **1** ser. **2** existencia.
● **for the time being** por ahora.

belated [bɪ'leɪtɪd] adj tardío,-a.

belch [beltʃ] n (pl -**es**) eructo.
► vi eructar.

Belgian ['beldʒən] adj-n belga.

Belgium ['beldʒəm] n Bélgica.

belief [bɪ'liːf] n (pl **beliefs**). **1** creencia. **2** fe.

believe [bɪ'liːv] vt **1** creer: *believe me*, créeme. **2** creer, suponer: *he is believed to be dead*, se cree que está muerto.
► vi **1** creer: *we believe in God*, creemos en Dios. **2** confiar. **3** ser partidario,-a: *they believe in free trade*, creen en el libre comercio.

believer [bɪ'liːvəʳ] n creyente.

belittle [bɪ'lɪtəl] vt menospreciar.

bell [bel] n **1** campana. **2** campanilla. **3** timbre: *to ring the bell*, tocar el timbre. **4** cencerro.
● **he was saved by the bell** se salvó por los pelos.
● **that rings a bell** me suena.

bellboy ['belbɔɪ] n botones.

bellhop ['belhɒp] n botones.

bellow ['beləʊ] n bramido.
► vi bramar.

bellows ['beləʊz] npl fuelle.

belly ['belɪ] n (pl -**ies**). **1** vientre, barriga. **2** panza.
■ **belly button** fam ombligo.
■ **belly laugh** carcajada.

bellyache ['belɪeɪk] n fam dolor de barriga.
► vi fam quejarse.

belong [bɪˈlɒŋ] vi **1** pertenecer. **2** ser socio,-a.

belongings [bɪˈlɒŋɪŋz] npl pertenencias.

beloved [(adj) bɪˈlʌvd(n) bɪˈlʌvɪd] adj querido,-a, amado,-a.
▶ n amado,-a.

below [bɪˈləʊ] prep debajo de, por debajo de: *the flat below ours*, el piso que hay debajo del nuestro.
▶ adv abajo: *who lives on the floor below?*, ¿quién vive en el piso de abajo?
● **below zero** bajo cero.
● **see below** véase más abajo.

belt [belt] n **1** cinturón. **2** correa. **3** zona.

to belt along vi ir a todo gas.

to belt up vi **1** GB fam callarse. **2** GB fam abrocharse el cinturón.

bemused [bɪˈmjuːzd] adj perplejo,-a.

bench [bentʃ] n (pl **-es**). **1** banco (asiento). **2** banquillo.

bend [bend] n **1** curva. **2** ángulo.
▶ vt (pt & pp **bent**). **1** doblar. **2** inclinar.
▶ vi **1** doblarse. **2** torcer.
● **round the bend** loco,-a perdido,-a.

to bend down vi agacharse.

to bend over vi inclinarse.

beneath [bɪˈniːθ] prep bajo, debajo de, por debajo de.
▶ adv abajo, debajo: *we looked down at the village beneath*, miramos el pueblo de abajo.

benefactor [ˈbenɪfæktəʳ] n benefactor.

benefactress [ˈbenɪfæktrəs] n (pl **-es**) benefactora.

beneficial [benɪˈfɪʃəl] adj beneficioso,-a, provechoso,-a.

beneficiary [benɪˈfɪʃərɪ] n (pl **-ies**) beneficiario,-a.

benefit [ˈbenɪfɪt] n **1** beneficio, provecho. **2** bien: *it's for your benefit*, es por tu bien. **3** subsidio.
▶ vt-vi (pt & pp **benefited** o **benefitted**, ger **benefiting** o **benefitting**) beneficiar(se).

benevolence [bɪˈnevələns] n benevolencia.

benevolent [bɪˈnevələnt] adj benévolo,-a.

benign [bɪˈnaɪn] adj benigno,-a.

bent [bent] pt-pp → bend.
▶ adj **1** torcido,-a, doblado,-a. **2** fam corrupto,-a. **3** sl de la acera de enfrente.

▶ n inclinación (**for**, por).
● **bent on** empeñado,-a en.

benzine [ˈbenziːn] n bencina.

bequeath [bɪˈkwiːð] vt legar.

bequest [bɪˈkwest] n legado.

bereaved [bɪˈriːvd] adj desconsolado,-a *(por la muerte de un ser querido)*.

bereavement [bɪˈriːvmənt] n **1** pérdida *(de un ser querido)*. **2** duelo.

beret [ˈbereɪ] n boina.

berk [bɜːk] n GB fam idiota.

berry [ˈberɪ] n (pl **-ies**) baya.

berserk [bəˈzɜːk] adj enloquecido,-a: *to go berserk*, enloquecer.

berth [bɜːθ] n **1** amarradero. **2** camarote, litera.
▶ vi atracar.

beseech [bɪˈsiːtʃ] vt (pt & pp **besought** [bɪˈsɔːt] o **beseeched**) implorar, suplicar.

beset [bɪˈset] vt (pt & pp **beset**, ger **besetting**) acosar.

beside [bɪˈsaɪd] prep al lado de, junto a.
● **beside oneself** fuera de sí.
● **beside oneself with joy** loco,-a de alegría.
● **that's beside the point** eso no viene al caso.

besides [bɪˈsaɪdz] prep **1** además de. **2** excepto: *no one came besides you*, no vino nadie salvo tú.
▶ adv además.

besiege [bɪˈsiːdʒ] vt **1** sitiar. **2** fig asediar.

besought [bɪˈsɔːt] pt-pp → beseech.

best [best] adj mejor.
▶ adv mejor.
▶ n lo mejor.
● **all the best!** ¡que te vaya bien!
● **as best you can** lo mejor que puedas.
● **at best** en el mejor de los casos.
● **the best part of** la mayor parte de.
● **to do one's best** esmerarse.
● **to make the best of** sacar el mejor partido, aprovecharse de.
■ **best man** padrino de boda.

best-seller [bestˈseləʳ] n best-seller, superventas.

bet [bet] n apuesta.
▶ vt-vi (pt & pp **bet**, ger **betting**) apostar.

betray [bɪˈtreɪ] vt traicionar.

betrayal [bɪˈtreɪəl] n traición.

better [ˈbetəʳ] adj mejor.
▶ adv mejor.
▶ vt **1** mejorar. **2** superar.

► *npl* **betters** superiores.
● **better late than never** más vale tarde que nunca.
● **better off 1** mejor: *you would be better off in the country*, estarías mejor en el campo. **2** más rico: *when I'm better off, I'll buy a new car*, cuando tenga más dinero, me compraré un coche nuevo.
● **had better** más vale que + *subj*: *we'd better be going*, más vale que nos vayamos, deberíamos irnos.
● **so much the better** tanto mejor.
● **to get better** mejorar, ponerse mejor.
■ **better half** media naranja.
betting ['betɪŋ] *n* apuestas.
● **what's the betting that ...?** ¿qué te apuestas a que ...?
bettor ['betəʳ] *n* apostante.
between [bɪ'twiːn] *prep* entre.
► *adv* en medio, entre medio.
● **between the lines** entre líneas.
● **between you and me** entre tú y yo, en confianza.
bevel ['bevəl] *n* **1** bisel, chaflán. **2** cartabón.
► *vt* (GB *pt & pp* **bevelled**, *ger* **bevelling**; US *pt & pp* **beveled**, *ger* **beveling**) biselar.
beverage ['bevərɪdʒ] *n* bebida.
beware [bɪ'weəʳ] *vi* tener cuidado.
bewilder [bɪ'wɪldəʳ] *vt* desconcertar, confundir.
bewitch [bɪ'wɪtʃ] *vt* hechizar, fascinar.
beyond [bɪ'jɒnd] *prep* más allá de, al otro lado de.
► *adv* más allá.
► *n* **the beyond** el más allá.
● **beyond belief** increíble.
● **beyond doubt** indudable.
● **it's beyond me** no lo entiendo.
bias ['baɪəs] *n* (*pl* **biases**). **1** parcialidad, prejuicio. **2** tendencia, inclinación.
► *vt* predisponer.
biased ['baɪəst] *adj* parcial.
bib [bɪb] *n* babero.
Bible ['baɪbəl] *n* Biblia.
bibliography [bɪblɪ'ɒgrəfɪ] *n* (*pl* -**ies**) bibliografía.
biceps ['baɪseps] *n* bíceps.
bicker ['bɪkəʳ] *vi* discutir, pelear.
bicycle ['baɪsɪkəl] *n* bicicleta.

bid [bɪd] *n* **1** puja. **2** intento. **3** oferta: *to make a bid*, hacer una oferta.
► *vt* (*pt* **bid** o **bade** [beɪd], *pp* **bid** o **bidden** ['bɪdən], *ger* **bidding**). Las formas **bade** y **bidden** se usan cuando significa *ordenar, mandar*. **1** pujar. **2** decir: *to bid farewell*, decir adiós. **3** ordenar, mandar: *do as you are bidden*, haz lo que se te ordena.
► *vi* pujar, hacer ofertas.
bidder ['bɪdəʳ] *n* postor,-ra.
bidding ['bɪdɪŋ] *n* puja.
bide [baɪd] *vt-vi* (*pt* **bode** [bəʊd] o **bided**, *pp* **bided**) .
● **to bide one's time** esperar el momento oportuno.
bidet ['biːdeɪ] *n* bidé.
biennial [baɪ'enɪəl] *adj* bienal.
bifocal [baɪ'fəʊkəl] *adj* bifocal.
► *npl* **bifocals** lentes bifocales.
big [bɪg] *adj* (*comp* **bigger**, *superl* **biggest**) grande, gran: *a big car*, un coche grande; *a big day*, un gran día.
● **too big for one's boots** muy fanfarrón,-ona.
■ **big brother** hermano mayor.
■ **big game** caza mayor.
■ **big noise** pez gordo.
■ **big shot** pez gordo.
■ **big sister** hermana mayor.
bigamy ['bɪgəmɪ] *n* bigamia.
bighead ['bɪghed] *n* sabihondo,-a, creído,-a.
bigheaded [bɪg'hedɪd] *adj* sabihondo,-a, creído,-a.
big-hearted [bɪg'hɑːtɪd] *adj* de buen corazón, generoso,-a.
bigmouth ['bɪgmaʊθ] *n* bocazas.
bigot ['bɪgət] *n* fanático,-a.
bigotry ['bɪgətrɪ] *n* fanatismo.
bigwig ['bɪgwɪg] *n fam* pez gordo.
bike [baɪk] *n* **1** *fam* bici. **2** *fam* moto.
bikini [bɪ'kiːnɪ] *n* biquini.
bilateral [baɪ'lætərəl] *adj* bilateral.
bile [baɪl] *n* bilis, hiel.
bilingual [baɪ'lɪŋgwəl] *adj* bilingüe.
bill¹ [bɪl] *n* **1** factura, cuenta. **2** proyecto de ley. **3** US billete de banco. **4** cartel, póster.
► *vt* **1** facturar. **2** anunciar.
● **to fit the bill** cumplir los requisitos.
● **to top the bill** encabezar el reparto.
■ **bill of exchange** letra de cambio.

bill² [bɪl] *n* pico *(de ave)*.
billboard ['bɪlbɔːd] *n* US valla publicitaria.
billiards ['bɪlɪədz] *n* billar.
billion ['bɪlɪən] *n* **1** billón. **2** mil millones.

> Actualmente, tanto en América como en Gran Bretaña, **a billion** son mil millones (1.000.000.000), pero antiguamenteañol, sólo en Gran Bretaña equivalía al **billón** español, o sea, a un millón de millones.

billow ['bɪləʊ] *n* **1** ola. **2** nube.
▶ *vi* **1** ondear. **2** hincharse.
billy goat ['bɪlɪɡəʊt] *n* macho cabrío.
bin [bɪn] *n* cubo de la basura, papelera.
binary ['baɪnərɪ] *adj* binario,-a.
bind [baɪnd] *vt* (*pt & pp* **bound** [baʊnd]).
1 atar. **2** ligar *(salsa)*. **3** obligar.
▶ *n fam* lata, coñazo.
binder ['baɪndə'] *n* carpeta.
binding ['baɪndɪŋ] *n* **1** ribete. **2** encuadernación.
▶ *adj* obligatorio,-a, vinculante.
binge [bɪndʒ] *n* **1** borrachera. **2** comilona.
bingo ['bɪŋɡəʊ] *n* bingo.
binoculars [bɪ'nɒkjʊlɑːz] *npl* gemelos.
biographer [baɪ'ɒɡrəfə'] *n* biógrafo,-a.
biographical [baɪə'ɡræfɪkəl] *adj* biográfico,-a.
biography [baɪ'ɒɡrəfɪ] *n* (*pl* -**ies**) biografía.
biological [baɪə'lɒdʒɪkəl] *adj* biológico,-a.
biologist [baɪ'ɒlədʒɪst] *n* biólogo,-a.
biology [baɪ'ɒlədʒɪ] *n* biología.
biopsy ['baɪɒpsɪ] *n* (*pl* -**ies**) biopsia.
biorhythm ['baɪərɪðəm] *n* biorritmo.
biosphere ['baɪəsfɪə'] *n* biosfera.
birch [bɜːtʃ] *n* (*pl* -**es**). **1** abedul. **2** vara.
▶ *vt* azotar.
bird [bɜːd] *n* **1** ave, pájaro. **2** GB tía.
● **a bird in the hand is worth two in the bush** más vale pájaro en mano que ciento volando.
● **to kill two birds with one stone** matar dos pájaros de un tiro.
■ **bird of prey** ave de rapiña.
birdie ['bɜːdɪ] *n* **1** pajarito. **2** birdie *(en golf)*.
birdseed ['bɜːdsiːd] *n* alpiste.
bird's-eye view [bɜːdz'aɪvjuː] *n* vista aérea, a vuelo de pájaro.
bird-watcher ['bɜːdwɒtʃə'] *n* observador,-ra de aves.
Biro® ['baɪrəʊ] *n* GB boli.

birth [bɜːθ] *n* **1** nacimiento. **2** parto. **3** linaje.
● **to give birth to** dar a luz a.
■ **birth certificate** partida de nacimiento.
■ **birth control** control de natalidad.
birthday ['bɜːθdeɪ] *n* cumpleaños.
birthmark ['bɜːθmɑːk] *n* antojo.
birthplace ['bɜːθpleɪs] *n* lugar de nacimiento.
biscuit ['bɪskɪt] *n* galleta.
bisect [baɪ'sekt] *vt* bisecar.
bisexual [baɪ'seksjʊəl] *adj* bisexual.
bishop ['bɪʃəp] *n* **1** obispo. **2** alfil (*en ajedrez)*.
bison ['baɪsən] *n* bisonte.
bit¹ [bɪt] *n* **1** trozo, pedacito. **2** poco: *I have a bit of money left*, me queda un poco de dinero.
● **a bit** un poco, algo: *it's a bit expensive*, es un poco caro; *could you turn the volume up a bit?*, ¿puedes subir un poco el volumen?
● **bit by bit** poco a poco.
● **bits and pieces 1** trastos. **2** retazos.
● **to come to bits** romperse.
● **to take to bits** desmontar.
● **to go to bits** ponerse histérico,-a.
bit² [bɪt] *n* bit.
bit³ [bɪt] *n* broca.
bit⁴ [bɪt] *pt* → bite.
bitch [bɪtʃ] *n* (*pl* -**es**). **1** hembra, perra. **2** *pej* bruja, arpía.
▶ *vi fam* quejarse, refunfuñar.
bite [baɪt] *n* **1** mordisco: *to take a bite*, dar un mordisco. **2** picadura. **3** mordedura. **4** bocado.
▶ *vt-vi* (*pt* **bit** [bɪt], *pp* **bitten** ['bɪtən]). **1** morder(se). **2** picar.
biting ['baɪtɪŋ] *adj* cortante, mordaz.
bitten ['bɪtən] *pp* → bite.
bitter ['bɪtə'] *adj* (*comp* **bitterer**, *superl* **bitterest**). **1** amargo,-a *(sabor)*. **2** glacial *(viento)*. **3** amargado,-a *(persona)*. **4** enconado,-a *(lucha)*.
▶ *n* cerveza amarga.
▶ *npl* **bitters** bíter.
bitterly ['bɪtəlɪ] *adv* con amargura: *bitterly disappointed*, terriblemente decepcionado,-a; *it's bitterly cold*, hace un frío glacial.
bitterness ['bɪtənəs] *n* **1** amargor. **2** amargura, rencor.

bizarre [bɪ'zɑː'] *adj* raro,-a, extraño,-a.

blab [blæb] *vi* (*pt & pp* **blabbed**, *ger* **blabbing**). **1** *fam* parlotear. **2** *fam* cantar, descubrir el pastel.

black [blæk] *adj* **1** negro,-a. **2** aciago,-a, negro,-a.
▶ *n* **1** (*color*) negro. **2** (*persona*) negro,-a.
● **black and white** blanco y negro.
● **to put down STH in black and white** poner algo por escrito.
■ **black coffee** café solo.
■ **black eye** ojo morado.
■ **black hole** agujero negro.
■ **black market** mercado negro.
■ **black sheep** oveja negra.

to black out *vt* apagar las luces de.
▶ *vi* desmayarse.

black-and-blue [blækən'bluː] *adj* amoratado,-a.

blackberry ['blækbəri] *n* (*pl* **-ies**) mora, zarzamora.

blackbird ['blækbɜːd] *n* mirlo.

blackboard ['blækbɔːd] *n* pizarra.

blackcurrant [blæk'kʌrənt] *n* grosella negra.

blacken ['blækən] *vt* **1** ennegrecer. **2** *fig* manchar (*reputación*).

blackhead ['blækhed] *n* espinilla.

blackish ['blækɪʃ] *adj* negruzco,-a.

blackleg ['blækleg] *n* esquirol.

blackmail ['blækmeɪl] *n* chantaje.
▶ *vt* hacer chantaje a, chantajear.

blackmailer ['blækmeɪlə'] *n* chantajista.

blackness ['blæknəs] *n* negrura, oscuridad.

blackout ['blækaʊt] *n* **1** apagón. **2** pérdida de conocimiento.

blacksmith ['blæksmɪθ] *n* herrero.

bladder ['blædə'] *n* vejiga.

blade [bleɪd] *n* **1** hoja, filo (*de cuchillo*). **2** cuchilla (*de patín*). **3** pala (*de remo*). **4** brizna (*de hierba*).

blame [bleɪm] *n* culpa.
▶ *vt* culpar, echar la culpa a.
● **to be to blame** tener la culpa.
● **to put the blame on** echar la culpa a.
● **to take the blame for STH** asumir la responsabilidad de algo.

blanch [blɑːntʃ] *vt* escaldar.
▶ *vi* palidecer.

bland [blænd] *adj* soso,-a.

blank [blæŋk] *adj* **1** en blanco (*página*). **2** vacío,-a (*mirada*). **3** virgen (*cinta*).
▶ *n* espacio en blanco.
● **my mind went blank** me quedé en blanco.
● **to draw a blank** no tener éxito.
■ **blank cartridge** cartucho de fogueo.
■ **blank cheque** cheque en blanco.

blanket ['blæŋkɪt] *n* manta.
▶ *adj* **1** general. **2** que lo cubre todo.

blare [bleə'] *n* estruendo.

to blare out *vi* sonar muy fuerte.

blaspheme [blæs'fiːm] *vi* blasfemar.

blasphemous ['blæsfəməs] *adj* blasfemo,-a.

blasphemy ['blæsfəmɪ] *n* (*pl* **-ies**) blasfemia.

blast [blɑːst] *n* **1** ráfaga (*de aire*). **2** chorro (*de agua*). **3** toque, pitido. **4** explosión, voladura. **5** onda expansiva.
▶ *vt* **1** volar, hacer volar. **2** criticar.
▶ *interj* ¡maldita sea!
● **at full blast** a todo volumen.
■ **blast furnace** alto horno.

blasted ['blɑːstɪd] *adj* maldito,-a.

blast-off ['blɑːstɒf] *n* (*pl* **blast-offs**) despegue.

blatant ['bleɪtənt] *adj* descarado,-a.

blaze [bleɪz] *n* **1** incendio. **2** fogata, hoguera.
▶ *vi* **1** arder, estar encendido. **2** brillar con fuerza.
● **like blazes** a toda pastilla, a todo gas.
● **to blaze a trail** abrir un camino.

blazer ['bleɪzə'] *n* chaqueta de club deportivo, blazer.

bleach [bliːtʃ] *n* (*pl* **-es**) lejía.
▶ *vt* blanquear, aclarar.

bleak [bliːk] *adj* **1** desolado,-a (*paisaje*). **2** desapacible (*tiempo*). **3** poco prometedor,-ra (*panorama*).

bleary ['blɪərɪ] *adj* (**-ier**, **-iest**). **1** nubloso,-a. **2** legañoso,-a.

bleat [bliːt] *n* balido.
▶ *vi* balar.

bled [bled] *pt-pp* → bleed.

bleed [bliːd] *vi* (*pt & pp* **bled** [bled]) sangrar.
● **to bleed SB dry** sacarle a ALGN hasta el último céntimo.
● **to bleed to death** morir desangrado,-a.

bleeding ['bliːdɪŋ] *adj* *vulg* puñetero,-a.

bleep [bliːp] *n* pitido.
▶ *vi* pitar.
▶ *vt* localizar (*con un busca*).

bleeper ['bliːpəʳ] n busca, buscapersonas.
blemish ['blemɪʃ] n (pl -es). 1 imperfección. 2 marca. 3 fig mancha.
blend [blend] n mezcla, combinación.
▶ vt-vi 1 mezclarse, combinarse. 2 matizarse, armonizarse.
blender ['blendəʳ] n batidora, minipímer®.
bless [bles] vt bendecir.
● bless you! ¡Jesús!
blessed ['blesɪd] adj 1 bendito,-a. 2 santo, dichoso.
blessing ['blesɪŋ] n bendición.
blew [bluː] pt → blow.
blight [blaɪt] n fig plaga.
blind [blaɪnd] adj ciego,-a.
▶ n persiana.
▶ vt 1 cegar, dejar ciego,-a. 2 deslumbrar.
● to be blind estar ciego,-a.
● to go blind quedarse ciego,-a.
blinders ['blaɪndəz] npl US anteojeras.
blindfold ['blaɪndfəʊld] n venda.
▶ vt vendar los ojos a.
▶ adj-adv con los ojos vendados.
blindly ['blaɪndlɪ] adv ciegamente, a ciegas.
blindness ['blaɪndnəs] n ceguera.
blink [blɪŋk] n parpadeo.
▶ vi parpadear.
● on the blink averiado,-a.
blinkers ['blɪŋkəz] npl anteojeras.
bliss [blɪs] n felicidad, dicha.
blister ['blɪstəʳ] n 1 ampolla. 2 burbuja.
blizzard ['blɪzəd] n tormenta de nieve.
bloated ['bləʊtɪd] adj hinchado,-a.
blob [blɒb] n 1 gota. 2 mancha.
bloc [blɒk] n bloque.
block [blɒk] n 1 bloque, taco (de madera). 2 edificio, bloque. 3 manzana: we walked round the block, dimos la vuelta a la manzana. 4 bloqueo.
▶ vt 1 obstruir, cegar. 2 bloquear.
■ block letters mayúsculas, letras de imprenta.
blockade [blɒ'keɪd] n bloqueo.
▶ vt bloquear.
blockage ['blɒkɪdʒ] n obstrucción.
blockhead ['blɒkhed] n zoquete.
bloke [bləʊk] n GB fam tipo, tío.
blond [blɒnd] adj-n rubio,-a.

Suele escribirse **blonde** cuando se refiere a una mujer.

blood [blʌd] n 1 sangre. 2 alcurnia.

■ blood group grupo sanguíneo.
■ blood pressure tensión arterial: high/low blood pressure, tensión alta/baja.
bloodcurdling ['blʌdkɜːdəlɪŋ] adj horripilante.
bloodhound ['blʌdhaʊnd] n sabueso.
bloodless ['blʌdləs] adj incruento,-a, sin derramamiento de sangre.
bloodshed ['blʌdʃed] n derramamiento de sangre.
bloodshot ['blʌdʃɒt] adj rojo,-a, inyectado,-a de sangre.
bloodstream ['blʌdstriːm] n torrente sanguíneo.
bloodthirsty ['blʌdθɜːstɪ] adj (-ier, -iest) sanguinario,-a.
bloody ['blʌdɪ] adj (-ier, -iest). 1 sangriento,-a. 2 fam puñetero,-a, condenado,-a.
bloody-minded [blʌdɪ'maɪndɪd] adj tozudo,-a.
bloom [bluːm] n flor.
▶ vi florecer.
bloomer ['bluːməʳ] n GB fam metedura de pata.
bloomers ['bluːməz] npl pololos.
blooper ['bluːpəʳ] n US fam metedura de pata.
blossom ['blɒsəm] n flor.
▶ vi florecer.

Se refiere a la flor de los árboles: *orange blossom*, flor de azahar.

blot [blɒt] n borrón.
▶ vt (pt & pp blotted, ger blotting). 1 manchar. 2 secar.
● to blot one's copybook manchar su reputación.
to blot out vt 1 ocultar, tapar. 2 borrar.
blotch [blɒtʃ] n (pl -es). 1 mancha. 2 borrón.
blotter ['blɒtəʳ] n 1 papel secante. 2 US registro.
blotting-paper ['blɒtɪŋpeɪpəʳ] n papel secante.
blouse [blaʊz] n blusa.
blow[1] [bləʊ] n golpe.
■ blow below the belt golpe bajo.
blow[2] [bləʊ] vi (pt blew [bluː], pp blown [bləʊn]). 1 soplar (viento). 2 sonar (silbato). 3 fundirse (fusible). 4 volar: his hat blew off, se le voló el sombrero.
▶ vt 1 tocar (cláxon, trompeta, etc). 2 lle-

varse *(el viento)*: **the wind blew his newspaper away**, el viento se llevó su periódico. **3** *fam* dilapidar, ventilar: **he blew
all his savings on a car**, se ventiló todo
los ahorros en un coche.
- **blow you!** ¡vete a hacer puñetas!
- **to blow one's nose** sonarse la nariz.
- **to blow one's top** salirse de sus casillas.
to blow out *vt-vi* apagarse.
to blow over *vi* **1** amainar. **2** olvidarse.
to blow up *vt* **1** hacer explotar. **2** hinchar, inflar. **3** ampliar *(foto)*.
- ▶ *vi* **1** explotar. **2** salirse de sus casillas.
blowlamp ['bləʊlæmp] *n* soplete.
blowout ['bləʊaʊt] *n* **1** reventón. **2** *fam*
comilona.
blowpipe ['bləʊpaɪp] *n* cerbatana.
blowtorch ['bləʊtɔːtʃ] *n (pl* -**es***)* soplete.
blue [bluː] *adj* **1** azul. **2** triste, deprimido,-a. **3** verde *(película)*.
- ▶ *n* azul.
- **once in a blue moon** de Pascuas a
  Ramos.
- **out of the blue** de forma inesperada,
  como llovido del cielo.
- ▪ **the blues 1** melancolía, depresión. **2**
  el blues *(música)*.
blueberry ['bluːbərɪ] *n (pl* -**ies***)* arándano.
blue-eyed ['bluːaɪd] *adj* de ojos azules.
- ▪ **blue-eyed boy** niño mimado.
blueprint ['bluːprɪnt] *n* **1** cianotipo. **2** *fig*
anteproyecto.
bluetit ['bluːtɪt] *n* herrerillo común.
bluff [blʌf] *n* farol, fanfarronada.
- ▶ *vi* tirarse un farol, fanfarronear.
bluish ['bluːɪʃ] *adj* azulado,-a.
blunder ['blʌndə'] *n* plancha, metedura
de pata.
- ▶ *vi* meter la pata.
blunt [blʌnt] *adj* **1** desafilado,-a, despun-
tado,-a. **2** franco,-a.
- ▶ *vt* desafilar, despuntar.
bluntly ['blʌntlɪ] *adv* sin rodeos.
blur [blɜː'] *n* borrón.
blurred [blɜːd] *adj* borroso,-a.
blurt out ['blɜːt'aʊt] *vt* espetar, soltar
bruscamente.
blush [blʌʃ] *n (pl* -**es***)* rubor, sonrojo.
- ▶ *vi* ruborizarse, sonrojarse.
bluster ['blʌstə'] *n* fanfarronadas.
- ▶ *vt* fanfarronear.
blustery ['blʌstərɪ] *adj* ventoso,-a.

boa ['bəʊə] *n* boa.
boar [bɔː'] *n* verraco.
- ▪ **wild boar** jabalí.
board [bɔːd] *n* **1** tabla, tablero. **2** comida,
pensión. **3** tablón de anuncios. **4** pizarra.
5 junta, consejo.
- ▶ *vt* subirse a, embarcar en.
- ▶ *vi* alojarse, embarcar, subir.
- **on board** a bordo.
- **above board** en regla, legal.
- **across the board** general.
- ▪ **board of directors** consejo de administración, junta directiva.
- ▪ **full board** pensión completa.
- ▪ **half board** media pensión.
boarder ['bɔːdə'] *n* **1** huésped,-da *(en casa
de huéspedes)*. **2** interno,-a *(en internado)*.
boarding ['bɔːdɪŋ] *n* **1** embarque. **2** pensión, alojamiento.
- ▪ **boarding card** tarjeta de embarque.
- ▪ **boarding house** casa de huéspedes.
- ▪ **boarding school** internado.
boast [bəʊst] *n* jactancia.
- ▶ *vi* jactarse.
- ▶ *vt* ostentar, presumir de.
boastful ['bəʊstfʊl] *adj* jactancioso,-a.
boat [bəʊt] *n* barco, barca, buque, lancha.
boating ['bəʊtɪŋ] *n* .
- **to go boating** dar un paseo en barca.
boatload ['bəʊtləʊd] *n fam* montón.
boatswain ['bəʊsən] *n* contramaestre.
bob[1] [bɒb] *n* pelo a lo chico.
- ▶ *vt (pt & pp* **bobbed***, ger* **bobbing***)* cortar a lo chico.
- **to bob up and down** moverse arriba
  y abajo.
bob[2] [bɒb] *n* GB *fam* chelín.
bobbin ['bɒbɪn] *n* bobina.
bobby ['bɒbɪ] *n (pl* -**ies***)* GB *fam* poli.
bode [bəʊd] *pt* → bide.
- ▶ *vt-vi* presagiar.
- **to bode ill/well** ser de buen/mal
  agüero.
bodice ['bɒdɪs] *n* **1** corpiño. **2** canesú.
bodily ['bɒdɪlɪ] *adj* físico,-a, corporal.
- ▶ *adv* **1** físicamente. **2** como un solo
  hombre.
body ['bɒdɪ] *n (pl* -**ies***)*. **1** cuerpo. **2** cadáver.
3 organismo, entidad. **4** cuerpo *(objeto)*.
body-building ['bɒdɪbɪldɪŋ] *n* culturismo.
bodyguard ['bɒdɪgɑːd] *n* guardaespaldas.
bodywork ['bɒdɪwɜːk] *n* carrocería.

bog [bɒg] *n* **1** pantano, cenagal. **2** *vulg* meódromo.

● **to get bogged down** atascarse, encallarse.

bogey[1] ['bəʊgɪ] *n sl* moco.

bogey[2] ['bəʊgɪ] *n* bogey *(en golf)*.

bogeyman[1] ['bəʊgɪmæn] *n* coco, hombre del saco.

bogus ['bəʊgəs] *adj* falso,-a.

bohemian [bəʊ'hiːmɪən] *adj-n* bohemio,-a.

boil[1] [bɔɪl] *n* furúnculo.

boil[2] [bɔɪl] *vt-vi* hervir, cocer(se).

● **to come to the boil** romper a hervir.

to boil down to *vt* reducirse a.

boiler ['bɔɪləʳ] *n* caldera.

boiling ['bɔɪlɪn] *adj* **1** hirviente, hirviendo, muy caliente *(comida, etc)*. **2** muy caluroso, de mucho calor *(tiempo)*.

■ **boiling point** punto de ebullición.

boisterous ['bɔɪstərəs] *adj* bullicioso,-a.

bold [bəʊld] *adj* **1** valiente, audaz, atrevido,-a. **2** descarado,-a. **3** fuerte, vivo *(color)*.

■ **bold type** negrita.

boldness ['bəʊldnəs] *n* **1** valor, audacia. **2** descaro.

Bolivia [bə'lɪvɪə] *n* Bolivia.

Bolivian [bə'lɪvɪən] *adj-n* boliviano,-a.

bolshie ['bɒlʃɪ] *adj* GB *fam* respondón,-ona.

bolshy ['bɒlʃɪ] *adj* (-**ier**, -**iest**) GB *fam* respondón,-ona.

bolster ['bəʊlstəʳ] *n* cabezal, travesaño.

▶ *vt* reforzar.

bolt [bəʊlt] *n* **1** cerrojo, pestillo. **2** perno, tornillo. **3** rayo.

▶ *vt* **1** cerrar con cerrojo. **2** sujetar con tornillos, atornillar. **3** *fam* engullir.

▶ *vi* escaparse, desbocarse.

● **bolt upright** tieso,-a.

● **to make a bolt for it** escaparse.

bomb [bɒm] *n* bomba.

▶ *vt* bombardear, colocar una bomba en.

■ **bomb scare** amenaza de bomba.

bombard [bɒm'bɑːd] *vt* bombardear.

bombastic [bɒm'bæstɪk] *adj* rimbombante, ampuloso,-a.

bomber ['bɒməʳ] *n* **1** bombardero. **2** terrorista que coloca bombas.

bombing ['bɒmɪn] *n* **1** bombardeo. **2** atentado con bomba.

bombproof ['bɒmpruːf] *adj* a prueba de bombas.

bombshell ['bɒmʃel] *n* **1** obús. **2** *fig* bomba. **3** *fam* mujer explosiva.

bona fide [bəʊnə'faɪdɪ] *adj* genuino,-a, auténtico,-a.

bond [bɒnd] *n* **1** lazo, vínculo. **2** bono, obligación. **3** fianza. **4** pacto.

▶ *vt-vi* pegarse.

bondage ['bɒndɪdʒ] *n* esclavitud, servidumbre.

bone [bəʊn] *n* **1** hueso. **2** espina *(de pescado)*.

▶ *vt* deshuesar.

■ **bone of contention** manzana de la discordia.

bone-idle [bəʊn'aɪdəl] *adj* holgazán,-ana.

bonfire ['bɒnfaɪəʳ] *n* hoguera.

En Gran Bretaña **Bonfire night** es la noche del cinco de noviembre en la que hay una celebración con hogueras y fuegos artificiales.

bonkers ['bɒnkəz] *adj* GB *fam* chalado,-a.

bonnet ['bɒnɪt] *n* **1** gorro, gorra. **2** capó.

bonny ['bɒnɪ] *adj* (-**ier**, -**iest**) hermoso,-a, lindo,-a.

bonus ['bəʊnəs] *n* (*pl* **bonuses**) prima.

bony ['bəʊnɪ] *adj* (-**ier**, -**iest**). **1** huesudo,-a. **2** lleno,-a de espinas.

boo [buː] *interj* ¡uh!

▶ *n* (*pl* **boos**) abucheo.

▶ *vt-vi* (*pt & pp* **booed**) abuchear.

boob[1] [buːb] *n fam* metedura de pata.

▶ *vi fam* meter la pata.

boob[2] [buːb] *n fam* teta.

booby prize ['buːbɪpraɪz] *n* premio de consolación.

booby trap ['buːbɪtræp] *n* trampa explosiva.

▶ *vt* **booby-trap** poner una bomba en.

book [bʊk] *n* libro.

▶ *vt* **1** reservar, contratar. **2** multar, amonestar.

▶ *npl* **books** libros, cuentas.

bookcase ['bʊkkeɪs] *n* librería, estantería.

booking ['bʊkɪn] *n* reserva.

■ **booking office** taquilla.

bookkeeping ['bʊkkiːpɪn] *n* teneduría de libros.

booklet ['bʊklət] *n* folleto.

bookmaker ['bʊkmeɪkəʳ] *n* GB corredor,-ra de apuestas.

bookseller ['bʊkseləʳ] *n* librero,-a.

bookshelf ['bʊkʃelf] *n* (*pl* **bookshelves**) estante.

▶ *npl* **bookshelves** librería, estantería.

bookshop ['bʊkʃɒp] *n* librería.

bookstore ['bʊkstɔːʳ] n librería.

bookworm ['bʊkwɜːm] n fig ratón de biblioteca.

boom¹ [buːm] n estampido, retumbo, estruendo.
▶ vi tronar, bramar.
▶ interj **boom!** ¡bum!

boom² [buːm] n fig boom, auge.
▶ vi estar en auge.

boomerang ['buːməræŋ] n bumerang.

boor [bʊəʳ] n patán.

boorish ['bʊərɪʃ] adj tosco,-a, zafio,-a.

boost [buːst] n 1 empuje. 2 fig estímulo.
▶ vt 1 aumentar, incrementar (ventas). 2 estimular, impulsar (producción).

boot [buːt] n 1 bota. 2 GB maletero.
▶ vt-vi arrancar (ordenador).
● **to boot** además.

to boot out vt echar, echar a patadas.

booth [buːð] n 1 cabina. 2 puesto (de mercado).

bootlegger ['buːtlegəʳ] n contrabandista.

booty ['buːtɪ] n botín.

booze [buːz] n fam bebida, alcohol.
▶ vi fam mamar.

boozer ['buːzəʳ] n 1 fam borracho,-a. 2 fam tasca.

bop [bɒp] n fam baile.
▶ vi (pt & pp **bopped**, ger **bopping**) fam bailar.

border ['bɔːdəʳ] n 1 frontera. 2 borde, margen. 3 ribete.

to border on vt 1 lindar con. 2 fig rayar en.

bore¹ [bɔːʳ] pt → bear.

bore² [bɔːʳ] n calibre.
▶ vt horadar, taladrar.
● **to bore a hole** abrir un agujero.

bore³ [bɔːʳ] n 1 pelmazo,-a, pesado,-a. 2 lata, rollo.

bored [bɔːd] adj aburrido,-a: *I'm bored*, estoy aburrido.
● **to get bored** aburrirse.

boredom ['bɔːdəm] n aburrimiento.

boring ['bɔːrɪŋ] adj aburrido,-a.

born [bɔːn] pp → bear.
▶ adj nato,-a: *he's a born loser*, es un perdedor nato.
● **to be born** nacer: *he was born in London*, nació en Londres.

borne [bɔːn] pp → bear.

borough ['bʌrə] n 1 distrito. 2 municipio.

borrow ['bɒrəʊ] vt tomar prestado,-a, pedir prestado,-a.

borrower ['bɒrəʊəʳ] n prestatario,-a.

bosom ['bʊzəm] n 1 pecho. 2 seno.
■ **bosom friend** amigo,-a del alma.

boss [bɒs] n (pl -es) jefe,-a.
▶ to boss vt mangonear.

bossy ['bɒsɪ] adj (-ier, -iest) mandón, -ona.

botanical [bəˈtænɪkəl] adj botánico,-a.

botanist ['bɒtənɪst] n botánico,-a.

botany ['bɒtənɪ] n botánica.

botch [bɒtʃ] n (pl -es) chapuza.
▶ vt hacer una chapuza de.

both [bəʊθ] adj-pron ambos,-as, los/las dos.
▶ conj a la vez: *it's both cheap and good*, es bueno y barato a la vez.
● **both ... and** tanto ... como: *both his father and his mother are doctors*, tanto su padre como su madre son médicos.

bother ['bɒðəʳ] n 1 molestia. 2 problemas.
▶ vt 1 molestar, fastidiar. 2 preocupar.
▶ vi 1 molestarse: *he didn't even bother to ring*, ni se molestó en llamar. 2 preocuparse.
● **not to be bothered** no apetecer: *I can not be bothered to go out*, no me apetece salir.

bottle ['bɒtəl] n 1 botella, frasco. 2 biberón. 3 GB fam agallas.
▶ vt embotellar, envasar.
■ **bottle bank** contenedor de vidrio.
■ **bottle opener** abrebotellas.

bottleneck ['bɒtəlnek] n fig cuello de botella.

bottom ['bɒtəm] n 1 fondo (del mar). 2 culo (de botella). 3 pie (de montaña). 4 bajo (de vestido). 5 bajos (de pantalón). 6 último,-a (de una cola). 7 final (de calle). 8 trasero, culo.
▶ adj de abajo.
● **to get to the bottom of STH** llegar al fondo de algo.

bottomless ['bɒtəmləs] adj sin fondo, insondable.

bough [baʊ] n rama.

bought [bɔːt] pt-pp → buy.

boulder ['bəʊldəʳ] n roca.

bounce [baʊns] n bote.
▶ vi 1 rebotar. 2 ser rechazado por el banco.
▶ vt hacer botar.

bouncer ['baʊnsəʳ] n fam portero, gorila.

bound[1] [baʊnd] *pt-pp* → bind.
▶ *adj* **1** atado,-a, ligado,-a. **2** obligado,-a. **3** encuadernado,-a.

bound[2] [baʊnd] *adj* seguro: *Sue's bound to win*, seguro que ganará Sue; *it's bound to happen*, tiene que pasar.
● **bound for** con destino a, con rumbo a.

bound[3] [baʊnd] *n* salto, brinco.
▶ *vi* saltar.

boundary ['baʊndəri] *n* (*pl* **-ies**) límite, frontera.

bounds [baʊndz] *npl* límites.

bouquet [buːˈkeɪ] *n* **1** ramillete. **2** aroma.

bourgeois ['bʊəʒwaːˈ] *adj-n* burgués, -esa.

bourgeoisie [bʊəʒwaːˈziː] *n* burguesía.

bout [baʊt] *n* **1** rato. **2** ataque *(enfermedad)*. **3** combate, encuentro *(de boxeo)*.

boutique [buːˈtiːk] *n* boutique, tienda.

bow[1] [baʊ] *n* reverencia.
▶ *vi* inclinarse, hacer una reverencia.

bow[2] [bəʊ] *n* **1** arco *(arma)*. **2** arco *(de violín)*. **3** lazo.
■ **bow tie** pajarita.

bow[3] [baʊ] *n* proa.

bowel ['baʊəl] *n* intestino.
▶ *npl* **bowels** entrañas.

bowl[1] [bəʊl] *n* **1** bol, tazón, cuenco. **2** palangana, barreño. **3** taza *(de váter)*.

bowl[2] [bəʊl] *vi* **1** jugar a las bochas. **2** lanzar la pelota *(en cricket)*.
▶ *n* bocha.

bow-legged ['bəʊlegd] *adj* estevado,-a, de piernas arqueadas.

bowler[1] ['bəʊləˈ] (También **bowler hat**) *n* bombín.

bowler[2] ['bəʊləˈ] *n* lanzador,-ra *(en cricket)*.

bowling ['bəʊlɪŋ] *n* bolos.
● **to go bowling** jugar a los bolos, jugar a las bochas.
■ **bowling alley** bolera.

bowls [bəʊlz] *npl* bochas.

box[1] [bɒks] *n* (*pl* **boxes**). **1** caja, cajón, cajetilla, estuche. **2** palco *(en teatro)*. **3** área del penalty *(fútbol)*. **4** GB *fam* caja tonta, tele.
▶ *vt* poner en cajas, encajonar.
■ **box office** taquilla.

box[2] [bɒks] *vi* boxear.

box[3] [bɒks] *n* (*pl* **boxes**) boj *(árbol)*.

boxer ['bɒksəˈ] *n* **1** boxeador,-ra. **2** bóxer *(perro)*.

boxing ['bɒksɪŋ] *n* boxeo.
■ **Boxing Day** GB 26 de diciembre, día de San Esteban.

boy [bɔɪ] *n* niño, chico, muchacho, joven.
■ **boy scout** explorador.

boycott ['bɔɪkɒt] *n* boicot.
▶ *vt* boicotear.

boyfriend ['bɔɪfrend] *n* novio, amigo.

boyhood ['bɔɪhʊd] *n* **1** niñez. **2** adolescencia.

boyish ['bɔɪɪʃ] *adj* **1** aniñado. **2** de niño.

bps ['biːˈpiːˈes] *abbr* (*bits per second*) bps.

bra [braː] *n* → brassiere.

brace [breɪs] *n* **1** abrazadera. **2** berbiquí. **3** aparato *(de dientes)*.
▶ *vt* reforzar.
▶ *npl* **braces** tirantes.
● **to brace oneself for** STH prepararse para algo.

bracelet ['breɪslət] *n* pulsera, brazalete.

bracing ['breɪsɪŋ] *adj* tonificante.

bracket ['brækɪt] *n* **1** paréntesis: *in brackets*, entre paréntesis. **2** soporte. **3** horquilla, banda *(grupo)*.

brag [bræg] *vi* (*pt & pp* **bragged**, *ger* **bragging**) fanfarronear, presumir, jactarse.

braid [breɪd] *n* US trenza.

Braille [breɪl] *n* Braille.

brain [breɪn] *n* cerebro.
▶ *npl* **brains** inteligencia.
■ **brain wave** idea genial.

brainy ['breɪnɪ] *adj* (**-ier**, **-iest**) *fam* inteligente.

brake [breɪk] *n* freno.
▶ *vt-vi* frenar.

bramble ['bræmbəl] *n* zarza.

bran [bræn] *n* salvado.

branch [braːntʃ] *n* (*pl* **-es**). **1** rama *(de árbol)*. **2** ramal *(de carretera)*. **3** sucursal.
▶ *vi* bifurcarse.

brand [brænd] *n* **1** marca. **2** clase. **3** hierro *(de marcar)*.
▶ *vt* marcar.

brandish ['brændɪʃ] *vt* blandir.

brand-new [bræn'njuː] *adj* flamante, completamente nuevo, de estreno.

brandy ['brændɪ] *n* (*pl* **-ies**) brandy.

brass [braːs] *n* (*pl* **-es**). **1** latón. **2** instrumentos de metal.

brassiere ['bræzɪəˈ] *n* sujetador, sostén.

brat [bræt] *n* *fam* mocoso,-a.

brave [breɪv] *adj* valiente.
▶ *vt* **1** desafiar. **2** hacer frente a.
bravery ['breɪvəri] *n* valentía.
bravo [brɑːˈvəʊ] *interj* ¡bravo!
brawl [brɔːl] *n* reyerta, pelea.
Brazil [brəˈzɪl] *n* Brasil.
Brazilian [brəˈzɪliən] *adj-n* brasileño,-a.
breach [briːtʃ] *n* (*pl* -**es**). **1** brecha, abertura. **2** incumplimiento (*de contrato*). **3** ruptura.
bread [bred] *n* **1** pan. **2** *sl* guita, pasta.
breadth [bredθ] *n* anchura.
break [breɪk] *n* **1** ruptura. **2** interrupción, pausa, descanso. **3** oportunidad.
▶ *vt* (*pt* **broke** [brəʊk], *pp* **broken** ['brəʊkən]). **1** romper. **2** batir (*récord*). **3** faltar a, no cumplir (*promesa*). **4** comunicar (*noticias*). **5** descifrar (*código*). **6** amortiguar (*caída*). **7** interrumpir (*viaje*).
▶ *vi* **1** romperse. **2** estallar (*tormenta*). **3** cambiar (*voz*). **4** quebrantarse (*salud*).
to break down *vt* **1** echar abajo, derribar. **2** desglosar.
▶ *vi* **1** averiarse, tener una avería. **2** estropearse.
to break in *vt* domar.
▶ *vi* entrar a robar, entrar por la fuerza.
to break into *vt* entrar por la fuerza en, forzar.
to break out *vi* **1** escaparse (*prisioneros*). **2** estallar (*guerra*).
to break up *vt* disolver (*multitud*).
▶ *vi* **1** disolverse (*multitud*). **2** separarse. **3** empezar las vacaciones.
breakdown ['breɪkdaʊn] *n* **1** fallo, avería. **2** crisis nerviosa. **3** ruptura. **4** análisis, desglose.
breakfast ['brekfəst] *n* desayuno.
▶ *vi* desayunar.
● **to have breakfast** desayunar.
break-in ['breɪkɪn] *n* entrada forzada, robo.
breakthrough ['breɪkθruː] *n* avance importante.
breakwater ['breɪkwɔːtəʳ] *n* rompeolas.
breast [brest] *n* **1** pecho. **2** pechuga (*de pollo*).
breast-feed ['brestfiːd] *vt* amamantar, dar el pecho a.
breaststroke ['breststrəʊk] *n* braza.
breath [breθ] *n* aliento.
● **out of breath** sin aliento.

● **to hold your breath** contener la respiración.
● **to take a deep breath** respirar hondo.
● **a breath of fresh air** un poco de aire fresco.
breathalyse ['breθəlaɪz] *vt* hacer la prueba del alcohol a.
Breathalyser ['breθəlaɪzəʳ] *n* alcoholímetro.
breathe [briːð] *vt-vi* respirar.
breathing ['briːðɪŋ] *n* respiración.
breathless ['breθləs] *adj* sin aliento, jadeante.
bred [bred] *pt-pp* → breed.
breeches ['brɪtʃiz] *npl* pantalones.
breed [briːd] *n* raza.
▶ *vt* (*pt & pp* **bred** [bred]) criar.
▶ *vi* reproducirse.
breeding ['briːdɪŋ] *n* **1** cría. **2** educación.
breeze [briːz] *n* brisa.
brew [bruː] *n* brebaje.
▶ *vt* **1** elaborar, hacer (*cerveza*). **2** preparar (*té*).
▶ *vi* reposar (*té*).
brewery ['brʊəri] *n* (*pl* -**ies**). **1** cervecería. **2** fábrica de cerveza.
bribe [braɪb] *n* soborno.
▶ *vt* sobornar.
bribery ['braɪbəri] *n* soborno.
bric-a-brac ['brɪkəbræk] *n* baratijas.
brick [brɪk] *n* **1** ladrillo. **2** cubo (*de madera*).
● **to drop a brick** GB *fam* meter la pata.
bricklayer ['brɪkleɪəʳ] *n* albañil.
bride [braɪd] *n* novia (*el día de la boda*).
bridegroom ['braɪdgruːm] *n* novio (*el día de la boda*).
bridesmaid ['braɪdzmeɪd] *n* dama de honor.
bridge [brɪdʒ] *n* **1** puente. **2** caballete (*de nariz*). **3** puente de mando (*en barco*). **4** bridge (*juego*).
▶ *vt* tender un puente sobre.
bridle ['braɪdəl] *n* brida.
▶ *vt* embridar.
▶ *vi* ofenderse.
brief [briːf] *adj* breve.
▶ *n* (*pl* **briefs**). **1** informe. **2** expediente. **3** instrucciones.
▶ *vt* **1** informar. **2** dar instrucciones a.
● **in brief** en resumen, en pocas palabras.
briefcase ['briːfkeɪs] *n* maletín, cartera.
briefs [briːfs] *npl* **1** calzoncillos. **2** bragas.

brigade [brɪˈɡeɪd] n brigada.
bright [braɪt] adj **1** brillante (luz). **2** soleado, despejado (día). **3** vivo,-a (color). **4** prometedor,-ra (futuro). **5** inteligente. **6** alegre, animado,-a. **7** brillante, genial (idea).
● **to get up bright and early** levantarse muy temprano.
brighten [ˈbraɪtən] vi animarse, alegrarse.
▶ vt **1** animar, alegrar. **2** despejar, aclarar.
to brighten up vi **1** despejarse. **2** animarse.
▶ vt animar, hacer más alegre.
brightness [ˈbraɪtnəs] n **1** luminosidad, brillo. **2** claridad. **3** viveza. **4** inteligencia.
brilliant [ˈbrɪljənt] adj **1** brillante, reluciente. **2** brillante, genial. **3** fam estupendo,-a, fantástico,-a.
brim [brɪm] n **1** borde. **2** ala (de sombrero).
▶ vi (pt & pp **brimmed**, ger **brimming**) rebosar.
bring [brɪŋ] vt (pt & pp **brought** [brɔːt]). **1** traer: *he brought his sister to the party*, trajo a su hermana a la fiesta. **2** conducir: *he was brought before the court*, fue llevado ante el tribunal; *this path brings you to the church*, este camino te lleva a la iglesia.
● **to bring a charge against SB** JUR acusar a ALGN.
to bring about vt provocar, causar.
to bring back vt **1** devolver. **2** volver a introducir: *to bring back memories of*, hacer recordar.
to bring down vt **1** derribar. **2** hacer bajar.
to bring forward vt adelantar.
to bring in vt **1** introducir. **2** producir, ingresar. **3** emitir (veredicto).
to bring off vt **1** conseguir, lograr. **2** llevar a cabo.
to bring on vt provocar.
to bring out vt sacar, publicar.
to bring round vt **1** persuadir, convencer. **2** hacer volver en sí.
to bring to vt hacer volver en sí.
to bring up vt **1** criar, educar. **2** plantear, sacar a colación. **3** devolver, vomitar.
brink [brɪŋk] n borde.
● **on the brink of** a punto de; al borde de: *on the brink of ruin*, al borde de la ruina.
brisk [brɪsk] adj enérgico,-a.

● **to go for a brisk walk** salir a caminar a paso ligero.
bristle [ˈbrɪsəl] n cerda.
▶ vi erizarse.
to bristle with vt fig estar lleno,-a de.
Britain [ˈbrɪtən] n Bretaña.
■ **Great Britain** Gran Bretaña.
British [ˈbrɪtɪʃ] adj británico,-a.
▶ npl **the British** los británicos.
brittle [ˈbrɪtəl] adj (comp **brittler**, superl **brittlest**) quebradizo,-a, frágil.
broad [brɔːd] adj **1** ancho,-a, amplio,-a, extenso,-a. **2** general, amplio,-a. **3** marcado,-a, cerrado,-a (acento).
● **in broad daylight** en pleno día.
■ **broad bean** haba.
broadcast [ˈbrɔːdkɑːst] n emisión, programa.
▶ vt (pt & pp **broadcast**). **1** emitir, transmitir. **2** difundir.
broadcasting [ˈbrɔːdkɑːstɪŋ] n **1** radiodifusión. **2** transmisión.
broaden [ˈbrɔːdən] vt-vi ensanchar(se).
● **to broaden the mind** ampliar los horizontes.
broadly [ˈbrɔːdlɪ] adv en términos generales.
broad-minded [brɔːdˈmaɪndɪd] adj liberal, tolerante.
broccoli [ˈbrɒkəlɪ] n brécol, brócoli.
brochure [ˈbrəʊʃə˞] n folleto.
broil [brɔɪl] vt US asar a la parrilla.
broiler [ˈbrɔɪlə˞] n pollo (para asar).
broke [brəʊk] pt → break.
▶ adj fam sin blanca.
● **to go broke** arruinarse.
broken [ˈbrəʊkən] pp → break.
▶ adj **1** roto,-a. **2** estropeado,-a (aparato). **3** fracturado,-a (hueso). **4** destrozado,-a (persona). **5** chapurreado,-a (lenguaje).
broker [ˈbrəʊkə˞] n corredor,-ra, broker, agente de bolsa.
brolly [ˈbrɒlɪ] n (pl -ies) GB fam paraguas.
bromide [ˈbrəʊmaɪd] n bromuro.
bromine [ˈbrəʊmaɪn] n bromo.
bronchitis [brɒŋˈkaɪtəs] n bronquitis.
bronze [brɒnz] n bronce.
▶ adj de bronce.
brooch [brəʊtʃ] n (pl -es) broche.
brood [bruːd] vi considerar, rumiar.
brook [brʊk] n arroyo, riachuelo.
broom [bruːm] n escoba.
broomstick [ˈbruːmstɪk] n palo de escoba.

Bros [brɒs] *abbr* (**Brothers**) Hermanos, Hnos: *Jones Bros*, Hnos Jones.

broth [brɒθ] *n* caldo.

brothel ['brɒθəl] *n* burdel.

brother ['brʌðəʳ] *n* hermano.

brotherhood ['brʌðəhʊd] *n* hermandad.

brother-in-law ['brʌðərɪnlɔː] *n* cuñado.

brotherly ['brʌðəlɪ] *adj* fraternal.

brought [brɔːt] *pt-pp* → bring.

brow [braʊ] *n* **1** ceja. **2** frente. **3** cresta, cima.

browbeat ['braʊbiːt] *vt* (*pt* **browbeat** ['braʊbiːt], *pp* **browbeaten** ['braʊbiːtən]) intimidar.

brown [braʊn] *adj* **1** marrón. **2** castaño,-a (*pelo*). **3** moreno,-a (*piel*). **4** integral (*arroz, pan*).
► *vt* dorar(se).

browse [braʊz] *vi* **1** pacer, ramonear. **2** mirar, hojear.
● **to browse the Web** navegar por la Web.

browser ['braʊzəʳ] *n* navegador (*programa*).

bruise [bruːz] *n* morado, magulladura, contusión.
► *vt-vi* magullar(se), contusionar(se).

brunette [bruː'net] *n* morena.
► *adj* moreno,-a.

brush [brʌʃ] *n* (*pl* **-es**). **1** cepillo. **2** pincel. **3** brocha. **4** maleza.
► *vt* **1** cepillar. **2** rozar.

to brush up *vt* refrescar, repasar.

brush-off ['brʌʃɒf] *n* (*pl* **brush-offs**) .
● **to give SB the brush-off** mandar a ALGN a paseo.

brusque [bruːsk] *adj* brusco,-a, áspero,-a.

Brussels ['brʌsəlz] *n* Bruselas.
■ **Brussels sprouts** coles de Bruselas.

brutal ['bruːtəl] *adj* brutal, cruel.

brutality [bruː'tælɪtɪ] *n* brutalidad, crueldad.

brute [bruːt] *adj* brutal, bruto,-a.
► *n* bruto,-a, bestia.

brutish ['bruːtɪʃ] *adj* brutal, bestial.

BSc ['biː'es'siː] *abbr* (**Bachelor of Science**) licenciado,-a en ciencias.

BSE ['biː'es'iː] *abbr* (**bovine spongiform encephalopathy**) encefalopatía espongiforme bovina.

Bt ['bærənət] *abbr* (**Baronet**) baronet.

BTA ['biː'tiː'eɪ] *abbr* (British Tourist Authority) organismo británico que regula el turismo.

bubble ['bʌbəl] *n* burbuja.
► *vi* burbujear, borbotear.
■ **bubble bath** gel de baño.
■ **bubble gum** chicle.

bubbly ['bʌblɪ] *adj* (-**ier**, -**iest**). **1** burbujeante. **2** vivaz.

buck[1] [bʌk] *n* US *fam* dólar.
● **to pass the buck to SB** echar el muerto a ALGN.

buck[2] [bʌk] *n* **1** macho de ciervo, liebre, conejo. **2** galán, señorito.
► *vi* corcovear.

to buck up *vt fam*: *buck your ideas up!*, ¡espabílate!
► *vi* animarse.

bucket ['bʌkɪt] *n* cubo.

buckle ['bʌkəl] *n* hebilla.
► *vt* abrochar (con hebilla).
► *vi* **1** torcerse, combarse. **2** doblarse (*piernas*).

bucolic [bjuː'kɒlɪk] *adj* bucólico,-a.

bud [bʌd] *n* yema, capullo (de planta).

Buddhism ['bʊdɪzəm] *n* budismo.

Buddhist ['bʊdɪst] *adj* budista.
► *n* budista.

budding ['bʌdɪŋ] *adj* en ciernes.

buddy ['bʌdɪ] *n* (*pl* -**ies**) US *fam* colega, amigo.

budge [bʌdʒ] *vt-vi* mover(se).
► *vi* ceder.

budgerigar ['bʌdʒərɪgɑːʳ] *n* periquito.

budget ['bʌdʒɪt] *n* presupuesto.
► *vt-vi* presupuestar.

buff [bʌf] *n* **1** color del ante. **2** aficionado,-a.
► *adj* de color del ante.

buffalo ['bʌfələʊ] *n* (*pl* **buffaloes**) búfalo.

buffer ['bʌfəʳ] *n* **1** tope (*para trenes*). **2** memoria intermedia.

buffet ['bʌfeɪ] *n* **1** bar, cantina, bar. **2** bufet libre.
■ **buffet car** vagón restaurante.

bug [bʌg] *n* **1** bicho. **2** *fam* microbio. **3** micrófono oculto. **4** error (*en programa*).
► *vt* (*pt & pp* **bugged**, *ger* **bugging**). **1** *fam* poner un micrófono oculto en. **2** *fam* molestar.

bugger ['bʌgəʳ] *n* **1** *vulg* cabrón,-ona. **2** *vulg* coñazo.
► *interj* **bugger!** *vulg* ¡joder!

to bugger about *vi vulg* hacer el gilipollas.

to bugger off *vi vulg* largarse.

to bugger up *vt vulg* joder, fastidiar.
bugle ['bjuːgəl] *n* corneta.
build [bɪld] *n* constitución, complexión: *a woman of slim build*, una mujer de constitución delgada.
▶ *vt* (*pt & pp* **built** [bɪlt]) construir.
to build up *vt-vi* acumular(se).
builder ['bɪldəʳ] *n* constructor,-ra.
building ['bɪldɪŋ] *n* **1** edificio. **2** construcción, edificación.
■ **building site** obra.
■ **building society** sociedad de ahorro para la vivienda.
build-up ['bɪldʌp] *n* **1** aumento. **2** acumulación.
built [bɪlt] *pt-pp* → build.
built-in [bɪltˈɪn] *adj* **1** empotrado,-a. **2** incorporado,-a.
built-up [bɪltˈʌp] *adj* urbanizado,-a.
bulb [bʌlb] *n* **1** bulbo. **2** bombilla.
Bulgaria [bʌlˈɡeərɪə] *n* Bulgaria.
Bulgarian [bʌlˈɡeərɪən] *adj* búlgaro,-a.
▶ *n* **1** búlgaro,-a (*persona*). **2** búlgaro (*lengua*).
bulge [bʌldʒ] *n* bulto.
▶ *vi* rebosar (**with**, de).
bulk [bʌlk] *n* **1** volumen, masa. **2** mayor parte.
● **in bulk** a granel, al por mayor.
bulky ['bʌlkɪ] *adj* (**-ier**, **-iest**) **1** voluminoso,-a. **2** corpulento.
bull [bʊl] *n* toro.
bulldog ['bʊldɒg] *n* buldog.
bulldozer ['bʊldəʊzəʳ] *n* bulldozer.
bullet ['bʊlɪt] *n* bala.
bulletin ['bʊlɪtɪn] *n* boletín.
bulletproof ['bʊlɪtpruːf] *adj* antibalas.
bullfight ['bʊlfaɪt] *n* corrida de toros.
bullfighter ['bʊlfaɪtəʳ] *n* torero,-a.
bullfighting ['bʊlfaɪtɪŋ] *n* los toros, tauromaquia.
bullion ['bʊljən] *n* lingotes (*de oro o plata*).
bullock ['bʊlək] *n* buey.
bullring ['bʊlrɪŋ] *n* plaza de toros.
bull's-eye ['bʊlzaɪ] *n* diana.
● **to score a bull's-eye** dar en el blanco.
bullshit ['bʊlʃɪt] *n vulg* chorradas.
bully ['bʊlɪ] *n* (*pl* **-ies**) matón.
▶ *vt* (*pt & pp* **-ied**) intimidar, atemorizar.
bum[1] [bʌm] *n* GB *fam* culo.
bum[2] [bʌm] *n* **1** US *fam* vagabundo,-a. **2** *fam* vago,-a.

▶ *vt* (*pt & pp* **bummed**, *ger* **bumming**) *fam* gorrear.
bumblebee ['bʌmbəlbiː] *n* abejorro.
bumbling ['bʌmblɪŋ] *adj* torpe, inútil.
bump [bʌmp] *n* **1** chichón, hinchazón. **2** bache (*en carretera*). **3** choque, batacazo, golpe.
▶ *vt-vi* chocar.
to bump into *vt* encontrar por casualidad, tropezar con.
to bump off *vt* matar.
bumper ['bʌmpəʳ] *adj* abundante.
▶ *n* parachoques.
bumpkin ['bʌmpkɪn] *n* paleto,-a.
bumpy ['bʌmpɪ] *adj* (**-ier**, **-iest**) lleno,-a de baches.
bun [bʌn] *n* **1** panecillo, bollo. **2** moño.
bunch [bʌntʃ] *n* (*pl* **-es**). **1** manojo. **2** ramo. **3** racimo. **4** grupo.
bundle ['bʌndəl] *n* **1** fardo. **2** haz. **3** fajo.
bung [bʌŋ] *n* tapón.
▶ *vt* **1** *fam* poner. **2** GB *fam* lanzar.
bungalow ['bʌŋgələʊ] *n* bungalow.
bungle ['bʌŋgəl] *vt* chapucear.
bungler ['bʌŋgələʳ] *n* chapucero,-a.
bunion ['bʌnjən] *n* juanete.
bunk [bʌŋk] *n* litera (*en un barco o tren*).
■ **bunk bed** litera (*en una habitación*).
bunker ['bʌŋkəʳ] *n* **1** carbonera. **2** búnker (*en golf*). **3** búnker.
bunny ['bʌnɪ] *n* (*pl* **-ies**). **1** *fam* conejito. **2** tía buena.
buoy [bɔɪ] *n* boya.
buoyant ['bɔɪənt] *adj* **1** flotante (*objeto*). **2** boyante (*economía*). **3** animado,-a (*persona*).
burden ['bɜːdən] *n* carga.
▶ *vt* cargar.
bureau ['bjʊərəʊ] *n* (*pl* **-s** o **bureaux**). **1** escritorio. **2** US cómoda. **3** oficina.
bureaucracy [bjʊəˈrɒkrəsɪ] *n* (*pl* **-ies**) burocracia.
bureaucrat ['bjʊərəkræt] *n* burócrata.
bureaucratic [bjʊərəˈkrætɪk] *adj* burocrático,-a.
burger ['bɜːgəʳ] *n* hamburguesa.
burglar ['bɜːgləʳ] *n* ladrón,-ona.
burglary ['bɜːglərɪ] *n* (*pl* **-ies**) robo.
burgle ['bɜːgəl] *vt* robar.
burial ['berɪəl] *n* entierro.
burly ['bɜːlɪ] *adj* (**-ier**, **-iest**) corpulento,-a.
burn [bɜːn] *n* quemadura.
▶ *vt* (*pt & pp* **burnt** [bɜːnt]) quemar.

► *vi* arder, quemarse.

● **to be burning hot** estar muy caliente.

● **to smell burning** oler a quemado.

to burn down *vt-vi* incendiar(se).

to burn out *vi* **1** extinguirse *(fuego)*. **2** gastarse *(máquina)*.

burner ['bɜːnəʳ] *n* quemador, fuego.

burning ['bɜːnɪŋ] *adj* **1** incendiado,-a, ardiendo. **2** ardiente *(deseo)*.

■ **burning question** cuestión candente.

burnt [bɜːnt] *pt-pp* → burn.

burp [bɜːp] *n fam* eructo.

► *vi fam* eructar.

burrow ['bʌrəʊ] *n* madriguera.

► *vi* excavar una madriguera.

burst [bɜːst] *n* **1** explosión, estallido. **2** reventón. **3** salva. **4** ráfaga *(de tiros)*.

► *vt-vi* (*pt & pp* **burst**) reventar(se).

● **to burst into tears** echarse a llorar.

● **to burst out crying/laughing** echarse a llorar/reír.

● **the river burst its banks** el río se desbordó.

bury ['beri] *vt* (*pt & pp* **-ied**) enterrar.

bus [bʌs] *n* (*pl* **buses**) autobús.

■ **bus stop** parada de autobús.

bush [bʊʃ] *n* (*pl* **-es**). **1** arbusto. **2** monte.

bushy ['bʊʃi] *adj* (**-ier**, **-iest**) espeso,-a, tupido,-a.

business ['bɪznəs] *n* (*pl* **-es**) **1** los negocios. **2** negocio, empresa. **3** asunto: *it's none of your business*, no es asunto tuyo.

● **to be in business** dedicarse a los negocios.

businesslike ['bɪznəslaɪk] *adj* formal, serio,-a.

businessman ['bɪznəsmən] *n* (*pl* **businessmen**) hombre de negocios, empresario.

businesswoman ['bɪznəswʊmən] *n* (*pl* **businesswomen**) mujer de negocios, empresaria.

busker ['bʌskəʳ] *n* GB músico,-a callejero,-a.

bust¹ [bʌst] *n* busto.

bust² [bʌst] *vt-vi fam* romper, romperse.

► *adj fam* roto,-a.

● **to go bust** quebrar.

bustle ['bʌsəl] *n* bullicio.

to bustle about *vi* ir y venir, no parar, trajinar.

busy ['bɪzi] *adj* (**-ier**, **-iest**) **1** ocupado,-a, atareado,-a *(persona)*. **2** concurrido,-a,

transitado,-a *(calle)*. **3** ajetreado,-a *(día)*. **4** que comunica *(teléfono)*.

● **to busy oneself doing** STH ocuparse en hacer algo.

busybody ['bɪzɪbɒdɪ] *n* (*pl* **-ies**) entremetido,-a.

but [bʌt] *conj* **1** pero: *it's cold, but dry*, hace frío, pero no llueve; *I'd like to, but I can't*, me gustaría, pero no puedo. **2** sino: *not two, but three*, no dos, sino tres.

► *adv* sólo: *had I but known ...*, si lo hubiese sabido ...; *she is but a child*, no es más que una niña.

► *prep* excepto, salvo, menos: *all but me*, todos menos yo.

● **but for** si no hubiese sido por, si no fuese por: *but for his help, we would have failed*, si no hubiese sido por su ayuda, habríamos fracasado.

butane ['bjuːteɪn] *n* butano.

butcher ['bʊtʃəʳ] *n* carnicero,-a.

butler ['bʌtləʳ] *n* mayordomo.

butt¹ [bʌt] *n* **1** colilla. **2** culata *(de rifle)*. **3** US *fam* culo.

butt² [bʌt] *n* blanco, objetivo.

butt³ [bʌt] *n* tonel.

butt⁴ [bʌt] *n* cabezazo.

► *vt* embestir.

to butt in *vi* entrometerse.

butter ['bʌtəʳ] *n* mantequilla.

► *vt* untar con mantequilla.

● **to look as if butter wouldn't melt in one's mouth** parecer una mosquita muerta.

to butter up *vt fam* dar coba a.

butterfingers ['bʌtəfɪŋgəz] *n* manazas.

butterfly ['bʌtəflaɪ] *n* (*pl* **-ies**) mariposa.

buttock ['bʌtək] *n* nalga.

button ['bʌtən] *n* botón.

► *vt-vi* abrocharse.

buttonhole ['bʌtənhəʊl] *n* ojal.

buttress ['bʌtrəs] *n* (*pl* **-es**) contrafuerte.

butty ['bʌti] *n* (*pl* **-ies**) GB *fam* bocata.

buy [baɪ] *vt* (*pt & pp* **bought** [bɔːt]). **1** comprar. **2** sobornar. **3** *fam* tragarse, creerse.

buyer ['baɪəʳ] *n* comprador,-ra.

buzz [bʌz] *n* zumbido.

► *vi* zumbar.

● **to give** SB **a buzz** dar un toque a ALGN, dar un telefonazo a ALGN.

buzzer ['bʌzəʳ] *n* timbre.

by [baɪ] *prep* **1** por: *painted by Fraser*, pintado por Fraser; *by air/road*, por avión/carretera. **2** en: *by car/train*, en coche/tren; *by hand*, a mano; *I won by 3 points*, gané por tres puntos; *better by far*, muchísimo mejor. **3** para: *I need it by ten*, lo necesito para las diez. **4** de: *a film by Woody Allen*, una película de Woody Allen; *he's a journalist by profession*, es periodista de profesión; *by day/night*, de día/noche; *by heart*, de memoria. **5** junto a, al lado de: *sit by me*, siéntate a mi lado. **6** según: *by the rules*, según las reglas. **7** por: *6 metres by 4*, 6 metros por 4; *paid by the hour*, pagado, -a por horas. **8** en: *we went by train*, fuimos en tren; *two by two*, de dos en dos. **9** con: *can I pay by credit card?*, ¿puedo pagar con tarjeta?

▶ *adv* de largo: *he passed by, he didn't stop*, pasó de largo, no se detuvo.

● **by and by** con el tiempo.

● **by oneself** solo,-a.

bye [baɪ] *interj fam* ¡adiós!, ¡hasta luego!

bylaw ['baɪlɔ:] *n* ordenanza municipal.

bypass ['baɪpɑːs] *n* (*pl* **-es**). **1** variante *(carretera)*. **2** by-pass.

by-product ['baɪprɒdʌkt] *n* subproducto, derivado.

bystander ['baɪstændə'] *n* **1** espectador, -ra. **2** alguien que está presente.

byte [baɪt] *n* byte.

C

c¹ ['sɜːkə] *abbr* (*circa*) hacia.

c² [sent] *abbr* (*cent*) centavo.

c³ ['kɒpɪraɪt] *abbr* (*copyright*) propiedad literaria, copyright.

c. ['sentʃərɪ] *abbr* siglo: *C18 literature*, la literatura del s. XVIII.

C of E ['siːəv'iː] *abbr* (*Church of England*) Iglesia Anglicana.

c/a [kərəntə'kaʊnt] *abbr* (*current account*) cuenta corriente, c/c.

cab [kæb] *n* **1** taxi. **2** cabina de conductor, cabina de maquinista. **3** cabriolé.

cabbage ['kæbɪdʒ] *n* col, repollo, berza.

cabin ['kæbɪn] *n* **1** cabaña. **2** camarote. **3** cabina.

cabinet ['kæbɪnət] *n* **1** gabinete. **2** armario, vitrina.

cable ['keɪbəl] *n* **1** cable (*eléctrico*). **2** cable, telegrama.
► *vt* cablegrafiar, telegrafiar.
■ **cable car** teleférico, telecabina.
■ **cable television** televisión por cable.

cache [kæʃ] *n* **1** alijo. **2** caché.
■ **cache memory** memoria caché.

cackle ['kækəl] *n* **1** cacareo. **2** risa socarrona.
► *vi* **1** cacarear. **2** reír socarronamente.

cactus ['kæktəs] *n* (*pl* **cacti** ['kæktaɪ] o **cactuses**) cactus.

CAD [kæd] *abbr* (*computer-aided design*) diseño con ayuda de ordenador.

caddie ['kædɪ] *n* cadi (*en golf*).

caddy ['kædɪ] *n* (*pl* **-ies**) cajita para el té.

cadet [kə'det] *n* cadete.

cadger ['kædʒəʳ] *n fam* gorrón,-ona.

café ['kæfeɪ] *n* cafetería.

cafeteria [kæfə'tɪərɪə] *n* (restaurante de) autoservicio.

caffeine ['kæfiːn] *n* cafeína.

cage [keɪdʒ] *n* jaula.
► *vt* enjaular.

cagey ['keɪdʒɪ] *adj* (-**ier**, -**iest**) *fam* cauteloso,-a, reservado,-a.

cagoule [kə'guːl] *n* chubasquero.

cake [keɪk] *n* pastel, tarta.
● **to sell like hot cakes** venderse como rosquillas.
● **it's a piece of cake** es pan comido, está chupado,-a.

calamity [kə'læmɪtɪ] *n* (*pl* **-ies**) calamidad.

calcium ['kælsɪəm] *n* calcio.

calculate ['kælkjəleɪt] *vt* calcular.
► *vi* hacer cálculos, calcular.

calculating ['kælkjəleɪtɪŋ] *adj* calculador,-ra.
■ **calculating machine** calculadora.

calculation [kælkjə'leɪʃən] *n* cálculo.

calculator ['kælkjəleɪtəʳ] *n* calculadora.

calculus ['kælkjələs] *n* cálculo.

calendar ['kælɪndəʳ] *n* calendario.

calf¹ [kɑːf] *n* (*pl* **calves**) ternero,-a, becerro,-a.

calf² [kɑːf] *n* (*pl* **calves**) pantorrilla.

calibre ['kælɪbəʳ] *n* (US **caliber**) *n* calibre.

call [kɔːl] *n* **1** grito: *nobody heard her calls*, nadie oyó sus gritos. **2** llamada: *there's a call for you*, tienes una llamada. **3** aviso, llamada: *last call for flight CH354*, última llamada para el vuelo CH354. **4** grito (*de animal*), reclamo (*de ave*). **5** demanda: *there's not much call for it*, no tiene mucha demanda. **6** llamada, llamamiento: *a call for calm*, un llamamiento a la calma. **7** visita: *we had a call from the police*, recibimos una visita de la policía.

▶ *vt* **1** llamar: *he called me into his office*, me llamó a su despacho; *what is he called?*, ¿cómo se llama?; *he called me a liar*, me llamó mentiroso. **2** llamar, telefonear: *call your mother*, llama a tu madre. **3** convocar, anunciar *(reunión)*.

▶ *vi* **1** llamar: *has anybody called?*, ¿ha llamado alguien? **2** pasar: *she called on her way to work*, pasó camino del trabajo; *call at the butcher's*, pásate por la carnicería. **3** efectuar parada: *this train calls at Selby and York*, este tren efectúa parada en Selby y York.

● **on call** de guardia.

● **to call into question** poner en duda.

● **to call to mind** traer a la memoria.

● **to pay a call on** visitar.

● **let's call it a day** dejémoslo por hoy.

■ **call box** GB cabina telefónica.

■ **call girl** prostituta.

to call for *vt* **1** pasar a buscar. **2** exigir, necesitar: *this calls for a celebration*, esto hay que celebrarlo.

to call off *vt* suspender, cancelar.

to call on *vt* **1** visitar. **2** *fml* instar: *he called on them to negotiate*, les instó a negociar.

to call out *vt* **1** sacar a la calle *(tropas)*. **2** avisar *(médico)*. **3** llamar a la huelga *(obreros)*.

▶ *vt-vi* gritar.

to call up *vt* **1** llamar a filas. **2** llamar *(por teléfono)*.

caller ['kɔːləʳ] *n* **1** visita, visitante. **2** persona que llama.

callipers ['kælɪpəz] *npl* **1** calibrador. **2** aparato ortopédico.

callous ['kæləs] *adj* duro,-a, insensible.

calm [kɑːm] *adj* **1** en calma, sereno,-a *(mar)*. **2** tranquilo,-a, sosegado,-a *(persona)*.

▶ *n* **1** calma *(del mar)*. **2** tranquilidad, serenidad *(de persona)*.

▶ *vt* tranquilizar, calmar.

to calm down *vt* tranquilizar, calmar.

calorie ['kælərɪ] *n* caloría.

camcorder ['kæmkɔːdəʳ] *n* videocámara.

came [keɪm] *pt* → come.

camel ['kæməl] *n* camello.

camera ['kæmərə] *n* cámara, máquina fotográfica.

● **in camera** a puerta cerrada.

cameraman ['kæmərəmæn] *n* (*pl* **cameramen**) cámara.

Cameroon [kæməˈruːn] *n* Camerún.

camomile ['kæməmaɪl] *n* manzanilla, camomila.

camouflage ['kæməflɑːʒ] *n* camuflaje.

▶ *vt* camuflar.

camp [kæmp] *n* campamento.

▶ *vi* acampar.

■ **camp bed** cama plegable.

■ **camp site** camping, campamento.

campaign [kæmˈpeɪn] *n* campaña.

▶ *vi* hacer campaña (*for,* **en favor de**).

camper ['kæmpəʳ] *n* **1** campista. **2** US caravana.

camping ['kæmpɪŋ] *n* .

● **to go camping** ir de camping.

■ **camping site** camping, campamento.

campus ['kæmpəs] *n* (*pl* **campuses**) campus.

can¹ [kæn] *aux* (*pt & cond* **could**). **1** poder: *can you come tomorrow?*, ¿puedes venir mañana? **2** saber: *he can swim*, sabe nadar; *can you speak Chinese?*, ¿sabes hablar chino? **3** poder: *you can sit down if you like*, puedes sentarte si quieres; *you can't park here*, no está permitido aparcar aquí. **4** poder: *he can not be here already!*, ¡no puede ser que ya haya llegado!; *what can it mean?*, ¿qué querrá decir?

can² [kæn] *n* **1** lata. **2** bidón.

▶ *vt* (*pt & pp* **canned**, *ger* **canning**) enlatar.

Canada ['kænədə] *n* Canadá.

Canadian [kəˈneɪdɪən] *adj* canadiense.

▶ *n* canadiense.

canal [kəˈnæl] *n* canal.

canary [kəˈneərɪ] *n* (*pl* **-ies**) canario.

Canary Islands [kəˈneərɪaɪləndz] *npl* Islas Canarias.

cancel ['kænsəl] *vt* (GB *pt & pp* **cancelled**, *ger* **cancelling**; US *pt & pp* **canceled**, *ger* **canceling**). **1** cancelar *(pedido)*. **2** anular *(contrato)*. **3** tachar.

cancellation [kænsəˈleɪʃən] *n* **1** cancelación *(de pedido)*. **2** anulación *(de contrato)*.

cancer ['kænsəʳ] *n* **1** cáncer *(enfermedad)*. **2 Cancer** Cáncer *(signo y constelación)*.

candid ['kændɪd] *adj* franco,-a, sincero,-a.

candidate ['kændɪdət] *n* **1** candidato,-a, aspirante. **2** examinando, opositor.

candle ['kændəl] *n* vela, cirio.

candlestick ['kændəlstɪk] n candelero, palmatoria.

candy ['kændɪ] n (pl -ies) US caramelo.

cane [keɪn] n 1 caña. 2 bastón, vara. 3 mimbre.
► vt azotar con la vara.

canine ['keɪnaɪn] adj canino,-a.

canister ['kænɪstə'] n bote, lata.

canned [kænd] adj 1 enlatado,-a. 2 fam mamado,-a.

cannibal ['kænɪbəl] adj caníbal.
► n caníbal.

cannon ['kænən] n cañón.

cannot ['kænɒt] aux → can.

Es la forma compuesta de **can** + **not**.

canoe [kə'nu:] n canoa, piragua.
► vi ir en canoa, ir en piragua.

canon[1] ['kænən] n canon.

canon[2] ['kænən] n canónigo.

canopy ['kænəpɪ] n (pl -ies). 1 dosel (de cama). 2 cubierta frondosa (de árboles).

can't [kɑːnt] aux contracción de **can** + **not**.

canteen [kæn'ti:n] n 1 cantina. 2 cubertería.

canter ['kæntə'] n medio galope.
► vi ir a medio galope.

canvas ['kænvəs] n (pl **canvases**). 1 lona. 2 lienzo.

canvass ['kænvəs] vi hacer propaganda política.

canyon ['kænjən] n cañón.

cap [kæp] n 1 gorro, gorra, cofia. 2 capuchón, chapa, tapa.
► vt (pt & pp **capped**, ger **capping**) cubrir, coronar.
● **to cap it all** para colmo.

capability [keɪpə'bɪlɪtɪ] n capacidad, aptitud, competencia.

capable ['keɪpəbəl] adj capaz: **he's capable of not coming**, es capaz de no venir.

capacity [kə'pæsɪtɪ] n (pl -ies). 1 capacidad, cabida (de un contenedor). 2 capacidad, aforo (de teatro). 3 capacidad (habilidad). 4 condición, calidad: **in his capacity as a judge**, en calidad de juez.
● **to be filled to capacity** estar al completo.

cape[1] [keɪp] n capa corta.

cape[2] [keɪp] n cabo (promontorio).

caper[1] ['keɪpə'] n alcaparra.

caper[2] ['keɪpə'] n travesura.

capital ['kæpɪtəl] adj 1 mayúscula: **it's written with a capital A**, se escribe con A mayúscula. 2 capital: **the capital city**, la capital.
► n 1 capital (ciudad): **the provincial capital**, la capital de la provincia. 2 capital (dinero). 3 mayúscula: **in capitals**, en mayúsculas.
■ **capital letter** mayúscula.
■ **capital punishment** pena capital.

capitalism ['kæpɪtəlɪzəm] n capitalismo.

capitalist ['kæpɪtəlɪst] adj capitalista.
► n capitalista.

capitulate [kə'pɪtjəleɪt] vi capitular.

capricious [kə'prɪʃəs] adj caprichoso,-a, antojadizo,-a.

Capricorn ['kæprɪkɔ:n] n Capricornio.

capsize [kæp'saɪz] vi volcar.
► vt hacer volcar.

capsule ['kæpsju:l] n cápsula.

captain ['kæptɪn] n capitán (de barco); comandante (de avión).

caption ['kæpʃən] n leyenda, pie de foto.

captivate ['kæptɪveɪt] vt cautivar, fascinar.

captive ['kæptɪv] adj-n cautivo,-a; prisionero,-a.

captivity [kæp'tɪvɪtɪ] n cautiverio, cautividad.
● **in captivity** en cautividad.

capture ['kæptʃə'] n 1 captura, apresamiento, toma. 2 presa.
► vt 1 capturar, apresar, tomar. 2 captar.

car [kɑ:'] n 1 coche, automóvil. 2 vagón, coche (de ferrocarril).
■ **car bomb** coche bomba.
■ **car park** aparcamiento.
■ **car wash** túnel de lavado.

caramel ['kærəmel] n 1 azúcar quemado. 2 caramelo.

carat ['kærət] n quilate.

caravan ['kærəvæn] n caravana.

carbohydrate [kɑ:bəʊ'haɪdreɪt] n hidrato de carbono.

carbon ['kɑ:bən] n carbono.
■ **carbon dioxide** dióxido de carbono.
■ **carbon monoxide** monóxido de carbono.
■ **carbon paper** papel carbón.

carburettor [kɑ:bə'retə'] n carburador.

carcass ['kɑ:kəs] n (pl **-es**) res muerta, animal muerto.

card [kɑ:d] n 1 carta, naipe. 2 tarjeta, felicitación. **3** ficha. **4** carnet, carné *(de socio)*. **5** cartulina.

● **to play cards** jugar a las cartas.

cardboard ['kɑːdbɔːd] *n* cartón.

cardiac ['kɑːdɪæk] *adj* cardíaco,-a.

■ **cardiac arrest** paro cardíaco.

cardigan ['kɑːdɪgən] *n* rebeca, chaqueta de punto.

cardinal ['kɑːdɪnəl] *adj* cardinal.

► *n* cardenal *(religioso)*.

■ **cardinal number** número cardinal.

cardphone ['kɑːdfəʊn] *n* teléfono de tarjeta.

care [keəʳ] *n* **1** cuidado: *she did it with great care*, lo hizo con mucho cuidado. **2** asistencia: *health care*, asistencia sanitaria. **3** preocupación, inquietud: *she was free of all cares*, no tenía preocupaciones. **4** custodia.

► *vi* **1** preocuparse: *he doesn't care about others*, no le importan los demás; *I don't care*, me tiene sin cuidado. **2** *fml* apetecer: *would you care to dance?*, ¿le apetecería bailar?

► *vt* importar: *I don't care what she says*, no me importa lo que diga.

● **take care!** ¡cuidado!

● **to take care of 1** cuidar, cuidar de. **2** ocuparse de, hacerse cargo de.

● **to take care to do STH** asegurarse de hacer algo, procurar hacer algo.

● **to take care not to do STH** tener cuidado de no hacer algo, guardarse mucho de hacer algo.

to care for *vt* **1** cuidar. **2** gustar, interesar. **3** querer.

career [kəˈrɪəʳ] *n* **1** carrera. **2** vida profesional.

careful ['keəfʊl] *adj* **1** cuidadoso,-a. **2** prudente: *a careful driver*, un conductor prudente.

● **to be careful** tener cuidado.

carefully ['keəfʊlɪ] *adv* cuidadosamente, con cuidado: *drive carefully*, conduce con cuidado.

careless ['keələs] *adj* **1** descuidado,-a, negligente *(persona)*. **2** poco cuidado. **3** imprudente *(conductor)*.

caress [kəˈres] *n (pl* **-es)** caricia.

► *vt* acariciar.

caretaker ['keəteɪkəʳ] *n* conserje.

cargo ['kɑːgəʊ] *n (pl* **-s** o **-es)** carga, cargamento.

Caribbean [kærɪˈbɪən, US kəˈrɪbɪən] *adj* caribeño,-a.

■ **the Caribbean** el Caribe.

caricature ['kærɪkətjʊəʳ] *n* caricatura.

► *vt* caricaturizar.

caries ['keərɪz] *n* caries.

carnation [kɑːˈneɪʃən] *n* clavel.

carnival ['kɑːnɪvəl] *n* carnaval.

carol ['kærəl] *n* villancico.

carp¹ [kɑːp] *n* carpa *(pez)*.

carp² [kɑːp] *vi* refunfuñar, quejarse.

carpenter ['kɑːpɪntəʳ] *n* carpintero.

carpentry ['kɑːpɪntrɪ] *n* carpintería.

carpet ['kɑːpɪt] *n* moqueta, alfombra.

► *vt* enmoquetar.

carriage ['kærɪdʒ] *n* **1** carruaje. **2** vagón, coche *(de ferrocarril)*. **3** transporte.

■ **carriage paid** portes pagados.

carriageway ['kærɪdʒweɪ] *n* GB carril.

carrier ['kærɪəʳ] *n* **1** transportista. **2** portador,-ra *(de enfermedad)*.

■ **carrier bag** bolsa *(de plástico o papel)*.

■ **carrier pigeon** paloma mensajera.

carrot ['kærət] *n* zanahoria.

carry ['kærɪ] *vt (pt & pp* **-ied)**. **1** llevar, llevar encima *(dinero)*. **2** transportar *(mercancía)*. **3** vender, tener en existencia. **4** conllevar *(responsabilidad)*. **5** publicar, cubrir *(historia)*. **6** aprobar *(voto)*. **7** ser portador,-ra *(de enfermedad)*.

► *vi* oírse.

● **to get carried away 1** exaltarse. **2** dejarse llevar.

to carry forward *vt* llevar a la columna siguiente, llevar a la página siguiente.

to carry off *vt* **1** realizar con éxito. **2** llevarse *(premio)*.

to carry on *vt* seguir, continuar.

to carry on with *vt (a person)* estar liado,-a con.

to carry out *vt* **1** llevar a cabo, realizar. **2** cumplir *(orden, amenaza)*.

carsick ['kɑːsɪk] *adj* mareado,-a.

● **to get carsick** marearse *(en un coche)*.

cart [kɑːt] *n* **1** carro. **2** carretilla.

cartel [kɑːˈtel] *n* cártel.

cartilage ['kɑːtɪlɪdʒ] *n* cartílago.

carton ['kɑːtən] *n* **1** envase de cartón. **2** cartón.

cartoon [kɑːˈtuːn] *n* **1** caricatura. **2** dibujos animados. **3** historieta, tira cómica.

cartridge ['kɑːtrɪdʒ] *n* **1** cartucho. **2** recambio *(para estilográfica)*.

cartwheel ['kɑːtwiːl] *n* voltereta.
carve [kɑːv] *vt* tallar *(madera)*. **2** esculpir *(piedra)*. **3** cortar, trinchar *(carne)*.
carving ['kɑːvɪŋ] *n* **1** talla *(de madera)*. **2** escultura *(de piedra)*.
■ **carving knife** trinchante, cuchillo de trinchar.
cascade [kæs'keɪd] *n* cascada.
case[1] [keɪs] *n* **1** caso. **2** causa, proceso *(criminal)*. **3** argumento, razones.
● **in any case** en todo caso, en cualquier caso.
● **in case** por si: *take your umbrella in case it rains*, lleva el paraguas por si llueve.
● **in case of** en caso de.
● **just in case** por si acaso.
case[2] [keɪs] *n* **1** maleta. **2** caja. **3** estuche, funda.
cash [kæʃ] *n* dinero en efectivo, metálico.
▶ *vt* cobrar *(talón)*.
● **cash down** al contado.
● **cash on delivery** contra reembolso.
● **to pay cash** pagar al contado, pagar en efectivo.
■ **cash desk** caja.
■ **cash dispenser** cajero automático.
■ **cash register** caja registradora.
cash-and-carry [kæʃən'kærɪ] *n* (*pl* -**ies**) autoservicio al por mayor.
cashew [kə'ʃuː] *n* anacardo.
cashier [kæ'ʃɪəʳ] *n* cajero,-a.
cashmere [kæʃ'mɪəʳ] *n* cachemira.
casino [kə'siːnəʊ] *n* (*pl* **casinos**) casino.
cask [kɑːsk] *n* tonel, barril.
casket ['kɑːskɪt] *n* cofre.
casserole ['kæsərəʊl] *n* **1** cazuela. **2** guisado.
cassette [kə'set] *n* casete.
■ **cassette player** casete.
■ **cassette recorder** casete.
cast [kɑːst] *n* **1** reparto *(de película, etc)*. **2** molde. **3** yeso, escayola *(uso médico)*.
▶ *vt* (*pt & pp* **cast**). **1** lanzar. **2** dar el papel de: *he was cast as Hamlet*, le dieron el papel de Hamlet. **3** moldear.
● **to be cast away** naufragar.
● **to cast a shadow** proyectar una sombra.
● **to cast a spell on** hechizar.
● **to cast a vote** emitir un voto.
● **to cast doubts on** poner en duda.
● **to cast suspicion on** levantar sospechas sobre.
■ **cast iron** hierro colado.

to cast off *vt* desechar.
▶ *vi* soltar amarras.
castaway ['kɑːstəweɪ] *n* náufrago,-a.
caste [kɑːst] *n* casta.
caster ['kɑːstəʳ] *n* ruedecilla.
■ **caster sugar** azúcar glasé.
Castile [kæ'stiːl] *n* Castilla.
Castilian [kæ'stɪlɪən] *adj* castellano,-a.
▶ *n* **1** castellano,-a *(persona)*. **2** castellano *(lengua)*.
castle ['kɑːsəl] *n* **1** castillo. **2** torre *(ajedrez)*.
castrate [kæ'streɪt] *vt* castrar, capar.
casual ['kæʒjʊəl] *adj* **1** fortuito,-a, casual *(encuentro)*. **2** informal *(ropa)*. **3** superficial: *a casual glance*, una ojeada. **4** ocasional *(trabajador)*. **5** despreocupado,-a *(comportamiento)*.
casually ['kæʒjʊəlɪ] *adv* sin darle importancia, con aire despreocupado.
casualty ['kæʒjʊəltɪ] *n* (*pl* -**ies**). **1** herido, -a, víctima. **2** baja *(soldado)*.
■ **casualty department** urgencias.
cat [kæt] *n* gato,-a.
● **to let the cat out of the bag** descubrir el pastel.
● **to put the cat among the pigeons** armar un revuelo.
Catalan ['kætəlæn] *adj* catalán,-ana.
▶ *n* **1** catalán,-ana *(persona)*. **2** catalán *(lengua)*.
catalogue ['kætəlɒg] (US **catalog**) *n* GB catálogo.
▶ *vt* GB catalogar.
Catalonia [kætə'ləʊnɪə] *n* Cataluña.
catalyst ['kætəlɪst] *n* catalizador.
catapult ['kætəpʌlt] *n* **1** catapulta. **2** tirachinas.
▶ *vt* catapultar.
cataract ['kætərækt] *n* **1** catarata, cascada salto de agua. **2** catarata *(del ojo)*.
catarrh [kə'tɑːʳ] *n* catarro.
catastrophe [kə'tæstrəfɪ] *n* catástrofe.
catch [kætʃ] *vt* (*pt & pp* **caught**). **1** coger, atrapar. **2** coger, tomar *(tren)*. **3** pillar, sorprender. **4** alcanzar: *I ran and caught him*, corrí y lo alcancé. **5** contraer, contagiarse: *to catch a cold*, coger un resfriado. **6** oír.
▶ *vi* engancharse *(ropa)*.
▶ *n* (*pl* -**es**). **1** parada *(de pelota)*. **2** pesca. **3** *fam* pega. **4** cierre, pestillo.

● **to catch fire** prender fuego, encenderse.

● **to catch hold of** agarrar, echar mano a.

● **to catch SB's eye** captar la atención de ALGN.

● **to catch sight of** entrever.

to catch on *vi* **1** caer en la cuenta. **2** hacerse popular. **3** pillar el truco.

to catch out *vt* pillar, sorprender.

to catch up *vt* **1** atrapar, alcanzar. **2** ponerse al día.

catching ['kætʃɪŋ] *adj* contagioso,-a.

catchy ['kætʃɪ] *adj* (**-ier, -iest**) pegadizo,-a.

catechism ['kætəkɪzəm] *n* catecismo.

categorical [kætə'ɡɒrɪkəl] *adj* categórico,-a.

category ['kætəɡərɪ] *n* (*pl* **-ies**) categoría.

cater ['keɪtə'] *vi* **1** proveer comida. **2** atender: *to cater for SB's needs*, atender a las necesidades de ALGN.

caterer ['keɪtərə'] *n* proveedor,-ra.

caterpillar ['kætəpɪlə'] *n* oruga.

cathedral [kə'θiːdrəl] *n* catedral.

Catholic ['kæθəlɪk] *adj-n* católico,-a.

Catholicism [kə'θɒlɪsɪzəm] *n* catolicismo.

cattle ['kætəl] *n* ganado vacuno.

caught [kɔːt] *pt-pp* → catch.

cauliflower ['kɒlɪflaʊə'] *n* coliflor.

cause [kɔːz] *n* **1** causa. **2** razón, motivo.

▶ *vt* causar.

● **to cause SB to do STH** hacer que ALGN haga algo.

caustic ['kɔːstɪk] *adj* cáustico,-a.

caution ['kɔːʃən] *n* **1** cautela, precaución. **2** aviso, advertencia.

▶ *vt* advertir, amonestar.

cautious ['kɔːʃəs] *adj* cauteloso,-a, prudente.

cavalry ['kævəlrɪ] *n* caballería.

cave [keɪv] *n* cueva.

■ **cave painting** pintura rupestre.

to cave in *vi* hundirse, derrumbarse.

caveman ['keɪvmæn] *n* (*pl* **cavemen**) cavernícola.

cavern ['kævən] *n* caverna.

caviar ['kævɪɑː'] *n* caviar.

cavity ['kævɪtɪ] *n* (*pl* **-ies**). **1** cavidad. **2** caries.

CBI ['siː'biː'aɪ] *abbr* GB (*Confederation of British Industry*) confederación británica de organizaciones empresariales.

cc[1] ['siː'siː] *abbr* (*cubic centimetre*) centímetro cúbico.

cc[2] ['siː'siː] *abbr* (*carbon copy*) copia a papel carbón.

CD ['siː'diː] *abbr* (*compact disc*) disco compacto, CD.

■ **CD player** reproductor de discos compactos.

CE ['siː'viː] *abbr* (*Church of England*) Iglesia Anglicana.

cease [siːs] *vt-vi* cesar, terminar.

● **to cease fire** hacer un alto el fuego.

cease-fire [siːs'faɪə'] *n* alto el fuego.

ceaseless ['siːsləs] *adj* incesante.

cedar ['siːdə'] *n* cedro.

ceiling ['siːlɪŋ] *n* **1** techo. **2** tope.

● **to hit the ceiling** ponerse histérico,-a.

celebrate ['selɪbreɪt] *vt-vi* celebrar.

celebrated ['selɪbreɪtɪd] *adj* célebre (*for*, por).

celebration [selɪ'breɪʃən] *n* celebración.

▶ *npl* **celebrations** festejos.

● **in celebration of** en conmemoración de.

celebrity [sə'lebrɪtɪ] *n* (*pl* **-ies**) celebridad, famoso,-a.

celery ['selərɪ] *n* apio.

cell [sel] *n* **1** celda. **2** célula. **3** elemento, pila.

cellar ['selə'] *n* **1** sótano. **2** bodega (*para vino*).

cellist ['tʃelɪst] *n* violoncelista.

cello ['tʃeləʊ] *n* (*pl* **cellos**) violoncelo.

cellophane® ['seləfeɪn] *n* celofán®.

cellphone ['selfəʊn] *n* teléfono móvil.

celluloid ['seljəlɔɪd] *n* celuloide.

cellulose ['seljələʊs] *n* celulosa.

Celt [kelt] *n* celta.

Celtic ['keltɪk] *adj* celta.

cement [sɪ'ment] *n* cemento.

▶ *vt* **1** unir con cemento. **2** cimentar.

■ **cement mixer** hormigonera.

cemetery ['semətrɪ] *n* (*pl* **-ies**) cementerio.

censor ['sensə'] *n* censor,-ra.

▶ *vt* censurar.

censorship ['sensəʃɪp] *n* censura.

censure ['senʃə'] *n* censura.

▶ *vt* censurar.

census ['sensəs] *n* (*pl* **censuses**) censo, padrón.

cent [sent] *n* centavo, céntimo.

● **per cent** por ciento.

centenary [sen'tiːnərɪ] *n* (*pl* **-ies**) centenario.

centennial [sen'tenɪəl] n centenario.
centigrade ['sentɪgreɪd] adj centígrado.
centimetre ['sentɪmiːtəʳ] (US **centimeter**) n centímetro.
centipede ['sentɪpiːd] n ciempiés.
central ['sentrəl] adj central.
■ **central heating** calefacción central.
■ **central processing unit** CPU.
centralize ['sentrəlaɪz] vt centralizar.
centre ['sentəʳ] (US **center**) n centro.
▶ vt-vi centrar, centrarse.
■ **centre forward** delantero centro.
■ **centre of gravity** centro de gravedad.
century ['sentʃərɪ] n (pl **-ies**) siglo.
ceramic [sə'ræmɪk] adj de cerámica.
▶ npl **ceramics** cerámica.
cereal ['sɪərɪəl] n 1 cereal. 2 cereales.
cerebral ['serɪbrəl] adj cerebral.
ceremonial [serɪ'məʊnɪəl] adj ceremonial.
ceremony ['serɪmənɪ] n (pl **-ies**) ceremonia.
certain ['sɜːtən] adj 1 seguro,-a: *she's certain to pass*, seguro que aprobará. 2 cierto,-a, alguno,-a: *in certain countries they drive on the left*, el algunos países se conduce por la izquierda. 3 cierto,-a: *a certain Mr Buck*, un tal Sr Buck.
● **for certain** con toda seguridad.
● **to a certain extent** hasta cierto punto.
● **to make certain of** asegurarse de.
certainly ['sɜːtənlɪ] adv 1 desde luego, por supuesto: *certainly not*, por supuesto que no. 2 ciertamente, no cabe duda de que: *she certainly works hard*, no cabe duda de que trabaja mucho.
certainty ['sɜːtəntɪ] n (pl **-ies**) certeza, seguridad.
● **it's a certainty that ...** es seguro que ....
certificate [sə'tɪfɪkət] n certificado.
certify ['sɜːtɪfaɪ] vt (pt & pp **-ied**) certificar.
cervix ['sɜːvɪks] n (pl **-es** o **cervices**). 1 cerviz. 2 cuello del útero.
cesspit ['sespɪt] n pozo negro.
Ceylon [sɪ'lɒn] n Ceilán.
cf. ['siː'ef] abbr (**confer**) compárese, cfr.
CFC ['siː'ef'siː] abbr (**chlorofluorocarbon**) clorofluorocarbono, CFC.
chafe [tʃeɪf] vt rozar, escoriar.
▶ vi irritarse.
chain [tʃeɪn] n 1 cadena. 2 cordillera. 3 serie.
▶ vt encadenar.
● **in chains** encadenado,-a.
● **to chain smoke** fumar un cigarrillo tras otro.
■ **chain reaction** reacción en cadena.
chair [tʃeəʳ] n 1 silla. 2 sillón. 3 presidencia. 4 cátedra.
▶ vt presidir.
■ **chair lift** telesilla.
chairman ['tʃeəmən] n (pl **chairmen**) presidente (de un comité u organización).
chairmanship ['tʃeəmənʃɪp] n presidencia (de un comité u organización).
chairperson ['tʃeəpɜːsən] n (pl **chairpeople**) presidente,-a (de un comité u organización).
chairwoman ['tʃeəwʊmən] n (pl **chairwomen**) presidenta (de un comité u organización).
chalet ['ʃæleɪ] n chalet, chalé.
chalice ['tʃælɪs] n cáliz.
chalk [tʃɔːk] n 1 creta. 2 tiza.
to chalk up vt fam apuntarse.
challenge ['tʃælɪndʒ] n reto, desafío.
▶ vt 1 retar, desafiar. 2 poner en duda, cuestionar.
challenger ['tʃælɪndʒəʳ] n contendiente, rival.
chamber ['tʃeɪmbəʳ] n cámara.
■ **chamber music** música de cámara.
■ **chamber of commerce** cámara de comercio.
chambermaid ['tʃeɪmbəmeɪd] n camarera.
chameleon [kə'miːlɪən] n camaleón.
champagne [ʃæm'peɪn] n champán.
champion ['tʃæmpɪən] n 1 campeón, -ona. 2 fig defensor,-ra.
▶ vt fig defender.
championship ['tʃæmpɪənʃɪp] n campeonato.
chance [tʃɑːns] n 1 azar. 2 oportunidad: *give me a chance, I won't disappoint you*, dame una oportunidad, no te decepcionaré. 3 posibilidad: *you have no chance of winning*, no tienes ninguna posibilidad de ganar.
▶ vt arriesgar.
● **by chance** por casualidad.
● **on the off chance** por si acaso.
● **to chance on STH** encontrar algo por casualidad.
● **to chance to do STH** hacer algo por casualidad.

● **to have a good chance of doing** STH tener buenas posibilidades de hacer algo.

● **to take a chance** arriesgarse.

chancellor [ˈtʃɑːnsələ^r] *n* **1** canciller. **2** GB rector,-ra *(de universidad)*.

■ **Chancellor of the Exchequer** GB ministro,-a de Economía y Hacienda.

chancy [ˈtsɑːnsɪ] *adj* (-**ier**, -**iest**) *fam* arriesgado,-a.

chandelier [ʃændəˈlɪə^r] *n* araña *(lámpara)*.

change [tʃeɪndʒ] *n* **1** cambio. **2** cambio, vuelta *(de dinero)*.

► *vt* cambiar: *he's changed jobs*, ha cambiado de trabajo.

► *vi* **1** cambiar: *things never change*, las cosas no cambian nunca. **2** cambiarse de ropa: *he showered and changed*, se duchó y se cambió de ropa.

● **for a change** para variar.

● **to change one's mind** cambiar de opinión.

● **to change into** convertirse en, transformarse en.

● **to change hands** cambiar de dueño.

■ **change of clothes** muda de ropa.

■ **change of heart** cambio de parecer.

changeable [ˈtʃeɪndʒəbəl] *adj* variable.

changing [ˈtʃeɪndʒɪŋ] *adj* cambiante.

■ **changing room** vestuario, probador.

channel [ˈtʃænəl] *n* **1** canal *(cauce de agua)*. **2** canal, cadena *(de televisión)*. **3** vía, conducto: *through the official channels*, por los conductos oficiales.

► *vt* (GB *pt & pp* **channelled**, *ger* **channelling**; US *pt & pp* **channeled**, *ger* **channeling**) canalizar, encauzar.

■ **the English Channel** el canal de la Mancha.

chant [tʃɑːnt] *n* **1** canto litúrgico. **2** consigna.

► *vt-vi* **1** cantar. **2** corear, gritar.

chaos [ˈkeɪɒs] *n* caos.

chaotic [keɪˈɒtɪk] *adj* caótico,-a.

chap [tʃæp] *n fam* tío, tipo.

chapel [ˈtʃæpəl] *n* capilla.

chaplain [ˈtʃæplɪn] *n* capellán.

chapter [ˈtʃæptə^r] *n* capítulo.

char[1] [tʃɑː^r] *vt-vi* carbonizar, carbonizarse.

char[2] [tʃɑː^r] *n* GB *fam* asistenta.

character [ˈkærəktə^r] *n* **1** carácter, personalidad, manera de ser. **2** personaje: *the main character of the play*, el protago-

nista de la obra. **3** *fam* tipo: *he's a nasty character*, es un mal tipo. **4** carácter, letra.

characteristic [kærəktəˈrɪstɪk] *adj* característico,-a.

► *n* característica.

characterize [ˈkærəktəraɪz] *vt* **1** caracterizar. **2** calificar.

charade [ʃəˈrɑːd] *n* farsa.

► *npl* **charades** charadas.

charcoal [ˈtʃɑːkəʊl] *n* **1** carbón vegetal. **2** carboncillo.

charge [tʃɑːdʒ] *n* **1** precio, coste. **2** cargo, acusación *(formal)*. **3** carga, ataque. **4** carga explosiva. **5** carga eléctrica.

► *vt* **1** cobrar. **2** acusar *(de delito)*. **3** cargar *(pistola, pila)*. **4** cargar contra, atacar *(tropas)*.

► *vi* **1** cargar, atacar *(tropas)*. **2** embestir, arremeter *(toro)*. **3** irrumpir, entrar o salir corriendo *(multitud)*.

● **to be in charge of** estar a cargo de.

● **to bring a charge against** SB formular una acusación contra ALGN.

● **to charge** SB **with murder** acusar a ALGN de asesinato.

● **to take charge of** hacerse cargo de.

charger [ˈtʃɑːdʒə^r] *n* cargador *(de batería)*.

chariot [ˈtʃærɪət] *n* carro de guerra.

charisma [kəˈrɪzmə] *n* carisma.

charismatic [kærɪzˈmætɪk] *adj* carismático,-a.

charitable [ˈtʃærɪtəbəl] *adj* **1** caritativo,-a *(persona)*. **2** benéfico,-a *(organización)*.

charity [ˈtʃærɪtɪ] *n* (*pl* -**ies**). **1** caridad. **2** organización benéfica.

charm [tʃɑːm] *n* **1** encanto. **2** amuleto *(de la suerte)*. **3** hechizo.

► *vt* cautivar, encantar.

● **to work like a charm** funcionar a las mil maravillas.

charming [ˈtʃɑːmɪŋ] *adj* encantador,-ra.

chart [tʃɑːt] *n* **1** tabla, gráfico, diagrama. **2** carta de navegación.

► *vt* hacer un mapa de, describir: *this book charts her rise to fame*, este libro describe su ascenso a la fama.

■ **the charts** los cuarenta principales.

charter [ˈtʃɑːtə^r] *n* **1** carta, estatutos. **2** flete.

► *vt* fletar.

■ **charter flight** vuelo chárter.

charwoman [ˈtʃɑːwʊmən] *n* (*pl* **charwomen**) asistenta.

chase [tʃeɪs] *n* persecución.
▶ *vt* perseguir.
chasm ['kæzəm] *n* sima, abismo.
chassis ['ʃæsɪ] *n* (*pl* **chassis** ['ʃæsɪz]) chasis.
chaste [tʃeɪst] *adj* casto,-a.
chastise [tʃæs'taɪz] *vt* reprender.
chastity ['tʃæstɪtɪ] *n* castidad.
chat [tʃæt] *n* charla.
▶ *vi* (*pt* & *pp* **chatted**, *ger* **chatting**). 1 charlar. 2 chatear, charlar.
■ **chat room** chat, sala de chat.
■ **chat show** programa de entrevistas.
to chat up *vt fam* intentar ligar con.
chatter ['tʃætə'] *n* 1 cháchara, parloteo. 2 castañeteo *(de dientes)*.
▶ *vi* 1 charlar, parlotear. 2 castañetear *(dientes)*.
chatterbox ['tʃætəbɒks] *n* (*pl* **chatterboxes**) parlanchín,-ina, charlatán,-ana.
chatty ['tʃætɪ] *adj* (**-ier**, **-iest**) parlanchín, -ina.
chauffeur ['ʃəʊfə'] *n* chófer.
chauvinism ['ʃəʊvɪnɪzəm] *n* chovinismo.
chauvinist ['ʃəʊvɪnɪst] *adj* chovinista.
▶ *n* chovinista.
cheap [tʃiːp] *adj* 1 barato,-a, económico, -a. 2 de mala calidad. 3 vil, bajo,-a.
● **to feel cheap** sentir vergüenza.
cheapen ['tʃiːpən] *vt* 1 abaratar. 2 *fig* degradar.
cheat [tʃiːt] *n* tramposo,-a.
▶ *vi* 1 hacer trampa. 2 copiar *(en un examen)*.
▶ *vt* engañar, timar.
check [tʃek] *n* 1 comprobación, verificación. 2 US → cheque. 3 US nota, cuenta. 4 jaque. 5 cuadro: *a check shirt*, una camisa a cuadros.
▶ *vt* 1 comprobar, revisar, verificar. 2 detener. 3 contener, refrenar. 4 dar jaque a.
● **to keep in check** contener.
to check in *vi* 1 facturar *(en aeropuerto)*. 2 dejar los datos *(en hotel)*.
checkbook ['tʃekbʊk] *n* US talonario de cheques.
checked [tʃekt] *adj* a cuadros, de cuadros.
checkers ['tʃekəz] *npl* US damas.
checkmate ['tʃekmeɪt] *n* jaque mate.
▶ *vt* dar mate a.
checkout ['tʃekaʊt] *n* caja.

checkup ['tʃekʌp] *n* chequeo, reconocimiento médico.
cheek [tʃiːk] *n* 1 mejilla. 2 *fig* descaro: *what a cheek!*, ¡qué cara!
cheekbone ['tʃiːkbəʊn] *n* pómulo.
cheeky ['tʃiːkɪ] *adj* (**-ier**, **-iest**) descarado,-a.
cheer [tʃɪə'] *n* viva, vítor.
▶ *vt-vi* vitorear, aclamar.
to cheer up *vt-vi* animar(se), alegrar(se).
cheerful ['tʃɪəfʊl] *adj* alegre.
cheers [tʃɪəz] *interj* 1 ¡salud! 2 ¡gracias! 3 ¡adiós!, ¡hasta luego!
cheese [tʃiːz] *n* queso.
cheesecake ['tʃiːzkeɪk] *n* tarta de queso.
cheesed off [tʃiːzd'ɒf] *adj* GB *fam* harto,-a.
cheetah ['tʃiːtə] *n* guepardo.
chef [ʃef] *n* (*pl* **chefs**) chef.
chemical ['kemɪkəl] *adj* químico,-a.
▶ *n* producto químico.
chemist ['kemɪst] *n* 1 químico,-a. 2 GB farmacéutico,-a.
chemistry ['kemɪstrɪ] *n* química.
chemist's ['kemɪsts] *n* farmacia.
cheque [tʃek] *n* cheque, talón.
chequebook ['tʃekbʊk] *n* talonario de cheques.
cherish ['tʃerɪʃ] *vt* 1 apreciar, valorar. 2 abrigar *(esperanza)*. 3 tener mucho cariño a *(persona)*.
cherry ['tʃerɪ] *n* (*pl* **-ies**) cereza.
■ **cherry tree** cerezo.
cherub ['tʃerəb] *n* (*pl* **-s** o **cherubim**) querubín.
chess [tʃes] *n* ajedrez.
chessboard ['tʃesbɔːd] *n* tablero de ajedrez.
chesspiece ['tʃespiːs] *n* pieza de ajedrez.
chest [tʃest] *n* 1 pecho. 2 cofre, arca.
● **to get STH off one's chest** desahogarse.
■ **chest of drawers** cómoda, cajonera.
chestnut ['tʃesnʌt] *n* 1 castaña *(fruto)*. 2 castaño *(color)*.
▶ *adj* castaño,-a, alazán,-ana.
■ **chestnut tree** castaño.
chew [tʃuː] *vt* mascar, masticar.
● **to chew STH over** darle vueltas a algo.
chewing gum ['tʃuːɪŋɡʌm] *n* goma de mascar, chicle.
chewy ['tʃuːɪ] *adj* (**-ier**, **-iest**) correoso,-a, duro,-a.
chic [ʃiːk] *adj* elegante.
chick [tʃɪk] *n* polluelo, pollito,-a.

chicken ['tʃɪkɪn] n 1 pollo (carne). 2 gallina (ave). 3 fam gallina (cobarde).
► adj fam gallina.
to chicken out vi fam rajarse.
chickenpox ['tʃɪkɪnpɒks] n varicela.
chickpea ['tʃɪkpiː] n garbanzo.
chicory ['tʃɪkərɪ] n achicoria.
chief [tʃiːf] adj principal, mayor.
► n (pl **chiefs**) jefe.
chiefly ['tʃiːflɪ] adv principalmente, sobre todo.
chieftain ['tʃiːftən] n cacique.
chihuahua [tʃɪ'wɑːwə] n chihuahua.
chilblain ['tʃɪlbleɪn] n sabañón.
child [tʃaɪld] n (pl **children**). 1 niño,-a. 2 hijo, hija.
■ **child minder** niñero,-a.
● **only child** hijo,-a único,-a.
childbirth ['tʃaɪldbɜːθ] n parto.
childhood ['tʃaɪldhʊd] n infancia, niñez.
childish ['tʃaɪldɪʃ] adj 1 infantil. 2 inmaduro,-a.
childlike ['tʃaɪldlaɪk] adj infantil, inocente.
children ['tʃɪldrən] npl → child.
Chile ['tʃɪlɪ] n Chile.
Chilean ['tʃɪlɪən] adj-n chileno,-a.
chill [tʃɪl] adj 1 frío,-a. 2 helado,-a.
► n 1 frío. 2 resfriado.
► vt-vi enfriar(se).
● **to catch/get a chill** resfriarse.
chilly ['tʃɪlɪ] adj (-ier, -iest) frío,-a.
● **to feel chilly** tener frío.
chime [tʃaɪm] n repique (de campanas), campanada (de reloj).
► vi sonar, repicar (campanas), dar la hora (reloj).
chimney ['tʃɪmnɪ] n chimenea.
■ **chimney sweep** deshollinador,-a.
chimpanzee [tʃɪmpæn'ziː] n chimpancé.
chin [tʃɪn] n barbilla, mentón.
china ['tʃaɪnə] n 1 loza, porcelana. 2 vajilla de porcelana.
China ['tʃaɪnə] n China.
Chinese [tʃaɪ'niːz] adj-n chino,-a.
► npl **the Chinese** los chinos.
chink[1] [tʃɪŋk] n grieta.
chink[2] [tʃɪŋk] n tintineo.
► vi tintinear.
chip [tʃɪp] n 1 patata frita. 2 chip. 3 astilla, lasca (de madera). 4 desportilladura (de plato, vaso). 5 ficha (en casino).
► vt-vi (pt & pp **chipped**, ger **chipping**). 1 astillarse (madera). 2 resquebrajarse

(piedra). 3 desportillarse (plato, vaso). 4 desconcharse (pintura).
chiropodist [kɪ'rɒpədɪst] n podólogo,-a, pedicuro,-a.
chirp [tʃɜːp] vi 1 gorjear (ave). 2 chirriar (insecto).
chisel ['tʃɪzəl] n 1 formón, escoplo (para madera). 2 cincel (para piedra).
► vt (GB pt & pp **chiselled**, ger **chiselling**; US pt & pp **chiseled**, ger **chiseling**). 1 tallar (madera). 2 labrar, cincelar (piedra).
chit [tʃɪt] n nota.
chitchat ['tʃɪttʃæt] n fam cháchara, charla.
chloride ['klɔːraɪd] n cloruro.
chlorine ['klɔːriːn] n cloro.
chloroform ['klɒrəfɔːm] n cloroformo.
chock [tʃɒk] n calzo, cuña.
chock-a-block [tʃɒkə'blɒk] adj fam hasta los topes, abarrotado,-a.
chock-full [tʃɒk'fʊl] adj fam hasta los topes.
chocolate ['tʃɒkələt] n 1 chocolate. 2 bombón.
choice [tʃɔɪs] n 1 elección. 2 surtido, selección. 3 opción, alternativa.
► adj selecto,-a.
● **to have no choice** no tener más remedio.
● **to make a choice** escoger.
choir ['kwaɪəʳ] n coro.
choke [tʃəʊk] n estárter.
► vt 1 ahogar, sofocar. 2 atascar.
► vi ahogarse, sofocarse, atragantarse.
to choke back vt contener.
cholera ['kɒlərə] n cólera.
choose [tʃuːz] vt (pt **chose** [tʃəʊz], pp **chosen** ['tʃəʊzən]). 1 escoger, elegir. 2 decidir por, optar por.
● **there's not much to choose between them** son muy parecidos,-as.
choosy ['tʃuːzɪ] adj (-ier, -iest) fam exigente, quisquilloso,-a.
chop [tʃɒp] n 1 hachazo, golpe. 2 chuleta (carne).
► vt (pt & pp **chopped**, ger **chopping**) cortar.
● **to get the chop** ser despedido,-a de un trabajo.
chop down vt talar.
chop up vt 1 cortar en trozos. 2 picar (carne, etc).

choppy ['tʃɒpɪ] *adj* (**-ier**, **-iest**) picado,-a *(mar)*.

chopsticks ['tʃɒpstɪks] *npl* palillos chinos.

choral ['kɔːrəl] *adj* coral.

chord[1] [kɔːd] *n* cuerda *(geometría)*.

chord[2] [kɔːd] *n* acorde *(música)*.

chore [tʃɔːʳ] *n* tarea, faena.

chorus ['kɔːrəs] *n* (*pl* **choruses**). **1** coro. **2** estribillo.

■ **chorus girl** corista.

chose [tʃəʊz] *pt* → choose.

chosen ['tʃəʊzən] *pp* → choose.

Christ [kraɪst] *n* Cristo.

christen ['krɪsən] *vt* bautizar.

christening ['krɪsənɪŋ] *n* bautizo.

Christian ['krɪstɪən] *adj-n* cristiano,-a.

■ **Christian name** nombre de pila.

Christmas ['krɪsməs] *n* (*pl* **Christmases**) Navidad.

● **Merry Christmas!** ¡Feliz Navidad!

■ **Christmas card** tarjeta de Navidad, christmas.

■ **Christmas carol** villancico.

■ **Christmas Eve** Nochebuena.

chrome [krəʊm] *n* cromo.

chromosome ['krəʊməsəʊm] *n* cromosoma.

chromium ['krəʊmɪəm] *n* cromo.

chronic ['krɒnɪk] *adj* crónico,-a.

chronicle ['krɒnɪkəl] *n* crónica.

chronological [krɒnə'lɒdʒɪkəl] *adj* cronológico,-a.

chronology [krə'nɒlədʒɪ] *n* (*pl* **-ies**) cronología.

chrysalis ['krɪsəlɪs] *n* (*pl* **chrysalises**) crisálida.

chrysanthemum [krɪ'sænθəməm] *n* crisantemo.

chubby ['tʃʌbɪ] *adj* (**-ier**, **-iest**) gordillo, regordete.

chuck [tʃʌk] *vt* tirar *(objeto)*. **2** abandonar, dejar *(novio, trabajo)*.

to chuck out *vt* **1** echar *(persona)*. **2** tirar *(objeto)*.

chuckle ['tʃʌkəl] *vi* reír para sus adentros.

▶ *n* risita.

chum [tʃʌm] *n fam* compinche.

chunk [tʃʌŋk] *n fam* cacho, pedazo.

church [tʃɜːtʃ] *n* (*pl* **-es**) iglesia.

churchyard ['tʃɜːtʃjɑːd] *n* cementerio.

churn [tʃɜːn] *n* **1** GB lechera. **2** mantequera.

▶ *vt* agitar, revolver.

to churn out *vt* producir en serie, hacer como churros.

chute [ʃuːt] *n* tobogán.

CIA ['siːaɪ'eɪ] *abbr (**Central Intelligence Agency**)* CIA.

cider ['saɪdəʳ] *n* sidra.

cig [sɪg] *n fam* cigarro.

cigar [sɪ'gɑːʳ] *n* puro.

cigarette [sɪgə'ret] *n* cigarro, cigarrillo.

■ **cigarette case** pitillera.

■ **cigarette holder** boquilla.

■ **cigarette lighter** encendedor.

cinch [sɪntʃ] *n* (*pl* **-es**) *fam* .

● **it's a cinch** está chupado, está tirado.

cinder ['sɪndəʳ] *n* ceniza.

cinema ['sɪnəmə] *n* cine.

cinnamon ['sɪnəmən] *n* canela.

cipher ['saɪfəʳ] *n* código.

circle ['sɜːkəl] *n* **1** círculo. **2** anfiteatro *(en teatro)*.

▶ *vt* **1** rodear. **2** trazar un círculo alrededor de.

▶ *vi* dar vueltas.

● **to come full circle** completar un ciclo.

● **to go round in circles** dar vueltas.

circuit ['sɜːkɪt] *n* **1** circuito. **2** vuelta. **3** pista.

circular ['sɜːkjələʳ] *adj* circular, redondo.

▶ *n* circular.

circulate ['sɜːkjəleɪt] *vi* circular.

▶ *vt* hacer circular.

circulation [sɜːkjə'leɪʃən] *n* **1** circulación. **2** tirada *(de periódico)*.

circumcise ['sɜːkəmsaɪz] *vt* circuncidar.

circumcision [sɜːkəm'sɪʒən] *n* circuncisión.

circumference [sə'kʌmfərəns] *n* circunferencia.

circumflex ['sɜːkəmfleks] *adj* circunflejo,-a.

circumstance ['sɜːkəmstəns] *n* circunstancia.

● **in/under the circumstances** dadas las circunstancias.

● **under no circumstances** en ningún caso, bajo ningún concepto.

circumstantial [sɜːkəm'stænʃəl] *adj* circunstancial.

circus ['sɜːkəs] *n* (*pl* **circuses**). **1** circo. **2** GB glorieta, rotonda.

cirrhosis [sɪ'rəʊsɪs] *n* cirrosis.

cistern ['sɪstən] *n* cisterna.

cite [saɪt] *vt* citar.

citizen ['sɪtɪzən] *n* ciudadano,-a.

citizenship ['sɪtɪzənʃɪp] n ciudadanía.

citric ['sɪtrɪk] adj cítrico,-a.

citrus fruit ['sɪtrəsfruːt] n cítrico.

city ['sɪtɪ] n (pl -ies) ciudad.
■ **the City** la City, *el centro financiero de Londres.*

civic ['sɪvɪk] adj 1 cívico,-a. 2 público,-a.
■ **civic centre** centro municipal.

civil ['sɪvəl] adj 1 civil. 2 cortés, educado,-a.
■ **civil law** derecho civil.
■ **civil rights** derechos civiles.
■ **civil servant** funcionario,-a.
■ **civil service** administración pública.
■ **civil war** guerra civil.

civilian [sɪˈvɪljən] adj civil.
▶ n civil.

civilization [sɪvɪlaɪˈzeɪʃən] n civilización.

civilize ['sɪvɪlaɪz] vt civilizar.

clad [klæd] pt-pp → clothe.
▶ adj vestido,-a.

claim [kleɪm] n 1 reclamación, reivindicación. 2 derecho. 3 afirmación, pretensión.
▶ vt 1 afirmar, sostener. 2 reclamar.
● **to lay claim to** reclamar el derecho a.

clam [klæm] n almeja.

to clam up ['klæm'ʌp] vi (pt & pp **clammed**, ger **clamming**) fam no decir ni mu.

clamber ['klæmbə'] vi trepar.

clammy ['klæmɪ] adj (-ier, -iest). 1 bochornoso,-a. 2 pegajoso,-a, sudoroso,-a.

clamour ['klæmə'] (US **clamor**) n clamor, griterío.
▶ vi clamar: *to clamour for STH,* pedir algo a gritos.

clamp [klæmp] n abrazadera.
▶ vt sujetar.

to clamp down on vt poner freno a.

clampdown ['klæmpdaʊn] n restricción.

clan [klæn] n clan.

clandestine [klænˈdestɪn] adj clandestino,-a.

clang [klæŋ] n sonido metálico fuerte, estruendo.
▶ vi sonar.
▶ vt hacer sonar.

clap [klæp] n 1 aplauso. 2 ruido seco: *a clap of thunder,* un trueno. 3 palmada.
▶ vt-vi (pt & pp **clapped**, ger **clapping**) aplaudir.
● **to clap eyes on** ver.
● **to clap one's hands** dar palmadas.

● **to clap SB on the back** dar una palmada en la espalda a ALGN.

clapping ['klæpɪŋ] n aplausos.

clarify ['klærɪfaɪ] vt-vi (pt & pp -**ied**) aclararse, clarificarse.

clarinet [klærɪˈnet] n clarinete.

clarity ['klærɪtɪ] n claridad.

clash [klæʃ] n (pl -es). 1 choque, enfrentamiento. 2 conflicto: *a clash of interests,* un conflicto de intereses. 3 estruendo.
▶ vi 1 chocar, tener un enfrentamiento *(fuerzas opuestas).* 2 coincidir *(fechas).* 3 desentonar *(colores).* 4 sonar *(espadas, platillos).*

clasp [klɑːsp] n 1 broche *(de collar).* 2 hebilla, cierre *(de cinturón).*
▶ vt asir, agarrar.

class [klɑːs] n (pl -es) clase.
▶ vt clasificar.

classic ['klæsɪk] adj clásico,-a.
▶ n clásico.

classical ['klæsɪkəl] adj clásico,-a.
■ **classical music** música clásica.

classification [klæsɪfɪˈkeɪʃən] n clasificación.

classified ['klæsɪfaɪd] adj 1 clasificado,-a. 2 secreto,-a, confidencial.
■ **classified advertisements** anuncios por palabras.

classify ['klæsɪfaɪ] vt (pt & pp -**ied**) clasificar.

classmate ['klɑːsmeɪt] n compañero,-a de clase.

classroom ['klɑːsruːm] n aula, clase.

classy ['klɑːsɪ] adj (-ier, -iest) fam con clase.

clatter ['klætə'] n ruido, estrépito.
▶ vi hacer ruido.

clause [klɔːz] n 1 cláusula. 2 oración.

claustrophobia [klɔːstrəˈfəʊbɪə] n claustrofobia.

claustrophobic [klɔːstrəˈfəʊbɪk] adj claustrofóbico,-a.

clavicle ['klævɪkəl] n clavícula.

claw [klɔː] n 1 garra *(de ave).* 2 uña *(de gato).* 3 pinza *(de cangrejo).*
▶ vt-vi arañar.

clay [kleɪ] n arcilla, barro.

clean [kliːn] adj limpio,-a.
▶ vt limpiar.

to clean out vt 1 limpiar a fondo. 2 fam dejar sin blanca a.

to clean up *vt* limpiar.
clean-cut [kliːnˈkʌt] *adj* definido,-a, nítido,-a.
cleaner [ˈkliːnəʳ] *n* **1** encargado,-a de la limpieza, limpiador,-ra. **2** limpiador *(producto)*.
cleaner's [ˈkliːnəz] *n* tintorería.
● **to take** SB **to the cleaner's** dejar a algn sin blanca.
cleanliness [ˈklenlɪnəs] *n* limpieza.
cleanse [klenz] *vt* limpiar.
clear [klɪəʳ] *adj* **1** claro,-a *(explicación)*. **2** transparente *(vidrio)*. **3** despejado,-a *(cielo, vista)*. **4** claro,-a *(voz, letra)*. **5** nítido,-a *(imagen)*. **6** lúcido,-a *(pensamiento, mente)*.
▶ *vt* **1** despejar *(habitación, carretera)*. **2** levantar, recoger *(mesa)*. **3** absolver *(acusado)*. **4** salvar *(obstáculo)*.
▶ *vi* despejarse.
● **to be clear about** STH tener algo claro.
● **to clear one's throat** aclararse la garganta.
● **to have a clear conscience** tener la conciencia tranquila.
● **to make oneself clear** explicarse con claridad.
● **in the clear 1** fuera de peligro. **2** fuera de toda sospecha.
to clear away *vt* quitar.
to clear off *vi fam* largarse.
to clear out *vi* largarse.
▶ *vt* **1** vaciar *(habitación)*. **2** tirar *(trastos)*.
to clear up *vt* **1** aclarar. **2** ordenar, recoger.
▶ *vi* mejorar, despejarse *(tiempo)*.
clearance [ˈklɪərəns] *n* **1** despeje. **2** espacio libre. **3** permiso, autorización.
■ **clearance sale** liquidación.
clear-cut [klɪəˈkʌt] *adj* bien definido,-a.
clear-headed [ˈklɪəˈhedɪd] *adj* lúcido,-a.
clearing [ˈklɪərɪŋ] *n* claro *(de bosque)*.
clearly [ˈklɪəlɪ] *adv* **1** claramente, con claridad. **2** evidentemente, obviamente.
clear-sighted [klɪəˈsaɪtɪd] *adj* clarividente, perspicaz.
cleavage [ˈkliːvɪdʒ] *n fam* escote.
clef [klef] *n* (*pl* **clefs**) clave *(música)*.
cleft [kleft] *n* hendidura, grieta.
clench [klentʃ] *vt* apretar *(puños)*.
clergy [ˈklɜːdʒɪ] *n* clero.
clergyman [ˈklɜːdʒɪmən] *n* (*pl* **clergymen**) clérigo, eclesiástico.

clerical [ˈklerɪkəl] *adj* **1** eclesiástico,-a. **2** de oficina, administrativo,-a.
clerk [klɑːk, US klɜːk] *n* **1** oficinista, administrativo,-a, empleado,-a. **2** US dependiente,-a.
■ **clerk of the court** secretario,-a de juez.
clever [ˈklevəʳ] *adj* (*comp* **cleverer**, *superl* **cleverest**). **1** listo,-a, espabilado,-a. **2** ingenioso,-a.
■ **clever Dick** sabelotodo.
cleverness [ˈklevənəs] *n* **1** inteligencia. **2** destreza, habilidad.
cliché [ˈkliːʃeɪ] *n* cliché.
click [klɪk] *n* **1** clic *(de cámara, puerta)*. **2** chasquido *(de lengua, dedos)*.
▶ *vt* chasquear *(lengua, dedos)*.
▶ *vi* **1** hacer clic. **2** caer en la cuenta: *suddenly, it clicked*, de pronto, lo entendí.
client [ˈklaɪənt] *n* cliente.
cliff [klɪf] *n* (*pl* **cliffs**) acantilado, precipicio.
cliffhanger [ˈklɪfhæŋəʳ] *n* película de suspense, historia de suspense.
climate [ˈklaɪmət] *n* clima.
climatic [klaɪˈmætɪk] *adj* climático,-a.
climax [ˈklaɪmæks] *n* (*pl* **climaxes**). **1** clímax, punto culminante. **2** orgasmo.
climb [klaɪm] *n* subida, escalada, ascensión.
▶ *vt* **1** subir *(escalera)*. **2** trepar a *(árbol)*. **3** escalar *(montaña)*.
▶ *vi* **1** subirse: *the road climbs steeply*, la carretera es muy empinada. **2** trepar *(planta)*.
to climb down *vi* **1** bajarse. **2** *fig* ceder.
climber [ˈklaɪməʳ] *n* alpinista, escalador,-ra.
clinch [klɪntʃ] *vt fam* cerrar *(trato)*.
cling [klɪŋ] *vi* (*pt & pp* **clung**) asirse, aferrarse.
clinic [ˈklɪnɪk] *n* clínica.
clinical [ˈklɪnɪkəl] *adj* clínico,-a.
clink[1] [klɪŋk] *n* tintineo.
▶ *vi* tintinear.
clink[1] [klɪŋk] *n* GB *sl* chirona.
clip[1] [klɪp] *n* clip, fragmento *(de película)*.
▶ *vt* (*pt & pp* **clipped**, *ger* **clipping**). **1** cortar *(barba)*. **2** *fam* dar un cachete.
clip[2] [klɪp] *n* **1** clic. **2** pasador *(para pelo)*.
▶ *vt* (*pt & pp* **clipped**, *ger* **clipping**) sujetar con un clip.
clippers [ˈklɪpəz] *npl* cortaúñas.
clipping [ˈklɪpɪŋ] *n* recorte de periódico.
clique [kliːk] *n* camarilla, pandilla.

clitoris [ˈklɪtərɪs] n (pl **clitorises**) clítoris.
cloak [kləʊk] n capa.
cloakroom [ˈkləʊkruːm] n **1** guardarropa. **2** GB servicios.
clock [klɒk] n **1** reloj. **2** fam cuentakilómetros.
● **against the clock** contra reloj.
● **round the clock** día y noche.
● **to put the clock back** atrasar los relojes.
● **to put the clock forward** adelantar los relojes.
to clock in on vi fichar a la entrada, entrar a trabajar.
to clock off/out vi fichar a la salida, salir de trabajar.
to clock up vt recorrer.
clockwise [ˈklɒkwaɪz] adj-adv en el sentido de las agujas del reloj.
clockwork [ˈklɒkwɜːk] n mecanismo de relojería.
● **like clockwork** como una seda, sobre ruedas.
clod [klɒd] n terrón.
clog [klɒg] n zueco.
▶ vt-vi (pt & pp **clogged**, ger **clogging**) obstruir(se).
cloister [ˈklɔɪstə'] n claustro.
clone [kləʊn] n clon.
close[1] [kləʊs] adj **1** cercano,-a (distancia). **2** íntimo,-a (amigo). **3** cercano,-a (pariente). **4** detenido,-a, detallado,-a (examen).
▶ adv cerca.
● **to keep a close watch on** vigilar estrechamente.
close[2] [kləʊz] vt cerrar: *close your eyes*, cierra los ojos.
▶ vi cerrarse, cerrar: *the shop closes at five*, la tienda cierra a las cinco.
▶ n fin, conclusión: *at the close of the day*, al final del día.
● **to bring to a close** concluir.
● **to close ranks** cerrar filas.
● **to draw to a close** tocar a su fin.
■ **close season** temporada de veda.
close down vt-vi cerrar definitivamente.
close in vi **1** acortarse (días). **2** caer (noche). **3** acercarse (enemigo).
closed [kləʊzd] adj cerrado,-a.
■ **closed circuit television** televisión por circuito cerrado.
close-fitting [kləʊsˈfɪtɪŋ] adj ceñido,-a.
close-knit [kləʊsˈnɪt] adj unido,-a.

closely [ˈkləʊslɪ] adv **1** estrechamente: *to be closely involved in STH*, estar muy metido en algo. **2** de cerca, atentamente: *to follow STH closely*, seguir algo de cerca.
closet [ˈklɒzɪt] n US armario.
close-up [ˈkləʊsʌp] n primer plano.
closing [ˈkləʊzɪŋ] n cierre.
■ **closing ceremony** acto de clausura.
■ **closing date** fecha límite.
■ **closing time** hora de cierre.
closure [ˈkləʊʒə'] n cierre.
clot [klɒt] n **1** coágulo. **2** GB fam tonto,-a.
▶ vi (pt & pp **clotted**, ger **clotting**) coagularse.
cloth [klɒθ] n **1** tela. **2** trapo.
clothe [kləʊð] vt (pt & pp **clothed** o **clad**) vestir.
clothes [kləʊðz] npl ropa: *these clothes are new*, esta ropa es nueva.
● **in plain clothes** de paisano,-a.
● **to put one's clothes on** vestirse.
● **to take one's clothes off** quitarse la ropa.
■ **clothes hanger** percha.
■ **clothes peg** pinza.
clothesline [ˈkləʊðzlaɪn] n cuerda de la ropa.
clothing [ˈkləʊðɪŋ] n ropa.
cloud [klaʊd] n nube.
● **every cloud has a silver lining** no hay mal que por bien no venga.
● **under a cloud** bajo sospecha.
to cloud over vi nublarse.
cloudy [ˈklaʊdɪ] adj (-ier, -iest). **1** nublado,-a. **2** turbio,-a.
clout [klaʊt] n **1** fam tortazo. **2** fam influencia.
▶ vt fam dar un tortazo a.
clove[1] [kləʊv] n clavo (especie).
clove[2] [kləʊv] n diente (de ajo).
clover [ˈkləʊvə'] n trébol.
clown [klaʊn] n payaso.
to clown about/around vi hacer el payaso.
club [klʌb] n **1** club, sociedad. **2** porra, garrote. **3** palo (de golf). **4** trébol (cartas).
▶ vt (pt & pp **clubbed**, ger **clubbing**) aporrear.
to club together vi hacer una recolecta.
cluck [klʌk] vi cloquear.
clue [kluː] n pista, indicio: *he hasn't got a clue*, no tiene ni idea.

clump [klʌmp] *n* **1** grupo *(de árboles)*. **2** mata *(de plantas)*. **3** terrón *(de tierra)*.
► *vi* andar pesada y ruidosamente.

clumsiness ['klʌmzɪnəs] *n* torpeza.

clumsy ['klʌmzɪ] *adj* (-**ier**, -**iest**) torpe.

clung [klʌŋ] *pt-pp* → cling.

cluster ['klʌstə'] *n* grupo.
► *vi* agruparse, apiñarse.

clutch [klʌtʃ] *n* (*pl* -**es**) embrague.
► *vt* agarrar, asir.
● **in SB's clutches** en las garras de ALGN.

to clutch at *vt* intentar agarrar.

clutter ['klʌtə'] *n* desorden, confusión.
► *vt* llenar, atestar: *cluttered with toys*, atestado,-a de juguetes, hasta arriba de juguetes.

c/o ['keərɒv] *abbr* (**care of**) en casa de, c/d.

Co[1] [kəʊ] *abbr* (**Company**) Compañía, Cía.

Co[2] [kəʊ] *abbr* (**County**) condado.

coach [kəʊtʃ] *n* (*pl* -**es**). **1** autocar. **2** carruaje, coche de caballos, carroza. **3** coche, vagón *(de tren)*. **4** profesor,-ra particular. **5** entrenador,-ra.
► *vt* preparar, entrenar.
■ **coach station** estación de autobuses.

coagulate [kəʊ'ægjəleɪt] *vi* coagularse.

coal [kəʊl] *n* carbón, hulla.
● **to haul SB over the coals** echar un rapapolvo a ALGN.
■ **coal mine** mina de carbón.
■ **coal mining** minería del carbón.

coalition [kəʊə'lɪʃən] *n* coalición.

coarse [kɔːs] *adj* **1** basto,-a *(material)*. **2** grosero,-a, ordinario,-a *(persona)*.

coast [kəʊst] *n* costa, litoral.
► *vi* **1** ir en punto muerto *(coche)*. **2** ir sin pedalear *(bicicleta)*.
● **the coast is clear** no hay moros en la costa.

coastal ['kəʊstəl] *adj* costero,-a.

coastguard ['kəʊstgɑːd] *n* guardacostas.

coastline ['kəʊstlaɪn] *n* costa, litoral.

coat [kəʊt] *n* **1** abrigo *(prenda)*. **2** capa, mano *(de pintura)*. **3** pelaje, pelo, lana *(de animal)*.
► *vt* cubrir.
■ **coat hanger** percha.
■ **coat hook** colgador.
■ **coat of arms** escudo de armas.

coating ['kəʊtɪŋ] *n* capa, baño.

coax [kəʊks] *vt* persuadir.
● **to coax STH out of SB** sonsacar algo a ALGN.

cob [kɒb] *n* mazorca.

cobalt ['kəʊbɔːlt] *n* cobalto.

cobble ['kɒbəl] *n* adoquín.

cobble together *vt* amañar, apañar.

cobbled ['kɒbəld] *adj* adoquinado,-a.

cobbler ['kɒblə'] *n* zapatero *(remendón)*.

cobweb ['kɒbweb] *n* telaraña.

cocaine [kə'keɪn] *n* cocaína.

cock [kɒk] *n* **1** gallo. **2** macho *(ave)*. **3** *vulg* polla.
► *vt* alzar, levantar.

to cock up *vt* GB *fam* fastidiar, jorobar.

cock-a-doodle-doo [kɒkəduːdl'duː] *interj* quiquiriquí.

cockatoo [kɒkə'tuː] *n* (*pl* **cockatoos**) cacatúa.

cockerel ['kɒkərəl] *n* gallo joven.

cockle ['kɒkəl] *n* berberecho.

cockney ['kɒknɪ] *adj* (-**ier**, -**iest**) cockney, de los barrios obreros del este de Londres.
► *n* **1** *habitante de los barrios obreros del este de Londres*. **2** *dialectos de estos barrios*.

cockpit ['kɒkpɪt] *n* cabina del piloto.

cockroach ['kɒkrəʊtʃ] *n* (*pl* -**es**) cucaracha.

cocktail ['kɒkteɪl] *n* cóctel.
■ **cocktail shaker** coctelera.

cockup ['kɒkʌp] *n* GB *vulg* chapuza.

cocky ['kɒkɪ] *adj* (-**ier**, -**iest**) *fam* creído, -a, chulo,-a.

cocoa ['kəʊkəʊ] *n* cacao.

coconut ['kəʊkənʌt] *n* coco.

cocoon [kə'kuːn] *n* capullo.

cod [kɒd] *n* bacalao.

COD ['siːˈəʊ'diː] *abbr* contra reembolso.

En Gran Bretaña significa **cash on delivery**, en EEUU **collect on delivery**.

code [kəʊd] *n* **1** código, clave. **2** prefijo *(para telefonear)*.
► *vt* poner en clave, codificar.
■ **code name** nombre en clave.
■ **code of practice** código de ética profesional.

coeducation [kəʊedjə'keɪʃən] *n* enseñanza mixta.

coffee ['kɒfɪ] *n* café.
■ **coffee cup** taza de café.
■ **coffee grinder** molinillo de café.
■ **coffee shop** cafetería.
■ **coffee table** mesa de centro.

coffeepot ['kɒfɪpɒt] *n* cafetera.

coffer ['kɒfə'] *n* arca.

coffin ['kɒfɪn] *n* ataúd, féretro.

cog [kɒg] n **1** diente de engranaje. **2** fig pieza.

cogent ['kəʊdʒənt] adj convincente.

cogwheel ['kɒgwiːl] n rueda dentada.

coherence [kəʊ'hɪərəns] n coherencia.

coherent [kəʊ'hɪərənt] adj coherente.

cohesion [kəʊ'hiːʒən] n cohesión.

cohesive [kəʊ'hiːsɪv] adj cohesivo,-a.

coil [kɔɪl] n **1** rollo (de cuerda). **2** rizo, moño (de pelo). **3** bobina (eléctrica). **4** espiral, DIU.
► vt-vi enrollarse, enroscarse.

coin [kɔɪn] n moneda.
► vt **1** acuñar. **2** fig inventar.

coincide [kəʊɪn'saɪd] vi coincidir.

coincidence [kəʊ'ɪnsɪdəns] n coincidencia, casualidad.

coke [kəʊk] n **1** fam refesco de cola. **2** sl coca.

colander ['kʌləndə'] n colador.

cold [kəʊld] adj frío,-a.
► n **1** frío. **2** resfriado, catarro.
● **to be cold 1** tener frío (persona). **2** estar frío,-a (objeto). **3** hacer frío (tiempo).
● **to catch a cold** resfriarse.
● **to feel the cold** ser friolero,-a.
● **to get cold** resfriarse.
● **to give SB the cold shoulder** hacerle el vacío a ALGN.
● **to have a cold** estar resfriado,-a.
● **to knock SB out cold** dejar a ALGN inconsciente.
■ **cold sore** herpes, pupa.
■ **cold war** guerra fría.

cold-blooded [kəʊld'blʌdɪd] adj **1** cruel, desalmado,-a (persona). **2** de sangre fría (animal). **3** a sangre fría (asesinato).

cold-hearted [kəʊld'hɑːtɪd] adj insensible, despiadado,-a.

coldness ['kəʊldnəs] n frialdad.

coleslaw ['kəʊlslɔː] n ensalada de col.

collaboration [kəlæbə'reɪʃən] n colaboración.

collapse [kə'læps] n **1** derrumbamiento (de edificio). **2** hundimiento (de suelo). **3** fracaso (de plan). **4** colapso (de persona).
► vi **1** derrumbarse (edificio). **2** hundirse (suelo). **3** desplomarse (persona). **4** venirse abajo (plan).

collapsible [kə'læpsəbəl] adj plegable.

collar ['kɒlə'] n **1** cuello (de camisa). **2** collar (de perro).
► vt fam pillar, pescar.

collarbone ['kɒləbəʊn] n clavícula.

collateral [kə'lætərəl] adj colateral.
► n garantía subsidiaria.

colleague ['kɒliːg] n colega, compañero de trabajo.

collect [kə'lekt] vt **1** reunir, juntar (objetos). **2** coleccionar (sellos). **3** recaudar (impuestos). **4** hacer una colecta. **5** ir a buscar, recoger (persona).
► vi **1** acumularse (objetos). **2** congregarse (personas).
● **to call collect** US llamar a cobro revertido.
● **to collect oneself** serenarse, recobrar el dominio de sí mismo.

collected [kə'lektɪd] adj tranquilo, dueño,-a de sí mismo,-a.

collection [kə'lekʃən] n **1** colección (de sellos). **2** colecta (con fines benéficos). **3** recogida (de correo). **4** recaudación (de impuestos).

collective [kə'lektɪv] adj colectivo,-a.
► n cooperativa.

collector [kə'lektə'] n coleccionista.

college ['kɒlɪdʒ] n **1** centro de educación superior. **2** escuela universitaria. **3** facultad.

collide [kə'laɪd] vi colisionar, chocar.

colliery ['kɒljərɪ] n (pl -ies) mina de carbón.

collision [kə'lɪʒən] n colisión, choque.

colloquial [kə'ləʊkwɪəl] adj familiar, coloquial.

cologne [kə'ləʊn] n colonia.

Colombia [kə'lʌmbɪə] n Colombia.

Colombian [kə'lʌmbɪən] adj-n colombiano,-a.

colon[1] ['kəʊlən] n (Anat) colon.

colon[2] ['kəʊlən] n dos puntos (signo de puntuación).

colonel ['kɜːnəl] n coronel.

colonial [kə'ləʊnɪəl] adj colonial.

colonialism [kə'ləʊnɪəlɪzəm] n colonialismo.

colonist ['kɒlənɪst] n colono, colonizador,-ra.

colonize ['kɒlənaɪz] vt colonizar.

colony ['kɒlənɪ] n (pl -ies) colonia.

color ['kʌlə'] n - vt - vi US → colour.

colossal [kə'lɒsəl] adj colosal.

colour ['kʌlə'] (US **color**) n color.
► vt **1** colorear, pintar. **2** fig influir.
► vi sonrojarse, ruborizarse.

► *npl* **colours** bandera, enseña.
● **in full colour** a todo color.
● **to be off colour** no encontrarse bien.
● **to lose colour** palidecer.
■ **colour bar** discriminación racial.
■ **colour blindness** daltonismo.
■ **colour film** película en color.
■ **colour television** televisión en color.
colour-blind ['kʌləblaɪnd] *adj* daltónico,-a.
coloured ['kʌləd] *adj* de color.
colourful ['kʌləfʊl] *adj* **1** lleno,-a de color. **2** vivo,-a, lleno,-a de colorido. **3** pintoresco,-a.
colouring ['kʌlərɪŋ] *n* **1** colorante *(substancia)*. **2** colorido.
colt [kəʊlt] *n* potro.
column ['kɒləm] *n* columna.
coma ['kəʊmə] *n* coma.
comb [kəʊm] *n* peine.
► *vt* **1** peinar *(pelo)*. **2** rastrear, peinar *(zona)*.
combat ['kɒmbæt] *n* combate.
► *vt-vi* combatir.
combatant ['kɒmbətənt] *n* combatiente.
combination [kɒmbɪ'neɪʃən] *n* combinación, mezcla.
combine [*(vb)* kəm'baɪn*(n)* 'kɒmbaɪn] *vt* combinar.
► *vi* **1** combinarse *(elementos)*. **2** unirse *(equipos)*. **3** fusionarse *(compañías)*.
► *n* grupo de empresas.
combustible [kəm'bʌstɪbəl] *adj* combustible.
combustion [kəm'bʌstʃən] *n* combustión.
■ **combustion engine** motor de combustión.
come [kʌm] *vi* (*pt* **came** [keɪm], *pp* **come** [kʌm]). **1** venir: *can I come with you?*, ¿puedo ir contigo?; *coming!*, ¡ya voy! **2** llegar. **3** *vulg* correrse.
● **come what may** pase lo que pase.
● **to come down in the world** venir a menos.
● **to come in handy** ser útil.
● **to come into fashion** ponerse de moda.
● **to come into force** entrar en vigor.
● **to come of age** llegar a la mayoría de edad.
● **to come out in favour of** declararse a favor de.
● **to come out against** declararse en contra de.

● **to come to an end** acabar, terminar.
● **to come together** juntarse.
● **to come to one's senses 1** volver en sí. **2** recobrar la razón.
● **to come to pass** acaecer.
● **to come true** hacerse realidad.
● **to come under attack** ser atacado,-a.
● **come again?** ¿cómo?
to come about *vi* ocurrir, suceder.
to come across *vt* encontrar por casualidad.
► *vi* causar una impresión: *to come across badly*, causar mala impresión; *to come across well*, causar buena impresión.
to come along *vi* **1** progresar, avanzar. **2** presentarse, aparecer.
to come apart *vi* romperse, partirse.
to come at *vt* atacar.
to come back *vi* volver, regresar.
to come before *vt* **1** preceder. **2** *fig* ser más importante que.
to come by *vt* conseguir.
to come down *vi* **1** caer *(avión)*. **2** bajar *(precios)*.
to come down with *vt fam* coger, pillar *(enfermedad)*.
to come forward *vi* **1** avanzar. **2** ofrecerse, presentarse.
to come from *vt* ser de: *I come from Spain*, soy de España.
to come in *vi* **1** entrar: *come in!*, ¡adelante! **2** llegar *(tren)*.
to come in for *vt* ser objeto de.
to come into *vt* heredar.
to come off *vi* **1** tener lugar. **2** tener éxito. **3** desprenderse, caerse *(pieza)*. **4** quitarse *(mancha)*.
to come on *vi* **1** progresar, avanzar. **2** *fam* empezar.
to come out *vi* **1** salir: *when the sun comes out*, cuando salga el sol. **2** quitarse *(mancha)*. **3** GB declararse en huelga. **4** salir del armario *(homosexual)*. **5** salir *(foto)*.
to come out with *vt* soltar.
to come round *vi* **1** volver en sí. **2** dejarse convencer, ceder. **3** visitar.
to come through *vi* llegar.
► *vt* sobrevivir.
to come to *vi* volver en sí.
► *vt* subir a, ascender a.

to come up vi **1** surgir (tema). **2** acercarse. **3** salir (sol).

to come up against vt topar con.

to come up to vt llegar a: **the water came up to my waist**, el agua me llegaba a la cintura.

to come up with vt **1** tener (idea). **2** encontrar (solución).

to come upon vt encontrar.

comeback ['kʌmbæk] n fam reaparición.

comedian [kə'miːdɪən] n cómico, humorista.

comedienne [kəmiːdɪ'en] n cómica, humorista.

comedy ['kɒmədɪ] n (pl -**ies**) comedia.

comet ['kɒmɪt] n cometa.

comfort ['kʌmfət] n **1** comodidad. **2** consuelo.
▶ vt consolar.

comfortable ['kʌmfətəbəl] adj **1** cómodo,-a (silla). **2** acomodado,-a (situación).
● **to make oneself comfortable** ponerse cómodo,-a.

comforting ['kʌmfətɪŋ] adj reconfortante.

comfy ['kʌmfɪ] adj (-**ier**, -**iest**) fam cómodo,-a.

comic ['kɒmɪk] adj-n cómico,-a.
▶ n tebeo, cómic.
■ **comic strip** tira cómica.

comical ['kɒmɪkəl] adj cómico,-a.

coming ['kʌmɪŋ] n **1** llegada. **2** advenimiento.
▶ adj **1** próximo,-a: **this coming Sunday**, el próximo domingo. **2** venidero,-a (año, generación).
■ **comings and goings** idas y venidas.

comma ['kɒmə] n coma.

command [kə'mɑːnd] n **1** orden. **2** mando: **under the command of the king**, bajo el mando del rey. **3** comando, instrucción. **4** dominio: **he has a good command of Greek**, tiene un buen conocimiento del griego.
▶ vt-vi **1** mandar, ordenar. **2** tener el mando, dirigir.

commander [kə'mɑːndə'] n comandante.

commandment [kə'mɑːndmənt] n mandamiento.

commando [kə'mɑːndəʊ] n (pl -**s** o -**es**) comando.

commemorate [kə'meməreɪt] vt conmemorar.

commemoration [kəmemə'reɪʃən] n conmemoración.

commemorative [kə'memərətɪv] adj conmemorativo,-a.

commend [kə'mend] vt **1** elogiar. **2** recomendar.

comment ['kɒment] n comentario: **no comment**, sin comentarios.
▶ vi comentar.

commentary ['kɒməntərɪ] n (pl -**ies**) comentario.

commentator ['kɒmənteɪtə'] n comentarista.

commerce ['kɒmɜːs] n comercio.

commercial [kə'mɜːʃəl] adj comercial.
▶ n anuncio.

commercialize [kə'mɜːʃəlaɪz] vt comercializar.

commission [kə'mɪʃən] n **1** comisión. **2** encargo.
▶ vt encargar, comisionar.

commissioner [kə'mɪʃənə'] n comisario.

commit [kə'mɪt] vt (pt & pp **committed**, ger **committing**) cometer.
● **to commit oneself** comprometerse.
● **to commit suicide** suicidarse.
● **to commit to memory** memorizar.
● **to commit to prison** encarcelar.

commitment [kə'mɪtmənt] n compromiso.

committee [kə'mɪtɪ] n comité, comisión.

commodity [kə'mɒdɪtɪ] n (pl -**ies**) producto, artículo.

common ['kɒmən] adj (comp **commoner**, superl **commonest**). **1** corriente, usual. **2** común. **3** vulgar, bajo,-a, ordinario,-a.
▶ n terreno común.
● **in common** en común.
● **to be common knowledge** ser de dominio público.
■ **common denominator** común denominador.
■ **common factor** factor común.
■ **Common Market** Mercado Común.
■ **common sense** sentido común.

commonplace ['kɒmənpleɪs] adj (normal y corriente), normal.

commotion [kə'məʊʃən] n alboroto, agitación.

communal ['kɒmjənəl] adj comunal, comunitario,-a.

commune[1] ['kɒmjuːn] *n* comuna, comunidad.

commune[2] [kə'mjuːn] *vi* comulgar, estar en comunión.

communicate [kə'mjuːnɪkeɪt] *vt-vi* comunicar(se).

communication [kəmjuːnɪ'keɪʃən] *n* **1** comunicación *(contacto)*. **2** comunicado *(mensaje)*.

communicative [kə'mjuːnɪkətɪv] *adj* comunicativo,-a.

communion [kə'mjuːnjən] *n* comunión.

communiqué [kə'mjuːnɪkeɪ] *n* comunicado.

communism ['kɒmjənɪzəm] *n* comunismo.

communist ['kɒmjənɪst] *adj* comunista.
▶ *n* comunista.

community [kə'mjuːnɪtɪ] *n* (*pl* -ies) comunidad.
■ **community centre** centro social.
■ **community spirit** civismo.

commute [kə'mjuːt] *vi* viajar diariamente de casa al lugar de trabajo.
▶ *vt* conmutar.

commuter [kə'mjuːtəʳ] *n persona que viaja diariamente al lugar de trabajo.*

compact [kəm'pækt] *adj* compacto,-a.
▶ *n* polvera de bolsillo.
■ **compact disc** disco compacto.

companion [kəm'pænjən] *n* compañero,-a.

company ['kʌmpənɪ] *n* (*pl* -ies). **1** compañía. **2** compañía, empresa. **3** *fam* visita.
● **to keep SB company** hacer compañía a algn.
● **to part company** separarse.

comparable ['kɒmpərəbəl] *adj* comparable.

comparative [kəm'pærətɪv] *adj* **1** comparativo,-a. **2** relativo,-a. **3** comparado,-a.

comparatively [kəm'pærətɪvlɪ] *adv* relativamente.

compare [kəm'peəʳ] *vt* comparar.
▶ *vi* compararse.
● **beyond compare** sin comparación.

comparison [kəm'pærɪsən] *n* comparación.
● **in comparison with/to** en comparación con.
● **there's no comparison** no hay punto de comparación.

compartment [kəm'pɑːtmənt] *n* compartimiento, compartimento.

compass ['kʌmpəs] *n* (*pl* -es). **1** brújula. **2** compás.

compassion [kəm'pæʃən] *n* compasión.

compassionate [kəm'pæʃənət] *adj* compasivo,-a.

compatible [kəm'pætɪbəl] *adj* compatible.

compel [kəm'pel] *vt* (GB *pt & pp* **compelled**, *ger* **compelling**; US *pt & pp* **compeled**, *ger* **compeling**) obligar, forzar, compeler.

compensate ['kɒmpənseɪt] *vt* **1** compensar. **2** indemnizar.

compensation [kɒmpən'seɪʃən] *n* **1** compensación. **2** indemnización.

compere ['kɒmpeəʳ] *n* GB presentador,-ra.
▶ *vt* GB presentar.

compete [kəm'piːt] *vi* competir.

competence ['kɒmpɪtəns] *n* competencia, aptitud.

competent ['kɒmpɪtənt] *adj* competente.

competition [kɒmpə'tɪʃən] *n* **1** concurso, competición. **2** competencia, rivalidad.

competitive [kəm'petɪtɪv] *adj* **1** de espíritu competitivo *(persona)*. **2** competitivo, -a *(precio)*.

competitor [kəm'petɪtəʳ] *n* **1** competidor,-ra. **2** participante, concursante.

complacent [kəm'pleɪsənt] *adj* pagado,-a de sí mismo,-a.

complain [kəm'pleɪn] *vt* quejarse.

complaint [kəm'pleɪnt] *n* **1** queja. **2** reclamación. **3** dolencia, afección, achaque.
● **to lodge a complaint** presentar una reclamación.

complement ['kɒmplɪmənt] *n* complemento.

complementary [kɒmplɪ'mentərɪ] *adj* complementario,-a.

complete [kəm'pliːt] *adj* **1** completo,-a. **2** acabado,-a, terminado,-a. **3** total *(fracaso)*.
▶ *vt* **1** completar. **2** acabar, terminar.

completely [kəm'pliːtlɪ] *adv* por completo, completamente.

completion [kəm'pliːʃən] *n* finalización, terminación.

complex ['kɒmpleks] *adj* complejo,-a.
▶ *n* (*pl* **complexes**) complejo.

complexion [kəm'plekʃən] *n* cutis, tez.

complexity [kəm'pleksɪtɪ] *n* (*pl* -ies) complejidad.

complicate ['kɒmplɪkeɪt] *vt* complicar.

complicated ['kɒmplɪkeɪtɪd] *adj* complicado,-a.

complication [kɒmplɪ'keɪʃən] *n* complicación.

compliment   [(n)   'kɒmplɪmənt(vb) 'kɒmplɪment] *n* cumplido.
▶ *vt* felicitar.
▶ *npl* **compliments** saludos: *my compliments to the chef*, felicite al cocinero de mi parte.
● **with the compliments of** ... obsequio de ....

comply [kəm'plaɪ] *vi* (*pt & pp* -**ied**) obedecer: *it complies with European standards*, cumple con la normativa europea.

component [kəm'pəʊnənt] *adj-n* componente.

compose [kəm'pəʊz] *vt* componer.
● **to be composed of** componerse de.
● **to compose oneself** calmarse, serenarse.

composed [kəm'pəʊzd] *adj* sereno,-a, sosegado,-a.

composer [kəm'pəʊzə'] *n* compositor,-ra.

composite ['kɒmpəzɪt] *adj* compuesto,-a.

composition [kɒmpə'zɪʃən] *n* **1** composición. **2** redacción.

compost ['kɒmpɒst] *n* abono.

composure [kəm'pəʊʒə'] *n* calma, serenidad.

compound¹   [(adj-n)   'kɒmpaʊnd(vb) kəm'paʊnd] *adj* compuesto,-a.
▶ *n* compuesto.
▶ *vt* agravar.

compound² ['kɒmpaʊnd] *n* recinto.

comprehend [kɒmprɪ'hend] *vt* comprender.

comprehension [kɒmprɪ'henʃən] *n* comprensión.

comprehensive [kɒmprɪ'hensɪv] *adj* **1** completo,-a, global. **2** amplio,-a, extenso,-a.
■ **comprehensive insurance** seguro a todo riesgo.
■ **comprehensive school** GB *instituto de enseñanza secundaria*.

compress ['kɒmpres] *n* (*pl* **compresses** [kəm'pres]) compresa.
▶ *vt* **1** comprimir. **2** reducir.

compression [kəm'preʃən] *n* compresión.

comprise [kəm'praɪz] *vt* **1** constar de. **2** componer, componerse.

compromise ['kɒmprəmaɪz] *n* arreglo, acuerdo.
▶ *vi* transigir, llegar a un acuerdo.
▶ *vt* comprometer.

compulsive [kəm'pʌlsɪv] *adj* **1** absorbente *(libro)*. **2** empedernido,-a, compulsivo,-a.

compulsory [kəm'pʌlsərɪ] *adj* obligatorio,-a.

computer [kəm'pjuːtə'] *n* ordenador.
■ **computer game** juego de ordenador.
■ **computer programmer** programador,-ra.
■ **computer science** informática.

computerize [kəm'pjuːtəraɪz] *vt* informatizar.

computing [kəm'pjuːtɪŋ] *n* informática.

comrade ['kɒmreɪd] *n* compañero,-a, camarada.

con [kɒn] *n fam* estafa, timo.
▶ *vt* (*pt & pp* **conned**, *ger* **conning**) *fam* estafar, timar.
■ **con man** *fam* estafador.

Con [kɒn] *abbr* GB (*Conservative*) conservador,-ra.

conceal [kən'siːl] *vt* ocultar.

concede [kən'siːd] *vt* reconocer, admitir.
▶ *vi* ceder.

conceit [kən'siːt] *n* vanidad, presunción.

conceited [kən'siːtɪd] *adj* engreído,-a, presuntuoso,-a.

conceivable [kən'siːvəbəl] *adj* concebible.

conceivably [kən'siːvəblɪ] *adv* posiblemente.

conceive [kən'siːv] *vt-vi* concebir.

concentrate ['kɒnsəntreɪt] *vt-vi* concentrar(se).

concentrated ['kɒnsəntreɪtɪd] *adj* **1** concentrado,-a *(zumo)*. **2** intenso,-a *(esfuerzo)*.

concentration [kɒnsən'treɪʃən] *n* concentración.
■ **concentration camp** campo de concentración.

concept ['kɒnsept] *n* concepto.

conception [kən'sepʃən] *n* **1** concepción. **2** concepto, idea.

concern [kən'sɜːn] *n* **1** preocupación, inquietud. **2** negocio, empresa.
▶ *vt* **1** afectar, concernir, importar a. **2** preocupar. **3** tener que ver con.
● **as far as I'm concerned** por lo que a mí se refiere.

- **it's no concern of mine** no es asunto mío.
- **there's no cause for concern** no hay por qué preocuparse.
- **to whom it may concern** a quien corresponda.

concerned [kənˈsɜːnd] *adj* preocupado,-a.

concerning [kənˈsɜːnɪŋ] *prep* referente a, sobre, acerca de.

concert [ˈkɒnsət] *n* concierto.
- **in concert** en concierto.
■ **concert house** sala de conciertos.

concerted [kənˈsɜːtɪd] *adj* en común, conjunto,-a.

concerto [kənˈtʃeətəʊ] *n* (*pl* **concertos**) concierto.

concession [kənˈseʃən] *n* concesión.

conciliation [kənsɪlɪˈeɪʃən] *n* conciliación.

concise [kənˈsaɪs] *adj* conciso,-a.

conclude [kənˈkluːd] *vt-vi* **1** concluir. **2** llegar a (*acuerdo*). **3** firmar (*tratado*). **4** cerrar (*trato*).
► *vi* terminar, concluir.

conclusion [kənˈkluːʒən] *n* **1** conclusión. **2** final.

conclusive [kənˈkluːsɪv] *adj* concluyente, definitivo.

concoct [kənˈkɒkt] *vt* **1** preparar (*salsa*). **2** inventar (*excusa*).

concourse [ˈkɒnkɔːs] *n* vestíbulo.

concrete [ˈkɒŋkriːt] *adj* concreto,-a, específico,-a.
► *n* hormigón.
■ **concrete mixer** hormigonera.

concur [kənˈkɜː] *vi* (*pt & pp* **concurred**, *ger* **concurring**) coincidir.

condemn [kənˈdem] *vt* **1** condenar. **2** declarar en estado de ruina (*edificio*).

condemnation [kɒndemˈneɪʃən] *n* condena.

condensation [kɒndenˈseɪʃən] *n* **1** condensación. **2** vaho.

condense [kənˈdens] *vt-vi* condensar(se).
■ **condensed milk** leche condensada.

condescend [kɒndɪˈsend] *vi* **1** dignarse. **2** tratar con condescendencia.

condescending [kɒndɪˈsendɪŋ] *adj* condescendiente.

condescension [kɒndɪˈsenʃən] *n* condescendencia.

condiment [ˈkɒndɪmənt] *n* condimento.

condition [kənˈdɪʃən] *n* **1** condición, estado. **2** circunstancia. **3** afección (*médica*).
► *vt* **1** condicionar, determinar. **2** acondicionar.
- **in bad condition** en mal estado.
- **in good condition** en buen estado.
- **on condition that** a condición de que.
- **to be out of condition** no estar en forma.

conditional [kənˈdɪʃənəl] *adj* condicional.
► *n* condicional.
- **to be conditional on/upon** depender de.

conditioner [kənˈdɪʃənəʳ] *n* suavizante.

condolences [kənˈdəʊlənsɪz] *npl* pésame.
- **please accept my condolences** le acompaño en el sentimiento.
- **to offer one's condolences** dar el pésame.

condom [ˈkɒndəm] *n* condón.

condone [kənˈdəʊn] *vt* consentir, aprobar.

condor [ˈkɒndɔːʳ] *n* cóndor.

conducive [kənˈdjuːsɪv] *adj* propicio,-a.

conduct [(*n*) ˈkɒndʌkt(*vb*) kənˈdʌkt] *n* **1** conducta, comportamiento. **2** dirección, gestión.
► *vt* **1** dirigir, llevar a cabo: *to conduct a survey*, realizar un sondeo. **2** comportarse: *to conduct oneself badly*, portarse mal. **3** ser conductor,-ra de (*calor*).
► *vt-vi* dirigir (*orquesta*).

conductor [kənˈdʌktəʳ] *n* **1** director,-ra (*de orquesta*). **2** cobrador (*de autobús*). **3** conductor (*de calor*).

conductress [kənˈdʌktrəs] *n* (*pl* **-es**) cobradora (*de autobús*).

cone [kəʊn] *n* **1** cono. **2** cucurucho. **3** piña.

confectionery [kənˈfekʃənəri] *n* dulces.

confederacy [kənˈfedərəsi] *n* (*pl* **-ies**) confederación.

confederation [kənfedəˈreɪʃən] *n* confederación.

confer [kənˈfɜːʳ] *vt* (*pt & pp* **conferred**) conferir, conceder (*premio*).
► *vi* consultar.

conference [ˈkɒnfərəns] *n* **1** congreso. **2** reunión.
- **to be in conference** estar reunido,-a.
■ **conference call** teleconferencia.

confess [kənˈfes] *vt-vi* confesar(se).

confession [kənˈfeʃən] *n* confesión.

confessional [kənˈfeʃənəl] *n* confesionario.

confidant [ˈkɒnfɪdænt] *n* confidente.

confidante ['kɒnfɪdænt] n confidenta.

confide [kən'faɪd] vt-vi confiar.

confidence ['kɒnfɪdəns] n **1** confianza: *I have confidence in him*, confío en él. **2** confianza, seguridad *(en sí mismo)*. **3** confidencia *(secreto)*.

confident ['kɒnfɪdənt] adj seguro,-a *(de sí mismo)*.

● **to be confident that...** estar seguro de que..., confiar en que....

confidential [kɒnfɪ'denʃəl] adj confidencial.

confidently ['kɒnfɪdəntlɪ] adv con seguridad.

confine [kən'faɪn] vt **1** limitar. **2** encerrar, recluir.

confinement [kən'faɪnmənt] n **1** reclusión, confinamiento: *to be in solitary confinement*, estar incomunicado. **2** parto.

confines ['kɒnfaɪnz] npl límites.

confirm [kən'fɜːm] vt confirmar.

confirmation [kɒnfə'meɪʃən] n confirmación.

confirmed [kən'fɜːmd] adj empedernido,-a, inveterado,-a.

confiscate ['kɒnfɪskeɪt] vt confiscar.

conflict [(n) 'kɒnflɪkt(vb) kən'flɪkt] n conflicto.
► vi chocar, estar en conflicto.

conflicting [kən'flɪktɪŋ] adj **1** contradictorio,-a *(pruebas)*. **2** contrario,-a *(opiniones)*.

conform [kən'fɔːm] vi **1** conformarse, avenirse. **2** ajustarse.

conformity [kən'fɔːmɪtɪ] n conformidad.
● **in conformity with** conforme a.

confront [kən'frʌnt] vt **1** afrontar *(peligro)*. **2** enfrentarse con *(enemigo)*.

confuse [kən'fjuːz] vt **1** desconcertar, desorientar. **2** confundir *(with, con)*. **3** complicar *(asunto)*.

confused [kən'fjuːzd] adj **1** confundido,-a *(persona)*. **2** confuso,-a *(explicación)*.
● **to get confused** confundirse.

confusing [kən'fjuːzɪŋ] adj confuso,-a.

confusion [kən'fjuːʒən] n confusión.

congeal [kən'dʒiːl] vi coagularse.

congenial [kən'dʒiːnɪəl] adj agradable.

congenital [kən'dʒenɪtəl] adj congénito,-a.

congested [kən'dʒestɪd] adj **1** colapsado,-a, congestionado,-a *(ciudad, calle)*. **2** congestionado,-a *(venas, etc)*.

congestion [kən'dʒestʃən] n congestión.

conglomerate [kən'glɒmərət] n conglomerado.

congratulate [kən'grætjəleɪt] vt felicitar.

congratulations [kəngrætjə'leɪʃəns] npl felicidades, enhorabuena.

congregate ['kɒŋgrɪgeɪt] vi congregarse.

congregation [kɒŋgrɪ'geɪʃən] n fieles.

congress ['kɒŋgres] n (pl **-es**) congreso.

conical ['kɒnɪkəl] adj cónico,-a.

conifer ['kɒnɪfəʳ] n conífera.

conjecture [kən'dʒektʃəʳ] n conjetura.
► vt conjeturar.

conjunction [kən'dʒʌŋkʃən] n conjunción.
● **in conjunction with** conjuntamente con.

conjure ['kʌndʒəʳ] vi hacer magia, hacer juegos de manos.
► vt hacer aparecer.

to conjure up vt evocar.

conjurer ['kʌndʒərəʳ] n mago,-a, prestidigitador,-ra.

conjuror ['kʌndʒərəʳ] n mago,-a, prestidigitador,-ra.

connect [kə'nekt] vt **1** conectar. **2** comunicar, unir. **3** relacionar, asociar. **4** pasar, poner *(al teléfono)*.
► vi enlazar *(vuelos)*.

connection [kə'nekʃən] n **1** conexión. **2** relación. **3** unión, enlace. **4** correspondencia, conexión *(vuelos)*.

connexion [kə'nekʃən] n **1** conexión. **2** relación. **3** unión, enlace. **4** correspondencia, conexión *(vuelos)*.

connoisseur [kɒnə'sɜːʳ] n entendido,-a.

connotation [kɒnə'teɪʃən] n connotación.

conquer ['kɒŋkəʳ] vt **1** conquistar. **2** vencer a.

conqueror ['kɒŋkərəʳ] n conquistador, -ra, vencedor,-ra.

conquest ['kɒŋkwest] n conquista.

conscience ['kɒnʃəns] n conciencia.

conscientious [kɒnʃɪ'enʃəs] adj concienzudo,-a.
■ **conscientious objector** objetor,-ra de conciencia.

conscious ['kɒnʃəs] adj consciente.

consciousness ['kɒnʃəsnəs] n **1** conciencia. **2** conocimiento.
● **to lose consciousness** perder el conocimiento.

● **to regain consciousness** recobrar el conocimiento.

conscript [(n) 'konskript(vb) kən'skript] n recluta.

► vt reclutar.

conscription [kən'skripʃən] n servicio militar obligatorio.

consecutive [kən'sekjətɪv] adj consecutivo,-a.

consent [kən'sent] n consentimiento.

► vi consentir.

consequence ['konsɪkwəns] n 1 consecuencia. 2 resultado.

● **it is of no consequence** no tiene importancia.

consequent ['konsɪkwənt] adj consiguiente.

consequently ['konsɪkwəntlɪ] adv por consiguiente.

conservation [konsə'veɪʃən] n conservación, protección.

conservationist [konsə'veɪʃənɪst] n conservacionista, ecologista.

conservatism [kən'sɜːvətɪzəm] n conservadurismo.

conservative [kən'sɜːvətɪv] adj conservador,-ra.

► n conservador,-ra.

conservatory [kən'sɜːvətrɪ] n (pl -ies). 1 invernadero. 2 conservatorio.

conserve [kən'sɜːv] vt 1 ahorrar (energía). 2 conservar, preservar (naturaleza).

► n conserva.

consider [kən'sɪdə'] vt considerar.

considerable [kən'sɪdərəbəl] adj importante, considerable.

considerably [kən'sɪdərəblɪ] adv bastante.

considerate [kən'sɪdərət] adj considerado,-a.

consideration [kənsɪdə'reɪʃən] n consideración.

● **to take into consideration** tener en cuenta.

considering [kən'sɪdərɪŋ] prep teniendo en cuenta.

► conj teniendo en cuenta que.

consign [kən'saɪn] vt 1 consignar. 2 confiar.

● **consigned to oblivion** relegado,-a al olvido.

consist [kən'sɪst] vi 1 consistir. 2 constar.

consistency [kən'sɪstənsɪ] n 1 consecuencia, coherencia. 2 consistencia.

consistent [kən'sɪstənt] adj 1 consecuente, coherente. 2 constante.

consolation [konsə'leɪʃən] n consolación, consuelo.

console[1] ['konsəʊl] n consola.

console[2] [kən'səʊl] vt consolar.

consolidate [kən'solɪdeɪt] vt-vi consolidar(se).

consonant ['konsənənt] n consonante.

conspicuous [kəns'pɪkjʊəs] adj llamativo,-a, visible.

conspiracy [kən'spɪrəsɪ] n (pl -ies) conspiración.

conspire [kən'spaɪə'] vi conspirar.

constable ['kʌnstəbəl] n policía, guardia.

constant ['konstənt] adj 1 constante. 2 continuo,-a. 3 leal.

► n constante.

constellation [konstə'leɪʃən] n constelación.

constipated ['konstɪpeɪtɪd] adj estreñido,-a.

constipation [konstɪ'peɪʃən] n estreñimiento.

constituency [kən'stɪtjʊənsɪ] n (pl -ies) circunscripción, distrito electoral.

constituent [kəns'tɪtjʊənt] adj 1 constitutivo,-a. 2 elector,-ra, votante.

► n componente.

constitute ['konstɪtjuːt] vt constituir.

constitution [konstɪ'tjuːʃən] n constitución.

constitutional [konstɪ'tjuːʃənəl] adj constitucional.

constrain [kəns'treɪn] vt forzar, obligar.

constraint [kən'streɪnt] n 1 coacción. 2 limitación.

constrict [kən'strɪkt] vt apretar, constreñir.

construct [kəns'trʌkt] vt construir.

construction [kən'strʌkʃən] n construcción.

constructive [kən'strʌktɪv] adj constructivo,-a.

construe [kən'struː] vt interpretar.

consul ['konsəl] n cónsul.

consulate ['konsjələt] n consulado.

consult [kən'sʌlt] vt-vi consultar.

consultant [kən'sʌltənt] n 1 asesor,-ra. 2 medico especialista.

consultation [konsəl'teɪʃən] n consulta.

consume [kən'sjuːm] vt consumir.

consumer [kən'sjuːmə'] n consumidor,-ra.

■ **consumer goods** bienes de consumo.

■ **consumer society** sociedad de consumo.

consummate [*(adj)* 'kɒnsəmət*(vb)* 'kɒnsəmeɪt] *adj* consumado,-a.
► *vt* consumar.

consumption [kən'sʌmpʃən] *n* **1** consumo. **2** tisis.

contact ['kɒntækt] *n* contacto.
► *vt* ponerse en contacto con, contactar con.

■ **contact lens** lentilla, lente de contacto.

contagious [kən'teɪdʒəs] *adj* contagioso,-a.

contain [kən'teɪn] *vt* contener.

container [kən'teɪnə'] *n* **1** recipiente, envase. **2** *(Comm)* conáiner.

contaminate [kən'tæmɪneɪt] *vt* contaminar.

contamination [kəntæmɪ'neɪʃən] *n* contaminación, polución.

contemplate ['kɒntempleɪt] *vt* **1** contemplar, meditar. **2** considerar.

contemporary [kən'tempərərɪ] *adj-n* contemporáneo,-a.

contempt [kən'tempt] *n* desprecio, menosprecio.
● **to hold in contempt** despreciar.
■ **contempt of court** desacato a la autoridad.

contend [kən'tend] *vi* **1** competir, luchar. **2** enfrentarse a *(problemas)*.
► *vt* sostener, afirmar.

content[1] ['kɒntent] *n* contenido.

content[2] [kən'tent] *adj* contento,-a, satisfecho,-a.
► *vt* contentar.
● **to content oneself with** contentarse con.

contented [kən'tentɪd] *adj* contento,-a, satisfecho,-a.

contention [kən'tenʃən] *n* **1** controversia, contienda. **2** parecer.

contentious [kən'tenʃəs] *adj* polémico,-a.

contents ['kɒntents] *npl* contenido.

contest [*(n)* 'kɒntest*(vb)* kən'test] *n* **1** concurso, competición. **2** contienda, lucha.
► *vt* **1** luchar por, competir por. **2** presentarse como candidato,-a *(en elecciones)*. **3** refutar, rebatir *(afirmación)*.

contestant [kən'testənt] *n* **1** concursante. **2** candidato,-a.

context ['kɒntekst] *n* contexto.

continent ['kɒntɪnənt] *n* continente.

continental [kɒntɪ'nentəl] *adj* **1** continental. **2** GB europeo,-a.
■ **continental breakfast** desayuno continental.

contingency [kən'tɪndʒənsɪ] *n* (*pl* -**ies**) contingencia, eventualidad.
■ **contingency plan** plan de emergencia.

contingent [kən'tɪndʒənt] *adj* supeditado,-a.
► *n* contingente.

continual [kən'tɪnjʊəl] *adj* continuo,-a, constante.

continuation [kəntɪnjʊ'eɪʃən] *n* continuación.

continue [kən'tɪnjuː] *vt-vi* continuar, seguir.

continuity [kɒntɪ'njuːɪtɪ] *n* continuidad.

continuous [kən'tɪnjʊəs] *adj* continuo,-a, constante.

contort [kən'tɔːt] *vt-vi* contorsionar(se).

contour ['kɒntʊə'] *n* contorno.
■ **contour line** curva de nivel.

contraband ['kɒntrəbænd] *n* contrabando.

contraception [kɒntrə'sepʃən] *n* anticoncepción.

contraceptive [kɒntrə'septɪv] *adj* anticonceptivo,-a.
► *n* anticonceptivo.

contract [*(n)* 'kɒntrækt*(vb)* kən'trækt] *n* contrato.
► *vi* contraerse.
► *vt* contraer *(enfermedad, matrimonio)*.

contraction [kən'trækʃən] *n* contracción.

contractor [kən'træktə'] *n* contratista.

contradict [kɒntrə'dɪkt] *vt* contradecir.

contradiction [kɒntrə'dɪkʃən] *n* contradicción.

contradictory [kɒntrə'dɪktərɪ] *adj* contradictorio,-a.

contrary [*(adj)* 'kɒntrərɪ*(n)* kən'treərɪ] *adj* contrario,a *(opinión)*.
► *n* contrario.
● **contrary to** en contra de, al contrario de: *contrary to what we expected*, al contrario de lo que esperábamos.
● **on the contrary** al contrario.

contrast [*(n)* 'kɒntræst*(vb)* kɒn'træst] *n* contraste.
► *vt-vi* contrastar.
● **in contrast to** a diferencia de.

contribute [kən'trɪbjuːt] *vt-vi* contribuir.
► *vi* colaborar *(en periódico)*.

contribution [kɒntrɪˈbjuːʃən] *n* **1** contribución, aportación. **2** colaboración *(en periódico)*.

contributor [kənˈtrɪbjətəʳ] *n* **1** contribuyente. **2** colaborador,-ra *(en periódico)*.

contrive [kənˈtraɪv] *vt* idear, inventar.

● **to contrive to do STH** arreglárselas para hacer algo.

contrived [kənˈtraɪvd] *adj* artificial, forzado,-a.

control [kənˈtrəʊl] *n* **1** control. **2** mando, control. **3** dominio.

▶ *vt* (GB *pt & pp* **controlled**, *ger* **controlling**; US *pt & pp* **controled**, *ger* **controling**). **1** controlar, tener el mando de. **2** dominar: *control yourself*, contrólate.

● **out of control** fuera de control.

● **to be in control** estar al mando.

● **to bring under control** conseguir controlar.

● **to go out of control** descontrolarse.

● **to lose control** perder el control.

● **under control** bajo control.

■ **control tower** torre de control.

controller [kənˈtrəʊləʳ] *n* **1** controlador, -ra. **2** director,-ra. **3** director,-ra de programación.

controversial [kɒntrəˈvɜːʃəl] *adj* controvertido,-a, polémico,-a.

controversy [kənˈtrɒvəsi] *n* (*pl* **-ies**) controversia, polémica.

convene [kənˈviːn] *vt* convocar.

▶ *vi* reunirse.

convenience [kənˈviːnɪəns] *n* conveniencia, comodidad.

■ **convenience food** plato precocinado.

convenient [kənˈviːnɪənt] *adj* **1** conveniente, oportuno,-a. **2** bien situado,-a *(lugar)*. **3** práctico,-a.

convent [ˈkɒnvənt] *n* convento.

convention [kənˈvenʃən] *n* convención.

conventional [kənˈvenʃənəl] *adj* convencional.

converge [kənˈvɜːdʒ] *vi* converger, convergir.

conversant [kənˈvɜːsənt] *adj* versado,-a.

conversation [kɒnvəˈseɪʃən] *n* conversación.

converse [ˈkɒnvɜːs] *adj* opuesto,-a, contrario,-a.

▶ *n* lo opuesto, lo contrario.

conversion [kənˈvɜːʃən] *n* conversión.

convert [(*n*) ˈkɒnvɜːt *(vb)* kənˈvɜːt] *n* converso,-a.

▶ *vt* convertir.

▶ *vi* convertirse *(a una religión)*.

convertible [kənˈvɜːtəbəl] *adj* convertible.

▶ *adj-n* descapotable *(coche)*.

convex [ˈkɒnveks] *adj* convexo,-a.

convey [kənˈveɪ] *vt* **1** llevar, transportar. **2** comunicar, expresar *(idea)*.

conveyor belt [kənˈveɪəbelt] *n* cinta transportadora.

convict [(*n*) ˈkɒnvɪkt *(vb)* kənˈvɪkt] *n* **1** preso,-a. **2** interno,-a.

▶ *vt* declarar culpable.

conviction [kənˈvɪkʃən] *n* **1** convicción. **2** condena.

convince [kənˈvɪns] *vt* convencer.

convincing [kənˈvɪnsɪŋ] *adj* convincente.

convoy [ˈkɒnvɔɪ] *n* convoy.

convulsion [kənˈvʌlʃən] *n* convulsión.

cook [kʊk] *n* cocinero,-ra.

▶ *vt* guisar, cocinar, preparar, hacer *(comida)*.

▶ *vi* quisarse, cocinarse, prepararse, hacerse.

to cook up *vt* **1** tramar *(plan)*. **2** inventar *(excusa)*.

cooker [ˈkʊkəʳ] *n* cocina: *an electric cooker*, una cocina eléctrica.

cookery [ˈkʊkəri] *n* cocina: *Spanish cookery*, la cocina española.

■ **cookery book** libro de cocina.

cookie [ˈkʊki] *n* US galleta.

cooking [ˈkʊkɪŋ] *n* cocina: *Spanish cooking*, cocina española.

● **to do the cooking** cocinar.

cool [kuːl] *adj* **1** fresco,-a *(bebida)*. **2** tranquilo,-a *(persona)*. **3** frío,-a *(acogida)*. **4** sl guay, genial.

▶ *vt* refrescar, enfriar.

▶ *vi* enfriarse.

● **to keep one's cool** mantener la calma.

● **to lose one's cool** perder la calma.

to cool down *vt-vi* **1** enfriar(se) *(comida)*. **2** calmar(se) *(persona)*.

coolness [ˈkuːlnəs] *n* **1** fresco, frescor. **2** frialdad *(de acogida)*. **3** serenidad *(de persona)*.

coop [kuːp] *n* gallinero.

to coop up *vt* encerrar.

cooperate [kəʊˈɒpəreɪt] *vi* cooperar, colaborar.

cooperation [kəʊɒpəˈreɪʃən] n cooperación, colaboración.

cooperative [kəʊˈɒpərətɪv] adj **1** cooperativo,-a. **2** cooperador,-ra, dispuesto,-a a colaborar.
▶ n cooperativa.

coordinate [kəʊˈɔːdɪneɪt] vt coordinar.

coordination [kəʊɔːdɪˈneɪʃən] n coordinación.

cop [kɒp] n fam poli.
● **it's not much cop** no es nada del otro mundo.

to cop out vi fam rajarse.

cope [kəʊp] vi arreglárselas: **I just can't cope!**, ¡es que no doy abasto!

to cope with vt poder con, hacer frente a.

copious [ˈkəʊpɪəs] adj copioso,-a.

copper [ˈkɒpəʳ] n **1** cobre. **2** GB fam pela, perra. **3** fam poli.

copy [ˈkɒpɪ] n (pl -ies). **1** copia. **2** ejemplar (de libro, disco).
▶ vt-vi (pt & pp -ied) copiar.

copycat [ˈkɒpɪkæt] n fam copión,-ona.

copyright [ˈkɒpɪraɪt] n derechos de autor.

coral [ˈkɒrəl] n coral.
■ **coral reef** arrecife de coral.

cord [kɔːd] n cuerda, cordón.
▶ npl **cords** fam pantalones de pana.

cordon [ˈkɔːdən] n cordón.
▶ vt acordonar.

corduroy [ˈkɔːdərɔɪ] n pana.

core [kɔːʳ] n **1** núcleo, centro. **2** corazón (de manzana).
● **to the core** hasta la médula.

cork [kɔːk] n corcho.
■ **cork oak** alcornoque.

corkscrew [ˈkɔːkskruː] n sacacorchos.

corn[1] [kɔːn] n **1** maíz. **2** cereales.
■ **corn on the cob** mazorca, maíz tierno (en mazorca).

corn[2] [kɔːn] n callo (dureza).

cornea [ˈkɔːnɪə] n córnea.

corner [ˈkɔːnəʳ] n **1** esquina. **2** rincón.
▶ vt arrinconar.
● **in a tight corner** en un aprieto.
● **just round the corner** a la vuelta de la esquina.
● **to corner the market** acaparar el mercado.
■ **corner kick** córner.

cornerstone [ˈkɔːnəstəʊn] n piedra angular.

cornet [ˈkɔːnɪt] n **1** corneta (instrumento). **2** GB cucurucho.

cornflakes [ˈkɔːnfleɪks] npl copos de maíz.

cornflour [ˈkɔːnflaʊəʳ] n harina de maíz, maicena.

cornstarch [ˈkɔːnstɑːtʃ] n harina de maíz, maicena.

corny [ˈkɔːnɪ] adj (-ier, -iest). **1** fam gastado,-a, sobado,-a (chiste). **2** fam cursi, sensiblero,-a.

corollary [kəˈrɒlərɪ] n (pl -ies) corolario.

coronation [kɒrəˈneɪʃən] n coronación.

coroner [ˈkɒrənəʳ] n juez de instrucción.

Corp [ˈkɔːpərəl] abbr (**corporal**) cabo.

corporal [ˈkɔːpərəl] n cabo (militar).
▶ adj corporal.

corporation [kɔːpəˈreɪʃən] n **1** corporación. **2** GB ayuntamiento, consistorio.

corps [kɔːʳ] n (pl **corps** [kɔːz]) cuerpo.

corpse [kɔːps] n cadáver.

corpuscle [ˈkɔːpəsəl] n glóbulo.
■ **red corpuscle** glóbulo rojo.
■ **white corpuscle** glóbulo blanco.

correct [kəˈrekt] adj **1** correcto,-a. **2** exacto,-a. **3** formal.
▶ vt corregir.

correction [kəˈrekʃən] n corrección.

correlation [kɒrəˈleɪʃən] n correlación.

correspond [kɒrɪsˈpɒnd] vi **1** coincidir, corresponderse. **2** escribirse, cartearse.

correspondence [kɒrɪsˈpɒndəns] n correspondencia.
■ **correspondence course** curso por correspondencia.

correspondent [kɒrɪsˈpɒndənt] n corresponsal.

corresponding [kɒrɪsˈpɒndɪŋ] adj correspondiente.

corridor [ˈkɒrɪdɔːʳ] n pasillo, corredor.

corrode [kəˈrəʊd] vt corroer.

corrosion [kəˈrəʊʒən] n corrosión.

corrosive [kəˈrəʊsɪv] adj corrosivo,-a.

corrugated [ˈkɒrəgeɪtɪd] vt ondulado,-a.

corrupt [kəˈrʌpt] adj corrompido,-a, corrupto,-a.
▶ vt-vi corromper.

corruption [kəˈrʌpʃən] n corrupción.

corset [ˈkɔːsɪt] n corsé.

Corsica [ˈkɔːsɪkə] n Córcega.

Corsican [ˈkɔːsɪkən] adj-n corso,-a.

cortisone [ˈkɔːtɪzəʊn] n cortisona.

cosh [kɒʃ] n (pl **coshes**) GB porra.
► vt GB dar un porrazo a.
cosmetic [kɒzˈmetɪk] n cosmético.
■ **cosmetic surgery** cirugía estética.
cosmetics [kɒzˈmetɪks] npl productos
cosméticos.
cosmic [ˈkɒzmɪk] adj cósmico,-a.
cosmopolitan [kɒzməˈpɒlɪtən] adj cos-
mopolita.
cosmos [ˈkɒzmɒs] n cosmos.
cost [kɒst] n coste, costo, precio.
► vi (pt & pp **cost**) costar, valer.
► npl **costs** costas (de juicio).
● **at all costs** a toda costa.
● **at the cost of** a costa de.
● **whatever the cost** cueste lo que
cueste.
■ **cost of living** coste de la vida.
Costa Rica [kɒstəˈriːkə] n Costa Rica.
Costa Rican [kɒstəˈriːkən] adj-n costarricense.
costly [ˈkɒstlɪ] adj (-**ier**, -**iest**) costoso,-a.
costume [ˈkɒstjuːm] n traje, disfraz: **the
national costume**, el traje típico del país.
■ **costume jewellery** bisutería.
cosy [ˈkəʊzɪ] adj (-**ier**, -**iest**) acogedor,-ra.
cot [kɒt] n cuna.
cottage [ˈkɒtɪdʒ] n casa de campo.
■ **cottage cheese** requesón.
cotton [ˈkɒtən] n 1 algodón. 2 hilo.
■ **cotton plant** algodonero.
■ **cotton wool** algodón hidrófilo.
to cotton on vi caer en la cuenta.
couch [kaʊtʃ] n (pl -**es**) canapé, sofá.
couchette [kuːˈʃet] n litera.
cough [kɒf] n tos.
► vi toser.
■ **cough mixture** jarabe para la tos.
to cough up vt soltar.
► vi fam desembolsar, aflojar la pasta.
could [kʊd, kəd] pt → can.
council [ˈkaʊnsəl] n 1 ayuntamiento. 2
consejo. 3 concilio.
councillor [ˈkaʊnsələʳ] n concejal.
counsel [ˈkaʊnsəl] n 1 consejo. 2 abogado,-a.
► vt (GB pt & pp **counselled**, ger **coun-
selling**; US pt & pp **counseled**, ger
counseling) aconsejar.
count¹ [kaʊnt] n conde.
count² [kaʊnt] n cuenta, recuento.
► vt 1 contar. 2 considerar: **count your-**

self lucky you weren't fined, suerte tienes de que no te multaran.
► vi contar.
● **to keep count** llevar la cuenta.
● **to lose count** perder la cuenta.
to count in vt fam incluir, contar con.
to count on vt contar con.
to count out vt 1 ir contando. 2 fam no
contar con.
countable [ˈkaʊntəbəl] adj contable.
countdown [ˈkaʊntdaʊn] n cuenta atrás.
countenance [ˈkaʊntənəns] n fml rostro,
semblante.
► vt fml aceptar, tolerar.
counter [ˈkaʊntəʳ] n 1 mostrador (de tienda). 2 ficha (de juego).
► vt 1 contrarrestar. 2 corresponder (a
ataque).
► vi contestar, replicar.
► adv en contra.
counteract [kaʊntəˈrækt] vt contrarrestar.
counterattack [ˈkaʊntərətæk] n contraataque.
► vt-vi contraatacar.
counterbalance [ˈkaʊntəbæləns] n contrapeso.
► vt contrapesar.
counterclockwise [kaʊntəˈklɒkwaɪz] adj-
adv US en sentido contrario al de las agujas del reloj.
counterespionage [kaʊntərˈespɪənɑːʒ] n
contraespionaje.
counterfeit [ˈkaʊntəfɪt] adj falso,-a, falsificado,-a.
► n falsificación.
► vt falsificar.
counterfoil [ˈkaʊntəfɔɪl] n matriz.
counterpane [ˈkaʊntəpeɪn] n colcha, cubrecama.
counterpart [ˈkaʊntəpɑːt] n 1 homólogo,-a. 2 equivalente.
counterproductive [kaʊntəprəˈdʌktɪv]
adj contraproducente.
countess [ˈkaʊntəs] n (pl -**es**) condesa.
countless [ˈkaʊntləs] adj incontable, innumerable.
country [ˈkʌntrɪ] n (pl -**ies**). 1 país. 2
campo. 3 tierra, región.
countryman [ˈkʌntrɪmən] n (pl **country-
men** [ˈkʌntrɪmən]). 1 campesino. 2 compatriota.
countryside [ˈkʌntrɪsaɪd] n 1 campo. 2
paisaje.

countrywoman [ˈkʌntrɪwʊmən] n (pl countrywomen [ˈkʌntrɪwɪmɪn]). 1 campesina. 2 compatriota.

county [ˈkaʊntɪ] n (pl -ies) condado.

coup [kuː] n golpe.

■ coup d'état golpe de estado.

couple [ˈkʌpəl] n 1 par (de cosas). 2 pareja (de personas): **a married couple**, un matrimonio.

► vt enganchar, conectar.

► vi aparearse.

coupon [ˈkuːpɒn] n cupón, vale, boleto.

courage [ˈkʌrɪdʒ] n valor, valentía.

courageous [kəˈreɪdʒəs] adj valeroso,-a, valiente.

courgette [kʊəˈʒet] n calabacín.

courier [ˈkʊərɪəʳ] n 1 mensajero,-a. 2 guía turístico,-a.

course [kɔːs] n 1 rumbo (de barco, avión). 2 curso (de río). 3 serie, ciclo. 4 curso: **a short course**, un cursillo. 5 plato. 6 campo (de golf).

● during the course of durante.

● in due course a su debido tiempo.

● in the course of time con el tiempo.

● of course desde luego, por supuesto.

■ first course primer plato.

■ main course plato principal.

court [kɔːt] n 1 tribunal, juzgado. 2 pista (de tenis). 3 patio. 4 corte (de rey).

► vt cortejar.

● to take SB to court llevar a ALGN a juicio.

courteous [ˈkɜːtɪəs] adj cortés.

courtesy [ˈkɜːtəsɪ] n (pl -ies) cortesía.

court-martial [kɔːtˈmɑːʃəl] n (pl courts martial) consejo de guerra.

courtship [ˈkɔːtʃɪp] n cortejo, noviazgo.

courtyard [ˈkɔːtjɑːd] n patio.

cousin [ˈkʌzən] n primo,-a.

cove [kəʊv] n cala, ensenada.

covenant [ˈkʌvənənt] n convenio, pacto.

cover [ˈkʌvəʳ] n 1 cubierta, funda. 2 tapa (de cazuela). 3 cubierta (de libro), portada (de revista). 4 cobertura (de seguro). 5 abrigo, protección.

► vt 1 cubrir. 2 tapar (con tapa). 3 asegurar (con seguro). 4 abarcar (tema). 5 cubrir, informar sobre.

● to take cover refugiarse.

● under cover of al amparo de, al abrigo de.

● under separate cover por separado.

■ cover charge precio del cubierto.

■ cover girl modelo de portada.

■ cover note GB seguro provisional.

to cover up vt 1 cubrir, tapar. 2 encubrir.

► vi cubrirse, taparse.

coverage [ˈkʌvərɪdʒ] n 1 reportaje. 2 cobertura (de seguro).

covering [ˈkʌvərɪŋ] n envoltura, capa.

covert [ˈkʌvət] adj secreto,-a.

cover-up [ˈkʌvərʌp] n encubrimiento.

covet [ˈkʌvət] vt codiciar.

cow [kaʊ] n vaca.

coward [ˈkaʊəd] n cobarde.

cowardice [ˈkaʊədɪs] n cobardía.

cowardly [ˈkaʊədlɪ] adj cobarde.

cowboy [ˈkaʊbɔɪ] n vaquero.

cowshed [ˈkaʊʃed] n establo.

coy [kɔɪ] adj (comp coyer, superl coyest) tímido,-a.

cpu [ˈsiːpiːˈjuː] abbr (**central processing unit**) CPU.

crab [kræb] n cangrejo.

■ crab apple manzana silvestre.

crack [kræk] vt 1 rajar, agrietar (suelo). 2 forzar (caja fuerte). 3 cascar (huevo, nuez). 4 chasquear, hacer restallar (látigo). 5 golpearse: **he cracked his head against the wall**, se golpeó la cabeza contra la pared. 6 soltar (chiste).

► vi 1 rajarse, agrietarse. 2 quebrarse (voz). 3 hundirse, venirse abajo (persona). 4 crujir.

► n 1 raja (en taza). 2 grieta (en pared). 3 restallido, chasquido (de látigo). 4 intento: **he had a crack at solving the problem**, intentó resolver el problema. 5 golpe (en la cabeza).

► adj fam de primera.

● to get cracking poner manos a la obra.

cracker [ˈkrækəʳ] n galleta salada.

crackle [ˈkrækəl] n chisporroteo.

► vi chisporrotear.

cradle [ˈkreɪdəl] n cuna.

► vt acunar.

craft [krɑːft] n 1 arte, oficio. 2 artesanía. 3 barco, embarcación. 4 maña.

■ a pleasure craft un barco de recreo.

craftsman [ˈkrɑːftsmən] n (pl craftsmen) artesano.

crafty [ˈkrɑːftɪ] adj (-ier, -iest) astuto,-a, taimado,-a.

crag [kræg] *n* risco, peñasco.

cram [kræm] *vt* (*pt & pp* **crammed**, *ger* **cramming**) llenar, atestar.
► *vi fam* empollar.

cramp[1] [kræmp] *n* calambre.
► *npl* retortijones.

cramp[2] [kræmp] *vt* limitar, restringir.
● **to cramp SB's style** cortarle las alas a ALGN.

crane [kreɪn] *n* **1** grulla común. **2** grúa.
► *vt-vi* estirar(se).

crank [kræŋk] *n* manivela.

cranky ['kræŋki] *adj* (-**ier**, -**iest**) *fam* chiflado,-a, excéntrico,-a.

crap [kræp] *n* **1** *fam* mierda. **2** *fam* gilipolleces.
► *vi* (*pt & pp* **crapped**, *ger* **crapping**) *fam* cagar.

crash [kræʃ] *vi* **1** chocar, estrellarse (*avión, coche*). **2** quebrar.
► *n* (*pl* -**es**). **1** estallido, estrépito (*ruido*). **2** choque, accidente: *a car crash*, un accidente de coche. **3** quiebra.
■ **a crash helmet** casco protector.
■ **a crash course** curso intensivo.

crass [kræs] *adj* burdo,-a.

crate [kreɪt] *n* caja.

crater ['kreɪtə'] *n* cráter.

crave [kreɪv] *vi* ansiar.

craving ['kreɪvɪŋ] *n* ansia, antojo.

crawfish ['krɔːfɪʃ] *n* (*pl* -**es**) langosta.

crawl [krɔːl] *vi* **1** arrastrarse (*adulto*), gatear (*bebé*). **2** avanzar lentamente (*coche*).
► *n* crol.
● **to crawl with** estar apestado,-a de.
● **to make SB's flesh crawl** poner los pelos de punta a ALGN.

crayfish ['kreɪfɪʃ] *n* (*pl* -**es**) cangrejo de río.

crayon ['kreɪɒn] *n* lápiz de color.

craze [kreɪz] *n* manía, moda.

crazy ['kreɪzi] *adj* (-**ier**, -**iest**) *fam* loco,-a, chiflado,-a.
● **to drive SB crazy** volver loco,-a a ALGN.

creak [kriːk] *vi* crujir, chirriar.
► *n* crujido, chirrido.

cream [kriːm] *n* **1** crema, nata. **2** crema (*cosmético*). **3 the cream** *fig* la flor y nata.
■ **cream cheese** queso crema.

crease [kriːs] *n* arruga, raya.
► *vt-vi* arrugar(se).

create [kriːˈeɪt] *vt* **1** crear. **2** producir, causar.

creation [kriːˈeɪʃən] *n* creación.

creative [kriːˈeɪtɪv] *adj* creativo,-a.

creature ['kriːtʃə'] *n* criatura.

crèche [kreʃ] *n* guardería.

credentials [krɪˈdenʃəlz] *npl* credenciales.

credibility [kredrˈbɪlətɪ] *n* credibilidad.

credible ['kredɪbəl] *adj* creíble.

credit ['kredɪt] *n* **1** mérito, reconocimiento. **2** crédito, haber: *credit and debit*, debe y haber.
► *vt* **1** creer, dar crédito a. **2** abonar, ingresar.
► *npl* **credits** créditos (*de película*).
● **on credit** a crédito.
● **to be in credit** tener un saldo positivo.
● **to do SB credit** honrar a ALGN.
● **to take credit for STH** atribuirse el mérito de algo.
■ **credit card** tarjeta de crédito.

creditor ['kredɪtə'] *n* acreedor,-ra.

creed [kriːd] *n* credo.

creek [kriːk] *n* **1** GB cala. **2** US riachuelo.

creep [kriːp] *vi* (*pt & pp* **crept**). **1** arrastrarse (*insecto*), deslizarse (*animal*). **2** trepar. **3** moverse lenta y silenciosamente: *he crept out of the room so as not to wake the baby*, salió silenciosamente de la habitación para no despertar al niño.
► *n fam* asqueroso,-a.
● **to give SB the creeps** ponerle a ALGN la piel de gallina.

creeper ['kriːpə'] *n* trepadora, enredadera.

cremation [krɪˈmeɪʃən] *n* incineración.

crematorium [kreməˈtɔːrɪəm] *n* (*pl* **crematoria**) crematorio.

crème caramel [kremkærəˈmel] *n* flan.

crept [krept] *pt-pp* → creep.

crescent ['kresənt] *adj* creciente.
► *n* medialuna.

crest [krest] *n* **1** cresta (*de gallo*). **2** cima, cumbre (*de columna*). **3** blasón (*heráldico*).

crestfallen ['krestfɔːlən] *adj* abatido,-a.

crevice ['krevɪs] *n* raja, grieta.

crew [kruː] *n* **1** tripulación. **2** equipo.
■ **crew cut** pelado al cero.

crib [krɪb] *n* cuna.
► *vt* (*pt & pp* **cribbed**, *ger* **cribbing**) *fam* copiar, plagiar.

crick [krɪk] *n* tortícolis.

cricket[1] ['krɪkɪt] *n* grillo (*insecto*).

cricket[2] ['krɪkɪt] *n* críquet (*deporte*).

crime [kraɪm] *n* **1** crimen. **2** delito. **3** delincuencia.

criminal ['krɪmɪnəl] *adj* criminal, delincuente.
▶ *n* criminal, delincuente.
■ **criminal record** antecedentes penales.
crimson ['krɪmzən] *adj* carmesí.
▶ *n* carmesí.
cringe [krɪndʒ] *vi* abatirse, encogerse.
crinkle ['krɪŋkəl] *vt-vi* arrugar(se).
cripple ['krɪpəl] *n* lisiado,-a, inválido,-a.
▶ *vt* **1** lisiar, tullir *(persona)*. **2** paralizar *(industria)*.
crisis ['kraɪsɪs] *n (pl* **crises** ['kraɪsiːz]) crisis.
crisp [krɪsp] *adj* **1** crujiente *(pan)*. **2** fresco,-a *(lechuga)*. **3** frío,-a y seco,-a *(tiempo)*.
▶ *n* GB patata frita *(de bolsa)*.
crisscross ['krɪskrɒs] *vt-vi* entrecruzar(se).
criterion [kraɪ'tɪərɪən] *n* criterio.
critic ['krɪtɪk] *n* crítico,-a.
critical ['krɪtɪkəl] *adj* crítico,-a.
● **in critical condition** grave.
● **to be critical of** STH criticar algo.
criticism ['krɪtɪsɪzəm] *n* crítica.
criticize ['krɪtɪsaɪz] *vt-vi* criticar.
croak [krəʊk] *n* **1** graznido *(de cuervo)*. **2** canto *(de rana)*. **3** voz ronca.
▶ *vi* **1** graznar *(cuervo)*. **2** croar *(rana)*. **3** hablar con voz ronca.
Croat ['krəʊæt] *adj* croata.
▶ *n* croata *(persona)*, croata *(lengua)*.
Croatia [krəʊ'eɪʃə] *n* Croacia.
Croatian [krəʊ'eɪʃən] *adj* croata.
▶ *n* croata *(persona)*, croata *(lengua)*.
crochet ['krəʊʃeɪ] *n* croché, ganchillo.
▶ *vi* hacer croché, hacer ganchillo.
crockery ['krɒkərɪ] *n* loza, vajilla.
crocodile ['krɒkədaɪl] *n* cocodrilo.
crocus ['krəʊkəs] *n (pl* **crocuses**) azafrán.
crony ['krəʊnɪ] *n (pl* **-ies**) compinche.
crook [krʊk] *n* **1** gancho. **2** cayado. **3** *fam* delincuente.
crooked ['krʊkɪd] *adj* **1** torcido,-a. **2** tortuoso,-a *(camino)*. **3** *fam* deshonesto,-a *(persona)*.
crop [krɒp] *n* **1** cultivo, cosecha. **2** pelado corto.
▶ *vt (pt & pp* **cropped,** *ger* **cropping). 1** pacer. **2** pelar al rape.
to crop up *vi fam* surgir.
croquet ['krəʊkeɪ] *n* croquet.
cross [krɒs] *adj* enojado,-a.
▶ *n (pl* **-es**). **1** cruz. **2** cruce, mezcla.
▶ *vt* cruzar, atravesar.

▶ *vi* cruzar, cruzarse.
● **it crossed my mind that ...** se me ocurrió que ....
● **to cross oneself** santiguarse.
to cross off *vt* borrar, tachar.
to cross out *vt* borrar, tachar.
to cross over *vt* pasar, atravesar.
crossbar ['krɒsbɑː'] *n* travesaño.
crossbow ['krɒsbəʊ] *n* ballesta.
crossbred ['krɒsbred] *adj-n* híbrido,-a.
cross-country [krɒs'kʌntrɪ] *adj-adv* campo través.
■ **cross-country race** cros.
cross-examine [krɒsɪg'zæmɪn] *vt* interrogar.
cross-eyed ['krɒsaɪd] *adj* bizco,-a.
crossing ['krɒsɪŋ] *n* **1** cruce *(de carretera)*. **2** travesía *(en barco)*.
cross-reference [krɒs'refərəns] *n* remisión.
crossroads ['krɒsrəʊdz] *n* encrucijada, cruce.
crosswise ['krɒswaɪz] *adv* en diagonal.
crossword ['krɒswɜːd] *n* crucigrama.
crotch [krɒtʃ] *n (pl* **-es**) entrepierna.
crotchet ['krɒtʃɪt] *n* negra *(nota)*.
crouch [kraʊtʃ] *vi* agacharse, agazaparse.
crow [krəʊ] *n* cuervo.
▶ *vi (pt* **crowed** o **crew**) cantar.
■ **crow's-feet** patas de gallo.
crowbar ['krəʊbɑː'] *n* palanca.
crowd [kraʊd] *n* **1** multitud, gentío. **2** público. **3** gente.
▶ *vt* **1** llenar, atestar. **2** empujar.
▶ *vi* apiñarse.
crowded ['kraʊdɪd] *adj* lleno,-a de gente, abarrotado,-a.
crown [kraʊn] *n* **1** corona *(de monarca)*. **2** copa *(de árbol, sombrero)*. **3** coronilla.
▶ *vt* coronar.
crucial ['kruːʃəl] *adj* crucial, decisivo,-a.
crucifix ['kruːsɪfɪks] *n (pl* **crucifixes**) crucifijo.
crude [kruːd] *n* **1** tosco,-a, grosero,-a *(chiste)*. **2** crudo,-a *(petróleo)*.
cruel ['kruːəl] *adj (comp* **crueller,** *superl* **cruellest**) cruel.
cruelty ['kruːəltɪ] *n (pl* **-ies**) crueldad.
cruet ['kruːɪt] *n* vinagreras.
cruise [kruːz] *vi* hacer un crucero.
▶ *n (viaje)* crucero.
cruiser ['kruːzə'] *n (barco)* crucero.
crumb [krʌm] *n* miga, migaja.

crumble ['krʌmbəl] *vt* desmenuzar, desmigar.
► *vi* desmoronarse, deshacerse.

crumple ['krʌmpəl] *vt-vi* arrugar(se).

crunch [krʌntʃ] *vt* 1 mascar. 2 hacer crujir.
► *vi* crujir.
► *n (pl* **-es)** crujido.

crusade [kruː'seɪd] *n* cruzada.

crush [krʌʃ] *n (pl* **-es). 1** aglomeración, gentío. 2 *fam* enamoramiento.
► *vt* 1 aplastar. 2 triturar.

crust [krʌst] *n* 1 corteza *(de pan).* 2 pasta. 3 corteza *(de la Tierra).*

crustacean [krʌ'steɪʃən] *n* crustáceo.

crutch [krʌtʃ] *n (pl* **-es)** muleta.
● **to be on crutches** llevar muletas.

crux [krʌks] *n (pl* **cruxes)** quid, meollo.

cry [kraɪ] *vt-vi (pt & pp* **-ied)** gritar.
► *vi* llorar, lamentarse.
► *n (pl* **-ies). 1** grito. 2 llanto.

crybaby ['kraɪbeɪbɪ] *n (pl* **-ies)** llorón,-ona.

to cry out *vi* gritar: *to cry out for STH,* pedir algo a gritos.

crying ['kraɪɪŋ] *n* llanto.
► *adj fig* apremiante.

crypt [krɪpt] *n* cripta.

cryptic ['krɪptɪk] *adj* enigmático,-a, críptico,-a.

crystal ['krɪstəl] *n* cristal.

crystallize ['krɪstəlaɪz] *vt-vi* cristalizar(se).

cub [kʌb] *n* cachorro,-a.
■ **bear cub** osezno.
■ **wolf cub** lobezno.

Cuba ['kjuːbə] *n* Cuba.

Cuban ['kjuːbən] *adj-n* cubano,-a.

cube [kjuːb] *n* 1 cubo *(figura).* 2 terrón *(de azúcar).*
► *vt* elevar al cubo.
■ **cube root** raíz cúbica.

cubic ['kjuːbɪk] *adj* cúbico,-a.

cubicle ['kjuːbɪkəl] *n* cubículo.

cuckoo ['kʊkuː] *n (pl* **cuckoos)** cuco común.

cucumber ['kjuːkʌmbə'] *n* pepino.

cuddle ['kʌdəl] *vt-vi* abrazar(se).
► *n* abrazo.

cue[1] [kjuː] *n* 1 señal. 2 pie *(en teatro).*

cue[2] [kjuː] *n* taco *(de billar).*

cuff[1] [kʌf] *n (pl* **cuffs)** puño.
■ **cuff links** gemelos *(de camisa).*

cuff[2] [kʌf] *vt* abofetear.

cul-de-sac ['kʌldəsæk] *n* calle sin salida.

culminate ['kʌlmɪneɪt] *vt* culminar.

culprit ['kʌlprɪt] *n* culpable.

cult [kʌlt] *n* culto.

cultivate ['kʌltɪveɪt] *vt* cultivar.

cultivated ['kʌltɪveɪtɪd] *adj* 1 culto,-a *(persona).* 2 cultivado,-a *(tierra).*

cultivation [kʌltɪ'veɪʃən] *n* cultivo.

culture ['kʌltʃə'] *n* cultura.

cultured ['kʌltʃəd] *adj* culto,-a.

cumbersome ['kʌmbəsəm] *adj* 1 voluminoso. 2 incómodo,-a.

cumin ['kʌmɪn] *n* comino.

cunning ['kʌnɪŋ] *adj* astuto,-a.
► *n* astucia, maña.

cup [kʌp] *n* 1 taza. 2 copa *(trofeo).*
● **it is not my cup of tea** no me va demasiado.

cupboard ['kʌbəd] *n* armario.

curable ['kjʊərəbəl] *adj* curable.

curate ['kjʊərət] *n* coadjutor.

curator [kjʊ'reɪtə'] *n* conservador,-ra *(de museo).*

curb [kɜːb] *n* freno, restricción.
► *vt* refrenar, contener.

curd [kɜːd] *n* cuajada.
■ **curd cheese** requesón.

curdle ['kɜːdəl] *vt-vi* 1 cuajar, cortar(se) *(leche).* 2 helar(se) *(sangre).*

cure [kjʊə'] *vt* curar.
► *n* cura.

curfew ['kɜːfjuː] *n* toque de queda.

curiosity [kjʊərɪ'bsətɪ] *n (pl* **-ies)** curiosidad.

curious ['kjʊərɪəs] *adj* 1 curioso,-a. 2 extraño.

curl [kɜːl] *vt-vi* rizar(se).
► *n* 1 rizo, bucle. 2 espiral.

curly ['kɜːlɪ] *adj (-ier, -iest)* rizado,-a.

currant ['kʌrənt] *n* pasa.

currency ['kʌrənsɪ] *n (pl* **-ies)** moneda.
■ **foreign currency** divisa.

current ['kʌrənt] *adj* 1 actual *(precio).* 2 en curso, corriente *(mes).* 3 corriente, común *(idea).* 4 último,-a *(problema).*
► *n* corriente.
■ **current account** cuenta corriente.
■ **current affairs** temas de actualidad.

curriculum [kə'rɪkjələm] *n (pl* **curriculms** o **curricula). 1** plan de estudios. 2 currículum.

curry ['kʌrɪ] *n (pl* **-ies)** curry.

curse [kɜːs] *n* 1 maldición, maleficio. 2 palabrota. 3 *fig* azote, desgracia.
► *vt-vi* maldecir.

● **to put a curse on** SB maldecir a ALGN.
cursor ['kɜːsəʳ] *n* cursor.
cursory ['kɜːsərı] *adj* rápido,-a, superficial.
curt [kɜːt] *adj* seco,-a, brusco,-a.
curtail [kɜːˈteɪl] *vt* reducir.
curtain ['kɜːtən] *n* **1** cortina. **2** telón.
● **to draw the curtains** correr las cortinas.
● **to drop the curtain** bajar el telón.
● **to raise the curtain** alzar el telón.
curve [kɜːv] *n* curva.
▶ *vi* torcer, hacer una curva.
cushion ['kʊʃən] *n* cojín, almohadón.
▶ *vt fig* suavizar, amortiguar.
custard ['kʌstəd] *n* natillas.
custody ['kʌstədɪ] *n* **1** custodia. **2** detención.
● **in custody** bajo custodia.
● **to take into custody** detener.
custom ['kʌstəm] *n* costumbre.
customary ['kʌstəmərɪ] *adj* acostumbrado,-a, habitual.
customer ['kʌstəməʳ] *n* cliente.
■ **customer services** servicio de atención al cliente.
customs ['kʌstəmz] *n* aduana.
■ **customs duties** derechos de aduana, aranceles.

> **customs** puede considerarse singular o plural.

cut [kʌt] *vt* (*pt & pp* **cut**, *ger* **cutting**). **1** cortar: *he cut the bread in half*, cortó el pan por la mitad. **2** tallar *(piedra, vidrio)*. **3** dividir. **4** recortar: *they want to cut arms spending*, quieren recortar los gastos de armamento.
▶ *n* **1** corte, incisión. **2** parte *(ganancias)*. **3** rebaja, reducción, recorte: *a wage cut*, un recorte salarial.
▶ *adj* cortado,-a.
● **to cut corners** simplificar.
■ **cold cuts** fiambres.

to cut down *vt* **1** talar, cortar. **2** *fig* reducir: *to cut down on smoking*, fumar menos.
to cut in *vi* interrumpir.
to cut off *vt* **1** cortar *(electricidad)*. **2** aislar: *after the storm, the town was cut off*, tras la tormenta, la ciudad quedó incomunicada.
to cut out *vt* **1** recortar, cortar. **2** eliminar, suprimir.
to cut up *vt* cortar en pedazos, trinchar.
cute [kjuːt] *adj* **1** mono,-a. **2** guapo,-a.
cutlery ['kʌtlərɪ] *n* cubiertos, cubertería.
cutlet ['kʌtlət] *n* chuleta.
cutting ['kʌtɪŋ] *n* **1** recorte. **2** esqueje.
▶ *adj* cortante *(viento)*.
cuttlefish ['kʌtəlfɪʃ] *n* (*pl* -**es**) jibia, sepia.
cv ['siːˈviː] *abbr (curriculum vitae)* currículum vitae.
cyanide ['saɪənaɪd] *n* cianuro.
cybercafé ['saɪbəkæfeɪ] *n* cibercafé.
cyberspace ['saɪbəspeɪs] *n* ciberespacio.
cycle ['saɪkəl] *n* **1** ciclo. **2** *(bicycle)* bicicleta.
▶ *vi* ir en bicicleta.
cycling ['saɪklɪŋ] *n* ciclismo.
cyclist ['saɪklɪst] *n* ciclista.
cyclone ['saɪkləʊn] *n* ciclón.
cylinder ['sɪlɪndəʳ] *n* **1** cilindro. **2** bombona.
cymbal ['sɪmbəl] *n* címbalo.
cynic ['sɪnɪk] *n* cínico,-a.
cynical ['sɪnɪkəl] *adj* cínico,-a.
cynicism ['sɪnɪsɪzəm] *n* cinismo.
cypress ['saɪprəs] *n* (*pl* -**es**) ciprés.
Cypriot ['sɪprɪət] *adj* chipriota,-a.
▶ *n* chipriota.
Cyprus ['saɪprəs] *n* Chipre.
cyst [sɪst] *n* quiste.
czar [zɑːʳ] *n* zar.
Czech [tʃek] *adj* checo,-a.
▶ *n* **1** checo,-a *(persona)*. **2** checo *(lengua)*.
■ **Czech Republic** República Checa.
Czechoslovak [tʃekəˈsləʊvæk] *adj-n* checoslovaco,-a.
Czechoslovakia [tʃekəʊsləˈvækɪə] *n* Checoslovaquia.

D

DA ['diː'eɪ] *abbr* US (*District Attorney*) fiscal.

dab [dæb] *n* **1** toque. **2** poquito.
► *vt* (*pt & pp* **dabbed**, *ger* **dabbing**). **1** tocar ligeramente. **2** aplicar *(pintura)*.

dabble ['dæbəl] *vi* entretenerse.

dad [dæd] *n fam* papá.

daddy ['dædɪ] *n* (*pl* -**ies**) *fam* papá.

daffodil ['dæfədɪl] *n* narciso.

daft [dɑːft] *adj fam* chalado,-a, tonto,-a.

dagger ['dægəʳ] *n* daga, puñal.

daily ['deɪlɪ] *adj* diario,-a, cotidiano,-a.
► *adv* diariamente.
► *n* (*pl* -**ies**) diario.

dainty ['deɪntɪ] *adj* (-**ier**, -**iest**). **1** delicado,-a. **2** refinado,-a.

dairy ['deərɪ] *n* (*pl* -**ies**). **1** vaquería. **2** lechería.
■ **dairy farming** industria lechera.

daisy ['deɪzɪ] *n* (*pl* -**ies**) margarita.

dam [dæm] *n* **1** dique. **2** embalse, presa.
► *vt* (*pt & pp* **dammed**, *ger* **damming**). **1** represar, embalsar. **2** construir un dique en.

damage ['dæmɪdʒ] *vt* **1** dañar, estropear. **2** *fig* perjudicar.
► *n* **1** daño, daños. **2** *fig* perjuicio.
► *npl* **damages** daños y perjuicios.

damaging ['dæmɪdʒɪŋ] *adj* perjudicial.

dame [deɪm] *n* **1** dama. **2** US *fam* tía.

damn [dæm] *interj fam* ¡maldito,-a sea!
► *adj fam* maldito,-a.
► *vt* condenar, maldecir.
● **I don't give a damn** me importa un bledo.

damned [dæmd] *adj* maldito,-a.

damp [dæmp] *adj* húmedo,-a, mojado,-a.
► *n* humedad.

dampen ['dæmpən] *vt* **1** humedecer. **2** *fig* apagar.

dance [dɑːns] *n* baile, danza.
► *vt-vi* bailar.

dancer ['dɑːnsəʳ] *n* **1** bailaor,-ra. **2** bailarín,-ina.

dandelion ['dændɪlaɪən] *n* diente de león.

dandruff ['dændrəf] *n* caspa.

Dane [deɪn] *n* danés,-esa.

danger ['deɪndʒəʳ] *n* peligro.
● **to be in danger of** correr el riesgo de.

dangerous ['deɪndʒərəs] *adj* peligroso,-a.

dangle ['dæŋgəl] *vt-vi* colgar.

Danish ['deɪnɪʃ] *adj* danés,-esa.
► *n* danés.
► *npl* **the Danish** los daneses.

dank [dæŋk] *adj* húmedo,-a y malsano,-a.

Danube ['dænjuːb] *n* Danubio.

dare [deəʳ] *vi* atreverse, osar.
► *vt* desafiar.
► *n* reto, desafío.
● **I dare say...** creo que.
● **don't you dare!** ¡ni se te ocurra!

daring ['deərɪŋ] *adj* audaz, osado,-a.
► *n* osadía, atrevimiento.

dark [dɑːk] *adj* **1** oscuro,-a. **2** moreno,-a *(pelo, piel)*. **3** *fig* triste, negro,-a *(días)*. **4** *fig* oscuro,-a, misterioso,-a *(secreto)*.
► *n* **1** oscuridad. **2** anochecer.
● **to be in the dark** estar a oscuras, no saber nada.
● **to grow dark** anochecer.

darken ['dɑːkən] *vt-vi* oscurecer(se).

darkness ['dɑːknəs] *n* oscuridad, tinieblas.
● **in darkness** a oscuras.

darling ['dɑːlɪŋ] *n* querido,-a, cariño.
► *adj* querido,-a.

darn[1] [dɑːn] *n* zurcido.
▶ *vt* zurcir.
darn[2] [dɑːn] *interj fam* ¡ostras!
dart [dɑːt] *n* **1** dardo. **2** movimiento rápido. **3** pinza *(en falda, pantalón)*.
▶ *vi* lanzarse, precipitarse.
dartboard ['dɑːtbɔːd] *n* diana.
dash [dæʃ] *n (pl* **-es)**. **1** poco, pizca *(de sol)*. **2** chorro *(de líquido)*.
▶ *vt* **1** romper, estrellar. **2** *fig* desvanecer *(esperanzas)*.
▶ *vi* correr, ir deprisa.
● **to make a dash for STH** precipitarse hacia algo.
to dash off *vt* escribir deprisa y corriendo.
▶ *vi* salir corriendo.
dashboard ['dæʃbɔːd] *n* salpicadero.
data ['deɪtə] *npl* datos, información.
■ **data base** base de datos.
■ **data processing** procesamiento de datos.
date[1] [deɪt] *n* **1** fecha. **2** cita, compromiso.
▶ *vt* **1** fechar, datar. **2** US *fam* salir con.
● **out of date 1** anticuado,-a. **2** pasado,-a de moda *(ropa)*. **3** desfasado,-a *(tecnología)*. **4** caducado,-a *(comida, billete)*.
● **up to date** actualizado,-a, al día.
● **to be up to date on STH** estar al corriente de algo.
■ **date of birth** fecha de nacimiento.
date[2] [deɪt] *n* dátil.
dated ['deɪtɪd] *adj* anticuado,-a.
daub [dɔːb] *n* revestimiento, capa.
▶ *vt* embadurnar, untar.
▶ *vi fam* pintarrajear.
daughter ['dɔːtəʳ] *n* hija.
daughter-in-law ['dɔːtərɪnlɔː] *n (pl* **daughters-in-law)** nuera.
daunt [dɔːnt] *vt* intimidar.
dawn [dɔːn] *n* **1** alba, aurora, amanecer. **2** *fig* albores.
▶ *vi* amanecer.
● **it dawned on me that ...** caí en la cuenta de que ....
day [deɪ] *n* **1** día. **2** jornada. **3** época, tiempo.
● **by day** de día.
● **the day after tomorrow** pasado mañana.
● **the day before yesterday** anteayer.
● **the following day** al día siguiente.
● **these days** hoy en día.
■ **day off** día libre.

daybreak ['deɪbreɪk] *n* amanecer, alba.
daydream ['deɪdriːm] *n* ensueño.
▶ *vi* soñar despierto,-a.
daylight ['deɪlaɪt] *n* luz de día.
daytime *n* día: *in the daytime*, de día.
daze [deɪz] *n* aturdimiento.
▶ *vt* aturdir.
dazzle ['dæzəl] *n* deslumbramiento.
▶ *vt* deslumbrar.
DEA ['diː'iː'eɪ] *abbr* US *(Drug Enforcement Administration)* agencia norteamericana contra el narcotráfico, DEA.
dead [ded] *adj* **1** muerto,-a. **2** dormido,-a, entumecido. **3** sordo,-a *(ruido)*. **4** total, absoluto,-a: *dead silence*, silencio total. **5** gastado,-a, agotado,-a.
▶ *n: in the dead of night/winter*, en plena noche/pleno invierno.
▶ *npl* **the dead** los muertos.
▶ *adv* **1** totalmente. **2** justo.
● **to stop dead** pararse en seco.
■ **dead end** callejón sin salida.
deadline ['dedlaɪn] *n* **1** fecha límite, hora límite. **2** plazo.
deadlock ['dedlɒk] *n* punto muerto.
deadly ['dedlɪ] *adj* (**-ier**, **-iest**). **1** mortal *(veneno)*. **2** mortífero,-a *(arma)*.
deaf [def] *adj* sordo,-a.
● **to turn a deaf ear** hacerse el sordo/la sorda.
deaf-and-dumb [defən'dʌm] *adj* sordomudo,-a.
deafen ['defən] *vt* ensordecer.
deafness ['defnəs] *n* sordera.
deal [diːl] *n* **1** trato, pacto. **2** cantidad: *a great deal of noise*, mucho ruido. **3** reparto *(de cartas)*.
▶ *vt (pt & pp* **dealt)**. **1** dar, asestar *(golpe)*. **2** repartir *(cartas)*.
▶ *vi* comerciar.
to deal with *vt* **1** tratar con. **2** abordar, ocuparse de *(problema)*. **3** tratar de *(tema)*.
dealer ['diːləʳ] *n* **1** comerciante, vendedor,-ra. **2** traficante *(de drogas)*.
dealings ['diːlɪŋz] *npl* **1** trato. **2** negocios.
dealt [delt] *pt-pp* → deal.
dean [diːn] *n* **1** deán. **2** decano,-a *(de universidad)*.
dear [dɪəʳ] *adj* **1** querido,-a, estimado,-a. **2** caro,-a *(precio)*.
▶ *n* querido,-a, cariño.
● **dear me!** ¡caramba!, ¡vaya por Dios!

● **Dear Sir** Muy señor mío, Estimado señor.
● **oh dear!** ¡caramba!, ¡vaya por Dios!
dearly ['dɪəlɪ] adv mucho.
death [deθ] n muerte.
● **on pain of death** bajo pena de muerte.
■ **death certificate** certificado de defunción.
■ **death penalty** pena de muerte.
deathly ['deθlɪ] adj sepulcral.
deathtrap ['deθtræp] n fam trampa mortal.
debate [dɪ'beɪt] n debate, discusión.
► vt-vi debatir, discutir.
debit ['debɪt] n débito.
► vt cargar en cuenta.
■ **debit balance** saldo negativo.
debris ['deɪbriː] n escombros.
debt [det] n deuda.
● **to get into debt** endeudarse, contraer deudas.
● **to pay off a debt** saldar una deuda.
● **to run up debts** endeudarse, contraer deudas.
debtor ['detəʳ] n deudor,-ra.
debug [diː'bʌg] vt depurar (programa informático).
debunk [diː'bʌŋk] vt fam desmitificar, desenmascarar, desacreditar (idea, creencia).
debut ['deɪbjuː] n estreno, debut.
decade ['dekeɪd] n década, decenio.
decadence ['dekədəns] n decadencia.
decadent ['dekədənt] adj decadente.
decaffeinated [diː'kæfɪneɪtɪd] adj descafeinado,-a.
decay [dɪ'keɪ] n 1 descomposición (de cuerpo). 2 deterioro (de edificio). 3 caries (de diente). 4 fig decadencia (de sociedad).
► vi 1 descomponerse (cuerpo). 2 deteriorarse (edificio). 3 cariarse (diente). 4 fig corromperse (sociedad).
deceased [dɪ'siːst] adj-n difunto,-a, fallecido,-a.
deceit [dɪ'siːt] n engaño, falsedad.
deceitful [dɪ'siːtfʊl] adj falso,-a, mentiroso,-a.
deceive [dɪ'siːv] vt engañar.
December [dɪ'sembəʳ] n diciembre.
decency ['diːsənsɪ] n decencia.
decent ['diːsənt] adj 1 decente. 2 adecuado,-a, razonable. 3 fam bueno,-a.
deception [dɪ'sepʃən] n engaño, mentira.

deceptive [dɪ'septɪv] adj engañoso,-a, falso,-a.
decibel ['desɪbel] n decibelio.
decide [dɪ'saɪd] vt-vi decidirse.
● **to decide on** optar por.
decided [dɪ'saɪdɪd] adj 1 decidido,-a, resuelto,-a. 2 marcado,-a, claro,-a.
decidedly [dɪ'saɪdɪdlɪ] adv decididamente, sin duda.
deciding [dɪ'saɪdɪŋ] adj decisivo,-a.
decimal ['desɪməl] adj decimal.
► n decimal.
■ **decimal place** cifra decimal.
■ **decimal point** coma decimal.
decipher [dɪ'saɪfəʳ] vt descifrar.
decision [dɪ'sɪʒən] n decisión.
decisive [dɪ'saɪsɪv] adj 1 decisivo,-a (factor). 2 decidido,-a, resuelto,-a (persona).
deck [dek] n 1 cubierta (de barco). 2 piso (de autobús). 3 US baraja.
deckchair ['dektʃeəʳ] n tumbona, silla de playa.
declaration [deklə'reɪʃən] n declaración.
declare [dɪ'kleəʳ] vt declarar.
► vi pronunciarse.
● **to declare war on** declarar la guerra a.
decline [dɪ'klaɪn] n 1 disminución. 2 deterioro, empeoramiento (de salud).
► vi 1 disminuir. 2 deteriorarse, empeorarse (salud).
► vt 1 rehusar, rechazar. 2 declinar (sustantivo).
decorate ['dekəreɪt] vt decorar, adornar.
► vt-vi pintar, empapelar.
decoration [dekə'reɪʃən] n 1 decoración. 2 condecoración.
decorative ['dekərətɪv] adj decorativo,-a.
decoy ['diːkɔɪ] n señuelo.
► vt atraer con señuelo.
decrease [dɪ'kriːs] n disminución, reducción.
► vt-vi disminuir, reducir.
decree [dɪ'kriː] n decreto.
► vt decretar.
dedicate ['dedɪkeɪt] vt dedicar, consagrar.
dedication [dedɪ'keɪʃən] n 1 dedicación, entrega. 2 dedicatoria.
deduce [dɪ'djuːs] vt deducir, inferir.
deduct [dɪ'dʌkt] vt restar, descontar, deducir.
deduction [dɪ'dʌkʃən] n deducción.
deed [diːd] n 1 acto, acción. 2 hazaña. 3 escritura (de propiedad).

deem [diːm] *vt* juzgar, considerar.
deep [diːp] *adj* **1** hondo,-a, profundo,-a: *it's ten metres deep*, tiene diez metros de profundidad. **2** grave *(sonido, voz)*. **3** oscuro,-a. **4** intenso,-a *(color)*.
▶ *adv* profundamente.
▶ *n* profundidad.
● **deep down** en el fondo.
● **to be deep in thought** estar absorto,-a.
deepen [ˈdiːpən] *vt* ahondar, profundizar.
▶ *vi* intensificarse *(color, emoción)*.
deeply [ˈdiːpli] *adv* profundamente.
deer [dɪəʳ] *n (pl* **deer***)* ciervo.
default [dɪˈfɔːlt] *n* **1** negligencia. **2** incumplimiento de pago. **3** incomparecencia.
▶ *vi* **1** faltar a un compromiso, incumplir. **2** no pagar *(una deuda)*. **3** no presentarse, no comparecer.
■ **default settings** valores por defecto.
defeat [dɪˈfiːt] *n* derrota.
▶ *vt* **1** derrotar, vencer. **2** *fig* frustrar *(planes)*.
● **to admit defeat** darse por vencido.
defect [*(n)* ˈdiːfekt*(vb)* dɪˈfekt] *n* defecto, desperfecto.
▶ *vi* desertar.
defective [dɪˈfektɪv] *adj* **1** defectuoso,-a. **2** defectivo,-a.
defence [dɪˈfens] *n* defensa.
defenceless [dɪˈfensləs] *adj* indefenso,-a.
defend [dɪˈfend] *vt* defender.
defendant [dɪˈfendənt] *n* demandado,-a, acusado,-a.
defender [dɪˈfendəʳ] *n* **1** defensor,-ra. **2** defensa *(en fútbol)*.
defending [dɪˈfendɪŋ] *adj* .
■ **defending counsel** abogado,-a defensor,-ra.
defensive [dɪˈfensɪv] *adj* defensivo,-a.
▶ *n* defensiva.
defer[1] [dɪˈfɜːʳ] *vt (pt & pp* **deferred***, ger* **deferring***)* aplazar, retrasar.
defer[2] [dɪˈfɜːʳ] *vi (pt & pp* **deferred***, ger* **deferring***)* deferir.
defiance [dɪˈfaɪəns] *n* desafío.
● **in defiance of** a despecho de.
defiant [dɪˈfaɪənt] *adj* desafiante, provocativo,-a.
deficiency [dɪˈfɪʃənsɪ] *n* deficiencia.
deficient [dɪˈfɪʃənt] *adj* deficiente.
● **to be deficient in STH** estar falto,-a de algo.

deficit [ˈdefɪsɪt] *n* déficit.
define [dɪˈfaɪn] *vt* definir.
definite [ˈdefɪnət] *adj* **1** definitivo,-a, concreto,-a. **2** seguro,-a. **3** claro,-a, preciso,-a.
■ **definite article** artículo determinado.
definitely [ˈdefɪnətlɪ] *adv* definitivamente.
definition [defɪˈnɪʃən] *n* **1** definición. **2** nitidez.
definitive [dɪˈfɪnɪtɪv] *adj* definitivo,-a.
deflate [dɪˈfleɪt] *vt-vi* desinflar(se), deshinchar(se).
deflect [dɪˈflekt] *vt-vi* desviar(se).
deform [dɪˈfɔːm] *vt* deformar, desfigurar.
deformed [dɪˈfɔːmd] *adj* deforme.
defrost [diːˈfrɒst] *vt-vi* descongelar(se).
deft [deft] *adj* diestro,-a, hábil.
defunct [dɪˈfʌŋkt] *adj* difunto,-a.
defy [dɪˈfaɪ] *vt* **1** desafiar *(persona)*. **2** desacatar, desobedecer *(ley)*. **3** retar.
degenerate [*(adj - n)* dɪˈdʒenərət*(vb)* dɪˈdʒenəreɪt] *adj-n* degenerado,-a.
▶ *vi* degenerar.
degeneration [dɪdʒenəˈreɪʃən] *n* degeneración.
degrade [dɪˈgreɪd] *vt* degradar, rebajar.
degrading [dɪˈgreɪdɪŋ] *adj* degradante.
degree [dɪˈgriː] *n* **1** grado. **2** punto, etapa. **3** título, licenciatura.
● **by degrees** poco a poco.
● **to some degree** hasta cierto punto.
● **to take a degree in STH** licenciarse en algo.
■ **honorary degree** doctorado "honoris causa".
dehydrate [diːhaɪˈdreɪt] *vt* deshidratar.
dejected [dɪˈdʒektɪd] *adj* abatido,-a, desanimado,-a.
delay [dɪˈleɪ] *n* retraso.
▶ *vt* aplazar, diferir.
▶ *vt-vi* **1** retrasar(se) *(tren, bus)*. **2** entretener(se) *(persona)*.
delegate [*(adj - n)* ˈdelɪgət*(vb)* ˈdelɪgeɪt] *adj-n* delegado,-a.
▶ *vt* delegar.
delegation [delɪˈgeɪʃən] *n* delegación.
delete [dɪˈliːt] *vt* borrar, suprimir.
deliberate [*(adj)* dɪˈlɪbərət*(vb)* dɪˈlɪbəreɪt] *adj* deliberado,-a, premeditado,-a.
▶ *vt-vi* deliberar.
delicacy [ˈdelɪkəsɪ] *n (pl* **-ies***)*. **1** delicadeza. **2** manjar *(exquisito)*.
delicate [ˈdelɪkət] *adj* **1** delicado,-a, fino,-a. **2** suave.

delicatessen [delɪkə'tesən] *n* charcutería selecta.

delicious [dɪ'lɪʃəs] *adj* delicioso,-a, exquisito,-a.

delight [dɪ'laɪt] *n* **1** placer, gusto. **2** encanto, delicia *(lugar, persona)*.
▶ *vt* deleitar, encantar, dar gusto.
▶ *vi* deleitarse.

delighted [dɪ'laɪtɪd] *adj* encantado,-a: *I am delighted to see you*, estoy encantado de verte.

delightful [dɪ'laɪtfʊl] *adj* encantador,-ra, ameno,-a.

delinquency [dɪ'lɪŋkwənsɪ] *n* delincuencia.

delinquent [dɪ'lɪŋkwənt] *adj* delincuente.
▶ *n* delincuente.

deliver [dɪ'lɪvə'] *vt* **1** entregar, repartir *(mercancía)*. **2** dar, asestar *(golpe, patada)*. **3** pronunciar *(discurso)*. **4** asistir al parto de, traer al mundo. **5** *fml* liberar.

delivery [dɪ'lɪvərɪ] *n (pl* **-ies***)*. **1** entrega, reparto *(de mercancía)*. **2** reparto *(de costos)*. **3** modo de hablar. **4** parto, alumbramiento.
● **cash on delivery** entrega contra reembolso.
■ **delivery man** repartidor.
■ **delivery note** albarán de entrega.
■ **delivery room** sala de partos.
■ **delivery van** GB furgoneta de reparto.

delta ['deltə] *n* delta.

delude [dɪ'luːd] *vt* engañar.

deluge ['deljuːdʒ] *n* **1** diluvio. **2** aluvión *(de cartas)*.
▶ *vt* inundar.

delusion [dɪ'luːʒən] *n* **1** error, idea equivocada. **2** falsa ilusión, espejismo.
■ **delusions of grandeur** delirios de grandeza.

de luxe [də'lʌks] *adj* de lujo.

demand [dɪ'mɑːnd] *n* **1** solicitud, reclamación, petición. **2** exigencia. **3** demanda: *there's a big demand for computers*, hay una gran demanda de ordenadores.
▶ *vt* exigir, reclamar.
● **on demand** a petición.

demanding [dɪ'mɑːndɪŋ] *adj* exigente.

demented [dɪ'mentɪd] *adj* demente.

demise [dɪ'maɪz] *n* **1** fallecimiento, defunción. **2** desaparición.

demist [diː'mɪst] *vt* desempañar.

democracy [dɪ'mɒkrəsɪ] *n (pl* **-ies***)* democracia.

democrat ['deməkræt] *n* demócrata.

democratic [demə'krætɪk] *adj* democrático,-a.
■ **Democratic party** US partido demócrata.

demolish [dɪ'mɒlɪʃ] *vt* derribar, demoler.

demolition [demə'lɪʃən] *n* demolición, derribo.

demon ['diːmən] *n* demonio, diablo.

demonstrate ['demənstreɪt] *vt* **1** demostrar, probar. **2** mostrar, enseñar.
▶ *vi* manifestarse.

demonstration [demən'streɪʃən] *n* **1** demostración. **2** manifestación.

demonstrative [dɪ'mɒnstrətɪv] *adj* **1** efusivo,-a, expresivo,-a. **2** demostrativo,-a *(adjetivo)*.

demonstrator ['demənstreɪtə'] *n* manifestante.

demoralize [dɪ'mɒrəlaɪz] *vt* desmoralizar.

den [den] *n* guarida.

denial [dɪ'naɪəl] *n* **1** mentís. **2** denegación, negativa.

denim ['denɪm] *n* tela vaquera.
▶ *adj* vaquero,-a, tejano,-a.

Denmark ['denmɑːk] *n* Dinamarca.

denomination [dɪnɒmɪ'neɪʃən] *n* **1** confesión *(grupo religioso)*. **2** valor *(de moneda)*. **3** denominación.

denominator [dɪ'nɒmɪneɪtə'] *n* denominador.

denounce [dɪ'naʊns] *vt* **1** denunciar *(ladrón)*. **2** censurar *(actitud)*.

dense [dens] *adj* **1** denso,-a, espeso,-a. **2** *fam* corto,-a *(persona)*.

density ['densɪtɪ] *n* densidad.

dent [dent] *n* abolladura, bollo, porrazo.
▶ *vt* abollar.

dental ['dentəl] *adj* dental.
■ **dental surgeon** odontólogo,-a.

dentist ['dentɪst] *n* dentista.

dentures ['dentʃəz] *npl* dentadura postiza.

deny [dɪ'naɪ] *vt* negar, desmentir.

deodorant [diː'əʊdərənt] *n* desodorante.

depart [dɪ'pɑːt] *vi* **1** *fml* partir, salir. **2** *fig* desviarse, apartarse.

department [dɪ'pɑːtmənt] *n* **1** departamento, sección *(en oficina, tienda)*. **2** ministerio.
■ **department store** grandes almacenes.

departure [dɪ'pɑːtʃə'] *n* **1** partida, marcha *(de persona)*. **2** salida *(de tren, avión)*. **3** *fig* desviación.

depend [dɪ'pend] *vi* depender.
● **that depends/it all depends** según, depende.
to depend on *vt* **1** confiar en, fiarse de. **2** depender de.
dependable [dɪ'pendəbəl] *adj* fiable.
dependence [dɪ'pəndəns] *n* dependencia.
dependent [dɪ'pendənt] *adj* dependiente.
● **to be dependent on** depender de.
depict [dɪ'pɪkt] *vt* **1** pintar, representar, retratar. **2** *fig* describir.
depilatory [dɪ'pɪlətərɪ] *n* depilatorio.
deplore [dɪ'plɔː'] *vt* deplorar, lamentar.
deploy [dɪ'plɔɪ] *vt fig* desplegar.
deport [dɪ'pɔːt] *vt* deportar.
deportation [diːpɔː'teɪʃən] *n* deportación.
depose [dɪ'pəʊz] *vt* deponer, destituir.
deposit [dɪ'pɒzɪt] *n* **1** sedimento, depósito. **2** yacimiento *(en mina)*. **3** poso *(en vino)*. **4** depósito *(en barco)*. **5** depósito, entrada, paga y señal.
▶ *vt* **1** depositar. **2** ingresar.
■ **deposit account** cuenta de ahorros.
depot ['depəʊ] *n* **1** almacén. **2** depósito *(der armas)*. **3** cochera *(de autobuses)*. **4** US estación de ferrocarriles.
depress [dɪ'pres] *vt* **1** deprimir. **2** reducir, disminuir.
depressing [dɪ'presɪŋ] *adj* deprimente.
depression [dɪ'preʃən] *n* depresión.
depressive [dɪ'presɪv] *adj* depresivo,-a.
deprivation [deprɪ'veɪʃən] *n* privación, pobreza.
deprive [dɪ'praɪv] *vt* privar.
depth [depθ] *n* **1** profundidad, fondo *(de armario)*. **2** gravedad *(de voz, sonido)*. **3** intensidad *(de emoción, color)*.
● **in depth** a fondo.
● **to be out of one's depth 1** no hacer pie, no tocar fondo *(en agua)*. **2** estar perdido,-a *(en tema, trabajo)*.
deputation [depjʊ'teɪʃən] *n* delegación.
deputy ['depjətɪ] *n (pl* **-ies)**. **1** sustituto,-a, suplente. **2** diputado,-a.
■ **deputy chairman** vicepresidente,-a.
deranged [dɪ'reɪndʒd] *adj fml* trastornado,-a, loco,-a.
derelict ['derɪlɪkt] *adj* abandonado,-a.
derivative [dɪ'rɪvətɪv] *adj pej* poco original.
▶ *n* derivado.
derive [dɪ'raɪv] *vt* derivar, sacar.
▶ *vi* derivarse.

derogatory [dɪ'rɒgətərɪ] *adj* despectivo,-a, peyorativo,-a.
derrick ['derɪk] *n* **1** grúa. **2** torre de perforación.
descend [dɪ'send] *vt-vi* descender, bajar.
to descend on/upon *vt* **1** atacar, abatirse *(sobre)*. **2** *fig* visitar: *they descended on us at supper time*, se dejaron caer por casa a la hora de cenar.
to descend to *vt* rebajarse a.
descendant [dɪ'sendənt] *n* descendiente.
descent [dɪ'sent] *n* **1** descenso, bajada. **2** pendiente. **3** ascendencia.
describe [dɪ'skraɪb] *vt* **1** describir. **2** describir, trazar *(círculo)*.
description [dɪ'skrɪpʃən] *n* descripción.
● **of some description** de alguna clase.
descriptive [dɪ'skrɪptɪv] *adj* descriptivo,-a.
desert[1] ['dezət] *n* desierto.
desert[2] [dɪ'zɜːt] *vt* abandonar, dejar.
▶ *vi* desertar.
deserve [dɪ'zɜːv] *vt* merecerse: *you deserve a rest*, te mereces un descanso.
deservedly [dɪ'zɜːvədlɪ] *adv* merecidamente, con toda razón.
deserving [dɪ'zɜːvɪŋ] *adj* **1** que vale, digno,-a. **2** meritorio,-a.
design [dɪ'zaɪn] *n* **1** diseño, creación. **2** dibujo, motivo, plano, proyecto. **3** *fig* plan, intención.
▶ *vt* **1** diseñar, crear. **2** concebir, idear.
▶ *vi* diseñar.
designate [(*vb*) 'dezɪgneɪt(*adj*) 'dezɪgnət] *vt* **1** *fml* indicar, señalar. **2** designar, nombrar.
▶ *adj* designado,-a.
designer [dɪ'zaɪnə'] *n* diseñador,-ra.
desirable [dɪ'zaɪərəbəl] *adj* deseable, atractivo,-a.
desire [dɪ'zaɪə'] *n* deseo.
▶ *vt* desear.
desk [desk] *n* **1** pupitre. **2** escritorio, mesa *(de trabajo)*.
■ **desk work** trabajo de oficina.
desktop ['desktɒp] *n* escritorio.
■ **desktop computer** ordenador de sobremesa.
■ **desktop publishing** autoedición.
desolate ['desələt] *adj* **1** desolado,-a, desierto,-a *(lugar)*. **2** triste, desconsolado,-a, solitario,-a *(persona)*.

desolation [desəˈleɪʃən] n 1 desolación *(de lugar)*. 2 desconsuelo, aflicción *(de persona)*.

despair [dɪsˈpeəʳ] n desesperación.
▸ vi desesperarse, perder la esperanza.

despatch [dɪsˈpætʃ] vt-n → dispatch.

desperate [ˈdespərət] adj desesperado,-a.
● **to be desperate for** necesitar desesperadamente.

desperately [ˈdesprətlɪ] adv desesperadamente.

desperation [despəˈreɪʃən] n desesperación.

despicable [dɪˈspɪkəbəl] adj despreciable, vil, bajo,-a.

despise [dɪˈspaɪz] vt despreciar, menospreciar.

despite [dɪˈspaɪt] prep a pesar de.

despondent [dɪˈspɒndənt] adj desalentado,-a, desanimado,-a.

despot [ˈdespɒt] n déspota.

despotism [ˈdespətɪzəm] n despotismo.

dessert [dɪˈzɜːt] n postre.

dessertspoon [dɪˈzɜːtspuːn] n 1 cuchara de postre. 2 cucharadita *(de postre)*.

destination [destɪˈneɪʃən] n destino *(de tren)*.

destined [ˈdestɪnd] adj 1 destinado,-a. 2 *fig* condenado,-a: *destined to fail*, condenado,-a al fracaso. 3 con destino.

destiny [ˈdestɪnɪ] n *(pl* -ies*)* destino.

destitute [ˈdestɪtjuːt] adj indigente.
● **destitute of** desprovisto,-a de.

destroy [dɪˈstrɔɪ] vt destruir.

destroyer [dɪˈstrɔɪəʳ] n 1 destructor *(buque)*. 2 destructor,-ra *(persona)*.

destruction [dɪˈstrʌkʃən] n destrucción.

destructive [dɪˈstrʌktɪv] adj destructor, -ra, destructivo,-a.

detach [dɪˈtætʃ] vt separar.

detached [dɪˈtætʃt] adj 1 separado,-a, suelto,-a. 2 desinteresado,-a, imparcial.
■ **detached house** casa independiente.
■ **detached retina** desprendimiento de retina.

detachment [dɪˈtætʃmənt] n 1 separación. 2 desapego, indiferencia. 3 destacamento *(militar)*.

detail [ˈdiːteɪl] n detalle, pormenor.
▸ vt 1 detallar, enumerar. 2 destacar *(tropas)*.
● **in detail** en detalle, detalladamente.
● **to go into detail** entrar en detalles.

detain [dɪˈteɪn] vt 1 detener. 2 retener, entretener.

detect [dɪˈtekt] vt detectar, descubrir.

detective [dɪˈtektɪv] n detective.
■ **detective story** novela policíaca.

detector [dɪˈtektəʳ] n detector.

detention [dɪˈtenʃən] n detención, arresto.
● **to get detention** quedarse castigado, -a *(en la escuela)*.

deter [dɪˈtɜː] vt *(pt & pp* **deterred**, *ger* **deterring**) disuadir.

detergent [dɪˈtɜːdʒənt] n detergente.

deteriorate [dɪˈtɪərɪəreɪt] vi deteriorarse, empeorar.

determination [dɪtɜːmɪˈneɪʃən] n decisión, firme propósito.

determine [dɪˈtɜːmɪn] vt determinar, decidir.

determined [dɪˈtɜːmɪnd] adj decidido,-a, resuelto,-a.

deterrent [dɪˈterənt] adj disuasivo,-a, disuasorio,-a.
▸ n fuerza disuasoria.

detest [dɪˈtest] vt detestar, odiar.

detonate [ˈdetəneɪt] vi estallar, detonar.
▸ vt hacer estallar.

detonator [ˈdetəneɪtəʳ] n detonador.

detour [ˈdiːtʊəʳ] n desvío.

detract [dɪˈtrækt] vt quitar mérito.

devaluation [diːvæljuːˈeɪʃən] n devaluación.

devalue [diːˈvæljuː] vt-vi devaluar(se).

devastate [ˈdevəsteɪt] vt devastar, asolar.

devastating [ˈdevəsteɪtɪŋ] adj devastador,-ra.

develop [dɪˈveləp] vt 1 desarrollar. 2 explotar *(recursos)*. 3 urbanizar *(zona)*. 4 revelar *(carrete)*. 5 elaborar *(plan)*.
▸ vi desarrollarse.
■ **developing country** país en vías de desarrollo.

development [dɪˈveləpmənt] n 1 desarrollo. 2 avance. 3 cambio, novedad. 4 explotación *(de recursos)*. 5 urbanización *(de zona)*. 6 revelado *(de carrete)*. 7 elaboración *(de planes)*.

deviate [ˈdiːvɪeɪt] vi desviarse.

device [dɪˈvaɪs] n 1 mecanismo, dispositivo. 2 ardid, estratagema.

devil [ˈdevəl] n diablo, demonio.

devious [ˈdiːvɪəs] adj tortuoso,-a, enrevesado,-a.

devise [dɪ'vaɪz] *vt* idear, concebir.
devoid [dɪ'vɔɪd] *adj* falto,-a, desprovisto,-a.
devote [dɪ'vəʊt] *vt* consagrar, dedicar.
devoted [dɪ'vəʊtɪd] *adj* fiel, leal.
devotion [dɪ'vəʊʃən] *n* **1** consagración, dedicación. **2** afecto, cariño. **3** devoción.
devour [dɪ'vaʊə'] *vt* devorar.
devout [dɪ'vaʊt] *adj* **1** devoto,-a, piadoso,-a. **2** sincero,-a.
dew [djuː] *n* rocío.
dexterity [dek'sterɪtɪ] *n* destreza, habilidad.
dexterous ['dekstrəs] *adj* diestro,-a, hábil.
diabetes [daɪə'biːtiːz] *n* diabetes.
diabetic [daɪə'betɪk] *adj-n* diabético,-a.
diabolical [daɪə'bɒlɪkəl] *adj* diabólico,-a.
diagnose ['daɪəgnəʊz] *vt* diagnosticar.
diagnosis [daɪəg'nəʊsɪs] *n* (*pl* **diagnoses** [daɪəg'nəʊsiːz]) diagnóstico.
diagnostic [daɪəg'nɒstɪk] *adj* diagnóstico,-a.
diagonal [daɪ'ægənəl] *adj* diagonal.
  ▶ *n* diagonal.
diagonally [daɪ'ægənəlɪ] *adv* en diagonal.
diagram ['daɪəgræm] *n* diagrama, esquema, gráfico.
dial ['daɪəl] *n* **1** esfera (*de reloj*). **2** dial (*de radio*). **3** teclado (*de teléfono*).
  ▶ *vt* marcar: *she dialled a wrong number*, marcó un número equivocado.
  ■ **dialling code** prefijo telefónico.
  ■ **dialling tone** señal de llamada.
dialect ['daɪəlekt] *n* dialecto.
dialogue ['daɪəlɒg] (US **dialog**) *n* diálogo.
diameter [daɪ'æmɪtə'] *n* diámetro.
diamond ['daɪəmənd] *n* diamante.
diaper ['daɪəpə'] *n* US pañal.
diaphragm ['daɪəfræm] *n* diafragma.
diarrhoea [daɪə'rɪə] *n* diarrea.
diary ['daɪərɪ] *n* **1** diario. **2** agenda.
dice [daɪs] *n* (*pl* **dice**) dado.
  ▶ *vt* cortar en dados.
dictate [dɪk'teɪt] *vt* **1** dictar (*carta*). **2** dictar, establecer, imponer.
  ▶ *vi* mandar.
  ▶ *n* mandato.
dictation [dɪk'teɪʃən] *n* dictado.
dictator [dɪk'teɪtə'] *n* dictador,-ra.
dictatorial [dɪktə'tɔːrɪəl] *adj* dictatorial.
dictatorship [dɪk'teɪtəʃɪp] *n* dictadura.
dictionary ['dɪkʃənərɪ] *n* (*pl* **-ies**) diccionario.

did [dɪd] *pt* → **do**.
didactic [dɪ'dæktɪk] *adj* didáctico,-a.
diddle ['dɪdəl] *vt fam* estafar, timar.
didn't ['dɪdənt] *aux* contracción de **did** + **not**.
die [daɪ] *vi* (*ger* **dying**) morir.
  ● **to be dying for/to** *fam* morirse de ganas de.
to die away *vi* desvanecerse.
to die down *vi* **1** extinguirse. **2** *fig* disminuir.
to die off *vi* morir uno tras otro.
to die out *vi* perderse, desaparecer.
diesel ['diːzəl] *n* gasóleo.
  ■ **diesel engine** motor diesel.
diet ['daɪət] *n* dieta, régimen.
  ● **to be on a diet** estar a régimen.
  ● **to go on a diet** ponerse a régimen.
differ ['dɪfə'] *vi* **1** diferir, diferenciarse. **2** discrepar.
difference ['dɪfərəns] *n* **1** diferencia. **2** desacuerdo.
  ● **to make no difference** dar lo mismo.
  ● **what difference does it make?** ¿qué más da?
different ['dɪfərənt] *adj* diferente, distinto,-a.
differentiate [dɪfə'renʃɪeɪt] *vt-vi* diferenciar(se), distinguir(se).
differently ['dɪfərəntlɪ] *adv* de otra manera.
difficult ['dɪfɪkəlt] *adj* difícil.
difficulty ['dɪfɪkəltɪ] *n* (*pl* **-ies**). **1** dificultad. **2** apuro, aprieto.
diffident ['dɪfɪdənt] *adj* retraído,-a.
diffuse [(*adj*) dɪ'fjuːs(*vb*) dɪ'fjuːz] *adj* difuso,-a.
  ▶ *vt-vi* difundir(se).
dig [dɪg] *vt* (*pt & pp* **dug**). **1** cavar (*hoyo*), excavar (*túnel*). **2** clavar, hincar (*con uñas*).
  ▶ *n fam* pulla.
  ▶ *npl* **digs** GB alojamiento.
to dig out/up *vt* desenterrar.
digest [(*n*) 'daɪdʒest(*vb*) dɪ'dʒest] *n* resumen, compendio.
  ▶ *vt-vi* digerir.
  ▶ *vt* resumir.
digestion [dɪ'dʒestʃən] *n* digestión.
digestive [daɪ'dʒestɪv] *adj* digestivo,-a.
  ■ **digestive tract** aparato digestivo.
digger ['dɪgə'] *n* excavadora.
digit ['dɪdʒɪt] *n* dígito.
dignified ['dɪgnɪfaɪd] *adj* solemne, serio,-a.

dignify ['dɪgnɪfaɪ] *vt* (*pt & pp* -**ied**) dignificar, enaltecer.

dignitary ['dɪgnɪtəri] *n* dignatario.

dignity ['dɪgnɪti] *n* dignidad.

dike [daɪk] *n* US → dyke.

dilapidated [dɪ'læpɪdeɪtɪd] *adj* **1** en estado ruinoso (*edificio*). **2** desvencijado,-a (*mueble*). **3** en muy mal estado (*coche*).

dilate [daɪ'leɪt] *vt-vi* dilatar(se).

dilemma [dɪ'lemə] *n* dilema.

diligence ['dɪlɪdʒəns] *n* diligencia.

diligent ['dɪlɪdʒənt] *adj* diligente.

dilute [daɪ'luːt] *vt* **1** diluir. **2** *fig* atenuar, suavizar.

dim [dɪm] *adj* **1** débil, difuso,-a, tenue. **2** oscuro,-a. **3** borroso,-a. **4** *fam* tonto,-a.
► *vt* **1** bajar, atenuar. **2** empañar. **3** *fig* borrar, difuminar.

dime [daɪm] *n* US moneda de diez centavos.

dimension [dɪ'menʃən] *n* dimensión.

diminish [dɪ'mɪnɪʃ] *vt* disminuir, reducir.
► *vi* disminuirse, reducirse.

diminutive [dɪ'mɪnjətɪv] *adj* diminuto,-a.
► *n* diminutivo.

dimple ['dɪmpəl] *n* hoyuelo.

din [dɪn] *n* alboroto, estrépito.

dine [daɪn] *vi* cenar.

diner ['daɪnə'] *n* **1** comensal. **2** US restaurante barato.

dinghy ['dɪŋgɪ] *n* (*pl* -**ies**) bote.

dingy ['dɪndʒɪ] *adj* (-**ier**, -**iest**). **1** sucio,-a, sórdido,-a (*habitación*). **2** deslucido,-a, deslustrado,-a (*ropa*).

dining car ['daɪnɪŋkɑː'] *n* coche restaurante.

dining room ['daɪnɪŋruːm] *n* comedor.

dinner ['dɪnə'] *n* comida, cena.
● **to have dinner** cenar.
■ **dinner jacket** esmoquin.
■ **dinner table** mesa de comedor.
■ **dinner service** vajilla.

dinosaur ['daɪnəsɔː'] *n* dinosaurio.

diocese ['daɪəsɪs] *n* diócesis.

dioxide [daɪ'ɒksaɪd] *n* dióxido.

dip [dɪp] *n* **1** declive, pendiente. **2** *fam* chapuzón.
► *vt* (*pt & pp* **dipped**, *ger* **dipping**) sumergir, bañar, mojar.
► *vi* bajar.
● **to dip the lights** poner las luces cortas.

to dip into *vt* **1** hojear (*libro*). **2** echar mano de (*ahorros*).

diphthong ['dɪfθɒŋ] *n* diptongo.

diploma [dɪ'pləʊmə] *n* diploma.

diplomacy [dɪ'pləʊməsɪ] *n* diplomacia.

diplomat ['dɪpləmæt] *n* diplomático,-a.

diplomatic [dɪplə'mætɪk] *adj* diplomático,-a.

dire ['daɪə'] *adj* **1** extremo,-a. **2** terrible.

direct [dɪ'rekt, daɪ'rekt] *adj* **1** directo,-a. **2** franco,-a, sincero,-a (*persona*).
► *adv* **1** directamente, directo (*vuelo*). **2** en directo (*programa de TV*).
► *vt* **1** dirigir, indicar. **2** *fml* mandar, ordenar.
■ **direct object** complemento directo.

direction [dɪ'rekʃən, daɪ'rekʃən] *n* dirección, sentido.
► *npl* **directions 1** señas (*de lugar*). **2** instrucciones de uso, modo de empleo.
● **to ask for directions** preguntar cómo se va.

directly [dɪ'rektlɪ, daɪ'rektlɪ] *adv* **1** directamente. **2** francamente, claro.

directness [dɪ'rektnəs, daɪ'rektnəs] *n* franqueza, sinceridad.

director [dɪ'rektə', daɪ'rektə'] *n* director,-ra.
■ **managing director** director,-ra, gerente.

directory [dɪ'rektərɪ, daɪ'rektərɪ] *n* (*pl* -**ies**). **1** guía telefónica. **2** callejero.

dirt [dɜːt] *n* **1** suciedad, mugre. **2** tierra.
● **to treat SB like dirt** tratar mal a ALGN.

dirty ['dɜːtɪ] *adj* (-**ier**, -**iest**). **1** sucio,-a. **2** indecente, verde (*chiste*). **3** *fam* bajo,-a, vil.
► *vt-vi* (*pt & pp* -**ied**) ensuciar(se).
● **to get dirty** ensuciarse.
● **to give SB a dirty look** fulminar a ALGN con la mirada.
■ **dirty trick** cochinada.
■ **dirty word** palabrota.

disability [dɪsə'bɪlɪtɪ] *n* (*pl* -**ies**) invalidez, discapacidad, minusvalía.

disabled [dɪs'eɪbəld] *adj* minusválido,-a, incapacitado,-a.

disadvantage [dɪsəd'vɑːntɪdʒ] *n* desventaja, inconveniente.

disadvantageous [dɪsædvɑːn'teɪdʒəs] *adj* desventajoso,-a, desfavorable.

disagree [dɪsə'griː] *vi* **1** discrepar. **2** sentar mal (*comida*).

disagreeable [dɪsə'grɪəbəl] *adj* desagradable.

disagreement [dɪsə'griːmənt] *n* desacuerdo.

● **to have a disagreement** discutir.

disappear [dɪsə'pɪəʳ] *vi* desaparecer.

disappearance [dɪsə'pɪərəns] *n* desaparición.

disappoint [dɪsə'pɔɪnt] *vt* decepcionar, defraudar.

disappointed [dɪsə'pɔɪntɪd] *adj* decepcionado,-a.

disappointing [dɪsə'pɔɪntɪŋ] *adj* decepcionante.

disappointment [dɪsə'pɔɪntmənt] *n* desilusión, decepción.

disapproval [dɪsə'pruːvəl] *n* desaprobación.

disapprove [dɪsə'pruːv] *vi* desaprobar.

disarm [dɪs'ɑːm] *vt-vi* desarmar(se).

disarmament [dɪs'ɑːməmənt] *n* desarme.

disaster [dɪ'zɑːstəʳ] *n* desastre.

disastrous [dɪ'zɑːstrəs] *adj* desastroso,-a, catastrófico,-a.

disbelief [dɪsbɪ'liːf] *n* incredulidad.

disc [dɪsk] *n* disco.

■ **disc jockey** disc-jockey.

discard [dɪs'kɑːd] *vt* desechar, deshacerse de.

discern [dɪ'sɜːn] *vt* percibir, discernir.

discerning [dɪ'sɜːnɪŋ] *adj* perspicaz, sagaz.

discharge [(*n*) 'dɪstʃɑːdʒ(*vb*) dɪs'tʃɑːdʒ] *n* **1** descarga *(eléctrica)*. **2** emisión *(de humo)*. **3** escape *(de gas)*. **4** liberación, puesta en libertad *(de preso)*. **5** alta *(de paciente)*. **6** licencia *(de soldado)*. **7** despido *(de empleado)*.
► *vt-vi* **1** verter *(residuos)*. **2** descargar *(carga)*. **3** emitir *(gas)*.
► *vt* **1** liberar, soltar *(preso)*. **2** dar de alta *(paciente)*. **3** licenciar *(soldado)*. **4** despedir *(empleado)*. **5** saldar *(deuda)*.

disciple [dɪ'saɪpəl] *n* discípulo,-a.

discipline ['dɪsɪplɪn] *n* disciplina.
► *vt* **1** disciplinar. **2** expedientar *(oficial)*.

disclose [dɪs'kləʊz] *vt* revelar.

disco ['dɪskəʊ] *n* (*pl* **discos**) *fam* discoteca, disco.

discolour [dɪs'kʌləʳ] (US **discolor**) *vt-vi* desteñir(se).

discomfort [dɪs'kʌmfət] *n* **1** incomodidad. **2** malestar, molestia.

disconnect [dɪskə'nekt] *vt* desconectar, cortar *(gas)*.

disconnected [dɪskə'nektɪd] *adj* **1** desconectado,-a. **2** cortado,-a *(gas)*. **3** *fig* deshilvanado,-a.

discontent [dɪskən'tent] *n* descontento.

discontinue [dɪskən'tɪnjuː] *vt* suspender, interrumpir.

discotheque ['dɪskətek] *n* discoteca.

discount [(*n*) 'dɪskaʊnt(*vb*) dɪs'kaʊnt] *n* descuento.
► *vt* **1** descontar, rebajar. **2** descartar.

discourage [dɪs'kʌrɪdʒ] *vt* **1** desanimar, desalentar. **2** disuadir.

discouragement [dɪs'kʌrɪdʒmənt] *n* **1** desaliento, desánimo. **2** disuasión.

discouraging [dɪs'kʌrɪdʒɪŋ] *adj* desalentador,-ra.

discover [dɪ'skʌvəʳ] *vt* descubrir.

discovery [dɪ'skʌvərɪ] *n* (*pl* **-ies**) descubrimiento.

discreet [dɪ'skriːt] *adj* discreto,-a.

discrepancy [dɪ'skrepənsɪ] *n* (*pl* **-ies**) discrepancia.

discretion [dɪ'skreʃən] *n* discreción.

● **at the discretion of** a juicio de.

discriminate [dɪ'skrɪmɪneɪt] *vi* **1** discriminar. **2** distinguir.

discrimination [dɪskrɪmɪ'neɪʃən] *n* discriminación.

discus ['dɪskəs] *n* disco.

discuss [dɪ'skʌs] *vt-vi* discutir.
► *vt* hablar de.

discussion [dɪ'skʌʃən] *n* discusión, debate.

disdain [dɪs'deɪn] *n* desdén, menosprecio.
► *vt* desdeñar, menospreciar.

disdainful [dɪs'deɪnful] *adj* desdeñoso,-a.

disease [dɪ'ziːz] *n* enfermedad.

disembark [dɪsɪm'bɑːk] *vt-vi* desembarcar.

disenchanted [dɪsɪn'tʃɑːntɪd] *adj* desencantado,-a.

disentangle [dɪsɪn'tæŋgəl] *vt* desenredar, desenmarañar.

disfigure [dɪs'fɪgəʳ] *vt* desfigurar.

disgrace [dɪs'greɪs] *n* **1** desgracia. **2** escándalo, vergüenza.
► *vt* deshonrar.

disgraceful [dɪs'greɪsful] *adj* vergonzoso,-a.

disguise [dɪs'gaɪz] *n* disfraz.
► *vt* **1** disfrazar. **2** *fig* disimular *(emoción)*.

● **in disguise** disfrazado,-a.

disgust [dɪsˈɡʌst] n asco, repugnancia.
► vt repugnar, dar asco.
disgusting [dɪsˈɡʌstɪŋ] adj **1** asqueroso,-a, repugnante. **2** intolerable, indignante.
dish [dɪʃ] n plato, fuente (para servir).
● **to do the dishes** lavar los platos.
to dish out vt fam repartir.
to dish up vt servir.
dishcloth [ˈdɪʃklɒθ] n paño de cocina.
dishearten [dɪsˈhɑːtən] vt desanimar, descorazonar.
dishevelled [dɪˈʃevəld] adj **1** despeinado, -a (pelo). **2** desaliñado,-a, desarreglado,-a (aspecto).
dishonest [dɪsˈɒnɪst] adj **1** deshonesto,-a, poco honrado,-a (persona). **2** fraudulento,-a (medios).
dishonesty [dɪsˈɒnɪstɪ] n **1** deshonestidad, falta de honradez. **2** fraude.
dishonour [dɪsˈɒnəʳ] (US **dishonor**) n deshonra.
► vt deshonrar.
dishwasher [ˈdɪʃwɒʃəʳ] n lavavajillas.
disillusion [dɪsɪˈluːʒən] vt desilusionar.
disinfect [dɪsɪnˈfekt] vt desinfectar.
disinfectant [dɪsɪnˈfektənt] n desinfectante.
disinherit [dɪsɪnˈherɪt] vt desheredar.
disintegrate [dɪsˈɪntɪɡreɪt] vt-vi desintegrar(se), disgregar(se).
disintegration [dɪsɪntɪˈɡreɪʃən] n desintegración.
disinterested [dɪsˈɪntrəstɪd] adj desinteresado,-a, imparcial.
disjointed [dɪsˈdʒɔɪntɪd] adj fig inconexo, -a.
disk [dɪsk] n disco.
diskette [dɪsˈket] n disquete.
dislike [dɪsˈlaɪk] n aversión, antipatía.
► vt **1** no gustar (objeto). **2** no gustar, tener antipatía a (persona).
dislocate [ˈdɪsləkeɪt] vt dislocar.
dislodge [dɪsˈlɒdʒ] vt desalojar, sacar.
disloyal [dɪsˈlɔɪəl] adj desleal.
dismal [ˈdɪzməl] adj triste, sombrío,-a, deprimente.
dismantle [dɪsˈmæntəl] vt-vi desmontar(se), desarmar(se).
dismay [dɪsˈmeɪ] n consternación.
► vt consternar, acongojar.
dismiss [dɪsˈmɪs] vt **1** despedir, destituir (empleado). **2** dar permiso para retirarse. **3** descartar, desechar. **4** desestimar, denegar.

dismissal [dɪsˈmɪsəl] n **1** despido, destitución (de empleado). **2** rechazo (de idea). **3** permiso para retirarse. **4** desestimación, denegación.
dismount [dɪsˈmaunt] vi desmontarse.
disobedience [dɪsəˈbiːdɪəns] n desobediencia.
disobedient [dɪsəˈbiːdɪənt] adj desobediente.
disobey [dɪsəˈbeɪ] vt-vi desobedecer.
disorder [dɪsˈɔːdəʳ] n desorden.
disorderly [dɪsˈɔːdəlɪ] adj **1** desordenado,-a. **2** alborotado,-a, escandaloso,-a.
disorganized [dɪsˈɔːɡənaɪzd] adj desorganizado,-a.
disorientate [dɪsˈɔːrɪənteɪt] vt desorientar.
disown [dɪsˈəun] vt no reconocer, renegar de.
dispatch [dɪˈspætʃ] n (pl **-es**). **1** despacho, parte, comunicado. **2** reportaje (de corresponsalía). **3** despacho, envío.
► vt enviar, expedir, despachar.
■ **dispatch rider** mensajero.
dispel [dɪˈspel] vt disipar.
dispensary [dɪˈspensərɪ] n dispensario.
dispense [dɪˈspens] vt **1** distribuir, repartir. **2** suministrar, administrar (medicamento).
to dispense with vt prescindir de, pasar sin.
dispenser [dɪˈspensəʳ] n máquina expendedora.
disperse [dɪˈspɜːs] vt-vi dispersar(se).
displace [dɪsˈpleɪs] vt **1** dislocar (hueso). **2** sustituir, reemplazar.
■ **displaced person** expatriado,-a.
display [dɪˈspleɪ] n **1** exposición, muestra (de artículos). **2** exhibición, despliegue (de fuerzas). **3** visualización (en pantalla).
► vt **1** exhibir, mostrar, exponer (artículos). **2** visualizar (en pantalla).
displease [dɪsˈpliːz] vt fml disgustar.
disposable [dɪˈspəuzəbəl] adj desechable.
disposal [dɪˈspəuzəl] n eliminación.
● **at SB's disposal** a la disposición de ALGN.
dispose [dɪˈspəuz] vt disponer, colocar.
to dispose of vt **1** tirar (basura). **2** deshacerse de (objetos).
disposition [dɪspəˈzɪʃən] n fml carácter, modo de ser.

dispossess [dɪspə'zes] *vt* desposeer, quitar.

disproportionate [dɪsprə'pɔ:ʃənət] *adj* desproporcionado,-a.

disprove [dɪs'pru:v] *vt* refutar.

dispute [(*n*) 'dɪspju:t/(*vb*) dɪ'spju:t] *n* discusión, controversia, disputa.

▶ *vt* cuestionar, poner en duda.

▶ *vt-vi* disputar, discutir.

● **beyond dispute** indiscutiblemente.

disqualification [dɪskwɒlɪfɪ'keɪʃən] *n* descalificación.

disqualify [dɪs'kwɒlɪfaɪ] *vt* (*pt & pp* -**ied**). **1** descalificar. **2** incapacitar, inhabilitar.

disregard [dɪsrɪ'gɑ:d] *n* indiferencia, despreocupación.

▶ *vt* no hacer caso de.

disrespect [dɪsrɪ'spekt] *n* falta de respeto, desacato.

disrespectful [dɪsrɪ'spektful] *adj* irrespetuoso,-a.

disrupt [dɪs'rʌpt] *vt* trastornar, desbaratar.

disruption [dɪs'rʌpʃən] *n* trastorno, molestias.

disruptive [dɪs'rʌptɪv] *adj* **1** perjudicial (*efecto*). **2** revoltoso,-a (*niño*).

dissatisfaction [dɪssætɪs'fækʃən] *n* insatisfacción, descontento.

dissatisfied [dɪs'sætɪsfaɪd] *adj* descontento,-a.

dissect [dɪ'sekt, daɪ'sekt] *vt* disecar.

disseminate [dɪ'semɪneɪt] *vt fml* diseminar.

dissent [dɪ'sent] *n* disentimiento.

▶ *vi* disentir.

dissertation [dɪsə'teɪʃən] *n* tesina.

dissident ['dɪsɪdənt] *adj-n* disidente.

dissimilar [dɪ'sɪmɪlə˞] *adj* diferente.

dissociate [dɪ'səʊsɪeɪt] *vt* disociar, separar.

dissolution [dɪsə'lu:ʃən] *n* disolución, rescisión (*de acuerdo*).

dissolve [dɪ'zɒlv] *vt* disolver.

▶ *vi* **1** disolverse. **2** *fig* deshacerse: ***to dissolve into tears/laughter***, deshacerse en lágrimas/risa.

dissuade [dɪ'sweɪd] *vt* disuadir.

dissuasion [dɪ'sweɪʒən] *n* disuasión.

distance ['dɪstəns] *n* distancia.

▶ *vt* distanciar.

● **from a distance** desde lejos.

● **in the distance** a lo lejos.

● **to keep one's distance** mantener la distancia.

distant ['dɪstənt] *adj* **1** remoto,-a, lejano, -a. **2** distante, frío,-a (*persona*).

distaste [dɪs'teɪst] *n* aversión.

distasteful [dɪs'teɪstful] *adj* **1** desagradable. **2** de mal gusto (*chiste*).

distend [dɪ'stend] *vt-vi* dilatar(se).

distil [dɪs'tɪl] *vt* destilar.

distillery [dɪ'stɪləri] *n* destilería.

distinct [dɪ'stɪŋkt] *adj* **1** distinto,-a. **2** marcado,-a, inconfundible, claro,-a.

distinction [dɪ'stɪŋkʃən] *n* **1** diferencia. **2** distinción, honor. **3** sobresaliente (*calificación*).

distinctive [dɪ'stɪŋktɪv] *adj* característico,-a, distintivo,-a.

distinguish [dɪ'stɪŋgwɪʃ] *vt-vi* distinguir(se).

distort [dɪ'stɔ:t] *vt* **1** deformar. **2** *fig* distorsionar.

distortion [dɪ'stɔ:ʃən] *n* **1** deformación. **2** *fig* distorsión.

distract [dɪ'strækt] *vt* distraer.

distracted [dɪ'stræktɪd] *adj* distraído,-a.

distraction [dɪ'strækʃən] *n* **1** distracción. **2** confusión.

● **to drive SB to distraction** sacar a ALGN de quicio.

distraught [dɪ'strɔ:t] *adj* angustiado,-a, turbado,-a.

distress [dɪ'stres] *n* angustia, dolor.

▶ *vt* afligir.

■ **distress call/signal** señal de socorro.

distressing [dɪ'stresɪŋ] *adj* penoso,-a.

distribute [dɪ'strɪbju:t] *vt* distribuir, repartir.

distribution [dɪstrɪ'bju:ʃən] *n* distribución.

district ['dɪstrɪkt] *n* distrito, barrio, región.

distrust [dɪs'trʌst] *n* desconfianza, recelo.

▶ *vt* desconfiar, recelar.

disturb [dɪ'stɜ:b] *vt* **1** molestar, interrumpir. **2** perturbar, inquietar.

disturbance [dɪ'stɜ:bəns] *n* **1** disturbio, alboroto, altercado. **2** molestia.

disturbed [dɪ'stɜ:bd] *adj* desequilibrado,-a, trastornado,-a.

disuse [dɪs'ju:s] *n* desuso.

ditch [dɪtʃ] *n* (*pl* -**es**). **1** zanja, foso, cuneta. **2** acequia (*para agua*).

▶ *vt fam* dejar tirado,-a, abandonado,-a.

dither ['dɪðə˞] *vi* vacilar, titubear.

ditto ['dɪtəʊ] *adv* ídem.

dive [daɪv] *n* **1** zambullida, inmersión *(al agua)*. **2** buceo *(bajo el agua)*. **3** picado *(pájaro, avión)*. **4** salto *(natación)*. **5** *fam* antro.
► *vi* (GB *pt & pp* **dived**; US *pt & pp* **dove** [dəʊv]). **1** zambullirse, tirarse de cabeza *(al agua)*. **2** bucear *(bajo el agua)*. **3** bajar en picado *(pájaro, avión)*. **4** saltar *(natación)*. **5** moverse rápidamente: *she dived for the phone*, se precipitó hacia el teléfono.

diver ['daɪvə'] *n* **1** buceador,-ra, buzo. **2** saltador,-ra *(de trampolín)*.

diverge [daɪ'vɜːdʒ] *vi* divergir, bifurcarse *(carreteras)*.

diverse [daɪ'vɜːs] *adj fml* diverso,-a.

diversify [daɪ'vɜːsɪfaɪ] *vt-vi* (*pt & pp* **-ied**) diversificar(se).

diversion [daɪ'vɜːʃən] *n* **1** desvío, desviación. **2** distracción.

diversity [daɪ'vɜːsɪtɪ] *n* diversidad.

divert [daɪ'vɜːt] *vt* **1** desviar. **2** distraer.

divide [dɪ'vaɪd] *vt* **1** dividir, separar: *divide the dough into three different parts*, divide la masa en tres partes iguales. **2** dividir: *32 divided by 8 is 4*, 32 dividido entre 8 son 4. **3** repartir.
► *vi* dividirse, separarse.

dividend ['dɪvɪdend] *n* **1** dividendo. **2** *fig* beneficio.

divine¹ [dɪ'vaɪn] *adj* divino,-a.

divine² [dɪ'vaɪn] *vt-vi* adivinar.

diving ['daɪvɪŋ] *n* **1** submarinismo. **2** saltos de trampolín.
■ **diving board** trampolín.

division [dɪ'vɪʒən] *n* división.

divisor [dɪ'vaɪzə'] *n* divisor.

divorce [dɪ'vɔːs] *n* divorcio.
► *vt-vi* divorciarse de: *he divorced her*, se divorció de ella.

divorcé [dɪ'vɔːseɪ] *n* divorciado.

divorcée [dɪvɔː'siː] *n* divorciada.

divulge [daɪ'vʌldʒ] *vt* divulgar, revelar.

DIY ['diːaɪ'waɪ] *abbr* GB (**do-it-yourself**) bricolaje.

dizziness ['dɪzɪnəs] *n* mareo, vértigo.

dizzy ['dɪzɪ] *adj* (**-ier**, **-iest**) mareado,-a.

DJ¹ ['diː'dʒeɪ] *abbr* GB *fam* (**dinner jacket**) esmoquin, smoking.

DJ² ['diː'dʒeɪ] *abbr fam* (**disc jockey**) disc-jockey.

DNA ['diː'en'eɪ] *abbr* (**deoxyribonucleic acid**) ADN.

do [duː] *aux* (*pt* **did**, *pp* **done**, *ger* **doing**). **1**: *do you smoke?*, ¿fumas?; *I don't want to dance*, no quiero bailar. **2**: *do come with us!*, ¡anda, vente con nosotros! **3**: *he likes them and so do I*, a él le gustan, y a mí también; *who went?*, ¿quién fue?, ¿yo. **4**: *you don't smoke, do you?*, no fumas, ¿verdad?
► *vt* **1** hacer, realizar: *what are you doing?*, ¿qué haces? **2** ser suficiente: *ten packets will do us*, con diez paquetes tenemos suficiente.
► *vi* **1** hacer: *do as I tell you*, haz lo que te digo. **2**: *how are you doing?*, ¿cómo te van las cosas?; *she did badly in the exams*, le fueron mal los exámenes. **3** bastar, servir: *that will do*, basta, así basta; *this cushion will do as/for a pillow*, este cojín servirá de almohada.
● **how do you do? 1** ¿cómo está usted? *(saludo)*. **2** mucho gusto, encantado,-a *(respuesta)*.
● **to do one's best** hacer todo lo posible.
● **to do one's hair** peinarse.
● **to do the cleaning** cocinar.
● **to do the cooking** limpiar.
● **to do you good** sentarse bien, irte bien.
● **well done!** *fam* ¡enhorabuena!
● **to do well** ir bien, tener éxito.
■ **do's and don'ts** lo que se debe y lo que no se debe hacer.
to do away with *vt* **1** abolir. **2** *fam* acabar con, eliminar.
to do in *vt* **1** *fam* matar, cargarse. **2** agotar: *I'm done in*, estoy hecho,-a polvo.
to do up *vt* **1** *fam* abrocharse, atar. **2** envolver. **3** arreglar, renovar.
to do with *vt* **1** necesitar: *I could do with a rest*, un descanso me vendría muy bien. **2** tener que ver: *it's nothing to do with me*, no tiene nada que ver conmigo.
to do without *vt* pasar sin, arreglárselas sin.

docile ['dəʊsaɪl] *adj* dócil, manso,-a *(animal)*.

dock¹ [dɒk] *n* **1** muelle, dársena *(en puerto)*. **2** banquillo *(de los acusados)*.
► *vt-vi* **1** atracar *(barco)*. **2** acoplar *(nave espacial)*.

dock² [dɒk] *vt* **1** cortar, recortar. **2** descontar *(de salario)*.

docker ['dɒkə'] *n* estibador.

dockyard ['dɒkjɑːd] *n* astillero.

doctor ['dɒktə'] *n* **1** médico,-a, doctor,-ra. **2** doctor,-ra.
► *vt* **1** falsificar, amañar. **2** capar, castrar.

doctrine ['dɒktrɪn] *n* doctrina.

document ['dɒkjəmənt] *n* documento.
► *vt* documentar.

documentary [dɒkjə'mentərɪ] *adj* (-ier, -iest) documental.
► *n* (*pl* -ies) documental.

doddery ['dɒdərɪ] *adj fam* renqueante.

doddle ['dɒdəl] *n fam* pan comido.

dodge [dɒdʒ] *n* **1** regate, evasión. **2** *fam* truco, astucia.
► *vi* esquivar *(golpe)*.
► *vt* **1** despistar, dar esquinazo a *(perseguidor)*. **2** evadir, eludir, evitar *(impuestos)*.

dodgy ['dɒdʒɪ] *adj* (-ier, -iest). **1** de poco fiar, poco fiable. **2** inestable.

doe [dəʊ] *n* **1** cierva. **2** coneja. **3** liebre hembra.

does [dʌz] *3rd pers sing pres* → do.

dog [dɒg] *n* perro,-a.
► *vt* (*pt & pp* **dogged**, *ger* **dogging**) acosar, perseguir.

dogged ['dɒgɪd] *adj* terco,-a, obstinado, -a.

doggy ['dɒgɪ] *n* (*pl* -ies) perrito,-a.

dogma ['dɒgmə] *n* dogma.

dogmatic [dɒg'mætɪk] *adj* dogmático,-a.

dogsbody ['dɒgzbɒdɪ] *n* (*pl* -ies) GB *fam* burro de carga.

do-it-yourself [duːɪtjɔː'self] *n* bricolaje.

doldrums ['dɒldrəmz] *npl* .
● **in the doldrums** abatido,-a, deprimido,-a.

dole [dəʊl] *n* GB *fam* subsidio de desempleo.
● **to be on the dole** estar en el paro.

to dole out *vt* repartir.

doll [dɒl] *n* muñeca.
● **to get dolled up** emperifollarse.

dollar ['dɒlə'] *n* dólar.

dolly ['dɒlɪ] *n* (*pl* -ies) muñeca.

dolphin ['dɒlfɪn] *n* delfín.

domain [də'meɪn] *n* **1** dominio, propiedad. **2** campo, esfera. **3** dominio.
■ **domain name** nombre de dominio.

dome [dəʊm] *n* cúpula *(de edificio)*.

domestic [də'mestɪk] *adj* **1** doméstico,-a *(animal)*. **2** hogareño,-a, casero,-a *(persona)*. **3** nacional *(vuelo)*.

dominant ['dɒmɪnənt] *adj* dominante.

dominate ['dɒmɪneɪt] *vt-vi* dominar.

domination [dɒmɪ'neɪʃən] *n* dominación.

domineering [dɒmɪ'nɪərɪŋ] *adj pej* dominante.

Dominica [dɒmɪ'niːkə] *n* Dominica.

Dominican [də'mɪnɪkən] *adj-n* dominicano,-a.
■ **Dominican Republic** República Dominicana.

domino ['dɒmɪnəʊ] *n* (*pl* **dominoes**) ficha de dominó.
► *npl* **dominoes** dominó.

donate [dəʊ'neɪt] *vt* donar, hacer un donativo de.

donation [dəʊ'neɪʃən] *n* **1** donación. **2** donativo.

done [dʌn] *pp* → do.
► *adj* **1** terminado,-a, acabado,-a: *the job is done*, el trabajo está terminado. **2** *fam* agotado,-a. **3** cocido,-a, hecho,-a.
● **done!** ¡trato hecho!
● **it isn't done to ...** es de mal gusto ....

donkey ['dɒŋkɪ] *n* burro,-a.

donor ['dəʊnə'] *n* donante.

don't [dəʊnt] *aux* contracción de *do* + *not*.

doodle ['duːdəl] *vi* garabatear, hacer garabatos.
► *n* garabato.

doom [duːm] *n* destino, perdición.
► *vt* condenar.

door [dɔː'] *n* **1** puerta. **2** portal.
● **(from) door to door** de puerta en puerta.
● **next door** (en) la casa de al lado.
● **by the back door** por la puerta falsa.
● **out of doors** al aire libre.
● **to answer the door** abrir la puerta.
● **to be on the door** *fam* hacer de portero,-a.

doorbell ['dɔːbel] *n* timbre: *to ring the doorbell*, llamar al timbre.

doorman ['dɔːmən] *n* (*pl* **doormen**) portero.

doorstep ['dɔːstep] *n* peldaño.
● **on your doorstep** a un paso, al lado de casa.

door-to-door [dɔːtə'dɔː] *adj* a domicilio.

doorway ['dɔːweɪ] *n* entrada, portal.

dope [dəʊp] *n* **1** *sl* droga. **2** *fam* imbécil.
► *vt* **1** *fam* poner droga en. **2** dopar.

dopey ['dəʊpɪ] *adj* **1** estúpido,-a. **2** *fam* grogui.

dormitory ['dɔːmɪtərɪ] *n* (*pl* -**ies**). **1** dormitorio. **2** US colegio mayor.

dosage ['dəʊsɪdʒ] *n* dosis, posología.

dose [dəʊs] *n* dosis.

doss down ['dɒs'daʊn] *vi* GB *sl* echarse a dormir, acostarse.

dossier ['dɒsɪeɪ] *n* expediente, dossier.

dot [dɒt] *n* punto.
  ▸ *vt* (*pt & pp* **dotted**, *ger* **dotting**). **1** poner el punto a. **2** salpicar.
  ● **on the dot** *fam* a la hora en punto.

dote [dəʊt] *vi* adorar.

double ['dʌbəl] *adj-adv* doble: *a double whisky*, un whisky doble.
  ▸ *n* **1** doble: *to earn double*, ganar el doble. **2** doble, viva imagen.
  ▸ *vt-vi* doblar(se), duplicar(se).
  ▸ *npl* **doubles** dobles.
  ● **to double as** hacer las veces de.
  ● **on the double** enseguida.
  ■ **double agent** agente doble.
  ■ **double bass** contrabajo.
  ■ **double bed** cama de matrimonio.
  ■ **double cream** nata para montar.
  ■ **double chin** papada.
  ■ **double meaning** doble sentido.
  ■ **double room** habitación doble.
  ■ **double talk** ambigüedades.

to double up *vt* retorcer, partir: *to be doubled up with laughter*, partirse de risa.
  ▸ *vi* doblarse.

double-cross [dʌbəl'krɒs] *vt* engañar, traicionar.

double-decker [dʌbəl'dekəʳ] *n* GB autobús de dos pisos.

doubly ['dʌblɪ] *adv* doblemente.

doubt [daʊt] *n* duda, incertidumbre.
  ▸ *vt* **1** dudar/desconfiar de. **2** dudar: *I doubt if she'll come*, dudo que venga.
  ● **beyond doubt** sin duda alguna.
  ● **no doubt** sin duda.

doubtful ['daʊtfʊl] *adj* **1** dudoso,-a, de duda (*mirada*). **2** improbable.

doubtless ['daʊtləs] *adv* sin duda.

dough [dəʊ] *n* **1** masa (*de pan*). **2** *fam* pasta, guita (*dinero*).

doughnut ['dəʊnʌt] *n* rosquilla, donut.

douse [daʊs] *vt* **1** apagar. **2** mojar, rociar.

dove[1] [dʌv] *n* paloma.

dove[2] [dəʊv] *pt* US → dive.

dowdy ['daʊdɪ] *adj* (-**ier**, -**iest**). **1** *pej* sin gracia (*vestido*). **2** *pej* mal vestido,-a (*persona*).

down[1] [daʊn] *prep* **1** abajo, hacia abajo: *down the street*, calle abajo; *they ran down the hill*, corrieron cuesta abajo. **2** por: *cut it down the middle*, córtalo por la mitad.
  ▸ *adv* **1** abajo, hacia abajo, al suelo, a tierra: *she fell down and broke her leg*, se cayó y se rompió la pierna. **2** abajo: *down here/there*, aquí/allí abajo. **3** reducido,-a, bajado,-a: *sales are down this year*, las ventas han bajado este año. **4** estropeado,-a: *the computer is down*, el ordenador está estropeado.
  ▸ *adj* *fam* depre, deprimido.
  ▸ *vt* **1** derribar, abatir. **2** tumbar, tirar al suelo. **3** *fam* tomarse de un trago.
  ● **down with ...!** ¡abajo ...!
  ● **face down** boca abajo.
  ■ **down payment** entrada.

down[2] [daʊn] *n* **1** plumón. **2** vello, pelusa, pelusilla.

downcast ['daʊnkɑːst] *adj* abatido,-a.

downfall ['daʊnfɔːl] *n* perdición, ruina.

downgrade [daʊn'greɪd] *vt* degradar.

downhearted [daʊn'hɑːtɪd] *adj* desanimado,-a.

downhill [daʊn'hɪl] *adv* cuesta abajo.
  ▸ *adj* en pendiente, de descenso.
  ● **to go downhill** ir cuesta abajo, empeorar.

download ['daʊn'ləʊd] *vt* bajar, descargar.

downpour ['daʊnpɔːʳ] *n* chaparrón.

downright ['daʊnraɪt] *adj* total: *downright liar*, mentiroso redomado.

downstairs [daʊn'steəz] *adv* abajo: *to go downstairs*, bajar la escalera, ir abajo.
  ▸ *adj* en la planta baja, de abajo.

downstream [daʊn'striːm] *adv* río abajo.

downtown [daʊn'taʊn] *adv* **1** US al centro de la ciudad. **2** en el centro de la ciudad.
  ▸ *adj* del centro de la ciudad.

downward ['daʊnwəd] *adj* **1** descendente. **2** a la baja.

downwards ['daʊnwədz] *adv* hacia abajo: *face downwards*, boca abajo.

dowry ['daʊərɪ] *n* (*pl* -**ies**) dote.

dowse [daʊs] *vt* → douse.

doz ['dʌzən] *abbr* (**dozen**) docena, doc.

doze [dəʊz] n cabezada.
▶ vi dormitar, echar una cabezada.
to doze off vi quedarse dormido,-a.
dozen ['dʌzən] n docena.
dozy ['dəʊzi] adj (-ier, -iest). 1 amodorra-do,-a. 2 idiota.
DPP ['diː'piː'piː] abbr GB (**Director of Public Prosecutions**) ~ Fiscal General del Estado.
Dr ['dɒktə'] abbr (**Doctor**) Doctor,-ra, Dr., Dra.
drab [dræb] adj (comp **drabber**, superl **drabbest**) monótono,-a, gris.
draft [drɑːft] n 1 borrador, esbozo. 2 letra de cambio, giro. 3 US servicio militar obligatorio. 4 US → draught.
▶ vt 1 hacer un borrador de, redactar. 2 US reclutar.
draftsman ['drɑːftsmən] n US → draughtsman.
drafty ['drɑːftɪ] adj US → draughty.
drag [dræg] n 1 resistencia. 2 fig estorbo. 3 fam lata, rollo. 4 fam calada, chupada.
▶ vt (pt & pp **dragged**, ger **dragging**). 1 arrastrar. 2 rastrear, dragar.
▶ vi 1 arrastrarse. 2 rezagarse.
● **in drag** vestido de mujer.
to drag on vi prolongarse.
to drag out vt alargar, prolongar.
to drag up vt fam sacar a relucir.
dragon ['drægən] n dragón.
drain [dreɪn] n 1 desagüe, alcantarilla. 2 fig desgaste, agotamiento: *the boys are a drain on her*, los niños la dejan agotada.
▶ vt 1 drenar (pantano). 2 desecar, avenar (lago). 3 apurar (vaso). 4 vaciar (depósito). 5 escurrir (verduras).
▶ vi escurrirse.
● **to go down the drain** echarse a perder, irse al traste.
drainpipe ['dreɪnpaɪp] n (tubería de) desagüe.
drama ['drɑːmə] n 1 obra de teatro, drama. 2 teatro, arte dramático. 3 fig drama.
dramatic [drə'mætɪk] adj 1 dramático,-a. 2 emocionante, espectacular.
dramatist ['dræmətɪst] n dramaturgo,-a.
drank [dræŋk] pt → drink.
drape [dreɪp] vt cubrir.
▶ npl **drapes** US cortinas.
drastic ['dræstɪk] adj drástico,-a.
draught [drɑːft] n 1 corriente de aire. 2 trago.

▶ npl **draughts** GB damas.
● **on draught** a presión, de barril.
draughtsman ['drɑːftsmən] n delineante.
draw [drɔː] n 1 sorteo. 2 empate. 3 atracción, gancho.
▶ vt (pt **drew** [druː], pp **drawn** [drɔːn]). 1 dibujar, trazar (línea, círculo). 2 arrastrar, tirar de. 3 descorrer, correr (cortinas). 4 sacar, desenvainar (espada). 5 cobrar (sueldo). 6 girar, librar (talón). 7 atraer. 8 aspirar (aire). 9 sacar (conclusión).
▶ vi 1 dibujar. 2 moverse: *the train drew into/out of the station*, el tren entró en/salió de la estación. 3 empatar: *they drew two all*, empataron a dos. 4 tirar (chimenea).
● **to draw apart** separarse.
● **to draw attention to** llamar la atención sobre.
● **to draw blood** hacer sangrar.
● **to draw near** acercarse.
● **it's the luck of the draw** toca a quien toca.
● **to draw the line** decir basta.
to draw back vi 1 retroceder. 2 echarse para atrás.
to draw in vi apartarse, echarse a un lado.
to draw on vt recurrir a, hacer uso de.
to draw out vt alargar.
to draw up vt 1 preparar (contrato). 2 esbozar (plan).
▶ vi llegar.
drawback ['drɔːbæk] n inconveniente, desventaja.
drawbridge ['drɔːbrɪdʒ] n puente levadizo.
drawer ['drɔːə'] n cajón.
drawing ['drɔːɪŋ] n dibujo.
■ **drawing pin** GB chincheta.
■ **drawing room** sala de estar, salón.
drawl [drɔːl] n voz cansina.
▶ vi hablar arrastrando las palabras.
drawn [drɔːn] pp → draw.
▶ adj 1 empatado,-a (partido). 2 ojeroso,-a (cara).
dread [dred] n temor, pavor.
▶ vt-vi temer, tener pavor a.
dreadful ['dredfʊl] adj 1 terrible, espantoso,-a. 2 fam fatal, horrible: *how dreadful!*, ¡qué horror!
dreadfully ['dredfʊlɪ] adv 1 horriblemen-

te, terriblemente. **2** *fam* enormemente:
he's dreadfully tired, está muy cansado.
dream [driːm] *n* **1** sueño. **2** *fam* maravilla.
▶ *vt-vi* (*pt & pp* **dreamed** o **dreamt**) soñar.
to dream up *vt fam* idear, inventarse.
dreamer ['driːməʳ] *n* soñador,-ra.
dreamt [dremt] *pt-pp* → dream.
dreary ['drɪərɪ] *adj* (**-ier, -iest**). **1** triste,
deprimente. **2** *fam* aburrido,-a, monótono,-a.
dredge [dredʒ] *vt-vi* dragar, rastrear.
drench [drentʃ] *vt* mojar, empapar.
dress [dres] *n* **1** vestido. **2** ropa, vestimenta.
▶ *vt* **1** vestir. **2** vendar *(herida)*. **3** aderezar, aliñar *(ensalada)*.
▶ *vi* vestirse.
■ **dress rehearsal** ensayo general *(con trajes)*.
■ **to get dressed** vestirse.
to dress down *vt* regañar.
to dress up *vi* disfrazarse, ponerse de tiros largos.
▶ *vt fig* disfrazar.
dresser ['dresəʳ] *n* **1** GB aparador. **2** US tocador.
dressing ['dresɪŋ] *n* **1** vendaje. **2** aliño *(de ensalada)*.
■ **dressing gown** bata.
■ **dressing table** tocador.
drew [druː] *pt* → draw.
dribble ['drɪbəl] *n* **1** gotas, hilo. **2** baba.
▶ *vi* **1** gotear *(líquido)*. **2** babear *(bebé)*.
▶ *vt* driblar, regatear *(en fútbol)*.
drier ['draɪəʳ] *n* → dryer.
drift [drɪft] *n* **1** flujo. **2** ventisquero *(de nieve)*. **3** montón *(de arena)*. **4** *fig* significado.
▶ *vi* **1** amontonarse *(nieve)*. **2** ir a la deriva *(barco)*. **3** *fig* vagar *(persona)*.
drill¹ [drɪl] *n* **1** taladro. **2** broca. **3** instrucción *(militar)*. **4** ejercicio. **5** fresa *(de dentista)*.
▶ *vt* **1** taladrar. **2** instruir *(tropas)*.
▶ *vi* **1** taladrar. **2** entrenarse *(tropas)*.
drill² [drɪl] *n* dril *(tela)*.
drink [drɪŋk] *n* bebida, copa.
▶ *vt-vi* (*pt* **drank** [dræŋk], *pp* **drunk** [drʌŋk]) beber.
● **to drink to** STH/SB brindar por algo/ALGN.
● **to have** STH **to drink** tomar algo.
to drink in *vt* absorber *(escena)*.

drinking ['drɪŋkɪŋ] *n* .
■ **drinking fountain** fuente *(de agua potable)*.
■ **drinking water** agua potable.
drip [drɪp] *n* **1** goteo. **2** gota a gota *(de suero)*. **3** *fam* soso,-a *(persona)*.
▶ *vi* (*pt & pp* **dripped**, *ger* **dripping**) gotear.
▶ *vt* dejar caer gota a gota.
drive [draɪv] *n* **1** paseo en coche. **2** camino de entrada. **3** golpe inicial *(golf)*. **4** drive *(tenis)*. **5** energía, ímpetu *(empuje)*. **6** campaña. **7** transmisión *(en motor)*. **8** tracción *(en coche)*. **9** unidad de disco.
▶ *vt* (*pt* **drove** [drəʊv], *pp* **driven** ['drɪvən]). **1** conducir. **2** llevar, acompañar: ***I'll drive you home***, te llevaré a casa. **3** impulsar. **4** arrear *(ganado)*. **5** mandar *(pelota)*. **6** clavar. **7** volver: ***you drive me mad***, me vuelves loco.
to drive at *vt fam* insinuar.
drivel ['drɪvəl] *n* tonterías.
driven ['drɪvən] *pp* → drive.
driver ['draɪvəʳ] *n* conductor,-ra: ***truck driver***, camionero.
driving ['draɪvɪŋ] *adj* .
■ **driving licence** carnet, permiso de conducir.
■ **driving school** autoescuela.
drizzle ['drɪzəl] *n* llovizna.
▶ *vi* lloviznar.
droll [drəʊl] *adj* gracioso,-a, curioso,-a.
dromedary ['drɒmədərɪ] *n* dromedario.
drone¹ [drəʊn] *n* zángano.
drone² [drəʊn] *n* zumbido.
▶ *vi* zumbar.
drool [druːl] *n* baba.
▶ *vi* babear.
droop [druːp] *n* caída, inclinación.
▶ *vi* **1** inclinarse, caerse. **2** marchitarse.
drop [drɒp] *n* **1** gota. **2** pastilla. **3** pendiente, desnivel. **4** caída.
▶ *vt* (*pt & pp* **dropped**, *ger* **dropping**). **1** dejar caer: ***he dropped the glass***, se le cayó el vaso. **2** *fam* dejar, romper con. **3** abandonar, dejar *(hábito)*. **4** comerse *(al hablar, al escribir)*. **5** no seleccionar, excluir *(de equipo)*. **6** soltar.
▶ *vi* **1** caerse *(persona)*. **2** bajar, caer *(precios, voz)*. **3** amainar *(viento)*.
● **to drop** SB **a line** escribir cuatro líneas a ALGN.
to drop away *vi* disminuir.

to drop by/in/round *vi* dejarse caer, pasar.

to drop off *vi* **1** *fam* quedarse dormido, -a. **2** disminuir.

to drop out *vi* **1** dejar los estudios. **2** retirarse *(de un partido)*.

dropper ['drɒpəʳ] *n* cuentagotas.

droppings ['drɒpɪŋz] *npl* excrementos, cagadas.

drought [draʊt] *n* sequía.

drove [drəʊv] *pt* → drive.

► *n* **1** manada. **2** multitud.

drown [draʊn] *vt-vi* ahogar(se).

drowse [draʊz] *vi* dormitar.

drowsiness ['draʊzɪnəs] *n* somnolencia, modorra.

drowsy ['draʊzɪ] *adj* (-**ier**, -**iest**) somnoliento,-a, soñoliento,-a.

● **to feel drowsy** estar amodorrado,-a.

drug [drʌg] *n* **1** medicamento, medicina. **2** droga, estupefaciente, narcótico.

► *vt* (*pt & pp* **drugged**, *ger* **drugging**) drogar.

● **to be on/take drugs** drogarse.

■ **drug addict** drogadicto,-a.

■ **drug pusher** traficante de drogas.

■ **drug squad** brigada de estupefacientes.

drugstore ['drʌgstɔːʳ] *n* US establecimiento donde se compran medicamentos, periódicos, comida etc.

drum [drʌm] *n* **1** tambor *(instrumento musical)*. **2** bidón *(contenedor)*. **3** tambor *(en máquina)*.

► *vi* (*pt & pp* **drummed**, *ger* **drumming**). **1** tocar el tambor. **2** tamborilear.

► *npl* **drums** batería.

drummer ['drʌməʳ] *n* tambor, batería *(músico)*.

drumstick ['drʌmstɪk] *n* **1** baqueta. **2** muslo *(de pollo)*.

drunk [drʌŋk] *pp* → drink.

► *adj-n* borracho,-a.

● **to get drunk** emborracharse.

drunkard ['drʌŋkəd] *n* borracho,-a.

drunken ['drʌŋkən] *adj* borracho,-a.

dry [draɪ] *adj* (-**ier**, -**iest**). **1** seco,-a. **2** aburrido,-a.

► *vt-vi* (-**ier**, -**iest**) secar(se).

dry-clean [draɪ'kliːn] *vt* limpiar en seco.

dry-cleaners [draɪ'kliːnəz] *n* tintorería.

dryer ['draɪəʳ] *n* secadora.

dryness ['draɪnəs] *n* sequedad.

dual ['djuːəl] *adj* dual, doble.

■ **dual carriageway** autovía, vía rápida.

dub [dʌb] *vt* (*pt & pp* **dubbed**, *ger* **dubbing**). **1** doblar *(película)*. **2** apodar, llamar.

dubious ['djuːbɪəs] *adj* dudoso,-a.

Dublin ['dʌblɪn] *n* Dublín.

Dubliner ['dʌblɪnəʳ] *n* dublinés,-esa.

duchess ['dʌtʃəs] *n* duquesa.

duck[1] [dʌk] *n* pato,-a.

duck[2] [dʌk] *vt-vi* agachar(se).

duckling ['dʌklɪŋ] *n* patito.

duct [dʌkt] *n* conducto.

dud [dʌd] *adj* **1** *fam* defectuoso,-a, inútil. **2** sin carga *(pila)*. **3** *fam* falso,-a.

► *n* **1** *bomba que no estalla*. **2** *fam* birria, porquería.

due [djuː] *adj* **1** debido,-a *(dinero)*. **2** pagadero,-a. **3** esperado,-a: *I'm due for a rise*, me toca una subida de sueldo; *she's due to arrive tomorrow*, está previsto que llegue mañana; *the train is due at five*, el tren debe llegar a las cinco.

► *n* merecido: *to give SB his/her due*, dar a ALGN su merecido.

► *adv* derecho hacia.

► *npl* **dues** cuota.

● **in due course/time** a su debido tiempo.

● **to be due to** deberse a.

■ **due date** plazo, vencimiento.

duel ['djuːəl] *n* duelo.

► *vi* batirse en duelo.

duet [djuː'et] *n* dúo.

duffle coat ['dʌfəlkəʊt] *n* trenca.

dug [dʌg] *pt-pp* → dig.

duke [djuːk] *n* duque.

dull [dʌl] *adj* **1** apagado,-a *(color)*. **2** gris *(día)*. **3** sordo,-a *(sonido)*. **4** torpe *(persona)*. **5** monótono,-a, pesado,-a *(película)*.

► *vt* **1** aliviar *(dolor)*. **2** amortiguar *(sonido)*.

duly ['djuːlɪ] *adv* **1** debidamente. **2** como era de esperar.

dumb [dʌm] *adj* **1** mudo,-a. **2** *fam* tonto,-a.

● **to be deaf and dumb** ser sordomudo.

dumbfound [dʌm'faʊnd] *vt* dejar sin habla.

dumbfounded [dʌm'faʊndɪd] *adj* pasmado,-a, mudo de asombro.

dumbly ['dʌmlɪ] *adv* sin decir nada.

dummy ['dʌmɪ] *n* (*pl* -**ies**). **1** imitación. **2** maniquí. **3** GB chupete. **4** *fam* imbécil.

dump [dʌmp] *n* **1** vertedero, basurero. **2** *fam* poblacho, pueblo de mala muerte. **3** *fam* antro, tugurio.
  ▶ *vt* **1** tirar, verter, dejar: *"No dumping"*, "Prohibido arrojar basuras". **2** abandonar, dejar. **3** volcar.
  ● **down in the dumps** pocho,-a, depre.

dumpling ['dʌmplɪŋ] *n* **1** bola de masa hervida para acompañar carnes, etc. **2** tipo de budín relleno.

dumpy ['dʌmpɪ] *adj* (-**ier**, -**iest**) *fam* rechoncho,-a.

dune [dju:n] *n* duna.

dung [dʌŋ] *n* estiércol.

dungarees [dʌŋgə'ri:z] *n* pantalones de peto, mono.

dungeon ['dʌndʒən] *n* mazmorra.

duo ['dju:əʊ] *n* (*pl* **duos**) dúo.

dupe [dju:p] *n* ingenuo,-a.
  ▶ *vt* embaucar, engañar.

duplicate [(*adj*) 'dju:plɪkət(n) 'dju:plɪkeɪt] *adj* duplicado,-a.
  ▶ *n* duplicado.
  ▶ *vt* duplicar.

durable ['djʊərəbəl] *adj* duradero,-a.

duration [djʊə'reɪʃən] *n* duración.

during ['djʊərɪŋ] *prep* durante.

dusk [dʌsk] *n* anochecer, crepúsculo: *at dusk*, al anochecer.

dust [dʌst] *n* polvo.
  ▶ *vt* **1** desempolvar, quitar el polvo a. **2** espolvorear.

dustbin ['dʌstbɪn] *n* GB cubo de la basura.

duster ['dʌstə'] *n* **1** paño, trapo. **2** borrador *(de pizarra)*.

dustman ['dʌstmən] *n* (*pl* **dustmen**) GB basurero.

dustpan ['dʌstpæn] *n* recogedor.

dusty ['dʌstɪ] *adj* (-**ier**, -**iest**) polvoriento,-a, lleno,-a de polvo.

Dutch [dʌtʃ] *adj* holandés,-esa, neerlandés,-esa.
  ▶ *n* holandés.
  ▶ *npl* **the Dutch** los holandeses.
  ■ **Dutch cap** diafragma.

duty ['dju:tɪ] *n* (*pl* -**ies**). **1** deber, obligación. **2** cometido. **3** impuesto. **4** guardia.
  ● **to be on/off duty** estar/no estar de servicio/guardia.
  ● **to do one's duty** cumplir con su deber.

duty-free ['dju:tɪfri:] *adj* libre de impuestos.
  ▶ *adv* sin pagar impuestos.
  ▶ *n* tienda de duty-free.

duvet ['du:veɪ] *n* edredón *m* nórdico.

DVD ['di:vi:'di:] *abbr* (*Digital Versatile Disk*) DVD.

dwarf [dwɔ:f] *n* (*pl* -**s** o **dwarves**) enano,-a.
  ▶ *vt* achicar, empequeñecer.

dwell [dwel] *vi* (*pt & pp* **dwelt**) *fml* habitar, morar.

to dwell on/upon *vt* insistir en.

dwelling ['dwelɪŋ] *n* morada.

dwelt [dwelt] *pt-pp* → dwell.

dwindle ['dwɪndəl] *vi* menguar, disminuir.

dye [daɪ] *n* tinte.
  ▶ *vt-vi* teñir(se).

dyke [daɪk] *n* **1** dique, barrera. **2** terraplén. **3** *sl* lesbiana, tortillera.

dynamic [daɪ'næmɪk] *adj* dinámico,-a.

dynamics [daɪ'næmɪks] *n* dinámica.

dynamite ['daɪnəmaɪt] *n* dinamita.

dynamo ['daɪnəməʊ] *n* (*pl* **dynamos**) dinamo.

dynasty ['dɪnəstɪ] *n* (*pl* -**ies**) dinastía.

dysentery ['dɪsəntrɪ] *n* disentería.

dyslexia [dɪs'leksɪə] *n* dislexia.

E

E [iːst] *abbr* **1** (*east*) E, este. **2** mi *(nota)*.
each [iːtʃ] *adj* cada: ***each day***, cada día, todos los días.
▶ *pron* cada uno,-a: ***each with his wife***, cada uno con su esposa.
▶ *adv* cada uno,-a: ***the apples cost 15p each***, las manzanas van a 15 peniques cada una.
● **each other** el/la uno,-a al/a la otro,-a: ***we love each other***, nos queremos.
eager [ˈiːgəʳ] *adj* ávido,-a, ansioso,-a, impaciente.
● **to be eager for SB to do STH** estar deseando que ALGN haga algo.
eagerly [ˈiːgəlɪ] *adv* con impaciencia, con afán.
eagle [ˈiːgəl] *n* águila.
ear[1] [ɪəʳ] *n* **1** oreja. **2** oído.
ear[2] [ɪəʳ] *n* espiga *(de trigo)*.
earache [ˈɪəreɪk] *n* dolor de oídos.
eardrum [ˈɪədrʌm] *n* tímpano.
early [ˈɜːlɪ] *adj* (-**ier**, -**iest**) temprano,-a: ***early in the morning/afternoon***, a primera hora de la mañana/tarde.
▶ *adv* temprano.
● **in the early morning** de madrugada.
earmark [ˈɪəmɑːk] *vt* destinar.
earn [ɜːn] *vt* **1** ganar *(dinero)*. **2** merecer(se).
earnest [ˈɜːnɪst] *adj* serio,-a, formal.
● **in earnest** en serio.
earnings [ˈɜːnɪŋz] *npl* ingresos.
earphones [ˈɪəfəʊnz] *npl* auriculares.
earplug [ˈɪəplʌg] *n* tapón *(para los oídos)*.
earring [ˈɪərɪŋ] *n* pendiente *(joya)*.
earth [ɜːθ] *n* tierra.
● **what/where on earth ...?** ¿qué/dónde demonios ...?

■ **the Earth** la Tierra.
earthly [ˈɜːθlɪ] *adj* terrenal.
● **not to have an earthly** no tener la más mínima posibilidad.
earthquake [ˈɜːθkweɪk] *n* terremoto.
earthworm [ˈɜːθwɜːm] *n* lombriz.
earwig [ˈɪəwɪg] *n* tijereta.
ease [iːz] *n* **1** facilidad. **2** tranquilidad. **3** comodidad.
▶ *vt* aliviar, calmar.
▶ *vi* disminuir.
● **at ease** relajado,-a.
● **to set SB's mind at ease** tranquilizar a ALGN.
to ease off *vi* disminuir.
easel [ˈiːzəl] *n* caballete.
easily [ˈiːzɪlɪ] *adv* **1** fácilmente. **2** con mucho.
east [iːst] *n* este, oriente.
▶ *adj* oriental, del este.
▶ *adv* hacia el este.
Easter [ˈiːstəʳ] *n* **1** Pascua *(de Resurrección)*. **2** Semana Santa.
easterly [ˈiːstəlɪ] *adj* **1** al este, hacia el este. **2** del este.
eastern [ˈiːstən] *adj* oriental, del este.
eastward [ˈiːstwəd] *adj* hacia el este.
eastwards [ˈiːstwədz] *adv* hacia el este.
easy [ˈiːzɪ] *adj* (-**ier**, -**iest**). **1** fácil, sencillo,-a. **2** cómodo,-a, holgado,-a *(vida)*.
● **take it easy!** ¡tranquilo,-a!
● **to take things easy** tomar las cosas con calma.
● **I'm easy** *fam* me es igual.
■ **easy chair** sillón.
■ **easy terms** facilidades de pago.
easy-going [iːzɪˈgəʊɪŋ] *adj* calmado,-a, tranquilo,-a.

eat [iːt] *vt-vi* (*pt* **ate** [eɪt, et], *pp* **eaten** ['iːtən]) comer.
to eat away *vt* desgastar, corroer *(metal)*.
to eat into *vt fig* consumir.
to eat out *vi* comer fuera.
to eat up *vt* comerse *(todo)*.
eaten ['iːtən] *pp* → eat.
eavesdrop ['iːvzdrɒp] *vi* **1** escuchar a escondidas. **2** estar pendiente de una conversación ajena.
ebb [eb] *n* reflujo.
   ▶ *vi* bajar, menguar.
   • **at a low ebb** en un punto bajo.
   ■ **ebb and flow 1** flujo y reflujo *(de la marea)*. **2** altibajos.
   ■ **ebb-tide** marea menguante.
ebony ['ebənɪ] *n* ébano.
eccentric [ɪk'sentrɪk] *adj-n* excéntrico,-a.
echo ['ekəʊ] *n* (*pl* **echoes**) eco.
   ▶ *vt* repetir.
   ▶ *vi* tener eco, resonar.
eclipse [ɪ'klɪps] *n* eclipse.
   ▶ *vt* eclipsar.
ecological [iːkə'lɒdʒɪkəl] *adj* ecológico,-a.
ecologist [ɪ'kɒlədʒɪst] *n* ecologista.
ecology [ɪ'kɒlədʒɪ] *n* ecología.
economic [iːkə'nɒmɪk] *adj* **1** económico,-a *(desarrollo, política)*. **2** rentable.
economical [iːkə'nɒmɪkəl] *adj* barato,-a, económico,-a.
economics [iːkə'nɒmɪks] *n* economía, ciencias económicas.

Es incontable y el verbo va en singular.

economist [ɪ'kɒnəmɪst] *n* economista.
economize [ɪ'kɒnəmaɪz] *vi* economizar, ahorrar.
economy [ɪ'kɒnəmɪ] *n* (*pl* **-ies**) economía.
ecosystem ['iːkəʊsɪstəm] *n* ecosistema.
ecstasy ['ekstəsɪ] *n* (*pl* **-ies**) éxtasis.
Ecuador ['ekwədɔːʳ] *n* Ecuador.
Ecuadorian [ekwə'dɔːrɪən] *adj-n* ecuatoriano,-a.
eczema ['eksɪmə] *n* eccema.
edge [edʒ] *n* **1** borde. **2** canto *(de moneda, escalón)*. **3** filo *(de navaja)*. **4** orilla *(de lago)*. **5** afueras *(de población)*.
   ▶ *vt* ribetear.
   • **on edge** nervioso,-a.
   • **to have the edge on/over** SB llevar ventaja a ALGN.
to edge forward *vi* avanzar lentamente.
edgy ['edʒɪ] *adj* (**-ier**, **-iest**) nervioso,-a.
edible ['edɪbəl] *adj* comestible.

edict ['iːdɪkt] *n* edicto.
Edinburgh ['edɪnbərə] *n* Edimburgo.
edit ['edɪt] *vt* **1** preparar para la imprenta. **2** corregir. **3** dirigir *(periódico)*. **4** montar, editar *(película)*.
edition [ɪ'dɪʃən] *n* edición.
editor ['edɪtəʳ] *n* **1** editor,-ra *(de libro)*. **2** director,-ra *(de periódico)*. **3** montador,-ra *(de película)*. **4** COMPUT editor.
editorial [edɪ'tɔːrɪəl] *adj* editorial.
   ▶ *n* editorial *(artículo)*.
   ■ **editorial staff** redacción.
educate ['edjʊkeɪt] *vt* educar.
educated ['edjʊkeɪtɪd] *adj* culto,-a.
education [edjʊ'keɪʃən] *n* **1** educación. **2** enseñanza. **3** estudios. **4** pedagogía.
educational [edjʊ'keɪʃənəl] *adj* educativo,-a.
eel [iːl] *n* anguila.
eerie ['ɪərɪ] *adj* misterioso,-a.
effect [ɪ'fekt] *n* efecto.
   ▶ *vt* efectuar.
   ▶ *npl* **effects** efectos.
   • **in effect** de hecho.
   • **to come into effect** entrar en vigor.
   • **to take effect 1** surtir efecto, hacer efecto *(medicamento, etc)*. **2** entrar en vigor *(ley)*.
   • **to the effect that** en el sentido de que.
effective [ɪ'fektɪv] *adj* **1** eficaz *(medicamento)*. **2** efectivo,-a, real. **3** impresionante.
effeminate [ɪ'femɪnət] *adj* afeminado,-a.
effervescent [efə'vesənt] *adj* efervescente.
efficiency [ɪ'fɪʃənsɪ] *n* **1** eficiencia, competencia *(de persona)*. **2** eficacia *(de producto)*. **3** rendimiento *(de máquina)*.
efficient [ɪ'fɪʃənt] *adj* **1** eficiente, competente *(persona)*. **2** eficaz *(producto)*. **3** de buen rendimiento *(máquina)*.
effort ['efət] *n* **1** esfuerzo. **2** intento.
EFL ['iːef'el] *abbr* (*English as a foreign language*) inglés como lengua extranjera.
egg [eg] *n* huevo.
   ■ **boiled egg** huevo pasado por agua.
   ■ **egg cup** huevera.
   ■ **fried egg** huevo frito.
   ■ **hard-boiled egg** huevo duro.
to egg on *vt* animar.
eggplant ['egplɑːnt] *n* berenjena.
ego ['iːgəʊ] *n* (*pl* **egos**). **1** yo. **2** *fam* amor propio.

egocentric [iːgəʊ'sentrɪk] *adj* egocéntrico,-a.

egoism ['iːgəʊɪzəm] *n* egoísmo.

egoist ['iːgəʊɪst] *n* egoísta.

Egypt ['iːdʒɪpt] *n* Egipto.

Egyptian [ɪ'dʒɪpʃən] *adj* egipcio,-a.
▶ *n* **1** egipcio,-a *(persona)*. **2** egipcio *(lengua)*.

eiderdown ['aɪdədaʊn] *n* edredón.

eight [eɪt] *num* ocho.

eighteen [eɪ'tiːn] *num* dieciocho.

eighteenth [eɪ'tiːnθ] *adj* decimoctavo,-a.
▶ *n* **1** decimoctavo. **2** decimooctavo, decimoctava parte *(fracción)*. **3** dieciocho *(en fechas)*.

eighth [eɪtθ] *adj* octavo,-a.
▶ *n* **1** octavo. **2** octavo, octava parte *(fracción)*. **3** ocho *(en fechas)*.

eightieth ['eɪtɪθ] *adj* octogésimo,-a.
▶ *n* octogésimo, octogésima parte *(fracción)*.

eighty ['eɪti] *num* ochenta.

Eire ['eərə] *n* Eire, Irlanda.

either ['aɪðə', 'iːðə'] *adj* **1** cualquiera: *either of them*, cualquiera de los dos. **2** ni el uno/la una ni el otro/la otra, ninguno,-a: *I don't like either of them*, no me gusta ninguno de los dos. **3** cada, los/las dos, ambos,-as: *with a gun in either hand*, con una pistola en cada mano.
▶ *conj* o: *either red or green*, o rojo o verde.
▶ *adv* tampoco: *Ann didn't come either*, tampoco vino Ana.
▶ *pron* cualquiera de los dos: *there's juice or milk- you can have either*, hay zumo o leche,- puedes tomar cualquiera de los dos.

eject [ɪ'dʒekt] *vt* expulsar.
▶ *vi* eyectar, eyectarse.

El Salvador [el'sælvədɔː'] *n* El Salvador.

elaborate [*(adj)* ɪ'læbərət *(vb)* ɪ'læbəreɪt] *adj* **1** detallado,-a. **2** complicado,-a, intrincado,-a.
▶ *vi* extenderse.

elastic [ɪ'læstɪk] *adj* elástico,-a.
▶ *n* elástico.
■ **elastic band** goma elástica.

elbow ['elbəʊ] *n* **1** codo. **2** recodo.
▶ *vt* dar un codazo a.

elder¹ ['eldə'] *adj* mayor: *he's my elder brother*, es mi hermano mayor.
▶ *n* mayor.

elder² ['eldə'] *n* saúco *(planta)*.

elderly ['eldəlɪ] *adj* mayor, anciano,-a: *the elderly*, los ancianos.

eldest ['eldɪst] *adj* mayor: *my eldest sister*, mi hermana mayor.

elect [ɪ'lekt] *adj* electo,-a.
▶ *vt* elegir.

election [ɪ'lekʃən] *n* elección.

electorate [ɪ'lektərət] *n* electorado.

electric [ɪ'lektrɪk] *adj* eléctrico,-a: *electric current*, corriente eléctrica.
■ **electric chair** silla eléctrica.
■ **electric shock** electrochoque, descarga eléctrica.

electrical [ɪ'lektrɪkəl] *adj* eléctrico,-a: *electrical fault*, fallo eléctrico.
■ **electrical appliance** electrodoméstico.

electrician [ɪlek'trɪʃən] *n* electricista.

electricity [ɪlek'trɪsɪtɪ] *n* electricidad.

electrocute [ɪ'lektrəkjuːt] *vt* electrocutar.

electrode [ɪ'lektrəʊd] *n* electrodo.

electron [ɪ'lektrɒn] *n* electrón.

electronic [ɪlek'trɒnɪk] *adj* electrónico,-a.
■ **electronic mail** correo electrónico.

electronics [ɪlek'trɒnɪks] *n* electrónica.
Es incontable y el verbo va en singular.

elegance ['elɪgəns] *n* elegancia.

elegant ['elɪgənt] *adj* elegante.

element ['elɪmənt] *n* **1** elemento. **2** componente. **3** resistencia *(para calentar)*.
▶ *npl* **elements** fundamentos.

elementary [elɪ'mentərɪ] *adj* elemental.
■ **elementary education** enseñanza primaria.

elephant ['elɪfənt] *n* elefante.

elevate ['elɪveɪt] *vt* **1** elevar. **2** ascender.

elevation [elɪ'veɪʃən] *n* **1** elevación. **2** ascenso. **3** altitud.

elevator ['elɪveɪtə'] *n* US ascensor.

eleven [ɪ'levən] *num* once.
▶ *n* equipo, once, selección.

eleventh [ɪ'levənθ] *adj* undécimo,-a.
▶ *n* **1** undécimo. **2** onceavo, onceava parte *(fracción)*. **3** once *(en fechas)*.

elf [elf] *n (pl* **elves)** elfo.

elicit [ɪ'lɪsɪt] *vt* sonsacar, obtener.

eligible ['elɪdʒəbəl] *adj* elegible.

eliminate [ɪ'lɪmɪneɪt] *vt* eliminar.

elk [elk] *n* alce.

elm [elm] *n* olmo.

eloquent ['eləkwənt] *adj* elocuente.

else [els] *adv* otro, más: *let's do something else*, hagamos otra cosa; *anything* *else?*, ¿algo más?; *nobody else*, nadie más; *someone else*, otra persona más.

● **or else** si no: *behave yourself or else*, pórtate bien, si no ya verás; *hurry up or else you'll be late*, date prisa o llegarás tarde.

elsewhere [els'weə'] *adv* en otro sitio.

elude [ɪ'luːd] *vt* eludir.

e-mail [iːmeɪl] *n* correo electrónico.
► *vt* **1** enviar un correo electrónico a. **2** enviar por correo electrónico.

■ **e-mail address** dirección de correo electrónico.

embankment [ɪm'bæŋkmənt] *n* **1** terraplén. **2** dique *(de río)*.

embargo [em'baːgəʊ] *n* (*pl* **embargoes**) embargo.
► *vt* **1** prohibir. **2** embargar.

embark [ɪm'baːk] *vt-vi* embarcar(se).

● **to embark on STH** emprender algo.

embarrass [ɪm'bærəs] *vt* avergonzar, turbar.

● **to be embarrassed** sentir vergüenza.

embarrassing [ɪm'bærəsɪŋ] *adj* embarazoso,-a, violento,-a.

embarrassment [ɪm'bærəsmənt] *n* **1** vergüenza. **2** molestia, estorbo.

embassy ['embəsɪ] *n* (*pl* **-ies**) embajada.

ember ['embə'] *n* ascua, rescoldo.

embrace [ɪm'breɪs] *n* abrazo.
► *vt* **1** abrazar. **2** abarcar.
► *vi* abrazarse.

embroider [ɪm'brɔɪdə'] *vt* bordar.

embroidery [ɪm'brɔɪdərɪ] *n* bordado.

embryo ['embrɪəʊ] *n* (*pl* **embryos**) embrión.

embryonic [embrɪ'ɒnɪk] *adj* embrionario,-a.

emerald ['emərəld] *n* esmeralda.
► *adj* de color esmeralda.

emerge [ɪ'mɜːdʒ] *vi* emerger, aparecer: *it emerged that...*, resultó que ....

emergency [ɪ'mɜːdʒənsɪ] *n* (*pl* **-ies**). **1** emergencia. **2** urgencia *(médica)*.

■ **emergency exit** salida de emergencia.

emery ['emərɪ] *n* esmeril.

■ **emery board** lima de uñas.

emigrate ['emɪgreɪt] *vi* emigrar.

emigration [emɪ'greɪʃən] *n* emigración.

eminence ['emɪnəns] *n* eminencia.

emirate ['emɪreɪt] *n* emirato.

■ **United Arab Emirates** Emiratos Árabes Unidos.

emission [ɪ'mɪʃən] *n* emisión.

emit [ɪ'mɪt] *vt* (*pt & pp* **emitted**, *ger* **emitting**) emitir *(sonido)*; despedir *(olor)*.

emotion [ɪ'məʊʃən] *n* emoción.

emotional [ɪ'məʊʃənəl] *adj* **1** emocional *(problemas)*. **2** emotivo,-a *(encuentro)*.

emperor ['empərə'] *n* emperador.

emphasis ['emfəsɪs] *n* (*pl* **emphases**) énfasis.

● **to place emphasis on** hacer hincapié en.

emphasize ['emfəsaɪz] *vt* enfatizar, hacer hincapié en, subrayar.

emphatic [em'fætɪk] *adj* enfático,-a, enérgico,-a.

empire ['empaɪə'] *n* imperio.

employ [ɪm'plɔɪ] *vt* emplear, dar trabajo.

employee [em'plɔɪiː, emplɔ'iː] *n* empleado,-a, trabajador,-ra.

employer [em'plɔɪə'] *n* patrón,-ona.

employment [em'plɔɪmənt] *n* empleo, trabajo.

empress ['emprəs] *n* (*pl* **-es**) emperatriz.

emptiness ['emptɪnəs] *n* vacío.

empty ['emptɪ] *adj* (**-ier**, **-iest**). **1** vacío,-a. **2** libre.
► *vt-vi* (*pt & pp* **-ied**) vaciar(se).

enable [ɪ'neɪbəl] *vt* permitir.

enact [ɪ'nækt] *vt* **1** promulgar *(ley)*. **2** representar *(obra de teatro)*.

enamel [ɪ'næməl] *n* esmalte.
► *vt* (GB *pt & pp* **enamelled**, *ger* **enamelling**; US *pt & pp* **enameled**, *ger* **enameling**) esmaltar.

enchanting [ɪn'tʃaːntɪŋ] *adj* encantador,-ra.

enchantment [ɪn'tʃaːntmənt] *n* encanto, hechizo.

encircle [ɪn'sɜːkəl] *vt* rodear, cercar.

enclose [ɪn'kləʊz] *vt* **1** cercar, rodear. **2** adjuntar: *please find enclosed...*, envío adjunto....

enclosure [ɪn'kləʊʒə'] *n* **1** cercado. **2** anexo, documento adjunto.

encore ['ɒŋkɔː'] *interj* ¡otra!
► *n* repetición.

encounter [ɪn'kaʊntə'] *n* encuentro.
► *vt* encontrar, encontrarse con.

encourage [ɪn'kʌrɪdʒ] *vt* **1** animar, alentar. **2** fomentar.

encouragement [ɪn'kʌrɪdʒmənt] *n* **1** aliento, ánimo. **2** fomento.

encouraging [ɪn'kʌrɪdʒɪŋ] *adj* alentador,-ra.

encyclopaedia [ensaɪkləˈpiːdɪə] *n* enciclopedia.

end [end] *n* **1** cabo *(de cuerda)*. **2** final *(de calle)*. **3** extremo *(de mesa)*. **4** punta *(de palo)*. **5** fin, final, conclusión. **6** objeto, objetivo.

▶ *vt-vi* acabar(se), terminar(se).

● **at the end of** al final de.

● **in the end** al final.

● **to come to an end** acabarse.

to end up *vi* acabar, terminar: *we ended up phoning for a taxi*, acabamos llamando un taxi.

endanger [ɪnˈdeɪndʒəʳ] *vt* poner en peligro.

endearing [ɪnˈdɪərɪŋ] *adj* simpático,-a, atrayente.

endeavour [ɪnˈdevəʳ] (US **endeavor**) *n* esfuerzo, empeño.

▶ *vi* esforzarse.

ending [ˈendɪŋ] *n* final.

endive [ˈendaɪv] *n* endibia.

endless [ˈendləs] *adj* **1** sin fin, interminable. **2** infinito.

endorse [ɪnˈdɔːs] *vt* **1** endosar *(talón)*. **2** aprobar.

endow [ɪnˈdaʊ] *vt* dotar.

endurance [ɪnˈdjʊərəns] *n* resistencia, aguante.

endure [ɪnˈdjʊəʳ] *vt* soportar, resistir.

▶ *vi* durar, perdurar.

enemy [ˈenəmɪ] *n (pl* **-ies**) enemigo,-a.

energetic [enəˈdʒetɪk] *adj* enérgico,-a.

energy [ˈenədʒɪ] *n (pl* **-ies**) energía.

enforce [ɪnˈfɔːs] *vt* hacer cumplir.

engage [ɪnˈgeɪdʒ] *vt* **1** contratar. **2** atraer *(atención)*. **3** engranar con.

● **to engage SB in conversation** entablar conversación con ALGN.

engaged [ɪnˈgeɪdʒd] *adj* **1** prometido,-a. **2** ocupado,-a *(servicio)*. **3** comunicando *(teléfono)*.

● **to get engaged** prometerse.

engagement [ɪnˈgeɪdʒmənt] *n* **1** petición de mano, noviazgo. **2** compromiso, cita.

engine [ˈendʒɪn] *n* **1** motor. **2** máquina, locomotora.

■ **engine driver** maquinista.

■ **engine room** sala de máquinas.

engineer [endʒɪˈnɪəʳ] *n* **1** ingeniero,-a. **2** US maquinista.

▶ *vt fig* maquinar.

engineering [endʒɪˈnɪərɪŋ] *n* ingeniería.

England [ˈɪŋglənd] *n* Inglaterra.

English [ˈɪŋglɪʃ] *adj* inglés,-esa.

▶ *n* **1** inglés,-esa *(persona)*. **2** inglés *(lengua)*.

▶ *npl* **the English** los ingleses.

■ **English Channel** Canal de la Mancha.

Englishman [ˈɪŋglɪʃmən] *n (pl* **Englishmen**) inglés.

Englishwoman [ˈɪŋglɪʃwʊmən] *n (pl* **Englishwomen**) inglesa.

engrave [ɪnˈgreɪv] *vt* grabar.

engrossed [ɪnˈgrəʊst] *adj* absorto,-a.

engulf [ɪnˈgʌlf] *vt* sumergir, sumir.

enhance [ɪnˈhɑːns] *vt* realzar.

enigma [ɪˈnɪgmə] *n* enigma.

enigmatic [enɪgˈmætɪk] *adj* enigmático,-a.

enjoy [ɪnˈdʒɔɪ] *vt* gozar de, disfrutar de: *did you enjoy the show?*, ¿te gustó el espectáculo?

● **to enjoy oneself** divertirse, pasarlo bien.

enjoyable [ɪnˈdʒɔɪəbəl] *adj* agradable, entretenido,-a, ameno,-a.

enjoyment [ɪnˈdʒɔɪmənt] *n* placer, gusto, goce, disfrute.

enlarge [ɪnˈlɑːdʒ] *vt-vi* aumentar(se), ampliar(se) *(fotografía)*.

to enlarge upon *vt* extenderse sobre.

enlargement [ɪnˈlɑːdʒmənt] *n* ampliación.

enlighten [ɪnˈlaɪtən] *vt* iluminar, aclarar.

● **to enlighten SB on STH** aclararle algo a ALGN.

enlist [ɪnˈlɪst] *vt-vi* alistar(se).

enormous [ɪˈnɔːməs] *adj* enorme.

enough [ɪˈnʌf] *adj* bastante, suficiente: *there's enough food for everyone*, hay suficiente comida para todos.

▶ *adv* bastante: *you are not tall enough to play basketball*, no eres lo suficientemente alto para jugar al baloncesto.

▶ *pron* suficiente: *more than enough*, más que suficiente.

● **that's enough!** ¡ya basta!

enquire [ɪŋˈkwaɪəʳ] *vi* **1** preguntar. **2** investigar.

enquiry [ɪŋˈkwaɪərɪ] *n (pl* **-ies**). **1** pregunta. **2** investigación.

● **to make an enquiry** preguntar.

enrage [ɪnˈreɪdʒ] *vt* enfurecer.

enrich [ɪnˈrɪtʃ] *vt* enriquecer.

enrol [ɪnˈrəʊl] *vt-vi* (GB *pt & pp* **enrolled**, *ger* **enrolling**; US *pt & pp* **enroled**, *ger* **enroling**) matricular(se).

enrolment [ɪnˈrəʊlmənt] n matrícula, inscripción.

ensue [ɪnˈsjuː] vi **1** seguir. **2** resultar.

ensure [ɪnˈʃʊəʳ] vt asegurar.

entail [ɪnˈteɪl] vt suponer, implicar, acarrear.

entangle [ɪnˈtæŋɡəl] vt enredar, enmarañar.

enter [ˈentəʳ] vt **1** entrar en *(habitación)*. **2** ingresar en *(organización)*. **3** inscribirse a, presentarse en *(competición)*. **4** anotar, apuntar *(información)*. **5** dar entrada a, introducir.
▶ vi entrar.

to enter into vt **1** iniciar *(negociaciones)*. **2** firmar *(contrato)*. **3** entablar *(conversación)*.

enterprise [ˈentəpraɪz] n **1** empresa. **2** energía, iniciativa, espíritu emprendedor.

entertain [entəˈteɪn] vt **1** entretener, divertir. **2** recibir, invitar. **3** considerar *(idea, propuesta)*.

entertainer [entəˈteɪnəʳ] n artista.

entertaining [entəˈteɪnɪŋ] adj divertido,-a, entretenido,-a.

entertainment [entəˈteɪnmənt] n entretenimiento, diversión.

enthral [ɪnˈθrɔːl] vt (GB pt & pp **enthralled**, ger **enthralling**; US pt & pp **enthraled**, ger **enthraling**) cautivar.

enthralling [ɪnˈθrɔːlɪŋ] adj cautivador,-ra.

enthusiasm [ɪnˈθjuːzɪæzəm] n entusiasmo.

enthusiast [ɪnˈθjuːzɪæst] n entusiasta.

enthusiastic [ɪnθjuːzɪˈæstɪk] adj entusiasta.

enthusiastically [ɪnθjuːzɪˈæstɪklɪ] adv con entusiasmo.

entice [ɪnˈtaɪs] vt atraer, seducir.

entire [ɪnˈtaɪəʳ] adj entero,-a, completo,-a, íntegro,-a.

entirely [ɪnˈtaɪəlɪ] adv completamente, totalmente.

entitle [ɪnˈtaɪtəl] vt dar derecho a.
● **to be entitled 1** titularse *(libro, etc)*. **2** tener derecho *(persona)*: *you are entitled to a discount*, tiene derecho a un descuento.

entity [ˈentɪtɪ] n (pl -ies) entidad.

entrails [ˈentreɪlz] npl entrañas, vísceras.

entrance[1] [ˈentrəns] n **1** entrada. **2** entrada en escena.

● **"No entrance"** "Se prohíbe la entrada".

■ **entrance examination** examen de ingreso.

entrance[2] [enˈtrɑːns] vt encantar, hechizar.

entrant [ˈentrənt] n participante.

entrepreneur [ɒntrəprəˈnɜːʳ] n empresario,-a.

entrust [ɪnˈtrʌst] vt confiar.

entry [ˈentrɪ] n (pl -ies). **1** entrada. **2** participante.

● **"No entry"** "Prohibida la entrada".

enunciate [ɪˈnʌnsɪeɪt] vt **1** pronunciar *(palabra)*. **2** expresar, enunciar *(idea)*.

envelop [ɪnˈveləp] vt envolver.

envelope [ˈenvələʊp] n sobre.

envious [ˈenvɪəs] adj envidioso,-a.

● **to be envious** tener envidia.

environment [ɪnˈvaɪrənmənt] n **1** medio ambiente. **2** ambiente, medio.

environmental [ɪnvaɪərənˈmentəl] adj medioambiental.

envisage [ɪnˈvɪzɪdʒ] vt **1** prever. **2** concebir, imaginar.

envoy [ˈenvɔɪ] n enviado,-a.

envy [ˈenvɪ] n (pl -ies) envidia.
▶ vt (pt & pp -**ied**) envidiar.

enzyme [ˈenzaɪm] n enzima.

ephemeral [ɪˈfemərəl] adj efímero,-a.

epic [ˈepɪk] adj épico,-a.
▶ n epopeya.

epidemic [epɪˈdemɪk] n epidemia.

epilepsy [ˈepɪlepsɪ] n epilepsia.

epileptic [epɪˈleptɪk] adj-n epiléptico,-a.

episode [ˈepɪsəʊd] n episodio.

epitaph [ˈepɪtɑːf] n epitafio.

epoch [ˈiːpɒk] n (pl **epochs**) época.

equal [ˈiːkwəl] adj igual.
▶ n igual: *he has no equal*, no tiene igual.
▶ vt (GB pt & pp **equalled**, ger **equalling**; US pt & pp **equaled**, ger **equaling**). **1** ser igual a, equivaler a: *2 plus 2 equals 4*, 2 más 2 son 4. **2** igualar.

● **all things being equal** en igualdad de condiciones.

● **to be equal to 1** estar a la altura de *(ocasión)*. **2** sentirse con fuerzas para *(tarea)*.

■ **equal rights** igualdad de derechos.

equality [ɪˈkwɒlɪtɪ] n (pl -ies) igualdad.

equalize ['iːkwəlaɪz] *vi* igualar el marcador, empatar.

equally ['iːkwəlɪ] *adv* igualmente, por igual.

equate [ɪ'kweɪt] *vt* equiparar, comparar.

equation [ɪ'kweɪʒən] *n* ecuación.

equator [ɪ'kweɪtəʳ] *n* ecuador.

equilibrium [iːkwɪ'lɪbrɪəm] *n* equilibrio.

equip [ɪ'kwɪp] *vt* (*pt & pp* **equipped**, *ger* **equipping**) equipar, proveer.

equipment [ɪ'kwɪpmənt] *n* **1** equipo, material, artículos. **2** equipamiento.

equitable ['ekwɪtəbəl] *adj* equitativo,-a.

equivalence [ɪ'kwɪvələns] *n* equivalencia.

equivalent [ɪ'kwɪvələnt] *adj* equivalente.
► *n* equivalente.
● **to be equivalent to** equivaler a.

era ['ɪərə] *n* era.

eradicate [ɪ'rædɪkeɪt] *vt* erradicar, extirpar, desarraigar.

erase [ɪ'reɪz] *vt* borrar.

eraser [ɪ'reɪzəʳ] *n* **1** US goma de borrar. **2** borrador *(de pizarra)*.

erect [ɪ'rekt] *adj* **1** derecho,-a, erguido,-a *(persona)*. **2** erecto,-a *(pene)*.
► *vt* **1** levantar, erigir *(monumento)*. **2** armar, montar *(tienda de campaña)*.

erection [ɪ'rekʃən] *n* **1** erección *(de pene)*. **2** construcción *(de edificio)*.

erode [ɪ'rəʊd] *vt* **1** erosionar *(roca)*. **2** corroer, desgastar *(metal)*. **3** *fig* mermar *(poder)*.

erosion [ɪ'rəʊʒən] *n* **1** erosión *(de roca)*. **2** corrosión, desgaste *(de metal)*.

erotic [ɪ'rɒtɪk] *adj* erótico,-a.

errand ['erənd] *n* encargo, recado.
● **to run errands** hacer recados.

erratic [ɪ'rætɪk] *adj* irregular, inconstante.

error ['erəʳ] *n* error.

erupt [ɪ'rʌpt] *vi* **1** entrar en erupción *(volcán)*. **2** estallar *(violencia)*.

eruption [ɪ'rʌpʃən] *n* **1** erupción *(de volcán)*. **2** estallido *(de violencia)*. **3** erupción *(cutánea)*.

escalate ['eskəleɪt] *vi* **1** intensificarse *(guerra)*. **2** aumentar *(precios)*.

escalation [eskə'leɪʃən] *n* **1** escalada *(de guerra)*. **2** subida, aumento *(de precios)*.

escalator ['eskəleɪtəʳ] *n* escalera mecánica.

escapade ['eskəpeɪd, eskə'peɪd] *n* aventura.

escape [ɪ'skeɪp] *n* **1** fuga, huida. **2** fuga, escape *(de gas)*.

► *vi* **1** escaparse, fugarse, huir. **2** escapar *(gas)*.
► *vt* evitar, librarse de.
● **to make one's escape** escaparse.

escort [(*n*) e'skɔːt(*vb*) ɪ'skɔːt] *n* **1** acompañante. **2** escolta.
► *vt* **1** acompañar. **2** escoltar.

ESP[1] ['iː'es'piː] *abbr* (**extrasensory perception**) percepción extrasensorial.

ESP[2] ['iː'es'piː] *abbr* (**English for Specific Purposes**) inglés para fines específicos.

especial [ɪ'speʃəl] *adj* especial, particular.

especially [ɪ'speʃəlɪ] *adv* especialmente, sobre todo.

espionage ['espɪənɑːʒ] *n* espionaje.

Esq. [ɪ'skwaɪəʳ] *abbr* GB Sr D.

essay ['eseɪ] *n* **1** redacción, trabajo. **2** ensayo.

essence ['esəns] *n* esencia.

essential [ɪ'senʃəl] *adj* **1** esencial. **2** vital, indispensable.

essentially [ɪ'senʃəlɪ] *adv* esencialmente.

EST ['iː'es'tiː] *abbr* US (**Eastern Standard Time**) hora del meridiano 75 al oeste de Greenwich.

establish [ɪ'stæblɪʃ] *vt* **1** establecer, fundar, crear. **2** demostrar *(inocencia)*.

establishment [ɪ'stæblɪʃmənt] *n* **1** establecimiento. **2** GB **the Establishment** el poder, el sistema.

estate [ɪ'steɪt] *n* **1** finca. **2** urbanización. **3** bienes.
■ **estate agent** agente inmobiliario,-a.
■ **estate agent's** agencia inmobiliaria.
■ **estate car** GB coche familiar.

esteem [ɪ'stiːm] *vt* **1** apreciar, estimar. **2** juzgar, considerar.
► *n* aprecio.
● **to hold SB in high esteem** apreciar mucho a ALGN.

estimate [(*n*) 'estɪmət(*vb*) 'estɪmeɪt] *n* **1** cálculo. **2** presupuesto.
► *vt* calcular.

estimation [estɪ'meɪʃən] *n* opinión, juicio.

Estonia [e'stəʊnɪə] *n* Estonia.

Estonian [e'stəʊnɪən] *adj* estonio,-a.
► *n* **1** estonio,-a *(persona)*. **2** estonio *(lengua)*.

estuary ['estjʊərɪ] *n* (*pl* **-ies**) estuario.

ETA ['iː'tiː'eɪ] *abbr* (**estimated time of arrival**) hora prevista de llegada.

etch [etʃ] *vt* grabar al aguafuerte.

etching ['etʃɪŋ] *n* aguafuerte.

eternal [ɪˈtɜːnəl] adj eterno,-a.
eternity [ɪˈtɜːnɪtɪ] n eternidad.
ether [ˈiːθəʳ] n éter.
ethic [ˈeθɪk] n ética.
ethical [ˈeθɪkəl] adj ético,-a.
Ethiopia [iːθɪˈəʊpɪə] n Etiopía.
Ethiopian [iːθɪˈəʊpɪən] adj etíope,-a.
► n etíope, etiope.
ethnic [ˈeθnɪk] adj étnico,-a.
ethyl [ˈiːθaɪl, ˈeθɪl] n etilo.
■ ethyl alcohol alcohol etílico.
etiquette [ˈetɪket] n protocolo, etiqueta.
eucalyptus [juːkəˈlɪptəs] n (pl eucalyptuses) eucalipto.
euphemism [ˈjuːfəmɪzəm] n eufemismo.
euphemistic [juːfɪˈmɪstɪk] adj eufemístico,-a.
euro [ˈjʊərəʊ] n euro.
Europe [ˈjʊərəp] n Europa.
European [jʊərəˈpɪən] adj-n europeo,-a.
■ European Community Comunidad Europea.
■ European Union Unión Europea.
euthanasia [juːθəˈneɪzɪə] n eutanasia.
evacuate [ɪˈvækjʊeɪt] vt 1 evacuar. 2 desalojar, desocupar.
evade [ɪˈveɪd] vt evadir, eludir, evitar.
evaluate [ɪˈvæljʊeɪt] vt 1 evaluar. 2 calcular.
evangelical [iːvænˈdʒelɪkəl] adj evangélico,-a.
evangelism [ɪˈvændʒəlɪzəm] n evangelismo.
evangelist [ɪˈvændʒəlɪst] n evangelista.
evaporate [ɪˈvæpəreɪt] vt-vi evaporar(se).
evasion [ɪˈveɪʒən] n evasión.
evasive [ɪˈveɪsɪv] adj evasivo,-a.
eve [iːv] n víspera, vigilia.
even [ˈiːvən] adj 1 llano,-a, liso,-a (superficie). 2 uniforme, regular (color). 3 igual, igualado,-a (puntuación). 4 par (número).
► adv 1 hasta, incluso: even John was there, hasta John estaba allí. 2 siquiera: not even John was there, ni siquiera John estaba allí. 3 aún, todavía: Monday was cold, but today it's even colder, el lunes hacía frío, pero hoy hace más aún.
► vt-vi igualar(se).
● even as mientras.
● even if aunque.
● even so incluso, aun así.
● even though aunque, aun cuando.
● to break even cubrir gastos.

● to get even with SB desquitarse con ALGN.
to even out vt-vi igualar.
evening [ˈiːvnɪŋ] n tarde, noche: yesterday evening, ayer por la tarde; tomorrow evening, mañana por la noche.
● good evening! ¡buenas tardes!, ¡buenas noches!
■ evening dress 1 vestido de noche. 2 traje de etiqueta.
evenly [ˈiːvənlɪ] adv 1 uniformemente, regularmente. 2 equitativamente (repartir).
event [ɪˈvent] n 1 suceso, acontecimiento. 2 prueba (deportiva).
● at all events en todo caso.
● in any event pase lo que pase.
● in the event of en caso de.
eventful [ɪˈventfʊl] adj lleno,-a de acontecimientos, memorable.
eventual [ɪˈventʃʊəl] adj final.
eventuality [ventʃʊˈælɪtɪ] n (pl -ies) eventualidad.
eventually [ɪˈventʃʊəlɪ] adv finalmente.
ever [ˈevəʳ] adv 1 nunca, jamás: nobody ever comes, no viene nunca nadie. 2 alguna vez: have you ever seen her?, ¿la has visto alguna vez? 3 desde: ever since the war, desde la guerra; they met 5 years ago and they've been friends ever since, se conocieron hace 5 años y son amigos desde entonces. 4: better than ever, mejor que nunca; the best ever, el mejor que se ha visto nunca. 5 demonios: what ever shall I do?, ¿qué demonios hago?
● ever so ... muy ....
● for ever (and ever) para siempre.
● hardly ever casi nunca.
evergreen [ˈevəgriːn] adj de hoja perenne.
■ evergreen oak encina.
everlasting [evəˈlɑːstɪŋ] adj eterno,-a.
every [ˈevrɪ] adj cada, todos,-as: every day, cada día, todos los días; every other day, un día sí y otro no.
● every now and then de vez en cuando.
everybody [ˈevrɪbɒdɪ] pron todos,-as, todo el mundo.
everyday [ˈevrɪdeɪ] adj diario,-a, cotidiano,-a, de todos los días.
everyone [ˈevrɪwʌn] pron → everybody.
everything [ˈevrɪθɪŋ] pron todo.

everywhere ['evrɪweə'] *adv* **1** en/por todas partes. **2** a todas partes.

evict [ɪ'vɪkt] *vt* desahuciar.

eviction [ɪ'vɪkʃən] *n* desahucio.

evidence ['evɪdəns] *n* **1** pruebas. **2** indicios.

• **to give evidence** prestar declaración.

evident ['evɪdənt] *adj* evidente, patente.

evidently ['evɪdəntlɪ] *adv* evidentemente, obviamente.

evil ['iːvəl] *adj (comp* **eviller** *o* **more evil**, *superl* **evillest** *o* **most evil**). **1** malo,-a, malvado,-a *(persona)*. **2** malo,-a, perjudicial *(cosa)*.

▶ *n* mal.

evocative [ɪ'vɒkətɪv] *adj* evocador,-ra.

evoke [ɪ'vəʊk] *vt* evocar.

evolution [iːvə'luːʃən] *n* evolución.

evolve [ɪ'vɒlv] *vt* desarrollar.

▶ *vi* evolucionar, desarrollarse.

ewe [juː] *n* oveja *(hembra)*.

exact [ɪg'zækt] *adj* exacto,-a.

▶ *vt* exigir, imponer.

exacting [ɪg'zæktɪŋ] *adj* exigente.

exactly [ɪg'zæktlɪ] *adv* exactamente.

exaggerate [ɪg'zædʒəreɪt] *vt-vi* exagerar.

exaggeration [ɪgzædʒə'reɪʃən] *n* exageración.

exalt [ɪg'zɔːlt] *vt* exaltar.

exam [ɪg'zæm] *n fam* examen.

examination [ɪgzæmɪ'neɪʃən] *n* **1** examen. **2** reconocimiento, revisión, chequeo. **3** interrogatorio.

examine [ɪg'zæmɪn] *vt* **1** inspeccionar, revisar. **2** examinar. **3** hacer un reconocimiento a. **4** interrogar.

examiner [ɪg'zæmɪnə'] *n* examinador,-ra.

example [ɪg'zɑːmpəl] *n* ejemplo.

• **for example** por ejemplo.

exasperate [ɪg'zɑːspəreɪt] *vt* exasperar, irritar.

excavate ['ekskəveɪt] *vt* excavar.

excavation [ekskə'veɪʃən] *n* excavación.

excavator ['ekskəveɪtə'] *n* excavadora.

exceed [ɪk'siːd] *vt* exceder, sobrepasar, superar.

exceedingly [ɪk'siːdɪŋlɪ] *adv* extremadamente, sumamente.

excel [ɪk'sel] *vt* (GB *pt & pp* **excelled**, *ger* **excelling**; US *pt & pp* **exceled**, *ger* **exceling**) aventajar, superar.

▶ *vi* sobresalir.

• **to excel oneself** superarse.

excellence ['eksələns] *n* excelencia.

excellent ['eksələnt] *adj* excelente.

except [ɪk'sept] *prep* excepto, salvo, a excepción de.

▶ *vt* excluir, exceptuar.

exception [ɪk'sepʃən] *n* excepción.

• **to take exception to** STH ofenderse por algo.

• **with the exception of** a excepción de.

exceptional [ɪk'sepʃənəl] *adj* excepcional.

excerpt ['eksɜːpt] *n* extracto, pasaje.

excess [ɪk'ses] *n (pl* **-es**) exceso.

• **in excess of** superior a.

excessive [ɪk'sesɪv] *adj* excesivo,-a.

exchange [ɪks'tʃeɪndʒ] *n* **1** cambio. **2** intercambio *(de ideas)*. **3** canje *m (de presos)*. **4** cambio *(de divisa)*. **5** lonja, bolsa. **6** central telefónica.

▶ *vt* **1** cambiar, intercambiar *(ideas)*. **2** canjear *(presos)*.

• **in exchange for** a cambio de.

▪ **exchange rate** tipo de cambio.

exchequer [ɪks'tʃekə'] *n* tesoro público.

excitable [ɪk'saɪtəbəl] *adj* excitable.

excite [ɪk'saɪt] *vt* **1** emocionar, entusiasmar. **2** excitar *(sexualmente)*. **3** provocar, despertar *(emoción, interés)*.

excited [ɪk'saɪtɪd] *adj* **1** emocionado,-a, entusiasmado,-a. **2** excitado,-a *(sexualmente)*.

excitement [ɪk'saɪtmənt] *n* **1** emoción. **2** agitación, alboroto.

exciting [ɪk'saɪtɪŋ] *adj* emocionante, apasionante.

exclaim [ɪk'skleɪm] *vt-vi* exclamar.

exclamation [eksklə'meɪʃən] *n* exclamación.

▪ **exclamation mark** signo de admiración.

exclude [ɪk'skluːd] *vt* excluir.

excluding [ɪk'skluːdɪŋ] *prep* excepto, menos.

exclusive [ɪk'skluːsɪv] *adj* **1** exclusivo,-a. **2** selecto,-a.

• **exclusive of** con exclusión de.

exclusively [ɪk'skluːsɪvlɪ] *adv* exclusivamente.

excommunicate [ekskə'mjuːnɪkeɪt] *vt* excomulgar.

excommunication [ekskəmjuːnɪ'keɪʃən] *n* excomunión.

excrement ['ekskrɪmənt] *n* excremento.

excrete [ɪk'skriːt] *vt* excretar.

excretion [ɪk'skriːʃən] n excreción.
excruciating [ɪk'skruːʃɪeɪtɪŋ] adj insoportable.
excursion [ɪk'skɜːʒən] n excursión.
excusable [ɪk'skjuːzəbəl] adj excusable.
excuse [(n) ɪk'skjuːs(vb) ɪk'skjuːz] n 1 disculpa. 2 excusa.
▶ vt 1 perdonar, disculpar. 2 justificar.
● **excuse me!** 1 ¡perdone!, ¡por favor! (al interrumpir). 2 ¡disculpe! (al marcharse).
● **to excuse SB from doing STH** eximir a ALGN de hacer algo.
execute ['eksɪkjuːt] vt 1 ejecutar, ajusticiar (reo). 2 ejecutar (plan). 3 cumplir (orden). 4 interpretar (música).
execution [eksɪ'kjuːʃən] n 1 ejecución. 2 cumplimiento (de orden). 3 interpretación (de música).
executioner [eksɪ'kjuːʃənə] n verdugo.
executive [ɪg'zekjətɪv] adj-n ejecutivo,-a.
executor [ɪg'zekjətə] n albacea.
exemplify [ɪg'zemplɪfaɪ] vt (pt & pp -ied) ejemplificar.
exempt [ɪg'zempt] adj exento,-a, libre.
▶ vt eximir.
exemption [ɪg'zempʃən] n exención.
exercise ['eksəsaɪz] n ejercicio.
▶ vt 1 ejercer (poder). 2 sacar de paseo (perro).
▶ vi hacer ejercicio.
■ **exercise book** cuaderno.
exert [ɪg'zɜːt] vt ejercer.
● **to exert oneself** esforzarse.
exhale [eks'heɪl] vt-vi espirar.
exhaust [ɪg'zɔːst] n gases de combustión.
▶ vt agotar.
■ **exhaust pipe** tubo de escape.
exhausted [ɪg'zɔːstɪd] adj agotado,-a.
exhausting [ɪg'zɔːstɪŋ] adj agotador,-ra.
exhaustion [ɪg'zɔːstʃən] n agotamiento.
exhibit [ɪg'zɪbɪt] n objeto en exposición.
▶ vt 1 exponer. 2 mostrar, dar muestras de, manifestar.
exhibition [eksɪ'bɪʃən] n 1 exposición. 2 demostración.
● **to make an exhibition of oneself** ponerse en ridículo.
exhibitor [ɪg'zɪbɪtə] n expositor,-ra.
exhilarating [ɪg'zɪləreɪtɪŋ] adj estimulante, emocionante.
exile ['eksaɪl] n 1 destierro, exilio. 2 desterrado,-a, exiliado,-a.
▶ vt desterrar, exiliar.

exist [ɪg'zɪst] vi 1 existir. 2 subsistir.
existence [ɪg'zɪstəns] n existencia.
● **to come into existence** nacer, crearse, fundarse.
existential [egzɪ'stenʃəl] adj existencial.
existing [egzɪ'stɪŋ] adj existente, actual.
exit ['eksɪt] n 1 salida. 2 mutis (de escenario).
▶ vi hacer mutis, salir de escena.
exorbitant [ɪg'zɔːbɪtənt] adj exorbitante, desorbitado,-a.
exotic [eg'zɒtɪk] adj exótico,-a.
expand [ɪk'spænd] vt-vi 1 ampliar(se) (negocio). 2 dilatar(se) (metal). 3 desarrollar(se) (comercio).
to expand on vt ampliar.
expanse [ɪk'spæns] n extensión.
expansion [ɪk'spænʃən] n 1 ampliación, expansión (de negocio). 2 dilatación (de metal). 3 desarrollo (de comercio).
expatriate [(adj - n) ek'spætrɪət(vb) eks'pætrɪeɪt] adj-n expatriado,-a.
▶ vt desterrar, expatriar.
expect [ɪk'spekt] vt 1 esperar. 2 suponer, imaginar.
● **to be expecting** fam estar embarazada.
expectancy [ɪk'spektənsɪ] n expectación.
expectant [ɪk'spektənt] adj expectante.
■ **expectant mother** futura madre.
expectation [ekspek'teɪʃən] n expectativa.
● **contrary to expectations** contrariamente a lo que se esperaba.
expedient [ɪk'spiːdɪənt] adj conveniente.
▶ n expediente, recurso.
expedition [ekspɪ'dɪʃən] n expedición.
expel [ɪk'spel] vt (pt & pp **expelled**, ger **expelling**) expulsar.
expend [ɪk'spend] vt 1 gastar (dinero). 2 consumir, agotar (recursos). 3 invertir (esfuerzos).
expendable [ɪk'spendəbəl] adj prescindible.
expenditure [ɪk'spendɪtʃə] n gasto, desembolso.
expense [ɪk'spens] n gasto, desembolso.
▶ npl **expenses** gastos.
● **to spare no expense** no escatimar gastos.
● **at the expense of** a expensas de, a costa de.
expensive [ɪk'spensɪv] adj caro,-a, costoso,-a.

experience [ɪk'spɪərɪəns] *n* experiencia.
► *vt* experimentar, tener *(dificultades)*.
experienced [ɪk'spɪərɪənst] *adj* experimentado,-a, con experiencia.
experiment [ɪk'sperɪmənt] *n* experimento.
► *vi* experimentar.
experimental [ɪksperɪ'mentəl] *adj* experimental.
expert ['ekspɜːt] *adj-n* experto,-a.
expertise [ekspɜː'tiːz] *n* pericia.
expire [ɪk'spaɪəʳ] *vi* **1** vencer *(contrato)*. **2** caducar *(pasaporte)*.
expiry [ɪk'spaɪərɪ] *n* vencimiento.
■ **expiry date** fecha de caducidad.
explain [ɪk'spleɪn] *vt-vi* **1** explicar. **2** aclarar.
● **to explain oneself** explicarse.
explanation [eksplə'neɪʃən] *n* **1** explicación. **2** aclaración. **3** disculpa.
explanatory [ɪk'splænətərɪ] *adj* explicativo,-a.
explicit [ɪk'splɪsɪt] *adj* explícito,-a.
explode [ɪk'spləʊd] *vt* hacer estallar, hacer explotar.
► *vi* estallar, explotar, hacer explosión.
exploit [(*n*) 'eksplɔɪt(*vb*) ɪk'splɔɪt] *n* hazaña, proeza.
► *vt* explotar.
exploitation [eksplɔɪ'teɪʃən] *n* explotación.
exploration [eksplə'reɪʃən] *n* exploración.
explore [ɪk'splɔː'] *vt* explorar.
explorer [ɪk'splɔːrəʳ] *n* explorador,-ra.
explosion [ɪk'spləʊʒən] *n* explosión, estallido.
explosive [ɪk'spləʊsɪv] *adj* explosivo,-a.
► *n* explosivo.
■ **explosive device** artefacto explosivo.
export [(*n*) 'ekspɔːt(*vb*) ɪk'spɔːt] *n* **1** exportación. **2** artículo de exportación.
► *vt* exportar.
exporter [ek'spɔːtəʳ] *n* exportador,-ra.
expose [ɪk'spəʊz] *vt* **1** exponer. **2** descubrir, poner al descubierto.
exposure [ɪk'spəʊʒəʳ] *n* **1** exposición. **2** descubrimiento. **3** fotografía.
● **to die of exposure** morir de frío.
express [ɪk'spres] *adj* **1** expreso,-a *(tren)*. **2** urgente *(correo)*.
► *n* (*pl* -**es**) expreso, tren expreso.
► *vt* expresar.
► *adv* urgente.
expression [ɪk'spreʃən] *n* expresión.

expressive [ɪk'spresɪv] *adj* expresivo,-a.
expulsion [ɪk'spʌlʃən] *n* expulsión.
exquisite [ek'skwɪzɪt, 'ekskwɪzɪt] *adj* exquisito,-a.
extend [ɪk'stend] *vt* **1** extender. **2** ampliar *(casa)*. **3** alargar *(carretera)*. **4** alargar *(estancia)*. **5** prorrogar *(visado)*. **6** alargar *(mano)*. **7** dar *(ayuda)*.
► *vi* **1** alargarse, extenderse. **2** sobresalir.
● **to extend an invitation to SB** invitar a ALGN.
extension [ɪk'stenʃən] *n* **1** extensión, ampliación. **2** prórroga. **3** extensión: *my extension number is 764*, mi extensión es 764.
extensive [ɪk'stensɪv] *adj* **1** extenso,-a, amplio,-a. **2** cuantioso *(daños)*.
extensively [ɪk'stensɪvlɪ] *adv* extensamente.
extent [ɪk'stent] *n* **1** extensión, alcance *(de problema, daños)*. **2** extensión *(tamaño)*.
● **to a certain extent** hasta cierto punto.
● **to a greater or lesser extent** en mayor o menor grado.
● **to a large extent** en gran parte.
● **to what extent?** ¿hasta qué punto?
extenuate [ɪk'stenjʊeɪt] *vt* atenuar, disminuir.
exterior [ɪk'stɪərɪəʳ] *adj* exterior.
► *n* exterior.
exterminate [ɪk'stɜːmɪneɪt] *vt* exterminar.
extermination [ɪkstɜːmɪ'neɪʃən] *n* exterminio.
external [ek'stɜːnəl] *adj* externo,-a, exterior.
extinct [ɪk'stɪŋkt] *adj* **1** extinto,-a. **2** extinguido,-a.
● **to become extinct** extinguirse.
extinction [ɪk'stɪŋkʃən] *n* extinción.
extinguish [ɪk'stɪŋgwɪʃ] *vt* extinguir, apagar.
extort [ɪk'stɔːt] *vt* obtener bajo amenaza, sacar.
extortion [ɪk'stɔːʃən] *n* extorsión.
extortionate [ɪk'stɔːʃənət] *adj* desorbitado,-a *(precio)*.
extra ['ekstrə] *adj* **1** extra, adicional, más: *two extra plates*, dos platos más. **2** de sobra: *have you got an extra pen?*, ¿tienes un boli de sobra?
► *adv* extra: *we paid extra*, pagamos un suplemento.

► *n* **1** extra. **2** suplemento. **3** extra, figurante.

■ **extra charge** suplemento.

■ **extra time** prórroga.

extract [(*n*) 'ekstrækt(*vb*) ɪk'strækt] *n* extracto.

► *vt* extraer.

extractor [ɪk'stræktə'] *n* extractor.

extradition [ekstrə'dɪʃən] *n* extradición.

extramarital [ekstrə'mærɪtəl] *adj* extramatrimonial.

extraordinary [ɪk'strɔːdənrɪ] *adj* extraordinario,-a.

extraterrestrial [ekstrətə'restrɪəl] *adj-n* extraterrestre.

extravagance [ɪk'strævəgəns] *n* **1** despilfarro, derroche. **2** extravagancia.

extravagant [ɪk'strævəgənt] *adj* **1** derrochador,-ra. **2** exagerado,-a, excesivo,-a.

extreme [ɪk'striːm] *adj* **1** extremo,-a, intenso, sumo. **2** excepcional *(caso)*.

► *n* extremo.

extremely [ɪk'striːmlɪ] *adv* sumamente, extremadamente.

extremist [ɪk'striːmɪst] *n* extremista.

extremity [ɪk'stremɪtɪ] *n (pl* -**ies)** extremidad.

extricate ['ekstrɪkeɪt] *vt* librar.

extrovert ['ekstrəvɜːt] *adj-n* extrovertido,-a.

exuberant [ɪg'zjuːbərənt] *adj* **1** eufórico,-a. **2** exuberante.

exude [ɪg'zjuːd] *vt-vi* **1** emanar *(felicidad)*. **2** exudar *(resina)*.

exultant [ɪg'zʌltənt] *adj* exultante, triunfante.

eye [aɪ] *n* ojo.

► *vt* observar, mirar con detenimiento.

● **to keep an eye on** vigilar, echar un ojo.

● **to see eye to eye** opinar igual, estar de acuerdo.

● **to turn a blind eye to** hacer la vista gorda a.

eyeball ['aɪbɔːl] *n* globo ocular.

eyebrow ['aɪbraʊ] *n* ceja.

eyelash ['aɪlæʃ] *n (pl* -**es)** pestaña.

eyelid ['aɪlɪd] *n* párpado.

eyeshadow ['aɪʃædəʊ] *n* sombra de ojos.

eyesight ['aɪsaɪt] *n* vista.

eyesore ['aɪsɔː'] *n* monstruosidad.

eyewitness ['aɪwɪtnəs] *n (pl* -**es)** testigo presencial.

F

f ['femɪnɪn] *abbr* fa *(nota)*.

F ['færənhaɪt] *abbr* (***Fahrenheit***) Fahrenheit, F.

FA ['eɪ] *abbr* GB (***Football Association***) Federación de Fútbol.

fable ['feɪbəl] *n* fábula.

fabric ['fæbrɪk] *n* **1** tela, tejido. **2** *fig* estructura.

fabulous ['fæbjələs] *adj* fabuloso,-a.

facade [fə'saːd] *n* fachada.

façade [fə'saːd] *n* fachada.

face [feɪs] *n* **1** cara, rostro, semblante: *she's got a pretty face*, tiene una cara bonita. **2** superficie. **3** cara: *the face of the moon*, la cara de la luna. **4** esfera: *a clock face*, una esfera de reloj. **5** *fig* faz: *to disappear off the face of the earth*, desaparecer de la faz de la tierra.
► *vt* **1** dar a: *the house faces west*, la casa da al oeste. **2** mirar hacia, hallarse frente a, encontrarse ante. **3** afrontar, enfrentarse con/a: *they're facing serious problems*, se enfrentan a serios problemas. **4** soportar.
► *vi* mirar hacia: *he sat down facing the door*, se sentó mirando hacia la puerta.
● **in the face of** ante.
● **to face the facts** afrontar la realidad.
● **to lose face** desprestigiarse.
● **to pull faces** hacer muecas, poner caras raras.
● **to save face** guardar las apariencias.
■ **face cream** crema facial.
■ **face value** valor nominal.
■ **face down** boca abajo.
■ **face up** boca arriba.

to face up to *vt* hacer cara a, afrontar.

faceless ['feɪsləs] *adj* anónimo,-a.

facelift ['feɪslɪft] *n* **1** lifting, estiramiento facial. **2** *fig* renovación.

facet ['fæsɪt] *n* faceta.

facial ['feɪʃəl] *adj* facial.

facilitate [fə'sɪlɪteɪt] *vt* facilitar.

facility [fə'sɪlɪtɪ] *n* (*pl* **-ies**) facilidad.
► *npl* **facilities** instalaciones, servicios: *sports facilities*, instalaciones deportivas.

facsimile [fæk'sɪmɪlɪ] *n* facsímil, facsímile.

fact [fækt] *n* hecho.
● **as a matter of fact** en realidad.
● **in fact** de hecho.
■ **the facts of life** los misterios de la vida, el sexo.

faction ['fækʃən] *n* facción.

factor ['fæktə] *n* factor.

factory ['fæktərɪ] *n* (*pl* **-ies**) fábrica.

factual ['fæktʃʊəl] *adj* factual.

faculty ['fækəltɪ] *n* (*pl* **-ies**). **1** facultad. **2** US profesorado.

fad [fæd] *n* **1** capricho. **2** moda.

fade [feɪd] *vt* desteñir.
► *vi* **1** desteñirse, perder el color. **2** apagarse.

to fade away *vi* desvanecerse.

faeces ['fiːsiːz] *npl* heces.

fag [fæg] *n* **1** *fam* lata, rollo. **2** GB *fam* pitillo. **3** US *fam* marica.

fail [feɪl] *n* suspenso.
► *vt-vi* **1** fallar: *he failed in his attempt to make peace*, fracasó en su intento de hacer las paces. **2** suspender: *he failed his driving test*, suspendió el examen de conducir.
► *vi* **1** fracasar: *their attempt to climb the mountain failed*, su intento de escalar la montaña fracasó. **2** quebrar, hacer bancarrota.

- **to fail to** no lograr, dejar de: *the alarm failed to go off*, la alarma no saltó.
- **without fail** sin falta.

failing ['feɪlɪŋ] *n* defecto, fallo.

▶ *prep* a falta de: *failing that, ask John if he knows how to do it*, si eso no resulta, pregunta a John si sabe hacerlo.

failure ['feɪljəʳ] *n* **1** fracaso. **2** quiebra. **3** fallo, avería: *engine failure*, fallo del motor. **4**: *her failure to answer*, el hecho de que no contestara.

faint [feɪnt] *adj* **1** débil: *a faint sound*, un sonido débil. **2** pálido,-a. **3** vago,-a: *a faint recollection*, un vago recuerdo.

▶ *vi* desmayarse.

fair[1] [feəʳ] *adj* **1** justo,-a, equitativo,-a: *it's not fair!*, ¡no es justo! **2** considerable: *he has a fair chance of getting the job*, tiene bastantes posibilidades de conseguir el trabajo. **3** rubio,-a, blanco,-a: *fair hair*, pelo rubio; *fair skin*, piel blanca. **4** *fml* bello,-a: *the fair sex*, el sexo débil.

- **fair and square** merecidamente.
- **fair enough** de acuerdo.
- **fair copy** copia en limpio.
- **fair play** juego limpio.

fair[2] [feəʳ] *n* feria, mercado.

fairground ['feəɡraʊnd] *n* recinto ferial, parque de atracciones.

fairly ['feəlɪ] *adv* **1** justamente. **2** bastante: *it's fairly good*, es bastante bueno.

fairness ['feənəs] *n* **1** justicia: *in fairness*, para ser justos. **2** color rubio, palidez, blancura.

fairy ['feərɪ] *n* (*pl* -ies). **1** hada. **2** *fam* marica.

- **fairy tale** cuento de hadas.

faith [feɪθ] *n* **1** fe: *the Christian faith*, la fe cristiana. **2** confianza: *you must have faith in yourself*, debes tener confianza en ti mismo.

- **in bad faith** de mala fe.
- **in good faith** de buena fe.

faithful ['feɪθfʊl] *adj* fiel.

faithfully ['feɪθfʊlɪ] *adv* fielmente.

- **yours faithfully** le saluda atentamente.

faithfulness ['feɪθfʊlnəs] *n* fidelidad.

fake [feɪk] *n* **1** falsificación. **2** impostor,-ra, farsante.

▶ *adj* falso,-a, falsificado,-a.

▶ *vt* **1** falsificar. **2** fingir.

falcon ['fɔːlkən] *n* halcón.

fall [fɔːl] *n* **1** caída: *a fall from that*

height could be fatal, una caída desde esa altura podría resultar mortal. **2** nevada. **3** descenso: *a fall in the temperature*, un descenso en la temperatura. **4** US otoño.

▶ *vi* (*pt* **fell** [fel], *pp* **fallen** ['fɔːlən]). **1** caer, caerse: *the leaves fall from the trees in autumn*, las hojas caen de los árboles en otoño. **2** bajar: *the price of fruit falls in summer*, el precio de la fruta baja en verano.

▶ *npl* **falls** cascada.

- **to fall asleep** dormirse.
- **to fall in love** enamorarse.
- **to fall short** no alcanzar.
- **to fall flat** salir mal, no funcionar.
- **to fall to pieces** hacerse pedazos.

to fall back *vi* retroceder.

to fall back on *vt* recurrir a, echar mano de.

to fall behind *vi* retrasarse.

to fall down *vt-vi* caer, caerse: *he fell down the stairs*, se cayó por la escalera.

to fall for *vt* **1** dejarse engañar por. **2** *fam* enamorarse de.

to fall off *vt-vi* caer, caerse: *he fell off his chair*, se cayó de la silla; *the button fell off*, se cayó el botón.

to fall out *vi* reñir, enfadarse.

to fall through *vi* fracasar: *my plans fell through*, mis planes fracasaron.

fallacy ['fæləsɪ] *n* (*pl* -ies) falacia.

fallen ['fɔːlən] *pp* → **fall**.

fallible ['fæləbəl] *adj* falible.

fall-out ['fɔːlaʊt] *n* lluvia radiactiva.

- **fall-out shelter** refugio atómico.

fallow ['fæləʊ] *adj* en barbecho.

false [fɔːls] *adj* falso,-a.

- **false alarm** falsa alarma.
- **false bottom** doble fondo.
- **false start** salida nula.
- **false teeth** dentadura postiza.

falsehood ['fɔːlshʊd] *n* falsedad.

falsely ['fɔːlslɪ] *adv* falsamente.

falsify ['fɔːlsɪfaɪ] *vt* (*pt & pp* -**ied**) falsificar.

falter ['fɔːltəʳ] *vi* vacilar, titubear.

fame [feɪm] *n* fama.

familiar [fəˈmɪlɪəʳ] *adj* **1** familiar: *the name sounds familiar*, el nombre me resulta familiar. **2** familiarizado. **3** íntimo,-a.

familiarity [fəmɪlɪˈærɪtɪ] *n* **1** familiaridad. **2** conocimientos: *his familiarity with* *the problem will be of great help*, sus conocimientos del problema nos serán de gran ayuda.

familiarize [fəˈmɪliəraɪz] *vt* familiarizar.

family [ˈfæmɪli] *n* (*pl* -**ies**) familia.
- **to run in the family** venir de familia.
- ■ **family doctor** médico,-a de cabecera.
- ■ **family film** película apta para todos los públicos.
- ■ **family name** apellido.
- ■ **family planning** planificación familiar.
- ■ **family tree** árbol genealógico.

famine [ˈfæmɪn] *n* hambre.

famished [ˈfæmɪʃt] *adj* muerto,-a de hambre.

famous [ˈfeɪməs] *adj* famoso,-a, célebre.

famously [ˈfeɪməslɪ] *adv fam* estupendamente.

fan [fæn] *n* **1** abanico. **2** ventilador *(eléctrico)*. **3** aficionado,-a, admirador,-ra, fan: *thousands of fans went to the concert*, miles de admiradores fueron al concierto; *a football fan*, un hincha.
► *vt* (*pt & pp* **fanned**, *ger* **fanning**). **1** abanicar, ventilar: *he fanned himself with his hat*, se abanicaba con el sombrero. **2** *fig* avivar: *to fan the flames*, avivar las llamas.
to fan out *vi* abrirse en abanico.

fanatic [fəˈnætɪk] *adj-n* fanático,-a.

fanciful [ˈfænsɪfʊl] *adj* **1** rocambolesco,-a: *he always has fanciful ideas*, siempre tiene ideas rocambolescas. **2** imaginativo,-a.

fancy [ˈfænsɪ] *n* (*pl* -**ies**). **1** fantasía, imaginación. **2** capricho, antojo.
► *adj* (-**ier**, -**iest**) elegante: *a fancy hotel*, un hotel elegante.
► *vt* (*pt & pp* -**ied**). **1** imaginarse, figurarse. **2** apetecer: *I fancy an ice cream*, me apetece un helado. **3** gustar: *my friend fancies you*, le gustas a mi amigo.
- **fancy that!** ¡figúrate!, ¡imagínate!
- **to take a fancy to** STH encapricharse con algo.
- ■ **fancy dress** disfraz: *a fancy dress party*, una fiesta de disfraces.

fancy-free [ˈfænsɪˈfriː] *adj* sin compromiso.

fanfare [ˈfænfeəʳ] *n* fanfarria.

fang [fæŋ] *n* colmillo.

fantastic [fænˈtæstɪk] *adj* fantástico,-a.

fantasy [ˈfæntəsɪ] *n* (*pl* -**ies**) fantasía.

FAO [ˈefeɪˈəʊ] *abbr* (*Food and Agriculture Organization*) Organización para la Agricultura y la Alimentación; *(abbreviation)* FAO.

far [fɑːʳ] *adj* (*comp* **farther** *o* **further**, *superl* **farthest** *o* **furthest**). **1** lejano,-a: *in a far country*, en un país lejano. **2** opuesto,-a, extremo,-a: *at the far end of the stadium*, en el otro extremo del estadio.
► *adv* **1** lejos: *how far is it?*, ¿a qué distancia está? **2** mucho: *far better*, mucho mejor; *it's far too expensive*, es demasiado caro.
- **as far as** hasta: *he ran as far as the church and came back*, corrió hasta la iglesia y volvió.
- **as/so far as I know** que yo sepa.
- **by far** con mucho.
- **far and wide** por todas partes.
- **far away** lejos.
- **in so far as ...** en la medida en que ....
- **so far 1** hasta ahora: *so far, everything's going well*, hasta ahora, todo ha ido bien. **2** hasta cierto punto: *he can only help so far*, sólo puede ayudar hasta cierto punto.

faraway [ˈfɑːrəweɪ] *adj* lejano,-a, remoto,-a, perdido,-a.

farce [fɑːs] *n* farsa.

farcical [ˈfɑːsɪkəl] *adj* absurdo,-a.

fare [feəʳ] *n* tarifa, precio del billete/viaje, pasaje: *have you got the bus fare?*, ¿tienes el dinero del autobús?
► *vi* desenvolverse: *he fared well in the exam*, le fue bien en el examen.

farewell [feəˈwel] *interj* ¡adiós!
► *n* despedida.
- **to bid/ say farewell** despedirse.

far-fetched [fɑːˈfetʃt] *adj* rebuscado,-a, inverosímil.

farm [fɑːm] *n* granja.
► *vt* cultivar, labrar.
► *vi* cultivar la tierra.
- ■ **farm labourer** jornalero,-a agrícola.

farmer [ˈfɑːməʳ] *n* agricultor,-ra, granjero,-a.

farmhouse [ˈfɑːmhaʊs] *n* granja.

farming [ˈfɑːmɪŋ] *n* agricultura, ganadería.
- ■ **farming industry** industria agropecuaria.

farmyard ['fɑːmjɑːd] *n* corral.

far-reaching [fɑː'riːtʃɪŋ] *adj* de gran alcance.

far-sighted [fɑː'saɪtɪd] *adj* previsor,-ra.

fart [fɑːt] *n fam* pedo.
► *vi fam* tirarse un pedo.

farther ['fɑːðəʳ] *adj-adv* → far.

farthest ['fɑːðɪst] *adj-adv* → far.

fascinate ['fæsɪneɪt] *vt* fascinar.

fascinating ['fæsɪneɪtɪŋ] *adj* fascinante.

fascination [fæsɪ'neɪʃən] *n* fascinación.

fascism ['fæʃɪzəm] *n* fascismo.

fascist ['fæʃɪst] *adj* fascista.
► *n* fascista.

fashion ['fæʃən] *n* **1** moda. **2** modo.
► *vt* formar, labrar.
● **in fashion** de moda.
● **out of fashion** pasado,-a de moda.

fashionable ['fæʃənəbəl] *adj* de moda.

fashionably ['fæʃənəblɪ] *adv* a la moda.

fast[1] [fɑːst] *adj* **1** rápido,-a: *a fast train*, un tren rápido. **2** sólido,-a, que no destiñe: *fast colours*, colores sólidos. **3** adelantado,-a: *my watch is fast*, mi reloj está adelantado.
► *adv* **1** rápidamente, deprisa: *how fast was he going?*, ¿a qué velocidad iba?; *she was driving very fast*, corría mucho. **2** firmemente: *fast asleep*, profundamente dormido,-a.
● **to stand fast** mantenerse firme.
● **not so fast!** *fam* ¡un momento!
■ **fast food** comida rápida.

fast[2] [fɑːst] *vi* ayunar.
► *n* ayuno.

fasten ['fɑːsən] *vt* **1** fijar, sujetar. **2** atar: *he didn't fasten his tie*, no se ató la corbata. **3** abrochar: *he fastened his coat*, se abrochó el abrigo.
► *vi* cerrarse, abrochar(se).

fastener ['fɑːsənəʳ] *n* cierre.

fastidious [fæ'stɪdɪəs] *adj* quisquilloso,-a.

fat [fæt] *adj* (*comp* **fatter**, *superl* **fattest**) gordo,-a.
► *n* grasa.
● **to get fat** engordar.

fatal ['feɪtəl] *adj* **1** fatídico: *a fatal mistake*, un error fatídico. **2** mortal: *a fatal wound*, una herida mortal.

fatality [fə'tælɪtɪ] *n* (*pl* **-ies**) víctima mortal.

fate [feɪt] *n* **1** destino. **2** suerte: *to tempt fate*, tentar a la suerte.

fated ['feɪtɪd] *adj* predestinado,-a.

fateful ['feɪtfʊl] *adj* fatídico,-a: *the fateful day*, el día fatídico.

father ['fɑːðəʳ] *n* padre.
► *vt* engendrar.
● **like father, like son** de tal palo, tal astilla.
■ **Father Christmas** Papá Noel.
■ **Our Father** Padre Nuestro.

father-in-law ['fɑːðərɪnlɔː] *n* (*pl* **fathers-in-law**) suegro.

fatherland ['fɑːðəlænd] *n* patria.

fatherly ['fɑːðəlɪ] *adj* paternal.

fathom ['fæðəm] *n* braza.
► *vt* penetrar en, comprender.

fatigue [fə'tiːg] *n* fatiga, cansancio.
► *vt fml* fatigar, cansar.

fatten ['fætən] *vt* **1** cebar. **2** engordar.

fatty ['fætɪ] *adj* (**-ier**, **-iest**). **1** graso,-a. **2** gordito,-a.

fatuous ['fætjʊəs] *adj* fatuo,-a.

faucet ['fɔːsɪt] *n* US grifo.

fault [fɔːlt] *n* **1** defecto, desperfecto: *a technical fault*, un fallo técnico. **2** culpa: *it's his fault*, es culpa suya. **3** error, falta: *there's a fault in the invoice*, hay un error en la factura. **4** falla (geológica). **5** falta (en deporte).
► *vt* criticar.
● **to be at fault** tener la culpa.
● **to find fault with** poner reparos a, criticar.

fault-finding ['fɔːltfaɪndɪŋ] *adj* criticón,-ona.

faultless ['fɔːltləs] *adj* perfecto,-a.

faulty ['fɔːltɪ] *adj* (**-ier**, **-iest**) defectuoso,-a.

fauna ['fɔːnə] *n* fauna.

faux pas [fəʊ'pɑː] *n* (*pl* **faux pas**) metedura de pata.

favour ['feɪvəʳ] (US **favor**) *n* favor: *will you do me a favour?*, ¿me puedes hacer un favor?
► *vt* **1** favorecer. **2** estar a favor de.
● **in favour of** partidario,-a de.

favourable ['feɪvərəbəl] (US **favorable**) *adj* favorable.

favourite ['feɪvərɪt] (US **favorite**) *adj-n* preferido,-a.

favouritism ['feɪvərɪtɪzəm] (US **favoritism**) *n* favoritismo.

fawn [fɔːn] *n* cervato.
► *adj-n* beige.

to fawn on *vt* adular, lisonjear.

fax [fæks] *n* (*pl* **faxes**) fax.
▶ *vt* enviar por fax.
FBI ['ef'biː'aɪ] *abbr* (*Federal Bureau of Investigation*) FBI.
FC ['ef'siː] *abbr* GB (*Football Club*) CF.
fear [fɪər] *n* miedo, temor: *he has a fear of snakes*, tiene miedo de las serpientes; *my fears were confirmed*, mis temores se confirmaron.
▶ *vt-vi* temer, tener miedo: *I feared that something had happened to you*, temí que te hubiera pasado algo.
fearful ['fɪəfʊl] *adj* **1** miedoso,-a: *he's so fearful he won't get near a dog*, es tan miedoso que no se acerca a los perros. **2** terrible, espantoso,-a, tremendo,-a: *he's a fearful liar*, es un mentiroso tremendo.
fearless ['fɪələs] *adj* intrépido,-a.
fearsome ['fɪəsəm] *adj* aterrador,-a.
feasible ['fiːzəbl] *adj* factible, viable.
feast [fiːst] *n* **1** festín, banquete. **2** fiesta de guardar.
● **to feast your eyes on STH** regalarse la vista con algo.
feat [fiːt] *n* proeza, hazaña.
feather ['feðər] *n* pluma.
feature ['fiːtʃər] *n* **1** rasgo, facción. **2** rasgo, característica. **3** reportaje.
▶ *vt* **1** poner de relieve. **2** tener como protagonista.
▶ *vi* figurar, constar.
■ **feature film** largometraje.
Feb [feb] *abbr* (*February*) febrero.
February ['februəri] *n* febrero.
fed [fed] *pt-pp* → feed.
federal ['fedərəl] *adj* federal.
federation [fedə'reɪʃən] *n* federación.
fed up [fed'ʌp] *adj* fam harto,-a: *I'm fed up with homework*, estoy harto de los deberes.
fee [fiː] *n* honorarios, cuota, tarifa.
feeble ['fiːbl] *adj* débil.
feed [fiːd] *n* pienso.
▶ *vt* (*pt & pp* **fed**). **1** alimentar, dar de comer a: *what do you feed your dog?*, ¿qué le das de comer a tu perro? **2** introducir: *to feed data*, introducir datos.
▶ *vi* alimentarse: *he fed on the vegetables from his garden*, se alimentaba de las verduras de su jardín.
feedback ['fiːdbæk] *n* **1** realimentación. **2** *fig* reacción, feedback.
feel [fiːl] *n* tacto, sensación.

▶ *vt* (*pt & pp* **felt**). **1** tocar, palpar: *she felt his forehead*, le tocó la frente. **2** sentir, notar, apreciar: *I can feel your heart beating*, noto cómo te late el corazón; *I felt myself blushing*, sentí que me ponía colorado. **3** creer: *I feel I ought to tell her*, creo que debería decírselo.
▶ *vi* **1** sentir(se), encontrarse: *do you feel ill?*, ¿te encuentras mal? **2** parecer: *it feels like leather*, parece piel. **3** opinar: *how do you feel about the new project?*, ¿qué te parece el nuevo proyecto?
● **to feel like** apetecer: *I feel like an ice cream*, me apetece un helado.
● **to feel like doing STH** tener ganas de hacer algo.
to feel for *vt* compadecer a, compadecerse de.
feeler ['fiːlər] *n* antena.
feeling ['fiːlɪŋ] *n* **1** sentimiento: *a feeling of guilt*, un sentimiento de culpa. **2** sensación: *a feeling of tiredness*, una sensación de cansancio. **3** impresión: *I have the feeling that something will happen*, tengo la impresión de que pasará algo. **4** sentir, opinión: *what are your feelings on that project?*, ¿qué piensas de ese proyecto?
▶ *adj* sensible, compasivo,-a.
● **no hard feelings** *fam* no nos guardemos rencor.
● **to hurt somebody's feelings** herir los sentimientos de alguien.
feet [fiːt] *npl* → foot.
feign [feɪn] *vt* fingir, aparentar.
feint [feɪnt] *n* *fml* finta.
feline ['fiːlaɪn] *adj-n* felino,-a.
fell¹ [fel] *vt* **1** talar. **2** derribar.
fell² [fel] *pt* → fall.
fellow ['feləʊ] *n* *fam* tipo, tío: *he's a nice fellow*, es buena gente.
▶ *adj* compañero,-a: *fellow citizen*, conciudadano,-a; *fellow student*, compañero,-a de estudios; *fellow worker*, compañero,-a de trabajo.
fellowship ['feləʊʃɪp] *n* **1** asociación, sociedad. **2** compañerismo. **3** beca.
felony ['feləni] *n* (*pl* -**ies**) crimen, delito grave.
felt¹ [felt] *pt-pp* → feel.
felt² [felt] *n* fieltro.
felt-tip pen ['felttɪp'pen] *n* rotulador.
female ['fiːmeɪl] *n* **1** hembra. **2** mujer,

chica: *a white female*, una mujer blanca.
► *adj* **1** femenino,-a: *the female sex*, el sexo femenino. **2** mujer: *a female singer*, una cantante. **3** hembra: *a female elephant*, un elefante hembra.
feminine ['feminin] *adj* femenino,-a.
► *n* femenino.
feminism ['feminizəm] *n* feminismo.
feminist ['feminist] *adj* feminista.
► *n* feminista.
fence [fens] *n* valla, cerca.
► *vi* practicar la esgrima.
► *vt* cercar: *they fenced the garden with wire*, cercaron el jardín con alambre.
● **to sit on the fence** ver los toros desde la barrera.
to fence off *vt* separar mediante cercas.
fencing ['fensɪŋ] *n* **1** esgrima. **2** material para cercas.
fend [fend] *vi* **to fend for oneself** valerse por sí mismo,-a.
to fend off *vt fig* parar, desviar, esquivar.
fender ['fendəʳ] *n* **1** pantalla. **2** US parachoques.
fennel ['fenəl] *n* hinojo.
ferment [*(n)* 'fɜːmənt*(vb)* fə'ment] *n* fermento.
► *vt-vi* fermentar.
fermentation [fɜːmen'teɪʃən] *n* fermentación.
fern [fɜːn] *n* helecho.
ferocious [fə'rəʊʃəs] *adj* feroz.
ferocity [fə'rɒsɪti] *n* ferocidad.
ferret ['ferɪt] *n* hurón.
to ferret out *vt* descubrir.
ferrous ['ferəs] *adj* ferroso,-a.
ferry ['feri] *n (pl* **-ies)** transbordador, ferry.
► *vt-vi (pt & pp* **-ied)** transportar.
fertile ['fɜːtaɪl] *adj* fértil, fecundo,-a: *fertile land*, tierra fértil.
fertility [fə'tɪlɪti] *n* fertilidad.
fertilize ['fɜːtɪlaɪz] *vt* **1** fertilizar, abonar. **2** fecundar.
fertilizer ['fɜːtɪlaɪzəʳ] *n* fertilizante, abono.
fervent ['fɜːvənt] *adj* ferviente, fervoroso,-a.
fervour ['fɜːvəʳ] (US **fervor**) *n* fervor.
fester ['festəʳ] *vi* enconarse: *a festering sore*, una llaga purulenta.
festival ['festɪvəl] *n* **1** festival: *a film festival*, un festival de cine. **2** fiesta: *Christmas is a religious festival*, la Navidad es una fiesta religiosa.

fetch [fetʃ] *vt* ir a por, ir a buscar, buscar: *will you fetch my slippers?*, ¿me traes las zapatillas, por favor?; *could you fetch the children from school?*, ¿puedes ir a buscar a los niños al colegio?
fête [feɪt] *n* fiesta.
► *vt* festejar.
fetid ['fetɪd] *adj* fétido,-a.
fetish ['fetɪʃ] *n (pl* **-es)** fetiche.
fetishist ['fetɪʃɪst] *n* fetichista.
fetter ['fetəʳ] *vt* encadenar.
► *npl* **fetters** grillo, grilletes, cadenas.
feud [fjuːd] *n* enemistad *(duradera)*.
feudal ['fjuːdəl] *adj* feudal.
feudalism ['fjuːdəlɪzəm] *n* feudalismo.
fever ['fiːvəʳ] *n* fiebre: *she has a high fever*, tiene mucha fiebre.
feverish ['fiːvərɪʃ] *adj* febril.
few [fjuː] *adj-pron* **1** pocos,-as: *there are few frogs in the lake*, hay pocas ranas en el lago; *we saw fewer people than expected*, vimos menos gente de la que esperábamos. **2 a few** unos,-as cuantos,-as, algunos,-as: *a few of them*, algunos de ellos; *a few days*, unos cuantos días.
● **as few as** solamente.
● **no fewer than** no menos de.
● **quite a few** un buen número, unos cuantos: *he wrote quite a few books*, escribió unos cuantos libros.
fiancé [fɪ'ænseɪ] *n* prometido.
fiancée [fɪ'ænseɪ] *n* prometida.
fiasco [fɪ'æskəʊ] *n (pl* **-s** o **-es)** fiasco, fracaso.
fib [fɪb] *n fam* bola.
► *vi (pt & pp* **fibbed**, *ger* **fibbing)** *fam* contar bolas.
fibre ['faɪbəʳ] (US **fiber**) *n* fibra.
fibreglass ['faɪbəglɑːs] (US **fiberglass**) *n* fibra de vidrio.
fibrous ['faɪbrəs] *adj* fibroso,-a.
fickle ['fɪkəl] *adj* inconstante, voluble.
fiction ['fɪkʃən] *n* **1** novela, narrativa. **2** ficción: *a work of fiction*, una obra de ficción.
fictional ['fɪkʃənəl] *adj* ficticio,-a.
fictitious [fɪk'tɪʃəs] *adj* ficticio,-a.
fiddle ['fɪdəl] *n* **1** *fam* violín. **2** *fam* estafa, trampa.
► *vi fam* juguetear: *don't fiddle with the stereo, you'll break it*, no juegues con el estéreo, lo vas a romper.
► *vt fam* falsificar.

to fiddle about/around vi fam perder el tiempo: *stop fiddling around and get down to work*, para de perder el tiempo y ponte a trabajar.

fiddler ['fɪdləʳ] n fam violinista.

fidelity [fɪ'delɪtɪ] n fidelidad.

fidget ['fɪdʒɪt] n persona inquieta.
  ▶ vi moverse, no poder estarse quieto,-a: *stop fidgeting!*, iestáte quieto!
  ● **to fidget with** jugar con.

fidgety ['fɪdʒɪtɪ] adj inquieto,-a.

field [fiːld] n 1 campo: *a field of wheat*, un campo de trigo. 2 campo, área, esfera: *he's a major expert in his field*, es un gran experto en su campo. 3 campo, terreno: *a football field*, un campo de fútbol. 4 yacimiento: *a coal field*, un yacimiento de carbón.

fiend [fiːnd] n 1 demonio, diablo. 2 fam fanático,-a.

fiendish ['fiːndɪʃ] adj diabólico,-a.

fierce [fɪəs] adj 1 feroz: *a fierce lion*, un león feroz. 2 fig fuerte, intenso,-a: *a fierce wind*, un fuerte viento.

fiery ['faɪərɪ] adj (-ier, -iest). 1 encendido,-a. 2 fig fogoso,-a.

fifteen [fɪf'tiːn] num quince.

fifteenth [fɪf'tiːnθ] adj decimoquinto,-a.
  ▶ n 1 decimoquinto. 2 decimoquinta parte. 3 quince (en fecha).

fifth [fɪfθ] adj quinto,-a.
  ▶ n 1 quinto. 2 quinta parte. 3 cinco (en fecha).

fiftieth ['fɪftɪəθ] adj quincuagésimo,-a.
  ▶ n 1 quincuagésimo. 2 quincuagésima parte.

fifty ['fɪftɪ] num cincuenta.

fifties ['fɪftɪz] n **the fifties** los años cincuenta, la década de los años cincuenta: *England in the fifties*, la Inglaterra de los años cincuenta; *she's in her fifties*, tiene cincuenta y tantos años.

fig [fɪg] n higo.
  ■ **fig tree** higuera.

fight [faɪt] n 1 lucha: *the fight for survival*, la lucha por la supervivencia. 2 pelea: *they had a fight*, se pelearon.
  ▶ vi (pt & pp fought) pelearse, discutir: *two boys were fighting*, dos chicos se pelearon.
  ▶ vt-vi 1 pelearse, luchar: *our soldiers are fighting the enemy*, nuestros soldados luchan contra el enemigo. 2 fig lu-

char, combatir: *they are fighting against the invaders*, luchan contra los invasores.

to fight back vi resistir, defenderse.

to fight off vt rechazar.

fighter ['faɪtəʳ] n 1 combatiente. 2 boxeador,-ra, púgil. 3 fig luchador,-ra.
  ■ **fighter plane** caza, avión de caza.

figurative ['fɪgərətɪv] adj figurado,-a.

figure ['fɪgəʳ] n 1 forma, figura: *a china figure*, una figura de porcelana. 2 figura, tipo: *she has a good figure*, tiene un buen tipo. 3 figura, personaje: *he's a public figure*, es un personaje público. 4 cifra, número: *a three figure number*, un número de tres cifras.
  ▶ vi figurar, constar: *the price doesn't figure in the list*, el precio no figura en la lista.
  ▶ vt US suponer: *I figure she'll come*, supongo que vendrá.
  ● **that figures!** iya me parecía a mí!
  ● **figure of speech** figura retórica.
  ■ **figure skating** patinaje artístico.

to figure out vt fam comprender, explicarse: *I can't figure out why she did it*, no me explico por qué lo hizo.

figurehead ['fɪgəhed] n 1 mascarón de proa. 2 fig figura decorativa.

filament ['fɪləmənt] n filamento.

file [faɪl] n 1 lima. 2 carpeta. 3 archivo, expediente. 4 archivo, fichero. 5 fila.
  ▶ vt 1 limar: *she files her nails*, se lima las uñas. 2 archivar, fichar. 3 presentar: *to file a demand*, presentar una demanda.
  ▶ vi desfilar: *the soldiers filed out*, los soldados salieron en fila.
  ● **in single file** en fila india.
  ● **to be on file** estar archivado,-a.

filigree ['fɪlɪgriː] n filigrana.

filing cabinet ['faɪlɪŋkæbɪnət] n archivador.

Filipino [fɪlɪ'piːnəʊ] adj-n filipino,-a.

fill [fɪl] vt 1 llenar: *please, fill the tank with petrol*, por favor, llene el depósito de gasolina. 2 rellenar. 3 empastar.
  ● **to have had one's fill** estar harto,-a.

to fill in vt 1 rellenar: *to fill in a form*, rellenar un impreso. 2 poner al corriente: *she filled him in on the latest events*, le puso al corriente de los últimos acontecimientos.

to fill in for vt sustituir a.

to fill out vi **1** rellenar: *to fill out a form*, rellenar un impreso. **2** engordar.

to fill up vt-vi llenar(se): *to fill up the tank*, llenar el depósito.

fillet ['fɪlɪt] n filete.

filling ['fɪlɪŋ] n **1** empaste. **2** relleno.

■ **filling station** gasolinera.

filly ['fɪlɪ] n (pl **-ies**) potra.

film [fɪlm] n **1** película, film, filme. **2** capa, película.
► vt rodar, filmar.

■ **film star** estrella de cine.

filter ['fɪltə'] n filtro.
► vt-vi filtrar(se): *we have to filter the water*, tenemos que filtrar el agua.

filth [fɪlθ] n **1** suciedad, porquería. **2** fig obscenidades.

filthy ['fɪlθɪ] adj (**-ier**, **-iest**) sucio,-a, asqueroso,-a.

fin [fɪn] n aleta.

final ['faɪnəl] adj **1** final, último,-a: *the final scene of the play*, la última escena de la obra. **2** definitivo,-a: *this is the final copy*, ésta es la copia definitiva.
► n final.
► npl **finals** exámenes finales.

finalist ['faɪnəlɪst] n finalista.

finalize ['faɪnəlaɪz] vt ultimar.

finally ['faɪnəlɪ] adv **1** por fin: *we finally managed to catch the thief*, por fin conseguimos atrapar al ladrón. **2** por último, finalmente: *finally, I must thank everybody for coming*, por último, debo dar las gracias a todos por haber venido.

finance ['faɪnæns] vt financiar.
► n finanzas: *the Minister of Finance*, el Ministro de Hacienda.
► npl **finances** fondos.

financial [faɪ'nænʃəl] adj financiero,-a, económico: *he has financial problems*, tiene problemas económicos.

financier [faɪ'nænsɪə'] n financiero,-a.

find [faɪnd] n hallazgo.
► vt (pt & pp **found**). **1** encontrar, hallar: *I can't find the exit*, no puedo encontrar la salida. **2** declarar: *he was found guilty*, lo declararon culpable.

● **to find one's way** encontrar el camino.

to find out vt-vi averiguar: *we must find out who did it*, debemos averiguar quién lo hizo.
► vi enterarse: *his boss found out about*

his stealing money, su jefe se enteró de que robaba dinero.

findings ['faɪndɪŋz] npl conclusiones, resultados.

fine[1] [faɪn] adj **1** bien: *how are you? - fine, thanks*, ¿cómo estás? -bien, gracias. **2** excelente, magnífico: *that's a fine building*, es un edificio magnífico. **3** bueno: *it's a fine day*, hace buen día. **4** fino, delgado: *fine wire*, alambre fino.
► adv fam muy bien: *everything's going fine*, todo va muy bien.

fine[2] [faɪn] n multa.
► vt multar, poner una multa: *he was fined £50*, le pusieron una multa de 50 libras.

finger ['fɪŋgə'] n dedo.
► vt tocar.

fingernail ['fɪŋgəneɪl] n uña.

fingerprint ['fɪŋgəprɪnt] n huella digital, huella dactilar.

fingertip ['fɪŋgətɪp] n punta del dedo, yema del dedo.

● **to have STH at one's fingertips 1** saberse algo al dedillo. **2** tener algo al alcance de la mano.

finicky ['fɪnɪkɪ] adj (**-ier**, **-iest**) remilgado,-a.

finish ['fɪnɪʃ] n (pl **-es**). **1** fin, final: *from start to finish*, de principio a fin. **2** acabado: *a matt finsh*, un acabado mate.
► vi acabar, terminar.
► vt acabar, terminar: *the party finished at 4 in the morning*, la fiesta acabó a las 4 de la mañana; *have you finished reading the paper?*, ¿has acabado de leer el periódico?; *finish your potatoes*, termínate las patatas.

● **to the finish** hasta el final.

■ **a close finish** un final muy reñido.

to finish off vt acabar, terminar: *I just want to finish off this letter*, sólo quiero terminar esta carta.

to finish with vt **1** acabar con. **2** romper con.

finishing ['fɪnɪʃɪŋ] adj final.

■ **finishing line** meta, línea de meta.

finite ['faɪnaɪt] adj finito,-a.

Finland ['fɪnlənd] n Finlandia.

Finn [fɪn] n finlandés,-esa.

Finnish ['fɪnɪʃ] adj finlandés,-a.
► n finlandés.
► npl **the Finnish** los finlandeses.

fir [fɜːʳ] *n* abeto.

fire ['faɪəʳ] *n* **1** fuego: *come and sit near the fire*, ven a sentarte cerca del fuego. **2** incendio, fuego: *a forest fire*, un incendio forestal. **3** estufa: *an electric fire*, una estufa eléctrica. **4** fuego: *open fire!*, ¡abran fuego!

▶ *vt* **1** disparar, lanzar: *he fired a shot at the thief*, disparó un tiro al ladrón. **2** *fam* despedir, echar: *his boss fired him this morning*, su jefe lo echó esta mañana.

▶ *vi* disparar: *the soldiers fired at the enemy*, los soldados dispararon al enemigo.

▶ *interj* ¡fuego!

● **to be on fire** estar ardiendo, estar en llamas.

● **to catch fire** incendiarse.

● **to set fire to** STH prender fuego a algo, incendiar algo.

■ **fire engine** coche de bomberos.

■ **fire escape** escalera de incendios.

■ **fire extinguisher** extintor.

■ **fire station** parque de bomberos.

■ **fire hydrant** boca de incendios.

firearm ['faɪərɑːm] *n* arma de fuego.

fireman ['faɪəmən] *n* (*pl* **firemen**) bombero.

fireplace ['faɪəpleɪs] *n* chimenea, hogar.

fireproof ['faɪəpruːf] *adj* incombustible, ignífugo, a prueba de fuego.

firewall ['faɪəwɔːl] *n* cortafuego.

firewood ['faɪəwʊd] *n* leña.

fireworks ['faɪəwɜːks] *npl* fuegos artificiales.

firing ['faɪərɪŋ] *n* tiroteo.

■ **firing squad** pelotón de fusilamiento.

■ **firing range** campo de tiro.

firm[1] [fɜːm] *n* empresa, firma.

firm[2] [fɜːm] *adj* firme: *firm ground*, terreno firme; *a firm offer*, una oferta en firme.

firmly ['fɜːmlɪ] *adv* firmemente.

firmness ['fɜːmnəs] *n* firmeza.

first [fɜːst] *adj* primero,-a: *it's the first time I come here*, es la primera vez que vengo aquí.

▶ *adv* **1** primero: *he came first in the race*, llegó el primero en la carrera; *you play later, first you must finish your lunch*, podrás jugar después, primero tienes que acabar de comer. **2** por primera vez: *I first saw her at university*, la vi por primera vez en la universidad.

▶ *n* **1** primero,-a. **2** sobresaliente.

● **at first** al principio.

● **at first sight** a primera vista.

● **first of all** en primer lugar.

■ **first aid** primeros auxilios.

■ **first aid kit** botiquín de primeros auxilios.

■ **first floor 1** GB primer piso. **2** US planta baja.

■ **first name** nombre de pila.

■ **first degree** licenciatura.

■ **first refusal** primera opción.

first-class ['fɜːstklɑːs] *adj* **1** de primera clase. **2** *fig* excelente.

▶ *adv* en primera.

firstly ['fɜːstlɪ] *adv* en primer lugar, ante todo.

first-rate ['fɜːstreɪt] *adj* excelente.

fiscal ['fɪskəl] *adj* fiscal.

fish [fɪʃ] *n* (*pl* **-es**). **1** pez. **2** pescado.

▶ *vi* pescar.

■ **fish and chips** pescado con patatas.

■ **fish finger** varita de pescado.

■ **fish shop** pescadería.

Cuando significa **pez**, *fish* es un nombre contable y su plural es *fish*, aunque también se puede emplear la forma menos frecuente *fishes*. Cuando significa **pescado**, es incontable y, por lo tanto, no tiene plural.

fisherman ['fɪʃəmən] *n* (*pl* **fishermen**) pescador.

fishing ['fɪʃɪŋ] *n* pesca.

● **to go fishing** ir de pesca.

■ **fishing boat** barca de pesca.

■ **fishing rod** caña de pescar.

fishmonger ['fɪʃmʌŋgəʳ] *n* GB pescadero,-a.

fishmonger's ['fɪʃmʌŋgəz] *n* pescadería.

fishy ['fɪʃɪ] *adj* (-**ier**, -**iest**). **1** a pescado: *it has a fishy taste*, sabe a pescado. **2** sospechoso,-a: *there's something fishy in that story*, hay algo sospechoso en esa historia.

fission ['fɪʃən] *n* fisión.

fissure ['fɪʃəʳ] *n* fisura, grieta.

fist [fɪst] *n* puño.

fistful ['fɪstfʊl] *n* puñado.

fit[1] [fɪt] *n* ataque, acceso: *a nervous fit*, un ataque de nervios; *a fit of coughing*, un ataque de tos.

fit[2] [fɪt] *vt* (*pt & pp* **fitted**, *ger* **fitting**). **1** ir bien a: *these shoes don't fit me, they're too big*, estos zapatos no me van bien,

me quedan grandes. **2** entrar: *this box won't fit in the boot*, esta caja no va a entrar en el maletero. **3** abrir: *this key fits both the doors*, esta llave abre las dos puertas. **4** poner, colocar: *the spy fitted a microphone under the table*, el espía puso un micrófono debajo de la mesa.
► *vi* **1** caber: *my clothes won't fit in the suitcase*, no me cabe la ropa en la maleta. **2** cuadrar.
► *adj* (*comp* **fitter**, *superl* **fittest**). **1** apto,-a, adecuado,-a: *he isn't fit to drive*, no está en condiciones de conducir. **2** en forma: *he's very fit because he goes running every day*, está muy en forma porque sale a correr todos los días.
● **by fits and starts** a trompicones.
● **to see fit** estimar oportuno.
to fit in *vi* **1** encajar: *I feel I don't fit in with these people*, siento que no encajo con esta gente. **2** cuadrar: *the evidence fits in with the theory*, las pruebas concuerdan con la teoría.
► *vt* encontrar un hueco para.
to fit out *vt* equipar.
fitness [ˈfɪtnəs] *n* buena forma *(física)*.
fitted [ˈfɪtɪd] *adj* empotrado,-a.
fitting [ˈfɪtɪŋ] *adj fml* apropiado,-a.
► *n* prueba *(de traje, etc)*.
► *npl* **fittings** accesorios.
■ **fitting room** probador.
five [faɪv] *num* cinco.
fix [fɪks] *vt* **1** fijar, sujetar: *he fixed the cupboard to the wall*, sujetó el armario a la pared. **2** arreglar: *the plumber has come to fix the tap*, ha venido el fontanero a arreglar el grifo. **3** decidir, fijar: *have you fixed a price for the house?*, ¿habéis fijado el precio de la casa? **4** US preparar: *let me fix you a drink*, te prepararé una copa.
► *n* (*pl* **fixes**). **1** *fam* apuro, aprieto. **2** *sl* pico.
● **to fix one's eyes on STH** fijar los ojos en algo.
to fix on *vt* decidir por, optar por.
to fix up *vt* proveer.
fixation [fɪkˈseɪʃən] *n* obsesión.
fixed [fɪkst] *adj* fijo,-a.
fixture [ˈfɪkstʃəʳ] *n* encuentro *(deportivo)*.
► *npl* **fixtures** muebles empotrados.
fizz [fɪz] *n* burbujeo.
► *vi* burbujear.

fizzle [ˈfɪzəl] *vi* chisporrotear.
to fizzle out *vi* ir perdiendo fuerza hasta quedarse en nada: *the fire fizzled out*, el fuego se apagó lentamente.
fizzy [ˈfɪzɪ] *adj* (**-ier**, **-iest**) gaseoso,-a, con gas, espumoso,-a.
flabbergasted [ˈflæbəgɑːstɪd] *adj* pasmado,-a, atónito,-a.
flabby [ˈflæbɪ] *adj* (**-ier**, **-iest**) fofo,-a.
flaccid [ˈflæksɪd] *adj* fláccido,-a.
flag[1] [flæg] *n* bandera.
flag[2] [flæg] *vi* (*pt & pp* **flagged**, *ger* **flagging**) decaer: *their interest in the project flagged at the end*, al final su interés en el proyecto decayó.
flagpole [ˈflægpəʊl] *n* asta, mástil.
flagship [ˈflægʃɪp] *n* buque insignia.
flagstone [ˈflægstəʊn] *n* losa.
flair [fleəʳ] *n* talento, don: *he has a flair for languages*, tiene talento para los idiomas.
flake [fleɪk] *n* **1** copo: *a snow flake*, un copo de nieve. **2** escama: *a flake of skin*, una escama de piel.
► *vi* **1** descamarse. **2** desconcharse.
flamboyant [flæmˈbɔɪənt] *adj* llamativo,-a, extravagante.
flame [fleɪm] *n* llama.
● **in flames** en llamas.
flamingo [fləˈmɪŋɡəʊ] *n* (*pl* **-s** o **-es**) flamenco *(ave)*.
flan [flæn] *n* tarta rellena.
flange [flændʒ] *n* brida, reborde.
flank [flæŋk] *n* **1** ijada, ijar. **2** flanco.
► *vt* flanquear, bordear.
flannel [ˈflænəl] *n* franela.
flap [flæp] *n* **1** solapa: *the flap on an envelope*, la solapa de un sobre. **2** faldón: *the flap of a jacket*, el faldón de una chaqueta.
► *vt* (*pt & pp* **flapped**, *ger* **flapping**) batir: *the bird flapped its wings*, el pájaro batió las alas.
► *vi* **1** agitarse. **2** ondear.
flare [fleəʳ] *n* **1** llamarada. **2** bengala.
► *vi* **1** llamear: *the candle flared*, la vela llameaba. **2** estallar: *her temper flared*, explotó, montó en cólera.
to flare up *vi* estallar.
flared [fleəd] *adj* acampanado,-a.
flash [flæʃ] *n* (*pl* **-es**). **1** destello: *a flash of light*, un destello de luz; *like a flash*,

como un rayo. **2** flash, noticia de última hora. **3** flash *(de cámara)*.
▶ *vi* **1** brillar, destellar: *the stars flashed in the sky*, las estrellas centelleaban en el cielo. **2** pasar como un rayo.
▶ *vt* dirigir *(luz)*: *he flashed his torch at his face*, le apuntó a la cara con la linterna.
■ **flash of lightning** relámpago.
flashback ['flæʃbæk] *n* escena retrospectiva, flashback.
flashlight ['flæʃlaɪt] *n* linterna.
flashy ['flæʃɪ] *adj* (-ier, -iest) llamativo,-a.
flask [flæsk] *n* termo.
flat[1] [flæt] *n* GB piso.
flat[2] [flæt] *adj* (*comp* **flatter**, *superl* **flattest**). **1** llano,-a, plano,-a: *flat land*, terreno llano. **2** desinflado,-a, deshinchado,-a: *a flat tyre*, un neumático deshinchado. **3** descargado,-a: *a flat battery*, una batería descargada. **4** que ha perdido el gas: *this beer's flat!*, ¡esta cerveza no tiene gas! **5** rotundo,-a, tajante: *a flat refusal*, una negativa tajante. **6** bemol.
▶ *n* superficie plana, llanura.
▶ *adv*: *in ten seconds flat*, en diez segundos justos.
■ **flat rate** precio fijo.
■ **flat roof** azotea.
flatly ['flætlɪ] *adv* rotundamente.
flatten ['flætən] *vt* **1** allanar. **2** aplastar.
flatter ['flætəʳ] *vt* **1** adular, halagar. **2** favorecer, sentar bien.
flattering ['flætərɪŋ] *adj* **1** lisonjero,-a, halagador,-a. **2** favorecedor,-ra.
flattery ['flætərɪ] *n* adulación, halago.
flatulence ['flætjʊləns] *n fml* flatulencia.
flaunt [flɔːnt] *vt* hacer alarde de.
flautist ['flɔːtɪst] *n* flautista.
flavour ['fleɪvəʳ] (US **flavor**) *n* **1** sabor. **2** *fig* atmósfera.
▶ *vt* sazonar, condimentar.
flavouring ['fleɪvərɪŋ] (US **flavoring**) *n* condimento.
flaw [flɔː] *n* defecto, desperfecto.
flawless ['flɔːləs] *adj* impecable.
flea [fliː] *n* pulga.
fleck [flek] *n* mota, punto.
flee [fliː] *vt* (*pt & pp* **fled** [fled]) huir de.
▶ *vi* huir.
fleece [fliːs] *n* lana, vellón.
▶ *vt fam* desplumar, robar.

fleet [fliːt] *n* **1** armada. **2** flota, parque móvil.
fleeting ['fliːtɪŋ] *adj* fugaz, efímero,-a.
flesh [fleʃ] *n* carne.
fleshy ['fleʃɪ] *adj* (-ier, -iest) gordo,-a.
flew [fluː] *pt* → fly.
flex [fleks] *n* (*pl* **flexes**) GB cable *(eléctrico)*.
▶ *vt* doblar, flexionar.
flexible ['fleksəbəl] *adj* flexible.
flick [flɪk] *n* movimiento rápido, movimiento brusco, coletazo, latigazo.
▶ *vt* **1** pulsar. **2** chasquear.
flicker ['flɪkəʳ] *n* **1** parpadeo. **2** *fig* indicio: *a flick of hope*, un rayo de esperanza.
▶ *vi* parpadear, vacilar: *a flickering light*, una luz titilante.
flight [flaɪt] *n* **1** vuelo. **2** bandada. **3** tramo: *flight of stairs*, tramo de escalera. **4** huida, fuga.
● **to take flight** darse a la fuga.
flighty ['flaɪtɪ] *adj* (-ier, -iest) *fig* frívolo,-a.
flimsy ['flɪmzɪ] *adj* (-ier, -iest). **1** fino,-a: *a flimsy material*, un tejido fino. **2** poco sólido,-a. **3** *fig* poco creíble: *that's a flimsy excuse*, eso es una excusa muy pobre.
flinch [flɪntʃ] *vi* **1** estremecerse. **2** retroceder: *he won't flinch from duty*, no se echará atrás ante el deber.
fling [flɪŋ] *n* **1** lanzamiento. **2** juerga. **3** lío *(amoroso)*.
▶ *vt* (*pt & pp* **flung**) arrojar, tirar, lanzar: *he flung himself to the ground*, se arrojó al suelo.
● **to have a fling** echar una cana al aire.
flint [flɪnt] *n* **1** pedernal. **2** piedra.
flip [flɪp] *n* voltereta.
▶ *vt* (*pt & pp* **flipped**, *ger* **flipping**). **1** echar *(al aire)*: *to flip a coin*, echar una moneda a cara o cruz. **2** dar la vuelta a.
▶ *vi fam* perder los estribos.
▶ *interj* **flip!** *fam* ¡ostras!
flippant ['flɪpənt] *adj* frívolo,-a, poco serio,-a.
flipper ['flɪpəʳ] *n* aleta.
flirt [flɜːt] *n* coqueto,-a.
▶ *vi* flirtear, coquetear.
flirtation [flɜːˈteɪʃən] *n* coqueteo.
float [fləʊt] *n* **1** flotador. **2** corcho. **3** carroza.
▶ *vi* flotar.
▶ *vt* hacer flotar.
flock [flɒk] *n* **1** rebaño, bandada: *a flock*

of sheep, un rebaño de ovejas. **2** *fam* tropel: *people came in flocks*, la gente vino en tropel. **3** grey, rebaño.

▶ *vi* acudir en masa: *the fans flocked to greet the football players*, los aficionados acudieron en masa a saludar a los jugadores de fútbol.

● **to flock together** congregarse.

flog [flɒg] *vt* (*pt & pp* **flogged**, *ger* **flogging**). **1** azotar. **2** GB *fam* vender.

flood [flʌd] *n* **1** inundación. **2** *fig* torrente, avalancha: *we received a flood of letters*, recibimos una avalancha de cartas.

▶ *vt* inundar.

▶ *vi* desbordarse.

floodlight [ˈflʌdlaɪt] *n* foco.

floor [flɔːʳ] *n* **1** suelo, piso: *there were carpets on the floor*, había alfombras en el suelo. **2** piso, planta: *my flat is on the fourth floor*, mi casa está en el cuarto piso.

▶ *vt* **1** derribar. **2** *fig* dejar perplejo,-a.

● **to give/ have the floor** dar/ tener la palabra.

flop [flɒp] *n fam* fracaso.

▶ *vi* (*pt & pp* **flopped**, *ger* **flopping**). **1** *fam* dejarse caer: *he flopped down on the bed*, se desplomó en la cama. **2** *fam* fracasar: *the show flopped*, el espectáculo fracasó.

floppy [ˈflɒpɪ] *adj* (-**ier**, -**iest**) blando,-a, flexible.

■ **floppy disk** disquete, disco flexible.

flora [ˈflɔːrə] *n* flora.

floral [ˈflɔːrəl] *adj* floral.

florid [ˈflɒrɪd] *adj pej* florido,-a, recargado,-a.

florist [ˈflɒrɪst] *n* florista.

■ **florist's** floristería.

flounce [flaʊns] *n* volante *(de vestido)*.

to flounce in *vi* entrar airadamente.

flounder [ˈflaʊndəʳ] *vi* **1** luchar. **2** *fig* vacilar.

flour [flaʊəʳ] *n* harina.

flourish [ˈflʌrɪʃ] *n* ademán, gesto.

▶ *vt* ondear, agitar: *he was flourishing a knife*, blandía un cuchillo.

▶ *vi* florecer.

flourishing [ˈflʌrɪʃɪŋ] *adj* floreciente, próspero,-a.

flow [fləʊ] *n* **1** flujo: *the flow of blood*, el flujo de la sangre. **2** corriente: *a flow of water*, una corriente de agua. **3** circula-

ción: *the flow of traffic*, la circulación del tráfico.

▶ *vi* **1** fluir, manar: *blood flows throughout veins*, la sangre fluye por la venas. **2** circular: *traffic is flowing*, el tráfico circula con fluidez. **3** correr, fluir: *the river flows through a beautiful valley*, el río discurre por un hermoso valle.

● **to flow into** desembocar en.

■ **flow chart** diagrama de flujo, organigrama.

flower [flaʊəʳ] *n* flor.

▶ *vi* florecer.

■ **flower bed** parterre.

flowerpot [ˈflaʊəpɒt] *n* maceta, tiesto.

flowery [ˈflaʊərɪ] *adj* (-**ier**, -**iest**). **1** de flores. **2** florido,-a.

flowing [ˈfləʊɪŋ] *adj* **1** que fluye. **2** fluido,-a, suelto,-a.

flown [fləʊn] *pp* → fly.

flu [fluː] *n* gripe.

fluctuate [ˈflʌktjʊeɪt] *vi* fluctuar.

fluency [ˈfluːənsɪ] *n* **1** fluidez. **2** dominio: *his fluency in French helped him a lot*, su dominio del francés le fue de gran ayuda.

fluent [ˈfluːənt] *adj* fluido,-a, suelto,-a: *she's fluent in French*, habla el francés con fluidez; *she speaks fluent Danish*, habla el danés con soltura.

fluently [ˈfluːəntlɪ] *adv* con soltura: *he speaks French fluently*, domina el francés, habla el francés con soltura.

fluff [flʌf] *n* pelusa, lanilla.

▶ *vt fam* pifiarla, equivocarse: *I fluffed the exam*, la pifié en el examen.

to fluff out/up *vt* encrespar, erizar.

▶ *vi* encresparse, erizarse.

fluffy [ˈflʌfɪ] *adj* (-**ier**, -**iest**) mullido,-a.

fluid [ˈfluːɪd] *adj* fluido,-a: *a fluid movement*, un movimiento fluido.

▶ *n* fluido, líquido.

fluke [fluːk] *n fam* chiripa.

flung [flʌŋ] *pt-pp* → fling.

fluorescent [flʊəˈresənt] *adj* fluorescente.

■ **fluorescent light** fluorescente.

flurry [ˈflʌrɪ] *n* (*pl* -**ies**). **1** ráfaga: *a flurry of rain*, un chaparrón. **2** *fig* oleada: *we received a flurry of objections to our plan*, recibimos un aluvión de objeciones a nuestro plan.

flush [flʌʃ] *n* (*pl* -**es**) rubor.

▶ *vt* **1** limpiar con agua. **2** *fig* hacer salir.

▶ *vi* ruborizarse.

● **to flush the lavatory** tirar de la cadena *(del wáter)*.

● **to be flush** *fam* andar bien de dinero.

fluster ['flʌstə'] *vt* poner nervioso,-a.

● **to get in a fluster** ponerse nervioso,-a.

flute [fluːt] *n* flauta.

flutter ['flʌtə'] *n* **1** agitación. **2** aleteo: *I heard the flutter of wings*, oí el aleteo de unas alas. **3** parpadeo. **4** *fam* apuesta.

▶ *vi* **1** ondear: *the flag fluttered in the breeze*, la bandera ondeaba con el aire. **2** revolotear: *butterflies fluttered from flower to flower*, las mariposas revoloteaban de flor en flor.

● **to be in a flutter** estar nervioso,-a.

● **to flutter one's eyelashes** parpadear.

fly¹ [flaɪ] *vi* (*pt* **flew**, *pp* **flown**, *ger* **flying**). **1** volar: *most birds can fly*, la mayoría de los pájaros vuelan. **2** ir en avión: *we flew from London to Edinburgh*, fuimos de Londres a Edimburgo en avión. **3** ondear: *the flag is flying in the wind*, la bandera ondea al viento. **4** irse volando: *he flew down the stairs*, bajó la escalera volando.

▶ *vt* **1** pilotar *(avión)*. **2** enviar por avión. **3** izar.

▶ *npl* **flies** bragueta.

fly² [flaɪ] *n* (*pl* **-ies**) mosca.

flying ['flaɪɪŋ] *n* **1** aviación. **2** vuelo.

▶ *adj* **1** volante. **2** rápido,-a.

● **to pass with flying colours** salir airoso,-a *(de un examen, etc)*.

■ **flying saucer** platillo volante.

■ **flying visit** visita relámpago.

flyover ['flaɪəʊvə'] *n* GB paso elevado.

FM ['efem] *abbr* (*Frequency Modulation*) FM.

FO ['efəʊ] *abbr* GB (*Foreign Office*) Ministerio de Asuntos Exteriores.

foal [fəʊl] *n* potro,-a.

foam [fəʊm] *n* espuma: *to foam at the mouth*, echar espuma por la boca.

▶ *vi* hacer espuma.

■ **foam rubber** gomaespuma.

foamy ['fəʊmi] *adj* (**-ier**, **-iest**) espumoso,-a.

fob [fɒb] *vt* (*pt* & *pp* **fobbed**, *ger* **fobbing**).

● **to fob off** embaucar, engañar.

● **to fob** SB **off with excuses** darle largas a ALGN.

focus ['fəʊkəs] *n* (*pl* **focuses**) foco.

▶ *vt* (*pt* & *pp* **focussed**, *ger* **focussing**) enfocar.

▶ *vi* centrarse.

● **in focus** enfocado,-a.

● **out of focus** desenfocado,-a.

foetus ['fiːtəs] *n* (*pl* **foetuses**) feto.

fog [fɒg] *n* niebla.

▶ *vt-vi* (*pt* & *pp* **fogged**, *ger* **fogging**) empañar.

foggy ['fɒgi] *adj* (**-ier**, **-iest**) de niebla: *it's foggy*, hay niebla; *a foggy day*, un día de niebla.

foglamp ['fɒglæmp] *n* faro antiniebla.

foible ['fɔɪbəl] *n* manía.

foil¹ [fɔɪl] *vt fml* frustrar.

foil² [fɔɪl] *n* papel de aluminio.

fold¹ [fəʊld] *n* redil, aprisco.

fold² [fəʊld] *n* pliegue: *a skirt with folds*, una falda con pliegues.

▶ *vt* doblar, plegar: *she folded the sheet of paper*, dobló la hoja de papel.

▶ *vi* doblarse, plegarse.

● **to fold one's arms** cruzar los brazos.

folder ['fəʊldə'] *n* carpeta.

folding ['fəʊldɪŋ] *adj* plegable: *a folding bed*, una cama plegable.

foliage ['fəʊlɪdʒ] *n fml* follaje.

folk [fəʊk] *adj* popular.

▶ *npl* **1** gente: *country folk*, gente del campo. **2 folks** *fam* familia.

■ **folk music** música popular.

■ **folk song** canción popular.

folklore ['fəʊklɔː'] *n* folclor, folclore.

follow ['fɒləʊ] *vt-vi* **1** seguir: *the detective followed the suspect*, el detective siguió al sospechoso; *follow the instructions*, siga las instrucciones. **2** entender, seguir: *I don't follow you*, no te entiendo.

▶ *vt* perseguir.

▶ *vi* deducirse: *it follows that he's innocent*, se deduce que es inocente.

to follow out *vt* ejecutar.

to follow through *vt* llevar a cabo: *he will follow through the project*, él llevará a cabo el proyecto.

to follow up *vt* seguir de cerca, profundizar en: *his boss said he would follow the case up*, su jefe dijo que seguiría el caso de cerca.

follower ['fɒləʊə'] *n* seguidor,-ra, discípulo,-a.

following ['fɒləʊɪŋ] *adj* siguiente: *the following day*, al día siguiente.
▶ *n* seguidores.
▶ *prep* tras: *following the elections*, tras las elecciones.

follow-up ['fɒləʊʌp] *n* **1** continuación. **2** seguimiento: *a follow-up study*, un estudio de seguimiento.

folly ['fɒlɪ] *n* (*pl* -ies) *fml* locura, desatino.

fond [fɒnd] *adj* **1** cariñoso,-a: *a fond look*, una mirada cariñosa. **2** ser aficionado,-a: *he's fond of photography*, le gusta mucho la fotografía.
● **to be fond of SB** tenerle cariño a ALGN: *she's very fond of Jim*, le tiene mucho cariño a Jim.

fondle ['fɒndəl] *vt* acariciar.

fondly ['fɒndlɪ] *adv* **1** cariñosamente. **2** ingenuamente.

fondness ['fɒndnəs] *n* **1** cariño. **2** afición.

font [fɒnt] *n* pila bautismal.

food [fuːd] *n* comida, alimento.
■ **food poisoning** intoxicación alimenticia.

foodstuffs ['fuːdstʌfs] *npl* alimentos, comestibles, productos alimenticios.

fool [fuːl] *n* **1** tonto,-a, imbécil: *don't be a fool*, no seas tonto,-a. **2** bufón,-ona.
▶ *vt* engañar: *you can't fool me!*, ¡a mí no me engañas!
▶ *vi* bromear: *it wasn't true, I was just fooling*, no era verdad, sólo bromeaba.
● **to make a fool of** poner en ridículo a.
● **to play the fool** hacer el tonto.

to fool about/around *vi* hacer el tonto: *you shouldn't fool around with a gun*, no deberías jugar con una pistola.

foolhardy ['fuːlhɑːdɪ] *adj* (-ier, -iest) imprudente, intrépido,-a.

foolish ['fuːlɪʃ] *adj* estúpido,-a.

foolishness ['fuːlɪʃnəs] *n* estupidez.

foolproof ['fuːlpruːf] *adj* infalible.

foot [fʊt] *n* (*pl* **feet**). **1** pie: *he's got big feet*, tiene los pies grandes; *at the foot of the mountain*, al pie de la montaña; *he's five feet tall*, mide cinco pies. **2** pata.
● **on foot** a pie: *we went on foot*, fuimos a pie.
● **to set foot in** entrar en.
● **to get off on the wrong foot** *fam* empezar con mal pie.
● **to put one's foot down 1** imponerse. **2** pisar a fondo.

● **to put one's feet up** descansar, relajarse.

| Un pie equivale aproximadamente a 30 centímetros. |

football ['fʊtbɔːl] *n* **1** fútbol: *they play football every Saturday*, juegan al fútbol todos los sábados. **2** balón.
■ **football pools** quinielas.

| En inglés americano, *football* es fútbol americano; el fútbol tal como se juega en Europa se llama *soccer*. |

footballer ['fʊtbɔːlə] *n* futbolista.

footlights ['fʊtlaɪts] *npl* candilejas.

footnote ['fʊtnəʊt] *n* nota a pie de página.

footpath ['fʊtpɑːθ] *n* sendero, camino.

footprint ['fʊtprɪnt] *n* huella, pisada.

footstep ['fʊtstep] *n* paso, pisada.

footwear ['fʊtweə] *n* calzado.

for [fɔː] *prep* **1** para: *it's for you*, es para ti. **2** para: *what's this for?*, ¿para qué sirve esto? **3** por: *do it for me*, hazlo por mí. **4** por: *he was fined for stealing*, le pusieron una multa por robar. **5** por, durante: *for two weeks*, durante dos semanas. **6**: *I walked for five miles*, caminé cinco millas. **7** para, hacia: *her feelings for him*, sus sentimientos hacia él. **8** por: *I got it for £500*, lo conseguí por 500 libras. **9** a favor de: *are you for the plan, or against?*, ¿estás a favor del plan, o en contra? **10** desde hace: *I have lived in Spain for twenty years*, vivo en España desde hace veinte años. **11** como: *what do they use for fuel?*, ¿qué utilizan como combustible? **12** de: *"T" for Tony*, "T" de Toni; *what is the word for "cheese" in Spanish?*, ¿cómo se dice "cheese" en español? **13** for + *object* + *inf*: *it's time for you to go*, es hora de que te marches.
▶ *conj* ya que.
● **as for me** por mi parte, en cuanto a mí.
● **for all I know** que yo sepa.
● **for good** para siempre.
● **for one thing** para empezar.
● **what for?** ¿para qué?

forage ['fɒrɪdʒ] *n* forraje.
▶ *vt* hurgar, fisgar.

forbade [fɔːˈbeɪd] *pt* → forbid.

forbid [fəˈbɪd] *vt* (*pt* **forbade**, *pp* **forbidden**, *ger* **forbidding**) prohibir: *smoking is forbidden*, está prohibido fumar.

forbidding [fəˈbɪdɪŋ] *adj* severo,-a.

force [fɔːs] *n* **1** fuerza: *the force of an explosion*, la fuerza de una explosión. **2** cuerpo: *the armed forces*, las fuerzas armadas.
▶ *vt* **1** forzar: *they forced a window open*, forzaron una ventana. **2** obligar: *he forced me to tell him*, me obligó a contárselo.
● **by force** a/por la fuerza.
● **to come into force** entrar en vigor.
forceful ['fɔːsfʊl] *adj* enérgico,-a.
forceps ['fɔːseps] *npl* fórceps.
ford [fɔːd] *n* vado.
▶ *vt* vadear.
forearm ['fɔːrɑːm] *n* antebrazo.
foreboding [fɔː'bəʊdɪŋ] *n* presentimiento.
forecast ['fɔːkɑːst] *n* pronóstico, previsión: *the weather forecast*, el pronóstico del tiempo.
▶ *vt* (*pt & pp* **forecast** *o* **forecasted** ['fɔːkɑːstɪd]) pronosticar.
forefathers ['fɔːfɑːðəz] *npl* antepasados.
forefinger ['fɔːfɪŋɡə'] *n* dedo índice.
forefront ['fɔːfrʌnt] *n* vanguardia.
forego [fɔː'ɡəʊ] *vt* (*pt* **forewent**, *pp* **foregone**) renunciar a, sacrificar.
foregoing [fɔː'ɡəʊɪŋ] *adj* precedente.
foregone [fɔː'ɡɒn] *pp* → forego.
foreground ['fɔːɡraʊnd] *n* primer plano.
forehead ['fɒrɪd, 'fɔːhed] *n* frente.
foreign ['fɒrɪn] *adj* **1** extranjero,-a: *a foreign tourist*, un turista extranjero. **2** exterior: *foreign policy*, política exterior. **3** ajeno,-a: *that's completely foreign to his nature*, es totalmente ajeno a su manera de ser.
■ **foreign exchange** divisas.
■ **Foreign Office** GB Ministerio de Asuntos Exteriores.
■ **foreign currency** divisa.
foreigner ['fɒrɪnə'] *n* extranjero,-a.
foreman ['fɔːmən] *n* (*pl* **foremen**) capataz.
foremost ['fɔːməʊst] *adj* principal: *he's one of the foremost artists of this century*, es uno de los artistas más importantes de este siglo.
▶ *adv* en primer lugar: *first and foremost*, ante todo, por encima de todo.
forensic [fə'rensɪk] *adj* forense.
forerunner ['fɔːrʌnə'] *n* precursor,-ra.
foresee [fɔː'siː] *vt* (*pt* **foresaw** [fɔː'sɔː], *pp* **foreseen** [fɔː'siːn]) prever.

foresight ['fɔːsaɪt] *n* previsión.
foreskin ['fɔːskɪn] *n* prepucio.
forest ['fɒrɪst] *n* bosque, selva.
■ **forest fire** incendio forestal.
forestall [fɔː'stɔːl] *vt* anticiparse a: *to forestall a question*, anticiparse a una pregunta.
forestry ['fɒrɪstrɪ] *n* silvicultura.
foretell [fɔː'tel] *vt* (*pt & pp* **foretold** [fɔː'təʊld]) presagiar, pronosticar.
forethought ['fɔːθɔːt] *n* previsión.
foretold [fɔː'təʊld] *pt-pp* → foretell.
forever [fə'revə'] *adv* **1** siempre. **2** para siempre: *he will live forever in my memory*, vivirá para siempre en mis recuerdos.
forewarn [fɔː'wɔːn] *vt* prevenir.
forewent [fɔː'went] *pp* → forego.
foreword ['fɔːwɜːd] *n* prólogo.
forfeit ['fɔːfɪt] *n* **1** pena, multa. **2** prenda: *to play forfeits*, jugar a las prendas.
▶ *vt* perder, renunciar a.
forgave [fə'ɡeɪv] *pt* → forgive.
forge [fɔːdʒ] *n* **1** fragua. **2** herrería.
▶ *vt* **1** falsificar: *somebody forged my signature*, alguien falsificó mi firma. **2** forjar, fraguar. **3** *fig* forjar: *the two countries forged an alliance against the enemy*, los dos países forjaron una alianza contra el enemigo.
forgery ['fɔːdʒərɪ] *n* (*pl* **-ies**) falsificación: *this painting is a forgery*, este cuadro es una falsificación.
forget [fə'ɡet] *vt* (*pt* **forgot**, *pp* **forgotten**, *ger* **forgetting**) olvidar, olvidarse de: *do not forget to send a postcard*, no te olvides de mandar una postal; *I've forgotten my swimming costume*, he olvidado mi bañador; *sorry, I forgot*, lo siento, se me olvidó.
● **forget it!** ¡olvídalo!, ¡déjalo!
● **to forget oneself** perder el control.
forgetful [fə'ɡetfʊl] *adj* despistado,-a.
forgive [fə'ɡɪv] *vt* (*pt* **forgave** [fə'ɡeɪv], *pp* **forgiven** [fə'ɡɪvən]) perdonar: *I'll never forgive you*, no te perdonaré nunca.
forgiveness [fə'ɡɪvnəs] *n* perdón.
forgo [fɔː'ɡəʊ] *vt* → forego.
forgone [fɔː'ɡɒn] *pp* → forego.
forgot [fə'ɡɒt] *pt* → forget.
forgotten [fə'ɡɒtən] *pp* → forget.
fork [fɔːk] *n* **1** tenedor. **2** horca, horquilla. **3** bifurcación: *there's a fork in the road*, hay una bifurcación en la carretera.

► *vi* bifurcarse: *when the road forks, turn right*, cuando la carretera se bifurque, tuerza a la dercha.

to fork out *vt fam* soltar, aflojar: *I had to fork out a lot of money for it*, tuve que soltar mucho dinero por él.

forlorn [fə'lɔːn] *adj* **1** triste, de tristeza. **2** desesperado,-a: *a forlorn attempt*, un intento desesperado.

■ **forlorn hope** esperanza vana.

form [fɔːm] *n* **1** forma: *a cake in the form of a heart*, una tarta en forma de corazón. **2** formas: *as a matter of form*, para guardar las formas. **3** impreso, formulario: *you have to fill in this application form*, tiene que rellenar esta solicitud. **4** curso: *I'm in the third form*, hago tercero.

► *vt* formar: *the dancers formed a circle*, los bailarines formaron un círculo; *to form a club*, formar un club.

► *vi* formarse: *ice formed on the surface of the lake*, se formó hielo en la superficie del lago.

● **off form** en baja forma.

● **on form** en forma.

■ **form of address** tratamiento.

formal ['fɔːməl] *adj* **1** formal: *a formal letter*, una carta formal. **2** de etiqueta: *formal clothes*, ropa de etiqueta. **3** ceremonioso,-a: *formal person*, persona ceremoniosa.

formality [fɔː'mælɪtɪ] *n* (*pl* **-ies**) formalidad.

formally ['fɔːməlɪ] *adv* formalmente.

format ['fɔːmæt] *n* formato.

► *vt* (*pt & pp* **formatted**, *ger* **formatting**) formatear.

formation [fɔː'meɪʃən] *n* formación.

former ['fɔːmə'] *adj* **1** primer,-a: *the former case*, el primer caso. **2** antiguo,-a, ex-: *the former champion*, el excampeón.

► *pron* **the former** aquél, aquélla.

● **in former times** antiguamente.

formerly ['fɔːməlɪ] *adv* antiguamente.

formidable ['fɔːmɪdəbəl] *adj* **1** formidable. **2** temible.

formula ['fɔːmjələ] *n* (*pl* **formulas** *o* **formulae** ['fɔːmjʊliː]) fórmula.

formulate ['fɔːmjəleɪt] *vt* formular.

fornicate ['fɔːnɪkeɪt] *vi fml* fornicar.

forsake [fə'seɪk] *vt* (*pt* **forsook** [fə'sʊk], *pp*

forsaken [fə'seɪkən]). **1** *fml* abandonar. **2** renunciar a.

fort [fɔːt] *n* fuerte, fortaleza.

forte ['fɔːteɪ] *n* fuerte.

forth [fɔːθ] *adv* en adelante: *from that day forth*, desde aquel día en adelante.

● **and so forth** y así sucesivamente.

forthcoming [fɔːθ'kʌmɪŋ] *adj* **1** próximo,-a: *the forthcoming elections*, las próximas elecciones. **2** disponible: *no reply was forthcoming*, no hubo respuesta.

fortieth ['fɔːtɪəθ] *adj* cuadragésimo,-a.

► *n* **1** cuadragésimo. **2** cuadragésima parte.

fortification [fɔːtɪfɪ'keɪʃən] *n* fortificación.

fortify ['fɔːtɪfaɪ] *vt* (*pt & pp* **-ied**). **1** fortificar. **2** *fig* fortalecer.

fortnight ['fɔːtnaɪt] *n* GB quincena, dos semanas: *a fortnight's holiday*, quince días de vacaciones.

fortnightly ['fɔːtnaɪtlɪ] *adj* quincenal.

► *adv* cada quince días.

fortress ['fɔːtrəs] *n* (*pl* **-es**) fortaleza.

fortunate ['fɔːtʃənət] *adj* afortunado,-a.

fortunately ['fɔːtʃənətlɪ] *adv* afortunadamente.

fortune ['fɔːtʃən] *n* **1** fortuna: *he made a fortune and spent it all*, hizo una fortuna y lo gastó todo. **2** suerte: *fortune smiled on her*, la suerte le sonrió.

● **to tell somebody's fortune** decirle la buenaventura a alguien.

fortune-teller ['fɔːtʃəntelə'] *n* adivino,-a.

forty ['fɔːtɪ] *num* cuarenta.

forward ['fɔːwəd] *adv* **1** hacia adelante: *to go forward*, ir hacia adelante. **2** en adelante: *from this day forward*, de ahora en adelante, de aquí en adelante.

► *adj* **1** hacia adelante: *a forward step*, un paso hacia adelante. **2** delantero,-a, frontal: *a forward position*, una posición delantera. **3** adelantado,-a: *forward planning*, planificación anticipada. **4** atrevido,-a, descarado,-a.

► *n* delantero,-a.

► *vt* **1** remitir: *please forward*, remítase al destinatario. **2** *fml* adelantar.

● **to bring** STH **forward** adelantar algo.

● **to put the clock forward** adelantar el reloj.

forwards ['fɔːwədz] *adv* → forward.

forwent [fɔː'went] *pt* → forego.

fossil ['fɒsəl] *n* fósil.
foster ['fɒstəʳ] *vt* acoger.
▶ *adj* adoptivo,-a.
■ **foster child** hijo,-a adoptivo,-a.
■ **foster mother** madre adoptiva.
fought [fɔːt] *pt-pp* → fight.
foul [faʊl] *adj* **1** asqueroso,-a: *a foul taste*, un sabor asqueroso. **2** fétido,-a: *a foul smell*, un olor asqueroso. **3** *fml* vil, atroz: *a foul crime*, un crimen atroz.
▶ *n* falta *(en deporte)*.
▶ *vt* **1** ensuciar. **2** cometer una falta contra.
▶ *vi* ensuciarse.
to foul up *vt fam* estropear, echar a perder: *he fouled up my plans*, me estropeó los planes.
foul-mouthed [faʊl'maʊðd] *adj* malhablado,-a.
found[1] [faʊnd] *vt* fundar.
found[2] [faʊnd] *pt-pp* → find.
foundation [faʊn'deɪʃən] *n* **1** fundación. **2** fundamento, base.
▶ *npl* **foundations** cimientos.
founder[1] ['faʊndəʳ] *vi* irse a pique.
founder[2] ['faʊndəʳ] *n* fundador,-ra.
foundry ['faʊndrɪ] *n (pl* **-ies)** fundición.
fountain ['faʊntən] *n* **1** fuente. **2** surtidor.
■ **fountain pen** pluma estilográfica.
four [fɔːʳ] *num* cuatro.
● **on all fours** a gatas, en cuatro patas.
fourteen [fɔː'tiːn] *num* catorce.
fourteenth [fɔː'tiːnθ] *adj* decimocuarto,-a.
▶ *n* **1** decimocuarto. **2** decimocuarta parte. **3** catorce *(en fecha)*.
fourth [fɔːθ] *adj* cuarto,-a.
▶ *n* cuarto, cuarta parte, cuatro.
fowl [faʊl] *n (pl* **fowl)** ave de corral.
fox [fɒks] *n (pl* **foxes)** zorro,-a.
▶ *vt fam* engañar.
foxy ['fɒksɪ] *adj* **(-ier,** **-iest)** *fam* astuto,-a.
foyer ['fɔɪeɪ, 'fɔɪəʳ] *n* vestíbulo.
fraction ['frækʃən] *n* fracción.
fracture ['fræktʃəʳ] *n* fractura.
▶ *vt-vi* fracturar(se): *he fractured a rib*, se fracturó una costilla.
fragile ['frædʒaɪl] *adj* **1** frágil. **2** *fig* delicado,-a.
fragility [frə'dʒɪlɪtɪ] *n* fragilidad.
fragment [(*n*) 'frægmənt(*vb*) fræg'ment] *n* fragmento.
▶ *vi* fragmentarse.
fragrance ['freɪgrəns] *n* fragancia.

frail [freɪl] *adj* frágil, delicado,-a.
frame [freɪm] *n* **1** armazón, armadura: *a tent frame*, un armazón de tienda; *a bed frame*, una armadura de cama. **2** cuadro: *a bicycle frame*, un cuadro de bicicleta. **3** montura: *glasses with a metal frame*, gafas de montura metálica. **4** marco: *a window frame*, un marco de ventana. **5** fotograma.
▶ *vt* **1** enmarcar: *she framed the photograph*, enmarcó la fotografía. **2** *fam* tender una trampa a ALGN para que parezca culpable.
■ **frame of mind** estado de ánimo.
framework ['freɪmwɜːk] *n* **1** armazón, estructura. **2** *fig* marco.
franc [fræŋk] *n* franco.
France [frɑːns] *n* Francia.
franchise ['fræntʃaɪz] *n* **1** concesión, licencia, franquicia. **2** derecho de voto.
frank [fræŋk] *adj* franco,-a.
frankness ['fræŋknəs] *n* franqueza.
frantic ['fræntɪk] *adj* frenético,-a.
fraternal [frə'tɜːnəl] *adj* fraternal.
fraternity [frə'tɜːnɪtɪ] *n (pl* **-ies).** **1** asociación, hermandad, cofradía. **2** fraternidad. **3** *US* asociación de estudiantes. **4** fraternidad.
fraternize ['frætənaɪz] *vi* confraternizar.
fraud [frɔːd] *n* **1** fraude. **2** impostor,-ra.
fraught [frɔːt] *adj* **1** lleno,-a, cargado,-a: *the plan was fraught with danger*, el plan era muy peligroso. **2** *fam* tenso,-a.
fray[1] [freɪ] *vi* **1** deshilacharse, desgastarse: *this cloth is fraying*, esta tela se está deshilachando. **2** *fig* crisparse.
fray[2] [freɪ] *n* combate.
freak [friːk] *n* **1** monstruo. **2** *sl* fanático, -a: *a film freak*, un fanático del cine.
▶ *adj* insólito,-a.
to freak out *vt-vi sl* flipar, alucinar.
freakish ['friːkɪʃ] *adj* insólito,-a.
freckle ['frekəl] *n* peca.
freckled ['frekəld] *adj* pecoso,-a.
free [friː] *adj* **1** libre: *you are free to do what you want*, eres libre de hacer lo que quieras; *are you free on Monday?*, ¿estás libre el lunes?; *I have lots of free time*, tengo mucho tiempo libre. **2** gratuito,-a: *they give you a free drink*, te dan una copa gratis.

▶ *adv* **1** gratis: ***they got in free***, entraron gratis. **2** suelto,-a.

▶ *vt* **1** poner en libertad, liberar: ***the hostages have been freed***, los rehenes han sido liberados. **2** soltar.

● **feel free!** ¡tú mismo,-a!

● **free and easy** despreocupado,-a.

● **free of charge** gratuito, gratuitamente.

● **to run free** andar suelto,-a.

● **to set SB free** liberar a ALGN, poner en libertad a ALGN.

■ **free speech** libertad de expresión.

■ **free trade** libre comercio.

■ **free will** libre albedrío.

freedom ['friːdəm] *n* libertad.

free-for-all ['friːfərɔːl] *n fam* pelea.

freelance ['friːlɑːns] *adj* autónomo,-a, freelance.

▶ *n* colaborador,-ra externo,-a, trabajador,-ra por cuenta propia.

freelancer ['friːlɑːnsəʳ] *n* colaborador,-ra externo,-a, trabajador,-ra por cuenta propia.

freely ['friːlɪ] *adv* **1** libremente. **2** gratis.

freemason ['friːmeɪsən] *n* francmasón,-ona.

free-range ['friːreɪndʒ] *adj* de corral: ***free-range eggs***, huevos de corral.

freestyle ['friːstaɪl] *n* estilo libre.

freeway ['friːweɪ] *n US* autopista.

freeze [friːz] *n* **1** helada. **2** congelación *(de precios)*.

▶ *vt-vi* (*pt* **froze** [frəʊz], *pp* **frozen** ['frəʊzən]) congelar(se): ***water freezes at nought degrees***, el agua se congela a cero grados.

▶ *vi fig* quedarse inmóvil: ***when he saw her, he froze***, cuando la vió, se quedó petrificado.

freezer ['friːzəʳ] *n* congelador.

freezing ['friːzɪŋ] *adj* helado: ***I'm freezing***, me muero de frío; ***it's freezing cold***, hace un frío que pela.

▶ *n* congelación.

■ **freezing point** punto de congelación.

freight [freɪt] *n* **1** transporte. **2** carga, flete.

■ **freight train** tren de mercancías.

French [frentʃ] *adj* francés,-a.

▶ *n* francés.

▶ *npl* **the French** los franceses.

■ **French bean** judía verde.

■ **French fries** patatas fritas.

frenzy ['frenzɪ] *n* (*pl* **-ies**) frenesí: ***a frenzy of activity***, una actividad frenética.

frequency ['friːkwənsɪ] *n* (*pl* **-ies**) frecuencia.

frequent [(*adj*) 'friːkwənt(*vb*) frɪ'kwent] *adj* frecuente.

▶ *vt* frecuentar.

frequently ['friːkwəntlɪ] *adv* frecuentemente.

fresco ['freskəʊ] *n* (*pl* **-s** o **-es**) fresco.

fresh [freʃ] *adj* **1** fresco,-a: ***fresh fruit***, fruta fresca. **2** *fig* nuevo,-a: ***I'll make a fresh pot of coffee***, haré otra cafetera; ***the police have found fresh evidence***, la policía ha encontrado nuevas pruebas.

● **in the fresh air** al aire libre.

■ **fresh water** agua dulce.

■ **fresh air** aire fresco.

freshen ['freʃən] *vt-vi* refrescar, refrescarse.

to freshen up *vt-vi* asear, asearse.

fresher ['freʃəʳ] *n* estudiante de primer curso.

freshly ['freʃlɪ] *adv* recién: ***freshly baked cake***, un pastel recién sacado del horno.

freshman ['freʃmən] *n* (*pl* **freshmen**) estudiante de primer curso.

freshness ['freʃnəs] *n* **1** frescura. **2** frescor. **3** novedad.

fret [fret] *vi* (*pt & pp* **fretted**, *ger* **fretting**) preocuparse: ***he's always fretting for her***, siempre está preocupado por ella.

fretful ['fretfʊl] *adj* preocupado,-a.

Fri ['fraɪdɪ] *abbr* (*Friday*) viernes.

friar [fraɪəʳ] *n* fraile.

friction ['frɪkʃən] *n* fricción.

Friday ['fraɪdɪ] *n* viernes.

fridge [frɪdʒ] *n* nevera, frigorífico.

fried [fraɪd] *adj* frito,-a: ***fried eggs***, huevos fritos.

friend [frend] *n* amigo,-a.

● **to make friends** hacerse amigo,-a.

friendly ['frendlɪ] *adj* (**-ier**, **-iest**). **1** simpático,-a: ***he's very friendly***, es muy simpático. **2** acogedor,-ra.

● **to become friendly** hacerse amigos,-as.

■ **friendly game/match** partido amistoso.

friendship ['frendʃɪp] *n* amistad.

frieze [friːz] *n* friso.

frigate ['frɪgət] *n* fragata.

fright [fraɪt] *n* **1** susto: ***he gave me a real***

fright, me dio un verdadero susto. **2** miedo.

● **to get a fright** pegarse un susto.

● **to take fright** asustarse.

● **to look a fright** *fam* estar hecho,-a un adefesio.

frighten ['fraɪtən] *vt* asustar, espantar: *dogs frighten him*, le dan miedo los perros.

to frighten away/off *vt* ahuyentar.

frightened ['fraɪtənd] *adj* asustado,-a.

● **to be frightened** tener miedo: *he's frightened of spiders*, le dan miedo las arañas.

frightening ['fraɪtənɪŋ] *adj* espantoso,-a, aterrador,-ra: *it was really frightening experience*, fue una experiencia terrorífica.

frightful ['fraɪtfʊl] *adj* espantoso,-a, horroroso,-a.

frightfully ['fraɪtfʊlɪ] *adv fam* muy, tremendamente.

frigid ['frɪdʒɪd] *adj* frígido,-a.

frill [frɪl] *n* **1** volante. **2** adorno.

● **with no frills** sencillo,-a.

fringe [frɪndʒ] *n* **1** fleco: *a tablecloth with a fringe*, un mantel con flecos. **2** flequillo: *she wears her hair in a fringe*, tiene flequillo. **3** borde.

frisk [frɪsk] *vt* registrar, cachear.

frisky ['frɪskɪ] *adj* (**-ier**, **-iest**) retozón,-ona, juguetón,-ona.

fritter ['frɪtər] *n* buñuelo.

to fritter away *vi pej* malgastar: *he frittered away his money on clothes*, malgastó su dinero en ropa.

frivolous ['frɪvələs] *adj* frívolo,-a.

frizzy ['frɪzɪ] *adj* (**-ier**, **-iest**) crespo,-a, rizado,-a: *frizzy hair*, pelo rizado.

fro [frəʊ] *phr* **to and fro** de un lado para otro.

frog [frɒg] *n* rana.

frogman ['frɒgmən] *n* (*pl* **frogmen**) hombre rana.

frolic ['frɒlɪk] *vi* (*pt & pp* **frolicked**, *ger* **frolicking**) juguetear, retozar.

from [frɒm] *prep* **1** de: *he's from Cardiff*, es de Cardiff; *the train from London to Edinburgh*, el tren de Londres a Edimburgo; *this letter is from my brother*, esta carta es de mi hermano; *a town 10 miles from here*, una ciudad a 10 millas de aquí; *I borrowed a book from the li-*

brary, saqué un libro de la biblioteca. **2** de, desde: *from Monday to Friday*, de lunes a viernes; *from January to June*, desde enero hasta junio. **3** de, con, a partir de: *butter is made from milk*, la mantequilla se saca de la leche; *wine is made from grapes*, el vino se obtiene de la uva. **4** según, por: *from experience*, por experiencia.

● **from now on** de ahora en adelante, a partir de ahora.

front [frʌnt] *n* **1** parte delantera: *the front of the car*, la parte delantera del coche. **2** frente, principio: *come to the front of the class*, ponte en la primera fila en clase; *he sits at the front*, se sienta delante. **3** principio: *the front of the queue*, el principio de la cola. **4** frente: *a cold front*, un frente frío. **5** fachada. **6** frente (*en guerra*). **7** *fig* tapadera.

▶ *adj* **1** delantero,-a, de delante: *children shouldn't sit in the front seat*, los niños no deben sentarse en el asiento delantero. **2** primero: *we sat in the front row*, nos pusimos en primera fila; *the front page of the paper*, la primera página del periódico.

▶ *vi* dar: *the window fronts onto the sea*, la ventana da al mar.

● **in front of** delante de: *I parked the car in front of the school*, aparqué el coche delante del colegio.

■ **front door** puerta principal, puerta de entrada.

frontal ['frʌntəl] *adj* frontal.

frontier ['frʌntɪər] *n* frontera.

frost [frɒst] *n* **1** escarcha. **2** helada.

▶ *vi* **to frost over** helarse, escarcharse.

frostbite ['frɒstbaɪt] *n* congelación.

frosted glass ['frɒstɪd] *adj* cristal esmerilado,-a.

frosty ['frɒstɪ] *adj* (**-ier**, **-iest**) helado,-a.

froth [frɒθ] *n* espuma.

▶ *vi* hacer espuma.

frothy ['frɒθɪ] *adj* (**-ier**, **-iest**) espumoso,-a.

frown [fraʊn] *vi* fruncir el ceño.

to frown upon *vt fig* desaprobar, censurar.

froze [frəʊz] *pt* → freeze.

frozen ['frəʊzən] *pp* → freeze.

frugal ['fruːgəl] *adj* frugal.

fruit [fruːt] *n* **1** fruta: *here you can buy*

fruit and vegetables, aquí puedes comprar fruta y verdura. **2** fruto.
▸ *vi* dar fruto.
■ **fruit dish** frutero: *fruit juice*, zumo de frutas.
■ **fruit machine** máquina tragaperras.
■ **fruit salad** macedonia.
fruitful ['fruːtful] *adj* fructífero,-a.
fruitless ['fruːtləs] *adj* infructuoso,-a.
frustrate [frʌ'streɪt] *vt* frustrar.
frustration [frʌ'streɪʃən] *n* frustración.
fry [fraɪ] *vt-vi* (*pt & pp* **fried**, *ger* **frying**) freír, freírse.
frying pan ['fraɪɪŋpæn] *n* sartén.
ft ['fʊt, 'fiːt] *abbr* (*footfeet*) pie, pies.
fuchsia ['fjuːʃə] *n* fucsia.
fuck [fʌk] *vt-vi vulg* joder, follar.
● **fuck (it)!** *vulg* ¡joder!
● **fuck off!** *vulg* ¡vete a la mierda!
fucking ['fʌkɪŋ] *adj vulg* jodido,-a: *you're a fucking idiot!*, ¡eres un gilipollas!
fudge [fʌdʒ] *n* dulce hecho con azúcar, leche y mantequilla.
fuel [fjʊəl] *n* combustible, carburante.
▸ *vt* **1** abastecer de combustible. **2** *fig* empeorar.
▸ *vi* abastecerse de combustible.
fugitive ['fjuːdʒɪtɪv] *adj-n* fugitivo,-a.
fulfil [fʊl'fɪl] *vt* (GB *pt & pp* **fulfilled**, *ger* **fulfilling**; US *pt & pp* **fulfiled**, *ger* **fulfiling**). **1** cumplir: *will the government fulfil its promises?*, ¿cumplirá el gobierno sus promesas? **2** realizar, efectuar: *to fulfil an ambition*, hacer realidad una ambición. **3** satisfacer: *the hospital fulfils the need of its patients*, el hospital satisface las necesidades de sus pacientes.
fulfilment [fʊl'fɪlmənt] *n* **1** realización. **2** cumplimiento. **3** satisfacción.
full [fʊl] *adj* **1** lleno,-a: *one bottle is full, but the other is empty*, una botella está llena, pero la otra está vacía; *I can't eat anymore, I'm full*, no puedo comer más, estoy lleno. **2** completo,-a: *what's your full name?*, ¿cuál es tu nombre completo?; *the hotel is full*, el hotel está completo.
▸ *adv* justo, de lleno: *the sun shone full in her face*, el sol le daba de lleno en la cara.
● **at full speed** a toda velocidad.
● **full well** perfectamente: *you know*

full well that that's not true, sabes perfectamente que eso no es verdad.
● **in full** en su totalidad: *write your address in full*, escriba su dirección completa.
● **to be full of oneself** ser un/una engreído,-a, estar pagado de sí mismo.
● **in full swing** *fam* en pleno auge.
■ **full house** lleno total.
■ **full moon** luna llena.
■ **full stop** punto y seguido.
■ **full time** a tiempo completo.
full-grown [fʊl'grəʊn] *adj* **1** crecido,-a. **2** adulto,-a.
full-length [fʊl'leŋθ] *adj* **1** de cuerpo entero: *a full-length mirror*, un espejo de cuerpo entero. **2** largo,-a: *a full-length coat*, un abrigo largo. **3** de largo metraje.
full-scale [fʊl'skeɪl] *adj* **1** de tamaño natural: *a full-scale model*, una maqueta a tamaño natural. **2** completo,-a, total: *a full-scale investigation*, una investigación profunda.
full-time [fʊl'taɪm] *adj* de jornada completa.
▸ *adv* a jornada completa: *he works full-time*, trabaja a jornada completa.
fully ['fʊlɪ] *adv* **1** completamente, enteramente. **2** con todo detalle.
fumble ['fʌmbəl] *vi* revolver torpemente.
fume [fjuːm] *vi* **1** echar humo. **2** *fig* subirse por las paredes.
▸ *npl* **fumes** humos, vapores.
fumigate ['fjuːmɪgeɪt] *vt* fumigar.
fun [fʌn] *n* diversión: *it was great fun at the fair*, lo pasamos muy bien en la feria.
▸ *adj* divertido,-a.
● **in/for fun** en broma: *we just did it for fun*, lo hicimos en broma.
● **to be fun** ser divertido,-a.
● **to have fun** divertirse, pasarlo bien: *we had a lot of fun*, nos divertimos mucho.
● **to make fun of** reírse de.
function ['fʌŋkʃən] *n* **1** función: *the function of the brain*, la función del cerebro. **2** acto, ceremonia.
▸ *vi* funcionar: *his heart is functioning properly*, su corazón funciona perfectamente.
functional ['fʌŋkʃənəl] *adj* funcional.
fund [fʌnd] *n* fondo.
▸ *vt* patrocinar.

fundamental [fʌndə'mentəl] *adj* fundamental.
► *npl* **fundamentals** fundamentos.
funeral ['fjuːnərəl] *n* entierro, funerales.
■ **funeral procession** cortejo fúnebre.
■ **funeral parlor** US funeraria.
funfair ['fʌnfeəʳ] *n* GB feria, parque de atracciones.
fungus ['fʌŋgəs] *n* (*pl* **funguses** *o* **fungi** ['fʌndʒaɪ]) hongo.
funnel ['fʌnəl] *n* **1** embudo. **2** chimenea *(de barco)*.
► *vt* (GB *pt & pp* **funnelled**, *ger* **funnelling**; US *pt & pp* **funneled**, *ger* **funneling**). **1** verter por un embudo. **2** *fig* encauzar.
funny ['fʌnɪ] *adj* (-**ier**, -**iest**). **1** gracioso,-a, divertido,-a: *that was a funny joke*, ése fue un chiste gracioso; *a funny film*, una película divertida. **2** raro,-a, extraño,-a, curioso,-a: *I can hear a funny noise*, oigo un ruido raro.
fur [fɜːʳ] *n* **1** pelo, pelaje: *my cat has black fur*, mi gato tiene el pelo negro. **2** piel. **3** sarro.
■ **fur coat** abrigo de pieles.
furious ['fjʊərɪəs] *adj* furioso,-a.
furnace ['fɜːnəs] *n* horno.
furnish ['fɜːnɪʃ] *vt* **1** amueblar. **2** *fml* suministrar, proporcionar, facilitar.
furnishings ['fɜːnɪʃɪŋz] *npl* **1** muebles, mobiliario. **2** accesorios.
furniture ['fɜːnɪtʃəʳ] *n* mobiliario, muebles.
● **a piece of furniture** un mueble.
■ **furniture van** camión de mudanzas.
furrow ['fʌrəʊ] *n* surco.
furry ['fɜːrɪ] *adj* (-**ier**, -**iest**) peludo,-a: *a furry kitten*, un gatito peludo.
further ['fɜːðəʳ] *adj-adv* → far.
► *adj* **1** nuevo,-a: *until further notice*, hasta nuevo aviso. **2** adicional: *we need further information*, necesitamos más información.

► *adv* **1** más: *further along*, más adelante; *we'll discuss this further tomorrow*, hablaremos más de esto mañana. **2** *fml* además.
► *vt* fomentar, promover.
furthermore [fɜːðə'mɔːʳ] *adv fml* además.
furthest ['fɜːðɪst] *adj-adv* → far.
furtive ['fɜːtɪv] *adj* furtivo,-a.
fury ['fjʊərɪ] *n* (*pl* -**ies**) furia, furor.
fuse [fjuːz] *n* **1** fusible, plomo. **2** mecha, espoleta.
► *vt-vi* **1** fusionar(se). **2** fundir(se).
■ **fuse box** caja de fusibles.
fusion ['fjuːʒən] *n* fusión.
fuss [fʌs] *n* (*pl* -**es**) alboroto, jaleo: *a lot of fuss about nothing*, mucho ruido y pocas nueces.
► *vi* preocuparse: *she's always fussing over the children*, siempre se está preocupando por los niños.
● **to kick up a fuss** armar un escándalo.
● **to make a fuss** quejarse.
fussy ['fʌsɪ] *adj* (-**ier**, -**iest**) quisquilloso,-a.
fusty ['fʌstɪ] *adj* (-**ier**, -**iest**). **1** mohoso,-a. **2** chapado,-a a la antigua.
futile ['fjuːtaɪl] *adj* vano,-a, inútil.
future ['fjuːtʃəʳ] *adj* futuro,-a.
► *n* **1** futuro, porvenir. **2** futuro: *the future tense*, el futuro.
● **in the future** en el futuro: *be more careful in the future*, ten más cuidado de ahora en adelante.
● **in the near future** en un futuro próximo.
fuzz [fʌz] *n* pelusa.
■ **the fuzz** *sl* la pasma.
fuzzy ['fʌzɪ] *adj* (-**ier**, -**iest**). **1** rizado,-a, crespo,-a. **2** borroso,-a.
fwd ['fɔːwəd] *abbr* (**forward**) adelante.
FYI ['efwaɪ'aɪ] *abbr* (**for your information**) para su información, para que lo sepa.

G

gab [gæb] *vi* (*pt & pp* **gabbed**, *ger* **gab-bing**) charlar.
● **to have the gift of the gab** tener mucha labia.
gabardine ['gæbədiːn] *n* gabardina.
gabble ['gæbəl] *n* farfulleo.
▶ *vt* farfullar, hablar atropelladamente.
gadget ['gædʒɪt] *n* aparato, chisme.
Gaelic ['geɪlɪk] *adj* gaélico,-a.
▶ *n* gaélico.
gaffe [gæf] *n* metedura de pata.
● **to make a gaffe** meter la pata.
gag [gæg] *n* **1** mordaza. **2** chiste, broma.
▶ *vt* (*pt & pp* **gagged**, *ger* **gagging**) amordazar.
gage [geɪdʒ] *n* US → gauge.
gaily ['geɪlɪ] *adv* alegremente.
gain [geɪn] *n* **1** ganancia, beneficio, provecho. **2** aumento.
▶ *vt* **1** lograr, conseguir. **2** engordar: *to gain 3 kilos*, engordar 3 kilos. **3** aumentar.
▶ *vi* **1** adelantarse (*reloj*). **2** subir (*acciones*). **3** engordar (*peso*).
● **to gain ground** ganar terreno.
gait [geɪt] *n* porte, andares.
gal [gæl] *abbr* (**gallon**) galón.
galactic [gə'læktɪk] *adj* galáctico,-a.
galaxy ['gæləksɪ] *n* (*pl* **-ies**) galaxia.
gale [geɪl] *n* vendaval.
■ **gales of laughter** carcajadas.
Galicia [gə'lɪsɪə] *n* Galicia.
Galician [gə'lɪsɪən] *adj* gallego,-a.
▶ *n* **1** gallego,-a (*persona*). **2** gallego (*lengua*).
gall¹ [gɔːl] *n fig* descaro.
gall² [gɔːl] *vt* irritar.
gallant ['gælənt] *adj* **1** valiente. **2** galante.

gallantry ['gæləntrɪ] *n* **1** valentía. **2** galantería.
galleon ['gælɪən] *n* galeón.
gallery ['gælərɪ] *n* (*pl* **-ies**). **1** galería. **2** galería, gallinero (*en teatro*).
galley ['gælɪ] *n* **1** galera. **2** cocina.
gallivant [gælɪ'vænt] *vi* callejear.
gallon ['gælən] *n* galón.

> Un *gallon* equivale a 4,5 litros aproximadamente.

gallop ['gæləp] *n* galope.
▶ *vi* galopar.
● **to go at a gallop** galopar.
gallows ['gæləʊz] *n* horca, patíbulo.
galore [gə'lɔː'] *adv* en abundancia.
galvanize ['gælvənaɪz] *vt* galvanizar.
gamble ['gæmbəl] *n* **1** jugada, empresa arriesgada. **2** apuesta.
▶ *vi* jugar.
▶ *vt* apostar, jugarse.
gambler ['gæmblə'] *n* jugador,-ra.
gambling ['gæmblɪŋ] *n* juego.
■ **gambling den** casa de juego.
gambol ['gæmbəl] *vi* (GB *pt & pp* **gambolled**, *ger* **gambolling**; US *pt & pp* **gamboled**, *ger* **gamboling**) brincar, retozar.
game [geɪm] *n* **1** juego. **2** partido (*de tenis, fútbol, etc*). **3** partida (*de cartas, ajedrez, etc*). **4** caza: *a restaurant that specializes in game*, un resturante especializado en platos de caza.
▶ *adj* dispuesto,-a, listo,-a.
▶ *npl* **games** educación física.
■ **game reserve** coto de caza.
gamekeeper ['geɪmkiːpə'] *n* guardabosque.
gammon ['gæmən] *n* jamón.

gamut ['gæmət] *n* gama, serie.

gander ['gændə'] *n* ganso.

gang [gæn] *n* **1** banda *(de delincuentes)*. **2** pandilla *(de amigos)*. **3** cuadrilla, brigada *(de obreros)*.

to gang up on *vt* unirse contra.

gangplank ['gænplænk] *n* plancha, pasarela *(en barco)*.

gangrene ['gængriːn] *n* gangrena.

gangster ['gænstə'] *n* gángster.

gangway ['gænweɪ] *n* **1** pasillo. **2** pasarela *(en barco)*.

gaol [dʒeɪl] *n* cárcel.

gap [gæp] *n* **1** abertura, hueco. **2** espacio. **3** blanco. **4** intervalo. **5** laguna *(de conocimientos)*.

gape [geɪp] *vi* **1** abrirse *(herida, agujero)*. **2** mirar boquiabierto,-a.

garage ['gærɑːʒ, 'gærɪdʒ] *n* **1** garaje. **2** taller mecánico. **3** gasolinera.

garbage ['gɑːbɪdʒ] *n* basura.

garbled ['gɑːbəld] *adj* confuso,-a, incomprensible.

garden ['gɑːdən] *n* jardín.
► *vi* trabajar en el jardín.

gardener ['gɑːdənə'] *n* jardinero,-a.

gardening ['gɑːdənɪŋ] *n* jardinería.

gargle ['gɑːgəl] *vi* hacer gárgaras.

garish ['geərɪʃ] *adj* chillón,-ona.

garlic ['gɑːlɪk] *n* ajo.

garment ['gɑːmənt] *n* prenda de vestir.

garnish ['gɑːnɪʃ] *n* (*pl* -**es**) guarnición.
► *vt* guarnecer.

garrison ['gærɪsən] *n* guarnición *(militar)*.
► *vt* guarnecer.

garrulous ['gærələs] *adj* locuaz.

garter ['gɑːtə'] *n* liga.

gas [gæs] *n* (*pl* **gases**). **1** gas. **2** US gasolina.
► *vt* (*pt & pp* **gassed**, *ger* **gassing**) asfixiar con gas.
■ **gas chamber** cámara de gas.
■ **gas mask** máscara antigás.
■ **gas station** gasolina.

gaseous ['gæsɪəs] *adj* gaseoso,-a.

gash [gæʃ] *n* (*pl* -**es**) raja, corte.
► *vt* rajar, cortar.

gasoline ['gæsəliːn] *n* US gasolina.

gasp [gɑːsp] *vi* dar un grito ahogado.
● **to gasp for air** hacer esfuerzos por respirar.

gassy ['gæsɪ] *adj* (-**ier**, -**iest**) gaseoso,-a.

gastric ['gæstrɪk] *adj* gástrico,-a.

gastronomy [gæs'trɒnəmɪ] *n* gastronomía.

gate [geɪt] *n* **1** puerta, verja. **2** puerta de embarque *(en aeropuerto)*.

gateau ['gætəʊ] *n* (*pl* **gateaux** ['gætəʊz]) pastel.

gatecrash ['geɪtkræʃ] *vt-vi fam* colarse.

gateway ['geɪtweɪ] *n* puerta.

gather ['gæðə'] *vt* **1** juntar, reunir *(personas)*. **2** recoger, coger *(flores, fruta)*. **3** recaudar *(impuestos)*. **4** ganar *(velocidad)*. **5** fruncir *(vestido, etc)*. **6** deducir, inferir.
► *vi* **1** reunirse *(personas)*. **2** acumularse *(nubes)*.

gathering ['gæðərɪŋ] *n* reunión.

gauche [gəʊʃ] *adj* torpe.

gaudy ['gɔːdɪ] *adj* (-**ier**, -**iest**) chillón,-ona.

gauge [geɪdʒ] *n* **1** indicador. **2** medida estándar. **3** calibre. **4** ancho de vía.
► *vt* **1** medir, calibrar. **2** *fig* juzgar.

gaunt [gɔːnt] *adj* demacrado,-a.

gauze [gɔːz] *n* gasa.

gave [geɪv] *pt* → give.

gawky ['gɔːkɪ] *adj* (-**ier**, -**iest**) desgarbado,-a.

gawp [gɔːp] *vi* mirar boquiabierto,-a.

gay [geɪ] *adj* **1** alegre. **2** vistoso,-a *(aspecto)*. **3** gay, homosexual.
► *n* gay, homosexual.

gaze [geɪz] *n* mirada fija.
► *vi* mirar fijamente.

gazelle [gə'zel] *n* gacela.

gazette [gə'zet] *n* gaceta.

GB ['dʒiː'biː] *abbr* GB *(Great Britain)* Gran Bretaña.

GCSE ['dʒiː'siː'es'iː] *abbr* GB *(General Certificate of Secondary Education)* Certificado de Enseñanza Secundaria.

GDP ['dʒiː'diː'piː] *abbr (gross domestic product)* PIB.

gear [gɪə'] *n* **1** engranaje. **2** marcha, velocidad: *reverse gear*, marcha atrás. **3** *fam* efectos personales, ropa, cosas, equipo.
■ **gear lever** palanca de cambio.

gearbox ['gɪəbɒks] *n* (*pl* **gearboxes**) caja de cambios.

gee [dʒiː] *interj* US ¡caramba!

geese [giːs] *npl* → goose.

gelatine ['dʒelətiːn] *n* gelatina.

gem [dʒem] *n* **1** gema, piedra preciosa. **2** *fig* joya.

Gemini ['dʒemɪnaɪ] *n* Géminis.

gen [dʒen] *n fam* información.

gender ['dʒendə'] n **1** género (gramatical). **2** sexo.

gene [dʒiːn] n gen.

genealogy [dʒiːnɪˈælədʒɪ] n (pl -ies) genealogía.

general ['dʒenərəl] adj general.
▶ n general (oficial).
● **in general** por lo general.
■ **general election** elecciones generales.
■ **general knowledge** cultura general.
■ **general practitioner** médico,-a de cabecera.
■ **the general public** el público.

generalization [dʒenərəlaɪˈzeɪʃən] n generalización.

generalize ['dʒenərəlaɪz] vt-vi generalizar.

generally ['dʒenərəlɪ] adv generalmente, en general.

generate ['dʒenəreɪt] vt generar, producir.

generation [dʒenəˈreɪʃən] n generación.
■ **generation gap** brecha generacional.

generator ['dʒenəreɪtə'] n generador.

generic [dʒəˈnerɪk] adj genérico,-a.

generosity [dʒenəˈrɒsətɪ] n generosidad.

generous ['dʒenərəs] adj **1** generoso,-a (persona). **2** abundante, copioso,-a (ración).

genetic [dʒəˈnetɪk] adj genético,-a.

genetics [dʒəˈnetɪks] n genética.

Es incontable y el verbo va en singular.

genial ['dʒiːnɪəl] adj simpático,-a, afable.

genital ['dʒenɪtəl] adj genital.
▶ npl **genitals** genitales.

genitive ['dʒenɪtɪv] adj genitivo,-a.
▶ n genitivo.

genius ['dʒiːnɪəs] n (pl **geniuses**) genio.

genocide ['dʒenəsaɪd] n genocidio.

genre ['ʒɑːnrə] n género.

gent [dʒent] n **1** fam caballero. **2** **gents** fam servicio de caballeros.

genteel [dʒenˈtiːl] adj **1** fino,-a. **2** pej cursi.

gentile ['dʒentaɪl] adj-n no judío,-a, gentil.

gentle ['dʒentəl] adj (comp **gentler**, superl **gentlest**). **1** amable (persona). **2** suave (brisa). **3** manso,-a (animal).

gentleman ['dʒentəlmən] n (pl **gentlemen**) caballero.

gently ['dʒentlɪ] adv **1** suavemente. **2** despacio.

genuine ['dʒenjʊɪn] adj **1** genuino,-a, auténtico,-a (objeto). **2** sincero,-a (sentimiento).

genuinely ['dʒenjʊɪnlɪ] adv **1** verdaderamente, realmente. **2** sinceramente.

genus ['dʒiːnəs] n (pl **genera** ['dʒenərə]) género.

geographical [dʒɪəˈgræfɪkəl] adj geográfico,-a.

geography [dʒɪˈɒgrəfɪ] n geografía.

geological [dʒɪəˈlɒdʒɪkəl] adj geológico,-a.

geology [dʒɪˈɒlədʒɪ] n geología.

geometrical [dʒɪəˈmetrɪkəl] adj geométrico,-a.

geometry [dʒɪˈɒmətrɪ] n geometría.

geranium [dʒəˈreɪnɪəm] n geranio.

geriatric [dʒerɪˈætrɪk] adj geriátrico,-a.

geriatrics [dʒerɪˈætrɪks] n geriatría.

Es incontable y el verbo va en singular.

germ [dʒɜːm] n germen, microbio.

German ['dʒɜːmən] adj alemán,-ana.
▶ n **1** alemán,-ana (persona). **2** alemán (lengua).

Germany ['dʒɜːmənɪ] n Alemania.

germinate ['dʒɜːmɪneɪt] vt-vi germinar.

gerund ['dʒerənd] n gerundio.

gesticulate [dʒesˈtɪkjəleɪt] vi gesticular.

gesticulation [dʒestɪkjəˈleɪʃən] n gesticulación.

gesture ['dʒestʃə'] n ademán, gesto.
▶ vi hacer un ademán, hacer gestos.
● **as a gesture of** en señal de.

get [get] vt (pt & pp **got**, ger **getting**). **1** obtener, conseguir: *I need to get a job*, necesito conseguir un trabajo; *she got £2,000 for her car*, le dieron 2.000 libras por su coche. **2** recibir: *he got a prize for his painting*, recibió un premio por su cuadro; *I got a bike for my birthday*, me regalaron una bici para mi cumpleaños. **3** traer: *can you get my slippers for me?*, ¿me traes las zapatillas? **4** coger: *he got the flu*, cogió la gripe. **5** tomar, coger: *will you get the bus or the train?*, ¿cogerás el autobús o el tren? **6** persuadir, convencer: *can you get him to help us?*, ¿puedes convencerlo para que nos ayude? **7** preparar, hacer: *can I get you a coffee?*, ¿te preparo un café? **8** fam entender: *he told me a joke, but I didn't get it*, me explicó un chiste, pero no lo entendí. **9** molestar, reventar: *what gets me is that he never does a stroke of*

work!, ilo que me revienta es que no pega golpe! **10** comprar: ***I'll get some cheese from the supermarket***, compraré queso en el supermercado. **11** buscar, recoger: ***I'm going to get the car from the garage***, voy a buscar el coche al taller.
▶ *vi* **1** ponerse, volverse: ***he got really angry***, se puso furioso; ***to get better***, mejorar; ***to get dirty***, ensuciarse; ***to get tired***, cansarse; ***to get wet***, mojarse. **2** ir: ***how do you get there?***, cómo se va hasta allí? **3** llegar: ***we got to Edinburgh at six o'clock***, llegamos a Edimburgo a las seis. **4** llegar a: ***you'll get to like it in the end***, acabará gustándote; ***I never got to see that film***, nunca llegué a ver esa película.
● **to get on one's nerves** irritar, poner nervioso,-a.
● **to get ready** preparar, prepararse.
● **to get rid of** deshacerse de.
● **to get to know SB** llegar a conocer a ALGN.

to get about *vi* moverse, viajar.
to get across *vt* **1** cruzar. **2** comunicar, transmitir.
to get ahead *vi* adelantar, progresar.
to get along *vi* **1** arreglárselas. **2** marcharse.
to get along with *vt* llevarse (bien) con.
to get around *vi* moverse, viajar.
to get around to *vt* encontrar el tiempo para.
to get at *vt* **1** alcanzar, llegar a. **2** insinuar: ***what are you getting at?***, ¿qué insinúas? **3** meterse con.
to get away *vi* escaparse.
to get away with *vt* salir impune de.
to get back *vi* volver, regresar.
▶ *vt* recuperar.
to get behind *vi* atrasarse.
to get by *vi* **1** arreglárselas. **2** pasar.
to get down *vt* deprimir.
▶ *vi* bajarse.
to get down to *vt* ponerse a.
to get in *vi* **1** llegar: ***I got in about ten***, llegué sobre las diez. **2** entrar, subir *(a un coche)*.
to get into *vt* **1** llegar a *(tren)*. **2** entrar en, subir a *(coche)*.
to get off *vt* **1** quitar. **2** bajarse de *(coche)*.
▶ *vi* **1** bajarse *(de coche)*. **2** salir *(de viaje)*. **3** comenzar. **4** escaparse, librarse.

to get off with *vt* ligar.
to get on *vt* **1** subir a, subirse a *(vehículo)*. **2** montar *(bicicleta)*.
▶ *vi* **1** progresar, avanzar, tener éxito. **2** llevarse bien. **3** seguir: ***get on with your work!***, iseguid con vuestro trabajo! **4** envejecer, hacerse tarde.
to get on for *vt* ser casi: ***it's getting on for five o'clock***, son casi las cinco.
to get onto *vt* **1** ponerse en contacto con *(persona)*. **2** empezar a hablar de *(tema)*. **3** subirse a *(vehículo)*.
to get out *vt* **1** sacar *(objeto)*. **2** quitar *(mancha)*.
▶ *vi* **1** salir: ***get out of here!***, isal de aquí! **2** escapar.
to get out of *vt* librarse de.
to get over *vt* **1** recuperarse de *(enfermedad)*. **2** sobreponerse a *(pérdida)*. **3** salvar *(obstáculo)*. **4** vencer *(dificultad)*. **5** comunicar *(idea)*.
to get over with *vt* acabar con.
to get round *vt* **1** salvar *(obstáculo)*. **2** soslayar *(ley)*. **3** convencer *(persona)*.
to get round to *vt* encontrar el tiempo para.
to get through *vi* **1** conseguir hablar *(por teléfono)*. **2** hacerse entender. **3** llegar.
▶ *vt* **1** acabar, gastar *(comida)*. **2** gastar *(dinero)*. **3** superar *(prueba)*, aprobar *(examen)*. **4** hacer entender, comunicar *(idea, mensaje)*.
to get together *vi* reunirse, juntarse.
to get up *vt-vi* levantar(se).
to get up to *vt* hacer: ***I wonder what they're getting up to***, me pregunto qué estarán haciendo.
getaway ['getəweɪ] *n* fuga.
get-together ['gettəgeðə'] *n* **1** *fam* reunión. **2** *fam* fiesta.
getup ['getʌp] *n fam* indumentaria.
ghastly ['gɑːstlɪ] *adj* (**-ier**, **-iest**) horrible, horroroso,-a.
gherkin ['gɜːkɪn] *n* pepinillo.
ghetto ['getəʊ] *n* (*pl* **-s** o **-es**) gueto.
ghost [gəʊst] *n* fantasma.
■ **Holy Ghost** Espíritu Santo.
ghoul [guːl] *n* persona de gustos macabros.
giant ['dʒaɪənt] *n* gigante,-a.
▶ *adj* gigante, gigantesco,-a.
gibberish ['dʒɪbərɪʃ] *n* galimatías.

gibe [dʒaɪb] *n* mofa.
▶ *vi* mofarse.
Gibraltar [dʒɪˈbrɔːltəʳ] *n* Gibraltar.
giddy [ˈgɪdɪ] *adj* (**-ier**, **-iest**) mareado,-a.
gift [gɪft] *n* **1** regalo, obsequio. **2** don, talento.
gifted [ˈgɪftɪd] *adj* dotado,-a, con talento.
gigantic [dʒaɪˈgæntɪk] *adj* gigantesco,-a.
giggle [ˈgɪgəl] *n* risa tonta.
▶ *vi* reírse tontamente.
• **to have the giggles** tener la risa tonta.
gild [gɪld] *vt* dorar.
• **to gild the pill** dorar la píldora.
gills [gɪlz] *npl* agallas.
gilt [gɪlt] *adj* dorado,-a.
▶ *n* dorado.
gimmick [ˈgɪmɪk] *n* reclamo, truco.
gin [dʒɪn] *n* ginebra.
ginger [ˈdʒɪndʒəʳ] *n* jengibre.
▶ *adj* pelirrojo,-a.
gingerly [ˈdʒɪndʒəlɪ] *adv* con mucho cuidado.
gipsy [ˈdʒɪpsɪ] *n* (*pl* **-ies**) gitano,-a.
giraffe [dʒɪˈrɑːf] *n* jirafa.
girdle [ˈgɜːdəl] *n* faja.
girl [gɜːl] *n* chica, muchacha, joven, niña.
girlfriend [ˈgɜːlfrend] *n* **1** novia. **2** US amiga, compañera.
girlish [ˈgɜːlɪʃ] *adj* de niña.
giro [ˈdʒaɪrəʊ] *n* (*pl* **giros**) giro.
gist [dʒɪst] *n* esencia: *I understood the gist of the message*, entendí la esencia del mensaje.
give [gɪv] *vt* (*pt* **gave** [geɪv], *pp* **given** [ˈgɪvən]). **1** dar: *give this letter to your parents*, da esta carta a tus padres. **2** dar, regalar, donar: *we gave her a mobile phone for her birthday*, por su cumpleaños le regalamos un móvil; *they gave me a present*, me hicieron un regalo. **3** dar, pagar: *how much did they give you for your car?*, ¿cuánto te dieron por el coche?
▶ *vi* dar de sí, ceder: *the shoes are tight now, but they'll give*, los zapatos aprietan ahora, pero darán de sí.
• **to give SB to understand that** dar a entender a ALGN que.
• **to give SB up for dead** dar por muerto,-a a ALGN.
• **to give the game away** descubrir el pastel.
• **to give way 1** ceder. **2** ceder el paso.
■ **give and take** toma y daca.

to give away *vt* **1** regalar. **2** delatar, traicionar.
to give back *vt* devolver.
to give in *vi* ceder, rendirse.
▶ *vt* entregar (*deberes*).
to give off *vt* desprender (*olor*).
to give out *vt* repartir, distribuir.
▶ *vi* acabarse, agotarse (*fuerzas*).
to give over *vi* parar: *give over!*, ¡basta ya!, ¡para ya!
to give up *vt* dejar: *to give up smoking*, dejar de fumar.
▶ *vi* rendirse, entregarse (*a la policía*).
glacial [ˈgleɪʃəl] *adj* glacial.
glacier [ˈglæsɪəʳ, ˈgleɪʃəʳ] *n* glaciar.
glad [glæd] *adj* (*comp* **gladder**, *superl* **gladdest**) feliz, contento,-a.
• **to be glad** alegrarse: *I'm glad to see you*, me alegro de verte.
• **to be glad of** agradecer.
• **to be glad to do STH** tener mucho gusto en hacer algo.
gladden [ˈglædən] *vt* alegrar.
gladly [ˈglædlɪ] *adv* de buena gana, con mucho gusto.
glamorize [ˈglæməraɪz] *vt* hacer más atractivo,-a.
glamorous [ˈglæmərəs] *adj* **1** atractivo,-a. **2** encantador,-ra.
glamour [ˈglæməʳ] (US **glamor**) *n* **1** atractivo. **2** encanto.
glance [glɑːns] *n* vistazo, mirada.
▶ *vi* echar un vistazo.
• **at first glance** a primera vista.
• **to take a glance** echar un vistazo.
gland [glænd] *n* glándula.
glare [gleəʳ] *n* **1** luz deslumbrante, brillo, resplandor. **2** deslumbramiento. **3** mirada enfurecida.
▶ *vi* **1** deslumbrar. **2** mirar enfurecido.
glaring [ˈgleərɪŋ] *adj* **1** deslumbrante (*luz*). **2** patente, evidente (*error*).
glass [glɑːs] *n* (*pl* **-es**). **1** vidrio, cristal. **2** vaso, copa.
▶ *npl* **glasses** gafas.
glassware [ˈglɑːsweəʳ] *n* cristalería.
glassy [ˈglɑːsɪ] *adj* (**-ier**, **-iest**) vidrioso,-a.
glaze [gleɪz] *n* **1** vidriado (*cerámica*). **2** glaseado.
▶ *vt* **1** vidriar, esmaltar (*cerámica*). **2** glasear.
■ **double glazing** doble acristalamiento.
gleam [gliːm] *n* destello.

► *vi* relucir, brillar.
• **a gleam of hope** un rayo de esperanza.
glean [gliːn] *vt* recoger.
glee [gliː] *n* regocijo.
glen [glen] *n* cañada.
glib [glɪb] *adj (comp* **glibber***, superl* **glibbest**) charlatán,-ana.
glide [glaɪd] *vi* **1** planear. **2** deslizarse.
glider [ˈglaɪdəʳ] *n* planeador.
glimmer [ˈglɪməʳ] *n* luz tenue.
► *vi* brillar con luz tenue.
• **a glimmer of hope** un rayo de esperanza.
glimpse [glɪmps] *n* visión fugaz.
► *vt* vislumbrar.
• **to catch a glimpse of** vislumbrar.
glint [glɪnt] *n* destello, centelleo.
► *vi* destellar, centellear.
glisten [ˈglɪsən] *vi* brillar, relucir.
glitter [ˈglɪtəʳ] *n* **1** brillo. **2** purpurina.
► *vi* brillar, relucir.
• **all that glitters is not gold** no es oro todo lo que reluce.
gloat [gləʊt] *vi* regocijarse.
global [ˈgləʊbəl] *adj* **1** mundial. **2** global.
■ **global warming** calentamiento global.
globe [gləʊb] *n* **1** globo. **2** globo terrestre.
■ **globe-trotter** trotamundos *mf sing.*
globule [ˈglɒbjuːl] *n* glóbulo.
gloom [gluːm] *n* **1** penumbra. **2** tristeza. **3** pesimismo.
gloomy [ˈgluːmɪ] *adj* (-ier, -iest). **1** lóbrego,-a, oscuro *(lugar)*. **2** tristón,-ona, melancólico,-a *(voz)*. **3** pesimista, poco prometedor *(pronóstico)*.
glorify [ˈglɔːrɪfaɪ] *vt (pt & pp* -ied) glorificar, ensalzar.
glorious [ˈglɔːrɪəs] *adj* **1** glorioso,-a. **2** espléndido,-a, magnífico,-a.
glory [ˈglɔːrɪ] *n (pl* -ies). **1** gloria. **2** *fig* esplendor.
► *vi (pt & pp* -ied) disfrutar.
gloss [glɒs] *n (pl* -es). **1** lustre, brillo. **2** glosa.
► *vt* glosar.
■ **gloss paint** esmalte brillante.
to gloss over *vt* omitir, pasar por alto.
glossary [ˈglɒsərɪ] *n (pl* -ies) glosario.
glossy [ˈglɒsɪ] *adj* (-ier, -iest) brillante, lustroso,-a.
glove [glʌv] *n* guante.

glow [gləʊ] *n* **1** luz suave: *the red glow of the fire*, la suave luz roja del fuego. **2** rubor. **3** *fig* sensación de bienestar, sensación de satisfacción.
► *vi* brillar.
glower [ˈglaʊəʳ] *vi* mirar con el ceño fruncido.
glowing [ˈgləʊɪŋ] *adj fig* entusiasta, favorable.
glucose [ˈgluːkəʊz] *n* glucosa.
glue [gluː] *n* cola, pegamento.
► *vt* encolar, pegar.
glum [glʌm] *adj (comp* **glummer***, superl* **glummest**) desanimado,-a.
glut [glʌt] *n* superabundancia, exceso.
glutton [ˈglʌtən] *n* glotón,-ona.
gluttony [ˈglʌtənɪ] *n* glotonería, gula.
glycerine [ˈglɪsəriːn] *n* glicerina.
GMT [ˈdʒiːˈemˈdiː] *abbr (***Greenwich Mean Time***)* GMT.
gnarled [nɑːld] *adj* lleno,-a de nudos.
gnash [næʃ] *vt* hacer rechinar.
gnat [næt] *n* mosquito.
gnaw [nɔː] *vt* roer.
GNP [ˈdʒiːˈenˈpiː] *abbr (***gross national product***)* PNB.
go [gəʊ] *vi (pt* **went***, pp* **gone***, ger* **going**). **1** ir: *I'm going to the cinema*, voy al cine; *they've gone shopping*, se han ido de compras. **2** marcharse, irse, salir: *it's late, I'm going*, es tarde, me marcho; *we arrived late and the bus had gone*, llegamos tarde y el autobús ya había salido. **3** desaparecer: *where's my car? - it's gone*, ¿dónde está mi coche? - ha desaparecido. **4** ir, funcionar: *the car's old, but it still goes well*, el coche es viejo, pero aún va bien. **5** ir, salir: *the exam went very well*, el examen me fue muy bien. **6** volverse, ponerse, quedarse: *he's gone deaf*, se ha vuelto sordo. **7** entrar, caber: *the car won't go in the garage*, el coche no entra en el garaje. **8** romperse, estropearse: *telly's gone again!*, ¡la tele ha vuelto a estropearse! **9** guardarse: *where do the plates go?*, ¿dónde se guardan los platos? **10** terminarse, acabarse: *all the cheese has gone*, se ha terminado todo el queso. **11** pasar: *time goes quickly when you're enjoying yourself*, el tiempo pasa rápido cuando te lo estás pasando bien.
► *vt* hacer: *it goes tick-tock*, hace tic-tac.

► *n* (*pl* **gos**). **1** energía, empuje: *the kids are so full of go*, los niños están llenos de energía. **2** turno: *it's my go now*, ahora me toca a mí. **3** intento: *let me have a go*, deja que lo intente yo.

● **to be going to do** STH ir a hacer algo: *I think it's going to snow*, creo que va a nevar.

● **to go about one's business** ocuparse de sus asuntos.

● **to go to sleep** dormirse.

● **to have a go at** SB criticar a ALGN.

● **to make a go of** STH tener éxito en algo.

to go after *vt* perseguir.

to go along with *vt* estar de acuerdo con.

to go around *vi* → go round.

to go away *vi* marcharse.

to go back *vi* volver.

to go back on *vt* romper, faltar a *(promesa)*.

to go by *vi* pasar *(el tiempo, personas)*.

to go down *vi* **1** bajar *(precios, temperatura)*. **2** deshincharse *(neumático)*.

to go down with *vt* coger, pillar *(enfermedad)*.

to go for *vt* **1** atacar. **2** ir a buscar *(trabajo)*. **3** *fam* gustar: *I don't go for flamenco much*, el flamenco no me gusta mucho. **4** *fam* valer para: *that goes for me too!*, ¡eso vale para mí también!

to go in *vi* entrar.

to go in for *vt* dedicarse a: *I don't go in for that sort of thing*, ese tipo de cosas no me va.

to go into *vt* **1** investigar. **2** entrar en.

to go off *vi* **1** irse, marcharse: *he went off with my girlfriend*, se fue con mi novia. **2** estallar *(bomba)*. **3** sonar *(alarma)*. **4** dispararse *(pistola)*. **5** apagarse *(luz)*. **6** estropearse *(comida)*.

► *vt* perder el gusto por, perder el interés por.

to go on *vi* **1** seguir: *go on with your work*, sigue trabajando. **2** pasar, suceder. **3** encenderse *(luz)*. **4** quejarse.

to go out *vi* **1** salir. **2** apagarse *(luz)*.

to go over *vt* revisar, repasar.

to go over to *vt* pasarse a.

to go round *vi* **1** dar vueltas, girar. **2** alcanzar, haber bastante: *I don't think the beer will go round*, no creo que haya bastante cerveza para todos. **3** salir, estar: *he goes round with a funny crowd*, se le ve con gente extraña. **4** circular, correr *(rumor)*.

to go through *vt* **1** pasar por *(túnel)*. **2** sufrir, padecer. **3** examinar, registrar, revisar.

► *vi* ser aprobado,-a *(ley)*.

to go through with *vt* llevar a cabo.

to go under *vi* **1** hundirse. **2** irse a la quiebra.

to go up *vi* **1** subir. **2** estallar.

to go without *vt* pasar sin, prescindir de.

goal [gəʊl] *n* **1** meta, portería. **2** gol, tanto. **3** fin, objeto.

● **to score a goal** marcar un gol.

goalkeeper [ˈgəʊlkiːpəˈ] *n* portero, guardameta.

goat [gəʊt] *n* cabra, macho cabrío.

gobble [ˈgɒbəl] *vt* engullir.

go-between [ˈgəʊbɪtwiːn] *n* intermediario,-a.

goblet [ˈgɒblət] *n* copa.

god [gɒd] *n* dios.

● **for God's sake!** ¡por Dios!

● **my God!** ¡Dios mío!

● **God willing** si Dios quiere.

godchild [ˈgɒdtʃaɪld] *n* (*pl* **godchildren**) ahijado,-a.

goddaughter [ˈgɒddɔːtəˈ] *n* ahijada.

goddess [ˈgɒdəs] *n* (*pl* **-es**) diosa.

godfather [ˈgɒdfɑːðəˈ] *n* padrino.

godforsaken [ˈgɒdfəseɪkən] *adj* dejado,-a de la mano de Dios.

godmother [ˈgɒdmʌðəˈ] *n* madrina.

godparents [ˈgɒdpeərənts] *npl* padrinos.

godsend [ˈgɒdsend] *n* regalo caído del cielo.

godson [ˈgɒdsʌn] *n* ahijado.

goggle [ˈgɒgəl] *vi* mirar con ojos desorbitados.

► *npl* **goggles** gafas para natación.

going [ˈgəʊɪŋ] *n* **1** ida, partida. **2** estado del camino.

► *adj* **1** actual. **2** que marcha bien.

going-over [gəʊɪŋˈəʊvəˈ] *n* **1** *fam* inspección. **2** *fam* paliza.

goings-on [gəʊɪŋzˈɒn] *npl fam* cosas: *there have been some strange goings-on next door*, han pasado cosas rasas en la casa de al lado.

gold [gəʊld] *n* oro.

► *adj* **1** de oro. **2** dorado: *a gold car*, un coche dorado.

■ **gold leaf** pan de oro.

golden ['gəʊldən] *adj* **1** de oro. **2** dorado,-a.

■ **golden jubilee** cincuenta aniversario.

■ **golden wedding** bodas de oro.

goldfish ['gəʊldfɪʃ] *n* (*pl* -**es**) pez de colores.

gold-plated ['gəʊld'pleɪtɪd] *adj* chapado,-a en oro.

goldsmith ['gəʊldsmɪθ] *n* orfebre.

golf [gɒlf] *n* golf.

■ **golf club 1** palo de golf. **2** club de golf.

■ **golf course** campo de golf.

golfer ['gɒlfəʳ] *n* jugador,-a de golf.

gone [gɒn] *pp* → go.

gong [gɒŋ] *n* gong.

good [gʊd] *adj* (*comp* **better**, *superl* **best**).
1 bueno,-a. **2** amable.

► *interj* ¡bien!

► *n* bien: *it's for your own good*, es por tu propio bien.

► *npl* **goods 1** bienes. **2** género, artículos.

● **as good as** prácticamente, como.

● **a good deal** bastante.

● **for good** para siempre.

● **good afternoon** buenas tardes.

● **good evening 1** buenas tardes. **2** buenas noches *(como saludo)*.

● **good for you!** ¡bien hecho!

● **Good Friday** Viernes Santo.

● **good morning** buenos días.

● **good night** buenas noches *(como despedida)*.

● **to be good at STH** tener facilidad para algo, ser bueno en algo.

● **to do good** hacer bien: *a walk will do you good*, un paseo te hará bien.

goodbye [gʊd'baɪ] *n* adiós.

► *interj* ¡adiós!

● **to say goodbye to** despedirse de.

good-for-nothing ['gʊdfənʌθɪŋ] *adj-n* inútil.

good-humoured [gʊd'hjuːməd] *adj* de buen humor.

good-looking [gʊd'lʊkɪŋ] *adj* (*comp* **better-looking**, *superl* **best-looking**) guapo,-a.

good-natured [gʊd'neɪtʃəd] *adj* bondadoso,-a, de buen corazón.

goodness ['gʊdnəs] *n* **1** bondad. **2** valor nutritivo.

● **for goodness' sake!** ¡por Dios!

● **my goodness!** ¡Dios mío!, ¡cielos!

goodwill [gʊd'wɪl] *n* buena voluntad.

goody ['gʊdɪ] *n* (*pl* -**ies**) *fam* el bueno: *he plays a goody in this film*, hace de bueno en esta película.

► *npl* **goodies** *fam* cosas buenas: *there were delicious goodies at the party*, en la fiesta había cosas riquísimas.

goody-goody ['gʊdɪgʊdɪ] *adj-n* *fam* santurrón,-ona.

goose [guːs] *n* (*pl* **geese**) ganso, oca.

■ **goose pimples** carne de gallina: *he came out in goose pimples*, se le puso la carne de gallina.

gooseberry ['gʊzbrɪ, 'guːsbərɪ] *n* (*pl* -**ies**) grosella espinosa.

gooseflesh ['guːsfleʃ] *n* piel de gallina.

gore[1] [gɔːʳ] *n* sangre derramada.

gore[2] [gɔːʳ] *vt* cornear.

gorge [gɔːdʒ] *n* desfiladero.

● **to gorge oneself** atiborrarse, hartarse.

gorgeous ['gɔːdʒəs] *adj* **1** magnífico,-a, espléndido,-a. **2** guapísimo,-a.

gorilla [gə'rɪlə] *n* gorila.

gory ['gɔːrɪ] *adj* (-**ier**, -**iest**) sangriento,-a.

gosh [gɒʃ] *interj* *fam* ¡cielos!

go-slow [gəʊ'sləʊ] *n* huelga de celo.

gospel ['gɒspəl] *n* evangelio.

gossip ['gɒsɪp] *n* **1** cotilleo, chismorreo *(conversación)*. **2** cotilla, chismoso,-a *(persona)*.

► *vi* (*pt & pp* **gossiped**, *ger* **gossiping**) cotillear, chismorrear.

■ **gossip column** crónica de sociedad.

got [gɒt] *pt-pp* → get.

gourmet ['gʊəmeɪ] *n* gastrónomo,-a.

gout [gaʊt] *n* gota *(enfermedad)*.

govern ['gʌvən] *vt* **1** gobernar. **2** regir.

governess ['gʌvənəs] *n* (*pl* -**es**) institutriz.

government ['gʌvnmənt] *n* gobierno.

governmental [gʌvən'mentəl] *adj* gubernamental.

governor ['gʌvənəʳ] *n* **1** gobernador,-ra. **2** director,-ra.

gown [gaʊn] *n* **1** vestido largo. **2** toga *(de juez)*. **3** bata *(de médico)*.

GP ['dʒiː'piː] *abbr* (*pl* **GPs**) *(general practioner)* médico,-a de cabecera.

GPO ['dʒiː'piː'əʊ] *abbr* GB *(General Post Office)* Correos.

grab [græb] *vt (pt & pp* **grabbed**, *ger* **grabbing**). **1** asir, coger, agarrar. **2** *fam* entusiasmar: *how does that grab you?*, ¿qué te parece eso?

grace [greɪs] *n* **1** gracia, elegancia. **2** plazo, demora: *3 days' grace*, 3 días de plazo.
  ▶ *vt* **1** adornar. **2** honrar.
  ● **to say grace** bendecir la mesa.

graceful ['greɪsfʊl] *adj* elegante.

gracious ['greɪʃəs] *adj* **1** cortés, amable. **2** elegante.
  ▶ *interj* ¡Dios mío!

grade [greɪd] *n* **1** grado. **2** clase, categoría. **3** US pendiente, cuesta. **4** US nota, calificación. **5** US clase.
  ▶ *vt* clasificar.
  ● **to make the grade** alcanzar el nivel.

gradient ['greɪdɪənt] *n* pendiente.

gradual ['grædjʊəl] *adj* gradual.

gradually ['grædjʊəlɪ] *adv* poco a poco, gradualmente.

graduate [(n) 'grædjʊət (vb) 'grædjʊeɪt] *n* graduado,-a, licenciado,-a.
  ▶ *vt* graduar.
  ▶ *vi* graduarse.

graduation [grædjʊ'eɪʃən] *n* graduación.

graffiti [grə'fiːtɪ] *npl* pintadas, grafiti.
  | Es incontable y el verbo va en singular. |

graft¹ [grɑːft] *n* injerto.
  ▶ *vt* injertar.

graft² [grɑːft] *n* **1** GB *fam* trabajo duro. **2** US *fam* corrupción.
  ▶ *vt* GB *fam* trabajar duro, currar.

grain [greɪn] *n* **1** grano *(de arena)*. **2** cereales: *the grain harvest*, la cosecha de cereales. **3** fibra. **4** veta *(en madera)*.

gram [græm] *n* gramo.

grammar ['græmər] *n* gramática.
  ■ **grammar school** GB instituto de enseñanza secundaria.

grammatical [grə'mætɪkəl] *adj* **1** gramatical. **2** gramaticalmente correcto,-a.

gramme [græm] *n* gramo.

granary ['grænərɪ] *n (pl* **-ies)** granero.

grand [grænd] *adj* **1** grandioso,-a, espléndido,-a. **2** *fam* fenomenal, estupendo,-a.
  ■ **grand piano** piano de cola.
  ■ **grand total** total.

grandchild ['græntʃaɪld] *n (pl* **grandchildren)** nieto,-a.

granddad ['grændæd] *n fam* abuelo.

granddaughter ['grændɔːtər] *n* nieta.

grandeur ['grændʒər] *n* grandeza.

grandfather ['grændfɑːðər] *n* abuelo.
  ■ **grandfather clock** reloj de caja.

grandiose ['grændɪəʊs] *adj* grandioso,-a.

grandma ['grænmɑː] *n fam* abuela.

grandmother ['grænmʌðər] *n* abuela.

grandpa ['grænpɑː] *n fam* abuelo.

grandparents ['grændpeərənts] *npl* abuelos.

grandson ['grændsʌn] *n* nieto.

grandstand ['grændstænd] *n* tribuna.

granite ['grænɪt] *n* granito.

granny ['grænɪ] *n (pl* **-ies)** *fam* abuela.

grant [grɑːnt] *n* **1** beca. **2** subvención.
  ▶ *vt* **1** conceder. **2** reconocer, admitir.
  ● **to take SB for granted** no valorar a ALGN.
  ● **to take STH for granted** dar algo por sentado.

granulated ['grænjʊleɪtɪd] *adj* granulado,-a.

grape [greɪp] *n* uva.

grapefruit ['greɪpfruːt] *n* pomelo.

grapevine ['greɪpvaɪn] *n* vid, parra.
  ● **to hear STH on the grapevine** enterarse de algo por un pajarito.

graph [grɑːf] *n* diagrama, tabla.
  ■ **graph paper** papel cuadriculado.

graphic ['græfɪk] *adj* gráfico,-a.

graphics ['græfɪks] *n* grafismo. Es incontable y el verbo va en singular.
  ▶ *npl* gráficas.

graphite ['græfaɪt] *n* grafito.

grapple ['græpəl] *vi* forcejear.
  ● **to grapple with 1** luchar con *(persona)*. **2** esforzarse por resolver *(problema)*.

grasp [grɑːsp] *n* **1** asimiento. **2** alcance: *it is in our grasp*, está a nuestro alcance. **3** comprensión.
  ▶ *vt* **1** asir, agarrar. **2** comprender.
  ● **to have a good grasp of** dominar.

grass [grɑːs] *n (pl* **-es)**. **1** hierba. **2** césped. **3** pasto. **4** *sl* hierba.
  ▶ *vi* delatar.
  ■ **grass roots** base, fundamento.

grasshopper ['grɑːshɒpər] *n* saltamontes.

grassland ['grɑːslænd] *n* pradera, tierra de pasto.

grassy ['grɑːsɪ] *adj* (**-ier**, **-iest**) cubierto,-a de hierba.

grate¹ [greɪt] *vt* rallar.
  ▶ *vi* rechinar, chirriar.

grate² [greɪt] *n* **1** rejilla, parrilla. **2** chimenea.

grateful ['greɪtful] *adj* agradecido,-a.
● **to be grateful for** agradecer.

grater ['greɪtə'] *n* rallador.

gratification [grætɪfɪ'keɪʃən] *n* **1** placer, satisfacción. **2** gratificación.

gratify ['grætɪfaɪ] *vt* (*pt & pp* **-ied**) complacer, satisfacer.

gratifying ['grætɪfaɪɪŋ] *adj* grato,-a, gratificante.

grating¹ ['greɪtɪŋ] *n* rejilla, reja.

grating² ['greɪtɪŋ] *adj* **1** chirriante. **2** irritante.

gratis ['grætɪs, 'grɑːtɪs] *adv* gratis.

gratitude ['grætɪtjuːd] *n* gratitud, agradecimiento.

gratuitous [grə'tjuːɪtəs] *adj* gratuito,-a.

gratuity [grə'tjuːɪtɪ] *n* (*pl* **-ies**) propina.

grave¹ [greɪv] *n* tumba.

grave² [greɪv] *adj* grave, serio,-a.

grave³ [grɑːv] *adj* grave (*acento*).

gravedigger ['greɪvdɪgə'] *n* sepulturero,-a, enterrador,-ra.

gravel ['grævəl] *n* grava, gravilla.

gravestone ['greɪvstəun] *n* lápida.

graveyard ['greɪvjɑːd] *n* cementerio.

gravitate ['grævɪteɪt] *vi* gravitar.

to gravitate towards *vt* sentirse atraído,-a por.

gravity ['grævɪtɪ] *n* gravedad.

gravy ['greɪvɪ] *n* salsa (*de carne*).

graze [greɪz] *n* roce, rasguño.
▶ *vt* rozar.
▶ *vi* pacer, pastar.

grease [griːs] *n* grasa.
▶ *vt* engrasar.

greasy ['griːsɪ] *adj* (**-ier**, **-iest**) grasiento,-a, graso,-a.

great [greɪt] *adj* **1** grande, gran: *a great crowd of people*, una gran multitud. **2** gran, importante: *she's a great writer*, es una gran escritora. **3** *fam* estupendo,-a, fantástico,-a: *we had a great holiday*, tuvimos unas vacaciones estupendas.

great-aunt [greɪt'ɑːnt] *n* tía abuela.

great-grandchild [greɪt'grænt]aɪld] *n* (*pl* **great-grandchildren**) bisnieto,-a.

great-granddaughter [greɪt'grændɔːtə'] *n* bisnieta.

great-grandfather [greɪt'grænfɑːðə'] *n* bisabuelo.

great-grandmother [greɪt'grænmʌðə'] *n* bisabuela.

great-grandson [greɪt'grændsʌn] *n* bisnieto.

great-great-grandfather [greɪtgreɪt'grænfɑːðə'] *n* tatarabuelo.

great-great-grandmother [greɪtgreɪt'grænmʌðə'] *n* tatarabuela.

greatly ['greɪtlɪ] *adv* muy, mucho: *I greatly enjoyed myself*, me divertí mucho.

greatness ['greɪtnəs] *n* grandeza.

Greece [griːs] *n* Grecia.

greed [griːd] *n* **1** codicia, avaricia. **2** gula, glotonería.

greediness ['griːdɪnəs] *n* **1** codicia, avaricia. **2** gula, glotonería.

greedy ['griːdɪ] *adj* (**-ier**, **-iest**). **1** codicioso,-a, avaro,-a. **2** glotón,-ona.

Greek [griːk] *adj* griego,-a.
▶ *n* **1** griego,-a (*persona*). **2** griego (*lengua*).

green [griːn] *adj* **1** verde. **2** novato,-a, ingenuo,-a.
▶ *n* **1** verde. **2** green (*en golf*).
▶ *npl* **greens** verduras.
● **to be green with envy** morirse de envidia.
■ **green bean** judía verde.

greenery ['griːnərɪ] *n* follaje.

greengrocer ['griːngrəusə'] *n* verdulero,-a.

greengrocer's ['griːngrəusəz] *n* verdulería.

greenhouse ['griːnhaus] *n* invernadero.
■ **greenhouse effect** efecto invernadero.

Greenland ['griːnlənd] *n* Groenlandia.

greet [griːt] *vt* **1** saludar, recibir (*persona*). **2** acoger, recibir (*propuesta*).

greeting ['griːtɪŋ] *n* **1** saludo. **2** recibimiento.
■ **greetings card** tarjeta de felicitación.
■ **greetings from...** recuerdos de....

gregarious [gre'geərɪəs] *adj* gregario,-a.

gremlin ['gremlɪn] *n* duende.

grenade [grə'neɪd] *n* granada.

grew [gruː] *pt* → grow.

grey [greɪ] *adj* **1** gris. **2** cano,-a (*pelo*). **3** gris, tristón,-ona.
▶ *n* gris.

greyhound ['greɪhaund] *n* galgo.

grid [grɪd] *n* **1** reja, parrilla. **2** red nacional eléctrica. **3** cuadrícula.

griddle ['grɪdəl] *n* plancha (*para cocinar*).

grief [griːf] *n* dolor, pena.
● **to come to grief 1** tener problemas,

sufrir un percance, acabar mal *(persona)*. **2** fracasar *(planes)*.

● **good grief!** ¡Dios mío!

grievance ['gri:vəns] *n* **1** queja. **2** reivindicación.

grieve [gri:v] *vt* afligir, apenar.

▶ *vi* llorar la pérdida de alguien; sufrir.

grievous ['gri:vəs] *adj* **1** doloroso,-a, penoso,-a *(pérdida)*. **2** muy grave *(error)*.

grill [grɪl] *n* **1** parrilla. **2** parrillada: **mixed grill**, parrillada de carne.

▶ *vt* **1** asar a la parrilla. **2** *fam* interrogar.

grille [grɪl] *n* rejilla.

grim [grɪm] *adj (comp* **grimmer**, *superl* **grimmest**). **1** terrible. **2** lúgubre, deprimente, triste *(lugar)*. **3** severo,-a, muy serio,-a *(persona)*. **4** ceñudo,-a *(expresión)*.

● **the grim truth** la cruda realidad.

grimace ['grɪməs] *n* mueca.

▶ *vi* hacer una mueca.

grime [graɪm] *n* mugre, suciedad.

grimy ['graɪmɪ] *adj* (-**ier**, -**iest**) mugriento,-a, sucio,-a.

grin [grɪn] *n* sonrisa.

▶ *vi (pt & pp* **grinned**, *ger* **grinning**) sonreír.

grind [graɪnd] *vt (pt & pp* **ground**). **1** moler *(café)*. **2** pulverizar *(piedra)*. **3** machacar, moler *(grano, harina)*. **4** afilar *(cuchillo)*. **5** hacer rechinar *(dientes)*.

▶ *n fam* rutina.

grinder ['graɪndə'] *n* molinillo.

grindstone ['graɪnstəun] *n* muela, piedra de afilar.

grip [grɪp] *vt (pt & pp* **gripped**, *ger* **gripping**) asir, agarrar, apretar *(mano)*.

▶ *n* **1** asimiento, apretón *(de manos)*. **2** adherencia *(sujección de neumático)*. **3** dominio, control.

● **to get a grip on STH** agarrar algo.

● **to get to grips with STH** enfrentarse con algo.

● **to lose one's grip** perder el control.

gripe [graɪp] *vi fam* quejarse.

▶ *n* queja.

gripping ['grɪpɪŋ] *adj* apasionante, fascinante.

grisly ['grɪzlɪ] *adj* (-**ier**, -**iest**) espeluznante.

grit [grɪt] *n* **1** arena, gravilla. **2** *fam* valor.

● **to grit one's teeth** apretar los dientes.

grizzly bear [grɪzlɪ'beə'] *n* oso pardo.

groan [grəun] *n* **1** gemido, quejido *(de do-*

lor). **2** *fam* gruñido *(de desaprobación)*.

▶ *vi* **1** gemir, quejarse *(de dolor)*. **2** crujir *(puerta)*. **3** *fam* quejarse, refunfuñar.

grocer ['grəusə'] *n* tendero,-a.

grocer's ['grəusəz] *n* tienda de comestibles.

groceries ['grəusərɪz] *npl* comestibles.

groggy ['grɒgɪ] *adj* (-**ier**, -**iest**). **1** *fam* grogui, atontado,-a. **2** *fam* débil.

groin [grɔɪn] *n* ingle.

groom [gru:m] *n* **1** novio. **2** mozo de cuadra.

▶ *vt* **1** almohazar, cepillar *(caballo)*. **2** cuidar, arreglar, asear *(persona)*. **3** preparar.

● **to groom o.s.** acicalarse.

groove [gru:v] *n* **1** ranura. **2** surco.

grope [grəup] *vi* andar a tientas.

▶ *vt sl* sobar.

● **to grope for** buscar a tientas.

gross [grəus] *adj* **1** obeso,-a. **2** grosero,-a, tosco,-a, basto,-a. **3** grave *(injusticia)*. **4** craso,-a *(error)*. **5** bruto,-a *(peso, cantidad)*.

▶ *vt* recaudar, ganar en bruto.

grossly ['grəuslɪ] *adv* enormemente.

grotesque [grəu'tesk] *adj* grotesco,-a.

grotty ['grɒtɪ] *adj* (-**ier**, -**iest**) GB *fam* asqueroso,-a, malísimo,-a.

grouch [grautʃ] *n (pl* -**es**). **1** *fam* gruñón, -ona. **2** *fam* queja.

▶ *vi fam* refunfuñar, quejarse.

grouchy ['grautʃɪ] *adj* (-**ier**, -**iest**) refunfuñón,-ona.

ground¹ [graund] *pt-pp* → grind.

▶ *n* **1** tierra, suelo. **2** terreno. **3** campo *(de fútbol, batalla)*.

▶ *vt* **1** obligar a quedarse en tierra. **2** fundamentar, basar en.

▶ *npl* **grounds 1** razón, motivo. **2** jardines, posos.

● **on the grounds of** con motivo de.

■ **ground floor** planta baja.

ground² [graund] *pt-pp* → grind.

▶ *adj* molido,-a.

grounding ['graundɪŋ] *n* base, conocimientos básicos.

groundnut ['graundnʌt] *n* GB cacahuete.

group [gru:p] *n* grupo, conjunto.

▶ *vt* agrupar.

▶ *vi* agruparse, juntarse.

grouse¹ [graus] *n* urogallo.

grouse² [graus] *vi fam* quejarse.

▶ *n* queja.

grove [grəuv] *n* arboleda.

grovel ['grɒvəl] *vi* (GB *pt & pp* **grovelled**, *ger* **grovelling**; US *pt & pp* **groveled**, *ger* **groveling**) arrastrarse, humillarse.

grow [grəʊ] *vi* (*pt* **grew** [gruː], *pp* **grown** [grəʊn]). **1** crecer. **2** hacerse, volverse: *to grow rich*, enriquecerse.
▶ *vt* **1** cultivar *(planta)*. **2** dejarse crecer *(pelo, bigote)*.

to grow into *vt* convertirse en.

to grow on *vt* gustar cada vez más.

to grow up *vi* criarse, crecer.

grower ['grəʊə'] *n* cultivador,-ra.

growl [graʊl] *n* gruñido.
▶ *vi* gruñir.

grown [grəʊn] *pp* → grow.

grown-up ['grəʊnʌp] *adj-n* adulto,-a, persona mayor.

growth [grəʊθ] *n* **1** crecimiento, aumento. **2** bulto, tumor.

grub [grʌb] *n* **1** larva. **2** *fam* manduca, papeo.

grubby ['grʌbɪ] *adj* (**-ier**, **-iest**) sucio,-a.

grudge [grʌdʒ] *n* resentimiento, rencor.
▶ *vt* **1** hacer a regañadientes. **2** envidiar.
● **to bear SB a grudge** guardar rencor a ALGN.

grudgingly ['grʌdʒɪŋlɪ] *adv* de mala gana.

gruelling ['gruːəlɪŋ] *adj* agotador,-ra.

gruesome ['gruːsəm] *adj* horrible, horripilante.

gruff [grʌf] *adj* **1** rudo,-a *(modales)*. **2** ronco,-a *(voz)*.

grumble ['grʌmbəl] *n* queja.
▶ *vi* refunfuñar, quejarse.

grumbler ['grʌmblə'] *n* refunfuñón,-ona.

grumpily ['grʌmpɪlɪ] *adv* de mal humor.

grumpy ['grʌmpɪ] *adj* (**-ier**, **-iest**) gruñón,-ona.

grunt [grʌnt] *n* gruñido.
▶ *vi* gruñir.

guarantee [gærən'tiː] *n* garantía.
▶ *vt* **1** garantizar. **2** asegurar.

guarantor [gærən'tɔ:'] *n* garante.

guard [gɑːd] *n* **1** guardia, vigilancia. **2** guardia, centinela. **3** guardia *(grupo de centinelas)*. **4** jefe de tren. **5** dispositivo de seguridad *(en máquina)*.
▶ *vt* **1** guardar, proteger, defender. **2** vigilar, custodiar *(preso)*.
● **off one's guard** desprevenido,-a.
● **on guard** de guardia.
● **on one's guard** en guardia.
● **to stand guard** montar guardia.

■ **guard dog** perro guardián.

guarded ['gɑːdɪd] *adj* cauteloso,-a.

guardian ['gɑːdɪən] *n* **1** guardián,-ana. **2** tutor,-ra *(de niño)*.

■ **guardian angel** ángel de la guarda.

Guatemala [gwəʊtə'mɑːlə] *n* Guatemala.

Guatemalan [gwætə'mɑːlən] *adj-n* guatemalteco,-a.

guerrilla [gə'rɪlə] *n* guerrillero,-a.

■ **guerrilla warfare** guerra de guerrillas.

guess [ges] *vt-vi* **1** adivinar: *guess what happened to me today*, adivina lo que me ha pasado hoy. **2** *fam* suponer: *I guess you're right*, supongo que tienes razón.
▶ *n* (*pl* **-es**). **1** conjetura: *have a guess!*, ¡a ver si lo adivinas!; *I'll give you three guesses*, te doy tres oportunidades para adivinarlo. **2** cálculo.

guesswork ['geswɜːk] *n* conjeturas *(pl)*.

guest [gest] *n* **1** invitado,-a. **2** cliente,-a, huésped,-a.

guesthouse ['gesthaʊs] *n* casa de huéspedes, pensión.

guffaw [gʌ'fɔː] *n* carcajada.
▶ *vi* reírse a carcajadas.

guidance ['gaɪdəns] *n* **1** orientación. **2** consejo.

guide [gaɪd] *n* **1** guía *(persona)*. **2** guía, manual *(libro)*.
▶ *vt* guiar, orientar.

guidebook ['gaɪdbʊk] *n* guía.

guideline ['gaɪdlaɪn] *n* pauta, directriz.

guild [gɪld] *n* gremio.

guile [gaɪl] *n* astucia.

guileless ['gaɪlləs] *adj* ingenuo,-a.

guillotine ['gɪləti:n] *n* guillotina.
▶ *vt* guillotinar.

guilt [gɪlt] *n* **1** culpa. **2** culpabilidad.

guilty ['gɪltɪ] *adj* (**-ier**, **-iest**) culpable.

guinea ['gɪnɪ] *n* guinea.

■ **guinea pig** conejillo de Indias.

guise [gaɪz] *n* apariencia.

guitar [gɪ'tɑ:'] *n* guitarra.

guitarist [gɪ'tɑːrɪst] *n* guitarrista.

gulf [gʌlf] *n* **1** golfo *(masa de agua)*. **2** *fig* abismo.

gull [gʌl] *n* gaviota.

gullible ['gʌlɪbəl] *adj* crédulo,-a.

gully ['gʌlɪ] *n* (*pl* **-ies**) barranco.

gulp [gʌlp] *n* trago.

► *vt* tragar.

► *vi* tragar saliva.

gum[1] [gʌm] *n* encía.

gum[2] [gʌm] *n* goma, pegamento.

► *vt* (*pt & pp* **gummed**, *ger* **gumming**) engomar, pegar con goma.

gumption ['gʌmpʃən] *n* sentido común.

gun [gʌn] *n* **1** arma de fuego. **2** pistola, revólver. **3** rifle, fusil. **4** escopeta. **5** cañón.

■ **gun dog** perro de caza.

to gun down *vt* matar a tiros.

gunfire ['gʌnfaɪəʳ] *n* **1** fuego, disparos. **2** cañonazos.

gunman ['gʌnmən] *n* (*pl* **gunmen**) pistolero.

gunner ['gʌnəʳ] *n* artillero.

gunpoint ['gʌnpɔɪnt] *phr* **at gunpoint** a punta de pistola.

gunpowder ['gʌnpaʊdəʳ] *n* pólvora.

gunrunner ['gʌnrʌnəʳ] *n* traficante de armas.

gunrunning ['gʌnrʌnɪŋ] *n* tráfico de armas.

gunshot ['gʌnʃɒt] *n* disparo.

gurgle ['gɜːgəl] *n* **1** gorgoteo *(de agua)*. **2** gorjeo *(de bebé)*.

► *vi* **1** gorgotear *(agua)*. **2** gorjear *(bebé)*.

guru ['guːruː] *n* gurú.

gush [gʌʃ] *n* chorro.

► *vi* **1** brotar a borbotones. **2** ser efusivo,-a.

gushing ['gʌʃɪŋ] *adj* **1** que sale a borbotones. **2** efusivo,-a.

gust [gʌst] *n* ráfaga, racha.

gusto ['gʌstəʊ] *n* entusiasmo.

gusty ['gʌstɪ] *adj* (**-ier**, **-iest**) racheado,-a.

gut [gʌt] *n* intestino, tripa.

► *vt* (*pt & pp* **gutted**, *ger* **gutting**). **1** destripar. **2** destruir el interior de.

► *npl* **guts 1** entrañas, vísceras. **2** *fam* agallas: *he didn't have the guts to tell her*, no tuvo agallas para decírselo.

● **to hate SB's guts** no poder ni ver a alguien.

gutter ['gʌtəʳ] *n* **1** cuneta, alcantarilla *(en calle)*. **2** canalón, desagüe *(en tejado)*. **3** *(Fig)* arroyo, bajos fondos.

■ **gutter press** prensa amarilla.

guy [gaɪ] *n fam* tipo, tío, individuo.

guzzle ['gʌzəl] *vt* zamparse, engullirse.

gym [dʒɪm] *n* **1** *fam* gimnasio. **2** gimnasia.

■ **gym shoes** zapatillas de deporte.

gymkhana [dʒɪmˈkɑːnə] *n* gincana, gymkhana.

gymnasium [dʒɪmˈneɪzɪəm] *n* gimnasio.

gymnast ['dʒɪmnæst] *n* gimnasta.

gymnastics [dʒɪmˈnæstɪks] *n* gimnasia. Es incontable y el verbo va en singular.

gynaecological [gaɪnəkəˈlɒdʒɪkəl] *adj* ginecológico,-a.

gynaecologist [gaɪnɪˈkɒlədʒɪst] *n* ginecólogo,-a.

gynaecology [gaɪnɪˈkɒlədʒɪ] *n* ginecología.

gypsy ['dʒɪpsɪ] *adj-n* gitano,-a.

gyrate [dʒaɪˈreɪt] *vi* girar, dar vueltas

H

habit ['hæbɪt] *n* **1** hábito, costumbre. **2** hábito *(prenda)*.
habitable ['hæbɪtəbəl] *adj* habitable.
habitat ['hæbɪtæt] *n* hábitat.
habitual [hə'bɪtʃʊəl] *adj* **1** habitual, acostumbrado,-a. **2** empedernido,-a.
hack [hæk] *vt* **1** tajar, cortar. **2** COMPUT piratear.
hacksaw ['hæksɔ:] *n* sierra para metales.
had [hæd] *pt-pp* → have.
haddock ['hædək] *n* eglefino.
haemorrhage ['hemərɪdʒ] *n* hemorragia.
haemorrhoids ['hemərɔɪdz] *npl* hemorroides.
hag [hæg] *n* bruja, arpía.
haggard ['hægəd] *adj* ojeroso,-a.
haggle ['hægəl] *vi* regatear.
hail¹ [heɪl] *vt* **1** llamar. **2** aclamar.
● **to hail from** ser de.
hail² [heɪl] *n* granizo, pedrisco.
▶ *vi* granizar.
hailstone ['heɪlstəʊn] *n* granizo.
hailstorm ['heɪlstɔ:m] *n* granizada.
hair [heə'] *n* **1** cabello, pelo. **2** vello.
hairbrush ['heəbrʌʃ] *n (pl* **-es**) cepillo para el pelo.
haircut ['heəkʌt] *n* corte de pelo.
● **to have a haircut** cortarse el pelo.
hairdo ['heədu:] *n (pl* **hairdos**) *fam* peinado.
hairdresser ['heədresə'] *n* peluquero,-a.
■ **hairdresser's** peluquería.
hairdryer ['heədraɪə'] *n* secador de pelo.
hairpiece ['heəpi:s] *n* peluquín.
hairpin ['heəpɪn] *n* horquilla.
hair-raising ['heəreɪzɪŋ] *adj* espeluznante.
hairspray ['heəspreɪ] *n* laca *(para el pelo)*.

hairstyle ['heəstaɪl] *n* peinado.
hairy ['heərɪ] *adj* (**-ier**, **-iest**). **1** peludo,-a. **2** *fig* espeluznante.
hake [heɪk] *n* merluza.
half [hɑ:f] *n (pl* **halves**). **1** mitad: *the second half*, la segunda mitad. **2** medio: *a kilo and a half*, un kilo y medio.
▶ *adj* medio,-a: *half a dozen*, media docena; *half an hour*, media hora.
▶ *adv* medio, a medias: *half dead*, medio muerto,-a.
▶ *pron* mitad: *that's too much; I can only eat half*, eso es demasiado; sólo puedo comer la mitad.
● **to go halves on** pagar a medias.
● **half past** y media: *it's half past two*, son las dos y media.
half-brother ['hɑ:fbrʌðə'] *n* hermanastro.
half-caste ['hɑ:fkɑ:st] *adj-n* mestizo,-a.
half-hearted [hɑ:f'hɑ:tɪd] *adj* poco entusiasta.
halfpenny ['heɪpnɪ] *n (pl* **-ies**) medio penique.
half-sister ['hɑ:fsɪstə'] *n* hermanastra.
half-time [hɑ:f'taɪm] *n* descanso *(en partido)*.
halfway ['hɑ:fweɪ] *adj* intermedio,-a.
▶ *adv* a medio camino, a mitad de camino.
half-wit ['hɑ:fwɪt] *n* imbécil.
hall [hɔ:l] *n* **1** vestíbulo, entrada. **2** sala *(de conciertos)*. **3** casa solariega.
■ **hall of residence** colegio mayor.
hallmark ['hɔ:lmɑ:k] *n* **1** contraste *(en metal precioso)*. **2** *fig* sello.
hallo [hə'ləʊ] *interj* → hello.
Halloween [hæləʊ'i:n] *n* víspera de Todos los Santos.

hallucination [həluːsɪˈneɪʃən] *n* alucinación.

halo [ˈheɪləʊ] *n* (*pl* **-s** o **-es**) halo, aureola.

halt [hɔːlt] *n* alto, parada.
▶ *vt-vi* parar(se), cesar.
● **halt!** ¡alto!
● **to come to a halt** detenerse.

halting [ˈhɔːltɪŋ] *adj* vacilante.

halve [hɑːv] *vt* **1** partir en dos. **2** reducir a la mitad.

ham [hæm] *n* jamón.
● **to ham it up** exagerar.

hamburger [ˈhæmbɜːgə'] *n* hamburguesa.

hammer [ˈhæmə'] *n* martillo.
▶ *vt* **1** clavar *(con un martillo)*. **2** dar una paliza a.
▶ *vi* **1** dar martillazos. **2** aporrear.

hammock [ˈhæmək] *n* hamaca.

hamper [ˈhæmpə'] *n* cesta.

hamper [ˈhæmpə'] *vt* estorbar.

hamster [ˈhæmstə'] *n* hámster.

hand [hænd] *n* **1** mano. **2** trabajador,-ra, operario,-a. **3** tripulante *(de barco)*. **4** manecilla *(de reloj)*. **5** letra, caligrafía. **6** mano *(de naipes)*.
▶ *vt* dar, entregar.
● **at first hand** de primera mano.
● **at hand** a mano.
● **by hand** a mano.
● **hands up!** ¡manos arriba!
● **on hand** disponible.
● **on the one hand** por una parte.
● **on the other hand** por otra parte.
● **to have the upper hand** llevar ventaja.
● **to hold hands** estar cogidos,-as de la mano.
● **to lend a hand** echar una mano.

to hand back *vt* devolver.

to hand in *vt* entregar, presentar.

to hand out *vt* repartir.

to hand over *vt* entregar.

to hand round *vt* ofrecer.

handbag [ˈhændbæg] *n* bolso.

handball [ˈhændbɔːl] *n* balonmano.

handbook [ˈhændbʊk] *n* manual.

handbrake [ˈhændbreɪk] *n* freno de mano.

handcuff [ˈhændkʌf] *vt* esposar.
▶ *npl* **handcuffs** esposas.

handful [ˈhændfʊl] *n* puñado.

handicap [ˈhændɪkæp] *n* **1** discapacidad, minusvalía. **2** desventaja, obstáculo. **3** hándicap.
▶ *vt* obstaculizar, estorbar.

handicapped [ˈhændɪkæpt] *adj* discapacitado,-a, minusválido,-a.

handicraft [ˈhændɪkrɑːft] *n* artesanía.

handkerchief [ˈhæŋkətʃiːf] *n* (*pl* **-chiefs** o **-chieves**) pañuelo.

handle [ˈhændəl] *n* **1** pomo, picaporte *(de puerta)*. **2** tirador *(de cajón)*. **3** asa *(de taza)*. **4** mango *(de cuchillo)*.
▶ *vt* **1** manejar, usar. **2** tratar *(gente, problema)*. **3** aguantar *(tensión)*.
▶ *vi* comportarse.

handlebar [ˈhændəlbɑː'] *n* manillar.

handmade [hændˈmeɪd] *adj* hecho,-a a mano.

handout [ˈhændaʊt] *n* **1** folleto. **2** material. **3** nota de prensa. **4** limosna.

handshake [ˈhændʃeɪk] *n* apretón de manos.

handsome [ˈhænsəm] *adj* (*comp* **handsomer**, *superl* **handsomest**) guapo,-a, de buen ver.

handwriting [ˈhændraɪtɪŋ] *n* letra.

handwritten [ˈhændrɪtən] *adj* escrito,-a a mano.

handy [ˈhændɪ] *adj* (**-ier**, **-iest**). **1** práctico,-a, útil. **2** a mano.

hang [hæŋ] *vt* (*pt & pp* **hung** [hʌŋ]). **1** colgar. **2** ahorcar. En esta acepción *pt & pp* **hanged**.
▶ *vi* **1** colgar, pender, flotar. **2** ser ahorcado,-a. En esta acepción *pt & pp* **hanged**.
▶ *n* caída.
● **to get the hang of** cogerle el tranquillo a.

to hang about, hang around *vi* **1** esperar. **2** perder el tiempo.

to hang back *vi* **1** quedarse atrás. **2** no decidirse.

to hang out *vt* tender.
▶ *vi fam* frecuentar: **he hangs out in sleazy bars**, frecuenta baretos sórdidos.

to hang up *vt-vi* colgar *(teléfono)*.

hangar [ˈhæŋə'] *n* hangar.

hanger [ˈhæŋə'] *n* percha.

hang-glider [ˈhæŋglaɪdə'] *n* ala delta.

hang-gliding [ˈhæŋglaɪdɪŋ] *n* vuelo con ala delta.

hanging [ˈhæŋɪŋ] *adj* colgante.
▶ *n* **1** ejecución en la horca. **2** colgadura.

hangman [ˈhæŋmən] *n* (*pl* **hangmen**). **1** verdugo. **2** el ahorcado *(juego)*.

hangout [ˈhæŋaʊt] *n fam* guarida.

hangover ['hæŋəʊvəʳ] *n* resaca.

hang-up ['hæŋʌp] *n fam* complejo, manía.

hanker ['hæŋkəʳ] *vi* to hanker after ansiar, anhelar.

hanky-panky [hæŋkɪ'pæŋkɪ] *n* 1 *fam* chanchullos. 2 ñacañaca.

haphazard [hæp'hæzəd] *adj* 1 desordenado,-a, caótico. 2 improvisado,-a *(planes)*.

happen ['hæpən] *vi* ocurrir, pasar, suceder: *what happened?*, ¿qué pasó?

● to happen to do STH hacer algo por casualidad: *if you happen to ...*, si por casualidad ....

happening ['hæpənɪŋ] *n* acontecimiento.

happily ['hæpɪlɪ] *adv* 1 felizmente. 2 afortunadamente.

happiness ['hæpɪnəs] *n* felicidad.

happy ['hæpɪ] *adj* (-ier, -iest). 1 feliz, alegre. 2 contento,-a: *happy birthday!*, ¡feliz cumpleaños!

harass ['hærəs] *vt* acosar, hostigar.

harassment ['hærəsmənt] *n* acoso.

harbour ['hɑːbəʳ] (US harbor) *n* puerto.
▶ *vt* 1 encubrir, proteger *(criminal)*. 2 abrigar *(dudas, temores)*.

hard [hɑːd] *adj* 1 duro,-a *(material)*. 2 difícil *(pregunta, tema)*. 3 severo,-a, duro,-a *(trato)*.
▶ *adv* 1 fuerte, duro: *hit him hard!*, ¡pégale duro! 2 mucho: *it's snowing hard*, está nevando mucho.

● hard of hearing duro,-a de oído.

● to work hard trabajar mucho.

● to be hard up *fam* estar sin blanca.

■ hard court pista rápida.

■ hard disk disco duro.

■ hard labour trabajos forzados.

■ hard shoulder arcén.

harden ['hɑːdən] *vt-vi* endurecer(se).

hard-headed ['hɑːd'hedɪd] *adj* práctico,-a, realista.

hardhearted ['hɑːd'hɑːtɪd] *adj* despiadado,-a, insensible.

hardly ['hɑːdlɪ] *adv* 1 apenas: *I can hardly hear what she says*, apenas oigo lo que dice. 2 casi: *he hardly ever gets angry*, casi nunca se enfada.

hardness ['hɑːdnəs] *n* 1 dureza. 2 dificultad.

hardship ['hɑːdʃɪp] *n* apuro, dificultad.

hardware ['hɑːdweəʳ] *n* 1 artículos de ferretería. 2 hardware, soporte físico.

■ hardware store ferretería.

hard-working ['hɑːd'wɜːkɪŋ] *adj* trabajador,-ra.

hardy ['hɑːdɪ] *adj* (-ier, -iest). 1 fuerte, robusto,-a *(persona)*. 2 resistente *(planta)*.

hare [heəʳ] *n* liebre.

harebrained ['heəbreɪnd] *adj* descabellado,-a *(idea)*.

harem ['hɑːriːm, 'heərəm] *n* harén.

haricot bean ['hærɪkəʊ'biːn] *n* alubia.

harlequin ['hɑːlɪkwɪn] *n* arlequín.

harlot ['hɑːlət] *n* ramera.

harm [hɑːm] *n* mal, daño, perjuicio.
▶ *vt* dañar, perjudicar, hacer daño.

● to come to no harm no pasarle nada a nadie.

● there's no harm in... no se pierde nada..., no es malo.

harmful ['hɑːmfʊl] *adj* dañino,-a, nocivo,-a, perjudicial.

harmless ['hɑːmləs] *adj* inofensivo,-a, inocuo,-a.

harmonic [hɑː'mɒnɪk] *adj* armónico,-a.
▶ *n* armónico.

harmonica [hɑː'mɒnɪkə] *n* armónica.

harmonious [hɑː'məʊnɪəs] *adj* armonioso,-a.

harmonize ['hɑːmənaɪz] *vt-vi* armonizar.

harmony ['hɑːmənɪ] *n* (*pl* -ies) armonía.

harness ['hɑːnəs] *n* (*pl* -es) arnés, arreos.
▶ *vt* 1 poner los arreos *(a un caballo)*. 2 aprovechar *(recursos)*.

harp [hɑːp] *n* arpa.

to harp on about *vt* insistir en.

harpoon [hɑː'puːn] *n* arpón.
▶ *vt* arponear.

harpsichord ['hɑːpsɪkɔːd] *n* clavicordio.

harrowing ['hærəʊɪŋ] *adj* angustioso,-a.

harry ['hærɪ] *vt* (*pt & pp* harried, *ger* harrying) acosar.

harsh [hɑːʃ] *adj* 1 cruel, severo,-a *(castigo)*. 2 fuerte *(color, luz)*. 3 áspero,-a *(voz)*. 4 duro,-a *(invierno)*.

harvest ['hɑːvɪst] *n* cosecha, vendimia.
▶ *vt* cosechar, vendimiar.

harvester ['hɑːvɪstəʳ] *n* 1 segador,-ra. 2 segadora.

has [hæz] *3rd pers sing pres* → have.

hash¹ [hæʃ] *n* picadillo.

● to make a hash of STH estropear algo.

hash² [hæʃ] *n fam* hachís.

144

hashish ['hæʃiːʃ] *n* hachís.
hassle ['hæsəl] *n fam* rollo, problema, lío: *it's a real hassle!*, ies una lata!
▸ *vt fam* molestar, fastidiar.
haste [heɪst] *n* prisa.
● **in haste** de prisa.
hasten ['heɪsən] *vt-vi* apresurar(se).
hasty ['heɪstɪ] *adj* (**-ier**, **-iest**). **1** apresurado,-a. **2** precipitado,-a.
hat [hæt] *n* sombrero.
hatch [hætʃ] *n* (*pl* **-es**) trampilla, escotilla (*de barco*).
▸ *vt* **1** empollar, incubar. **2** *fig* idear, tramar.
▸ *vi* salir del huevo, romper el cascarón.
hatchet ['hætʃɪt] *n* hacha.
hate [heɪt] *n* odio.
▸ *vt* **1** odiar, detestar. **2** lamentar: *I hate to disturb you, but...*, lamento molestarte, pero....
hateful ['heɪtfʊl] *adj* odioso,-a.
hatred ['heɪtrəd] *n* odio.
haughty ['hɔːtɪ] *adj* (**-ier**, **-iest**) arrogante.
haul [hɔːl] *n* **1** botín. **2** redada (*de peces*).
▸ *vt* tirar de, arrastrar.
● **a long haul** un largo camino.
haulage ['hɔːlɪdʒ] *n* transporte.
haulier ['hɔːljəʳ] *n* transportista.
haunch [hɔːntʃ] *n* (*pl* **-es**) cadera y muslo.
haunt [hɔːnt] *n* sitio preferido.
▸ *vt* **1** frecuentar, aparecer en (*fantasma*). **2** obsesionar, atormentar (*recuerdo, pensamiento*).
haunted ['hɔːntɪd] *adj* encantado,-a.
have [hæv] *vt* (*pt & pp* **had**). **1** tener, poseer: *he has lots of momey*, tiene mucho dinero. **2** comer, beber, fumar: *to have breakfast*, desayunar; *to have lunch*, comer; *to have tea*, merendar; *to have dinner*, cenar. **3** tomar: *to have a bath*, bañarse; *to have a shower*, ducharse. **4** tener: *she has flu*, tiene la gripe. **5** hacer, celebrar: *are you having a birthday party?*, ¿harás una fiesta de cumpleaños? **6** tener, dar a luz: *Anna's had a baby girl*, Anna ha dado a luz a una niña. **7** hacer, mandar: *he had the house painted*, hizo pintar la casa. **8** permitir, consentir: *I won't have it!*, ¡no lo consentiré!
▸ *aux* haber: *I have seen a ghost*, he visto un fantasma; *I had seen the film before*, había visto la película antes.

● **had better** más vale que: *you'd better come alone*, más vale que vengas solo,-a.
● **have got** GB tener: *he's got a new bike*, tiene una bici nueva.
● **to have done with** acabar con.
● **to have had it 1** estar estropeado,-a (*objeto*). **2** estar apañado,-a (*persona*).
● **to have just** acabar de: *I have just seen him*, acabo de verlo.
● **to have sb on** tomarle el pelo a ALGN: *to have sth done*, hacerse algo; *they're having a house built*, les están construyendo una casa.
● **to have sth on** tener algo planeado, tener algo que hacer.
● **to have it in for sb** tenerla tomada con ALGN.
● **to have it out with sb** ajustar las cuentas con ALGN.
● **to have to do sth** tener que hacer algo.
● **to have to do with** tener que ver con.
● **to have it away, have it off** *vulg* echar un polvo.
to have on *vt* **1** llevar puesto,-a (*prenda*). **2** tomar el pelo.
to have out *vt* **1** sacarse (*muela*). **2** operarse de (*apendicitis, amígdalas*).
haven ['heɪvən] *n fig* refugio.
haversack ['hævəsæk] *n* mochila.
havoc ['hævək] *n* estragos.
● **to play havoc** causar estragos.
hawk [hɔːk] *n* halcón.
hay [heɪ] *n* heno.
hay-fever ['heɪfiːvəʳ] *n* fiebre del heno, alergia.
haywire ['heɪwaɪəʳ] *adj* loco,-a.
● **to go haywire** descontrolarse.
hazard ['hæzəd] *n* riesgo, peligro.
▸ *vt* aventurar, atreverse a hacer: *to hazard a guess*, atreverse a dar una opinión.
hazardous ['hæzədəs] *adj* arriesgado,-a, peligroso,-a.
haze [heɪz] *n* neblina.
hazel ['heɪzəl] *n* avellano.
▸ *adj* avellana (*color*).
hazelnut ['heɪzəlnʌt] *n* avellana.
hazy ['heɪzɪ] *adj* (**-ier**, **-iest**). **1** brumoso,-a: *it's hazy*, hay neblina. **2** *fig* vago,-a, confuso,-a.
he [hiː] *pron* él: *he came yesterday*, vino ayer.

▶ *adj* varón, macho: *a he bear*, un oso macho.

head [hed] *n* **1** cabeza. **2** cabezal *(de casete)*. **3** cabecera *(de cama, mesa)*. **4** principio *(de página)*. **5** espuma *(de cerveza)*. **6** director,-ra *(de escuela)*. **7** res, cabeza *(de ganado)*.
▶ *vt* **1** encabezar *(procesión)*. **2** rematar de cabeza. **3** dirigir *(organización)*.
● **heads or tails?** ¿cara o cruz?

to head for *vt* dirigirse hacia.

headache ['hedeɪk] *n* dolor de cabeza.

header ['hedəʳ] *n* cabezazo.

heading ['hedɪŋ] *n* **1** encabezamiento. **2** membrete.

headlamp ['hedlæmp] *n* faro.

headland ['hedlənd] *n* cabo.

headlight ['hedlaɪt] *n* faro.

headline ['hedlaɪn] *n* titular.

headlong ['hedlɒŋ] *adj* de cabeza.

headmaster [hed'mɑːstəʳ] *n* director.

headmistress [hed'mɪstrəs] *n (pl -es)* directora.

headphones ['hedfəʊnz] *npl* auriculares.

headquarters ['hedkwɔːtəz] *npl* **1** sede, oficina principal. **2** cuartel general.

headstrong ['hedstrɒŋ] *adj* obstinado,-a, testarudo,-a.

headteacher [hed'tiːtʃəʳ] *n* director,-ra *(de colegio)*.

headway ['hedweɪ] *n* .
● **to make headway** avanzar.

headword ['hedwɜːd] *n* entrada.

heal [hiːl] *vt-vi* curar(se).

health [helθ] *n* **1** salud. **2** sanidad.
■ **health centre** centro de salud, ambulatorio.

healthy ['helθɪ] *adj (-ier, -iest)*. **1** sano,-a. **2** saludable.

heap [hiːp] *n* montón.
▶ *vt* amontonar.

hear [hɪəʳ] *vt-vi (pt & pp **heard** [hɜːd])* oír.
● **to hear from** tener noticias de.
● **to hear of** oír hablar de.

hearer ['hɪərəʳ] *n* oyente.

hearing ['hɪərɪŋ] *n* **1** oído. **2** vista *(ante tribunal)*.
■ **hearing aid** audífono.

hearsay ['hɪəseɪ] *n* rumores.

hearse [hɜːs] *n* coche fúnebre.

heart [hɑːt] *n* **1** corazón. **2** valor. **3** cogollo *(de lechuga)*. **4** quid *(de problema)*.

▶ *npl* **hearts** corazones, copas *(de baraja española)*.
● **by heart** de memoria.
● **to lose heart** desanimarse.
● **to take heart** animarse.
● **with all your heart** de todo corazón.
■ **heart attack** ataque al corazón, infarto de miocardio.

heartbeat ['hɑːtbiːt] *n* latido del corazón.

heartbreaking ['hɑːtbreɪkɪŋ] *n* desgarrador,-ora.

heartbroken ['hɑːtbrəʊkən] *adj* desconsolado,-a.
● **to be heartbroken** tener el corazón destrozado.

hearten ['hɑːtən] *vt* animar.

hearth [hɑːθ] *n* hogar, chimenea.

heartless ['hɑːtləs] *adj* cruel, despiadado,-a.

heart-throb ['hɑːtθrɒb] *n* ídolo.

hearty ['hɑːtɪ] *adj (-ier, -iest)*. **1** campechano,-a *(persona)*. **2** cordial *(recibimiento)*. **3** abundante *(comida)*.

heat [hiːt] *n* **1** calor. **2** calefacción. **3** eliminatoria *(en deporte)*.
▶ *vt-vi* calentar(se).
● **on heat** en celo.

heated ['hiːtɪd] *adj* **1** climatizado,-a. **2** *fig* acalorado,-a.

heater ['hiːtəʳ] *n* estufa, calefactor.

heath [hiːθ] *n* brezal.

heathen ['hiːðən] *adj-n* pagano,-a.

heather ['heðəʳ] *n* brezo.

heating ['hiːtɪŋ] *n* calefacción.

heatwave ['hiːtweɪv] *n* ola de calor.

heave [hiːv] *n* tirón.
▶ *vt* **1** tirar, arrastrar. **2** *fam* lanzar.
▶ *vi* **1** subir y bajar. **2** respirar con dificultad. **3** hacer arcadas.

heaven ['hevən] *n* cielo.

heavenly ['hevənlɪ] *adj (-ier, -iest)*. **1** celestial. **2** *fig* divino,-a.
■ **heavenly body** cuerpo celeste.

heavily ['hevɪlɪ] *adv* **1** mucho: *it was raining heavily*, llovía mucho. **2** fuertemente: *they were heavily armed*, van fuertemente armados.

heavy ['hevɪ] *adj (-ier, -iest)*. **1** pesado,-a. **2** fuerte *(lluvia, golpe)*. **3** denso,-a *(tráfico)*. **4** profundo,-a *(sueño)*. **5** abundante *(cosecha)*.
● **to be a heavy smoker** fumar mucho.

heavyweight ['hevɪweɪt] n peso pesado.
heckle ['hekəl] vt interrumpir.
hectare ['hektɑːˈ] n hectárea.
hectic ['hektɪk] adj agitado,-a, ajetreado,-a.
hedge [hedʒ] n 1 seto vivo. 2 fig protección.
▶ vi contestar con evasivas.
hedgehog ['hedʒhɒg] n erizo.
heed [hiːd] n atención.
▶ vt prestar atención a.
● **to pay heed to** SB hacer caso a ALGN.
● **to take heed of** STH tener algo en cuenta.
heel [hiːl] n 1 talón. 2 tacón.
hefty ['heftɪ] adj (-ier, -iest). 1 corpulento, fuerte. 2 abundante, enorme.
heifer ['hefəˈ] n vaquilla.
height [haɪt] n 1 altura (de objeto). 2 altitud. 3 estatura (de persona). 4 fig punto álgido, cumbre.
heighten ['haɪtən] vt fig intensificar.
heinous ['heɪnəs] adj atroz.
heir [eəˈ] n heredero.
heiress ['eəres] n (pl -es) heredera.
heirloom ['eəluːm] n reliquia de familia.
held [held] pt-pp → hold.
helicopter ['helɪkɒptəˈ] n helicóptero.
helium ['hiːlɪəm] n helio.
hell [hel] n infierno.
● **a hell of a 1** fam estupendo,-a, fantástico,-a. 2 fatal, horrible.
hellish ['helɪʃ] adj fam infernal.
hello [heˈləʊ] interj 1 ¡hola! 2 ¡diga!, ¡dígame! (por teléfono).
helm [helm] n timón.
helmet ['helmɪt] n casco.
help [help] n ayuda.
▶ interj ¡socorro!
▶ vt 1 ayudar. 2 evitar: I couldn't help laughing, no pude contener la risa.
● **help yourself** sírvete tú mismo,-a.
● **I can't help it** no lo puedo evitar.
● **it can't be helped** no hay nada que hacer.
helper ['helpəˈ] n ayudante.
helpful ['helpfʊl] adj 1 útil (consejo). 2 amable, servicial (persona).
helping ['helpɪŋ] n ración.
helpless ['helpləs] adj 1 indefenso,-a (persona). 2 impotente (mirada).
helter-skelter [heltəˈskeltəˈ] adv atropelladamente.
▶ n tobogán.

hem [hem] n dobladillo.
▶ vt (pt & pp **hemmed**, ger **hemming**) hacer un dobladillo en.
to hem in vt cercar, rodear.
he-man ['hiːmæn] n (pl **he-men**) machote.
hemisphere ['hemɪsfɪəˈ] n hemisferio.
hemp [hemp] n cáñamo.
hen [hen] n gallina.
hence [hens] adv 1 por eso. 2 de aquí a: **five years hence**, de aquí a cinco años.
henceforth [hensˈfɔːθ] adv de ahora en adelante.
henchman ['hentʃmən] n (pl **henchmen**) secuaz, esbirro.
hepatitis [hepəˈtaɪtəs] n hepatitis.
her [hɜːˈ] pron 1 la (complemento directo): **I love her**, la quiero. 2 le, se (complemento indirecto): **give her the money**, dale el dinero; **give it to her**, dáselo. 3 ella (después de preposición): **go with her**, vete con ella.
▶ adj su, sus, de ella: **her dog**, de ella.
herald ['herəld] n heraldo.
▶ vt anunciar.
heraldry ['herəldrɪ] n heráldica.
herb [hɜːb] n hierba.
herbal ['hɜːbəl] adj de hierbas.
■ **herbal tea** infusión de hierbas.
herbalist ['hɜːbəlɪst] n herbolario,-a.
herbivorous [hɜːˈbɪvərəs] adj herbívoro,-a.
herd [hɜːd] n 1 manada (de ganado). 2 rebaño (de cabras). 3 piara (de cerdos).
▶ vt juntar en manada, juntar en rebaño.
here [hɪəˈ] adv aquí.
● **here and there** aquí y allá.
● **here you are** aquí tienes.
hereafter [hɪərˈɑːftəˈ] adv de ahora en adelante.
hereby [hɪəˈbaɪ] adv por la presente.
hereditary [hɪˈredɪtərɪ] adj hereditario,-a.
heredity [hɪˈredɪtɪ] n herencia.
heresy ['herəsɪ] n (pl -ies) herejía.
heretic ['herətɪk] n hereje.
heritage ['herɪtɪdʒ] n herencia, patrimonio.
hermaphrodite [hɜːˈmæfrədaɪt] adj hermafrodita.
▶ n hermafrodita.
hermetic [hɜːˈmetɪk] adj hermético,-a.
hermit ['hɜːmɪt] n ermitaño.
hernia ['hɜːnɪə] n hernia.
hero ['hɪərəʊ] n (pl **heroes**) héroe.
heroic [hɪˈrəʊɪk] adj heroico,-a.

heroin ['herəʊɪn] n heroína *(droga)*.
■ **heroin addict** heroinómano,-a.
heroine ['herəʊɪn] n heroína *(persona)*.
heroism ['herəʊɪzəm] n heroísmo.
herring ['herɪŋ] n arenque.
hers [hɜːz] pron (el) suyo, (la) suya, (los) suyos, (las) suyas.
herself [hɜː'self] pron **1** se, ella misma: *she bought herself a new dress*, se compró un vestido nuevo. **2** ella misma, sí misma: *she only thinks of herself*, sólo piensa en sí misma.
● **by herself** sola.
hesitant ['hezɪtənt] adj indeciso,-a.
hesitate ['hezɪteɪt] vi vacilar, dudar.
hesitation [hezɪ'teɪʃən] n duda.
heterogeneous [hetərəʊ'dʒiːnɪəs] adj heterogéneo,-a.
heterosexual [hetərəʊ'seksjʊəl] adj heterosexual.
► n heterosexual.
hexagon ['heksəgən] n hexágono.
hey [heɪ] interj ¡oye!, ¡oiga!
heyday ['heɪdeɪ] n auge, apogeo.
HGV [eɪtʃdʒiː'viː] abbr GB *(heavy goods vehicle)* vehículo pesado.
hi [haɪ] interj ¡hola!
hibernate ['haɪbəneɪt] vi hibernar.
hibernation [haɪbə'neɪʃən] n hibernación.
hiccough ['hɪkʌp] n hipo.
► vi tener hipo.
hiccup ['hɪkʌp] n hipo.
► vi (pt & pp **hiccupped**, ger **hiccupping**) tener hipo.
hid [hɪd] pt-pp → hide.
hidden ['hɪdən] pp → hide.
► adj escondido,-a, oculto,-a.
hide [haɪd] vt (pt **hid** [hɪd], pp **hidden** ['hɪdən]) esconder.
► vi esconderse.
hide [haɪd] n piel, cuero.
hide-and-seek [haɪdən'siːk] n escondite.
hideous ['hɪdɪəs] adj horroroso,-a, espantoso,-a.
hiding ['haɪdɪŋ] n paliza.
● **to go into hiding** esconderse.
hierarchy ['haɪərɑːkɪ] n (pl **-ies**) jerarquía.
hieroglyph ['haɪərəglɪf] n jeroglífico.
high [haɪ] adj **1** alto,-a: *it's 6 metres high*, mide 6 metros de altura. **2** elevado,-a *(ideales, principios)*. **3** agudo,-a *(voz)*. **4** fuerte *(viento)*. **5** sl colocado,-a.
► n punto máximo.

● **high and low** por todas partes.
■ **high court** tribunal supremo.
■ **high chair** silla alta.
■ **high fidelity** alta fidelidad.
■ **high jump** salto de altura.
■ **high school** instituto de enseñanza secundaria.
■ **high street** calle mayor.
■ **high tide** pleamar.
highbrow ['haɪbraʊ] adj intelectual.
higher ['haɪə'] adj superior.
■ **higher education** enseñanza superior.
high-heeled ['haɪhiːld] adj de tacón alto.
highlands ['haɪləndz] npl tierras altas.
highlight ['haɪlaɪt] vt hacer resaltar, poner de relieve.
highly ['haɪlɪ] adv muy: *it's highly enjoyable*, es muy divertido.
● **to speak highly of** SB hablar bien de alguien.
● **to think highly of** SB tener buena opinión de alguien.
Highness ['haɪnəs] n Alteza.
high-pitched ['haɪpɪtʃt] adj agudo,-a.
high-speed ['haɪspiːd] adj de gran velocidad.
highway ['haɪweɪ] n US autovía.
■ **Highway Code** GB código de la circulación.
highwayman ['haɪweɪmən] n (pl **highwaymen**) salteador de caminos, bandolero.
hijack ['haɪdʒæk] n secuestro.
► vt secuestrar.
hijacker ['haɪdʒækə'] n secuestrador,-ra.
hike [haɪk] n excursión.
► vi ir de excursión.
hiker ['haɪkə'] n excursionista.
hilarious [hɪ'leərɪəs] adj graciosísimo,-a, divertidísimo,-a.
hill [hɪl] n **1** colina. **2** cuesta, pendiente.
hillside ['hɪlsaɪd] n ladera.
hilly ['hɪlɪ] adj (**-ier, -iest**) montañoso,-a.
hilt [hɪlt] n empuñadura.
● **up to the hilt 1** al máximo. **2** hasta el cuello.
him [hɪm] pron **1** lo *(complemento directo)*: *I love him*, lo quiero. **2** le, se *(complemento indirecto)*: *give him the money*, dale el dinero; *give it to him*, dáselo. **3** él *(después de preposición)*: *we went with him*, fuimos con él.

Himalayas [ˌhɪməˈleɪəz] *npl* **the Himalayas** el Himalaya.

himself [hɪmˈself] *pron* **1** se, sí mismo: *he bought himself a new suit*, se compró un traje nuevo. **2** él mismo, sí mismo: *he only thinks of himself*, sólo piensa en sí mismo.

● **by himself** solo: *he was sitting by himself*, estaba sentado solo.

hind [haɪnd] *adj* trasero,-a.

hinder [ˈhɪndəʳ] *vt-vi* entorpecer, estorbar.

hindrance [ˈhɪndrəns] *n* estorbo, obstáculo.

hindsight [ˈhaɪndsaɪt] *n* retrospectiva: *with hindsight*, en retrospectiva.

Hindu [hɪnˈduː, ˈhɪnduː] *adj-n* hindú.

hinge [hɪndʒ] *n* bisagra, gozne.

● **to hinge on** depender de.

hint [hɪnt] *n* **1** insinuación, indirecta. **2** consejo. **3** pista, indicio.

▶ *vt* insinuar.

▶ *vi* lanzar indirectas.

hinterland [ˈhɪntəlænd] *n* interior.

hip [hɪp] *n* cadera.

● **hip hip hooray!** ¡hurra!, ¡viva!

hippie [ˈhɪpi] *adj fam* hippie.

▶ *n fam* hippie.

hippo [ˈhɪpəʊ] *n* (*pl* **hippos**) hipopótamo.

hippopotamus [hɪpəˈpɒtəməs] *n* (*pl* **hippopotamuses**) hipopótamo.

hippy [ˈhɪpi] *adj fam* hippie.

▶ *n* (*pl* **-ies**) *fam* hippie.

hire [ˈhaɪəʳ] *n* alquiler: *boats for hire*, se alquilan barcos.

▶ *vt* **1** alquilar. **2** contratar.

● **on hire purchase** a plazos.

his [hɪz] *adj* **1** su, sus: *his dog*, su perro. **2** de él.

▶ *pron* (el) suyo, (la) suya, (los) suyos, (las) suyas.

hiss [hɪs] *n* (*pl* **-es**). **1** siseo, silbido. **2** silbido *(de protesta)*.

▶ *vi* **1** sisear, silbar. **2** silbar *(para protestar)*.

historian [hɪˈstɔːriən] *n* historiador,-ra.

historic [hɪˈstɒrɪk] *adj* histórico,-a.

historical [hɪˈstɒrɪkəl] *adj* histórico,-a.

history [ˈhɪstəri] *n* (*pl* **-ies**) historia.

hit [hɪt] *n* **1** golpe. **2** éxito. **3** acierto. **4** visita *(a página web)*.

▶ *vt* (*pt & pp* **hit**, *ger* **hitting**). **1** golpear, pegar: *he hit his head on the door*, dio con la cabeza contra la puerta. **2** chocar

contra: *the car hit a tree*, el coche chocó contra un árbol. **3** afectar *(huelga)*. **4** alcanzar *(bala)*.

● **to hit it off with** llevarse bien con.

● **to score a direct hit** dar en el blanco.

hit-and-miss [ˈhɪtənˈmɪs] *adj* a la buena de Dios.

hitch [hɪtʃ] *n* (*pl* **-es**) tropiezo, dificultad.

▶ *vt* enganchar, atar.

▶ *vi fam* hacer autoestop, ir a dedo.

hitchhike [ˈhɪtʃhaɪk] *vi* hacer autoestop.

hitchhiker [ˈhɪtʃhaɪkəʳ] *n* autoestopista.

hitherto [hɪðəˈtuː] *adv (fml)* hasta ahora.

HIV [ˈeɪtʃaɪˈviː] *abbr* **(human immunodeficiency virus)** VIH.

● **to be diagnosed HIV negative** dar negativo,-a en la prueba del sida.

● **to be HIV positive** ser seropositivo,-a, ser portador,-ra del virus del sida.

■ **HIV carrier** seropositivo,-a, portador,-ra del virus del sida.

hive [haɪv] *n* colmena.

HMS [ˈeɪtʃemˈes] *abbr* GB *(His/Her Majesty's Ship)* barco de su majestad.

HNC [ˈeɪtʃenˈsiː] *abbr* GB **(Higher National Certificate)** título de formación profesional.

HND [ˈeɪtʃenˈdiː] *abbr* GB **(Higher National Diploma)** título de formación profesional.

hoard [hɔːd] *n* **1** provisión. **2** tesoro *(dinero)*.

▶ *vt* **1** acumular, acaparar. **2** atesorar *(dinero)*.

hoarding [ˈhɔːdɪŋ] *n* valla.

hoarse [hɔːs] *adj* ronco,-a, áspero,-a.

hoax [həʊks] *n* (*pl* **hoaxes**) trampa, engaño.

▶ *vt* engañar.

hobble [ˈhɒbəl] *vi* cojear.

hobby [ˈhɒbi] *n* (*pl* **-ies**) afición, hobby.

hockey [ˈhɒki] *n* hockey.

hog [hɒg] *n* cerdo.

▶ *vt* (*pt & pp* **hogged**, *ger* **hogging**) acaparar.

hoist [hɔɪst] *n* **1** grúa. **2** montacargas.

▶ *vt* **1** levantar. **2** izar *(bandera)*.

hold [həʊld] *n* **1** agarro, asimiento: *to have a firm hold on STH*, tener algo bien agarrado. **2** dominio central. **3** bodega *(de barco, avión)*.

▶ *vt* (*pt & pp* **held**). **1** aguantar, sostener, agarrar *(con la mano)*. **2** dar cabida a, tener capacidad para. **3** celebrar *(reunión)*. **4** mantener *(conversación)*. **5** creer, consi-

derar. **6** guardar *(secreto)*. **7** ostentar *(título)*.
▶ *vi fig* resistir, seguir siendo válido,-a.
● **to get hold of** STH asir, hacerse con algo.
● **hold it!** ¡espera!
● **to get hold of** SB localizar a ALGN.
● **to hold the line** no colgar el teléfono.
to hold back *vt* **1** retener. **2** ocultar.
to hold forth *vi* hablar largo y tendido.
to hold on *vi* **1** agarrar fuerte. **2** esperar, no colgar *(por teléfono)*.
to hold out *vt* tender *(mano)*.
▶ *vi* durar, resistir, aguantar *(persona)*.
to hold over *vt* aplazar.
to hold up *vt* **1** atracar, asaltar. **2** retrasar. **3** levantar *(mano)*.
▶ *vi* resistir.
to hold with *vt* estar de acuerdo con.
holder ['həʊldə'] *n* **1** poseedor,-ra, titular *(de pasaporte)*. **2** recipiente, soporte.
holding ['həʊldɪŋ] *n* **1** posesión. **2** holding *(empresa)*.
hold-up ['həʊldʌp] *n* **1** atraco. **2** retraso. **3** atasco, embotellamiento *(de tráfico)*.
hole [həʊl] *n* **1** agujero, hoyo. **2** hoyo *(en golf)*. **3** bache *(en carretera)*.
holiday ['hɒlɪdeɪ] *n* **1** fiesta. **2** vacaciones.
● **to be on holidays** estar de vacaciones.
● **to go on holiday** ir de vacaciones.
holiday-maker ['hɒlɪdɪmeɪkə'] *n* turista, veraneante.
holiness ['həʊlɪnəs] *n* santidad.
Holland ['hɒlənd] *n* Holanda.
hollow ['hɒləʊ] *adj (comp* **hollower**, *superl* **hollowest**). **1** hueco,-a. **2** *fig* falso,-a, poco sincero,-a.
▶ *n* **1** hueco. **2** hondonada, depresión.
holly ['hɒlɪ] *n (pl* **-ies**) acebo.
holocaust ['hɒləkɔːst] *n* holocausto.
holster ['həʊlstə'] *n* pistolera.
holy ['həʊlɪ] *adj* (**-ier**, **-iest**). **1** santo,-a, sagrado,-a. **2** bendito,-a.
homage ['hɒmɪdʒ] *n* homenaje.
home [həʊm] *n* **1** hogar, casa. **2** asilo, residencia.
▶ *adj* **1** casero,-a *(cocina)*. **2** del hogar, familiar. **3** nacional.
● **at home** en casa.
● **make yourself at home** póngase cómodo,-a.
● **to feel at home** estar a gusto.

● **to go home** irse a casa.
● **to leave home** irse de casa.
■ **home help** asistenta.
■ **Home Office** Ministerio del Interior.
■ **home page** **1** página web. **2** página inicial.
■ **Home Secretary** Ministro,-a del Interior.
homeland ['həʊmlænd] *n* patria.
homeless ['həʊmləs] *adj* sin techo, sin hogar.
▶ *npl* **the homeless** los sin techo.
homely ['həʊmlɪ] *adj* (**-ier**, **-iest**). **1** sencillo,-a, casero,-a. **2** US feo,-a.
home-made ['həʊm'meɪd] *adj* casero,-a, hecho,-a en casa.
homesick ['həʊmsɪk] *adj* nostálgico,-a.
● **to be homesick** tener morriña.
homesickness ['həʊmsɪknəs] *n* añoranza, morriña.
homework ['həʊmwɜːk] *n* deberes.
homicidal [hɒmɪ'saɪdəl] *adj* homicida.
homicide ['hɒmɪsaɪd] *n* **1** homicidio. **2** homicida.
homogeneous [hɒmə'dʒiːnɪəs] *adj* homogéneo,-a.
homosexual [həʊməʊ'seksjʊəl] *adj-n* homosexual.
Honduran [hɒn'djʊərən] *adj-n* hondureño,-a.
Honduras [hɒn'djʊərəs] *n* Honduras.
honest ['ɒnɪst] *adj* **1** honrado,-a, honesto,-a. **2** sincero,-a, franco,-a.
honestly ['ɒnɪstlɪ] *adv* **1** honradamente. **2** con franqueza, a decir verdad.
honesty ['ɒnɪstɪ] *n* honradez, rectitud.
honey ['hʌnɪ] *n* **1** miel. **2** US cariño.
honeymoon ['hʌnɪmuːn] *n* luna de miel.
honk [hɒŋk] *n* **1** graznido. **2** bocinazo.
▶ *vi* **1** graznar. **2** tocar la bocina.
honour ['ɒnə'] (US **honor**) *n* honor, honra.
▶ *vt* **1** honrar. **2** pagar, satisfacer *(deuda)*. **3** cumplir *(promesa, acuerdo)*.
■ **Your Honour** Su Señoría.
honourable ['ɒnərəbəl] (US **honorable**) *adj* **1** honrado,-a, honorable. **2** honroso,-a.
Hons ['hɒnəz] *abbr* GB (**Honours**) licenciado,-a.
hood [hʊd] *n* **1** capucha. **2** capota *(de coche)*. **3** US capó *(de coche)*.
hoof [huːf] *n (pl* **-s** o **hooves**). **1** pezuña. **2** casco *(de caballo)*.

hook [hʊk] *n* **1** gancho, percha. **2** anzuelo *(para pescar)*. **3** gancho *(en boxeo)*.
▶ *vt* enganchar.
● **off the hook 1** descolgado,-a *(teléfono)*. **2** a salvo, salvado,-a, liberado,-a *(persona)*.

to hook up *vt* conectar.

hooked [hʊkt] *adj* **1** aquilino,-a *(nariz)*. **2** enganchado,-a, obsesionado,-a.

hooligan [ˈhuːlɪɡən] *n* gamberro,-a.

hooliganism [ˈhuːlɪɡənɪzəm] *n* gamberrismo.

hoop [huːp] *n* aro.

hoorah [hʊˈrɑː] *interj* ¡hurra!, ¡viva!

hooray [hʊˈreɪ] *interj* ¡hurra!, ¡viva!

hoot [huːt] *n* **1** ululato *(de búho)*. **2** grito. **3** bocinazo.
▶ *vi* **1** ulular *(búho)*. **2** gritar. **3** dar un bocinazo, tocar la bocina.
● **hoots of laughter** risotadas, carcajadas.

hooter [ˈhuːtəʳ] *n* **1** sirena, bocina. **2** *fam* napias.

hoover [ˈhuːvəʳ] *n* aspiradora.
▶ *vt-vi* pasar la aspiradora (por).

hop[1] [hɒp] *n* salto.
▶ *vi* (*pt & pp* **hopped**, *ger* **hopping**). **1** saltar a la pata coja. **2** dar saltitos.

hop[2] [hɒp] *n* lúpulo.

hope [həʊp] *n* esperanza.
▶ *vt-vi* esperar.
● **to give up hope** perder las esperanzas.
● **to hope for the best** esperar que la suerte nos acompañe.

hopeful [ˈhəʊpfʊl] *adj* **1** esperanzado,-a, confiado,-a. **2** prometedor,-ra, esperanzador,-ra.
● **to be hopeful** tener la esperanza.

hopefully [ˈhəʊpfʊlɪ] *adv* **1** con esperanza, con ilusión. **2** con un poco de suerte.

hopeless [ˈhəʊpləs] *adj* **1** inútil, imposible, desesperado,-a. **2** *fam* inútil, negado en: *I'm hopeless at maths*, soy negado para las matemáticas.

horizon [həˈraɪzən] *n* horizonte.

horizontal [hɒrɪˈzɒntəl] *adj* horizontal.

hormone [ˈhɔːməʊn] *n* hormona.

horn [hɔːn] *n* **1** asta, cuerno. **2** bocina, cláxon. **3** trompa *(instrumento)*.

horny [ˈhɔːnɪ] *adj* (-**ier**, -**iest**). **1** calloso,-a. **2** *fam* cachondo,-a, caliente.

horoscope [ˈhɒrəskəʊp] *n* horóscopo.

horrible [ˈhɒrɪbəl] *adj* horrible.

horrid [ˈhɒrɪd] *adj* horroroso,-a.

horrific [həˈrɪfɪk] *adj* horrendo,-a, espantoso,-a.

horrify [ˈhɒrɪfaɪ] *vt* (*pt & pp* -**ied**) horrorizar.

horror [ˈhɒrəʳ] *n* horror.
■ **horror film** película de terror.

hors d'oeuvre [ɔːˈdɜːvʳ] *n* entremés.

horse [hɔːs] *n* caballo.
■ **horse show** concurso hípico.
■ **to go horse riding** montar a caballo.

horseman [ˈhɔːsmən] *n* (*pl* **horsemen**) jinete.

horsemanship [ˈhɔːsmənʃɪp] *n* equitación.

horsepower [ˈhɔːspaʊəʳ] *n* caballo *(de vapor)*.

horseshoe [ˈhɔːsʃuː] *n* herradura.

horsewoman [ˈhɔːswʊmən] *n* (*pl* **horsewomen**) amazona.

horticultural [hɔːtɪˈkʌltʃərəl] *adj* hortícola.

horticulture [ˈhɔːtɪkʌltʃəʳ] *n* horticultura.

hose[1] [həʊz] *n* manguera.

hose[2] [həʊz] *npl* calcetines, medias.

hospitable [hɒˈspɪtəbəl] *adj* hospitalario,-a.

hospital [ˈhɒspɪtəl] *n* hospital.

hospitality [hɒspɪˈtælɪtɪ] *n* hospitalidad.

host[1] [həʊst] *n* **1** anfitrión, -ona. **2** presentador, -ra *(de programa)*.
▶ *vt* **1** ser el anfitrión de. **2** presentar *(programa)*.

host[2] [həʊst] *n* multitud.

Host [həʊst] *n* hostia.

hostage [ˈhɒstɪdʒ] *n* rehén.

hostel [ˈhɒstəl] *n* **1** hostal, albergue. **2** residencia *(en universidad)*.

hostess [ˈhəʊstəs] *n* (*pl* -**es**). **1** anfitriona. **2** azafata *(de avión, programa)*. **3** camarera.

hostile [ˈhɒstaɪl] *adj* hostil.

hostility [hɒˈstɪlɪtɪ] *n* (*pl* -**ies**) hostilidad.

hot [hɒt] *adj* (*comp* **hotter**, *superl* **hottest**). **1** caliente *(bebida, comida, etc)*. **2** caluroso,-a, cálido,-a *(día, tiempo)*. **3** picante *(comida)*: *hot peppers*, pimientos picantes. **4** de última hora *(noticias)*.
● **to be hot 1** tener calor: *I'm very hot*, tengo mucho calor. **2** hacer calor: *it's hot today*, hoy hace calor.
■ **hot dog** perrito caliente.

hotchpotch ['hɒtʃpɒtʃ] n (pl -es) fam revoltijo.

hotel [həʊ'tel] n hotel.

hotelier [həʊ'telɪeɪ] n hotelero,-a.

hot-headed ['hɒthedɪd] adj impetuoso,-a.

hothouse ['hɒthaʊs] n invernadero.

hotplate ['hɒtpleɪt] n placa de cocina.

hound [haʊnd] n perro de caza.
► vt acosar.

hour [aʊəʳ] n **1** hora. **2** horario: *office hours*, horario de oficina.
■ **hour hand** aguja horaria.
● **on the hour** a la hora en punto.

hourly ['aʊəlɪ] adj cada hora.
► adv a cada hora.

house [(n) haʊs(vb) haʊz] n casa.
► vt alojar.
● **it's on the house** es cortesía de la casa, paga la casa.
■ **House of Commons** Cámara de los Comunes.
■ **House of Lords** Cámara de los Lores.
■ **Houses of Parliament** Parlamento.

housebreaking ['haʊsbreɪkɪŋ] n allanamiento de morada.

household ['haʊshəʊld] n casa, hogar.

householder ['haʊshəʊldəʳ] n dueño,-a de la casa.

housekeeper ['haʊskiːpəʳ] n ama de llaves.

housekeeping ['haʊskiːpɪŋ] n **1** administración de la casa. **2** dinero para los gastos de la casa.

house-trained ['haʊstreɪnd] adj adiestrado,-a.

housewife ['haʊswaɪf] n (pl **housewives**) ama de casa.

housework ['haʊswɜːk] n tareas de la casa.

housing ['haʊzɪŋ] n vivienda.
■ **housing development** conjunto residencial, urbanización.
■ **housing estate** conunto residencial, urbanización.

hovel ['hɒvəl] n cuchitril, tugurio.

hover ['hɒvəʳ] vi **1** permanecer inmóvil, planear (en el aire). **2** cernerse (ave).

hovercraft ['hɒvəkrɑːft] n hovercraft.

how [haʊ] adv **1** cómo: *how does this machine work?*, ¿cómo funciona esta máquina? **2** qué: *how beautiful you look!*, ¡qué guapa estás!
● **how about...?** ¿qué tal si...?, ¿qué te parece si...?

● **how are you?** ¿cómo estás?
● **how do you do?** ¿cómo está usted?
● **how much** cuánto,-a: *how much did it cost?*, ¿cuánto costó?
● **how many** cuántos,-as.
● **how old are you?** ¿cuántos años tienes?

however [haʊ'evəʳ] conj sin embargo, no obstante.
► adv: *however much*, por más que, por mucho que.

howl [haʊl] n aullido.
► vi aullar.

HP ['eɪtʃ'piː] abbr **1** GB (*hire-purchase*) compra a plazos. **2** (*horsepower*) caballos de vapor.

hr [aʊəʳ] abbr (*hour*) hora, h.

HTML ['eɪtʃtiː'em'el] abbr (*hypertext mark-up language*) HTML.

HTTP ['eɪtʃtiː'tiː'piː] abbr (*hypertext transfer protocol*) HTTP.

hub [hʌb] n **1** cubo (de rueda). **2** fig centro, eje.

hubbub ['hʌbʌb] n bullicio, jaleo.

huddle ['hʌdəl] n montón, grupo.
► vi **1** acurrucarse. **2** apiñarse.

hue [hjuː] n matiz, tinte.
● **hue and cry** protesta.

huff [hʌf] n enfado, enojo: *to be in a huff*, estar enojado,-a.

hug [hʌg] n abrazo.
► vt (pt & pp **hugged**, ger **hugging**) abrazar.

huge [hjuːdʒ] adj enorme, inmenso,-a.

hulk [hʌlk] n **1** buque viejo. **2** mole (persona).

hull [hʌl] n casco (de barco).

hullabaloo [hʌləbə'luː] n barullo.

hullo [hʌ'ləʊ] interj → hello.

hum [hʌm] n **1** zumbido (de abejas). **2** murmullo (de voces).
► vi (pt & pp **hummed**, ger **humming**) zumbar.
► vt-vi tararear, canturrear.

human ['hjuːmən] adj humano,-a.
► n humano.
■ **human being** ser humano.

humane [hjuː'meɪn] adj humano,-a.

humanism ['hjuːmənɪzəm] n humanismo.

humanitarian [hjuːmænɪ'teərɪən] adj humanitario,-a.

humanity [hjuː'mænɪtɪ] n (pl -ies). **1** humanidad. **2** género humano.

humble ['hʌmbəl] *adj* (*comp* **humbler**, *superl* **humblest**) humilde.
► *vt* humillar.
humbleness ['hʌmbəlnəs] *n* humildad.
humdrum ['hʌmdrʌm] *adj* monótono,-a, aburrido,-a.
humid ['hjuːmɪd] *adj* húmedo,-a.
humidity [hjuːˈmɪdɪti] *n* humedad.
humiliate [hjuːˈmɪlieɪt] *vt* humillar.
humiliation [hjuːmɪliˈeɪʃən] *n* humillación.
humility [hjuːˈmɪlɪti] *n* humildad.
hummingbird ['hʌmɪŋbɜːd] *n* colibrí.
humorist ['hjuːmərɪst] *n* humorista.
humorous ['hjuːmərəs] *adj* gracioso,-a, humorístico,-a.
humour ['hjuːməʳ] (US **humor**) *n* humor: *a good sense of humour*, buen sentido del humor.
► *vt* complacer.
hump [hʌmp] *n* giba, joroba.
► *vt* cargar.
hunch [hʌntʃ] *n* (*pl* **-es**) presentimiento, corazonada.
► *vt-vi* encorvar(se).
hundred ['hʌndrəd] *num* cien, ciento.
► *n* cien, ciento.
hundredth ['hʌndrədθ] *adj-n* centésimo,-a.
► *n* **1** centésimo, cien. **2** centésima parte (*fracción*).
hundredweight ['hʌndrədweɪt] *n* quintal.

En Gran Bretaña equivale a 50,8 kg; en Estados Unidos equivale a 45,4 kg.

hung [hʌŋ] *pt-pp* → hang.
Hungarian [hʌŋˈɡeərɪən] *adj* húngaro,-a.
► *n* **1** húngaro,-a (*persona*). **2** húngaro (*lengua*).
Hungary ['hʌŋɡəri] *n* Hungría.
hunger ['hʌŋɡəʳ] *n* hambre.
● **to hunger for** ansiar, anhelar.
■ **hunger strike** huelga de hambre.
hungry ['hʌŋɡri] *adj* (**-ier**, **-iest**) hambriento,-a.
● **to be hungry** tener hambre.
hunk [hʌŋk] *n* **1** *fam* pedazo (*grande*). **2** *fam* tío cachas.
hunt [hʌnt] *n* **1** caza. **2** búsqueda.
► *vt-vi* cazar.
● **to hunt for** buscar.
hunter ['hʌntəʳ] *n* cazador.
hunting ['hʌntɪŋ] *n* caza, montería.
● **to go hunting** ir de caza.

huntress ['hʌntrəs] *n* (*pl* **-es**) cazadora.
hurdle ['hɜːdəl] *n* **1** valla. **2** *fig* obstáculo.
hurl [hɜːl] *vt* lanzar, arrojar.
hurly-burly ['hɜːlɪbɜːli] *n* bullicio.
hurrah [huˈrɑː] *interj* ¡hurra!, ¡viva!
hurray [huˈreɪ] *interj* ¡hurra!, ¡viva!
hurricane ['hʌrɪkən, 'hʌrɪkeɪn] *n* huracán.
hurried ['hʌrɪd] *adj* apresurado,-a, hecho,-a de prisa.
hurry ['hʌri] *n* (*pl* **-ies**) prisa.
► *vt* (*pt & pp* **-ied**) dar prisa a, apresurar.
► *vi* apresurarse, darse prisa.
● **to be in a hurry** tener prisa.
to hurry up *vi* darse prisa.
hurt [hɜːt] *n* daño, dolor, mal.
► *adj* **1** herido,-a. **2** dolido,-a, ofendido,-a.
► *vt* (*pt & pp* **hurt**). **1** lastimar, hacer daño. **2** herir, ofender.
► *vi* doler: *my back hurts*, me duele la espalda.
● **to get hurt** hacerse daño.
● **to hurt SB's feelings** herir los sentimientos de ALGN, ofender a ALGN.
hurtful ['hɜːtfʊl] *adj* hiriente, cruel.
hurtle ['hɜːtəl] *vi* precipitarse.
husband ['hʌzbənd] *n* marido, esposo.
hush [hʌʃ] *n* (*pl* **-es**) quietud, silencio.
► *vt* hacer callar.
hush-hush [hʌʃˈhʌʃ] *adj* *fam* confidencial.
husk [hʌsk] *n* cáscara.
huskiness ['hʌskɪnəs] *n* ronquera.
husky ['hʌski] *adj* (**-ier**, **-iest**) ronco,-a.
husky ['hʌski] *n* (*pl* **-ies**) husky.
hustle ['hʌsəl] *n* bullicio.
► *vt* dar prisa a.
► *vi* apresurarse.
■ **hustle and bustle** bullicio.
hustler ['hʌsləʳ] *n* **1** estafador,-ra. **2** US *sl* puta (*mujer*). **3** US *sl* chapero (*hombre*).
hut [hʌt] *n* **1** cabaña. **2** cobertizo.
hutch [hʌtʃ] *n* (*pl* **-es**) conejera.
hyaena [haɪˈiːnə] *n* hiena.
hybrid ['haɪbrɪd] *adj* híbrido,-a.
► *n* híbrido.
hydrant ['haɪdrənt] *n* boca de riego: *fire hydrant*, boca de incendios.
hydraulic [haɪˈdrɔːlɪk] *adj* hidráulico,-a.
hydrochloric [haɪdrəˈklɒrɪk] *adj* clorhídrico,-a.
hydroelectric [haɪdrəʊɪˈlektrɪk] *adj* hidroeléctrico,-a.
hydrofoil ['haɪdrəfɔɪl] *n* hidroala.
hydrogen ['haɪdrədʒən] *n* hidrógeno.

hydroplane ['haɪdrəpleɪn] *n* hidroavión.
hyena [haɪˈiːnə] *n* hiena.
hygiene ['haɪdʒiːn] *n* higiene.
hygienic [haɪˈdʒiːnɪk] *adj* higiénico,-a.
hymen ['haɪmən] *n* himen.
hymn [hɪm] *n* himno.
■ **hymn book** cantoral.
hyperbola [haɪˈpɜːbələ] *n* hipérbola.
hyperbole [haɪˈpɜːbəlɪ] *n* hipérbole.
hypermarket ['haɪpəmɑːkɪt] *n* hipermercado.
hyphen ['haɪfən] *n* guión.
hyphenate ['haɪfəneɪt] *vt* separar con guión.
hypnosis [hɪpˈnəʊsɪs] *n* hipnosis.
hypnotic [hɪpˈnɒtɪk] *adj* hipnótico,-a.
hypnotism ['hɪpnətɪzəm] *n* hipnotismo.
hypnotist ['hɪpnətɪst] *n* hipnotizador,-a.
hypnotize ['hɪpnətaɪz] *vt* hipnotizar.

hypochondriac [haɪpəˈkɒndriæk] *n* hipocondríaco,-a.
hypocrisy [hɪˈpɒkrɪsɪ] *n* hipocresía.
hypocrite ['hɪpəkrɪt] *n* hipócrita.
hypocritical [hɪpəˈkrɪtɪkəl] *adj* hipócrita.
hypodermic [haɪpəˈdɜːmɪk] *adj* hipodérmico,-a.
hypotenuse [haɪˈpɒtənjuːz] *n* hipotenusa.
hypothesis [haɪˈpɒθəsɪs] *n* (*pl* **hypotheses**) hipótesis.
hypothetical [haɪpəˈθetɪkəl] *adj* hipotético,-a.
hysterectomy [hɪstəˈrektəmɪ] *n* (*pl* -**ies**) histerectomía.
hysteria [hɪˈstɪərɪə] *n* histeria.
hysterical [hɪˈsterɪkəl] *adj* histérico,-a.
hysterics [hɪˈsterɪks] *n* **1** histeria. **2** ataque de histeria.

Es incontable y el verbo va en singular.

I

I [aɪ] *pron* yo.
Iberian [aɪˈbɪərɪən] *adj* ibero,-a, íbero,-a, ibérico,-a.
▶ *n* **1** ibero,-a, íbero,-a *(persona)*. **2** ibero, íbero *(lengua)*.
■ **Iberian Peninsula** Península Ibérica.
ice [aɪs] *n* **1** hielo. **2** helado.
▶ *vt* glasear.
■ **ice cube** cubito.
■ **ice lolly** polo.
■ **ice rink** pista de (patinaje sobre) hielo.
to ice over/up *vi* helarse.
iceberg [ˈaɪsbɜːg] *n* iceberg.
icebox [ˈaɪsbɒks] *n (pl* **iceboxes)** nevera.
ice-cream [ˈaɪskriːm] *n* helado.
Iceland [ˈaɪslənd] *n* Islandia.
Icelander [ˈaɪsləndə'] *n* islandés,-esa.
Icelandic [aɪsˈlændɪk] *adj* islandés,-esa.
▶ *n* islandés *(lengua)*.
ice-skate [ˈaɪsskeɪt] *vi* patinar sobre hielo.
▶ *n* patín de hielo.
ice-skating [ˈaɪskeɪtɪŋ] *n* patinaje sobre hielo.
icicle [ˈaɪsɪkəl] *n* carámbano.
icing [ˈaɪsɪŋ] *n* glaseado.
■ **icing sugar** azúcar glas.
icon [ˈaɪkən] *n* icono.
icy [ˈaɪsɪ] *adj* (**-ier, -iest**). **1** helado,-a. **2** glacial.
ID [ˈaɪˈdiː] *abbr (**identification**)* identificación.
■ **ID card** documento nacional de identidad, DNI.
idea [aɪˈdɪə] *n* **1** idea. **2** opinión.
● **to have no idea** no tener ni idea.
ideal [aɪˈdiːl] *adj-n* ideal.
idealize [aɪˈdɪəlaɪz] *vt* idealizar.

ideally [aɪˈdɪəlɪ] *adv* **1** idealmente. **2** preferiblemente.
identical [aɪˈdentɪkəl] *adj* idéntico,-a.
identification [aɪdentɪfɪˈkeɪʃən] *n* **1** identificación. **2** documentación.
■ **identification parade** rueda de identificación.
identify [aɪˈdentɪfaɪ] *vt (pt & pp* **-ied)** identificar.
identity [aɪˈdentɪtɪ] *n (pl* **-ies)** identidad.
■ **identity card** carnet de identidad.
ideology [aɪdɪˈɒlədʒɪ] *n (pl* **-ies)** ideología.
idiom [ˈɪdɪəm] *n* **1** locución, modismo. **2** lenguaje.
idiot [ˈɪdɪət] *n* idiota.
idiotic [ɪdɪˈɒtɪk] *adj* idiota.
idle [ˈaɪdəl] *adj (comp* **idler,** *superl* **idlest)**. **1** perezoso,-a. **2** parado,-a *(máquina)*. **3** frívolo,-a *(cotilleo)*. **4** fútil, vano *(promesa)*.
to idle away *vt* desperdiciar.
idol [ˈaɪdəl] *n* ídolo.
i.e. [ˈaɪˈiː] *abbr (id est)* esto es, a saber, i.e.
if [ɪf] *conj* **1** si: **if I were you,** yo de ti; **if you want,** si quieres. **2** aunque: *a clever if rather talkative child,* un niño inteligente aunque demasiado hablador.
● **as if** como si.
● **if I were you** yo en tu lugar, yo que tú.
● **if only** ojalá, si: **if only I knew his name!,** ¡ojalá supiera cómo se llama!
● **if so** de ser así.
igloo [ˈɪgluː] *n (pl* **igloos)** iglú.
ignition [ɪgˈnɪʃən] *n* **1** ignición. **2** encendido *(de motor)*.
■ **ignition key** llave de contacto.
ignorance [ˈɪgnərəns] *n* ignorancia.
ignorant [ˈɪgnərənt] *adj* ignorante.

• **to be ignorant of** desconocer, ignorar.
ignore [ɪgˈnɔːʳ] vt **1** ignorar. **2** no hacer caso *(de orden, advertencia, persona)*. **3** pasar por alto *(conducta)*.
ill [ɪl] adj *(comp* **worse***, superl* **worst**). **1** enfermo,-a: *to be taken ill,* enfermar. **2** malo,-a, mal.
  ▶ n mal.
  ▶ adv mal: *I can ill afford it,* mal me lo puedo permitir.
• **ill at ease** incómodo,-a.
■ **ill health** mala salud.
■ **ill will** rencor.
illegal [ɪˈliːgəl] adj ilegal.
illegible [ɪˈledʒɪbəl] adj ilegible.
illegitimate [ɪlɪˈdʒɪtɪmət] adj ilegítimo,-a.
illicit [ɪˈlɪsɪt] adj ilícito,-a.
illiterate [ɪˈlɪtərət] adj-n **1** analfabeto,-a. **2** inculto,-a.
illness [ˈɪlnəs] n *(pl* **-es**) enfermedad.
illogical [ɪˈlɒdʒɪkəl] adj ilógico,-a.
illuminate [ɪˈluːmɪneɪt] vt iluminar.
illusion [ɪˈluːʒən] n ilusión: *optical illusion,* ilusión óptica.
• **to be under the illusion that ...** engañarse pensando que ....
illustrate [ˈɪləstreɪt] vt ilustrar.
illustration [ɪləsˈtreɪʃən] n **1** ilustración. **2** ejemplo.
image [ˈɪmɪdʒ] n imagen.
• **to be the image of** SB ser el vivo retrato de ALGN.
imaginary [ɪˈmædʒɪnərɪ] adj imaginario,-a.
imagination [ɪmædʒɪˈneɪʃən] n imaginación.
imaginative [ɪˈmædʒɪnətɪv] adj imaginativo,-a.
imagine [ɪˈmædʒɪn] vt imaginar.
imbalance [ɪmˈbæləns] n desequilibrio.
IMF [ˈaɪˈemˈef] abbr *(International Monetary Fund)* Fondo Monetario Internacional, FMI.
imitate [ˈɪmɪteɪt] vt imitar.
imitation [ɪmɪˈteɪʃən] n imitación.
immaculate [ɪˈmækjʊlət] adj inmaculado,-a, impecable.
immature [ɪməˈtjʊəʳ] adj inmaduro,-a.
immediate [ɪˈmiːdɪət] adj **1** inmediato,-a. **2** directo,-a, cercano,-a *(pariente)*.
immediately [ɪˈmiːdɪətlɪ] adv **1** inmediatamente, de inmediato, en seguida. **2** directamente.
  ▶ conj en cuanto, tan pronto como.

immense [ɪˈmens] adj inmenso,-a.
immerse [ɪˈmɜːs] vt sumergir.
immigrant [ˈɪmɪgrənt] adj inmigrante.
  ▶ n inmigrante.
immigration [ɪmɪˈgreɪʃən] n inmigración.
imminent [ˈɪmɪnənt] adj inminente.
immobile [ɪˈməʊbaɪl] adj inmóvil.
immobilize [ɪˈməʊbɪlaɪz] vt inmovilizar.
immoral [ɪˈmɒrəl] adj inmoral.
immortal [ɪˈmɔːtəl] adj **1** inmortal *(alma)*. **2** *fig* imperecedero,-a *(fama)*.
immortality [ɪmɔːˈtælɪtɪ] n inmortalidad.
immune [ɪˈmjuːn] adj inmune.
immunity [ɪˈmjuːnɪtɪ] n inmunidad.
immunize [ˈɪmjənaɪz] vt inmunizar.
imp [ɪmp] n **1** diablillo. **2** *fig* pillo.
impact [ˈɪmpækt] n **1** impacto. **2** choque.
impair [ɪmˈpeəʳ] vt **1** dañar. **2** debilitar.
impartial [ɪmˈpɑːʃəl] adj imparcial.
impassive [ɪmˈpæsɪv] adj impasible, imperturbable.
impatience [ɪmˈpeɪʃəns] n impaciencia.
impatient [ɪmˈpeɪʃənt] adj impaciente.
• **to get impatient** impacientarse.
impending [ɪmˈpendɪŋ] adj inminente.
imperative [ɪmˈperətɪv] adj esencial, imprescindible.
  ▶ n imperativo.
imperfect [ɪmˈpɜːfekt] adj defectuoso,-a.
  ▶ n imperfecto *(tiempo verbal)*.
imperfection [ɪmpəˈfekʃən] n imperfección.
imperial [ɪmˈpɪərɪəl] adj imperial.
imperialism [ɪmˈpɪərɪəlɪzəm] n imperialismo.
impersonal [ɪmˈpɜːsənəl] adj impersonal.
impersonate [ɪmˈpɜːsəneɪt] vt **1** hacerse pasar por. **2** imitar.
impersonation [ɪmpɜːsəˈneɪʃən] n imitación.
impertinent [ɪmˈpɜːtɪnənt] adj impertinente.
implant [ɪmˈplɑːnt] vt implantar.
implausible [ɪmˈplɔːzəbəl] adj inverosímil, poco convincente.
implement [*(n)* ˈɪmpləmənt *(vb)* ˈɪmplɪment] n instrumento, utensilio, herramienta.
  ▶ vt **1** llevar a cabo, poner en práctica. **2** aplicar *(ley)*.
implicate [ˈɪmplɪkeɪt] vt implicar, involucrar.
implication [ɪmplɪˈkeɪʃən] n implicación, consecuencia.

implicit [ɪmˈplɪsɪt] *adj* **1** implícito,-a. **2** absoluto,-a, incondicional.
implied [ɪmˈplaɪd] *adj* implícito,-a.
implore [ɪmˈplɔ:ˈ] *vt* implorar.
imply [ɪmˈplaɪ] *vt* (*pt & pp* **-ied**). **1** implicar, suponer. **2** significar. **3** insinuar, dar a entender.
impolite [ɪmpəˈlaɪt] *adj* maleducado,-a.
import[1] [ˈɪmpɔ:t] *n* **1** artículo de importación. **2** importación.
   ▶ *vt* importar.
import[2] [ˈɪmpɔ:t] *n* **1** *fml* significado. **2** *fml* importancia.
importance [ɪmˈpɔ:təns] *n* importancia.
important [ɪmˈpɔ:tənt] *adj* importante.
impose [ɪmˈpəʊz] *vt* imponer.
   ● **to impose on** abusar de.
impossibility [ɪmpɒsəˈbɪlɪtɪ] *n* (*pl* **-ies**) imposibilidad.
impossible [ɪmˈpɒsɪbəl] *adj* imposible.
impotence [ˈɪmpətəns] *n* impotencia.
impotent [ˈɪmpətənt] *adj* impotente.
impractical [ɪmˈpræktɪkəl] *adj* poco práctico,-a.
imprecise [ɪmprəˈsaɪs] *adj* impreciso,-a.
imprecision [ɪmprəˈsɪʒən] *n* imprecisión.
impress [ɪmˈpres] *vt* **1** impresionar: *I was favourably/unfavourably impressed*, me causó una buena/mala impresión. **2** subrayar, recalcar: *to impress STH on SB*, recalcarle algo a ALGN.
impression [ɪmˈpreʃən] *n* **1** impresión. **2** imitación.
   ● **to be under the impression that...** tener la impresión de que....
   ● **to do an impression on SB** causarle a ALGN una buena impresión.
impressive [ɪmˈpresɪv] *adj* impresionante.
imprisonment [ɪmˈprɪzənmənt] *n* **1** encarcelamiento. **2** cárcel.
improbable [ɪmˈprɒbəbəl] *adj* **1** improbable (*hecho*). **2** inverosímil (*historia*).
impromptu [ɪmˈprɒmptju:] *adj* improvisado,-a.
   ▶ *adv* de improviso, improvisadamente.
improper [ɪmˈprɒpəˈ] *adj* **1** impropio,-a. **2** inadecuado,-a. **3** deshonesto,-a.
improve [ɪmˈpru:v] *vt* mejorar.
   ▶ *vi* mejorar, mejorarse.
to improve on *vt* mejorar respecto a.
improvement [ɪmˈpru:vmənt] *n* **1** mejora, mejoría. **2** reforma.

   ● **to be an improvement on** ser mejor que.
improvise [ˈɪmprəvaɪz] *vt-vi* improvisar.
impulse [ˈɪmpʌls] *n* impulso.
   ● **on impulse** sin pensar, llevado,-a por un impulso.
impulsive [ɪmˈpʌlsɪv] *adj* impulsivo,-a.
in[1] [ɪntʃ] *abbr* (*inch*) pulgada.
in[2] [ɪn] *prep* **1** en, dentro de: *in May*, en mayo; *in the box*, en la caja; *in the morning*, por la mañana; *we'll be back in twenty minutes*, estaremos de vuelta dentro de veinte minutos. **2** en: *put it in your pocket*, métetelo en el bolsillo; *we arrived in Bonn*, llegamos a Bonn. **3** en, vestido,-a de: *the man in black*, el hombre vestido de negro. **4** en: *in public*, en público; *written in Greek*, escrito en griego. **5** por: *in the afternoon*, por la tarde. **6** al: *in doing that*, al hacer eso. **7** de: *the biggest in the world*, el más grande del mundo.
   ▶ *adv* **1** dentro: *put the clothes in*, mete la ropa dentro. **2** en casa: *is Judith in?*, ¿está Judith in? **3** de moda: *short skirts are in*, las faldas cortas están de moda. **4** en el poder.
   ● **in so far as** en la medida en que.
   ● **to be in for STH** estar a punto de recibir algo, esperarle algo a ALGN.
   ● **to be in on STH** estar enterado,-a de algo.
   ● **to be in with SB** llevarse bien con ALGN.
   ● **in all** en total.
   ■ **ins and outs** detalles, pormenores.
inability [ɪnəˈbɪlɪtɪ] *n* incapacidad.
inaccurate [ɪnˈækjərət] *adj* inexacto,-a, incorrecto,-a.
inadequacy [ɪnˈædɪkwəsɪ] *n* (*pl* **-ies**). **1** insuficiencia. **2** ineptitud, incapacidad (*de persona*).
inadequate [ɪnˈædɪkwət] *adj* **1** insuficiente. **2** inepto,-a, incapaz (*persona*).
inappropriate [ɪnəˈprəʊprɪət] *adj* **1** poco apropiado,-a, inadecuado,-a (*comentario*). **2** inoportuno,-a (*momento*).
inaugural [ɪˈnɔ:gjʊrəl] *adj* inaugural.
inaugurate [ɪˈnɔ:gjʊreɪt] *vt* **1** inaugurar (*edificio*). **2** investir (*presidente*).
inborn [ˈɪnbɔ:n] *adj* innato,-a.
inbred [ˈɪnbred] *adj* innato,-a.
Inc [ɪnˈkɔ:pəreɪtɪd] *abbr* US (*Incorporated*) sociedad anónima, S.A..

incapable [ɪn'keɪpəbəl] *adj* incapaz.
incapacitate [ɪnkə'pæsɪteɪt] *vt* incapacitar.
incapacity [ɪnkə'pæsɪtɪ] *n* incapacidad.
incense¹ ['ɪnsens] *n* incienso.
incense² ['ɪnsens] *vt* enfurecer.
incentive [ɪn'sentɪv] *n* incentivo.
incessant [ɪn'sesənt] *adj* incesante.
incessantly [ɪn'sesəntlɪ] *adv* sin cesar.
incest ['ɪnsest] *n* incesto.
inch [ɪntʃ] *n* (*pl* -**es**) pulgada.
incidence ['ɪnsɪdəns] *n* **1** índice *(frecuencia)*. **2** incidencia *(efecto)*.
incident ['ɪnsɪdənt] *n* incidente.
incidental [ɪnsɪ'dentəl] *adj* accesorio,-a, secundario,-a.
incidentally [ɪnsɪ'dentəlɪ] *adv* a propósito, por cierto.
incinerate [ɪn'sɪnəreɪt] *vt* incinerar.
incinerator [ɪn'sɪnəreɪtəʳ] *n* incinerador.
incision [ɪn'sɪʒən] *n* incisión.
incisive [ɪn'saɪsɪv] *adj* **1** incisivo,-a *(comentario)*. **2** penetrante *(mente)*. **3** agudo,-a *(voz)*.
incisor [ɪn'saɪzəʳ] *n (diente)* incisivo.
incite [ɪn'saɪt] *vt* incitar.
inclination [ɪnklɪ'neɪʃən] *n* inclinación, tendencia.
incline [*(n)* 'ɪnklaɪn/*(vb)* ɪn'klaɪn] *n* pendiente, cuesta.
▶ *vt* inclinar.
▶ *vi* **1** tender: *he's inclined to be late,* tiene tendencia a llegar tarde. **2** inclinarse.
include [ɪn'kluːd] *vt* incluir.
including [ɪn'kluːdɪŋ] *prep* incluso, inclusive, incluido.
inclusion [ɪn'kluːʒən] *n* inclusión.
inclusive [ɪn'kluːsɪv] *adj* inclusivo,-a.
● **to be inclusive of** incluir.
incoherence [ɪnkəʊ'hɪərəns] *n* incoherencia.
incoherent [ɪnkəʊ'hɪərənt] *adj* incoherente.
income ['ɪnkʌm] *n* ingresos, renta.
■ **income tax** impuesto sobre la renta.
■ **income tax return** declaración de la renta.
incoming ['ɪnkʌmɪŋ] *adj* entrante.
incompatible [ɪnkəm'pætəbəl] *adj* incompatible.
incompetence [ɪn'kɒmpətəns] *n* incompetencia, ineptitud.

incompetent [ɪn'kɒmpətənt] *adj* incompetente, inepto,-a.
incomplete [ɪnkəm'pliːt] *adj* incompleto,-a.
incomprehensible [ɪnkɒmprɪ'hensəbəl] *adj* incomprensible.
inconceivable [ɪnkən'siːvəbəl] *adj* inconcebible.
inconclusive [ɪnkən'kluːsɪv] *adj* no concluyente.
incongruous [ɪn'kɒŋgruəs] *adj* incongruente.
inconsequential [ɪnkɒnsɪ'kwenʃəl] *adj* de poca importancia, sin trascendencia.
inconsiderate [ɪnkən'sɪdərət] *adj* desconsiderado,-a.
inconsistent [ɪnkən'sɪstənt] *adj* inconsecuente, contradictorio,-a: *it's inconsistent with the facts,* no concuerda con los hechos.
inconspicuous [ɪnkən'spɪkjuəs] *adj* que pasa desapercibido,-a, que no llama la atención.
inconvenience [ɪnkən'viːnɪəns] *n* inconveniente, molestia.
▶ *vt* causar molestia a, molestar.
inconvenient [ɪnkən'viːnɪənt] *adj* **1** poco adecuado,-a, mal situado,-a *(lugar)*. **2** inoportuno,-a *(momento)*.
incorporate [ɪn'kɔːpəreɪt] *vt* incorporar.
incorrect [ɪnkə'rekt] *adj* incorrecto,-a.
increase [*(n)* 'ɪnkriːs/*(vb)* ɪn'kriːs] *n* aumento, incremento.
▶ *vt-vi* aumentar, subir.
● **to be on the increase** ir en aumento.
increasing [ɪn'kriːsɪŋ] *adj* creciente.
increasingly [ɪn'kriːsɪŋlɪ] *adv* cada vez más.
incredible [ɪn'kredɪbəl] *adj* increíble.
incredulous [ɪn'kredjələs] *adj* incrédulo,-a.
increment ['ɪnkrɪmənt] *n* incremento, aumento.
incriminate [ɪn'krɪmɪneɪt] *vt* incriminar.
incriminating [ɪn'krɪmɪneɪtɪŋ] *adj* incriminatorio,-a.
incubate ['ɪnkjʊbeɪt] *vt-vi* incubar.
incubator ['ɪnkjʊbeɪtəʳ] *n* incubadora.
incur [ɪn'kɜːʳ] *vt (pt & pp* incurred, *ger* incurring)*. **1** incurrir en *(críticas)*. **2** contraer *(deuda)*.
incurable [ɪn'kjʊərəbəl] *adj* incurable.
Ind [ɪndɪ'pendənt] *abbr* GB *(Independent)* independiente.

indebted [ɪnˈdetɪd] *adj* **1** endeudado,-a. **2** *fig* agradecido,-a.

indecent [ɪnˈdiːsənt] *adj* indecente.

indecisive [ɪndɪˈsaɪsɪv] *adj* indeciso,-a.

indeed [ɪnˈdiːd] *adv* **1** en efecto, efectivamente: *did you really hit him?- I did indeed*, ¿es verdad que le pegaste?- Efectivamente. **2** realmente, de veras: *he works very hard indeed*, realmente trabaja muchísimo; *thank you very much indeed*, muchísimas gracias.

indefinite [ɪnˈdefɪnət] *adj* indefinido,-a.

indefinitely [ɪnˈdefɪnətlɪ] *adv* indefinidamente.

indelible [ɪnˈdelɪbəl] *adj* indeleble, imborrable.

indemnity [ɪnˈdemnɪtɪ] *n* (*pl* -**ies**). **1** indemnidad. **2** indemnización.

independence [ɪndɪˈpendəns] *n* independencia.

independent [ɪndɪˈpendənt] *adj* independiente.
● **to become independent** independizarse.

in-depth [ɪnˈdepθ] *adj* exhaustivo,-a, a fondo.

indescribable [ɪndɪˈskraɪbəbəl] *adj* indescriptible.

indestructible [ɪndɪˈstrʌktəbəl] *adj* indestructible.

index [ˈɪndeks] *n* (*pl* **indexes**) índice.
▶ *vt* poner un índice a, catalogar.
■ **index finger** dedo índice.

India [ˈɪndɪə] *n* India.

Indian [ˈɪndɪən] *adj-n* indio,-a.
■ **the Indian Ocean** el océano Índico.

indicate [ˈɪndɪkeɪt] *vt* indicar.
▶ *vi* indicar, poner el intermitente.

indication [ɪndɪˈkeɪʃən] *n* indicio, señal.

indicative [ɪnˈdɪkətɪv] *adj* indicativo,-a.
▶ *n* indicativo.

indicator [ˈɪndɪkeɪtəʳ] *n* **1** indicador. **2** intermitente *(de coche)*.

indictment [ɪnˈdaɪtmənt] *n* **1** acusación. **2** *fig* crítica feroz.

indifference [ɪnˈdɪfərəns] *n* indiferencia.

indifferent [ɪnˈdɪfərənt] *adj* **1** indiferente. **2** mediocre, regular.

indigenous [ɪnˈdɪdʒənəs] *adj* indígena.

indigestion [ɪndɪˈdʒestʃən] *n* indigestión.

indignant [ɪnˈdɪgnənt] *adj* **1** indignado,-a *(persona)*. **2** de indignación *(mirada)*.

indignation [ɪndɪgˈneɪʃən] *n* indignación.

indirect [ɪndɪˈrekt] *adj* indirecto,-a.

indiscreet [ɪndɪˈskriːt] *adj* indiscreto,-a.

indiscretion [ɪndɪˈskreʃən] *n* indiscreción.

indiscriminate [ɪndɪˈskrɪmɪnət] *adj* indiscriminado,-a.

indispensable [ɪndɪˈspensəbəl] *adj* indispensable, imprescindible.

indisposed [ɪndɪˈspəʊzd] *adj* indispuesto,-a.

indisputable [ɪndɪˈspjuːtəbəl] *adj* **1** indiscutible *(ganador, argumento)*. **2** irrefutable *(prueba)*.

indistinct [ɪndɪˈstɪŋkt] *adj* **1** vago,-a *(recuerdo)*. **2** borroso,-a, poco definido,-a *(forma)*.

individual [ɪndɪˈvɪdjʊəl] *adj* **1** individual. **2** particular, personal *(estilo)*.
▶ *n* individuo.

indoctrination [ɪndɒktrɪˈneɪʃən] *n* adoctrinamiento.

Indonesia [ɪndəˈniːzɪə] *n* Indonesia.

Indonesian [ɪndəˈniːzɪən] *adj-n* indonesio,-a.

indoor [ˈɪndɔːʳ] *adj* **1** interior, de estar por casa *(ropa)*. **2** cubierto,-a *(pista de tenis)*.
■ **indoor football** fútbol sala.
■ **indoor pool** piscina cubierta.

indoors [ɪnˈdɔːz] *adv* dentro: *come indoors, it's cold outside*, entra, fuera hace frío.
● **to stay indoors** quedarse en casa.

induce [ɪnˈdjuːs] *vt* **1** inducir, provocar. **2** causar, producir.

indulge [ɪnˈdʌldʒ] *vt* **1** satisfacer *(capricho)*. **2** complacer *(persona)*. **3** mimar *(niño)*.
● **to indulge in** permitirse o darse el lujo de.

indulgence [ɪnˈdʌldʒəns] *n* **1** indulgencia. **2** pequeño lujo.

indulgent [ɪnˈdʌldʒənt] *adj* indulgente.

industrial [ɪnˈdʌstrɪəl] *adj* industrial.
■ **industrial accident** accidente laboral.
■ **industrial action** protesta laboral.
■ **industrial dispute** conflicto laboral.
■ **industrial estate** polígono industrial.

industrialist [ɪnˈdʌstrɪəlɪst] *n* industrial, empresario,-a.

industrialize [ɪnˈdʌstrɪəlaɪz] *vt-vi* industrializar(se).

industrious [ɪnˈdʌstrɪəs] *adj* trabajador,-ra, aplicado,-a.

industry [ˈɪndəstrɪ] *n* (*pl* -**ies**). **1** industria. **2** diligencia, aplicación.

inedible [ɪn'edəbəl] *adj* no comestible.

ineffective [ɪnɪ'fektɪv] *adj* **1** ineficaz, inútil. **2** incompetente, inepto,-a *(persona)*.

ineffectual [ɪnɪ'fektʃʊəl] *adj* **1** ineficaz, inútil. **2** incompetente, inepto,-a *(persona)*.

inefficiency [ɪnɪ'fɪʃənsɪ] *n* **1** ineficacia. **2** incompetencia, ineptitud *(de persona)*.

inefficient [ɪnɪ'fɪʃənt] *adj* **1** ineficaz, ineficiente. **2** incompetente, inepto,-a *(persona)*.

inept [ɪ'nept] *adj* inepto,-a.

inequality [ɪnɪ'kwɒlətɪ] *n* (*pl* -**ies**) desigualdad.

inert [ɪ'nɜːt] *adj* inerte.

inertia [ɪ'nɜːʃə] *n* inercia.

inescapable [ɪnɪ'skeɪpəbəl] *adj* ineludible.

inevitable [ɪn'evɪtəbəl] *adj* inevitable.

inexact [ɪnɪg'zækt] *adj* inexacto,-a.

inexpensive [ɪnɪk'spensɪv] *adj* barato,-a, económico,-a.

inexperience [ɪnɪk'spɪərɪəns] *n* inexperiencia.

inexperienced [ɪnɪk'spɪərɪənst] *adj* inexperto,-a.

inexpert [ɪn'ekspɜːt] *adj* inexperto,-a.

inexplicable [ɪnɪk'splɪkəbəl] *adj* inexplicable.

inexpressive [ɪnɪk'spresɪv] *adj* inexpresivo,-a.

infallible [ɪn'fæləbəl] *adj* infalible.

infamous ['ɪnfəməs] *adj* infame.

infancy ['ɪnfənsɪ] *n* infancia.

infant ['ɪnfənt] *n* niño,-a.

infantile ['ɪnfəntaɪl] *adj* infantil.

infantry ['ɪnfəntrɪ] *n* infantería.

infatuated [ɪn'fætjʊeɪtɪd] *adj* encaprichado,-a.

infect [ɪn'fekt] *vt* **1** infectar. **2** contagiar.

infection [ɪn'fekʃən] *n* **1** infección. **2** contagio.

infectious [ɪn'fekʃəs] *adj* infeccioso,-a, contagioso,-a.

infer [ɪn'fɜːʳ] *vt* (*pt & pp* **inferred**, *ger* **inferring**) inferir, deducir.

inferior [ɪn'fɪərɪəʳ] *adj* inferior.

   ▶ *n* inferior.

inferiority [ɪnfɪərɪ'ɒrətɪ] *n* inferioridad.

infertile [ɪn'fɜːtaɪl] *adj* estéril.

infest [ɪn'fest] *vt* infestar.

infidelity [ɪnfɪ'delətɪ] *n* (*pl* -**ies**) infidelidad.

infiltrate ['ɪnfɪltreɪt] *vt* infiltrarse en.

infinite ['ɪnfɪnət] *adj* infinito,-a.

infinitive [ɪn'fɪnɪtɪv] *n* infinitivo.

infinity [ɪn'fɪnɪtɪ] *n* **1** infinito. **2** *fig* infinidad.

infirm [ɪn'fɜːm] *adj* débil, enfermizo,-a.

infirmary [ɪn'fɜːmərɪ] *n* (*pl* -**ies**). **1** hospital. **2** enfermería.

inflammable [ɪn'flæməbəl] *adj* **1** inflamable. **2** *fig* explosivo,-a.

inflammation [ɪnflə'meɪʃən] *n* inflamación.

inflate [ɪn'fleɪt] *vt-vi* inflar(se), hinchar(se).

inflation [ɪn'fleɪʃən] *n* inflación.

inflexible [ɪn'fleksɪbəl] *adj* inflexible.

inflict [ɪn'flɪkt] *vt* **1** infligir *(derrota)*. **2** imponer *(idea)*. **3** causar, ocasionar *(daño)*.

influence ['ɪnflʊəns] *n* influencia.

   ▶ *vt* influir en.

influential [ɪnflʊ'enʃəl] *adj* influyente.

influenza [ɪnflʊ'enzə] *n* gripe.

influx ['ɪnflʌks] *n* (*pl* **influxes**) afluencia.

info ['ɪnfəʊ] *n fam* información.

inform [ɪn'fɔːm] *vt* informar.

   ● **to inform on SB** delatar a ALGN, denunciar a ALGN.

informal [ɪn'fɔːməl] *adj* informal, coloquial.

informality [ɪnfɔː'mælɪtɪ] *n* (*pl* -**ies**) informalidad.

informant [ɪn'fɔːmənt] *n* informante, informador,-a.

information [ɪnfə'meɪʃən] *n* información.

informative [ɪn'fɔːmətɪv] *adj* informativo,-a.

informer [ɪn'fɔːməʳ] *n* delator,-ra.

infrared [ɪnfrə'red] *adj* infrarrojo,-a.

infrastructure ['ɪnfrəstrʌktʃəʳ] *n* infraestructura.

infrequent [ɪn'friːkwənt] *adj* infrecuente.

infringe [ɪn'frɪndʒ] *vt* infringir, transgredir.

   ● **to infringe on** violar, invadir.

infuriate [ɪn'fjʊərɪeɪt] *vt* enfurecer.

infuriating [ɪn'fjʊərɪeɪtɪŋ] *adj* exasperante, irritante.

ingenious [ɪn'dʒiːnɪəs] *adj* ingenioso,-a.

ingenuity [ɪndʒɪ'njuːɪtɪ] *n* ingenio, inventiva.

ingot ['ɪŋgət] *n* lingote.

ingrained [ɪn'greɪnd] *adj* **1** incrustado,-a *(suciedad)*. **2** arraigado,-a *(costumbre)*.

ingredient [ɪn'griːdɪənt] *n* ingrediente.

inhabit [ɪn'hæbɪt] *vt* habitar, vivir en.

inhabitant [ɪn'hæbɪtənt] *n* habitante.

inhale [ɪnˈheɪl] vt **1** aspirar. **2** inhalar.
▶ vi tragarse el humo.
inherit [ɪnˈherɪt] vt heredar.
inheritance [ɪnˈherɪtəns] n herencia.
inhibit [ɪnˈhɪbɪt] vt inhibir, impedir.
inhibition [ɪnhɪˈbɪʃən] n inhibición.
inhuman [ɪnˈhjuːmən] adj inhumano,-a.
inimitable [ɪˈnɪmɪtəbəl] adj inimitable.
initial [ɪˈnɪʃəl] adj inicial.
▶ n inicial.
▶ vt (pt & pp **initialled**, ger **initialling**) firmar con las iniciales.
initially [ɪˈnɪʃəlɪ] adv inicialmente, al principio.
initiate [ɪˈnɪʃɪeɪt] vt iniciar.
initiative [ɪˈnɪʃɪətɪv] n iniciativa.
inject [ɪnˈdʒekt] vt inyectar.
injection [ɪnˈdʒekʃən] n inyección.
injure [ˈɪndʒəˈ] vt herir.
injured [ˈɪndʒəd] adj herido,-a, lesionado,-a, ofendido,-a (mirada).
injury [ˈɪndʒərɪ] n (pl -**ies**) herida, lesión.
■ **injury time** tiempo de descuento (en partido).
injustice [ɪnˈdʒʌstɪs] n injusticia.
● **to do SB an injustice** ser injusto con ALGN.
ink [ɪŋk] n tinta.
inkjet printer [ˈɪŋkdʒetˈprɪntəˈ] n impresora de chorro de tinta.
inkling [ˈɪŋklɪŋ] n **1** noción, vaga idea. **2** sospecha, presentimiento.
inland [(adj) ˈɪnlənd(adv) ɪnˈlænd] adj de tierra adentro, del interior.
▶ adv tierra adentro, en el interior.
■ **Inland Revenue** GB Hacienda Pública.
inlet [ˈɪnlet] n **1** cala, ensenada. **2** entrada (de río, mar).
inmate [ˈɪnmeɪt] n **1** residente. **2** preso,-a, recluso,-a (en cárcel). **3** enfermo,-a (en hospital). **4** interno,-a (en asilo).
inn [ɪn] n **1** posada, fonda, mesón. **2** taberna.
innate [ɪˈneɪt] adj innato,-a.
inner [ˈɪnəˈ] adj interior.
■ **inner tube** cámara.
innermost [ˈɪnəməʊst] adj **1** más interior. **2** más íntimo,-a (pensamientos).
innocence [ˈɪnəsəns] n inocencia.
innocent [ˈɪnəsənt] adj-n inocente.
innovation [ɪnəˈveɪʃən] n innovación.
innovative [ˈɪnəvətɪv] adj innovador,-ra.

innuendo [ɪnjʊˈendəʊ] n (pl -**s** o -**es**) insinuación.
innumerable [ɪˈnjuːmərəbəl] adj innumerable.
inoculate [ɪˈnɒkjʊleɪt] vt inocular.
inpatient [ˈɪnpeɪʃənt] n paciente hospitalizado,-a.
input [ˈɪnpʊt] n **1** entrada, inversión (de dinero). **2** input, entrada (de datos).
▶ vt (pt & pp **inputted**, ger **inputting**) entrar, introducir (datos).
inquest [ˈɪnkwest] n **1** investigación judicial. **2** fam investigación.
inquire [ɪnˈkwaɪəˈ] vt preguntar.
● **"Inquire within"** "Razón aquí".
● **to inquire about STH** preguntar por algo.
● **to inquire into STH** investigar algo.
inquiry [ɪnˈkwaɪərɪ] n (pl -**ies**). **1** pregunta. **2** investigación, pesquisa.
● **"Inquiries"** "Información".
inquisition [ɪnkwɪˈzɪʃən] n inquisición, interrogatorio.
inquisitive [ɪnˈkwɪzɪtɪv] adj curioso,-a.
insane [ɪnˈseɪn] adj demente, loco,-a.
● **to go insane** volverse loco,-a.
insanity [ɪnˈsænɪtɪ] n locura, demencia.
inscribe [ɪnˈskraɪb] vt inscribir, grabar.
inscription [ɪnˈskrɪpʃən] n inscripción.
insect [ˈɪnsekt] n insecto.
insecticide [ɪnˈsektɪsaɪd] n insecticida.
insecure [ɪnsɪˈkjʊəˈ] adj inseguro,-a.
insecurity [ɪnsɪˈkjʊərɪtɪ] n inseguridad.
insensitive [ɪnˈsensətɪv] adj insensible.
inseparable [ɪnˈsepərəbəl] adj inseparable.
insert [ɪnˈsɜːt] vt insertar, introducir.
inside [ɪnˈsaɪd] n interior: **from the inside**, desde dentro.
▶ npl **insides** tripas, entrañas.
▶ adj interior, interno,-a.
▶ adv **1** dentro (posición). **2** adentro (movimiento): **come inside!**, ¡entrad!
▶ prep dentro de: **it is inside the box**, está dentro de la caja.
● **inside out** de dentro afuera, al revés, del revés.
insider [ɪnˈsaɪdəˈ] n persona enterada.
insight [ˈɪnsaɪt] n **1** perspicacia, penetración. **2** idea.
insignificant [ɪnsɪgˈnɪfɪkənt] adj insignificante.
insincere [ɪnsɪnˈsɪəˈ] adj falso,-a.
insinuate [ɪnˈsɪnjʊeɪt] vt insinuar.

insist [ɪnˈsɪst] *vi* insistir.

insistence [ɪnˈsɪstəns] *n* insistencia.

insistent [ɪnˈsɪstənt] *adj* insistente.

insolent [ˈɪnsələnt] *adj* insolente.

insomnia [ɪnˈsɒmnɪə] *n* insomnio.

inspect [ɪnˈspekt] *vt* **1** revisar, inspeccionar. **2** registrar *(equipaje)*. **3** pasar revista a *(tropas)*.

inspection [ɪnˈspekʃən] *n* **1** inspección. **2** registro *(a equipaje)*. **3** revista *(a tropas)*.

inspector [ɪnˈspektə] *n* **1** inspector,-ra. **2** revisor,-ra *(en tren)*.

inspiration [ɪnspɪˈreɪʃən] *n* inspiración.

inspire [ɪnˈspaɪə] *vt* **1** inspirar. **2** animar.

instability [ɪnstəˈbɪlɪtɪ] *n* inestabilidad.

install [ɪnˈstɔːl] *vt* instalar.

installation [ɪnstəˈleɪʃən] *n* instalación.

instalment [ɪnˈstɔːlmənt] *n* **1** plazo *(de pago)*. **2** entrega, fascículo *(de libro)*. **3** episodio, capítulo *(de serie)*.

instance [ˈɪnstəns] *n* ejemplo, caso.
- **for instance** por ejemplo.
- **in the first instance** en primer lugar.

instant [ˈɪnstənt] *n* instante, momento: *it will be ready in an instant*, estará listo en un instante.
▶ *adj* **1** inmediato,-a. **2** instantáneo,-a *(café)*.

instantaneous [ɪnstənˈteɪnɪəs] *adj* instantáneo,-a.

instantly [ˈɪnstəntlɪ] *adv* al instante, inmediatamente.

instead [ɪnˈsted] *adv* en cambio, en vez de eso: *the theatre was full, so we went to the cinema instead*, el teatro estaba lleno, así que fuimos al cine.
- **instead of** en lugar de, en vez de: *would you like coffee instead of tea?*, ¿quieres café en lugar de té?

instep [ˈɪnstep] *n* empeine.

instigate [ˈɪnstɪgeɪt] *vt* instigar.

instinct [ˈɪnstɪŋkt] *n* instinto.

instinctive [ɪnˈstɪŋktɪv] *adj* instintivo,-a.

institute [ˈɪnstɪtjuːt] *n* instituto.
▶ *vt* instituir, iniciar.

institution [ɪnstɪˈtjuːʃən] *n* **1** institución. **2** asilo.

instruct [ɪnˈstrʌkt] *vt* **1** instruir, enseñar. **2** ordenar, mandar.

instruction [ɪnˈstrʌkʃən] *n* instrucción.
▶ *npl* **instructions** instrucciones, indicaciones.

instructor [ɪnˈstrʌktə] *n* **1** instructor,-ra.

2 profesor,-ra *(de conducir)*. **3** monitor,-ra *(de deporte)*.

instrument [ˈɪnstrəmənt] *n* instrumento.

instrumental [ɪnstrəˈmentəl] *adj* instrumental.
- **to be instrumental in** contribuir decisivamente a.

insufficient [ɪnsəˈfɪʃənt] *adj* insuficiente.

insular [ˈɪnsjʊlə] *adj* insular.

insulate [ˈɪnsjəleɪt] *vt* aislar.

insulation [ɪnsjəˈleɪʃən] *n* aislamiento.

insulin [ˈɪnsjəlɪn] *n* insulina.

insult [*(n)* ˈɪnsʌlt *(vb)* ɪnˈsʌlt] *n* **1** insulto *(palabras)*. **2** afrenta, ofensa *(acción)*.
▶ *vt* insultar.

insurance [ɪnˈʃʊərəns] *n* seguro.
- **insurance policy** póliza de seguro.

insure [ɪnˈʃʊə] *vt* asegurar.

intact [ɪnˈtækt] *adj* intacto,-a.

intake [ˈɪnteɪk] *n* **1** consumo *(de comida)*. **2** número de admitidos *(de estudiantes)*.

integral [ˈɪntɪgrəl] *adj* **1** integral, esencial. **2** integral *(ecuación)*. **3** entero *(número)*.
▶ *n* integral.

integrate [ˈɪntɪgreɪt] *vt-vi* integrar(se).

integration [ɪntɪˈgreɪʃən] *n* integración.

integrity [ɪnˈtegrətɪ] *n* integridad.

intellect [ˈɪntəlekt] *n* intelecto, inteligencia.

intellectual [ɪntəˈlektjʊəl] *adj-n* intelectual.

intelligence [ɪnˈtelɪdʒəns] *n* inteligencia.

intelligent [ɪnˈtelɪdʒənt] *adj* inteligente.

intend [ɪnˈtend] *vt* tener la intención de, proponerse.

intended [ɪnˈtendɪd] *adj* **1** deseado,-a, buscado,-a. **2** intencionado,-a, deliberado,-a.
- **intended for** para, dirigido,-a a.

intense [ɪnˈtens] *adj* **1** intenso,-a. **2** muy serio,-a *(persona)*.

intensify [ɪnˈtensɪfaɪ] *vt-vi (pt & pp* **-ied)** intensificar(se), aumentar(se).

intensity [ɪnˈtensɪtɪ] *n (pl* **-ies)** intensidad.

intensive [ɪnˈtensɪv] *adj* intensivo,-a.
- **intensive care** cuidados intensivos.

intent [ɪnˈtent] *adj* atento,-a.
▶ *n* intención.
- **to all intents and purposes** para todos los efectos.
- **to be intent on** estar decidido,-a a, estar empeñado,-a en.
- **with intent to** con la intención de.

intention [ɪn'tenʃən] *n* intención.
intentional [ɪn'tenʃənəl] *adj* intencional.
intentionally [ɪn'tenʃənəlɪ] *adv* adrede.
interactive [ɪntər'æktɪv] *adj* interactivo,-a.
intercede [ɪntə'siːd] *vi* interceder.
● **to intercede on SB's behalf** interceder por ALGN.
intercept [ɪntə'sept] *vt* interceptar.
interchange ['ɪntətʃeɪndʒ] *n* **1** intercambio. **2** enlace *(en la carretera)*.
intercom ['ɪntəkɒm] *n* interfono.
intercourse ['ɪntəkɔːs] *n* **1** trato. **2** coito, relaciones sexuales.
interest ['ɪntrəst] *n* **1** interés. **2** participación *(en negocio)*.
▶ *vt* interesar.
● **in the interests of ...** en pro de ....
● **to be of interest** interesar.
● **to take an interest** interesarse por.
■ **interest rate** tipo de interés.
interested ['ɪntrəstɪd] *adj* interesado,-a.
interesting ['ɪntrəstɪŋ] *adj* interesante.
interface ['ɪntəfeɪs] *n* interfaz.
interfere [ɪntə'fɪə'] *vi* entrometerse, interferir.
● **to interfere with** dificultar, estorbar, obstaculizar.
interference [ɪntə'fɪərəns] *n* **1** intromisión, injerencia. **2** interferencia.
interfering [ɪntə'fɪərɪŋ] *adj* entrometido,-a.
interior [ɪn'tɪərɪə'] *adj-n* interior.
interjection [ɪntə'dʒekʃən] *n* **1** interjección. **2** comentario.
interloper ['ɪntələʊpə'] *n* intruso,-a.
interlude ['ɪntəluːd] *n* **1** intermedio, descanso. **2** interludio *(en música)*.
intermediate [ɪntə'miːdɪət] *adj* intermedio,-a.
intermission [ɪntə'mɪʃən] *n* intermedio, descanso.
intern [*(n)* 'ɪntɜːn*(vb)* ɪn'tɜːn] *n* US interno,-a *(médico)*.
▶ *vt* internar.
internal [ɪn'tɜːnəl] *adj* interior, interno,-a.
■ **internal flight** vuelo nacional.
■ **Internal Revenue** US Hacienda Pública.
international [ɪntə'næʃənəl] *adj* internacional.
Internet ['ɪntənet] *n* Internet.
■ **Internet access provider** proveedor de acceso a Internet.
■ **Internet service provider** proveedor de Internet.

interplay ['ɪntəpleɪ] *n* interacción.
Interpol ['ɪntəpɒl] *abbr (International Criminal Police Organization)* Interpol.
interpret [ɪn'tɜːprət] *vt* interpretar.
▶ *vi* hacer de intérprete.
interpretation [ɪntɜːprə'teɪʃən] *n* interpretación.
interpreter [ɪn'tɜːprətə'] *n* intérprete.
interrogate [ɪn'terəgeɪt] *vt* interrogar.
interrogation [ɪnterə'geɪʃən] *n* interrogatorio.
interrogative [ɪntə'rɒgətɪv] *adj* interrogativo,-a.
▶ *n* forma interrogativa, oración interrogativa.
interrupt [ɪntə'rʌpt] *vt-vi* interrumpir.
interruption [ɪntə'rʌpʃən] *n* interrupción.
intersection [ɪntə'sekʃən] *n* cruce, intersección.
interval ['ɪntəvəl] *n* **1** intervalo. **2** descanso, intermedio *(en teatro, etc)*.
● **at regular intervals** con regularidad.
intervene [ɪntə'viːn] *vi* **1** intervenir. **2** sobrevenir, ocurrir *(acontecimiento)*. **3** transcurrir *(tiempo)*.
intervention [ɪntə'venʃən] *n* intervención.
interview ['ɪntəvjuː] *n* entrevista.
▶ *vt* entrevistar.
interviewer ['ɪntəvjuːə'] *n* entrevistador,-ra.
intestine [ɪn'testɪn] *n* intestino.
intimacy ['ɪntɪməsɪ] *n* intimidad.
intimate[1] ['ɪntɪmət] *adj* íntimo,-a, personal.
intimate[2] ['ɪntɪmeɪt] *vt* dar a entender, insinuar.
intimidate [ɪn'tɪmɪdeɪt] *vt* intimidar.
intimidating [ɪn'tɪmɪdeɪtɪŋ] *adj* intimidante, amenazador,-ra.
into ['ɪntu] *prep* **1** en, dentro de: *they went into the shop*, entraron en la tienda. **2** dividido entre: *five into twenty goes four*, veinte dividido entre cinco son cuatro.
● **to be into STH 1** *fam* apetecerle algo a ALGN. **2** ser aficionado,-a a algo.
intolerable [ɪn'tɒlərəbəl] *adj* intolerable.
intolerance [ɪn'tɒlərəns] *n* intolerancia.
intolerant [ɪn'tɒlərənt] *adj* intolerante.
intonation [ɪntə'neɪʃən] *n* entonación.
intoxicated [ɪn'tɒksɪkeɪtɪd] *adj* ebrio,-a.
intoxication [ɪntɒksɪ'keɪʃən] *n* embriaguez.
intranet ['ɪntrənet] *n* intranet.

intransitive [ɪn'trænsɪtɪv] *adj* intransitivo,-a.

intrigue [ɪn'triːg] *n* intriga.
▶ *vt-vi* intrigar.

introduce [ɪntrə'djuːs] *vt* **1** introducir. **2** presentar *(persona)*. **3** promulgar *(ley)*.

introduction [ɪntrə'dʌkʃən] *n* **1** introducción. **2** presentación *(de persona)*. **3** promulgación *(de ley)*.

introductory [ɪntrə'dʌktəri] *adj* introductorio,-a, preliminar *(palabras)*.

introvert ['ɪntrəvɜːt] *n* introvertido,-a.

introverted ['ɪntrəvɜːtɪd] *adj* introvertido,-a.

intrude [ɪn'truːd] *vi* **1** entrometerse, inmiscuirse. **2** molestar, estorbar.

intruder [ɪn'truːdə'] *n* intruso,-a.

intrusion [ɪn'truːʒən] *n* **1** intrusión. **2** invasión, intromisión.

intuition [ɪntjuː'ɪʃən] *n* intuición.

intuitive [ɪn'tjuːɪtɪv] *adj* intuitivo,-a.

invade [ɪn'veɪd] *vt* invadir.

invader [ɪn'veɪdə'] *n* invasor,-ra.

invalid[1] ['ɪnvəlɪd] *n* inválido,-a, enfermo,-a.

invalid[2] [ɪn'vælɪd] *adj* inválido,-a, nulo,-a.

invalidate [ɪn'vælɪdeɪt] *vt* invalidar, anular.

invaluable [ɪn'væljuəbəl] *adj* inestimable.

invasion [ɪn'veɪʒən] *n* invasión.

invent [ɪn'vent] *vt* inventar.

invention [ɪn'venʃən] *n* **1** invento *(cosa)*. **2** invención *(acción)*.

inventor [ɪn'ventə'] *n* inventor,-ra.

inventory ['ɪnvəntri] *n* (*pl* **-ies**) inventario.

inversion [ɪn'vɜːʒən] *n* inversión.

invert [ɪn'vɜːt] *vt* invertir.

invertebrate [ɪn'vɜːtɪbrət] *adj-n* invertebrado,-a.

inverted [ɪn'vɜːtɪd] *adj* invertido,-a.
■ **inverted commas** comillas: *in inverted commas*, entre comillas.

invest [ɪn'vest] *vt* invertir.
▶ *vi* invertir dinero.

investigate [ɪn'vestɪgeɪt] *vt-vi* investigar.

investigation [ɪnvestɪ'geɪʃən] *n* investigación.

investigator [ɪn'vestɪgeɪtə'] *n* investigador,-ra.

investment [ɪn'vestmənt] *n* inversión.

investor [ɪn'vestə'] *n* inversor,-ra.

invincible [ɪn'vɪnsəbəl] *adj* invencible.

invisible [ɪn'vɪzəbəl] *adj* invisible.
■ **invisible ink** tinta simpática.

invitation [ɪnvɪ'teɪʃən] *n* invitación.

invite [ɪn'vaɪt] *vt* **1** invitar. **2** pedir, solicitar *(comentarios)*. **3** provocar *(problemas)*.

inviting [ɪn'vaɪtɪŋ] *adj* tentador,-ra, atractivo,-a.

invoice ['ɪnvɔɪs] *n* factura.
▶ *vt* facturar.

involuntary [ɪn'vɒləntəri] *adj* involuntario,-a.

involve [ɪn'vɒlv] *vt* **1** involucrar, comprometer: *don't involve me in your schemes*, no me mezcles en tus planes. **2** tener que ver con, afectar a. **3** suponer, implicar: *it involves working at the weekends*, supone trabajar los fines de semana.

involved [ɪn'vɒlvd] *adj* complicado,-a, enrevesado,-a.
● **to get involved in** meterse en, enredarse en.
● **to get involved with SB** liarse con ALGN.

involvement [ɪn'vɒlvmənt] *n* **1** participación. **2** complicidad *(en crimen)*. **3** relación.

inward ['ɪnwəd] *adj* interior.
▶ *adv* hacia adentro: *the windows open inward*, las ventanas se abren hacia dentro.

inwards ['ɪnwədz] *adv* hacia adentro.

iodine ['aɪədiːn] *n* yodo.

ion [aɪən] *n* ion.

IOU ['aɪ'əʊ'juː] *abbr (I owe you)* pagaré.

IQ ['aɪ'kjuː] *abbr (intelligence quotient)* CI.

IRA ['aɪ'ɑːr'eɪ] *abbr (Irish Republican Army)* IRA.

Iran [ɪ'rɑːn] *n* Irán.

Iranian [ɪ'reɪnɪən] *adj-n* iraní.

Iraq [ɪ'rɑːk] *n* Irak.

Iraqi [ɪ'rɑːkɪ] *adj* iraquí.
▶ *n* iraquí.

irate [aɪ'reɪt] *adj* furioso,-a.

Ireland ['aɪələnd] *n* Irlanda.
■ **Northern Ireland** Irlanda del norte.

iris ['aɪərɪs] *n* (*pl* **irises**). **1** iris *(del ojo)*. **2** lirio.

Irish ['aɪrɪʃ] *adj* irlandés,-esa.
▶ *n* irlandés *(lengua)*.
▶ *npl* **the Irish** los irlandeses.
● **Northern Irish** norirlandés,-esa.
■ **Irish Sea** Mar de Irlanda.

iron ['aɪən] *n* **1** hierro. **2** plancha.
▶ *vt* planchar.
■ **Iron Age** Edad de Hierro.

ironic [aɪ'rɒnɪk] *adj* irónico,-a.

ironing ['aɪənɪŋ] *n* **1** ropa por planchar. **2** ropa planchada.
● **to do the ironing** planchar.
■ **ironing board** tabla de planchar.
ironmonger ['aɪənmʌŋgəʳ] *n* ferretero,-a.
ironmonger's ['aɪənmʌŋgəz] *n* ferretería.
irony ['aɪrəni] *n* (*pl* -**ies**) ironía.
irrational [ɪ'ræʃənəl] *adj* irracional.
irregular [ɪ'regjələʳ] *adj* irregular.
irregularity [ɪregjə'lærɪti] *n* (*pl* -**ies**) irregularidad.
irrelevant [ɪ'relɪvənt] *adj* irrelevante, que no viene al caso.
irresistible [ɪrɪ'zɪstəbəl] *adj* irresistible.
irresponsible [ɪrɪ'spɒnsəbəl] *adj* irresponsable.
irrigate ['ɪrɪgeɪt] *vt* regar, irrigar.
irrigation [ɪrɪ'geɪʃən] *n* riego, irrigación.
irritable ['ɪrɪtəbəl] *adj* irritable.
irritate ['ɪrɪteɪt] *vt* irritar.
irritating ['ɪrɪteɪtɪŋ] *adj* irritante, molesto,-a.
irritation [ɪrɪ'teɪʃən] *n* irritación.
is [ɪz] *3rd pers sing pres* → be.
Islam ['ɪzlɑːm] *n* Islam.
Islamic [ɪz'læmɪk] *adj* islámico,-a.
island ['aɪlənd] *n* isla.
isle [aɪl] *n* isla.
isolate ['aɪsəleɪt] *vt* aislar.
isolation [aɪsə'leɪʃən] *n* aislamiento.
ISP ['aɪ'es'piː] *abbr* (*Internet Service Provider*) proveedor de servicios Internet, proveedor de Internet, PSI.
Israel ['ɪzreɪl] *n* Israel.
Israeli [ɪz'reɪli] *adj-n* israelí.
Israelite ['ɪzrɪəlaɪt] *adj-n* israelita.
issue ['ɪʃuː] *n* **1** asunto, tema. **2** edición (*de libro*). **3** número (*de revista*). **4** emisión (*de sellos, acciones*). **5** expedición (*de pasaporte*). **6** *fml* descendencia (*hijos*).
► *vt* **1** publicar (*libro*). **2** emitir (*sellos, acciones*). **3** expedir (*pasaporte*). **4** dar (*orden*), promulgar (*decreto*).

isthmus ['ɪsməs] *n* (*pl* **isthmuses**) istmo.
it [ɪt] *pron* **1** él, ella, ello (*sujeto*): *where's my shirt? it's not in my room*, ¿dónde está mi camisa?, no está en mi habitación. **2** lo, la (*complemento directo*): *I've lost my wallet, I can't find it*, he perdido mi cartera, no la encuentro. **3** le (*complemento indirecto*): *the dog's thirsty - Give it some water*, el perro tiene sed - Dale agua. **4** él, ella, ello (*después de preposición*).
IT ['aɪ'tiː] *abbr* (*information technology*) informática.
Italian [ɪ'tæliən] *adj* italiano,-a.
► *n* **1** italiano,-a (*persona*). **2** italiano (*lengua*).
italics [ɪ'tælɪks] *npl* cursiva.
Italy ['ɪtəli] *n* Italia.
itch [ɪtʃ] *n* (*pl* -**es**) picazón, picor.
► *vi* picar: *my leg itches*, me pica la pierna.
● **to be itching to do STH** estar impaciente por hacer algo.
itchy ['ɪtʃi] *adj* (-**ier**, -**iest**) que pica.
item ['aɪtəm] *n* **1** artículo, cosa. **2** asunto (*en agenda*). **3** partida (*en factura*). **4** noticia.
itemize ['aɪtəmaɪz] *vt* **1** hacer una lista de. **2** detallar.
itinerary [aɪ'tɪnərəri] *n* (*pl* -**ies**) itinerario.
its [ɪts] *adj* su, sus.
itself [ɪt'self] *pron* **1** se (*reflexivo*): *the cat washed itself*, el gato se lavó. **2** él mismo, ello mismo, ella misma (*enfático*): *the town itself is lovely*, el pueblo en sí es bonito. **3** sí, sí mismo,-a (*después de preposición*).
● **by itself** solo: *the dog opened the door by itself*, el perro abrió la puerta solo.
ITV ['aɪ'tiː'viː] *abbr* GB (*Independent Television*) cadena de televisión privada.
ivory ['aɪvəri] *n* marfil.
ivy ['aɪvi] *n* hiedra

J

jab [dʒæb] *n* pinchazo, inyección.
▶ *vt* (*pt & pp* **jabbed**, *ger* **jabbing**) pinchar, clavar.
jabber ['dʒæbər] *vi-vt* farfullar.
jack [dʒæk] *n* **1** gato (*para coche*). **2** jota, sota.
jackal ['dʒækɔːl] *n* chacal.
jackass ['dʒækæs] *n* (*pl* **-es**) burro.
jacket ['dʒækɪt] *n* **1** chaqueta, americana. **2** cazadora. **3** sobrecubierta (*de libro*).
jack-knife ['dʒæknaɪf] *n* (*pl* **jack-knifves**) navaja.
jack-of-all-trades ['dʒækəvɔːltreɪdz] *n* (*pl* **jacks-of-all-trades**) persona de muchos oficios, manitas.
jackpot ['dʒækpɒt] *n* premio gordo.
jade [dʒeɪd] *n* jade.
jaded ['dʒeɪdɪd] *adj* agotado,-a, cansado,-a.
jagged ['dʒægɪd] *adj* dentado,-a.
jaguar ['dʒægjuə'] *n* jaguar.
jail [dʒeɪl] *n* cárcel, prisión.
▶ *vt* encarcelar.
jailer ['dʒeɪlə'] *n* carcelero,-a.
jam¹ [dʒæm] *n* confitura, mermelada.
jam² [dʒæm] *n* **1** aprieto, apuro. **2** embotellamiento, atasco: *a traffic jam*, un atasco.
▶ *vt* (*pt & pp* **jammed**, *ger* **jamming**). **1** atestar, apiñar: *the room was jammed with children*, la sala estaba atestada de niños. **2** embutir, meter: *he jammed his clothes into the case*, metió la ropa en la maleta.
▶ *vi* atascarse, bloquearse: *the lock has jammed*, se ha atascado la cerradura.
Jamaica [dʒə'meɪkə] *n* Jamaica.
Jamaican [dʒə'meɪkən] *adj-n* jamaicano,-a.

jamboree [dʒæmbə'riː] *n* **1** juerga. **2** reunión de muchachos exploradores.
jammy ['dʒæmɪ] *adj* (**-ier**, **-iest**) *fam* suertudo,-a.
jam-packed [dʒæm'pækt] *adj fam* atestado,-a, a tope.
jangle ['dʒæŋgəl] *vi* sonar de un modo discordante.
▶ *vt* hacer sonar de un modo discordante.
janitor ['dʒænɪtə'] *n* portero.
January ['dʒænjuərɪ] *n* enero.
Japan [dʒə'pæn] *n* Japón.
Japanese [dʒæpə'niːz] *adj* japonés,-esa.
▶ *n* **1** japonés,-esa (*persona*). **2** japonés (*lengua*).
▶ *npl* **the Japanese** los japoneses.
jar [dʒɑː'] *n* tarro, pote.
▶ *vt* (*pt & pp* **jarred**, *ger* **jarring**) golpear, sacudir.
▶ *vi* chirriar.
jargon ['dʒɑːgən] *n* jerga, jerigonza.
jasmin ['dʒæzmɪn] *n* jazmín.
jaundice ['dʒɔːndɪs] *n* ictericia.
jaundiced ['dʒɔːndɪst] *adj fig* amargado,-a.
jaunt [dʒɔːnt] *n* excursión, viaje.
javelin ['dʒævəlɪn] *n* jabalina.
jaw [dʒɔː] *n* mandíbula.
jay [dʒeɪ] *n* arrendajo común.
jaywalker ['dʒeɪwɔːlkə'] *n* peatón imprudente.
jazz [dʒæz] *n* jazz.
to jazz up *vt* animar, alegrar.
jazzy ['dʒæzɪ] *adj* (**-ier**, **-iest**) *fam* llamativo,-a.
jealous ['dʒeləs] *adj* celoso,-a.
● **to be jealous of** SB tener celos de ALGN.
jealousy ['dʒeləsɪ] *n* (*pl* **-ies**) celos.

jeans [dʒiːnz] *npl* vaqueros.

jeep [dʒiːp] *n* jeep, vehículo todoterreno.

jeer [dʒɪə'] *vi* **1** burlarse. **2** abuchear.
► *n* **1** burla. **2** abucheo.

Jehovah [dʒɪˈhəʊvə] *n* Jehová.
■ **Jehova's Witness** testigo de Jehová.

jelly [ˈdʒelɪ] *n* (*pl* **-ies**). **1** jalea. **2** gelatina.

jellyfish [ˈdʒelɪfɪʃ] *n* (*pl* **-es**) medusa.

jeopardize [ˈdʒepədaɪz] *vt* poner en peligro.

jeopardy [ˈdʒepədɪ] *n* peligro.

jerk [dʒɜːk] *n* **1** tirón, sacudida. **2** *fam* imbécil.
► *vt* sacudir, tirar de.
► *vi* dar una sacudida.

to jerk off *vi vulg* hacerse una paja.

jerkin [ˈdʒɜːkɪn] *n* chaleco.

jerry-built [ˈdʒerɪbɪlt] *adj* mal construido,-a.

jersey [ˈdʒɜːzɪ] *n* jersey, suéter.

jest [dʒest] *n* broma.
● **in jest** en broma.

jet [dʒet] *n* **1** reactor, jet. **2** chorro.
► *vi* (*pt & pp* **jetted**, *ger* **jetting**). **1** salir disparado,-a. **2** *fam* viajar en avión.

jet-lag [ˈdʒetlæg] *n* jet-lag.

jet-set [ˈdʒetset] *n* jetset.

jetty [ˈdʒetɪ] *n* (*pl* **-ies**) malecón.

Jew [dʒuː] *n* judío.

jewel [ˈdʒuːəl] *n* **1** joya, alhaja. **2** piedra preciosa.

jeweller [ˈdʒuːələ'] *n* joyero,-a.
■ **jeweller's** joyería.

jewellery [ˈdʒuːəlrɪ] *n* joyas.

Jewish [ˈdʒuːɪʃ] *adj* judío,-a.

jibe [dʒaɪb] *n-vi* → gibe.

jiffy [ˈdʒɪfɪ] *n fam* instante: *it'll only take a jiffy*, en un momento está hecho.
● **in a jiffy** en un santiamén.

jigsaw [ˈdʒɪgsɔː] *n* rompecabezas.

jilt [dʒɪlt] *vt* dejar plantado,-a.

jingle [ˈdʒɪŋgəl] *n* **1** tintineo. **2** melodía (*de anuncio*).
► *vi* tintinear.

jingoism [ˈdʒɪŋgəʊɪzəm] *n* patriotería.

jinx [dʒɪŋks] *n* (*pl* **jinxes**) gafe.

jitters [ˈdʒɪtəz] *npl fam* nervios.
● **to get the jitters** ponerse como un flan.

jittery [ˈdʒɪtərɪ] *adj* nervioso,-a.

job [dʒɒb] *n* trabajo.
● **it's a good job that ...** menos mal que ....
● **out of a job** parado,-a, sin trabajo.

jobless [ˈdʒɒbləs] *adj* parado,-a, sin trabajo.

jockey [ˈdʒɒkɪ] *n* jockey.

jockstrap [ˈdʒɒkstræp] *n* suspensorio.

jog [dʒɒg] *n* trote.
► *vt* (*pt & pp* **jogged**, *ger* **jogging**) empujar, sacudir.
► *vi* hacer footing, correr.
● **to go for a jog** hacer footing.

jogging [ˈdʒɒgɪŋ] *n* footing.

join [dʒɔɪn] *vt* **1** juntar, unir: *he joined the beds*, juntó las camas. **2** reunirse con: *he said he'd join us after work*, dijo que se reuniría con nosotros después del trabajo. **3** acompañar: *I'm going for a coffee, will you join me?*, voy a tomar un café, ¿quieres acompañarme? **4** alistarse (*en ejército*); ingresar (*en policía*). **5** hacerse socio,-a (*de un club*). **6** afiliarse a (*partido, sindicato*). **7** incorporarse (*a empresa*).
► *vi* **1** juntarse. **2** confluir (*ríos*).

to join in *vi* participar.

joiner [ˈdʒɔɪnə'] *n* carpintero.

joint [dʒɔɪnt] *n* **1** junta, juntura, unión, ensambladura. **2** articulación (*de rodilla, cadera*). **3** corte de carne. **4** *sl* porro. **5** *sl* antro.
► *adj* conjunto,-a, compartido,-a.
■ **joint account** cuenta conjunta.
■ **joint ownership** propiedad compartida.
■ **joint venture** empresa conjunta.

jointly [ˈdʒɔɪntlɪ] *adv* conjuntamente.

joke [dʒəʊk] *n* **1** chiste. **2** broma.
► *vi* bromear.
● **to crack a joke** contar un chiste.
● **to play a joke on** gastar una broma a.

joker [ˈdʒəʊkə'] *n* **1** bromista. **2** comodín.

jolly [ˈdʒɒlɪ] *adj* (**-ier**, **-iest**) alegre.
► *adv* muy.
● **jolly good!** ¡estupendo!

jolt [dʒəʊlt] *n* **1** sacudida. **2** sorpresa, susto.
► *vt* sacudir.
► *vi* dar una sacudida.

Jordan [ˈdʒɔːdən] *n* **1** Jordania. **2 the Jordan** el Jordán.

jostle [ˈdʒɒsəl] *vt* empujar.
► *vi* dar empujones.

jot [dʒɒt] *n* pizca.
● **not to care a jot**: *I don't care a jot*, no me importa lo más mínimo.

to jot down *vt* apuntar.

jotter [ˈdʒɒtə'] *n* GB bloc.

journal [ˈdʒɜːnəl] *n* **1** revista, publicación (*especializada*). **2** diario.

journalism ['dʒɜːnəlɪzəm] *n* periodismo.
journalist ['dʒɜːnəlɪst] *n* periodista.
journey ['dʒɜːnɪ] *n* **1** viaje. **2** trayecto: *a 20 mile journey*, un trayecto de 20 millas.
jowl [dʒaʊl] *n* carrillo.
joy [dʒɔɪ] *n* gozo, júbilo, alegría.
joyful ['dʒɔɪfʊl] *adj* jubiloso,-a, alegre.
joyous ['dʒɔɪəs] *adj* de júbilo.
joyride ['dʒɔɪraɪd] *n fam* paseo en un coche robado.
joystick ['dʒɔɪstɪk] *n* palanca de mando, joystick.
JP ['dʒeɪ'piː] *abbr* (**Justice of the Peace**) juez de paz.
jubilant ['dʒuːbɪlənt] *adj* jubiloso,-a.
jubilee ['dʒuːbɪliː] *n* aniversario.
Judaism ['dʒuːdeɪɪzəm] *n* judaísmo.
judder ['dʒʌdəʳ] *vi* dar sacudidas, vibrar.
judge [dʒʌdʒ] *n* juez, jueza.
► *vt-vi* juzgar.
► *vt* calcular, evaluar.
judgement ['dʒʌdʒmənt] *n* **1** juicio, criterio: *an error of judgement*, un error de criterio. **2** juicio, opinión: *in my judgement*, a mi juicio. **3** fallo.
■ **judgement day** día del juicio.
judicial [dʒuː'dɪʃəl] *adj* judicial.
judicious [dʒuː'dɪʃəs] *adj* juicioso,-a.
judo ['dʒuːdəʊ] *n* judo.
jug [dʒʌg] *n* jarro.
juggernaut ['dʒʌgənɔːt] *n* GB camión pesado.
juggle ['dʒʌgəl] *vi* hacer juegos malabares.
juggler ['dʒʌgləʳ] *n* malabarista.
juice [dʒuːs] *n* **1** jugo. **2** zumo.
juicy ['dʒuːsɪ] *adj* (-ier, -iest). **1** jugoso,-a. **2** *fam* picante.
jukebox ['dʒuːkbɒks] *n* (*pl* **jukeboxes**) máquina de discos.
July [dʒuː'laɪ] *n* julio.
jumble ['dʒʌmbəl] *n* revoltijo, confusión.
► *vt* mezclar.
■ **jumble sale** rastro benéfico, mercadillo.
jumbo ['dʒʌmbəʊ] *adj* gigante.
► *n* (*pl* **jumbos**) jumbo.
jump [dʒʌmp] *n* salto.
► *vt-vi* saltar.
► *vi* dar un salto.
● **to jump to one's feet** ponerse de pie.
to jump at *vt* aceptar sin pensarlo.
jumper ['dʒʌmpəʳ] *n* **1** GB jersey. **2** US pichi.

jump-suit ['dʒʌmpsuːt] *n* mono.
jumpy ['dʒʌmpɪ] *adj* (-ier, -iest) nervioso,-a.
junction ['dʒʌŋkʃən] *n* **1** salida, acceso *(en autopista)*. **2** cruce.
juncture ['dʒʌŋktʃəʳ] *n* coyuntura.
June [dʒuːn] *n* junio.
jungle ['dʒʌŋgəl] *n* jungla, selva.
junior ['dʒuːnɪəʳ] *adj* **1** menor, más joven. **2** subalterno,-a.
► *n* **1** menor. **2** subalterno,-a. **3** GB alumno,-a de básica. **4** US hijo,-a.
juniper ['dʒuːnɪpəʳ] *n* enebro.
junk¹ [dʒʌŋk] *n* trastos.
■ **junk food** comida basura.
■ **junk mail** propaganda *(que se recibe por correo)*.
junk² [dʒʌŋk] *n* junco.
junkie ['dʒʌŋkɪ] *n sl* yonqui.
Jupiter ['dʒuːpɪtəʳ] *n* Júpiter.
jurisdiction [dʒʊərɪs'dɪkʃən] *n* jurisdicción.
juror ['dʒʊərəʳ] *n* jurado.
jury ['dʒʊərɪ] *n* (*pl* **-ies**) jurado.
just¹ [dʒʌst] *adj* justo,-a.
just² [dʒʌst] *adv* **1** exactamente, justo: *that's just what I expected*, eso es exactamente lo que esperaba. **2** solamente: *there's just one left*, sólo queda uno. **3** justo ahora: *I'm just about to leave*, estoy a punto de salir. **4** justo: *I arrived just in time*, llegué justo a tiempo.
● **just about** prácticamente.
● **just in case** por si acaso.
● **just now** ahora mismo.
● **to have just done** STH acabar de hacer algo: *I've just arrived*, acabo de llegar.
● **just yet** todavía: *it's not ready just yet*, todavía no está listo.
justice ['dʒʌstɪs] *n* justicia.
■ **Justice of the Peace** juez de paz.
justifiable [dʒʌstɪ'faɪəbəl] *adj* justificable.
justification [dʒʌstɪfɪ'keɪʃən] *n* justificación.
justified ['dʒʌstɪfaɪd] *adj* justificado,-a.
justify ['dʒʌstɪfaɪ] *vt* (*pt & pp* **-ied**) justificar.
jut [dʒʌt] *vi* (*pt & pp* **jutted**, *ger* **jutting**) sobresalir.
jute [dʒuːt] *n* yute.
juvenile ['dʒuːvɪnaɪl] *adj* **1** juvenil. **2** infantil.
► *n* menor.
juxtapose ['dʒʌkstəpəʊz] *vt* yuxtaponer.

K

kaftan ['kæftæn] *n* caftán.

kaleidoscope [kə'laɪdəskəʊp] *n* calidoscopio.

kamikaze [kæmɪ'kɑːzɪ] *adj-n* kamikaze.

kangaroo [kæŋɡə'ruː] *n* (*pl* **kangaroos**) canguro.

kaput [kə'pʊt] *adj fam* roto,-a, estropeado,-a.

karate [kə'rɑːtɪ] *n* kárate.

kayak ['kaɪæk] *n* kayac.

kebab [kɪ'bæb] *n* pincho moruno.

keel [kiːl] *n* quilla.

to keel over *vi* **1** zozobrar *(barco)*. **2** desplomarse *(persona)*.

keen [kiːn] *adj* **1** entusiasta, muy aficionado,-a: *he's a keen golfer*, es muy aficionado al golf. **2** agudo,-a *(mente)*. **3** penetrante *(mirada)*. **4** cortante *(viento)*. **5** fuerte *(competencia)*. **6** competitivo,-a *(precio)*.

● **keen on** aficionado,-a a: *I'm not very keen on it*, no me gusta demasiado.

● **to be keen to do STH** tener muchas ganas de hacer algo.

● **to take a keen interest in** mostrar un gran interés por.

keep [kiːp] *n* **1** sustento, manutención *f.* **2** torreón, torre del homenaje *(de castillo)*. ▶ *vt* (*pt & pp* **kept** [kept]). **1** quedarse, guardar *(no devolver)*. **2** guardar, tener guardado,-a: *you should keep eggs in the fridge*, deberías guardar los huevos en la nevera. **3** retener, detener, entretener: *sorry to keep you waiting*, discúlpeme por hacerlo esperar. **4** tener *(tienda, negocio)*. **5** tener, vender *(artículos)*. **6** llevar *(cuentas)*. **7** escribir, llevar *(diario)*. **8** mantener *(orden)*. **9** cumplir *(promesa)*. **10** guardar *(secreto)*. **11** acudir a, no faltar a *(cita)*. **12** mantener *(persona)*. **13** criar *(gallinas, cerdos)*. **14** mantener: *keep your room tidy*, mantén tu habitación limpia. ▶ *vi* **1** seguir, continuar: *keep straight*, siga todo recto. **2** conservarse bien: *cheese keeps well in the fridge*, el queso se conserva bien en la nevera.

● **keep the change** quédese con la vuelta.

● **to keep doing STH** seguir haciendo algo: *don't stop, keep talking*, no pares, sigue hablando; *I keep losing my keys*, siempre pierdo las llaves.

● **to keep going** seguir, seguir adelante.

● **to keep one's head** no perder la cabeza.

● **to keep quiet** callarse, no hacer ruido.

● **to keep SB company** hacerle compañía a ALGN.

● **to keep STH clean** conservar algo limpio,-a.

● **to keep STH to oneself** guardar algo para sí.

to keep away *vt-vi* mantener(se) a distancia.

to keep back *vt* **1** reservar, guardar *(dinero)*. **2** ocultar, no dar *(información)*. **3** tener a raya *(enemigo)*.

to keep back from *vi* mantenerse lejos de.

to keep down *vt* oprimir, contener.

to keep in *vt* no dejar salir.

to keep on *vi* seguir, continuar: *he kept on talking*, siguió hablando. ▶ *vt* no quitarse *(ropa)*.

to keep out *vt* no dejar entrar. ▶ *vi* no entrar: *keep out!*, prohibida la entrada.

to keep up *vi* mantener el ritmo.
▶ *vt* mantener despierto,-a, tener en vela.
keeper ['ki:pə'] *n* **1** guardián,-ana *(de zoo)*. **2** guarda *(de parque)*.
keeping ['ki:pɪŋ] *n* cuidado, custodia.
● **in keeping with** en consonancia con.
keg [keg] *n* barril.
kennel ['kenəl] *n* perrera, caseta para perros.
▶ *npl* **kennels** residencia canina.
Kenya ['kenjə] *n* Kenia.
Kenyan ['kenjən] *adj-n* keniano,-a.
kept [kept] *pt-pp* → keep.
kerb [kɜːb] *n* bordillo.
kerfuffle [kə'fʌfəl] *n fam* jaleo.
kernel ['kɜːnəl] *n* **1** semilla *(de nuez, fruta)*. **2** *fig* núcleo.
ketchup ['ketʃəp] *n* ketchup, catsup.
kettle ['ketəl] *n* hervidor.
key [ki:] *n* **1** llave *(de cerradura)*. **2** clave *(de misterio)*. **3** tecla *(de teclado)*. **4** tono *(música)*. **5** soluciones, respuestas *(de ejercicios)*.
▶ *adj* clave.
▶ *vt* teclear.
■ **key ring** llavero.
to key in *vt* introducir, entrar *(textos, datos)*.
keyboard ['ki:bɔːd] *n* teclado.
keyed up [ki:d'ʌp] *adj* nervioso,-a, excitado,-a.
keyhole ['ki:həʊl] *n* ojo de la cerradura.
khaki ['kɑːkɪ] *adj-n* caqui.
kick [kɪk] *n* **1** puntapié, patada *(de persona)*. **2** coz *(de animal)*. **3** emoción, sensación: *I get a kick out of flying*, me emociona viajar.
▶ *vt* **1** dar un puntapié a, dar una patada a *(persona)*. **2** dar coces a *(animal)*.
● **for kicks** para divertirse.
● **to kick the bucket** *fam* estirar la pata.
● **to kick up a fuss** *fam* armar un escándalo.
to kick out *vt* echar.
kick-off ['kɪkɒf] *n (pl* **kick-offs***)* saque inicial *(en fútbol, rugby)*.
kid[1] [kɪd] *n* **1** cabrito *(animal)*. **2** cabritilla *(piel)*. **3** *fam* niño,-a, chico,-a.
kid[2] [kɪd] *vt (pt & pp* **kidded***, ger* **kidding***)* tomar el pelo a.
▶ *vi* estar de broma: *you must be kidding!*, ¡debes de estar de broma!

kidnap ['kɪdnæp] *vt (pt & pp* **kidnapped***, ger* **kidnapping***)* secuestrar.
kidnapper ['kɪdnæpə'] *n* secuestrador,-ra.
kidnapping ['kɪdnæpɪŋ] *n* secuestro.
kidney ['kɪdnɪ] *n* riñón.
kill [kɪl] *vt* matar.
● **to kill two birds with one stone** matar dos pájaros de un tiro.
to kill off *vt* exterminar.
killer ['kɪlə'] *n* asesino,-a.
killing ['kɪlɪŋ] *n* **1** matanza *(de animal)*. **2** asesinato *(de persona)*.
● **to make a killing** hacer su agosto, forrarse.
killjoy ['kɪldʒɔɪ] *n* aguafiestas *mf inv*.
kiln [kɪln] *n* horno.
kilo ['ki:ləʊ] *n (pl* **kilos***)* kilo.
kilogram ['kɪləgræm] *n* kilogramo.

También **kilogramme**.

kilometre [kɪ'lɒmɪtə'] *(US* **kilometer***) n* kilómetro.
kilowatt ['kɪləwɒt] *n* kilovatio.
kilt [kɪlt] *n* falda escocesa.
kin [kɪn] *n* parientes, familia.
kind [kaɪnd] *adj* simpático,-a, amable.
▶ *n* tipo, género, clase.
● **in kind 1** en especie *(pago)*. **2** con la misma moneda *(trato)*.
● **a kind of** una especie de.
● **to be so kind as to** tener la bondad de.
kindergarten ['kɪndəgɑːtən] *n* parvulario, jardín de infancia.
kind-hearted [kaɪnd'hɑːtɪd] *adj* bondadoso,-a, de buen corazón.
kindle ['kɪndəl] *vt* encender.
kindly ['kaɪndlɪ] *adj (-***ier***, -***iest***)* bondadoso,-a, amable.
▶ *adv* **1** amablemente. **2** por favor: *will you kindly let me talk?*, ¿sería tan amable de dejarme hablar?
kindness ['kaɪndnəs] *n* **1** bondad, amabilidad. **2** favor.
kinetic [kɪ'netɪk] *adj* cinético,-a.
kinetics [kɪ'netɪks] *n* cinética.

Es incontable y el verbo va en singular.

king [kɪŋ] *n* rey.
kingdom ['kɪŋdəm] *n* reino.
kink [kɪŋk] *n* **1** rizo *(de pelo)*. **2** *fig* vicio, manía.
kinky ['kɪŋkɪ] *adj (-***ier***, -***iest***)* *fam* pervertido,-a *(sexual)*.
kinship ['kɪnʃɪp] *n* parentesco.

kiosk ['kiːɒsk] *n* **1** quiosco. **2** cabina telefónica.

kip [kɪp] *vi* (*pt & pp* **kipped**, *ger* **kipping**) *fam* dormir.

● **to have a kip** dormir.

kipper ['kɪpə'] *n* arenque ahumado.

kiss [kɪs] *n* (*pl* **-es**) beso.

▶ *vt-vi* besar(se).

kit [kɪt] *n* **1** equipo. **2** petate. **3** maqueta, kit.

kitchen ['kɪtʃɪn] *n* cocina.

kite [kaɪt] *n* cometa.

kitten ['kɪtən] *n* gatito,-a.

kitty ['kɪtɪ] *n* (*pl* **-ies**). **1** *fam* minino,-a. **2** *fam* bote (*de dinero*).

kiwi ['kiːwiː] *n* kiwi.

kleptomania [kleptə'meɪnɪə] *n* cleptomanía.

kleptomaniac [kleptə'meɪnɪæk] *n* cleptómano,-a.

km [kɪ'lɒmɪtə', 'kɪləmiːtə'] *abbr* (*pl* **km** o **kms**) *(kilometre)* kilómetro, km.

knack [næk] *n* maña, truquillo.

knacker ['nækə'] *n* matarife.

▶ *npl* **knackers** *vulg* cojones.

knackered ['nækəd] *adj* **1** *fam* reventado,-a, hecho,-a polvo (*persona*). **2** *fam* escoñado,-a, jodido,-a (*objeto*).

knapsack ['næpsæk] *n* mochila.

knead [niːd] *vt* amasar.

knee [niː] *n* rodilla.

● **on one's knees** de rodillas.

kneecap ['niːkæp] *n* rótula.

kneel [niːl] *vi* (*pt & pp* **knelt**) arrodillarse, ponerse de rodillas.

knelt [nelt] *pt-pp* → kneel.

knew [njuː] *pt* → know.

knickers ['nɪkəz] *npl* bragas: *a pair of knickers*, unas bragas.

knick-knack ['nɪknæk] *n* chuchería.

knife [naɪf] *n* (*pl* **knives**) cuchillo.

▶ *vt* (*pt & pp* **knived**, *ger* **kniving**) apuñalar.

knight [naɪt] *n* **1** caballero. **2** caballo (*ajedrez*).

▶ *vt* armar caballero a.

knit [nɪt] *vt* (*pt & pp* **knit** o **knitted**, *ger* **knitting**) tejer.

▶ *vi* **1** hacer punto, hacer calceta, tricotar. **2** soldarse (*huesos*).

knitting ['nɪtɪŋ] *n* punto, calceta.

■ **knitting needle** aguja de hacer punto.

knob [nɒb] *n* **1** pomo (*de puerta*). **2** tirador (*de cajón*). **3** puño (*de palo*). **4** bulto, protuberancia. **5** botón (*de radio*).

knobbly ['nɒblɪ] *adj* (**-ier**, **-iest**) nudoso,-a.

knock [nɒk] *n* **1** golpe: *there was a knock on the door*, llamaron a la puerta. **2** revés (*de la fortuna*).

▶ *vt* **1** golpear: *he knocked his head on the ceiling*, se dio con la cabeza contra el techo. **2** criticar.

▶ *vi* llamar: *someone knocked on the door*, alguien llamó a la puerta.

to knock back *vt* beber de un trago, pimplarse.

to knock down *vt* **1** derribar (*edificio*). **2** atropellar (*persona*).

to knock off *vt* **1** tirar. **2** *fam* birlar, mangar. **3** *fam* liquidar (*persona*). **4** rebajar (*cantidad*).

▶ *vi* acabar, salir del trabajo.

to knock out *vt* dejar sin conocimiento, dejar fuera de combate (*en boxeo*).

to knock over *vt* volcar (*vaso*), atropellar (*persona*).

to knock up *vt* **1** GB *fam* despertar. **2** US *fam* dejar preñada.

▶ *vi* pelotear (*en tenis*).

knocker ['nɒkə'] *n* aldaba.

▶ *npl* **knockers** *fam* tetas.

knock-kneed ['nɒkniːd] *adj* patizambo,-a.

knockout ['nɒkaʊt] *n* **1** knock-out, nocáut, K.O., fuera de combate. **2** *fam* maravilla.

■ **knockout competition** eliminatoria.

knot [nɒt] *n* nudo: *to tie a knot*, hacer un nudo.

▶ *vt* (*pt & pp* **knotted**, *ger* **knotting**) anudar.

knotty ['nɒtɪ] *adj* (**-ier**, **-iest**). **1** nudoso,-a. **2** difícil, espinoso,-a (*problema*).

know [nəʊ] *vt-vi* (*pt* **knew** [njuː], *pp* **known** [nəʊn]). **1** conocer: *do you know Colin?*, ¿conoces a Colin? **2** saber: *I do not know the answer*, no sé la respuesta.

● **as far as I know** que yo sepa.

● **to know by sight** conocer de vista.

● **to know how to do STH** saber hacer algo.

know-all ['nəʊɔːl] *n* sabelotodo.

know-how ['nəʊhaʊ] *n* conocimientos *mpl* prácticos.

knowing ['nəʊɪŋ] *adj* de complicidad (*mirada, sonrisa*).

knowingly ['nəʊɪŋlɪ] *adv* intencionadamente, a sabiendas, adrede.
knowledge ['nɒlɪdʒ] *n* **1** conocimiento. **2** conocimientos.
● **to have a good knowledge of** conocer bien.
knowledgeable ['nɒlɪdʒəbəl] *adj* erudito, -a, entendido,-a.
known [nəʊn] *pp* → know.
knuckle ['nʌkəl] *n* nudillo.
to knuckle down *vi fam* ponerse a trabajar en serio.
to knuckle under *vi* pasar por el aro, doblegarse.

KO ['keɪ'əʊ] *abbr (knockout)* fuera de combate, KO.
koala [kəʊ'ɑːlə] *n* koala.
Koran [kɔː'rɑːn] *n* Corán.
Korea [kə'rɪə] *n* Corea: *North Korea*, Corea del Norte; *South Korea*, Corea del Sur.
Korean [kə'rɪən] *adj* coreano,-a.
▶ *n* **1** coreano,-a *(persona)*. **2** coreano *(lengua)*: *North Korean*, norcoreano,-a; *South Korean*, surcoreano,-a.
kph ['keɪ'piː'eɪtʃ] *abbr (kilometres per hour)* kilómetros por hora, km/h.
Kuwait [kʊ'weɪt] *n* Kuwait.
Kuwaiti [kʊ'weɪtɪ] *adj-n* kuwaití.

L

L¹ [el] *abbr* (*Learner driver*) conductor en prácticas

L² [el] *abbr* (*large size*) talla grande, G.

Lab ['leɪbə] *abbr* (*Labour*) laborista.

label ['leɪbəl] *n* etiqueta.
  ► *vt* (GB *pt & pp* **labelled**, *ger* **labelling**; US *pt & pp* **labeled**, *ger* **labeling**) etiquetar.

laboratory [lə'bɒrətəri] *n* (*pl* -ies) laboratorio.

laborious [lə'bɔːrɪəs] *adj* laborioso,-a.

labour ['leɪbə] (US **labor**) *n* **1** trabajo. **2** tarea, faena. **3** mano de obra.
  ► *vt* insistir en.
  ● **to go into labour** ponerse de parto.
  ■ **Labour Party** partido laborista.

labourer ['leɪbərə] (US **laborer**) *n* peón, obrero,-a.

labyrinth ['læbərɪnθ] *n* laberinto.

lace [leɪs] *n* **1** cordón (*de zapato*). **2** encaje.
  ► *vt* atar.

lack [læk] *n* falta, carencia.
  ► *vt* faltar, carecer de.

lacking ['lækɪŋ] *adj* carente de.

lacquer ['lækə] *n* laca, fijador.
  ► *vt* lacar, poner laca a.

lad [læd] *n* muchacho, chaval.

ladder ['lædə] *n* **1** escalera de mano. **2** carrera (*en medias*).

laden ['leɪdən] *adj* cargado,-a, lleno,-a.

lading ['leɪdɪŋ] *n* embarque.

ladle ['leɪdəl] *n* cucharón.

lady ['leɪdɪ] *n* (*pl* -ies) señora, dama.

ladybird ['leɪdɪbɜːd] *n* mariquita.

ladylike ['leɪdɪlaɪk] *adj* delicado,-a, elegante.

lag [læg] *n* retraso, demora.
  ► *vi* (*pt & pp* **lagged**, *ger* **lagging**) rezagarse: *you're lagging behind*, te estás rezagando.

lager ['lɑːgə] *n* cerveza rubia.

lagoon [lə'guːn] *n* laguna.

laid [leɪd] *pt-pp* → lay.

lain [leɪn] *pp* → lie.

lair [leə] *n* guarida.

lake [leɪk] *n* lago.

lamb [læm] *n* **1** cordero. **2** carne de cordero.

lame [leɪm] *adj* cojo,-a.

lameness ['leɪmnəs] *n* cojera.

lament [lə'ment] *n* lamento.
  ► *vt-vi* lamentar(se).

lamentable ['læməntəbəl] *adj* lamentable.

laminate [(*n*) 'læmɪnət(*vb*) 'læmɪneɪt] *n* laminado.
  ► *vt* laminar.

lamp [læmp] *n* lámpara.

lampoon [læm'puːn] *n* pasquín.
  ► *vt* satirizar.

lamp-post ['læmppəʊst] *n* farola.

lampshade ['læmpʃeɪd] *n* pantalla (*de lámpara*).

lance [lɑːns] *n* **1** lanza. **2** lanceta (*de cirujano*).

land [lænd] *n* **1** tierra: *by land and sea*, por tierra y por mar. **2** suelo, tierra: *he lives off the land*, vive de la tierra. **3** terreno, finca. **4** país.
  ► *vi* **1** aterrizar, tomar tierra (*avión*). **2** caer (*pelota*).
  ► *vt* *fig* conseguir (*trabajo, dinero*).
  ► *vt-vi* desembarcar.

landing ['lændɪŋ] *n* **1** aterrizaje (*de avión*). **2** descansillo, rellano (*en escalera*). **3** desembarco (*de personas*).

landlady ['lændleɪdɪ] *n* (*pl* -ies) **1** propietaria, casera *(de vivienda)*. **2** dueña *(de pensión)*.

landlocked ['lændlɒkt] *adj* sin salida al mar.

landlord ['lænlɔːd] *n* **1** propietario, casero *(de vivienda)*. **2** dueño *(de pensión)*.

landmark ['lændmɑːk] *n* **1** lugar muy conocido, edificio muy conocido. **2** *fig* hito.

landowner ['lændəʊnə'] *n* propietario,-a, terrateniente.

landscape ['lændskeɪp] *n* paisaje.

landslide ['lændslaɪd] *n* desprendimiento de tierras.

lane [leɪn] *n* **1** camino. **2** carril *(de autopista)*. **3** calle *(en atletismo, natación)*.

language ['læŋgwɪdʒ] *n* **1** lenguaje: ***scientific language***, lenguaje científico. **2** lengua, idioma.

● **to use bad language** decir palabrotas.

languid ['læŋgwɪd] *adj* lánguido,-a.

languish ['læŋgwɪʃ] *vi* languidecer.

lank [læŋk] *adj* lacio,-a.

lanky ['læŋkɪ] *adj* (**-ier**, **-iest**) larguirucho,-a.

lanolin ['lænəlɪn] *n* lanolina.

lantern ['læntən] *n* linterna, farol.

Lao [laʊ] *n* laosiano.

Laos [laʊz, laʊs] *n* Laos.

Laotian ['laʊʃɪən] *adj-n* laosiano,-a.

lap¹ [læp] *n* regazo, rodillas.

lap² [læp] *n* **1** vuelta *(de carrera)*. **2** etapa *(de viaje)*.

▶ *vt* (*pt & pp* **lapped**, *ger* **lapping**) doblar *(en carrera)*.

lap³ [læp] *vt* (*pt & pp* **lapped**, *ger* **lapping**) lamer, beber lamiendo.

lapel [lə'pel] *n* solapa.

lapse [læps] *n* **1** transcurso, lapso *(de tiempo)*. **2** desliz, lapsus, fallo.

▶ *vi* **1** cometer un desliz. **2** caducar, vencer *(contrato)*. **3** desaparecer, extinguirse *(costumbre)*.

● **to lapse into** STH sumirse, caer en: *he lapsed into silence*, se quedó callado.

laptop ['læptɒp] *n* ordenador portátil.

larceny ['lɑːsənɪ] *n* latrocinio.

lard [lɑːd] *n* manteca de cerdo.

larder ['lɑːdə'] *n* despensa.

large [lɑːdʒ] *adj* **1** grande, gran. **2** importante *(suma)*.

● **at large** suelto,-a, en libertad.

largely ['lɑːdʒlɪ] *adv* en gran parte.

large-scale ['lɑːdʒskeɪl] *adj* a gran escala, en gran escala.

lark [lɑːk] *n* alondra.

to lark about/around *vi* hacer tonterías, hacer el indio.

laryngitis [lærɪn'dʒaɪtɪs] *n* laringitis.

larynx ['lærɪŋks] *n* (*pl* **larynxes**) laringe.

lascivious [lə'sɪvɪəs] *adj* lascivo,-a.

laser ['leɪzə'] *n* láser.

lash [læʃ] *n* (*pl* **-es**). **1** latigazo, azote. **2** pestaña.

▶ *vt* **1** azotar. **2** atar.

to lash out *vi* **1** atacar, arremeter contra. **2** despilfarrar.

to lash out at *vt* criticar, arremeter contra.

to lash out on *vt* gastar mucho dinero en.

lass [læs] *n* (*pl* **-es**) chica, chavala, muchacha.

lasso [læ'suː] *n* (*pl* **-s** o **-es**) lazo.

last [lɑːst] *adj* **1** último,-a: *the last train*, el último tren; *over the last few years*, en los últimos años. **2** pasado,-a: *last Monday*, el lunes pasado; *last night*, anoche.

▶ *adv* **1** por última vez: *when did you last see your father?*, ¿cuándo fue la última vez que viste a tu padre? **2** en último lugar, en última posición: *he arrived last*, llegó el último.

▶ *n* el/la último,-a.

▶ *vt-vi* durar.

● **at last** al fin, por fin.

● **last but one** penúltimo,-a.

● **the night before last** anteanoche.

● **to the last** hasta el final.

lasting ['lɑːstɪŋ] *adj* duradero,-a, perdurable.

lastly ['lɑːstlɪ] *adv* finalmente.

latch [lætʃ] *n* (*pl* **-es**) picaporte, pestillo.

late [leɪt] *adj* **1**: *in late May*, a finales de Mayo; *in the late afternoon*, a media tarde; *she's in her late forties*, tiene casi cincuenta años, ronda los cincuenta. **2** difunto,-a.

▶ *adv* **1** tarde: *he went to bed late*, se fue a dormir tarde. **2** con retraso: *the train arrived an hour late*, el tren llegó con una hora de retraso.

● **to be late** llegar tarde: *you're late!*, ¡llegas tarde!

● **to get late** hacerse tarde.

● **to work late** trabajar hasta tarde.

lately ['leɪtlɪ] *adv* últimamente.

latent ['leɪtənt] *adj* latente.

later ['leɪtə'] *adj* posterior *(fecha, edición)*.

▶ *adv* **1** más tarde. **2** después, luego.

● **later on** más tarde, después.

lateral ['lætərəl] *adj* lateral.

latest ['leɪtɪst] *adj* último,-a.

● **at the latest** a más tardar, como muy tarde.

latex ['leɪteks] *n* látex.

lathe [leɪð] *n* torno.

lather ['lɑːðə'] *n* espuma.

▶ *vt* enjabonar.

▶ *vi* hacer espuma.

Latin ['lætɪn] *adj* latino,-a.

▶ *n* **1** latino,-a *(persona)*. **2** latín *(lengua)*.

latitude ['lætɪtjuːd] *n* latitud.

latter ['lætə'] *adj* último,-a.

▶ *pron* **the latter** éste,-a, este,-a último,-a.

lattice ['lætɪs] *n* celosía, enrejado.

laudable ['lɔːdəbəl] *adj* laudable.

laugh [lɑːf] *n* risa.

▶ *vi* reír, reírse.

● **to have a laugh** reírse.

● **to laugh at** reírse de.

laughable ['lɑːfəbəl] *adj* ridículo,-a, risible.

laughing ['lɑːfɪŋ] *adj* risueño,-a.

▶ *n* risas.

■ **laughing gas** gas hilarante.

laughing-stock ['lɑːfɪŋstɒk] *n* hazmerreír.

laughter ['lɑːftə'] *n* risas.

launch [lɔːntʃ] *n* *(pl* **-es**). **1** lanzamiento *(de producto, misil)*. **2** botadura *(de barco)*. **3** estreno *(de película)*. **4** lancha.

▶ *vt* **1** lanzar *(producto, misil)*. **2** botar *(barco)*. **3** estrenar *(película)*.

launder ['lɔːndə'] *vt* **1** lavar y planchar *(ropa)*. **2** blanquear *(dinero)*.

launderette [lɔːndə'ret] *n* lavandería automática.

laundry ['lɔːndrɪ] *n* *(pl* **-ies**). **1** lavandería. **2** colada, ropa lavada.

laurel ['lɒrəl] *n* laurel.

lava ['lɑːvə] *n* lava.

lavatory ['lævətərɪ] *n* *(pl* **-ies**). **1** wáter. **2** lavabo, baño. **3** servicios, aseo *(público)*.

lavender ['lævɪndə'] *n* espliego, lavanda.

lavish ['lævɪʃ] *adj* **1** pródigo,-a, generoso,-a. **2** abundante. **3** lujoso,-a.

▶ *vt* prodigar.

law [lɔː] *n* **1** ley. **2** derecho *(carrera)*. **3 the law** *fam* la poli, la pasma.

● **to break the law** violar la ley.

● **to go against the law** ser ilegal, ir en contra de la ley.

■ **law and order** orden público.

■ **law court** tribunal de justicia.

law-abiding ['lɔːəbaɪdɪŋ] *adj* que observa la ley, respetuoso,-a de la ley.

law-breaker ['lɔːbreɪkə'] *n* infractor,-ra de la ley.

lawful ['lɔːfʊl] *adj* legal, legítimo,-a, lícito,-a.

lawless ['lɔːləs] *adj* **1** sin ley *(región)*. **2** rebelde *(persona)*.

lawn [lɔːn] *n* césped.

lawnmower ['lɔːnməʊə'] *n* cortacésped.

lawsuit ['lɔːsjuːt] *n* pleito.

lawyer ['lɔːjə'] *n* abogado,-a.

lax [læks] *adj* **1** laxo,-a *(moral)*. **2** descuidado,-a *(persona)*.

laxative ['læksətɪv] *adj-n* laxante.

lay¹ [leɪ] *adj* **1** laico,-a, seglar. **2** lego,-a, no profesional.

lay² [leɪ] *vt* *(pt & pp* **laid** [leɪd]; *ger* **laying**). **1** poner, colocar. **2** tender *(cable)*. **3** echar *(cimientos)*. **4** poner *(huevos)*. **5** *vulg* tirarse, follarse.

● **to be laid up** tener que guardar cama.

● **to lay one's hands on SB** pillar a ALGN.

● **to lay the table** poner la mesa.

lay³ [leɪ] *pt* → lie.

to lay down *vt* **1** dejar *(herramientas)*. **2** deponer *(armas)*. **3** guardar *(vino)*.

to lay in *vt* proveerse de.

to lay into *vt* atacar, arremeter contra.

to lay off *vt* **1** despedir *(empleado)*. **2** *fam* dejar en paz.

to lay on *vt* proveer.

to lay out *vt* **1** extender, tender *(mapa, tela)*. **2** hacer el trazado de *(población)*. **3** diseñar *(jardín)*. **4** *fam* dejar fuera de combate.

to lay up *vt* almacenar.

layabout ['leɪəbʊt] *n* *fam* holgazán,-ana.

lay-by ['leɪbaɪ] *n* *(pl* **-ies**) área de descanso.

layer ['leɪə'] *n* capa, estrato *(de rocas)*.

layman ['leɪmən] *n* *(pl* **laymen**). **1** laico. **2** profano, lego,-a.

layout ['leɪaʊt] *n* **1** disposición, distribución *(de casa)*. **2** trazado *(de ciudad, jardín)*.

laziness ['leɪzɪnəs] *n* pereza.

lazy ['leɪzɪ] *adj* (**-ier**, **-iest**) perezoso,-a.

lb [paʊnd] *abbr* (*pl* **lb** o **lbs**) (*pound*) libra.

LCD [elsiː'diː] *abbr* (*of* **liquid crystal display**) pantalla de cristal líquido.

lead¹ [led] *n* **1** plomo (*metal*). **2** mina (*de lápiz*).

lead² [liːd] *n* **1** delantera, cabeza (*en competición*). **2** ejemplo. **3** correa (*de perro*). **4** primer papel, papel principal. **5** cable (*eléctrico*). **6** pista.

▶ *vt* (*pt & pp* **led** [led]). **1** llevar, conducir (*sendero, guía*). **2** liderar, dirigir. **3** ocupar el primer puesto en, llevar (*vida*).

▶ *vi* **1** ir primero,-a, llevar la delantera (*en carrera*). **2** tener el mando. **3** conducir (*camino*): **where does this path lead?**, ¿a dónde conduce este camino?; **this door leads into the kitchen**, esta puerta da a la cocina.

● **to be in the lead** ir en cabeza.

● **to follow SB's lead** seguir el ejemplo de alguien.

● **to lead SB on** engañar a ALGN.

● **to lead SB to believe STH** llevar a ALGN a creer algo.

● **to lead the way** enseñar el camino.

● **to take the lead** tomar la delantera.

leader ['liːdəʳ] *n* **1** líder, dirigente. **2** líder (*de carrera*). **3** editorial (*de periódico*).

leadership ['liːdəʃɪp] *n* **1** liderato, liderazgo (*posición*). **2** dotes de mando (*cualidad*). **3** dirección, dirigentes (*personas*).

lead-free ['ledfriː] *adj* sin plomo.

leading ['liːdɪŋ] *adj* destacado,-a, principal.

leaf [liːf] *n* (*pl* **leaves**) hoja.

leaflet ['liːflət] *n* folleto.

leafy ['liːfɪ] *adj* (**-ier**, **-iest**) frondoso,-a.

league [liːg] *n* liga.

leak [liːk] *n* **1** escape, fuga (*de gas, agua*). **2** filtración (*de información*). **3** agujero (*en recipiente*). **4** gotera (*en tejado*). **5** *fam* meada.

▶ *vi* **1** escaparse (*gas, agua*). **2** filtrarse (*información*). **3** tener un agujero (*recipiente*). **4** tener un escape (*tubería*). **5** dejar entrar agua (*zapatos, tejado*). **6** gotear (*tejado*).

leaky ['liːkɪ] *adj* (**-ier**, **-iest**). **1** que tiene escapes (*tubería*). **2** que tiene agujeros (*recipiente*). **3** que deja entrar agua (*zapato*). **4** que tiene goteras (*tejado*).

lean¹ [liːn] *adj* **1** delgado,-a, flaco,-a. **2** magro,-a.

lean² [liːn] *vt* apoyar: **she leaned the ladder against the wall**, apoyó la escalera contra la pared.

▶ *vi* **1** apoyarse. **2** inclinarse (*curva, pendiente*).

leaning ['liːnɪŋ] *adj* inclinado,-a.

▶ *n* inclinación, tendencia.

to lean out *vt-vi* asomar(se).

leant [lent] *pt-pp* → **lean**.

leap [liːp] *n* salto, brinco.

▶ *vi* (*pt & pp* **leapt**) saltar, brincar.

■ **leap year** año bisiesto.

leapfrog ['liːpfrɒg] *n*.

● **to play leapfrog** jugar a pídola.

leapt [lept] *pt-pp* → **leap**.

learn [lɜːn] *vt-vi* (*pt & pp* **learnt**) aprender.

▶ *vt* enterarse de.

learned ['lɜːnɪd] *adj* erudito,-a.

learner ['lɜːnəʳ] *n* estudiante.

■ **learner driver** conductor,-ra en prácticas.

learning ['lɜːnɪŋ] *n* conocimientos, saber.

learnt [lɜːnt] *pt-pp* → **learn**.

lease [liːs] *n* contrato de arrendamiento.

▶ *vt* arrendar.

leash [liːʃ] *n* (*pl* **-es**) correa.

least [liːst] *adj* más mínimo,-a, menor: **I haven't the least idea**, no tengo ni la más mínima idea, no tengo ni la menor idea.

▶ *adv* menos: **this is the least expensive model**, este es el modelo menos caro.

▶ *n* **the least** lo menos: **it's the least you can do for him**, es lo menos que puedes hacer por él.

● **at least** por lo menos.

● **least of all** y menos, y menos todavía.

● **not in the least** en lo más mínimo.

leather ['leðəʳ] *n* piel, cuero.

leave¹ [liːv] *vt* (*pt & pp* **left**). **1** dejar (*gen*). **2** dejar, abandonar (*esposa, hogar*). **3** salir de (*lugar*). **4** dejarse, olvidarse.

▶ *vi* salir, marcharse, irse, partir (*persona*).

● **to be left** quedar: **there are three books left**, quedan tres libros.

● **to leave behind** dejar, olvidar.

leave² [liːv] *n* permiso, vacaciones.

● **to be on leave** estar de permiso.

● **to take one's leave of** despedirse de.

to leave out *vt* omitir.

Lebanese [lebə'niːz] *adj-n* libanés,-esa.
► *npl* **the Lebanese** los libaneses.
Lebanon ['lebənən] *n* Líbano.
lecherous ['letʃərəs] *adj* lujurioso,-a, lascivo,-a.
lectern ['lektən] *n* atril.
lecture ['lektʃə'] *n* **1** conferencia: *to give a lecture*, dar una conferencia. **2** clase *(en universidad)*. **3** sermón.
► *vi* **1** dar una conferencia. **2** dar clase *(en universidad)*. **3** sermonear.
► *vt* sermonear, echar un sermón a.
lecturer ['lektʃərə'] *n* **1** conferenciante. **2** profesor,-ra *(universitario)*.
led [led] *pt-pp* → lead.
ledge [ledʒ] *n* **1** repisa, alféizar *(de ventana)*. **2** saliente *(de montaña)*.
ledger ['ledʒə'] *n* libro de contabilidad.
leech [liːtʃ] *n (pl* **-es***)* sanguijuela.
leek [liːk] *n* puerro.
leer [lɪə'] *vi* mirar con lascivia.
► *n* mirada lasciva.
left[1] [left] *adj* **1** izquierdo,-a. **2** de izquierdas, izquierdista.
► *n* izquierda.
► *adv* a la izquierda, hacia la izquierda: *turn left*, gira a la izquierda.
● **on the left** a la izquierda, a mano izquierda: *my house is on the left*, mi casa está a la izquierda.
left[2] [left] *pt-pp* → leave.
● **to be left over** quedar, sobrar.
left-hand ['lefthænd] *adj* de la izquierda, izquierdo,-a: *the left-hand side*, el lado izquierdo.
left-handed [left'hændɪd] *adj* zurdo,-a.
leftist ['leftɪst] *adj-n* izquierdista.
left-luggage office [left'lʌgɪdʒ ɒfɪs] *n* consigna.
leftover *adj* sobrante.
left-wing ['leftwɪŋ] *adj* de izquierdas.
leg [leg] *n* **1** pierna *(de persona)*. **2** pata *(de animal, mueble)*. **3** pierna *(de cordero)*, muslo *(de pollo)*. **4** pernera *(de pantalón)*.
● **to pull SB's leg** tomar el pelo a ALGN.
legacy ['legəsɪ] *n (pl* **-ies***)* legado, herencia.
legal ['liːgəl] *adj* **1** legal, legítimo,-a, lícito,-a. **2** legal, jurídico,-a *(asesoría, sistema)*.
■ **legal tender** moneda de curso legal.
legalize ['liːgəlaɪz] *vt* legalizar.
legend ['ledʒənd] *n* leyenda.

legendary ['ledʒəndərɪ] *adj* legendario,-a.
leggings ['legɪŋz] *npl* mallas.
legible ['ledʒəbəl] *adj* legible.
legion ['liːdʒən] *n* legión.
legislate ['ledʒɪsleɪt] *vi* legislar.
legislation [ledʒɪs'leɪʃən] *n* legislación.
legislature ['ledʒɪsleɪtʃə'] *n* asamblea legislativa, cuerpo legislativo.
legitimate [lɪ'dʒɪtɪmət] *adj* legítimo,-a.
legitimize [lɪ'dʒɪtɪmaɪz] *vt* legitimar.
leisure ['leʒə'] *n* ocio, tiempo libre.
■ **leisure centre** centro recreativo.
leisurely ['leʒəlɪ] *adj* sin prisa, relajado,-a.
lemon ['lemən] *n* limón.
■ **lemon tree** limonero.
lemonade [lemə'neɪd] *n* limonada.
lend [lend] *vt (pt & pp* **lent***)* dejar, prestar.
● **to lend a hand** echar una mano.
length [leŋθ] *n* **1** largo, longitud: *it's 5 metres in length*, mide 5 metros de largo. **2** duración *(de espectáculo, discurso)*. **3** trozo *(de cuerda, madera)*. **4** tramo *(de carretera)*. **5** largo *(de piscina)*.
lengthen ['leŋθən] *vt-vi* alargar(se).
lengthy ['leŋθɪ] *adj (***-ier***, ***-iest***)* largo,-a.
lenient ['liːnɪənt] *adj* indulgente, benévolo,-a.
lens [lenz] *n (pl* **lenses***)*. **1** lente *(de gafas)*. **2** objetivo *(de cámara)*.
lent [lent] *pt-pp* → lend.
Lent [lent] *n* Cuaresma.
lentil ['lentɪl] *n* lenteja.
Leo [liːəʊ] *n* Leo.
leopard ['lepəd] *n* leopardo.
leotard ['liːətɑːd] *n* malla.
leper ['lepə'] *n* leproso,-a.
leprosy ['leprəsɪ] *n* lepra.
lesbian ['lezbɪən] *adj* lesbiano,-a.
► *n* lesbiana.
less [les] *adj-adv-prep* menos.
● **less and less** cada vez menos.
● **less...than...** menos...que....
lessen ['lesən] *vt-vi* disminuir(se).
lesser ['lesə'] *adj* menor.
● **to a lesser extent** en menor grado.
lesson ['lesən] *n* lección, clase.
lest [lest] *conj fml* para que no.
let [let] *vt (pt & pp* **let***)*. **1** dejar, permitir. **2** arrendar, alquilar: *"to let"*, se alquila.
► *aux*: *let this be a warning*, que esto sirva de advertencia; *let us pray*, oremos; *let's go!*, ¡vamos!
● **let alone ...** y mucho menos ....

● **to let alone** dejar en paz, no tocar.
● **to let go of** soltar.
● **to let loose** soltar, desatar.
● **to let off steam** desfogarse.
● **to let SB in on STH** revelar algo a ALGN.
● **to let SB know** hacer saber a ALGN.

to let down vt **1** deshinchar, desinflar. **2** alargar (dobladillo). **3** defraudar.

to let in vt dejar entrar, dejar pasar.

to let off vt **1** hacer explotar (bomba). **2** hacer estallar (fuegos artificiales). **3** perdonar.

to let on vi fam descubrir el pastel: *you won't let on, will you?*, no dirás nada, ¿verdad?

to let out vt **1** dejar salir, soltar. **2** alquilar. **3** soltar (sonido).

to let through vt dejar pasar.

to let up vi cesar (calor, lluvia).

letdown ['letdaun] n decepción.

lethal ['li:θəl] adj letal, mortal.

lethargic [lɪ'θɑːdʒɪk] adj aletargado,-a.

lethargy ['leθədʒɪ] n letargo.

letter ['letə'] n **1** letra. **2** carta.
■ **letter box** buzón.

lettuce ['letɪs] n lechuga.

leukaemia [luːˈkiːmɪə] n leucemia.

level ['levəl] adj (comp **leveller**, superl **levellest**). **1** llano,-a, plano,-a (suelo). **2** a nivel, nivelado,-a (en altura). **3** empatado,-a.
▶ n nivel.
▶ vt (GB pt & pp **levelled**, ger **levelling**; US pt & pp **leveled**, ger **leveling**) nivelar.
● **on the level** fam de fiar, honrado,-a, legal.
■ **level crossing** paso a nivel.

lever ['liːvə'] n palanca.

levitate ['levɪteɪt] vi levitar.

levy ['levɪ] n (pl -**ies**) recaudación.
▶ vt (pt & pp -**ied**) recaudar.

lewd [luːd] adj **1** lascivo,-a (mirada). **2** obsceno,-a (canción).

lexicographer [leksɪˈkɒgrəfə'] n lexicógrafo,-a.

lexicography [leksɪˈkɒgrəfɪ] n lexicografía.

liability [laɪəˈbɪlɪtɪ] n (pl -**ies**) responsabilidad.
▶ npl **liabilities** COMM pasivo.

liable ['laɪəbəl] adj **1** responsable. **2** propenso,-a.

● **to be liable to do STH** tener tendencia a hacer algo.

liaison [lɪ'eɪzən] n **1** enlace. **2** amorío.

liar ['laɪə'] n mentiroso,-a.

libel ['laɪbəl] n libelo, difamación.
▶ vt (GB pt & pp **libelled**, ger **libelling**; US pt & pp **libeled**, ger **libeling**) difamar.

liberal ['lɪbərəl] adj **1** liberal. **2** abundante.
▶ n POL liberal.

liberalize ['lɪbərəlaɪz] vt liberalizar.

liberate ['lɪbəreɪt] vt liberar.

liberation [lɪbəˈreɪʃən] n liberación.

liberator ['lɪbəreɪtə'] n libertador,-ra.

liberty ['lɪbətɪ] n (pl -**ies**) libertad.

Libra ['liːbrə] n Libra.

librarian [laɪˈbreərɪən] n bibliotecario,-a.

library ['laɪbrərɪ] n (pl -**ies**) biblioteca.

Libya ['lɪbɪə] n Libia.

Libyan ['lɪbɪən] adj-n libio,-a.

lice [laɪs] npl → louse.

licence ['laɪsəns] n licencia, permiso.

license ['laɪsəns] vt autorizar.

licensee [laɪsənˈsiː] n **1** concesionario,-a. **2** dueño,-a (de bar).

licentious [laɪˈsenʃəs] adj licencioso,-a.

lichen ['laɪkən] n liquen.

lick [lɪk] n lamedura, lametón.
▶ vt lamer.

licking ['lɪkɪŋ] n fam paliza.

licorice ['lɪkərɪs] n regaliz.

lid [lɪd] n tapa, tapadera.

lie¹ [laɪ] n mentira: *to tell lies*, decir mentiras.
▶ vi mentir.

lie² [laɪ] vi (pt **lay** [leɪ], pp **lain** [leɪn], ger **lying**). **1** acostarse, tumbarse. **2** estar acostado,-a, estar tumbado,-a. **3** yacer (muerto). **4** estar situado,-a, encontrarse. **5** quedarse, permanecer.
● **to lie low** estar escondido,-a.

to lie back vi recostarse.

to lie down vi acostarse, tumbarse.

lie-down ['laɪdaun] n siesta.

lieu [luː] phr **in lieu of** en lugar de.

lieutenant [lefˈtenənt] n teniente.

life [laɪf] n (pl **lives**) vida.
● **for life** de por vida, para toda la vida.
● **to come to life** cobrar vida.
■ **life belt** salvavidas.
■ **life imprisonment** cadena perpetua.
■ **life jacket** chaleco salvavidas.
■ **life sentence** cadena perpetua.

life-boat ['laɪfbəʊt] *n* **1** bote salvavidas *(en barco)*. **2** lancha de salvamento.
lifeguard ['laɪfgɑːd] *n* socorrista.
lifelike ['laɪflaɪk] *adj* natural, realista.
lifelong [laɪflɒŋ] *adj* de toda la vida.
life-sized ['laɪfsaɪzd] *adj* de tamaño natural.
lifestyle ['laɪfstaɪl] *n* estilo de vida.
lifetime ['laɪftaɪm] *n* vida: *this will last you a lifetime*, esto te durará toda la vida.
lift [lɪft] *n* GB ascensor.
  ▶ *vt-vi* levantar.
  ▶ *vt fam* afanar, birlar.
  • **to give SB a lift** llevar a ALGN en coche.
lift-off ['lɪftɒf] *n (pl* **lift-offs**) despegue.
ligament ['lɪgəmənt] *n* ligamento.
light¹ [laɪt] *n* **1** luz. **2** luz, lámpara. **3** fuego *(para cigarrillo)*.
  ▶ *vt-vi (pt & pp* **lighted** *o* **lit** [lɪt]) encender(se) *(llama, fuego)*.
  ▶ *vt* iluminar, alumbrar.
  ▶ *adj* **1** claro,-a *(color)*. **2** con mucha claridad, luminoso,-a *(habitación)*.
  • **in the light of** en vista de.
  • **to come to light** salir a la luz.
  ■ **light bulb** bombilla.
  ■ **light switch** interruptor.
  ■ **light year** año luz.
light² [laɪt] *adj* **1** ligero,-a *(peso)*. **2** suave *(brisa)*.
  • **to travel light** viajar con poco equipaje.
lighten¹ ['laɪtən] *vt-vi* aclarar(se).
  ▶ *vt* iluminar *(habitación)*.
lighten² ['laɪtən] *vt* aligerar *(peso)*.
  ▶ *vi* alegrarse.
lighter ['laɪtə'] *n* encendedor, mechero.
light-fingered ['laɪtfɪŋgəd] *adj* de dedos largos, amigo,-a de lo ajeno.
light-headed [laɪt'hedɪd] *adj* mareado,-a.
lighthouse ['laɪthaʊs] *n* faro.
lighting ['laɪtɪŋ] *n* **1** iluminación. **2** alumbrado.
lightly ['laɪtlɪ] *adv* **1** ligeramente. **2** a la ligera.
lightning ['laɪtnɪŋ] *n* rayo, relámpago.
like¹ [laɪk] *adj* semejante, parecido,-a.
  ▶ *prep* como: *what did it look like?*, ¿cómo era?; *he sings like Pavarotti*, canza como Pavarotti; *his car is like new*, su coche está como nuevo.
  • **and the like** y cosas así.
  • **like father, like son** de tal palo tal astilla.
  • **like this** así.
like² [laɪk] *vt*: *I like wine*, me gusta el vino; *do you like him?*, ¿te gusta?; *would you like me to leave?*, ¿quieres que me vaya?
  ▶ *npl* **likes** gustos.
  • **as you like** como quieras.
likeable ['laɪkəbəl] *adj* simpático,-a, agradable.
likelihood ['laɪklɪhʊd] *n* probabilidad.
likely ['laɪklɪ] *adj* (**-ier, -iest**) probable.
  ▶ *adv* probablemente.
liken ['laɪkən] *vt* comparar.
likeness ['laɪknəs] *n (pl* **-es**) semejanza, parecido.
likewise ['laɪkwaɪz] *adv* **1** también. **2** lo mismo: *watch what I do and do likewise*, mira lo que hago y haz lo mismo.
liking ['laɪkɪŋ] *n* gusto, preferencia.
  • **to be to SB's liking** gustarle a ALGN, ser del gusto de ALGN.
Lilo ['laɪləʊ] *n* colchoneta.
lilt [lɪlt] *n* melodía.
lily ['lɪlɪ] *n (pl* **-ies**) lirio, azucena.
limb [lɪmb] *n* miembro.
limber up [lɪmbər'ʌp] *vi* calentar, hacer ejercicios de calentamiento.
lime¹ [laɪm] *n* cal.
lime² [laɪm] *n* lima *(fruto)*.
lime³ [laɪm] *n* tilo *(árbol)*.
limelight ['laɪmlaɪt] *n* foco.
  • **to be in the limelight** ser el centro de atención, estar en el candelero.
limestone ['laɪmstəʊn] *n* piedra caliza.
limit ['lɪmɪt] *n* límite.
  ▶ *vt* limitar.
limitation [lɪmɪ'teɪʃən] *n* limitación.
limited ['lɪmɪtɪd] *adj* limitado,-a.
  ■ **limited company** sociedad anónima.
limousine [lɪmə'ziːn] *n* limusina.
limp¹ [lɪmp] *n* cojera.
  ▶ *vi* cojear.
limp² [lɪmp] *adj* **1** flojo,-a, fláccido,-a. **2** débil.
limpet ['lɪmpɪt] *n* lapa.
limpid ['lɪmpɪd] *adj* límpido,-a.
linchpin ['lɪntʃpɪn] *n fig* eje.
linden ['lɪndən] *n* tilo.

line[1] [laɪn] n **1** línea. **2** raya *(en papel)*. **3** línea *(de texto)*. **4** cuerda, cordel. **5** sedal *(de pesca)*. **6** US cola. **7** fila, hilera *(de árboles)*. **8** tendedero. **9** línea *(de teléfono)*: *the line is busy*, está comunicando.
► *vt* alinear.

line[2] [laɪn] *vt* forrar, revestir, ead.

to line up *vt* **1** poner en fila. **2** *fam* preparar, organizar.
► *vi* ponerse en fila.

linear [ˈlɪnɪəʳ] *adj* lineal.

lined[1] [laɪnd] *adj* **1** rayado,-a *(papel)*. **2** arrugado,-a *(cara)*.

lined[2] [laɪnd] *adj* forrado,-a *(prenda)*.

linen [ˈlɪnɪn] n **1** lino. **2** ropa blanca.

liner [ˈlaɪnəʳ] n transatlántico.

linesman [ˈlaɪnzmən] n *(pl* **linesmen)** juez de línea.

linger [ˈlɪŋgəʳ] *vi* **1** quedarse. **2** persistir, perdurar.

lingerie [ˈlɑːnʒəriː] n lencería.

lingering [ˈlɪŋgərɪŋ] *adj* **1** lento,-a. **2** persistente.

linguist [ˈlɪŋgwɪst] n **1** lingüista. **2** políglota.

linguistic [lɪŋˈgwɪstɪk] *adj* lingüístico,-a.

linguistics [lɪŋˈgwɪstɪks] n lingüística.

Es incontable y el verbo va en singular.

lining [ˈlaɪnɪŋ] n forro.

link [lɪŋk] *vt* **1** unir, conectar. **2** *fig* vincular, relacionar.
► n **1** eslabón *(de cadena)*. **2** enlace, conexión. **3** *fig* vínculo, lazo, relación.
► *npl* **links** campo de golf.

linkage [ˈlɪŋkɪdʒ] n conexión.

linoleum [lɪˈnəʊlɪəm] n linóleo.

lintel [ˈlɪntəl] n dintel.

lion [ˈlaɪən] n león.

lioness [ˈlaɪənəs] n *(pl* **-es)** leona.

lip [lɪp] n labio.

lip-read [ˈlɪpriːd] *vt-vi* leer los labios *(a)*.

lipstick [ˈlɪpstɪk] n pintalabios, barra de labios, lápiz de labios.

liquefy [ˈlɪkwɪfaɪ] *vt-vi* (*pt & pp* **-ied)** licuar(se).

liqueur [lɪˈkjʊəʳ] n licor.

liquid [ˈlɪkwɪd] *adj* líquido,-a.
► n líquido.

liquidate [ˈlɪkwɪdeɪt] *vt* liquidar.

liquidize [ˈlɪkwɪdaɪz] *vt* licuar.

liquor [ˈlɪkəʳ] n alcohol, bebida alcohólica.

liquorice [ˈlɪkərɪs] n regaliz.

lisp [lɪsp] n ceceo.
► *vi* cecear.

list [lɪst] n lista.
► *vt* hacer una lista de.

listen [ˈlɪsən] *vi* **1** escuchar. **2** hacer caso.

listener [ˈlɪsənəʳ] n oyente, radioyente.
● **to be a good listener** saber escuchar.

listless [ˈlɪstləs] *adj* decaído,-a, apático.

lit [lɪt] *pt-pp* → light.

literacy [ˈlɪtərəsɪ] n alfabetización.

literal [ˈlɪtərəl] *adj* literal.

literally [ˈlɪtərəlɪ] *adv* literalmente.

literary [ˈlɪtərərɪ] *adj* literario,-a.

literate [ˈlɪtərət] *adj* alfabetizado,-a.

literature [ˈlɪtərɪtʃəʳ] n **1** literatura. **2** folletos, información.

lithe [laɪð] *adj* ágil.

lithography [lɪˈθɒgrəfɪ] n *(pl* **-ies)** litografía.

litigate [ˈlɪtɪgeɪt] *vi* litigar.

litigation [lɪtɪˈgeɪʃən] n litigio.

litre [ˈliːtəʳ] (US **liter**) n litro.

litter [ˈlɪtəʳ] n **1** basura, papeles. **2** camada.
► *vt* ensuciar, dejar en desorden: *littered with books*, lleno de libros, cubierto de libros.

little [ˈlɪtəl] (El comparativo y superlativo son **less** y **least**, excepto en la primera acepción) *adj* **1** pequeño,-a: *a little boy*, un niño pequeño. En esta acepción, se suele formar el comparativo y superlativo con **smaller** y **smallest**. **2** poco,-a: *we have very little money*, tenemos muy poco dinero.
► *pron* poco: *I only want a little*, sólo quiero un poco.
► *adv* poco: *I sleep very little*, duermo muy poco.
● **little by little** poco a poco.

liturgy [ˈlɪtədʒɪ] n *(pl* **-ies)** liturgia.

live[1] [lɪv] *vt-vi* vivir.
● **to live it up** pasárselo bomba.

live[2] [laɪv] *adj* **1** vivo,-a. **2** en directo *(programa, transmisión)*. **3** con corriente *(cable, circuito)*.

to live down *vt* lograr que se olvide.

to live on *vt* vivir de, alimentarse de.
► *vi* sobrevivir.

livelihood [ˈlaɪvlɪhʊd] n sustento.

liveliness [ˈlaɪvlɪnəs] n vivacidad, animación.

lively [ˈlaɪvlɪ] *adj* (**-ier, -iest**). **1** vivo,-a *(persona)*. **2** animado,-a *(fiesta)*.

liven up [laɪvənˈʌp] *vt-vi* animar(se).
liver [ˈlɪvəʳ] *n* hígado.
livestock [ˈlaɪvstɒk] *n* ganado.
livid [ˈlɪvɪd] *adj* **1** lívido. **2** *fam* furioso,-a.
living [ˈlɪvɪŋ] *adj* vivo,-a, viviente.
▶ *n* medio de vida: *what do you do for a living?*, ¿cómo te ganas la vida?
■ **living room** sala de estar.
lizard [ˈlɪzəd] *n* lagarto *(grande)*, lagartija *(pequeño)*.
llama [ˈlɑːmə] *n* llama *(animal)*.
load [ləʊd] *n* carga.
▶ *vt-vi* cargar.
● **loads of ...** montones de ....
loaded [ˈləʊdɪd] *adj* **1** cargado,-a *(arma)*. **2** tendencioso,-a *(pregunta)*. **3** *fam* forrado, -a *(persona)*.
loaf [ləʊf] *n* (*pl* **loaves**) pan, barra.
loafer [ˈləʊfəʳ] *n* vago,-a.
loan [ləʊn] *n* préstamo.
▶ *vt* prestar.
loath [ləʊθ] *adj* reacio,-a.
loathe [ləʊð] *vt* detestar, odiar.
loathing [ˈləʊðɪŋ] *n* odio.
loathsome [ˈləʊðsəm] *adj* odioso,-a.
lobby [ˈlɒbɪ] *n* (*pl* **-ies**). **1** vestíbulo. **2** POL grupo de presión.
▶ *vt* (*pt & pp* **lobbied**, *ger* **lobbying**) POL presionar, ejercer presión sobre.
lobe [ləʊb] *n* lóbulo.
lobster [ˈlɒbstəʳ] *n* bogavante.
■ **spiny lobster** langosta.
local [ˈləʊkəl] *adj* **1** local. **2** del barrio, del pueblo, de la ciudad *(persona)*. **3** municipal, regional *(gobierno)*.
▶ *n* **1** lugareño,-a. **2** GB *fam* bar del barrio.
locality [ləʊˈkælɪtɪ] *n* (*pl* **-ies**) localidad.
locate [ləʊˈkeɪt] *vt* **1** localizar. **2** situar, ubicar.
location [ləʊˈkeɪʃən] *n* **1** lugar. **2** ubicación. **3** localización.
loch [lɒk] *n* (*pl* **lochs**) lago.
lock[1] [lɒk] *n* **1** cerradura *(de puerta)*. **2** esclusa *(en canal)*.
▶ *vt* cerrar con llave.
lock[2] [lɒk] *n* mecha, mechón *(de pelo)*.
locker [ˈlɒkəʳ] *n* taquilla, armario.
locket [ˈlɒkɪt] *n* guardapelo, relicario.
lockout [ˈlɒkaʊt] *n* cierre patronal.
locksmith [ˈlɒksmɪθ] *n* cerrajero.
locomotive [ləʊkəˈməʊtɪv] *n* locomotora.
locum [ˈləʊkəm] *n* suplente.

locust [ˈləʊkəst] *n* langosta.
locution [ləˈkjuːʃən] *n* locución.
lodge [lɒdʒ] *n* **1** casita *(del guarda)*. **2** portería. **3** logia *(masónica)*.
▶ *vi* alojarse, hospedarse.
▶ *vt* presentar *(queja)*.
lodger [ˈlɒdʒəʳ] *n* huésped.
lodging [ˈlɒdʒɪŋ] *n* alojamiento.
loft [lɒft] *n* desván.
log [lɒg] *n* **1** tronco, leño *(para fuego)*. **2** cuaderno de bitácora. **3** diario de vuelo. **4** COMPUT registro.
▶ *vt* (*pt & pp* **logged**, *ger* **logging**) registrar, anotar.
to log in/log on *vi* COMPUT entrar *(en sistema)*.
to log off/log out *vi* COMPUT salir *(del sistema)*.
logarithm [ˈlɒgərɪðəm] *n* logaritmo.
loggerheads [ˈlɒgəhedz] *npl* .
● **to be at loggerheads** tener malas relaciones.
logic [ˈlɒdʒɪk] *n* lógica.
logical [ˈlɒdʒɪkəl] *adj* lógico,-a.
logistic [ləˈdʒɪstɪk] *adj* logístico,-a.
loin [lɔɪn] *n* **1** lomo *(de cerdo)*. **2** solomillo *(de ternera)*.
loincloth [ˈlɔɪnklɒθ] *n* taparrabos.
loiter [ˈlɔɪtəʳ] *vi* **1** holgazanear. **2** merodear.
loll [lɒl] *vi* repantigarse.
lollipop [ˈlɒlɪpɒp] *n* **1** piruleta, pirulí. **2** polo.
lolly [ˈlɒlɪ] *n* (*pl* **-ies**). **1** *fam* piruleta, pirulí. **2** *fam* polo. **3** *fam* pasta *(dinero)*.
London [ˈlʌndən] *n* Londres.
Londoner [ˈlʌndənəʳ] *n* londinense.
lone [ləʊn] *adj* **1** solo,-a. **2** solitario,-a.
loneliness [ˈləʊnlɪnəs] *n* soledad.
lonely [ˈləʊnlɪ] *adj* (**-ier**, **-iest**). **1** solo,-a, solitario,-a. **2** aislado,-a *(lugar)*.
long[1] [lɒŋ] *adj* largo,-a: *a long journey*, un viaje largo; *how long is the film?*, ¿cuánto dura la película?; *the garden is 30 metres long*, el jardín mide 30 metros de largo.
▶ *adv* **1** mucho, mucho tiempo: *I won't be long*, no tardaré mucho; *how long have you had this problem?*, ¿desde cuándo tienes este problema? **2 no longer, not any longer**: *he couldn't wait any longer and he left*, ya no podía esperar más y se marchó; *she doesn't*

work here any longer, ya no trabaja aquí.
- **a long time** mucho tiempo.
- **a long way** lejos.
- **as long as** mientras, con tal de que.
- **how long...?** ¿cuánto tiempo?
- **in the long run** a la larga.
- **long ago** hace mucho tiempo.
- **so long** hasta la vista.
- **long jump** salto de longitud.

long² [lɒŋ] *vi* **1 to long for** anhelar. **2 to long to** tener muchas ganas de.
longbow ['lɒŋbəʊ] *n* arco.
long-distance [lɒŋ'dɪstəns] *adj* **1** de larga distancia *(llamada)*. **2** de fondo *(corredor)*.
longhand ['lɒŋhænd] *n* escritura a mano.
longing ['lɒŋɪŋ] *n* **1** ansia, anhelo. **2** nostalgia.
longitude ['lɒndʒɪtjuːd] *n* longitud.
long-playing [lɒŋ'pleɪɪŋ] *adj* de larga duración.
long-range [lɒŋ'reɪndʒ] *adj* **1** de largo alcance *(distancia)*. **2** a largo plazo *(tiempo)*.
long-sighted [lɒŋ'saɪtɪd] *adj* hipermétrope.
long-standing [lɒŋ'stændɪŋ] *adj* antiguo,-a.
long-suffering [lɒŋ'sʌfərɪŋ] *adj* sufrido,-a.
long-term [lɒŋ'tɜːm] *adj* a largo plazo.
longways ['lɒŋweɪz] *adv* a lo largo.
loo [luː] *n (pl* **loos)** *fam* wáter, servicio.
look [lʊk] *vi* **1** mirar. **2** parecer: *it looks easy*, parece fácil; *that steak looks good*, ese filete tiene buen aspecto.
▶ *n* **1** mirada, vistazo. **2** aspecto, apariencia. **3** expresión *(de cara)*.
- **to have a look at** STH, **take a look at** STH echar un vistazo a algo.
- **good looks** belleza.
to look after *vt* **1** ocuparse de. **2** cuidar.
to look ahead *vi* mirar al futuro.
to look at *vt* **1** mirar. **2** examinar.
to look down on *vt* despreciar.
to look for *vt* buscar.
to look forward to *vt* esperar *(con ansia)*.
to look into *vt* investigar.
to look like *vt* **1** parecer, ser: *what does Sarah look like?*, ¿cómo es Sarah? **2** parecerse a: *he looks like his father*, se parece a su padre.
to look on *vi* mirar, observar.

to look onto *vt* dar a.
to look out *vi* vigilar, ir con cuidado.
- **look out!** ¡ten cuidado!
to look round *vi* **1** volver la cabeza. **2** mirar *(en tienda)*.
▶ *vt* visitar *(ciudad)*.
to look through *vt* examinar, revisar, hojear *(libro)*.
to look up *vi* **1** mejorar. **2** alzar la vista.
▶ *vt* **1** buscar. **2** ir a visitar.
lookalike ['lʊkəlaɪk] *n* doble, sosia.
lookout ['lʊkaʊt] *n* **1** vigía *(persona)*. **2** atalaya *(lugar)*.
- **to be on the lookout for** estar al acecho de.
loom¹ [luːm] *n* telar.
loom² [luːm] *vi* vislumbrarse.
loony ['luːnɪ] *adj* (**-ier, -iest)** *fam* chalado,-a.
loop [luːp] *n* **1** lazo. **2** curva. **3** COMPUT bucle.
loophole ['luːphəʊl] *n fig* escapatoria.
loose [luːs] *adj* **1** suelto,-a: *there's a tiger loose!*, ¡hay un tigre suelto! **2** flojo,-a *(nudo)*. **3** holgado,-a *(ropa)*. **4** desatado,-a.
▶ *vt* soltar.
- **on the loose** suelto,-a.
loosen ['luːsən] *vt-vi* soltar(se), aflojar(se).
loot [luːt] *n* **1** botín. **2** *fam* pasta.
▶ *vt-vi* saquear.
lop [lɒp] *vt (pt & pp* **lopped,** *ger* **lopping)** podar.
lope [ləʊp] *vi* andar con paso largo.
lopsided [lɒp'saɪdɪd] *adj* torcido,-a, ladeado.
loquacious [lə'kweɪʃəs] *adj* locuaz.
lord [lɔːd] *n* **1** señor. **2** lord.
- **the Lord** el Señor.
- **the Lord's Prayer** el padrenuestro.
lordship ['lɔːdʃɪp] *n* señoría.
lore [lɔːˈ] *n* saber popular.
lorry ['lɒrɪ] *n (pl* **-ies)** camión.
lose [luːz] *vt-vi (pt & pp* **lost). 1** perder. **2** atrasarse *(reloj)*.
- **to lose one's way** perderse.
loser ['luːzəˈ] *n* perdedor,-a.
- **to be a bad loser** no saber perder.
- **to be a good loser** saber perder.
loss [lɒs] *n (pl* **-es)** pérdida.
lost [lɒst] *pt-pp* → lose.
▶ *adj* perdido,-a.
- **to get lost** perderse.
- **lost property** objetos perdidos.

lot [lɒt] *n* **1** suerte. **2** US solar, terreno. **3** lote *(en subasta)*. **4** cantidad: *a lot*, mucho, muchísimo; *a lot of ...*, muchísimo,-a, muchísimos,-as; *lots of ...*, cantidad de ....

● **to cast lots** echar suertes.

lotion [ˈləʊʃən] *n* loción.

lottery [ˈlɒtərɪ] *n* (*pl* -**ies**) lotería.

loud [laʊd] *adj* **1** fuerte *(sonido)*. **2** alto,-a *(voz)*. **3** chillón,-ona *(color)*. **4** vulgar, ordinario,-a *(conducta)*.

▶ *adv* fuerte, alto.

loudmouth [ˈlaʊdmaʊθ] *n pej* bocazas *mf inv*.

loudspeaker [laʊdˈspiːkəˈ] *n* altavoz.

lounge [laʊndʒ] *n* salón, sala de estar.

▶ *vi* no hacer nada, holgazanear.

louse [laʊs] *n* (*pl* **lice**). **1** piojo. **2** *fam* canalla.

lousy [ˈlaʊzɪ] *adj* (-**ier**, -**iest**) *fam* fatal, malísimo,-a, asqueroso,-a.

lout [laʊt] *n* gamberro,-a.

lovable [ˈlʌvəbəl] *adj* adorable.

love [lʌv] *n* **1** amor. **2** cero *(en tenis)*.

▶ *vt* **1** amar, querer. **2**: *I love fish*, me encanta el pescado, me gusta muchísimo el pescado; *she loves reading*, le encanta leer.

● **not for love or money** por nada del mundo.

● **to be in love with** estar enamorado, -a de.

● **to make love** hacer el amor.

■ **love affair** aventura amorosa.

■ **love at first sight** amor a primera vista.

lovely [ˈlʌvlɪ] *adj* (-**ier**, -**iest**) maravilloso,-a, hermoso,-a, precioso,-a, encantador,-ra.

lover [ˈlʌvəˈ] *n* amante.

loving [ˈlʌvɪŋ] *adj* afectuoso,-a, cariñoso, -a.

low [ləʊ] *adj* **1** bajo,-a *(pared, temperatura)*. **2** abatido,-a, deprimido,-a. **3** grave *(sonido)*.

▶ *adv* bajo.

■ **low tide** bajamar.

lowdown [ˈləʊdaʊn] *n fam*: **to give SB the lowdown on STH**, explicar algo a alguien con todo lujo de detalles.

lower [ˈləʊəˈ] *adj* inferior.

▶ *vt* **1** bajar *(voz, precios)*. **2** arriar *(bandera)*.

■ **lower case** caja baja, minúscula.

lower-class [ləʊəˈklɑːs] *adj* de clase baja.

low-fat [ˈləʊˈfæt] *adj* bajo,-a en grasas.

lowly [ˈləʊlɪ] *adj* (-**ier**, -**iest**) humilde, modesto,-a.

low-necked [ləʊˈnekt] *adj* escotado,-a.

loyal [ˈlɔɪəl] *adj* leal, fiel.

loyalty [ˈlɔɪəltɪ] *n* (*pl* -**ies**) lealtad, fidelidad.

lozenge [ˈlɒzɪndʒ] *n* **1** pastilla. **2** rombo.

LP [elˈpiː] *abbr (**long-player**)* disco de larga duración, elepé, LP.

LSD [eles'diː] *abbr (**lysergic acid diethylamide**)* dietilamida del ácido lisérgico, LSD.

Ltd [ˈlɪmɪtd] *abbr* GB (**Limited**) Limitada, Ltda.

lubricant [ˈluːbrɪkənt] *n* lubricante.

lubricate [ˈluːbrɪkeɪt] *vt* lubricar.

lubrication [luːbrɪˈkeɪʃən] *n* lubricación.

lucid [ˈluːsɪd] *adj* lúcido,-a.

luck [lʌk] *n* suerte: *good luck!*, ¡suerte!

luckily [ˈlʌkɪlɪ] *adv* afortunadamente.

luckless [ˈlʌkləs] *adj* desafortunado,-a.

lucky [ˈlʌkɪ] *adj* (-**ier**, -**iest**) afortunado,-a, con suerte.

● **to be lucky** tener suerte.

■ **lucky charm** amuleto.

lucrative [ˈluːkrətɪv] *adj* lucrativo,-a.

ludicrous [ˈluːdɪkrəs] *adj* ridículo,-a.

lug[1] [lʌg] *vt* (*pt & pp* **lugged**, *ger* **lugging**) *fam* cargar con.

lug[2] [lʌg] *n* GB *fam* oreja.

luggage [ˈlʌgɪdʒ] *n* equipaje.

■ **luggage rack** portaequipajes.

lugubrious [ləˈgjuːbrɪəs] *adj* lúgubre.

lukewarm [ˈluːkwɔːm] *adj* templado,-a, tibio,-a.

lull [lʌl] *n* momento de calma.

▶ *vt* adormecer, arrullar.

lullaby [ˈlʌləbaɪ] *n* (*pl* -**ies**) canción de cuna, nana.

lumbago [lʌmˈbeɪgəʊ] *n* lumbago.

lumber [ˈlʌmbəˈ] *n* **1** madera. **2** trastos viejos.

▶ *vi* moverse pesadamente.

▶ *vt* cargar.

lumberjack [ˈlʌmbədʒæk] *n* leñador.

luminous [ˈluːmɪnəs] *adj* luminoso,-a.

lump [lʌmp] *n* **1** pedazo, trozo. **2** terrón *(de azúcar)*. **3** bulto *(en cuerpo)*. **4** grumo *(en salsa)*.

- **to lump it** *fam* apechugar.
- **lump sum** suma global.

to lump together *vt* juntar.

lumpy ['lʌmpɪ] *adj* (-**ier**, -**iest**). **1** lleno,-a de bultos. **2** grumoso,-a.

lunacy ['luːnəsɪ] *n* locura.

lunar ['luːnə'] *adj* lunar.

lunatic ['luːnətɪk] *adj-n* loco,-a.

lunch [lʌntʃ] *n* (*pl* -**es**) comida, almuerzo.
  ▶ *vi* comer, almorzar.

- **to have lunch** comer, almozar.
- **lunch break** hora de comer.

luncheon ['lʌntʃən] *n fml* almuerzo.

lunchtime ['lʌntʃtaɪm] *n* hora de comer.

lung [lʌŋ] *n* pulmón.

lunge [lʌndʒ] *vi* arremeter, embestir.

lurch [lɜːtʃ] *n* (*pl* -**es**) sacudida, tumbo, bandazo.
  ▶ *vi* **1** dar sacudidas, dar bandazos. **2** tambalearse.

- **to leave in the lurch** dejar en la estacada.

lure [ljʊə'] *n* **1** señuelo. **2** *fig* atractivo.
  ▶ *vt* atraer.

lurid ['ljuərɪd] *adj* **1** chillón,-ona *(color)*. **2** horripilante, espeluznante *(detalles)*.

lurk [lɜːk] *vi* estar al acecho.

luscious ['lʌʃəs] *adj* delicioso,-a, exquisito,-a.

lush [lʌʃ] *adj* exuberante.

lust [lʌst] *n* **1** codicia. **2** lujuria.

to lust after *vt* **1** codiciar. **2** desear *(sexualmente)*.

lustful ['lʌstfʊl] *adj* lujurioso,-a.

lustre ['lʌstə'] (US **luster**) *n* lustre, brillo.

lusty ['lʌstɪ] *adj* (-**ier**, -**iest**) fuerte, robusto,-a.

lute [luːt] *n* laúd.

Luxembourg ['lʌksəmbɜːg] *n* Luxemburgo.

luxurious [lʌgˈzjuərɪəs] *adj* lujoso,-a.

luxury ['lʌkʃərɪ] *n* (*pl* -**ies**) lujo.

- **luxury goods** artículos de lujo.

LW ['lɒŋweɪv] *abbr (long wave)* onda larga, OL.

lying ['laɪɪŋ] *adj* mentiroso,-a.
  ▶ *n* mentiras.

lymphatic [lɪmˈfætɪk] *adj* linfático,-a.

lynch [lɪntʃ] *vt* linchar.

lynching ['lɪntʃɪŋ] *n* linchamiento.

lynx [lɪŋks] *n* (*pl* **lynxes**) lince.

lyre ['laɪə'] *n* lira *(instrumento)*.

lyric ['lɪrɪk] *adj* lírico,-a.
  ▶ *npl* **lyrics** letra *(de canción)*.

lyrical ['lɪrɪkəl] *adj* lírico,-a.

lyricist ['lɪrɪsɪst] *n* letrista.

M

M¹ ['mɪlɪən] *abbr (million)* millón: *£24M*, veinticuatro millones de libras.

M² ['miːdɪəm] *abbr (medium size)* talla mediana, M.

M³ [em] *abbr* GB *(motorway)* autopista: *there are roadworks on the M18*, hay obras en la autopista M18.

MA ['em'eɪ] *abbr (Master of Arts)* máster de humanidades.

ma'am [mæm, mɑːm] *n fml* señora.

mac [mæk] *n* impermeable.

macabre [mə'kɑːbrə] *adj* macabro,-a.

macaroni [mækə'rəʊnɪ] *n* macarrones.
> Es incontable y el verbo va en singular.

machine [mə'ʃiːn] *n* máquina, aparato.
- **machine gun** ametralladora.

machinery [mə'ʃiːnərɪ] *n* maquinaria.

mackerel ['mækrəl] *n* caballa.

mackintosh ['mækɪntɒʃ] *n (pl* **-es**) impermeable.

mad [mæd] *adj (comp* **madder***, superl* **maddest**). **1** loco,-a. **2** disparatado,-a, insensato,-a *(idea, plan).* **3** furioso,-a, muy enfadado,-a *(persona).* **4** rabioso,-a *(perro).*
- **like mad** a toda pastilla: *he was running like mad*, corría a toda pastilla.
- **to be mad** estar enfadado,-a.
- **to be mad about** estar loco,-a por.
- **to drive SB mad** volver loco,-a a ALGN.
- **to go mad** volverse loco,-a.
- **mad cow disease** enfermedad de las vacas locas.

madam ['mædəm] *n fml* señora.

madden ['mædən] *vt* enfurecer.

made [meɪd] *pt-pp* → make.

made-up ['meɪdʌp] *adj* **1** maquillado,-a *(cara).* **2** pintado,-a *(ojos).* **3** inventado,-a.

madhouse ['mædhaʊs] *n fam* casa de locos, manicomio.

madly ['mædlɪ] *adv* **1** locamente. **2** precipitadamente. **3** *fam* terriblemente: *to be madly in love*, estar locamente enamorado,-a.

madman ['mædmən] *n (pl* **madmen**) loco.

madness ['mædnəs] *n* locura.

magazine [mægə'ziːn] *n* revista.

maggot ['mægət] *n* larva, gusano.

magic ['mædʒɪk] *n* magia.
▶ *adj* mágico,-a.
- **as if by magic** como por arte de magia.
- **magic wand** varita mágica.

magical ['mædʒɪkəl] *adj* mágico,-a.

magician [mə'dʒɪʃən] *n* prestidigitador, -ra, mago,-a.

magistrate ['mædʒɪstreɪt] *n* juez.

magnet ['mægnət] *n* imán.

magnetic [mæg'netɪk] *adj* magnético,-a.
- **magnetic field** campo magnético.
- **magnetic tape** cinta magnética.

magnificent [mæg'nɪfɪsənt] *adj* magnífico,-a, espléndido,-a.

magnify ['mægnɪfaɪ] *vt (pt & pp* **-ied**). **1** aumentar, ampliar. **2** exagerar.

magnifying glass ['mægnɪfaɪɪŋglɑːs] *n (pl* **-es**) lupa.

magnitude ['mægnɪtjuːd] *n* magnitud.

mahogany [mə'hɒgənɪ] *n* caoba.

maid [meɪd] *n* **1** criada, sirvienta. **2** camarera *(en hotel).*
- **maid of honour** dama de honor.

maiden ['meɪdən] *n* doncella.
▶ *adj* **1** soltera. **2** inaugural.
- **maiden name** apellido de soltera.

mail [meɪl] *n* correo.
▶ *vt* **1** US echar al buzón. **2** enviar por correo.
■ **mail order** venta por correo.
■ **mail train** tren correo.
mailbox ['meɪlbɒks] *n* (*pl* **mailboxes**) US buzón.
mailman ['meɪlmæn] *n* (*pl* **mailmen**) US cartero.
maim [meɪm] *vt* mutilar, lisiar.
main [meɪn] *adj* **1** principal. **2** esencial.
▶ *n* **1** tubería principal, cañería principal, conducto principal. **2** red eléctrica.
■ **main beam** viga maestra.
■ **main office** oficina central.
■ **main street** calle mayor.
mainland ['meɪnlənd] *n* continente.
mainly ['meɪnlɪ] *adv* principalmente.
maintain [meɪn'teɪn] *vt* mantener.
maintenance ['meɪntənəns] *n* **1** mantenimiento. **2** pensión alimenticia.
maisonette [meɪzə'net] *n* dúplex.
maize [meɪz] *n* maíz.
majesty ['mædʒəstɪ] *n* (*pl* **-ies**) majestad.
major ['meɪdʒəʳ] *adj* **1** mayor, principal. **2** importante, considerable. **3** MUS mayor.
▶ *n* comandante.
Majorca [mə'dʒɔːkə] *n* Mallorca.
majority [mə'dʒɒrɪtɪ] *n* (*pl* **-ies**) mayoría.
■ **majority rule** gobierno mayoritario.
make [meɪk] *vt* (*pt & pp* **made** [meɪd]). **1** hacer: *she made me a cake*, me hizo un pastel; *he made a phone call*, hizo una llamada. **2** hacer: *the film made me cry*, la película me hizo llorar; *the traffic made me late*, el tráfico hizo que llegara tarde, llegué tarde por el tráfico. **3** obligar: *they made him move his car*, le obligaron a retirar su coche. **4** ganar: *how much do you make a year?*, ¿cuánto ganas al año? **5** conseguir: *I made it!*, ¡lo conseguí! **6** ser: *three plus nine makes twelve*, tres más nueve son doce.
▶ *n* marca.
● **to be made of** ser de, estar hecho,-a de.
● **to make a decision** tomar una decisión.
● **to make a living** ganarse la vida.
● **to make a mistake** equivocarse.
● **to make a speech** pronunciar un discurso.

● **to make a start** empezar.
● **to make believe** fingir.
● **to make do** arreglárselas.
● **to make friends with** SB hacerse amigo de ALGN.
● **to make fun of** burlarse de.
● **to make it** conseguir llegar a tiempo; alcanzar el éxito.
● **to make it up with** SB hacer las paces.
● **to make love to** SB hacer el amor con ALGN.
● **to make sense** tener sentido.
● **to make** SB **angry** enfadar a ALGN.
● **to make** STH **clear** aclarar algo.
● **to make** STH **known** dar a conocer algo.
● **to make sure** asegurarse.
● **to make the best/most of** STH sacar el máximo provecho de algo.
● **to make up one's mind** decidirse.
to make for *vt* **1** dirigirse hacia. **2** contribuir a.
to make out *vt* **1** hacer (*lista*). **2** extender (*talón*). **3** distinguir, descifrar (*escritura*). **4** entender (*persona*). **5** pretender: *she makes out she's tough*, se las da de dura.
▶ *vi* arreglárselas.
to make up *vt* **1** inventar. **2** hacer, preparar (*cama, paquete*). **3** completar (*cantidad*). **4** componer, formar. **5** maquillar.
▶ *vi* **1** maquillarse. **2** hacer las paces, reconciliarse.
to make up for *vt* compensar.
make-believe ['meɪkbɪliːv] *n* fantasía, invención.
maker ['meɪkəʳ] *n* fabricante.
makeshift ['meɪkʃɪft] *adj* provisional.
make-up ['meɪkʌp] *n* **1** maquillaje. **2** composición. **3** carácter (*de persona*). **4** compaginación (*de libro*). **5** confección (*de ropa*).
■ **make-up remover** desmaquillador.
making ['meɪkɪŋ] *n* **1** fabricación. **2** creación.
● **to have the makings of** STH tener madera de algo.
malaria [mə'leərɪə] *n* malaria, paludismo.
Malay [mə'leɪ] *adj* malayo,-a.
▶ *n* **1** malayo,-a (*persona*). **2** malayo (*lengua*).
Malaysia [mə'leɪzɪə] *n* Malaisia.
Malaysian [mə'leɪzɪən] *adj-n* malasio,-a.

male [meɪl] *adj-n* macho.
► *adj* **1** varón: *a male child*, un hijo varón. **2** masculino,-a.
► *n* varón.
■ **male chauvinism** machismo.
■ **male chauvinist** machista.
malfunction [mæl'fʌŋkʃən] *n* funcionamiento defectuoso.
► *vi* funcionar mal.
malice ['mælɪs] *n* malicia, maldad.
● **to bear** SB **malice** guardar rencor a ALGN.
malicious [mə'lɪʃəs] *adj* malévolo,-a, malicioso,-a.
malignant [mə'lɪgnənt] *adj* **1** malvado,-a *(persona)*. **2** maligno,-a *(tumor)*.
malnutrition [mælnjuː'trɪʃən] *n* desnutrición.
malpractice [mæl'præktɪs] *n* negligencia, mala práctica.
malt [mɔːlt] *n* malta.
mammal ['mæməl] *n* mamífero.
mammoth ['mæməθ] *n* mamut.
► *adj* gigantesco,-a, descomunal.
man [mæn] *n (pl* **men** [men]). **1** hombre. **2 Man** el hombre.
► *vt (pt & pp* **manned**, *ger* **manning**). **1** tripular *(nave)*. **2** servir.
● **man and wife** marido y mujer.
● **the man in the street** el ciudadano de a pie.
Man [mæn] *n* **Isle of Man** Isla de Man.
manage ['mænɪdʒ] *vt* **1** dirigir, llevar *(negocio)*. **2** administrar *(propiedad)*. **3** llevar *(casa)*. **4** manejar *(niño)*.
► *vi* **1** poder: *can you manage with that box?*, ¿puedes con esa caja? **2** arreglárselas, apañarse: *I can manage by myself*, puedo arreglármelas solo. **3** conseguir: *I don't know how he managed to persuade her*, no sé cómo consiguió convencerla.
manageable ['mænɪdʒəbəl] *adj* manejable.
management ['mænɪdʒmənt] *n* **1** dirección, administración, gestión. **2** junta directiva, consejo de administración.
manager ['mænɪdʒəʳ] *n* **1** director,-ra, gerente *(de empresa)*. **2** administrador,-ra *(de propiedad)*. **3** encargado,-a *(de restaurante)*. **4** empresario,-a *(de teatro)*. **5** representante, mánager *(de actor)*. **6** entrenador, mánager *(de deportista)*.
manageress [mænɪdʒə'res] *n (pl* **-es**). **1**

directora, gerente *(de empresa)*. **2** encargada, jefa *(de tienda, etc)*.
mandate ['mændeɪt] *n* mandato.
mane [meɪn] *n* **1** crin *(de caballo)*. **2** melena *(de león)*.
mangle[1] ['mæŋgəl] *n* escurridor, rodillo.
► *vt* escurrir.
mangle[2] ['mæŋgəl] *vt* **1** destrozar. **2** aplastar.
mango ['mæŋgəʊ] *n (pl* **-s** o **-es**) mango.
manhood ['mænhʊd] *n* madurez.
● **to reach manhood** llegar a la edad viril.
mania ['meɪnɪə] *n* manía.
maniac ['meɪnɪæk] *n* **1** maníaco,-a. **2** *fam* fanático,-a. **3** *fam* loco,-a.
manicure ['mænɪkjʊəʳ] *n* manicura.
► *vt* hacer la manicura a.
manifesto [mænɪ'festəʊ] *n (pl* **-s** o **-es**) manifiesto.
manipulate [mə'nɪpjʊleɪt] *vt* manipular.
mankind [mæn'kaɪnd] *n* la humanidad, el género humano.
manly ['mænlɪ] *adj* (**-ier**, **-iest**) varonil, viril, macho.
man-made [mæn'meɪd] *adj* **1** artificial. **2** sintético,-a.
manner ['mænəʳ] *n* **1** manera, modo. **2** forma de ser, comportamiento.
► *npl* **manners** maneras, modales.
● **in a manner of speaking** por decirlo así.
● **in this manner** de esta manera, así.
● **to be bad manners** ser de mala educación.
● **to be good manners** ser de buena educación.
mannerism ['mænərɪzəm] *n* peculiaridad.
manoeuvre [mə'nuːvəʳ] (US **maneuver**) *n* maniobra.
► *vt-vi* maniobrar.
manor ['mænəʳ] *n* señorío.
■ **manor house** casa solariega.
manpower ['mænpaʊəʳ] *n* mano de obra.
mansion ['mænʃən] *n* mansión, casa solariega.
manslaughter ['mænslɔːtəʳ] *n* homicidio involuntario.
mantelpiece ['mæntəlpiːs] *n* repisa de chimenea.

manual [ˈmænjʊəl] adj-n manual.

manually [ˈmænjʊəlɪ] adv a mano.

manufacture [mænjʊˈfæktʃəʳ] n 1 fabricación. 2 confección (de ropa). 3 elaboración (de comida).
▶ vt 1 fabricar. 2 confeccionar (ropa). 3 elaborar (comida).

manufacturer [mænjʊˈfæktʃərəʳ] n fabricante.

manure [məˈnjʊəʳ] n abono, estiércol.

manuscript [ˈmænjʊskrɪpt] n manuscrito.

many [ˈmenɪ] adj-pron (comp more, superl most) muchos,-as: *many children can can play an instrument*, muchos niños tocan un instrumento; *many people never go on holiday*, mucha gente nunca tiene vacaciones.
● as many ... as tantos,-as ... como.
● how many? ¿cuántos,-as?
● not many pocos,-as.
● too many demasiados,-as.

map [mæp] n 1 mapa (de país, región). 2 plano (de ciudad).
▶ vt (pt & pp mapped, ger mapping) trazar un mapa, trazar un plano.
■ map of the world mapamundi.

to map out vt proyectar, planear.

maple [ˈmeɪpəl] n arce.

Mar [mɑːtʃ] abbr (March) marzo.

marathon [ˈmærəθən] n maratón.
▶ adj maratoniano,-a.

marble [ˈmɑːbəl] n 1 mármol. 2 canica.
▶ adj de mármol.

march [mɑːtʃ] n (pl -es). 1 marcha, caminata. 2 manifestación.
▶ vi 1 marchar, hacer una marcha, caminar. 2 hacer una manifestación, manifestarse.
● to march SB off llevarse a ALGN (a la fuerza).

to march past vi desfilar.

March [mɑːtʃ] n marzo.

mare [meəʳ] n yegua.

margarine [mɑːdʒəˈriːn] n margarina.

margin [ˈmɑːdʒɪn] n margen.

marginal [ˈmɑːdʒɪnəl] adj marginal.

marigold [ˈmærɪɡəʊld] n maravilla, caléndula.

marine [məˈriːn] adj marino,-a, marítimo,-a.
▶ n soldado de infantería de marina.

marionette [mærɪəˈnet] n marioneta, títere.

marital [ˈmærɪtəl] adj matrimonial.
■ marital status estado civil.

maritime [ˈmærɪtaɪm] adj marítimo,-a.

mark¹ [mɑːk] n marco (moneda).

mark² [mɑːk] n 1 huella, señal. 2 mancha. 3 señal, marca. 4 nota, calificación.
▶ vt 1 marcar. 2 manchar. 3 señalar. 4 corregir, puntuar, calificar.
● mark my words! ¡verás como tengo razón!
● on your marks! ¡preparados!
● to get good marks sacar buenas notas.
● to hit the mark dar en el blanco.
● to make one's mark distinguirse.
● to mark time hacer tiempo.

to mark down vt 1 rebajar (precio). 2 bajar la nota a. 3 anotar, apuntar.

to mark out vt delimitar (zona).

marked [mɑːkt] adj marcado,-a, apreciable.

marker [ˈmɑːkəʳ] n 1 jalón. 2 rotulador.

market [ˈmɑːkɪt] n mercado.
▶ vt vender, poner en venta.
● to be on the market estar a la venta, estar en venta.

marketing [ˈmɑːkɪtɪŋ] n márketing, mercadotecnia.

marksman [ˈmɑːksmən] n (pl marksmen) tirador.

marmalade [ˈmɑːməleɪd] n mermelada (de cítricos).

maroon¹ [məˈruːn] vt aislar, abandonar.

maroon² [məˈruːn] adj granate.
▶ n granate.

marquee [mɑːˈkiː] n carpa, entoldado.

marriage [ˈmærɪdʒ] n 1 matrimonio. 2 boda.

married [ˈmærɪd] adj casado,-a.
● to get married casarse.
■ married couple matrimonio.
■ married name apellido de casada.

marrow [ˈmærəʊ] n 1 tuétano, médula. 2 calabacín.

marry [ˈmærɪ] vt (pt & pp -ied). 1 casarse con. 2 casar.
● to marry into money emparentar con una familia adinerada.

marsh [mɑːʃ] n (pl -es). 1 pantano, ciénaga. 2 marisma.

marshal [ˈmɑːʃəl] n 1 mariscal. 2 oficial de justicia. 3 US jefe,-a de policía.

martial [ˈmɑːʃəl] adj marcial.
■ martial law ley marcial.

martyr ['mɑːtə'] n mártir.
marvel ['mɑːvəl] n maravilla.
▶ vi (GB pt & pp **marvelled**, ger **marvelling**; US pt & pp **marveled**, ger **marveling**) maravillarse.
marvellous ['mɑːvələs] adj maravilloso, -a, estupendo,-a.
Marxism ['mɑːksɪzəm] n marxismo.
marzipan ['mɑːzɪpæn] n mazapán.
mascara [mæ'skɑːrə] n rímel.
mascot ['mæskɒt] n mascota.
masculine ['mɑːskjʊlɪn] adj masculino,-a.
▶ n masculino.
mash [mæʃ] vt triturar.
▶ n fam puré de patatas.
mask [mɑːsk] n 1 máscara. 2 mascarilla.
▶ vt enmascarar.
■ **masked ball** baile de disfraces.
masochism ['mæsəkɪzəm] n masoquismo.
mason ['meɪsən] n albañil.
mass¹ [mæs] n (pl -es). 1 masa. 2 montón, gran cantidad.
▶ vi congregarse, reunirse.
● **the masses** las masas.
● **to mass produce** fabricar en serie.
■ **mass media** medios de comunicación de masas.
■ **mass production** fabricación en serie.
mass² [mæs] n (pl -es) misa.
massacre ['mæsəkə'] n masacre, carnicería, matanza.
▶ vt masacrar.
massage ['mæsɑːʒ] n masaje.
▶ vt dar masajes a.
massive ['mæsɪv] adj 1 macizo,-a, sólido,-a. 2 enorme, descomunal.
mast [mɑːst] n mástil.
master ['mɑːstə'] n 1 señor, amo (de casa, criados). 2 dueño (de animal). 3 maestro, profesor de instituto. 4 maestro, experto.
▶ vt 1 dominar, controlar (situación). 2 llegar a dominar (técnica).
■ **master bedroom** dormitorio principal.
■ **master builder** maestro de obras, contratista.
■ **master key** llave maestra.
■ **master of ceremonies** maestro de ceremonias.

masterpiece ['mɑːstəpiːs] n obra maestra.
masturbate ['mæstəbeɪt] vt-vi masturbar(se).
mat [mæt] n 1 alfombrilla, estera, felpudo. 2 salvamanteles.
match¹ [mætʃ] n (pl -es) cerilla, fósforo.
match² [mætʃ] n (pl -es) partido, encuentro.
▶ vt 1 igualar: *nobody can match him*, nadie lo iguala. 2 hacer juego con, combinar con.
▶ vi hacer juego, combinar (ropa, colores).
● **to be a good match 1** hacer juego, ir bien juntos (cosas). 2 hacer buena pareja (personas).
● **to be a match for SB** estar a la altura de alguien.
● **to be no match for SB** no estar a la altura de alguien.
● **to match up to** estar a la altura de.
● **to meet one's match** encontrar uno la horma de su zapato.
matchbox ['mætʃbɒks] n (pl **matcboxes**) caja de cerillas.
matching ['mætʃɪŋ] adj que hace juego.
mate¹ [meɪt] n mate (en ajedrez).
mate² [meɪt] n 1 compañero,-a, colega. 2 pareja (persona), macho, hembra (animal). 3 oficial de cubierta.
▶ vt-vi aparear(se).
material [mə'tɪərɪəl] adj 1 material. 2 importante, substancial.
▶ n 1 materia: *raw material*, materia prima. 2 tela, tejido. 3 material.
▶ npl **materials** material, materiales.
materialism [mə'tɪərɪəlɪzəm] n materialismo.
materialize [mə'tɪərɪəlaɪz] vi realizarse, materializarse.
maternity [mə'tɜːnɪtɪ] n maternidad.
■ **maternity hospital** maternidad.
■ **maternity leave** baja por maternidad.
mathematics [mæθə'mætɪks] n matemáticas.
Es incontable y el verbo va en singular.
maths [mæθs] n fam mates.
Es incontable y el verbo va en singular.
matron ['meɪtrən] n 1 enfermera jefe, enfermera jefa. 2 ama de llaves.
matt [mæt] adj mate.
matter ['mætə'] n 1 materia. 2 asunto, cuestión.

▶ *vi* importar: *it doesn't matter to me*, no me importa, me da igual.

● **as a matter of fact** en realidad, de hecho.

● **it's a matter of ...** es cuestión de ....

● **no matter ...**: *I never win, no matter what I do*, nunca gano, haga lo que haga; *no matter where you go*, vayas donde vayas; *no matter how busy he is*, por muy ocupado que esté.

● **the matter**: *what's the matter?*, ¿qué pasa?, ¿qué ocurre?; *there's nothing the matter*, no pasa nada; *what's the matter with you?*, ¿qué te pasa?

● **to make matters worse** para colmo de desgracias.

matter-of-fact [mætərəv'fækt] *adj* práctico,-a, realista.

mattress ['mætrəs] *n* (*pl* **-es**) colchón.

mature [mə'tʃʊəʳ] *adj* **1** maduro,-a. **2** vencido,-a (*bono, póliza*).

▶ *vt-vi* madurar.

▶ *vi* vencer (*bono, póliza*).

maturity [mə'tʃʊərɪtɪ] *n* madurez.

mauve [məʊv] *adj* malva.

▶ *n* malva.

max [mæks, 'mæksɪməm] *abbr* (*maximum*) máximo, max.

maximum ['mæksɪməm] *adj* máximo,-a.

▶ *n* máximo.

● **as a maximum** como máximo.

● **to the maximum** al máximo.

may [meɪ] *aux* **1** poder, ser posible: *he may come*, es posible que venga, puede que venga. **2** poder: *may I go?*, ¿puedo irme? **3**: *may it be so*, ojalá sea así; *may he rest in peace*, que en paz descanse.

● **come what may** pase lo que pase.

● **may as well**: *you may as well buy the big one*, ya puestos, cómprate el grande; *I may as well tell you, you'll find out anyway*, más vale que te lo diga, te enterarás de todas maneras.

May [meɪ] *n* mayo.

maybe ['meɪbiː] *adv* quizá, quizás, tal vez: *maybe it'll rain*, tal vez llueva.

mayonnaise [meɪə'neɪz] *n* mayonesa, mahonesa.

mayor [meəʳ] *n* alcalde.

maze [meɪz] *n* laberinto.

MB ['megəbaɪt] *abbr* (*megabyte*) megabyte, Mb.

MC¹ ['em'siː] *abbr* (*Master of Ceremonies*) maestro de ceremonias.

MC² ['em'siː] *abbr* (*musicassette*) casete.

MD ['em'diː] *abbr* (*Doctor of Medicine*) doctor,-a en Medicina, Dr.,-ra. en Medicina.

me [miː] *pron* **1** me, mí: *can you see me?*, ¿me ves?; *follow me*, sígueme; *it's for me*, es para mí. **2** yo: *it's me!*, ¡soy yo!

● **with me** conmigo.

meadow ['medəʊ] *n* prado, pradera.

meagre ['miːgəʳ] (US **meager**) *adj* escaso,-a.

meal [miːl] *n* comida.

● **to have a meal** comer.

mean¹ [miːn] *adj* **1** tacaño,-a, mezquino,-a. **2** malo,-a, cruel. **3** medio,-a: *mean temperature*, temperatura media.

mean² [miːn] *vt* (*pt & pp* **meant**). **1** querer decir: *what does this world mean?*, ¿qué quiere decir esta palabra? **2** significar: *this means a lot to me*, esto significa mucho para mí. **3** querer, tener intención de: *I didn't mean to do it*, lo hice sin querer. **4** suponer, implicar. **5** destinar.

● **I mean** quiero decir, o sea.

● **to mean it** decirlo en serio.

● **to mean well** tener buenas intenciones.

● **what do you mean?** ¿qué quieres decir?

mean³ [miːn] *n* media.

meaning ['miːnɪŋ] *n* sentido, significado.

meaningful ['miːnɪŋfʊl] *adj* significativo,-a.

meaningless ['miːnɪŋləs] *adj* sin sentido.

means [miːnz] *n* medio, manera: *there is no means of knowing*, no hay manera de saberlo.

▶ *npl* medios, recursos económicos.

● **a man of means** un hombre acaudalado.

● **by all means!** ¡naturalmente!

● **by means of** por medio de, mediante.

● **by no means** de ninguna manera, de ningún modo.

■ **means of transport** medio de transporte.

meant [ment] *pt-pp* → mean.

meantime ['miːntaɪm] *phr* **in the meantime** mientras tanto, entretanto.

meanwhile ['miːnwaɪl] *adv* mientras tanto, entretanto.

measles ['miːzəlz] *n* sarampión.
■ **German measles** rubeola.

Es incontable y el verbo va en singular.

measure ['meʒəʳ] *n* **1** medida. **2** MUS compás.
► *vt* **1** medir *(zona)*. **2** tomar las medidas de *(persona)*.
► *vi* medir.
● **in some measure** hasta cierto punto.
● **to take measures** tomar medidas.
to measure up *vi* estar a la altura.
measurement ['meʒəmənt] *n* **1** medición *(acción)*. **2** medida.
meat [miːt] *n* carne.
■ **meat pie** empanada de carne.
meatball ['miːtbɔːl] *n* albóndiga.
mechanic [mɪ'kænɪk] *n* mecánico,-a.
mechanical [mɪ'kænɪkəl] *adj* mecánico,-a.
mechanics [mɪ'kænɪks] *n* mecánica. Es incontable y el verbo va en singular.
► *npl* mecanismos.
mechanism ['mekənɪzəm] *n* mecanismo.
mechanize ['mekənaɪz] *vt* mecanizar.
medal ['medəl] *n* medalla.
medallion [mɪ'dælɪən] *n* medallón.
meddle ['medəl] *vi* entrometerse.
media ['miːdɪə] *npl* medios de comunicación.

Ver también **medium**.

mediaeval [medɪ'iːvəl] *adj* medieval.
mediate ['miːdɪeɪt] *vi* mediar.
mediator ['miːdɪeɪtəʳ] *n* mediador,-ra.
medical ['medɪkəl] *adj* médico,-a.
► *n fam* chequeo, reconocimiento médico.
■ **medical record** historial médico.
■ **medical student** estudiante de medicina.
medication [medɪ'keɪʃən] *n* medicación.
medicine ['medsɪn] *n* **1** medicina. **2** medicamento.
medieval [medɪ'iːvəl] *adj* medieval.
mediocre [miːdɪ'əʊkəʳ] *adj* mediocre.
meditate ['medɪteɪt] *vi* meditar, reflexionar.
meditation [medɪ'teɪʃən] *n* meditación.
Mediterranean [medɪtə'reɪnɪən] *adj-n* mediterráneo,-a.
● **the Mediterranean** el mar Mediterráneo.
medium ['miːdɪəm] *n* (*pl* **media** o **me-**

diums). **1** medio. **2** medio de comunicación. **3** medio ambiente. **4** médium *(persona)*.
► *adj* mediano,-a.
medley ['medlɪ] *n* **1** popurrí. **2** mezcla.
meek [miːk] *adj* manso,-a, dócil.
meet [miːt] *vt* (*pt & pp* **met**). **1** encontrar, encontrarse con *(por casualidad)*. **2** reunirse con, verse con. **3** conocer. **4** ir a buscar, venir a buscar: *I'll meet you at the station*, te iré a buscar a la estación. **5** encontrar *(peligro, muerte)*. **6** satisfacer *(condiciones)*. **7** cubrir *(gastos)*.
► *vi* **1** encontrarse *(por casualidad)*. **2** reunirse, verse. **3** conocerse. **4** unirse, confluir *(ríos)*; empalmar *(carreteras)*.
► *n* **1** SP encuentro. **2** partida de caza.
● **pleased to meet you!** ¡encantado,-a de conocerle!
● **to make ends meet** *fam* llegar a fin de mes.
to meet up *vi fam* quedar.
to meet with *vt* **1** tropezar con *(dificultad)*; tener *(éxito)*. **2** reunirse con, encontrarse con *(persona)*.
meeting ['miːtɪŋ] *n* **1** reunión. **2** junta *(de accionistas)*. **3** POL mitin. **4** encuentro. **5** cita. **6** SP encuentro.
■ **meeting point** lugar de encuentro.
megaphone ['megəfəʊn] *n* megáfono, altavoz.
melancholy ['melənkəlɪ] *n* melancolía.
► *adj* melancólico,-a.
mellow ['meləʊ] *adj* **1** maduro,-a *(fruta)*. **2** añejo,-a *(vino)*. **3** suave *(color, voz)*. **4** sereno,-a *(persona)*.
► *vt-vi* **1** madurar *(fruta)*. **2** suavizar(se) *(color, voz)*. **3** serenar(se) *(persona)*.
melodrama ['melədrɑːmə] *n* melodrama.
melody ['melədɪ] *n* (*pl* **-ies**) melodía.
melon ['melən] *n* melón.
melt [melt] *vt-vi* **1** derretir(se) *(hielo, nieve)*. **2** fundir(se) *(metal)*. **3** *fig* atenuar(se), disipar(se) *(ira)*.
● **to melt into tears** deshacerse en lágrimas.
to melt away *vi* **1** derretirse *(hielo, nieve)*. **2** desaparecer *(dinero, gente)*. **3** desvanecerse *(sentimiento)*.
member ['membəʳ] *n* **1** miembro. **2** socio,-a *(de club)*. **3** POL afiliado,-a. **4** miembro *(del cuerpo)*.
■ **member of staff** empleado,-a.

■ **Member of Parliament** diputado,-a.

membership ['membəʃıp] n **1** calidad de miembro,-a, calidad de socio,-a. **2** número de miembros, número de socios.

■ **membership card** tarjeta de socio.

■ **membership fee** cuota de socio.

memo ['meməʊ] n (pl **memos**) → memorandum.

memoirs ['memwɑː'z] npl memorias.

memorable ['memərəbəl] adj memorable.

memorandum [memə'rændəm] n (pl **-s** o **memoranda** [memə'rændə]). **1** memorándum. **2** nota, apunte.

memorial [mə'mɔːrɪəl] adj conmemorativo,-a.

▶ n monumento conmemorativo.

memorize ['meməraız] vt memorizar, aprender de memoria.

memory ['memərı] n (pl **-ies**). **1** memoria. **2** recuerdo.

● **from memory** de memoria.

● **in memory of SB** en memoria de ALGN.

men [men] npl → man.

menace ['menəs] n **1** amenaza. **2** peligro.

▶ vt amenazar.

menacing ['menəsıŋ] adj amenazador,-ra.

mend [mend] n remiendo.

▶ vt **1** reparar, arreglar. **2** remendar (ropa).

▶ vi mejorar, mejorarse.

● **to mend one's ways** reformarse.

menopause ['menəupɔːz] n menopausia.

menstruation [menstrʊ'eıʃən] n menstruación, regla.

menswear ['menzweə'] n ropa de caballero.

mental ['mentəl] adj **1** mental. **2** fam chalado,-a, tocado,-a.

■ **mental asylum** manicomio.

■ **mental hospital** hospital psiquiátrico.

mention ['menʃən] n mención.

▶ vt mencionar, hacer mención de.

● **don't mention it!** ¡de nada!, ¡no hay de qué!

● **to make mention of STH** mencionar algo.

menu ['menjuː] n **1** carta (en restaurante). **2** COMPUT menú.

MEP ['em'iː'piː] abbr (**Member of the Eu-**

ropean Parliament) miembro del Parlamento Europeo.

mercenary ['mɜːsənərı] adj-n mercenario,-a.

merchandise ['mɜːtʃəndaız] n mercancías, géneros.

merchant ['mɜːtʃənt] n comerciante.

■ **merchant navy** marina mercante.

merciless ['mɜːsıləs] adj despiadado,-a.

mercury ['mɜːkjʊrı] n mercurio.

mercy ['mɜːsı] n (pl **-ies**) misericordia, clemencia, compasión.

● **at the mercy of** a la merced de.

● **to have mercy on SB** tener compasión de ALGN.

mere [mıə'] adj mero,-a, simple.

merely ['mıəlı] adv solamente, simplemente.

merge [mɜːdʒ] vt unir, empalmar (carreteras).

▶ vi confluir, unirse, empalmar (carreteras).

▶ vt-vi fusionar(se) (empresas).

merger ['mɜːdʒə'] n fusión.

meringue [mə'ræŋ] n merengue.

merit ['merıt] n mérito.

▶ vt merecer.

mermaid ['mɜːmeıd] n sirena.

merry ['merı] adj (**-ier**, **-iest**) alegre.

● **merry Christmas!** ¡feliz Navidad!

merry-go-round ['merıgəʊraʊnd] n tiovivo, caballitos.

mesh [meʃ] n (pl **-es**). **1** malla. **2** engranaje.

▶ vi engranar.

mesmerize ['mezməraız] vt hipnotizar.

mess [mes] n (pl **-es**). **1** desorden, lío, follón. **2** suciedad, porquería. **3** comedor (militar).

● **to look a mess** fam estar horroroso,-a.

● **to make a mess of** fam estropear.

to mess about/around vi **1** gandulear. **2** hacer el tonto.

▶ vt fastidiar.

to mess up vt **1** fam desordenar (habitación). **2** estropear (planes). **3** ensuciar (ropa).

message ['mesıdʒ] n mensaje.

● **to get the message** fam entender, enterarse.

messenger ['mesındʒə'] n mensajero,-a.

Messrs ['mesəz] abbr (**messieurs**) Señores, Sres.

messy ['mesɪ] *adj* (-**ier**, -**iest**). **1** desordenado,-a. **2** sucio,-a.

met [met] *pt-pp* → meet.

metabolism [me'tæbəlɪzəm] *n* metabolismo.

metal ['metəl] *n* metal.

▶ *adj* metálico,-a, de metal.

metallic [mə'tælɪk] *adj* **1** metálico,-a. **2** metalizado,-a.

metaphor ['metəfɔːʳ] *n* metáfora.

meteor ['miːtɪəʳ] *n* meteoro, bólido.

meteorite ['miːtɪəraɪt] *n* meteorito.

meter¹ ['miːtəʳ] *n* US → metre.

meter² ['miːtəʳ] *n* contador.

method ['meθəd] *n* método.

methodical [mə'θɒdɪkəl] *adj* metódico,-a.

meticulous [mə'tɪkjʊləs] *adj* meticuloso,-a.

metre ['miːtəʳ] (US **meter**) *n* metro.

metric ['metrɪk] *adj* métrico,-a.

mew [mjuː] *n* maullido.

▶ *vi* maullar.

Mexican ['meksɪkən] *adj-n* mexicano,-a, mejicano,-a.

Mexico ['meksɪləʊ] *n* México, Méjico.

■ **New Mexico** Nuevo México.

mezzanine ['mezəniːn] *n* entresuelo.

MHz ['megəhɜːts] *abbr* (*megahertz*) megahercio, MHz.

miaow [mɪ'aʊ] *n* miau.

▶ *vi* maullar.

mice [maɪs] *npl* → mouse.

microbe ['maɪkrəʊb] *n* microbio.

microchip ['maɪkrəʊtʃɪp] *n* microchip.

microphone ['maɪkrəfəʊn] *n* micrófono.

microprocessor [maɪkrəʊ'prəʊsesəʳ] *n* microprocesador.

microscope ['maɪkrəskəʊp] *n* microscopio.

microwave ['maɪkrəʊweɪv] *n* microonda, microondas.

■ **microwave oven** horno microondas.

midday [mɪd'deɪ] *n* mediodía.

● **at midday** al mediodía.

middle ['mɪdəl] *adj* **1** del medio, central. **2** mediano,-a.

▶ *n* **1** medio, centro (*de habitación*). **2** mitad: *in the middle of the night*, en mitad de la noche, en plena noche. **3** *fam* cintura.

● **to be in the middle of** estar en medio de, estar metido,-a en (*actividad*).

■ **middle age** mediana edad.

■ **middle class** clase media.

■ **middle name** segundo nombre.

middleman ['mɪdəlmən] *n* (*pl* **middlemen**) intermediario.

middle-of-the-road [mɪdələvðəˈrəʊd] *adj* *fig* moderado,-a.

midget ['mɪdʒɪt] *n* enano,-a.

midnight ['mɪdnaɪt] *n* medianoche.

midway ['mɪdweɪ] *adv* a medio camino.

midweek ['mɪdwiːk] *adj* de entre semana.

▶ *adv* entre semana.

midwife ['mɪdwaɪf] *n* (*pl* **midwifves**) comadrona.

might¹ [maɪt] *n* poder, fuerza.

● **with all one's might** con todas sus fuerzas.

might² [maɪt] *aux* → may.

mighty ['maɪtɪ] *adj* (-**ier**, -**iest**) fuerte, poderoso,-a.

migraine ['maɪɡreɪn] *n* jaqueca, migraña.

migrant ['maɪɡrənt] *adj* **1** migratorio,-a (*ave*). **2** emigrante (*persona*).

migrate [maɪ'ɡreɪt] *vi* emigrar.

mike [maɪk] *n* *fam* micro.

mild [maɪld] *adj* **1** apacible (*persona*). **2** suave (*clima*).

mildew ['mɪldjuː] *n* **1** moho. **2** añublo (*en plantas*).

mildly ['maɪldlɪ] *adv* **1** suavemente. **2** ligeramente.

mile [maɪl] *n* milla.

● **it's miles away** *fam* está lejísimos.

milestone ['maɪlstəʊn] *n* hito.

militant ['mɪlɪtənt] *adj* militante.

military ['mɪlɪtərɪ] *adj* militar.

▶ *n* **the military** los militares, las fuerzas armadas.

■ **military takeover** golpe militar.

milk [mɪlk] *n* leche.

▶ *vt* ordeñar.

● **to milk SB of STH** *fam* quitarle algo a ALGN.

■ **milk chocolate** chocolate con leche.

■ **milk products** productos lácteos.

■ **milk shake** batido.

milkman ['mɪlkmən] *n* (*pl* **milkmen**) lechero, repartidor de la leche.

milky ['mɪlkɪ] *adj* (-**ier**, -**iest**). **1** con mucha leche. **2** lechoso,-a, pálido,-a.

■ **Milky Way** Vía Láctea.

mill [mɪl] *n* **1** molino. **2** molinillo *(de café)*. **3** fábrica.

▶ *vt* moler.

to mill about/around *vi* arremolinarse.

millennium [mɪ'lenɪəm] *n* milenio.

millimetre ['mɪlɪmiːtəʳ] (US **millimeter**) *n* milímetro.

million ['mɪljən] *n* millón: *one million dollars*, un millón de dólares.

millionaire [mɪljə'neəʳ] *n* millonario,-a.

millionth ['mɪljənθ] *adj* millonésimo,-a.

▶ *n* millonésimo, millonésima parte.

mime [maɪm] *n* **1** mímica, mimo. **2** mimo *(persona)*.

▶ *vt* imitar.

▶ *vi* hacer mimo, hacer mímica.

mimic ['mɪmɪk] *n* mimo.

▶ *vt (pt & pp* **mimicked***, ger* **mimicking***)* imitar.

mince [mɪns] *n* GB carne picada.

▶ *vt* picar.

● **not to mince one's words** no tener pelos en la lengua, no andarse con rodeos.

mincemeat ['mɪnsmiːt] *n* conserva de picadillo de fruta.

● **to make mincemeat of SB** hacer picadillo a ALGN.

mind [maɪnd] *n* **1** mente. **2** mentalidad. **3** pensamientos.

▶ *vt* **1** hacer caso de: *don't mind him*, no le hagas caso. **2** cuidar. **3** tener cuidado con.

▶ *vt-vi* importar: *do you mind if I close the window?*, ¿le importa que cierre la ventana?; *I don't mind staying*, no tengo inconveniente en quedarme.

● **mind out!** ¡ojo!, ¡cuidado!

● **mind you ...** ten en cuenta que ..., te advierto que....

● **mind your own business** no te metas en lo que no te importa.

● **never mind** no importa, da igual.

● **to bear STH in mind** tener algo en cuenta.

● **to change one's mind** cambiar de opinión.

● **to have STH in mind** estar pensando en algo.

● **to lose one's mind** perder el juicio.

● **to make up one's mind** decidirse.

● **to speak one's mind** hablar sin rodeos.

mindless ['maɪndləs] *adj* absurdo,-a, estúpido,-a.

mine[1] [maɪn] *n* mina.

▶ *vt* **1** extraer *(minerales)*. **2** sembrar minas en *(carretera)*. **3** volar con minas, minar *(barco)*.

mine[2] [maɪn] *pron* (el) mío, (la) mía, (los) míos, (las) mías: *she's a friend of mine*, es amiga mía; *these keys are mine*, estas llaves son mías.

miner ['maɪnəʳ] *n* minero,-a.

mineral ['mɪnərəl] *adj* mineral.

▶ *n* mineral.

■ **mineral water** agua mineral.

mingle ['mɪŋgəl] *vt-vi* mezclar(se).

miniature ['mɪnɪtʃəʳ] *n* miniatura.

▶ *adj* en miniatura.

minibus ['mɪnɪbʌs] *n (pl* **minibuses***)* minibús.

minimal ['mɪnɪməl] *adj* mínimo,-a.

minimum ['mɪnɪməm] *adj* mínimo,-a.

▶ *n* mínimo.

mining ['maɪnɪŋ] *n* minería, explotación de minas.

■ **mining industry** industria minera.

minister ['mɪnɪstəʳ] *n* **1** ministro,-a. **2** pastor,-ra *(cura)*.

ministry ['mɪnɪstrɪ] *n (pl* **-ies***)*. **1** ministerio. **2** sacerdocio.

mink [mɪŋk] *n* visón.

minor ['maɪnəʳ] *adj* **1** pequeño,-a, de poca importancia *(daños, herida)*. **2** secundario,-a *(papel, carretera)*.

▶ *n* menor de edad.

Minorca [mɪ'nɔːkə] *n* Menorca.

minority [maɪ'nɒrɪtɪ] *n (pl* **-ies***)* minoría.

▶ *adj* minoritario,-a.

mint[1] [mɪnt] *vt* acuñar.

● **in mint condition** en perfecto estado.

● **the Mint** la Casa de la Moneda.

mint[2] [mɪnt] *n* **1** menta. **2** pastilla de menta.

minus ['maɪnəs] *prep* menos: *four minus three*, cuatro menos tres; *minus five degrees*, cinco grados bajo cero.

▶ *adj* negativo,-a.

■ **minus sign** signo menos.

minute[1] ['maɪnjuːt] *adj* **1** diminuto,-a. **2** minucioso,-a.

minute[2] ['mɪnɪt] *n* **1** minuto. **2** momento: *just a minute!*, ¡un momentito!, ¡un segundo!

▶ *npl* **minutes** actas.

● **at the last minute** al último momento.

● **the minute (that)** ... en cuanto ....

■ **minute hand** minutero.

miracle ['mɪrəkəl] *n* milagro.

● **to work miracles** hacer milagros.

miraculous [mɪ'rækjʊləs] *adj* milagroso,-a.

miraculously [mɪ'rækjʊləslɪ] *adv* de milagro.

mirage [mɪ'rɑːʒ] *n* espejismo.

mirror ['mɪrəʳ] *n* espejo; retrovisor *(de coche)*.

▶ *vt* reflejar.

misbehave [mɪsbɪ'heɪv] *vi* portarse mal.

miscalculate [mɪs'kælkjʊleɪt] *vt-vi* calcular mal.

miscarriage [mɪs'kærɪdʒ] *n* aborto *(espontáneo)*.

miscellaneous [mɪsɪ'leɪnɪəs] *adj* diverso, -a, variado,-a.

mischief ['mɪstʃɪf] *n* travesura, travesuras.

● **to get up to mischief** hacer travesuras.

mischievous ['mɪstʃɪvəs] *adj* **1** travieso,-a *(persona)*. **2** pícaro,-a *(mirada)*.

misconception [mɪskən'sepʃən] *n* idea equivocada, concepto erróneo.

misconduct [mɪs'kɒndʌkt] *n* mala conducta.

▶ *vi* gestionar mal.

misdemeanour [mɪsdɪ'miːnəʳ] (US **misdemeanor**) *n* **1** fechoría. **2** delito menor.

miser ['maɪzəʳ] *n* avaro,-a.

miserable ['mɪzərəbəl] *adj* **1** triste, deprimido,-a. **2** desagradable, horrible *(tiempo)*. **3** miserable.

misery ['mɪzərɪ] *n (pl* **-ies**). **1** tristeza, desdicha. **2** sufrimiento: *a life of misery*, una vida de sufrimiento. **3** miseria.

misfire [mɪs'faɪəʳ] *vi* fallar.

misfortune [mɪs'fɔːtʃən] *n* infortunio, desgracia.

misgiving [mɪs'gɪvɪŋ] *n* duda, recelo.

misguided [mɪs'gaɪdɪd] *adj* equivocado,-a.

mishap ['mɪshæp] *n* percance, contratiempo.

misinterpret [mɪsɪn'tɜːprət] *vt* malinterpretar.

misjudge [mɪs'dʒʌdʒ] *vt* juzgar mal.

mislaid [mɪs'leɪd] *pt-pp* → mislay.

mislay [mɪs'leɪ] *vt (pt & pp* **mislaid**) extraviar, perder.

mislead [mɪs'liːd] *vt* engañar, inducir a error.

misled [mɪs'led] *pt-pp* → mislead.

mismanagement [mɪs'mænɪdʒmənt] *n* mala administración.

misplace [mɪs'pleɪs] *vt* perder, extraviar.

misprint ['mɪsprɪnt] *n* errata, error de imprenta.

miss[1] [mɪs] *n (pl* **-es**) señorita: *Miss Brown*, la señorita Brown.

miss[2] [mɪs] *n (pl* **-es**) fallo, tiro errado.

▶ *vt-vi* no acertar, fallar, errar: *to miss the target*, no dar en el banco.

▶ *vt* **1** perder: *he missed the train*, perdió el tren. **2** no entender. **3** echar de menos, añorar. **4** echar en falta. **5** no ver; no oír.

▶ *vi* faltar: *nobody is missing*, no falta nadie.

● **to miss class** faltar a clase.

● **to miss the boat** perder la ocasión, perder el tren.

● **to give STH a miss** *fam* pasar de algo, no hacer algo.

to miss out *vt* saltarse.

to miss out on *vi* dejar pasar, perderse.

missile ['mɪsaɪl] *n* misil.

■ **missile launcher** lanzamisiles.

missing ['mɪsɪŋ] *adj* **1** perdido,-a, extraviado,-a *(objeto)*. **2** desaparecido,-a *(persona)*.

mission ['mɪʃən] *n* misión.

missionary ['mɪʃənərɪ] *n (pl* **-ies**) misionero,-a.

mist [mɪst] *n* **1** neblina, bruma. **2** vaho.

to mist over/up *vi* **1** empañarse. **2** cubrirse de neblina.

mistake [mɪs'teɪk] *n* **1** equivocación, error. **2** falta *(en examen)*.

▶ *vt (pt* **mistook** [mɪs'tʊk], *pp* **mistaken** [mɪs'teɪkən]). **1** entender mal. **2** confundir.

● **by mistake** por error, por equivocación.

● **to make a mistake** equivocarse.

mister ['mɪstəʳ] *n* señor.

mistletoe ['mɪzəltəʊ] *n* muérdago.

mistook [mɪs'tʊk] *pt* → mistake.

mistreat [mɪs'triːt] *vt* maltratar.

mistress ['mɪstrəs] *n (pl* **-es**). **1** ama, señora *(de casa)*. **2** amante *(querida)*.

mistrust [mɪs'trʌst] *n* desconfianza, recelo.
► *vt* desconfiar de.

misty ['mɪstɪ] *adj* (**-ier**, **-iest**) neblinoso, -a, con neblina.

misunderstand [mɪsʌndə'stænd] *vt-vi* (*pt & pp* **misunderstood** [mɪsʌndə'stʊd]) entender mal, malinterpretar.

misunderstanding [mɪsʌndə'stændɪŋ] *n* malentendido.

misunderstood [mɪsʌndə'stʊd] *pt-pp →* misunderstand.

misuse [(*n*) mɪs'juːs(*vb*) mɪs'juːz] *n* **1** mal uso. **2** abuso (*de poder*).
► *vt* **1** emplear mal. **2** abusar de (*de poder*).

mitten ['mɪtən] *n* manopla.

mix [mɪks] *n* (*pl* **mixes**) mezcla.
► *vt* mezclar.
► *vi* **1** mezclarse. **2** relacionarse.

to mix up *vt* **1** mezclar (*ingredientes*). **2** confundir (*conceptos*). **3** revolver, desordenar.

mixed [mɪkst] *adj* **1** variado,-a. **2** contradictorio,-a (*sentimientos*). **3** mixto,-a (*de ambos sexos*).

mixer ['mɪksə'] *n* batidora.

mixture ['mɪkstʃə'] *n* mezcla.

mix-up ['mɪksʌp] *n fam* lío, confusión.

moan [məʊn] *n* gemido, quejido.
► *vi* **1** gemir. **2** *pej* quejarse.

moat [məʊt] *n* foso.

mob [mɒb] *n* **1** muchedumbre, gentío. **2** banda.
► *vt* (*pt & pp* **mobbed**, *ger* **mobbing**) acosar, asediar.

mobile ['məʊbaɪl] *adj-n* móvil.
■ **mobile home** caravana, remolque.
■ **mobile phone** móvil, teléfono móvil.

moccasin ['mɒkəsɪn] *n* mocasín.

mock [mɒk] *adj* **1** falso, de imitación. **2** de prueba, simulado,-a: *a mock battle*, un simulacro de batalla.
► *vt* burlarse de.
► *vi* burlarse.

mockery ['mɒkərɪ] *n* (*pl* **-ies**). **1** burla, mofa. **2** farsa.
● **to make a mockery of STH** poner en ridículo algo.

MOD ['en'əʊ'diː] *abbr* GB (***Ministry of Defence***) Ministerio de Defensa.

model ['mɒdəl] *n* **1** modelo. **2** modelo, maniquí. **3** maqueta.
► *adj* **1** en miniatura, a escala. **2** ejemplar, modelo.
► *vt* (GB *pt & pp* **modelled**, *ger* **modelling**; US *pt & pp* **modeled**, *ger* **modeling**). **1** modelar. **2** presentar (*en pase de modelos*).
■ **model aeroplane** maqueta de avión, aeromodelo.
■ **model home** casa piloto.

modem ['məʊdəm] *n* módem.

moderate ['mɒdərət] *adj* **1** moderado,-a, módico,-a (*precio*). **2** mediano,-a, regular.
► *n* POL moderado,-a.
► *vt-vi* moderar(se).

moderately ['mɒdərətlɪ] *adv* medianamente.

moderation [mɒdə'reɪʃən] *n* moderación.
● **in moderation** con moderación.

modern ['mɒdən] *adj* **1** moderno,-a. **2** contemporáneo,-a (*literatura, arte*).

modernize ['mɒdənaɪz] *vt* modernizar, actualizar.

modest ['mɒdɪst] *adj* **1** modesto,-a. **2** discreto,-a (*éxito*); módico,-a (*precio*).

modesty ['mɒdɪstɪ] *n* modestia.

modify ['mɒdɪfaɪ] *vt* (*pt & pp* **-ied**) modificar.

module ['mɒdjuːl] *n* módulo.

moist [mɔɪst] *adj* **1** húmedo,-a. **2** ligeramente mojado,-a.

moisten ['mɔɪsən] *vt* **1** humedecer. **2** mojar ligeramente.

moisture ['mɔɪstʃə'] *n* humedad.

moisturizer ['mɔɪstʃəraɪzə'] *n* hidratante.

molar ['məʊlə'] *n* muela.

mold [məʊld] *n* US → mould.

moldy ['məʊldɪ] *adj* (**-ier**, **-iest**) US → mouldy.

mole¹ [məʊl] *n* lunar.

mole² [məʊl] *n* topo (*animal*).

molecule ['mɒləkjuːl] *n* molécula.

molest [mə'lest] *vt* **1** hostigar, acosar. **2** agredir sexualmente.

mom [mɒm] *n* US *fam* mamá.

moment ['məʊmənt] *n* momento, instante.
● **at any moment** de un momento a otro.
● **at every moment** constantemente.
● **at the last moment** a última hora.
● **at the moment** de momento.
● **for the moment** de momento.
● **just a moment** un momento.

momentarily [məʊmən'terɪlɪ] *adv* momentáneamente.

momentum [məʊ'mentəm] *n* **1** PHYS momento. **2** *fig* ímpetu, impulso.

Mon ['mʌndɪ] *abbr (Monday)* lunes, lun.

Monaco ['mɒnəkəʊ] *n* Mónaco.

monarch ['mɒnək] *n (pl* **monarchs)** monarca.

monarchy ['mɒnəkɪ] *n (pl* **-ies)** monarquía.

monastery ['mɒnəstərɪ] *n (pl* **-ies)** monasterio.

Monday ['mʌndɪ] *n* lunes.

Monegasque ['mɒnəgæsk] *adj-n* monegasco,-a.

monetary ['mʌnɪtərɪ] *adj* monetario,-a.

money ['mʌnɪ] *n* dinero.
- **to be in the money** *fam* ser rico,-a.
- **to get one's money's worth** sacar partido del dinero.
- **to make money 1** ganar dinero *(persona).* **2** ser rentable, rendir *(negocio).*
■ **money order** giro postal.

moneybox ['mʌnɪbɒks] *n (pl* **moneyboxes)** hucha.

moneyed ['mʌnɪd] *adj* adinerado,-a.

mongrel ['mʌŋɡrəl] *n* perro cruzado.

monitor ['mɒnɪtə'] *n* **1** monitor. **2** responsable, encargado,-a.
► *vt* **1** escuchar. **2** seguir de cerca, controlar.

monk [mʌŋk] *n* monje.

monkey ['mʌŋkɪ] *n* mono.
■ **monkey wrench** llave inglesa.

monologue ['mɒnəlɒɡ] (US **monolog**) *n* monólogo.

monopolize [mə'nɒpəlaɪz] *vt* monopolizar.

monopoly [mə'nɒpəlɪ] *n (pl* **-ies)** monopolio.

monotonous [mə'nɒtənəs] *adj* monótono,-a.

monotony [mə'nɒtənɪ] *n* monotonía.

monster ['mɒnstə'] *n* monstruo.
► *adj* enorme.

monstrosity [mɒn'strɒsɪtɪ] *n (pl* **-ies)** monstruosidad.

monstrous ['mɒnstrəs] *adj* enorme, monstruoso,-a.

month [mʌnθ] *n* mes.

monthly ['mʌnθlɪ] *adj* mensual.
► *adv* mensualmente, cada mes.
■ **monthly instalment** mensualidad.

monument ['mɒnjʊmənt] *n* monumento.

monumental [mɒnjʊ'mentəl] *adj* monumental.

moo [muː] *n (pl* **moos)** mugido.
► *vi (pt & pp* **mooed,** *ger* **mooing)** mugir.

mood¹ [muːd] *n* humor.
- **to be in a bad mood** estar de mal humor.
- **to be in a good mood** estar de buen humor.
- **to be in the mood for** tener ganas de, estar de humor para.

mood² [muːd] *n* modo: *the subjunctive mood,* el modo subjuntivo.

moody ['muːdɪ] *adj* **(-ier, -iest)** malhumorado,-a.

moon [muːn] *n* luna.
- **once in a blue moon** de Pascuas a Ramos.
- **to be over the moon** estar en el séptimo cielo.
■ **moon landing** alunizaje.

moonlight ['muːnlaɪt] *n* luz de luna, claro de luna.
► *vi fam* estar pluriempleado,-a.

moor¹ [mʊə'] *n* páramo, brezal.

moor² [mʊə'] *vt* amarrar, anclar.

Moor [mʊə'] *n* moro,-a.

mop [mɒp] *n* **1** fregona. **2** *fam* mata de pelo, pelambrera.
► *vt (pt & pp* **mopped,** *ger* **mopping)** fregar, pasar la fregona por.

to mop up *vt* limpiar.

mope [məʊp] *vi* estar deprimido,-a, estar abatido,-a.

moped ['məʊped] *n* ciclomotor.

moral ['mɒrəl] *adj* moral.
► *n* moraleja.
► *npl* **morals** moral.

morale [mə'rɑːl] *n* moral.

morality [mə'rælɪtɪ] *n* moral.

moratorium [mɒrə'tɔːrɪəm] *n (pl* **moratoria)** moratoria.

morbid ['mɔːbɪd] *adj* enfermizo,-a, morboso,-a.

more [mɔː'] *adj-adv* más: *more than twenty people,* más de veinte personas; *more expensive,* más caro.
- **... any more** ya no ...: *I don't live here any more,* ya no vivo aquí.
- **more and more expensive** cada vez más caro,-a.

● **more or less** más o menos.

● **once more** una vez más.

● **the more he has, the more he wants** cuanto más tiene más quiere.

● **would you like some more?** ¿quieres más?

Ver también **many** y **much**.

moreover [mɔːˈrəʊvəʳ] *adv fml* además, por otra parte.

morgue [mɔːg] *n* depósito de cadáveres.

morning [ˈmɔːnɪŋ] *n* mañana.

▶ *adj* matutino,-a, de la mañana.

● **good morning!** ¡buenos días!

● **in the morning** por la mañana: *at eight o'clock in the morning*, a las ocho de la mañana.

● **tomorrow morning** mañana por la mañana.

Moroccan [məˈrɒkən] *adj-n* marroquí.

Morocco [məˈrɒkəʊ] *n* Marruecos.

moron [ˈmɔːrɒn] *n pej* imbécil, idiota.

morphine [ˈmɔːfiːn] *n* morfina.

morsel [ˈmɔːsəl] *n* bocado.

mortal [ˈmɔːtəl] *adj-n* mortal.

mortality [mɔːˈtælɪti] *n* (*pl* **-ies**) mortalidad.

mortally [ˈmɔːtəli] *adv* mortalmente, de muerte.

mortar [ˈmɔːtəʳ] *n* mortero.

mortgage [ˈmɔːgɪdʒ] *n* hipoteca.

▶ *vt* hipotecar.

■ **mortgage loan** préstamo hipotecario.

■ **mortgage rate** tipo de interés hipotecario.

mosaic [məˈzeɪɪk] *adj* mosaico.

Moslem [ˈmɒzləm] *adj-n* musulmán,-ana.

mosque [mɒsk] *n* mezquita.

mosquito [məsˈkiːtəʊ] *n* (*pl* **-s** o **-es**) mosquito.

■ **mosquito net** mosquitero.

moss [mɒs] *n* (*pl* **-es**) musgo.

most [məʊst] *adj* **1** más: *he's got the most points*, él tiene más puntos. **2** la mayoría: *most people live in flats*, la mayoría de la gente vive en pisos.

▶ *adv* más: *the most difficult question*, la pregunta más difícil.

▶ *pron* **1** la mayor parte. **2** la mayoría: *most of the people*, la mayoría de la gente.

● **at most** como máximo.

● **for the most part** por lo general.

● **most likely** muy probablemente.

● **to make the most of** STH aprovechar algo al máximo.

Ver también **many** y **much**.

mostly [ˈməʊstli] *adv* principalmente.

MOT [ˈemˈəʊˈtiː] *abbr* GB (*Ministry of Transport*) Ministerio de Trasporte.

■ **MOT test** inspección técnica de vehículos, ITV.

motel [məʊˈtel] *n* motel.

moth [mɒθ] *n* **1** mariposa nocturna. **2** polilla.

mother [ˈmʌðəʳ] *n* madre.

▶ *vt* **1** dar a luz. **2** cuidar como una madre, mimar.

■ **mother country** patria, madre patria.

■ **mother tongue** lengua materna.

motherhood [ˈmʌðəhʊd] *n* maternidad.

mother-in-law [ˈmʌðərɪnlɔː] *n* (*pl* **mothers-in-law**) suegra.

motif [məʊˈtiːf] *n* (*pl* **motifs**). **1** motivo, adorno, dibujo. **2** MUS tema.

motion [ˈməʊʃən] *n* **1** movimiento. **2** gesto, ademán. **3** moción.

▶ *vi* hacer señas.

▶ *vt* indicar con señas.

● **in motion** en marcha.

● **in slow motion** a cámara lenta.

■ **motion picture** película.

motivation [məʊtɪˈveɪʃən] *n* motivación.

motive [ˈməʊtɪv] *n* **1** motivo, razón. **2** móvil (*de crimen*).

motor [ˈməʊtəʳ] *n* **1** motor. **2** *fam* coche.

■ **motor racing** carreras de coches.

■ **motor show** salón del automóvil.

motorbike [ˈməʊtəbaɪk] *n fam* moto.

motorboat [ˈməʊtəbəʊt] *n* lancha motora.

motorcycle [ˈməʊtəsaɪkəl] *n* motocicleta, moto.

motorist [ˈməʊtərɪst] *n* automovilista.

motorway [ˈməʊtəweɪ] *n* GB autopista.

motto [ˈmɒtəʊ] *n* (*pl* **-s** o **-es**) lema.

mould¹ [məʊld] *n* moho.

mould² [məʊld] *n* molde.

▶ *vt* moldear, modelar (*arcilla*).

mouldy [ˈməʊldi] *adj* (**-ier**, **-iest**) mohoso,-a, enmohecido,-a.

mound [maʊnd] *n* **1** montón. **2** montículo.

mount¹ [maʊnt] *n* monte.

mount² [maʊnt] *n* **1** montura (*animal*). **2** montura, marco (*de foto*).

▶ vt 1 subirse a (caballo),. 2 montar en (bicicleta). 3 fml subir (montaña). 4 enmarcar (foto). 5 montar (joya).

to mount up vi acumularse.

mountain ['maʊntən] n montaña.
▶ adj de montaña, montañés,-esa.
■ mountain bike bicicleta de montaña.
■ mountain range cordillera, sierra.

mountaineer [maʊntə'nɪəʳ] n montañero,-a.

mountaineering [maʊntə'nɪərɪŋ] n alpinismo.

mountainous ['maʊntənəs] adj montañoso,-a.

mourn [mɔːn] vt 1 llorar la muerte de. 2 echar de menos.

mourning ['mɔːnɪŋ] n luto, duelo.
● to be in mourning estar de luto.

mouse [maʊs] n (pl mice) ratón.

mousetrap ['maʊstræp] n ratonera.

moustache [məs'tɑːʃ] n bigote.

mouth [maʊθ] n 1 boca. 2 desembocadura (de río). 3 entrada (de túnel).
● by word of mouth de palabra.
● down in the mouth deprimido,-a.
● to keep one's mouth shut no decir esta boca es mía.
■ mouth organ armónica.

mouthful ['maʊθfʊl] n 1 bocado. 2 trago. 3 bocanada.

mouth-organ ['maʊθɔːgən] n armónica.

mouthpiece ['maʊθpiːs] n 1 boquilla (de instrumento). 2 micrófono (de teléfono).

move [muːv] n 1 movimiento. 2 turno, jugada (en juego): it's your move, es tu turno, te toca a ti. 3 mudanza (de casa).
▶ vt 1 mover, cambiar de sitio, apartar. 2 conmover. 3 convencer, inducir.
▶ vi 1 moverse. 2 trasladarse: they are moving to a new flat, se están trasladando a un piso nuevo. 3 jugar.
● to make a move dar un paso, irse.
● to move house mudarse de casa.
● to get a move on fam darse prisa.

to move along vi avanzar.

to move away vi 1 apartarse, alejarse. 2 mudarse de casa, trasladarse.

to move forward vt-vi avanzar.
▶ vt adelantar (reloj).

to move in vi 1 instalarse (en casa nueva). 2 intervenir (policía).

to move on vi 1 seguir (viaje). 2 pasar a, cambiar.

to move over vt-vi correr(se): move over a bit, córrete un poco.

movement ['muːvmənt] n 1 movimiento. 2 traslado (de objetos). 3 desplazamiento (de tropas). 4 mecanismo.

movie ['muːvi] n US película.
● to go to the movies ir al cine.

moving ['muːvɪŋ] adj 1 móvil. 2 en movimiento. 3 conmovedor,-ra.
■ moving staircase escalera mecánica.

mow [maʊ] vt (pt mowed [maʊd], pp mown [mən]) segar, cortar.

mower ['maʊəʳ] n cortacésped.

MP ['em'piː] abbr 1 (Member of Parliament) miembro de la Cámara de los Comunes, diputado,-a. 2 (Military Police) policía militar.

mph ['em'piː'eɪtʃ] abbr (miles per hour) millas por hora.

MSc ['em'es'siː] abbr (Master of Science) máster en ciencias.

much [mʌtʃ] adj (comp more [mɔːʳ], superl most [məʊst]) mucho,-a: there isn't much time, no hay mucho tiempo.
▶ adv-pron mucho: did it rain much?, ¿llovió mucho?
● as much ... as tanto,-a ... como.
● how much? ¿cuánto?
● so much tanto.
● very much muchísimo.
● to make much of STH dar mucha importancia a algo.

muck [mʌk] n 1 suciedad, porquería. 2 estiércol.

to muck about/around vi perder el tiempo, hacer el indio.

to muck in vi fam echar una mano.

to muck up vt 1 ensuciar. 2 echar a perder, fastidiar.

mucus ['mjuːkəs] n (pl mucuses) mucosidad.

mud [mʌd] n barro, lodo.

muddle ['mʌdəl] n 1 desorden. 2 embrollo, lío.
▶ vt confundir.
● to be in a muddle 1 estar hecho,-a un lío (persona). 2 estar en desorden (papeles, etc).

to muddle through vi arreglárselas.

muddy ['mʌdɪ] adj (-ier, -iest). 1 fangoso,-a, lodoso,-a (sendero). 2 cubierto,-a de barro, lleno,-a de barro (persona). 3 turbio,-a (río).

mudguard ['mʌdgɑːd] *n* guardabarros.

muffler ['mʌflə'] *n* **1** bufanda. **2** US silenciador *(de coche)*.

mug[1] [mʌg] *n* **1** taza. **2** jarra.

mug[2] [mʌg] *n* GB *fam* primo,-a, ingenuo,-a.
► *vt* (*pt & pp* **mugged**, *ger* **mugging**) atracar.

mugger ['mʌgə'] *n* atracador,-ra.

mugging ['mʌgɪŋ] *n* atraco.

muggy ['mʌgɪ] *adj* (**-ier**, **-iest**) bochornoso,-a.

mule [mjuːl] *n* mulo,-a.

multinational [mʌltɪ'næʃənəl] *adj* multinacional.
► *n* multinacional.

multiple ['mʌltɪpəl] *adj* múltiple.
► *n* múltiplo.

multiplication [mʌltɪplɪ'keɪʃən] *n* multiplicación.

multiply ['mʌltɪplaɪ] *vt-vi* (*pt & pp* **-ied**) multiplicar(se).

multitude ['mʌltɪtjuːd] *n* multitud.

mum [mʌm] *n* GB *fam* mamá.

mumble ['mʌmbəl] *vt-vi* murmurar, musitar.

mummy[1] ['mʌmɪ] *n* (*pl* **-ies**) momia.

mummy[2] ['mʌmɪ] *n* (*pl* **-ies**) GB *fam* mamá.

mumps [mʌmps] *n* paperas.

munch [mʌntʃ] *vt-vi* mascar.

municipal [mjuː'nɪsɪpəl] *adj* municipal.

murder ['mɜːdə'] *n* asesinato, homicidio.
► *vt* asesinar.

murderer ['mɜːdərə'] *n* asesino,-a, homicida.

murky ['mɜːkɪ] *adj* (**-ier**, **-iest**). **1** oscuro,-a, tenebroso,-a *(lugar, noche)*. **2** turbio,-a *(asunto)*.

murmur ['mɜːmə'] *n* **1** murmullo *(de voz, río)*. **2** susurro *(de viento)*. **3** rumor *(de tráfico)*.
► *vt-vi* murmurar.
● **without a murmur** sin rechistar.

muscle ['mʌsəl] *n* músculo.
● **she didn't move a muscle** ni se inmutó.

muscular ['mʌskjʊlə'] *adj* **1** muscular *(tejido)*. **2** musculoso,-a *(persona)*.

muse[1] [mjuːz] *vi* meditar, reflexionar.

muse[2] [mjuːz] *n* musa.

museum [mjuː'zɪəm] *n* museo.

mushroom ['mʌʃrʊm] *n* seta, hongo, champiñón.

► *vi* crecer rápidamente.

music ['mjuːzɪk] *n* música.
● **to face the music** dar la cara.
■ **music hall** teatro de variedades.
■ **music score** partitura.
■ **music stand** atril.

musical ['mjuːzɪkəl] *adj* **1** musical. **2** dotado,-a para la música, aficionado,-a a la música.
► *n* musical.

musician [mjuː'zɪʃən] *n* músico,-a.

musk [mʌsk] *n* almizcle.

musketeer [mʌskə'tɪə'] *n* mosquetero.

Muslim ['mʌzlɪm] *adj-n* musulmán,-ana.

mussel ['mʌsəl] *n* mejillón.

must[1] [mʌst] *aux* **1** deber, tener que: *I must leave*, debo marcharme; *you must never do that again*, nunca vuelvas a hacer eso. **2** deber de: *she must be ill*, debe de estar enferma; *he must have got lost*, debe de haberse perdido. **3** tener que: *you must come round to dinner*, tienes que venir a cenar a casa.
► *n fam* cosa imprescindible: *a visit to the palace is a must*, una visita al palacio es imprescindible.

must[2] [mʌst] *n* mosto.

mustard ['mʌstəd] *n* mostaza.

musty ['mʌstɪ] *adj* (**-ier**, **-iest**). **1** rancio,-a *(comida)*. **2** que huele a cerrado *(habitación)*.

mute [mjuːt] *adj-n* mudo,-a.

muted ['mjuːtɪd] *adj* **1** apagado,-a, sordo,-a *(sonido)*. **2** apagado,-a, suave *(color)*.

mutilate ['mjuːtɪleɪt] *vt* mutilar.

mutineer [mjuːtɪ'nɪə'] *n* amotinado,-a.

mutiny ['mjuːtɪnɪ] *n* (*pl* **-ies**) motín.
► *vi* (*pt & pp* **-ied**) amotinarse.

mutter ['mʌtə'] *n* refunfuño.
► *vt* decir entre dientes, mascullar.
► *vi* refunfuñar.

mutton ['mʌtən] *n* carne de oveja.

mutual ['mjuːtʃʊəl] *adj* mutuo,-a, recíproco,-a.
● **by mutual consent** de común acuerdo.

mutually ['mjuːtʃʊəlɪ] *adv* mutuamente.

muzzle ['mʌzəl] *n* **1** hocico. **2** bozal. **3** boca *(de pistola)*.
► *vt* **1** poner bozal a. **2** *fig* amordazar.

MW ['miːdɪəmweɪv] *abbr* (**medium wave**) onda media, OM.

my [maɪ] *adj* mi, mis: *my book*, mi libro; *my friends*, mis amigos.

► *interj* ¡caramba!

myopia [maɪˈəʊpɪə] *n* miopía.

myself [maɪˈself] *pron* **1** me: *I cut myself,* me corté. **2** mí: *I kept it for myself,* lo guardé para mí.

• **by myself** yo mismo,-a, yo solo,-a: *I did it by myself,* lo hice yo mismo.

mysterious [mɪˈstɪərɪəs] *adj* misterioso,-a.

mystery [ˈmɪstərɪ] *n* (*pl* -**ies**) misterio.

mystic [ˈmɪstɪk] *adj-n* místico,-a.

mystify [ˈmɪstɪfaɪ] *vt* (*pt & pp* -**ied**) dejar perplejo,-a, desconcertar.

mystique [mɪsˈtiːk] *n* misterio.

myth [mɪθ] *n* mito.

mythology [mɪˈθɒlədʒɪ] *n* mitología.

N

N [nɔːθ] *abbr* (*north*) norte; *(abbreviation)* N.

nab [næb] *vt* (*pt & pp* **nabbed**, *ger* **nabbing**) *fam* pescar, pillar.

nag [næg] *vt* (*pt & pp* **nagged**, *ger* **nagging**) dar la tabarra a: *she's always nagging me to buy her a mink coat*, siempre me da la tabarra para que le compre un abrigo de visón.
▸ *vi* quejarse.

nail [neɪl] *n* **1** uña. **2** clavo.
▸ *vt* clavar, fijar con clavos.
■ **nail file** lima de uñas.
■ **nail varnish** esmalte de uñas.
■ **nail varnish remover** quitaesmaltes.

naive [naɪˈiːv] *adj* ingenuo,-a.

naked [ˈneɪkɪd] *adj* desnudo,-a: *stark naked*, en cueros.
● **with the naked eye** a simple vista.

name [neɪm] *n* **1** nombre. **2** apellido.
▸ *vt* **1** poner nombre a, llamar: *my name is Jim*, me llamo Jim; *they named their daughter Sue*, le pusieron Sue a su hija. **2** nombrar.
● **in sb's name** a nombre de ALGN.
● **in the name of** en nombre de.
● **what's your name?** ¿cómo te llamas?

nameless [ˈneɪmləs] *adj* **1** anónimo,-a. **2** sin nombre.

namely [ˈneɪmlɪ] *adv* a saber.

namesake [ˈneɪmseɪk] *n* tocayo,-a.

nanny [ˈnænɪ] *n* (*pl* **-ies**) niñera.

nap [næp] *n* siesta.
▸ *vi* (*pt & pp* **napped**, *ger* **napping**) dormir la siesta.
● **to catch napping** coger desprevenido,-a.
● **to have a nap, take a nap** echarse una siesta.

nape [neɪp] *n* nuca, cogote.

napkin [ˈnæpkɪn] *n* servilleta.

nappy [ˈnæpɪ] *n* (*pl* **-ies**) pañal.

narcotic [nɑːˈkɒtɪk] *adj* narcótico,-a.
▸ *n* narcótico.

narrate [nəˈreɪt] *vt* narrar.

narrative [ˈnærətɪv] *adj* narrativo,-a.
▸ *n* **1** narración. **2** narrativa.

narrow [ˈnærəʊ] *adj* (*comp* **narrower**, *superl* **narrowest**). **1** estrecho,-a, angosto, -a. **2** reducido,-a, restringido,-a, limitado,-a.
▸ *vt* estrechar.
▸ *vi* estrecharse.

to narrow down *vt* reducir.

narrowly [ˈnærəʊlɪ] *adv* por poco.

narrow-minded [nærəʊˈmaɪndɪd] *adj* estrecho,-a de miras.

NASA [ˈnæsə] *abbr* US (*National Aeronautics and Space Administration*) Administración Nacional de Aeronáutica y del Espacio; *(abbreviation)* NASA.

nasal [ˈneɪzəl] *adj* nasal.

nasty [ˈnɑːstɪ] *adj* (**-ier**, **-iest**). **1** desagradable, repugnante, asqueroso,-a. **2** malo,a, malintencionado,-a, cruel. **3** serio,a, feo,-a, grave: *he had a nasty fall*, tuvo una caída seria. **4** peliagudo,-a, difícil, complicado,-a.

nation [ˈneɪʃən] *n* nación.

national [ˈnæʃnəl] *adj* nacional.
▸ *n* súbdito,-a.
■ **national anthem** himno nacional.
■ **national service** servicio militar.
■ **National Health Service** Sanidad pública británica.
■ **National Insurance** Seguridad Social.

nationalism ['næʃnəlɪzəm] n nacionalismo.
nationalist ['næʃnəlɪst] adj-n nacionalista.
nationality [næʃə'nælɪti] n (pl -ies) nacionalidad.
nationalize [næʃnə'laɪz] vt nacionalizar.
nationwide [(adj) 'neɪʃənwaɪd(adv) neɪʃən'waɪd] adj a escala nacional.
▶ adv por todo el país.
native ['neɪtɪv] adj 1 natal. 2 originario,-a. 3 materno.
▶ n 1 natural, nativo,-a. 2 indígena.
Nativity [nə'tɪvɪti] n Natividad.
NATO ['neɪtəʊ] abbr (North Atlantic Treaty Organization) Organización del Tratado del Atlántico Norte; (abbreviation) OTAN.
También se escribe **Nato**.
natter ['nætə'] vi fam charlar.
natty ['næti] adj (-ier, -iest) elegante.
natural ['nætʃərəl] adj 1 natural. 2 nato, -a: he's a natural leader, es un líder nato. 3 normal: it's natural for a dog to bark, es normal que un perro ladre.
naturalist ['nætʃərəlɪst] n naturalista.
naturally ['nætʃərəli] adv 1 naturalmente, por supuesto: naturally you can think it over before you decide, por supuesto se lo puede pensar antes de decidirse. 2 con naturalidad: act naturally, actúa con naturalidad. 3 por naturaleza: he's naturally optimistic, es optimista por naturaleza.
nature ['neɪtʃə'] n 1 naturaleza. 2 carácter: he has a good nature, tiene buen carácter. 3 índole, naturaleza.
● **by nature** por naturaleza.
naturist ['neɪtʃərɪst] n naturista.
naught [nɔːt] n nada.
naughty ['nɔːti] adj (-ier, -iest). 1 travieso,-a. 2 atrevido,-a.
nausea ['nɔːzɪə] n náuseas fpl.
nauseating ['nɔːzɪeɪtɪŋ] adj nauseabundo,-a.
nautical ['nɔːtɪkəl] adj náutico,-a.
naval ['neɪvəl] adj naval.
nave [neɪv] n nave.
navel ['neɪvəl] n ombligo.
navigate ['nævɪgeɪt] vt 1 navegar por. 2 gobernar.
▶ vi guiar: I'll drive the car, you get the

map and navigate, conduzco yo, tú coge el mapa y guíanos.
navigation [nævɪ'geɪʃən] n navegación.
navigator ['nævɪgeɪtə'] n navegante.
navy ['neɪvi] n (pl -ies) marina de guerra, armada.
■ **navy blue** azul marino.
Nazi ['nɑːtsi] adj-n nazi.
NB ['en'biː] abbr (nota bene) fíjate bien; (abbreviation) N.B.
También se escribe **nb, N.B.** y **n.b.**
NBA ['en'biː'eɪ] abbr US (National Basketball Association) asociación nacional de baloncesto; (abbreviation) NBA.
NE [nɔː'θiːst] abbr (northeast) nordeste; (abbreviation) NE.
near [nɪə'] adj 1 cercano,-a: she went to the nearest house, fue a la casa más cercana. 2 próximo,-a: in the near future, en un futuro próximo. 3: it was near chaos, fue casi un caos.
▶ adv 1 cerca: do you live near?, ¿vives cerca? 2 a punto de: she was near to tears, estaba al borde de las lágrimas.
▶ prep cerca de: he's too near the fire, está demasiado cerca del fuego.
▶ vt acercarse a.
■ **Near East** Oriente Próximo.
nearby ['nɪəbaɪ] adj cercano,-a: we went to eat at a nearby restaurant, fuimos a comer a un restaurante cercano.
▶ adv cerca: is there a bank nearby?, ¿hay un banco cerca?
nearly ['nɪəli] adv casi: it's nearly three o'clock, son casi las tres; I nearly fell, por poco me caigo.
neat [niːt] adj 1 ordenado,-a: the room was neat and tidy, la habitación estaba limpia y ordenada. 2 pulcro,-a. 3 claro,-a: her handwriting is very neat, tiene una letra muy clara. 4 hábil. 5 solo,-a: he drank a bottle of neat whisky, se bebió una botella de whisky solo.
neatly ['niːtli] adv con cuidado, con pulcritud.
necessarily [nesə'serɪli] adv necesariamente.
necessary ['nesɪsəri] adj 1 necesario,-a. 2 inevitable.
necessitate [nɪ'sesɪteɪt] vt exigir.
necessity [nɪ'sesɪti] n (pl -ies). 1 necesidad. 2 requisito indispensable.
● **of necessity** por necesidad.

neck [nek] *n* cuello.
▶ *vi fam* besuquearse.
● **to be up to one's neck in STH** estar hasta el cuello de algo.
necklace ['nekləs] *n* collar.
neckline ['neklaɪn] *n* escote.
nectar ['nektəʳ] *n* néctar.
née [neɪ] *adj* de soltera.
need [niːd] *n* necesidad: *there's no need to shout*, no hace falta que grites; *we must not forget the needs of others*, no debemos olvidar las necesidades de los demás.
▶ *vt* **1** necesitar: *do you need any money?*, ¿necesitas dinero?; *you don't need a new car*, no necesitas un coche nuevo. **2** tener que: *you don't need to come tomorrow*, no hace falta que vengas mañana; *I need to talk to you*, tengo que hablar contigo.
▶ *aux* tener que: *you needn't do it if you don't want to*, no tienes que hacerlo si no quieres; *Need I go?*, ¿tengo que ir?
● **in need** necesitado: *people in need*, la gente necesitada.
● **to be in need of** necesitar: *children are in need of love*, los niños necesitan amor.

Cuando **need** se usa como verbo principal, siempre va seguido de infinitivo con **to**, pero cuando es un verbo modal no le sigue la preposición y requiere el auxiliar **do** en las oraciones interrogativas y negativas. **Needn't have** seguido del participio pasado se usa para cuando algo se hizo sin que hubiese ninguna necesidad de hacerlo: *you needn't have bought any cheese; there's plenty in the fridge*, no hacía falta que compraras queso; hay mucho en la nevera.

---

needful ['niːdful] *adj* necesario,-a.
needle ['niːdəl] *n* aguja.
▶ *vt fam* pinchar.
needless ['niːdləs] *adj* innecesario,-a.
● **needless to say** huelga decir.
needy ['niːdɪ] *adj* (**-ier, -iest**) necesitado,-a.
negation [nɪ'geɪʃən] *n* negación.
negative ['negətɪv] *adj* negativo,-a: *his answer was negative*, su respuesta fue negativa.
▶ *n* **1** negación. **2** negativa. **3** negativo *(de foto)*.

neglect [nɪ'glekt] *n* descuido, negligencia.
▶ *vt* descuidar, desatender.
neglectful [nɪ'glektful] *adj* negligente, descuidado,-a.
negligée ['neglɪdʒeɪ] *n* salto de cama.
negligence ['neglɪdʒəns] *n* negligencia.
negligent ['neglɪdʒənt] *adj* negligente.
negligible ['neglɪdʒɪbəl] *adj* insignificante.
negotiate [nɪ'gəʊʃɪeɪt] *vt-vi* negociar.
▶ *vt* salvar *(obstáculo)*.
negotiation [nɪgəʊʃɪ'eɪʃən] *n* negociación.
negro ['niːgrəʊ] *adj-n* negro,-a.
neigh [neɪ] *n* relincho.
▶ *vi* relinchar.
neighbour ['neɪbəʳ] (US **neighbor**) *n* vecino,-a.
neighbourhood ['neɪbəhʊd] (US **neighborhood**) *n* **1** barrio. **2** zona.
● **in the neighbourhood of** cerca de.
neighbouring ['neɪbərɪŋ] (US **neighboring**) *adj* vecino,-a.
neighbourly ['neɪbəlɪ] (US **neighborly**) *adj* amable.
neither ['naɪðəʳ, 'niːðəʳ] *adj-pron* ninguno de los dos, ninguna de las dos: *neither of us*, ninguno de los dos; *neither car is his*, ninguno de los coches es suyo.
▶ *adv-conj* **1** ni: *it's neither good nor bad*, no es ni bueno ni malo. **2** tampoco: *I can't swim- Neither can I*, No sé nadar- Yo tampoco.
● **neither ... nor...** ni ... ni ....
neolithic [niːə'lɪθɪk] *adj* neolítico,-a.
neon ['niːən] *n* neón.
Nepal [nə'pɔːl] *n* Nepal.
Nepalese [nepə'liːz] *adj* nepalés,-esa, nepalí.
▶ *n* **1** nepalés,-esa, nepalí *(persona)*. **2** nepalés, nepalí *(lengua)*.
▶ *npl* **the Nepalese** los nepaleses, los nepalíes.
nephew ['nevjuː] *n* sobrino: *he has two nephews and three nieces*, tiene dos sobrinos y tres sobrinas.
nerve [nɜːv] *n* **1** nervio: *he's a bundle of nerves*, es un manojo de nervios. **2** valor: *it takes some nerve to do something like that*, hay que tener valor para hacer algo así. **3** descaro: *you've got a nerve!*, ¡qué cara tienes!
● **nerves** nervios, nerviosismo.
● **to get on SB's nerves** poner nervioso,-a a ALGN.

nervous ['nɜːvəs] *adj* nervioso,-a: *he was nervous about the exam*, estaba nervioso por el examen.
■ **nervous breakdown** depresión nerviosa.

nervousness ['nɜːvəsnəs] *n* **1** nerviosismo, nerviosidad. **2** miedo.

nest [nest] *n* nido.
▶ *vi* anidar.

nestle ['nesəl] *vi* acomodarse.

net[1] [net] *n* **1** red. **2 the Net** la Red.
▶ *vt (pt & pp* **netted***, ger* **netting)** coger con red.
■ **Net user** internauta.

net[2] [net] *adj* neto,-a.
▶ *vt (pt & pp* **netted***, ger* **netting)** ganar neto,-a.

netball ['netbɔːl] *n* especie debaloncesto femenino.

Netherlands ['neðələndʒ] *n* **the Netherlands** los Países Bajos.

netting ['netɪŋ] *n* malla.

nettle ['netəl] *n* ortiga.
▶ *vt* irritar.

network ['netwɜːk] *n* red: *a new road network*, una nueva red de carreteras.

neurotic [njʊˈrɒtɪk] *adj-n* neurótico,-a.

neuter ['njuːtəʳ] *adj* neutro,-a.
▶ *n* neutro.

neutral ['njuːtrəl] *adj* **1** neutro,-a. **2** POL neutral.
▶ *n* punto muerto *(marchas)*.

neutralize ['njuːtrəlaɪz] *vt* neutralizar.

never ['nevəʳ] *adv* nunca, jamás: *I'll never forget you*, nunca te olvidaré.

never-ending [nevəˈrendɪŋ] *adj* interminable.

nevertheless [nevəðəˈles] *adv* sin embargo.

new [njuː] *adj* nuevo,-a.
● **as good as new** como nuevo.
● **new to STH** nuevo en algo: *I'm still new to this company*, aún soy nuevo en esta empresa.
■ **New Year** Año Nuevo.
■ **New Year's Eve** Nochevieja.

newborn ['njuːbɔːn] *adj* recién nacido,-a.

newcomer ['njuːkʌməʳ] *n* recién llegado,-a.

newly ['njuːlɪ] *adv* recién, recientemente.

newlywed ['njuːlɪwed] *n* recién casado,-a.

news [njuːz] *n* noticias.
● **to break the news to SB** dar la noticia a ALGN.
■ **a piece of news** una noticia.

■ **news bulletin** boletín informativo.

Es incontable y el verbo va en singular: *if the news is bad, I don't want to hear it*, si las noticias son malas, no quiero oírlas.

newsagent ['njuːzeɪdʒənt] *n* vendedor, -ra de periódicos.
■ **newsagent's** quiosco de periódicos.

newsflash ['njuːzflæʃ] *n (pl* -**es)** noticia de última hora.

newsgroup ['njuːzgruːp] *n* grupo de noticias.

newsletter ['njuːzletəʳ] *n* hoja informativa.

newspaper ['njuːspeɪpəʳ] *n* diario, periódico.

newsreader ['njuːzriːdəʳ] *n* presentador,-ra del informativo.

newsworthy ['njuːzwɜːðɪ] *adj* de interés periodístico.

newt [njuːt] *n* tritón.

next [nekst] *adj* **1** próximo,-a, siguiente: *I'll tell him next time I see him*, se lo diré la próxima vez que lo vea. **2** próximo,-a: *next year*, el año que viene. **3** de al lado: *he lives next door*, vive en la casa de al lado.
▶ *adv* luego, después, a continuación: *what did you say next?*, ¿qué dijiste luego?
● **next door** de al lado: *our next door neighbours*, nuestros vecinos de al lado.
● **next to** al lado de: *the post office is next to the bank*, la oficina de correos está al lado del banco.
● **next to nothing** casi nada.
● **next to useless** casi inútil.
■ **next of kin** pariente(s) más cercano(s).

NGO ['endʒiːˈəʊ] *abbr (Non-Governmental Organization)* Organización no gubernamental; *(abbreviation)* ONG.

NHS ['enˈeɪtʃes] *abbr* GB *(National Health Service)* sanidad pública británica.

nib [nɪb] *n* plumilla.

nibble ['nɪbəl] *n* **1** mordisco. **2** bocadito.
▶ *vt-vi* mordisquear.

Nicaragua [nɪkəˈrægjʊə] *n* Nicaragua.

Nicaraguan [nɪkəˈrægjʊən] *adj-n* nicaragüense.

nice [naɪs] *adj* **1** amable, simpático,-a, majo,-a: *what a nice man!*, ¿qué hombre más simpático! **2** bueno,-a, agradable: *it's a really nice day*, hace un día muy bueno. **3** bonito,-a, mono,-a, guapo,-a: *that's a nice dress!*, ¡qué vestido más bonito!

nicely ['naɪslɪ] *adv* **1** bien: *the geraniums are growing nicely*, los geranios están creciendo bien. **2** amablemente: *if you ask nicely she'll say yes*, si se lo pides amablemente, dirá que sí.

niche [niːʃ] *n* nicho, hornacina.

nick [nɪk] *n* **1** mella, muesca. **2** GB *sl* chirona.

▶ *vt* **1** mellar. **2** *fam* birlar, mangar. **3** *fam* pillar, trincar: *he got nicked*, lo trincaron.
● **in good nick** en buenas condiciones.
● **in the nick of time** justo a tiempo.

nickel ['nɪkəl] *n* **1** níquel. **2** US moneda de cinco centavos.

nickname ['nɪkneɪm] *n* apodo.
▶ *vt* apodar.

niece [niːs] *n* sobrina: *I have two nephews and one niece*, tengo dos sobrinos y una sobrina.

niggle ['nɪgəl] *n* **1** duda. **2** preocupación.
▶ *vi* preocupar.

night [naɪt] *n* noche.
● **at night, by night** de noche.
● **good night** buenas noches *(despedida)*.
● **last night** anoche.

nightclub ['naɪtklʌb] *n* discoteca.

nightdress ['naɪtdres] *n (pl -es)* camisón.

nightgown ['naɪtgaʊn] *n* camisón.

nightingale ['naɪtɪŋgeɪl] *n* ruiseñor.

nightlife ['naɪtlaɪf] *n* vida nocturna.

nightly ['naɪtlɪ] *adv* cada noche.

nightmare ['naɪtmeəˈ] *n* pesadilla.

nil [nɪl] *n* nada, cero: *we lost two goals to nil*, perdimos dos goles a cero.

Nile [naɪl] *n* **the Nile** el Nilo.

nimble ['nɪmbəl] *adj* ágil.

nine [naɪn] *num* nueve.

ninepins ['naɪnpɪnz] *n juego de bolos.*

nineteen [naɪn'tiːn] *num* diecinueve.

nineteenth [naɪn'tiːnθ] *adj* decimonoveno,-a, decimonono,-a.
▶ *n* **1** decimonoveno. **2** decimonovena parte. **3** diecinueve *(en fecha)*.

ninetieth ['naɪntɪəθ] *adj* nonagésimo,-a.
▶ *n* nonagésimo, nonagésima parte.

ninety ['naɪntɪ] *num* noventa.

ninth [naɪnθ] *adj* noveno,-a, nono,-a.
▶ *n* **1** noveno. **2** novena parte. **3** nueve *(en fecha)*.

nip [nɪp] *n* **1** pellizco. **2** mordisco. **3** trago.
▶ *vt-vi (pt & pp* **nipped***, ger* **nipping**). **1** pellizcar. **2** mordisquear.
▶ *vi* ir *(en un momento)*.
● **to nip in the bud** cortar de raíz.

nipper ['nɪpəˈ] *n fam* chaval,-la.

nipple ['nɪpəl] *n* **1** pezón. **2** tetilla. **3** boquilla.

nippy ['nɪpɪ] *adj (*-**ier***,* -**iest***)*. **1** *fam* rápido,-a. **2** *fam* fresquito,-a: *it's a bit nippy this morning*, hace fresquito esta mañana.

nit [nɪt] *n* **1** liendre. **2** *fam* imbécil.

nite [naɪt] *n* US → night.

nitrogen ['naɪtrədʒən] *n* nitrógeno.

No ['nʌmbəˈ] *abbr (**number**)* número; *(abbreviation)* n°, núm.

no [nəʊ] *adv* no: *Is it raining? No, it's snowing*, ¿Llueve? No, nieva.
▶ *adj* **1** ninguno,-a, ningún: *I have no time*, no tengo tiempo; *there are no children in the classroom*, no hay ningún niño en la clase. **2** no: *he's no friend of mine*, no es amigo mío.
● **no smoking** prohibido fumar.

nobility [nəʊ'bɪlɪtɪ] *n* nobleza.

noble ['nəʊbəl] *adj (comp* **nobler***, superl* **noblest***)* noble.
▶ *n* noble.

nobleman ['nəʊbəlmən] *n (pl* **noblemen***)* noble.

nobody ['nəʊbədɪ] *pron* nadie: *there is nobody in the park*, no hay nadie en el parque.
▶ *n (pl* -**ies***)* don nadie: *he's a nobody*, es un don nadie.

nocturnal [nɒk'tɜːnəl] *adj* nocturno,-a.

nod [nɒd] *n* **1** saludo *(con la cabeza)*. **2** señal de asentimiento.
▶ *vi (pt & pp* **nodded***, ger* **nodding***)*. **1** saludar *(con la cabeza)*. **2** asentir *(con la cabeza)*: *he didn't speak, he just nodded*, no dijo nada, sólo asintió con la cabeza.

to nod off *vi* dormirse.

nohow ['nəʊhaʊ] *adv* de ninguna manera.

noise [nɔɪz] *n* ruido, sonido.
● **to make a noise** armar ruido.

noiseless ['nɔɪzləs] *adj* silencioso,-a.

noisy ['nɔɪzɪ] *adj (*-**ier***,* -**iest***)* ruidoso,-a.

nomad ['nəʊmæd] *adj-n* nómada.

nominal ['nɒmɪnəl] *adj* **1** nominal. **2** simbólico,-a *(precio)*.

nominate ['nɒmɪneɪt] *vt* **1** nombrar. **2** proponer.

nomination [nɒmɪ'neɪʃən] *n* **1** nombramiento. **2** propuesta.

nonchalant ['nɒnʃələnt] *adj* **1** despreocupado. **2** impasible.

noncommittal [nɒnkə'mɪtəl] *adj* no comprometedor,-ra, evasivo.

nonconformist [nɒnkən'fɔːmɪst] *adj-n* inconformista.

nondescript ['nɒndɪskrɪpt] *adj* **1** anodino,-a, insulso,-a. **2** indefinido,-a.

none [nʌn] *pron* **1** ninguno,-a: *none of those answers are correct*, ninguna de estas respuestas es correcta. **2** nadie: *none could afford it*, nadie podía pagarlo. **3** nada: *I wanted some butter, but there was none left*, quería mantequilla, pero ya no quedaba nada; *none of this is mine*, nada de esto es mío.
► *adv*: *he is none the wiser*, no ha entendido nada; *none too soon*, justo a tiempo, en buena hora.

nonentity [nɒ'nentɪtɪ] *n* (*pl* **-ies**) nulidad.

nonetheless [nʌnðə'les] *adv* no obstante.

nonexistent [nɒnɪg'zɪstənt] *adj* inexistente.

nonplussed [nɒn'plʌst] *adj* perplejo,-a.

nonsense ['nɒnsəns] *n* tonterías.

> Es incontable, no tiene plural: *don't talk nonsense!*, ¡no digas tonterías!

nonsmoker [nɒn'sməʊkəʳ] *n* no fumador,-ra.

nonstick [nɒn'stɪk] *adj* antiadherente.

nonstop [nɒn'stɒp] *adj* directo,-a: *a nonstop flight*, un vuelo directo.
► *adv* sin parar: *he worked nonstop to finish on time*, trabajó sin parar para acabar a tiempo.

noodle ['nuːdəl] *n* fideo.

nook [nʊk] *n* rincón.

noon [nuːn] *n* mediodía.

no-one ['nəʊwʌn] *pron* nadie.

noose [nuːs] *n* **1** lazo. **2** soga.

nor [nɔːʳ] *conj* **1** ni: *neither you nor I*, ni tú ni yo. **2** tampoco: *nor do I*, yo tampoco.

norm [nɔːm] *n* norma.

normal ['nɔːməl] *adj* normal.

normality [nɔː'mælɪtɪ] *n* normalidad.

normally ['nɔːməlɪ] *adv* normalmente.

north [nɔːθ] *n* norte: *Oviedo is in the north of Spain*, Oviedo está en el norte de España.
► *adj* del norte: *north winds*, vientos del norte.
► *adv* al norte: *we travelled north*, viajamos hacia el norte.
■ **North Pole** Polo Norte.
■ **North Sea** Mar del norte.

northeast [nɔːθ'iːst] *n* nordeste, noreste.
► *adj* del nordeste, del noreste.
► *adv* al nordeste, hacia el nordeste.

northerly ['nɔːðəlɪ] *adj* del norte, septentrional.

northern ['nɔːðən] *adj* del norte, septentrional.

northerner ['nɔːðənəʳ] *n* norteño,-a.

northwest [nɔːθ'west] *n* noroeste.
► *adj* del noroeste.
► *adv* al noroeste, hacia el noroeste.

Norway ['nɔːweɪ] *n* Noruega.

Norwegian [nɔː'wiːdʒən] *adj* noruego,-a.
► *n* **1** noruego,-a (*persona*). **2** noruego (*lengua*).

nose [nəʊz] *n* **1** nariz,. **2** hocico, morro. **3** olfato.
● **to nose about** curiosear.
● **to keep one's nose out of** STH no meter las narices en algo.
● **under** SB's **nose** delante de las narices de alguien.

nosebleed ['nəʊzbliːd] *n* hemorragia nasal.

nosey ['nəʊzɪ] *adj* (**-ier**, **-iest**) *fam* curioso,-a, entrometido,-a.

nosey-parker [nəʊzɪ'pɑːkəʳ] *n* *fam* entrometido,-a, metomentodo.

nosh [nɒʃ] *n* *sl* papeo.

nostalgia [nɒ'stældʒɪə] *n* nostalgia.

nostril ['nɒstrɪl] *n* fosa nasal.

not [nɒt] *adv* no: *this is not the first time*, no es la primera vez; *can you play bridge? I'm afraid not*, ¿sabes jugar al bridge? Me temo que no; *not always*, no siempre.
● **thanks, —not at all** gracias, —de nada.

> **Not** acompaña al auxiliar del verbo en las oraciones negativas. En el inglés hablado y en los textos escritos informales se suele contraer a **-n't**: *she isn't English*; *he doesn't like it*. También se usa para la forma negativa de los verbos subordinados: *he told me not to go*, me dijo que no fuera.

notable ['nəʊtəbəl] *adj* notable.

notation [nəʊ'teɪʃən] *n* notación.

notch [nɒtʃ] *n* (*pl* -es) muesca.

▶ *vt* hacer muescas en.

note [nəʊt] *vt* 1 notar, observar. 2 apuntar, anotar.

▶ *n* 1 nota. 2 billete.

▶ *npl* **notes** apuntes.

● **of note** de importancia.

● **to note down** apuntar, tomar nota: *I noted the number down in my book*, apunté el número en mi libro.

● **to take note of** tomar nota de.

notebook ['nəʊtbʊk] *n* 1 libreta, cuaderno. 2 ordenador *m* portátil.

noted ['nəʊtɪd] *adj* conocido,-a, célebre.

notepaper ['nəʊtpeɪpə'] *n* papel de cartas.

noteworthy ['nəʊtwɜːðɪ] *adj* digno,-a de mención.

nothing ['nʌθɪŋ] *pron* nada: *I have nothing to say*, no tengo nada que decir.

● **for nothing 1** gratis, gratuitamente. **2** en vano, en balde: *he worked for nothing*, trabajaba sin cobrar; *all this effort for nothing*, todo este esfuerzo para nada.

● **if nothing else** al menos.

● **nothing but** tan sólo.

notice ['nəʊtɪs] *n* 1 letrero: *the notice says "No smoking"*, en el letrero pone "Prohibido fumar". 2 anuncio: *I never look at the notices on the board*, nunca miro los anuncios en el tablón. 3 atención. 4 aviso: *there's a notice in the newspaper about forest fires*, hay un aviso en el periódico sobre los incendios forestales.

▶ *vt* notar, fijarse en, darse cuenta de: *did you notice his tie?*, ¿te fijaste en su corbata?

● **to take no notice of** no hacer caso de.

● **until further notice** hasta nuevo aviso.

noticeable ['nəʊtɪsəbəl] *adj* que se nota, evidente.

noticeboard ['nəʊtɪsbɔːd] *n* tablón de anuncios.

notify ['nəʊtɪfaɪ] *vt* (*pt & pp* -ied) notificar, avisar.

notion ['nəʊʃən] *n* noción, idea, concepto.

▶ *npl* **notions** US artículos de mercería.

notorious [nəʊ'tɔːrɪəs] *adj pej* célebre.

notwithstanding [nɒtwɪθ'stændɪŋ] *adv* no obstante.

▶ *prep* a pesar de.

nougat ['nuːgaː] *n* turrón blando.

nought [nɔːt] *n* cero: *nought point six six*, cero coma sesenta y seis.

noun [naʊn] *n* nombre, sustantivo.

nourish ['nʌrɪʃ] *vt* nutrir, alimentar.

nourishing ['nʌrɪʃɪŋ] *adj* nutritivo,-a.

nourishment ['nʌrɪʃmənt] *n* nutrición.

Nov ['nəʊvembə'] *abbr* (*November*) noviembre.

novel ['nɒvəl] *adj* original.

▶ *n* novela.

novelist ['nɒvəlɪst] *n* novelista.

novelty ['nɒvəltɪ] *n* (*pl* -ies) novedad.

November [nəʊ'vembə'] *n* noviembre.

novice ['nɒvɪs] *n* 1 novato,-a. 2 novicio,-a.

now [naʊ] *adv* 1 ahora. 2 hoy en día, actualmente. 3 ya: *I can't wait, I want it now*, no puedo esperar, ¡lo quiero ya!

● **from now on** de ahora en adelante.

● **now and then** de vez en cuando.

● **now that** ahora que.

nowadays ['naʊədeɪz] *adv* hoy día, hoy en día.

nowhere ['nəʊweə'] *adv* ninguna parte: *where are you going? Nowhere*, ¿adónde vas? A ninguna parte; *he had nowhere to hide*, no tenía ningún sitio donde esconderse.

● **nowhere else** en ninguna otra parte.

noxious ['nɒkʃəs] *adj* nocivo,-a.

nozzle ['nɒzəl] *n* boquilla.

NT ['næʃənəl'trʌst] *abbr* GB (*National Trust*) organización que vela por el patrimonio nacional, tanto natural como arquitectónico.

nuance [njuː'ɑːns] *n* matiz.

nuclear ['njuːklɪə'] *adj* nuclear.

■ **nuclear bomb** bomba nuclear.

■ **nuclear energy** energía nuclear.

nucleus ['njuːklɪəs] *n* (*pl* **nuclei**) núcleo.

nude [njuːd] *adj* desnudo,-a.

▶ *n* desnudo.

nudge [nʌdʒ] *n* codazo.

▶ *vt* dar un codazo a.

nudist ['njuːdɪst] *adj-n* nudista.

nudity ['njuːdɪtɪ] *n* desnudez.

nugget ['nʌgɪt] *n* pepita.

nuisance ['njuːsəns] *n* 1 molestia, fastidio, lata: *the train is late. What a nuisance!*, el tren llega tarde. ¡Qué fastidio!

2 pesado,-a: *he's a real nuisance*, es muy pesado.

null [nʌl] *adj* nulo,-a.

numb [nʌm] *adj* entumecido,-a.

▶ *vt* entumecer.

number ['nʌmbə'] *n* número.

▶ *vt* **1** numerar: *the seats are numbered*, los asientos están numerados. **2** contar: *his days are numbered*, tiene los días contados.

● **large numbers** muchos: *large numbers of people demonstrated in the street*, muchas personas se manifestaron en la calle.

● **a number of** varios: *a number of people asked where I had bought my hat*, varias personas me preguntaron dónde me había comprado el sombrero.

numberplate ['nʌmbəpleɪt] *n* GB placa de la matrícula.

numbness ['nʌmnəs] *n* entumecimiento.

numeral ['njuːmərəl] *n* número, cifra.

numerate ['njuːmərət] *adj* que tiene conocimientos de matemáticas.

numerical [njuːmerɪkəl] *adj* numérico,-a.

numerous ['njuːmərəs] *adj* numeroso,-a.

nun [nʌn] *n* monja, religiosa.

nunnery ['nʌnərɪ] *n* (*pl* -**ies**) convento (*de monjas*).

nuptial ['nʌpʃəl] *adj* nupcial.

nurse [nɜːs] *n* **1** enfermero,-a. **2** niñera.

▶ *vt* **1** cuidar: *she nursed him back to health*, lo estuvo cuidando hasta que se recuperó. **2** amamantar. **3** guardar: *to nurse a grudge against SB*, guardar rencor a ALGN.

nursery ['nɜːsrɪ] *n* (*pl* -**ies**). **1** cuarto de los niños. **2** guardería, parvulario. **3** vivero.

■ **nursery school** parvulario.

nursing ['nɜːsɪŋ] *n* enfermería.

■ **nursing home 1** hogar de ancianos. **2** clínica de maternidad.

nurture ['nɜːtʃə'] *vt* criar.

nut [nʌt] *n* **1** fruto seco. **2** tuerca. **3** *fam* forofo,-a, fanático,-a. **4** *fam* chalado,-a.

nutcase ['nʌtkeɪs] *n fam* chalado,-a.

nutcracker ['nʌtkrækə'] *n* cascanueces.

nutmeg ['nʌtmeg] *n* nuez moscada.

nutrient ['njuːtrɪənt] *n* sustancia nutritiva, nutriente.

nutrition [njuːtrɪʃən] *n* nutrición.

nutritious [njuːtrɪʃəs] *adj* nutritivo,-a.

nutshell ['nʌtʃel] *n* cáscara.

● **in a nutshell** en pocas palabras.

nutter ['nʌtə'] *n fam* chalado,-a.

nuzzle ['nʌzəl] *vt* rozar con el hocico.

● **to nuzzle up against** acurrucarse contra.

NW [nɔːθ'west] *abbr* (*northwest*) noroeste; (*abbreviation*) NO.

nylon ['naɪlɒn] *n* nilón, nailon.

▶ *npl* **nylons** medias de nilón.

nymph [nɪmf] *n* ninfa.

nymphomaniac [nɪmfə'meɪnɪæk] *n* ninfómana.

O

O [əʊ] *n* **1** o. **2** cero.

oaf [əʊf] *n* (*pl* **oafs**) palurdo,-a, zoquete.

oak [əʊk] *n* roble.

OAP ['əʊ'eɪ'piː] *abbr* GB (*old-age pensioner*) pensionista.

oar [ɔː'] *n* remo.

oarsman ['ɔːzmən] *n* (*pl* **oarsmen**) remero.

oasis [əʊ'eɪsɪs] *n* (*pl* **oases**) oasis.

oath [əʊθ] *n* **1** juramento. **2** palabrota.
● **on oath, under oath** bajo juramento.

oats [əʊts] *npl* avena.

obedience [ə'biːdɪəns] *n* obediencia.

obedient [ə'biːdɪənt] *adj* obediente.

obelisk ['ɒbɪlɪsk] *n* obelisco.

obese [əʊ'biːs] *adj* obeso,-a.

obesity [əʊ'biːsɪtɪ] *n* obesidad.

obey [ə'beɪ] *vt* obedecer.

obituary [ə'bɪtjʊərɪ] *n* (*pl* -**ies**) necrología, obituario.

object [(*n*) 'ɒbdʒɪkt(*vb*) əb'dʒekt] *n* **1** objeto. **2** objetivo, propósito. **3** complemento, objeto.
▶ *vt* objetar.
▶ *vi* oponerse.
● **money is no object** el dinero no importa.

objection [əb'dʒekʃən] *n* objeción, reparo.
● **to have no objection** no tener ninguna objeción.

objectionable [əb'dʒekʃənəbəl] *adj* desagradable.

objective [əb'dʒektɪv] *adj* objetivo,-a.
▶ *n* objetivo.

objector [əb'dʒektə'] *n* objetor,-ra.

obligation [ɒblɪ'geɪʃən] *n* obligación.

obligatory [ɒ'blɪgətərɪ] *adj* obligatorio,-a.

oblige [ə'blaɪdʒ] *vt* **1** obligar. **2** hacer un favor a, complacer.
● **much obliged** muy agradecido,-a.

obliging [ə'blaɪdʒɪŋ] *adj* complaciente, atento.

obliterate [ə'blɪtəreɪt] *vt* borrar.

oblivion [ə'blɪvɪən] *n* olvido.

oblivious [ə'blɪvɪəs] *adj* inconsciente: **he was oblivious of the danger**, no era consciente del peligro.

oblong ['ɒblɒŋ] *adj* oblongo,-a, alargado.
▶ *n* rectángulo.

obnoxious [əb'nɒkʃəs] *adj* repugnante.

oboe ['əʊbəʊ] *n* oboe.

obscene [ɒb'siːn] *adj* obsceno,-a.

obscenity [əb'senɪtɪ] *n* (*pl* -**ies**) obscenidad.

obscure [əbs'kjʊə'] *adj* **1** oscuro,-a. **2** poco conocido,-a.
▶ *vt* oscurecer, esconder.

obscurity [əb'skjʊərɪtɪ] *n* oscuridad.

observant [əb'zɜːvənt] *adj* observador,-ra.

observation [ɒbzə'veɪʃən] *n* **1** observación: **the patient is still in observation**, el paciente sigue en observación. **2** vigilancia: **the suspect is under police observation**, el sospechoso está bajo vigilancia policial. **3** comentario: **could I make an observation?**, ¿puedo hacer un comentario?

observatory [əb'zɜːvətrɪ] *n* (*pl* -**ies**) observatorio.

observe [əb'zɜːv] *vt* **1** observar. **2** cumplir (*la ley*).

observer [əb'zɜːvə'] *n* observador,-ra.

obsess [əb'ses] *vt* obsesionar.

obsession [əb'seʃən] *n* obsesión.

obsolete ['ɒbsəliːt] *adj* obsoleto,-a.

obstacle ['ɒbstəkəl] *n* obstáculo.

■ **obstacle race** carrera de obstáculos.

obstetrics [ɒb'stetrɪks] *n* obstetricia.

Es incontable y el verbo va en singular.

obstinacy ['ɒbstɪnəsɪ] *n* obstinación.

obstinate ['ɒbstɪnət] *adj* obstinado,-a, testarudo,-a, terco,-a.

obstruct [əb'strʌkt] *vt* **1** obstruir, bloquear. **2** obstaculizar, entorpecer.

obstruction [əb'strʌkʃən] *n* **1** obstrucción. **2** obstáculo.

obtain [əb'teɪn] *vt* obtener, conseguir.

obtrusive [əb'truːsɪv] *adj* molesto,-a.

obtuse [əb'tjuːs] *adj* obtuso,-a.

obvious ['ɒbvɪəs] *adj* obvio,-a, evidente.

obviously ['ɒbvɪəslɪ] *adv* obviamente, evidentemente.

occasion [ə'keɪʒən] *n* **1** vez, ocasión. **2** acontecimiento.

▶ *vt* ocasionar.

● **on one occasion** una vez, en una ocasión.

● **on the occasion of** con motivo de.

occasional [ə'keɪʒənəl] *adj* esporádico,-a: *he smokes the occasional cigarette*, de vez en cuando fuma un cigarrillo.

occasionally [ə'keɪʒənəlɪ] *adv* de vez en cuando, ocasionalmente.

occult ['ɒkʌlt] *adj* oculto,-a.

● **the occult** las ciencias ocultas.

occupant ['ɒkjʊpənt] *n* **1** ocupante *(de silla, vehículo)*. **2** inquilino,-a.

occupation [ɒkjʊ'peɪʃən] *n* **1** ocupación, empleo. **2** pasatiempo.

occupier ['ɒkjʊpaɪə'] *n* → occupant.

occupy ['ɒkjʊpaɪ] *vt* (*pt & pp* -**ied**) ocupar.

● **to occupy oneself (in doing STH)** entretenerse (haciendo algo).

occur [ə'kɜː'] *vi* (*pt & pp* **occurred**). **1** ocurrir, suceder. **2** ocurrirse: *nothing occurs to me*, no se me ocurre nada.

occurrence [ə'kʌrəns] *n* hecho, suceso: *a common occurrence*, un caso frecuente.

ocean ['əʊʃən] *n* océano.

Oceania [əʊʃɪ'ɑːnɪə] *n* Oceanía.

oceanic [əʊʃɪ'ænɪk] *adj* oceánico,-a.

ochre ['əʊkə'] (US **ocher**) *adj* ocre.

▶ *n* ocre.

o'clock [ə'klɒk] *adv*: *it's one o'clock*, es la una; *it's two o'clock*, son las dos.

octave ['ɒktɪv] *n* octava.

October [ɒk'təʊbə'] *n* octubre.

octopus ['ɒktəpəs] *n* (*pl* **octopuses**) pulpo.

odd [ɒd] *adj* **1** extraño,-a, raro,-a. **2** impar. **3**: *thirty odd*, treinta y pico, treinta y tantos. **4** suelto,-a. **5** desparejado,-a *(fascículo, calcetín)*. **6** ocasional, esporádico,-a: *he has the odd cigar*, fuma un puro de vez en cuando.

● **the odd one out** el que es distinto, la excepción.

oddity ['ɒdɪtɪ] *n* (*pl* -**ies**) rareza.

odds [ɒdz] *npl* probabilidades: *the odds are that …*, lo más probable es que …

● **it makes no odds** lo mismo da.

● **to be at odds with SB** estar reñido,-a con ALGN.

● **to fight against the odds** luchar contra las fuerzas superiores.

● **to succeed against the odds** triunfar a pesar de las dificultades.

■ **odds and ends** cositas, cosas sueltas.

odontology [ɒdɒn'tɒlədʒɪ] *n* odontología.

odour ['əʊdə'] (US **odor**) *n* olor.

oesophagus [iː'sɒfəgəs] (US **esophagus**) *n* (*pl* **oesophagi**) esófago.

of [ɒv, unstressed əv] *prep* de: *the wings of a plane*, las alas de un avión; *a friend of Pauline's*, una amiga de Pauline; *there are four of us*, somos cuatro.

off [ɒf] *prep* **1** de: *it fell off the wall*, se cayó de la pared. **2**: *I'm off coffee*, he perdido el gusto por el café. **3** cerca de: *off the coast*, cerca de la costa. **4**: *there's a button off your coat*, a tu abrigo le falta un botón. **5**: *there's 15% off the price*, hay un descuento del 15%.

▶ *adv* **1**: *he ran off*, se fue corriendo. **2**: *two days off*, dos días libres.

▶ *adj* **1** ausente, de baja. **2** apagado,-a *(aparato)*. **3** suspendido,-a *(partido)*. **4** malo,-a, pasado,-a, agrio,-a.

● **to be off work** estar de baja.

● **to be off one's food** estar desganado.

off-colour ['ɒfkʌlə'] (US **off-color**) *adj* indispuesto,-a.

offence [ə'fens] *n* **1** ofensa. **2** infracción, delito.

● **to take offence** ofenderse.

offend [ə'fend] *vt* ofender.

offender [ə'fendə'] *n* delincuente.

offensive [ə'fensɪv] *adj* ofensivo,-a.

▶ *n* ofensiva.

offer ['ɒfə'] *n* oferta.

► *vt* ofrecer.

● **on offer** de oferta.

● **to offer to ...** ofrecerse para ...

offering ['ɒfərɪŋ] *n* **1** ofrecimiento. **2** ofrenda.

offhand [ɒf'hænd] *adv* de improviso.

► *adj* descortés, brusco,-a.

office ['ɒfɪs] *n* **1** despacho, oficina. **2** cargo.

● **in office** en el poder.

● **to take office** tomar posesión del cargo.

■ **office hours** horas de oficina.

■ **office worker** oficinista.

officer ['ɒfɪsə'] *n* **1** oficial *(militar)*. **2** agente, policía.

official [ə'fɪʃəl] *adj* oficial.

► *n* funcionario,-a.

officially [ə'fɪʃəlɪ] *adv* oficialmente.

off-key [ɒf'kiː] *adj* desafinado,-a.

off-licence ['ɒflaɪsəns] *n* GB tienda de bebidas alcohólicas.

off-line ['ɒflaɪn] *adj* COMPUT desconectado,-a.

off-peak ['ɒfpiːk] *adj* de tarifa reducida.

offset [ɒf'set] *vt* (*pt & pp* **offset**) compensar, contrarrestar.

offshoot [ɒf'ʃuːt] *n* vástago, retoño *(de planta, árbol)*.

offside [ɒf'saɪd] *adj-adv* fuera de juego.

offspring ['ɒːfsprɪŋ] *n* (*pl* **offspring**) descendiente.

often ['ɒfən] *adv* a menudo, frecuentemente.

● **every so often** de vez en cuando.

● **how often...?** ¿cada cuánto...? ¿con qué frecuencia...?

● **more often than not** la mayoría de las veces.

oh [əʊ] *interj* ¡oh!, ¡ah!, ¡ay!

oil [ɔɪl] *n* **1** aceite. **2** petróleo. **3** óleo, pintura al óleo.

► *vt* engrasar, lubricar, lubrificar.

■ **oil industry** industria petrolera.

■ **oil paint** pintura al óleo.

■ **oil rig** plataforma petrolífera.

■ **oil slick** marea negra, mancha de petróleo.

■ **oil tanker** petrolero.

■ **oil well** pozo petrolífero.

oilcan ['ɔɪlkæn] *n* aceitera.

oilcloth ['ɔɪlklɒθ] *n* hule.

oilfield ['ɔɪlfiːld] *n* yacimiento petrolífero.

oily ['ɔɪlɪ] *adj* (-**ier**, -**iest**). **1** aceitoso,-a, grasiento,-a. **2** graso,-a.

ointment ['ɔɪntmənt] *n* ungüento.

okay [əʊ'keɪ] *interj* ¡vale!, ¡de acuerdo!

► *adj-adv* **1** bien: *the film was okay*, el film estaba bien. **2** vale, de acuerdo: *do you want a cup of tea?...Ok*, ¿quieres una taza de té?- Vale.

► *n* visto bueno.

► *vt* dar el visto bueno a.

old [əʊld] *adj* **1** viejo,-a *(cosa)*. **2** mayor, viejo,-a *(persona)*. **3** antiguo,-a.

● **how old are you?** ¿cuántos años tienes?

● **to be... years old** tener...años.

■ **old age** vejez, senectud.

■ **old boy** antiguo alumno.

■ **old girl** antigua alumna.

■ **old maid** solterona.

■ **old people's home** residencia de ancianos.

■ **Old Testament** Antiguo Testamento.

old-fashioned [əʊld'fæʃənd] *adj* anticuado,-a.

olive ['ɒlɪv] *n* **1** olivo. **2** aceituna, oliva.

■ **olive oil** aceite de oliva.

■ **olive tree** olivo.

Olympiad [ə'lɪmpɪæd] *n* Olimpíada, Olimpiada.

Olympic [ə'lɪmpɪk] *adj* olímpico,-a.

● **Olympic Games** Juegos Olímpicos.

omelette ['ɒmlət] *n* (US **omelet**) tortilla.

omen ['əʊmən] *n* agüero, presagio.

ominous ['ɒmɪnəs] *adj* de mal agüero, siniestro,-a.

omission [əʊ'mɪʃən] *n* **1** omisión. **2** olvido, descuido.

omit [əʊ'mɪt] *vt* (*pt & pp* **omitted**, *ger* **omitting**). **1** omitir. **2** pasar por alto. **3** olvidar.

omnibus ['ɒmnɪbəs] *n* (*pl* **omnibuses**) antología.

■ **omnibus edition** *todos los capítulos de la semana de una serie seguidos.*

omnipotent [ɒm'nɪpətənt] *adj* omnipotente.

on [ɒn] *prep* **1** en: *there were a lot of people on the train*, había mucha gente en el tren. **2** sobre, encima de, en: *on the floor*, en el suelo; *on the table*, sobre la mesa. **3** sobre: *a talk on birds*, una charla sobre las aves. **4:** *on my birthday*, el día de mi cumpleaños; *on Sunday*, el domingo; *on Sundays*, los domingos. **5:**

he got on the bus, se subió al autobús. **6**: *he's on the phone*, está al teléfono.

▶ *adv* **1** conectado,-a, puesto,-a, encendido,-a *(luz, aparato)*. **2** abierto,-a *(grifo)*. **3** puesto,-a: *what dress did she have on?*, ¿qué vestido llevaba? **4**: *the match is on after all*, el partido se celebra según lo previsto. **5** adelante, sin parar: *the policeman told him to stop, but he drove on*, el policía le dijo que se parara, pero siguió adelante.

● **and so on** y así sucesivamente.
● **it's on the house** invita la casa.
● **on and off** de vez en cuando.
● **on and on** sin parar: *he talked on and on*, no paró de hablar.

On seguido de un gerundio se traduce al español por *al* más infinitivo: *on arriving, she phoned her mother*, al llegar, llamó a su madre.

once [wʌns] *adv* **1** una vez: *once a week*, una vez por semana. **2** antes, anteriormente.
▶ *conj* una vez que, cuando.
● **all at once** repentinamente.
● **at once 1** enseguida, inmediatamente. **2** a la vez, al mismo tiempo. **3** de una vez.
● **once and for all** de una vez para siempre.
● **once more** una vez más.
● **once upon a time** érase una vez.
once-over [wʌns'əuvə'] *n fam* vistazo.
● **to give** STH **the once-over** dar un repaso a algo.
oncoming ['ɒnkʌmɪŋ] *adj* que viene de frente.
one [wʌn] *adj* **1** un, una. **2** único,-a: *it's my one chance*, es mi única oportunidad.
▶ *num* uno.
▶ *pron* uno,-a: *a red one*, uno,-a rojo,-a; *one has to be careful*, hay que ir con cuidado; *the one who*, el que, la que; *this one*, éste,-a; *the blue one*, el azul.
● **one another** el uno al otro, los unos a los otros, mutuamente.
one-armed [wʌnɑːmd] *adj* manco,-a.
■ **one-armed bandit** máquina tragaperras.
one-eyed [wʌnaɪd] *adj* tuerto,-a.
one-off [wʌnɒf] *adj fam* único,-a.
onerous ['ɒnərəs] *adj* oneroso,-a.

oneself [wʌn'self] *pron* uno,-a mismo,-a, sí mismo,-a: *to enjoy oneself*, divertirse.
● **by oneself** solo.
one-sided [wʌnsaɪdɪd] *adj* **1** desigual. **2** parcial.
one-time [wʌntaɪm] *adj* antiguo,-a.
one-way [wʌnweɪ] *adj* **1** de sentido único *(calle)*. **2** de ida *(billete)*.
ongoing ['ɒngəuɪŋ] *adj* que sigue, en curso.
onion ['ʌnɪən] *n* cebolla.
on-line ['ɒn'laɪn] *adj* COMPUT conectado,-a, en línea.
onlooker ['ɒnlukə'] *n* espectador,-ra.
only ['əunlɪ] *adj* único,-a.
▶ *adv* sólo, solamente, únicamente.
▶ *conj* pero: *I would go, only I'm too tired*, iría, pero estoy muy cansado.
● **if only** ojalá.
● **only just** apenas, por los pelos: *I only just caught the bus*, cogí el autobús por los pelos.

Only just con el presente perfecto se traduce por *acabar de* más infinitivo: *I've only just got home*, acabo de llegar a casa.

onrush ['ɒnrʌʃ] *n (pl -es)* arremetida, avalancha.
onset ['ɒnset] *n* principio.
onslaught ['ɒnslɔːt] *n* ataque violento.
onto ['ɒntu] *prep* **1** sobre: *the cat jumped onto the table*, el gato saltó sobre la mesa. **2**: *the police are onto the thieves*, la policía está siguiendo la pista de los ladrones.
onus ['əunəs] *n (pl onuses)* responsabilidad.
onwards ['ɒnwədz] *adv* **1** adelante, hacia adelante: *the soldiers marched onwards*, los soldados marcharon hacia adelante. **2** en adelante, a partir de: *from May onwards*, a partir de mayo.
● **from now onwards** de ahora en adelante.
onyx ['ɒnɪks] *n (pl onyxes)* ónice.
oops [uːps] *interj* ¡uy!
ooze¹ [uːz] *n* fango, cieno.
ooze² [uːz] *vi* rezumar.
▶ *vt* desprender, irradiar.
opal ['əupəl] *n* ópalo.
opaque [əu'peɪk] *adj* opaco,-a.
OPEC ['əupek] *abbr (Organization of Petroleum Exporting Countries)* Organi-

zación de los Países Exportadores de Petróleo; *(abbreviation)* OPEP.
open [ˈəʊpən] *adj* abierto,-a.
► *vt-vi* abrir(se).
● **in the open air** al aire libre.
■ **open season** temporada de caza.
open-air [ˈəʊpəneəˈ] *adj* al aire libre.
opener [ˈəʊpənəˈ] *n* abridor.
opening [ˈəʊpənɪŋ] *n* **1** comienzo. **2** abertura, brecha. **3** oportunidad. **4** vacante.
■ **opening hours** horario de apertura.
■ **opening night** noche de estreno.
openly [ˈəʊpənlɪ] *adv* abiertamente.
open-minded [əʊpənˈmaɪndɪd] *adj* tolerante, abierto.
opera [ˈɒpərə] *n* ópera.
■ **opera house** ópera, teatro de la ópera.
operate [ˈɒpəreɪt] *vt* **1** hacer funcionar, accionar *(máquina)*. **2** dirigir *(empresa)*.
► *vi* **1** funcionar *(máquina, sistema)*. **2** operar *(a paciente)*: **they're operating on him tomorrow**, le operan mañana.
■ **operating theatre** quirófano.
operation [ɒpəˈreɪʃən] *n* **1** operación: *a military operation*, una operación militar. **2** funcionamiento *(de máquina)*. **3** operación, intervención quirúrgica.
operational [ɒpəˈreɪʃənəl] *adj* **1** operativo,-a. **2** en funcionamiento.
operative [ˈɒpərətɪv] *adj* vigente.
► *n* operario,-a.
● **the operative word** la palabra clave.
operator [ˈɒpəreɪtəˈ] *n* **1** operador,-a, telefonista. **2** operario,-a.
opinion [əˈpɪnɪən] *n* opinión.
● **in my opinion** a mi juicio, en mi opinión.
● **to have a high opinion of SB** tener buen concepto de ALGN.
● **to have a low opinion of SB** tener mal concepto de ALGN.
opinionated [əˈpɪnɪəneɪtɪd] *adj* dogmático,-a.
opium [ˈəʊpɪəm] *n* opio.
opponent [əˈpəʊnənt] *n* adversario,-a.
opportune [ˈɒpətjuːn] *adj* oportuno,-a.
opportunity [ɒpəˈtjuːnɪtɪ] *n* (*pl* -**ies**) oportunidad.
● **to take the opportunity to do STH** aprovechar la oportunidad para hacer algo.
oppose [əˈpəʊz] *vt* oponerse a.

opposed [əˈpəʊzd] *adj* opuesto,-a, contrario,-a.
● **as opposed to** en vez de, en lugar de.
● **to be opposed to...** oponerse a...
opposing [əˈpəʊzɪŋ] *adj* contrario,-a, adversario,-a.
opposite [ˈɒpəzɪt] *adj* **1** de enfrente: *the house opposite*, la casa de enfrente. **2** opuesto,-a, contrario,-a: *in opposite direction*, en dirección contraria.
► *prep* enfrente de, frente a.
► *adv* enfrente.
► *n* antítesis, contrario.
■ **opposite sex** sexo opuesto.
opposition [ɒpəˈzɪʃən] *n* oposición.
oppress [əˈpres] *vt* oprimir.
oppression [əˈpreʃən] *n* opresión.
oppressor [əˈpresəˈ] *n* opresor,-ra.
opt [ɒpt] *vi* optar.
optical [ˈɒptɪkəl] *adj* óptico,-a.
■ **optical fibre** fibra óptica.
■ **optical illusion** ilusión óptica.
optician [ɒpˈtɪʃən] *n* óptico,-a.
● **optician's** óptica.
optimism [ˈɒptɪmɪzəm] *n* optimismo.
optimist [ˈɒptɪmɪst] *n* optimista.
optimistic [ɒptɪˈmɪstɪk] *adj* optimista.
optimize [ˈɒptɪmaɪz] *vt* optimizar.
optimum [ˈɒptɪməm] *adj* óptimo,-a.
► *n* grado óptimo.
option [ˈɒpʃən] *n* opción.
optional [ˈɒpʃənəl] *adj* opcional, optativo,-a.
opulence [ˈɒpjʊləns] *n* opulencia.
opulent [ˈɒpjʊlənt] *adj* opulento,-a.
or [ɔːˈ] *conj* **1** o: *would you like meat or fish?*, ¿quieres carne o pescado? **2** ni: *he doesn't smoke or drink*, no fuma ni bebe.
● **or else** de lo contrario, si no.
oracle [ˈɒrəkəl] *n* oráculo.
oral [ˈɔːrəl] *adj* oral.
► *n* examen oral.
orange [ˈɒrɪndʒ] *n* **1** naranja *(fruta)*. **2** naranja *(color)*.
► *adj* naranja, de color naranja.
■ **orange blossom** azahar.
■ **orange tree** naranjo.
orang-outan [ɔːræŋuːˈtæn] *n* orangután.
orator [ˈɒrətəˈ] *n* orador,-ra.
oratory[1] [ˈɒrətrɪ] *n* (*pl* -**ies**) oratoria.
oratory[2] [ˈɒrətrɪ] *n* (*pl* -**ies**) oratorio, capilla.

orb [ɔːb] n esfera.
orbit ['ɔːbɪt] n órbita.
▶ vt girar alrededor de.
orchard ['ɔːtʃəd] n huerto.
orchestra ['ɔːkɪstrə] n orquesta.
■ orchestra pit foso de la orquesta.
orchestral [ɔːˈkestrəl] adj orquestal.
orchid ['ɔːkɪd] n orquídea.
ordain [ɔːˈdeɪn] vt 1 ordenar (cura). 2 decretar.
ordeal [ɔːˈdiːl] n fig calvario.
order ['ɔːdə'] n 1 orden: to give an order, dar una orden. 2 pedido. 3 orden (religioso).
▶ vt 1 ordenar, mandar. 2 ordenar. 3 pedir, encargar.
● in order 1 en orden: in alphabetical order, en orden alfabético. 2 bien.
● in order to para, a fin de.
● "Out of order" "No funciona".
■ order form hoja de pedido.
orderly ['ɔːdəlɪ] adj 1 ordenado,-a, metódico,-a. 2 disciplinado,-a.
▶ n (pl -ies). 1 auxiliar, ayudante. 2 ordenanza.
ordinal ['ɔːdɪnəl] adj ordinal.
▶ n ordinal.
ordinance ['ɔːdɪnəns] n fml ordenanza.
ordinary ['ɔːdɪnərɪ] adj normal, corriente.
● out of the ordinary fuera de lo común.

Ordinary no tiene el matiz despectivo de ordinario en español.

ordination [ɔːdɪˈneɪʃən] n ordenación.
ore [ɔː'] n mineral, mena.
oregano [ɒrɪˈɡɑːnəʊ] n orégano.
organ ['ɔːɡən] n órgano.
organic [ɔːˈɡænɪk] adj orgánico,-a.
organism ['ɔːɡənɪzəm] n organismo.
organist ['ɔːɡənɪst] n organista.
organization [ɔːɡənaɪˈzeɪʃən] n organización.
■ organization chart organigrama.
organize ['ɔːɡənaɪz] vt-vi organizar(se).
orgasm ['ɔːɡæzəm] n orgasmo.
orgy ['ɔːdʒɪ] n (pl -ies) orgía.
Orient ['ɔːrɪənt] n Oriente.
oriental [ɔːrɪˈentəl] adj oriental.
▶ n oriental.

El término oriental se considera racista.

orientate ['ɔːrɪənteɪt] vt orientar.
orientation [ɔːrɪenˈteɪʃən] n orientación.

orifice ['ɒrɪfɪs] n orificio.
origin ['ɒrɪdʒɪn] n origen.
original [əˈrɪdʒɪnəl] adj 1 original. 2 primero, originario: the original owner, el primer propietario.
▶ n original.
● in the original en versión original.
originality [ərɪdʒɪˈnælɪtɪ] n originalidad.
originally [əˈrɪdʒɪnəlɪ] adv originariamente, al principio.
originate [əˈrɪdʒɪneɪt] vt originar, crear.
▶ vi tener su origen.
ornament ['ɔːnəmənt] n ornamento, adorno.
ornamental [ɔːnəˈmentəl] adj ornamental, decorativo,-a.
ornate [ɔːˈneɪt] adj recargado,-a, ornamentado,-a.
ornithology [ɔːnɪˈθɒlədʒɪ] n ornitología.
orphan ['ɔːfən] n huérfano,-a.
● to be orphaned quedar huérfano,-a.
orphanage ['ɔːfənɪdʒ] n orfanato.
orthodox ['ɔːθədɒks] adj ortodoxo,-a.
orthodoxy ['ɔːθədɒksɪ] n ortodoxia.
orthography [ɔːˈθɒɡrəfɪ] n ortografía.
orthopaedic [ɔːθəʊˈpiːdɪk] adj ortopédico,-a.
oscillate ['ɒsɪleɪt] vi oscilar.
ostensible [ɒˈstensɪbəl] adj aparente.
ostensibly [ɒˈstensɪblɪ] adv aparentemente.
ostentation [ɒstenˈteɪʃən] n ostentación.
ostentatious [ɒstenˈteɪʃəs] adj ostentoso,-a.
ostracize ['ɒstrəsaɪz] vt condenar al ostracismo, hacer el vacío a.
ostrich ['ɒstrɪtʃ] n (pl -es) avestruz.
other ['ʌðə'] adj-pron otro,-a.
● every other day días alternos.
● other than aparte de, salvo.
● the others los demás.
otherwise ['ʌðəwaɪz] adv 1 de otra manera, de manera distinta. 2 por lo demás, aparte de eso: my leg hurts, but otherwise I'm fine, me duele la pierna, pero aparte de eso estoy bien.
▶ conj si no, de lo contrario: take the umbrella, otherwise you'll get wet, llévate el paraguas, si no, te mojarás.
otter ['ɒtə'] n nutria.
ouch [aʊtʃ] interj ¡ay!

ought [ɔːt] *aux* **1** deber: *I ought to write-to thank her*, debería escribir para darle las gracias. **2**: *you ought to get the job*, seguramente conseguirás el trabajo.

ounce [aʊns] *n* onza.

Equivale a 28,35 g.

our [ˈaʊəʳ] *adj* nuestro,-a, nuestros,-as.

ours [ˈaʊəz] *pron* (el) nuestro, (la) nuestra, (los) nuestros, (las) nuestras: *a friend of ours*, un amigo nuestro; *their car hit ours*, su coche chocó contra el nuestro.

ourselves [aʊəˈselvz] *pron* **1** nos: *we bought ourselves sweets*, nos compramos caramelos. **2** nosotros,-as mismos, -as: *we did it ourselves*, lo hicimos nosotros mismos.

● **by ourselves** solos, sin ayuda: *we painted the room by ourselves*, pintamos la habitación sin ayuda.

oust [aʊst] *vt* echar.

out [aʊt] *adv* **1** fuera, afuera: *he ran out*, salió corriendo. **2** fuera: *he's out at the moment*, ha salido un momento. **3** equivocado,-a: *my calculation was out by £50*, mi cálculo tenía un error de 50 libras. **4**: *white socks are out*, los calcetines blancos ya no se llevan. **5** inconsciente. **6** en huelga. **7** apagado,-a *(luz)*. **8** fuera, eliminado,-a *(jugador)*. **9** publicado,-a: *the band has a new record out*, el grupo acaba de sacar un nuevo disco. **10**: *the sun is out*, ha salido el sol. **11** despedido,-a: *the boss said he was out*, el jefe dijo que estaba despedido.

▶ *prep* **out of 1** fuera de: *he was out of the country*, estaba fuera del país. **2** de: *made out of wood*, hecho,-a de madera. **3** de: *out of a tin*, de una lata. **4** por: *out of spite*, por despecho. **5** sin: *we're out of tea*, se nos ha acabado el té. **6** sobre: *five out of ten in French*, cinco sobre diez en francés. **7** de cada: *eight women out of ten*, ocho de cada diez mujeres.

● **out of date 1** anticuado,-a *(ropa)*. **2** caducado,-a *(pasaporte)*.

● **out of doors** al aire libre.

● **out of favour** en desgracia.

● **out of print** descatalogado,-a.

● **out of sorts** indispuesto,-a.

● **out of this world** extraordinario,-a.

● **out of work** parado,-a.

● **out to win** decidido,-a a vencer.

Cuando **out** acompaña a un verbo, modifica el significado del mismo: *don't let the baby out*, no dejes que se escape el bebé; *she took her purse out*, sacó el monedero; *my father is in, but my mother has gone out*, mi padre está en casa, pero mi madre ha salido.

outboard [ˈaʊtbɔːd] *adj* fueraborda.

outbreak [ˈaʊtbreɪk] *n* **1** estallido *(de guerra)*. **2** comienzo *(de hostilidades)*. **3** brote *(de epidemia)*.

outbuilding [ˈaʊtbɪldɪŋ] *n* dependencia.

outburst [ˈaʊtbɜːst] *n* explosión, arranque.

outcast [ˈaʊtkɑːst] *n* marginado,-a.

outcome [ˈaʊtkʌm] *n* resultado.

outcry [ˈaʊtkraɪ] *n* (*pl* -**ies**) protestas.

outdated [aʊtˈdeɪtɪd] *adj* anticuado,-a.

outdo [aʊtˈduː] *vt* (*pt* **outdid** [aʊtˈdɪd], *pp* **outdone** [aʊtˈdʌn]) superar, aventajar.

● **not to be outdone** para no ser menos.

outdoor [aʊtˈdɔːʳ] *adj* al aire libre.

▶ *adv* **outdoors** fuera, al aire libre.

outer [ˈaʊtəʳ] *adj* exterior, externo,-a.

■ **outer space** espacio exterior.

outfit [ˈaʊtfɪt] *n* **1** conjunto, traje. **2** equipo, grupo.

outgoing [aʊtˈgəʊɪŋ] *adj* **1** saliente, cesante. **2** sociable, extrovertido.

▶ *npl* **outgoings** gastos.

outgrow [aʊtˈgrəʊ] *vt* (*pt* **outgrew** [aʊtˈgruː], *pp* **outgrown** [aʊtˈgrəʊn]): *he's outgrown his shoes*, se le han quedado pequeños los zapatos.

outing [ˈaʊtɪŋ] *n* salida, excursión: *to go on an outing*, ir de excursión.

outlandish [aʊtˈlændɪʃ] *adj* extravagante.

outlaw [ˈaʊtlɔː] *n* forajido,-a, proscrito,-a.

▶ *vt* prohibir, ilegalizar.

outlay [ˈaʊtleɪ] *n* desembolso.

outlet [ˈaʊtlet] *n* **1** salida. **2** desagüe.

outline [ˈaʊtlaɪn] *n* **1** contorno, perfil. **2** resumen, esbozo.

▶ *vt* **1** perfilar. **2** resumir, esbozar.

outlive [aʊtˈlɪv] *vt* sobrevivir a.

outlook [ˈaʊtlʊk] *n* **1** vista. **2** punto de vista. **3** perspectiva.

outlying [ˈaʊtlaɪŋ] *adj* **1** alejado,-a, remoto. **2** periférico,-a.

outnumber [aʊtˈnʌmbəʳ] *vt* exceder en número, ser más que.

outpatient [ˈaʊtpeɪʃənt] *n* paciente externo,-a.

outpost ['aʊtpəʊst] *n* avanzada.

output ['aʊtpʊt] *n* **1** producción, rendimiento. **2** COMPUT salida.

outrage ['aʊtreɪdʒ] *n* **1** indignación, atropello. **2** atrocidad, escándalo.
► *vt* ultrajar, atropellar.

outrageous [aʊt'reɪdʒəs] *adj* **1** escandaloso,-a, indignante. **2** extravagante.

outright [(*adv*) aʊt'raɪt(*adj*) 'aʊtraɪt] *adv* **1** abiertamente, directamente a. **2** instantáneamente. **3** categóricamente, totalmente. **4** claramente.
► *adj* absoluto,-a, total.

outset ['aʊtset] *n* principio.
● **at the outset** al principio.
● **from the outset** desde el principio.

outside [(*n*) aʊt'saɪd(*prep*) 'aʊtsaɪd] *n* exterior, parte exterior: *from the outside*, desde fuera.
► *prep* fuera de.
► *adv* fuera, afuera: *to go outside*, ir fuera.
► *adj* exterior.
● **at the outside** como máximo.

outsider [aʊt'saɪdəʳ] *n* forastero,-a.

outskirts ['aʊtskɜːts] *npl* afueras.

outspoken [aʊt'spəʊkən] *adj* directo,-a, franco,-a: *to be outspoken*, no tener pelos en la lengua.

outstanding [aʊt'stændɪŋ] *adj* **1** destacado,-a, sobresaliente. **2** pendiente *(trabajo)*.

outstretched [aʊt'stretʃt] *adj* extendido,-a.

outstrip [aʊt'strɪp] *vt* dejar atrás, aventajar.

outward ['aʊtwəd] *adj* **1** exterior, externo,-a. **2** de ida *(viaje)*.
► *adv* **outward** o **outwards** hacia fuera, hacia afuera.

outweigh [aʊt'weɪ] *vt* pesar más que.

outwit [aʊt'wɪt] *vt* (*pt & pp* **outwitted**, *ger* **outwitting**) ser más listo,-a que.

oval ['əʊvəl] *adj* oval, ovalado,-a.
► *n* óvalo.

ovary ['əʊvərɪ] *n* (*pl* **-ies**) ovario.

ovation [əʊ'veɪʃən] *n* ovación.

oven ['ʌvən] *n* horno.

over ['əʊvəʳ] *adv* **1**: *come over here*, ven aquí; *over there*, allí; *come over for supper sometime*, ven a casa a cenar algún día. **2**: *he fell over*, se cayó; *she knocked the bottle over with her elbow*, tiró la botella con el codo. **3**: *children of twelve and over*, niños mayores de doce años. **4**: *we had to start all over again*, tuvimos que volver a empezar; *over and over again*, una y otra vez.
► *adj* acabado,-a: *the class is over*, la clase ha acabado.
► *prep* **1** encima de, por encima de: *there's a sign over the door*, hay un letrero encima de la puerta; *he jumped over the fence*, saltó por encima de la valla. **2** sobre, encima de: *she wore a red shawl over the dress*, llevaba un chal rojo sobre el vestido; *he put his hand over his mouth*, se tapó la boca con la mano. **3** más de: *there were over a hundred*, había más de cien. **4** al otro lado de: *they live over the road*, viven al otro lado de la calle, viven enfrente. **5** durante: *over the holidays*, durante las vacaciones. **6**: *are you over your illness yet?*, ¿ya te has recuperado de tu enfermedad? **7** por: *over the phone*, por teléfono. **8** por: *they had an argument over a woman*, discutieron por una mujer.
● **all over** en todas partes: *all over the world*, en todo el mundo.
● **all over again** de nuevo, otra vez.
● **over and over again** una y otra vez.
● **over here** aquí.
● **over there** allí.

> **Over** también combina con muchos otros verbos: *she leant over and took the money*, se inclinó y cogió el dinero; *she crossed over the other side of the road*, cruzó la calle; *I knocked the bottle over with my elbow*, tiré la botella con el codo; *he fell over and broke his leg*, se cayó y se rompió la pierna; *I'd like to think it over*, me gustaría pensármelo.

overall [(*adj*) 'əʊvərɔːl(*adv*) əʊvər'ɔːl] *adj* **1** global, total. **2** general.
► *adv* **1** en total. **2** en conjunto.
► *npl* **overalls** mono.

overbearing [əʊvə'beərɪŋ] *adj* dominante, despótico,-a.

overboard ['əʊvəbɔːd] *adv* por la borda.
● **to go overboard** *fam* pasarse.

overcame [əʊvə'keɪm] *pt* → overcome.

overcast ['əʊvəkɑːst] *adj* cubierto,-a, nublado,-a.

overcharge [əʊvə'tʃɑːdʒ] *vt* cobrar demasiado.

overcoat ['əʊvəkəʊt] *n* abrigo.

overcome [əʊvə'kʌm] *vt* (*pt* **overcame**, *pp* **overcome**). **1** vencer, superar. **2** abrumar.

overcrowded [əʊvə'kraʊdɪd] *adj* atestado,-a.

overdo [əʊvə'duː] *vt* (*pt* **overdid** [əʊvə'dɪd], *pp* **overdone** [əʊvə'dʌn]). **1** exagerar. **2** cocer demasiado.

overdose ['əʊvədəʊs] *n* sobredosis.

overdraft ['əʊvədrɑːft] *n* descubierto.

overdue [əʊvə'djuː] *adj* **1** atrasado,-a. **2** vencido,-a y sin pagar *(factura)*.

overestimate [əʊvər'estɪmeɪt] *vt* sobreestimar.

overexposed [əʊvərɪk'spəʊzd] *adj* sobreexpuesto,-a.

overflow [(*n*) 'əʊvəfləʊ(*vb*) əʊvə'fləʊ] *n* **1** desbordamiento. **2** desagüe.
▶ *vi* desbordarse.

overgrown [əʊvə'grəʊn] *adj* **1** cubierto,-a de maleza. **2** demasiado,-a grande.

overhaul [(*n*) 'əʊvəhɔːl(*vb*) əʊvə'hɔːl] *n* revisión general.
▶ *vt* repasar, revisar.

overhead [(*adj*) 'əʊvəhed(*adv*) əʊvə'hed] *adj* aéreo,-a, elevado,-a.
▶ *adv* en lo alto, por encima.
▶ *npl* **overheads** gastos generales.

overhear [əʊvə'hɪə'] *vt* (*pt & pp* **overheard** [əʊvə'hɜːd]) oír por casualidad.

overheat [əʊvə'hiːt] *vi* recalentarse.

overjoyed [əʊvə'dʒɔɪd] *adj* encantadísimo,-a.

overland ['əʊvəlænd] *adj-adv* por tierra.

overlap [əʊvə'læp] *vi* (*pt & pp* **overlapped**, *ger* **overlapping**) superponerse.

overleaf [əʊvə'liːf] *adv* al dorso, a la vuelta.

overlook [əʊvə'lʊk] *vt* **1** pasar por alto, no notar, no tener en cuenta. **2** hacer la vista gorda a, disculpar, dejar pasar. **3** dar a, tener vistas a.

overnight [əʊvə'naɪt] *adj* **1** de noche, de una noche. **2** de la noche a la mañana.
▶ *adv* **1** durante la noche, por la noche. **2** de la noche a la mañana.
● **to stay overnight** pasar la noche.

overpower [əʊvə'paʊə'] *vt* **1** dominar. **2** abrumar.

overran [əʊvə'ræn] *pt* → overrun.

overrate [əʊvə'reɪt] *vt* sobrevalorar.

override [əʊvə'raɪd] *vt* (*pt* **overrode**

[əʊvə'rəʊd], *pp* **overridden** [əʊvə'rɪdən]). **1** anteponerse a. **2** desautorizar.

overrule [əʊvə'ruːl] *vt* **1** denegar, invalidar. **2** desautorizar, anular.

overrun [əʊvə'rʌn] *vt* (*pt* **overran**, *pp* **overrun**, *ger* **overrunning**) invadir.
▶ *vi* durar más de lo previsto.

overseas [əʊvə'siːz] *adj* de ultramar, del extranjero.
▶ *adv* en ultramar, en el extranjero.

oversee [əʊvə'siː] *vt* (*pt* **oversaw** [əʊvə'sɔː], *pp* **overseen** [əʊvə'siːn]) supervisar, inspeccionar.

overseer ['əʊvəsɪə'] *n* supervisor,-ra.

overshadow [əʊvə'ʃædəʊ] *vt fig* eclipsar, ensombrecer.

oversight ['əʊvəsaɪt] *n* descuido.

oversleep [əʊvə'sliːp] *vi* (*pt & pp* **overslept** [əʊvə'slept]) dormirse, quedarse dormido.

overstep [əʊvə'step] *vt* sobrepasar, pasar de.
● **to overstep the mark** pasarse de la raya.

overt ['əʊvɜːt, əʊ'vɜːt] *adj* declarado,-a, abierto,-a.

overtake [əʊvə'teɪk] *vt* (*pt* **overtook** [əʊvə'tʊk], *pp* **overtaken** [əʊvə'teɪkən]) adelantar.

overthrow [əʊvə'θrəʊ] *vt* (*pt* **overthrew** [əʊvə'θruː], *pp* **overthrown** [əʊvə'θrəʊn]) derribar, derrocar.

overtime ['əʊvətaɪm] *n* horas extraordinarias, horas extra.

overture ['əʊvətjʊə'] *n* obertura.

overturn [əʊvə'tɜːn] *vt-vi* volcar.

overweight [əʊvə'weɪt] *adj* demasiado gordo,-a.
● **to be overweight** tener exceso de peso.

overwhelm [əʊvə'welm] *vt* **1** arrollar, aplastar. **2** *fig* abrumar.

overwhelming [əʊvə'welmɪŋ] *adj* aplastante, arrollador,-ra.

overwork [əʊvə'wɜːk] *vi* trabajar demasiado.
▶ *vt* hacer trabajar demasiado.

overwrought [əʊvə'rɔːt] *adj* muy nervioso,-a.

ovulation [ɒvjʊ'leɪʃən] *n* ovulación.

ovum ['əʊvəm] *n* (*pl* **ova** ['əʊvə]) óvulo.

owe [əʊ] *vt* deber.

owing ['əʊɪŋ] *adj* que se debe.

owl

• **owing to** debido a, a causa de.
owl [aʊl] *n* búho, mochuelo, lechuza.

> **Owl** es el nombre en general de varias aves diferentes que se parecen algo entre sí.

own [əʊn] *adj* propio,-a: *he has his own car*, tiene su propio coche.
▶ *pron*: *my/your/his own*, lo mío/tuyo/suyo; *a room of my own*, una habitación para mí solo.
▶ *vt* poseer, ser dueño,-a de, tener.
• **on one's own** solo, sin ayuda: *can you do it on your own?*, ¿puedes hacerlo solo?
to own up *vi* confesar.

owner ['əʊnə'] *n* dueño,-a, propietario,-a, poseedor,-ra.
ownership ['əʊnəʃɪp] *n* propiedad, posesión.
ox [ɒks] *n* (*pl* **oxen** ['ɒksən]) buey.
oxide ['ɒksaɪd] *n* óxido.
oxidize ['ɒksɪdaɪz] *vt-vi* oxidar(se).
oxygen ['ɒksɪdʒən] *n* oxígeno.
■ **oxygen mask** máscara de oxígeno.
oyster ['ɔɪstə'] *n* ostra.
oz [aʊns, 'aʊnsɪz] *abbr* (**ounce**) onza.

> *pl* **oz** o **ozs**.

ozone ['əʊzəʊn] *n* ozono.
■ **ozone layer** capa de ozono.

P

p¹ [piː, 'penɪ, pens] *abbr* GB *fam (penny, pence)* penique, peniques.

p² [peɪdʒ] *abbr (page)* página, p., pág.

P *abbr (Parking, car park)* aparcamiento, P.

p and p ['piːən'piː] *abbr* GB *(postage and packing)* gastos de embalaje y envío.

PA¹ ['piː'eɪ] *abbr (public address)* megafonía, sistema de megafonía.

PA² ['piː'eɪ] *abbr (personal assistant)* ayudante personal.

pace [peɪs] *n* **1** paso. **2** marcha, ritmo.
- **to keep pace with SB** seguir el ritmo de ALGN.
- **to keep pace with STH** mantenerse al corriente de algo.
- **to pace up and down** ir de un lado al otro.

pacemaker ['peɪsmeɪkə'] *n* **1** liebre *(en carrera)*. **2** marcapasos.

pacific [pə'sɪfɪk] *adj* pacífico,-a.

Pacific [pə'sɪfɪk] *adj* del Pacífico.
- **the Pacific** el Pacífico.

pacifist ['pæsɪfɪst] *adj-n* pacifista.

pacify ['pæsɪfaɪ] *vt (pt & pp -ied)* pacificar, apaciguar.

pack [pæk] *n* **1** paquete. **2** baraja. **3** banda *(de ladrones)*. **4** manada *(de lobos)*. **5** jauría *(de perros)*. **6** sarta *(de mentiras)*.
- ▶ *vt* **1** empaquetar. **2** hacer *(maleta)*. **3** atestar, abarrotar. **4** apretar.
- ▶ *vi* hacer las maletas.

to pack up *vi* **1** terminar de trabajar. **2** estropearse. **3** hacer las maletas.

package ['pækɪdʒ] *n* paquete.
- ▶ *vt* empaquetar, envasar.
- ▪ **package tour** viaje organizado.

packaging ['pækɪdʒɪŋ] *n* embalaje.

packed [pækt] *adj* lleno,-a, abarrotado,-a.

packet ['pækɪt] *n* paquete.
- ● **to cost a packet** costar un ojo de la cara.

packing ['pækɪŋ] *n* embalaje.

pact [pækt] *n* pacto.

pad [pæd] *n* **1** almohadilla. **2** taco, bloc *(de papel)*. **3** *fam* casa, piso.
- ▶ *vt (pt & pp padded, ger padding)* acolchar.

padded ['pædɪd] *adj* acolchado,-a.

padding ['pædɪŋ] *n* **1** relleno, acolchado *(de silla)*. **2** paja *(en discurso)*.

paddle¹ ['pædəl] *n* pala *(para remar)*.
- ▶ *vt-vi* remar con pala.

paddle² ['pædəl] *vi* chapotear.

paddock ['pædək] *n* cercado, prado.

padlock ['pædlɒk] *n* candado.
- ▶ *vt* cerrar con candado.

pagan ['peɪgən] *adj-n* pagano,-a.

page¹ [peɪdʒ] *n* página.
- ▶ *vt* avisar por megafonía.

page² [peɪdʒ] *n* **1** botones. **2** paje.

pageboy ['peɪdʒbɔɪ] *n* paje.

paid [peɪd] *pt-pp* → pay.

pail [peɪl] *n* cubo.

pain [peɪn] *n* **1** dolor. **2** pesado,-a.
- ● **on pain of** so pena de.
- ● **to be a pain in the neck 1** ser un plomo *(persona)*. **2** ser una lata *(cosa)*.
- ● **to take pains to** esforzarse en.

painful ['peɪnfʊl] *adj* doloroso,-a.

painkiller ['peɪnkɪlə'] *n* calmante, analgésico.

painless ['peɪnləs] *adj* indoloro,-a.

painstaking ['peɪnzteɪkɪŋ] *adj* meticuloso,-a, minucioso,-a.

paint [peɪnt] *n* pintura.
▶ *vt-vi* pintar.
paintbrush ['peɪntbrʌʃ] *n* (*pl* -**es**). **1** brocha. **2** pincel.
painter ['peɪntə'] *n* pintor,-ra.
painting ['peɪntɪŋ] *n* **1** pintura. **2** cuadro.
pair [peə'] *n* **1** par: *a pair of scissors*, unas tijeras; *a pair of trousers*, un pantalón. **2** pareja: *a pair of lovers*, una pareja de amantes.
to pair off *vi* formar pareja.
to pair up *vt-vi* emparejar(se).
pajamas [pə'dʒæməz] *npl* US pijama.
Pakistan [pɑːkɪ'staːn] *n* Paquistán.
Pakistani [pɑːkɪ'staːn] *adj-n* paquistaní.
pal [pæl] *n fam* camarada, colega.
palace ['pæləs] *n* palacio.
palate ['pælət] *n* paladar.
pale [peɪl] *adj* **1** pálido,-a *(rostro)*. **2** claro, -a *(color)*.
▶ *vi* palidecer.
Palestine ['pælɪstaɪn] *n* Palestina.
Palestinian [pælɪ'stɪnɪən] *adj-n* palestino,-a.
pall[1] [pɔːl] *n* **1** nube *(de humo)*. **2** paño mortuorio.
pall[2] [pɔːl] *vi* aburrir, cansar.
palm [pɑːm] *n* palma *(de la mano)*.
● **to palm STH off on SB** endosar algo a ALGN.
palm[2] [pɑːm] *n* palmera *(árbol)*.
■ **Palm Sunday** Domingo de Ramos.
paltry ['pɔːltrɪ] *adj* (-**ier**, -**iest**) mísero,-a, mezquino,-a.
pamper ['pæmpə'] *vt* mimar.
pamphlet ['pæmflət] *n* **1** folleto *(publicitario)*. **2** panfleto *(político)*.
pan [pæn] *n* cazo, olla.
■ **frying pan** sartén.
Panama ['pænəmɑː] *n* Panamá.
■ **Panama Canal** Canal de Panamá.
Panamanian [pænə'meɪnɪən] *adj-n* panameño,-a.
pancake ['pænkeɪk] *n* crepe, tortita.
pancreas ['pæŋkrɪəs] *n* (*pl* **pancreases**) páncreas.
panda ['pændə] *n* oso panda, panda.
■ **panda car** coche patrulla.
pander ['pændə'] *vi* **to pander to** hacerle el juego *(a alguien)*, consentir, complacer.
pane [peɪn] *n* cristal, vidrio.
panel ['pænəl] *n* **1** panel *(en pared, puerta)*. **2** tablero, cuadro *(de instrumentos)*. **3** gru-

po, equipo *(de personas)*. **4** jurado, comisión.
pang [pæŋ] *n* punzada, dolor agudo.
panic ['pænɪk] *n* pánico.
▶ *vi* (*pt & pp* **panicked**, *ger* **panicking**) entrar el pánico, aterrarse.
panic-striken ['pænɪkstrɪkən] *adj* aterrorizado,-a.
pansy ['pænzɪ] *n* (*pl* -**ies**). **1** pensamiento *(flor)*. **2** *fam* mariquita.
pant [pænt] *n* jadeo, resuello.
▶ *vi* jadear, resollar.
panther ['pænθə'] *n* pantera.
panties ['pæntɪz] *npl* bragas.
pantomime ['pæntəmaɪm] *n* **1** pantomima. **2** GB representación teatral navideña basada en cuentos infantiles.
pantry ['pæntrɪ] *n* (*pl* -**ies**) despensa.
pants [pænts] *npl* **1** calzoncillos. **2** bragas. **3** US pantalones.
papa [pə'pɑː] *n fam* papá.
paper ['peɪpə'] *n* **1** papel. **2** diario, periódico. **3** examen. **4** estudio, ensayo.
▶ *npl* **papers** documentación.
▶ *vt* empapelar.
● **on paper** por escrito.
■ **paper money** papel moneda.
■ **paper shop** quiosco de periódicos.
paperback ['peɪpəbæk] *n* libro en rústica.
paperclip ['peɪpəklɪp] *n* clip.
paperweight ['peɪpəweɪt] *n* pisapapeles.
paperwork ['peɪpəwɜːk] *n* papeleo.
paprika ['pæprɪkə] *n* paprika, pimentón dulce.
par [pɑː'] *n* par *(en golf)*.
● **on a par with** al mismo nivel que.
parable ['pærəbəl] *n* parábola.
parabolic [pærə'bɒlɪk] *adj* parabólico,-a.
parachute ['pærəʃuːt] *n* paracaídas.
▶ *vi* lanzarse en paracaídas.
parachutist ['pærəʃuːtɪst] *n* paracaidista.
parade [pə'reɪd] *n* desfile.
▶ *vi* desfilar.
paradise ['pærədaɪs] *n* paraíso.
paradox ['pærədɒks] *n* (*pl* **paradoxes**) paradoja.
paraffin ['pærəfɪn] *n* parafina.
paragraph ['pærəgrɑːf] *n* párrafo.
Paraguay [pærə'gwaɪ] *n* Paraguay.
Paraguayan [pærə'gwaɪən] *adj-n* paraguayo,-a.
parakeet ['pærəkiːt] *n* periquito.
parallel ['pærəlel] *adj* paralelo,-a.

▶ *n* **1** paralelo. **2** paralela. **3** paralelismo.

▶ *vt* ser análogo,-a a.

paralyse ['pærəlaɪz] *vt* paralizar.

paralysis [pə'rælɪsɪs] *n* (*pl* **paralyses**) parálisis.

paralytic [pærə'lɪtɪk] *adj-n* paralítico,-a.

paramilitary [pærə'mɪlɪtəri] *adj* paramilitar.

paramount ['pærəmaʊnt] *adj* supremo,-a, vital, fundamental: *of paramount importance*, de suma importancia.

paranoia [pærə'nɔɪə] *n* paranoia.

paranoic [pærə'nɔɪk] *adj-n* paranoico,-a.

paranoid ['pærənɔɪd] *adj-n* paranoico,-a.

paraphrase ['pærəfreɪz] *n* paráfrasis.

▶ *vt* parafrasear.

parasite ['pærəsaɪt] *n* parásito,-a.

parasol [pærə'sɒl] *n* sombrilla.

paratrooper ['pærətruːpə'] *n* paracaidista *(del ejército)*.

parcel ['pɑːsəl] *n* paquete.

to parcel out *vt* repartir, dividir.

to parcel up *vt* empaquetar.

parched [pɑːtʃt] *adj* **1** abrasado,-a, reseco,-a *(tierra)*. **2** muerto,-a de sed *(persona)*.

parchment ['pɑːtʃmənt] *n* pergamino.

pardon ['pɑːdən] *n* **1** perdón. **2** indulto, amnistía.

▶ *vt* **1** perdonar. **2** indultar.

● **I beg your pardon** le ruego me disculpe, perdón.

● **pardon?** ¿perdón?, ¿cómo dice?

● **pardon me!** ¡perdón!, ¡disculpe!

pare [peə'] *vt* **1** pelar *(fruta)*. **2** cortar *(uñas)*.

parent ['peərənt] *n* padre, madre.

▶ *npl* **parents** padres.

parenthesis [pə'renθəsɪs] *n* (*pl* **parentheses**) paréntesis.

parish ['pærɪʃ] *n* (*pl* **-es**) parroquia.

parishioner [pə'rɪʃənə'] *n* feligrés,-esa.

park [pɑːk] *n* parque.

▶ *vt-vi* aparcar.

parking ['pɑːkɪŋ] *n* aparcamiento.

● **no parking** prohibido aparcar.

■ **parking lot** US aparcamiento.

■ **parking meter** parquímetro.

■ **parking place** sitio para aparcar.

■ **parking ticket** multa por aparcamiento indebido.

parliament ['pɑːləmənt] *n* parlamento.

parliamentary [pɑːlə'mentəri] *adj* parlamentario,-a.

parlour ['pɑːlə'] (US **parlor**) *n* salón.

parody ['pærədɪ] *n* (*pl* **-ies**) parodia.

▶ *vt* (*pt & pp* **-ied**) parodiar.

parole [pə'rəʊl] *n* libertad condicional.

● **on parole** en libertad condicional.

parquet ['pɑːkeɪ] *n* parqué.

parrot ['pærət] *n* loro.

parsley ['pɑːslɪ] *n* perejil.

parsnip ['pɑːsnɪp] *n* chirivía.

parson ['pɑːsən] *n* párroco, cura.

part [pɑːt] *n* **1** parte. **2** pieza *(de máquina)*. **3** papel *(en obra, etc)*.

▶ *vt* **1** separar. **2** peinar con raya: *she parts her hair down the middle*, se peina con la raya al medio.

▶ *vi* separarse.

● **for my part** por mi parte.

● **in part** en parte.

● **to take an important part in** desempeñar un papel importante.

● **to take part in** participar en.

partial ['pɑːʃəl] *adj* parcial.

● **to be partial to** ser aficionado,-a a.

partiality [pɑːʃɪ'ælɪtɪ] *n* **1** parcialidad. **2** afición.

partially ['pɑːʃəlɪ] *adv* parcialmente.

participant [pɑː'tɪsɪpənt] *n* participante.

participate [pɑː'tɪsɪpeɪt] *vi* participar.

participation [pɑːtɪsɪ'peɪʃən] *n* participación.

participle ['pɑːtɪsɪpəl] *n* participio.

particle ['pɑːtɪkəl] *n* partícula.

particular [pə'tɪkjʊlə'] *adj* **1** particular, concreto,-a. **2** especial: *for no particular reason*, por ninguna razón especial. **3** exigente.

▶ *npl* **particulars** detalles, datos.

● **in particular** en particular.

particularly [pə'tɪkjʊləlɪ] *adv* especialmente.

parting ['pɑːtɪŋ] *n* **1** despedida. **2** raya *(en pelo)*.

partisan [pɑːtɪ'zæn] *n* **1** partidario,-a. **2** partisano,-a.

partition [pɑː'tɪʃən] *n* **1** partición, división. **2** tabique.

▶ *vt* partir, dividir.

partly ['pɑːtlɪ] *adv* parcialmente, en parte.

partner ['pɑːtnə'] *n* **1** compañero,-a. **2** socio,-a *(en negocio)*. **3** pareja *(en deporte)*. **4** cónyuge.

partridge ['pɑːtrɪdʒ] *n* perdiz pardilla.

part-time [pɑːt'taɪm] *adj* de media jornada.
► *adv* a tiempo parcial.

party ['pɑːtɪ] *n* (*pl* **-ies**). **1** fiesta. **2** partido (*político*). **3** grupo (*de gente*). **4** parte (*en contrato, etc*).

pass [pɑːs] *n* (*pl* **-es**). **1** puerto (*de montaña*). **2** pase (*documento*). **3** aprobado. **4** SP pase.
► *vt-vi* **1** pasar. **2** adelantar. **3** aprobar.
● **to make a pass at** SB insinuarse a ALGN.
● **to pass judgment on** juzgar.
● **to pass water** orinar.

to pass away *vi* pasar a mejor vida.

to pass by *vi* pasar, pasar cerca.

to pass off *vt* hacer pasar por.

to pass on *vt* pasar: *he passed on the information to his colleagues*, pasó la información a sus colegas; *I'll pass you on to her secretary*, le paso con su secretaria.
► *vi* pasar a mejor vida.

to pass out *vi* desmayarse.

to pass over *vt* hacer caso omiso de.

to pass through *vi* estar de paso.

to pass up *vt* dejar pasar, dejar escapar.

passable ['pɑːsəbəl] *adj* **1** pasable, aceptable. **2** transitable.

passage ['pæsɪdʒ] *n* **1** pasaje, pasadizo (*calle*). **2** pasillo (*en casa*). **3** paso (*de vehículo, tiempo*). **4** travesía, viaje (*por mar*). **5** pasaje (*de texto*).

passageway ['pæsɪdʒweɪ] *n* **1** pasillo (*en casa*). **2** pasaje, pasadizo.

passé [pæ'seɪ] *adj* pasado,-a de moda.

passenger ['pæsɪndʒəʳ] *n* viajero,-a, pasajero,-a.

passer-by [pɑːsə'baɪ] *n* (*pl* **passers-by**) transeúnte.

passing ['pɑːsɪŋ] *adj* **1** pasajero,-a (*moda*). **2** de pasada (*comentario*).
● **to say** STH **in passing** decir algo de pasada.

passion ['pæʃən] *n* pasión.

passionate ['pæʃənət] *adj* apasionado,-a.

passive ['pæsɪv] *adj* pasivo,-a.
► *n* voz pasiva.
■ **passive smoker** fumador,-a pasivo,-a.

passover ['pɑːsəʊvəʳ] *n* Pascua judía.

passport ['pɑːspɔːt] *n* pasaporte.

password ['pɑːswɜːd] *n* contraseña.

past [pɑːst] *adj* **1** pasado,-a: *over the past week*, durante la semana pasada. **2** último,-a: *the past few days*, los últimos días. **3** acabado,-a, terminado,-a: *the danger is now past*, ya pasó el peligro. **4** antiguo,-a, anterior: *based on past experience*, basado en experiencias anteriores.
► *adv* por delante: *he walked past*, pasó corriendo.
► *n* pasado.
► *prep* **1** más allá de: *it's just past the cinema*, está un poco más allá del cine. **2** por delante de: *she ran past me*, pasó por mi lado corriendo. **3** y: *five past six*, las seis y cinco. **4** más de: *it's past nine o'clock*, son más de las nueve, son las nueve pasadas.
● **to be past caring** traerle a ALGN sin cuidado.
■ **past participle** participio pasado.
■ **past tense** pasado.

pasta ['pæstə] *n* pasta.

paste [peɪst] *n* **1** pasta. **2** engrudo; cola.
► *vt* pegar.

pastel ['pæstəl] *n* pastel.

pasteurized ['pɑːstʃəraɪzd] *adj* pasteurizado,-a.

pastime ['pɑːstaɪm] *n* pasatiempo.

pastor ['pɑːstəʳ] *n* pastor (*sacerdote*).

pastoral ['pɑːstərəl] *adj* **1** pastoril, bucólico,-a. **2** pastoral.

pastry ['peɪstrɪ] *n* (*pl* **-ies**). **1** masa. **2** pastel, pasta.

pasture ['pɑːstʃəʳ] *n* pasto.

pasty[1] ['pæstɪ] *n* (*pl* **-ies**) empanada.

pasty[2] ['peɪstɪ] *adj* (**-ier**, **-iest**) pálido,-a.

pat[1] [pæt] *n* **1** golpecito, palmadita. **2** porción (*de mantequilla*).
► *vt* (*pt & pp* **patted**, *ger* **patting**) dar golpecitos a, dar palmaditas a.

pat[2] [pæt] *adv* de memoria, al dedillo.
● **to know** STH **off pat** saberse algo al dedillo.

patch [pætʃ] *n* (*pl* **-es**). **1** remiendo. **2** parche (*del ojo*). **3** trozo, parcela (*de tierra*). **4** mancha (*de humedad*).
► *vt* remendar, poner un parche a.
● **not to be a patch on** no tener ni punto de comparación con.
● **to go through a bad patch** pasar por una mala racha.

pâté ['pætei] *n* paté.

patent ['peɪtənt] *adj* 1 patente, evidente.
2 patentado.
▶ *n* patente.
▶ *vt* patentar.
■ **patent leather** charol.

paternal [pə'tɜ:nəl] *adj* 1 paternal *(amor, actitud)*. 2 paterno,-a *(abuelo)*.

paternalistic [pətɜ:nə'lɪstɪk] *adj* paternalista.

paternity [pə'tɜ:nɪtɪ] *n* paternidad.

path [pɑ:θ] *n* 1 camino, sendero. 2 trayectoria *(de bala)*.
● **on the right path** bien encaminado,-a.

pathetic [pə'θetɪk] *adj* 1 patético,-a. 2 malísimo,-a.

pathway ['pɑ:θweɪ] *n* camino, sendero.

patience ['peɪʃəns] *n* 1 paciencia. 2 solitario *(juego de cartas)*.
● **to try SB's patience** poner a prueba la paciencia de ALGN.

patient ['peɪʃənt] *adj* paciente.
▶ *n* paciente, enfermo,-a.

patio ['pætɪəʊ] *n (pl* **patios**) patio.

patriarch ['peɪtrɪɑ:k] *n (pl* **patriarchs**) patriarca.

patrimony ['pætrɪmənɪ] *n* patrimonio.

patriot ['peɪtrɪət] *n* patriota.

patriotic [pætrɪ'ɒtɪk] *adj* patriótico,-a.

patriotism ['pætrɪətɪzəm] *n* patriotismo.

patrol [pə'trəʊl] *n* patrulla.
▶ *vi-vt (pt & pp* **patrolled**, *ger* **patrolling**) patrullar.
● **on patrol** de patrulla.
■ **patrol car** coche patrulla.

patron ['peɪtrən] *adj* 1 patrocinador,-ra. 2 cliente,-a habitual. 3 mecenas.
■ **patron saint** patrón,-ona, santo,-a patrón,-ona.

patronage ['pætrənɪdʒ] *n* patrocinio.

patronize ['pætrənaɪz] *vt* 1 ser cliente,-a habitual de, frecuentar *(tienda)*. 2 patrocinar, auspiciar. 3 *pej* tratar con condescendencia.

patter¹ ['pætə'] *n* 1 tamborileo *(de lluvia)*. 2 pasitos *(de pies)*.
▶ *vt* 1 golpetear, tamborilear *(lluvia)*. 2 corretear *(pies)*.

patter² ['pætə'] *n fam* labia.

pattern ['pætən] *n* 1 modelo. 2 patrón *(en costura)*. 3 dibujo, diseño *(en tela)*. 4 pauta, tendencia.

pause [pɔ:z] *n* pausa.
▶ *vi* 1 hacer una pausa. 2 detenerse.

pave [peɪv] *vt* pavimentar, adoquinar.
● **to pave the way** preparar el terreno.

pavement ['peɪvmənt] *n* acera.

pavillion [pə'vɪlɪən] *n* pabellón.

paw [pɔ:] *n* 1 pata *(de animal)*. 2 garra, zarpa *(de tigre)*.
▶ *vt* manosear, sobar.

pawn¹ [pɔ:n] *n* peón *(en ajedrez)*.

pawn² [pɔ:n] *vt* empeñar.

pawnbroker ['pɔ:nbrəʊkə'] *n* prestamista.

pawnshop ['pɔ:nʃɒp] *n* casa de empeños.

pay [peɪ] *n* paga, sueldo.
▶ *vt-vi (pt & pp* **paid** [peɪd]) pagar.
▶ *vi* 1 ser rentable. 2 valer la pena.
● **to pay attention** prestar atención.
● **to pay a visit** hacer una visita.
■ **pay packet** sobre del sueldo, paga.
■ **pay phone** teléfono público.

to pay back *vt* devolver.

to pay in *vt* ingresar.

to pay off *vt* 1 saldar *(deuda)*. 2 acabar de pagar *(hipoteca)*. 3 dar el finiquito a *(empleado)*.
▶ *vi* salir bien.

payable ['peɪəbəl] *adj* pagadero,-a.

payday ['peɪdeɪ] *n* día de paga.

PAYE ['piː'eɪ'waɪ'iː] *abbr* GB *(pay as you earn)* recaudación de impuestos mediante retenciones practicadas sobre el sueldo.

payee [peɪ'iː] *n* beneficiario,-a.

payment ['peɪmənt] *n* pago.

payroll ['peɪrəʊl] *n* nómina.

payslip ['peɪslɪp] *n* nómina.

pc¹ [pɜ'sent] *abbr (per cent)* por ciento, p.c.

pc² ['piː'siː] *abbr (personal computer)* ordenador personal, PC.

PC ['piː'siː] *abbr* GB *(Police Constable)* agente de policía.

PE ['piː'iː] *abbr (physical education)* educación física.

pea [piː] *n* guisante.

peace [piːs] *n* 1 paz. 2 tranquilidad.
● **at peace, in peace** en paz.
● **to make one's peace with SB** hacer las paces con ALGN.
■ **peace of mind** tranquilidad de espíritu.

peaceful ['piːsfʊl] *adj* 1 pacífico,-a. 2 tranquilo,-a.

peace-keeping ['piːskiːpɪŋ] *adj* de pacificación.

peach [piːtʃ] *n* (*pl* **-es**) melocotón.
■ **peach tree** melocotonero.

peacock ['piːkɒk] *n* pavo real.

peak [piːk] *n* **1** cima, pico *(de montaña)*. **2** apogeo. **3** visera *(de gorra)*.
► *adj* máximo,-a.
► *vi* alcanzar su punto máximo.
■ **peak hour** hora punta.
■ **peak period** período de tarifa máxima.
■ **peak season** temporada alta.

peal [piːl] *n* **1** repique *(de campanas)*. **2** estrépito, estruendo *(de trueno)*.
► *vt-vi* repicar *(campanas)*.

peanut ['piːnʌt] *n* cacahuete.
■ **peanut butter** mantequilla de cacahuete.

pear [peəʳ] *n* pera.
■ **pear tree** peral.

pearl [pɜːl] *n* perla.

peasant ['pezənt] *n* **1** campesino,-a. **2** *pej* inculto,-a, palurdo,-a.

peat [piːt] *n* turba.

pebble ['pebəl] *n* guijarro, china, guija.

peck [pek] *n* **1** picotazo. **2** *fam* beso.
► *vt* picotear.

peckish ['pekɪʃ] *adj* algo hambriento,-a.

pectoral ['pektərəl] *adj-n* pectoral.

peculiar [pɪˈkjuːlɪəʳ] *adj* **1** extraño,-a, raro,-a. **2** peculiar, propio,-a.

peculiarity [pɪkjuːlɪˈærɪtɪ] *n* (*pl* **-ies**). **1** rareza. **2** característica, peculiaridad.

pedagogical [pedəˈɡɒdʒɪkəl] *adj* pedagógico,-a.

pedagogy ['pedəɡɒdʒɪ] *n* pedagogía.

pedal ['pedəl] *n* pedal.
► *vi* (GB *pt & pp* **pedalled**, *ger* **pedalling**; US *pt & pp* **pedaled**, *ger* **pedaling**) pedalear.

peddle ['pedəl] *vt-vi* **1** vender *(de puerta en puerta)*. **2** traficar con.

peddler ['pedləʳ] *n* **1** vendedor,-ra ambulante. **2** pequeño,-a traficante *(de drogas)*.

pedestrian [pɪˈdestrɪən] *n* peatón.
► *adj* pedestre.
■ **pedestrian crossing** paso de peatones.
■ **pedestrian precinct** zona peatonal.

pediatrician [piːdɪəˈtrɪʃən] *n* pediatra.

pediatrics [piːdɪˈætrɪks] *n* pediatría.

Es incontable y el verbo va en singular.

pedigree ['pedɪɡriː] *n* pedigrí.
► *adj* de raza.

pee [piː] *n fam* pis.
► *vi fam* hacer pis.

peek [piːk] *n* ojeada.
► *vi* mirar a hurtadillas, espiar.
● **to have a peek at** echar una ojeada a.

peel [piːl] *n* **1** piel. **2** corteza *(de naranja, limón)*.
► *vt* pelar, mondar.
► *vi* **1** pelarse *(piel)*. **2** desconcharse *(pintura)*. **3** desprenderse, despegarse *(papel pintado)*.

peep[1] [piːp] *n* pío *(ruido)*.

peep[2] [piːp] *n* ojeada, vistazo.
► *vi* mirar, echar una ojeada.
● **to have a peep at** echar una ojeada a.

peep-hole ['piːphəʊl] *n* mirilla.

peeping Tom [piːpɪŋˈtɒm] *n* mirón.

peer[1] [pɪəʳ] *n* **1** igual. **2** noble, par.
■ **peer group** grupo paritario.

peer[2] [pɪəʳ] *vi* mirar atentamente.

peeved [piːvd] *adj fam* molesto,-a.

peg [peɡ] *n* **1** pinza *(de colgar ropa)*. **2** percha, colgador.
► *vt* (*pt & pp* **pegged**, *ger* **pegging**) fijar *(precios)*.

pejorative [pəˈdʒɒrətɪv] *adj* peyorativo, -a, despectivo,-a.

pelican ['pelɪkən] *n* pelícano.

pellet ['pelɪt] *n* **1** pelotilla, bolita. **2** perdigón.

pelt[1] [pelt] *n* piel, pellejo.

pelt[2] [pelt] *vt* tirar, lanzar: *they pelted him with eggs*, le tiraron huevos.
► *vi* **1** llover a cántaros. **2** correr a toda pastilla.

pelvis ['pelvɪs] *n* (*pl* **pelvises**) pelvis.

pen[1] [pen] *n* **1** bolígrafo. **2** pluma, estilográfica. **3** rotulador.

pen[2] [pen] *n* corral, aprisco *(para ganado)*.

penal ['piːnəl] *adj* penal.

penalize ['piːnəlaɪz] *vt* penalizar, castigar.

penalty ['penltɪ] *n* (*pl* **-ies**). **1** pena, castigo. **2** penalización, penalti.
■ **penalty area** área de castigo.

penance ['penəns] *n* penitencia.

pence [pens] *npl* → penny.

penchant ['pɒnʃɒn] *n* inclinación, tendencia.

pencil ['pensəl] *n* lápiz.
■ **pencil case** plumier, estuche.

■ **pencil sharpener** sacapuntas.
pendant ['pendənt] *n* colgante.
pending ['pendɪŋ] *adj* pendiente.
  ▶ *prep* en espera de.
pendulum ['pendjʊləm] *n* péndulo.
penetrate ['penɪtreɪt] *vt* penetrar.
penetrating ['penɪtreɪtɪŋ] *adj* **1** penetrante *(mirada)*. **2** perspicaz *(mente)*.
penetration [penɪ'treɪʃən] *n* penetración.
penfriend ['penfrend] *n* amigo,-a por correspondencia.
penguin ['peŋgwɪn] *n* pingüino.
penicillin [penɪ'sɪlɪn] *n* penicilina.
peninsula [pə'nɪnsjʊlə] *n* península.
penis ['piːnɪs] *n* (*pl* **penises**) pene.
penitent ['penɪtənt] *adj* arrepentido,-a.
  ▶ *n* penitente.
penitentiary [penɪ'tenʃərɪ] *n* (*pl* **-ies**) US penitenciaría.
penknife ['pennaɪf] *n* (*pl* **penknifves**). **1** cortaplumas. **2** navaja.
pennant ['penənt] *n* banderín.
penniless ['penɪləs] *adj* sin dinero.
penny ['penɪ] *n* (*pl* **-ies**). **1** GB penique. **2** US centavo.
  ● **to spend a penny** *fam* ir al servicio.
pension ['penʃən] *n* pensión.
  ● **to pension SB off** jubilar a ALGN.
  ■ **pension fund** fondo de pensiones.
  ■ **pension plan** plan de pensiones.
pensioner ['penʃənəʳ] *n* jubilado,-a, pensionista.
pentagon ['pentəgən] *n* pentágono.
pentathlon [pen'tæθlən] *n* pentatlón.
Pentecost ['pentɪkɒst] *n* Pentecostés.
penthouse ['penthaʊs] *n* ático.
penultimate [pɪ'nʌltɪmət] *adj* penúltimo,-a.
people ['piːpəl] *npl* (*pl* **persons** o **people**) gente, personas: *there are some people waiting*, hay gente esperando.
  ▶ *n* pueblo.
  ▶ *vt* poblar.
pep [pep] *n* *fam* energía, brío, empuje.
pepper ['pepəʳ] *n* **1** pimienta. **2** pimiento.
  ▶ *vt* sazonar con pimienta.
peppermint ['pepəmɪnt] *n* menta.
per [pɜːʳ] *prep* por: *it costs five pounds per kilo*, cuesta cinco libras el kilo.
  ● **as per** según: *as per instructions*, según las instrucciones.
  ● **per cent** por ciento.
  ● **per person** por persona.

perceive [pə'siːv] *vt* percibir, ver, distinguir.
percentage [pə'sentɪdʒ] *n* porcentaje.
perceptible [pə'septɪbəl] *adj* perceptible.
perception [pə'sepʃən] *n* percepción.
perch[1] [pɜːtʃ] *n* (*pl* **-es**). **1** percha *(para pájaro)*. **2** posición privilegiada.
  ▶ *vi* posarse *(pájaro)*.
perch[2] [pɜːtʃ] *n* (*pl* **-es**) perca.
percolator ['pɜːkəleɪtəʳ] *n* cafetera de filtro.
percussion [pɜː'kʌʃən] *n* percusión.
perennial [pə'renɪəl] *adj* perenne.
perfect [(*adj*) 'pɜːfɪkt(*vb*) pə'fekt] *adj* **1** perfecto,-a, ideal. **2** total, absoluto,-a, completo,-a: *a perfect idiot*, un idiota redomado.
  ▶ *vt* perfeccionar.
perfection [pə'fekʃən] *n* perfección.
perfectly ['pɜːfɪktlɪ] *adv* **1** perfectamente, a la perfección. **2** absolutamente, totalmente.
perforate ['pɜːfəreɪt] *vt* perforar.
perform [pə'fɔːm] *vt* **1** hacer, ejecutar, realizar. **2** interpretar *(música)*. **3** representar *(obra de teatro)*.
  ▶ *vi* **1** actuar *(actor)*. **2** funcionar, rendir *(máquina)*.
performance [pə'fɔːməns] *n* **1** ejecución, realización. **2** interpretación, actuación *(de cantante, actor)*. **3** representación *(de obra de teatro)*. **4** funcionamiento *(de máquina)*. **5** rendimiento *(de alumno)*.
performer [pə'fɔːməʳ] *n* **1** actor, actriz. **2** intérprete *(de pieza musical)*.
perfume ['pɜːfjuːm] *n* perfume.
  ▶ *vt* perfumar.
perhaps [pə'hæps] *adv* quizá, quizás, tal vez.
perimeter [pə'rɪmɪtəʳ] *n* perímetro.
period ['pɪərɪəd] *n* **1** período, periodo, época. **2** clase. **3** US punto final.
  ▶ *adj* de época.
periodic [pɪərɪ'ɒdɪk] *adj* periódico,-a.
periodical [pɪərɪ'ɒdɪkəl] *adj* periódico,-a.
  ▶ *n* revista.
peripheral [pə'rɪfərəl] *adj* **1** secundario,-a. **2** periférico.
  ▶ *n* COMPUT unidad periférica.
periphery [pə'rɪfərɪ] *n* (*pl* **-ies**) periferia.
periscope ['perɪskəʊp] *n* periscopio.
perish ['perɪʃ] *vi* perecer, fenecer.
perishable ['perɪʃəbəl] *adj* perecedero,-a.

► *npl* **perishables** productos perecederos.

perjury ['pɜːdʒərɪ] *n (pl* **-ies**) perjurio.

perk [pɜːk] *n fam* beneficio.

to perk up *vi* animarse, reanimarse.

perky ['pɜːkɪ] *adj* (**-ier**, **-iest**) animado,-a.

perm [pɜːm] *n fam* permanente.

► *vt fam: to perm SB's hair,* hacer la permanente a ALGN; *to have one's hair permed,* hacerse la permanente.

permanent ['pɜːmənənt] *adj* permanente, fijo,-a.

permeate ['pɜːmɪeɪt] *vt-vi* penetrar, impregnar.

permission [pəˈmɪʃən] *n* permiso.

permissive [pəˈmɪsɪv] *adj* permisivo,-a.

permit ['pɜːmɪt] *n* **1** permiso, autorización. **2** pase.

► *vt (pt & pp* **permitted**, *ger* **permitting**) permitir.

perpendicular [pɜːpənˈdɪkjʊləʳ] *adj-n* perpendicular.

perpetrate ['pɜːpɪtreɪt] *vt* perpetrar.

perpetual [pəˈpetjʊəl] *adj* **1** perpetuo,-a. **2** constante, incesante.

perpetuate [pəˈpetjʊeɪt] *vt* perpetuar.

perplexed [pəˈplekst] *adj* perplejo,-a.

persecute ['pɜːsɪkjuːt] *vt* perseguir.

persecution [pɜːsɪˈkjuːʃən] *n* persecución.

persevere [pɜːsɪˈvɪəʳ] *vi* perseverar.

Persia ['pɜːʒə] *n* Persia.

Persian ['pɜːʒən] *adj* persa.

► *n* **1** persa *(persona)*. **2** persa *(lengua)*.

■ **Persian Gulf** golfo Pérsico.

persist [pəˈsɪst] *vi* persistir.

● **to persist in doing STH** empeñarse en hacer algo.

persistent [pəˈsɪstənt] *adj* persistente.

person ['pɜːsən] *n (pl* **people**) persona.

● **in person** en persona.

El plural suele ser **people**.

personal ['pɜːsənəl] *adj* **1** personal. **2** personal, privado,-a *(carta, problema)*.

■ **personal computer** ordenador personal.

■ **personal organizer** agenda personal.

■ **personal property** bienes personales.

personality [pɜːsəˈnælɪtɪ] *n (pl* **-ies**) personalidad.

personify [pɜːˈsɒnɪfaɪ] *vt (pt & pp* **-ied**) personificar.

personnel [pɜːsəˈnel] *n* personal.

perspective [pəˈspektɪv] *n* perspectiva.

perspiration [pɜːspɪˈreɪʃən] *n* transpiración, sudor.

perspire [pəˈspaɪəʳ] *vt-vi* transpirar, sudar.

persuade [pəˈsweɪd] *vt* persuadir, convencer.

● **to persuade SB to do STH** convencer a ALGN para que haga algo.

persuasion [pəˈsweɪʒən] *n* **1** persuasión. **2** persuasiva. **3** creencia, opinión: *people of all persuasions,* gente de todas las creencias.

persuasive [pəˈsweɪsɪv] *adj* persuasivo, -a, convincente.

pert [pɜːt] *adj* **1** coqueto,-a *(sombrero)*. **2** fresco,-a, descarado,-a *(persona)*.

pertinent ['pɜːtɪnənt] *adj* pertinente, oportuno,-a.

perturb [pəˈtɜːb] *vt* perturbar, inquietar.

Peru [pəˈruː] *n* Perú.

Peruvian [pəˈruːvɪən] *adj-n* peruano,-a.

pervade [pɜːˈveɪd] *vt* impregnar.

perverse [pəˈvɜːs] *adj* perverso,-a.

perversion [pəˈvɜːʃən] *n* **1** perversión. **2** tergiversación.

pervert [*(n)* ˈpɜːvɜːt/*(vb)* pəˈvɜːt] *n* pervertido,-a.

► *vt* **1** pervertir. **2** tergiversar *(verdad, etc)*.

pessimism ['pesɪmɪzəm] *n* pesimismo.

pessimist ['pesɪmɪst] *n* pesimista.

pessimistic [pesɪˈmɪstɪk] *adj* pesimista.

pest [pest] *n* **1** insecto nocivo, plaga. **2** *fam* pelma, pesado,-a.

pester ['pestəʳ] *vt* molestar.

pesticide ['pestɪsaɪd] *n* pesticida.

pestle ['pesəl] *n* mano de mortero.

pet [pet] *n* **1** animal doméstico. **2** favorito,-a *(persona)*.

► *adj* **1** domesticado,-a *(animal)*. **2** favorito,-a *(persona)*.

► *vt (pt & pp* **petted**, *ger* **petting**) acariciar.

► *vi fam* besuquearse.

petal ['petəl] *n* pétalo.

peter out ['piːtəraʊt] *vi* acabarse, agotarse.

petition [pəˈtɪʃən] *n* petición, solicitud.

► *vt* presentar una solicitud a.

petrify ['petrɪfaɪ] *vt (pt & pp* **-ied**) petrificar.

petrol ['petrəl] *n* gasolina.

■ **petrol pump** surtidor de gasolina.

■ **petrol station** gasolinera.

■ **petrol tank** depósito de gasolina.

petroleum [pəˈtrəʊlɪəm] *n* petróleo.
petticoat [ˈpetɪkəʊt] *n* **1** enaguas. **2** combinación.
petty [ˈpetɪ] *adj* (**-ier, -iest**). **1** insignificante. **2** mezquino,-a.
■ **petty cash** dinero para gastos menores.
■ **petty officer** suboficial de marina.
pew [pjuː] *n* banco *(de iglesia)*.
pewter [ˈpjuːtəʳ] *n* peltre.
phallic [ˈfælɪk] *adj* fálico,-a.
phallus [ˈfæləs] *n* (*pl* **phalluses**) falo.
phantom [ˈfæntəm] *n* fantasma.
pharmaceutical [fɑːməˈsjuːtɪkəl] *adj* farmacéutico,-a.
pharmacist [ˈfɑːməsɪst] *n* farmacéutico,-a.
pharmacy [ˈfɑːməsɪ] *n* (*pl* **-ies**) farmacia.
phase [feɪz] *n* fase.
to phase in *vt* introducir progresivamente.
to phase out *vt* retirar progresivamente.
PhD [ˈpiːˈeɪtʃˈdiː] *abbr* **1** (*Doctor of Philosophy*) doctor,-ra *(en cualquier especialidad académica)*. **2** doctorado.
pheasant [ˈfezənt] *n* faisán.
phenomenon [fɪˈnɒmɪnən] *n* (*pl* **phenomena**) fenómeno.
philanthropist [fɪˈlænθrəpɪst] *n* filántropo,-a.
philharmonic [fɪlɑːˈmɒnɪk] *adj* filarmónico,-a.
Philippine [ˈfɪlɪpiːn] *adj* filipino,-a.
■ **Philippine Sea** Mar de Filipinas.
Philippines [ˈfɪlɪpiːnz] *n* Filipinas.
philosopher [fɪˈlɒsəfəʳ] *n* filósofo,-a.
philosophical [fɪləˈsɒfɪkəl] *adj* filosófico,-a.
philosophy [fɪˈlɒsəfɪ] *n* (*pl* **-ies**) filosofía.
phlegm [flem] *n* flema.
phlegmatic [flegˈmætɪk] *adj* flemático,-a.
phobia [ˈfəʊbɪə] *n* fobia.
phone [fəʊn] *n-vt-vi fam* → telephone.
● **to be on the phone** estar hablando por teléfono.
■ **phone book** listín telefónico.
■ **phone box** cabina telefónica.
■ **phone call** llamada telefónica.
■ **phone line** línea telefónica.
■ **phone number** número de teléfono.
phonecard [ˈfəʊnkɑːd] *n* tarjeta telefónica.

phonetic [fəˈnetɪk] *adj* fonético,-a.
phonetics [fəˈnetɪks] *n* fonética.
> Es incontable y el verbo va en singular.

phoney [ˈfəʊnɪ] *adj* (**-ier, -iest**) *fam* falso,-a.
phony [ˈfəʊnɪ] *adj* (**-ier, -iest**) *fam* falso,-a.
phosphate [ˈfɒsfeɪt] *n* fosfato.
phosphorus [ˈfɒsfərəs] *n* fósforo.
photo [ˈfəʊtəʊ] *n* (*pl* **photos**) *fam* foto.
● **to take a photo of** SB hacerle una foto a ALGN.
photocopier [ˈfəʊtəʊkɒpɪəʳ] *n* fotocopiadora.
photocopy [ˈfəʊtəʊkɒpɪ] *n* (*pl* **-ies**) fotocopia.
▶ *vt* (*pt & pp* **-ied**) fotocopiar.
photograph [ˈfəʊtəgrɑːf] *n* fotografía.
▶ *vt-vi* fotografiar.
photographer [fəˈtɒgrəfəʳ] *n* fotógrafo,-a.
photographic [fəʊtəˈgræfɪk] *adj* fotográfico,-a.
photography [fəˈtɒgrəfɪ] *n* (*pl* **-ies**) fotografía.
phrasal verb [freɪzəlˈvɜːb] *n* verbo con partícula, verbo frasal.
phrase [freɪz] *n* frase.
▶ *vt* expresar.
phrasebook [ˈfreɪzbʊk] *n* manual de conversación.
physical [ˈfɪzɪkəl] *adj* físico,-a.
■ **physical education** educación física.
■ **physical examination** examen médico.
physician [fɪˈzɪʃən] *n* médico,-a.
physicist [ˈfɪzɪsɪst] *n* físico,-a.
physics [ˈfɪzɪks] *n* física.
> Es incontable y el verbo va en singular.

physiological [fɪzɪəˈlɒdʒɪkəl] *adj* fisiológico,-a.
physiology [fɪzɪˈɒlədʒɪ] *n* (*pl* **-ies**) fisiología.
physiotherapy [fɪzɪəʊˈθerəpɪ] *n* fisioterapia.
physique [fɪˈziːk] *n* físico.
pianist [ˈpɪənɪst] *n* pianista.
piano [pɪˈænəʊ] *n* (*pl* **pianos**) piano.
pick¹ [pɪk] *n* pico, piqueta.
pick² [pɪk] *n* pico, piqueta.
▶ *vt* **1** escoger, elegir, seleccionar. **2** coger *(flores, fruta)*. **3** forzar *(cerradura)*.
● **take your pick** escoge el/la que quieras.
● **to pick a fight with** buscar camorra con.

- **to pick holes in** encontrar defectos en.
- **the pick of** la flor y nata de, lo mejor de.
- **to pick one's nose** hurgarse la nariz.
- **to pick one's teeth** escarbarse los dientes.
- **to pick SB's pocket** robarle la cartera a ALGN.

to pick off vt matar uno a uno.
to pick on vt meterse con.
to pick out vt **1** escoger. **2** distinguir.
to pick up vt **1** coger, recoger. **2** ir a buscar. **3** captar (emisora de radio). **4** aprender (lengua). **5** fam ligarse.
pickaxe ['pɪkæks] n pico, piqueta.
picket ['pɪkɪt] n piquete.
 ▶ vt formar un piquete en.
pickle ['pɪkəl] n **1** encurtido, escabeche. **2** aprieto.
 ▶ vt encurtir, escabechar.
pick-me-up ['pɪkmiːʌp] n tónico.
pickpocket ['pɪkpɒkɪt] n carterista.
pick-up ['pɪkʌp] n **1** brazo del tocadiscos, fonocaptor. **2** furgoneta.
picnic ['pɪknɪk] n merienda, picnic.
 ▶ vi (pt & pp picnicked, ger picnicking) ir de picnic, hacer un picnic.
pictorial [pɪk'tɔːrɪəl] adj **1** ilustrado,-a (revista). **2** pictórico,-a (representación).
picture ['pɪktʃəʳ] n **1** pintura, cuadro. **2** retrato. **3** dibujo. **4** fotografía. **5** lámina. **6** película. **7** imagen.
 ▶ vt **1** pintar, retratar. **2** imaginar, imaginarse.
- **to take a picture** hacer una foto.
picturesque [pɪktʃəˈresk] adj pintoresco,-a.
piddling ['pɪdəlɪŋ] adj fam insignificante.
pidgin ['pɪdʒɪn] n pidgin.
pie [paɪ] n **1** pastel, tarta (dulce). **2** pastel, empanada (salado).
piece [piːs] n **1** trozo, pedazo. **2** pieza. **3** moneda.
- **to take to pieces** desmontar.
- **in one piece 1** sano y salvo (persona). **2** intacto,-a (objeto).
- **it's a piece of cake** fam es pan comido.

Sirve para individualizar los nombres incontables: *an interesting piece of news*, una noticia interesante.

to piece together vt **1** reconstruir (pasado). **2** juntar (ideas).
piecemeal ['piːsmiːl] adv poco a poco.
piecework ['piːswɜːk] n trabajo a destajo.
pier [pɪəʳ] n **1** muelle, embarcadero. **2** pilar.
pierce [pɪəs] vt perforar, agujerear.
piercing ['pɪəsɪŋ] adj **1** penetrante (mirada). **2** desgarrador,-a (grito).
piety ['paɪətɪ] n (pl -ies) piedad.
pig [pɪg] n **1** cerdo,-a. **2** glotón,-ona. **3** sl madero.
- **to make a pig of oneself** darse un atracón.
■ **pig farm** granja porcina.
pigeon ['pɪdʒɪn] n paloma.
pigeonhole ['pɪdʒɪnhəʊl] n casilla.
pig-headed [pɪg'hedɪd] adj testarudo,-a.
piglet ['pɪglət] n cochinillo, lechón.
pigment ['pɪgmənt] n pigmento.
pigsty ['pɪgstaɪ] n (pl -ies) pocilga.
pigtail ['pɪgteɪl] n trenza.
pike[1] [paɪk] n pica.
pike[2] [paɪk] n lucio.
pile [paɪl] n montón, pila.
 ▶ vt amontonar, apilar.
to pile up vt-vi amontonar(se), apilar(se).
pile-up ['paɪlʌp] n choque en cadena.
piles [paɪlz] npl almorranas, hemorroides.
pilfer ['pɪlfəʳ] vt-vi hurtar.
pilgrim ['pɪlgrɪm] n peregrino,-a.
pilgrimage ['pɪlgrɪmɪdʒ] n peregrinación.
pill [pɪl] n píldora, pastilla.
- **to be on the pill** tomar la píldora.
pillar ['pɪləʳ] n pilar, columna.
pillow ['pɪləʊ] n almohada.
pilot ['paɪlət] adj-n piloto.
 ▶ vt pilotar.
pimento [pɪ'mentəʊ] n (pl pimentos) pimiento morrón.
pimp [pɪmp] n chulo, macarra.
pimple ['pɪmpəl] n grano.
pin [pɪn] n **1** alfiler. **2** clavija.
 ▶ vt (pt & pp pinned, ger pinning). **1** prender, sujetar (con alfileres). **2** clavar (cartel).
to pin down vt **1** definir, precisar. **2** inmovilizar.
pinafore ['pɪnəfɔːʳ] n delantal.
pincers ['pɪnsəz] npl **1** tenazas. **2** pinzas (de cangrejo).

pinch [pɪntʃ] *n* (*pl* **-es**). **1** pellizco. **2** pizca.
► *vt* **1** pellizcar. **2** apretar *(zapatos)*. **3** *fam* birlar, afanar.
pine[1] [paɪn] *n* pino.
■ **pine cone** piña.
■ **pine nut** piñón.
pine[2] [paɪn] *vi* **to pine (away)** consumirse.
pineapple ['paɪnæpəl] *n* piña.
ping [pɪŋ] *n* sonido metálico.
► *vi* hacer un sonido metálico.
ping-pong ['pɪŋpɒŋ] *n* tenis de mesa, pimpón.
pinion ['pɪnɪən] *n* piñón *(rueda dentada)*.
pink [pɪŋk] *adj* rosa, de color rosa, rosado,-a.
► *n* **1** rosa *(color)*. **2** clavel, clavellina.
pinnacle ['pɪnəkəl] *n* **1** pináculo. **2** cima, cumbre *(de montaña)*.
pinpoint ['pɪnpɔɪnt] *vt* señalar, determinar.
pint [paɪnt] *n* pinta.

En Gran Bretaña equivale a 0,57 litros; en Estados Unidos equivale a 0,47 litros.

pioneer [paɪə'nɪəʳ] *n* pionero,-a.
► *vt* iniciar.
pious [paɪəs] *adj* pío,-a.
pip [pɪp] *n* pepita.
● **to be pipped at the post** perder por los pelos.
pipe [paɪp] *n* **1** tubería, cañería *(de agua, gas)*. **2** pipa *(para fumar)*. **3** caramillo *(instrumento)*.
► *npl* **pipes** gaita.
► *vt* llevar por tubería, conducir por tubería.
to pipe down *vi* callarse.
pipeline ['paɪplaɪn] *n* **1** tubería. **2** gasoducto. **3** oleoducto.
● **in the pipeline** en trámite.
piper ['paɪpəʳ] *n* gaitero,-a.
piping ['paɪpɪŋ] *n* tuberías.
● **piping hot** muy caliente.
piracy ['paɪərəsɪ] *n* piratería.
piranha [pɪ'rɑːnə] *n* piraña.
pirate ['paɪərət] *n* pirata.
► *vt* piratear.
Pisces ['paɪsiːz] *n* Piscis.
piss [pɪs] *n fam* meada.
► *vi fam* mear.
● **to take the piss** cachondearse.

● **to piss down** *fam* llover a cántaros.
to piss off *vi sl* largarse.
► *vt sl* cabrear, poner de mala leche.
pissed [pɪst] *adj* **1** GB *fam* trompa, pedo. **2** US *fam* harto,-a.
pistachio [pɪs'tɑːʃɪəʊ] *n* (*pl* **pistachios**) pistacho.
pistol ['pɪstəl] *n* pistola.
piston ['pɪstən] *n* pistón, émbolo.
pit[1] [pɪt] *n* **1** hoyo, foso. **2** mina. **3** foso de la orquesta. **4** marca, señal, cicatriz.
► *vt* (*pt & pp* **pitted**, *ger* **pitting**) picar.
● **to pit one's strength against, pit one's wits against** medirse con.
pit[2] [pɪt] *n* US hueso *(de fruta)*.
► *vt* (*pt & pp* **pitted**, *ger* **pitting**) deshuesar.
pitch[1] [pɪtʃ] *n* (*pl* **-es**). **1** MUS tono. **2** campo, terreno *(de juego)*. **3** lanzamiento. **4** grado, nivel. **5** pendiente.
► *vt* **1** tirar, arrojar, lanzar. **2** plantar, armar *(tienda de campaña)*.
■ **pitched battle** batalla campal.
pitch[2] [pɪtʃ] *n* pez, brea.
to pitch in *vi* colaborar, ayudar.
to pitch into *vt* **1** ponerse *(a hacer algo)*: **he pitched into his work**, se puso a trabajar. **2** atacar, arremeter contra.
pitch-black[2] [pɪtʃ'blæk] *adj* negro,-a como la boca del lobo.
pitcher[1] ['pɪtʃəʳ] *n* **1** GB cántaro. **2** US jarro.
pitcher[2] ['pɪtʃəʳ] *n* US lanzador,-ra *(de béisbol)*.
pitchfork ['pɪtʃfɔːk] *n* horca.
pitfall ['pɪtfɔːl] *n* escollo.
pith [pɪθ] *n* **1** médula. **2** meollo.
pitiful ['pɪtɪfʊl] *adj* **1** lastimoso,-a. **2** lamentable, penoso,-a.
pitiless ['pɪtɪləs] *adj* despiadado,-a.
pittance ['pɪtəns] *n* miseria.
pity ['pɪtɪ] *n* (*pl* **-ies**) pena, lástima.
► *vt* (*pt & pp* **-ied**) compadecerse de.
● **to take pity on** SB apiadarse de ALGN.
● **what a pity!** ¡qué lástima!
pivot ['pɪvət] *n* pivote, eje.
► *vi* girar.
pizza ['piːtsə] *n* pizza.
■ **pizza parlour** pizzería.
placard ['plækɑːd] *n* pancarta.
placate [plə'keɪt] *vt* aplacar, apaciguar.
place [pleɪs] *n* **1** lugar, sitio. **2** asiento, sitio. **3** plaza *(en escuela, etc)*. **4** posición *(en carretera, etc)*. **5** *fam* casa, piso.

▸ *vt* **1** colocar, poner, situar. **2** recordar.
● **all over the place** en todas partes.
● **in place** en su sitio.
● **in place of** en vez de.
● **in the first place** en primer lugar.
● **out of place** fuera de lugar.
● **to place an order** hacer un pedido.
● **to take place** tener lugar.
● **to take the place of** sustituir.
■ **place mat** mantel individual.
■ **place name** topónimo.

placenta [pləˈsentə] *n* placenta.

plague [pleɪg] *n* **1** plaga. **2** peste.
▸ *vt* asediar, acosar, importunar.

plaice [pleɪs] *n* platija.

plaid [plæd] *n* tejido escocés.

plain [pleɪn] *adj* **1** claro,-a, evidente: *the plain truth*, la pura verdad. **2** sencillo,-a. **3** sin atractivo. **4** franco,-a, directo,-a *(discurso)*. **5** liso,-a *(tejido)*. **6** sin leche *(chocolate)*.
▸ *n* llanura.
● **in plain clothes** vestido,-a de paisano.
● **to make STH plain** dejar algo bien claro.
■ **plain yoghurt** yogur natural.

plain-spoken [pleɪnˈspəʊkən] *adj* franco,-a.

plaintiff [ˈpleɪntɪf] *n (pl* **plaintiffs)** demandante.

plait [plæt] *n* trenza.
▸ *vt* trenzar.

plan [plæn] *n* **1** plan, programa. **2** plano *(de ciudad)*.
▸ *vt (pt & pp* **planned**, *ger* **planning)** planear, planificar.
▸ *vi* hacer planes.

plane¹ [pleɪn] *n* **1** plano *(superficie)*. **2** aeroplano, avión.

plane² [pleɪn] *n* cepillo, garlopa *(para madera)*.

plane³ [pleɪn] *n* plátano *(árbol)*.

planet [ˈplænət] *n* planeta.

plank [plæŋk] *n* tablón, tabla.

plankton [ˈplæŋktən] *n* plancton.

planning [ˈplænɪŋ] *n* planificación.
■ **planning permission** permiso de obras.

plant¹ [plɑːnt] *n* planta.
▸ *vt* **1** plantar, sembrar. **2** colocar *(bomba)*.
■ **plant pot** maceta, tiesto.

plant² [plɑːnt] *n* **1** equipo, maquinaria *(industrial)*. **2** fábrica, planta.

plantation [plænˈteɪʃən] *n* plantación.

plaque [plæk] *n* placa.

plasma [ˈplæzmə] *n* plasma.

plaster [ˈplɑːstəʳ] *n* **1** yeso. **2** MED escayola. **3** esparadrapo, tirita®.
▸ *vt* **1** enyesar. **2** cubrir.
■ **plaster cast** escayola.

plastic [ˈplæstɪk] *adj* plástico,-a.
▸ *n* plástico.

plasticine® [ˈplæstɪsiːn] *n* plastilina®.

plate [pleɪt] *n* **1** plato. **2** placa. **3** grabado, lámina.
▸ *vt* chapar.

plateau [ˈplætəʊ] *n (pl* **-s** o **plateaux)** meseta.

platform [ˈplætfɔːm] *n* **1** plataforma. **2** tarima, tribuna, estrado. **3** andén. **4** POL programa.

platinum [ˈplætɪnəm] *n* platino.

platonic [pləˈtɒnɪk] *adj* platónico,-a.

platoon [pləˈtuːn] *n* pelotón.

plausible [ˈplɔːzɪbəl] *adj* verosímil, plausible.

play [pleɪ] *n* **1** juego. **2** obra de teatro. **3** juego, movimiento.
▸ *vt-vi* **1** jugar. **2** tocar: *he plays the piano*, toca el piano.
▸ *vt* **1** interpretar, hacer el papel de. **2** jugar a: *she plays tennis*, juega al tenis. **3** jugar contra *(equipo, adversario)*. **4** poner *(disco)*.
● **to play a trick on** hacer una mala jugada a.
● **to play for time** tratar de ganar tiempo.
● **to play hard to get** hacerse de rogar.
● **to play the fool** hacer el indio.
● **to play truant** hacer novillos.
● **to play it by ear** decidir sobre la marcha.
■ **play on words** juego de palabras.

to play along *vi* seguir la corriente.
to play down *vt* quitar importancia a.
to play on *vt* aprovecharse de.
to play up *vt* causar problemas a.
▸ *vi* **1** no funcionar bien *(máquina)*. **2** dar guerra *(niño)*.

playboy [ˈpleɪbɔɪ] *n* playboy.

player [ˈpleɪəʳ] *n* **1** jugador,-ra. **2** actor, actriz. **3** músico,-a: *a piano player*, un pianista.

playful ['pleɪfʊl] *adj* juguetón,-ona.

playground ['pleɪgraʊnd] *n* patio de recreo.

playhouse ['pleɪhaʊs] *n* teatro.

playing field ['pleɪŋgfiːld] *n* campo de juego.

playmate ['pleɪmeɪt] *n* compañero,-a de juego.

play-off ['pleɪɒf] *n* (*pl* **play-offs**) partido de desempate.

plaything ['pleɪθɪŋ] *n* juguete.

playtime ['pleɪtaɪm] *n* recreo.

playwright ['pleɪraɪt] *n* dramaturgo,-a.

PLC ['piːˈelˈsiː] *abbr* GB (*Public Limited Company*) Sociedad Anónima, S.A..
> También se escribe **plc**.

plea [pliː] *n* petición, súplica, ruego.
● **to enter a plea of guilty** declararse culpable.
● **to enter a plea of not guilty** declararse inocente.

plead [pliːd] *vi* suplicar.
▶ *vt* alegar.
● **to plead guilty** declararse culpable.
● **to plead not guilty** declararse inocente.

pleasant ['plezənt] *adj* (*comp* **pleasanter**, *superl* **pleasantest**). **1** agradable *(tiempo)*. **2** simpático,-a, amable *(persona)*.

please [pliːz] *vt-vi* agradar, gustar, placer, complacer.
▶ *interj* por favor.
● **as you please** como quieras.
● **please yourself** haz lo que quieras.

pleased [pliːzd] *adj* contento,-a, satisfecho,-a.
● **pleased to meet you!** ¡encantado,-a!, ¡mucho gusto!
● **to be pleased to do STH** alegrarse de hacer algo, tener el placer de hacer algo.

pleasing ['pliːzɪŋ] *adj* agradable.

pleasurable ['pleʒərəbəl] *adj* agradable.

pleasure ['pleʒəʳ] *n* placer.
● **it gives me great pleasure to ...** me complace ....
● **it's my pleasure** de nada, no hay de qué.
● **with pleasure** con mucho gusto.

pleat [pliːt] *n* pliegue.
▶ *vt* plisar.

pledge [pledʒ] *n* **1** promesa. **2** prenda, señal.

▶ *vt-vi* prometer.

plentiful ['plentɪfʊl] *adj* abundante.

plenty ['plentɪ] *n* abundancia.
▶ *pron* **1** muchos,-as: *plenty of reasons*, muchas razones. **2** de sobra, en abundancia: *don't run, there's plenty of time*, no corras, hay tiempo de sobra.

pliable ['plaɪəbəl] *adj* flexible.

pliers ['plaɪəz] *npl* alicates.

plight [plaɪt] *n* situación grave.

plimsolls ['plɪmsəlz] *npl* GB playeras.

plod [plɒd] *vi* (*pt & pp* **plodded**, *ger* **plodding**). **1** andar pesadamente. **2** trabajar laboriosamente.

plonk[1] [plɒŋk] *vt* dejar caer.

plonk[2] [plɒŋk] *n fam* vino peleón.

plot[1] [plɒt] *n* **1** conspiración, complot. **2** trama, argumento.
▶ *vt* (*pt & pp* **plotted**, *ger* **plotting**). **1** tramar, urdir. **2** trazar *(rumbo)*.
▶ *vi* conspirar, intrigar.

plot[2] [plɒt] *n* parcela, terreno.

plough [plaʊ] *n* arado.
▶ *vt-vi* arar, labrar.

plow [plaʊ] *n-vt-vi* US → **plough**.

pluck [plʌk] *n* valor.
▶ *vt* **1** arrancar *(flor)*. **2** desplumar *(ave)*.
● **to pluck one's eyebrows** depilarse las cejas.
● **to pluck up courage** armarse de valor.

plug [plʌg] *n* **1** tapón. **2** enchufe, clavija *(macho)*, enchufe, toma *(hembra)*. **3** bujía.
▶ *vt* (*pt & pp* **plugged**, *ger* **plugging**) tapar, rellenar.

to plug in *vt-vi* enchufar(se).

plughole ['plʌghəʊl] *n* desagüe.

plum [plʌm] *n* ciruela.
■ **plum tree** ciruelo.

plumage ['pluːmɪdʒ] *n* plumaje.

plumb [plʌm] *n* plomada.
▶ *adj-adv* a plomo.
▶ *adv* **1** US completamente. **2** US justo: *plumb in the middle*, justo en el centro.
▶ *vt* sondar, sondear.

plumber ['plʌməʳ] *n* fontanero,-a.

plumbing ['plʌmɪŋ] *n* fontanería.

plume [pluːm] *n* penacho.

plummet ['plʌmɪt] *vi* caer en picado.

plump [plʌmp] *adj* rechoncho,-a, rollizo,-a.

plump for ['plʌmpfɔːʳ] *vt* optar por.

plunder ['plʌndə'] *n* **1** pillaje, saqueo. **2** botín.

▶ *vt* saquear.

plunge [plʌndʒ] *n* **1** zambullida. **2** caída vertiginosa.

▶ *vi* **1** zambullirse, tirarse de cabeza. **2** caer en picado.

▶ *vt* **1** sumergir *(en agua)*. **2** hundir *(cuchillo)*.

● **to take the plunge** dar el paso decisivo.

plunger ['plʌndʒə'] *n* desatascador.

pluperfect [plu:'pɜːfekt] *n* pluscuamperfecto.

plural ['plʊərəl] *adj-n* plural.

plus [plʌs] *prep* más: *five plus three is eight*, cinco más tres son ocho.

▶ *conj* además de que.

▶ *n* (*pl* **pluses**) ventaja.

■ **plus sign** signo de más.

plush [plʌʃ] *adj fam* lujoso,-a.

ply [plaɪ] *vi* (*pt & pp* **-ied**) hacer el trayecto, navegar.

● **to ply one's trade** ejercer su oficio.

● **to ply SB with STH** no parar de ofrecer algo a ALGN.

plywood ['plaɪwʊd] *n* contrachapado.

pm ['piː'em] *abbr* (*post meridiem*) después del mediodía: *at 4 pm*, a las cuatro de la tarde.

En Estados Unidos también se escribe **PM**.

PM ['piː'em] *abbr* GB (*Prime Minister*) Primer,-a Ministro,-a.

PMT ['piː'em'tiː] *abbr* (*premenstrual tension*) tensión premenstrual.

pneumatic [njuːˈmætɪk] *adj* neumático,-a.

pneumonia [njuːˈməʊnɪə] *n* neumonía, pulmonía.

PO[1] ['pəʊstɒfɪs] *abbr* (*Post Office*) correos.

PO[2] ['pəʊstələːdə'] *abbr* (*postal order*) giro postal, g.p..

poach[1] [pəʊtʃ] *vt-vi* **1** cazar en vedado. **2** pescar en vedado.

poach[2] [pəʊtʃ] *vt* **1** hervir. **2** escalfar *(huevos)*.

pocket ['pɒkɪt] *n* bolsillo.

▶ *vt* **1** embolsar(se). **2** meterse en el bolsillo.

■ **pocket money** dinero de bolsillo.

pocketbook ['pɒkɪtbʊk] *n* **1** US bolso. **2** libreta. **3** US libro en rústica.

pod [pɒd] *n* vaina.

podgy ['pɒdʒɪ] *adj* (**-ier, -iest**) regordete,-a.

podium ['pəʊdɪəm] *n* podio.

poem ['pəʊəm] *n* poema, poesía.

poet ['pəʊət] *n* poeta.

poetic [pəʊˈetɪk] *adj* poético,-a.

poetry ['pəʊətrɪ] *n* poesía.

poignant ['pɔɪnjənt] *adj* conmovedor,-ra.

point [pɔɪnt] *n* **1** punta *(de aguja, etc)*. **2** punto *(en espacio)*. **3** punto, momento *(en el tiempo)*. **4** punto: *freezing point*, punto de congelación. **5** punto, tanto *(en puntuación)*. **6** punto, cuestión: *the point is...*, la cuestión es.... **7** coma: *5 point 66*, cinco coma sesenta y seis. **8** sentido: *what's the point of arguing?*, ¿de qué sirve discutir? **9 points** agujas.

▶ *vi* **1** indicar: *the sign points right*, la señal indica hacia la derecha. **2** señalar *(con el dedo)*.

▶ *vt* apuntar: *he pointed a gun at me*, me apuntó con una pistola.

● **on the point of** a punto de.

● **there's no point in ...** no vale la pena ....

● **to be beside the point** no venir al caso.

● **to come to the point** ir al grano.

● **up to a point** hasta cierto punto.

■ **point of view** punto de vista.

■ **weak point** punto débil.

to point out *vt* señalar.

point-blank [pɔɪnt'blæŋk] *adj* **1** categórico,-a *(rechazo)*. **2** a quemarropa *(disparo)*.

▶ *adv* **1** categóricamente *(rechazar)*. **2** a quemarropa *(disparar)*.

pointed ['pɔɪntɪd] *adj* **1** puntiagudo,-a *(objeto)*. **2** intencionado,-a *(comentario)*.

pointer ['pɔɪntə'] *n* **1** indicador. **2** perro de muestra, pointer.

pointless ['pɔɪntləs] *adj* sin sentido.

poise [pɔɪz] *n* porte, elegancia.

poison ['pɔɪzən] *n* veneno.

▶ *vt* envenenar.

poisonous ['pɔɪzənəs] *adj* venenoso,-a.

poke [pəʊk] *n* **1** empujón, empellón. **2** codazo.

▶ *vt* **1**: *he poked me in the arm*, me dio con el dedo en el brazo; *she poked him in the ribs*, le dio un codazo en las costillas. **2** atizar *(fuego)*. **3** asomar: *he poked his head out of the window*, asomó la cabeza por la ventana.

poker¹ ['pəʊkə'] *n* póquer.
poker² ['pəʊkə'] *n* atizador.
Poland ['pəʊlənd] *n* Polonia.
polar ['pəʊlə'] *adj* polar.
■ **polar bear** oso polar.
polarize ['pəʊləraɪz] *vt* polarizar.
▶ *vi* polarizarse.
pole¹ [pəʊl] *n* **1** palo, poste: *telegraph pole*, poste telegráfico. **2** pértiga.
■ **pole vault** salto con pértiga.
pole² [pəʊl] *n* polo.
● **to be poles apart** ser polos opuestos.
■ **pole star** estrella polar.
Pole [pəʊl] *n* polaco,-a.
polemic [pə'lemɪk] *adj* polémico,-a.
▶ *n* polémica.
police [pə'liːs] *npl* policía.
▶ *vt* vigilar.
■ **police car** coche patrulla.
■ **police officer** agente de policía.
■ **police record** antecedentes policiales.
■ **police station** comisaría de policía.
policeman [pə'liːsmən] *n* (*pl* **policemen**) policía, guardia.
policewoman [pə'liːswʊmən] *n* (*pl* **policewomen**) mujer policía.
policy ['pɒlɪsɪ] *n* (*pl* **-ies**). **1** política: *foreign policy*, política exterior. **2** póliza (*de seguros*).
polish ['pɒlɪʃ] *n* (*pl* **-es**). **1** cera (*para muebles*). **2** betún (*para zapatos*). **3** esmalte (*para uñas*). **4** lustre, brillo.
▶ *vt* **1** abrillantar, sacar brillo a. **2** pulir (*estilo*).
● **to give STH a polish** sacar brillo a algo.
to polish off *vt* **1** despachar (*trabajo*). **2** zamparse (*comida*).
Polish ['pəʊlɪʃ] *adj* polaco,-a.
▶ *n* **1** polaco,-a (*persona*). **2** polaco (*lengua*).
polite [pə'laɪt] *adj* (*comp* **politer**, *superl* **politest**) cortés, bien educado,-a.
politeness [pə'laɪtnəs] *n* cortesía, educación.
political [pə'lɪtɪkəl] *adj* político,-a.
■ **political asylum** asilo político.
politician [pɒlɪ'tɪʃən] *n* político,-a.
politics ['pɒlɪtɪks] *n* política. Es incontable y el verbo va en singular.
▶ *npl* opiniones políticas.
poll [pəʊl] *n* **1** votación. **2** encuesta, sondeo.

▶ *vt* obtener.
pollen ['pɒlən] *n* polen.
pollutant [pə'luːtənt] *n* contaminante.
pollute [pɒ'luːt] *vt* contaminar.
pollution [pɒ'luːʃən] *n* contaminación.
polo ['pəʊləʊ] *n* polo.
■ **polo neck** cuello alto.
polyester [pɒlɪ'estə'] *n* poliéster.
polygon ['pɒlɪɡɒn] *n* polígono.
polystyrene [pɒlɪ'staɪriːn] *n* poliestireno.
polytechnic [pɒlɪ'teknɪk] *n* escuela politécnica.
polyurethane [pɒlɪ'jʊərəθeɪn] *n* poliuretano.
pomegranate ['pɒmɪɡrænət] *n* granada (*fruta*).
pomp [pɒmp] *n* pompa.
pompom ['pɒmpɒm] *n* pompón.
pompous ['pɒmpəs] *adj* pomposo,-a.
pond [pɒnd] *n* estanque.
ponder ['pɒndə'] *vt* ponderar, considerar.
pong [pɒŋ] *n fam* tufo.
▶ *vt fam* apestar.
pontoon¹ [pɒn'tuːn] *n* veintiuna (*juego de naipes*).
pontoon² [pɒn'tuːn] *n* pontón.
pony ['pəʊnɪ] *n* (*pl* **-ies**) poni.
ponytail ['pəʊnɪteɪl] *n* cola de caballo.
poodle ['puːdəl] *n* caniche.
poof [pʊf] *n* (*pl* **poofs**) *sl* marica.
pooh-pooh [puː'puː] *vt* despreciar.
pool¹ [puːl] *n* **1** charco. **2** estanque. **3** piscina.
pool² [puːl] *n* **1** fondo común. **2** billar americano.
▶ *vt* reunir, juntar, poner en común.
▶ *npl* **the pools** las quinielas.
poor [pʊə'] *adj* **1** pobre. **2** malo,-a, de mala calidad.
poorly ['pʊəlɪ] *adj* (**-ier, -iest**) mal, malo,-a.
▶ *adv* mal: *poorly paid workers*, trabajadores mal pagados.
pop¹ [pɒp] *n* **1** estallido (*sonido*). **2** tapanazo. **3** *fam* gaseosa, refresco.
▶ *vt* (*pt & pp* **popped**, *ger* **popping**) poner: *pop it in your pocket*, métetelo en el bolsillo.
▶ *vt-vi* reventar, estallar.
pop² [pɒp] *n fam* papá.
to pop in *vi* (*pt & pp* **popped**, *ger* **popping**) entrar un momento.

to pop out *vi* salir un momento.

to pop up *vi* aparecer de repente.

popcorn ['pɒpkɔːn] *n* palomitas *(de maíz)*, rosetas *(de maíz)*.

pope [pəʊp] *n* papa.

poplar ['pɒplə'] *n* álamo, chopo.

poppy ['pɒpɪ] *n (pl* **-ies)** amapola.

popular ['pɒpjʊlə'] *adj* popular.

popularity [pɒpjʊ'lærɪtɪ] *n* popularidad.

popularize ['pɒpjʊlaraɪz] *vt* popularizar.

populate ['pɒpjʊleɪt] *vt* poblar.

population [pɒpjʊ'leɪʃən] *n* población, habitantes.

■ **population explosion** explosión demográfica.

porcelain ['pɔːsəlɪn] *n* porcelana.

porch [pɔːtʃ] *n (pl* **-es)** pórtico, entrada.

porcupine ['pɔːkjʊpaɪn] *n* puerco espín.

pore [pɔː'] *n* poro.

pore over ['pɔːr'əʊvə'] *vt* estudiar detenidamente.

pork [pɔːk] *n* carne de cerdo.

■ **pork chop** chuleta de cerdo.

pornographic [pɔːnə'græfɪk] *adj* pornográfico,-a.

pornography [pɔː'nɒgrəfɪ] *n* pornografía.

porpoise ['pɔːpəs] *n* marsopa.

porridge ['pɒrɪdʒ] *n* gachas de avena.

port[1] [pɔːt] *n* puerto *(de mar)*.

port[2] [pɔːt] *n* babor.

port[3] [pɔːt] *n* oporto *(vino)*.

portable ['pɔːtəbəl] *adj* portátil.

portal ['pɔːtəl] *n* COMPUT portal.

porter ['pɔːtə'] *n* **1** portero,-a. **2** mozo.

portfolio [pɔːt'fəʊlɪəʊ] *n (pl* **portfolios). 1** carpeta. **2** POL cartera.

porthole ['pɔːthəʊl] *n* portilla.

portion ['pɔːʃən] *n* **1** porción, parte. **2** ración *(de comida)*.

to portion out *vt* repartir.

portly ['pɔːtlɪ] *adj* **(-ier,** **-iest)** corpulento,-a.

portrait ['pɔːtreɪt] *n* retrato.

portray [pɔː'treɪ] *vt* **1** retratar. **2** describir, representar.

Portugal ['pɔːtjʊgəl] *n* Portugal.

Portuguese [pɔːtjʊ'giːz] *adj* portugués,-esa.

▶ *n* **1** portugués,-esa *(persona)*. **2** portugués *(lengua)*.

▶ *npl* **the Portuguese** los portugueses.

pose [pəʊz] *n* **1** actitud, postura. **2** afectación, pose.

▶ *vt* **1** plantear *(problema)*. **2** representar *(amenaza)*.

▶ *vi* **1** adoptar una pose. **2** posar *(como modelo)*.

● **to pose as** hacerse pasar por.

posh [pɒʃ] *adj* **1** GB *fam* elegante, de lujo *(lugar)*. **2** GB *fam* afectado,-a, pijo,-a *(persona)*.

position [pə'zɪʃən] *n* **1** sitio, posición. **2** postura, actitud: *I'm sitting in an uncomfortable position*, estoy sentado en una posición incómoda. **3** puesto, empleo. **4** situación: *it was an awkward position*, era una situación incómoda.

▶ *vt* colocar.

positive ['pɒzɪtɪv] *adj* **1** positivo,-a. **2** seguro,-a: *I'm positive that I saw him*, seguro que lo vi. **3** *fam* auténtico,-a.

possess [pə'zes] *vt* **1** poseer, tener. **2** apoderarse de: *jealousy possessed him*, los celos se apoderaron de él.

possession [pə'zeʃən] *n* posesión.

possessive [pə'zesɪv] *adj* posesivo,-a.

possibility [pɒsɪ'bɪlɪtɪ] *n (pl* **-ies)** posibilidad.

possible ['pɒsɪbəl] *adj* posible.

● **as much as possible** todo lo posible.

● **as soon as possible** cuanto antes.

possibly ['pɒsɪblɪ] *adv* posiblemente.

post[1] [pəʊst] *n* poste, estaca, palo.

post[2] [pəʊst] *n* **1** puesto, cargo. **2** puesto *(militar)*.

▶ *vt* enviar, destinar *(subordinado)*.

post[3] [pəʊst] *n* correo.

▶ *vt* **1** echar al correo *(carta)*. **2** poner *(anuncio)*.

■ **post office** oficina de correos.

■ **post office box** apartado de correos.

postage ['pəʊstɪdʒ] *n* franqueo, porte.

■ **postage and packing** gastos de envío.

■ **postage stamp** sello de correos.

postal ['pəʊstəl] *adj* postal.

■ **postal district** distrito postal.

■ **postal order** giro postal.

postbox ['pəʊstbɒks] *n (pl* **postboxes)** buzón.

postcard ['pəʊstkɑːd] *n* tarjeta postal, postal.

postcode ['pəʊstkəʊd] *n* código postal.

poster ['pəʊstə'] *n* póster, cartel.

posterior [pɒ'stɪərɪə'] *adj* posterior.

▶ *n fam* trasero.

posterity [pɒs'terɪtɪ] *n* posteridad.

postgraduate [pəʊst'grædjʊət] *n* postgra-
duado,-a.
posthumous ['pɒstjʊməs] *adj* póstumo,-a.
postman ['pəʊstmən] *n* (*pl* **postmen**)
cartero.
postmark ['pəʊstmɑːk] *n* matasellos.
postmortem [pəʊst'mɔːtəm] *n* autopsia.
postpone [pəs'pəʊn] *vt* aplazar, posponer.
postponement [pəs'pəʊnmənt] *n* aplazamiento.
postscript ['pəʊstskrɪpt] *n* posdata.
posture ['pɒstʃəʳ] *n* postura.
postwoman ['pəʊstwʊmən] *n* (*pl* **post-
women**) cartera.
pot¹ [pɒt] *n* **1** pote, tarro (*de mermelada*).
2 bote (*de pintura*). **3** tetera. **4** cafetera. **5**
olla. **6** maceta, tiesto.
● **to go to pot** *fam* irse al traste.
pot² [pɒt] *n sl* maría, hierba.
potassium [pə'tæsɪəm] *n* potasio.
potato [pə'teɪtəʊ] *n* (*pl* **potatoes**) patata.
potent ['pəʊtənt] *adj* potente.
potential [pə'tenʃəl] *adj-n* potencial.
pothole ['pɒthəʊl] *n* **1** cueva. **2** bache (*de
carretera*).
potluck [pɒt'lʌk] *n* .
● **to take potluck** comer de lo que haya.
potted ['pɒtɪd] *adj* **1** en conserva. **2** en
maceta, en tiesto.
potter¹ ['pɒtəʳ] *n* alfarero,-a.
potter² ['pɒtəʳ] *vi* entretenerse, hacer cositas, pasar el rato haciendo algo: *he pot-
ters around in the garden quite a lot*, se
entretiene bastante tarbajando en el jardín.
pottery ['pɒtərɪ] *n* **1** alfarería. **2** cerámica.
potty¹ ['pɒtɪ] *n* (*pl* **-ies**) orinal (*de niño*).
potty² ['pɒtɪ] *adj* (**-ier**, **-iest**) *fam* chiflado,-a.
pouch [paʊtʃ] *n* (*pl* **-es**) **1** bolsa. **2** petaca
(*de tabaco*).
poultice ['pəʊltɪs] *n* cataplasma.
poultry ['pəʊltrɪ] *n* aves de corral.
pounce [paʊns] *vi* abalanzarse.
pound¹ [paʊnd] *n* libra (*moneda, unidad
de peso*).
pound² [paʊnd] *vt* **1** machacar. **2** golpear,
aporrear.
▶ *vi* palpitar (*corazón*).

pound³ [paʊnd] *n* **1** perrera. **2** depósito
municipal (*de coches*).
pour [pɔːʳ] *vt* **1** verter, echar (*líquido*). **2**
echar arroz, harina.
▶ *vi* **1** correr, fluir: *refugees poured into
the country*, grandes cantidades de refugiados entraron en el país. **2** llover a cántaros.
pout [paʊt] *n* puchero.
▶ *vi* hacer pucheros.
poverty ['pɒvətɪ] *n* pobreza.
POW ['piː'əʊ'dʌbəljuː] *abbr* (*prisioner of
war*) prisionero,-a de guerra.
powder ['paʊdəʳ] *n* polvo.
▶ *vt* empolvar.
power ['paʊəʳ] *n* **1** fuerza (*física*). **2** poder,
capacidad. **3** capacidad, facultad. **4** fuerza, corriente (*eléctrica*). **5** poder, autoridad. **6** energía: *nuclear power*, energía
nuclear. **7** potencia (*nación*). **8** potencia:
to the power of four, elevado a la cuarta
potencia.
▶ *vt* mover, propulsar.
● **in power** en el poder.
■ **power cut** apagón.
■ **power point** toma de corriente.
■ **power station** central eléctrica.
powerful ['paʊəfʊl] *adj* **1** poderoso,-a
(*país*). **2** fuerte (*golpe, brazos*). **3** potente,
eficaz (*medicamento*).
powerless ['paʊələs] *adj* impotente.
pp ['peɪdʒɪz] *abbr* (*pages*) páginas, pgs.
PR ['piː'ɑː] *abbr* (*public relations*) relaciones públicas.
practicable ['præktɪkəbəl] *adj* factible.
practical ['præktɪkəl] *adj* práctico,-a.
practically ['præktɪkəlɪ] *adv* casi, prácticamente.
practice ['præktɪs] *n* **1** práctica: *theory
and practice*, teoría y práctica. **2** entrenamiento. **3** costumbre. **4** ejercicio (*de
profesión*). **5** consulta (*de médico*). **6** bufete
(*de abogados*).
▶ *vt-vi* US → practise.
● **in practice** en la práctica.
● **to be out of practice** faltar práctica,
haber perdido práctica.
● **to put into practice** lleva a la práctica.
practise ['præktɪs] *vt-vi* **1** practicar. **2** ejercer (*profesión*). **3** practicar (*religión*).
▶ *vi* entrenar (*deportes*).

practitioner [præk'tɪʃənəʳ] *n* médico,-a.
pragmatic [præg'mætɪk] *adj* pragmáti-co,-a.
prairie ['preərɪ] *n* pradera, llanura.
praise [preɪz] *n* alabanza, elogio.
▶ *vt* alabar.
pram [præm] *n* GB cochecito de niño.
prank [præŋk] *n* travesura, broma.
prattle ['prætəl] *n* charla, parloteo.
▶ *vi* charlar, parlotear.
prawn [prɔːn] *n* gamba.
pray [preɪ] *vi* orar, rezar.
prayer [preəʳ] *n* oración, plegaria.
■ **prayer book** misal.
preach [priːtʃ] *vt-vi* predicar.
preacher ['priːtʃəʳ] *n* predicador,-ra.
precarious [prɪ'keərɪəs] *adj* precario,-a, inseguro,-a.
precaution [prɪ'kɔːʃən] *n* precaución.
precede [prɪ'siːd] *vt-vi* preceder.
precedence ['presɪdəns] *n* precedencia, prioridad.
precedent ['presɪdənt] *adj* precedente.
precept ['priːsept] *n* precepto.
precinct ['priːsɪŋkt] *n* distrito, zona.
▶ *npl* **precincts** recinto.
precious ['preʃəs] *adj* **1** precioso,-a, valioso,-a. **2** querido,-a, preciado,-a.
▶ *adv* muy: *precious little*, muy poco.
■ **precious stone** piedra preciosa.
precipice ['presɪpɪs] *n* precipicio.
precipitate [(adj) prɪ'sɪpɪtət (vb) prɪ'sɪpɪteɪt] *adj* precipitado,-a.
▶ *vt* precipitar.
precise [prɪ'saɪs] *adj* **1** preciso,-a, exacto,-a. **2** meticuloso,-a *(persona)*.
precisely [prɪ'saɪslɪ] *adv* precisamente.
precision [prɪ'sɪʒən] *n* precisión, exactitud.
preclude [prɪ'kluːd] *vt* excluir, descartar.
precocious [prɪ'kəʊʃəs] *adj* precoz.
preconceived [priːkən'siːvd] *adj* preconcebido,-a.
precooked [priː'kʊkt] *vt* precocinado,-a.
predator ['predətəʳ] *n* depredador.
predecessor ['priːdɪsesəʳ] *n* predecesor,-ra.
predestination [priːdestɪ'neɪʃən] *n* predestinación.
predestine [priː'destɪn] *vt* predestinar.
predetermine [priːdɪ'tɜːmɪn] *vt* predeterminar.
predicament [prɪ'dɪkəmənt] *n* apuro, aprieto.

predict [prɪ'dɪkt] *vt* predecir, vaticinar, pronosticar.
predictable [prɪ'dɪktəbəl] *adj* previsible.
prediction [prɪ'dɪkʃən] *n* predicción, vaticinio, pronóstico.
predispose [priːdɪs'pəʊz] *vt* predisponer.
predominant [prɪ'dɒmɪnənt] *adj* predominante.
predominate [prɪ'dɒmɪneɪt] *vi* predominar.
pre-eminent [priː'emɪnənt] *adj* preeminente.
pre-empt [priː'empt] *vt* adelantarse a.
prefabricated [priː'fæbrɪkeɪtɪd] *adj* prefabricado,-a.
preface ['prefəs] *n* prefacio, prólogo.
prefect ['priːfekt] *n* **1** prefecto. **2** GB monitor,-ra *(en colegio)*.
prefer [prɪ'fɜː'] *vt (pt & pp* **preferred***, ger* **preferring***)* preferir.
preferable ['prefərəbəl] *adj* preferible.
preference ['prefərəns] *n* preferencia.
preferential [prefə'renʃəl] *adj* preferente.
prefix ['priːfɪks] *n (pl* **prefixes***)* prefijo.
pregnancy ['pregnənsɪ] *n (pl* **-ies***)* embarazo.
■ **pregnancy test** prueba del embarazo.
pregnant ['pregnənt] *adj-n* embarazada, preñada.
● **to be pregnant by** SB quedarse embarazada de ALGN.
● **to get pregnant** quedarse embarazada.
prehistoric [priːhɪ'stɒrɪk] *n* prehistórico,-a.
prejudge [priː'dʒʌdʒ] *vt* prejuzgar.
prejudice ['predʒədɪs] *n* prejuicio.
▶ *vt* **1** predisponer. **2** perjudicar, dañar.
prejudiced ['predʒədɪst] *adj* con prejuicios.
● **to be prejudiced** tener prejuicios.
prejudicial [predʒə'dɪʃəl] *adj* perjudicial.
preliminary [prɪ'lɪmɪnərɪ] *adj-n (pl* **-ies***)* preliminar.
prelude ['preljuːd] *n* preludio.
premature [premə'tjʊəʳ] *adj* prematuro,-a.
premeditated [priː'medɪteɪtɪd] *adj* premeditado,-a.
premier ['premɪəʳ] *adj* primero,-a, principal.
▶ *n* primer,-ra ministro,-a.

première ['premɪeəʳ] *n* estreno.
premise ['premɪs] *n* premisa.
▸ *npl* **premises** local.
premium ['priːmɪəm] *n* prima.
premonition [priːməˈnɪʃən] *n* premonición.
preoccupation [priːɒkjʊˈpeɪʃən] *n* preocupación.
preoccupy [priːˈɒkjʊpaɪ] *vt* (*pt & pp* **-ied**) preocupar.
prepaid [priːˈpeɪd] *adj* pagado,-a por adelantado.
preparation [prepəˈreɪʃən] *n* **1** preparación. **2** preparado.
▸ *npl* **preparations** preparativos.
preparatory [prɪˈpærətərɪ] *adj* preparatorio,-a, preliminar.
prepare [prɪˈpeəʳ] *vt-vi* preparar(se).
prepared [prɪˈpeəd] *adj* **1** listo,-a, preparado,-a. **2** dispuesto,-a.
preposition [prepəˈzɪʃən] *n* preposición.
prepossessing [priːpəˈzesɪŋ] *adj* atractivo,-a.
preposterous [prɪˈpɒstərəs] *adj* absurdo,-a, descabellado,-a.
prerequisite [priːˈrekwɪzɪt] *n* requisito previo.
prerogative [prɪˈrɒgətɪv] *n* prerrogativa.
Presbyterian [prezbɪˈtɪərɪən] *adj-n* presbiteriano,-a.
preschool [priːˈskuːl] *adj* preescolar.
prescribe [prɪsˈkraɪb] *vt* **1** prescribir, ordenar: *prescribed reading*, lecturas obligatorias. **2** recetar.
prescription [prɪsˈkrɪpʃən] *n* receta médica.
● **on prescription** con receta médica.
presence ['prezəns] *n* presencia.
present[1] ['prezənt] *adj* **1** presente: *were you present at the trial?*, ¿estuvo usted presente durante el juicio? **2** actual: *the present government*, el gobierno actual.
▸ *n* **1** presente, actualidad. **2** presente *(tiempo verbal)*.
● **at present** actualmente.
● **at the present time** actualmente.
● **for the present** por ahora.
● **to be present** estar presente, asistir.
■ **present continuous** presente continuo.
■ **present perfect** presente perfecto.
■ **present tense** presente.
present[2] [*(n)* 'prezənt(*vb*) prɪ'zent] *n* regalo, presente, obsequio.

▸ *vt* **1** presentar *(a persona)*. **2** entregar, presentar, dar. **3** representar *(obra)*. **4** presentar *(programa)*.
● **to present a problem** representar un problema.
presentable [prɪˈzentəbəl] *adj* presentable.
● **to make oneself presentable** arreglarse.
presentation [prezənˈteɪʃən] *n* **1** presentación. **2** entrega *(de premio)*.
presenter [prɪˈzentəʳ] *n* **1** locutor,-ra. **2** presentador,-ra.
presently ['prezəntlɪ] *adv* **1** GB pronto, dentro de poco. **2** US ahora.
preservation [prezəˈveɪʃən] *n* conservación, preservación.
preservative [prɪˈzɜːvətɪv] *n* conservante.
preserve [prɪˈzɜːv] *n* **1** conserva *(de fruta, verdura)*. **2** confitura. **3** coto, vedado.
▸ *vt* conservar, preservar.
preside [prɪˈzaɪd] *vi* presidir.
president ['prezɪdənt] *n* presidente,-a.
press [pres] *n* (*pl* **-es**). **1** prensa. **2** prensa *(máquina)*. **3** imprenta.
▸ *vt* **1** pulsar, apretar *(botón)*. **2** prensar *(uvas, olivas)*. **3** planchar *(ropa)*. **4** presionar *(persona)*.
▸ *vi* apretar.
■ **press briefing** rueda de prensa.
■ **press release** comunicado de prensa.
to press ahead/on *vi* seguir adelante.
to press for *vt* exigir, reclamar.
pressing ['presɪŋ] *adj* urgente, apremiante.
press-up ['presʌp] *n* flexión.
pressure ['preʃəʳ] *n* **1** presión. **2** tensión. **3** presionar.
● **to put pressure on** presionar a.
■ **pressure cooker** olla a presión.
■ **pressure group** grupo de presión.
pressurize ['preʃəraɪz] *vt* **1** presurizar. **2** presionar.
prestige [presˈtiːʒ] *n* prestigio.
prestigious [presˈtɪdʒəs] *adj* prestigioso,-a.
presumably [prɪˈzjuːməblɪ] *adv* se supone que.
presume [prɪˈzjuːm] *vt-vi* suponer.
presumption [prɪˈzʌmpʃən] *n* **1** suposición. **2** presunción.
presumptuous [prɪˈzʌmptjʊəs] *adj* presuntuoso,-a.

presuppose [priːsəˈpəʊz] *vt* presuponer.
pretence [prɪˈtens] *n* **1** fingimiento, simulación. **2** pretensión.

● **under false pretences** con engaño, fraudulentamente.

pretend [prɪˈtend] *vt-vi* **1** aparentar, fingir. **2** pretender. **3** jugar: *let's pretend we're astronauts*, juguemos a astronautas.

► *vi* pretender.

pretentious [prɪˈtenʃəs] *adj* pretencioso, -a, presumido,-a.
pretext [ˈpriːtekst] *n* pretexto.
pretty [ˈprɪtɪ] *adj* (-**ier**, -**iest**) bonito,-a, mono,-a.

► *adv* bastante.

● **pretty much** más o menos.
● **pretty well** casi.

prevail [prɪˈveɪl] *vi* **1** predominar, imperar. **2** prevalecer.

● **to prevail upon** convencer, persuadir.

prevailing [prɪˈveɪlɪŋ] *adj* predominante.
prevalent [ˈprevələnt] *adj* predominante.
prevaricate [prɪˈværɪkeɪt] *vi* andarse con evasivas.
prevent [prɪˈvent] *vt* impedir, evitar.
prevention [prɪˈvenʃən] *n* prevención.
preventive [prɪˈventɪv] *adj* preventivo,-a.
preview [ˈpriːvjuː] *n* preestreno.
previous [ˈpriːvɪəs] *adj* previo,-a, anterior.

● **previous to** antes de.
■ **previous convictions** antecedentes penales.

previously [ˈpriːvɪəslɪ] *adv* previamente, con anterioridad.
prey [preɪ] *n* presa.

● **to fall prey to** ser víctima de.

to prey on *vt* **1** cazar, alimentarse de. **2** atormentar: *fear preyed on his mind*, el miedo hizo presa en él.
price [praɪs] *n* precio, importe.

► *vt* poner un precio a.

● **at any price** a toda costa.

priceless [ˈpraɪsləs] *adj* que no tiene precio.
pricey [ˈpraɪsɪ] *adj* (-**ier**, -**iest**) *fam* caro,-a.
prick [prɪk] *n* **1** pinchazo. **2** *vulg* gilipollas *mf inv*. **3** *vulg* polla.

► *vt* pinchar.

● **to prick up one's ears** aguzar el oído.

prickle [ˈprɪkəl] *n* **1** pincho, púa, espina. **2** picor.

► *vt-vi* pinchar, picar.

prickly [ˈprɪklɪ] *adj* (-**ier**, -**iest**). **1** espinoso,-a, con púas, con pinchos. **2** irritable.
pricy [ˈpraɪsɪ] *adj* (-**ier**, -**iest**) *fam* caro,-a.
pride [praɪd] *n* **1** orgullo. **2** amor propio.

● **to pride oneself on** enorgullecerse de.
● **to take pride in** enorgullecerse de.

priest [priːst] *n* sacerdote.
priestess [ˈpriːstes] *n* (*pl* -**es**) sacerdotisa.
prig [prɪg] *n* mojigato,-a.
prim [prɪm] *adj* (*comp* **primmer**, *superl* **primmest**) remilgado,-a.
primarily [praɪˈmerɪlɪ] *adv* ante todo.
primary [ˈpraɪmərɪ] *adj* **1** principal, primordial. **2** primario,-a.

■ **primary colour** color primario.
■ **primary school** escuela primaria.

primate[1] [ˈpraɪmeɪt] *n* primate *(simio)*.
primate[2] [ˈpraɪmət] *n* primado *(de la Iglesia)*.
prime [praɪm] *adj* **1** primero,-a, principal. **2** selecto,-a, de primera.

■ **Prime Minister** primer,-a ministro,-a.
■ **prime number** número primo.
■ **prime of life** flor de la vida.
■ **prime time** franja de mayor audiencia.

primitive [ˈprɪmɪtɪv] *adj* primitivo,-a.
primrose [ˈprɪmrəʊz] *n* **1** primavera, prímula.
prince [prɪns] *n* príncipe.
princess [ˈprɪnses] *n* (*pl* -**es**) princesa.
principal [ˈprɪnsɪpəl] *adj* principal.

► *n* director,-ra *(de colegio)*; rector,-ra *(de universidad)*.

principle [ˈprɪnsɪpəl] *n* principio.

● **in principle** en principio.
● **on principle** por principio.

print [prɪnt] *n* **1** impresión, huella. **2** letra. **3** copia *(fotografía)*. **4** grabado. **5** estampado *(de tela)*.

► *vt* **1** imprimir *(libro)*. **2** publicar. **3** sacar una copia de *(fotografía)*. **4** escribir con letra de imprenta. **5** estampar *(tela)*.

● **in print** en catálogo.
● **out of print** descatalogado,-a.

to print out *vt* imprimir.
printer [ˈprɪntəʳ] *n* **1** impresor,-ra *(persona)*. **2** impresora *(máquina)*.
printing [ˈprɪntɪŋ] *n* **1** impresión *(acción)*. **2** imprenta *(arte)*.

print-out ['prɪntaʊt] *n* impresión, copia impresa.

prior[1] ['praɪəʳ] *adj* anterior, previo,-a.
● **prior to** antes de.
■ **prior knowledge** conocimiento previo.

prior[2] ['praɪəʳ] *n* prior *(religioso)*.

priority [praɪˈɒrɪtɪ] *n (pl* **-ies**) prioridad.

prise [praɪz] *vt: to prise STH off*, quitar haciendo palanca; *to prise STH open*, abrir haciendo palanca.

prism ['prɪzəm] *n* prisma.

prison ['prɪzən] *n* prisión, cárcel.
■ **prison camp** campamento de prisioneros.

prisoner ['prɪzənəʳ] *n* **1** preso,-a, recluso,-a. **2** prisionero,-a.
● **to be taken prisoner** ser hecho prisionero,-a.

privacy ['praɪvəsɪ] *n* intimidad.

private ['praɪvət] *adj* **1** privado,-a. **2** personal, particular: *for your private use*, para su uso personal. **3** confidencial, íntimo,-a. **4** privado,-a, de pago. **5** reservado,-a *(persona)*.
► *n* soldado raso.
● **in private** en privado.
■ **private enterprise** empresa privada.
■ **private eye** detective privado.
■ **private income** renta personal.

privately ['praɪvətlɪ] *adv* **1** en privado. **2** de forma privada.
● **privately owned** de propiedad privada.

privatize ['praɪvətaɪz] *vt* privatizar.

privilege ['prɪvɪlɪdʒ] *n* privilegio.

privileged ['prɪvɪlɪdʒd] *adj* privilegiado,-a.

privy ['prɪvɪ] *adj* enterado,-a.

prize[1] [praɪz] *n* premio.
► *adj* de primera.

prize[2] [praɪz] *vt* apreciar.

prize[3] [praɪz] *vt* US → prise.

pro[1] [prəʊ] *n (pl* **pros**) pro: *the pros and cons*, los pros y los contras.

pro[2] [prəʊ] *n (pl* **pros**) profesional.

probability [prɒbəˈbɪlɪtɪ] *n (pl* **-ies**) probabilidad.

probable ['prɒbəbəl] *adj* probable.

probably ['prɒbəblɪ] *adv* probablemente: *they will probably call*, es probable que llamen; *John probably told them*, se lo habrá dicho John.

probation [prəˈbeɪʃən] *n* libertad condicional.

probe [prəʊb] *n* **1** sonda. **2** investigación.
► *vt* **1** sondar, sondear. **2** investigar.

problem ['prɒbləm] *n* problema.

problematic [prɒbləˈmætɪk] *adj* problemático,-a.

problematical [prɒbləˈmætɪkəl] *adj* problemático,-a.

procedure [prəˈsiːdʒəʳ] *n* procedimiento, trámite.

proceed [prəˈsiːd] *vi* **1** continuar, proseguir, seguir. **2** proceder.

proceedings [prəˈsiːdɪŋz] *npl* **1** actas. **2** acto.
● **to take proceedings against SB** JUR proceder contra ALGN.

proceeds ['prəʊsiːdz] *npl* beneficios.

process ['prəʊses] *n (pl* **-es**). **1** proceso, procedimiento *(método)*. **2** proceso: *the industrial process*, el proceso industrial.
► *vt* **1** procesar. **2** revelar.
● **to be in the process of doing STH** estar en vías de hacer algo.

processing ['prəʊsesɪŋ] *n* procesamiento.

procession [prəˈseʃən] *n* desfile, procesión.

proclaim [prəˈkleɪm] *vt* proclamar.

procrastinate [prəˈkræstɪneɪt] *vi* dejar las cosas para más tarde.

prod [prɒd] *n* empujón, pinchazo.
► *vt (pt & pp* **prodded***, ger* **prodding***)* empujar, pinchar.

prodigal ['prɒdɪgəl] *adj* pródigo,-a.

prodigious [prəˈdɪdʒəs] *adj* prodigioso,-a.

prodigy ['prɒdɪdʒɪ] *n (pl* **-ies**) prodigio.

produce [*(vb)* prəˈdjuːs*(n)* 'prɒdjuːs] *vt* **1** producir, fabricar. **2** enseñar, sacar *(pistola)*. **3** dar, producir: *this land produces good wine*, esta tierra da buen vino. **4** realizar *(programa)*. **5** producir *(película)*. **6** dirigir *(obra de teatro)*.
► *n* productos *(agrícolas)*.

producer [prəˈdjuːsəʳ] *n* **1** productor,-ra. **2** realizador,-ra *(de programa)*. **3** director,-ra *(de película)*.

product ['prɒdʌkt] *n* **1** producto. **2** resultado, fruto.

production [prəˈdʌkʃən] *n* **1** producción. **2** realización *(de programa)*. **3** producción *(de película)*. **4** representación *(de obra)*.
■ **production line** cadena de producción.

productive [prəˈdʌktɪv] *adj* productivo,-a.
productivity [prɒdʌkˈtɪvɪti] *n* productividad.
Prof [prəˈfesəʳ] *abbr* (**Professor**) catedráti-co,-a de universidad.
profane [prəˈfeɪn] *adj* sacrílego,-a.
▶ *vt* profanar.
profess [prəˈfes] *vt* **1** profesar, declarar. **2** pretender.
profession [prəˈfeʃən] *n* profesión.
professional [prəˈfeʃənəl] *adj-n* profesio-nal.
professor [prəˈfesəʳ] *n* GB catedrático,-a de universidad.
proficiency [prəˈfɪʃənsi] *n* competencia, habilidad.
proficient [prəˈfɪʃənt] *adj* hábil, compe-tente: *she's proficient in French*, tiene un buen nivel de francés.
profile [ˈprəʊfaɪl] *n* perfil.
● **in profile** de perfil.
● **to have a high profile** estar en el can-delero.
profit [ˈprɒfɪt] *n* **1** ganancia, beneficio. **2** provecho.
▶ *vi*: *to profit from*, sacar provecho de.
● **to make a profit** obtener beneficios.
■ **profit and loss** ganancias y pérdidas.
profitable [ˈprɒfɪtəbəl] *adj* **1** rentable. **2** provechoso,-a, beneficioso,-a.
profound [prəˈfaʊnd] *adj* profundo,-a.
profuse [prəˈfjuːs] *adj* profuso,-a.
profusely [prəˈfjuːsli] *adv* profusamente.
profusion [prəˈfjuːʒən] *n* profusión.
progeny [ˈprɒdʒəni] *n* progenie.
program [ˈprəʊɡræm] *n* US programa.
▶ *vt* (*pt & pp* **programmed**, *ger* **pro-gramming**) US programar.

Esta grafía se usa también en informática.

programme [ˈprəʊɡræm] *n* GB programa.
▶ *vt* GB programar.
programmer [ˈprəʊɡræməʳ] *n* programa-dor,-ra.
progress [(*n*) ˈprəʊɡres(*vb*) prəʊˈɡres] *n* progreso, avance: *scientific progress*, avances científicos.
▶ *vi* progresar, avanzar.
● **in progress** en curso.
● **to make progress** avanzar.
progressive [prəˈɡresɪv] *adj* **1** progresi-vo,-a. **2** progresista.
▶ *n* progresista.

prohibit [prəˈhɪbɪt] *vt* prohibir.
prohibition [prəʊɪˈbɪʃən] *n* prohibición.
project [(*n*) ˈprɒdʒekt(*vb*) prəˈdʒekt] *n* **1** proyecto. **2** trabajo.
▶ *vt* proyectar.
▶ *vi* sobresalir.
projectile [prəˈdʒektaɪl] *n* proyectil.
projector [prəˈdʒektəʳ] *n* proyector.
proletarian [prəʊləˈtɲərɪən] *adj* proleta-rio,-a.
prolific [prəˈlɪfɪk] *adj* prolífico,-a.
prologue [ˈprəʊlɒɡ] (US **prolog**) *n* prólogo.
prolong [prəˈlɒŋ] *vt* prolongar, alargar.
promenade [prɒməˈnɑːd] *n* paseo marí-timo.
prominence [ˈprɒmɪnəns] *n* **1** prominen-cia. **2** importancia.
prominent [ˈprɒmɪnənt] *adj* **1** prominen-te, destacado,-a. **2** importante.
promiscuous [prəˈmɪskjʊəs] *adj* promis-cuo,-a.
promise [ˈprɒmɪs] *n* promesa.
▶ *vt-vi* prometer.
● **to make a promise** hacer una prome-sa.
promising [ˈprɒmɪsɪŋ] *adj* prometedor,-ra.
promote [prəˈməʊt] *vt* **1** ascender, pro-mover (*empleado*). **2** promover, fomen-tar. **3** promocionar (*producto*).
● **to be promoted** SP subir de categoría.
promotion [prəˈməʊʃən] *n* **1** promoción, fomento. **2** ascenso.
■ **promotion drive** campaña de promo-ción.
prompt [prɒmpt] *adj* **1** inmediato, -a, rá-pido,-a (*servicio, acción*). **2** puntual (*perso-na*).
▶ *adv* en punto.
▶ *vt* **1** inducir, impulsar, incitar. **2** apun-tar (*en teatro*).
prompter [ˈprɒmptəʳ] *n* apuntador,-ra.
prone [prəʊn] *adj* boca abajo.
● **prone to** propenso,-a a.
prong [prɒŋ] *n* diente, punta.
pronoun [ˈprəʊnaʊn] *n* pronombre.
pronounce [prəˈnaʊns] *vt* **1** pronunciar. **2** declarar.
● **to pronounce sentence** dictar sen-tencia.
pronounced [prəˈnaʊnst] *adj* pronuncia-do,-a, marcado,-a.

pronunciation [prənʌnsɪ'eɪʃən] *n* pronunciación.

proof [pru:f] *n* (*pl* **proofs**). **1** prueba. **2** graduación *(alcohólica)*.

prop[1] [prɒp] *n* **1** puntal *(objeto)*. **2** apoyo, sostén *(persona)*.

prop[2] [prɒp] *n* accesorio *(attrezzo)*.

to prop up *vt* **1** apuntalar *(techo)*. **2** apoyar, sostener *(persona)*.

propaganda [prɒpə'gændə] *n* propaganda.

propagate ['prɒpəgeɪt] *vt-vi* propagar(se).

propel [prə'pel] *vt* (GB *pt & pp* **propelled**, *ger* **propelling**; US *pt & pp* **propeled**, *ger* **propeling**) propulsar, impulsar.

propeller [prə'pelə'] *n* hélice.

propensity [prə'pensɪti] *n* (*pl* **-ies**) propensión.

proper ['prɒpə'] *adj* **1** adecuado,-a *(procedimiento)*. **2** correcto,-a *(respuesta, conducta)*. **3** decente. **4** propiamente dicho,-a *(después de sustantivo)*. **5** *fam* auténtico,-a, correcto,-a, digno,-a, en condiciones.
■ **proper noun** nombre propio.

properly ['prɒpəlɪ] *adv* bien, correctamente.

property ['prɒpətɪ] *n* (*pl* **-ies**) propiedad.

prophecy ['prɒfəsɪ] *n* (*pl* **-ies**) profecía.

prophesy ['prɒfəsaɪ] *vt-vi* (*pt & pp* **-ied**) profetizar.

prophet ['prɒfɪt] *n* profeta.

prophetic [prə'fetɪk] *adj* profético,-a.

proportion [prə'pɔ:ʃən] *n* proporción.
● **out of proportion** desproporcionado,-a.

proportional [prə'pɔ:ʃənəl] *adj* proporcional.

proportionate [prə'pɔ:ʃənət] *adj* proporcionado,-a.

proposal [prə'pəʊzəl] *n* propuesta.

propose [prə'pəʊz] *vt* **1** proponer *(sugerencia)*. **2** pensar, tener la intención de.
▶ *vi* pedir la mano, declararse.

proposition [prɒpə'zɪʃən] *n* proposición, propuesta.

proprietor [prə'praɪətə'] *n* propietario,-a, dueño,-a.

propriety [prə'praɪətɪ] *n* (*pl* **-ies**). **1** corrección, decencia. **2** conveniencia, oportunidad.

propulsion [prə'pʌlʃən] *n* propulsión.

prose [prəʊz] *n* prosa.

prosecute ['prɒsɪkju:t] *vt* procesar, enjuiciar.

prosecution [prɒsɪ'kju:ʃən] *n* **1** proceso, juicio *(acción)*. **2** acusación *(persona)*.

prosecutor ['prɒsɪkju:tə'] *n* fiscal, abogado,-a de la acusación.

prospect [(*n*) 'prɒspekt *(vb)* prə'spekt] *n* **1** perspectiva. **2** probabilidad.
▶ *vt* explorar.
▶ *vi* buscar.

prospective [prə'spektɪv] *adj* **1** futuro,-a. **2** posible.

prospectus [prə'spektəs] *n* (*pl* **prospectuses**) prospecto.

prosper ['prɒspə'] *vi* prosperar.

prosperity [prɒ'sperɪtɪ] *n* prosperidad.

prosperous ['prɒspərəs] *adj* próspero,-a.

prostate ['prɒsteɪt] *n* próstata.

prostitute ['prɒstɪtju:t] *n* prostituta.

prostitution [prɒstɪ'tju:ʃən] *n* prostitución.

prostrate [(*adj*) 'prɒstreɪt *(vb)* prɒ'streɪt] *adj* postrado,-a.
▶ *vt* postrar.

protagonist [prəʊ'tægənɪst] *n* **1** protagonista. **2** defensor,-ra, partidario,-a.

protect [prə'tekt] *vt* proteger.

protection [prə'tekʃən] *n* protección.

protective [prə'tektɪv] *adj* protector,-ra.

protector [prə'tektə'] *n* protector,-ra.

protégé ['prəʊtəʒeɪ] *n* protegido.

protégée ['prəʊtəʒeɪ] *n* protegida.

protein ['prəʊti:n] *n* proteína.

protest [(*n*) 'prəʊtest *(vb)* prə'test] *n* protesta.
▶ *vt-vi* protestar.
■ **protest march** manifestación.

Protestant ['prɒtɪstənt] *adj-n* protestante.

protocol ['prəʊtəkɒl] *n* protocolo.

prototype ['prəʊtətaɪp] *n* prototipo.

protracted [prə'træktɪd] *vt* prolongado,-a.

protrude [prə'tru:d] *vi* sobresalir.

protruding [prə'tru:dɪŋ] *adj* saliente, prominente.

proud [praʊd] *adj* orgulloso,-a.
● **to be proud of** enorgullecerse de.
● **to be proud to** tener el honor de.

prove [pru:v] *vt* (*pt* **proved**, *pp* **proved** *o* **proven** ['pru:vən]) probar, demostrar.
▶ *vi* resultar: *the exam proved to be very difficult*, el examen resultó ser muy difícil.

● **to prove SB right** demostrar que ALGN tiene razón.

● **to prove SB wrong** demostrar que ALGN está equivocado,-a.

proverb ['prɒvɜːb] n proverbio, refrán.

proverbial [prə'vɜːbɪəl] adj proverbial.

provide [prə'vaɪd] vt **1** proporcionar, facilitar, suministrar. **2** estipular (ley).

to provide for vt **1** mantener (familia). **2** prevenir, tomar medidas para.

provided [prə'vaɪdɪd] conj **provided (that)** siempre que, con tal de que.

providence ['prɒvɪdəns] n providencia.

provident ['prɒvɪdənt] adj previsor,-ra.

providential [prɒvɪ'denʃəl] adj providencial.

providing [prə'vaɪdɪŋ] conj → provided.

province ['prɒvɪns] n provincia.

● **it's not my province** no es de mi competencia.

provincial [prə'vɪnʃəl] adj **1** provincial. **2** pej provinciano,-a.

provision [prə'vɪʒən] n **1** suministro, provisión. **2** disposición.

● **to make provision for** prever.

provisional [prə'vɪʒənəl] adj provisional.

proviso [prə'vaɪzəʊ] n (pl **provisos**) condición.

provocative [prə'vɒkətɪv] adj **1** provocativo,-a (vestido). **2** provocador,-a (gesto).

provoke [prə'vəʊk] vt provocar.

provoking [prə'vəʊkɪŋ] adj provocador,-ra.

prow [praʊ] n proa.

prowess ['praʊəs] n destreza, habilidad.

prowl [praʊl] vi merodear, rondar.

proximity ['prɒksɪmɪtɪ] n proximidad.

proxy ['prɒksɪ] n (pl **-ies**) representante, apoderado,-a.

● **by proxy** por poder, por poderes.

prude [pruːd] n remilgado,-a, mojigato,-a.

prudence ['pruːdəns] n prudencia.

prudent ['pruːdənt] adj prudente.

prudish ['pruːdɪʃ] adj remilgado,-a, mojigato,-a.

prune[1] [pruːn] n ciruela pasa.

prune[2] [pruːn] vt podar.

pry [praɪ] vi (pt & pp **-ied**) husmear, fisgonear.

▶ vt → prise.

PS ['piː'es] abbr (**postscript**) posdata, P.D, P.S.

psalm [sɑːm] n salmo.

pseudonym ['suːdənɪm] n seudónimo.

psyche ['saɪkɪ] n psique.

psychiatrist [saɪ'kaɪətrɪst] n psiquiatra.

psychiatry [saɪ'kaɪətrɪ] n psiquiatría.

psychoanalysis [saɪkəʊə'nælɪsɪs] n psicoanálisis.

psychoanalyst [saɪkəʊ'ænəlɪst] n psicoanalista.

psychological [saɪkə'lɒdʒɪkəl] adj psicológico,-a.

psychologist [saɪ'kɒlədʒɪst] n psicólogo,-a.

psychology [saɪ'kɒlədʒɪ] n psicología.

psychopath ['saɪkəʊpæθ] n psicópata.

psychosis [saɪ'kəʊsɪs] n (pl **psychoses**) psicosis.

pt[1] [paɪnt] abbr (**pint**) pinta.

pt[2] [pɑːt] abbr (**part**) parte.

PTA ['piː'tiː'eɪ] abbr (**Parent-Teacher Association**) asociación de padres de alumnos y profesores.

PTO ['piː'tiː'əʊ] abbr (**please turn over**) sigue.

pub [pʌb] n bar, pub.

puberty ['pjuːbətɪ] n pubertad.

pubic ['pjuːbɪk] adj púbico,-a.

public ['pʌblɪk] adj público,-a.

▶ n público.

■ **public convenience** GB aseos públicos.

■ **public holiday** fiesta nacional.

■ **public house** bar, pub.

■ **public prosecutor** fiscal.

■ **public school** colegio privado (en GB), colegio público (en EEUU).

■ **public servant** funcionario,-a.

■ **public utility** servicio público.

■ **public works** obras públicas.

publication [pʌblɪ'keɪʃən] n publicación.

publicity [pʌ'blɪsɪtɪ] n publicidad.

publicize [pʌblɪ'saɪz] vt **1** divulgar, hacer público,-a. **2** promocionar, promover.

publish ['pʌblɪʃ] vt publicar, editar.

publisher ['pʌblɪʃə'] n **1** editor,-ra. **2** editorial.

pudding ['pʊdɪŋ] n **1** budín, pudín. **2** GB postre.

puddle ['pʌdəl] n charco.

Puerto Rican ['pweətəʊ 'riːkən] adj-n puertorriqueño,-a, portorriqueño,-a.

Puerto Rico ['pweətəʊ 'riːkəʊ] n Puerto Rico.

puff [pʌf] n (pl **puffs**). **1** soplo, resoplido. **2** calada (de cigarrillo). **3** ráfaga (de viento). **4** bocanada (de humo).
► vi **1** dar caladas. **2** jadear.
■ **puff pastry** hojaldre.
to puff up vt-vi hinchar(se).
puke ['pjuːk] vi fam echar la papa, devolver, vomitar.
pull [pʊl] n **1** tirón. **2** atracción. **3** fam influencia.
► vt **1** tirar de, dar un tirón a: *he pulled his hair*, le tiró del pelo. **2** arrastrar, tirar de: *the cart was pulled by a donkey*, un burro tiraba de la carreta. **3** fam atraer.
► vi tirar.
● **to pull a face** hacer una mueca.
● **to pull a fast one on SB** fam hacer una mala jugada a ALGN.
● **to pull a gun on SB** amenazar a ALGN con una pistola.
● **to pull oneself together** serenarse.
● **to pull SB's leg** tomar el pelo a ALGN.
● **to pull strings** tocar muchas teclas, mover hilos.
● **to pull to pieces** hacer pedazos, destrozar.
to pull apart vt desmontar.
to pull away vi alejarse.
to pull down vt **1** bajar. **2** derribar (edificio).
to pull in vi entrar en la estación (tren).
to pull off vt **1** llevar a cabo. **2** quitar, sacar (ropa).
to pull out vt sacar, arrancar (muela).
► vi **1** salir de la estación (tren); alejarse (coche). **2** retirarse.
to pull through vi reponerse.
to pull together vi trabajar como equipo, cooperar.
to pull up vt **1** subir (calcetín). **2** arrancar (planta).
► vi detenerse, parar.
pulley ['pʊlɪ] n polea.
pullover ['pʊləʊvəʳ] n jersey, suéter.
pulp [pʌlp] n **1** pulpa. **2** pasta (de papel).
pulpit ['pʊlpɪt] n púlpito.
pulsate [pʌl'seɪt] vi palpitar, latir.
pulse¹ [pʌls] n **1** pulsación. **2** pulso.
► vi palpitar, latir.
pulse² [pʌls] n legumbre.
puma ['pjuːmə] n puma.
pumice stone ['pʌmɪsstəʊn] n piedra pómez.

pump¹ [pʌmp] n **1** bomba (de aire, líquido). **2** surtidor (de gasolina).
► vt **1** bombear (líquido). **2** fam sonsacar (persona).
► vi latir (corazón).
pump² [pʌmp] n **1** GB zapatilla deportiva, playera. **2** zapatilla de ballet. **3** US zapato de salón.
pumpkin ['pʌmpkɪn] n calabaza.
pump up ['pʌmp'ʌp] vt hinchar, inflar.
pun [pʌn] n juego de palabras.
punch¹ [pʌntʃ] n (pl -es). **1** puñetazo. **2** empuje.
► vt dar un puñetazo a.
punch² [pʌntʃ] n (pl -es) ponche (bebida).
punch³ [pʌntʃ] n (pl -es). **1** punzón. **2** perforadora (para billetes).
► vt **1** perforar. **2** picar (billete).
punch-up ['pʌntʃʌp] n fam riña, pelea.
punctual ['pʌŋktjʊəl] adj puntual.
punctuality [pʌŋktjʊ'ælɪtɪ] n puntualidad.
punctuate ['pʌŋktjʊeɪt] vt puntuar.
punctuation [pʌŋktjʊ'eɪʃən] n puntuación.
■ **punctuation mark** signo de puntuación.
puncture ['pʌŋktʃəʳ] n pinchazo.
► vt-vi pinchar(se).
pungent ['pʌndʒənt] adj **1** acre (olor). **2** mordaz (comentario).
punish ['pʌnɪʃ] vt castigar.
punishment ['pʌnɪʃmənt] n castigo.
punk [pʌŋk] n **1** punk, punki (persona). **2** punk (música). **3** US fam gamberro,-a.
punt [pʌnt] n batea.
► vi ir en batea.
punter ['pʌntəʳ] n **1** fam apostante. **2** fam cliente,-a.
puny ['pjuːnɪ] adj (-ier, -iest) endeble, canijo,-a.
pup [pʌp] n cría, cachorro,-a.
pupil¹ ['pjuːpɪl] n alumno,-a.
pupil² ['pjuːpɪl] n pupila (de ojo).
puppet ['pʌpɪt] n títere, marioneta.
■ **puppet show** teatro de títeres.
puppy ['pʌpɪ] n (pl -ies) cachorro,-a.
purchase ['pɜːtʃəs] n compra, adquisición.
► vt comprar, adquirir.
■ **purchasing power** poder adquisitivo.
purchaser ['pɜːtʃəsəʳ] n comprador,-ra.

pure ['pjʊəʳ] *adj* puro,-a.

purée ['pjʊəreɪ] *n* puré.

purely ['pjʊəlɪ] *adv* simplemente, puramente.

purge [pɜːdʒ] *n* purga.
► *vt* purgar.

purifier ['pjʊərɪfaɪəʳ] *n* purificador.

Puritan ['pjʊərɪtən] *adj-n* puritano,-a.

purity ['pjʊərɪtɪ] *n* (*pl* **-ies**) pureza.

purple ['pɜːpəl] *adj* púrpura, morado,-a.
► *n* púrpura, morado.

purport [pɜːˈpɔːt] *n* significado.
► *vt* pretender, dar a entender.

purpose ['pɜːpəs] *n* **1** propósito, motivo, intención. **2** utilidad: *what is the purpose of this?*, ¿para qué sirve esto?
● **on purpose** a propósito.
● **to no purpose** en vano.

purposely ['pɜːpəslɪ] *adv* a propósito, intencionadamente, adrede.

purr [pɜːʳ] *n* ronroneo.
► *vi* ronronear.

purse [pɜːs] *n* **1** GB monedero. **2** US bolso. **3** premio.
► *vt* apretar, fruncir *(labios)*.

pursue [pəˈsjuː] *vt* **1** perseguir. **2** proseguir, seguir con.

pursuit [pəˈsjuːt] *n* **1** persecución. **2** búsqueda. **3** actividad, pasatiempo.

purveyor [pɜːˈveɪəʳ] *n* proveedor,-ra.

pus [pʌs] *n* pus.

push [pʊʃ] *n* (*pl* **-es**) empujón, empuje.
► *vt-vi* empujar.
► *vt* **1** pulsar, apretar *(botón)*. **2** *fam* promocionar *(artículo)*. **3** *fam* presionar *(persona)*. **4** *sl* vender, pasar *(droga)*.
● **to give SB the push 1** romper con ALGN *(novio)*. **2** poner a ALGN de patitas en la calle *(empleado)*.
● **to push one's luck** arriesgarse, tentar la suerte.

to push around *vt* dar órdenes a, mandonear.

to push off *vi fam* largarse.

to push on *vi* seguir, continuar.

pushchair ['pʊʃtʃeəʳ] *n* cochecito de niño.

pusher ['pʊʃəʳ] *n fam* camello *(de drogas)*.

pushover ['pʊʃəʊvəʳ] *n fam* cosa fácil.
● **it's a pushover** está chupado.

pushy ['pʊʃɪ] *adj* (**-ier, -iest**) *fam* insistente.

pussy ['pʊsɪ] *n* (*pl* **-ies**) gatito, minino.

put [pʊt] *vt* (*pt & pp* **put**, *ger* **putting**). **1**
poner, colocar: *she put the money on the table*, puso el dinero en la mesa; *he put his hand in his pocket*, se metió la mano en el bolsillo. **2** expresar: *try to put it in French*, intenta expresarlo en francés. **3** escribir: *what can I put?*, ¿qué escribo?
● **put together** juntos,-as.
● **to be hard put to do STH**: *I'd be hard put to find a better example*, me sería muy difícil encontrar un ejemplo mejor.
● **to put an end to** acabar con.
● **to put a question to SB** hacerle una pregunta a ALGN.
● **to put it about that** hacer correr la voz que.
● **to put one over on SB** engañar a ALGN.
● **to put right** arreglar.
● **to put SB up to STH** incitar a ALGN a hacer algo.
● **to put the blame on** echar la culpa a.
● **to put the clocks back** retrasar la hora.
● **to put the clocks forward** adelantar la hora.
● **to put to bed** acostar.
● **to put to death** ejecutar.
● **to put to sea** zarpar.
● **to put to the vote** someter a votación.
● **to put two and two together** atar cabos.
● **to put up a fight** ofrecer resistencia.
● **to put up for sale** poner en venta.
● **to put paid to** *fam* acabar con, echar por tierra.
● **to stay put** *fam* quedarse quieto,-a.

to put across *vt* comunicar, transmitir.

to put aside *vt* **1** ahorrar, guardar *(dinero)*. **2** dejar a un lado *(trabajo)*.

to put away *vt* **1** guardar *(objeto)*. **2** encerrar *(persona)*.

to put back *vt* **1** aplazar, retrasar. **2** atrasar *(reloj)*. **3** devolver a su sitio.

to put down *vt* **1** dejar: *she put her suitcase down*, dejó la maleta en el suelo. **2** sofocar *(rebelión)*. **3** sacrificar *(animal)*. **4** apuntar, escribir. **5** *fam* humillar.

to put down to *vt* atribuir a.

to put forward *vt* **1** proponer *(plan)*. **2** adelantar *(reloj)*.

to put in *vt* **1** dedicar *(tiempo)*. **2** presentar *(queja)*.

to put in for *vt* solicitar.

to put off *vt* **1** aplazar. **2** distraer. **3** desanimar: *the mere thought of it puts me off*, sólo con pensarlo se me quitan las ganas.

to put on *vt* **1** poner, encender *(luz, radio)*. **2** ponerse *(ropa)*. **3** ganar *(peso, velocidad)*. **4** montar *(obra, espectáculo)*.

to put out *vt* **1** sacar. **2** apagar *(fuego, luz)*. **3** molestar.

to put over *vt* comunicar, transmitir.

to put through *vt* conectar *(por teléfono)*.

to put to *vt* proponer, sugerir.

to put together *vt* **1** reunir, juntar *(equipo)*. **2** montar, armar *(máquina)*.

to put up *vt* **1** levantar *(mano)*. **2** alojar. **3** armar *(tienda de campaña)*. **4** construir *(edificio)*. **5** colgar *(cuadro)*. **6** aumentar, subir *(precios, impuestos)*.

to put up with *vt* soportar, aguantar.

putrid ['pjuːtrɪd] *adj* pútrido,-a.

putt [pʌt] *n* tiro al hoyo.

▶ *vt-vi* tirar al hoyo.

putty ['pʌtɪ] *n* masilla.

puzzle ['pʌzəl] *n* **1** rompecabezas. **2** misterio.

▶ *vt* dejar perplejo,-a, desconcertar.

● **to puzzle about** STH, **puzzle over** STH dar vueltas a algo *(en la cabeza)*.

to puzzle out *vt* descifrar, resolver.

puzzled ['pʌzəld] *adj* perplejo,-a, desconcertado,-a.

puzzling ['pʌzəlɪŋ] *adj* desconcertante.

PVC ['piːˈviːˈsiː] *abbr (polyvinyl chloride)* policloruro de vinilo, PVC.

pygmy ['pɪgmɪ] *adj-n* pigmeo,-a.

pyjamas [pəˈdʒɑːməz] *npl* pijama.

pylon ['paɪlən] *n* torre *(de tendido eléctrico)*.

pyramid ['pɪrəmɪd] *n* pirámide.

Pyrenees [pɪrəˈniːz] *n* **the Pyrenees** los Pirineos.

Q

quack [kwæk] n 1 graznido. 2 curandero,-a.
► vi graznar.
quadrangle ['kwɒdræŋgəl] n patio interior.
quadrant ['kwɒdrənt] n cuadrante.
quadraphonic [kwɒdrə'fɒnɪk] adj cua-
drafónico,-a.
quadruped ['kwɒdrəped] n cuadrúpedo.
quadruple ['kwɒdrʊpəl] adj cuádruple.
► vt-vi cuadruplicar(se).
quadruplet ['kwɒdrʊplət] n cuatrillizo,-a.
quagmire ['kwɒgmaɪə'] n cenagal.
quail [kweɪl] n codorniz.
► vi acobardarse.
quaint [kweɪnt] adj 1 pintoresco,-a, típico,-a (lugar). 2 singular, original (costumbre).
quake [kweɪk] n fam terremoto.
► vi temblar.
Quaker ['kweɪkə'] adj-n cuáquero,-a.
qualification [kwɒlɪfɪ'keɪʃən] n 1 requisito (para empleo). 2 diploma, título. 3 sal-
vedad, reserva.
qualified ['kwɒlɪfaɪd] adj 1 capacitado,-a,
cualificado,-a. 2 titulado,-a.
qualify ['kwɒlɪfaɪ] vt (pt & pp -ied). 1 capacitar, dar derecho. 2 modificar, matizar (declaración).
► vi 1 reunir las condiciones necesarias.
2 obtener el título. 3 clasificarse, pasar a
la siguiente ronda. 4 tener derecho.
qualitative ['kwɒlɪtətɪv] adj cualitativo,-a.
quality ['kwɒlɪtɪ] n (pl -ies). 1 calidad. 2
cualidad.
qualm [kwɑːm] n duda, inquietud.
● to have no qualms about doing STH
no tener escrúpulos en hacer algo.

quandary ['kwɒndərɪ] n (pl -ies) dilema.
quantify ['kwɒntɪfaɪ] vt (pt & pp -ied)
cuantificar.
quantity ['kwɒntɪtɪ] n (pl -ies) cantidad.
■ quantity surveyor aparejador,-ra.
quarantine ['kwɒrəntiːn] n cuarentena.
► vt poner en cuarentena.
quarrel ['kwɒrəl] n riña, pelea.
► vi (GB pt & pp quarrelled, ger quarrel-
ling; US pt & pp quarreled, ger quar-
reling) reñir, pelear.
quarrelsome ['kwɒrəlsəm] adj penden-
ciero,-a.
quarry ['kwɒrɪ] n (pl -ies). 1 cantera. 2
presa.
► vt (pt & pp -ied) extraer.
quart [kwɔːt] n cuarto de galón.

En Gran Bretaña equivale a 1,14 litros;
en Estados Unidos equivale a 0,95 litros.

quarter ['kwɔːtə'] n 1 cuarto, cuarta parte: a quarter of a kilo, un cuarto de kilo.
2 cuarto: a quarter past five, las cinco y
cuarto. 3 barrio. 4 trimestre. 5 US veinticinco centavos.
► npl quarters alojamiento.
● from all quarters de todas partes.
● to give no quarter no dar cuartel.
quarterfinal [kwɔːtə'faɪnəl] n cuarto de
final.
quarterly ['kwɔːtəlɪ] adj trimestral.
► adv trimestralmente.
► n (pl -ies) revista trimestral.
quartermaster ['kwɔːtəmɑːstə'] n oficial
de intendencia.
quartet [kwɔː'tet] n cuarteto.
quartz [kwɔːts] n cuarzo.

quash [kwɒʃ] vt 1 sofocar. 2 (sentencia, veredicto) anular.

quaver ['kweɪvə'] n 1 corchea. 2 trémolo.
► vi temblar.

quay [kiː] n muelle.

queasy ['kwiːzɪ] adj (-ier, -iest) mareado,-a.

queen [kwiːn] n 1 reina (monarca). 2 reina, dama (en ajedrez, naipes). 3 sl loca, maricona.
■ queen bee abeja reina.
■ queen mother reina madre.

queer [kwɪə'] adj 1 raro,-a, extraño,-a. 2 fam gay.
► n fam gay.

quell [kwel] vt reprimir, sofocar.

quench [kwentʃ] vt 1 saciar (sed). 2 apagar (fuego).

querulous ['kwerjʊləs] adj quejumbroso,-a.

query ['kwɪərɪ] n (pl -ies) pregunta, duda.
► vt (pt & pp -ied) poner en duda.

quest [kwest] n búsqueda.

question ['kwestʃən] n 1 pregunta. 2 cuestión, problema, asunto.
► vt 1 hacer preguntas a, interrogar. 2 cuestionar, poner en duda.
● out of the question imposible.
● to call into question poner en duda.
■ question mark interrogante.

questionable ['kwestʃənəbəl] adj 1 cuestionable, discutible. 2 dudoso,-a, sospechoso,-a.

questionnaire [kwestʃə'neə'] n cuestionario.

queue [kjuː] n cola.
► vi hacer cola.

quibble ['kwɪbəl] n pega.
► vi poner pegas.

quick [kwɪk] adj 1 rápido,-a: be quick!, ¡date prisa! 2 espabilado,-a, despierto,-a.
► adv rápido, rápidamente.
● to cut to the quick herir en lo vivo.
● to have a quick temper tener mucho genio.

quicken ['kwɪkən] vt-vi acelerar(se).

quickie ['kwɪkɪ] n fam uno,-a rápido,-a.

quicksand ['kwɪksænd] n arenas movedizas.

quick-tempered [kwɪk'tempəd] adj de genio vivo.

quick-witted [kwɪk'wɪtɪd] adj agudo,-a, listo,-a.

quid [kwɪd] n (pl quid) GB libra: you owe me ten quid, me debes diez libras.

quiet ['kwaɪət] adj (comp quieter, superl quietest). 1 callado,-a, silencioso,-a: be quiet!, ¡cállate! 2 tranquilo,-a (lugar).
► n 1 silencio. 2 tranquilidad, calma.
► vt-vi US → quieten.
● on the quiet a la chita callando.

quieten ['kwaɪətən] vt-vi 1 callar(se). 2 tranquilizar(se).

quietly ['kwaɪətlɪ] adv 1 bajo, en voz baja (hablar). 2 sin hacer ruido (moverse).

quietness ['kwaɪətnəs] n 1 silencio. 2 tranquilidad.

quill [kwɪl] n 1 pluma. 2 púa.

quilt [kwɪlt] n colcha, edredón.

quince [kwɪns] n membrillo.

quinine ['kwɪniːn] n quinina.

quintessence [kwɪn'tesəns] n quintaesencia.

quintet [kwɪn'tet] n quinteto.

quintuplet [kwɪn'tjʊplət] n quintillizo,-a.

quip [kwɪp] n ocurrencia, chiste.
► vi (pt & pp quipped, ger quipping) bromear.

quirk [kwɜːk] n 1 manía. 2 avatar, vicisitud.

quirky ['kwɜːkɪ] adj (-ier, -iest) raro,-a.

quit [kwɪt] vt (pt & pp quitted, ger quitting). 1 dejar, abandonar (trabajo). 2 dejar de: to quit smoking, dejar de fumar.
► vi marcharse.
● to call it quits hacer las paces.

quite [kwaɪt] adv 1 bastante: he's quite tall, es bastante alto. 2 completamente, realmente, verdaderamente: I quite understand, lo entiendo perfectamente.

quiver ['kwɪvə'] n temblor, estremecimiento.
► vi temblar, estremecerse.

quiz [kwɪz] n concurso (televisivo, etc).
► vt (pt & pp quizzed, ger quizzing) preguntar, interrogar.

quoit [kwɔɪt] n aro.

quorum ['kwɔːrəm] n quórum.

quota ['kwəʊtə] n 1 cuota. 2 cupo.

quotation [kwəʊ'teɪʃən] n 1 cita (de libro). 2 cotización. 3 presupuesto.
■ quotation marks comillas.

quote [kwəʊt] n cita.
► vt 1 citar. 2 dar el precio de. 3 cotizar.

quotient ['kwəʊʃənt] n cociente.

R

RA ['aːr'eɪ] *abbr* **1** GB *(Royal Academy)* Real Academia de las Artes. **2** GB *(Royal Academician)* miembro de la Real Academia de las Artes.

rabbi ['ræbaɪ] *n* rabino, rabí.

rabbit ['ræbɪt] *n* conejo.
● **to rabbit on** no parar de hablar.

rabble ['ræbəl] *n* populacho.

rabid ['ræbɪd] *adj* rabioso,-a.

rabies ['reɪbiːz] *n* rabia.

RAC ['aːr'eɪ'siː] *abbr* GB *(Royal Automobile Club)* automóvil club británico.

raccoon [rə'kuːn] *n* mapache.

race¹ [reɪs] *n* raza.

race² [reɪs] *n* carrera.
▶ *vi* correr, competir.

racecourse ['reɪskɔːs] *n* GB hipódromo.

racehorse ['reɪhɔːs] *n* caballo de carreras.

racial ['reɪʃəl] *adj* racial.

racing ['reɪsɪŋ] *n* carreras.
■ **horse racing** carreras de caballos.
■ **racing car** coche de carreras.
■ **racing driver** piloto de carreras.

racism ['reɪsɪzəm] *n* racismo.

racist ['reɪsɪst] *adj-n* racista.

rack [ræk] *n* **1** estante. **2** baca *(de coche)*. **3** rejilla *(en tren)*. **4** escurreplatos. **5** potro *(de tortura)*.
▶ *vt* atormentar.
● **to rack one's brains** devanarse los sesos.

racket¹ ['rækɪt] *n* raqueta.

racket² ['rækɪt] *n* **1** alboroto, ruido. **2** *fam* timo.

racoon [rə'kuːn] *n* mapache.

racy ['reɪsɪ] *adj* (**-ier, -iest**) atrevido,-a.

radar ['reɪdaːʳ] *n* radar.

radiant ['reɪdɪənt] *adj* radiante.

radiate ['reɪdɪeɪt] *vt-vi* irradiar.

radiation [reɪdɪ'eɪʃən] *n* radiación.

radiator ['reɪdɪeɪtəʳ] *n* radiador.

radical ['rædɪkəl] *adj-n* radical.

radio ['reɪdɪəʊ] *n* (*pl* **radios**) radio: *I heard it on the radio*, lo oí por la radio.

radioactive [reɪdɪəʊ'æktɪv] *adj* radiactivo,-a.

radioactivity [reɪdɪəʊæk'tɪvɪtɪ] *n* radiactividad.

radio-controlled [reɪdɪəʊkɒn'trəʊld] *adj* teledirigido,-a.

radish ['rædɪʃ] *n* (*pl* **-es**) rábano.

radium ['reɪdɪəm] *n* radio.

radius ['reɪdɪəs] *n* (*pl* **radii** ['reɪdɪaɪ]) radio.

RAF ['aːr'eɪ'ef] *abbr* GB *(Royal Air Force)* fuerzas aéreas británicas.

raffle ['ræfəl] *n* rifa.
▶ *vt-vi* rifar, sortear.

raft [raːft] *n* balsa.

rafter ['raːftəʳ] *n* viga.

rag [ræg] *n* **1** harapo, andrajo, pingajo. **2** trapo. **3** *fam* periódico malo.
● **in rags** harapiento,-a, andrajoso,-a.

rage [reɪdʒ] *n* rabia, furor, cólera.
▶ *vi* **1** rabiar, estar furioso, -a *(persona)*. **2** hacer estragos *(epidemia)*.
● **to be all the rage** hacer furor.
● **to fly into a rage** montar en cólera.

ragged ['rægɪd] *adj* **1** andrajoso,-a, harapiento,-a *(persona)*. **2** roto,-a, deshilachado,-a *(ropa)*.

raid [reɪd] *n* **1** incursión, ataque, razia. **2** redada. **3** atraco, asalto.
▶ *vt* **1** hacer una incursión o ataque. **2** hacer una redada. **3** atracar, asaltar.

rail¹ [reɪl] *n* **1** barra. **2** pasamano, barandilla. **3** raíl, carril, riel.

- **by rail** por ferrocarril.
- **rail strike** huelga de ferroviarios.

rail² [reɪl] *vi* despotricar.

railings ['reɪlɪŋz] *npl* verja.

railroad ['reɪlrəʊd] *n* ferrocarril.

railway ['reɪlweɪ] *n* **1** ferrocarril. **2** vía férrea.

- **railway line** vía férrea.
- **railway station** estación de ferrocarril.

rain [reɪn] *n* lluvia.

- ▶ *vi* llover: *it's raining*, llueve.
- **in the rain** bajo la lluvia.
- **rain forest** selva tropical.

rainbow ['reɪnbəʊ] *n* arco iris.

raincoat ['reɪnkəʊt] *n* impermeable.

raindrop ['reɪndrɒp] *n* gota de lluvia.

rainfall ['reɪnfɔːl] *n* **1** precipitación. **2** pluviosidad.

rainy ['reɪnɪ] *adj* (**-ier, -iest**) lluvioso,-a.

raise [reɪz] *vt* **1** levantar. **2** subir, aumentar *(precios, temperatura)*. **3** provocar *(risas)*. **4** criar, educar *(niños)*. **5** plantear *(asunto, problema)*. **6** recaudar, conseguir *(fondos)*.

- ▶ *n* aumento de sueldo.

raisin ['reɪzən] *n* pasa.

rake¹ [reɪk] *n* rastrillo.

- ▶ *vt* rastrillar.
- **to be raking it in** estar forrándose.
- **to rake up the past** desenterrar el pasado.

rake² [reɪk] *n* libertino.

rake-off ['reɪkɒf] *n* (*pl* **rake-offs**) *sl* tajada.

rally ['rælɪ] *n* (*pl* **-ies**). **1** reunión. **2** POL. mitin. **3** rally. **4** intercambio de golpes *(tenis)*.

- ▶ *vi* (*pt & pp* **-ied**). **1** reponerse, recuperarse. **2** reunirse.

to rally round *vi* unirse, formar piña.

ram [ræm] *n* carnero.

- ▶ *vt* (*pt & pp* **rammed**, *ger* **ramming**). **1** apretar, embutir. **2** chocar contra.

RAM [ræm] *abbr* (*random access memory*) memoria de acceso aleatorio, RAM.

ramble ['ræmbəl] *n* excursión.

- ▶ *vi* **1** ir de excursión. **2** divagar.

rambler ['ræmblə'] *n* excursionista.

rambling ['ræmblɪŋ] *adj* **1** enmarañado, -a *(discurso)*. **2** laberíntico,-a *(casa)*.

ramp [ræmp] *n* rampa.

rampage [ræm'peɪdʒ] *vi* comportarse como un loco, desmandarse.

rampant ['ræmpənt] *adj* incontrolado,-a.

ramshackle ['ræmʃækəl] *adj* destartalado,-a.

ran [ræn] *pt* → run.

ranch [rɑːntʃ] *n* (*pl* **-es**) rancho, hacienda.

rancid ['rænsɪd] *adj* rancio,-a.

random ['rændəm] *adj* fortuito,-a.

- **at random** al azar.

randy ['rændɪ] *adj* (**-ier, -iest**) *fam* cachondo,-a.

rang [ræŋ] *pp* → ring.

range [reɪndʒ] *n* **1** gama, surtido *(de productos)*. **2** alcance *(de misil, telescopio)*. **3** cordillera, sierra.

- ▶ *vi* variar, oscilar: *they range from ... to...*, van desde ... hasta ....

rank¹ [ræŋk] *n* **1** fila. **2** graduación, grado *(militar)*. **3** categoría.

- ▶ *vi* figurar, estar.
- ▶ *vt* considerar, clasificar.

rank² [ræŋk] *adj* **1** fétido,-a. **2** total, completo,-a, absoluto,-a.

ranking ['ræŋkɪŋ] *n* clasificación, ranking.

ransack ['rænsæk] *vt* **1** saquear, desvalijar. **2** registrar a fondo.

ransom ['rænsəm] *n* rescate.

- ▶ *vt* rescatar.
- **to hold SB to ransom** pedir rescate por ALGN.

rap [ræp] *n* **1** golpe seco. **2** rap *(música)*.

- ▶ *vi* (*pt & pp* **rapped**, *ger* **rapping**) golpear.
- **to take the rap** pagar el pato.

rape¹ [reɪp] *n* violación.

- ▶ *vt* violar.

rape² [reɪp] *n* colza.

rapid ['ræpɪd] *adj* rápido,-a.

- ▶ *npl* **rapids** rápidos.

rapist ['reɪpɪst] *n* violador,-ra.

rapport [ræ'pɔː'] *n* compenetración.

rapt [ræpt] *adj* arrebatado,-a, absorto,-a.

rare [reə'] *adj* **1** poco común, raro,-a. **2** poco hecho,-a *(carne)*.

rarely ['reəlɪ] *adv* raras veces.

rascal ['rɑːskəl] *n* bribón, pillo.

rash¹ [ræʃ] *n* (*pl* **-es**) sarpullido.

rash² [ræʃ] *adj* imprudente.

rasher ['ræʃə'] *n* loncha.

rasp [rɑːsp] *n* escofina.

- ▶ *vt* **1** raspar. **2** decir con voz áspera.

raspberry ['rɑːzbərɪ] n (pl -ies). **1** frambuesa. **2** fam pedorreta.

rat [ræt] n **1** rata. **2** fam canalla.
- **to rat on 1** chivarse de, delatar (persona). **2** romper (promesa).
- **to smell a rat** olerse algo raro.

rate [reɪt] vt **1** considerar. **2** tasar, estimar.
► n **1** tasa, índice, tipo. **2** velocidad, ritmo. **3** tarifa, precio.
► npl **rates** GB contribución urbana.
- **at any rate** de todos modos.
- **at the rate of** a razón de.
- **first rate** de primera categoría.
- **second rate** de segunda categoría.
■ **rate of exchange** tipo de cambio.

ratepayer ['reɪtpeɪəʳ] n GB contribuyente.

rather ['rɑːðəʳ] adv bastante, algo, un tanto.
- **I would rather** preferiría.
- **or rather** o mejor dicho.
- **rather than** en vez de, mejor que.

rating ['reɪtɪŋ] n **1** clasificación. **2** posición.
► npl **ratings** índice de audiencia.

ratio ['reɪʃɪəʊ] n (pl **ratios**) razón, relación, proporción.

ration ['ræʃən] n ración.
► vt racionar.

rational ['ræʃənəl] adj racional.

rattle ['rætəl] n **1** sonajero. **2** carraca, matraca. **3** traqueteo.
► vi sonar.
► vt **1** hacer sonar. **2** fam poner nervioso,-a.

to rattle off vt decir a toda prisa, escribir a toda prisa.

to rattle on vi hablar sin parar.

to rattle through vt despachar rápidamente.

rattlesnake ['rætəlsneɪk] n serpiente de cascabel.

ravage ['rævɪdʒ] vt asolar, devastar.
► npl **ravages** estragos.

rave [reɪv] vi **1** despotricar. **2** deshacerse en alabanzas.
► n juerga.

raven ['reɪvən] n cuervo.

ravenous ['rævənəs] adj voraz.

rave-up ['reɪvʌp] n fam juerga.

ravine [rəˈviːn] n barranco.

raving ['reɪvɪŋ] adj-adv de atar.
- **raving mad** loco,-a de atar.

ravish ['rævɪʃ] vt extasiar.

ravishing ['rævɪʃɪŋ] adj deslumbrante, magnífico,-a.

raw [rɔː] adj **1** crudo,-a. **2** bruto,-a, sin refinar. **3** novato,-a, primerizo. **4** crudo,-a (tiempo).
■ **raw material** materia prima.

ray[1] [reɪ] n rayo (de luz).

ray[2] [reɪ] n raya (pez).

ray[3] [reɪ] n re (nota musical).

rayon ['reɪɒn] n rayón.

razor ['reɪzəʳ] n **1** navaja de afeitar. **2** maquinilla de afeitar.
■ **razor blade** cuchilla de afeitar.

RC ['ɑːˈsiː, ˌrəʊmənˈkæθəlɪk] abbr (**Roman Catholic**) católico,-a.

Rd [rəʊd] abbr (**Road**) calle, c/.

re[1] [riː] prep respecto a, con referencia a.

re[2] [reɪ] n re (nota).

reach [riːtʃ] n (pl -es) alcance.
► vt **1** llegar a (lugar). **2** alcanzar, llegar a (objeto). **3** contactar, localizar. **4** alcanzar (decisión, acuerdo).
► vi **1** llegar, extenderse (lugar). **2** alcanzar, llegar: I can't reach, no alcanzo.
- **within reach of** al alcance de.
■ **out of reach** fuera del alcance.

to reach out vi alargar la mano.

react [rɪˈækt] vi reaccionar.

reaction [rɪˈækʃən] n reacción.

reactionary [rɪˈækʃənərɪ] adj-n reaccionario,-a.

read [riːd] vt (pt & pp **read** [red]). **1** leer. **2** interpretar. **3** estudiar, cursar (en universidad).
► vi **1** indicar, marcar (instrumento). **2** decir, poner (cartel, anuncio).
- **to read back** volver a leer, releer.
- **to read out** leer en voz alta.

to read up on vt investigar, buscar datos sobre.

reader ['riːdəʳ] n lector,-ra.

readily ['redɪlɪ] adv **1** fácilmente. **2** de buena gana.

reading ['riːdɪŋ] n lectura.

ready ['redɪ] adj (-ier, -iest). **1** preparado,-a, listo,-a. **2** dispuesto,-a.
- **to get ready** preparar(se).
- **ready, steady, go!** preparados, listos, ¡ya!

ready-made [redɪˈmeɪd] adj hecho,-a, confeccionado,-a.

real [rɪəl] adj **1** real, verdadero,-a. **2** genuino,-a, auténtico,-a.

► *adv fam* muy.
■ **real estate** bienes inmuebles.
realism ['rɪəlɪzəm] *n* realismo.
realistic [rɪə'lɪstɪk] *adj* realista.
reality [rɪ'ælɪtɪ] *n* (*pl* **-ies**) realidad.
realization [rɪəlaɪ'zeɪʃən] *n* **1** realización. **2** comprensión.
realize ['rɪəlaɪz] *vt* **1** darse cuenta de. **2** realizar, llevar a cabo *(plan)*. **3** realizar *(bienes, activos)*.
really ['rɪəlɪ] *adv* realmente, verdaderamente.
realm [relm] *n* **1** reino. **2** campo, esfera.
reap [riːp] *vt* cosechar.
reappear [riːə'pɪə'] *vi* reaparecer.
rear[1] [rɪə'] *adj* trasero,-a, de atrás.
► *n* **1** parte de atrás. **2** fondo. **3** *fam* trasero, culo.
rear[2] [rɪə'] *vt* **1** criar. **2** levantar.
► *vi* **to rear (up)** encabritarse.
rearmament [riː'ɑːməmənt] *n* rearme.
rearrange [riːə'reɪndʒ] *vt* **1** colocar de otra manera. **2** volver a concertar *(reunión)*.
rear-view ['rɪəvjuː] *adj* .
■ **rear-view mirror** retrovisor.
reason ['riːzən] *n* **1** razón, motivo. **2** razón, sentido común.
► *vi* razonar.
● **it stands to reason** es lógico.
● **within reason** dentro de lo razonable.
reasonable ['riːzənəbəl] *adj* razonable.
reasoning ['riːzənɪŋ] *n* razonamiento.
reassurance [riːə'ʃʊərəns] *n* tranquilidad, consuelo.
reassure [riːə'ʃʊə'] *vt* tranquilizar.
reassuring [riːə'ʃʊərɪŋ] *adj* tranquilizador,-ra.
rebate ['riːbeɪt] *n* **1** devolución, reembolso. **2** bonificación.
rebel ['rebəl rɪ'bel] *adj-n* rebelde.
► *vi* (*pt & pp* **rebelled**, *ger* **rebelling**) rebelarse.
rebellion [rɪ'beljən] *n* rebelión.
rebellious [rɪ'beljəs] *adj* rebelde.
rebound [(*n*) 'riːbaʊnd(*vb*) rɪ'baʊnd] *n* rebote.
► *vi* rebotar.
● **on the rebound** de rebote.
rebuff [rɪ'bʌf] *n* (*pl* **rebuffs**) repulsa, desaire.
► *vt* repulsar, desairar.
rebuild [riː'bɪld] *vt* (*pt & pp* **rebuilt** [riː'bɪlt]) reconstruir.

rebuke [rɪ'bjuːk] *n* reproche, reprimenda.
► *vt* reprender.
recall [rɪ'kɔːl] *n* memoria.
► *vt* **1** llamar. **2** retirar *(embajador)*. **3** recordar.
recapture [riː'kæptʃə'] *vt* **1** reconquistar. **2** *fig* hacer revivir, reproducir.
receipt [rɪ'siːt] *n* recibo.
► *npl* **receipts 1** entradas, ingresos. **2** recaudación *(en taquilla)*.
receive [rɪ'siːv] *vt* recibir.
receiver [rɪ'siːvə'] *n* **1** receptor,-ra *(persona)*. **2** receptor *(de radio)*. **3** auricular *(de teléfono)*.
recent ['riːsənt] *adj* reciente.
recently ['riːsəntlɪ] *adv* recientemente.
reception [rɪ'sepʃən] *n* **1** recepción. **2** acogida. **3** banquete.
■ **reception desk** recepción.
receptionist [rɪ'sepʃənɪst] *n* recepcionista.
recess ['riːses] *n* (*pl* **-es**). **1** hueco. **2** descanso. **3** POL período de vacaciones.
recession [rɪ'seʃən] *n* recesión.
recharge [riː'tʃɑːdʒ] *vt* recargar.
rechargeable [riː'tʃɑːdʒəbəl] *adj* recargable.
recipe ['resəpɪ] *n* receta.
recipient [rɪ'sɪpɪənt] *n* receptor,-ra.
reciprocal [rɪ'sɪprəkəl] *adj* recíproco,-a.
reciprocate [rɪ'sɪprəkeɪt] *vi* corresponder.
► *vt* devolver.
recital [rɪ'saɪtəl] *n* recital.
recite [rɪ'saɪt] *vt-vi* recitar.
reckless ['rekləs] *adj* **1** precipitado,-a. **2** temerario,-a, imprudente.
reckon ['rekən] *vt-vi* **1** contar. **2** calcular.
► *vt* creer, considerar.
to reckon on *vt* contar con.
to reckon with *vt* **1** tener en cuenta. **2** vérselas con.
reckoning ['rekənɪŋ] *n* cálculos.
● **by my reckoning** según mis cálculos.
reclaim [rɪ'kleɪm] *vt* **1** reclamar, reivindicar. **2** recuperar. **3** reciclar.
recline [rɪ'klaɪn] *vt-vi* reclinar(se).
recognition [rekəg'nɪʃən] *n* reconocimiento.
recognize ['rekəgnaɪz] *vt* reconocer.
recoil [(*n*) 'riːkɔɪl(*vb*) rɪ'kɔɪl] *n* retroceso.
► *vi* retroceder.
recollect [rekə'lekt] *vt* recordar.

recollection [rekə'lekʃən] *n* recuerdo.
recommend [rekə'mend] *vt* recomendar.
recommendation [rekəmen'deɪʃən] *n* recomendación.
recompense ['rekəmpens] *n* recompensa.
► *vt* recompensar.
reconcile ['rekənsaɪl] *vt* **1** reconciliar *(personas)*. **2** conciliar *(ideas)*.
● **to reconcile oneself to** resignarse a.
reconciliation [rekənsɪlɪ'eɪʃən] *n* **1** reconciliación *(de personas)*. **2** conciliación *(de ideas)*.
reconsider [ri:kən'sɪdəʳ] *vt* reconsiderar.
reconstruct [ri:kəns'trʌkt] *vt* reconstruir.
record [*(n)* 'rekɔːd*(vb)* rɪ'kɔːd] *n* **1** constancia escrita, registro, documento. **2** historial, expediente. **3** disco *(música)*. **4** récord, marca.
► *vt* **1** hacer constar. **2** anotar. **3** grabar.
● **off the record** confidencialmente.
● **to beat the record** batir el récord.
■ **record player** tocadiscos.
recorder [rɪ'kɔːdəʳ] *n* flauta dulce.
recording [rɪ'kɔːdɪŋ] *n* grabación.
recount [rɪ'kaʊnt 'riːkaʊnt] *vt* **1** contar, relatar. **2** volver a contar.
► *n* recuento.
recourse [rɪ'kɔːs] *n* recurso.
● **to have recourse to** recurrir a.
recover [rɪ'kʌvəʳ] *vt-vi* recuperar(se).
recovery [rɪ'kʌvərɪ] *n* *(pl* -**ies**) recuperación.
recreation [rekrɪ'eɪʃən] *n* esparcimiento, pasatiempo, recreo.
recruit [rɪ'kruːt] *n* recluta.
► *vt* reclutar.
rectangle ['rektæŋgəl] *n* rectángulo.
rectangular [rekt'æŋgjʊləʳ] *adj* rectangular.
rectify ['rektɪfaɪ] *vt* *(pt & pp* -**ied**) rectificar, corregir.
recuperate [rɪk'uːpəreɪt] *vi* recuperar(se).
recuperation [rɪk'uːpəreɪʃən] *n* recuperación.
recur [rɪ'kɜːʳ] *vi* *(pt & pp* **recurred**, *ger* **recurring**) repetirse, reproducirse.
recycle [riː'saɪkəl] *vt* reciclar.
recycling [riː'saɪkəlɪŋ] *n* reciclaje.
red [red] *adj* *(comp* **redder**, *superl* **reddest**) **1** rojo,-a. **2** pelirrojo,-a *(pelo)*.
► *n* rojo.
● **to be in the red** estar en números rojos.

● **to turn red** ponerse colorado,-a, sonrojarse.
■ **red tape** papeleo burocrático.
■ **red wine** vino tinto.
■ **Red Cross** Cruz Roja.
reddish ['redɪʃ] *adj* rojizo,-a.
redeem [rɪ'diːm] *vt* **1** rescatar, recuperar. **2** redimir, salvar. **3** cumplir *(promesa)*.
red-handed [red'hændɪd] *adj* con las manos en la masa, in fraganti.
redhead ['redhed] *n* pelirrojo,-a.
red-hot [red'hɒt] *adj* al rojo vivo.
redress [rɪ'dres] *n* reparación, desagravio.
► *vt* reparar, corregir.
reduce [rɪ'djuːs] *vt-vi* reducir(se).
reduction [rɪ'dʌkʃən] *n* reducción.
redundancy [rɪ'dʌndənsɪ] *n* *(pl* -**ies**) despido.
redundant [rɪ'dʌndənt] *adj* **1** redundante. **2** despedido,-a.
● **to be made redundant** perder el empleo, ser despedido,-a.
reed [riːd] *n* **1** caña, junco. **2** lengüeta *(de instrumento)*.
reef [riːf] *n* *(pl* **reefs**) arrecife.
reek [riːk] *n* tufo.
► *vi* apestar.
reel[1] [riːl] *n* carrete *(de película)*.
reel[2] [riːl] *vi* **1** tambalear, tambalearse. **2** dar vueltas *(cabeza)*.
ref ['refərəns] *abbr (reference)* referencia, ref.
refer [rɪ'fɜːʳ] *vt* *(pt & pp* **referred**, *ger* **referring**) remitir, enviar.
► *vi* **1** referirse. **2** consultar.
referee [refə'riː] *n* **1** árbitro. **2** garante, avalador,-ra.
► *vt* arbitrar.
reference ['refərəns] *n* referencia.
● **with reference to** referente a.
■ **reference book** libro de consulta.
referendum [refə'rendəm] *n* *(pl* -**s** o **referenda** [refə'rendə]) referéndum.
refill [*(n)* 'riːfɪl*(vb)* riː'fɪl] *n* recambio.
► *vt* rellenar.
refine [rɪ'faɪn] *vt* refinar.
refined [rɪ'faɪnd] *adj* refinado,-a.
refinement [rɪ'faɪnmənt] *n* refinamiento.
refinery [rɪ'faɪnərɪ] *n* *(pl* -**ies**) refinería.
reflect [rɪ'flekt] *vt* reflejar.
► *vi* reflexionar.
reflection [rɪ'flekʃən] *n* **1** reflejo. **2** reflexión.

reflector [rɪ'flektə'] n catafaro, reflector.
reflex ['riːfleks] adj reflejo,-a.
reflexive [rɪ'fleksɪv] adj reflexivo,-a.
reform [rɪ'fɔːm] n reforma.
▶ vt reformar.
refrain[1] [rɪ'freɪn] n estribillo.
refrain[2] [rɪ'freɪn] vi abstenerse.
refresh [rɪ'freʃ] vt refrescar.
refreshing [rɪ'freʃɪŋ] adj refrescante.
refreshments [rɪ'freʃmənts] npl refrigerio.
refrigerate [rɪ'frɪdʒəreɪt] vt refrigerar.
refrigerator [rɪ'frɪdʒəreɪtə'] n frigorífico, nevera.
refuel [riː'fjʊəl] vt-vi repostar.
refuge ['refjuːdʒ] n refugio.
● **to take refuge** refugiarse.
refugee [refjuː'dʒiː] n refugiado,-a.
refund [(n) 'riːfʌnd(vb) riː'fʌnd] n reembolso.
▶ vt reembolsar.
refusal [rɪ'fjuːzəl] n 1 negativa. 2 rechazo, denegación.
refuse[1] ['refjuːs] n basura.
refuse[2] [rɪ'fjuːz] vt rehusar, rechazar.
▶ vi negarse.
regain [rɪ'geɪn] vt recobrar, recuperar.
regard [rɪ'gɑːd] vt considerar: *he is regarded as a hero*, se le considera un héroe.
▶ n respeto, consideración.
▶ npl **regards** recuerdos.
● **as regards...** en lo que se refiere a....
● **with regard to** con respecto a.
● **without regard to** sin hacer caso de.
regarding [rɪ'gɑːdɪŋ] prep tocante a, respecto a, en relación con.
regardless [rɪ'gɑːdləs] adv a pesar de todo.
▶ prep **regardless of** sin tener en cuenta.
regime [reɪ'ʒiːm] n régimen.
regiment ['redʒɪmənt] n regimiento.
region ['riːdʒən] n región.
register ['redʒɪstə'] n registro, lista.
▶ vi 1 registrarse *(en hotel)*. 2 matricularse *(para clases)*. 3 inscribirse.
▶ vt 1 certificar *(carta)*. 2 inscribir en el registro *(boda, nacimiento)*. 3 indicar, registrar *(temperatura)*.
■ **registered post** correo certificado.
registrar [redʒɪs'trɑː'] n 1 registrador,-ra.

2 secretario,-a *(en universidad)*. 3 GB médico,-a *(en hospital)*.
registration [redʒɪs'treɪʃən] n 1 registro. 2 facturación. 3 matriculación.
■ **registration number** matrícula *(de coche)*.
registry ['redʒɪstrɪ] n *(pl -ies)* registro.
■ **registry office** registro civil.
regret [rɪ'gret] n 1 remordimiento. 2 pesar.
▶ vt *(pt & pp* **regretted**, *ger* **regretting**). 1 lamentar. 2 arrepentirse de.
● **to have no regrets** no arrepentirse.
regretful [rɪ'gretfʊl] adj arrepentido,-a.
regrettable [rɪ'gretəbəl] adj lamentable.
regular ['regjʊlə'] adj 1 regular. 2 habitual *(cliente)*. 3 normal.
▶ n fam cliente habitual.
regularity [regjʊ'lærətɪ] n *(pl -ies)* regularidad.
regulate ['regjʊleɪt] vt regular.
regulation [regjʊ'leɪʃən] n 1 regulación. 2 regla, norma.
rehabilitate [riːhə'bɪlɪteɪt] vt rehabilitar.
rehearsal [rɪ'hɜːsəl] n ensayo.
rehearse [rɪ'hɜːs] vt ensayar.
reign [reɪn] n reinado.
▶ vi reinar.
reimburse [riːɪm'bɜːs] vt reembolsar.
rein [reɪn] n rienda.
▶ npl **reins** andadores.
reindeer ['reɪndɪə'] n *(pl reindeer)* reno.
reinforce [riːɪn'fɔːs] vt reforzar.
■ **reinforced concrete** hormigón armado.
reinforcement [riːɪn'fɔːsmənt] n refuerzo.
reinstate [riːɪn'steɪt] vt readmitir, reincorporar.
reject [(n) 'riːdʒekt(vb) rɪ'dʒekt] n desecho.
▶ vt rechazar, rehusar.
rejection [rɪ'dʒekʃən] n rechazo.
rejoice [rɪ'dʒɔɪs] vi alegrarse, regocijarse.
rejuvenate [rɪ'dʒuːvəneɪt] vt rejuvenecer.
relapse [rɪ'læps] n 1 recaída. 2 reincidencia.
▶ vi 1 recaer. 2 reincidir.
relate [rɪ'leɪt] vt 1 relatar, contar. 2 relacionar.
▶ vi 1 estar relacionado,-a. 2 identificarse, entenderse.
related [rɪ'leɪtɪd] adj 1 relacionado,-a. 2 emparentado,-a.

relation [rɪˈleɪʃən] *n* **1** relación. **2** pariente,-a, familiar.
● **in relation to** en relación a.
relationship [rɪˈleɪʃənʃɪp] *n* **1** relación. **2** relaciones *(entre personas)*.
relative [ˈrelətɪv] *adj* relativo,-a.
▶ *n* pariente,-a.
relax [rɪˈlæks] *vt-vi* relajar(se).
relaxation [riːlækˈseɪʃən] *n* **1** relajación, esparcimiento. **2** descanso.
relaxed [rɪˈlækst] *adj* relajado,-a.
relaxing [rɪˈlæksɪŋ] *adj* relajante.
relay [ˈriːleɪ] *n* **1** relevo: *a relay race*, una carrera de relevos. **2** relé.
▶ *vt* retransmitir *(señal)*.
release [rɪˈliːs] *n* **1** liberación, puesta en libertad. **2** estreno *(de película)*. **3** disco recién salido.
▶ *vt* **1** liberar, poner en libertad. **2** estrenar *(película)*. **3** sacar *(disco)*. **4** soltar.
relegate [ˈrelɪɡeɪt] *vt* relegar.
● **to be relegated** SP descender.
relent [rɪˈlent] *vi* ceder, amainar.
relevant [ˈreləvənt] *adj* pertinente.
reliable [rɪˈlaɪəbəl] *adj* **1** fiable, de fiar *(persona)*. **2** fidedigno,-a *(noticia)*. **3** seguro,-a *(máquina)*.
reliance [rɪˈlaɪəns] *n* dependencia.
relic [ˈrelɪk] *n* reliquia.
relief [rɪˈliːf] *n* **1** alivio. **2** auxilio, socorro. **3** relevo *(persona)*. **4** relieve.
relieve [rɪˈliːv] *vt* **1** aliviar. **2** alegrar. **3** relevar.
religion [rɪˈlɪdʒən] *n* religión.
religious [rɪˈlɪdʒəs] *adj* religioso,-a.
relinquish [rɪˈlɪŋkwɪʃ] *vt* renunciar a.
relish [ˈrelɪʃ] *n* gusto, deleite.
▶ *vt* disfrutar de: *I don't relish the idea*, no me gusta la idea.
reluctance [rɪˈlʌktəns] *n* reticencia.
reluctant [rɪˈlʌktənt] *adj* reacio,-a.
rely [rɪˈlaɪ] *vi* **rely on** *(pt & pp* **relied***, ger* **relying***)* confiar en, contar con.
remain [rɪˈmeɪn] *vi* **1** quedarse, permanecer. **2** quedar, sobrar.
▶ *npl* **remains** restos.
remainder [rɪˈmeɪndəʳ] *n* resto.
remaining [rɪˈmeɪnɪŋ] *adj* restante.
remark [rɪˈmɑːk] *n* observación, comentario.
▶ *vt* observar, comentar.

remarkable [rɪˈmɑːkəbəl] *adj* notable, extraordinario,-a.
remedy [ˈremədɪ] *n* *(pl* **-ies***)* remedio.
▶ *vt* *(pt & pp* **remedied***, ger* **remedying***)* remediar.
remember [rɪˈmembəʳ] *vt* recordar, acordarse de: *remember to buy bread*, acuérdate de comprar pan; *I remember talking to her*, recuerdo haber hablado con ella.
● **remember me to ...** recuerdos a ... de mi parte.
remind [rɪˈmaɪnd] *vt* recordar: *remind her to phone me*, recuérdale que me llame.
reminder [rɪˈmaɪndəʳ] *n* recordatorio.
reminisce [remɪˈnɪs] *vi* rememorar.
reminiscent [remɪˈnɪsənt] *adj* lleno,-a de recuerdos.
● **reminiscent of ...** que recuerda ....
remit [rɪˈmɪt] *vt* *(pt & pp* **remitted***, ger* **remitting***)* remitir.
remittance [rɪˈmɪtəns] *n* giro.
remnant [ˈremnənt] *n* **1** resto. **2** retal.
remorse [rɪˈmɔːs] *n* remordimiento.
remorseful [rɪˈmɔːsful] *adj* arrepentido,-a.
remote [rɪˈməʊt] *adj* remoto,-a, aislado,-a.
● **not the remotest idea** ni la más mínima idea.
■ **remote control** mando a distancia.
removal [rɪˈmuːvəl] *n* **1** eliminación, retirada. **2** traslado, mudanza. **3** extracción. **4** extirpación.
remove [rɪˈmuːv] *vt* **1** quitar, eliminar. **2** quitar, sacar. **3** despedir. **4** extirpar.
▶ *vi* trasladarse, mudarse.
Renaissance [rəˈneɪsəns] *n* Renacimiento.
render [ˈrendəʳ] *vt* **1** dar, prestar *(ayuda, favor)*. **2** hacer, convertir en. **3** cantar *(canción)*. **4** interpretar *(música)*.
rendezvous [ˈrɒndɪvuː] *n* *(pl* **rendezvous***)*. **1** cita. **2** lugar de reunión.
rendition [renˈdɪʃən] *n* interpretación.
renew [rɪˈnjuː] *vt* **1** renovar. **2** reanudar.
renewable [rɪˈnjuːəbəl] *adj* renovable.
renewal [rɪˈnjuːəl] *n* **1** renovación. **2** reanudación.
renounce [rɪˈnaʊns] *vt* renunciar.
renovate [ˈrenəveɪt] *vt* restaurar.
renovation [renəˈveɪʃən] *n* restauración.
renown [rɪˈnaʊn] *n* renombre, fama.
renowned [rɪˈnaʊnd] *adj* renombrado,-a, famoso,-a.

rent[1] [rent] *n* alquiler.
► *vt* alquilar, arrendar.
rent[2] [rent] *pt-pp* → **rend**.
rental ['rentəl] *n* alquiler.
reopen [riː'əʊpən] *vt-vi* reabrir(se).
reorganization [riːɔːgənaɪ'zeɪʃən] *n* reorganización.
reorganize [riː'ɔːgənaɪz] *vt* reorganizar.
repair [rɪ'peəˈ] *n* reparación.
► *vt* reparar, arreglar.
● **in good repair** en buen estado.
repatriate [riː'pætrɪeɪt] *vt* repatriar.
repay [riː'peɪ] *vt* (*pt & pp* **repaid**) devolver.
repayment [riː'peɪmənt] *n* devolución, reembolso.
repeal [rɪ'piːl] *n* abrogación, revocación.
► *vt* abrogar, revocar.
repeat [rɪ'piːt] *n* repetición.
► *vt* repetir.
repeatedly [rɪ'piːtɪdlɪ] *adv* repetidamente.
repel [rɪ'pel] *vt* (*pt & pp* **repelled**, *ger* **repelling**). **1** repeler. **2** repugnar.
repellent [rɪ'pelənt] *adj* repelente.
► *n* repelente de insectos.
repent [rɪ'pent] *vt-vi* arrepentirse (*de*).
repercussion [riːpə'kʌʃən] *n* repercusión.
repertoire ['repətwɑːˈ] *n* repertorio.
repetition [repə'tɪʃən] *n* repetición.
repetitive [rɪ'petɪtɪv] *adj* repetitivo,-a.
replace [rɪ'pleɪs] *vt* **1** devolver a su sitio. **2** reemplazar, substituir.
replacement [rɪ'pleɪsmənt] *n* **1** sustitución. **2** sustituto,-a, suplente. **3** pieza de cambio, repuesto.
replay [(*n*) 'riːpleɪ(*vb*) riː'pleɪ] *n* **1** repetición. **2** partido de desempate.
► *vt* repetir.
reply [rɪ'plaɪ] *n* (*pl* **-ies**) respuesta, contestación.
► *vi* (*pt & pp* **-ied**) responder, contestar.
report [rɪ'pɔːt] *n* **1** informe (*escrito o verbal*). **2** noticia. **3** reportaje. **4** boletín de evaluación, boletín escolar.
► *vt* **1** informar sobre, dar parte de. **2** denunciar (*crimen*).
► *vi* presentarse: *you must report to the headmaster*, debes presentarte al director.
■ **reported speech** estilo indirecto.
reporter [rɪ'pɔːtəˈ] *n* reportero,-a, periodista.

repose [rɪ'pəʊz] *n* reposo.
► *vi* reposar, descansar.
represent [reprɪ'zent] *vt* representar.
representation [reprɪzen'teɪʃən] *n* representación.
representative [reprɪ'zentətɪv] *adj* representativo,-a.
► *n* **1** representante. **2** US diputado,-a.
repress [rɪ'pres] *vt* reprimir.
repression [rɪ'preʃən] *n* represión.
repressive [rɪ'presɪv] *adj* represivo,-a.
reprieve [rɪ'priːv] *n* **1** indulto. **2** *fig* respiro, tregua.
► *vt* indultar.
reprimand ['reprɪmɑːnd] *n* reprimenda, reprensión.
► *vt* reprender.
reprint [(*n*) 'riːprɪnt (*vb*) riː'prɪnt] *n* reimpresión.
► *vt* reimprimir.
reprisal [rɪ'praɪzəl] *n* represalia.
reproach [rɪ'prəʊtʃ] *n* (*pl* **-es**) reproche.
► *vt* reprochar.
reproduce [riːprə'djuːs] *vt-vi* reproducir(se).
reproduction [riːprə'dʌkʃən] *n* reproducción.
reproductive [riːprə'dʌktɪv] *adj* reproductor,-ra.
reptile ['reptaɪl] *n* reptil.
republic [rɪ'pʌblɪk] *n* república.
republican [rɪ'pʌblɪkən] *adj-n* republicano,-a.
repudiate [rɪ'pjuːdɪeɪt] *vt* rechazar.
repugnant [rɪ'pʌgnənt] *adj* repugnante.
repulse [rɪ'pʌls] *vt* rechazar.
repulsive [rɪ'pʌlsɪv] *adj* repulsivo,-a.
reputable ['repjʊtəbəl] *adj* **1** acreditado, -a. **2** de confianza (*persona*).
reputation [repjʊ'teɪʃən] *n* reputación, fama.
repute [rɪ'pjuːt] *n* reputación, fama.
reputed [rɪ'pjuːtɪd] *adj* reputado,-a: *to be reputed to be...*, tener fama de ser....
reputedly [rɪ'pjuːtɪdlɪ] *adv* según se dice.
request [rɪ'kwest] *n* solicitud, petición.
► *vt* pedir, solicitar.
require [rɪ'kwaɪəˈ] *vt* **1** requerir, exigir. **2** necesitar.
requirement [rɪ'kwaɪəmənt] *n* **1** requisito, condición. **2** necesidad.
requisite ['rekwɪzɪt] *adj* requerido,-a, necesario,-a.

rescue ['reskjuː] *n* rescate, salvamento: *a rescue operation*, una operación de rescate.
▶ *vt* rescatar, salvar.

rescuer ['reskjʊə'] *n* salvador,-ra.

research [rɪ'sɜːtʃ] *n* (*pl* **-es**) investigación.
▶ *vt-vi* investigar.

researcher [rɪ'sɜːtʃə'] *n* investigador,-ra.

resemblance [rɪ'zembləns] *n* parecido, semejanza.

resemble [rɪ'zembəl] *vt* parecerse a.

resent [rɪ'zent] *vt* ofenderse por, tomar a mal.

resentful [rɪ'zentfʊl] *adj* resentido,-a, ofendido,-a.

resentment [rɪ'zentmənt] *n* resentimiento, rencor.

reservation [rezə'veɪʃən] *n* reserva.

reserve [rɪ'zɜːv] *n* reserva.
▶ *vt* reservar.

reserved [rɪ'zɜːvd] *adj* reservado,-a.

reservoir ['rezəvwɑː'] *n* embalse.

reshuffle [riː'ʃʌfəl] *n* remodelación, reorganización (de Gobierno).
▶ *vt* **1** remodelar, reorganizar (Gobierno). **2** volver a barajar.

reside [rɪ'zaɪd] *vi* residir.

residence ['rezɪdəns] *n* residencia.

resident ['rezɪdənt] *adj-n* residente.

residential [rezɪ'denʃəl] *adj* residencial.

residue ['rezɪdjuː] *n* residuo.

resign [rɪ'zaɪn] *vt-vi* dimitir.
● **to resign oneself to** STH resignarse a algo.

resignation [rezɪg'neɪʃən] *n* **1** dimisión. **2** resignación.

resilient [rɪ'zɪlɪənt] *adj* **1** elástico,-a (material). **2** fuerte, resistente (persona).

resin ['rezɪn] *n* resina.

resist [rɪ'zɪst] *vt* **1** resistir, oponerse (a cambios). **2** oponer resistencia (a enemigo). **3** resistir (tentación).

resistance [rɪ'zɪstəns] *n* resistencia.

resistant [rɪ'zɪstənt] *adj* resistente.

resolute ['rezəluːt] *adj* resuelto,-a, decidido,-a.

resolution [rezə'luːʃən] *n* resolución.

resolve [rɪ'zɒlv] *n* resolución.
▶ *vt* **1** resolver, decidir, acordar. **2** resolver (disputa).

resort [rɪ'zɔːt] *n* **1** lugar de vacaciones: *a ski resort*, una estación de esquí. **2** recurso.
▶ *vi* recurrir.

resound [rɪ'zaund] *vi* resonar.

resounding [rɪ'zaundɪŋ] *adj* **1** resonante, clamoroso,-a. **2** *fig* enorme, importante.

resource [rɪ'zɔːs] *n* recurso.

resourceful [rɪ'zɔːsfʊl] *adj* ingenioso,-a, con recursos.

respect [rɪ'spekt] *n* **1** respeto. **2** sentido, respecto: *in some respects*, en algunos sentidos.
▶ *vt* respetar.
● **with respect to** con respeto a.

respectable [rɪ'spektəbəl] *adj* respetable.

respectful [rɪ'spektfʊl] *adj* respetuoso,-a.

respective [rɪ'spektɪv] *adj* respectivo,-a.

respiratory ['respərətərɪ] *adj* respiratorio,-a.

respite ['respaɪt] *n* respiro, alivio.

respond [rɪ'spɒnd] *vi* responder, reaccionar.
● **to respond to a treatment** responder a un tratamiento.

response [rɪ'spɒns] *n* respuesta, reacción.

responsibility [rɪspɒnsɪ'bɪlɪtɪ] *n* (*pl* **-ies**) responsabilidad.

responsible [rɪ'spɒnsəbəl] *adj* responsable.

responsive [rɪ'spɒnsɪv] *adj* receptivo,-a.

rest[1] [rest] *n* **1** descanso, reposo: *to have a rest*, descansar. **2** paz, tranquilidad. **3** soporte.
▶ *vt-vi* descansar.
▶ *vt* apoyar.

rest[2] [rest] *n* resto: *the rest*, lo demás, los demás; *the rest of...*, el resto de....

to rest with *vi* corresponder a, depender de.

restaurant ['restərɒnt] *n* restaurante.

restful ['restfʊl] *adj* tranquilo,-a.

restive ['restɪv] *adj* inquieto,-a.

restless ['restləs] *adj* inquieto,-a, agitado,-a.

restoration [restə'reɪʃən] *n* **1** restauración. **2** devolución.

restore [rɪ'stɔː'] *vt* **1** restaurar (monarquía). **2** devolver (salud). **3** restablecer (orden).

restrain [rɪ'streɪn] *vt* contener, reprimir.

restraint [rɪ'streɪnt] *n* **1** limitación, restricción. **2** moderación, comedimiento.

restrict [rɪ'strɪkt] *vt* restringir, limitar.

restriction [rɪ'strɪkʃən] *n* restricción.

restrictive [rɪ'strɪktɪv] *adj* restrictivo,-a.

result [rɪ'zʌlt] n resultado: **as a result...**, como resultado....
▸ vi to result from, resultar de.
to result in vt tener como resultado.
resume [rɪ'zjuːm] vt-vi reanudar(se).
● **to resume one's seat** volver a sentarse.
résumé ['rezjuːmeɪ] n resumen.
resurrect [rezə'rekt] vt resucitar.
resurrection [rezə'rekʃən] n resurrección.
resuscitate [rɪ'sʌsɪteɪt] vt-vi resucitar.
retail ['riːteɪl] n venta al detall, venta al por menor.
▸ vt-vi vender(se) al por menor.
■ **retail price** precio de venta al público.
retailer ['riːteɪləʳ] n detallista.
retain [rɪ'teɪn] vt **1** retener, conservar. **2** guardar.
retaliate [rɪ'tælɪeɪt] vi vengarse, tomar represalias.
retaliation [rɪtælɪ'eɪʃən] n represalias.
retarded [rɪ'tɑːdɪd] adj retrasado, -a.
retch [retʃ] vi tener arcadas.
retention [rɪ'tenʃən] n retención.
reticent ['retɪsənt] adj reticente.
retina ['retɪnə] n retina.
retire [rɪ'taɪəʳ] vt jubilar.
▸ vi **1** jubilarse. **2** retirarse. **3** acostarse.
retired [rɪ'taɪəd] adj jubilado,-a.
retirement [rɪ'taɪəmənt] n jubilación.
retiring [rɪ'taɪərɪŋ] adj **1** retraído,-a, tímido,-a. **2** que está a punto de jubilarse.
retort [rɪ'tɔːt] n réplica, contestación.
▸ vt replicar, contestar.
retrace [rɪ'treɪs] vt desandar, volver sobre.
● **to retrace one's steps** volver sobre sus pasos.
retract [rɪ'trækt] vt **1** retractarse de (promesa). **2** retraer (garras). **3** replegar (tren de aterrizaje).
retreat [rɪ'triːt] n **1** retirada. **2** retiro, refugio.
▸ vi retirarse.
● **to beat a retreat** batirse en retirada.
retrial [riː'traɪəl] n nuevo juicio.
retribution [retrɪ'bjuːʃən] n justo castigo.
retrieval [rɪ'triːvəl] n recuperación.
retrieve [rɪ'triːv] vt recuperar.
retrograde ['retrəgreɪd] adj retrógrado,-a.
retrospect ['retrəspekt] phr **in retrospect** retrospectivamente.
retrospective [retrə'spektɪv] adj **1** retrospectivo,-a. **2** retroactivo,-a.

return [rɪ'tɜːn] n **1** vuelta, regreso, retorno. **2** devolución. **3** beneficio.
▸ vi volver, regresar.
▸ vt **1** devolver. **2** elegir (candidato). **3** pronunciar (veredicto).
● **in return for** a cambio de.
● **many happy returns (of the day)!** ¡feliz cumpleaños!
■ **return ticket** billete de ida y vuelta.
reunion [riː'juːnɪən] n reunión, reencuentro.
reunite [riːjuː'naɪt] vt-vi reunir(se).
revalue [riː'væljuː] vt revalorizar.
reveal [rɪ'viːl] vt revelar, descubrir.
reveille [rɪ'vælɪ] n diana (toque de corneta).
revel in ['revəl ɪn] vi (GB pt & pp **revelled**, ger **revelling**; US pt & pp **reveled**, ger **reveling**) disfrutar mucho con.
revelation [revə'leɪʃən] n revelación.
revelry ['revəlrɪ] n (pl **-ies**) juerga.
revenge [rɪ'vendʒ] n venganza.
▸ vt vengar.
● **to revenge oneself** vengarse.
revenue ['revənjuː] n ingresos.
reverberate [rɪ'vɜːbəreɪt] vi **1** resonar, retumbar (sonido). **2** fig tener repercusiones.
reverberation [rɪvɜːbə'reɪʃən] n **1** resonancia, retumbo (sonido). **2** fig repercusiones.
revere [rɪ'vɪəʳ] vt reverenciar.
reverence ['revərəns] n reverencia.
reverend ['revərənd] adj reverendo,-a.
reverent ['revərənt] adj reverente.
reverie ['revərɪ] n ensueño.
reversal [rɪ'vɜːsəl] n **1** inversión (de orden). **2** cambio completo (de opinión).
reverse [rɪ'vɜːs] adj inverso,-a, contrario,-a.
▸ n **1** lo contrario: **he did the reverse of what I expected**, hizo lo contrario de lo que esperaba. **2** reverso (de moneda). **3** revés (de tela). **4** marcha atrás: **he put the car into reverse**, dio marcha atrás. **5** revés, contratiempo.
▸ vt **1** invertir (orden). **2** volver al revés. **3** revocar (decisión).
▸ vi poner marcha atrás, dar marcha atrás.
● **to reverse the charges** llamar a cobro revertido.
■ **reverse gear** marcha atrás.
revert [rɪ'vɜːt] vi volver.

review [rɪ'vjuː] n **1** revista. **2** examen. **3** crítica.
▶ vt **1** pasar revista a *(tropas)*. **2** examinar. **3** hacer una crítica *(de libro, película)*.

reviewer [rɪ'vjuːəʳ] n crítico,-a.

revile [rɪ'vaɪl] vt injuriar, vilipendiar.

revise [rɪ'vaɪz] vt **1** revisar. **2** corregir. **3** modificar.
▶ vt-vi repasar, hacer repaso *(para examen)*.

revision [rɪ'vɪʒən] n **1** revisión. **2** corrección. **3** modificación. **4** repaso *(para examen)*.

revitalize [riː'vaɪtəlaɪz] vt revitalizar, revivificar.

revival [rɪ'vaɪvəl] n **1** renacimiento. **2** reactivación *(de economía)*. **3** reestreno, reposición *(de obra de teatro)*.

revive [rɪ'vaɪv] vt **1** reanimar, reavivar, despertar. **2** reactivar *(economía)*. **3** reestrenar, reponer *(obra de teatro)*. **4** hacer volver en sí.
▶ vi volver en sí.

revoke [rɪ'vəʊk] vt revocar.

revolt [rɪ'vəʊlt] n revuelta, rebelión.
▶ vi sublevarse, rebelarse.
▶ vt repugnar, dar asco a.

revolting [rɪmær'ɪvəʊltɪŋ] adj repugnante.

revolution [revəˈluːʃən] n revolución.

revolutionary [revəˈluːʃənərɪ] adj-n revolucionario,-a.

revolve [rɪ'vɒlv] vi girar, dar vueltas.

revolver [rɪ'vɒlvəʳ] n revólver.

revolving [rɪ'vɒlvɪŋ] adj giratorio,-a.

revulsion [rɪ'vʌlʃən] n revulsión.

reward [rɪ'wɔːd] n recompensa.
▶ vt recompensar.

rewarding [rɪ'wɔːdɪŋ] adj gratificador,-ra.

rewind [riː'waɪnd] vt *(pt & pp rewound)* rebobinar.

rhetoric ['retərɪk] n retórica.

rheumatic [ruː'mætɪk] adj reumático,-a.

rheumatism ['ruːmətɪzəm] n reumatismo, reuma.

rhinoceros [raɪ'nɒsərəs] n *(pl rhinoceroses)* rinoceronte.

rhubarb ['ruːbɑːb] n ruibarbo.

rhyme [raɪm] n **1** rima. **2** verso, poema.
▶ vt-vi rimar.
● **without rhyme or reason** sin ton ni son.

rhythm ['rɪðəm] n ritmo.

rhythmic ['rɪðmɪk] adj rítmico,-a.

rib [rɪb] n costilla.

ribbon ['rɪbən] n cinta.

rice [raɪs] n arroz.
■ **rice field** arrozal.
■ **rice pudding** arroz con leche.

rich [rɪtʃ] adj **1** rico,-a: *to become rich*, enriquecerse. **2** suntuoso,-a, lujoso,-a. **3** fértil *(tierra)*. **4** fuerte, pesado,-a *(comida)*. **5** sonoro,-a *(voz)*.

riches ['rɪtʃɪz] npl riqueza.

rickets ['rɪkɪts] npl raquitismo.

rickety ['rɪkətɪ] adj *(-ier, -iest)* desvencijado,-a, tambaleante.

ricochet ['rɪkəʃeɪ] n rebote.
▶ vi rebotar.

rid [rɪd] vt *(pt & pp ridded, ger ridding)* librar.
● **to get rid of** deshacerse de, desembarazarse de.

ridden ['rɪdən] pp → ride.

riddle ['rɪdəl] n **1** acertijo, adivinanza. **2** enigma.

ride [raɪd] n paseo, viaje, vuelta: *to go for a ride*, ir a dar una vuelta.
▶ vi *(pt rode [rəʊd], pp ridden ['rɪdən], ger riding)*. **1** montar a caballo. **2** viajar, ir: *we rode to London in a jeep*, fuimos a Londres en jeep.
▶ vt **1** montar *(a caballo)*. **2** montar en, andar en *(moto, bicicleta)*.
● **to take SB for a ride** tomar el pelo a ALGN.

to ride on vt depender de.

to ride out vt aguantar hasta el final de.

rider ['raɪdəʳ] n **1** jinete, amazona. **2** ciclista. **3** motorista.

ridge [rɪdʒ] n **1** cresta *(de montaña)*. **2** caballete *(de tejado)*.

ridicule ['rɪdɪkjuːl] n ridículo.
▶ vt ridiculizar, poner en ridículo.

ridiculous [rɪ'dɪkjʊləs] adj ridículo,-a.

riding ['raɪdɪŋ] n equitación.

rife [raɪf] adj abundante.
● **to be rife** abundar.

riffraff ['rɪfræf] n chusma.

rifle[1] ['raɪfəl] n rifle, fusil.

rifle[2] ['raɪfəl] vt **1** revolver, hurgar. **2** desvalijar.

rift [rɪft] n **1** hendedura, grieta. **2** *fig* ruptura, desavenencia.

rig [rɪg] n plataforma petrolífera.
▶ vt *(pt & pp rigged, ger rigging)*. **1** aparejar. **2** *fam* amañar.

to rig up vt improvisar, armar.
rigging ['rɪgɪŋ] n jarcias fpl.
right [raɪt] adj **1** derecho,-a (mano). **2** correcto,-a: *have you got the right time?*, ¿tienes la hora buena? **3** justo,-a: *that's not right!*, ¡no es justo! **4** apropiado,-a, adecuado,-a (momento). **5** fam auténtico,-a, total: *he's a right idiot*, es un perfecto idiota.
▶ adv **1** a la derecha, hacia la derecha: *he turned right*, torció a la derecha. **2** bien, correctamente: *he spelt her name right*, escribió bien su nombre. **3** inmediatamente: *he'll be right back*, enseguida vuelve. **4** GB fam muy: *I was right fed up*, estaba superharto.
▶ n **1** derecha. **2** derecho: *we believe in equal rights*, creemos en la igualdad de derechos. **3** bien: *right and wrong*, el bien y el mal.
▶ vt **1** corregir. **2** enderezar, poner derecho,-a.
● **all right!** ¡bien!, ¡conforme!, ¡vale!
● **right away** enseguida.
● **right now** ahora mismo.
● **to be right** tener razón.
● **to put right** arreglar.
● **to serve SB right** estarle bien empleado a ALGN.
■ **right angle** ángulo recto.
■ **right of way 1** derecho de paso (por un camino). **2** prioridad (respecto a otro vehículo).
■ **right wing** derecha (política).
righteous ['raɪtʃəs] adj **1** recto,-a, justo,-a (persona). **2** justificado,-a (ira).
rightful ['raɪtfʊl] adj legítimo,-a (heredero).
right-hand ['raɪthænd] adj derecho,-a.
rightly ['raɪtlɪ] adv con razón, correctamente.
right-wing ['raɪtwɪŋ] adj de derechas.
rigid ['rɪdʒɪd] adj rígido,-a.
rigour ['rɪgə'] (US **rigor**) n rigor.
rile [raɪl] vt fam poner nervioso,-a, irritar.
rim [rɪm] n **1** borde, canto. **2** llanta.
rind [raɪnd] n corteza.
ring[1] [rɪŋ] n **1** anillo, sortija. **2** anilla, aro. **3** círculo, corro (de personas). **4** pista, arena. **5** ring, cuadrilátero (de boxeo).
▶ vt (pt & pp **ringed**). **1** anillar (pájaro). **2** rodear.
■ **ring road** cinturón de ronda, carretera de circunvalación.
ring[2] [rɪŋ] n **1** tañido; toque (de campana). **2** llamada (de teléfono, al timbre).

▶ vi (pt **rang**; pp **rung**). **1** sonar, tañer, repicar (campana). **2** sonar (teléfono, timbre). **3** zumbar (oídos).
▶ vt **1** llamar (por teléfono). **2** tocar (timbre).
ringing ['rɪŋɪŋ] n **1** tañido, repique. **2** timbre (de teléfono). **3** zumbido (de oídos).
ringleader ['rɪŋliːdə'] n cabecilla.
ringlet ['rɪŋlət] n rizo.
ringside ['rɪŋsaɪd] adj de primera fila.
▶ n primera fila.
rink [rɪŋk] n pista de patinaje.
rinse [rɪns] vt **1** aclarar. **2** enjuagar.
riot ['raɪət] n **1** disturbio. **2** motín.
▶ vi amotinarse.
rioter ['raɪətə'] n **1** amotinado,-a. **2** alborotador,-ra.
rip [rɪp] n rasgadura.
▶ vt-vi (pt & pp **ripped**, ger **ripping**) rasgar.
to rip off vi arrancar.
▶ vt fam timar.
RIP ['ɑːr'aɪ'piː] abbr (**rest in peace, requiescat in pace**) en paz descanse, E.P.D.
ripe [raɪp] adj maduro,-a.
ripen ['raɪpən] vt-vi madurar.
ripeness ['raɪpnəs] n madurez.
rip-off ['rɪpɒf] n (pl **rip-offs**) fam timo.
ripple ['rɪpəl] n **1** onda, rizo (en agua). **2** murmullo (de risas, aplausos).
▶ vt-vi rizar(se).
rise [raɪz] n **1** ascenso, subida. **2** aumento (de sueldo). **3** subida, cuesta (en montaña).
▶ vi (pt **rose**, pp **risen**). **1** ascender, subir. **2** aumentar (precios). **3** ponerse de pie. **4** levantarse (de la cama). **5** salir (sol, luna). **6** nacer (río). **7** crecer (nivel del río). **8** elevarse (montañas). **9** alzarse (voz).
● **to give rise to** dar origen a.
● **to rise to the occasion** ponerse a la altura de las circunstancias.
rising ['raɪzɪŋ] n levantamiento.
▶ adj **1** creciente. **2** naciente (sol).
risk [rɪsk] n riesgo, peligro.
▶ vt arriesgar.
● **to risk doing STH** exponerse a hacer algo.
● **to take a risk** arriesgarse, correr un riesgo.
risky ['rɪskɪ] adj (**-ier, -iest**) arriesgado,-a.
rite [raɪt] n rito.
ritual ['rɪtjʊəl] adj-n ritual.

rival ['raɪvəl] *adj-n* competidor,-ra, rival.
► *vt* (GB *pt & pp* **rivalled**, *ger* **rivalling**; US *pt & pp* **rivaled**, *ger* **rivaling**) competir con, rivalizar con.

rivalry ['raɪvəlrɪ] *n* (*pl* **-ies**) rivalidad, competencia.

river ['rɪvə'] *n* río.

river-bank ['rɪvəbæŋk] *n* ribera, orilla.

river-bed ['rɪvəbed] *n* lecho.

riverside ['rɪvəsaɪd] *n* ribera, orilla.

rivet ['rɪvɪt] *n* remache.
► *vt* **1** remachar. **2** fascinar: *they were riveted to the screen*, tenían los ojos pegados a la pantalla.

riveting ['rɪvɪtɪŋ] *adj* fascinante.

rly ['reɪlweɪ] *abbr* (**railway**) ferrocarril, FC.

road [rəʊd] *n* **1** carretera. **2** camino.
● **by road** por carretera.
● **in the road** *fam* estorbando.
■ **road sweeper** barrendero,-a.
■ **road safety** seguridad vial.
■ **road sign** señal de tráfico.

roadblock ['rəʊdblɒk] *n* control policial.

roadway ['rəʊdweɪ] *n* calzada.

roadworthy ['rəʊdwɜːðɪ] *adj* apto para circular (*vehículo*).

roam [rəʊm] *vt* vagar por, recorrer.
► *vi* vagar.

roar [rɔː'] *n* **1** bramido. **2** rugido (*de león*). **3** griterío, clamor (*de multitud*). **4** estruendo (*de tráfico*).
► *vi* rugir, bramar.

roaring ['rɔːrɪŋ] *adj*: *a roaring success*, un éxito tremendo; *a roaring fire*, un fuego muy vivo.
● **to do a roaring trade** hacer su agosto, hacer muy buen negocio.

roast [rəʊst] *adj* asado,-a.
► *n* asado.
► *vt* **1** asar (*carne*). **2** tostar (*café, nueces*).
► *vi* asarse (*persona*).

roasting ['rəʊstɪŋ] *adj* abrasador,-ra.
► *n* sermón, bronca.
● **to give SB a roasting** echar un rapapolvo a ALGN.

rob [rɒb] *vt* (*pt & pp* **robbed**, *ger* **robbing**). **1** robar. **2** atracar (*banco*).

robber ['rɒbə'] *n* **1** ladrón,-ona. **2** atracador,-ra (*de banco*).

robbery ['rɒbərɪ] *n* (*pl* **-ies**). **1** robo. **2** atraco (*de banco*).

robe [rəʊb] *n* **1** bata. **2** vestidura, toga.

robin ['rɒbɪn] *n* petirrojo.

robot ['rəʊbɒt] *n* robot.

robust [rəʊ'bʌst] *adj* robusto,-a, fuerte.

rock [rɒk] *n* **1** roca. **2** rock (*música*).
► *vt-vi* mecer(se).
► *vt* **1** acunar. **2** sacudir.
● **on the rocks 1** arruinado,-a (*matrimonio, negocio*). **2** con hielo (*bebida*).

rock-climbing ['rɒkklaɪmɪŋ] *n* alpinismo.

rocker ['rɒkə'] *n* balancín.
● **off one's rocker** *fam* mal de la cabeza.

rocket ['rɒkɪt] *n* cohete.
► *vi* dispararse.

Rockies ['rɒkɪz] *n* **the Rockies** las Montañas Rocosas.

rocking-chair ['rɒkɪŋtʃeə'] *n* mecedora.

rocky ['rɒkɪ] *adj* (**-ier**, **-iest**) rocoso,-a.

rod [rɒd] *n* **1** vara. **2** barra.

rode [rəʊd] *pt* → **ride**.

rodent ['rəʊdənt] *n* roedor.

roe [rəʊ] *n* hueva (*de pescado*).

rogue [rəʊg] *n* pícaro, bribón.

role [rəʊl] *n* papel.

roll [rəʊl] *n* **1** rollo. **2** lista. **3** bollo, panecillo.
► *vt* **1** hacer rodar. **2** enroscar. **3** enrollar (*papel*). **4** liar (*cigarrillo*).
► *vi* **1** rodar. **2** enroscarse. **3** enrollarse (*papel*).
● **to roll up one's sleeves** arremangarse.
● **to be rolling in it** *fam* estar forrado,-a.

to roll out *vt* extender.

to roll up *vt-vi* **1** enrollar(se). **2** enroscar(se).

roller ['rəʊlə'] *n* **1** rodillo. **2** ola grande. **3** rulo.
■ **roller coasting** montaña rusa.
■ **roller skates** patines de ruedas.
■ **roller skating** patinaje sobre ruedas.

roller-skate ['rəʊləskeɪt] *vi* patinar sobre ruedas.

rolling ['rəʊlɪŋ] *adj* ondulante.
■ **rolling pin** rodillo (*de cocina*).
■ **rolling stock** material rodante.

ROM [rɒm] *abbr* (**read-only memory**) memoria sólo de lectura, ROM.

Roman ['rəʊmən] *adj-n* romano,-a.

romance [rəʊ'mæns] *n* **1** romance, libro de caballerías. **2** novela romántica. **3** romanticismo. **4** idilio, aventura.

Romania [ruː'meɪnɪə] *n* Rumanía.

Romanian [ruː'meɪnɪən] *adj* rumano,-a.
► *n* **1** rumano,-a (*persona*). **2** rumano (*lengua*).

romantic [rəʊ'mæntɪk] *adj* romántico,-a.

romp [rɒmp] *vi* jugar, retozar.

rompers ['rɒmpəz] *npl* pelele.

roof [ruːf] *n* (*pl* **roofs**). **1** tejado, techado. **2** cielo *(de boca)*. **3** techo *(de coche)*.
► *vt* techar.

roof-rack ['ruːfræk] *n* baca.

rook [rʊk] *n* **1** grajo. **2** torre *(en ajedrez)*.

room [ruːm] *n* **1** cuarto, habitación. **2** espacio, sitio.
● **to take up room** ocupar sitio.

roomy ['ruːmɪ] *adj* (**-ier**, **-iest**) espacioso,-a, amplio,-a.

roost [ruːst] *n* percha *(de ave)*.
► *vi* posarse.

rooster ['ruːstə'] *n* gallo.

root [ruːt] *n* raíz.
► *vi* buscar, hurgar.
● **to take root** arraigar.

rope [rəʊp] *n* cuerda.
► *vt* atar, amarrar.

to rope in *vt fam* enganchar.

rosary ['rəʊzərɪ] *n* (*pl* **-ies**) rosario.

rose¹ [rəʊz] *n* rosa.

rosé² [rəʊz] *pt* → rise.

rosé ['rəʊzeɪ] *n* vino rosado.

rosemary ['rəʊzmərɪ] *n* romero.

rosette [rəʊ'zet] *n* escarapela.

roster ['rɒstə'] *n* lista.

rosy ['rəʊzɪ] *adj* (**-ier**, **-iest**). **1** rosado,-a, sonrosado,-a. **2** prometedor,-ra.

rot [rɒt] *n* putrefacción.
► *vt-vi* (*pt* & *pp* **rotted**, *ger* **rotting**) pudrir(se).

rota ['rəʊtə] *n* → roster.

rotate [rəʊ'teɪt] *vt* hacer girar, dar vueltas a.
► *vi* girar, dar vueltas.
► *vt-vi fig* alternar.

rotten ['rɒtən] *adj* **1** podrido,-a. **2** picado,-a *(diente)*. **3** *fam* malísimo,-a.

rotter ['rɒtə'] *n fam* sinvergüenza.

rouge [ruːʒ] *n* colorete.

rough [rʌf] *adj* **1** áspero,-a, basto,-a *(superficie)*. **2** lleno,-a de baches *(carretera)*. **3** desigual *(suelo)*. **4** escabroso,-a *(terreno)*. **5** agitado,-a *(mar)*. **6** tempestuoso,-a *(tiempo)*. **7** áspero,-a *(vino)*. **8** rudo,-a, tosco,-a *(persona, modales)*. **9** violento,-a *(viento, comportamiento)*. **10** aproximado,-a *(presupuesto)*. **11** *fam* fatal.
● **to rough it** vivir sin comodidades.
● **to sleep rough** dormir al raso.

■ **rough copy** borrador.

■ **rough sea** marejada.

■ **rough version** borrador.

roughen ['rʌfən] *vt* poner áspero,-a.

roughly ['rʌflɪ] *adv* **1** aproximadamente. **2** bruscamente, violentamente.

roughness ['rʌfnəs] *n* **1** aspereza. **2** violencia.

roulette [ruː'let] *n* ruleta.

round [raʊnd] *adj* redondo,-a.
► *n* **1** círculo. **2** serie, tanda, ronda *(de conversaciones)*. **3** ronda, asalto *(en boxeo)*. **4** ronda *(de policía)*. **5** ronda *(de copas)*. **6** bala, cartucho.
► *adv* **1** por ahí. **2**: *they came round to see me*, vinieron a verme.
► *prep* **1** alrededor de: *she had flowers round her neck*, llevaba flores alrededor del cuello. **2** a la vuelta de: *it's just round the corner*, está a la vuelta de la esquina.
► *vt* dar la vuelta a, doblar *(esquina)*.
● **all the year round** durante todo el año.
● **round the clock** día y noche.
● **round the corner** a la vuelta de la esquina.
● **the other way round** al revés.
● **to go round** dar vueltas.
● **to turn round** dar la vuelta.

to round off *vt* completar, acabar.

to round up *vt* **1** redondear *(cifra)*. **2** acorralar *(ganado)*. **3** reunir *(personas)*.

roundabout ['raʊndəbaʊt] *adj* indirecto,-a.
► *n* **1** tiovivo. **2** rotonda.

rounders ['raʊndəz] *n* especie de béisbol infantil.

round-up ['raʊndʌp] *n* **1** rodeo *(de ganado)*. **2** redada *(de policía)*. **3** resumen.

rouse [raʊz] *vt-vi* despertar(se).
► *vt* provocar.

rousing ['raʊzɪŋ] *adj* **1** apasionante. **2** conmovedor,-ra.

rout [raʊt] *n* derrota.
► *vt* derrotar.

route [ruːt] *n* **1** ruta, camino, vía. **2** línea, trayecto *(de autobús)*.

routine [ruː'tiːn] *n* rutina.
► *adj* rutinario,-a.

rove [rəʊv] *vi* vagar, errar.

row¹ [raʊ] *n* **1** riña, pelea. **2** jaleo, ruido.
► *vi* pelearse.

row² [rəʊ] n fila, hilera.
● in a row 1 en fila. 2 seguidos: *three in a row*, tres seguidos.
row³ [rəʊ] n paseo en bote.
▶ vi-vi remar.
rowdy ['raʊdɪ] adj (-ier, -iest). 1 alborotador,-ra. 2 ruidoso,-a.
rowing ['rəʊɪŋ] n remo.
■ rowing boat bote de remos.
royal ['rɔɪəl] adj real.
royalist ['rɔɪəlɪst] adj-n monárquico,-a.
royalty ['rɔɪəltɪ] n (pl -ies). 1 realeza. 2 miembros de la familia real.
▶ npl royalties derechos (de autor).
RRP ['aːrɑːr'piː] abbr (recommended retail price) precio recomendado de venta al público.
RSPCA ['aːres'piː'siː'eɪ] abbr GB (Royal Society for the Prevention of Cruelty to Animals) sociedad protectora de animales.
RSVP ['aːres'viː'piː] abbr (répondez s'il vous plaît) se ruega contestación, S. R. C.
Rt. Hon [raɪt'ɒnərəbəl] abbr GB (Right Honourable) su Señoría.
rub [rʌb] n friega.
▶ vt (pt & pp rubbed, ger rubbing) frotar, restregar.
▶ vi rozar.
● to rub it in fam restregarlo por las narices a ALGN.
to rub out vt borrar.
rubber ['rʌbəʳ] n 1 caucho, goma. 2 goma de borrar. 3 US fam goma (preservativo).
■ rubber band goma elástica.
■ rubber ring flotador.
rubbish ['rʌbɪʃ] n 1 basura. 2 fam birria, porquería: *that film's rubbish*, esa película es una porquería. 3 tonterías: *don't talk rubbish*, no digas tonterías.
rubble ['rʌbəl] n escombros.
rubella [ruːˈbelə] n rubeola, rubéola.
ruby ['ruːbɪ] n (pl -ies) rubí.
RUC ['aːjuːˈsiː] abbr GB (Royal Ulster Constabulary) cuerpo de policía de Irlanda del Norte.
rucksack ['rʌksæk] n mochila.
ructions ['rʌkʃənz] npl fam follón.
rudder ['rʌdəʳ] n timón.
ruddy ['rʌdɪ] adj (-ier, -iest) colorado,-a.
rude [ruːd] adj 1 maleducado,-a, descortés: *it's rude to point*, es de mala educa-

ción señalar con el dedo. 2 rudo,-a, tosco,-a.
rudeness ['ruːdnəs] n 1 falta de educación, descortesía. 2 rudeza, tosquedad.
rudimentary [ruːdɪˈmentrɪ] adj rudimentario,-a.
ruffle ['rʌfəl] vt 1 agitar, perturbar (agua). 2 erizar, encrespar (plumas). 3 despeinar, alborotar (pelo). 4 irritar, enervar (persona).
rug [rʌg] n alfombra, alfombrilla.
rugby ['rʌgbɪ] n rugby.
rugged ['rʌgɪd] adj escabroso,-a, accidentado,-a.
ruin [ruːɪn] n ruina.
▶ vt 1 arruinar. 2 estropear.
ruined ['ruːɪnd] adj 1 arruinado,-a (persona). 2 estropeado,-a (aparato). 3 en ruinas (castillo).
rule [ruːl] n 1 regla, norma. 2 dominio, gobierno, mandato. 3 reinado.
▶ vt-vi 1 gobernar, mandar. 2 reinar. 3 decretar.
● as a rule por regla general.
● to be against the rules ir contra las reglas.
to rule out vt excluir, descartar.
ruler ['ruːləʳ] n 1 gobernante, dirigente. 2 soberano,-a. 3 regla.
ruling ['ruːlɪŋ] adj dirigente.
▶ n fallo (de tribunal).
rum [rʌm] n ron.
Rumania [ruːˈmeɪnɪə] n → Romania.
Rumanian [ruːˈmeɪnɪən] adj-n → Romanian.
rumble ['rʌmbəl] n retumbo, ruido sordo.
▶ vi 1 retumbar, hacer un ruido sordo. 2 hacer ruidos (estómago).
ruminant ['ruːmɪnənt] adj-n rumiante.
ruminate ['ruːmɪneɪt] vt-vi rumiar.
rummage ['rʌmɪdʒ] vt-vi hurgar, rebuscar.
rumour ['ruːməʳ] (US rumor) n rumor.
▶ vt rumorear.
rump [rʌmp] n 1 ancas. 2 trasero (de persona).
rumple ['rʌmpəl] vt 1 arrugar (ropa). 2 despeinar (pelo).
rumpus ['rʌmpəs] n (pl rumpuses) fam jaleo, escándalo.
run [rʌn] vi (pt ran [ræn], pp run [rʌn], ger running). 1 correr. 2 correr, discurrir (sendero). 3 gotear (nariz). 4 funcionar

(aparato, organización). **5** presentarse *(a elecciones).* **6** durar. **7** circular *(autobús, tren).* **8** desteñirse *(color).*

▶ *vt* **1** correr en. **2** llevar *(en coche, moto).* **3** llevar, dirigir, regentar *(organización).* **4** organizar, montar *(negocio).* **5** hacer funcionar *(aparato).* **6** ejecutar *(macro, programa).*

▶ *n* **1** carrera. **2** viaje, paseo. **3** racha. **4** pista *(de esquí).* **5** carrera *(en media).*

● **in the long run** a la larga.

● **to be on the run** haberse fugado de la justicia.

to run after *vt* perseguir.

to run along *vi* irse.

to run away *vi* escaparse.

to run down *vt* **1** atropellar. **2** criticar. **3** agotar *(batería).*

▶ *vi* **1** agotarse *(batería).* **2** pararse *(reloj).*

to run in *vt* **1** rodar *(coche).* **2** detener *(delincuente).*

to run into *vt* **1** chocar con *(coche).* **2** tropezar con, encontrarse con *(persona).*

to run off *vi* escaparse.

▶ *vt* imprimir.

to run off with *vt* escaparse con, fugarse con.

to run out *vi* acabarse: *I've run out of sugar,* se me ha acabado el azúcar.

to run over *vt* atropellar.

▶ *vi* **1** rebosar. **2** derramar.

to run through *vt* **1** ensayar. **2** echar un vistazo a.

to run up *vt* **1** acumular *(deudas).* **2** izar *(bandera).*

runaway ['rʌnəweɪ] *adj* incontrolado,-a.

▶ *adj-n* fugitivo,-a.

rung [rʌŋ] *n* escalón.

▶ *pp* → ring.

runner ['rʌnəʳ] *n* corredor,-ra.

■ **runner bean** judía verde.

runner-up [rʌnərˈʌp] *n (pl* **runners-up)** subcampeón,-ona.

running ['rʌnɪŋ] *n* **1** atletismo. **2** organización. **3** funcionamiento.

▶ *adj* **1** corriente *(agua).* **2** continuo,-a,

seguido,-a: *three years running,* tres años seguidos.

● **in the running** con posibilidades de ganar.

● **out of the running** sin posibilidades de ganar.

■ **running costs** gastos de mantenimiento.

runny ['rʌnɪ] *adj* (**-ier, -iest**) blando,-a, líquido,-a.

● **to have a runny nose** tener mocos.

run-of-the-mill [rʌnəvðəˈmɪl] *adj* corriente y moliente.

run-up ['rʌnʌp] *n* etapa preliminar.

runway ['rʌnweɪ] *n* pista de aterrizaje.

rupture ['rʌptʃəʳ] *n* ruptura.

▶ *vt* romper.

● **to rupture oneself** herniarse.

rural ['rʊərəl] *adj* rural.

rush [rʌʃ] *n (pl* **-es**). **1** prisa, precipitación. **2** movimiento impetuoso, avance impetuoso.

▶ *vt* **1** apresurar, dar prisa a. **2** llevar rápidamente: *he was rushed to hospital,* lo llevaron rápidamente al hospital.

▶ *vi* precipitarse, apresurarse.

● **to be in a rush** tener prisa.

● **to be rushed off one's feet** ir de culo.

■ **rush hour** hora punta.

rusk [rʌsk] *n* galleta *(para bebé).*

Russia ['rʌʃə] *n* Rusia.

Russian ['rʌʃən] *adj* ruso,-a.

▶ *n* **1** ruso,-a *(persona).* **2** ruso *(lengua).*

rust [rʌst] *n* óxido.

▶ *vt-vi* oxidar(se).

rustic ['rʌstɪk] *adj* rústico,-a.

rustle ['rʌsəl] *n* **1** crujido *(de papel).* **2** susurro *(de hojas).*

▶ *vt* hacer crujir *(papel).*

▶ *vi* **1** susurrar *(hojas).* **2** crujir *(papel).*

rusty ['rʌstɪ] *adj* (**-ier, -iest**) oxidado,-a.

rut [rʌt] *n* surco.

● **in a rut** esclavo,-a de la rutina.

ruthless ['ruːθləs] *adj* cruel, despiadado,-a.

rye [raɪ] *n* centeno.

S

S [sauθ] *abbr (south)* sur, S.

sabbatical [sə'bætɪkəl] *adj* sabático.
▶ *n* año sabático.

sabotage ['sæbətɑːʒ] *n* sabotaje.
▶ *vt* sabotear.

sack [sæk] *n* saco.
▶ *vt fam* despedir a, echar del trabajo a.
● **to get the sack** *fam* ser despedido,-a.
● **to hit the sack** *fam* irse al catre.

sacred ['seɪkrəd] *adj* sagrado,-a.
■ **sacred music** música sacra.

sacrifice ['sækrɪfaɪs] *n* sacrificio.
▶ *vt* sacrificar.

sacrilege ['sækrɪlɪdʒ] *n* sacrilegio.

sad [sæd] *adj (comp* **sadder***, superl* **saddest***)* triste.

saddle ['sædəl] *n* **1** silla *(de montar)*. **2** sillín *(de bicicleta)*.
▶ *vt* ensillar.

sadism ['seɪdɪzəm] *n* sadismo.

sadly ['sædli] *adv* **1** tristemente. **2** desgraciadamente, lamentablemente.

sadness ['sædnəs] *n* tristeza.

safe [seɪf] *adj* **1** ileso,-a. **2** a salvo, fuera de peligro. **3** inocuo,-a. **4** seguro,-a, no peligroso,-a.
▶ *n* caja fuerte.
● **safe and sound** sano,-a y salvo,-a.
● **safe from** a salvo de.
● **to be on the safe side** para mayor seguridad.

safeguard ['seɪfgɑːd] *n* salvaguarda.
▶ *vt* salvaguardar.

safely ['seɪfli] *adv* **1** con toda seguridad. **2** sin contratiempos, sin percances. **3** sin peligro, con seguridad, tranquilamente.

safety ['seɪftɪ] *n* seguridad.
■ **safety belt** cinturón de seguridad.

■ **safety drill** instrucciones de seguridad.
■ **safety pin** imperdible.
■ **safety valve** válvula de seguridad.

saffron ['sæfrən] *n* azafrán.

sag [sæg] *vi (pt & pp* **sagged***, ger* **sagging***)*. **1** combarse *(moneda, hierro)*. **2** hundirse *(tejado)*. **3** pandear *(pared)*. **4** *fig* flaquear, decaer.

Sagittarius [sædʒɪ'teərɪəs] *n* Sagitario.

said [sed] *pt-pp* → say.

sail [seɪl] *n* **1** vela *(de lona)*. **2** paseo en barco.
▶ *vt* navegar.
▶ *vi* **1** ir en barco. **2** zarpar.
● **to set sail** zarpar.
● **to sail through** STH hacer algo con facilidad.

sailing ['seɪlɪŋ] *n* **1** navegación. **2** vela *(deporte)*: *to go sailing*, ir a navegar, hacer vela.
■ **sailing boat** velero, barco de vela.
■ **sailing ship** velero, buque de vela.

sailor ['seɪlə'] *n* marinero.

saint [seɪnt] *n* san, santo,-a.

sake [seɪk] *n* bien.
● **for old times' sake** por los viejos tiempos.
● **for the sake of** por, por el bien de.
● **for God's/goodness'/Heaven's sake!** ¡por el amor de Dios!

salad ['sæləd] *n* ensalada.
■ **salad bowl** ensaladera.
■ **salad dressing** aliño, aderezo.

salary ['sælərɪ] *n (pl* **-ies***)* salario, sueldo.

sale [seɪl] *n* **1** venta. **2** liquidación, rebajas. **3** subasta.
● **for sale** en venta.

- **on sale 1** a la venta. **2** rebajado,-a, en liquidación.
- **sales manager** jefe,-a de ventas, director,-ra comercial.

salesclerk ['seɪlzklɑːk] *n* dependiente,-a.

salesman ['seɪlzmən] *n (pl* **salesmen**). **1** vendedor. **2** dependiente *(en tienda)*. **3** representante, viajante.

saleswoman ['seɪlzwʊmən] *n (pl* **saleswomen**). **1** vendedora. **2** dependienta *(en tienda)*. **3** representante, viajante.

saliva [sə'laɪvə] *n* saliva.

salmon ['sæmən] *n (pl* **salmon**) salmón.

salon ['sælɒn] *n* salón.

salt [sɔːlt] *n* sal.
- ▶ *vt* **1** curar. **2** salar, echar sal en.
- **salt beef** cecina.
- **salt pork** tocino.
- **the salt of the earth** la sal de la tierra.

saltwater ['sɔːltwɔːtə'] *adj* de agua salada.

salty ['sɔːltɪ] *adj* (**-ier, -iest**) salado,-a.

salute [sə'luːt] *n* saludo.
- ▶ *vt-vi* saludar.

Salvadorian [sælvə'dɔːrɪən] *adj-n* salvadoreño,-a.

salvage ['sælvɪdʒ] *n* **1** salvamento, rescate. **2** objetos recuperados.
- ▶ *vt* salvar, rescatar.

salvation [sæl'veɪʃən] *n* salvación.

same [seɪm] *adj* mismo,-a: *we have the same car*, tenemos el mismo coche.
- ▶ *pron* **the same** lo mismo: *I want the same as you*, quiero lo mismo que tú.
- ▶ *adv* igual, del mismo modo: *the two words are pronounced the same*, las dos palabras se pronuncian igual.
- **all the same** a pesar de todo.
- **at the same time** a la vez, al mismo tiempo.
- **same here** *fam* yo también.
- **the same to you!** *fam* ¡igualmente!

sample ['sɑːmpəl] *n* muestra.
- ▶ *vt* probar, catar *(vino)*.

sanatorium [sænə'tɔːrɪəm] *n (pl* **-s** o **sanatoria** [sænə'tɔːrɪə]) sanatorio.

sanction ['sæŋkʃən] *n* sanción.
- ▶ *vt* sancionar.

sanctuary ['sæŋktjʊərɪ] *n (pl* **-ies**). **1** santuario. **2** asilo, refugio. **3** reserva *(de animales)*.

sand [sænd] *n* arena.
- ▶ *npl* **sands** playa.
- **sand dune** duna.

sandal ['sændəl] *n* sandalia.

sandbank ['sændbæŋk] *n* banco de arena.

sandpaper ['sændpeɪpə'] *n* papel de lija.
- ▶ *vt* lijar.

sandstone ['sændstəʊn] *n* arenisca.

sandwich ['sænwɪdʒ] *n (pl* **-es**) sandwich, emparedado.

sandy ['sændɪ] *adj* (**-ier, -iest**). **1** arenoso,-a. **2** rubio rojizo *(pelo)*.

sane [seɪn] *adj* **1** cuerdo,-a. **2** sensato,-a.

sang [sæŋ] *pt* → sing.

sanitary ['sænɪtərɪ] *adj* **1** sanitario,-a, de sanidad. **2** higiénico,-a.
- **sanitary towel** compresa.

sanitation [sænɪ'teɪʃən] *n* sanidad pública.

sanity ['sænɪtɪ] *n* **1** cordura, juicio. **2** sensatez.

sank [sæŋk] *pt* → sink.

sap¹ [sæp] *n* savia.

sap² [sæp] *vt (pt & pp* **sapped,** *ger* **sapping)** *fig* minar, debilitar.

sapphire ['sæfaɪə'] *n* zafiro.

sarcasm ['sɑːkæzəm] *n* sarcasmo, sorna.

sarcastic [sɑː'kæstɪk] *adj* sarcástico,-a.

sardine [sɑː'diːn] *n* sardina.

Sardinia [sɑː'dɪnɪə] *n* Cerdeña.

Sardinian [sɑː'dɪnɪən] *adj-n* sardo,-a.

sash¹ [sæʃ] *n (pl* **-es**) marco *(de ventana)*.
- **sash window** ventana de guillotina.

sash² [sæʃ] *n (pl* **-es**) faja.

sat [sæt] *pt-pp* → sit.

Sat ['sætdɪ] *abbr* **(Saturday)** sábado.

satchel ['sætʃəl] *n* cartera *(de colegial)*.

satellite ['sætəlaɪt] *n* satélite.
- **by satellite** por vía satélite.
- **satellite dish aerial** antena parabólica.
- **satellite television** televisión por satélite.

satin ['sætɪn] *n* satén, raso.

satire ['sætaɪə'] *n* sátira.

satirical [sə'tɪrɪkəl] *adj* satírico,-a.

satisfaction [sætɪs'fækʃən] *n* satisfacción.

satisfactory [sætɪs'fæktərɪ] *adj* satisfactorio,-a.

satisfied ['sætɪsfaɪd] *adj* satisfecho,-a.

satisfy ['sætɪsfaɪ] *vt (pt & pp* **-ied**). **1** satisfacer *(deseo)*. **2** cumplir *(condiciones)*. **3** convencer.

saturate ['sætʃəreɪt] *vt* **1** saturar. **2** empapar.

Saturday ['sætədɪ] *n* sábado.
sauce [sɔːs] *n* salsa.
■ **sauce boat** salsera.
saucepan ['sɔːspən] *n* **1** cazo, cacerola. **2** olla.
saucer ['sɔːsə'] *n* platillo.
Saudi ['saʊdɪ] *adj* saudí, saudita.
▶ *n* saudí, saudita.
■ **Saudi Arabia** Arabia Saudita.
sauna ['sɔːnə] *n* sauna.
saunter ['sɔːntə'] *vi* pasearse.
sausage ['sɒsɪdʒ] *n* **1** salchicha. **2** embutido.
savage ['sævɪdʒ] *adj* **1** feroz, salvaje *(animal)*. **2** brutal, violento *(ataque)*. **3** salvaje *(tribu)*.
▶ *n* salvaje.
▶ *vt* embestir, atacar con ferocidad.
save [seɪv] *vt* **1** salvar *(vida)*. **2** guardar *(comida, fuerzas)*. **3** ahorrar, ahorrarse *(dinero)*. **4** guardar, archivar *(en ordenador)*. **5** evitar: *it'll save us a lot of trouble*, nos evitará muchos problemas. **6** parar *(pelota)*.
▶ *vi* ahorrar.
▶ *prep fml* salvo, a excepción de.
saving ['seɪvɪŋ] *n* ahorro, economía.
▶ *npl* **savings** ahorros.
■ **savings account** cuenta de ahorros.
■ **savings bank** caja de ahorros.
saviour ['seɪvɪə'] (US **savior**) *n* salvador, -ra.
savour ['seɪvə'] (US **savor**) *n* sabor.
▶ *vt* saborear.
savoury ['seɪvərɪ] (US **savory**) *adj* salado,-a.
▶ *n* (*pl* -**ies**) canapé, entremés.
saw[1] [sɔː] *n* sierra.
▶ *vt-vi* (*pt* **sawed** [sɔːd], *pp* **sawn** [sɔːn]) serrar.
saw[2] [sɔː] *pt* → see.
sawdust ['sɔːdʌst] *n* serrín.
sawn [sɔːn] *pp* → saw.
saxophone ['sæksəfəʊn] *n* saxofón.
say [seɪ] *vt* (*pt & pp* **said** [sed]). **1** decir: *he says he's innocent*, dice que es inocente. **2** marcar *(reloj)*. **3** poner, suponer: *let's say it costs about £20*, pongamos que cuesta unas 20 libras.
● **it is said that ...** dicen que ..., se dice que ....
● **that is to say** es decir.

● **to have one's say** dar su opinión.
● **to say the least** como mínimo.
● **you don't say!** *fam* ¡no me digas!
saying ['seɪɪŋ] *n* dicho, decir.
scab [skæb] *n* **1** costra, postilla. **2** *pej* esquirol.
scaffold ['skæfəʊld] *n* **1** andamio. **2** patíbulo.
scaffolding ['skæfəldɪŋ] *n* andamiaje.
scald [skɔːld] *n* escaldadura.
▶ *vt* **1** escaldar. **2** calentar.
scale[1] [skeɪl] *n* escama *(de pez)*.
scale[2] [skeɪl] (Se usa también en plural **scales**) *n* balanza, báscula.
scale[3] [skeɪl] *n* **1** escala. **2** tamaño, escala.
▶ *vt* **1** escalar. **2** escamar.
● **on a large scale** a gran escala.
● **on a small scale** a pequeña escala.
● **to scale** a escala.
■ **scale drawing** dibujo a escala.
■ **scale model** maqueta.
to scale down *vt* reducir.
to scale up *vt* ampliar.
scalp [skælp] *n* cuero cabelludo.
scalpel ['skælpəl] *n* bisturí.
scamper ['skæmpə'] *vi* corretear.
scampi ['skæmpɪ] *n* gambas a la gabardina.
scan [skæn] *vt* (*pt & pp* **scanned**, *ger* **scanning**). **1** escrutar. **2** echar un vistazo a, examinar.
▶ *n* ecografía.
scandal ['skændəl] *n* **1** escándalo. **2** chismes.
Scandinavia [skændɪ'neɪvɪə] *n* Escandinavia.
Scandinavian [skændɪ'neɪvɪən] *adj-n* escandinavo,-a.
scant [skænt] *adj* escaso,-a.
scapegoat ['skeɪpgəʊt] *n fig* cabeza de turco, chivo expiatorio.
scar [skɑː'] *n* cicatriz.
▶ *vt* (*pt & pp* **scarred**, *ger* **scarring**) dejar cicatriz en.
scarce [skeəs] *adj* escaso,-a.
● **to be scarce** escasear.
scarcely ['skeəslɪ] *adv* apenas.
● **scarcely anyone** casi nadie.
● **scarcely ever** casi nunca.
scarcity ['skeəsɪtɪ] *n* escasez.
scare [skeə'] *n* susto, sobresalto.
▶ *vt-vi* asustar(se), espantar(se).
▶ *vt* dar miedo.

to scare away/off *vt* espantar, ahuyentar.

scarecrow ['skeəkrəʊ] *n* espantapájaros.

scared [skeəd] *adj* asustado,-a.
- **to be scared** tener miedo: *he's scared of dogs*, tiene miedo a los perros.

scarf [skɑːf] *n* (*pl* **-s** o **scarves**). **1** pañuelo. **2** bufanda.

scarlet ['skɑːlət] *adj-n* escarlata.
- **scarlet fever** escarlatina.

scary ['skeərɪ] *adj* (**-ier**, **-iest**). **1** espeluznante, que da miedo. **2** de miedo *(película)*.

scatter ['skætə'] *vt-vi* **1** dispersar(se). **2** esparcir, derramar.

scavenge ['skævɪndʒ] *vi* hurgar, escarbar.
▶ *vt* buscar en la basura.

scenario [sɪˈnɑːrɪəʊ] *n* (*pl* **scenarios**). **1** guión. **2** perspectiva, panorama, escenario.

scene [siːn] *n* **1** escena. **2** escenario. **3** vista, panorama. **4** lugar: *the scene of the accident*, el lugar del accidente.
- **behind the scenes** entre bastidores.
- **the scene of the crime** el lugar del crimen.
- **to make a scene** armar un escándalo.

scenery ['siːnərɪ] *n* **1** paisaje. **2** decorado *(en teatro)*.

scent [sent] *n* **1** olor, fragancia. **2** perfume. **3** pista, rastro.
▶ *vt* **1** olfatear, presentir. **2** perfumar.

schedule ['ʃedjuːl, 'skedjuːl] *n* **1** programa. **2** lista. **3** US horario.
▶ *vt* programar, fijar.
- **on schedule** a la hora prevista.
- **to be ahead of schedule** ir adelantado,-a.
- **to be behind schedule** ir retrasado,-a.
- **scheduled flight** vuelo regular.

scheme [skiːm] *n* **1** plan, programa. **2** intriga, ardid.
▶ *vi* conspirar, tramar.

schizophrenia [ˌskɪtsəʊˈfriːnɪə] *n* esquizofrenia.

scholar ['skɒlə'] *n* **1** erudito,-a. **2** becario,-a.

scholarship ['skɒləʃɪp] *n* **1** beca. **2** erudición.

school[1] [skuːl] *n* **1** escuela, colegio, instituto.
▶ *vt* enseñar, instruir.

- **school book** libro de texto.
- **school of thought** corriente de pensamiento.
- **school year** año escolar.

school[2] [skuːl] *n* banco *(de peces)*.

schoolchild ['skuːltʃaɪld] *n* (*pl* **schoolchildren**) alumno,-a.

schooling ['skuːlɪŋ] *n* estudios.

schoolmaster ['skuːlmɑːstə'] *n* **1** profesor. **2** maestro.

schoolmistress ['skuːlmɪstrəs] *n* (*pl* **-es**). **1** profesora. **2** maestra.

science ['saɪəns] *n* **1** ciencia. **2** ciencias *(asignatura)*.
- **science fiction** ciencia ficción.

scientific [ˌsaɪənˈtɪfɪk] *adj* científico,-a.

scientist ['saɪəntɪst] *n* científico,-a.

scissors ['sɪzəz] *npl* tijeras.
- **a pair of scissors** unas tijeras.

scoff[1] [skɒf] *vi* mofarse, burlarse.

scoff[2] [skɒf] *vt fam* zamparse.

scold [skəʊld] *vt* reñir, regañar.

scoop [skuːp] *n* **1** pala *(para azúcar)*. **2** cucharón *(para helado)*. **3** cucharada *(de azúcar)*. **4** bola *(de helado)*. **5** exclusiva.

to scoop out *vt* sacar con pala, sacar con cucharón.

scooter ['skuːtə'] *n* **1** Vespa®, moto. **2** patinete.

scope [skəʊp] *n* **1** alcance, ámbito. **2** posibilidades: *there isn't much scope for improvement*, no hay muchas posibilidades de mejorar.

scorch [skɔːtʃ] *vt* **1** chamuscar. **2** abrasar.

score [skɔː'] *n* **1** tanteo, puntuación *(en golf, naipes)*. **2** resultado. **3** partitura, música *(de película)*.
▶ *vt-vi* marcar *(gol, etc)*.
▶ *vi* obtener una puntuación.
▶ *vt* lograr, conseguir.
- **on that score** a ese respecto.
- **to keep the score** seguir el marcador, llevar la cuenta de los tantos.
- **what's the score?** ¿cómo van?

scoreboard ['skɔːbɔːd] *n* marcador.

scorn [skɔːn] *n* desdén, desprecio.
▶ *vt* desdeñar, despreciar.

Scorpio ['skɔːpɪəʊ] *n* Escorpión, Escorpio.

scorpion ['skɔːpɪən] *n* escorpión.

Scot [skɒt] *n* escocés,-esa.

Scotland ['skɒtlənd] *n* Escocia.

Scots [skɒts] *adj* escocés,-esa.

Scottish ['skɒtɪʃ] *adj* escocés,-esa.
► *npl* **the Scottish** los escoceses.
scoundrel ['skaʊndrəl] *n* canalla, sinvergüenza.
scour¹ ['skaʊəʳ] *vt* recorrer, registrar.
scour² ['skaʊəʳ] *vt* fregar, restregar.
scout [skaʊt] *n* explorador,-ra.
scowl [skaʊl] *n* ceño fruncido.
► *vi* fruncir el ceño.
scramble ['skræmbəl] *n* lucha.
► *vi* **1** trepar. **2** pelearse: **to scramble for seats**, pelearse por encontrar asiento.
► *vt* revolver, mezclar.
■ **scrambled eggs** huevos revueltos.
scrap [skræp] *vt* (*pt & pp* **scrapped**, *ger* **scrapping**) desechar.
► *n* trozo, pedazo.
► *npl* **scraps** restos, sobras (*de comida*).
■ **scrap metal** chatarra.
■ **scrap paper** papel borrador.
scrape [skreɪp] *n* **1** raspado. **2** lío, apuro: **he always got into scrapes**, siempre se metía en líos.
► *vt* **1** rascar. **2** hacerse un rasguño en, rasparse.
to scrape along *vi* ir tirando.
to scrape through *vt* aprobar por los pelos.
scratch [skrætʃ] *n* (*pl* **-es**) rasguño, arañazo, raya.
► *vt* **1** arañar, rayar. **2** rascar.
● **to be up to scratch** dar la talla.
● **to start from scratch** partir de cero.
■ **scratch team** equipo improvisado.
scream [skriːm] *n* grito, chillido.
► *vt-vi* gritar, chillar.
● **it was a scream** *fam* fue la monda.
screech [skriːtʃ] *n* (*pl* **-es**) **1** chillido (*de persona*). **2** chirrido (*de neumáticos, etc*).
► *vi* **1** chillar (*persona*). **2** chirriar (*neumáticos, etc*).
screen [skriːn] *n* **1** biombo. **2** pantalla (*de cine, televisión*). **3** *fig* cortina: **a screen of trees**, una cortina de árboles.
► *vt* **1** proteger. **2** ocultar, tapar. **3** examinar. **4** proyectar (*película*).
■ **screen test** prueba cinematográfica.
■ **screen door** puerta de tela metálica.
■ **screen saver** protector de pantalla.
screw [skruː] *n* tornillo.
► *vt* atornillar.
► *vt-vi vulg* joder.
● **to screw money out of SB** *fam* sacarle dinero a ALGN.

to screw up *vt* **1** arrugar (*papel*). **2** hacer una mueca (*cara*). **3** *sl* jorobar, fastidiar.
screwdriver ['skruːdraɪvəʳ] *n* destornillador.
scribble ['skrɪbəl] *n* garabatos.
► *vt-vi* garabatear.
script [skrɪpt] *n* **1** guión. **2** escritura. **3** letra, caligrafía.
scrounge [skraʊndʒ] *vi* gorronear, vivir de gorra.
► *vt* gorronear.
● **to scrounge off SB** vivir a costa de ALGN.
scrub [skrʌb] *n* **1** maleza. **2** fregado.
► *vt* (*pt & pp* **scrubbed**, *ger* **scrubbing**) fregar.
scruff [skrʌf] *n* (*pl* **scruffs**) cogote.
scruffy ['skrʌfɪ] *adj* (**-ier**, **-iest**). **1** desaliñado,-a. **2** destartalado,-a.
scruple ['skruːpəl] *n* escrúpulo.
scrupulous ['skruːpjʊləs] *adj* escrupuloso,-a.
scrutinize ['skruːtɪnaɪz] *vt* escudriñar, examinar a fondo.
scuba diving ['skuːbədaɪvɪŋ] *n* submarinismo.
sculptor ['skʌlptəʳ] *n* escultor,-ra.
sculptress ['skʌlptrəs] *n* (*pl* **-es**) escultora.
sculpture ['skʌlptʃəʳ] *n* escultura.
scum [skʌm] *n* **1** espuma. **2** *fig* escoria.
scurry ['skʌrɪ] *vi* (*pt & pp* **-ied**) correr, salir corriendo.
to scurry away/off *vi* escabullirse.
scuttle ['skʌtəl] *vt* echar a pique, hundir adrede (*barco*).
to scuttle away/off *vi* escabullirse.
SE [saʊθˈiːst] *abbr* (**southeast**) SE.
sea [siː] *n* mar.
● **at sea 1** en el mar. **2** desorientado,-a.
● **by the sea** a orillas del mar.
■ **sea creature** animal marino.
■ **sea level** nivel del mar.
■ **sea lion** león marino.
■ **sea trout** trucha de mar, reo.
seafood ['siːfuːd] *n* marisco.
seafront ['siːfrʌnt] *n* paseo marítimo.
seagull ['siːgʌl] *n* gaviota.
sea-horse ['siːhɔːs] *n* caballito de mar.
seal¹ [siːl] *n* foca.
seal² [siːl] *n* sello.
► *vt* sellar, tapar, cerrar.

■ **seal of approval** visto bueno, aprobación.

to seal off *vt* **1** cerrar. **2** cerrar el acceso a.

seam [siːm] *n* **1** costura. **2** juntura, junta. **3** veta *(de mineral)*.

seamstress ['semstrəs] *n (pl* **-es)** costurera.

search [sɜːtʃ] *n (pl* **-es). 1** búsqueda. **2** registro *(de edificio, persona)*.

► *vi* buscar.

► *vt* **1** registrar *(edificio)*. **2** registrar, cachear *(persona)*.

● **in search of** en busca de.

■ **search engine** buscador.

■ **search party** equipo de búsqueda.

■ **search warrant** orden de registro.

searchlight ['sɜːtʃlaɪt] *n* reflector, proyector.

seasick ['siːsɪk] *adj* mareado,-a.

seaside ['siːsaɪd] *n* playa, costa.

■ **seaside resort** centro turístico en la costa.

season ['siːzən] *n* **1** estación *(del año)*. **2** época. **3** temporada *(para deporte, etc)*.

► *vt* sazonar.

● **in season 1** en sazón *(fruta)*. **2** en celo *(animal)*. **3** en temporada alta *(turismo)*.

● **out of season 1** fuera de temporada *(fruta)*. **2** en temporada baja *(turismo)*.

■ **season ticket** abono *(de temporada)*.

seashore ['siːʃɔːʳ] *n* orilla del mar.

seat [siːt] *n* **1** asiento. **2** localidad *(en teatro, etc)*. **3** sillín *(de bicicleta)*. **4** sede, centro. **5** escaño *(en Parlamento)*.

► *vt* **1** sentar. **2** tener cabida para.

● **to take a seat** sentarse, tomar asiento.

■ **seat belt** cinturón de seguridad.

seaweed ['siːwiːd] *n* alga.

secluded [sɪ'kluːdɪd] *adj* aislado,-a, apartado,-a.

second¹ ['sekənd] *adj-n* segundo,-a.

► *adv* segundo, en segundo lugar.

► *vt* apoyar, secundar.

► *npl* **seconds** artículos defectuosos, artículos con tara.

● **to have second thoughts about** STH dudar de algo.

■ **second class** segunda clase.

■ **second name** apellido.

second² ['sekənd] *n* segundo *(de tiempo)*.

■ **second hand** segundero.

secondary ['sekəndərɪ] *adj* secundario,-a.

■ **secondary school** escuela de enseñanza secundaria.

second-class ['sekəndklɑːs] *adj* de segunda clase.

second-hand ['sekəndhænd] *adj* de segunda mano.

secondly ['sekəndlɪ] *adv* en segundo lugar.

secrecy ['siːkrəsɪ] *n* secreto.

secret ['siːkrət] *adj* secreto,-a.

► *n* secreto.

● **in secret** en secreto.

■ **secret service** servicio secreto.

secretary ['sekrətərɪ] *n (pl* **-ies)** secretario,-a.

■ **Secretary of State 1** ministro,-a con cartera *(en GB)*. **2** ministro,-a de Asuntos Exteriores *(en EEUU)*.

secrete [sɪ'kriːt] *vt* secretar, segregar.

secretly ['siːkrətlɪ] *adv* en secreto, a escondidas.

sect [sekt] *n* secta.

section ['sekʃən] *n* sección, parte.

► *vt* cortar, seccionar.

sector ['sektə] *n* sector.

secular ['sekjʊlə'] *adj* **1** laico,-a *(educación)*. **2** profano,-a *(arte, música)*.

secure [sɪ'kjʊə'] *adj* **1** seguro,-a. **2** firme, bien sujeto,-a.

► *vt* **1** sujetar, fijar, asegurar *(ventana, etc)*. **2** proteger. **3** obtener, conseguir *(acuerdo, votos, etc)*.

security [sɪ'kjʊərɪtɪ] *n* **1** seguridad. **2** fianza, aval.

► *npl* **securities** COMM valores.

■ **security guard** guardia de seguridad.

sedative ['sedətɪv] *adj* sedante.

► *n* calmante, sedante.

sedentary ['sedəntərɪ] *adj* sedentario,-a.

sediment ['sedɪmənt] *n* sedimento.

seduce [sɪ'djuːs] *vt* seducir.

see¹ [siː] *vt-vi (pt* **saw** [sɔː], *pp* **seen** [siːn]). **1** ver. **2** procurar: *see that you arrive on time*, procura llegar a la hora. **3** acompañar: *he saw her to the door*, la acompañó a la puerta. **4** entender, ver: *I don't see why we can't go in*, no entiendo por qué no podemos entrar.

● **let's see** a ver, vamos a ver.

● **see you later!** ¡hasta luego!

● **to be seeing things** ver visiones.

● **to see red** ponerse hecho,-a una furia.

● **we'll see** ya veremos.

see² [siː] n sede *(religiosa)*.

to see about vt ocuparse de.

to see off vt despedirse de.

to see out vt acompañar hasta la puerta.

to see through vt calar a, verle el plumero a.

to see to vt ocuparse de.

seed [siːd] n 1 semilla *(de planta)*. 2 pepita *(de fruta)*. 3 cabeza de serie *(tenis)*.

seedy ['siːdɪ] adj (-ier, -iest) sórdido,-a.

seek [siːk] vt (pt & pp sought [sɔːt]). 1 buscar. 2 solicitar.

to seek out vt buscar.

seem [siːm] vi parecer: *it seems to me that ...*, me parece que ....

● **so it seems** eso parece.

seeming ['siːmɪŋ] adj aparente.

seemingly ['siːmɪŋlɪ] adv aparentemente, al parecer.

seen [siːn] pp → see.

seep [siːp] vi filtrarse.

seesaw ['siːsɔː] n balancín.

see-through ['siːθruː] adj transparente.

segment ['segmənt] n segmento.

segregate ['segrɪgeɪt] vt segregar.

segregation [segrɪ'geɪʃən] n segregación.

seize [siːz] vt 1 asir, agarrar, coger. 2 incautar, embargar. 3 tomar, apoderarse de.

to seize up vi agarrotarse.

seizure ['siːʒəʳ] n 1 incautación, embargo *(de bienes)*. 2 ataque *(de apoplejía)*.

seldom ['seldəm] adv raramente, rara vez.

select [sɪ'lekt] vt 1 escoger, elegir. 2 seleccionar.

▶ adj selecto,-a, escogido,-a, exclusivo,-a.

selection [sɪ'lekʃən] n 1 selección. 2 elección. 3 surtido.

selective [sɪ'lektɪv] adj selectivo,-a.

self [self] n (pl selves) yo, identidad propia: *my other self*, mi otro yo; *Jane will soon be her usual self again*, Jane pronto volverá a ser la misma de siempre.

self-assured [selfə'ʃʊəd] adj seguro,-a de sí mismo,-a.

self-centred [self'sentəd] adj egocéntrico,-a.

self-confidence [self'kɒnfɪdəns] n confianza en sí mismo,-a.

self-conscious [self'kɒnʃəs] adj cohibido,-a, tímido,-a.

self-defence [selfdɪ'fens] n defensa personal, autodefensa.

● **in self-defence** en defensa propia.

self-employed [selfɪm'plɔɪd] adj autónomo,-a, que trabaja por cuenta propia.

self-government [self'gʌvənmənt] n autonomía, autogobierno.

selfish ['selfɪʃ] adj egoísta.

selfishness ['selfɪʃnəs] n egoísmo.

self-portrait [self'pɔːtreɪt] n autorretrato.

self-respect [selfrɪ'spekt] n amor propio, dignidad.

self-righteous [self'raɪtʃəs] adj con superioridad moral.

self-service [self'sɜːvɪs] adj de autoservicio.

▶ n autoservicio.

sell [sel] vt-vi (pt & pp sold [səʊld]) vender.

● **to be sold on STH** fam estar entusiasmado por algo.

to sell off vt liquidar.

▶ vi venderse.

to sell out vi claudicar, venderse.

▶ vt agotarse: *the tickets are sold out*, las localidades están agotadas.

to sell up vi venderlo todo.

sell-by date ['selbaɪdeɪt] n fecha de caducidad.

seller ['seləʳ] n vendedor,-ra.

Sellotape® ['seləteɪp] n Celo®, cinta adhesiva.

semen ['siːmən] n semen.

semester [sɪ'mestəʳ] n semestre.

semicircle ['semɪsɜːkəl] n semicírculo.

semicolon [semɪ'kəʊlən] n punto y coma.

semidetached [semɪdɪ'tætʃt] adj adosado,-a.

▶ n casa adosada.

semifinal [semɪ'faɪnəl] n semifinal.

seminar ['semɪnɑːʳ] n seminario.

senate ['senət] n senado.

senator ['senətəʳ] n senador,-ra.

send [send] vt (pt & pp sent [sent]). 1 enviar, mandar: *send me the results*, envíeme los resultados. 2 volver: *the noise sent her mad*, el ruido la volvió loca.

● **to send SB packing** fam mandar a ALGN a freír espárragos.

● **to send STH flying** hacer saltar algo por los aires.

● **to send word** mandar recado.

to send away *vt* despachar.

to send away for *vt* pedir algo por correo.

to send back *vt* **1** devolver *(artículos, etc)*. **2** hacer volver *(persona)*.

to send for *vt* **1** mandar llamar a *(persona)*. **2** pedir por correo.

to send in *vt* **1** mandar, enviar *(por correo)*. **2** hacer pasar *(visita)*.

to send off *vt* **1** enviar *(por correo)*. **2** expulsar *(jugador)*.

to send on *vt* **1** hacer seguir *(carta)*. **2** mandar por adelantado *(equipaje)*.

sender ['sendə'] *n* remitente.

send-off ['sendɒf] *n* *(pl* **send-offs)** *fam* despedida.

senile ['siːnaɪl] *adj* senil.

senior ['siːniə'] *adj* **1** mayor *(por edad)*. **2** superior *(por rango)*. **3** de más antigüedad. **4** padre: *John Smith Senior*, John Smith, padre.

▸ *n* **1** mayor *(por edad)*. **2** superior *(por rango)*.

■ **senior citizen** jubilado,-a, persona de la tercera edad.

sensation [sen'seɪʃən] *n* sensación.

● **to be a sensation** ser todo un éxito.

sensational [sen'seɪʃənəl] *adj* **1** sensacional. **2** sensacionalista.

sense [sens] *n* **1** sentido: *sense of taste*, sentido del gusto. **2** sentimiento, sensación. **3** juicio, sentido común. **4** sentido, significado.

▸ *vt* sentir, percibir.

● **in a sense** en cierto modo.

● **there's no sense in ...** ¿de qué sirve ...?

● **to come to one's senses** recobrar el juicio.

● **to make sense** tener sentido, ser sensato,-a.

● **to make sense of STH** entender algo.

■ **sense of humour** sentido del humor.

senseless ['sensləs] *adj* **1** inconsciente. **2** absurdo,-a, insensato,-a.

sensibility [sensɪ'bɪlɪtɪ] *n* *(pl* **-ies)** sensibilidad.

sensible ['sensɪbəl] *adj* sensato,-a, razonable.

sensitive ['sensɪtɪv] *adj* **1** sensible. **2** susceptible. **3** confidencial *(documentos)*.

sensual ['sensjʊel] *adj* sensual.

sent [sent] *pt-pp* → send.

sentence ['sentəns] *n* **1** frase, oración. **2** sentencia, fallo, condena.

▸ *vt* condenar.

● **to pass sentence on SB** imponer una pena a ALGN.

sentimental [sentɪ'mentəl] *adj* sentimental.

sentry ['sentrɪ] *n* *(pl* **-ies)** centinela.

Sep [sep'tembə'] *abbr* **(September)** septiembre, setiembre.

separate [*(vb)* 'sepəreɪt(adj) 'sepərət] *vt* **1** separar. **2** dividir.

▸ *vi* separarse.

▸ *adj* **1** separado,-a: *they sleep in separate rooms*, duermen en habitaciones separadas. **2** distinto,-a.

separately ['seprətlɪ] *adv* por separado.

separation [sepə'reɪʃən] *n* separación.

September [səp'tembə'] *n* septiembre, setiembre.

sequel ['siːkwəl] *n* **1** secuela. **2** continuación *(de película, libro)*.

sequence ['siːkwəns] *n* **1** secuencia. **2** sucesión, serie.

serene [sə'riːn] *adj* sereno,-a, tranquilo,-a.

sergeant ['sɑːdʒənt] *n* sargento.

■ **sergeant major** sargento mayor, brigada.

serial ['sɪərɪəl] *n* serial, novela por entregas.

■ **serial killer** asesino,-a en serie.

■ **serial number** número de serie.

series ['sɪəriːz] *n* *(pl* **-ies).** **1** serie. **2** ciclo, programa.

serious ['sɪərɪəs] *adj* **1** serio,-a. **2** grave *(accidente)*.

● **seriously wounded** herido,-a de gravedad.

● **to be serious** hablar en serio.

seriously ['sɪərɪəslɪ] *adv* **1** en serio. **2** seriamente, gravemente.

● **to take seriously** tomarse en serio.

seriousness ['sɪərɪəsnəs] *n* seriedad, gravedad.

sermon ['sɜːmən] *n* sermón.

servant ['sɜːvənt] *n* criado,-a.

serve [sɜːv] *vt-vi* **1** servir: *he served the company for thirty years*, sirvió a la empresa durante treinta años. **2** servir *(comida, bebida)*. **3** despachar, servir *(en tienda)*. **4** sacar *(en tenis)*.

▸ *vt* **1** equipar. **2** cumplir *(condena)*.

▶ *n* saque *(en tenis)*.
● **to serve time** cumplir una condena.
● **it serves him** *etc* **right** *fam* lo tiene bien merecido.
service ['sɜːvɪs] *n* **1** servicio. **2** revisión, puesta a punto *(de coche)*. **3** oficio *(religioso)*. **4** juego, servicio *(de platos)*. **5** saque, servicio *(tenis)*.
● **at your service** a su disposición.
● **in service** en funcionamiento.
● **out of service** fuera de servicio.
■ **service station** estación de servicio.
serviceman ['sɜːvɪsmən] *n* (*pl* **servicemen**) militar.
serviette [sɜːvɪˈet] *n* GB servilleta.
session ['seʃən] *n* sesión.
set¹ [set] *n* **1** juego, colección *(de libros, etc)*. **2** conjunto. **3** set *(tenis)*. **4** aparato *(televisor, radio)*.
set² [set] *n* **1** plató *(de televisión)*. **2** escenario, decorado.
▶ *adj* **1** fijo,-a *(cantidad)*. **2** rígido,-a, inflexible *(opinión)*. **3** listo,-a: **are you all set to go?**, ¿estáis todos listos para salir?
▶ *vt* (*pt & pp* **set**). **1** poner, colocar, tender *(trampa)*. **2** poner *(mesa)*. **3** fijar *(fecha)*. **4** ajustar, poner *(reloj)*. **5** poner *(deberes)*. **6** montar *(joya)*. **7** marcar *(pelo)*.
▶ *vi* **1** ponerse *(sol)*. **2** cuajar *(líquido)*. **3** endurecerse *(cemento)*.
● **to set (oneself) up** establecerse.
● **to be set on doing** STH estar empeñado,-a en hacer algo.
● **to set an example** dar ejemplo.
● **to set fire to** STH prender fuego a algo.
● **to set** SB **free** poner a ALGN en libertad.
● **to set the pace** marcar el paso.
● **to set to work** ponerse a trabajar.
■ **set lunch** menú del día.
■ **set phrase** frase hecha.
■ **set price** precio fijo.
to set about *vt* empezar a: **they set about cleaning the house**, se pusieron a limpiar la casa.
to set aside *vt* **1** guardar, reservar. **2** dejar de lado.
to set back *vt* **1** apartar: **the house is set back from the road**, la casa está apartada de la carretera. **2** retrasar. **3** *fam* costar.
to set down *vt* **1** poner por escrito. **2** GB dejar.

to set in *vi* **1** comenzar *(mal tiempo)*. **2** surgir *(problemas)*.
to set off *vi* salir, ponerse en camino.
▶ *vt* **1** hacer estallar *(bomba)*. **2** hacer sonar, hacer saltar *(alarma)*.
to set out *vi* **1** partir, salir. **2** proponerse, pretender.
▶ *vt* disponer, exponer.
to set up *vt* **1** levantar *(monumento)*. **2** montar *(tienda de campaña)*. **3** crear, montar *(organización)*. **4** planear, convocar.
setback ['setbæk] *n* revés, contratiempo.
settee [seˈtiː] *n* sofá.
setting ['setɪŋ] *n* **1** engaste *(de joya)*. **2** marco, escenario *(de película)*. **3** posición *(de máquina)*.
settle ['setəl] *vt* **1** acordar *(precio)*. **2** resolver *(disputa)*. **3** calmar, tranquilizar. **4** pagar *(deuda)*. **5** colonizar, poblar.
▶ *vi* **1** posarse *(pájaro)*. **2** depositarse, asentarse *(polvo)*. **3** acomodarse. **4** afincarse, establecerse. **5** calmarse, tranquilizarse *(persona)*. **6** estabilizarse *(tiempo)*.
● **to settle out of court** JUR llegar a un acuerdo amistoso.
to settle down *vi* **1** instalarse, afincarse. **2** sentar la cabeza. **3** adaptarse.
to settle for *vt* conformarse con.
to settle in *vi* **1** adaptarse *(a trabajo)*. **2** instalarse *(en casa)*.
to settle on *vt* decidirse por.
settlement ['setəlmənt] *n* **1** poblado, colonia. **2** acuerdo. **3** pago.
● **to reach a settlement** llegar a un acuerdo.
settler ['setləʳ] *n* poblador,-ra, colono.
setup ['setʌp] *n* **1** sistema, organización. **2** *fam* montaje.
seven ['sevən] *num* siete.
seventeen [sevənˈtiːn] *num* diecisiete.
seventeenth [sevənˈtiːnθ] *adj* decimoséptimo,-a.
▶ *n* **1** decimoséptimo. **2** decimoséptima parte. **3** diecisiete *(en fecha)*.
seventh ['sevənθ] *adj-n* séptimo,-a.
▶ *n* **1** séptimo. **2** séptima parte. **3** siete *(en fecha)*.
seventieth ['sevəntɪəθ] *adj-n* septuagésimo,-a.
▶ *n* **1** septuagésimo. **2** septuagésima parte.

seventy ['sevəntı] *num* setenta.

sever ['sevər] *vt* **1** cortar *(cuerda)*. **2** romper *(relación)*.

several ['sevərəl] *adj-pron* varios,-as.

severe [sɪ'vɪər] *adj* **1** severo,-a *(castigo)*. **2** agudo,-a, intenso *(dolor)*. **3** grave *(enfermedad)*. **4** duro,-a *(clima)*.

severely [sɪ'vɪəlɪ] *adv* **1** severamente *(castigar)*. **2** gravemente *(enfermar)*.

sew [səʊ] *vt-vi* (*pt* **sewed** [səʊd], *pp* **sewn** [səʊn]) coser.

sewage ['sjuːɪdʒ] *n* aguas residuales.

■ **sewage system** alcantarillado.

sewer [sjʊər] *n* alcantarilla, cloaca.

sewing ['səʊɪŋ] *n* costura.

■ **sewing machine** máquina de coser.

sewn [səʊn] *pp* → sew.

sex [seks] *n* (*pl* **sexes**) sexo.

● **to have sex with** tener relaciones sexuales con.

■ **sex appeal** atractivo sexual.

sexist ['seksɪst] *adj-n* sexista.

sexual ['seksjʊəl] *adj* sexual.

sexuality [seksjʊ'ælɪtɪ] *n* sexualidad.

sexy ['seksɪ] *adj* (**-ier**, **-iest**) sexy.

shabby ['ʃæbɪ] *adj* (**-ier**, **-iest**). **1** raído,-a, desharrapado,-a *(ropa)*. **2** mal vestido,-a *(persona)*. **3** mezquino,-a *(conducta)*.

shack [ʃæk] *n* choza.

shade [ʃeɪd] *n* **1** sombra. **2** pantalla *(de lámpara)*. **3** matiz *(de color)*.
    ▶ *vt* **1** proteger contra el sol o la luz *(ojos)*. **2** dar sombra *(lugar)*.

shadow ['ʃædəʊ] *n* sombra.
    ▶ *vt fig* seguir la pista a.
● **without a shadow of doubt** sin lugar a dudas.

shady ['ʃeɪdɪ] *adj* (**-ier**, **-iest**). **1** a la sombra *(lugar)*. **2** *fam* sospechoso,-a *(persona)*.

shaft [ʃɑːft] *n* **1** mango *(de herramienta)*. **2** astil *(de flecha)*. **3** eje. **4** pozo *(de mina)*. **5** hueco *(de ascensor)*. **6** rayo *(de luz)*.

shaggy ['ʃægɪ] *adj* (**-ier**, **-iest**). **1** desgreñado,-a *(persona)*. **2** peludo,-a *(perro)*.

shake [ʃeɪk] *n* **1** sacudida. **2** batido *(bebida)*.
    ▶ *vt* (*pt* **shook** [ʃʊk], *pp* **shaken** ['ʃeɪkən]). **1** sacudir, agitar, hacer temblar *(edificio, etc)*. **2** trastornar, conmocionar.
    ▶ *vi* temblar.
● **to shake hands** darse la mano.
● **to shake one's head** negar con la cabeza.

to shake off *vt* **1** sacudirse. **2** quitarse de encima.

to shake up *vt* **1** agitar *(líquido)*. **2** conmocionar. **3** reorganizar *(sistema, equipo)*.

shake-up ['ʃeɪkʌp] *n fig* reorganización.

shaky ['ʃeɪkɪ] *adj* (**-ier**, **-iest**). **1** tembloroso,-a, inestable, poco firme *(escalera)*. **2** débil, malo,-a *(salud)*. **3** *fig* sin fundamento *(argumento)*.

shall [ʃæl, unstressed ʃəl] *aux* **1** indica un tiempo futuro: *I shall go tomorrow*, iré mañana; *we shall see them on Sunday*, los veremos el domingo. **2** indica ofrecimiento: *shall I close the window?*, ¿cierro la ventana? **3** indica una sugerencia: *shall we go to the cinema?*, ¿vamos al cine? **4** indica una promesa: *you shall have everything you want, my dear*, tendrás todo lo que desees, cariño. **5** uso enfático, una orden: *you shall stop work immediately*, debes parar de trabajar enseguida.

shallow ['ʃæləʊ] *adj* (*comp* **shallower**, *superl* **shallowest**). **1** poco profundo,-a *(agua)*. **2** *fig* superficial *(persona)*.

sham [ʃæm] *n* farsa.
    ▶ *adj* falso,-a.
    ▶ *vt-vi* (*pt & pp* **shammed**, *ger* **shamming**) fingir.

shambles ['ʃæmbəlz] *n* desorden, confusión.
● **in a shambles** patas arriba.

shame [ʃeɪm] *n* **1** vergüenza. **2** lástima, pena.
    ▶ *vt* avergonzar.
● **to put to shame** dejar en mal lugar.
● **what a shame!** ¡qué pena!, ¡qué lástima!

shameful ['ʃeɪmfʊl] *adj* vergonzoso,-a.

shameless ['ʃeɪmləs] *adj* desvergonzado,-a.

shampoo [ʃæm'puː] *n* (*pl* **shampoos**) champú.
    ▶ *vt* (*pt & pp* **shampooed**, *ger* **shampooing**) lavar con champú.

shandy ['ʃændɪ] *n* (*pl* **-ies**) GB clara, cerveza con gaseosa.

shape [ʃeɪp] *n* **1** forma, figura, silueta. **2** estado: *he's in great shape*, está en muy buena forma.
    ▶ *vt* **1** dar forma a, modelar *(arcilla)*. **2** determinar, formar *(carácter)*.
    ▶ *vi* **to shape (up)** desenvolverse.
● **out of shape 1** desentrenado,-a, en

baja forma *(persona)*. **2** deforme *(objeto)*.

● **to get into shape** ponerse en forma.
● **to give shape** dar forma.

shapeless ['ʃeɪpləs] *adj* informe, sin forma.
share [ʃeəʳ] *n* **1** parte. **2** acción *(en bolsa)*.
▶ *vt-vi* compartir.
▶ *vt* repartir, dividir.
● **to do one's share** hacer uno su parte.
shareholder ['ʃeəhəʊldəʳ] *n* accionista.
shark[1] [ʃɑːk] *n* tiburón.
shark[2] [ʃɑːk] *n fam* estafador,-ra, timador,-ra.
sharp [ʃɑːp] *adj* **1** afilado,-a *(cuchillo)*. **2** puntiagudo,-a *(palo, aguja)*. **3** avispado,-a, espabilado,-a *(persona)*. **4** fuerte, agudo,-a *(dolor)*. **5** brusco,-a, repentino *(subida, giro)*. **6** definido,-a, nítido,-a *(imagen)*. **7** mordaz *(crítica)*. **8** severo,-a *(reprimenda)*. **9** sostenido,-a: **F sharp**, fa sostenido. **10** cerrado,-a *(curva)*.
▶ *adv* en punto: **at ten o'clock sharp**, a las diez en punto.
sharpen ['ʃɑːpən] *vt* **1** afilar *(cuchillo)*. **2** sacar punta a *(lápiz)*. **3** *fig* agudizar.
sharpener ['ʃɑːpənəʳ] *n* **1** afilador *(para cuchillos)*. **2** sacapuntas *(para lápices)*.
shatter ['ʃætəʳ] *vt* **1** romper, hacer añicos. **2** destrozar, destruir. **3** agotar.
▶ *vi* romperse, hacerse añicos.
● **to be shattered** estar destrozado,-a.
shave [ʃeɪv] *n* afeitado.
▶ *vt-vi* afeitar(se).
● **to have a close shave** salvarse por los pelos.
● **to have a shave** afeitarse.
shaver ['ʃeɪvəʳ] *n* máquina de afeitar.
shaving ['ʃeɪvɪŋ] *n* **1** afeitado. **2** viruta.
■ **shaving brush** brocha de afeitar.
■ **shaving foam** espuma de afeitar.
shawl [ʃɔːl] *n* chal.
she [ʃiː] *pron* ella.
shear [ʃɪəʳ] *vt (pt* **sheared,** *pp* **sheared** o **shorn)** esquilar.
▶ *npl* **shears** tijeras *(de esquilar o podar)*.
sheath [ʃiːθ] *n (pl* **sheaths** [ʃiːðz]). **1** vaina *(para espada)*. **2** funda *(para cuchillo)*. **3** preservativo.
shed[1] [ʃed] *n* **1** cobertizo *(en jardín)*. **2** barraca.
shed[2] [ʃed] *vt (pt & pp* **shed,** *ger* **shedding). 1** derramar *(lágrimas)*. **2** despojar-

se de, quitarse *(ropa)*. **3** deshacerse de *(preocupaciones)*.
● **to shed its skin** mudar de piel.
sheep [ʃiːp] *n (pl* **sheep)** oveja.
sheer [ʃɪəʳ] *adj* **1** escarpado,-a *(acantilado)*. **2** fino,-a *(medias)*.
sheet [ʃiːt] *n* **1** sábana. **2** hoja *(de papel)*. **3** lámina *(de metal)*. **4** capa *(de hielo)*.
■ **sheet metal** metal en lámina.
■ **sheet music** partitura.
shelf [ʃelf] *n (pl* **shelves)** estante.
▶ *npl* **shelves** estantería.
shell [ʃel] *n* **1** cáscara *(de huevo,nuez)*. **2** vaina *(de guisante)*. **3** caparazón *(de tortuga)*. **4** concha *(de caracola)*. **5** armazón, esqueleto *(de edificio)*. **6** obús, proyectil.
▶ *vt* **1** descascarar *(nuez)*. **2** desvainar *(guisante)*. **3** bombardear.
to shell out *vt fam* soltar, pagar.
shellfish ['ʃelfɪʃ] *n (pl* **shellfish)** marisco.
shelter ['ʃeltəʳ] *n* **1** abrigo, protección. **2** refugio. **3** asilo.
▶ *vt* abrigar, amparar, proteger.
▶ *vi* refugiarse, ponerse al abrigo, resguardarse.
● **to take shelter** refugiarse.
shelve [ʃelv] *vt* **1** poner en la estantería. **2** *fig* dar carpetazo, archivar.
shepherd ['ʃepəd] *n* pastor.
sherry ['ʃerɪ] *n (pl* **-ies)** jerez, vino de jerez.
shield [ʃiːld] *n* **1** escudo. **2** pantalla protectora.
▶ *vt* proteger.
shift [ʃɪft] *n* **1** cambio. **2** turno *(de trabajo)*.
▶ *vt* cambiar(se), cambiar(se) de sitio, desplazar(se).
shilling ['ʃɪlɪŋ] *n* chelín.
shimmer ['ʃɪməʳ] *n* luz trémula.
▶ *vi* rielar.
shin [ʃɪn] *n* espinilla.
shine [ʃaɪn] *n* brillo, lustre.
▶ *vi (pt & pp* **shone** [ʃɒn]). **1** brillar *(sol)*. **2** relucir *(metal)*. **3** *fig* sobresalir.
▶ *vt* **1** dirigir *(luz)*. **2** sacar brillo a *(zapatos)*.
shingle ['ʃɪŋgəl] *n* guijarros.
shingles ['ʃɪŋgəlz] *npl* herpes, culebrilla.
shining ['ʃaɪnɪŋ] *adj* **1** brillante, reluciente. **2** destacado,-a.
shiny ['ʃaɪnɪ] *adj (* **-ier,** **-iest)** brillante.
ship [ʃɪp] *n* barco, buque.
▶ *vt (pt & pp* **shipped,** *ger* **shipping)** enviar, enviar por barco.

● **on board ship** a bordo.

shipment ['ʃɪpmənt] *n* **1** cargamento. **2** envío.

shipping ['ʃɪpɪŋ] *n* **1** barcos. **2** envío, transporte.

shipwreck ['ʃɪprek] *n* naufragio.

● **to be shipwrecked** naufragar.

shipyard ['ʃɪpjɑːd] *n* astillero.

shirt [ʃɜːt] *n* camisa.

● **in shirt sleeves** en mangas de camisa.

shit [ʃɪt] *n vulg* mierda.

▶ *vi* (*pt & pp* **shitted**, **shit** o **shat**, ger **shitting**) *vulg* cagar.

shiver ['ʃɪvəʳ] *n* escalofrío.

▶ *vi* **1** tiritar, estremecerse. **2** temblar.

shock [ʃɒk] *n* **1** choque, sacudida. **2** golpe, conmoción. **3** susto. **4** shock.

▶ *vt* **1** conmocionar, trastornar. **2** asustar.

shocking ['ʃɒkɪŋ] *adj* **1** espantoso,-a, horroroso,-a. **2** escandaloso,-a, chocante. **3** chillón: ***shocking pink***, rosa chillón.

shod [ʃɒd] *pt-pp* → shoe.

shoddy ['ʃɒdɪ] *adj* (**-ier**, **-iest**) chapucero,-a.

shoe [ʃuː] *n* **1** zapato. **2** herradura.

▶ *vt* (*pt & pp* **shod**, ger **shoeing**) herrar.

■ **shoe polish** betún.

■ **shoe shop** zapatería.

shoehorn ['ʃuːhɔːn] *n* calzador.

shoelace ['ʃuːleɪs] *n* cordón de zapato.

shoemaker ['ʃuːmeɪkəʳ] *n* zapatero,-a.

shone [ʃɒn] *pt-pp* → shine.

shook [ʃʊk] *pt* → shake.

shoot [ʃuːt] *n* **1** brote, retoño. **2** rodaje (*de película*). **3** GB cacería.

▶ *vt* (*pt & pp* **shot**). **1** pegar un tiro a: ***to shoot SB dead***, matar a ALGN a tiros. **2** lanzar (*misil*). **3** disparar (*flecha, bala*). **4** rodar, filmar (*película*). **5** fotografiar. **6** chutar (*pelota*).

▶ *vi* disparar.

■ **shooting star** estrella fugaz.

to shoot down *vt* **1** derribar (*avión*). **2** matar a tiros (*persona*).

to shoot out *vi* salir disparado,-a.

to shoot past *vi* pasar volando.

to shoot up *vi* **1** salir (*llamas*). **2** dispararse (*precios*). **3** crecer rápidamente (*planta, niño*). **4** *sl* chutarse.

shop [ʃɒp] *n* **1** tienda. **2** comercio, negocio. **3** taller.

▶ *vi* (*pt & pp* **shopped**, ger **shopping**) hacer compras, ir de compras.

● **to set up shop** abrir un negocio.

● **to talk shop** hablar del trabajo.

■ **shop assistant** dependiente,-a.

■ **shop floor** obreros, trabajadores.

■ **shop window** escaparate.

shoplifting ['ʃɒplɪftɪŋ] *n* hurto (*en tiendas*).

shopper ['ʃɒpəʳ] *n* comprador,-ra.

shopping ['ʃɒpɪŋ] *n* compras.

● **to do the shopping** hacer la compra.

● **to go shopping** ir de compras.

■ **shopping arcade** galerías comerciales.

■ **shopping centre** centro comercial.

shore¹ [ʃɔːʳ] *n* orilla, costa (*de lago, mar*).

● **on shore** en tierra.

shore² [ʃɔːʳ] *vt* apuntalar.

shorn [ʃɔːn] *pp* → shear.

short [ʃɔːt] *adj* **1** corto,-a (*pantalón, pelo*). **2** bajo,-a (*estatura, persona*). **3** breve, corto,-a (*duración*). **4** seco,-a, brusco,-a (*modales*).

▶ *adv* bruscamente.

▶ *n* **1** bebida corta, copa. **2** cortometraje. **3** cortocircuito.

▶ *npl* **shorts** pantalón corto.

● **at short notice** con poca antelación.

● **in short** en pocas palabras.

● **for short** para abreviar.

● **shortly after** poco después.

● **to be short of** andar escaso,-a de, andar mal de.

● **to be STH short** faltar algo: ***we're a chair short***, nos falta una silla.

● **to cut short** interrumpir.

● **to stop short** frenar en seco.

■ **short circuit** cortocircuito.

■ **short cut** atajo.

■ **short story** cuento, relato.

shortage ['ʃɔːtɪdʒ] *n* falta, escasez.

shortcomings ['ʃɔːtkʌmɪŋz] *npl* defectos.

shorten ['ʃɔːtən] *vt* acortar, abreviar, reducir.

▶ *vi* acortarse.

shorthand ['ʃɔːthænd] *n* taquigrafía.

■ **shorthand typing** taquimecanografía.

shortly ['ʃɔːtlɪ] *adv* dentro de poco, en breve.

● **shortly after** poco después.

● **shortly before** poco antes.

short-sighted [ʃɔːt'saɪtɪd] *adj* corto,-a de vista, miope.

short-term ['ʃɔːttɜːm] *adj* a corto plazo.

shot¹ [ʃɒt] *n* **1** tiro, disparo, balazo *(de pistola)*. **2** bala, proyectil. **3** tirador,-ra *(persona)*. **4** tiro *(a gol)*. **5** chute *(fútbol)*. **6** intento. **7** inyección, pinchazo. **8** trago. **9** foto. **10** toma *(en cine)*.

● **to be off like a shot** salir disparado,-a.

● **to have a shot at STH** intentar hacer algo.

● **not by a long shot** ni mucho menos, ni de lejos.

shot² [ʃɒt] *pt-pp* → shoot.

shotgun ['ʃɒtɡʌn] *n* escopeta.

should [ʃʊd] *aux* **1** deber *(para expresar sugerencias)*: **you should see the dentist**, deberías ir al dentista. **2** deber de *(para expresar probabilidad)*: **the clothes should be dry now**, la ropa ya debe de estar seca.

● **I should like to ask a question** quisiera hacer una pregunta.

● **I should think so** me imagino que sí.

shoulder ['ʃəʊldəʳ] *n* **1** hombro *(de persona)*. **2** espalda *(de carne)*.

▶ *vt* cargar con.

● **shoulder to shoulder** hombro con hombro.

● **to give SB the cold shoulder** volver la espalda a ALGN.

■ **shoulder bag** bolso *(de bandolera)*.

■ **shoulder blade** omoplato, omóplato.

shout [ʃaʊt] *n* grito.

▶ *vt-vi* gritar.

to shout down *vt* hacer callar a gritos.

shove [ʃʌv] *n* empujón.

▶ *vt-vi* empujar.

to shove off *vi fam* largarse.

shovel ['ʃʌvəl] *n* pala.

▶ *vt* (GB *pt & pp* **shovelled**, *ger* **shovelling**; US *pt & pp* **shoveled**, *ger* **shoveling**) mover con pala, quitar con pala.

show [ʃəʊ] *n* **1** espectáculo, función. **2** programa *(televisivo, de radio)*. **3** exposición, feria. **4** demostración, muestra.

▶ *vt* (*pt* **showed** [ʃəʊd], *pp* **shown** [ʃəʊn]). **1** mostrar, enseñar. **2** exponer. **3** indicar, marcar, señalar. **4** demostrar. **5** llevar, acompañar: **he showed her to the door**, la acompañó a la puerta.

▶ *vt-vi* poner *(película)*: **what's showing?**, ¿qué ponen?

▶ *vi* notarse, verse: **the stain doesn't show**, no se ve la mancha.

● **time will show** el tiempo lo dirá.

● **to be on show** estar expuesto,-a.

● **to make a show of** hacer gala de, hacer alarde de.

● **to show SB in** hacer pasar a ALGN.

● **to steal the show** llevarse la palma.

■ **show business** el mundo del espectáculo.

■ **show of hands** votación a mano alzada.

to show off *vi* fardar, fanfarronear.

to show up *vt* **1** hacer resaltar, destacar. **2** dejar en ridículo.

▶ *vi fam* presentarse, aparecer.

showdown ['ʃəʊdaʊn] *n* enfrentamiento.

shower ['ʃaʊəʳ] *n* **1** ducha. **2** chubasco, chaparrón.

▶ *vt* **1** *fig* inundar, colmar. **2** regar.

▶ *vi* ducharse.

● **to have a shower** ducharse.

shown [ʃəʊn] *pp* → show.

show-off ['ʃəʊɒf] *n* (*pl* **show-offs**) *fam* fanfarrón,-ona.

showroom ['ʃəʊrʊm] *n* sala de exposiciones.

showy ['ʃəʊɪ] *adj* (-**ier**, -**iest**) ostentoso, -a, llamativo,-a.

shrank [ʃræŋk] *pt* → shrink.

shrapnel ['ʃræpnəl] *n* metralla.

shred [ʃred] *n* **1** triza, jirón *(de tela)*. **2** tira *(de papel)*. **3** *fig* pizca.

▶ *vt* (*pt & pp* **shredded**, *ger* **shredding**). **1** hacer trizas *(papel)*. **2** hacer jirones *(tela)*. **3** rallar *(verduras)*. **4** desmenuzar *(pollo)*.

● **to tear STH to shreds** romper en pedazos, hacer trizas.

shrewd [ʃruːd] *adj* astuto,-a, perspicaz.

shriek [ʃriːk] *n* chillido, grito.

▶ *vi* chillar, gritar.

● **to shriek with laughter** reírse a carcajadas.

shrill [ʃrɪl] *adj* agudo,-a, chillón,-ona.

shrimp [ʃrɪmp] *n* **1** camarón, gamba. **2** *pej* enano,-a.

shrine [ʃraɪn] *n* **1** santuario. **2** capilla, ermita.

shrink [ʃrɪŋk] *vt-vi* (*pt* **shrank** [ʃræŋk], *pp* **shrunk** [ʃrʌŋk]) encoger(se).

▶ *n fam* médico de los nervios, psiquiatra.

• **to shrink from doing** STH no tener valor para hacer algo.
to shrink away from *vi* retroceder, echarse atrás.
shrivel ['ʃrɪvəl] *vi* (GB *pt & pp* **shrivelled**, *ger* **shrivelling**; US *pt & pp* **shriveled**, *ger* **shriveling**) marchitarse.
shroud [ʃraʊd] *n* **1** mortaja, sudario. **2** velo: *a shroud of mistery*, un velo de misterio.
► *vt fig* envolver.
shrub [ʃrʌb] *n* arbusto.
shrug [ʃrʌg] *vi* (*pt & pp* **shrugged**, *ger* **shrugging**) encogerse de hombros.
• **to give a shrug** encogerse de hombros.
• **to shrug one's shoulders** encogerse de hombros.
to shrug off *vt* quitar importancia a.
shrunk [ʃrʌnk] *pp* → shrink.
shudder ['ʃʌdəʳ] *n* **1** escalofrío, estremecimiento. **2** sacudida.
► *vi* **1** estremecerse, temblar. **2** dar sacudidas.
shuffle ['ʃʌfəl] *n* **1**: *he walks with a shuffle*, anda arrastrando los pies. **2**: *give the cards a shuffle*, baraja las cartas.
► *vt* **1** barajar *(cartas)*. **2** revolver *(papeles)*.
► *vi* andar arrastrando los pies.
shush! [ʃʊʃ] *interj* ¡chis!, ¡chitón!
shut [ʃʌt] *vt-vi* (*pt & pp* **shut**, *ger* **shutting**) cerrar(se).
to shut away *vt* **1** encerrar. **2** guardar bajo llave.
to shut down *vt* cerrar.
► *vi* cerrarse.
to shut off *vt* **1** cortar, cerrar. **2** aislar.
to shut up *vt* **1** cerrar. **2** *fam* hacer callar.
► *vi fam* callar, callarse.
shutdown ['ʃʌtdaʊn] *n* cierre.
shutter ['ʃʌtəʳ] *n* **1** postigo, contraventana *(de ventana)*. **2** obturador *(de máquina de fotos)*.
shuttle ['ʃʌtəl] *n* **1** puente aéreo *(de avión)*. **2** servicio regular *(de bus, tren)*. **3** transbordador espacial.
► *vt* transportar.
► *vi* ir y venir.
shy [ʃaɪ] *adj* (-**ier**, -**iest**) tímido,-a.
► *vi* (*pt & pp* **shied**, *ger* **shying**) espantarse.
• **to be shy to do** STH no atreverse a hacer algo.

• **to shy away from** STH huir de algo.
shyness ['ʃaɪnəs] *n* timidez.
Sicily ['sɪsɪlɪ] *n* Sicilia.
sick [sɪk] *adj* **1** enfermo,-a. **2** mareado,-a. **3** morboso,-a.
• **to be sick** vomitar, estar harto,-a.
• **it makes me sick** *fam* me pone enfermo,-a.
■ **sick leave** baja por enfermedad.
■ **sick pay** subsidio por enfermedad.
sicken ['sɪkən] *vt* **1** poner enfermo,-a. **2** dar asco.
sickening ['sɪkənɪŋ] *adj* repugnante, asqueroso,-a.
sickly ['sɪklɪ] *adj* (-**ier**, -**iest**). **1** enfermizo,-a. **2** pálido,-a. **3** empalagoso,-a *(olor, sabor)*. **4** horrible *(color)*.
sickness ['sɪknəs] *n* **1** enfermedad. **2** náusea, mareo.
side [saɪd] *n* **1** lado. **2** costado *(de persona)*. **3** ijar, ijada *(de animal)*. **4** borde *(de mesa)*. **5** orilla *(de lago)*. **6** bando, lado *(en guerra)*. **7** equipo. **8** parte: *on my father's side*, por parte de mi padre.
► *vi* ponerse del lado.
• **side by side** juntos,-as, uno,-a al lado de otro,-a.
• **to look on the bright side** ver el lado bueno de las cosas.
• **to put** STH **to one side** apartar algo.
• **to take sides with** SB ponerse de parte de ALGN.
■ **side dish** acompañamiento.
■ **side door** puerta lateral.
■ **side entrance** entrada lateral.
■ **side effect** efecto secundario.
■ **side street** bocacalle, callejuela.
sideboard ['saɪdbɔːd] *n* aparador.
► *npl* **sideboards** patillas.
sideburns ['saɪdbɜːnz] *npl* patillas.
sidelight ['saɪdlaɪt] *n* luz de posición.
sideline ['saɪdlaɪn] *n* **1** línea de banda. **2** empleo suplementario.
sidelong ['saɪdlɒŋ] *adj* de soslayo.
► *adv* de lado.
sidetrack ['saɪdtræk] *vt* despistar, distraer.
sidewalk ['saɪdwɔːk] *n* US acera.
sideways ['saɪdweɪz] *adj* **1** lateral *(movimiento)*. **2** de soslayo *(mirada)*.
► *adv* **1** de lado *(movimiento)*. **2** de soslayo *(mirada)*.

siege [siːdʒ] *n* sitio, cerco.
● **to lay siege to** sitiar, cercar.
sieve [sɪv] *n* **1** tamiz *(para harina)*. **2** criba *(para granos)*. **3** colador *(para líquidos)*.
► *vt* **1** tamizar *(harina)*. **2** cribar *(granos)*. **3** colar *(líquidos)*.
sift [sɪft] *vt* tamizar, cribar.
● **to sift through** examinar cuidadosamente.
sigh [saɪ] *n* suspiro.
► *vi* suspirar.
sight [saɪt] *n* **1** vista. **2** espectáculo. **3** imagen. **4** mira *(de escopeta)*.
► *vt* observar, ver, divisar.
► *npl* **sights** atracciones, monumentos.
► *adv* **a sight** *fam* mucho: *a sight cheaper*, mucho más barato.
● **at first sight** a primera vista.
● **in sight** a la vista.
● **to catch sight of** ver, divisar.
● **to come into sight** aparecer.
● **to disappear out of sight** perderse de vista.
● **to know SB by sight** conocer a ALGN de vista.
● **to lose sight of** perder de vista.
● **to see the sights** visitar la ciudad.
sightseeing ['saɪtsiːɪŋ] *n* visita turística, turismo.
sign [saɪn] *n* **1** signo. **2** señal, gesto. **3** letrero, anuncio, aviso. **4** rastro, huella.
► *vt-vi* firmar.
● **as a sign of** como muestra de.
to sign away *vt* ceder.
to sign in *vi* firmar el registro.
to sign on/up *vt* **1** contratar *(empleado)*. **2** fichar *(jugador)*.
signal ['sɪɡnəl] *n* señal.
► *vi* (GB *pt & pp* **signalled**, *ger* **signalling**; US *pt & pp* **signaled**, *ger* **signaling**). **1** hacer señales *(con manos)*. **2** señalizar, poner el intermitente: *signal before you turn*, pon el intermitente antes de girar.
► *vt* indicar, señalar.
signature ['sɪɡnɪtʃəʳ] *n* firma.
significance [sɪɡ'nɪfɪkəns] *n* trascendencia, importancia.
significant [sɪɡ'nɪfɪkənt] *adj* significativo,-a.
signify ['sɪɡnɪfaɪ] *vt* (*pt & pp* **-ied**). **1** significar. **2** mostrar, indicar.
signpost ['saɪnpəʊst] *n* señal indicadora, poste indicador.

silence ['saɪləns] *n* silencio.
► *vt* acallar, hacer callar.
● **in silence** en silencio.
silent ['saɪlənt] *adj* **1** silencioso,-a. **2** callado,-a. **3** mudo,-a *(película)*.
● **to be silent** callarse.
silently ['saɪləntlɪ] *adv* silenciosamente, en silencio.
silhouette [sɪluːˈet] *n* silueta.
silk [sɪlk] *n* seda.
silkworm ['sɪlkwɜːm] *n* gusano de la seda.
silky ['sɪlkɪ] *adj* (**-ier**, **-iest**) sedoso,-a.
sill [sɪl] *n* alféizar, antepecho.
silly ['sɪlɪ] *adj* (**-ier**, **-iest**) tonto,-a, necio,-a.
● **to do STH silly** hacer una tontería.
silver ['sɪlvəʳ] *n* **1** plata. **2** monedas de plata. **3** vajilla de plata, plata.
► *adj* de plata, plateado,-a.
■ **silver foil** papel de plata.
■ **silver jubilee** veinticinco aniversario.
■ **silver wedding** bodas de plata.
silversmith ['sɪlvəsmɪθ] *n* platero,-a.
similar ['sɪmɪləʳ] *adj* parecido,-a, similar, semejante.
similarity [sɪmɪ'lærɪtɪ] *n* (*pl* **-ies**) semejanza, parecido.
similarly ['sɪmɪləlɪ] *adv* igualmente, del mismo modo.
simmer ['sɪməʳ] *vt-vi* cocer(se) a fuego lento.
simple ['sɪmpəl] *adj* (*comp* **simpler**, *superl* **simplest**). **1** sencillo,-a, simple. **2** simple, tonto,-a *(persona)*.
simplicity [sɪm'plɪsɪtɪ] *n* **1** sencillez. **2** simpleza.
simplify ['sɪmplɪfaɪ] *vt* (*pt & pp* **-ied**) simplificar.
simplistic [sɪm'plɪstɪk] *adj* simplista.
simply ['sɪmplɪ] *adv* simplemente.
simulate ['sɪmjʊleɪt] *vt* simular.
simultaneous [sɪməl'teɪnɪəs] *adj* simultáneo,-a.
simultaneously [sɪməl'teɪnɪəslɪ] *adv* simultáneamente, a la vez.
sin [sɪn] *n* pecado: *the seven deadly sins*, los siete pecados capitales.
► *vi* (*pt & pp* **sinned**, *ger* **sinning**) pecar.
since [sɪns] *adv* desde entonces: *we met at the party and I haven't seen him since*, nos encontramos en la fiesta y desde entonces no lo he vuelto a ver.

▶ *prep* desde: *I've been here since four o'clock*, llevo aquí desde las cuatro.

▶ *conj* **1** desde que: *you've learned a lot since you joined the company*, has aprendido mucho desde que entraste en la empresa. **2** ya que, puesto que.

sincere [sɪn'sɪə'] *adj* sincero,-a.

sincerely [sɪn'sɪəlɪ] *adv* sinceramente.

● **yours sincerely** atentamente *(en carta)*.

sincerity [sɪn'serɪtɪ] *n* sinceridad.

sinful ['sɪnfʊl] *adj* **1** pecador,-ra. **2** pecaminoso,-a.

sing [sɪŋ] *vt-vi (pt* **sang** [sæŋ], *pp* **sung** [sʌŋ]) cantar.

Singapore [sɪŋɡə'pɔː'] *n* Singapur.

singer ['sɪŋə'] *n* cantante.

singing ['sɪŋɪŋ] *n* canto, cantar.

single ['sɪŋɡəl] *adj* **1** solo,-a. **2** único,-a. **3** individual *(cama)*. **4** soltero,-a.

▶ *n* **1** GB billete sencillo, billete de ida. **2** single *(disco)*.

▶ *npl* **singles** individuales.

● **every single ...** todos los ...: *every single day*, todos los días.

● **in single file** en fila india.

■ **single bed** cama individual.

■ **single parent** madre soltera, padre soltero.

■ **single room** habitación individual.

to single out *vt* **1** escoger, elegir. **2** destacar.

single-handed [sɪŋɡəl'hændɪd] *adj-adv* sin ayuda, solo,-a.

singly ['sɪŋɡlɪ] *adv* por separado, uno por uno.

singular ['sɪŋɡjʊlə'] *adj* **1** singular. **2** *fml* excepcional.

▶ *n* singular.

sinister ['sɪnɪstə'] *adj* siniestro,-a.

sink [sɪŋk] *n* **1** fregadero, pila *(de cocina)*. **2** US lavabo *(de cuarto de baño)*.

▶ *vt (pt* **sank**, *pp* **sunk**). **1** hundir, echar a pique *(barco)*. **2** hundir, acabar con *(plan)*. **3** cavar *(agujero)*. **4** abrir, perforar *(pozo)*. **5** hincar, clavar *(el diente)*: *she sank her teeth into his arm*, le pegó un mordisco en el brazo. **6** invertir.

▶ *vi* **1** hundirse *(barco)*. **2** ponerse *(sol, luna)*. **3** bajar, descender.

to sink in *vi* **1** caer en la cuenta de. **2** *fig* causar impresión.

sinner ['sɪnə'] *n* pecador,-ra.

sip [sɪp] *n* sorbo.

▶ *vt (pt & pp* **sipped**, *ger* **sipping**) beber a sorbos.

sir [sɜː'] *n* **1** *fml* señor: *yes, sir*, sí, señor. **2** sir: *Sir Winston Churchill*, sir Winston Churchill.

● **Dear Sir** muy señor mío, estimado señor.

siren ['saɪərən] *n* sirena.

sirloin ['sɜːlɔɪn] *n* solomillo.

sister ['sɪstə'] *n* **1** hermana. **2** GB enfermera jefe. **3** hermana, monja, sor.

sister-in-law ['sɪstərɪnlɔː] *n (pl* **sisters-in-law**) cuñada.

sit [sɪt] *vi (pt & pp* **sat** [sæt], *ger* **sitting**). **1** sentarse: *he's sitting in my chair*, está sentado en mi silla. **2** posar *(para artista)*. **3** ser miembro: *he sits on a jury*, es miembro de un jurado. **4** reunirse.

▶ *vt* GB presentarse a *(examen)*.

to sit about/around *vi fam* no hacer nada.

to sit down *vi* sentarse.

to sit in for *vt* sustituir a.

to sit on *vt* **1** formar parte de *(comisión)*. **2** *fam* retener, no tramitar.

to sit out/through *vt* aguantar *(hasta el final)*.

to sit up *vi* **1** incorporarse. **2** quedarse levantado,-a.

site [saɪt] *n* **1** emplazamiento, zona. **2** terreno.

sit-in ['sɪtɪn] *n* sentada, protesta.

sitting ['sɪtɪŋ] *n* **1** turno *(de comidas)*. **2** sesión.

■ **sitting member** POL miembro activo.

■ **sitting room** sala de estar, salón.

situated ['sɪtjʊeɪtɪd] *adj* situado,-a, ubicado,-a.

situation [sɪtjʊ'eɪʃən] *n* situación.

■ **"Situations vacant"** "Ofertas de trabajo".

six [sɪks] *adj-n* seis.

sixteen [sɪks'tiːn] *adj* dieciséis.

▶ *n* dieciséis.

sixteenth [sɪks'tiːnθ] *adj-n* decimosexto,-a.

▶ *n* **1** decimosexto. **2** decimosexta parte. **3** dieciséis *(en fecha)*.

sixth [sɪksθ] *adj-n* sexto,-a.

▶ *n* **1** sexto. **2** sexta parte. **3** seis *(en fecha)*.

sixtieth ['sɪkstɪəθ] *adj-n* sexagésimo,-a.

▶ *n* sexagésimo, sexagésima parte.

sixty ['sɪkstɪ] *adj-n* sesenta.

size [saɪz] *n* **1** tamaño. **2** talla *(de prenda de vestir)*. **3** número *(de zapatos)*. **4** magnitud.

● **to cut SB down to size** bajarle los humos a ALGN.

to size up *vt* evaluar.

skate [skeɪt] *n* patín.

▶ *vi* patinar.

skateboard ['skeɪtbɔːd] *n* monopatín.

skating ['skeɪtɪŋ] *n* patinaje.

■ **skating rink** pista de patinaje.

skeleton ['skelɪtən] *n* **1** esqueleto. **2** armazón.

▶ *adj* reducido,-a.

■ **skeleton key** llave maestra.

sketch [sketʃ] *n* (*pl* **-es**). **1** boceto, bosquejo, esbozo. **2** esquema. **3** sketch.

▶ *vt* bosquejar, esbozar.

■ **sketch map** croquis.

ski [skiː] *n* esquí.

▶ *vi* esquiar.

■ **ski instructor** monitor,-ra de esquí.

■ **ski lift** telesquí, telesilla.

■ **ski resort** estación de esquí.

skid [skɪd] *n* patinazo, derrape.

▶ *vi* (*pt & pp* **skidded**, *ger* **skidding**) patinar, derrapar.

skier ['skɪə'] *n* esquiador,-ra.

skiing ['skɪŋ] *n* esquí.

skilful ['skɪlfʊl] *adj* diestro,-a, hábil.

skilfully ['skɪlfʊlɪ] *adv* hábilmente, con destreza.

skill [skɪl] *n* **1** habilidad, destreza. **2** técnica, arte.

skilled [skɪld] *adj* **1** cualificado,-a, especializado,-a. **2** hábil, experto,-a.

skim [skɪm] *vt* (*pt & pp* **skimmed**, *ger* **skimming**). **1** desnatar, descremar *(leche)*. **2** rozar.

skin [skɪn] *n* **1** piel, cutis, tez. **2** pellejo *(de animal)*. **3** monda, mondadura *(de naranja)*. **4** capa *(de pintura)*. **5** nata.

▶ *vt* (*pt & pp* **skinned**, *ger* **skinning**). **1** desollar, despellejar *(animal)*. **2** pelar *(fruta)*. **3** hacer un rasguño en *(rodilla)*.

● **to get under one's skin** irritarle a uno.

● **to save one's skin** *fam* salvar el pellejo.

skin-diving ['skɪndaɪvɪŋ] *n* buceo, submarinismo.

skinhead ['skɪnhed] *n* cabeza rapada.

skinny ['skɪnɪ] *adj* (**-ier**, **-iest**) *fam* flaco,-a.

skip¹ [skɪp] *n* salto, brinco.

▶ *vi* (*pt & pp* **skipped**, *ger* **skipping**) saltar, dar brincos.

▶ *vt* *fig* saltarse.

■ **skipping rope** comba.

skip² [skɪp] *n* contenedor, container.

skipper ['skɪpə'] *n* capitán *(de barco)*.

skirmish ['skɜːmɪʃ] *n* (*pl* **-es**) escaramuza, refriega, pelea.

skirt [skɜːt] *n* falda.

▶ *vt* **1** bordear, rodear. **2** evitar, eludir.

■ **skirting board** GB zócalo, rodapié.

skittle ['skɪtəl] *n* bolo.

▶ *npl* **skittles** bolos, boliche.

skull [skʌl] *n* cráneo, calavera.

sky [skaɪ] *n* (*pl* **-ies**) cielo.

sky-diving ['skaɪdaɪvɪŋ] *n* paracaidismo.

skylight ['skaɪlaɪt] *n* tragaluz, claraboya.

skyscraper ['skaɪskreɪpə'] *n* rascacielos.

slab [slæb] *n* **1** losa *(de piedra)*. **2** trozo *(de pastel)*. **3** tableta *(de chocolate)*.

slack [slæk] *adj* **1** flojo,-a, poco apretado,-a. **2** descuidado,-a *(persona)*. **3** flojo,-a *(actividad)*. **4** bajo,-a *(temporada)*.

▶ *n* parte floja.

▶ *vi* *pej* gandulear.

slacken ['slækən] *vt* aflojar.

▶ *vi* **1** aflojarse. **2** reducirse, disminuir.

slag [slæg] *n* **1** escoria. **2** GB *sl* fulana.

slain [sleɪn] *pp* → slay.

slam [slæm] *n* **1** golpe *(ruido)*. **2** portazo.

▶ *vt* (*pt & pp* **slammed**, *ger* **slamming**). **1** cerrar de golpe. **2** *fig* criticar duramente.

▶ *vi* cerrarse de golpe.

● **to slam on the brakes** AUTO dar un frenazo.

● **to slam the door** dar un portazo.

slander ['slɑːndə'] *n* difamación, calumnia.

▶ *vt* difamar, calumniar.

slang [slæŋ] *n* argot, jerga.

slant [slɑːnt] *n* **1** inclinación, pendiente. **2** punto de vista.

▶ *vt* **1** inclinar, ladear. **2** *pej* enfocar subjetivamente.

▶ *vi* inclinarse, ladearse.

slap [slæp] *n* **1** palmadita *(en la espalda)*. **2** cachete, bofetada.

► *adv fam* justo, de lleno: *slap in the middle*, justo en el medio.
► *vt* (*pt & pp* **slapped**, *ger* **slapping**). **1** pegar *(con la mano)*. **2** abofetear, dar una bofetada a *(en la cara)*. **3** dar una palmada *(en la espalda)*.

slash [slæʃ] *n* (*pl* **-es**). **1** tajo *(con espada)*. **2** cuchillada, navajazo. **3** barra oblicua. **4** *sl* meada.
► *vt* **1** dar un tajo a *(con espada)*. **2** acuchillar, cortar. **3** *fig* rebajar, reducir.
● **to have a slash** *vulg* mear.

slate[1] [sleɪt] *n* pizarra.

slate[2] [sleɪt] *vt* GB criticar duramente.

slaughter ['slɔːtə^r] *n* **1** matanza *(de animales)*. **2** carnicería *(de personas)*.
► *vt* **1** matar *(animales)*. **2** masacrar *(personas)*. **3** *fam* dar una paliza a.

slaughterhouse ['slɔːtəhaʊs] *n* matadero.

Slav [slɑːv] *n* eslavo,-a.

slave [sleɪv] *n* esclavo,-a.
■ **slave trade** trata de esclavos.

slavery ['sleɪvərɪ] *n* esclavitud.

slay [sleɪ] *vt* (*pt* **slew**, *pp* **slain**) matar, asesinar.

sledge [sledʒ] *n* trineo.

sleek [sliːk] *adj* **1** liso,-a, lustroso,-a *(pelo)*. **2** impecable, elegante *(aspecto)*.

sleep [sliːp] *n* **1** sueño. **2** legañas.
► *vt-vi* (*pt & pp* **slept**) dormir.
► *vi fam* entumecerse.
► *vt* tener camas para.
● **to go to sleep** irse a dormir.
● **to sleep on STH** consultar algo con la almohada.
● **to sleep it off** *fam* dormir la mona.
● **to sleep like a log/top** dormir como un tronco.
● **to sleep with** acostarse con.

to sleep in *vi* quedarse en la cama, dormir hasta tarde.

to sleep through *vt* no oír, no despertarse con.

sleeping ['sliːpɪŋ] *adj* durmiente, dormido,-a.
■ **sleeping bag** saco de dormir.
■ **sleeping car** coche-cama.
■ **sleeping pill** somnífero, pastilla para dormir.

sleepwalker ['sliːpwɔːkə^r] *n* sonámbulo,-a.

sleepy ['sliːpɪ] *adj* (**-ier**, **-iest**) soñoliento,-a.

● **to be sleepy** tener sueño.
● **to make sleepy** dar sueño.

sleet [sliːt] *n* aguanieve.
► *vi* caer aguanieve.

sleeve [sliːv] *n* **1** manga *(de prenda de vestir)*. **2** funda *(de disco)*.
● **to have STH up one's sleeve** guardarse un as en la manga.

sleigh [sleɪ] *n* trineo.

slender ['slendə^r] *adj* **1** delgado,-a, esbelto,-a. **2** escaso,-a.

slept [slept] *pt-pp* → sleep.

slew [sluː] *pt* → slay.

slice [slaɪs] *n* **1** rebanada *(de pan)*. **2** loncha *(de jamón)*. **3** tajada *(de carne)*. **4** rodaja *(de limón)*. **5** porción, trozo *(de pastel)*. **6** *fig* parte. **7** pala, paleta *(herramienta)*.
► *vt* cortar a rebanadas/lonchas *etc.*
► *vi* dar efecto a la pelota.

to slice off/through *vt* cortar.

slick [slɪk] *adj* **1** hábil. **2** *pej* despabilado,-a.
► *n* marea negra.

slide [slaɪd] *n* **1** deslizamiento, desliz, resbalón. **2** tobogán. **3** *fig* bajada, caída *(de precios)*. **4** diapositiva. **5** portaobjetos *(de microscopio)*.
► *vi* (*pt & pp* **slid** [slɪd]). **1** deslizarse. **2** resbalar.
► *vt* deslizar.
● **to let STH slide** no ocuparse de algo.
■ **slide projector** proyector de diapositivas.
■ **slide rule** regla de cálculo.
■ **sliding door** puerta corredera.

slight [slaɪt] *adj* **1** ligero,-a, leve. **2** delicado,-a *(persona)*.
► *n* desaire.
► *vt* despreciar.

slightly ['slaɪtlɪ] *adv* ligeramente, un poco.

slim [slɪm] *adj* (*comp* **slimmer**, *superl* **slimmest**). **1** delgado,-a, esbelto,-a. **2** *fig* remoto,-a *(posibilidad)*.
► *vi* (*pt & pp* **slimmed**, *ger* **slimming**) adelgazar.

slime [slaɪm] *n* **1** lodo, cieno. **2** baba *(de caracol)*.

sling [slɪŋ] *n* **1** cabestrillo. **2** honda.
► *vt* (*pt & pp* **slung**). **1** tirar, arrojar. **2** colgar.

slink [slɪŋk] *vi* (*pt & pp* **slunk**) desplazarse sigilosamente.

to slink away o **off** *vi* escabullirse.

slip[1] [slɪp] *n* **1** resbalón, traspié. **2** *fig* error, desliz. **3** combinación *(prenda femenina)*.

▶ *vi* (*pt & pp* **slipped**, *ger* **slipping**). **1** resbalar. **2** escabullirse, escurrirse.

▶ *vt* **1** pasar, meter, deslizar: *he slipped the key into the lock*, metió la llave en la cerradura. **2** dar a escondidas.

● **to give SB the slip** dar esquinazo a ALGN.

● **to let a chance slip** dejar escapar una oportunidad.

● **to slip one's memory/mind** írsele a uno de la memoria.

■ **slip of the pen/tongue** lapsus.

slip[2] [slɪp] *n* **1** papel, papelito. **2** ficha.

to slip away/by *vi* pasar volando.

to slip into/on *vt* ponerse rápidamente.

to slip off *vt* quitarse.

to slip out *vi* **1** escabullirse. **2** escaparse: *I'm sorry, it just slipped out*, lo siento, se me escapó.

to slip up *vi* cometer un desliz, equivocarse.

slipper ['slɪpəʳ] *n* zapatilla.

slippery ['slɪpəri] *adj* **1** resbaladizo,-a *(suelo)*. **2** escurridizo,-a *(persona)*.

slit [slɪt] *n* abertura, hendedura, corte.

▶ *vt* (*pt & pp* **slit**, *ger* **slitting**) cortar, rajar, hender.

sliver ['slɪvəʳ] *n* astilla.

slob [slɒb] *n* *fam* dejado,-a.

slog [slɒg] *n* GB *fam* paliza.

▶ *vi* (*pt & pp* **slogged**, *ger* **slogging**) GB *fam* currar.

slogan ['sləʊgən] *n* eslogan, lema.

slop [slɒp] *vt* (*pt & pp* **slopped**, *ger* **slopping**) derramar.

▶ *vi* derramarse, verterse.

slope [sləʊp] *n* cuesta, pendiente *(de montaña)*.

▶ *vi* inclinarse.

● **to be on a slippery slope** ir cuesta abajo.

sloppy ['slɒpi] *adj* (**-ier**, **-iest**). **1** descuidado,-a *(persona)*. **2** chapucero,-a *(trabajo)*.

sloshed [slɒʃt] *adj fam* borracho,-a.

● **to get sloshed** pillar una trompa.

slot [slɒt] *n* **1** abertura. **2** ranura *(para monedas)*. **3** muesca.

▶ *vt* (*pt & pp* **slotted**, *ger* **slotting**) meter, introducir.

■ **slot machine** máquina expendedora, tragaperras.

slouch [slaʊtʃ] *vi* andar con los hombros caídos, sentarse con los hombros caídos.

slow [sləʊ] *adj* **1** lento,-a, atrasado,-a *(reloj)*. **2** flojo,-a *(negocio)*. **3** lento,-a, torpe *(persona)*.

▶ *adv* despacio, lentamente.

● **in slow motion** a cámara lenta.

to slow down *vi* ir más despacio, reducir la velocidad.

slug [slʌg] *n* babosa.

sluggish ['slʌgɪʃ] *adj* **1** lento,-a. **2** COMM inactivo,-a.

slum [slʌm] *n* **1** barrio bajo. **2** chabola, tugurio.

slump [slʌmp] *n* crisis económica, bajón.

▶ *vi* **1** hundirse *(economía)*. **2** desplomarse *(precios)*. **3** caer en picado *(demanda)*. **4** caer: *she slumped to the floor*, se desmayó y se cayó al suelo.

slung [slʌŋ] *pt-pp* → sling.

slunk [slʌŋk] *pt-pp* → slink.

slur [slɜːʳ] *n* calumnia, difamación.

▶ *vt* (*pt & pp* **slurred**, *ger* **slurring**) comerse, pronunciar mal.

slush [slʌʃ] *n* **1** nieve medio derretida. **2** *fam* sentimentalismo.

slut [slʌt] *n pej* fulana, ramera.

sly [slaɪ] *adj* (**-ier**, **-iest**). **1** astuto,-a, taimado,-a. **2** furtivo,-a *(mirada)*.

● **on the sly** a escondidas, a hurtadillas.

smack[1] [smæk] *n* bofetada, cachete.

▶ *vt* dar una bofetada a, abofetear, golpear.

● **to smack one's lips** relamerse.

smack[2] [smæk] *n sl* caballo *(heroína)*.

to smack of *vt fig* oler a.

small [smɔːl] *adj* **1** pequeño,-a, chico,-a. **2** insignificante *(asunto)*.

● **a small table** una mesita.

● **small wonder that ...** no me extraña que ....

● **in the small hours** a altas horas de la noche.

■ **small ads** anuncios por palabras.

■ **small change** cambio, suelto.

■ **small fry** gente de poca monta.

■ **small letter** minúscula.

small-minded [smɔːl'maɪndɪd] *adj* de miras estrechas.

smallpox ['smɔːlpɒks] *n* viruela.
smart [smɑːt] *adj* **1** elegante, fino,-a. **2** US listo,-a, inteligente. **3** rápido,-a.
▸ *vi* picar, escocer.
■ **the smart set** la gente bien.
smash [smæʃ] *n (pl* **-es**). **1** estrépito. **2** choque violento. **3** smash, mate *(en tenis)*.
▸ *vt* **1** romper, hacer pedazos. **2** aplastar. **3** pegar, golpear.
▸ *vi* romperse, hacerse pedazos.
■ **smash hit** gran éxito, exitazo.
to smash into *vt-vi* chocar, estrellar(se): *the car smashed into a wall*, el coche se estrelló contra un muro.
smashing ['smæʃɪŋ] *adj* GB *fam* estupendo,-a, fenomenal.
smattering ['smætərɪŋ] *n* nociones: *he has a smattering of French*, tiene nociones de francés.
smear [smɪəʳ] *n* **1** mancha. **2** calumnia, difamación.
▸ *vt* **1** untar. **2** manchar. **3** calumniar, difamar.
smell [smel] *n* **1** olfato. **2** olor.
▸ *vt (pt & pp* **smelled** o **smelt** [smelt]). **1** oler. **2** *fig* olfatear.
▸ *vi* oler: *it smells good*, huele bien; *it smells of lemon*, huele a limón.
smelly ['smelɪ] *adj* (**-ier**, **-iest**) apestoso, -a, pestilente: *it's smelly*, huele mal.
smelt[1] [smelt] *vt* fundir.
smelt[2] [smelt] *pt-pp* → smell.
smile [smaɪl] *n* sonrisa.
▸ *vi* sonreír.
smirk [smɜːk] *n* sonrisa de satisfacción.
▸ *vi* sonreír satisfecho,-a.
smock [smɒk] *n* bata.
smog [smɒg] *n* niebla tóxica, smog.
smoke [sməʊk] *n* humo.
▸ *vt-vi* fumar.
▸ *vt* ahumar.
▸ *vi* echar humo.
● **"No smoking"** "Prohibido fumar".
● **to have a smoke** *fam* fumarse un cigarrillo.
■ **smoke screen** cortina de humo.
smoked [sməʊkt] *adj* ahumado,-a.
smoker ['sməʊkəʳ] *n* fumador,-ra.
smoky ['sməʊkɪ] *adj* (**-ier**, **-iest**). **1** humeante *(fuego)*. **2** lleno,-a de humo *(habitación)*. **3** ahumado,-a *(color, color)*.
smooth [smuːð] *adj* **1** liso,-a. **2** llano,-a

(carretera). **3** sin grumos *(líquido)*. **4** suave *(vino)*. **5** *fig* agradable, tranquilo,-a. **6** *pej* zalamero,-a, meloso,-a *(persona)*.
▸ *vt* alisar.
● **to smooth the path** allanar el camino.
● **to smooth things over** limar asperezas.
to smooth back/down/out *vt* alisar.
smoothly ['smuːðlɪ] *adv* **1** suavemente. **2** sin complicaciones.
smother ['smʌðəʳ] *vt* **1** asfixiar. **2** cubrir.
▸ *vi* asfixiarse.
smoulder ['sməʊldəʳ] *vi* **1** arder sin llama. **2** arder.
smudge [smʌdʒ] *n* borrón.
▸ *vt* ensuciar, emborronar.
▸ *vi* emborronarse.
smug [smʌg] *adj* (*comp* **smugger**, *superl* **smuggest**) engreído,-a, satisfecho,-a.
smuggle ['smʌgəl] *vt* pasar de contrabando.
smuggler ['smʌgləʳ] *n* contrabandista.
snack [snæk] *n* bocado, tentempié, merienda.
● **to have a snack** picar algo, comer algo ligero.
■ **snack bar** cafetería, bar.
snag [snæg] *n fig* pega, problema.
snail [sneɪl] *n* caracol.
snake [sneɪk] *n* serpiente, culebra.
▸ *vi fig* serpentear.
snap [snæp] *n* **1** ruido seco, chasquido *(con dedos)*. **2** foto, instantánea.
▸ *adj* instantáneo,-a, rápido,-a *(decisión)*.
▸ *vt (pt & pp* **snapped**, *ger* **snapping**). **1** partir *(en dos)*. **2** chasquear *(los dedos)*. **3** decir bruscamente.
▸ *vi* **1** partirse *(en dos)*. **2** perder los nervios. **3** hablar bruscamente.
● **to snap shut** cerrarse de golpe.
● **to snap out of it** *fam* animarse.
to snap up *vt* no dejar escapar.
snapshot ['snæpʃɒt] *n* foto instantánea.
snarl [snɑːl] *n* gruñido.
▸ *vi* gruñir.
snatch [snætʃ] *n (pl* **-es**). **1** *fam* robo, hurto. **2** trozo, fragmento.
▸ *vt* **1** coger, agarrar, asir. **2** *fam* robar, secuestrar.
● **to snatch an opportunity** aprovechar una ocasión.
● **to snatch some sleep** sacar tiempo para dormir.

sneak [sniːk] *n fam* chivato,-a, soplón, -ona.
► *vt fam* chivarse.
to sneak away/off *vi* escabullirse.
to sneak in *vi* entrar a hurtadillas.
to sneak out *vi* salir a hurtadillas.
to sneak up *vt* acercarse sigilosamente.
sneakers ['sniːkrz] *npl* US zapatillas de deporte.
sneer [snɪə'] *n* **1** mueca de desprecio. **2** comentario desdeñoso.
► *vi* burlarse.
sneeze [sniːz] *n* estornudo.
► *vi* estornudar.
sniff [snɪf] *n* **1** inhalación, olfateo. **2** husmeo *(de perro)*.
► *vt-vi* oler, olfatear, husmear.
► *vi* sorberse los mocos.
snip [snɪp] *vt* (*pt & pp* **snipped**, *ger* **snipping**) cortar.
to snip off *vt* cortar con tijeras.
sniper ['snaɪpə'] *n* francotirador,-ra.
snob [snɒb] *n* esnob, snob.
snobbish ['snɒbɪʃ] *adj* esnob, snob.
snooker ['snuːkə'] *n* snooker.
snooze [snuːz] *n fam* cabezada.
► *vi* dormitar.
● **to have a snooze** *fam* echar una cabezada.
snore [snɔː'] *n* ronquido.
► *vi* roncar.
snorkel ['snɔːkəl] *n* tubo de bucear.
snort [snɔːt] *vi* resoplar.
snout [snaʊt] *n* hocico.
snow [snəʊ] *n* nieve.
► *vi* nevar.
● **to be snowed in/up** quedar aislado, -a por la nieve.
● **to be snowed under with work** estar agobiado,-a de trabajo.
snowball ['snəʊbɔːl] *n* bola de nieve.
snowfall ['snəʊfɔːl] *n* nevada.
snowflake ['snəʊfleɪk] *n* copo de nieve.
snowman ['snəʊmæn] *n* (*pl* **snowmen**) muñeco de nieve.
Snr ['siːnɪə'] *abbr* (**senior**) padre.
snub [snʌb] *n* desaire.
► *vt* (*pt & pp* **snubbed**, *ger* **snubbing**) desairar, rechazar.
snuff [snʌf] *n* rapé.
snuff out ['snʌfaʊt] *vt* sofocar, apagar.
snug [snʌg] *adj* (*comp* **snugger**, *superl*

snuggest). **1** cómodo,-a, acogedor,-a, calentito,-a. **2** ajustado,-a, ceñido,-a.
so [səʊ] *adv* **1** tan, tanto,-a: *she's so tired that...*, está tan cansada que...; *you're so right that...*, tienes tanta razón que.... **2** mucho: *I miss you so*, te echo mucho de menos. **3** así: *It's Mary – So it is!*, Es María, – ¡Así es! **4** que sí, que no: *I guess so*, supongo que sí; *I don't think so*, creo que no. **5** también: *I went to the demonstration and so did David*, fui a la manifestación y David también.
► *conj* **1** así que, por lo tanto. **2** para: *they went early so as to get good seats*, fueron pronto para conseguir buenos asientos.
● **and so on** y así sucesivamente.
● **an hour or so** una hora más o menos.
● **if so** en ese caso.
● **not so... as...** no tan... como....
● **or so** más o menos: *the journey takes an hour or so*, el viaje dura más o menos una hora.
● **so far** hasta ahora.
● **so long!** ¡hasta luego!
● **so many** tantos,-as.
● **so much** tanto,-a.
● **so (that) ...** para (que) ....
● **so what?** *fam* ¿y qué?
soak [səʊk] *vt* **1** poner en remojo, remojar. **2** empapar.
► *vi* estar en remojo.
● **soaked to the skin** calado,-a hasta los huesos.
● **to get soaked** empaparse.
to soak through *vi* penetrar, calar.
to soak up *vt* absorber.
soap [səʊp] *n* jabón.
► *vt* enjabonar, jabonar.
■ **soap opera** telenovela, culebrón, radionovela.
■ **soap powder** detergente en polvo.
soapy ['səʊpɪ] *adj* (**-ier, -iest**) jabonoso,-a.
soar [sɔː'] *vi* **1** remontar el vuelo *(pájaro, avión)*. **2** *fig* crecer, aumentar *(precios)*.
sob [sɒb] *n* sollozo.
► *vi* (*pt & pp* **sobbed**, *ger* **sobbing**) sollozar.
sober ['səʊbə'] *adj* **1** sobrio,-a. **2** sensato,-a, serio,-a. **3** discreto,-a *(color)*.
to sober up *vi* pasársele a uno la borrachera.
so-called ['səʊkɔːld] *adj* supuesto,-a, llamado,-a.

soccer ['sɒkəʳ] n fútbol.
sociable ['səʊʃəbəl] adj sociable.
social ['səʊʃəl] adj 1 social. 2 sociable.
■ social climber arribista.
■ social event acto social.
■ social science ciencias sociales.
■ social security seguridad social.
■ social worker asistente,-a social.
■ Social Democrat socialdemócrata.
socialism ['səʊʃəlɪzəm] n socialismo.
socialist ['səʊʃəlɪst] adj-n socialista.
socialize ['səʊʃəlaɪz] vi relacionarse, alternar.
society [sə'saɪətɪ] n (pl -ies). 1 sociedad. 2 compañía. 3 asociación, sociedad.
■ society column ecos de sociedad.
sociology [səʊsɪ'ɒlədʒɪ] n sociología.
sock [sɒk] n calcetín.
socket ['sɒkɪt] n 1 cuenca (del ojo). 2 enchufe, toma de corriente.
sod¹ [sɒd] n terrón, tepe.
sod² [sɒd] n 1 fam cabrón,-ona. 2 fam desgraciado,-a.
● sod it! fam ¡maldito,-a sea!
soda ['səʊdə] n 1 soda. 2 US gaseosa.
■ soda water soda, sifón.
sofa ['səʊfə] n sofá.
■ sofa bed sofá cama.
soft [sɒft] adj 1 blando,-a (cojín). 2 suave (música). 3 débil.
■ soft drink refresco.
soften ['sɒfən] vt-vi 1 ablandar(se). 2 suavizar(se).
softly ['sɒftlɪ] adv suavemente.
software ['sɒftweəʳ] n software.
■ software package paquete de software.
soggy ['sɒgɪ] adj (-ier, -iest) empapado, -a.
soil [sɔɪl] n tierra.
► vt ensuciar, manchar.
solar ['səʊləʳ] adj solar.
sold [səʊld] pt-pp → sell.
solder ['sɒldəʳ] n soldadura.
► vt soldar.
soldier ['səʊldʒəʳ] n soldado.
sole¹ [səʊl] n 1 planta (del pie). 2 suela (de zapato).
sole² [səʊl] n lenguado (pez).
sole³ [səʊl] adj único,-a.
solely ['səʊllɪ] adv solamente, únicamente.

solemn ['sɒləm] adj solemne.
solicitor [sə'lɪsɪtəʳ] n 1 abogado,-a, procurador,-ra. 2 notario,-a.
solid ['sɒlɪd] adj 1 sólido,-a (alimentos). 2 macizo,-a (oro). 3 fuerte, macizo,-a. 4 entero,-a: we waited for two solid hours, esperamos dos horas enteras. 5 puro,-a (metal).
► n sólido.
solidarity [sɒlɪ'dærɪtɪ] n solidaridad.
solidify [sə'lɪdɪfaɪ] vt-vi (pt & pp -ied) solidificar(se).
solidity [sə'lɪdɪtɪ] n solidez.
solitary ['sɒlɪtərɪ] adj 1 solitario,-a. 2 solo,-a.
solitude ['sɒlɪtjuːd] n soledad.
solo ['səʊləʊ] n (pl solos) solo.
► adj en solitario.
► adv solo,-a, a solas.
solution [sə'luːʃən] n solución.
solve [sɒlv] vt resolver, solucionar.
sombre ['sɒmbəʳ] (US somber) adj 1 sombrío,-a (color). 2 lúgubre, umbrío,-a (lugar).
some [sʌm] adj 1 unos,-as, algunos,-as (con sust pl): there were some flowers in a vase, había unas flores en un jarrón. 2 un poco (de) (con sust sing): would you like some coffee?, ¿quieres un poco de café? 3 cierto,-a, alguno,-a: some cars are better than others, algunos coches son mejores que otros. 4 algún,-una: some day, algún día. 5 bastante: it cost him some money, le costó bastante dinero.
► pron 1 algunos,-as, unos,-as: some danced and others sang, algunos bailaron y otros cantaron. 2 algo, un poco: can I have some?, ¿puedo coger un poco?
● in some ways en cierto modo, en cierta manera.
● some ... or other algún,-una ... que otro,-a.
● some other time en otro momento.
somebody ['sʌmbədɪ] pron alguien.
● somebody else otro,-a, otra persona.
somehow ['sʌmhaʊ] adv 1 de algún modo. 2 por alguna razón.
someone ['sʌmwʌn] pron → somebody.
somersault ['sʌməsɔːlt] n 1 salto mortal, voltereta. 2 vuelta de campana (de coche).

something ['sʌmθɪŋ] *n* algo.
● **something else** otra cosa.
sometime ['sʌmtaɪm] *adv* un día, algún día.
▶ *adj* antiguo,-a, ex-.
● **sometime or other** un día de éstos.
sometimes ['sʌmtaɪmz] *adv* a veces, de vez en cuando.
somewhat ['sʌmwɒt] *adv* algo, un tanto.
somewhere ['sʌmweəʳ] *adv* en alguna parte, a alguna parte.
▶ *pron* un lugar, un sitio.
● **somewhere else** en otra parte.
son [sʌn] *n* hijo.
song [sɒŋ] *n* 1 canción. 2 canto.
● **to burst into song** ponerse a cantar.
son-in-law ['sʌnɪnlɔː] *n* (*pl* **sons-in-law**) yerno.
soon [suːn] *adv* 1 pronto, dentro de poco. 2 pronto, temprano.
● **as soon as** en cuanto.
● **as soon as possible** cuanto antes.
● **I would as soon ...** preferiría ....
● **soon afterwards** poco después.
sooner ['suːnəʳ] *adv* más temprano.
● **I would sooner** preferiría.
● **no sooner ...** nada más ...: *no sooner did he call than ...*, acababa de llamar cuando ....
● **sooner or later** tarde o temprano.
● **the sooner the better** cuanto antes mejor.
soot [sʊt] *n* hollín.
soothe [suːð] *vt* 1 calmar *(nervios)*. 2 aliviar *(dolor)*.
sophisticated [səˈfɪstɪkeɪtɪd] *adj* sofisticado,-a.
soprano [səˈprɑːnəʊ] *n* (*pl* **sopranos**) soprano.
sorcerer ['sɔːsərəʳ] *n* hechicero, brujo.
sordid ['sɔːdɪd] *adj* sórdido,-a.
sore [sɔːʳ] *adj* 1 dolorido,-a, inflamado,-a. 2 *fam* enfadado,-a.
▶ *n* llaga, úlcera.
● **to have a sore throat** tener dolor de garganta.
■ **sore point** asunto delicado.
sorely ['sɔːlɪ] *adv* profundamente, muy.
sorrow ['sɒrəʊ] *n* pena, pesar, dolor.
sorry ['sɒrɪ] *adj* (**-ier**, **-iest**) triste, lamentable.
▶ *interj* ¡perdón!, ¡disculpe!
● **to be sorry** sentirlo: *I'm sorry*, lo sien-

to; *I'm sorry about your father*, siento lo de tu padre; *I'm sorry I'm late*, siento haber llegado tarde; *he's sorry for all the trouble he caused*, está arrepentido de todos los problemas que ha causado.
● **to feel sorry for SB** compadecer a ALGN.
● **to say sorry** disculparse.
sort [sɔːt] *n* 1 clase, tipo. 2 *fam* tipo.
▶ *vt* clasificar.
● **a sort of** una especie de.
● **all sorts of** todo tipo de.
● **of sorts** de alguna clase.
● **out of sorts** pachucho,-a, de mal humor.
● **sort of** un poco, más o menos.
● **to be sort of ...** *fam* estar como ....
to sort out *vt* 1 clasificar, ordenar. 2 arreglar, solucionar *(problema)*.
so-so ['səʊsəʊ] *adv fam* así así, regular.
sought [sɔːt] *pt-pp* → seek.
soul [səʊl] *n* alma.
● **not a soul** ni un alma.
sound[1] [saʊnd] *n* 1 sonido. 2 ruido, volumen.
▶ *vt* tocar, hacer sonar.
▶ *vi* 1 sonar: *it sounds like Mozart*, suena a Mozart. 2 sonar *(sirena)*. 3 *fig* parecer: *she sounded angry*, parecía enojada.
■ **sound barrier** barrera del sonido.
■ **sound wave** onda sonora.
sound[2] [saʊnd] *n* estrecho, brazo *(de agua)*.
sound[3] [saʊnd] *adj* 1 sano,-a: *safe and sound*, sano y salvo. 2 en buen estado. 3 razonable. 4 fuerte, robusto,-a. 5 profundo,-a.
● **to be sound asleep** estar profundamente dormido,-a.
soundproof ['saʊndpruːf] *adj* insonorizado,-a.
▶ *vt* insonorizar.
soundtrack ['saʊndtræk] *n* banda sonora.
soup [suːp] *n* 1 sopa. 2 caldo, consomé.
■ **soup plate** plato hondo, plato sopero.
■ **soup spoon** cuchara sopera.
sour ['saʊəʳ] *adj* 1 ácido,-a, agrio,-a *(fruta)*. 2 cortado,-a, agrio,-a *(leche)*. 3 *fig* amargado,-a *(persona)*.
source [sɔːs] *n* 1 fuente *(de información)*. 2 fuente, origen, causa *(de problema)*.

south [saʊθ] *n* sur.
► *adj* del sur.
► *adv* hacia el sur, al sur.
southeast [saʊθ'iːst] *n* sudeste.
► *adj* del sudeste.
► *adv* hacia el sudeste, al sudeste.
southern ['sʌðən] *adj* del sur, meridional.
southwest [saʊθ'west] *n* sudoeste.
► *adj* del sudoeste.
► *adv* hacia el sudoeste, al sudoeste.
souvenir [suːvə'nɪə'] *n* recuerdo.
sovereign ['sɒvrɪn] *adj-n* soberano,-a.
sow¹ [saʊ] *n* cerda, puerca.
sow² [səʊ] *vt* (*pt* sowed [səʊd], *pp* sown [səʊn]) sembrar.
space [speɪs] *n* 1 espacio: *the first man in space*, el primer hombre en el espacio. 2 sitio, lugar. 3 espacio *(tiempo)*.
► *vt* espaciar.
■ **space age** era espacial.
■ **space shuttle** transbordador espacial.
spacecraft ['speɪskrɑːft] *n* nave espacial.
spaceship ['speɪsʃɪp] *n* nave espacial.
spacious ['speɪʃəs] *adj* espacioso,-a, amplio,-a.
spade¹ [speɪd] *n* pala *(de cavar)*.
spade² [speɪd] *n* 1 pica *(naipes)*. 2 espada *(baraja española)*.
Spain [speɪn] *n* España.
span [spæn] *n* 1 lapso, espacio *(de tiempo)*. 2 envergadura *(de alas)*. 3 luz. 4 ojo *(de arco)*.
► *vt* (*pt & pp* spanned, *ger* spanning). 1 atravesar *(puente)*. 2 abarcar *(vida)*.
Spaniard ['spænjəd] *n* español,-la.
Spanish ['spænɪʃ] *adj* español,-la.
► *n* 1 español,-la *(persona)*. 2 español, castellano *(lengua)*.
► *npl* the Spanish los españoles.
spank [spæŋk] *vt* zurrar, pegar.
spanner ['spænə'] *n* llave de tuerca.
spare [speə'] *adj* 1 de sobra, de más, libre: *there's a spare seat*, hay un asiento libre. 2 de recambio, de repuesto: *a spare wheel*, una rueda de repuesto.
► *n* recambio, pieza de recambio.
► *vt* 1 prescindir de, pasar sin. 2 escatimar: *they spared no effort*, no escatimaron esfuerzos. 3 ahorrar: *you can spare the details*, puedes ahorrarte los detalles. 4 perdonar *(vida)*.
● **can you spare five minutes?** ¿tienes cinco minutos?

● **...to spare** ... de sobra: *we have lots of time to spare*, tenemos tiempo de sobra.
■ **spare room** habitación de invitados.
■ **spare time** tiempo libre.
sparing ['speərɪŋ] *adj* frugal.
sparingly ['speərɪŋlɪ] *adv* en poca cantidad, con moderación.
spark [spɑːk] *n* chispa.
► *vi* echar chispas.
► *vt* provocar.
■ **spark plug** bujía.
to spark off *vt* provocar.
sparkle ['spɑːkəl] *n* 1 centelleo, brillo *(de ojos)*. 2 viveza *(de persona)*.
► *vi* 1 centellear, destellar *(ojos)*. 2 brillar *(persona)*.
sparrow ['spærəʊ] *n* gorrión.
sparse [spɑːs] *adj* escaso,-a.
spasm ['spæzəm] *n* 1 espasmo. 2 acceso *(de tos, ira)*.
spat [spæt] *pt-pp* → spit.
spate [speɪt] *n* 1 avalancha *(de cartas)*. 2 racha, serie *(de accidentes)*.
spatter ['spætə'] *vt* salpicar, rociar.
speak [spiːk] *vi* (*pt* spoke [spəʊk], *pp* spoken ['spəʊkən]). 1 hablar. 2 pronunciar un discurso.
► *vt* 1 decir: *he spoke the truth*, dijo la verdad. 2 hablar *(idioma)*.
● **generally speaking** en términos generales.
● **so to speak** por así decirlo.
● **speaking of ...** hablando de ....
● **to be nothing to speak of** no ser nada especial.
● **to speak one's mind** hablar claro, hablar sin rodeos.
to speak out *vi* hablar claro.
to speak up *vi* hablar más fuerte.
to speak up for *vi* salir en defensa de.
speaker ['spiːkə'] *n* 1 persona que habla, el/la que habla. 2 interlocutor,-ra *(en diálogo)*. 3 conferenciante, orador,-ra. 4 hablante *(de idioma)*. 5 altavoz.
spear [spɪə'] *n* 1 lanza. 2 arpón.
special ['speʃəl] *adj* 1 especial. 2 particular, en particular *(interés)*. 3 extraordinario,-a *(edición)*.
► *n* 1 tren especial. 2 programa especial.
■ **special delivery** correo urgente.
■ **special offer** oferta especial.
specialist ['speʃəlɪst] *n* especialista.

speciality [speʃɪˈælɪtɪ] *n* (*pl* -**ies**) especialidad.

specialize [ˈspeʃəlaɪz] *vi* especializarse.

specially [ˈspeʃəlɪ] *adv* especialmente.

species [ˈspiːʃiːz] *n* (*pl* -**ies**) especie.

specific [spəˈsɪfɪk] *adj* **1** específico,-a *(caso)*. **2** preciso,-a, exacto,-a *(número)*.
▶ *npl* **specifics** datos concretos.

specifically [spəˈsɪfɪklɪ] *adv* concretamente, en concreto.

specifications [spesɪfɪˈkeɪʃənz] *npl* datos específicos.

specify [ˈspesɪfaɪ] *vt* (*pt & pp* -**ied**) especificar, precisar.

specimen [ˈspesɪmən] *n* espécimen, muestra, ejemplar.

speck [spek] *n* **1** mota *(de polvo)*. **2** pizca. **3** punto. **4** manchita *(de suciedad)*.

spectacle [ˈspektəkəl] *n* espectáculo.
▶ *npl* **spectacles** gafas.

spectacular [spekˈtækjʊlə] *adj* espectacular.
▶ *n* superproducción.

spectator [spekˈteɪtə] *n* espectador,-ra.

spectre [ˈspektə] (US **specter**) *n* espectro, fantasma.

speculate [ˈspekjʊleɪt] *vi* especular.

speculation [spekjʊˈleɪʃən] *n* especulación.

sped [sped] *pt-pp* → speed.

speech [spiːtʃ] *n* (*pl* -**es**). **1** habla. **2** pronunciación. **3** discurso.
● **to lose the power of speech** perder el habla.
● **to make a speech** pronunciar un discurso.

speechless [ˈspiːtʃləs] *adj* mudo,-a, boquiabierto,-a.

speed [spiːd] *n* velocidad.
▶ *vi* (*pt & pp* **speeded** o **sped** [sped]). **1** ir corriendo, ir a toda prisa. **2** exceder el límite de velocidad permitido.
● **at speed** a gran velocidad.
● **at top speed** a gran velocidad.
● **speed limit** límite de velocidad.

to speed past *vi* pasar volando.

to speed up *vt-vi* **1** acelerar *(coche)*. **2** apresurar(se) *(persona)*.

speedometer [spɪˈdɒmɪtə] *n* velocímetro.

speedy [ˈspiːdɪ] *adj* (-**ier**, -**iest**) rápido,-a, veloz.

spell¹ [spel] *n* hechizo, encanto.

● **to put a spell on SB** hechizar a ALGN.

spell² [spel] *n* **1** período, temporada, racha. **2** tanda, turno.

spell³ [spel] *vt-vi* (*pt & pp* **spelt** [spelt]). **1** deletrear. **2** escribir correctamente.
▶ *vt fig* representar, significar, implicar.

spelling [ˈspelɪŋ] *n* ortografía.
■ **spelling mistake** falta de ortografía.

spelt [spelt] *pt-pp* → spell.

spend [spend] *vt* (*pt & pp* **spent** [spent]). **1** gastar *(dinero)*. **2** pasar: *we spent two days there*, pasamos allí dos días. **3** dedicar: *she spends a lot of time with her baby*, dedica mucho tiempo a su bebé.

spending [ˈspendɪŋ] *n* gasto.
■ **spending power** poder adquisitivo.

spent [spent] *pt-pp* → spend.

sperm [spɜːm] *n* esperma.

sphere [sfɪə] *n* esfera.

spice [spaɪs] *n* **1** especia. **2** *fig* sazón, sal.
▶ *vt* sazonar, condimentar.

spicy [ˈspaɪsɪ] *adj* (-**ier**, -**iest**). **1** sazonado,-a, picante. **2** *fig* picante *(historia)*.

spider [ˈspaɪdə] *n* araña.
■ **spider's web** telaraña.

spike [spaɪk] *n* **1** punta, púa. **2** pincho. **3** clavo *(en zapatos)*. **4** espiga. **5** estaca.

spiky [ˈspaɪkɪ] *adj* (-**ier**, -**iest**). **1** puntiagudo,-a. **2** *fam* de punta *(pelo)*.

spill [spɪl] *n* derrame.
▶ *vt-vi* (*pt & pp* **spilt** [spɪlt]) derramar(se), verter(se).
● **to spill the beans** *fam* descubrir el pastel.

to spill over *vt* desbordarse.

spin [spɪn] *n* **1** vuelta, giro. **2** centrifugado *(de lavadora)*. **3** efecto *(de pelota)*. **4** *fam* garbeo.
▶ *vt* (*pt & pp* **spun** [spʌn], *ger* **spinning**). **1** hacer girar, dar vueltas *(a)*. **2** centrifugar.
▶ *vi* girar, dar vueltas *(a)*.
▶ *vt-vi* hilar.
● **to go for a spin** dar una vuelta *(en coche o moto)*.
● **to spin SB a yarn** *fam* soltarle un rollo a ALGN.

to spin out *vt* prolongar.

spinach [ˈspɪnɪdʒ] *n* espinacas.

spinal [ˈspaɪnəl] *adj* espinal, vertebral.
■ **spinal column** columna vertebral.
■ **spinal cord** médula espinal.

spin-dryer [spɪnˈdraɪə] *n* secadora.

spine [spaɪn] n **1** columna vertebral, espina dorsal. **2** lomo *(de libro)*. **3** púa *(de erizo)*.

spinning ['spɪnɪŋ] n hilado, hilandería.

■ **spinning top** peonza, trompo.

■ **spinning wheel** rueca, torno de hilar.

spinster ['spɪnstə'] n soltera.

● **to be an old spinster** ser una vieja solterona.

spiral ['spaɪərəl] adj espiral.

▶ n espiral.

▶ vi (GB pt & pp **spiralled**, ger **spiralling**; US pt & pp **spiraled**, ger **spiraling**) moverse en espiral.

■ **spiral staircase** escalera de caracol.

spire ['spaɪə'] n aguja, chapitel.

spirit[1] ['spɪrɪt] n alcohol.

▶ npl **spirits** licores.

■ **spirit level** nivel de burbuja.

spirit[2] ['spɪrɪt] n **1** espíritu, alma. **2** fantasma. **3** vigor, ánimo, carácter.

▶ npl **spirits** humor, moral.

● **to be in high spirits** estar animado,-a.

● **to be in low spirits** estar desanimado,-a.

■ **the Holy Spirit** el Espíritu Santo.

to spirit away/off vt llevarse como por arte de magia.

spiritual ['spɪrɪtjʊəl] adj espiritual.

▶ n espiritual negro.

spit[1] [spɪt] n asador, espetón.

spit[2] [spɪt] n saliva, esputo.

▶ vt-vi (pt & pp **spat** [spæt], ger **spitting**) escupir.

to spit out vt escupir.

spite [spaɪt] n rencor, ojeriza.

▶ vt fastidiar.

● **in spite of** a pesar de, pese a.

● **out of spite** por despecho.

spiteful ['spaɪtfʊl] adj rencoroso,-a, malévolo,-a.

spitefully ['spaɪtfʊlɪ] adv **1** con rencor. **2** por despecho.

splash [splæʃ] n (pl -**es**). **1** chapoteo. **2** salpicadura. **3** fig mancha *(de luz)*.

▶ vt salpicar, rociar.

▶ vi chapotear.

▶ interj ¡plaf!

● **to make a splash** causar sensación.

to splash out vi fam derrochar dinero.

splendid ['splendɪd] adj espléndido,-a, maravilloso,-a.

splendour ['splendə'] (US **splendor**) n esplendor.

splint [splɪnt] n tablilla.

splinter ['splɪntə'] n **1** astilla *(de madera)*. **2** esquirla *(de metal)*. **3** fragmento *(de vidrio)*.

▶ vt-vi astillar(se), hacer(se) astillas.

■ **splinter group** POL grupo disidente, facción.

split [splɪt] n **1** grieta, hendidura *(en madera)*. **2** desgarrón *(en tela)*. **3** división, ruptura. **4** escisión.

▶ adj **1** partido,-a, hendido,-a. **2** dividido,-a.

▶ vt-vi (pt & pp **split**, ger **splitting**). **1** agrietar(se). **2** partir(se), dividir(se). **3** rajar(se), rasgar(se).

▶ vi **1** escindirse. **2** sl largarse.

● **in a split second** en una fracción de segundo.

to split up vt partir, dividir.

▶ vi dispersarse, separarse *(pareja)*.

spoil [spɔɪl] vt (pt & pp **spoiled** o **spoilt** [spɔɪlt]). **1** estropear, echar a perder. **2** mimar, malcriar.

▶ vi estropearse, echarse a perder.

▶ npl **spoils** botín.

spoke[1] [spəʊk] pt → speak.

spoke[2] [spəʊk] n radio *(de rueda)*.

spoken ['spəʊkən] pp → speak.

spokesman ['spəʊksmən] n (pl **spokesmen**) portavoz.

sponge [spʌndʒ] n esponja.

▶ vt lavar/limpiar con una esponja.

▶ vi pej vivir de gorra, gorronear.

■ **sponge cake** bizcocho.

to sponge off vt pej vivir a costa de.

sponger ['spʌndʒə'] n pej gorrón,-ona, sablista.

sponsor ['spɒnsə'] n **1** patrocinador,-ra. **2** padrino, madrina.

▶ vt **1** patrocinar. **2** apadrinar.

spontaneous [spɒn'teɪnɪəs] adj espontáneo,-a.

spoof [spuːf] n (pl **spoofs**) parodia.

spooky ['spuːkɪ] adj (-**ier**, -**iest**) fam escalofriante.

spool [spuːl] n carrete, bobina.

spoon [spuːn] n cuchara, cucharilla, cucharita.

spoonful ['spuːnfʊl] n (pl -**s** o **spoonsful**) cucharada.

sport [spɔːt] n deporte.

► *vt* lucir.
● **to be a good sport** *fam* ser buena persona.
■ **sports car** coche deportivo.
■ **sports jacket** chaqueta de sport.
sportsman ['spɔːtsmən] *n* (*pl* **sportsmen**) deportista.
sportswear ['spɔːtsweəʳ] *n* ropa deportiva.
sportswoman ['spɔːtswumən] *n* (*pl* **sportswomen**) deportista.
spot [spɒt] *n* **1** lunar, punto (*en tela*). **2** mancha. **3** grano (*en cara*). **4** sitio, lugar. **5** aprieto, apuro. **6** spot *publicitario*. **7** *fam* poquito.
► *vt* (*pt & pp* **spotted**, *ger* **spotting**). **1** descubrir, encontrar. **2** darse cuenta de. **3** notar.
● **to be on the spot** estar allí, estar presente.
● **to put SB on the spot** poner a ALGN en un aprieto.
spotless ['spɒtləs] *adj* **1** limpísimo,-a, impecable (*ropa*). **2** *fig* intachable (*reputación*).
spotlight ['spɒtlaɪt] *n* foco.
● **to be in the spotlight** ser el centro de atención.
spotty ['spɒtɪ] *adj* (-ier, -iest) lleno,-a de granos.
spouse [spauz] *n* cónyuge.
spout [spaut] *n* **1** pico (*de jarra*). **2** surtidor (*de fuente*). **3** canalón, chorro (*de tejado*).
► *vt* echar, arrojar.
► *vi* salir a chorros.
sprain [spreɪn] *n* torcedura.
► *vt* torcerse: *she sprained her ankle*, se torció el tobillo.
sprang [spræŋ] *pt* → spring.
sprawl [sprɔːl] *vi* **1** tumbarse, repantigarse (*persona*). **2** extenderse (*ciudad*).
spray[1] [spreɪ] *n* **1** rociada (*de agua*). **2** espuma (*del mar*). **3** pulverización (*de lata*). **4** spray, atomizador.
► *vt* **1** rociar (*agua*). **2** atomizar (*perfume*). **3** pulverizar (*insecticida*).
■ **spray can** aerosol, spray.
■ **spray paint** pintura en aerosol.
spray[2] [spreɪ] *n* rama (*de flores*).
spread [spred] *n* **1** extensión. **2** difusión (*de ideas*). **3** propagación (*de enfermedad*). **4** envergadura (*de alas*). **5** pasta (*para untar*): *cheese spread*, queso para untar. **6** *fam* comilona.
► *vt-vi* (*pt & pp* **spread**). **1** extender(se). **2** desplegar(se) (*alas*). **3** difundir(se) (*rumor*). **4** propagar(se) (*fuego*).
► *vt* untar (*mantequilla*).
spreadsheet ['spredʃiːt] *n* hoja de cálculo.
spree [spriː] *n* juerga, parranda.
● **to go on a spree** ir de juerga, irse de marcha.
spring [sprɪŋ] *n* **1** primavera. **2** manantial, fuente. **3** muelle (*de mueble*). **4** resorte (*de reloj*). **5** ballesta (*de coche*). **6** elasticidad.
► *vi* (*pt* **sprang** [spræŋ], *pp* **sprung** [sprʌŋ]) saltar.
► *vt* *fig* espetar, soltar de pronto: *he sprang the news on me*, me espetó la noticia.
● **to spring a leak** hacer agua.
● **to spring to one's feet** levantarse de un salto.
■ **spring onion** cebolleta.
■ **spring roll** rollito de primavera.
to spring up *vi* aparecer, surgir.
springboard ['sprɪŋbɔːd] *n* trampolín.
springtime ['sprɪŋtaɪm] *n* primavera.
sprinkle ['sprɪŋkəl] *vt* **1** rociar, salpicar (*con agua*). **2** espolvorear (*con harina*).
sprinkler ['sprɪŋkələʳ] *n* aspersor.
sprint [sprɪnt] *n* esprint, sprint, carrera corta.
► *vi* esprintar, correr a toda velocidad.
sprout [spraut] *n* brote, retoño.
► *vi* **1** brotar (*plantar*). **2** *fig* crecer rápidamente.
■ **Brussels sprouts** coles de Bruselas.
sprung [sprʌŋ] *pp* → spring.
spun [spʌn] *pt-pp* → spin.
spur [spɜːʳ] *n* **1** espuela (*de jinete*). **2** espolón. **3** aguijón, estímulo.
► *vt* (*pt & pp* **spurred**, *ger* **spurring**). **1** espolear (*caballo*). **2** estimular, incitar.
● **on the spur of the moment** sin pensarlo.
spurt [spɜːt] *n* **1** chorro (*de líquido*). **2** racha, ataque (*de esfuerzo, velocidad*). **3** esfuerzo, sprint final.
► *vi* **1** chorrear, salir a chorros. **2** acelerar.
spy [spaɪ] *n* (*pl* -ies) espía.
► *vi* (*pt & pp* -ied) espiar.

sq [skweə⁺] *abbr* (*square*) cuadrado,-a.

Sq [skweə⁺] *abbr* (*Square*) Plaza, Pl., Plza..

squabble ['skwɒbəl] *n* disputa, riña.
► *vi* disputar, reñir.

squad [skwɒd] *n* 1 pelotón *(tropas)*. 2 brigada *(de policía)*.
■ **squad car** coche patrulla.

squadron ['skwɒdrən] *n* 1 escuadrón. 2 escuadrilla.

squalid ['skwɒlɪd] *adj* 1 sucio,-a, mugriento,-a. 2 miserable.

squalor ['skwɒlə⁺] *n* 1 suciedad, mugre. 2 miseria.

squander ['skwɒndə⁺] *vt* derrochar, malgastar.

square [skweə⁺] *n* 1 cuadrado *(forma)*. 2 cuadro *(en tela)*. 3 casilla *(en tablero)*. 4 plaza. 5 *fam* carroza, carca.
► *adj* 1 cuadrado,-a. 2 bueno,-a, decente *(comida)*.
► *adv* justo, exactamente: **square in the middle**, justo en el medio.
► *vt-vi* cuadrar.
► *vt* 1 elevar al cuadrado. 2 ajustar, arreglar.
● **to get a square deal** recibir un trato justo.
■ **square brackets** corchetes.
■ **square metre** metro cuadrado.
■ **square root** raíz cuadrada.
■ **squared paper** papel cuadriculado.

to square up *vi fam* ajustar las cuentas.

squash¹ [skwɒʃ] *n (pl* -**es***)*. 1 apiñamiento, agolpamiento. 2 zumo. 3 squash.
► *vt* 1 aplastar. 2 *fig* apabullar, hacer callar *(persona)*.
► *vi* aplastarse, chafarse.

squash² [skwɒʃ] *n (pl* -**es***)* calabaza.

squat [skwɒt] *adj* rechoncho,-a, achaparrado,-a.
► *vi (pt & pp* **squatted***, ger* **squatting***)*. 1 agacharse, sentarse en cuclillas. 2 ocupar ilegalmente.

squatter ['skwɒtə⁺] *n* okupa, ocupante ilegal.

squawk [skwɔːk] *n* graznido, chillido.
► *vi* graznar, chillar.

squeak [skwiːk] *n* 1 chillido *(de animal)*. 2 chirrido *(de neumático)*.
► *vi* 1 chillar *(animal)*. 2 chirriar, rechinar *(neumático)*.

squeal [skwiːl] *n* chillido.
► *vi* 1 chillar *(persona, animal)*. 2 chirriar *(frenos)*. 3 *fam* cantar, chivarse.

squeamish ['skwiːmɪʃ] *adj* aprensivo,-a, impresionable.

squeeze [skwiːz] *n* 1 apretón *(de manos)*. 2 aprieto, apuro.
► *vt* 1 apretar. 2 exprimir *(limón)*. 3 estrujar *(esponja)*.

to squeeze in *vt-vi* meter(se) con dificultad.

squeezer ['skwiːzə⁺] *n* exprimidor.

squid [skwɪd] *n* calamar, chipirón.

squint [skwɪnt] *n* 1 bizquera. 2 *fam* vistazo, ojeada.
► *vi* 1 bizquear, ser bizco,-a. 2 entrecerrar los ojos.

squirm [skwɜːm] *vi* retorcerse.

squirrel ['skwɪrəl] *n* ardilla.

squirt [skwɜːt] *n* 1 chorro. 2 *fam* mequetrefe.
► *vt* lanzar a chorro.

to squirt out *vi* salir a chorro.

Sr ['siːnɪə⁺] *abbr* (*Senior*) → Snr.

st [stəʊn] *abbr* GB (*stone*) unidad de peso que equivale a 6,350 kg.

St¹ [seɪnt] *abbr* (*Saint*) San, Santo, Santa, S., Sto., Sta.

St² [striːt] *abbr* (*Street*) calle, c/.

stab [stæb] *n* puñalada, navajazo.
► *vt-vi (pt & pp* **stabbed***, ger* **stabbing***)* apuñalar, acuchillar.
■ **stab of pain** punzada de dolor.

stability [stəˈbɪlɪtɪ] *n* estabilidad.

stabilize ['steɪbəlaɪz] *vt-vi* estabilizar(se).

stable¹ ['steɪbəl] *adj (comp* **stabler***, superl* **stablest***)*. 1 estable. 2 equilibrado,-a *(persona)*.

stable² ['steɪbəl] *n* cuadra, caballeriza, establo.

stack [stæk] *n* montón, pila.
► *vt* apilar, amontonar.

stadium ['steɪdɪəm] *n* estadio.

staff [stɑːf] *n* 1 personal, empleados. Es incontable y el verbo va en singular. 2 bastón, báculo. pl **staffs** o **staves**.
► *vt* proveer de personal: **the office is staffed by volunteers**, los que trabajan en el despacho son voluntarios.
■ **staff room** sala de profesores.

stag [stæg] *n* ciervo, venado.
■ **stag party** despedida de soltero.

stage [steɪdʒ] *n* 1 etapa, fase. 2 escenario, escena.
► *vt* 1 poner en escena, representar. 2 llevar a cabo.

- **by this stage** a estas alturas.
- **in stages** por etapas.
- **on stage** en escena.
- **to go on stage** salir al escenario.
- **stage manager** director,-ra de escena.

stagger ['stægə'] *vi* tambalearse.
▶ *vt* **1** escalonar. **2** dejar atónito,-a.

stain [stem] *n* mancha.
▶ *vt-vi* manchar(se).
- **stained glass** vidrio de colores.
- **stained glass window** vidriera.
- **stain remover** quitamanchas.

stainless ['stemləs] *adj* inoxidable.
- **stainless steel** acero inoxidable.

stair [steə'] *n* escalón, peldaño.
▶ *npl* **stairs** escalera.

staircase ['steəkeis] *n* escalera.

stake[1] [steik] *n* **1** apuesta, puesta. **2** intereses.
▶ *vt* apostar.
- **at stake** en juego, en peligro.

stake[2] [steik] *n* estaca, palo.

to stake out *vt* delimitar.

stale [steil] *adj* **1** duro,-a *(pan)*. **2** pasado, -a *(comida)*. **3** a cerrado *(olor)*. **4** gastado,- a *(broma)*.

stalemate ['steilmeit] *n* **1** tablas *(en ajedrez)*. **2** punto muerto.

stalk[1] [stɔːk] *n* **1** tallo *(de planta)*. **2** rabo, rabillo *(de fruta)*.

stalk[2] [stɔːk] *vt* acechar.
▶ *vi* andar con paso airado.

stall[1] [stɔːl] *n* **1** puesto *(de mercado)*. **2** caseta *(de feria)*.
▶ *npl* **stalls** platea.

stall[2] [stɔːl] *vi* **1** calarse, pararse *(motor)*. **2** *fam* andarse con rodeos *(persona)*.
▶ *vt* **1** calar, parar *(motor)*. **2** *fam* entretener *(persona)*.

stallion ['stæliən] *n* semental.

stammer ['stæmə'] *n* tartamudeo.
▶ *vi* tartamudear.

stamp [stæmp] *n* **1** sello, timbre. **2** sello de goma, tampón.
▶ *vt* **1** poner sello a. **2** sellar.
▶ *vi* patear, patalear, zapatear.
- **to stamp one's feet** patalear, zapatear *(bailando)*.
- **stamp collecting** filatelia.

to stamp out *vt fig* acabar con, erradicar.

stampede [stæm'piːd] *n* estampida, desbandada.

▶ *vi* salir en estampida.

stance [stæns] *n* postura.

stand [stænd] *n* **1** posición, postura. **2** pie *(de lámpara)*. **3** puesto *(de mercado)*. **4** stand, pabellón *(de feria)*. **5** plataforma. **6** tribuna.
▶ *vi* *(pt & pp* **stood** [stud]*)*. **1** estar de pie, ponerse de pie, levantarse, quedarse de pie. **2** estar, encontrarse: *the church stands on a hill*, la iglesia está en una colina. **3** seguir en pie *(oferta)*. **4** estar: *the house stands empty*, la casa está vacía. **5** presentarse a *(elecciones)*.
▶ *vt* **1** poner, colocar. **2** *fam* aguantar: *I can't stand him*, no lo aguanto.
- **as things stand** tal como están las cosas.
- **stand still!** ¡estáte quieto!
- **to stand to reason** ser lógico,-a.

to stand back *vi* apartarse, alejarse.

to stand by *vi* **1** quedarse sin hacer nada, cruzarse de brazos. **2** estar preparado,-a.
▶ *vt* **1** respaldar a *(persona)*. **2** atenerse a *(decisión)*.

to stand for *vt* **1** significar. **2** tolerar. **3** defender, representar.

to stand in for *vt* suplir, sustituir a.

to stand out *vi* destacar.

to stand up *vi* ponerse de pie, levantarse.
▶ *vt fam* dejar plantado,-a.

to stand up for *vt fig* defender.

to stand up to *vt* **1** resistir, aguantar. **2** hacer frente, plantar cara.

standard ['stændəd] *n* **1** nivel. **2** criterio, valor. **3** norma. **4** estandarte. **5** patrón.
▶ *adj* normal, corriente, estándar.
- **to be below standard** no satisfacer los requisitos.
- **to be up to standard** satisfacer los requisitos.
- **standard of living** nivel de vida.
- **standard time** hora oficial.

standby ['stændbai] *n* *(pl* **-ies**) sustituto,-a.
- **to be on standby 1** estar en lista de espera *(pasajero)*. **2** estar de retén *(soldado)*. **3** estar en estado de alerta *(bomberos, policía)*.

standing ['stændiŋ] *adj* **1** de pie. **2** permanente *(comisión)*.

▶ n **1** rango, estatus. **2** duración.

■ **standing invitation** invitación abierta.

■ **standing order** FIN domiciliación de pago.

■ **standing ovation** ovación con el público en pie.

■ **standing start** SP salida parada.

standpoint ['stændpɔɪnt] n punto de vista.

standstill ['stændstɪl] n paralización.

● **at a standstill 1** parado,-a *(tráfico)*. **2** paralizado,-a *(industria)*.

stank [stæŋk] pt → stink.

staple[1] ['steɪpəl] n producto básico.

▶ adj básico,-a *(alimento, dieta)*.

staple[2] ['steɪpəl] n grapa.

▶ vt grapar.

stapler ['steɪpələˈ] n grapadora.

star [stɑːˈ] n estrella.

▶ adj estelar.

▶ vi (pt & pp **starred**, ger **starring**) protagonizar.

▶ vt tener como protagonista a.

■ **star sign** signo del zodiaco.

starboard ['stɑːbəd] n estribor.

starch [stɑːtʃ] n *(pl* **-es***)* almidón, fécula.

stardom ['stɑːdəm] n estrellato.

stare [steəˈ] n mirada fija.

▶ vi mirar fijamente, clavar la vista.

● **to stare into space** mirar al vacío.

starfish ['stɑːfɪʃ] n *(pl* **-es***)* estrella de mar.

stark [stɑːk] adj **1** desolado,-a *(paisaje)*. **2** sobrio,-a, austero,-a *(decoración)*. **3** fig crudo,-a, puro,-a *(verdad)*.

▶ adv completamente.

● **stark mad** loco,-a de remate.

● **stark naked** fam en cueros.

starry ['stɑːrɪ] adj (-ier, -iest) estrellado,-a.

start [stɑːt] n **1** principio, comienzo. **2** salida *(de carrera)*. **3** ventaja. **4** susto, sobresalto.

▶ vt-vi **1** empezar, comenzar. **2** arrancar *(coche)*.

▶ vi sobresaltarse, asustarse.

● **for a start** para empezar.

● **from the start** desde el principio.

● **to make an early start** empezar a primera hora, salir a primera hora.

■ **starting point** punto de partida.

to start back vi emprender la vuelta.

to start off/out vi **1** empezar. **2** salir, partir.

to start up vt-vi arrancar *(coche)*.

starter ['stɑːtəˈ] n **1** juez de salida. **2** motor de arranque. **3** primer plato.

● **for starters 1** para empezar. **2** como primer plato.

startle ['stɑːtəl] vt asustar, sobresaltar.

starvation [stɑːˈveɪʃən] n hambre, inanición.

starve [stɑːv] vi **1** pasar hambre. **2** tener mucha hambre: *I'm starving!*, ¡me muero de hambre!

▶ vt matar de hambre, hacer pasar hambre.

● **to starve to death** morirse de hambre.

state [steɪt] n **1** estado, condición. **2** POL estado.

▶ adj POL estatal, del Estado.

▶ vt **1** afirmar. **2** exponer *(hechos)*. **3** fijar *(fecha)*.

● **to be in a state about** STH tener los nervios de punta por algo.

● **to lie in state** estar de cuerpo presente.

■ **state education** enseñanza pública.

■ **state of mind** estado de ánimo.

■ **state visit** visita oficial.

stately ['steɪtlɪ] adj (-ier, -iest) majestuoso,-a.

statement ['steɪtmənt] n **1** declaración, afirmación. **2** comunicado *(oficial, formal)*. **3** extracto de cuentas.

● **to make a statement 1** prestar declaración *(a policía)*. **2** hacer una declaración *(a la prensa)*.

statesman ['steɪtsmən] n *(pl* **statesmen***)* estadista, hombre de Estado.

station ['steɪʃən] n **1** estación *(de autobuses, tren)*. **2** emisora *(de radio)*. **3** canal *(de TV)*. **4** puesto.

▶ vt **1** estacionar, destinar, destacar *(tropas)*. **2** situar, colocar, ubicar *(posición)*.

stationary ['steɪʃənərɪ] adj **1** inmóvil. **2** estacionario,-a.

stationery ['steɪʃənərɪ] n **1** papel de carta. **2** artículos de escritorio.

statistics [stəˈtɪstɪks] n estadística. Es incontable y el verbo va en singular.

▶ npl estadísticas.

statue ['stætjuː] n estatua.

status ['steɪtəs] n **1** estado, condición. **2** estatus, prestigio.

■ **status quo** statu quo.

statute ['stætjuːt] n estatuto.
staunch [stɔːntʃ] adj fiel, leal.
stave [steɪv] n pentagrama.
to stave off vt 1 evitar (derrota). 2 aplazar (hambre).
stay [steɪ] n estancia.
▶ vi 1 quedarse, permanecer. 2 alojarse (en hotel).
● to stay away from STH no acercarse a algo.
to stay in vi quedarse en casa, no salir.
to stay on vi quedarse.
to stay out vi quedarse fuera.
to stay up vi no acostarse: *to stay up late*, acostarse tarde.
steadily ['stedɪlɪ] adv constantemente.
steady ['stedɪ] adj (-ier, -iest). 1 firme, seguro,-a, estable (mesa). 2 constante, regular (movimiento). 3 sereno,-a (voz). 4 estable, serio,-a (persona). 5 fijo,-a (empleo).
▶ vt-vi (pt & pp -ied) estabilizar(se).
● to steady SB's nerves calmarle a ALGN los nervios.
steak [steɪk] n bistec, filete.
steal [stiːl] vt-vi (pt stole [stəʊl], pp stolen ['stəʊlən]). 1 robar, hurtar. 2 entrar, salir etc sigilosamente: *she stole out without anybody noticing*, salió sigilosamente sin que nadie se diera cuenta.
● to steal the show acaparar la atención de todos.
to steal away vi escabullirse.
steam [stiːm] n vapor.
▶ vt cocer al vapor.
▶ vi echar vapor, humear (sopa).
■ steam engine máquina de vapor.
■ steam iron plancha de vapor.
to steam up vi empañarse.
steamer ['stiːmə'] n → steamship.
steamroller ['stiːmrəʊlə'] n apisonadora.
steamship ['stiːmʃɪp] n buque de vapor, vapor.
steel [stiːl] n acero.
● to steel oneself armarse de valor.
■ steel industry industria siderúrgica.
■ steel wool estropajo de aluminio.
steep¹ [stiːp] adj 1 empinado,-a, escarpado,-a (colina). 2 fig excesivo,-a (precio).
steep² [stiːp] vt remojar.
steeple ['stiːpəl] n aguja, chapitel.
steer [stɪə'] vt 1 dirigir. 2 conducir (vehículo). 3 gobernar (barco). 4 fig llevar (conversación).

steering ['stɪərɪŋ] n dirección.
■ steering wheel volante.
stem [stem] n 1 tallo (de planta). 2 pie (de vaso). 3 raíz (de palabra).
▶ vt (pt & pp stemmed, ger stemming) contener, detener.
to stem from vt derivarse de.
stench [stentʃ] n (pl -es) hedor, peste.
step [step] n 1 paso. 2 escalón, peldaño. 3 gestión, trámite.
▶ vi (pt & pp stepped, ger stepping) dar un paso, andar.
▶ npl steps 1 escalinata (exterior). 2 escalera (interior).
● step by step paso a paso, poco a poco.
● to step on STH pisar algo.
● to take steps tomar medidas.
● to watch one's step ir con cuidado.
to step aside vi apartarse.
to step back vi 1 retroceder, dar un paso atrás. 2 distanciarse.
to step down vi renunciar.
to step in vi intervenir.
to step out vi salir.
to step up vt fam aumentar.
stepbrother ['stepbrʌðə'] n hermanastro.
stepchild ['steptʃaɪld] n (pl stepchildren) hijastro,-a.
stepdaughter ['stepdɔːtə'] n hijastra.
stepfather ['stepfɑːðə'] n padrastro.
stepladder ['steplædə'] n escalera de mano, escalera de tijera.
stepmother ['stepmʌðə'] n madrastra.
stepsister ['stepsɪstə'] n hermanastra.
stepson ['stepsʌn] n hijastro.
stereo ['stɪərɪəʊ] n (pl stereos). 1 equipo estereofónico. 2 estéreo (sonido).
▶ adj estereofónico,-a.
stereotype ['stɪərətaɪp] n estereotipo.
▶ vt estereotipar.
sterile ['steraɪl] adj 1 estéril (mujer). 2 esterilizado,-a (leche).
sterling ['stɜːlɪŋ] n libra esterlina.
▶ adj puro,-a, de ley: *sterling silver*, plata de ley.
stern¹ [stɜːn] adj austero,-a, severo,-a.
stern² [stɜːn] n popa.
stew [stjuː] n estofado, guisado.
▶ vt 1 estofar, guisar (carne). 2 cocer (verdura).
steward ['stjuːəd] n 1 camarero (de barco). 2 auxiliar de vuelo (de avión).

stewardess ['stjuːədes] *n* (*pl* **-es**). **1** camarera *(de barco)*. **2** azafata *(de avión)*.

stick[1] [stɪk] *n* **1** palo. **2** bastón *(para caminar)*. **3** rama *(de apio)*.

● **to get hold of the wrong end of the stick** *fam* coger el rábano por las hojas.

stick[2] [stɪk] *vt* (*pt & pp* **stuck**). **1** clavar, hincar *(punta)*. **2** *fam* poner, meter. **3** pegar *(con pegamento)*. **4** *fam* aguantar.

▶ *vi* **1** pegarse *(con pegamento)*. **2** atascarse, atrancarse, encasquillarse.

● **to stick one's neck out** jugarse el tipo.

to stick around *vi fam* quedarse.

to stick at *vt* seguir con.

to stick by *vt* **1** *fam* apoyar *(amigo)*. **2** *fam* cumplir con *(promesa)*.

to stick out *vi* **1** sobresalir. **2** *fam* saltar a la vista.

▶ *vt* sacar.

to stick to *vt* **1** atenerse a *(decisión)*. **2** cumplir con *(promesa)*.

to stick up *vi* **1** salir, sobresalir. **2** estar de punta *(pelo)*.

to stick up for *vt fam* defender.

sticker ['stɪkə'] *n* **1** etiqueta adhesiva. **2** pegatina.

sticky ['stɪkɪ] *adj* (**-ier**, **-iest**). **1** pegajoso,-a. **2** bochornoso,-a *(tiempo)*. **3** *fam* difícil *(situación)*.

stiff [stɪf] *adj* **1** rígido,-a, tieso,-a. **2** entumecido,-a *(articulación)*. **3** espeso,-a. **4** frío,-a, estirado,-a *(modales)*. **5** *fig* difícil, duro,-a *(condiciones)*. **6** *fam* fuerte, cargado,-a *(bebida)*.

● **to feel stiff** tener agujetas.

● **to keep a stiff upper lip** poner a mal tiempo buena cara.

● **to be scared stiff** *fam* estar muerto,-a de miedo.

stiffen ['stɪfən] *vt* **1** reforzar *(tela)*. **2** almidonar *(cuello)*. **3** endurecer *(pasta)*.

▶ *vi* **1** ponerse rígido,-a *(persona)*. **2** entumecerse *(articulación)*.

▶ *vt-vi* fortalecer(se).

stifle ['staɪfəl] *vt* ahogar.

▶ *vi* ahogarse, sofocarse.

stigma ['stɪgmə] *n* estigma.

still [stɪl] *adj* **1** quieto,-a. **2** tranquilo,-a *(lago)*. **3** sin gas *(agua)*.

▶ *adv* **1** todavía, aún: *I can still hear it*, todavía lo oigo. **2** aun así: *he was ill, but*

he still went to work, estaba enfermo, pero aún así fue a trabajar. **3** sin embargo.

● **to keep still** estarse quieto,-a.

● **to stand still** no moverse.

■ **still life** ART naturaleza muerta, bodegón.

stillborn ['stɪlbɔːn] *adj* nacido,-a muerto,-a.

stillness ['stɪlnəs] *n* calma, quietud.

stilt [stɪlt] *n* zanco.

stilted ['stɪltɪd] *adj* afectado,-a.

stimulant ['stɪmjʊlənt] *n* estimulante.

stimulate ['stɪmjʊleɪt] *vt* estimular.

stimulus ['stɪmjʊləs] *n* (*pl* **stimuli** ['stɪmjʊliː]) estímulo.

sting [stɪŋ] *n* **1** aguijón *(de avispa)*. **2** picadura *(herida)*. **3** escozor, picazón. **4** *fig* punzada *(de remordimientos)*.

▶ *vt-vi* (*pt & pp* **stung**) picar.

▶ *vt fig* herir en lo más hondo.

stingy ['stɪndʒɪ] *adj* (**-ier**, **-iest**) tacaño,-a, roñoso,-a.

stink [stɪŋk] *n* peste, hedor.

▶ *vi* (*pt* **stank** [stæŋk], *pp* **stunk** [stʌŋk]) apestar, heder.

stint [stɪnt] *n* período, temporada.

▶ *vt* escatimar.

stipulate ['stɪpjʊleɪt] *vt* estipular.

stir [stɜː'] *vt* (*pt & pp* **stirred**, *ger* **stirring**). **1** remover *(café)*. **2** mover, agitar. **3** conmover, estimular. **4** provocar.

▶ *vi* moverse, levantarse.

▶ *n fig* revuelo, conmoción.

● **to stir to action** incitar a la acción.

to stir up *vt* **1** provocar. **2** remover *(agua)*.

stirrup ['stɪrəp] *n* estribo.

stitch [stɪtʃ] *n* (*pl* **-es**). **1** puntada *(al coser)*. **2** punto *(de media)*. **3** punto *(de sutura)*.

▶ *vt* **1** coser. **2** suturar.

● **to be in stitches** *fam* troncharse de risa.

stock [stɒk] *n* **1** reserva, surtido. **2** COMM existencias, stock. **3** capital social. **4** ganado. **5** caldo. **6** linaje.

▶ *adj* **1** *pej* consabido,-a, muy visto,-a. **2** COMM normal, de serie.

▶ *vt* **1** tener *(en el almacén)*. **2** surtir. **3** llenar.

● **in stock** en el almacén.

● **to be out of stock** estar agotado,-a.

● **to take stock of** evaluar.

■ **stock exchange** bolsa.

■ **stock market** bolsa de valores, mercado de valores.

to **stock up** vi abastecerse.

stockbroker ['stɒkbrəʊkə'] n corredor,-ra de bolsa.

stocking ['stɒkɪŋ] n media.

stocky ['stɒkɪ] adj (-**ier**, -**iest**) robusto,-a, fornido,-a.

stoke [stəʊk] vt atizar, avivar.

to **stoke up** vi fig atiborrarse.

stole[1] [stəʊl] pt → steal.

stole[2] [stəʊl] n estola.

stolen ['stəʊlən] pp → steal.

stolid ['stɒlɪd] adj impasible.

stomach ['stʌmək] n (pl **stomachs**) estómago, barriga.

▶ vt fig aguantar, tragar.

● **on an empty stomach** en ayunas.

■ **stomach ache** dolor de estómago.

stone [stəʊn] n **1** piedra. **2** hueso (de cereza, aceituna). **3** piedra, 6,348 kg: *she weighs 9 stone*, pesa 57 kilos.

▶ adj de piedra.

▶ vt apedrear.

● **at a stone's throw** a tiro de piedra.

■ **Stone Age** Edad de Piedra.

stone-cold [stəʊn'kəʊld] adj helado,-a.

stoned [stəʊnd] adj **1** sl flipado,-a, colocado,-a. **2** fam trompa.

stony ['stəʊnɪ] adj (-**ier**, -**iest**). **1** pedregoso,-a. **2** frío,-a, glacial (mirada).

stood [stʊd] pt-pp → stand.

stool [stuːl] n taburete.

stoop [stuːp] n encorvamiento.

▶ vi **1** inclinarse, agacharse. **2** ser cargado,-a de espaldas.

to **stoop to** vt fig rebajarse a.

stop [stɒp] n **1** parada, alto. **2** punto (signo de puntuación). **3** parada (de autobús).

▶ vt (pt & pp **stopped**, ger **stopping**). **1** parar (autobús). **2** impedir, evitar: *I tried to stop him from coming*, traté de evitar que viniera. **3** paralizar (producción). **4** poner fin a, poner término a, acabar con (injusticia). **5** suspender (pago). **6** dejar de: *stop smoking!*, ideja de fumar!

▶ vi **1** pararse, detenerse. **2** terminar.

▶ interj ipare!, ¡alto!

● **stop it!** ¡basta ya!

● **to come to a stop** pararse.

■ **stop sign** señal de stop.

to **stop by** vi fam pasar.

to **stop off** vi hacer una parada.

to **stop up** vt tapar, taponar.

stopover ['stɒpəʊvə'] n parada, escala (de avión).

stoppage ['stɒpɪdʒ] n **1** interrupción, paro (de trabajo). **2** huelga. **3** deducción. **4** obstrucción.

stopper ['stɒpə'] n tapón.

stopwatch ['stɒpwɒtʃ] n (pl -**es**) cronómetro.

storage ['stɔːrɪdʒ] n almacenaje, almacenamiento.

■ **storage heater** acumulador.

■ **storage unit** armario.

store [stɔː'] n **1** provisión, reserva. **2** tienda, almacén.

▶ vt almacenar, guardar.

● **in store** de reserva.

to **store up** vt acumular.

storey ['stɔːrɪ] n piso, planta.

stork [stɔːk] n cigüeña.

storm [stɔːm] n **1** tormenta, tempestad (en mar). **2** borrasca (con viento). **3** fig revuelo.

● **to storm in/out/off** entrar/salir/marcharse furiosamente.

stormy ['stɔːmɪ] adj (-**ier**, -**iest**). **1** tormentoso,-a (tiempo). **2** acalorado,-a, tempestuoso,-a (pelea).

story ['stɔːrɪ] n (pl -**ies**). **1** historia, cuento, relato. **2** artículo. **3** anécdota, chiste. **4** argumento, trama (de película). **5** rumor, mentira.

stout [staʊt] adj **1** gordo,-a, robusto,-a. **2** sólido,-a. **3** firme, resuelto,-a.

▶ n cerveza negra.

stove [stəʊv] n **1** estufa. **2** cocina, hornillo.

stow [stəʊ] vt guardar.

stowaway ['stəʊəweɪ] n polizón.

straddle ['strædəl] vt sentarse a horcajadas sobre.

straggle ['strægəl] vi **1** desparramarse. **2** rezagarse.

straight [streɪt] adj **1** recto,-a, derecho,-a (línea). **2** liso,-a (pelo). **3** seguido,-a: *eight hours straight*, ocho horas seguidas. **4** honrado,-a, de confianza. **5** sincero,-a (respuesta). **6** solo,-a (bebida). **7** fam hetero. **8** sl carca.

▶ adv **1** en línea recta. **2** directamente: *he went straight to the office*, fue direc-

tamente al despacho. **3** enseguida. **4** francamente. **5** con claridad *(pensar)*.
► *n* recta *(en carrera)*.
● **straight ahead** todo recto.
● **straight off** sin pensarlo.
● **to get things straight** dejar las cosas claras.
● **to keep a straight face** aguantarse la risa.

straightaway [streɪtəˈweɪ] *adv* en seguida.
straighten [ˈstreɪtən] *vt* **1** enderezar, poner bien, arreglar. **2** estirar.
to straighten out *vt-vi* resolver(se).
to straighten up *vt* **1** ordenar. **2** poner derecho,-a.
► *vi* ponerse derecho,-a.
straightforward [streɪtˈfɔːwəd] *adj* franco,-a, honrado,-a.
strain [streɪn] *n* **1** presión, tensión. **2** estrés, tensión. **3** torcedura.
► *vt* **1** estirar, tensar *(cuerda)*. **2** torcerse, hacerse un esguince *(músculo)*. **3** forzar *(vista, voz)*. **4** colar, filtrar.
► *vi* tirar.
strainer [ˈstreɪnəˈ] *n* colador.
strait [streɪt] *n* GEOG estrecho.
● **in dire straits** en un gran aprieto.
straitjacket [ˈstreɪtdʒækɪt] *n* camisa de fuerza.
strand[1] [strænd] *n* **1** hebra, hilo. **2** ramal *(de cuerda)*. **3** mechón. **4** sarta *(de perlas)*.
strand[2] [strænd] *vt* **1** varar *(barco)*. **2** *fig* abandonar: **he was left stranded**, lo dejaron plantado.
strange [streɪndʒ] *adj* **1** extraño,-a, raro, -a. **2** desconocido,-a.
strangely [ˈstreɪndʒlɪ] *adv* extrañamente: **strangely enough**, aunque parezca extraño.
stranger [ˈstreɪndʒəˈ] *n* extraño,-a, desconocido,-a.
strangle [ˈstræŋɡəl] *vt* estrangular.
strap [stræp] *n* **1** correa *(de reloj)*. **2** tirante *(de vestido)*.
► *vt* (*pt & pp* **strapped**, *ger* **strapping**). **1** atar con correa, sujetar con correa. **2** azotar con una correa.
strategic [strəˈtiːdʒɪk] *adj* estratégico,-a.
strategy [ˈstrætədʒɪ] *n* (*pl* **-ies**) estrategia.
straw [strɔː] *n* **1** paja: **straw hat**, sombrero de paja. **2** paja, pajita *(para beber)*.
● **that's the last straw!** *fam* ¡eso el colmo!

strawberry [ˈstrɔːbərɪ] *n* (*pl* **-ies**) fresa, fresón.
stray [streɪ] *adj* perdido,-a.
► *n* animal extraviado.
► *vi* extraviarse, perderse.
streak [striːk] *n* **1** raya, lista. **2** mecha, mechón *(de pelo)*. **3** veta. **4** *fig* vena *(de locura)*. **5** *fig* racha *(de suerte)*.
streaky [ˈstriːkɪ] *adj* (**-ier**, **-iest**). **1** con mechas *(pelo)*. **2** entreverado,-a *(beicon)*.
stream [striːm] *n* **1** arroyo, riachuelo. **2** corriente. **3** flujo *(de agua)*. **4** chorro *(de sangre)*. **5** *fig* oleada, torrente *(de gente)*.
► *vi* **1** manar, correr, chorrear. **2** *fig* desfilar *(gente)*.
streamer [ˈstriːməˈ] *n* serpentina.
streamline [ˈstriːmlaɪn] *n* línea aerodinámica.
► *vt* **1** aerodinamizar. **2** racionalizar.
street [striːt] *n* calle.
■ **street lamp** farola.
streetlamp [ˈstriːtlæmp] *n* farola.
strength [streŋθ] *n* **1** fuerza. **2** valor *(de moneda)*. **3** intensidad *(de emoción, color)*. **4** poder, potencia.
● **in strength** en gran número.
● **on the strength of** basándose en.
■ **strength of will** fuerza de voluntad.
strengthen [ˈstreŋθən] *vt-vi* **1** fortalecer(se), reforzar(se). **2** intensificar(se).
strenuous [ˈstrenjʊəs] *adj* fatigoso,-a, agotador,-ra.
stress [stres] *n* (*pl* **-es**). **1** tensión nerviosa, estrés. **2** tensión. **3** hincapié, énfasis. **4** acento tónico.
► *vt* **1** recalcar, subrayar. **2** acentuar.
● **to be under stress** estar estresado,-a.
● **to lay great stress on** STH hacer hincapié en algo, poner énfasis en algo.
stressful [ˈstresfʊl] *adj* estresante.
stretch [stretʃ] *n* (*pl* **-es**). **1** extensión. **2** elasticidad. **3** trecho, tramo *(de terreno)*. **4** período, intervalo *(de tiempo)*.
► *vt-vi* **1** extender(se) *(terreno)*. **2** estirar(se) *(elástico)*; ensanchar(se) *(zapatos)*.
► *vt* desperezarse.
● **to stretch one's legs** estirar las piernas.
● **at a stretch** de un tirón.
to stretch out *vt* **1** estirar *(piernas)*. **2** alargar *(mano)*.
► *vi* **1** estirarse, tumbarse. **2** alargarse.

stretcher ['stretʃə'] n camilla.

stretchy ['stretʃi] adj (-ier, -iest) elástico,-a.

stricken ['strɪkən] adj 1 afligido,-a (de dolor). 2 afectado,-a (por catástrofe).

strict [strɪkt] adj estricto,-a.

● in the strictest confidence en el más absoluto secreto.

● strictly speaking en sentido estricto.

stride [straɪd] n zancada, trancada.
▶ vi (pt strode [strəʊd], pp stridden ['strɪdən]) andar a zancadas.

● to take STH in one's stride tomarse las cosas con calma.

strident ['straɪdənt] adj estridente.

strife [straɪf] n conflictos, luchas.

strike [straɪk] n 1 huelga. 2 golpe. 3 hallazgo. 4 ataque, golpe.
▶ vt (pt & pp struck). 1 pegar, golpear. 2 chocar contra, alcanzar (rayo, bala). 3 descubrir (oro, petróleo). 4 acuñar (moneda). 5 encender (cerilla). 6 dar, tocar (reloj). 7 cerrar (trato). 8 parecer: she strikes me as very nice, me parece muy simpática.
▶ vi 1 atacar. 2 hacer huelga. 3 dar la hora, tocar la hora.

● it strikes me that ... se me ocurre que ....

● to be on strike estar en huelga.

● to go on strike declararse en huelga.

● to be struck dumb quedarse mudo, -a.

● to strike out on one's own volar con sus propias alas.

● to strike it rich fam hacerse rico,-a.

to strike back vi devolver el golpe.

to strike down vt abatir.

to strike off vt 1 tachar. 2 suspender.

to strike up vt entablar.

striker ['straɪkə'] n 1 huelguista. 2 delantero,-a (en fútbol).

striking ['straɪkɪŋ] adj llamativo,-a, impresionante.

string [strɪŋ] n 1 cuerda, cordón. 2 ristra (de ajos, mentiras). 3 serie (de acontecimientos).
▶ vt (pt & pp strung [strʌŋ]). 1 ensartar. 2 encordar.

● to pull strings for SB mover hilos para ayudar a ALGN.

■ string bean judía verde.

to string along vi seguir la corriente.

stringent ['strɪndʒənt] adj severo,-a, estricto,-a.

strip¹ [strɪp] n 1 tira (de papel, cuero). 2 franja (de tierra). 3 historieta.

strip² [strɪp] vt (pt & pp stripped, ger stripping). 1 quitar (pintar). 2 vaciar (habitación). 3 desnudar (persona).
▶ vi desnudarse.

● to strip SB of STH despojar a ALGN de algo.

to strip down vt desmontar.

to strip off vi desnudarse, quitarse (una prenda).

stripe [straɪp] n 1 raya, lista. 2 galón (de oficial).

striped [straɪpt] adj a rayas.

strive [straɪv] vi (pt strove [strəʊv], pp striven ['strɪvən]) esforzarse.

strode [strəʊd] pt → stride.

stroke [strəʊk] n 1 golpe. 2 brazada (en natación). 3 campanada. 4 tiempo (de motor). 5 pincelada, trazo (de pluma). 6 apoplejía, derrame cerebral.
▶ vt acariciar.

■ stroke of luck golpe de suerte.

stroll [strəʊl] n paseo.
▶ vi pasear, dar un paseo.

● to take a stroll dar una vuelta.

strong [strɒŋ] adj 1 fuerte. 2 firme, acérrimo,-a. 3 fuerte, resistente (material).
▶ adv fuerte.

● to be ... strong contar con ... miembros: the army was 2000 strong, el ejército contaba con 2000 personas.

■ strong room cámara acorazada.

strongly ['strɒŋlɪ] adv fuertemente.

strong-minded [strɒŋ'maɪndɪd] adj resuelto,-a, decidido,-a.

stroppy ['strɒpɪ] adj (-ier, -iest) GB fam borde, de mala uva.

strove [strəʊv] pt → strive.

struck [strʌk] pt-pp → strike.

structural ['strʌktʃərəl] adj estructural.

structure ['strʌktʃə'] n 1 estructura. 2 construcción.
▶ vt estructurar.

struggle ['strʌgəl] n 1 lucha. 2 pelea, forcejeo.
▶ vi 1 luchar. 2 forcejear.

strung [strʌŋ] pt-pp → string.

strut [strʌt] n puntal, riostra.
▶ vi (pt & pp strutted, ger strutting) pavonearse.

stub [stʌb] n 1 colilla (de cigarrillo). 2 cabo

(de lápiz, vela). **3** matriz *(de talón)*. **4** resguardo *(de recibo)*.

stubble ['stʌbəl] *n* **1** rastrojo. **2** barba *(incipiente)*.

stubborn ['stʌbən] *adj* terco,-a, testarudo,-a, obstinado,-a.

stuck [stʌk] *pt-pp* → stick.

● **to get stuck** atascarse.

stuck-up [stʌk'ʌp] *adj fam* creído,-a.

stud[1] [stʌd] *n* **1** tachón *(en ropa)*. **2** tachuela *(en mueble)*.

▶ *vt (pt & pp* **studded**, *ger* **studding)** tachonar.

stud[2] [stʌd] *n* semental.

student ['stjuːdənt] *n* alumno,-a, estudiante.

■ **student teacher** profesor,-ra en prácticas.

studied ['stʌdɪd] *adj* **1** estudiado,-a, pensado,-a. **2** *pej* afectado,-a.

studio ['stjuːdɪəʊ] *n (pl* **studios)** estudio, taller *(de artista)*.

■ **studio flat** estudio.

studious ['stjuːdɪəs] *adj* estudioso,-a, aplicado,-a.

study ['stʌdɪ] *n (pl* **-ies)**. **1** estudio: *he wants to continue his studies*, quiere seguir con los estudios. **2** despacho.

▶ *vt-vi (pt & pp* **-ied)** estudiar.

▶ *vt* analizar, examinar.

stuff [stʌf] *n* **1** *fam* cosas, trastos, bártulos. **2** cosa: *what's that stuff on the table?*, ¿qué es eso que hay en la mesa?

▶ *vt* **1** rellenar. **2** disecar. **3** atiborrar.

● **to do one's stuff** *fam* hacer uno lo suyo.

● **to stuff oneself** *fam* hartarse de comida.

■ **stuffed shirt** *fam* persona estirada.

■ **stuffed toy** muñeco de peluche.

stuffing ['stʌfɪŋ] *n* relleno.

stuffy ['stʌfɪ] *adj (*-ier, -iest). **1** cargado,-a, mal ventilado,-a. **2** estirado,-a *(persona)*.

stumble ['stʌmbəl] *n* tropezón, traspié.

▶ *vi* tropezar, dar un traspié.

■ **stumbling block** escollo, tropiezo.

stump [stʌmp] *n* **1** tocón *(de árbol)*. **2** cabo *(de lápiz, vela)*. **3** muñón, chueca *(de pierna)*. **4** estaca *(en críquet)*.

▶ *vt fam* desconcertar.

▶ *vi* andar pisando fuerte.

stun [stʌn] *vt (pt & pp* **stunned**, *ger* **stunning)**. **1** aturdir, atontar. **2** sorprender. **3** pasmar, dejar pasmado.

stung [stʌŋ] *pt-pp* → sting.

stunk [stʌŋk] *pt-pp* → stink.

stunning ['stʌnɪŋ] *adj* **1** pasmoso. **2** estupendo,-a, impresionante.

stunt[1] [stʌnt] *n* **1** escena peligrosa. **2** truco.

stunt[2] [stʌnt] *vt* atrofiar.

stuntman ['stʌntmæn] *n (pl* **stuntmen** ['stʌntmen]) doble, especialista.

stuntwoman ['stʌntwʊmən] *n (pl* **stuntwomen** ['stʌntwɪmɪn]) doble, especialista.

stupid ['stjuːpɪd] *adj-n (comp* **stupider**, *superl* **stupidest)** tonto,-a, imbécil.

stupidity [stjuː'pɪdɪtɪ] *n* estupidez.

stupor ['stjuːpə'] *n* estupor.

sturdy ['stɜːdɪ] *adj (*-ier, -iest) robusto,-a, fuerte.

stutter ['stʌtə'] *n* tartamudeo.

▶ *vi* tartamudear.

stutterer ['stʌtərə'] *n* tartamudo,-a.

sty [staɪ] *n (pl* -ies) pocilga.

style [staɪl] *n* **1** estilo. **2** peinado. **3** moda.

stylish ['staɪlɪʃ] *adj* **1** elegante. **2** a la moda.

suave [swɑːv] *adj* refinado.

subconscious [sʌb'kɒnʃəs] *adj-n* subconsciente.

subdivide [sʌbdɪ'vaɪd] *vt* subdividir.

subdue [səb'djuː] *vt* **1** someter, dominar. **2** contener *(sentimientos)*. **3** atenuar, suavizar *(color)*.

subject [*(n-adj)* 'sʌbdʒekt*(vb)* səb'dʒekt] *n* **1** tema. **2** asignatura. **3** súbdito. **4** sujeto.

▶ *adj* **1** sujeto,-a. **2** expuesto,-a. **3** susceptible.

▶ *vt* someter.

● **subject to approval** previa aprobación.

subjective [səb'dʒektɪv] *adj* subjetivo,-a.

subjunctive [səb'dʒʌŋktɪv] *adj* subjuntivo,-a.

▶ *n* subjuntivo.

sublet [sʌb'let] *vt-vi (pt & pp* **sublet**, *ger* **subletting)** realquilar, subarrendar.

sublime [sə'blaɪm] *adj* sublime.

submarine [sʌbmə'riːn] *n* submarino.

submerge [səb'mɜːdʒ] *vt-vi* sumergir(se).

submission [səb'mɪʃən] *n* **1** sumisión. **2** presentación *(de documentos)*.

submissive [səb'mɪsɪv] *adj* sumiso,-a.

submit [səb'mɪt] *vt* (*pt & pp* **submitted**, *ger* **submitting**). **1** someter *(persona)*. **2** presentar *(solicitud)*.
▸ *vi* someterse.

subordinate [(*adj-n*) sə'bɔːdɪnət(*vb*) sə'bɔːdɪneɪt] *adj-n* subordinado,-a.
▸ *vt* subordinar.

subscribe [səb'skraɪb] *vi* **1** subscribirse *(a revista)*. **2** estar de acuerdo, suscribir *(opinión)*.

subscriber [səb'scraɪbəʳ] *n* **1** subscriptor, -ra *(de revista)*. **2** abonado,-a *(de servicio)*.

subscription [səb'skɪpʃən] *n* **1** subscripción *(de revista)*. **2** abono *(de servicio)*.

subsequent ['sʌbsɪkwənt] *adj* subsiguiente, posterior.

subsequently ['sʌbsɪkwəntlɪ] *adv* posteriormente.

subside [səb'saɪd] *vi* **1** hundirse *(suelo)*. **2** amainar, apaciguarse *(tiempo, ira)*.

subsidiary [səb'sɪdɪərɪ] *adj* secundario,-a.
▸ *n* (*pl* -**ies**) filial, sucursal.

subsidize ['sʌbsɪdaɪz] *vt* subvencionar.

subsidy ['sʌbsɪdɪ] *n* (*pl* -**ies**) subvención, subsidio.

subsist [səb'sɪst] *vi* subsistir.
● **to subsist on ...** subsistir a base de ....

subsistence [səb'sɪstəns] *n* subsistencia.
■ **subsistence wage** sueldo miserable.

substance ['sʌbstəns] *n* **1** sustancia. **2** *fig* esencia.

substantial [səb'stænʃəl] *adj* **1** importante, sustancial. **2** sólido,-a *(construcción)*. **3** abundante *(comida)*.

substitute ['sʌbstɪtjuːt] *n* **1** substituto,-a, suplente *(persona)*. **2** sucedáneo *(alimento)*.
▸ *vt* sustituir.

substitution [sʌbstɪ'tjuːʃən] *n* **1** sustitución. **2** suplencia.

subterranean [sʌbtə'reɪnɪən] *adj* subterráneo,-a.

subtitle ['sʌbtaɪtəl] *n* subtítulo.
▸ *vt* subtitular.

subtle ['sʌtəl] *adj* (*comp* **subtler**, *superl* **subtlest**). **1** sutil. **2** delicado,-a *(sabor)*. **3** agudo,-a *(comentario)*.

subtly ['sʌtlɪ] *adv* sutilmente.

subtract [səb'trækt] *vt* restar.

subtraction [səb'trækʃən] *n* resta.

suburb ['sʌbɜːb] *n* barrio periférico, barrio residencial.
■ **the suburbs** las afueras.

subversive [sʌb'vɜːsɪv] *adj-n* subversivo,-a.

subway ['sʌbweɪ] *n* **1** GB paso subterráneo. **2** US metro.

succeed [sək'siːd] *vi* **1** tener éxito, triunfar. **2** salir bien *(plan)*.
▸ *vt* suceder a.
● **to succeed in doing** STH conseguir hacer algo.

success [sək'ses] *n* (*pl* -**es**) éxito.
● **to be a success** tener éxito.

successful [sək'sesfʊl] *adj* **1** que tiene éxito,de éxito *(persona, película)*. **2** acertado,-a *(plan)*. **3** próspero,-a *(negocio)*. **4** feliz *(matrimonio)*.

successfully [sək'sesfʊlɪ] *adv* con éxito.

succession [sək'seʃən] *n* sucesión, serie.

successive [sək'sesɪv] *adj* sucesivo,-a.

successor [sək'sesəʳ] *n* sucesor,-ra.

succumb [sə'kʌm] *vi* sucumbir.

such [sʌtʃ] *adj* **1** tal, semejante: *there's no such thing*, no existe tal cosa; *how could you do such a thing?*, ¿cómo pudiste hacer algo así? **2** tan ... como, tanto,-a ... que: *he's not such a nice person as his brother*, no es tan buena persona como su hermano; *he was in such a hurry that he forgot his briefcase*, tenía tanta prisa que se olvidó el maletín.
▸ *adv* muy, mucho,-a, tan, tanto,-a: *she's such a clever woman*, es una mujer muy inteligente, ¡es una mujer tan inteligente!; *there were such a lot of books*, había muchos libros.
● **at such and such a time** a tal hora.
● **in such a way that ...** de tal manera que ....

suck [sʌk] *n* chupada.
▸ *vt-vi* chupar, mamar.
▸ *vt* **1** aspirar *(aspiradora)*. **2** tragar, succionar *(remolino)*.
● **to suck up to** SB *fam* dar coba a ALGN.

sucker ['sʌkəʳ] *n* **1** ventosa. **2** chupón. **3** *fam* primo,-a, bobo,-a.

suckle ['sʌkəl] *vt* amamantar.
▸ *vi* mamar.

suction ['sʌkʃən] *n* succión.
■ **suction pump** bomba de aspiración.

sudden ['sʌdən] *adj* **1** repentino,-a. **2** inesperado,-a, imprevisto,-a.
● **all of a sudden** de repente, de pronto.

suddenly ['sʌdənlɪ] *adv* de repente, de pronto.

suds [sʌdz] *npl* jabonaduras, espuma.
sue [suː] *vt-vi* demandar.
suede [sweɪd] *n* ante, gamuza.
▶ *adj* de ante, de gamuza.
suffer [ˈsʌfə'] *vt-vi* sufrir.
▶ *vt* aguantar, soportar.
suffering [ˈsʌfərɪŋ] *n* **1** sufrimiento. **2** dolor.
sufficient [səˈfɪʃənt] *adj* suficiente, bastante.
sufficiently [səˈfɪʃəntlɪ] *adv* suficientemente.
suffix [ˈsʌfɪks] *n* (*pl* **suffixes**) sufijo.
suffocate [ˈsʌfəkeɪt] *vt* asfixiar.
▶ *vi* asfixiarse, ahogarse.
sugar [ˈʃʊgə'] *n* azúcar.
■ **sugar bowl** azucarero.
■ **sugar cane** caña de azúcar.
■ **suggar lump** terrón de azúcar.
sugarbeet [ˈʃʊgəbiːt] *n* remolacha azucarera.
sugary [ˈʃʊgərɪ] *adj* (**-ier**, **-iest**). **1** azucarado,-a. **2** almibarado,-a, meloso,-a.
suggest [səˈdʒest] *vt* **1** sugerir. **2** aconsejar. **3** implicar.
suggestion [səˈdʒestʃən] *n* **1** sugerencia. **2** insinuación. **3** sombra, traza.
suggestive [səˈdʒestɪv] *adj* **1** indicativo, -a. **2** provocativo,-a, insinuante.
suicidal [sjuːɪˈsaɪdəl] *adj* suicida.
suicide [ˈsjuːɪsaɪd] *n* suicidio.
● **to commit suicide** suicidarse.
suit [sjuːt] *n* **1** traje (*de hombre*). **2** traje de chaqueta (*de mujer*). **3** pleito. **4** palo (*de naipes*).
▶ *vt* **1** convenir a, venir bien a. **2** sentar bien: *the cold doesn't suit me*, el frío no me sienta bien. **3** favorecer: *red really suits you*, el rojo te favorece mucho. **4** satisfacer.
● **suit yourself!** ¡como quieras!
● **suits me!** ¡a mí me está bien!
● **to follow suit** seguir el ejemplo.
suitable [ˈsjuːtəbəl] *adj* **1** conveniente. **2** adecuado,-a, apto,-a: *suitable for children*, apto,-a para niños.
suitcase [ˈsuːtkeɪs] *n* maleta.
suite [swiːt] *n* **1** juego (*de muebles*). **2** suite (*musical, de hotel*).
suitor [ˈsjuːtə'] *n* pretendiente.
sulk [sʌlk] *vi* enfurruñarse, estar de mal humor.
sulky [ˈsʌlkɪ] *adj* (**-ier**, **-iest**) malhumorado,-a.

sullen [ˈsʌlən] *adj* hosco,-a, huraño,-a.
sulphur [ˈsʌlfə'] *n* azufre.
sultana [sʌlˈtɑːnə] *n* pasa sultana.
sultry [ˈsʌltrɪ] *adj* (**-ier**, **-iest**). **1** bochornoso,-a, sofocante. **2** sensual.
sum [sʌm] *n* **1** suma. **2** importe (*de factura*).
● **in sum** en suma, en resumen.
■ **sum total** suma, total.
to sum up *vt* resumir.
summarize [ˈsʌməraɪz] *vt* resumir.
summary [ˈsʌmərɪ] *n* (*pl* **-ies**) resumen.
summer [ˈsʌmə'] *n* verano.
▶ *adj* **1** de verano. **2** veraniego,-a.
summertime [ˈsʌmətaɪm] *n* verano.
summit [ˈsʌmɪt] *n* cumbre.
summon [ˈsʌmən] *vt* llamar.
● **to summon up one's strength** armarse de valor.
summons [ˈsʌmənz] *n* (*pl* **summonses**). **1** llamamiento, llamada. **2** citación.
▶ *vt* citar.
sun [sʌn] *n* sol.
● **in the sun** al sol.
● **to sun oneself** tomar el sol.
Sun [ˈsʌndɪ] *abbr* (**Sunday**) domingo.
sunbathe [ˈsʌnbeɪð] *vi* tomar el sol.
sunburnt [ˈsʌnbɜːnt] *adj* quemado,-a por el sol.
● **to get sunburnt** quemarse.
Sunday [ˈsʌndeɪ] *n* domingo.
■ **Sunday school** catequesis.
sundial [ˈsʌndaɪəl] *n* reloj de sol.
sunflower [ˈsʌnflaʊə'] *n* girasol.
sung [sʌŋ] *pp* → sing.
sunglasses [ˈsʌnglɑːsɪz] *npl* gafas de sol.
sunk [sʌŋk] *pp* → sink.
sunlight [ˈsʌnlaɪt] *n* luz del sol.
sunny [ˈsʌnɪ] *adj* (**-ier**, **-iest**) soleado,-a.
● **to be sunny** hacer sol.
sunrise [ˈsʌnraɪz] *n* salida del sol, amanecer.
● **at sunrise** al amanecer.
sunset [ˈsʌnset] *n* puesta del sol, ocaso.
● **at sunset** al atardecer.
sunshade [ˈsʌnʃeɪd] *n* **1** sombrilla. **2** toldo.
sunshine [ˈsʌnʃaɪn] *n* luz del sol.
sunstroke [ˈsʌnstrəʊk] *n* insolación.
suntan [ˈsʌntæn] *n* bronceado.
■ **suntan lotion** bronceador.
super [ˈsuːpə'] *adj fam* fenomenal, de primera.

superb [suːˈpɜːb] *adj* estupendo,-a, magnífico,-a.

superficial [suːpəˈfɪʃəl] *adj* superficial.

superfluous [suːˈpɜːfluəs] *adj* superfluo,-a.

superhuman [suːpəˈhjuːmən] *adj* sobrehumano,-a.

superintendent [suːpərɪnˈtendənt] *n* inspector,-ra, supervisor,-ra.

superior [suːˈpɪərɪəʳ] *adj* **1** superior. **2** altanero,-a.
► *n* superior,-ra.

superiority [suːpɪərɪˈɒrɪtɪ] *n* superioridad.

superlative [suːˈpɜːlətɪv] *adj* superlativo,-a.
► *n* superlativo.

supermarket [suːpəˈmɑːkɪt] *n* supermercado.

supernatural [suːpəˈnætʃərəl] *adj* sobrenatural.

superpower [ˈsuːpəpaʊəʳ] *n* superpotencia.

supersonic [suːpəˈsɒnɪk] *adj* supersónico,-a.

superstition [suːpəˈstɪʃən] *n* superstición.

superstitious [sjuːpəˈstɪʃəs] *adj* supersticioso,-a.

supervise [ˈsuːpəvaɪz] *vt* **1** supervisar. **2** vigilar.

supervision [suːpəˈvɪʒən] *n* supervisión, vigilancia.

supervisor [ˈsuːpəvaɪzəʳ] *n* supervisor,-ra.

supper [ˈsʌpəʳ] *n* cena.
● **to have supper** cenar.

supple [ˈsʌpəl] *adj* flexible.

supplement [*(n)* ˈsʌplɪmənt *(vb)* ˈsʌplɪment] *n* suplemento.
► *vt* complementar.

supplementary [sʌplɪˈmentərɪ] *adj* suplementario,-a, adicional.

supplier [səˈplaɪəʳ] *n* suministrador,-ra, proveedor,-ra.

supply [səˈplaɪ] *vt* (*pt & pp* **-ied**). **1** suministrar, abastecer, proveer *(persona, empresa)*. **2** aprovisionar *(tropas)*. **3** facilitar *(información)*.
► *n* (*pl* **-ies**). **1** suministro, abastecimiento. **2** surtido, existencias.
► *npl* **supplies** víveres, provisiones.
● **supply and demand** la oferta y la demanda.

support [səˈpɔːt] *n* **1** apoyo. **2** ayuda económica.
► *vt* **1** sostener *(peso)*. **2** apoyar, respaldar *(causa)*. **3** seguir *(equipo)*. **4** mantener: *he has to support his family*, tiene que mantener a su familia.
● **to support oneself** ganarse la vida.

supporter [səˈpɔːtəʳ] *n* **1** POL partidario, -a. **2** seguidor,-ra, hincha, forofo,-a.

supportive [səˈpɔːtɪv] *adj* comprensivo,-a.

suppose [səˈpəʊz] *vt* suponer, imaginarse: *I suppose she'll arrive tomorrow*, supongo que llegará mañana; *suppose there was a war*, imagínate que hubiese una guerra.
● **I suppose so/not** supongo que sí/no.
● **to be supposed to ...** **1** se supone que ... *(suposición)*. **2** deber ... *(obligación)*: *you're supposed to be in bed*, deberías estar en la cama.

supposed [səˈpəʊzd] *adj* supuesto,-a.

supposedly [səˈpəʊzədlɪ] *adv* supuestamente.

suppository [səˈpɒzɪtərɪ] *n* (*pl* **-ies**) supositorio.

suppress [səˈpres] *vt* **1** suprimir *(texto)*. **2** reprimir *(sentimientos, revuelta)*.

suppression [səˈpreʃən] *n* **1** supresión *(de texto)*. **2** represión *(de sentimientos, revuelta)*.

supremacy [suːˈpreməsɪ] *n* supremacía.

supreme [suːˈpriːm] *adj* supremo,-a.
■ **supreme court** JUR tribunal supremo.

supremely [suːˈpriːmlɪ] *adv* sumamente.

surcharge [ˈsɜːtʃɑːdʒ] *n* recargo.

sure [ʃʊəʳ] *adj* seguro,-a, cierto,-a: *I'm sure she told the truth*, estoy seguro de que dijo la verdad.
► *adv* **1** claro. **2** seguro. **3** realmente, de verdad: *he sure is handsome*, ¡qué guapo es!
● **sure enough** efectivamente.
● **to be sure to ...** no olvidarse de ....
● **to make sure** asegurarse.

surely [ˈʃʊəlɪ] *adv* seguramente, sin duda.

surf [sɜːf] *n* **1** oleaje. **2** espuma.
► *vi* hacer surf.
● **to surf the Net** navegar por Internet.

surface [ˈsɜːfəs] *n* **1** superficie. **2** firme.
► *vt* revestir.
► *vi* **1** salir a la superficie *(submarino)*. **2** surgir *(problemas)*.

surge [sɜːdʒ] *n* **1** oleaje. **2** alza, aumento *(de ventas)*. **3** oleada *(de gente)*. **4** arranque, arrebato *(de emociones)*.
► *vi* agitarse, encresparse.

surgeon [ˈsɜːdʒən] *n* cirujano,-a.

surgery ['sɜːdʒərɪ] *n* (*pl* -**ies**). **1** cirugía. **2** GB consultorio, consulta.

surgical ['sɜːdʒɪkəl] *adj* quirúrgico,-a.

surly ['sɜːlɪ] *adj* (-**ier**, -**iest**) hosco,-a, arisco,-a.

surname ['sɜːneɪm] *n* apellido.

surpass [sɜːˈpɑːs] *vt* superar, sobrepasar.

surplus ['sɜːpləs] *adj* sobrante.
► *n* (*pl* **surpluses**). **1** sobrante, excedente. **2** superávit.

surprise [səˈpraɪz] *n* sorpresa.
► *adj* inesperado,-a, sorpresa *(ataque)*.
► *vt* sorprender.
● **to give SB a surprise** dar una sorpresa a ALGN.
● **to take SB by surprise** coger desprevenido,-a a ALGN.

surprising [səˈpraɪzɪŋ] *adj* sorprendente.

surreal [səˈrɪəl] *adj* surrealista.

surrealism [səˈrɪəlɪzəm] *n* surrealismo.

surrender [səˈrendəʳ] *n* rendición, entrega *(de armas)*.
► *vt-vi* rendir(se), entregar(se).

surround [səˈraʊnd] *vt* rodear.

surrounding [səˈraʊndɪŋ] *adj* circundante.
► *npl* **surroundings 1** alrededores. **2** entorno.

surveillance [sɜːˈveɪləns] *n* vigilancia.

survey [(*n*) 'sɜːveɪ(*vb*) səˈveɪ] *n* **1** sondeo *(de opinión)*. **2** encuesta, estudio *(de tendencias)*. **3** reconocimiento *(edificio, tierra)*. **4** medición *(en topografía)*. **5** panorama, visión general.
► *vt* **1** contemplar. **2** estudiar, analizar. **3** inspeccionar *(edificio, tierra)*.

surveyor [səˈveɪəʳ] *n* agrimensor,-ra, topógrafo,-a.

survival [səˈvaɪvəl] *n* **1** supervivencia. **2** vestigio, reliquia.

survive [səˈvaɪv] *vt* sobrevivir a.
► *vi* sobrevivir.

survivor [səˈvaɪvəʳ] *n* superviviente.

susceptible [səˈseptɪbəl] *adj* **1** susceptible, sensible *(a ataques)*. **2** propenso,-a *(a enfermedades)*.

suspect [(*adj-n*) 'sʌspekt(*vb*) səˈspekt] *adj-n* sospechoso,-a.
► *vt* **1** sospechar. **2** imaginar.

suspend [səˈspend] *vt* **1** suspender *(partido)*. **2** expulsar *(alumno)*. **3** sancionar *(jugador)*. **4** suspender, colgar.
■ **suspended sentence** JUR condena condicional.

suspender [səˈspendəʳ] *n* liga.
► *npl* **suspenders** tirantes.

suspense [səsˈspens] *n* **1** incertidumbre. **2** suspense, tensión.
● **to keep SB in suspense** tener a alguien en suspenso.

suspension [səˈspenʃən] *n* **1** suspensión *(de partido)*. **2** expulsión *(de alumno)*. **3** sanción *(de jugador)*.
■ **suspension bridge** puente colgante.

suspicion [səˈspɪʃən] *n* **1** sospecha. **2** recelo, desconfianza.

suspicious [səˈspɪʃəs] *adj* **1** sospechoso,-a. **2** desconfiado,-a.

suspiciously [sʌˈspɪʃəslɪ] *adv* **1** de modo sospechoso. **2** con recelo.

sustain [səˈsteɪn] *vt* **1** sostener. **2** sustentar *(con comida, bebida)*. **3** sufrir *(lesión)*.

SW[1] ['ʃɔːtweɪv] *abbr* (*short wave*) onda corta.

SW[2] [saʊθˈwest] *abbr* (*southwest*) sudoeste, suroeste, SO.

swagger ['swægəʳ] *vi* contonearse.

swallow[1] ['swɒləʊ] *n* **1** trago *(de bebida)*. **2** bocado *(de comida)*.
► *vt-vi* tragar(se).

swallow[2] ['swɒləʊ] *n* golondrina *(ave)*.

swam [swæm] *pt* → swim.

swamp [swɒmp] *n* pantano, ciénaga.
► *vt* **1** inundar *(tierra)*. **2** hundir *(barco)*. **3** abrumar.

swan [swɒn] *n* cisne.

swap [swɒp] *vt-vi* (*pt & pp* **swapped**, *ger* **swapping**) *fam* intercambiar, cambiar.
to swap round *vt* cambiar de sitio.

swarm [swɔːm] *n* **1** enjambre *(de abejas)*. **2** nube *(de moscas)*.
► *vi fig* rebosar.

swarthy ['swɔːðɪ] *adj* (-**ier**, -**iest**) moreno,-a, atezado,-a.

swat [swɒt] *vt* (*pt & pp* **swatted**, *ger* **swatting**) aplastar.

sway [sweɪ] *n* **1** balanceo, vaivén *(movimiento)*. **2** dominio *(influencia)*.
► *vt* **1** balancear, mecer. **2** convencer, persuadir, influir.
► *vi* **1** balancearse, mecerse. **2** tambalearse.
● **to hold sway over SB** dominar a ALGN.

swear [sweəʳ] *vt-vi* (*pt* **swore** [swɔːʳ], *pp* **sworn** [swɔːn]) jurar.
► *vi* decir palabrotas, jurar, blasfemar.

● **to be sworn in** jurar el cargo.

to swear by *vt fam* tener entera confianza en.

swearword ['sweəwɜːd] *n* palabrota, taco.

sweat [swet] *n* **1** sudor. **2** *fam* trabajo duro.
▶ *vt-vi* sudar.

● **to sweat it out** *fam* aguantar.

sweater ['swetər] *n* suéter, jersey.

sweatshirt ['swetʃɜːt] *n* sudadera.

Swede [swiːd] *n* sueco,-a.

Sweden ['swiːdən] *n* Suecia.

Swedish ['swiːdɪʃ] *adj* sueco,-a.
▶ *n* **1** sueco,-a *(persona)*. **2** sueco *(lengua)*.
▶ *npl* **the Swedish** los suecos.

sweep [swiːp] *n* **1** barrido *(de escoba)*. **2** movimiento amplio, gesto amplio *(de brazo)*. **3** redada, batida *(de policía)*. **4** *fam* deshollinador,-ra.
▶ *vt-vi* *(pt & pp* **swept** [swept]*)* barrer *(con escoba)*.
▶ *vt* **1** barrer *(viento, olas)*. **2** recorrer, extenderse por. **3** arrastrar.

● **to sweep in/out/past** entrar/salir/pasar rápidamente.

● **to sweep SB off his/her feet** hacer volver loco a ALGN.

● **to make a clean sweep of things** hacer tabla rasa.

to sweep aside *vt* **1** aparcar bruscamente. **2** *fig* rechazar.

sweeper ['swiːpər] *n* **1** barrendero,-a *(persona)*. **2** barredora *(máquina)*.

sweeping ['swiːpɪŋ] *adj* **1** amplio,-a *(curva)*. **2** arrollador,-ra *(victoria)*.

sweet [swiːt] *adj* **1** dulce *(sabor)*. **2** agradable *(sensación)*. **3** fragante *(olor)*.
▶ *n* **1** caramelo, golosina. **2** postre.

● **to have a sweet tooth** ser goloso,-a.

■ **sweet corn** maíz.

■ **sweet pea** guisante de olor.

■ **sweet potato** boniato.

sweetcorn ['swiːtkɔːn] *n* maíz dulce.

sweeten ['swiːtən] *vt* endulzar, azucarar.

sweetener ['swiːtənər] *n* edulcorante.

sweetheart ['swiːthɑːt] *n* **1** cariño. **2** novio,-a.

swell [swel] *n* marejada, oleaje.
▶ *adj* US *fam* fenomenal.
▶ *vi* *(pt* **swelled** [sweld]*, pp* **swollen** ['swəulən]*)*. **1** levantarse *(mar)*. **2** crecer *(río, ventas)*. **3** hincharse *(cuerpo)*.

swelling ['swelɪŋ] *n* hinchazón.

swept [swept] *pt-pp* → sweep.

swerve [swɜːv] *n* viraje *(brusco)*.
▶ *vt-vi* desviar(se) bruscamente.

swift [swɪft] *adj fml* rápido,-a, veloz.
▶ *n* vencejo común.

swim [swɪm] *n* baño.
▶ *vi* *(pt* **swam** [swæm]*, pp* **swum** [swʌm]*, ger* **swimming***)* nadar.

● **to go for a swim** ir a nadar, ir a bañarse.

swimmer ['swɪmər] *n* nadador,-ra.

swimming ['swɪmɪŋ] *n* natación.

■ **swimming baths** piscina *(pública cubierta)*.

■ **swimming costume** bañador.

■ **swimming pool** piscina.

■ **swimming trunks** bañador.

swimsuit ['swɪmsuːt] *n* bañador, traje de baño.

swindle ['swɪndəl] *n* estafa, timo.
▶ *vt* estafar, timar.

swindler ['swɪndlər] *n* estafador,-ra, timador,-ra.

swine [swaɪn] *n* **1** cerdo *(animal)*. *pl* **swine**. **2** *fam* cerdo,-a, canalla *(persona)*. *pl* **swines**.

swing [swɪŋ] *n* **1** balanceo, oscilación. **2** columpio. **3** giro, cambio. **4** swing *(golf, tenis)*. **5** swing *(música)*.
▶ *vt* *(pt & pp* **swung** [swʌŋ]*)*. **1** balancear. **2** menear *(brazos)*. **3** columpiar. **4** hacer girar.
▶ *vi* **1** balancearse. **2** menearse *(brazos)*. **3** columpiarse.
▶ *vt-vi fig* girar, virar.

● **in full swing** en pleno apogeo, en pleno desarrollo.

swipe [swaɪp] *n* golpe.
▶ *vt* **1** golpear, pegar. **2** *fam* birlar, mangar.

swirl [swɜːl] *n* **1** remolino. **2** voluta *(de humo)*. **3** vuelo *(de falda)*.
▶ *vi* **1** arremolinarse. **2** dar vueltas *(persona)*.

Swiss [swɪs] *adj-n* suizo,-a.
▶ *npl* **the Swiss** los suizos.

switch [swɪtʃ] *n* *(pl* **-es***)*. **1** interruptor, llave. **2** cambio repentino. **3** intercambio, canje.
▶ *vt* **1** cambiar de. **2** desviar *(tren, atención, apoyo)*.

● **to switch one's attention to** desviar la atención a.

to switch off *vt* **1** apagar *(radio, TV)*. **2** cortar *(corriente)*.

to switch on vt **1** encender *(luz)*. **2** poner *(radio, TV)*.

to switch over vi cambiar.

switchboard ['swɪtʃbɔːd] n centralita.

■ **switchboard operator** telefonista.

Switzerland ['swɪtsələnd] n Suiza.

swivel ['swɪvəl] vt-vi (GB pt & pp **swivelled**, ger **swivelling**; US pt & pp **swiveled**, ger **swiveling**) girar(se).

■ **swivel chair** silla giratoria.

swollen ['swəʊlən] pp → swell.

swoop [swuːp] vi **1** abalanzarse *(ave)*. **2** bajar en picado *(avión)*. **3** hacer una redada *(policía)*.

sword [sɔːd] n espada.

swordfish ['sɔːdfɪʃ] n (pl -**es**) pez espada.

swore [swɔː'] pt → swear.

sworn [swɔːn] pp → swear.

swot [swɒt] n fam empollón,-ona.

▶ vi (pt & pp **swotted**, ger **swotting**) fam empollar.

swum [swʌm] pp → swim.

swung [swʌŋ] pt-pp → swing.

sycamore ['sɪkəmɔː'] n sicomoro.

syllable ['sɪləbəl] n sílaba.

syllabus ['sɪləbəs] n (pl **syllabuses**). **1** plan de estudios. **2** programa de estudios.

symbol ['sɪmbəl] n símbolo.

symbolic [sɪm'bɒlɪk] adj simbólico,-a.

symmetrical [sɪ'metrɪkəl] adj simétrico,-a.

symmetry ['sɪmɪtrɪ] n simetría.

sympathetic [sɪmpə'θetɪk] adj **1** compasivo,-a. **2** comprensivo,-a. **3** favorable, bien dispuesto.

sympathize ['sɪmpəθaɪz] vi **1** compadecerse. **2** comprender.

sympathizer ['sɪmpəθaɪzə'] n simpatizante.

sympathy ['sɪmpəθɪ] n (pl -**ies**). **1** compasión, lástima. **2** condolencia, pésame. **3** comprensión.

● **to express one's sympathy** dar el pésame.

symphony ['sɪmfənɪ] n (pl -**ies**) sinfonía.

symptom ['sɪmptəm] n síntoma.

synagogue ['sɪnəgɒg] (US **synagog**) n sinagoga.

synchronize ['sɪŋkrənaɪz] vt sincronizar.

syndicate ['sɪndɪkət] n **1** organización, agrupación. **2** agencia *de prensa*.

syndrome ['sɪndrəʊm] n síndrome.

synonym ['sɪnənɪm] n sinónimo.

synonymous [sɪ'nɒnɪməs] adj sinónimo,-a.

syntax ['sɪntæks] n sintaxis.

synthesis ['sɪnθəsɪs] n (pl **syntheses** ['sɪnθəsiːz]) síntesis.

synthesize ['sɪnθəsaɪz] vt sintetizar.

synthetic [sɪn'θetɪk] adj sintético,-a.

▶ n fibra sintética.

syringe [sɪ'rɪndʒ] n jeringa, jeringuilla.

syrup ['sɪrəp] n **1** jarabe. **2** almíbar.

system ['sɪstəm] n sistema.

■ **systems analyst** analista de sistemas.

systematic [sɪstə'mætɪk] adj sistemático,-a.

systematize ['sɪstɪmətaɪz] vt sistematizar.

T

ta [tɑː] *interj* GB *fam* ¡gracias!
tab [tæb] *n* **1** lengüeta. **2** etiqueta *(en ropa)*.
table ['teɪbəl] *n* **1** mesa. **2** tabla, cuadro.
► *vt* presentar.
● **to clear the table** quitar la mesa.
● **to lay the table** poner la mesa.
■ **table football** futbolín.
■ **table tennis** tenis de mesa.
tablecloth ['teɪbəlklɒθ] *n* mantel.
tablespoon ['teɪbəlspuːn] *n* cucharón.
tablet ['tæblət] *n* **1** pastilla. **2** lápida.
tabloid ['tæblɔɪd] *n* periódico.
taboo [təˈbuː] *adj* tabú.
► *n (pl* **taboos**) tabú.
tacit ['tæsɪt] *adj* tácito,-a.
tack [tæk] *n* **1** tachuela. **2** táctica.
► *vt* **1** clavar con tachuelas. **2** hilvanar.
● **to change tack** cambiar de táctica.
tackle ['tækəl] *n* **1** equipo, aparejos. **2** polea. **3** entrada *(fútbol)*. **4** placaje *(rugby)*.
► *vt* **1** abordar, hacer frente *(problema)*. **2** entrarle a *(jugador)*. **3** placar *(rugby)*.
tacky ['tækɪ] *adj* (**-ier**, **-iest**). **1** pegajoso, -a. **2** hortera.
tact [tækt] *n* tacto.
tactful ['tæktful] *adj* discreto,-a, diplomático,-a.
tactics ['tæktɪks] *npl* táctica.
tactless ['tæktləs] *adj* falto,-a de tacto, indiscreto,-a.
tadpole ['tædpəʊl] *n* renacuajo.
tag [tæg] *n* **1** etiqueta. **2** pillapilla *(juego)*. **3** coletilla *(frase)*.
► *vt* (*pt & pp* **tagged**, *ger* **tagging**) etiquetar.
to tag on *vt* **1** añadir. **2** pegarse a.
tail [teɪl] *vt* seguir.

► *n* cola, rabo.
► *npl* **tails** cruz *(de moneda)*.
tailback ['teɪlbæk] *n* caravana, cola.
tailor ['teɪlə'] *n* sastre,-a.
► *vt fig* adaptar.
tailor-made [teɪləˈmeɪd] *adj* hecho,-a a medida.
taint [teɪnt] *vt* mancillar.
Taiwan [taɪˈwæn] *n* Taiwan.
take [teɪk] *vt* (*pt* **took** [tʊk], *pp* **taken** ['teɪkən]). **1** tomar, coger. **2** tomar *(comida, bebida)*. **3** aceptar: *he refused to take the money*, se negó a aceptar el dinero. **4** llevar: *she took me to the airport*, me llevó al aeropuerto. **5** requerir, necesitar: *it took two men to carry it*, tuvieron que llevarlo entre dos hombres. **6** apuntar, anotar. **7** ocupar: *this chair is taken*, esta silla está ocupada. **8** aguantar: *he can't take a joke*, no sabe aceptar una broma. **9** suponer. **10** llevar, tardar: *it will take two weeks*, tardará dos semanas.
► *n* toma *(filmando)*.
● **to take it out on SB** tomarla con ALGN: *she took it out on me*, la tomó conmigo.
● **to take STH up with SB** tratar algo con ALGN.
● **to take to one's heels** darse a la fuga.
to take after *vt* parecerse a.
to take away *vt* **1** llevarse. **2** quitar, sacar. **3** restar.
to take back *vt* **1** devolver. **2** retractarse: *he took back what he said*, se retractó de lo dicho.
to take down *vt* **1** desmontar *(piezas)*. **2** descolgar *(abrigo)*. **3** apuntar.

to take in *vt* **1** dar cobijo a. **2** engañar. **3** asimilar *(datos)*. **4** incluir *(correcciones)*. **5** meter *(ropa)*.

to take off *vt* **1** quitarse *(ropa)*. **2** imitar. ▶ *vi* despegar *(avión)*.

to take on *vt* **1** hacerse cargo de. **2** aceptar *(empleo)*. **3** contratar, emplear *(empleado)*.

to take out *vt* **1** sacar. **2** invitar a salir. **3** hacer *(seguro)*.

to take over *vt* apoderarse de *(país)*. ▶ *vi* tomar el poder.

to take over from *vt* relevar.

to take to *vt* **1** tomar cariño a *(persona)*. **2** engancharse a *(vicio)*. **3** empezar a.

to take up *vt* **1** ocupar *(tiempo, espacio)*. **2** continuar *(historia)*. **3** aceptar *(oferta)*. **4** empezar a: *he's taken up the guitar*, ha empezado a tocar la guitarra.

takeaway ['teɪkəweɪ] *n* establecimiento que vende comida para llevar.

taken ['teɪkən] *pp* → take.

takeoff ['teɪkɒf] *n* despegue.

takeover ['teɪkəʊvəʳ] *n* **1** toma de posesión *(de gobierno)*. **2** adquisición, absorción *(de empresa)*.

takings ['teɪkɪŋz] *npl* recaudación.

talcum powder ['tælkəmpaʊdəʳ] *n* polvos de talco.

tale [teɪl] *n* cuento.

● **to tell tales** contar cuentos.

talent ['tælənt] *n* talento.

■ **talent scout** cazatalentos *mf inv*.

talented ['tæləntɪd] *adj* de talento.

talk [tɔːk] *vt-vi* hablar.

▶ *n* **1** conversación, charla. **2** rumor.

● **to talk SB into STH** convencer a ALGN para que haga algo.

● **to talk SB out of STH** disuadir a ALGN de hacer algo.

■ **talk show** programa de entrevistas.

to talk over *vt* discutir.

to talk round *vt* convencer.

talkative ['tɔːkətɪv] *adj* hablador,-ra.

talker ['tɔːkəʳ] *n* hablador,-ra.

talking-to ['tɔːkɪŋtuː] *n* *(pl* **talkings-to)** *fam* bronca.

tall [tɔːl] *adj* alto,-a: *how tall are you?*, ¿cuánto mides?; *it's 5 metres tall*, mide 5 metros de alto.

■ **tall story** cuento chino.

tally ['tælɪ] *n* *(pl* **-ies)** cuenta.

▶ *vi* *(pt & pp* **tallied**, *ger* **tallying)** concordar.

tambourine [tæmbəˈriːn] *n* pandereta.

tame [teɪm] *adj* **1** manso,-a, dócil. **2** domesticado,-a. **3** *fig* soso,-a.

▶ *vt* domar, domesticar.

tamper with ['tæmpəwɪð] *vt* **1** interferir en, manipular. **2** falsificar. **3** estropear.

tampon ['tæmpɒn] *n* tampón.

tan [tæn] *n* **1** color canela. **2** bronceado.

▶ *vt* *(pt & pp* **tanned**, *ger* **tanning)**. **1** curtir *(cuero)*. **2** broncear, poner moreno, -a *(piel)*.

▶ *vi* broncearse, ponerse moreno,-a *(piel)*.

tangent ['tændʒənt] *n* tangente.

● **to go off at a tangent** salirse por la tangente.

tangerine [tændʒəˈriːn] *n* mandarina.

tangle ['tæŋgəl] *n* enredo.

▶ *vt* enredar.

▶ *vi* enredarse, enmarañarse.

to tangle with *vt* meterse con.

tango ['tæŋgəʊ] *n* *(pl* **tangos)** tango.

tank [tæŋk] *n* **1** depósito, tanque. **2** tanque, carro de combate.

tanker ['tæŋkəʳ] *n* **1** buque cisterna. **2** petrolero. **3** camión cisterna.

tantamount to ['tæntəmaʊnt tʊ] *prep* equivalente a.

tantrum ['tæntrəm] *n* berrinche, rabieta.

tap¹ [tæp] *n* grifo.

▶ *vt* *(pt & pp* **tapped**, *ger* **tapping)**. **1** explotar *(recursos)*. **2** pinchar, intervenir *(teléfono)*.

● **to turn the tap off** cerrar el grifo.

● **to turn the tap on** abrir el grifo.

tap² [tæp] *n* golpecito.

▶ *vt* *(pt & pp* **tapped**, *ger* **tapping)** golpear suavemente.

tap³ [tæp] *n* claqué.

■ **tap dancer** bailador,-ra de claqué.

tape [teɪp] *n* cinta.

▶ *vt* **1** pegar con cinta. **2** grabar.

■ **tape measure** cinta métrica.

■ **tape recorder** magnetófono, grabadora.

tapestry ['tæpəstrɪ] *n* *(pl* **-ies)** tapiz.

tar [tɑːʳ] *n* alquitrán.

target ['tɑːgɪt] *n* **1** blanco, objetivo. **2** meta.

tariff ['tærɪf] *n* *(pl* **tariffs)** **1** tarifa. **2** arancel.

tarmac ['tɑːmæk] *n* asfalto.

tarnish ['tɑːnɪʃ] *vt* **1** deslustrar *(plata)*. **2** empañar *(reputación)*.

► *vi* deslustrarse *(plata).*

tart [tɑːt] *adj* **1** acre, agrio,-a *(sabor).* **2** mordaz *(réplica).*

► *n* **1** tarta, pastel. **2** *sl* fulana.

tartan ['tɑːtən] *n* tartán.

task [tɑːsk] *n* tarea, labor.

taste [teɪst] *n* **1** gusto: *he has a terrible taste in clothes,* tiene muy mal gusto con la ropa. **2** sabor, gusto. **3** afición, gusto.

► *vt* **1** probar *(comida).* **2** catar *(vino).*

► *vi* saber: *this chocolate tastes of almonds,* este chocolate sabe a almendras.

● **in bad taste** de mal gusto.

● **in good taste** de buen gusto.

● **to have good taste in STH** tener buen gusto para algo.

tasteful ['teɪstfʊl] *adj* de buen gusto.

tasteless ['teɪstləs] *adj* **1** de mal gusto. **2** insípido,-a, soso,-a.

tasty ['teɪsti] *adj* (-ier, -iest) sabroso,-a.

ta-ta [tæ'tɑː] *interj* GB *fam* ¡adiós!

tattered ['tætəd] *adj* harapiento,-a, andrajoso,-a.

tatters ['tætəz] *npl* harapos, andrajos.

● **in tatters** andrajoso,-a, hecho jirones.

tattoo [tə'tuː] *n* (*pl* **tattoos**) tatuaje.

► *vt* tatuar.

tatty ['tæti] *adj* (-ier, -iest) **1** en mal estado *(mueble).* **2** raído,-a *(ropa).*

taught [tɔːt] *pt-pp* → teach.

taunt [tɔːnt] *n* mofa, pulla.

► *vt* mofarse de.

Taurus ['tɔːrəs] *n* Tauro.

taut [tɔːt] *adj* tirante, tieso,-a.

tavern ['tævən] *n* taberna, mesón.

tax [tæks] *n* (*pl* **taxes**) **1** impuesto, tasa. **2** contribución.

► *vt* **1** gravar *(artículo).* **2** cobrar impuestos a *(persona).*

■ **tax avoidance** evasión de impuestos.

■ **tax evasion** fraude fiscal.

■ **tax free** libre de impuestos.

■ **tax return** declaración de la renta.

taxation [tæk'seɪʃən] *n* impuestos.

taxi ['tæksi] *n* taxi.

■ **taxi driver** taxista.

taxpayer ['tækspeɪə'] *n* contribuyente.

TB ['tiː'biː] *abbr* (**tuberculosis**) tuberculosis.

tbsp ['teɪblspuːn] *abbr* (**tablespoon**) cucharada.

| pl **tbsps**. |

tea [tiː] *n* **1** té. **2** merienda. **3** cena.

■ **tea set** juego de té.

■ **tea spoon** cucharilla.

teach [tiːtʃ] *vt* (*pt & pp* **taught**). **1** enseñar. **2** dar clases de *(asignatura).*

► *vi* dar clases.

teacher ['tiːtʃə'] *n* maestro,-a, profesor,-ra.

teaching ['tiːtʃɪŋ] *n* enseñanza.

■ **teaching staff** profesorado, cuerpo docente.

teacloth ['tiːklɒθ] *n* paño de cocina.

teacup ['tiːkʌp] *n* taza de té.

team [tiːm] *n* equipo.

teapot ['tiːpɒt] *n* tetera.

tear¹ [tɪə'] *n* lágrima.

● **in tears** llorando.

● **to burst into tears** romper a llorar.

■ **tear gas** gas lacrimógeno.

tear² [teə'] *n* enganchón, rotura, siete.

► *vt* (*pt* **tore** [tɔː'], *pp* **torn** [tɔːn]) rasgar, romper: *I tore my trousers on a nail,* me hice un enganchón en el pantalón con un clavo.

to tear down *vt* derribar.

to tear into *vt* arremeter contra.

to tear up *vt* romper en pedazos.

teardrop ['tɪədrɒp] *n* lágrima.

tearful ['tɪəfʊl] *adj* lloroso,-a.

tease [tiːz] *vt* burlarse, tomar el pelo a.

teaspoon ['tiːspuːn] *n* cucharilla.

teaspoonful ['tiːspuːnfʊl] *n* cucharadita.

teat [tiːt] *n* **1** teta. **2** tetina *(de botella).*

technical ['teknɪkəl] *adj* técnico,-a.

■ **technical college** instituto superior de formación profesional.

technician [tek'nɪʃən] *n* técnico,-a.

technique [tek'niːk] *n* técnica.

technological [teknə'lɒdʒɪkəl] *adj* tecnológico,-a.

technology [tek'nɒlədʒɪ] *n* tecnología.

teddy bear ['tedɪbeə'] *n* osito de peluche.

tedious ['tiːdɪəs] *adj* tedioso,-a, aburrido,-a.

teem [tiːm] *vi* abundar en, estar lleno,-a: *the lake teems with fish,* el lago está lleno de peces; *the streets were teeming,* las calles estaban abarrotadas.

teenage ['tiːneɪdʒ] *adj* adolescente.

teenager ['tiːneɪdʒə'] *n* adolescente *(de 13 a 19 años).*

teeny ['tiːnɪ] *adj* (-ier, -iest) *fam* chiquitín,-ina.

| También **teeny-weeny**. |

tee-shirt ['tiːʃɜːt] *n* camiseta.

teeter ['tiːtə'] *vi* balancearse.

teeth [tiːθ] *npl* → tooth.

teethe [tiːð] *vi* echar los dientes.

teetotaller [tiːˈtəʊtlə'] *n* abstemio,-a.

TEFL ['tefəl, ˌtiːˈiːefˈel] *abbr (Teaching of English as a Foreign Language)* enseñanza del inglés como lengua extranjera.

tel [tel, 'telifəʊn] *abbr (telephone)* teléfono, tel.

telecommunications ['telikəmjuːnɪˈkeɪʃənz] *npl* telecomunicaciones.

telegram ['teligræm] *n* telegrama.

telegraph ['teligrɑːf] *n* telégrafo.
▸ *vt-vi* telegrafiar.
■ **telegraph pole** poste telegráfico.

telepathy [tɪˈlepəθɪ] *n* telepatía.

telephone ['telifəʊn] *n* teléfono.
▸ *vt-vi* telefonear, llamar por teléfono.
■ **telephone box** cabina telefónica.
■ **telephone directory** guía telefónica.
■ **telephone number** número de teléfono.
■ **telephone operator** operador,-ra, telefonista.

telephoto lens [telɪfəʊtəʊˈlenz] *n (pl lenses)* teleobjetivo.

telescope ['teliskəʊp] *n* telescopio.

televise ['telivaɪz] *vt* televisar.

television ['telivɪʒən] *n* **1** televisión: *to watch television*, ver la televisión. **2** televisor.
● **on television** en televisión: *what's on television?*, ¿qué echan por la televisión?
■ **television set** televisor.

telex ['teleks] *n (pl telexes)* télex.
▸ *vt* enviar por télex a.

tell [tel] *vt (pt & pp told* [təʊld]). **1** decir. **2** contar *(historia)*. **3** distinguir: *to tell right from wrong*, distinguir el bien del mal.
▸ *vi* saber: *you never can tell*, nunca se sabe.
● **I told you so** ya te lo dije.
● **to tell tales** contar cuentos.

to tell apart *vt* distinguir.

to tell off *vt* echar una bronca a, reñir.

to tell on *vt* **1** afectar a. **2** chivar.

teller ['telə'] *n* cajero,-a.

telling-off [telɪŋˈɒf] *n (pl tellings-off)* *fam* bronca.

telltale ['telteɪl] *n* chivato,-a, acusica.

telly ['telɪ] *n (pl -ies)* *fam* tele.

temper ['tempə'] *n* **1** humor. **2** mal genio. **3** temperamento.
▸ *vt* templar, suavizar.
● **to be in a temper** estar de mal humor.
● **to lose one's temper** enfadarse, perder los estribos.

temperament ['tempərəmənt] *n* temperamento.

temperate ['tempərət] *adj* **1** moderado,-a *(persona)*. **2** templado,-a *(clima)*.

temperature ['tempərətʃə'] *n* temperatura.
● **to have a temperature** tener fiebre.

tempest ['tempəst] *n* tempestad.

temple ['tempəl] *n* **1** templo. **2** sien.

tempo ['tempəʊ] *n (pl tempos)*. **1** tempo. **2** *fig* ritmo.

temporary ['tempərərɪ] *adj* temporal, provisional.

tempt [tempt] *vt* tentar.

temptation [tempˈteɪʃən] *n* tentación.

tempting ['temptɪŋ] *adj* tentador,-ra.

ten [ten] *adj* diez.
▸ *n* diez.

tenacious [təˈneɪʃəs] *adj* tenaz.

tenacity [təˈnæsɪtɪ] *n* tenacidad.

tenant ['tenənt] *n* inquilino,-a, arrendatario,-a.

tend [tend] *vi* tender a, tener tendencia a.
▸ *vt* cuidar, atender.

tendency ['tendənsɪ] *n (pl -ies)* tendencia.

tender[1] ['tendə'] *adj (comp tenderer, superl tenderest)*. **1** tierno,-a *(carne)*. **2** tierno,-a, cariñoso,-a *(persona)*. **3** dolorido,-a *(herida)*.

tender[2] ['tendə'] *n* oferta.
▸ *vt* presentar.

tender[3] ['tendə'] *n* **1** ténder *(de tren)*. **2** lancha auxiliar.

tenderhearted ['tendəhɑːtɪd] *adj* compasivo,-a, bondadoso,-a.

tenderness ['tendənəs] *n* ternura.

tendon ['tendən] *n* tendón.

tenement ['tenəmənt] *n* bloque de pisos.

tennis ['tenɪs] *n* tenis.
■ **tennis court** pista de tenis.
■ **tennis player** tenista.

tenor ['tenə'] *n* tenor.

tense [tens] *adj* tenso,-a.
► *n* tiempo *(de verbo).*
► *vt-vi* tensar(se).

tension ['tenʃən] *n* tensión.

tent [tent] *n* tienda de campaña.

tentacle ['tentəkəl] *n* tentáculo.

tentative ['tentətɪv] *adj* **1** de prueba, provisional *(plan).* **2** indeciso,-a *(persona).*

tenth [tenθ] *adj-n* décimo,-a.
► *n* **1** décimo. **2** décima parte. **3** diez *(en fecha).*

tenuous ['tenjʊəs] *adj* tenue, sutil.

tenure ['tenjə'] *n* tenencia, posesión.

tepid ['tepɪd] *adj* tibio,-a.

term [tɜːm] *vt* calificar de, llamar.
► *n* **1** trimestre. **2** período, plazo. **3** término, expresión: *a scientific term*, un término científico.
► *npl* **terms 1** condiciones. **2** relaciones.
● **in terms of** por lo que se refiere a, desde el punto de vista de.
● **in the long/short term** a largo/corto plazo.
● **to be on good terms with** tener buenas relaciones con.
● **to come to terms with STH** aceptar algo.

terminal ['tɜːmɪnəl] *adj* terminal.
► *n* terminal *(de ordenador, aeropuerto).*

terminate ['tɜːmɪneɪt] *vt-vi* terminar.

terminology [tɜːmɪ'nɒlədʒɪ] *n (pl* **-ies)** terminología.

terminus ['tɜːmɪnəs] *n (pl* **-es** o **termini** ['tɜːmɪnaɪ])** terminal *(estación).*

termite ['tɜːmaɪt] *n* termita.

terrace ['terəs] *n* **1** terraza. **2** hilera *(de cosas adosadas).*
► *npl* **terraces** gradas.

terrain [tə'reɪn] *n* terreno.

terrestrial [tə'restrɪəl] *adj* terrestre.

terrible ['terɪbəl] *adj* **1** terrible. **2** *fam* fatal.

terribly ['terɪblɪ] *adv* **1** terriblemente. **2** muy mal, fatal.

terrific [tə'rɪfɪk] *adj* fabuloso,-a, estupendo,-a.

terrify ['terɪfaɪ] *vt (pt & pp* **-ied)** aterrar, aterrorizar.

terrifying ['terɪfaɪɪŋ] *adj* aterrador,-ra.

territory ['terɪtərɪ] *n (pl* **-ies)** territorio.

terror ['terə'] *n* terror, espanto.

terrorism ['terərɪzəm] *n* terrorismo.

terrorist ['terərɪst] *adj-n* terrorista.

terrorize ['terəraɪz] *vt* aterrorizar.

terse [tɜːs] *adj* lacónico,-a.

test [test] *n* **1** prueba. **2** examen, test. **3** análisis.
► *vt* probar, poner a prueba.
■ **test tube** tubo de ensayo.
■ **test tube baby** niño,-a probeta.

testament ['testəmənt] *n* testamento.

testicle ['testɪkəl] *n* testículo.

testify ['testɪfaɪ] *vt (pt & pp* **-ied)** declarar, testificar.
► *vi* prestar declaración, declarar.

testimony ['testɪmənɪ] *n (pl* **-ies)** testimonio.

tetanus ['tetənəs] *n* tétanos.

tether ['teðə'] *vt* atar.
● **to be at the end of one's tether** no poder aguantar más.

text [tekst] *n* texto.

textbook ['tekstbʊk] *n* libro de texto.

textile ['tekstaɪl] *adj* textil.
► *n* textil, tejido.

texture ['tekstʃə'] *n* textura.

Thai [taɪ] *adj* tailandés,-esa.
► *n* **1** tailandés,-esa *(persona).* **2** tailandés *(lengua).*

Thailand ['taɪlænd] *n* Tailandia.

Thames [temz] *n* el Támesis.

than [ðæn, ŋʊð.ɒɪʊɐmə.ɒnecursmʊnstressednʊð.ɒɪʊɐmɐɸ.ɒnecursm̩ ðən] *conj* **1** que: *he is taller than you*, él es más alto que tú. **2** de: *more than once*, más de una vez.

thank [θæŋk] *vt* dar las gracias a, agradecer.
► *npl* **thanks** gracias.
● **thank God!** ¡gracias a Dios!
● **thanks to** gracias a.
● **thank you** gracias.

thankful ['θæŋkfʊl] *adj* agradecido,-a.

thanksgiving [θæŋks'gɪvɪŋ] *n* acción de gracias.

that [ðæt] *adj* ese, esa, aquel, aquella: *look at that cow*, mira esa vaca.
► *pron (pl* **those).** **1** ése, ésa, aquél, aquélla: *this is mine, that is yours*, ésta es mía, ésa es tuya. **2** eso, aquello: *what's that?*, ¿qué es eso? **3** *que (relativo): the car (that) he drives*, el coche que conduce. **4** que, el/la que, el/la cual *(con preposición): the door (that) he went through*, la puerta por la que/cual pasó.
► *conj* que: *I know (that) it's true*, sé que es verdad.

▶ *adv fam* tan: *it's not that dear!*, ino es tan caro!

● **that is** es decir.

● **that's it!** ibasta!, ise acabó!

● **that much** tanto,-a.

● **that's right** eso es.

thatch [θætʃ] *n* tejado de paja.

thaw [θɔː] *n* deshielo.

▶ *vt-vi* deshelar(se), descongelar(se).

the [ðə] *det* el, la, los, las.

▶ *adv*: *the more you have the more you want*, cuanto más se tiene más se quiere; *the sooner, the better*, cuanto antes mejor.

Delante de una vocal se pronuncia [ði] con énfasis [ðiː].

theatre ['θɪətə'] (US **theater**) *n* **1** teatro. **2** quirófano. **3** sala *(de cine)*.

theatrical [θɪ'ætrɪkəl] *adj* teatral.

theft [θeft] *n* robo, hurto.

their [ðeə'] *adj* su, sus.

theirs [ðeəz] *pron* (el) suyo, (la) suya, (los) suyos, (las) suyas: *our flat is like theirs*, nuestro piso es como el suyo.

them [ðem, *unstressed* ðəm] *pron* **1** los, las *(comp directo)*: *I'll phone them later*, las llamaré después. **2** les *(comp indirecto)*. **3** ellos, ellas *(con preposisición)*: *why don't you go with them?*, ¿por qué no vas con ellos?

theme [θiːm] *n* tema.

■ **theme park** parque temático.

themselves [ðəm'selvz] *pron* **1** ellos mismos, ellas mismas *(sujeto)*. **2** se: *they enjoyed themselves*, se divirtieron. **3** ellos mismos, ellas mismas: *they did it by themselves*, lo hicieron ellos solos.

then [ðen] *adv* **1** entonces: *we'll see you then*, nos veremos entonces. **2** entonces, luego, después: *I'll have soup first and then steak*, primero tomaré sopa y luego un filete. **3** pues, en ese caso. **4** en aquella época, entonces: *life was harder then*, entonces la vida era más dura.

▶ *adj* (de) entonces.

● **now and then** de vez en cuando.

● **now then** pues bien.

● **then again** también: *he may come and then again he may not*, puede que venga, y también puede que no.

theology [θɪ'ɒlədʒɪ] *n (pl* **-ies**) teología.

theorem ['θɪərəm] *n* teorema.

theoretical [θɪə'retɪcəl] *adj* teórico,-a.

theorize ['θɪəraɪz] *vi* teorizar.

theory ['θɪərɪ] *n (pl* **-ies**) teoría.

therapeutic [θerə'pjuːtɪk] *adj* terapéutico,-a.

therapy ['θerəpɪ] *n (pl* **-ies**) terapia.

there [ðeə'] *adv* allí, allá, ahí.

● **there is/are** hay.

● **there was/were** había.

● **there you are** ahí tienes.

thereabouts [ðeərə'bauts] *adv* por ahí.

thereafter [ðeə'ræftə'] *adv* a partir de entonces.

thereby ['ðeəbaɪ] *adv* de ese modo.

therefore ['ðeəfɔː'] *adv* por lo tanto.

thermal ['θɜːməl] *adj* **1** termal. **2** térmico,-a.

■ **thermal springs** fuentes termales, termas.

thermometer [θe'mɒmɪtə'] *n* termómetro.

thermos® ['θɜːmɒs] *n* termo.

También **thermos flask**.

thermostat ['θɜːməstæt] *n* termostato.

thesaurus [θɪ'sɔːrəs] *n (pl* **-es** o **thesauri** [θɪ'sɔːraɪ]) diccionario ideológico, tesauro.

these [ðiːz] *adj* estos,-as.

▶ *pron* éstos,-as.

thesis ['θiːsɪs] *n (pl* **theses** ['θiːsiːz]) tesis.

they [ðeɪ] *pron* ellos,-as.

● **they say that** dicen que, se dice que.

thick [θɪk] *adj* **1** grueso,-a: *two inches thick*, de dos pulgadas de grueso. **2** espeso,-a, denso *(líquido, bosque)*. **3** denso,-a *(gas)*. **4** poblado,-a, tupido,-a *(barba)*. **5** *fam* corto,-a de alcances, de pocas luces *(persona)*.

thicken ['θɪkən] *vt-vi* espesar(se).

thickness ['θɪknəs] *n* espesor, grueso, grosor.

thief [θiːf] *n (pl* **thieves**) ladrón,-ona.

thieve [θiːv] *vt - vi* robar, hurtar.

thigh [θaɪ] *n* muslo.

thimble ['θɪmbəl] *n* dedal.

thin [θɪn] *adj (comp* **thinner**, *superl* **thinnest**). **1** delgado,-a, flaco,-a *(persona)*. **2** fino,-a *(rebanada, material)*. **3** ralo,-a *(pelo, vegetación)*. **4** claro,-a, poco espeso,-a *(líquido)*.

▶ *vt (pt & pp* **thinned**, *ger* **thinning**) diluir.

to thin down vt aclarar.
► vi adelgazar.
thing [θɪŋ] n cosa.
• for one thing entre otras cosas.
• poor thing! ¡pobrecito,-a!
• the thing is ... el caso es que ....
think [θɪŋk] vt - vi (pt & pp thought [θɔːt]). 1 pensar. 2 pensar, imaginar: I thought so, me lo imaginaba. 3 pensar, opinar, parecer: what do you think of my new jacket?, ¿qué te parece mi chaqueta nueva?
► vt pensar, creer.
• think nothing of it no tiene importancia.
• to think better of it pensárselo mejor.
to think back vi recordar, hacer memoria.
to think over vt meditar, reflexionar.
to think up vt inventar, idear.
thinker ['θɪŋkəʳ] n pensador,-ra.
thinking ['θɪŋkɪŋ] n opinión, parecer.
third [θɜːd] adj tercero,-a.
► n 1 tercero,-a. 2 tercio, tercera parte (fracción). 3 tres (en fecha).
■ third party tercera persona.
■ third party insurance seguro a terceros.
■ Third World Tercer Mundo.
thirst [θɜːst] n sed.
thirsty ['θɜːstɪ] adj (-ier, -iest) sediento,-a.
• to be thirsty tener sed.
thirteen [θɜːˈtiːn] adj-n trece.
thirteenth [θɜːˈtiːnθ] adj - n decimotercero,-a.
► n 1 decimotercero. 2 decimotercera parte. 3 trece (en fecha).
thirtieth ['θɜːtɪəθ] adj - n trigésimo,-a.
► n 1 trigésimo. 2 trigésima parte. 3 treinta (en fecha).
thirty ['θɜːtɪ] adj-n treinta.
this [ðɪs] adj (pl these) este, esta.
► pron éste, ésta, esto.
► adv así: it was this big, era así de grande.
• like this así.
thistle ['θɪsəl] n cardo.
thong [θɒŋ] n correa.
thorn [θɔːn] n espina, pincho.
thorny ['θɔːnɪ] adj (-ier, -iest) espinoso,-a.

thorough ['θʌrə] adj 1 profundo,-a, a fondo (investigación). 2 cuidadoso,-a, minucioso,-a (persona). 3 total, completo,-a (idiota).
thoroughfare ['θʌrəfeəʳ] n vía pública.
thoroughly ['θʌrəlɪ] adv 1 a fondo, a conciencia, minuciosamente (examinar). 2 totalmente, absolutamente.
those [ðəʊz] adj esos,-as, aquellos,-as.
► pron ésos,-as, aquéllos,-as.
though [ðəʊ] conj 1 aunque, si bien: though I love her, I cannot marry her, aunque la quiero, no puedo casarme con ella. 2 pero: the restaurant was full, we got a table though, el restaurante estaba lleno, pero conseguimos una mesa.
► adv sin embargo.
• as though como si.
• even though aunque.
thought [θɔːt] pt/pp → think.
► n 1 pensamiento. 2 idea: I've just had a thought, se me acaba de ocurrir una idea. 3 consideración.
thoughtful ['θɔːtfʊl] adj 1 pensativo,-a, meditabundo,-a. 2 considerado,-a, atento,-a.
thoughtfulness ['θɔːtfʊlnəs] n 1 meditación. 2 consideración, atención.
thoughtless ['θɔːtləs] adj 1 desconsiderado,-a. 2 irreflexivo,-a.
thoughtlessness ['θɔːtləsnəs] n irreflexión, falta de consideración.
thousand ['θaʊzənd] adj-n mil.
thousandth ['θaʊzənθ] adj - n milésimo,-a.
► n 1 milésimo. 2 milésima parte.
thrash [θræʃ] vt 1 azotar, dar una paliza a. 2 derrotar.
► vi revolcarse, agitarse.
thrashing ['θræʃɪŋ] n zurra, paliza.
thread [θred] n 1 hilo. 2 rosca (de tornillo).
► vt 1 enhebrar (aguja). 2 ensartar (cuentas).
threat [θret] n amenaza.
threaten ['θretən] vt - vi amenazar.
threatening ['θretənɪŋ] adj amenazador,-ra.
three [θriː] adj-n tres.
three-dimensional [θriːdɪˈmenʃənəl] adj tridimensional.
thresh [θreʃ] vt - vi trillar.
threshold ['θreʃəʊld] n umbral.

threw [θruː] *pt* → throw.

thrifty ['θrɪftɪ] *adj* (-**ier**, -**iest**) económico,-a, frugal.

thrill [θrɪl] *n* emoción.
► *vt-vi* emocionar(se).
● **to get a thrill out of STH** emocionarse con algo.

thriller ['θrɪləʳ] *n* novela de suspense, película de suspense.

thrilling ['θrɪlɪŋ] *adj* emocionante.

thrive [θraɪv] *vi* (*pt* **thrived** o **throve** [θrəʊv], *pp* **thrived** o **thriven** ['θrɪvən]). **1** crecer *(planta)*. **2** prosperar *(industria)*.

thriving ['θraɪvɪŋ] *adj* próspero,-a, floreciente.

throat [θrəʊt] *n* garganta.
● **to be at each other's throats** tirarse los platos a la cabeza.

throb [θrɒb] *n* latido, palpitación.
► *vi* (*pt & pp* **throbbed**, *ger* **throbbing**) latir, palpitar.

thrombosis [θrɒm'bəʊsɪs] *n* (*pl* **thromboses**) trombosis.

throne [θrəʊn] *n* trono.

throng [θrɒŋ] *n* muchedumbre, tropel.
► *vi* apiñarse, agolparse.
► *vt* atestar.

throttle ['θrɒtəl] *n* válvula reguladora.
► *vt* estrangular.

through [θruː] *prep* **1** por, a través de: *through the door*, por la puerta. **2** por, a causa de: *off work through illness*, de baja por enfermedad. **3** durante todo,-a: *we danced through the night*, bailamos durante toda la noche. **4** hasta el final de: *he read through the book*, leyó todo el libro. **5** a través de: *I found out through a friend*, me enteré a través de un amigo.
► *adv* **1** de un lado a otro: *he let me through*, me dejó pasar. **2** hasta el final: *he read the book through*, leyó todo el libro.
► *adj* directo,-a.
● **to be through with** haber acabado con.
● **through and through** de arriba abajo.

throughout [θruː'aʊt] *prep* **1** por, en todo,-a: *throughout the world*, en todo el mundo. **2** durante todo,-a, a lo largo de: *throughout the year*, durante todo el año.

► *adv* **1** por todas partes, en todas partes. **2** completamente. **3** todo el tiempo.

throve [θrəʊv] *pt* → thrive.

throw [θrəʊ] *n* **1** lanzamiento, tiro. **2** tirada *(de dados)*.
► *vt* (*pt* **threw**, *pp* **thrown**). **1** tirar, arrojar, lanzar. **2** poner: *she threw a blanket over him*, le puso una manta encima.

to throw away *vt* **1** tirar *(basura)*. **2** desaprovechar *(oportunidad)*.

to throw back *vt* devolver.

to throw in *vt fam* incluir *(gratis)*.

to throw off *vt* librarse de.

to throw out *vt* **1** echar *(persona)*. **2** rechazar *(propuesta)*.

to throw up *vi* vomitar.

thru [θruː] *prep - adv* US → through: *Monday thru Friday*, de lunes a viernes.

thrush [θrʌʃ] *n* (*pl* -**es**) tordo.

thrust [θrʌst] *n* **1** empuje. **2** estocada *(de espada)*.
► *vt* **1** empujar. **2** clavar *(espada)*.

thud [θʌd] *n* ruido sordo.
► *vt* (*pt & pp* **thudded**, *ger* **thudding**) hacer un ruido sordo.

thug [θʌg] *n* matón, gamberro.

thumb [θʌm] *n* pulgar.

thumbtack ['θʌmtæk] *n* US chincheta.

thump [θʌmp] *n* golpe.
► *vt* golpear.

thunder ['θʌndəʳ] *n* trueno.
► *vi* tronar.

thunderstorm ['θʌndəstɔːm] *n* tormenta.

Thurs ['θɜːzdɪ] *abbr* (**Thursday**) jueves.
| También se escribe **Thur**. |

Thursday ['θɜːzdɪ] *n* jueves.

thus [ðʌs] *adv* así, de este modo.

thwart [θwɔːt] *vt* desbaratar, frustrar.

thyme [taɪm] *n* tomillo.

tic [tɪk] *n* tic.

tick¹ [tɪk] *n* garrapata.

tick² [tɪk] *n* **1** tictac *(ruido)*. **2** marca, señal.
► *vi* hacer tictac *(reloj)*.
► *vt* señalar, marcar *(con señal)*.

to tick off *vt* **1** marcar. **2** regañar.

ticket ['tɪkɪt] *n* **1** billete *(de bus, etc)*. **2** entrada *(de cine, etc)*. **3** etiqueta, resguardo. **4** *fam* multa.
■ **ticket collector** revisor,-ra.
■ **ticket machine** máquina expendedora de billetes.
■ **ticket office** taquilla.

ticking-off [ˈtɪkɪŋˈɒf] *n* (*pl* **tickings-off**) *fam* rapapolvo.

tickle [ˈtɪkəl] *vt* hacer cosquillas a.
▶ *vi* tener cosquillas.

ticklish [ˈtɪkəlɪʃ] *adj* .
● **to be ticklish 1** tener cosquillas *(persona)*. **2** ser delicado,-a *(situación)*.

tick-tock [ˈtɪktɒk] *n* tic-tac.

tide [taɪd] *n* **1** marea *(de mar)*. **2** *fig* corriente *(de opinión)*.
● **to swim against the tide** ir contracorriente.
● **to swim with the tide** dejarse llevar por la corriente.

to tide over *vt* ayudar, sacar de un apuro.

tidy [ˈtaɪdɪ] *adj* (**-ier**, **-iest**). **1** ordenado,-a *(habitación, persona)*. **2** arreglado,-a *(aspecto)*.

to tidy up *vt* **1** ordenar, arreglar *(habitación)*. **2** arreglar, acicalar *(persona)*: **tidy yourself up a bit**, arréglate un poco.
▶ *vi* poner las cosas en orden, recoger.

tie [taɪ] *n* **1** corbata. **2** lazo, vínculo. **3** empate. **4** atadura.
▶ *vt* atar, hacer *(nudo)*.
▶ *vi* empatar.

to tie down *vt* sujetar.

to tie up *vt* atar.

tier [tɪəʳ] *n* **1** grada, fila *(de asientos)*. **2** piso *(de pastel)*.

tiff [tɪf] *n* (*pl* **tiffs**) *fam* desavenencia.

tiger [ˈtaɪgəʳ] *n* tigre.

tight [taɪt] *adj* **1** apretado,-a *(ropa)*. **2** tirante, tenso,-a *(cuerda)*. **3** ajustado,-a, ceñido,-a *(ropa)*. **4** estricto,-a, riguroso,-a. **5** apretado,-a *(agenda)*. **6** reñido,-a *(partido)*. **7** *fam* agarrado,-a, tacaño,-a. **8** *fam* escaso,-a.
▶ *adv* con fuerza: **hold tight!**, ¡agárrate fuerte!
■ **tight spot** aprieto, brete.

tighten [ˈtaɪtən] *vt* **1** apretar. **2** tensar *(cuerda)*.
▶ *vi* **1** apretarse. **2** tensarse *(cuerda)*.

tightfisted [taɪtˈfɪstɪd] *adj* tacaño,-a.

tightrope [ˈtaɪtrəʊp] *n* cuerda floja.
● **to be on a tightrope** andar en la cuerda floja.
■ **tightrope walker** funámbulo,-a.

tights [taɪts] *npl* **1** panties, medias. **2** leotardos.

tile [taɪl] *n* **1** azulejo *(de pared)*. **2** baldosa *(de suelo)*. **3** teja *(de tejado)*.

till [tɪl] *prep* hasta: **it won't be ready till Thursday**, no estará listo hasta el jueves.
▶ *conj* hasta que: **we won't start until everyone arrives**, no empezaremos hasta que llegue todo el mundo.
▶ *n* caja registradora.

tilt [tɪlt] *n* inclinación, ladeo.
▶ *vt* inclinar.
▶ *vi* inclinarse, ladearse.
● **at full tilt** a toda velocidad.

timber [ˈtɪmbəʳ] *n* **1** madera *(de construcción)*. **2** viga. **3** árboles maderables.

time [taɪm] *n* **1** tiempo: **time flies**, el tiempo vuela. **2** rato: **it was a long time before he came**, pasó mucho tiempo antes de que viniera. **3** hora: **it's time to go**, es hora de irse; **what time is it?**, ¿qué hora es? **4** época: **at that time**, en aquella época. **5** vez: **how many times?**, ¿cuántas veces?; **two at a time**, de dos en dos. **6** compás *(ritmo)*.
▶ *vt* **1** medir la duración de, cronometrar. **2** fijar la hora de. **3** elegir el mejor momento para: **she timed her entrance perfectly**, eligió el momento más oportuno para entrar.
▶ *prep* **times** por, multiplicado por: **five times three**, cinco por tres.
● **all the time** todo el tiempo, constantemente.
● **at any time** en cualquier momento.
● **at no time** nunca.
● **at the same time** al mismo tiempo.
● **at times** a veces.
● **behind the times** anticuado.
● **for the time being** de momento.
● **from time to time** de vez en cuando.
● **in time** con tiempo, a tiempo.
● **it's about time** ya va siendo hora.
● **just in time** justo a tiempo.
● **on time** puntualmente.
● **to have a good time** divertirse, pasarlo bien.
● **to play for time** intentar ganar tiempo.
● **to take your time** tomarte el tiempo necesario.
● **to tell the time** decir la hora.
■ **time bomb** bomba de relojería.

timely [ˈtaɪmlɪ] *adj* (**-ier**, **-iest**) oportuno,-a.

timer [ˈtaɪməʳ] *n* temporizador.

timetable ['taɪmteɪbəl] *n* horario: *a bus timetable*, un horario de autobuses.

timid ['tɪmɪd] *adj* (*comp* **timider**, *superl* **timidest**) tímido,-a.

timing ['taɪmɪŋ] *n* **1** momento elegido. **2** cronometraje.

tin [tɪn] *n* **1** estaño. **2** lata, bote. **3** molde *(de tarta)*.
▶ *vt* (*pt & pp* **tinned**, *ger* **tinning**) enlatar.
■ **tin opener** abrelatas.

tinfoil ['tɪnfɔɪl] *n* papel de estaño.

tinge [tɪndʒ] *n* tinte, matiz.
▶ *vt* teñir.

tingle ['tɪŋgəl] *n* hormigueo.
▶ *vi* sentir hormigueo.

tinker ['tɪŋkəʳ] *n* hojalatero,-a.
▶ *vi* **tinker with** tratar de arreglar.

tinkle ['tɪŋkəl] *n* tintineo.
▶ *vi* tintinear.
● **to give SB a tinkle** GB *fam* llamar a ALGN por teléfono.

tinned [tɪnd] *adv* enlatado,-a, en conserva.

tinny ['tɪnɪ] *adj* (**-ier**, **-iest**) **1** metálico,-a *(sonido)*. **2** poco sólido,-a.

tinsel ['tɪnsəl] *n* espumillón.

tint [tɪnt] *n* tinte, matiz.
▶ *vt* teñir, matizar.

tiny ['taɪnɪ] *adj* (**-ier**, **-iest**) diminuto,-a.

tip[1] [tɪp] *n* extremo, punta.

tip[2] [tɪp] *n* **1** propina. **2** consejo.
▶ *vt* (*pt & pp* **tipped**, *ger* **tipping**) dar una propina a.

tip[3] [tɪp] *n* vertedero, basurero.
▶ *vt* (*pt & pp* **tipped**, *ger* **tipping**) verter, tirar *(basura)*.
▶ *vi* inclinarse, ladearse.

to tip off *vt* dar un soplo a.

to tip over/up *vt* volcar.
▶ *vi* volcarse.

tip-off ['tɪpɒf] *n* (*pl* **tip-offs**) *fam* soplo.

tipsy ['tɪpsɪ] *adj* (**-ier**, **-iest**) achispado,-a.

tiptoe ['tɪptəʊ] *vi* ir de puntillas.
● **on tiptoe** de puntillas.

tiptop ['tɪptɒp] *adj fam* de primera.

TIR ['tiː'aɪɑːʳ] *abbr* (***transport international routier***) TIR.

tire[1] ['taɪəʳ] *vt* cansar.
▶ *vi* cansarse, fatigarse.
● **to be tired of STH** estar harto de algo.
● **to get tired** cansarse.

tire[2] ['taɪəʳ] *n* US neumático.

to tire out *vt* agotar, cansar.

tired ['taɪəd] *adj* cansado,-a.

tireless ['taɪələs] *adj* incansable.

tiresome ['taɪəsəm] *adj* molesto,-a, pesado,-a.

tiring ['taɪərɪŋ] *adj* cansado,-a, agotador,-ra.

tissue ['tɪʃuː] *n* **1** pañuelo de papel. **2** tejido.
■ **a tissue of lies** una sarta de mentiras.
■ **tissue paper** papel de seda.

tit [tɪt] *n fam* teta.
● **tit for tat** donde las dan las toman.

titbit ['tɪtbɪt] *n* golosina.

title ['taɪtəl] *n* título.
■ **title deed** título de propiedad.
■ **title page** portada.

titter ['tɪtəʳ] *n* risita ahogada.
▶ *vi* reírse disimuladamente.

tittle-tattle ['tɪtəltætəl] *n* chismes.

tizzy ['tɪzɪ] *n* (*pl* **-ies**) *fam* .
● **to get into a tizzy** ponerse nervioso,-a.

TM ['treɪdmɑːk] *abbr* (***trademark***) marca registrada.

TNT ['tiːˈenˈtiː] *abbr* (***trinitrotoluene***) TNT.

to [tʊ, unstressed tə] *prep* **1** a: *give it to me*, dámelo a mí. **2** hacia, a: *go to the left*, ve hacia la izquierda; *we're going to the coast*, vamos a la costa. **3** a, hasta: *to count to ten*, contar hasta diez; *she works from nine to five*, trabaja de nueve a cinco. **4** menos: *ten to two*, las dos menos diez. **5** para, a fin de: *he's doing it to help you*, lo hace para ayudarte. **6** a, para: *I wrote a letter to my friend*, escribí una carta a mi amigo.
● **to and fro** de acá para allá.

toad [təʊd] *n* sapo.

toadstool ['təʊdstuːl] *n* seta venenosa.

toast [təʊst] *n* **1** pan tostado: *a piece of toast*, una tostada. **2** brindis.
▶ *vt* **1** tostar *(pan)*. **2** brindar por.
● **to drink a toast to** hacer un brindis por, brindar por.

toaster ['təʊstəʳ] *n* tostador.

tobacco [təˈbækəʊ] *n* (*pl* **-s** o **-es**) tabaco.

tobacconist [təˈbækənɪst] *n* estanquero,-a.
■ **tobacconist's** estanco.

toboggan [təˈbɒgən] *n* trineo.
▶ *vi* ir en trineo.

today [tə'deɪ] n hoy.
► adv 1 hoy. 2 hoy en día.
toddler ['tɒdlə'] n niño,-a que empieza a andar.
to-do [tə'duː] n (pl to-dos) lío, jaleo.
toe [təʊ] n 1 dedo del pie. 2 puntera (de zapato).
toenail ['təʊneɪl] n uña del dedo del pie.
toffee ['tɒfɪ] n toffee, caramelo masticable.
together [tə'geðə'] adv 1 junto, juntos,-as: *we sat together*, nos sentamos juntos. 2 a la vez, al mismo tiempo: *the two bombs exploded together*, las dos bombas estallaron al mismo tiempo.
● all together todos,-as juntos,-as.
● to come together juntarse.
● together with junto con.
togs [tɒgz] npl fam ropa.
toil [tɔɪl] n trabajo, esfuerzo.
► vi afanarse, esforzarse.
toilet ['tɔɪlət] n 1 váter, lavabo (en casa). 2 servicios (públicos). 3 aseo, arreglo personal.
■ toilet bag neceser.
■ toilet paper papel higiénico.
token ['təʊkən] n 1 señal, prueba. 2 vale. 3 ficha.
► adj simbólico,-a.
● by the same token del mismo modo, igualmente.
told [təʊld] pt pp → tell.
tolerance ['tɒlərəns] n tolerancia.
tolerant ['tɒlərənt] adj tolerante.
tolerate ['tɒləreɪt] vt tolerar.
toll¹ [təʊl] n 1 peaje. 2 número: *the death toll*, el número de víctimas mortales.
toll² [təʊl] n tañido (de campana).
► vt - vi tañer, doblar.
tomato [tə'mɑːtəʊ, US tə'meɪtəʊ] n (pl tomatoes) tomate.
tomb [tuːm] n tumba, sepulcro.
tomboy ['tɒmbɔɪ] n marimacho.
tombstone ['tuːmstəʊn] n lápida.
tomcat ['tɒmkæt] n gato macho.
tomorrow [tə'mɒrəʊ] adv mañana.
► n mañana.
■ the day after tomorrow pasado mañana.
■ tomorrow morning mañana por la mañana.
ton [tʌn] n tonelada.
● tons of un montón de.

tone [təʊn] n tono.
to tone down vt atenuar, suavizar.
tone-deaf [təʊn'def] adj duro,-a de oído.
tongs [tɒŋz] npl tenacillas, pinzas.
tongue [tʌŋ] n lengua.
● to have a loose tongue hablar más de la cuenta.
● to hold one's tongue callarse.
● to stick your tongue out sacar la lengua.
■ tongue twister trabalenguas.
tonic ['tɒnɪk] adj tónico,-a.
► n tónico.
tonight [tə'naɪt] adv-n esta noche.
tonnage ['tʌnɪdʒ] n tonelaje.
tonne [tʌn] n tonelada.
tonsil ['tɒnsəl] n amígdala.
tonsillitis [tɒnsə'laɪtəs] n amigdalitis.
too [tuː] adv 1 demasiado, mucho: *it's too hot*, hace demasiado calor. 2 también: *can I come too?*, ¿puedo ir yo también?
● too many demasiados,-as.
● too much demasiado,-a.
took [tʊk] pt → take.
tool [tuːl] n herramienta, instrumento, aparato.
toot [tuːt] n bocinazo.
► vt tocar (bocina).
► vi tocar la bocina.
tooth [tuːθ] n (pl teeth [tiːθ]). 1 diente, muela. 2 púa (de peine). 3 diente (de sierra).
● to be fed up to the back teeth with STH estar hasta la coronilla de algo.
toothache ['tuːθeɪk] n dolor de muelas.
toothbrush ['tuːθbrʌʃ] n (pl -es) cepillo de dientes.
toothless ['tuːθləs] adj sin dientes, desdentado,-a.
toothpaste ['tuːθpeɪst] n pasta de dientes.
toothpick ['tuːθpɪk] n mondadientes, palillo (de dientes).
top¹ [tɒp] n 1 parte superior, parte de arriba: *at the top of the page*, en la parte de arriba de la hoja. 2 cumbre (de montaña). 3 copa (de árbol). 4 tapón, tapa (de botella). 5 cabeza (de lista). 6 top, blusa (corta).
► adj 1 de arriba, superior, más alto,-a (estante, piso). 2 mejor (notas).
► vt (pt & pp topped, ger topping). 1 encabezar. 2 superar.

- **at the top of one's voice** a voz en grito.
- **at top speed** a toda velocidad.
- **from top to bottom** de arriba abajo.
- **on top of 1** encima de. **2** admás de: *on top of that*, encima, por si fuera poco.
- **to be top of the class** ser el primero de la clase.
- **to go over the top** pasarse de la raya.
■ **top hat** chistera.

top² [tɒp] *n* peonza *(juguete)*.

to top up *vt* llenar hasta arriba.

topic ['tɒpɪk] *n* tema, asunto.

topical ['tɒpɪkəl] *adj* de actualidad.

topless ['tɒpləs] *adj* desnudo,-a de cintura para arriba.

topple ['tɒpəl] *vt* **1** volcar. **2** *fig* derribar, derrocar *(gobierno)*.
► *vi* caer.

top-secret [tɒp'siːkrət] *adj* ultrasecreto,-a.

torch [tɔːtʃ] *n (pl* -es). **1** antorcha. **2** linterna *(eléctrica)*.

tore [tɔːʳ] *pt* → tear.

torment [(n) 'tɔːment(vb) tɔː'ment] *n* tormento, tortura.
► *vt* atormentar, torturar.

torn [tɔːn] *pp* → tear.
► *adj* rasgado,-a, roto,-a.

tornado [tɔː'neɪdəʊ] *n (pl* **tornados**) tornado.

torpedo [tɔː'piːdəʊ] *n (pl* **torpedoes**) torpedo.
► *vt* torpedear.

torrent ['tɒrənt] *n* torrente.

torso ['tɔːsəʊ] *n (pl* **torsos**) torso.

tortoise ['tɔːtəs] *n* tortuga *(de tierra)*.

tortuous ['tɔːtjʊəs] *adj* tortuoso,-a.

torture ['tɔːtʃə] *n* tortura, tormento.
► *vt* torturar, atormentar.

Tory ['tɔːrɪ] *adj - n* GB conservador,-a.

toss [tɒs] *n (pl* -es). **1** sacudida *(de cabeza)*. **2** sorteo a cara o cruz *(de moneda)*.
► *vt* **1** sacudir, menear *(cabeza)*. **2** arrojar, lanzar *(pelota)*. **3** agitar, mover.
► *vi* moverse, agitarse.

to toss up for *vt* echar a cara y cruz.

toss-up ['tɒsʌp] *n*: *it's a toss-up who'll win*, tanto puede ganar uno como otro.

tot [tɒt] *n* **1** chiquitín,-na. **2** *fam* trago.

to tot up *vt* sumar.

total ['təʊtəl] *adj - n* total.

► *vt - vi* (GB *pt & pp* **totalled**, *ger* **totalling**; US *pt & pp* **totaled**, *ger* **totaling**) sumar.
- **in total** en total.

totalitarian [təʊtælɪ'teərɪən] *adj* totalitario,-a.

totally ['təʊtəlɪ] *adv* totalmente.

totter ['tɒtə] *vi* tambalearse.

touch [tʌtʃ] *n (pl* -es). **1** toque: *a touch of colour*, un toque de color. **2** tacto: *it's hard to the touch*, es duro al tacto. **3** detalle. **4** *fam* habilidad.
► *vt-vi* conmover(se).
► *vt* **1** conmover. **2** igualar.
- **to get in touch with** ponerse en contacto con.
- **to keep in touch** mantenerse en contacto.

to touch down *vi* **1** aterrizar *(avión)*. **2** hacer un ensayo *(en rugby)*.

to touch off *vt* provocar.

to touch up *vt* retocar.

touchdown ['tʌtʃdaʊn] *n* **1** aterrizaje. **2** amerizaje. **3** ensayo *(en rugby)*.

touched [tʌtʃt] *adj* **1** conmovido,-a. **2** tocado,-a, chiflado,-a.

touchiness ['tʌtʃɪnəs] *n* susceptibilidad.

touching ['tʌtʃɪŋ] *adj* conmovedor,-ra.

touchy ['tʌtʃɪ] *adj* (-**ier**, -**iest**) susceptible.

tough [tʌf] *adj* **1** fuerte, resistente *(persona)*. **2** difícil, duro,-a *(examen)*. **3** duro,-a *(carne)*.
■ **tough luck** mala suerte.

toughen ['tʌfən] *vt-vi* endurecer(se).

toughness ['tʌfnəs] *n* **1** dureza, resistencia. **2** dificultad. **3** severidad.

toupee ['tuːpeɪ] *n* peluquín.

tour [tʊə] *n* **1** viaje. **2** visita *(de edificio)*. **3** gira.
► *vt* **1** recorrer *(país)*. **2** visitar *(edificio)*.

tourism ['tʊərɪzəm] *n* turismo.

tourist ['tʊərɪst] *n* turista.
■ **tourist office** oficina de turismo.

tournament ['tʊənəmənt] *n* torneo.

tout [taʊt] *n* revendedor,-ra.
► *vt* revender.
► *vi* intentar captar clientes.

tow [təʊ] *vt* remolcar.
- **on tow** a remolque.
- **to give a tow** remolcar.

towards [tə'wɔːdz] *prep* **1** hacia *(dirección)*: *he came slowly towards me*, vino lentamente hacia mí. **2** hacia, alrededor de *(tiempo)*: **towards the end of the year**, hacia finales de año. **3** para con *(actitud, responsabilidad)*. **4** para: **he gave me some money towards the present**, me dio dinero para el regalo.

También **toward**.

towel ['tavəl] *n* toalla.
tower ['tavə'] *n* torre.
▶ *vi* elevarse.
■ **tower block** bloque de pisos.
to tower above/over *vt* alzarse por encima de, ser más alto que.
towering ['tavərɪŋ] *adj* alto,-a.
town [tavn] *n* **1** ciudad. **2** población, municipio, pueblo. **3** centro *(de ciudad)*.
● **on the town** de juerga.
● **to paint the town red** ir de juerga.
■ **town clerk** secretario,-a del ayuntamiento.
■ **town council** ayuntamiento.
■ **town hall** ayuntamiento.
■ **town planning** urbanismo.
toxic ['tɒksɪk] *n* tóxico,-a.
toy [tɔɪ] *n* juguete.
to toy with *vt* **1** juguetear. **2** contemplar, darle vueltas a *(idea)*.
toyshop ['tɔɪʃɒp] *n* juguetería.
trace [treɪs] *n* indicio, rastro.
▶ *vt* **1** trazar, esbozar. **2** calcar. **3** seguir la pista de, localizar, encontrar. **4** buscar el origen de.
tracing ['treɪsɪŋ] *n* calco.
■ **tracing paper** papel de calcar.
track [træk] *n* **1** pista, huellas. **2** camino, senda. **3** pista, calle *(atletismo)*. **4** circuito *(de carreras)*. **5** vía *(de ferrocarril)*.
▶ *vt* seguir la pista de.
to track down *vt* localizar, encontrar.
tracksuit ['træksuːt] *n* chándal.
tract¹ [trækt] *n* **1** extensión *(de tierra)*. **2** tracto *(anatomía)*.
tract² [trækt] *n* **1** tratado. **2** panfleto.
traction ['trækʃən] *n* tracción.
tractor ['træktə'] *n* tractor.
trade [treɪd] *n* **1** oficio: **he's a carpenter by trade**, es carpintero de oficio. **2** negocio, ramo, industria. **3** comercio.
▶ *vi* comerciar.
▶ *vt* cambiar, trocar.
■ **trade union** sindicato obrero.
trademark ['treɪdmɑːk] *n* marca registrada.
trader ['treɪdə'] *n* comerciante.

tradesman ['treɪdzmən] *n (pl* **tradesmen)** **1** comerciante. **2** trabajador,-ra manual.
trading ['treɪdɪŋ] *n* comercio.
■ **trading estate** polígono comercial.
tradition [trə'dɪʃən] *n* tradición.
traditional [trə'dɪʃənəl] *adj* tradicional.
traffic ['træfɪk] *n* **1** tráfico, circulación. **2** tráfico.
▶ *vi (pt & pp* **trafficked***, ger* **trafficking)** traficar.
■ **traffic jam** embotellamiento, atasco.
■ **traffic light** semáforo.
■ **traffic sign** señal de tráfico.
■ **traffic warden** vigilante *mf* de zona azul.
trafficker ['træfɪkə'] *n* traficante.
tragedy ['trædʒədɪ] *n (pl* **-ies)** tragedia.
tragic ['trædʒɪk] *adj* trágico,-a.
trail [treɪl] *n* **1** rastro, pista. **2** camino, sendero. **3** estela *(de cometa, avión)*.
▶ *vt* **1** seguir, seguir la pista de. **2** arrastrar.
▶ *vi* **1** arrastrarse. **2** rezagarse. **3** arrastrarse *(planta)*.
trailer ['treɪlə'] *n* **1** remolque. **2** tráiler, avance *(película)*.
train [treɪn] *n* **1** tren. **2** cola *(de vestido)*.
▶ *vt* **1** entrenar. **2** formarse, estudiar.
▶ *vt* **1** entrenar *(deportista)*. **2** formar *(discípulo)*. **3** adiestrar *(animal)*.
● **by train** en tren.
■ **train station** estación de tren.
trainee [treɪ'niː] *n* aprendiz,-za.
trainer ['treɪnə'] *n* **1** entrenador,-ra, preparador,-ra. **2** amaestrador,-ra, cuidador,-ra *(de perros)*. **3** zapatilla *(de deporte)*.
training ['treɪnɪŋ] *n* **1** formación *(para trabajo)*. **2** entrenamiento. **3** amaestramiento *(de perros)*.
trait [treɪt] *n* rasgo.
traitor ['treɪtə'] *n* traidor,-ra.
tram [træm] *n* tranvía.
tramp [træmp] *n* vagabundo,-a.
▶ *vi* caminar *(con pasos pesados)*.
trample ['træmpəl] *vt* pisotear.
trampoline ['træmpəliːn] *n* cama elástica.
trance [trɑːns] *n* trance.
● **in a trance** en trance.
tranquillize ['træŋkwɪlaɪz] *vt* tranquilizar.
tranquillizer ['træŋkwɪlaɪzə'] *n* tranquilizante, calmante.
transaction [træn'zækʃən] *n* operación, transacción.

transatlantic [trænzət'læntɪk] *adj* transatlántico,-a.

transcend [træn'send] *vt* sobrepasar, trascender.

transcribe [træn'skraɪb] *vt* transcribir.

transcript ['trænskrɪpt] *n* transcripción.

transfer [(*n*) 'trænsfɜː'(*vb*) træns'fɜː'] *n* **1** transferencia *(de dinero).* **2** traslado *(de empleado).* **3** traspaso *(de bienes, poderes).*
▶ *vt* **1** transferir *(dinero).* **2** traspasar *(bienes, poderes).*
▶ *vi* hacer trasbordo.

transform [træns'fɔːm] *vt-vi* transformar(se).

transformation [trænsfə'meɪʃən] *n* transformación.

transformer [træns'fɔːmə'] *n* transformador.

transfusion [træns'fjuːʒən] *n* transfusión.

transient ['trænzɪənt] *adj* transitorio,-a.

transistor [træn'zɪstə'] *n* transistor.

transit ['trænsɪt] *n* tránsito, paso.

transition [træn'zɪʃən] *n* transición.

transitive ['trænsɪtɪv] *adj* transitivo,-a.

translate [træns'leɪt] *vt* traducir.

translation [træns'leɪʃən] *n* traducción.

translator [træns'leɪtə'] *n* traductor,-ra.

translucent [trænz'luːsənt] *adj* translúcido,-a.

transmission [trænz'mɪʃən] *n* transmisión.

transmit [trænz'mɪt] *vt* transmitir.

transmitter [trænz'mɪtə'] *n* transmisor.

transparency [træns'peərensɪ] *n* (*pl* **-ies**). **1** transparencia *(de material).* **2** diapositiva, transparencia.

transparent [træns'peərənt] *adj* transparente.

transpiration [trænspɪ'reɪʃən] *n* transpiración.

transpire [træns'paɪə'] *vt - vi* transpirar.
▶ *vi* **1** resultar: *it transpires that ...*, resulta que .... **2** ocurrir, pasar.

transplant [(*n*) 'trænsplɑːnt(*vb*) træns'plɑːnt] *n* trasplante.
▶ *vt* trasplantar.

transport [(*n*) 'trænspɔːt(*vb*) træns'pɔːt] *n* transporte.
▶ *vt* transportar.

transportation [trænspɔː'teɪʃən] *n* transporte.

transporter [træns'pɔːtə'] *n* transportador.

transvestite [trænz'vestaɪt] *n* travestido, -a, travesti, travestí.

trap [træp] *n* trampa.
▶ *vt* (*pt & pp* **trapped**, *ger* **trapping**) atrapar.
● **to be trapped** quedar atrapado.
● **to fall into a trap** caer en una trampa.
● **to set a trap** tender una trampa.

trapeze [trə'piːz] *n* trapecio.

trapper ['træpə'] *n* trampero,-a.

trash [træʃ] *n* US basura.

trashy ['træʃɪ] *adj* (**-ier**, **-iest**) de pacotilla.

traumatic [trɔː'mætɪk] *adj* traumático,-a.

travel ['trævəl] *n* viajes.
▶ *vi* (GB *pt & pp* **travelled**, *ger* **travelling**; US *pt & pp* **traveled**, *ger* **traveling**). **1** viajar. **2** ir, circular: *the car was travelling at 100 km/h*, el coche circulaba a 100 km/h.
■ **travel agency** agencia de viajes.
■ **travel brochure** folleto de viajes.

traveller ['trævələ'] *n* **1** viajero,-a. **2** viajante, representante.
■ **traveller's cheque** cheque de viaje.

travelling ['trævəlɪŋ] *adj* ambulante.
■ **travelling expenses** gastos de viaje.

travel-sick ['trævəlsɪk] *adj* mareado,-a.

travel-sickness ['trævəlsɪknəs] *n* mareo.

travesty ['trævəstɪ] *n* (*pl* **-ies**) parodia.

trawl [trɔːl] *n* red de arrastre.
▶ *vi* pescar al arrastre.

trawler ['trɔːlə'] *n* barco de arrastre.

tray [treɪ] *n* bandeja.

treacherous ['tretʃərəs] *adj* **1** traidor,-ra, traicionero,-a. **2** muy peligroso,-a.

tread [tred] *n* **1** paso. **2** banda, dibujo *(en neumático).*
▶ *vt - vi* (*pt* **trod** [trɒd], *pp* **trodden** ['trɒdən]) pisar.
● **to tread carefully** andar con pies de plomo.

treason ['triːzən] *n* traición.

treasure ['treʒə'] *n* tesoro.
▶ *vt* **1** guardar como oro en paño. **2** apreciar mucho.

treasurer ['treʒərə'] *n* tesorero,-a.

treasury ['treʒərɪ] *n* (*pl* **-ies**) tesorería.
■ **The Treasury** Ministerio de Hacienda.

treat [triːt] *n* **1** regalo. **2** placer, deleite.
▶ *vt* **1** tratar. **2** convidar, invitar. **3** darse el gusto, permitirse el lujo.

treatise ['triːtɪs] *n* tratado.

treatment ['triːtmənt] *n* **1** tratamiento. **2** trato, conducta.

treaty ['triːtɪ] *n* (*pl* **-ies**) tratado.

treble ['trebəl] *adj* **1** triple. **2** de tiple.
▶ *vt-vi* triplicar(se).

tree [triː] *n* árbol.

trek [trek] *n* **1** viaje (*largo y difícil*). **2** caminata (*a pie*).
▶ *vi* (*pt & pp* **trekked**, *ger* **trekking**) caminar.

tremble ['trembəl] *vi* temblar, estremecerse.

tremendous [trɪ'mendəs] *adj* **1** tremendo,-a, inmenso,-a. **2** *fam* fantástico,-a, estupendo,-a.

tremor ['tremə'] *n* temblor.

trench [trentʃ] *n* (*pl* **-es**). **1** zanja. **2** trinchera.

trend [trend] *n* tendencia.

trendy ['trendɪ] *adj* (**-ier**, **-iest**) *fam* moderno,-a, de moda.

trespass ['trespəs] *n* (*pl* **-es**) entrada ilegal.
▶ *vi* entrar ilegalmente.
● **"No trespassing"** "Prohibido el paso".

trestle ['tresəl] *n* caballete.

trial ['traɪəl] *n* **1** proceso, juicio. **2** prueba. **3** aflicción.
● **on trial** a prueba.
■ **trial run** ensayo.

triangle ['traɪæŋgəl] *n* triángulo.

triangular [traɪ'æŋgjʊlə'] *adj* triangular.

tribal ['traɪbəl] *adj* tribal.

tribe [traɪb] *n* tribu.

tribulation [trɪbjʊ'leɪʃən] *n* tribulación.

tribunal [traɪ'bjuːnəl] *n* tribunal.

tributary ['trɪbjʊtərɪ] *n* (*pl* **-ies**) afluente.

tribute ['trɪbjuːt] *n* **1** homenaje. **2** tributo (*pago*).
● **to pay tribute to SB** rendir homenaje a ALGN.

trice [traɪs] *n* .
● **in a trice** en un santiamén.

trick [trɪk] *n* **1** truco, número. **2** ardid, engaño. **3** broma.
▶ *vt* **1** engañar. **2** timar, estafar.
● **to play a trick on 1** gastar una broma a. **2** gastarle una faena a.

trickery ['trɪkərɪ] *n* artimañas, engaño.

trickle ['trɪkəl] *n* goteo, hilo.
▶ *vi* gotear, correr, resbalar.

tricky ['trɪkɪ] *adj* (**-ier**, **-iest**). **1** taimado, -a, astuto,-a (*persona*). **2** difícil, delicado, -a (*situación*).

tricycle ['traɪsɪkəl] *n* triciclo.

trident ['traɪdənt] *n* tridente.

trifle ['traɪfəl] *n* **1** fruslería, bagatela, nimiedad. **2** GB postre de bizcocho borracho, fruta, gelatina, crema y nata.
▶ *vi* jugar.

trifling ['traɪflɪŋ] *adj* insignificante.

trigger ['trɪgə'] *n* **1** disparador, botón (*de máquina de fotos*). **2** gatillo (*de pistola*).
▶ *vt* desencadenar.

to trigger off *vt* provocar, desencadenar.

trigonometry [trɪgə'nɒmətrɪ] *n* trigonometría.

trill [trɪl] *n* trino.
▶ *vt - vi* trinar.

trillion ['trɪlɪən] *n* **1** billón. **2** GB trillón (*antiguamente*).

trilogy ['trɪlədʒɪ] *n* (*pl* **-ies**) trilogía.

trim [trɪm] *adj* (*comp* **trimmer**, *superl* **trimmest**). **1** bien arreglado,-a, aseado, -a. **2** esbelto,-a, elegante.
▶ *n* **1** recorte (*de pelo*). **2** poda (*de planta*). **3** adorno.
▶ *vt* (*pt & pp* **trimmed**, *ger* **trimming**). **1** recortar (*pelo, bigote*). **2** decorar.
● **in trim** en forma.

trimmings ['trɪmɪŋs] *npl* **1** adornos, decoración. **2** guarnición.

trinket ['trɪŋkɪt] *n* baratija.

trio ['triːəʊ] *n* (*pl* **trios**) trío.

trip [trɪp] *n* **1** viaje. **2** excursión. **3** *sl* viaje (*con drogas*).
▶ *vi* (*pt & pp* **tripped**, *ger* **tripping**) tropezar.
▶ *vt* **trip (up)** poner la zancadilla a.

to trip over *vt - vi* tropezar (*y caerse*).

tripe [traɪp] *n* **1** callos (*plato*). **2** *fam* bobadas.

triple ['trɪpəl] *adj* triple.
▶ *vt-vi* triplicar(se).

triplet ['trɪplət] *n* trillizo,-a.

triplicate ['trɪplɪkət] *adj* triplicado,-a.
● **in triplicate** por triplicado.

tripod ['traɪpɒd] *n* trípode.

trite [traɪt] *adj* gastado,-a, trillado,-a.

triumph ['traɪəmf] *n* triunfo.
▶ *vi* triunfar.

triumphal [traɪ'ʌmfəl] *adj* triunfal.

triumphant [traɪ'ʌmfənt] *adj* triunfante.

trivial ['trɪvɪəl] *adj* trivial, insignificante.

trod [trɒd] *ptpp* → **tread**.

trodden ['trɒdən] *pp* → tread.

trolley ['trɒlɪ] *n* carro, carrito.

trombone [trɒm'bəʊn] *n* trombón.

troop [truːp] *n* grupo, banda *(de gente)*.
  ► *vi* marchar en masa, ir en masa.
  ► *npl* **troops** tropas.

trooper ['truːpə'] *n* soldado de caballería.

trophy ['trəʊfɪ] *n (pl* -**ies**) trofeo.

tropic ['trɒpɪk] *n* trópico.

tropical ['trɒpɪkəl] *adj* tropical.

trot [trɒt] *n* trote.
  ► *vi (pt & pp* **trotted**, *ger* **trotting**) trotar.
  ● **on the trot** seguidos,-as: *four times on the trot*, cuatro veces seguidas.

trotter ['trɒtə'] *n* manita, pie *(de cerdo)*.

trouble ['trʌbəl] *n* **1** problema, dificultad. **2** preocupación. **3** ansiedad, pena. **4** molestia.
  ► *vt* **1** preocupar. **2** molestar.
  ► *vi* molestarse.
  ► *npl* **troubles 1** preocupaciones. **2** conflictos, disturbios.
  ● **to be in trouble** estar en un apuro, tener problemas.
  ● **it's not worth the trouble** no vale la pena.
  ● **to get into trouble** meterse en un lío.
  ● **to get SB into trouble** *fam* dejar embarazada a ALGN.
  ● **to take the trouble to do STH** tomarse la molestia de hacer algo.
  ■ **trouble spot** punto conflictivo.

trouble-free ['trʌbəlfriː] *adj* sin problemas.

troublemaker ['trʌbəlmeɪkə'] *n* alborotador,-ra.

troubleshooter ['trʌbəlʃuːtə'] *n* conciliador,-ra, mediador,-ra.

troublesome ['trʌbəlsəm] *adj* molesto,-a, fastidioso,-a.

trough [trɒf] *n* **1** abrevadero *(para agua)*. **2** comedero *(para comida)*. **3** depresión, área de bajas presiones.

trounce [traʊns] *vt* zurrar.

troupe [truːp] *n* compañía *(de teatro)*.

trousers ['traʊzəz] *npl* pantalón.

trousseau ['truːsəʊ] *n (pl* -**s** o **trousseaux**) ajuar.

trout [traʊt] *n* trucha.

trowel ['traʊəl] *n* **1** paleta *(para cemento)*. **2** desplantador, trasplantador *(de jardinería)*.

truant ['truːənt] *n* alumno,-a que hace novillos.
  ● **to play truant** hacer novillos.

truce [truːs] *n* tregua.

truck [trʌk] *n* **1** GB vagón. **2** US camión.
  ■ **truck driver** camionero,-a.

trucker ['trʌkə'] *n* US camionero,-a.

trudge [trʌdʒ] *vi* andar penosamente.

true [truː] *adj* **1** verdadero,-a, cierto,-a *(historia)*. **2** auténtico,-a, genuino,-a *(intención)*. **3** fiel, leal *(amigo)*. **4** exacto,-a *(copia)*.
  ● **it's true** es verdad.
  ● **to come true** hacerse realidad.

truffle ['trʌfəl] *n* trufa.

truly ['truːlɪ] *adv* verdaderamente.
  ● **yours truly** atentamente.

trump [trʌmp] *n* triunfo.
  ► *vt* matar con un triunfo.
  ■ **trump card** baza.

to trump up *vt* inventar.

trumpet ['trʌmpɪt] *n* trompeta.
  ■ **trumpet player** trompetista.

truncheon ['trʌntʃən] *n* porra.

trunk [trʌŋk] *n* **1** tronco *(de árbol)*. **2** baúl. **3** trompa *(de elefante)*. **4** US maletero.
  ► *npl* **trunks** bañador.
  ■ **trunk call** llamada interurbana.

truss [trʌs] *n (pl* -**es**) braguero.

trust [trʌst] *n* **1** confianza, fe. **2** responsabilidad: *he occupies a position of trust*, ocupa un cargo de responsabilidad. **3** trust.
  ► *vt* **1** confiar en, fiarse de. **2** esperar.
  ● **to put one's trust in** depositar la confianza en.

trustee [trʌs'tiː] *n* fideicomisario,-a, depositario,-a.

trustful ['trʌstfʊl] *adj* confiado,-a.

trusting ['trʌstɪŋ] *adj* confiado,-a.

trustworthy ['trʌstwɜːðɪ] *adj* **1** digno,-a de confianza. **2** fidedigno,-a.

truth [truːθ] *n* verdad.
  ● **to tell the truth** decir la verdad.

truthful ['truːθfʊl] *adj* **1** verídico,-a. **2** veraz: *he wasn't totally truthful*, no decía toda la verdad.

try [traɪ] *n (pl* -**ies**). **1** intento, tentativa. **2** ensayo *(en rugby)*.
  ► *vt - vi (pt & pp* -**ied**) intentar, tratar de.
  ► *vt* **1** probar *(comida)*. **2** juzgar, someter a juicio. **3** probar, poner a prueba.
  ● **to have a try at STH** intentar hacer algo.

to try on *vt* probarse *(prenda de vestir)*.

to try out *vt* probar.

trying ['traɪɪŋ] *adj* pesado,-a, difícil.

T-shirt ['tiːʃɜːt] *n* camiseta.

tsp [tiːspuːn] *abbr* **(teaspoon)** cucharadita.
  pl **tsps**.

tub [tʌb] *n* **1** tina. **2** bañera, baño. **3** tarrina.

tuba ['tjuːbə] *n* tuba.

tubby ['tʌbɪ] *adj* (**-ier**, **-iest**) rechoncho,-a.

tube [tjuːb] *n* **1** tubo. **2** GB metro.
  ● **by tube** en metro.
  ■ **tube station** estación de metro.

tuber ['tjuːbə'] *n* tubérculo.

tuberculosis [tjʊbɜːkjʊ'ləʊsɪs] *n* tuberculosis.

tubular ['tjuːbjʊlə'] *adj* tubular.

tuck [tʌk] *n* pliegue.

to tuck in *vi* comer con apetito.
  ► *vt* **1** meter por dentro *(sábanas, camisa)*. **2** arropar *(persona)*.

Tues ['θjuːzdɪ] *abbr* **(Tuesday)** martes.

Tuesday ['tjuːzdɪ] *n* martes.

tuft [tʌft] *n* **1** mechón *(de pelo)*. **2** mata *(de hierba)*. **3** copete *(plumas)*.

tug [tʌg] *n* **1** tirón, estirón. **2** remolcador.
  ► *vt* (*pt & pp* **tugged**, *ger* **tugging**). **1** tirar de, arrastrar. **2** remolcar.

tugboat ['tʌgbəʊt] *n* remolcador.

tug-of-war [tʌgʌv'wɔː'] *n* **1** juego de tirar la cuerda. **2** tira y afloja.

tuition [tjʊ'ɪʃən] *n* enseñanza, instrucción.

tulip ['tjuːlɪp] *n* tulipán.

tumble ['tʌmbəl] *n* caída.
  ► *vi* caer, caerse.
  ■ **tumble dryer** secadora.

tumbler ['tʌmblə'] *n* vaso.

tummy ['tʌmɪ] *n* (*pl* **-ies**) *fam* barriga.

tumour ['tjuːmə'] *n* (US **tumor**) *n* tumor.

tuna ['tjuːnə] *n* (*pl* **tuna** o **tunas**) atún, bonito.

tundra ['tʌndrə] *n* tundra.

tune [tjuːn] *n* melodía.
  ► *vt* **1** afinar *(piano, etc)*. **2** poner a punto *(motor)*. **3** sintonizar *(radio, etc)*.
  ● **in tune** afinado,-a.
  ● **out of tune** desafinado,-a.
  ● **to sing out of tune** desafinar.

to tune in to *vt* sintonizar *(emisora)*.

tuneful ['tjuːnfʊl] *adj* melodioso,-a.

tuner ['tjuːnə'] *n* **1** afinador,-ra *(de pianos, etc)*. **2** sintonizador *(aparato)*.

tunic ['tjuːnɪk] *n* túnica.

tuning fork ['tjuːnɪŋfɔːk] *n* diapasón.

Tunis ['tjuːnɪs] *n* Túnez.

Tunisia [tjuː'nɪsɪə] *n* Túnez, Tunicia.

Tunisian [tjuː'nɪsɪən] *adj* - *n* tunecino,-a.

tunnel ['tʌnəl] *n* túnel.
  ► *vt* (GB *pt & pp* **tunnelled**, *ger* **tunnelling**; US *pt & pp* **tunneled**, *ger* **tunneling**) abrir un túnel.

tunny ['tʌnɪ] *n* (*pl* **-ies**) atún, bonito.

turban ['tɜːbən] *n* turbante.

turbine ['tɜːbaɪn] *n* turbina.

turbojet ['tɜːbəʊdʒet] *n* turborreactor.

turbot ['tɜːbət] *n* (*pl* **turbot** o **turbots**) rodaballo.

turbulence ['tɜːbjʊləns] *n* turbulencia.

turbulent ['tɜːbjʊlənt] *adj* turbulento,-a.

tureen [tə'riːn] *n* sopera.

turf [tɜːf] *n* césped.
  ■ **the turf** las carreras de caballos.

to turf out *vt* *fam* poner de patitas en la calle.

Turk [tɜːk] *n* turco,-a.

turkey ['tɜːkɪ] *n* pavo.

Turkey ['tɜːkɪ] *n* Turquía.

Turkish ['tɜːkɪʃ] *adj* turco,-a.
  ► *n* turco *(lengua)*.

turmoil ['tɜːmɔɪl] *n* confusión, alboroto.

turn [tɜːn] *n* **1** vuelta, giro. **2** vuelta *(de rueda)*. **3** curva, recodo *(de río)*. **4** turno: *whose turn is it?*, ¿a quién le toca? **5** calle, bocacalle. **6** *fam* susto.
  ► *vt* **1** girar *(pomo)*. **2** dar la vuelta a *(silla)*. **3** doblar *(esquina)*. **4** pasar *(página)*.
  ► *vi* **1** girar, dar vueltas. **2** volverse, dar la vuelta *(persona)*. **3** torcer, girar: *the car turned left*, el coche giró a la izquierda. **4** hacerse, ponerse, volverse: *his face turned red*, se le puso la cara colorada.
  ● **by turns** sucesivamente.
  ● **to do a good turn** hacer un favor.
  ● **to take turns** turnarse.

to turn away *vt* no dejar entrar.
  ► *vi* apartarse.

to turn back *vt* hacer retroceder.
  ► *vi* volver, volverse.

to turn down *vt* **1** rechazar *(propuesta)*. **2** bajar *(radio, etc)*.

to turn in *vt* entregar a la policía.
  ► *vi* *fam* acostarse.

to turn into *vt* convertir, transformar:

they turned the bedroom into an office, convirtieron el dormitorio en un despacho.

to turn off vt **1** desconectar *(electricidad)*. **2** apagar *(luz, gas)*. **3** cerrar *(agua)*. **4** parar *(máquina)*. **5** salir de *(carretera)*.

to turn on vt **1** conectar *(electricidad)*. **2** encender *(luz)*. **3** abrir *(gas, grifo)*. **4** poner en marcha *(máquina)*. **5** atacar. **6** fam excitar.

to turn out vt **1** apagar *(gas, luz)*. **2** producir. **3** vaciar.
▶ vi **1** salir, resultar. **2** acudir. **3** salir a la calle.

to turn over vt **1** dar la vuelta a. **2** dar vueltas a *(idea)*. **3** entregar. **4** facturar.
▶ vi darse la vuelta, volcarse.

to turn to vt **1** recurrir. **2** buscar *(página)*.

to turn up vi **1** aparecer. **2** presentarse, llegar.
▶ vt subir *(volumen)*.

turncoat ['tɜːnkəʊt] n tránsfuga.

turning ['tɜːnɪŋ] n bocacalle, esquina.
■ **turning point** punto decisivo.

turnip ['tɜːnɪp] n nabo.

turnout ['tɜːnaʊt] n asistencia, concurrencia.

turnover ['tɜːnəʊvəʳ] n facturación, volumen de negocio.

turnpike ['tɜːnpaɪk] n US autopista de peaje.

turntable ['tɜːnteɪbəl] n **1** plato giratorio. **2** tocadiscos.

turn-up ['tɜːnʌp] n GB vuelta.

turpentine ['tɜːpəntaɪn] n trementina, aguarrás.

turquoise ['tɜːkwɔɪz] n **1** turquesa *(piedra)*. **2** azul turquesa *(color)*.
▶ adj de color turquesa.

turret ['tʌrət] n torrecilla.

turtle ['tɜːtəl] n tortuga.

turtleneck ['tɜːtəlnek] n cuello de cisne, cuello alto.

tusk [tʌsk] n colmillo.

tussle ['tʌsəl] n pelea.
▶ vi pelearse.

tutor ['tjuːtəʳ] n **1** profesor,-ra particular. **2** tutor,-ra.

tutorial [tjuːˈtɔːrɪəl] n tutoría, clase con grupo reducido.

tuxedo [tʌkˈsiːdəʊ] n *(pl* **tuxedos***)* US esmoquin.

TV ['tiːˈviː] abbr *(**television**)* televisión, TV.

twaddle ['twɒdəl] n fam tonterías.

twang [twæŋ] n **1** sonido vibrante. **2** gangueo *(voz)*.

tweed [twiːd] n tweed.

tweet [twiːt] n pío pío.
▶ vi piar.

tweezers ['twiːzəz] npl pinzas.

twelfth [twelfθ] adj - n duodécimo,-a.
▶ n **1** duodécimo. **2** duodécima parte. **3** doce *(en fecha)*.
■ **twelfth night** Noche de Reyes.

twelve [twelv] num doce.

twentieth ['twentɪəθ] adj - n vigésimo,-a.
▶ n **1** vigésimo. **2** vigésima parte. **3** veinte *(en fecha)*.

twenty ['twentɪ] num veinte.

twice [twaɪs] adv dos veces: *twice as big as this one*, el doble de grande que éste.

twiddle ['twɪdəl] vt dar vueltas a.

twig [twɪg] n ramita.

twilight ['twaɪlaɪt] n crepúsculo.

twin [twɪn] n gemelo,-a, mellizo,-a.
■ **twin room** habitación con dos camas.

twine [twaɪn] n cordel.
▶ vt enroscar.

twinge [twɪndʒ] n punzada.

twinkle ['twɪŋkəl] n centelleo, brillo.
▶ vi **1** centellear, destellar. **2** brillar *(ojos)*.

twirl [twɜːl] vt - vi **1** girar rápidamente, dar vueltas a. **2** retorcer.

twist [twɪst] n **1** recodo, vuelta *(de carretera)*. **2** torsión *(movimiento)*. **3** torcedura. **4** twist *(baile)*.
▶ vt **1** torcer. **2** girar *(tapa)*.
▶ vi **1** torcerse *(tobillo)*. **2** serpentear *(río)*. **3** bailar el twist.

twit [twɪt] n fam tonto,-a.

twitch [twɪtʃ] n *(pl* **-es***)*. **1** tirón. **2** tic nervioso.
▶ vt tirar de, dar un tirón a.
▶ vi moverse nerviosamente.

twitter ['twɪtəʳ] n gorjeo.
▶ vi gorjear.

two [tuː] adj - n dos.

twofaced [tuːˈfeɪst] adj hipócrita.

two-piece ['tuːpiːs] adj de dos piezas.

tycoon [taɪˈkuːn] n magnate.

type [taɪp] n **1** tipo, clase. **2** letra, carácter.
▶ vt escribir a máquina, mecanografiar.

typewriter ['taɪpraɪtəʳ] n máquina de escribir.

typewritten ['taɪprɪtən] adj escrito,-a a máquina.

typhoid ['taɪfɔɪd] n fiebre tifoidea.
typhoon [taɪ'fuːn] n tifón.
typical ['tɪpɪkəl] adj típico,-a.
typify ['tɪpɪfaɪ] vt (pt & pp -ied) tipificar.
typing ['taɪpɪŋ] n mecanografía.
typist ['taɪpɪst] n mecanógrafo,-a.

tyrannical [tɪ'rænɪkəl] adj tiránico,-a.
tyrannize ['tɪrənaɪz] vt tiranizar.
tyranny ['tɪrənɪ] n (pl -ies) tiranía.
tyrant ['taɪərənt] n tirano,-a.
tyre ['taɪəʳ] (US tire) n neumático, llanta.

U

udder ['ʌdəʳ] *n* ubre.

UEFA [juːˈeɪfə] *abbr (Union of European Football Associations)* UEFA.

UFO ['juːefəʊ] *abbr (unidentified flying object)* OVNI.

ugly ['ʌglɪ] *adj* (-**ier**, -**iest**). 1 feo,-a. 2 desagradable.

UHF ['juːeɪtʃˈef] *abbr (ultra high frequency)* UHF.

UHT ['juːeɪtˈtiː] *abbr* uperisado,-a, uperizado,-a.

■ **UHT milk** leche uperisada.

■ **UHT treatment** uperisación, uperización.

UK ['juːkeɪ] *abbr (United Kingdom)* Reino Unido, R.U.

ulcer ['ʌlsəʳ] *n* 1 llaga. 2 úlcera *(de estómago)*.

ultimate ['ʌltɪmət] *adj* 1 último,-a, final. 2 máximo,-a.

ultimately ['ʌltɪmətlɪ] *adv* 1 finalmente. 2 en el fondo.

ultimatum [ʌltɪˈmeɪtəm] *n* ultimátum.

umbrella [ʌmˈbrelə] *n* paraguas.

umpire ['ʌmpaɪəʳ] *n* árbitro.

▶ *vt* arbitrar.

umpteen [ʌmpˈtiːn] *adj fam* la tira de, un montón de.

umpteenth [ʌmpˈtiːnθ] *adj* enésimo,-a.

UN ['juːen] *abbr (United Nations Organization)* Organización de las Naciones Unidas, ONU.

unable [ʌnˈeɪbəl] *adj* incapaz.

● **to be unable to** ser incapaz de, no poder.

unabridged [ʌnəˈbrɪdʒd] *adj* íntegro,-a.

unacceptable [ʌnəkˈseptəbəl] *adj* inaceptable.

unaccompanied [ʌnəˈkʌmpənɪd] *adj* 1 solo,-a. 2 sin acompañamiento.

unadulterated [ʌnəˈdʌltəreɪtɪd] *adj* puro,-a, sin adulterar.

unadvisable [ʌnədˈvaɪzəbəl] *adj* poco aconsejable.

unanimous [juːˈnænɪməs] *adj* unánime.

unarmed [ʌnˈɑːmd] *adj* desarmado,-a.

unassuming [ʌnəˈsjuːmɪŋ] *adj* modesto, -a, sin pretensiones.

unattainable [ʌnəˈteɪnəbəl] *adj* inasequible.

unattended [ʌnəˈtendɪd] *adj* sin vigilar.

unauthorized [ʌnˈɔːθəraɪzd] *adj* no autorizado,-a.

unavailable [ʌnəˈveɪləbəl] *adj* no disponible.

unavoidable [ʌnəˈvɔɪdəbəl] *adj* inevitable, ineludible.

unaware [ʌnəˈweəʳ] *adj* inconsciente.

● **to be unaware of** ignorar, no ser consciente de.

unawares [ʌnəˈweəz] *adv* sin darse cuenta, desprevenido,-a.

unbalanced [ʌnˈbælənst] *adj* desequilibrado,-a.

unbearable [ʌnˈbeərəbəl] *adj* insoportable.

unbeatable [ʌnˈbiːtəbəl] *adj* 1 invencible, insuperable *(rival)*. 2 inmejorable *(precio)*.

unbelievable [ʌnbɪˈliːvəbəl] *adj* increíble.

unbiassed [ʌnˈbaɪəst] *adj* imparcial.

unborn [ʌnˈbɔːn] *adj* 1 aún no nacido,-a. 2 *fig* nonato,-a.

unbreakable [ʌnˈbreɪkəbəl] *adj* irrompible.

unbutton [ʌnˈbʌtən] *vt* desabrochar, desbotonar.

uncanny [ʌnˈkænɪ] *adj* (**-ier, -iest**) misterioso,-a, extraño,-a.

uncertain [ʌnˈsɜːtən] *adj* 1 incierto,-a, dudoso,-a *(futuro)*. 2 indeciso,-a *(persona)*.

uncertainty [ʌnˈsɜːtəntɪ] *n* (*pl* **-ies**) incertidumbre.

unchanged [ʌnˈtʃeɪndʒd] *adj* igual, sin alterar.

uncivilized [ʌnˈsɪvɪlaɪzd] *adj* incivilizado,-a.

uncle [ˈʌŋkəl] *n* tío.

unclear [ʌnˈklɪəʳ] *adj* poco claro,-a.

uncomfortable [ʌnˈkʌmfətəbəl] *adj* incómodo,-a.

uncommon [ʌnˈkɒmən] *adj* 1 poco común. 2 insólito,-a.

uncommonly [ʌnˈkɒmənlɪ] *adv* extraordinariamente.

uncompromising [ʌnˈkɒmprəmaɪzɪŋ] *adj* inflexible, intransigente.

unconcerned [ʌnkənˈsɜːnd] *adj* indiferente, despreocupado,-a.

unconditional [ʌnkənˈdɪʃənəl] *adj* incondicional.

unconscious [ʌnˈkɒnʃəs] *adj* inconsciente.

unconstitutional [ʌnkɒnstɪˈtjuːʃənəl] *adj* inconstitucional.

uncontrollable [ʌnkənˈtrəʊləbəl] *adj* incontrollable.

unconventional [ʌnkənˈvenʃənəl] *adj* poco convencional.

uncooperative [ʌnkəʊˈɒpərətɪv] *adj* poco cooperativo,-a, poco dispuesto,-a a ayudar.

uncork [ʌnˈkɔːk] *vt* descorchar.

uncouth [ʌnˈkuːθ] *adj* 1 tosco,-a, inculto,-a *(modales)*. 2 ordinario,-a *(persona)*.

uncover [ʌnˈkʌvəʳ] *vt* 1 destapar, descubrir. 2 revelar *(secreto)*.

undecided [ʌndɪˈsaɪdɪd] *adj* 1 indeciso,-a. 2 no resuelto,-a, pendiente *(problema)*.

undeniable [ʌndɪˈnaɪəbəl] *adj* innegable, indiscutible.

under [ˈʌndəʳ] *prep* 1 bajo, debajo de: **she sat under a tree**, se sentó bajo un árbol. 2 menos de: **you can get one for under £5**, se pueden conseguir por menos de 5 libras. 3 bajo: **under Cromwell**, bajo Cromwell.

▶ *adv* abajo, debajo.

underclothes [ˈʌndəkləʊðz] *npl* ropa interior.

undercoat [ˈʌndəkəʊt] *n* primera mano *(de pintura)*.

undercover [ʌndəˈkʌvəʳ] *adj* clandestino,-a, secreto,-a.

undercurrent [ˈʌndəkʌrənt] *n* 1 corriente submarina. 2 *fig* corriente subyacente.

underdeveloped [ʌndədɪˈveləpt] *adj* subdesarrollado,-a.

underdog [ˈʌndədɒg] *n* probable perdedor,-ra.

underdone [ʌndəˈdʌn] *adj* poco hecho,-a.

underestimate [(n) ʌndərˈestɪmət(vb) ʌndərˈestɪmeɪt] *n* infravaloración.

▶ *vt* subestimar, infravalorar.

undergo [ʌndəˈgəʊ] *vt* (*pt* **underwent**, *pp* **undergone** [ʌndəˈgɒn]). 1 experimentar, sufrir *(cambio, dificultades)*. 2 hacer, someterse a *(operación)*.

undergraduate [ʌndəˈgrædjʊət] *n* estudiante universitario,-a no licenciado,-a.

underground [(adj) ˈʌndəgraʊnd(n) ʌndəˈgraʊnd] *adj* 1 subterráneo. 2 *fig* clandestino,-a.

▶ *n* 1 metro. 2 resistencia, movimiento clandestino.

▶ *adv* 1 bajo tierra. 2 en secreto.

undergrowth [ˈʌndəgrəʊθ] *n* maleza.

underhand [ˈʌndəhænd] *adj* deshonesto,-a.

underline [ʌndəˈlaɪn] *vt* subrayar.

undermine [ʌndəˈmaɪn] *vt* 1 minar, debilitar *(salud)*. 2 socavar *(cimientos)*.

underneath [ʌndəˈniːθ] *prep* debajo de.

▶ *adv* debajo.

▶ *n* parte inferior.

underpaid [ʌndəˈpeɪd] *vt* mal pagado,-a.

underpants [ˈʌndəpænts] *npl* calzoncillos, eslip.

underpass [ˈʌndəpæs] *n* (*pl* **-es**) paso subterráneo.

underrated [ʌndəˈreɪtɪd] *adj* infravalorado,-a.

underskirt [ˈʌndəskɜːt] *n* enagua.

understand [ʌndəˈstænd] *vt* (*pt & pp* **understood** [ʌndəˈstʊd]). 1 entender, comprender. 2 tener entendido.

● **to give to understand** dar a entender.

understandable [ʌndəˈstændəbəl] *adj* comprensible.

understanding [ʌndəˈstændɪŋ] *n* 1 en-

tendimiento, comprensión. **2** acuerdo, arreglo. **3** interpretación.
▶ *adj* comprensivo,-a.
● **on the understanding that...** a condición de que.

understatement [ʌndə'steɪtmənt] *n* atenuación: *it's an understatement to say that ...*, decir...es quedarse corto.

understood [ʌndə'stud] *pt-pp* → understand.
● **to make oneself understood** hacerse entender.

undertake [ʌndə'teɪk] *vt* (*pt* **undertook**, *pp* **undertaken** [ʌndə'teɪkən]). **1** emprender *(tarea)*. **2** asumir *(responsabilidad)*. **3** comprometerse *(a promesa)*.

undertaker ['ʌndəteɪkə'] *n* **1** empresario,-a de pompas fúnebres. **2** empleado,-a de la funeraria.

undertone ['ʌndətəʊn] *n* **1** voz baja. **2** matiz.

undertook [ʌndə'tʊk] *pt* → undertake.

underwater [ʌndə'wɔːtə'] *adj* submarino,-a.
▶ *adv* bajo el agua.

underwear ['ʌndəwɜːə'] *n* ropa interior.

underwent [ʌndə'went] *pt* → undergo.

underworld ['ʌndəwɜːld] *n* **1** hampa, bajos fondos. **2** el Hades.

undeserved [ʌndɪ'zɜːvd] *adj* inmerecido,-a.

undesirable [ʌndɪ'zaɪərəbəl] *adj-n* indeseable.

undeveloped [ʌndɪ'veləpt] *adj* **1** sin desarrollar. **2** sin edificar.

undid [ʌn'dɪd] *pt* → undo.

undisciplined [ʌn'dɪsɪplɪnd] *adj* indisciplinado,-a.

undisputed [ʌndɪs'pjuːtɪd] *adj* indiscutible, incuestionable.

undo [ʌn'duː] *vt* (*pt* **undid**, *pp* **undone**, *ger* **undoing**). **1** deshacer *(nudo)*. **2** desabrochar *(botón)*. **3** abrir *(paquete)*. **4** anular, deshacer.
● **to leave STH undone** dejar algo sin hacer.

undoubted [ʌn'daʊtɪd] *adj* indudable.

undress [ʌn'dres] *vt-vi* desnudar(se), desvestir(se).
● **to get undressed** desvestirse, desnudarse.

undue [ʌn'djuː] *adj* indebido,-a, excesivo,-a.

unduly [ʌn'djuːlɪ] *adv* indebidamente, excesivamente.

unearth [ʌn'ɜːθ] *vt* desenterrar, sacar a la luz.

uneasy [ʌn'iːzɪ] *adj* (**-ier**, **-iest**) intranquilo,-a, inquieto,-a.

uneconomical [ʌniːkə'nɒmɪkəl] *adj* poco rentable.

uneducated [ʌn'edjʊkeɪtɪd] *adj* inculto,-a, ignorante.

unemployed [ʌnɪm'plɔɪd] *adj* parado,-a, desempleado,-a.

unemployment [ʌnɪm'plɔɪmənt] *n* paro, desempleo.
■ **unemployment benefit** subsidio de desempleo.

unequal [ʌn'iːkwəl] *adj* desigual.

UNESCO [juːˈneskəʊ] *abbr* (*United Nations Educational, Scientific and Cultural Organization*) UNESCO.

uneven [ʌn'iːvən] *adj* **1** desigual. **2** irregular *(superficie)*. **3** lleno,-a de baches *(carretera)*.

uneventful [ʌnɪ'ventfʊl] *adj* sin incidentes, tranquilo,-a.

unexpected [ʌnɪk'spektɪd] *adj* inesperado,-a.

unfair [ʌn'feə'] *adj* injusto,-a.

unfaithful [ʌn'feɪθfʊl] *adj* infiel.

unfaithfulness [ʌn'feɪθfʊlnəs] *n* infidelidad.

unfamiliar [ʌnfə'mɪlɪə'] *adj* desconocido,-a.
● **to be unfamiliar with** desconocer.

unfashionable [ʌn'fæʃənəbəl] *adj* pasado,-a de moda.

unfasten [ʌn'fɑːsən] *vt* **1** desabrochar *(botón)*. **2** desatar *(nudo)*. **3** abrir *(puerta)*.

unfavourable [ʌn'feɪvərəbəl] *adj* desfavorable, adverso,-a.

unfinished [ʌn'fɪnɪʃt] *adj* inacabado,-a, incompleto,-a.

unfit [ʌn'fɪt] *adj* (*comp* **unfitter**, *superl* **unfittest**). **1** no apto,-a, inadecuado,-a. **2** desentrenado,-a *(físicamente)*: *to be unfit*, no estar en forma. **3** lesionado,-a. **4** incompetente.

unfold [ʌn'fəʊld] *vt-vi* desplegar(se), abrir(se).

unforeseeable [ʌnfɔː'siːəbəl] *adj* imprevisible.

unforeseen [ʌnfɔː'siːn] *adj* imprevisto,-a.

unforgettable [ʌnfə'getəbəl] *adj* inolvidable.

unforgivable [ʌnfə'gɪvəbəl] adj imperdonable.

unforgiving [ʌnfə'gɪvɪŋ] adj implacable.

unfortunate [ʌn'fɔːtʃənət] adj 1 desgraciado,-a *(accidente)*. 2 desafortunado,-a *(comentario)*.

unfortunately [ʌn'fɔːtʃənətlɪ] adv degraciadamente, desafortunadamente.

unfounded [ʌn'faʊndɪd] adj infundado,-a, sin base.

unfriendly [ʌn'frendlɪ] adj (-ier, -iest) poco amistoso, antipático,-a.

unfurnished [ʌn'fɜːnɪʃt] adj sin amueblar.

ungainly [ʌn'geɪnlɪ] adj (-ier, -iest) desgarbado,-a, torpe.

ungrateful [ʌn'greɪtfʊl] adj desagradecido,-a.

unhappily [ʌn'hæpɪlɪ] adv 1 desgraciadamente. 2 tristemente.

unhappiness [ʌn'hæpɪnəs] n infelicidad, tristeza.

unhappy [ʌn'hæpɪ] adj (-ier, -iest). 1 infeliz, triste. 2 desafortunado,-a *(comentario)*.

unharmed [ʌn'hɑːmd] adj ileso,-a.

unhealthy [ʌn'helθɪ] adj (-ier, -iest). 1 malsano,-a *(alimento)*. 2 enfermizo,-a, de mala salud *(persona)*. 3 morboso,-a *(interés)*.

unheard-of [ʌn'hɜːdəv] adj inaudito,-a.

unhinge [ʌn'hɪndʒ] vt desquiciar, sacar de quicio.

unhook [ʌn'hʊk] vt 1 desenganchar. 2 descolgar. 3 desabrochar *(vestido)*.

unhurt [ʌn'hɜːt] adj ileso,-a.

UNICEF ['juːnɪsef] abbr (United Nations Children's Fund) UNICEF.

unicorn ['juːnɪkɔːn] n unicornio.

unidentified [ʌnaɪ'dentɪfaɪd] adj no identificado,-a.

unification [juːnɪfɪ'keɪʃən] n unificación.

uniform ['juːnɪfɔːm] adj-n uniforme.

unify ['juːnɪfaɪ] vt (pt & pp -ied) unificar.

unilateral [juːnɪ'lætərəl] adj unilateral.

unimaginative [ʌnɪ'mædʒɪnətɪv] adj poco imaginativo,-a.

unimportant [ʌnɪm'pɔːtənt] adj insignificante, sin importancia.

uninhabited [ʌnɪn'hæbɪtɪd] adj deshabitado,-a.

unintelligible [ʌnɪn'telɪdʒəbəl] adj ininteligible.

unintentional [ʌnɪn'tenʃənəl] adj involuntario,-a.

uninterested [ʌn'ɪntrəstɪd] adj no interesado,-a.

uninteresting [ʌn'ɪntrəstɪŋ] adj sin interés.

uninterrupted [ʌnɪntə'rʌptɪd] adj ininterrumpido,-a, continuo,-a.

union ['juːnɪən] n 1 unión. 2 sindicato.

unique [juːˈniːk] adj único,-a.

unisex ['juːnɪseks] adj unisex.

unison ['juːnɪsən] phr in unison al unísono.

unit ['juːnɪt] n unidad.

unite [juːˈnaɪt] vt-vi unir(se).

unity ['juːnɪtɪ] n unidad.

universal [juːnɪ'vɜːsəl] adj universal.

universe ['juːnɪvɜːs] n universo.

university [juːnɪ'vɜːsɪtɪ] n (pl -ies) universidad.

► adj universitario,-a.

unjust [ʌn'dʒʌst] adj injusto,-a.

unjustifiable [ʌndʒʌstɪ'faɪəbəl] adj injustificable.

unjustified [ʌn'dʒʌstɪfaɪd] adj injustificado,-a.

unkempt [ʌn'kempt] adj 1 descuidado,-a, desaliñado. 2 despeinado,-a.

unkind [ʌn'kaɪnd] adj 1 poco amable *(persona)*. 2 cruel *(comentario)*.

unknown [ʌn'nəʊn] adj desconocido,-a.

■ unknown quantity incógnita.

unlawful [ʌn'lɔːfʊl] adj ilegal.

unleash [ʌn'liːʃ] vt 1 soltar *(animal)*. 2 fig desatar.

unless [ən'les] conj a menos que, a no ser que, si no: **don't do anything unless I tell you**, no hagas nada si no te lo digo yo.

unlike [ʌn'laɪk] adj diferente.

► prep a diferencia de.

unlikely [ʌn'laɪklɪ] adj (-ier, -iest) improbable, poco probable.

unlimited [ʌn'lɪmɪtɪd] adj ilimitado,-a.

unload [ʌn'ləʊd] vt descargar.

unlock [ʌn'lɒk] vt abrir *(con llave)*.

unlucky [ʌn'lʌkɪ] adj (-ier, -iest) desafortunado,-a, desgraciado,-a.

● to be unlucky 1 tener mala suerte, ser gafe. 2 traer mala suerte.

unmade [ʌn'meɪd] adj sin hacer *(cama)*.

unmanageable [ʌn'mænɪdʒəbəl] adj ingobernable, indomable.

unmanned [ʌn'mænd] *adj* no tripulado, -a *(nave espacial)*.

unmarried [ʌn'mærid] *adj* soltero,-a.

unmask [ʌn'mɑːsk] *vt* desenmascarar.

unmistakable [ʌnmɪs'teɪkəbəl] *adj* inconfundible, inequívoco,-a.

unmoved [ʌn'muːvd] *adj* impasible.

unnatural [ʌn'nætʃərəl] *adj* **1** poco natural. **2** antinatural.

unnecessary [ʌn'nesəsəri] *adj* innecesario,-a.

unnerve [ʌn'nɜːv] *vt* desconcertar, poner nervioso,-a.

unnoticed [ʌn'nəʊtɪst] *adj* inadvertido,-a, desapercibido,-a.

UNO ['juː'en'əʊ] *abbr* (**United Nations Organization**) ONU.

unobtainable [ʌnəb'teɪnəbəl] *adj* imposible de conseguir.

unobtrusive [ʌnɒb'truːsɪv] *adj* discreto,-a.

unoccupied [ʌn'ɒkjʊpaɪd] *adj* **1** deshabitado,-a *(casa)*. **2** desocupado,-a *(persona)*. **3** vacante *(empleo)*.

unofficial [ʌnə'fɪʃəl] *adj* extraoficial, oficioso,-a.

unorthodox [ʌn'ɔːθədɒks] *adj* **1** poco ortodoxo,-a. **2** heterodoxo,-a.

unpack [ʌn'pæk] *vt* **1** desempaquetar, desembalar. **2** deshacer *(maleta)*.
▶ *vi* deshacer las maletas.

unpaid [ʌn'peɪd] *adj* **1** sin pagar. **2** no retribuido,-a *(trabajo)*.

unpalatable [ʌm'pælətəbəl] *adj* desagradable.

unparalleled [ʌn'pærəleld] *adj* incomparable.

unperturbed [ʌnpə'tɜːbd] *adj* impertérrito,-a, impasible.

unpleasant [ʌn'plezənt] *adj* **1** desagradable. **2** desagradable, antipático,-a *(persona)*.

unplug [ʌn'plʌg] *vt* (*pt & pp* **unplugged**, *ger* **unplugging**) desenchufar.

unpolluted [ʌnpə'luːtɪd] *adj* no contaminado,-a.

unpopular [ʌn'pɒpjʊləʳ] *adj* impopular, que no gusta.

unprecedented [ʌn'presɪdentɪd] *adj* sin precedentes, inaudito,-a.

unpredictable [ʌnprɪ'dɪktəbəl] *adj* imprevisible.

unprejudiced [ʌn'predʒʊdɪst] *adj* imparcial.

unpretentious [ʌnprɪ'tenʃəs] *adj* modesto,-a, sin pretensiones.

unprincipled [ʌn'prɪnsɪpəld] *adj* sin escrúpulos.

unprofessional [ʌnprə'feʃənəl] *adj* poco profesional, inexperto,-a.

unprofitable [ʌn'prɒfɪtəbəl] *adj* poco rentable.

unprovoked [ʌnprə'vəʊkt] *adj* no provocado,-a.

unpublished [ʌn'pʌblɪʃt] *adj* inédito,-a.

unqualified [ʌn'kwɒlɪfaɪd] *adj* **1** sin título. **2** incondicional.

unquestionable [ʌn'kwestʃənəbəl] *adj* incuestionable, indiscutible.

unravel [ʌn'rævəl] *vt-vi* (GB *pt & pp* **unravelled**, *ger* **unravelling**; US *pt & pp* **unraveled**, *ger* **unraveling**) desenmarañar(se).

unreadable [ʌn'riːdəbəl] *adj* ilegible.

unreal [ʌn'rɪəl] *adj* irreal.

unrealistic [ʌnrɪə'lɪstɪk] *adj* poco realista.

unreasonable [ʌn'riːzənəbəl] *adj* **1** poco razonable. **2** desmesurado,-a, excesivo.

unrecognizable [ʌnrekəg'naɪzəbəl] *adj* irreconocible.

unrelenting [ʌnrɪ'lentɪŋ] *adj* inexorable.

unreliable [ʌnrɪ'laɪəbəl] *adj* **1** informal, de poca confianza *(persona)*. **2** poco fiable *(máquina)*. **3** poco fidedigno,-a *(noticia)*.

unrepentant [ʌnrɪ'pentənt] *adj* impenitente.

unrest [ʌn'rest] *n* **1** malestar, intranquilidad. **2** disturbios.

unripe [ʌn'raɪp] *adj* verde, inmaduro,-a.

unroll [ʌn'rəʊl] *vt-vi* desenrollar(se).

unruly [ʌn'ruːlɪ] *adj* (**-ier**, **-iest**). **1** revoltoso,-a, indisciplinado,-a. **2** rebelde *(pelo)*.

unsafe [ʌn'seɪf] *adj* **1** inseguro,-a. **2** peligroso,-a.

unsatisfactory [ʌnsætɪs'fæktərɪ] *adj* insatisfactorio,-a.

unsatisfied [ʌn'sætɪsfaɪd] *adj* insatisfecho,-a.

unsavoury [ʌn'seɪvərɪ] *adj* desagradable.

unscathed [ʌn'skeɪðd] *adj* indemne, ileso,-a.

unscrew [ʌn'skruː] *vt* **1** desatornillar. **2** desenroscar.

unscrupulous [ʌn'skruːpjʊləs] *adj* sin escrúpulos.

unseasonable [ʌn'siːzənəbəl] *adj* atípico,-a.

unselfish [ʌnˈselfɪʃ] *adj* desinteresado,-a, generoso,-a.

unsettle [ʌnˈsetəl] *vt* **1** perturbar, inquietar. **2** desestabilizar.

unsettled [ʌnˈsetəld] *adj* inestable.

unshaven [ʌnˈʃeɪvən] *adj* sin afeitar.

unsightly [ʌnˈsaɪtlɪ] *adj* (-**ier**, -**iest**) feo,-a.

unskilled [ʌnˈskɪld] *adj* **1** no cualificado,-a *(obrero)*. **2** no especializado,-a *(trabajo)*.

unsociable [ʌnˈsəʊʃəbəl] *adj* insociable, poco sociable.

unsophisticated [ʌnsəˈfɪstɪkeɪtɪd] *adj* ingenuo,-a, sencillo,-a.

unspeakable [ʌnˈspiːkəbəl] *adj* indecible.

unstable [ʌnˈsteɪbəl] *adj* inestable.

unsteady [ʌnˈstedɪ] *adj* (-**ier**, -**iest**) inseguro,-a, inestable.

unstuck [ʌnˈstʌk] *phr* **to come unstuck** **1** despegarse, desprenderse. **2** fracasar, fallar.

unsuccessful [ʌnsəkˈsesfʊl] *adj* fracasado,-a, sin éxito.

● **to be unsuccessful** no tener éxito, fracasar.

unsuitable [ʌnˈsuːtəbəl] *adj* **1** poco apropiado,-a *(persona)*. **2** inoportuno, inconveniente.

unsuited [ʌnˈsuːtɪd] *adj* **1** no apto,-a. **2** incompatible *(personas)*.

unsure [ʌnˈʃʊəʳ] *adj* inseguro,-a, no seguro,-a.

unsurmountable [ʌnsəˈmaʊntəbəl] *adj* insuperable.

unsuspected [ʌnsəsˈpektɪd] *adj* insospechado,-a.

unsuspecting [ʌnsəsˈpektɪŋ] *adj* confiado,-a.

untangle [ʌnˈtæŋgəl] *vt* desenmarañar.

unthinkable [ʌnˈθɪŋkəbəl] *adj* impensable, inconcebible.

untidiness [ʌnˈtaɪdɪnəs] *n* **1** desorden *(de habitación)*. **2** desaliño, desaseo *(de persona)*.

untidy [ʌnˈtaɪdɪ] *adj* (-**ier**, -**iest**). **1** desordenado,-a *(habitación)*. **2** desaliñado,-a, desaseado,-a *(persona)*.

untie [ʌnˈtaɪ] *vt* **1** desatar *(nudo)*. **2** soltar *(animal)*.

until [ənˈtɪl] *prep* hasta.

▶ *conj* hasta que.

untimely [ʌnˈtaɪmlɪ] *adj* (-**ier**, -**iest**). **1** inoportuno,-a. **2** prematuro,-a.

untold [ʌnˈtəʊld] *adj* **1** no contado,-a *(his-toria)*. **2** no revelado,-a *(secreto)*. **3** *fig* incalculable, indecible.

untouchable [ʌnˈtʌtʃəbəl] *adj-n* intocable.

untrained [ʌnˈtreɪnd] *adj* **1** inexperto,-a. **2** sin formación profesional.

untrue [ʌnˈtruː] *adj* **1** falso,-a. **2** infiel.

untrustworthy [ʌnˈtrʌstwɜːðɪ] *adj* poco fiable.

untruthful [ʌnˈtruːθfʊl] *adj* mentiroso,-a.

unused [(adj) ʌnˈjuːzd(adj) ʌnˈjuːst] *adj* **1** no usado,-a, sin usar, nuevo. **2** no acostumbrado,-a.

unusual [ʌnˈjuːʒʊəl] *adj* raro,-a, inusual.

unusually [ʌnˈjuːʒʊəlɪ] *adv* excepcionalmente, extraordinariamente.

unveil [ʌnˈveɪl] *vt* **1** descubrir *(monumento)*. **2** revelar *(secreto)*.

unwanted [ʌnˈwɒntɪd] *adj* **1** indeseado,-a. **2** no deseado,-a *(hijo)*.

unwarranted [ʌnˈwɒrəntɪd] *adj* injustificado,-a.

unwelcome [ʌnˈwelkəm] *adj* inoportuno,-a, molesto,-a.

unwell [ʌnˈwel] *adj* indispuesto,-a.

unwieldy [ʌnˈwiːldɪ] *adj* (-**ier**, -**iest**) engorroso,-a, difícil de manejar.

unwilling [ʌnˈwɪlɪŋ] *adj* reacio,-a, poco dispuesto,-a.

● **to be unwilling to do** STH no querer hacer algo.

unwillingness [ʌnˈwɪlɪŋnəs] *n* desgana, falta de voluntad.

unwind [ʌnˈwaɪnd] *vt* (*pt & pp* **unwound** [ʌnˈwaʊnd]) desenrollar.

▶ *vi* **1** desenrollarse. **2** *fam* relajarse.

unwise [ʌnˈwaɪz] *adj* imprudente, poco aconsejable.

unwitting [ʌnˈwɪtɪŋ] *adj* inconsciente.

unwittingly [ʌnˈwɪtɪŋlɪ] *adv* inconscientemente.

unworthy [ʌnˈwɜːðɪ] *adj* indigno,-a.

unwound [ʌnˈwaʊnd] *pt-pp* → unwind.

unwrap [ʌnˈræp] *vt* (*pt & pp* **unwrapped**, *ger* **unwrapping**) desenvolver, abrir.

up [ʌp] *adv* **1** arriba, hacia arriba: *to sit up in bed*, incorporarse; *to walk up*, subir andando. **2** levantado,-a: *he isn't up yet*, aún no se ha levantado. **3** hacia: *he came up and ...*, se acercó y .... **4** hacia el norte: *we went up to Scotland*, fuimos a Escocia. **5** más alto,-a: *turn the radio up*, sube la radio. **6** acabado,-a: *eat it up*,

acábatelo, cómetelo todo. **7** a trozos, a porciones, a raciones.
▶ *prep* **1**: *to go up the stairs*, subir la escalera; *to run up the street*, ir corriendo calle arriba. **2** en lo alto de: *up a tree*, en lo alto de un árbol.
▶ *vt* (*pt & pp* **upped**, *ger* **upping**) *fam* subir, aumentar.
● **close up** muy cerca.
● **to be up to** STH estar haciendo algo, estar tramando algo.
● **to feel up to doing** STH sentirse con fuerzas para hacer algo.
● **up to** hasta: *the plane can carry up to 150 people*, el avión puede llevar hasta 150 personas; *up to now*, hasta ahora.
● **well up in** STH saber mucho de algo.
● **it's not up to much** *fam* no vale gran cosa.
● **it's up to you** *fam* es cosa tuya.
● **to be on the up and up** *fam* ir cada vez mejor.
● **to up and go** *fam* coger e irse.
● **what's up?** *fam* ¿qué pasa?
● **up and down** de arriba a abajo, de un lado al otro.
● **up yours!** ¡vete a la mierda!
■ **ups and downs** altibajos.
up-and-coming [ʌpən'kʌmɪŋ] *adj* prometedor,-ra.
upbringing ['ʌpbrɪŋɪŋ] *n* educación, crianza.
update [*(n)* 'ʌpdeɪt*(vb)* 'ʌpdeɪt] *n* actualización, puesta al día.
▶ *vt* actualizar, poner al día.
upgrade ['ʌpgreɪd] *vt* **1** ascender *(persona)*. **2** mejorar, mejorar la calidad de. **3** modernizar, actualizar.
▶ *n* modernización, actualización.
upheaval [ʌp'hiːvəl] *n* trastorno, agitación.
upheld [ʌp'held] *pt-pp* → uphold.
uphill [*(adj)* 'ʌphɪl*(adv)* ʌp'hɪl] *adj* **1** ascendente. **2** *fig* difícil.
▶ *adv* cuesta arriba.
uphold [ʌp'həʊld] *vt* (*pt & pp* **upheld** [ʌp'held]) sostener, apoyar.
upholster [ʌp'həʊlstə'] *vt* tapizar.
upholstery [ʌp'həʊlstəri] *n* tapicería, tapizado.
upkeep ['ʌpkiːp] *n* mantenimiento.
uplift ['ʌplɪft] *vt* edificar, inspirar.
upon [ə'pɒn] *prep* → on.
upper ['ʌpə'] *adj* superior, de arriba.

■ **upper case** mayúsculas, caja alta.
■ **upper class** clase alta.
■ **upper house** cámara alta.
uppermost ['ʌpəməʊst] *adj* **1** más alto,-a. **2** *fig* principal.
upright ['ʌpraɪt] *adj* **1** derecho,-a, vertical *(posición)*. **2** recto,-a, honrado,-a *(persona)*.
▶ *adv* derecho: *sit upright*, siéntate derecho.
▶ *n* poste *(de portería)*.
uprising [ʌp'raɪzɪŋ] *n* sublevación, rebelión.
uproar ['ʌprɔː'] *n* alboroto, tumulto.
uproot [ʌp'ruːt] *vt* desarraigar.
upset [ʌp'set] *adj* disgustado,-a, ofendido,-a.
▶ *vt* (*pt & pp* **upset** ['ʌpset], *ger* **upsetting**). **1** contrariar, preocupar, disgustar. **2** desbaratar *(planes)*. **3** volcar *(barco)*. **4** derramar *(recipiente)*.
▶ *n* revés, contratiempo.
● **to have an upset stomach** estar mal del estómago.
upshot ['ʌpʃɒt] *n* resultado.
upside down [ʌpsaɪd'daʊn] *adv* al revés.
upstairs [*(adv)* ʌp'steəz*(n)* 'ʌpsteəz] *adv* **1** en el piso de arriba *(situación)*. **2** al piso de arriba *(movimiento)*.
▶ *n* piso de arriba.
▶ *adj* de arriba.
upstanding [ʌp'stændɪŋ] *adj* honrado,-a.
upsurge ['ʌpsɜːdʒ] *n* subida.
up-to-date [ʌptə'deɪt] *adj* **1** al día, actualizado. **2** moderno,-a, a la última.
upward ['ʌpwəd] *adj* hacia arriba, ascendente.
▶ *adv* hacia arriba.
upwards ['ʌpwədz] *adv* hacia arriba.
uranium [jʊ'reɪnɪəm] *n* uranio.
urban ['ɜːbən] *adj* urbano,-a.
urge [ɜːdʒ] *n* impulso, ganas.
▶ *vt* encarecer, recomendar vivamente: *to urge* SB *to do* STH, instar a ALGN a hacer algo.
urgency ['ɜːdʒənsi] *n* urgencia.
urgent ['ɜːdʒənt] *adj* urgente.
urinal [jʊ'raɪnəl] *n* urinario.
urine ['jʊərɪn] *n* orina.
URL ['juːɑːr'el] *abbr (uniform resource locator)* URL.
urn [ɜːn] *n* **1** urna. **2** tetera grande.
Uruguay ['jʊərəgwaɪ] *n* Uruguay.

Uruguayan [jʊərəˈgwaɪən] *adj-n* uruguayo,-a.

us [ʌs, *unstressed* əz] *pron* **1** nos, nosotros,-as: *give us your gun*, danos tu pistola; *come with us*, ven con nosotros; *it's us*, somos nosotros,-as. **2** *fam* me: *give us a kiss*, dame un beso.

US [ˈjuːˈes] *abbr* (*United States*) EE.UU.

USA[1] [ˈjuːˈesˈeɪ] *abbr* (*United States of America*) EE.UU..

USA[2] [ˈjuːˈesˈɑːmɪ] *abbr* (*United States Army*) Ejército de los Estados Unidos.

usage [ˈjuːzɪdʒ] *n* uso.

use [*(n)* juːs *(vb)* juːz] *n* **1** uso, empleo. **2** utilidad.
► *vt* **1** usar, utilizar, emplear. **2** usar, aprovecharse de.
● **used to** soler, acostumbrar *(se refiere solo al pasado)*: *I used to be fat*, antes estaba gorda; *there didn't use to be so many shops here*, antes aquí no había tantas tiendas; *there used to be a cinema here*, antes había aquí un cine; *he used to get up early*, solía levantarse temprano; *we always used to go to church on Sunday*, los domingos siempre íbamos a misa.
● **in use** en uso.
● **"Not in use"** "No funciona".
● **of use** útil.
● **out of use** en desuso.
● **what's the use of ...?** ¿de qué sirve ... ?
to use up *vt* terminar, gastar, agotar.

used [juːst] *adj* usado,-a.
● **to be used to** STH estar acostumbrado,-a a algo.
● **to get used to** STH acostumbrarse a algo.
useful [ˈjuːsfʊl] *adj* útil, provechoso,-a.
usefulness [ˈjuːsfʊlnəs] *n* utilidad.
useless [ˈjuːsləs] *adj* inútil.
user [ˈjuːzə] *n* usuario,-a.
usher [ˈʌʃə] *n* **1** ujier. **2** acomodador,-ra *(en cine)*.
to usher in *vt* hacer pasar.
usual [ˈjuːʒʊəl] *adj* usual, habitual, normal.
● **as usual** como de costumbre, como siempre.
usually [ˈjuːʒʊəlɪ] *adv* normalmente.
utensil [juːˈtensəl] *n* utensilio.
● **kitchen utensils** batería de cocina.
utility [juːˈtɪlɪtɪ] *n* (*pl* -**ies**). **1** utilidad. **2** empresa de servicio público.
utilize [ˈjuːtɪlaɪz] *vt* utilizar.
utmost [ˈʌtməʊst] *adj* sumo,-a, extremo,-a, mayor.
● **to do one's utmost** hacer todo lo posible.
utopia [juːˈtəʊpɪə] *n* utopía.
utter [ˈʌtə] *adj* absoluto,-a, total.
► *vt* pronunciar, articular.
utterly [ˈʌtəlɪ] *adv* totalmente, completamente.
U-turn [ˈjuːtɜːn] *n* cambio de sentido, giro de 180 grados

V

v¹ [vɜːs] *abbr* (**verse**) verso.

v² [vɜːsəs] *abbr* (**versus**) contra.

vacancy ['veɪkənsɪ] *n* (*pl* **-ies**). **1** vacante (*puesto de trabajo*): *we have a vacancy for a secretary*, tenemos una vacante para un puesto de secretaria. **2** habitación libre: *have you got any vacancies?*, ¿tiene habitaciones libres?
• **"No vacancies"** "Completo".

vacant ['veɪkənt] *adj* **1** vacío: *the building is vacant*, el edificio está vacío. **2** vacante: *there are several posts vacant*, hay varios puestos vacantes. **3** libre: *there are no rooms vacant*, no hay habitaciones libres.

vacate [vəˈkeɪt] *vt* **1** abandonar, dejar vacante. **2** desocupar: *the police told them to vacate the premises*, la policía les dijo que desocuparan el local.

vacation [vəˈkeɪʃən] *n* vacaciones: *we're on vacation*, estamos de vacaciones.

vaccinate ['væksɪneɪt] *vt* vacunar.

vaccine ['væksiːn] *n* vacuna.

vacuum ['vækjʊəm] *n* vacío.
▶ *vt* pasar la aspiradora por.
■ **vacuum cleaner** aspiradora.
■ **vacuum flask** termo.

vacuum-packed ['vækjʊəmpækt] *adj* envasado,-a al vacío.

vagina [vəˈdʒaɪnə] *n* vagina.

vague [veɪg] *adj* vago,-a, indefinido,-a: *I have vague memories of the accident*, tengo vagos recuerdos del accidente.

vain [veɪn] *adj* **1** vanidoso,-a. **2** vano,-a, inútil: *a vain attempt*, un intento inútil.
• **in vain** en vano: *he tried hard, but it was all in vain*, lo intentó en serio, pero todo fue inútil.

valentine ['væləntaɪn] *n* **1** tarjeta de enamorados (*enviada por la festividad de San Valentín*). **2** novio,-a.

valiant ['væljənt] *adj* valiente.

valid ['vælɪd] *adj* **1** válido,-a: *a valid argument*, un argumento válido. **2** válido,-a, valedero,-a: *a valid passport*, un pasaporte válido.

valley ['vælɪ] *n* valle.

valuable ['væljʊəbəl] *adj* valioso,-a: *thank you for your valuable help*, gracias por su valiosa ayuda.
▶ *npl* **valuables** objetos de valor.

valuation [væljʊˈeɪʃən] *n* valoración.

value ['væljuː] *n* valor: *a painting of great value*, un cuadro de gran valor.
▶ *vt* **1** valorar, tasar: *the house is valued at 75,000*, la casa está valorada en 75.000. **2** valorar, apreciar: *we value your friendship*, valoramos tu amistad.
• **it's good value for money** está bien de precio para lo que es.

valve [vælv] *n* válvula.

vampire ['væmpaɪəʳ] *n* vampiro.

van [væn] *n* **1** camioneta, furgoneta. **2** GB furgón.

vandal ['vændəl] *n* vándalo,-a.

vandalism ['vændəlɪzəm] *n* vandalismo.

vandalize ['vændəlaɪz] *vt* destrozar, causar destrozos: *they broke into the school and vandalized it*, entraron en el colegio y causaron destrozos.

vanguard ['vængɑːd] *n* vanguardia: *he's in the vanguard of the arts*, está en la vanguardia de las artes.

vanilla [vəˈnɪlə] *n* vainilla.

vanish ['vænɪʃ] *vi* desaparecer: *the man*

vanished into thin air, el hombre desapareció sin dejar rastro.

vanity ['vænɪtɪ] *n* (*pl* -**ies**) vanidad.

vapour ['veɪpə'] (US **vapor**) *n* vapor, vaho.

variable ['veərɪəbəl] *adj* variable.

▶ *n* variable.

variance ['veərɪəns] *n* discrepancia.

● **to be at variance 1** no concordar (*versiones*). **2** estar en desacuerdo (*personas*).

variant ['veərɪənt] *n* variante.

variation [veərɪ'eɪʃən] *n* variación.

varied ['veərɪd] *adj* variado,-a.

variety [və'raɪətɪ] *n* (*pl* -**ies**). **1** variedad, diversidad: *variety is the spice of life*, en la variedad está el gusto. **2** clase, variedad: *a new variety of apple*, una nueva variedad de manzanas.

● **a variety of** varios, muchos, diversos: *we have a variety of styles and colours*, tenemos varios estilos y colores.

■ **variety show** espectáculo de variedades.

various ['veərɪəs] *adj* **1** diversos,-as, distintos,-as. **2** varios,-as.

varnish ['vɑːnɪʃ] *n* (*pl* -**es**) barniz.

▶ *vt* barnizar.

vary ['veərɪ] *vt-vi* (*pt & pp* -**ied**) variar: *the prices vary according to the size*, los precios varían según el tamaño.

vase [vɑːz] *n* jarrón, florero.

vasectomy [væ'sektəmɪ] *n* (*pl* -**ies**) vasectomía.

vast [vɑːst] *adj* vasto,-a, inmenso,-a, enorme: *the vast majority of people*, la inmensa mayoría de la gente.

vat [væt] *n* tina, cuba.

VAT [væt, ˌviːeɪ'tiː] *abbr* (*value added tax*) IVA.

Vatican ['vætɪkən] *n* **the Vatican** el Vaticano.

▶ *adj* vaticano,-a.

■ **Vatican City** Ciudad del Vaticano.

■ **Vatican Council** Concilio Vaticano.

vault[1] [vɔːlt] *n* **1** bóveda (*de techo*). **2** cámara acorazada (*de banco*). **3** panteón, cripta (*de iglesia*).

vault[2] [vɔːlt] *n* salto.

▶ *vt-vi* saltar.

VCR [ˌviːsiː'ɑː'] *abbr* (*video cassette recorder*) grabador de vídeo, vídeo.

VD [ˌviː'diː] *abbr* (*venereal disease*) enfermedad venérea.

VDU [ˌviːdiː'juː] *abbr* (*visual display unit*) pantalla.

veal [viːl] *n* ternera.

veer [vɪə'] *vi* virar, girar, desviarse.

vegetable ['vedʒɪtəbəl] *adj* vegetal.

▶ *n* **1** vegetal. **2** hortaliza, verdura, legumbre.

vegetarian [vedʒɪ'teərɪən] *adj-n* vegetariano,-a.

vegetate ['vedʒɪteɪt] *vi* vegetar.

vegetation [vedʒɪ'teɪʃən] *n* vegetación.

vehemence ['vɪəmən] *n* vehemencia.

vehement ['vɪəmənt] *adj* vehemente.

vehicle ['viːəkəl] *n* vehículo.

veil [veɪl] *n* velo.

vein [veɪn] *n* **1** vena. **2** vena, nervio (*de hoja*). **3** vena, toque: *there was a vein of irony in his remark*, había un toque de ironía en su comentario.

velocity [və'lɒsɪtɪ] *n* (*pl* -**ies**) velocidad.

velvet ['velvɪt] *n* terciopelo.

vending machine ['vendɪŋməʃiːn] *n* máquina expendedora.

vendor ['vendə'] *n* vendedor,-ra.

veneer [və'nɪə'] *n* **1** chapa. **2** apariencia.

▶ *vt* chapar.

venerable ['venərəbəl] *adj* venerable.

venerate ['venəreɪt] *vt* venerar, reverenciar.

Venezuela [venɪ'zweɪlə] *n* Venezuela.

Venezuelan [venɪ'zweɪlən] *adj-n* venezolano,-a.

vengeance ['vendʒəns] *n* venganza.

● **with a vengeance** a rabiar, con ganas.

vengeful ['vendʒfʊl] *adj* vengativo,-a.

venison ['venɪsən] *n* carne de venado.

venom ['venəm] *n* **1** veneno. **2** odio.

vent [vent] *n* **1** abertura. **2** orificio, respiradero. **3** rejilla de ventilación.

▶ *vt* descargar: *he vented his anger on her*, se desahogó con ella.

● **to give vent to one's feelings** desahogarse.

ventilate ['ventɪleɪt] *vt* ventilar.

ventilation [ventɪ'leɪʃən] *n* ventilación.

ventilator ['ventɪleɪtə'] *n* ventilador.

venture ['ventʃə'] *n* empresa arriesgada, aventura.

▶ *vt* arriesgar, aventurar: *he ventured into the woods*, se aventuró a entrar en el bosque.

▶ *vi* aventurarse.

venue ['venjuː] *n* lugar.

veranda [vəˈrændə] *n* veranda, terraza.

También se escribe **verandah**.

verb [vɜːb] *n* verbo.

verbal [ˈvɜːbəl] *adj* verbal.

verdict [ˈvɜːdɪkt] *n* **1** veredicto. **2** opinión.

verge [vɜːdʒ] *n* borde, margen.
- **on the verge of** a punto de: *she was on the verge of crying*, estaba a punto de llorar.

to verge on *vt* rayar en: *this is verging on madness*, esto raya en la locura.

verification [verɪfɪˈkeɪʃən] *n* verificación, comprobación.

verify [ˈverɪfaɪ] *vt* (*pt & pp* **-ied**) verificar, comprobar.

veritable [ˈverɪtəbəl] *adj* verdadero,-a.

vermin [ˈvɜːmɪn] *n* (*pl* **vermin**). **1** alimaña. **2** bichos, sabandijas.

verruca [vəˈruːkə] *n* verruga.

versatile [ˈvɜːsətaɪl] *adj* versátil.

versatility [vɜːsəˈtɪlɪtɪ] *n* versatilidad.

verse [vɜːs] *n* **1** estrofa, versículo: *I learnt the first verse by heart*, me aprendí la primera estrofa de memoria. **2** verso, poesía: *Shakespeare wrote in verse*, Shakespeare escribió en verso.

versed [vɜːst] *adj* experto,-a, versado,-a: *he was well versed in history*, estaba versado en historia.

version [ˈvɜːʒən] *n* versión.

versus [ˈvɜːsəs] *prep* contra: *the Scotland versus Wales match*, el partido de Escocia contra Gales.

vertebra [ˈvɜːtɪbrə] *n* (*pl* **vertebrae** [ˈvɜːtɪbriː]) vértebra.

vertebrate [ˈvɜːtɪbrət] *adj* vertebrado,-a.
- ► *n* vertebrado.

vertical [ˈvɜːtɪkəl] *adj* vertical.

vertigo [ˈvɜːtɪgəʊ] *n* vértigo.

verve [vɜːv] *n* brío, empuje.

very [ˈverɪ] *adv* **1** muy: *you look very pretty*, estás muy guapa; *a very tall building*, un edificio muy alto; *at the very latest*, a más tardar; *at the very end*, al final de todo. **2** mucho: *it's very cold*, hace mucho frío; *I'm very sorry*, lo siento mucho; *thank you very much*, muchas gracias; *the very best*, el mejor posible; *the very last time*, la última vez; *the very same place*, el mismísimo sitio; *his very own boat*, su propio barco.
- ► *adj* mismo,-a, mismísimo,-a: *at that very moment*, en aquel mismo instante.

vessel [ˈvesəl] *n* **1** nave, buque, barco: *a merchant vessel*, un buque mercante. **2** recipiente, vasija: *a clay vessel*, una vasija de barro. **3** vaso: *a blood vessel*, un vaso sanguíneo.

vest [vest] *n* **1** camiseta *(interior)*. **2** US chaleco.
- ■ **vested interests** intereses creados.

to vest with *vt* conferir a.

vet [vet] *n fam* veterinario,-a.
- ► *vt* (*pt & pp* **vetted**, *ger* **vetting**) GB investigar, examinar.

veteran [ˈvetərən] *adj-n* veterano,-a.

veterinarian [vetərɪˈneərɪən] *n* US veterinario,-a.

veterinary [ˈvetərɪnərɪ] *adj* veterinario,-a.

veto [ˈviːtəʊ] *n* (*pl* **vetoes**) veto.
- ► *vt* vetar, prohibir.

VHF [ˈviːeɪtʃˈef] *abbr* (*very high frequency*) VHF.

VHS [ˈviːeɪtʃˈes] *abbr* (*Video Home System*) VHS.

via [vaɪə] *prep* vía, por vía de, por: *there is no direct flight, you have to go via Rome*, no hay vuelo directo, hay que ir vía Roma.

viable [ˈvaɪəbəl] *adj* viable, factible.

viaduct [ˈvaɪədʌkt] *n* viaducto.

vibrate [vaɪˈbreɪt] *vt* hacer vibrar.
- ► *vi* vibrar.

vibration [vaɪˈbreɪʃən] *n* vibración.

vicar [ˈvɪkə'] *n* **1** párroco. **2** vicario.

vicarious [vɪˈkeərɪəs] *adj* experimentado, -a por otro, indirecto,-a.

vice[1] [vaɪs] *n* vicio.

vice[2] [vaɪs] *n* tornillo de banco.

vice versa [vaɪsˈvɜːsə] *adv* viceversa.

vicinity [vɪˈsɪnɪtɪ] *n* vecindad, inmediaciones: *there are a few shops in the vicinity of the station*, hay algunas tiendas en la inmediaciones de la estación.

vicious [ˈvɪʃəs] *adj* **1** cruel: *a vicious murder*, un asesinato despiadado. **2** violento,-a, brutal: *it was a vicious beating*, fue una paliza brutal. **3** peligroso,-a, fiero: *a vicious dog*, un perro fiero.
- ■ **vicious circle** círculo vicioso.

victim [ˈvɪktɪm] *n* víctima.

victor [ˈvɪktə'] *n* vencedor,-ra.

victorious [vɪkˈtɔːrɪəs] *adj* victorioso,-a.

victory [ˈvɪktərɪ] *n* (*pl* **-ies**) victoria, triunfo.

video [ˈvɪdɪəʊ] *n* (*pl* **videos**) vídeo.
- ■ **video camera** videocámara.

- **video cassette** videocasete.
- **video game** videojuego.
- **video shop** videoclub.
- **video recorder** vídeo.

videotape [ˈvɪdɪəʊteɪp] *vt* grabar en vídeo.
▶ *n* videocinta, cinta de vídeo.
vie [vaɪ] *vi* competir.
Vietnam [vɪetˈnæm] *n* Vietnam.
Vietnamese [vɪetnəˈmiːz] *adj-n* vietnamita.
▶ *npl* **the Vietnamese** los vietnamitas.
view [vjuː] *n* **1** vista, panorama: *the view from the hotel is beautiful*, la vista desde el hotel es hermosa. **2** parecer, opinión, punto de vista: *what's your view on this?*, ¿cuál es tu opinión de esto?
▶ *vt* mirar, ver.
- **in my view** en mi opinión.
- **in view of** en vista de.
- **with a view to** con el propósito de.
- **to take a poor view of** *fam* ver con malos ojos.

viewer [ˈvjuːəʳ] *n* telespectador,-ra, televidente.
viewpoint [ˈvjuːpɔɪnt] *n* punto de vista.
vigil [ˈvɪdʒɪl] *n* vigilia.
- **to keep vigil** velar.

vigilant [ˈvɪdʒɪlənt] *adj* vigilante, atento,-a.
vigorous [ˈvɪgərəs] *adj* vigoroso,-a.
vigour [ˈvɪgəʳ] (US **vigor**) *n* vigor, energía.
vile [vaɪl] *adj* **1** vil: *a vile crime*, un vil crimen. **2** *fam* malísimo,-a: *a vile taste*, un sabor asqueroso.
villa [ˈvɪlə] *n* chalet.
village [ˈvɪlɪdʒ] *n* pueblo, aldea.
villager [ˈvɪlɪdʒəʳ] *n* aldeano,-a.
villain [ˈvɪlən] *n* **1** malo,-a: *Nicholson plays the villain*, Nicholson hace de malo. **2** GB *fam* criminal, delincuente.
vinaigrette [vɪnəˈgret] *n* vinagreta.
vindicate [ˈvɪndɪkeɪt] *vt* **1** justificar. **2** reivindicar.
vindictive [vɪnˈdɪktɪv] *adj* vengativo,-a.
vine [vaɪn] *n* vid, parra.
vinegar [ˈvɪnɪgəʳ] *n* vinagre.
vineyard [ˈvɪnjɑːd] *n* viña, viñedo.
vintage [ˈvɪntɪdʒ] *n* cosecha.
- **vintage car** coche antiguo, coche de época construido entre 1919 y 1930.
- **vintage wine** vino añejo.

vinyl [ˈvaɪnɪl] *n* vinilo.
viola [vɪˈəʊlə] *n* viola.
violate [ˈvaɪəleɪt] *vt* violar: *he violated the code of professional ethics*, violó el código deontológico.
violation [vaɪəˈleɪʃən] *n* violación: *the violation of the law*, la violación de la lay.
violence [ˈvaɪələns] *n* violencia.
violent [ˈvaɪələnt] *adj* violento,-a: *it was a violent film*, era una película violenta.
violet [ˈvaɪələt] *n* violeta *(flor, color)*.
▶ *adj* violeta, de color violeta.
violin [vaɪəˈlɪn] *n* violín.
violinist [vaɪəˈlɪnɪst] *n* violinista.
VIP [viːaɪˈpiː] *abbr (very important person)* VIP.
- **VIP lounge** sala VIP.
- **VIP treatment** tratamiento VIP.

viper [ˈvaɪpəʳ] *n* víbora.
virgin [ˈvɜːdʒɪn] *adj* virgen.
▶ *n* virgen.
virginity [vɜːˈdʒɪnɪtɪ] *n* virginidad.
Virgo [ˈvɜːgəʊ] *n* Virgo.
virile [ˈvɪraɪl] *adj* viril, varonil.
virility [vɪˈrɪlɪtɪ] *n* virilidad.
virtual [ˈvɜːtjʊəl] *adj* virtual.
- **virtual reality** realidad virtual.

virtually [ˈvɜːtjʊəlɪ] *adv* casi, prácticamente.
virtue [ˈvɜːtjuː] *n* virtud.
- **by virtue of** en virtud de.

virulent [ˈvɪrʊlənt] *adj* virulento,-a.
virus [ˈvaɪərəs] *n (pl* **viruses**) virus.
- **virus checker** antivirus.

visa [ˈviːzə] *n* visado.
vise [vaɪs] *n* US tornillo de banco.
visibility [vɪzɪˈbɪlɪtɪ] *n* visibilidad.
visible [ˈvɪzɪbəl] *adj* visible.
vision [ˈvɪʒən] *n* **1** visión: *to see a vision*, tener una visión. **2** vista: *a pilot must have a perfect vision*, un piloto debe tener la vista perfecta.
visit [ˈvɪzɪt] *n* visita.
▶ *vt* visitar.
- **to pay a visit** visitar: *my aunt paid us a visit*, mi tía nos hizo una visita.

visitor [ˈvɪzɪtəʳ] *n* **1** visita: *you've got a visitor*, tenéis una visita. **2** visitante: *there are many visitors in the museum*, hay muchos visitantes en el museo.
visor [ˈvaɪzəʳ] *n* visera.
vista [ˈvɪstə] *n* vista, panorama.
visual [ˈvɪzjʊəl] *adj* visual.
- **visual display unit** pantalla.

visualize [ˈvɪzjʊəlaɪz] *vt* imaginar.
vital [ˈvaɪtəl] *adj* **1** vital: *John's a very vi-*

tal person, John es una persona muy vital. **2** esencial, fundamental: *this is of vital importance*, esto es de una importancia vital.

▶ *npl* **vitals** órganos vitales.

vitality [vaɪˈtælɪtɪ] *n* vitalidad.

vitally [ˈvaɪtəlɪ] *adv* sumamente: *it is vitally important that...*, es fundamental que....

vitamin [ˈvɪtəmɪn] *n* vitamina.

vivacious [vɪˈveɪʃəs] *adj* vivaz, animado,-a.

vivid [ˈvɪvɪd] *adj* **1** vivo,-a, intenso,-a. **2** gráfico,-a.

vixen [ˈvɪksən] *n* zorra.

vocabulary [vəˈkæbjʊlərɪ] *n* (*pl* **-ies**) vocabulario, léxico.

vocal [ˈvəʊkəl] *adj* **1** vocal: *vocal organs*, órganos vocales. **2** ruidoso,-a: *the party has few members but they are vocal*, el partido tiene pocos miembros pero se hacen oír.

■ **vocal chords** cuerdas vocales.

vocalist [ˈvəʊkəlɪst] *n* cantante, vocalista.

vocation [vəʊˈkeɪʃən] *n* vocación.

vocational [vəʊˈkeɪʃənəl] *adj* vocacional.

■ **vocational guidance** orientación profesional.

■ **vocational training** formación profesional.

vociferous [vəˈsɪfərəs] *adj* vociferante.

vodka [ˈvɒdkə] *n* vodka.

vogue [vəʊg] *n* boga, moda.

● **to be in vogue** estar de moda.

voice [vɔɪs] *n* voz.

▶ *vt* **1** expresar, manifestar. **2** sonorizar.

● **to lose one's voice** quedarse afónico,-a.

● **to keep one's voice down** no levantar la voz.

● **to raise/lower one's voice** elevar/bajar la voz.

● **voice mail** buzón de voz.

void [vɔɪd] *adj* **1** vacío,-a. **2** nulo,-a, inválido,-a.

▶ *n* vacío: *her absence left a great void*, su ausencia dejó un gran vacío.

● **to make STH void** anular.

vol [vɒl, ˈvɒljuːm] *abbr* (*volume - book*) tomo; (*- loudness*) volumen.

volatile [ˈvɒlətaɪl] *adj* volátil.

volcanic [vɒlˈkænɪk] *adj* volcánico,-a.

volcano [vɒlˈkeɪnəʊ] *n* (*pl* **-s** o **-es**) volcán.

volition [vəˈlɪʃən] *n* volición, voluntad: *of one's own volition*, por voluntad propia.

volley [ˈvɒlɪ] *n* **1** descarga: *a volley of shots*, una descarga cerrada; *a volley of applause*, una salva de aplausos. **2** volea.

▶ *vi* volear.

volleyball [ˈvɒlibɔːl] *n* balonvolea, voleibol.

volt [vəʊlt] *n* voltio.

voltage [ˈvəʊltɪdʒ] *n* voltaje, tensión.

voluble [ˈvɒljʊbəl] *adj* locuaz, hablador,-ra.

volume [ˈvɒljuːm] *n* **1** tomo: *an encyclopaedia in ten volumes*, una enciclopedia en diez volúmenes. **2** volumen: *turn the volume of the TV down*, baja el volumen de la televisión. **3** capacidad, volumen: *how do you calculate the volume of a cylinder?*, ¿cómo se calcula el volumen de un cilindro?

voluminous [vəˈljuːmɪnəs] *adj* voluminoso,-a.

voluntarily [vɒlənˈterɪlɪ] *adv* voluntariamente, por voluntad propia.

voluntary [ˈvɒləntərɪ] *adj* voluntario,-a.

■ **voluntary organization** organización benéfica.

volunteer [vɒlənˈtɪəʳ] *n* voluntario,-a.

▶ *vt* ofrecer.

▶ *vi* ofrecerse: *he volunteered for a dangerous mission*, se ofreció voluntario para una misión peligrosa.

● **to volunteer to do STH** ofrecerse (*voluntario*) para hacer algo.

voluptuous [vəˈlʌptjʊəs] *adj* voluptuoso,-a.

vomit [ˈvɒmɪt] *n* vómito.

▶ *vt-vi* vomitar.

voracious [vəˈreɪʃəs] *adj* voraz.

vortex [ˈvɔːteks] *n* (*pl* **-es** o **vortices** [ˈvɔːtɪsiːz]). **1** vórtice. **2** *fig* vorágine.

vote [vəʊt] *n* **1** voto: *the winning candidate got 87 votes*, el candidato ganador obtuvo 87 votos. **2** votación: *we decided to take a vote on it*, decidimos someterlo a votación.

▶ *vt-vi* votar.

▶ *vt* elegir (*por votación*): *I voted for the independent candidate*, voté por el candidato independiente; *the union voted in favour of a strike*, el sindicato votó a favor de una huelga.

voter [ˈvəʊtəʳ] *n* votante.

vouch [vaʊtʃ] vi .
● **to vouch for** responder de: *I can vouch for him*, respondo de él.
voucher [ˈvaʊtʃəʳ] n vale, bono.
vow [vaʊ] n promesa solemne, voto.
▶ vt jurar, prometer solemnemente.
vowel [ˈvaʊəl] n vocal.
voyage [ˈvɔɪdʒ] n viaje.
▶ vi viajar.
voyager [ˈvɔɪədʒəʳ] n viajero,-a.

VTR [ˌviːtiːˈɑːʳ] abbr *(video tape recorder)* grabador de videocinta.
vulgar [ˈvʌlgəʳ] adj ordinario,-a, grosero, -a, vulgar.
vulgarity [vʌlˈgænti] n (pl -**ies**) ordinariez, grosería, vulgaridad.
vulnerable [ˈvʌlnərəbəl] adj vulnerable.
vulture [ˈvʌltʃəʳ] n buitre.
vulva [ˈvʌlvə] n (pl -**s** o **vulvae** [ˈvʌlviː]) vulva.

W

W [west] *abbr* (*west*) O.
wad [wɒd] *n* **1** taco (*de papel*). **2** fajo (*de dinero*).
wade [weɪd] *vi* andar por el agua: *to wade across a river*, vadear un río.
wafer ['weɪfə^r] *n* **1** barquillo, galleta, oblea. **2** hostia.
waffle¹ ['wɒfəl] *n* gofre.
waffle² ['wɒfəl] *n* GB *fam* palabrería.
▶ *vi* GB *fam* hablar mucho sin decir nada.
waft [wɒft] *vi* moverse por el aire, flotar.
wag [wæg] *n* meneo.
▶ *vt-vi* (*pt & pp* **wagged**, *ger* **wagging**) menear(se).
wage [weɪdʒ] *n* sueldo, salario.
● **to wage war on** hacer la guerra a.
wager ['weɪdʒə^r] *n* apuesta.
▶ *vt* apostar.
wagon ['wægən] *n* **1** carro, carromato. **2** vagón (*de tren*).

| También se escribe **waggon**. |

wail [weɪl] *n* lamento, gemido.
▶ *vi* lamentarse, gemir.
waist [weɪst] *n* cintura, talle.
waistcoat ['weɪskəʊt] *n* chaleco.
waistline ['weɪstlaɪn] *n* cintura.
wait [weɪt] *n* espera.
▶ *vi* esperar: *wait for me!*, ¡espérame!
● **to wait up for** SB esperar a ALGN levantado.
waiter ['weɪtə^r] *n* camarero.
waiting ['weɪtɪŋ] *n* espera.
■ **waiting list** lista de espera.
■ **waiting room** sala de espera.
waitress ['weɪtrəs] *n* (*pl* **-es**) camarera.
waive [weɪv] *vt* renunciar a.
wake¹ [weɪk] *n* velatorio.

▶ *vt* (*pt* **woke** [wəʊk], *pp* **woken** ['wəʊkən]) despertar.
wake² [weɪk] *n* estela (*de barco*).
● **in the wake of** tras, después de.
to wake up *vt-vi* despertar(se).
waken ['weɪkən] *vt-vi* despertar(se).
Wales [weɪlz] *n* (País de) Gales.
walk [wɔːk] *n* **1** paseo, caminata. **2** paseo (*ruta*). **3** andares, manera de caminar.
▶ *vi* andar, caminar: *I'll walk there*, iré andando, iré a pie.
▶ *vt* **1** pasear (*perro*). **2** acompañar (*persona*).
● **to go for a walk** dar un paseo.
● **to walk all over** SB tratar a ALGN a patadas.
● **to walk into a trap** caer en una trampa.
■ **walk of life** condición social.
to walk off with *vt* **1** ganar con facilidad. **2** *fam* mangar, birlar.
to walk out *vi* **1** marcharse. **2** ir a la huelga.
to walk out on *vt* abandonar.
walkie-talkie [wɔːkɪˈtɔːkɪ] *n* walkie-talkie.
walking stick ['wɔːkɪŋstɪk] *n* bastón.
Walkman® ['wɔːkmən] *n* Walkman®.
walkout ['wɔːkaʊt] *n* huelga.
walkover ['wɔːkəʊvə^r] *n* *fam* paseo.
wall [wɔːl] *n* **1** muro (*exterior*). **2** pared (*interior*). **3** muralla. **4** tapia (*de jardín*).
walled [wɔːld] *adj* amurallado,-a.
wallet ['wɒlɪt] *n* cartera.
wallop ['wɒləp] *n* *fam* porrazo, golpe fuerte.
▶ *vt* *fam* pegar fuerte.
wallpaper ['wɔːlpeɪpə^r] *n* papel pintado.
▶ *vt* empapelar.

wally [ˈwɒlɪ] n (pl **-ies**) fam inútil, imbécil.
walnut [ˈwɔːlnʌt] n nuez.
■ **walnut tree** nogal.
walrus [ˈwɔːlrəs] n (pl **walruses**) morsa.
waltz [wɔːls] n vals.
▶ vi bailar el vals, valsar.
wand [wɒnd] n varita.
wander [ˈwɒndəʳ] vi vagar, deambular.
▶ vt vagar por, recorrer.
● **to wander from the point** divagar, irse por las ramas.
wanderer [ˈwɒndərəʳ] n viajero,-a.
wandering [ˈwɒndərɪŋ] adj errante.
▶ npl **wanderings** viajes, andanzas.
wane [weɪn] vi menguar, disminuir.
wangle [ˈwæŋgəl] vt fam agenciarse, conseguir.
wank [wæŋk] n vulg paja.
▶ vi vulg hacerse una paja.
wanker [ˈwæŋkəʳ] n vulg gilipollas mf inv.
want [wɒnt] n **1** necesidad, deseo. **2** falta, carencia. **3** miseria, pobreza.
▶ vt **1** querer: *I want you to come with me*, quiero que me acompañes. **2** fam necesitar.
● **for want of** por falta de.
● **to be in want** estar necesitado,-a.
wanted [ˈwɒntɪd] adj **1** necesario,-a: *"Boy wanted"*, "Se necesita chico". **2** buscado,-a (por la policía): *"Wanted"*, "Se busca".
war [wɔːʳ] n guerra.
● **to be at war with** estar en guerra con.
warble [ˈwɔːbəl] vt-vi gorjear.
ward [wɔːd] n **1** sala (de hospital). **2** GB distrito electoral.
to ward off vt **1** prevenir, evitar (peligro). **2** parar (golpe).
warden [ˈwɔːdən] n **1** vigilante, guardián,-ana (de castillo, museo). **2** US alcaide (de cárcel).
wardrobe [ˈwɔːdrəʊb] n **1** armario (ropero), guardarropa. **2** vestuario.
warehouse [ˈweəhaʊs] n almacén.
wares [weəz] npl género, mercancías.
warfare [ˈwɔːfeəʳ] n guerra.
warhead [ˈwɔːhed] n cabeza (de misil).
warily [ˈweərɪlɪ] adv con cautela, cautelosamente.
warlike [ˈwɔːlaɪk] adj belicoso,-a.
warm [wɔːm] adj **1** caliente. **2** tibio,-a, templado,-a. **3** cálido,-a (clima). **4** caluroso,-a (día). **5** de abrigo (ropa).

▶ vt calentar.
● **to be warm 1** tener calor (persona). **2** hacer calor (clima).
● **to warm to SB** coger simpatía a ALGN.
to warm up vt calentar.
▶ vi **1** calentarse. **2** hacer ejercicios de calentamiento.
warm-blooded [wɔːmˈblʌdɪd] adj de sangre caliente.
warm-hearted [wɔːmˈhɑːtɪd] adj afectuoso,-a.
warmth [wɔːmθ] n **1** calor. **2** afecto, cordialidad, calidez.
warn [wɔːn] vt avisar, advertir, prevenir: *he warned me not to touch it*, me advirtió que no lo tocara; *he warned her about the strike*, le advirtió de la huelga.
warning [ˈwɔːnɪŋ] n **1** aviso, advertencia. **2** amonestación.
warp [wɔːp] n **1** urdimbre (de tela). **2** alabeo (de madera).
▶ vt-vi alabear(se), combar(se) (madera).
warrant [ˈwɒrənt] n orden judicial.
▶ vt justificar.
warranty [ˈwɒrəntɪ] n (pl **-ies**) garantía.
warren [ˈwɒrən] n **1** madriguera. **2** fig laberinto.
warrior [ˈwɒrɪəʳ] n guerrero,-a.
warship [ˈwɔːʃɪp] n buque de guerra.
wart [wɔːt] n verruga.
● **warts and all** con todos sus defectos.
wary [ˈweərɪ] adj (**-ier**, **-iest**) cauto,-a, cauteloso,-a.
was [wɒz, unstressed wəz] pt → be.
wash [wɒʃ] n (pl **-es**). **1** lavado. **2** ropa sucia, colada. **3** estela (de barco, avión). **4** enjuague (bucal).
▶ vt **1** lavar, lavarse (manos, pelo). **2** fregar, lavar (platos). **3** llevar, arrastrar.
● **to be in the wash** estar para lavar.
● **to have a wash** lavarse.
● **that won't wash!** fam ¡eso no cuela!
to wash out vt quitar lavando.
to wash up vt fregar (platos).
▶ vi **1** fregar los platos, lavar los platos. **2** US lavarse.
washable [ˈwɒʃəbəl] adj lavable.
washbasin [ˈwɒʃbeɪsən] n lavabo.
washbowl [ˈwɒʃbəʊl] n lavabo.
washed-out [wɒʃˈaʊt] adj agotado,-a.
washer [ˈwɒʃəʳ] n **1** arandela. **2** lavadora.
washing [ˈwɒʃɪŋ] n **1** lavado. **2** ropa sucia. **3** colada.

- **to do the washing** hacer la colada.
- **washing line** cuerda de tender la ropa.
- **washing machine** lavadora.

washing-up [wɒʃɪŋˈʌp] *n* **1** fregado. **2** platos.
- **to do the washing up** fregar los platos, lavar los platos.
- **washing-up liquid** lavavajillas.

washout [ˈwɒʃaʊt] *n fam* fracaso.

washroom [ˈwɒʃruːm] *n* US servicios, lavabo.

wasp [wɒsp] *n* avispa.
- **wasps' nest** avispero.

WASP [wɒsp] *abbr* US *(White, Anglo-Saxon, Protestant)* blanco, anglosajón, protestante.

waste [weɪst] *n* **1** desperdicio. **2** derroche, despilfarro *(de dinero)*. **3** desechos, desperdicios *(productos)*.
▶ *adj* **1** desechado,-a. **2** yermo,-a, baldío,-a *(tierra)*.
▶ *vt* **1** desperdiciar, malgastar *(comida, oportunidad)*. **2** despilfarrar, derrochar *(dinero)*.
- **it's a waste of time** es una pérdida de tiempo.

wasteful [ˈweɪstfʊl] *adj* despilfarrador,-ra, derrochador,-ra.

wastepaper basket [weɪstˈpeɪpəbɑːskɪt] *n* papelera.

watch [wɒtʃ] *n (pl -es)*. **1** reloj *(de pulsera)*. **2** vigilancia. **3** cuerpo de guardia.
▶ *vt* **1** mirar, ver *(televisión, película)*. **2** observar. **3** vigilar. **4** tener cuidado con, prestar atención a.
- **watch out!** ¡ojo!, ¡cuidado!

watchdog [ˈwɒtʃdɒg] *n* **1** perro guardián. **2** guardián,-ana.

watchful [ˈwɒtʃfʊl] *adj* vigilante, atento,-a.

watchmaker [ˈwɒtʃmeɪkə'] *n* relojero,-a.

watchman [ˈwɒtʃmən] *n (pl* **watchmen)** vigilante.

watchword [ˈwɒtʃwɜːd] *n* **1** contraseña, santo y seña. **2** consigna, lema.

water [ˈwɔːtə'] *n* agua.
▶ *vt* regar.
▶ *vi* **1** llorar *(ojos)*. **2** hacerse agua *(boca)*.
- **to get into hot water** meterse en un buen lío.
- **to hold water** hacer aguas *(argumento)*.
- **to keep one's head above water** mantenerse a flote.

- **to pass water** orinar.
- **under water 1** inundado,-a. **2** bajo el agua.
- **water bottle** cantimplora.
- **water lily** nenúfar.
- **water polo** waterpolo.

to water down *vt* **1** aguar, diluir. **2** *fig* descafeinar.

watercolour [ˈwɔːtəkʌlə'] (US **watercolor**) *n* acuarela.

watercress [ˈwɔːtkres] *n* berros.

waterfall [ˈwɔːtəfɔːl] *n* cascada, salto de agua, catarata.

watering [ˈwɔːtərɪŋ] *n* riego.
- **watering can** regadera.

waterlogged [ˈwɔːtəlɒgd] *adj* empapado,-a, anegado,-a.

watermelon [ˈwɔːtəmelən] *n* sandía.

watermill [ˈwɔːtəmɪl] *n* molino de agua.

waterproof [ˈwɔːtəpruːf] *adj* **1** impermeable *(tela)*. **2** sumergible *(reloj)*.
▶ *vt* impermeabilizar.

watershed [ˈwɔːtəʃed] *n* punto decisivo.

water-ski [ˈwɔːtəskiː] *n* esquí acuático.
▶ *vi* hacer esquí acuático.

water-skiing [ˈwɔːtəskiːɪŋ] *n* esquí acuático.

watertight [ˈwɔːtətaɪt] *adj* **1** hermético,-a *(cierre)*. **2** estanco,-a *(barco)*. **3** irrebatible, irrefutable *(argumento)*.

waterway [ˈwɔːtəweɪ] *n* vía fluvial.

watery [ˈwɔːtərɪ] *adj (-ier, -iest)*. **1** acuoso,-a. **2** aguado,-a *(sopa, bebida)*.

watt [wɒt] *n* vatio.

wave [weɪv] *n* **1** ola *(de mar)*. **2** onda. **3** ademán, movimiento *(de mano)*. **4** ola, oleada *(de crímenes)*.
▶ *vi* **1** saludar *(con la mano)*. **2** ondear *(bandera)*.
▶ *vt* **1** agitar. **2** marcar, ondular *(pelo)*.
- **to make waves** causar problemas.

wavelength [ˈweɪvleŋθ] *n* longitud de onda.
- **to be on different wavelengths** *fam* no estar en la misma onda.

waver [ˈweɪvə'] *vi* **1** oscilar. **2** temblar *(llama)*. **3** vacilar, dudar.

wavy [ˈweɪvɪ] *adj (-ier, -iest)*. **1** ondulado,-a. **2** ondulante.

wax [wæks] *n (pl* **waxes)** cera.
▶ *vt* encerar.

way [weɪ] *n* **1** camino: *which way did you go?*, ¿por dónde fuisteis? **2** dirección:

on the way to work, yendo al trabajo, camino del trabajo; **which way is the harbour?**, ¿dónde cae el puerto? **3** manera, modo: **we'll do it her way**, lo haremos a su manera.

▶ *adv fam* muy: **way back**, hace muchísimo.

● **a long way from** lejos de.
● **by the way** a propósito.
● **by way of** vía, por vía de.
● **on the way** por el camino, en camino.
● **on the way down** bajando.
● **on the way up** subiendo.
● **the right way round** bien puesto.
● **the wrong way round** al revés.
● **to find your way** encontrar el camino.
● **to get out of the way** apartarse del camino, quitarse de en medio.
● **to get under way** empezar, ponerse en marcha.
● **to give way** ceder, ceder el paso *(al conducir)*.
● **to lose one's way** perderse.
● **to stand in the way of** obstaculizar, obstruir el paso.
● **in a bad way** *fam* mal.

we [wiː, unstressed wɪ] *pron* nosotros,-as.

weak [wiːk] *adj* débil, flojo,-a.

weaken [ˈwiːkən] *vt* debilitar.

weakness [ˈwiːknəs] *n* (*pl* **-es**). **1** debilidad. **2** fallo, defecto.

● **to have a weakness for STH** tener debilidad por algo.

wealth [welθ] *n* riqueza.

wealthy [ˈwelθɪ] *adj* (**-ier**, **-iest**) rico,-a, adinerado,-a.

wean [wiːn] *vt* destetar.

weapon [ˈwepən] *n* arma.

wear [weəʳ] *n* **1** uso. **2** desgaste, deterioro. **3** ropa.

▶ *vt* (*pt* **wore** [wɔːʳ], *pp* **worn** [wɔːn]). **1** llevar puesto,-a. **2** vestir, ponerse *(ropa)*. **3** calzar *(zapatos)*. **4** desgastar.

▶ *vi* desgastarse.

● **to wear well** dar buen resultado: **this material wears well**, esta tela da buen resultado.

■ **wear and tear** desgaste.

to wear away *vt-vi* erosionar(se).

to wear off *vi* desaparecer.

to wear out *vi* gastarse, desgastarse.

▶ *vt* **1** agotar *(persona)*. **2** gastar *(ropa, zapatos)*.

weary [ˈwɪərɪ] *adj* (**-ier**, **-iest**) cansado,-a.

▶ *vt* (*pt* & *pp* **-ied**) cansar.

weasel [ˈwiːzəl] *n* comadreja.

weather [ˈweðəʳ] *n* tiempo: **what's the weather like?**, ¿qué tiempo hace?

▶ *vt* **1** aguantar *(crisis)*. **2** erosionar *(roca)*.

● **to be under the weather** no encontrarse muy bien.

● **to weather the storm** capear el temporal.

■ **weather forecast** pronóstico del tiempo, parte meteorológico.

weathercock [ˈweðəkɒk] *n* veleta.

weave [wiːv] *n* tejido.

▶ *vt-vi* (*pt* **wove**, *pp* **woven**). **1** tejer. **2** serpentear, zigzaguear.

▶ *vt* *fig* tramar.

weaver [ˈwiːvəʳ] *n* tejedor,-ra.

web [web] *n* **1** telaraña. **2** *fig* red. **3** Internet.

■ **web page** página web.

website [ˈwebsaɪt] *n* sitio web.

wed [wed] *vt* (*pt* & *pp* **wedded**, *ger* **wedding**) casarse con.

Wed [ˈwenzdɪ] *abbr* (**Wednesday**) miércoles.

wedding [ˈwedɪŋ] *n* boda.

■ **wedding cake** tarta de boda.

■ **wedding day** día de la boda.

■ **wedding dress** vestido de novia.

■ **wedding present** regalo de boda.

■ **wedding ring** alianza, anillo de boda.

wedge [wedʒ] *n* cuña, calce.

▶ *vt* acuñar, calzar.

Wednesday [ˈwenzdɪ] *n* miércoles.

wee[1] [wiː] *adj* pequeñito,-a,.

wee[2] [wiː] *n* *fam* pipí.

▶ *vi* hacer pipí.

weed [wiːd] *n* **1** mala hierba. **2** *fam* canijo,-a.

▶ *vt-vi* escardar.

weedkiller [ˈwiːdkɪləʳ] *n* herbicida.

weedy [ˈwiːdɪ] *adj* (**-ier**, **-iest**) *pej* debilucho,-a, enclenque.

week [wiːk] *n* semana.

● **a week today** dentro de una semana, dentro de ocho días.

weekday [ˈwiːkdeɪ] *n* día laborable.

weekend [ˈwiːkend] *n* fin de semana.

weekly [ˈwiːklɪ] *adj* semanal.

▶ *adv* semanalmente.

▶ *n* (*pl* **-ies**) semanario.

weep [wiːp] *vi* (*pt* & *pp* **wept**) llorar.

weigh [weɪ] *vt* **1** pesar. **2** sopesar.
● **to weigh anchor** levar anclas.
to weigh down *vt* **1** sobrecargar. **2** *fig* abrumar, agobiar.
to weigh up *vt* evaluar.
weight [weɪt] *n* **1** peso. **2** pesa.
▶ *vt* cargar con peso.
● **to lose weight** perder peso.
● **to put on weight** engordar.
weightlifting [ˈweɪtlɪftɪŋ] *n* levantamiento de pesas, halterofilia.
weir [wɪəʳ] *n* presa *(de río)*.
weird [wɪəd] *adj* raro,-a, extraño,-a.
weirdo [ˈwɪədəʊ] *n* (*pl* **weirdoes**) *fam* tipo raro.
welcome [ˈwelkəm] *adj* **1** bienvenido,-a *(invitado, visita)*. **2** grato,-a, agradable *(cambio, vista)*.
▶ *n* bienvenida, acogida.
▶ *vt* **1** acoger, recibir, dar la bienvenida a *(invitado, visita)*. **2** aplaudir, acoger con agrado *(cambio)*.
● **welcome home!** ¡bienvenido,-a a casa!
● **you're welcome** de nada, no hay de qué.
weld [weld] *n* soldadura.
▶ *vt* soldar.
welder [ˈweldəʳ] *n* soldador,-ra.
welfare [ˈwelfeəʳ] *n* bienestar.
■ **welfare state** estado de bienestar.
well[1] [wel] *adj-adv* bien.
▶ *interj* **1** bueno, pues. **2** ¡vaya!
● **as well** también.
● **as well as** además de.
● **it would be as well to ...** no estaría de más + *inf*.
● **just as well** menos mal.
● **pretty well** casi.
● **to do well** tener éxito, prosperar.
● **to get well** reponerse.
● **well done 1** bien hecho,-a *(bistec, etc)*. **2** ¡muy bien! *(para felicitar)*.
well[2] [wel] *n* pozo.
▶ *vi* manar, brotar.
well-behaved [welbɪˈheɪvd] *adj* bien educado,-a, formal.
well-being [welˈbiːɪŋ] *n* bienestar.
well-built [welˈbɪlt] *adj* **1** de construcción sólida *(casa)*. **2** fornido,-a *(persona)*.
well-heeled [welˈhiːld] *adj fam* adinerado,-a.
wellington [ˈwelɪŋtən] *n* bota de goma.

well-intentioned [welɪnˈtenʃənd] *adj* bien intencionado,-a.
well-known [welˈnəʊn] *adj* conocido,-a, famoso,-a.
well-meaning [welˈmiːnɪŋ] *adj* bien intencionado,-a.
well-off [welˈɒf] *adj* rico,-a, acomodado,-a.
well-timed [welˈtaɪmd] *adj* oportuno,-a.
well-to-do [weltəˈduː] *adj* acomodado,-a.
Welsh [welʃ] *adj* galés,-esa.
▶ *n* galés *(lengua)*.
▶ *npl* **the Welsh** los galeses.
went [went] *pt* → go.
wept [wept] *pt-pp* → weep.
were [wɜːʳ] *pt* → be.
west [west] *n* oeste, occidente.
▶ *adj* del oeste, occidental.
▶ *adv* al oeste, hacia el oeste.
■ **the West** Occidente.
westbound [ˈwestbaʊnd] *adj* en dirección al oeste.
westerly [ˈwestəlɪ] *adj* del oeste.
western [ˈwestən] *adj* del oeste, occidental.
▶ *n* western, película del oeste.
westward [ˈwestwəd] *adj* hacia el oeste.
westwards [ˈwestwəds] *adv* hacia el oeste.
wet [wet] *adj* (*comp* **wetter**, *superl* **wettest**). **1** mojado,-a. **2** húmedo,-a. **3** lluvioso,-a *(tiempo)*. **4** fresco,-a *(pintura)*. **5** *fam* soso,-a.
▶ *n* **1** humedad. **2** lluvia.
▶ *vt* (*pt & pp* **wetted**, *ger* **wetting**) mojar, humedecer.
● **to get wet** mojarse.
● **to wet oneself** orinarse.
● **"Wet paint"** "Recién pintado".
■ **wet blanket** aguafiestas *mf inv*.
wetness [ˈwetnəs] *n* humedad.
whack [wæk] *n* **1** golpe, porrazo. **2** *fam* parte.
▶ *vt* pegar, golpear.
whacked [wækt] *adj fam* agotado,-a.
whacking [ˈwækɪŋ] *adj fam* enorme.
whale [weɪl] *n* ballena.
● **to have a whale of time** *fam* pasárselo bomba.
wharf [wɔːf] *n* (*pl* **-s** o **wharves**) muelle, embarcadero.
what [wɒt] *adj* **1** qué *(preguntas)*: **what time is it?**, ¿qué hora es?; **I don't know what time it is**, no sé qué hora es. **2** qué,

menudo *(exclamaciones)*: **what a (smart) car!**, ¡menudo coche (más elegante)! **3**: **what oil we have is here**, todo el aceite que tenemos está aquí.

▶ *pron* **1** qué *(preguntas)*: **what is it?**, ¿qué es?; **I don't know what it is**, no sé qué es. **2** lo que *(subordinadas)*: **that's what he said**, eso es lo que dijo.

▶ *interj* ¡cómo!: **what!, you've lost it!**, ¡cómo! ¡lo has perdido!

whatever [wɒtˈevəʳ] *adj* **1** cualquiera que: **whatever colour you like**, el color que tú quieras. **2** en absoluto: **with no money whatever**, sin absolutamente nada de dinero.

▶ *pron* (todo) lo que: **whatever you like**, (todo) lo que tú quieras; **whatever you do**, hagas lo que hagas.

whatsoever [wɒtsəʊˈevəʳ] *adj* → whatever.

wheat [wiːt] *n* trigo.

wheedle [ˈwiːdəl] *vt* engatusar.

● **to wheedle SB into doing STH** engatusar a ALGN para que haga algo.

wheel [wiːl] *n* **1** rueda. **2** volante.

▶ *vt* empujar *(bicicleta)*.

▶ *vi* **1** girar, dar vueltas. **2** revolotear *(pájaros)*.

■ **wheel clamp** cepo.

wheelbarrow [ˈwiːlbærəʊ] *n* carretilla de mano.

wheelchair [ˈwiːltʃeəʳ] *n* silla de ruedas.

wheeze [wiːz] *n* **1** resuello. **2** respiración asmática.

▶ *vi* resollar.

when [wen] *adv* cuándo: **when did it happen?**, ¿cuándo pasó?; **tell me when**, dime cuándo.

▶ *conj* cuando: **when I arrived**, cuando llegué yo.

▶ *pron* cuando: **that was when it broke**, fue entonces cuando se rompió.

whenever [wenˈevəʳ] *conj* cuando quiera que, siempre que: **come whenever you want**, ven cuando quieras.

▶ *adv* **1** cuando sea: **we can go to the beach today or whenever**, podemos ir a la playa hoy o cuando sea. **2** cuándo.

where [weəʳ] *adv* **1** dónde, adónde: **where is it?**, ¿dónde está?; **where did you go?**, ¿adónde fuiste?; **tell me where it is**, dime dónde está. **2** en cualquier parte, donde sea.

▶ *pron* donde: **this is where it all happened**, aquí es donde pasó todo.

whereabouts [(n) ˈweərəbaʊts(adv) weərəˈbaʊts] *n* paradero.

▶ *adv* dónde, adónde.

whereas [weərˈæz] *conj* mientras que.

whereby [weəˈbaɪ] *adv* por el/la/lo cual.

wherever [weərˈevəʳ] *adv* dónde, adónde: **wherever did you put it**, ¿dónde diablos lo pusiste?

▶ *conj* dondequiera que.

whether [ˈweðəʳ] *conj* si: **I'm not sure whether I like it or not**, no sé si me gusta o no; **whether it rains or not**, llueva o no llueva.

which [wɪtʃ] *adj* qué: **which size do you want?**, ¿qué tamaño quieres?; **tell me which size you want**, dime qué tamaño quieres.

▶ *pron* **1** cuál, cuáles *(en interrogativas)*: **which do you want?**, ¿cuál quieres?; **ask him which they are**, pregúntale cuáles son. **2** que *(en subordinadas)*: **the shoes which I bought**, los zapatos que compré. **3** el/la/lo que, el/la/lo cual *(con preposición)*, los/las que, los/las cuales: **the shop in which ...**, la tienda en la que/cual .... **4** el/la cual, los/las cuales: **two glasses, one of which was dirty**, dos copas, una de las cuales estaba sucia. **5** lo que/cual: **he lost, which was a shame**, perdió, lo cual fue una lástima.

whichever [wɪtʃˈevər] *adj* (no importa) el/la/los/las que: **whichever model you choose**, no importa el modelo que elijas.

▶ *pron* cualquiera, el/la/los/las que: **take whichever you want**, coge el que quieras.

whiff [wɪf] *n (pl* **whiffs**). **1** soplo. **2** olorcillo.

while [waɪl] *n* rato, tiempo.

▶ *conj* **1** mientras. **2** aunque. **3** mientras que.

● **after a while** al cabo de un rato.

● **for a while** un rato.

● **once in a while** de vez en cuando.

● **to be worth one's while** valer la pena.

● **to while away the time** pasar el rato.

whilst [waɪlst] *conj* → while.

whim [wɪm] *n* antojo, capricho.

whimper [ˈwɪmpər] *n* gemido.

▶ *vi* lloriquear, gemir.

whine [waɪn] *n* **1** quejido *(de persona)*. **2** gemido *(de perro)*.

▶ *vi* **1** quejarse *(persona)*. **2** gemir *(perro)*.

whip [wɪp] *n* **1** látigo, fusta. **2** azote. **3** POL oficial encargado,-a de la disciplina de partido.

▶ *vt (pt & pp* **whipped**, *ger* **whipping)**. **1** fustigar *(caballo)*. **2** azotar, zurrar *(persona)*. **3** batir, montar *(nata, etc)*. **4** *fam* birlar.

● **to whip past** pasar deprisa.

■ **whipped cream** nata montada.

to whip off *vt* quitar deprisa.

whipping [wɪpɪŋ] *n* paliza, tunda.

■ **whipping cream** nata para montar.

whip-round [wɪpraʊnd] *n fam* colecta.

whirl [wɜːl] *n* **1** giro, vuelta. **2** remolino, torbellino *(de polvo)*.

▶ *vi* girar, dar vueltas rápidamente.

▶ *vt* hacer girar, dar vueltas a.

whirlpool [wɜːlpuːl] *n* remolino.

whirlwind [wɜːlwɪnd] *n* torbellino.

whirr [wɜː] *n* zumbido.

▶ *vi* zumbar.

whisk [wɪsk] *n* **1** batidor. **2** batidora *(eléctrica)*. **3** movimiento brusco.

▶ *vt* **1** montar *(nata, claras)*. **2** sacudir. **3** hacer algo rápidamente: *he whisked off his coat*, se quitó rápidamente el abrigo; *she whisked out her pen*, sacó rápidamente su bolígrafo.

whisker [wɪskə^r] *n* pelo *(de bigote)*.

▶ *npl* **whiskers** **1** patillas *(de persona)*. **2** bigotes *(de gato)*.

whiskey [wɪskɪ] *n* whisky, güisqui.

whisky [wɪskɪ] *n (pl* -ies) whisky, güisqui.

whisper [wɪspə^r] *n* susurro, cuchicheo.

▶ *vt-vi* susurrar, cuchichear.

whistle [wɪsəl] *n* **1** silbato, pito *(instrumento)*. **2** silbido, pitido *(sonido)*.

▶ *vt-vi* silbar.

white [waɪt] *adj* blanco,-a.

▶ *n* **1** blanco *(color)*. **2** clara *(de huevo)*.

■ **white coffee** café con leche.

■ **white lie** mentira piadosa.

■ **White House** Casa Blanca.

whitebait [waɪtbeɪt] *n* chanquetes.

white-collar [waɪtkɒlə^r] *adj* administrativo,-a, de cuello blanco.

whiteness [waɪtnəs] *n* blancura.

whitewash [waɪtwɒʃ] *n* **1** cal. **2** tapadera, encubrimiento.

▶ *vt* **1** encalar. **2** encubrir.

Whitsuntide [wɪtsʌntaɪd] *n* Pentecostés.

> También **Whitsun**.

whittle [wɪtəl] *vt* tallar.

to wittle away *vt* ir reduciendo.

whizz [wɪz] *n* zumbido.

▶ *vi* zumbar, silbar.

● **to whizz past** pasar zumbando.

whizz-kid [wɪzkɪd] *n fam* lince, hacha.

who [huː] *pron* **1** quién, quiénes *(en interrogativas directas e indirectas)*: *who did it?*, ¿quién lo hizo?; *I don't know who they are*, no sé quiénes son. **2** que *(en subordinadas-objeto)*: *those who want to go*, los que quieran ir; *the boy who she loves*, el chico al que quiere. **3** quien, quienes, el/la cual, los/las cuales, que *(en subordinadas-sujeto)*: *the workers, who were on strike, ...*, los trabajadores, quienes estaban en huelga, ...

WHO [dʌbəljuːeɪtʃˈəʊ] *abbr (World Health Organization)* OMS.

whoever [huːevə^r] *pron* **1** quien: *whoever scores most points wins*, gana quien saque más puntos. **2** quienquiera que, cualquiera que: *I don't like her, whoever she is*, quienquiera que sea, no me gusta.

whole [həʊl] *adj* **1** entero,-a: *the whole day*, todo el día. **2** intacto,-a.

▶ *n* conjunto, todo.

● **as a whole** en conjunto.

● **on the whole** en general.

● **the whole of** todo,-a.

■ **whole milk** leche entera.

wholemeal [həʊlmiːl] *adj* integral.

wholesale [həʊlseɪl] *adj-adv* COMM al por mayor.

▶ *adv* fig en masa.

▶ *adj* masivo,-a.

▶ *n* venta al por mayor.

wholesaler [həʊlseɪlə^r] *n* mayorista.

wholesome [həʊlsəm] *adj* sano,-a, saludable.

wholly [həʊlɪ] *adv* enteramente.

whom [huːm] *pron* **1** *fml* a quién, a quiénes *(en interrogativas)*: *whom did he kill?*, ¿a quién mató?; *with whom?*, ¿con quién? **2** a quien, a quienes *(en subordinadas)*: *students whom I have taught*, alumnos a quienes he dado clase; *the man with whom she was seen*, el hombre con quien la vieron, el hombre con el que la vieron.

whoop [hu:p] *n* grito, alarido.
▶ *vi* gritar.

whooping cough [ˈhu:pɪŋkɒf] *n* tos ferina.

whopper [ˈwɒpəʳ] *n* **1** *fam* cosa enorme: *it's a real whopper!*, ¡es enorme! **2** *fam* trola, bola.

whopping [wɒpɪŋ] *adj fam* enorme.

whore [hɔːʳ] *n* puta.

whose [hu:z] *pron* de quién, de quiénes: *whose is this?*, ¿de quién es esto?; *I know whose it is*, yo sé de quién es.
▶ *adj* **1** de quién, de quiénes: *whose dog is this?*, ¿de quién es este perro? **2** cuyo,-a, cuyos,-as: *the woman whose car was stolen*, la mujer cuyo coche robaron, la mujer a quien le robaron el coche.

why [waɪ] *adv* por qué: *why not?*, ¿por qué no?
▶ *interj* ¡vaya!, ¡toma!
▶ *n* porqué, causa.

wick [wɪk] *n* mecha.

wicked [wɪkɪd] *adj* (*comp* **wickeder**, *superl* **wickedest**) malo,-a.

wicker [wɪkəʳ] *n* mimbre.
▶ *adj* de mimbre.

wide [waɪd] *adj* **1** ancho,-a: *two feet wide*, dos pies de ancho. **2** amplio,-a, extenso,-a: *a wide range of products*, una amplia gama de productos.
• **wide apart** bien separados,-as.
• **wide open** abierto,-a de par en par.

widely [waɪdlɪ] *adv* mucho, generalmente.

widen [waɪdən] *vt-vi* **1** ensanchar(se) *(carretera, río)*. **2** extender(se) *(horizonte)*.

widespread [waɪdspred] *adj* generalizado,-a.

widow [wɪdəʊ] *n* viuda.

widowed [wɪdəʊd] *adj* viudo,-a.

widower [wɪdəʊəʳ] *n* viudo.

width [wɪdθ] *n* **1** ancho, anchura: *in width*, de ancho. **2** ancho *(de material, piscina)*.

wield [wi:ld] *vt* **1** manejar, empuñar *(arma)*. **2** ejercer *(poder)*.

wife [waɪf] *n* (*pl* **wives** [waɪvz]) esposa, mujer.

wig [wɪg] *n* peluca.

wiggle [wɪgəl] *vt-vi* menear(se).

wild [waɪld] *adj* **1** salvaje *(animal)*. **2** silvestre, campestre *(planta)*. **3** agreste *(paisaje)*. **4** violento,-a. **5** salvaje. **6** descontrolado,-a *(fiesta)*. **7** al azar *(adivinanza)*.
▶ *n* tierra virgen.
• **in the wild** en estado salvaje.
• **to be wild about** estar loco,-a por.

wildcat [waɪldkæt] *n* gato montés.
■ **wildcat strike** huelga salvaje.

wilderness [wɪldənəs] *n* (*pl* **-es**) yermo, desierto.

wildfire [waɪldfaɪəʳ] *n* .
• **to spread like wildfire** correr como la pólvora.

wildfowl [waɪldfaʊl] *npl* aves de caza.

wildlife [waɪldlaɪf] *n* fauna.

wilful [wɪlfʊl] *adj* **1** terco,-a, testarudo,-a. **2** premeditado,-a.

will[1] [wɪl] *aux* **1** *se usa para formar el futuro de los verbos*: *she will be here tomorrow*, estará aquí mañana; *we won't finish today*, no acabaremos hoy. **2** *indica voluntad*: *will you help me?, no I won't*, ¿quieres ayudarme? —no quiero; *he won't open the door*, se niega a abrir la puerta; *the car won't start*, el coche no arranca. **3** *indica insistencia*: *he will leave the door open*, es que no hay manera de que cierre la puerta. **4** poder: *this phone will accept credit cards*, este teléfono acepta tarjetas de crédito. **5** *indica una suposición*: *that will be the house*, aquélla será la casa, aquélla debe de ser la casa; *it won't rain, will it?*, ¿no lloverá, ¿verdad?

will[2] [wɪl] *n* **1** voluntad. **2** testamento.
▶ *vt* **1** desear, querer. **2** ordenar, mandar. **3** legar, dejar en testamento.

willing [wɪlɪŋ] *adj* complaciente.
• **willing to do** STH dispuesto,-a a hacer algo.

willingly [wɪlɪŋlɪ] *adv* de buena gana.

willingness [wɪlɪŋnəs] *n* buena voluntad.

willow [wɪləʊ] *n* sauce.

willpower [wɪlpaʊəʳ] *n* fuerza de voluntad.

willy-nilly [wɪlɪˈnɪlɪ] *adv* **1** a la buena de Dios. **2** a la fuerza.

wilt [wɪlt] *vi* marchitarse.

win [wɪn] *n* victoria, éxito.
▶ *vt-vi* (*pt & pp* **won**) ganar.

to win over/round *vt* convencer, persuadir.

wince [wɪns] *n* mueca de dolor.
▶ *vi* hacer una mueca de dolor.

winch [wɪntʃ] n (pl -**es**) torno, cabrestante.

wind[1] [wɪnd] n **1** viento, aire. **2** gases, flato. **3** aliento, resuello.

► vt dejar sin aliento.

● **to break wind** ventosear.

● **to get wind of** olerse.

● **to get the wind up** fam ponerse nervioso,-a.

■ **wind instrument** instrumento de viento.

■ **wind power** energía eólica.

wind[2] [waɪnd] vt (pt & pp **wound**). **1** envolver. **2** arrollar, devanar, enrollar. **3** dar cuerda a (reloj). **4** dar vueltas a (palanca).

► vi serpentear.

to wind down [waɪnd'daʊn] vi **1** quedarse sin cuerda (reloj). **2** relajarse (persona).

► vt bajar (ventanilla, persiana).

to wind up [waɪnd'ʌp] vt **1** dar cuerda a (reloj). **2** subir (ventanilla, persiana).

► vt-vi concluir.

► vi fam acabar: **he wound up in jail**, dio con los huesos en la cárcel.

windbag [wɪndbæg] n fam charlatán,-ana.

windbreak [wɪndbreɪk] n abrigadero (del viento).

windfall [wɪndfɔːl] n ganacia inesperada.

winding [waɪndɪŋ] adj sinuoso,-a, tortuoso,-a.

windmill [wɪndmɪl] n molino de viento.

window [wɪndəʊ] n **1** ventana. **2** ventanilla (de vehículo). **3** ventanilla (de banco, oficina, etc). **4** escaparate (de tienda).

■ **window cleaner** limpiacristales mf inv.

window-shopping [wɪndəʊʃɒpɪŋ] n .

● **to go window-shopping** ir a mirar escaparates.

windowsill [wɪndəʊsɪl] n alféizar.

windpipe [wɪndpaɪp] n tráquea.

windscreen [wɪndskriːn] n parabrisas.

■ **windscreen wiper** limpiaparabrisas.

wind-shield [wɪndʃiːld] n US parabrisas.

■ **wind-shield wiper** limpiaparabrisas.

windy [wɪndɪ] adj (-**ier**, -**iest**) ventoso,-a.

● **it's windy** hace viento.

wine [waɪn] n vino.

wing [wɪŋ] n **1** ala. **2** aleta (de coche). **3** banda (fútbol).

► npl **wings** bastidores: **in the wings**, entre bastidores.

wink [wɪŋk] n guiño.

► vi guiñar el ojo.

winkle [wɪŋkəl] n bígaro.

winner [wɪnəʳ] n **1** ganador,-ra (de premio, concurso, competición). **2** vencedor,-ra (de batalla).

winning [wɪnɪŋ] adj **1** ganador,-ra (equipo, caballo). **2** premiado,-a (billete). **3** atractivo,-a, encantador,-ra.

► npl **winnings** ganancias.

winter [wɪntəʳ] n invierno.

► vi invernar.

wipe [waɪp] vt **1** limpiar, pasar un trapo a. **2** secar, enjugar.

to wipe out vt **1** aniquilar, exterminar. **2** borrar.

wiper [waɪpəʳ] n limpiaparabrisas.

wire [waɪəʳ] n **1** alambre. **2** cable. **3** US telegrama.

► vt **1** hacer la instalación eléctrica de. **2** US enviar un telegrama a.

wiring [waɪrɪŋ] n cableado, instalación eléctrica.

wiry [waɪərɪ] adj (-**ier**, -**iest**) nervudo,-a.

wisdom [wɪzdəm] n **1** sabiduría. **2** prudencia, juicio.

■ **wisdom tooth** muela del juicio.

wise [waɪz] adj **1** sabio,-a. **2** juicioso,-a, prudente, sensato,-a.

■ **the Three Wise Men** los Reyes Magos.

wish [wɪʃ] n (pl -**es**) deseo.

► vt-vi **1** desear: **she wished me happy birthday**, me deseó un feliz cumpleaños. **2** querer. **3** ojalá: **I wish you were here**, ojalá estuvieras aquí.

● **I wish to ...** quisiera ....

● **to make a wish** pedir un deseo.

● **to wish SB good luck** desear buena suerte a ALGN.

● **(with) best wishes** muchos recuerdos.

wishful [wɪʃfʊl] adj **wishful thinking** ilusiones, confundir los deseos con la realidad.

wishy-washy [wɪʃɪwɒʃɪ] adj fam soso,-a, insípido,-a.

wisp [wɪsp] n **1** brizna (de hierba). **2** mechón (de pelo). **3** voluta (de humo).

wit [wɪt] n **1** agudeza, ingenio. **2** inteligencia.

● **to be at one's wits end** estar para volverse loco,-a.

● **to collect one's wits** serenarse.

witch [wɪtʃ] n (pl -**es**) bruja.

■ **witch doctor** hechicero.

witchcraft [wɪtʃkrɑːft] n brujería.

with [wɪð] *prep* **1** con: *come with me*, ven conmigo; *cut it with a knife*, córtalo con un cuchillo. **2** de: *he was blind with rage*, estaba ciego de ira.

withdraw [wɪð'drɔː] *vt* (*pt* **withdrew** [wɪð'druː], *pp* **withdrawn** [wɪð'drɔːn]). **1** retirar, sacar. **2** retractar *(palabras)*.
▶ *vi* retirarse.

withdrawal [wɪð'drɔːəl] *n* **1** retirada *(de tropas, apoyo)*. **2** reintegro *(de dinero)*. **3** retractación *(de palabras)*.

withdrawn [wɪð'drɔːn] *pp* → withdraw.
▶ *adj* introvertido,-a.

withdrew [wɪð'druː] *pt* → withdraw.

wither [wɪðəʳ] *vt-vi* marchitar(se), secar(se).

within [wɪ'ðɪn] *prep* **1** dentro de: *within these walls*, entre estas paredes. **2** al alcance de: *within hearing*, al alcance del oído. **3** a menos de: *within 3 miles of*, a menos de tres millas de. **4** antes de: *you must pay the fine within 2 weeks*, debes pagar la multa antes de 2 semanas.
▶ *adv* dentro, en el interior.

without [wɪ'ðaʊt] *prep* sin.

withstand [wɪð'stænd] *vt* (*pt & pp* **withstood** [wɪð'stʊd]) resistir, aguantar.

witness [wɪtnəs] *n* (*pl* **-es**) testigo.
▶ *vt* **1** presenciar. **2** firmar como testigo.
● **to bear witness to** dar fe de, atestiguar.
■ **witness box** tribuna de los testigos.

witty [wɪtɪ] *adj* (**-ier, -iest**) ingenioso,-a, agudo,-a.

wizard [wɪzəd] *n* **1** brujo, hechicero. **2** *fam* genio, lince.

wobble [wɒbəl] *n* tambaleo, bamboleo.
▶ *vi* tambalearse, bambolearse.

woe [wəʊ] *n* aflicción, desgracia.

woke [wəʊk] *pt* → wake.

woken [wəʊkən] *pp* → wake.

wolf [wʊlf] *n* (*pl* **wolves** [wʊlvz]) lobo.
to wolf down *vt* zamparse.

woman [wʊmən] *n* (*pl* **women** [wɪmɪn]) mujer.
■ **old woman** vieja, anciana.
■ **women's lib** *fam* movimiento feminista.

womanhood [wʊmənhʊd] *n* edad adulta *(de mujer)*.

womb [wuːm] *n* útero, matriz.

won [wʌn] *pt-pp* → win.

wonder [wʌndəʳ] *n* **1** maravilla: *the sev-*

en wonders of the world, las siete maravillas del mundo. **2** admiración, asombro.
▶ *vi* **1** preguntarse: *I wonder where he is, me pregunto dónde estará*, ¿dónde debe de estar? **2** asombrarse, maravillarse.
● **I shouldn't wonder if ...** no me sorprendería que + *subj*.
● **it makes you wonder** te da en qué pensar.
● **no wonder (that) ...** no es de extrañar que ....
● **to wonder about STH** pensar en algo.

wonderful [wʌndəfʊl] *adj* maravilloso,-a.

wonky [wɒŋkɪ] *adj* (**-ier, -iest**). **1** GB *fam* poco firme. **2** torcido,-a.

wood [wʊd] *n* **1** madera. **2** leña *(para fuego)*. **3** bosque.

woodcut [wʊdkʌt] *n* grabado en madera.

woodcutter [wʊdkʌtəʳ] *n* leñador,-ra.

wooden [wʊdən] *adj* de madera.
■ **wooden spoon** cuchara de palo.

woodland [wʊdlənd] *n* bosque, arbolado.

woodpecker [wʊdpekəʳ] *n* pájaro carpintero.

woodwork [wʊdwɜːk] *n* **1** carpintería. **2** artesanía de madera. **3** maderaje, maderamen.

woodworm [wʊdwɜːm] *n* carcoma.

woody [wʊdɪ] *adj* (**-ier, -iest**). **1** arbolado,-a *(zona)*. **2** leñoso,-a *(textura)*.

woof! [wʊf] *interj* ¡guau!

wool [wʊl] *n* lana: *all wool*, pura lana.
● **to pull the wool over SB's eyes** darle a ALGN gato por liebre.

woolen [wʊlən] *adj-n* → woollen.

woollen [wʊlən] *adj* **1** de lana *(jersey)*. **2** lanero,-a *(industria)*.
▶ *npl* **woollens** géneros de punto.

woolly [wʊlɪ] *adj* (**-ier, -iest**). **1** de lana. **2** lanoso,-a. **3** confuso,-a.

word [wɜːd] *n* palabra.
▶ *vt* expresar.
● **by word of mouth** oralmente.
● **from the word go** desde el principio.
● **in a word** en pocas palabras.
● **in other words** en otras palabras, o sea.
● **to give one's word** dar su palabra.
● **to have a word with SB** hablar con ALGN.

- **to have words with** SB discutir con ALGN.
- **to keep one's word** cumplir su palabra.
- **to take** SB's **word** aceptar lo que dice alguien.
- **word for word** palabra por palabra.
- ■ **word processing** procesamiento de textos.
- ■ **word processor** procesador de textos.

wording [ˈwɜːdɪŋ] n términos.

wore [wɔːʳ] pt → wear.

work [wɜːk] vt-vi trabajar.
   ▶ vi **1** funcionar (máquina, plan). **2** surtir efecto (medicamento).
   ▶ n **1** trabajo. **2** empleo, trabajo. **3** obra (literaria, artística).
   ▶ npl **works 1** fábrica. **2** mecanismo.
- **at work** trabajando, en el trabajo.
- **out of work** sin trabajo, parado,-a.
- **to get worked up** exaltarse, excitarse.
- **to have one's work cut out to do** STH vérselas y deseárselas para hacer algo.
- **to make short work of** STH despachar algo deprisa.
- **to set to work** ponerse a trabajar.
- **to work loose** soltarse, aflojarse.
- **to work to rule** hacer huelga de celo.
- **to work wonders** hacer maravillas.
- **work of art** obra de arte.

to work out vt **1** calcular (porcentaje). **2** planear, pensar (plan). **3** solucionar, resolver (problema).
   ▶ vi **1** salir: *it worked out well*, salió bien. **2** ir bien, salir bien (plan). **3** hacer ejercicios.

to work up vt **1** exaltar. **2** hacer, desarrollar.

workbench [ˈwɜːkbentʃ] n (pl -es) banco de trabajo.

workbook [ˈwɜːkbʊk] n **1** cuaderno. **2** libro de ejercicios.

workday [ˈwɜːkdeɪ] n día laborable.

worker [ˈwɜːkəʳ] n **1** trabajador,-ra. **2** obrero,-a, operario,-a.

workforce [ˈwɜːkfɔːs] n mano de obra.

working [ˈwɜːkɪŋ] adj **1** de trabajo (horas, ropa). **2** laboral (semana, vida). **3** laborable (día). **4** que trabaja (persona).
   ▶ npl **workings** funcionamiento.
- ■ **working class** clase obrera.

■ **working knowledge** conocimientos básicos.

workman [ˈwɜːkmən] n (pl **workmen**) obrero.

workmanship [ˈwɜːkmənʃɪp] n **1** habilidad. **2** trabajo.

workmate [ˈwɜːkmeɪt] n compañero,-a de trabajo.

workout [ˈwɜːkaʊt] n entrenamiento.

workshop [ˈwɜːkʃɒp] n taller.

worktop [ˈwɜːktɒp] n encimera.

work-to-rule [wɜːktəˈruːl] n huelga de celo.

world [wɜːld] n mundo.
- **all over the world** en todo el mundo.
- **it's a small world** el mundo es un pañuelo.
- **out of this world** fenomenal, estupendo,-a.
- **to have the best of both worlds** tenerlo todo.
- **to think the world of** adorar.
- ■ **world cup** copa del mundo, mundial (de fútbol).
- ■ **world war** guerra mundial.

world-class [wɜːldˈklɑːs] adj de categoría mundial.

worldly [ˈwɜːldlɪ] adj (-ier, -iest) mundano,-a.

worldwide [ˈwɜːldwaɪd] adj mundial, universal.

worm [wɜːm] n **1** gusano. **2** lombriz.

worn [wɔːn] pp → wear.

worn-out [wɔːnˈaʊt] adj **1** gastado,-a (ropa, neumático). **2** rendido,-a, agotado,-a (persona).

worried [ˈwʌrɪd] adj inquieto,-a, preocupado,-a.

worry [ˈwʌrɪ] n (pl -ies) inquietud, preocupación.
   ▶ vt-vi (pt & pp -ied) inquietar(se), preocupar(se).

worse [wɜːs] adj-adv peor.
   ▶ n lo peor.
- **for the worse** para peor.
- **to get worse** empeorar.
- **to get worse and worse** ir de mal en peor.

worsen [ˈwɜːsən] vt-vi empeorar.

worship [ˈwɜːʃɪp] n **1** adoración. **2** culto: *a place of worship*, un lugar de culto.
   ▶ vt (pt & pp **worshipped**, ger **worshipping**) adorar, rendir culto a.

worst [wɜːst] *adj-adv* peor: *the worst thing is...*, lo peor es que....
► *n* lo peor.
● **at the worst** en el peor de los casos.
worth [wɜːθ] *n* valor.
► *adj* que vale, que tiene un valor de: *it's worth £10, but I got it for £5*, vale diez libras pero yo pagué sólo cinco; *it's worth seeing*, vale la pena verlo.
● **to be worth** valer.
● **to be worth it** valer la pena.
worthless [wɜːθləs] *adj* **1** sin valor *(objeto)*. **2** despreciable *(persona)*.
worthwhile [wɜːθwaɪl] *adj* que vale la pena.
worthy [wɜːðɪ] *adj* (**-ier**, **-iest**) digno,-a, merecedor,-ra.
would [wʊd] *aux* **1** *(condicional)*: *she would tell you if she knew*, te lo diría si lo supiese. **2** *(disponibilidad)*: *he wouldn't help me*, se negó a ayudarme, no quiso ayudarme. **3** *(suposición)*: *that would have been Jim*, ese debió de ser Jim, ese sería Jim. **4** soler: *we would often go out together*, salíamos juntos a menudo, solíamos salir juntos. **5** *(insistencia)*: *he would go by car*, insistió en que teníamos que ir en coche.
● **would like** querer: *would you like a cup of tea?*, ¿quieres una taza de té?
would-be [wʊdbiː] *adj* supuesto,-a, aspirante a.
wound¹ [wuːnd] *n* herida.
► *vt* herir.
wound² [waʊnd] *pt-pp* → wind.
wounded [wuːndɪd] *adj* herido,-a.
wove [wəʊv] *pt* → weave.
woven [wəʊvən] *pp* → weave.
wow [waʊ] *interj fam* ¡caramba!
WPC [ˈdʌbəljuːpiːˈsiː] *abbr* GB **(Woman Police Constable)** agente de policía, mujer policía.
wpm [wɜːdzpəˈmɪnɪt] *abbr* **(words per minute)** palabras por minuto.
wrangle [ˈræŋgəl] *n* riña.
► *vi* reñir.
wrap [ræp] *vt* (*pt & pp* **wrapped**, *ger* **wrapping**) envolver.
● **to be wrapped up in** estar absorto,-a en.
to wrap up *vi* abrigarse.
wrapper [ˈræpəʳ] *n* envoltorio.
wrapping [ˈræpɪŋ] *n* envoltorio.

■ **wrapping paper** papel de envolver, papel de regalo.
wrath [rɒθ] *n* cólera, ira.
wreath [riːθ] *n* corona *(de flores)*.
wreck [rek] *n* **1** naufragio. **2** barco naufragado. **3** restos *(de coche)*. **4** ruinas *(de edificio)*. **5** ruina *(persona)*.
► *vt* **1** hacer naufragar. **2** destrozar, destruir, arruinar.
wreckage [ˈrekɪdʒ] *n* **1** restos *(de coche)*. **2** ruinas *(de edificio)*.
wrench [rentʃ] *n* (*pl* **-es**). **1** tirón. **2** torcedura. **3** separación dolorosa. **4** llave inglesa.
► *vt* arrancar *(de un tirón)*.
wrestle [ˈresəl] *vi* luchar.
wrestler [ˈresləʳ] *n* luchador,-ra.
wrestling [ˈreslɪŋ] *n* lucha.
wretch [retʃ] *n* (*pl* **-es**) desgraciado,-a.
wretched [ˈretʃɪd] *adj* **1** desgraciado,-a, infeliz, desdichado,-a. **2** *fam* horrible, malísimo,-a.
wriggle [ˈrɪgəl] *vt* menear, mover.
► *vi* retorcerse, menearse.
● **to wriggle out of** STH escaparse de algo.
wring [rɪŋ] *vt* (*pt & pp* **wrung** [rʌŋ]). **1** torcer, retorcer. **2** escurrir *(ropa)*.
● **to wring** SB's **neck** retorcerle el pescuezo a ALGN.
● **to wring** STH **out of** SB arrancarle algo a ALGN.
wringing wet [ˈrɪŋɪŋwet] *adj* empapado,-a.
wrinkle [ˈrɪŋkəl] *n* arruga.
► *vt-vi* arrugar(se).
wrist [rɪst] *n* muñeca.
wristwatch [ˈrɪstwɒtʃ] *n* (*pl* **-es**) reloj de pulsera.
writ [rɪt] *n* orden judicial.
write [raɪt] *vt-vi* (*pt* **wrote** [rəʊt], *pp* **written** [ˈrɪtən]) escribir.
► *vt* extender *(cheque)*.
to write back *vi* contestar *(por carta)*.
to write down *vt* anotar, apuntar.
to write off *vt* **1** anular *(deuda)*. **2** dar por perdido,-a *(proyecto)*. **3** escrribir rápidamente.
to write off for *vt* pedir por correo.
to write out *vt* **1** escribir *(en su forma completa)*. **2** extender *(cheque)*.
to write up *vt* redactar, escribir.

write-off ['raɪtɒf] *n* (*pl* **write-offs**). **1** siniestro total. **2** cancelación.

writer ['raɪtə'] *n* escritor,-ra, autor,-ra.

write-up ['raɪtʌp] *n fam* crítica, reseña.

writing ['raɪtɪŋ] *n* **1** escritura, escribir. **2** letra. **3** profesión de autor.
➤ *npl* **writings** obras.
■ **writing desk** escritorio.
■ **writing paper** papel de escribir, papel de cartas.

written ['rɪtən] *pp* → write.
➤ *adj* escrito,-a.

wrong [rɒŋ] *adj* **1** equivocado,-a, incorrecto,-a, erróneo,-a *(respuesta)*. **2** malo, -a *(acción)*. **3** injusto,-a. **4** malo,-a, inadecuado,-a, inoportuno,-a.
➤ *adv* mal, incorrectamente, equivocadamente.
➤ *n* **1** mal. **2** injusticia.

➤ *vt* ser injusto,-a con.
● **to be in the wrong** no tener razón, tener la culpa.
● **to be wrong** estar equivocado,-a, equivocarse.
● **to go wrong 1** equivocarse *(persona)*. **2** estropearse *(máquina)*, fallar *(plan)*.

wrong-doer ['rɒŋduə'] *n* malhechor,-ra.

wrongly ['rɒŋlɪ] *adv* **1** mal, sin razón, equivocadamente. **2** injustamente.

wrote [rəʊt] *pt* → write.

wrought [rɔːt] *adj* forjado,-a.

wrung [rʌŋ] *pt-pp* → wring.

wry [raɪ] *adj* (-**ier**, -**iest**). **1** irónico,-a. **2** retorcido.

WWF ['wɜːldwaɪldlaɪffʌnd] *abbr* (*World Wildlife Fund*) Fondo Mundial para la Naturaleza

X

xenophobia [zenə'fəubɪə] n xenofobia.
xenophobic [zenə'fəubɪk] adj xenófobo,-a.
Xerox ['zɪərɒks] (Es marca registrada) n
xerocopia.
► vt xerocopiar.
XL ['eks'el] abbr (*extra large*) muy grande.

Xmas ['eksməs, 'krɪsməs] n → Christmas.
X-ray ['eksreɪ] n 1 rayo X. 2 radiografía.
► vt radiografiar.
xylophone ['zaɪləfəʊn] n xilófono.
xylophonist [zaɪ'lɒfənɪst] n xilofonista.

Y

yacht [jɒt] *n* **1** barco de vela. **2** yate.
yachting ['jɒtɪŋ] *n* **1** deporte de la vela. **2** navegación a vela.
yachtsman ['jɒtsmən] *n* (*pl* **yachtsmen**) deportista de vela, aficionado a la vela.
yak [jæk] *n* yac, yak.
yam [jæm] *n* ñame.
yank [jæŋk] *n fam* tirón.
► *vt fam* tirar de.
Yank [jæŋk] *n pej* yanqui.
Yankee ['jæŋkɪ] *adj-n pej* yanqui.
yap [jæp] *n* ladrido (*agudo*).
► *vt* (*pt & pp* **yapped**, *ger* **yapping**) ladrar.
yard [jɑːd] *n* **1** patio. **2** US jardín. **3** yarda.
La medida equivale a 0,914 metros.
yardstick ['jɑːdstɪk] *n fig* criterio, patrón.
yarn [jɑːn] *n* **1** hilo. **2** cuento, rollo.
yawn [jɔːn] *n* bostezo.
► *vi* bostezar.
yd [jɑːd] *abbr* (**yard**) yarda.
pl **yds**.
yeah [jeə] *adv fam* sí.
year [jɪəˈ] *n* **1** año. **2** curso.
yearly ['jɪəlɪ] *adj* anual.
► *adv* anualmente.
yearn [jɜːn] *vi* anhelar.
yearning ['jɜːnɪŋ] *n* anhelo.
yeast [jiːst] *n* levadura.
yell [jel] *n* grito, alarido.
► *vi* gritar, dar alaridos.
yellow ['jeləʊ] *adj* (*comp* **yellower**, *superl* **yellowest**). **1** amarillo,-a. **2** *fam* miedica, gallina.
► *n* amarillo.
► *vt* volver amarillo.
► *vi* amarillear.

■ **yellow press** prensa amarilla, prensa sensacionalista.
yelp [jelp] *n* gañido. chillido.
► *vi* dar un gañido.
yen [jen] *n* **1** deseo, ganas. **2** yen (*moneda*).
yeoman ['jəʊmən] *n* (*pl* **yeomen**) pequeño terrateniente.
■ **yeoman of the guard** alabardero de la Torre de Londres.
yes [jes] *adv* sí.
► *n* sí.
● **to say yes** decir que sí.
yes-man ['jesmæn] *n* (*pl* **yes-men**) cobista: *he's a yes-man*, a todo dice que sí.
yesterday ['jestədɪ] *adv* ayer.
■ **the day before yesterday** anteayer.
yet [jet] *adv* **1** todavía, aún: *the taxi hasn't arrived yet*, aún no ha llegado el taxi. **2** ya: *has the taxi arrived yet?*, ¿ya ha llegado el taxi?
► *conj* no obstante, sin embargo.
yeti ['jetɪ] *n* yeti.
yew [juː] *n* tejo.
yield [jiːld] *n* **1** rendimiento. **2** cosecha. **3** rédito.
► *vt* **1** producir, dar. **2** rendir.
► *vi* **1** rendirse, ceder. **2** ceder (*estante, cerradura*).
yippee [jɪˈpiː] *interj fam* ¡yupi!
YMCA ['wɑːrˈemˈsiːˈeɪ] *abbr* (**Young Men's Christian Association**) asociación de jóvenes cristianos.
■ **YMCA hostel** albergue para jóvenes.
yob [jɒb] *n fam* gamberro,-a.
yobbo ['jɒbəʊ] *n* (*pl* **yobbos**) *fam* gamberro,-a.
yodel ['jəʊdəl] *vi* (GB *pt & pp* **yodelled**,

ger **yodelling**; US pt & pp **yodeled**, ger **yodeling**) cantar a la tirolesa.
yoga ['iəʊgə] n yoga.
yoghurt ['jɒgət] n yogur.
yoke [jəʊk] n yugo.
▶ vt uncir.
yokel ['jəʊkəl] n palurdo.
yolk [jəʊk] n yema.
yonder ['jɒndə'] adj aquel, aquella, aquellos,-as.
▶ adv allá.
you [juː] pron **1** tú, vosotros,-as. **2** usted, ustedes. **3** se (sujeto-impersonal). **4** ti (complemento). **5** te (antes del verbo). **6** vosotros,-as (plural). **7** os (antes del verbo). **8** usted (complemento). **9** le (antes del verbo). **10** ustedes (plural). **11** les (antes del verbo). **12** (complemento - impersonal) te: **they treat you well**, te tratan bien.
young [jʌŋ] adj joven.
■ **the young** los jóvenes.
youngster ['jʌŋstə'] n joven.
your [jɔː'] adj **1** tu, tus, vuestro,-a, vuestros,-as. **2** su, sus.
yours [jɔːz] pron **1** (el) tuyo, (la) tuya, (los) tuyos, (las) tuyas, (el) vuestro, (la) vuestra, (los) vuestros, (las) vuestras. **2** (el) suyo, (la) suya, (los) suyos, (las) suyas.
yourself [jɔː'self] pron **1** te, tú mismo,-a. **2** se, usted mismo,-a.
yourselves [jɔː'selvz] pron **1** os, vosotros,-as mismos,-as. **2** se, ustedes mismos,-as.
youth [juːθ] n **1** juventud. **2** joven.
■ **youth hostel** albergue de juventud.
youthful ['juːθfʊl] adj joven, juvenil.
yo-yo® ['iəʊiəʊ] n yoyo, yoyó.
YTS ['waɪ'tiː'es] abbr (**Youth Training Scheme**) plan de empleo juvenil que combina la formación profesional con la experiencia laboral.
yucky ['jʌkɪ] adj (-ier, -iest) fam asqueroso,-a.
Yugoslav ['juːgəslɑːv] n yugoslavo,-a.
Yugoslavia [juːgəʊ'slɑːvɪə] n Yugoslavia.
yule [juːl] n Navidad.
yummy ['jʌmɪ] adj (-ier, -iest) fam riquísimo, de rechupete.
YWCA ['waɪ'dʌbəljuː'siː'eɪ] abbr (**Young Women's Christian Association**) asociación de jóvenes cristianas

Z

Zaire [zɑːˈɪə] n Zaire.

Zambia [ˈzæmbɪə] n Zambia.

Zambian [ˈzæmbɪən] adj zambiano,-a.
▶ n zambiano,-a.

zany [ˈzeɪnɪ] adj (-ier, -iest). 1 fam estrafalario,-a. 2 chiflado,-a.

zeal [ziːl] n celo, entusiasmo.

zealot [ˈzelət] n fanático,-a.

zealous [ˈzeləs] adj celoso,-a, entusiasta.

zebra [ˈziːbrə, ˈzebrə] n cebra.
■ zebra crossing paso de peatones, paso de cebra.

zenith [ˈzenɪθ] n 1 cenit. 2 fig apogeo.

zeppelin [ˈzepəlɪn] n zepelín.

zero [ˈzɪərəʊ] n (pl -s o -es) cero.

zest [zest] n entusiasmo.

zigzag [ˈzɪgzæg] n zigzag.
▶ vi (pt & pp zigzagged, ger zigzagging) zigzaguear.

Zimbabwe [zɪmˈbɑːbweɪ] n Zimbabwe.

Zimbabwean [zɪmˈbɑːbwɪən] adj zimbabwense.
▶ n zimbabwense.

zinc [zɪŋk] n cinc, zinc.

zip [zɪp] n cremallera.
▶ vi (pt & pp zipped, ger zipping) ir como un rayo.
■ zip code US código postal.

to zip up vt cerrar con cremallera.

zipper [ˈzɪpr] n US cremallera.

zodiac [ˈzəʊdɪæk] n zodiaco, zodíaco.

zombie [ˈzɒmbɪ] n zombi.

zone [zəʊn] n zona.

zoo [zuː] n (pl zoos) zoo, zoológico.

zoological [zʊəˈlɒdʒɪkəl] adj zoológico,-a.

zoology [zʊˈblədʒɪ] n zoología.

zoom [zuːm] n 1 zumbido. 2 zoom, teleobjetivo.
▶ vt-vi pasar zumbando: *a sports car zoomed past me*, un coche deportivo me pasó zumbando.
■ zoom lens teleobjetivo.

SPANISH GRAMMAR

Main spelling difficulties

The letters *b* and *v*

These two letters are pronounced in exactly the same way. The letter *b* is used in all words in which this sound is followed by a consonant: *bruma, abstenerse*, but the letter *v* is used after *b, d* and *n*: *obvio, advertir, convencer*. Apart from this there are no general rules which govern their use; in case of doubt check in the dictionary.

The letters *c, k,* and *q*

These three letters are used to represent the sound [k]. Before the vowels *a, o, u*, before a consonant, and in some cases at the end of a word *c* is used: *casa, color, cuna, frac*. Before *e* or *i*, *qu* is written: *querer, quitar*. The letter *k* is used in words of foreign origin in which the original spelling has been maintained: *kitsch*.

The letters *c* and *z*

These two letters are used to represent the sound [θ]. Before the vowels *e* and *i* the letter *c* is used; before the vowels *a, o, u* and at the end of a word *z* is used: *cero, cima, zapato, azote, zurra, pez*. There are a few exceptions to this rule: *zigzag, zipizape, ¡zis, zas!* Some words may also be written with either *c* or *z*: *ácimo/ázimo, acimut/azimut, eccema/eczema, ceta/zeta, cinc/zinc*. Note that a final *z* changes to *c* in the plural: *pez → peces*.

The letters *g* and *j*

The letter *j* is always pronounced [x] (as in the Scottish "loch").

The letter *g* is pronounced [x] when it is followed by the vowels *e* and *i*, but [g] (as in "golf", "get") when it is followed by the vowels *a, o* or *u*.

In the group *gu + e/i* the *u* is silent and the pronunciation is [g], but when *gu* is followed by *a* or *o* the *u* is pronounced giving the sound [gw].

The group *güi*, with a dieresis over the *u*, is written only before *e* or *i*, and is pronounced [gw].

To summarize:

the sound [x] is written	*j*	before *a, o* and *u*
	j or *g*	before *e* and *i*
the sound [g] is written	*g*	before *a, o, u*
	gu	before *i* and *e*
the sound [gw] is written	*gu*	before *a* and *o*
	gü	before *e* and *i*.

The letters *r* and *rr*

The letter *r* is used to represent two different sounds: the one-tap [r] sound when it appears either in the middle of a word or in the final position: *carta, ardor*; and the multiple vibrant [rr] when it appears in initial position or follows the consonants *l, n* or *s*: *roca, honra*.

The double **rr** always represents the multiple vibrant [rr] sound and is written only between vowels: **barro, borrar**.

Stress in Spanish

The written accent

Words stressed on the final syllable require a written accent on that syllable when they end in a vowel or the consonants **n** or **s**: **vendrá, café, jabalí, miró, tabú, sillón, Tomás**.

but   **calor, carril, merced, sagaz, carcaj**.

Words stressed on the penultimate syllable require a written accent on that syllable whenever the word does not end in a vowel or the consonants **n** or **s**: **árbol, inútil, fémur, Gómez, fútbol**.

but   **cosa, venden, acento, examen, pisos**.

Words stressed on the antepenultimate syllable or earlier always require a written accent on the stressed syllable: **pájaro, carámbano, cómpratelo, pagándoselas**.

Generally speaking, monosyllabic words do not require written accents, but in some cases one is used to distinguish two different words with the same spelling: **él** (he, him) - **el** (the); **té** (tea) - **te** (the letter T). These will be found in the dictionary.

Note that in the case of adverbs ending in **-mente** any written accent in the root adjective is retained: **fácil** → **fácilmente; económico** → **económicamente**.

Diphthongs, triphthongs and hiatus

A group of two vowels that make one syllable is called a diphthong; a group of three is called a triphthong. A diphthong is formed by one weak vowel (**i** or **u**) in combination with one strong vowel (**a, e** or **o**). A triphthong is one strong vowel be tween two weak ones. As far as stress is concerned the general rules apply, with both diphthongs and triphthongs being treated as if they were one syllable. If a stressed dipththong or triphthong requires a written accent (following the rules above), this is placed above the strong vowel: **miércoles, acariciéis**.

Hiatus occurs when groups of consecutive vowels do not form diphthongs or triphthongs. In these cases the group is usually made up of strong vowels; the stressed vowel will carry a written accent or not in accordance with the rules above: **neón, tebeo, traéis**. However, when the stressed vowel is a weak vowel, it is the weak vowel which carries the written accent in order to distinguish the group from a diphthong or triphthong: **María, reían, frío**.

The combination **ui** is always considered a diphthong: **contribuir, ruin**.

The article

	definite		indefinite	
	masculine	femenine	masculine	masculine
singular	*el*	*la*	*un*	*una*
plural	*los*	*las*	*unos*	*unas*

Observations

With reflexive verbs the definite article is equivalent to an English possessive adjective in sentences such as:

me lavo la cara *(I wash my face)*   **cámbiate de ropa** *(change your clothes)*

The definite article may acquire the pronominal value of the English "the one" or "the ones": **el del traje azul** *(the one in the blue suit)*.

The masculine article (**el, un**) is used with feminine nouns which begin with a stressed **a-** or **ha-**, when these are used in the singular: **el agua, un hacha**. Note however that the plural forms are regular: **las aguas, unas hachas**. These nouns are marked in the dictionary.

The prepositions **a** and **de** and the article **el** contract to give the forms **al** and **del**.

There is also a neuter article **lo** which may be used with an adjective to signify a general quality:

me gusta lo bello   *(I like all that is beautiful)*
lo extraño es que...   *(the strange thing is that ...)*

The noun

Gender indication in the dictionary

Unlike their English counterparts, Spanish nouns have grammatical gender. In this dictionary the gender of every Spanish headword is given, but in the translations on the English-Spanish side, unmarked nouns ending in **-o** are to be taken to be masculine and those ending in **-a** are to be taken to be feminine; gender is marked in those cases where this does not apply.

Masculine and feminine forms

In many cases gender is shown by the ending which is added to the root. Nouns denoting men or male animals commonly end in **-o** while their counterparts denoting women and female animals end in **-a**: **chico → chica, gato → gata**.

Masculine nouns ending in a consonant add **-a** to form the feminine: **señor → señora**.

Some nouns denoting persons have the same form for both sexes. In these cases the gender is indicated only by the article used: **un pianista** *(a male pianist)*; **una pianista** *(a female pianist)*.

In the case of some nouns denoting animals gender is not indicated by the article but by placing the word **macho** or **hembra** after the noun: **una serpiente** (a snake); **una serpiente macho** (a male snake); **una serpiente hembra** (a female snake).

In some cases a change in gender signifes a change in meaning. For example, **la cólera** means "anger" and **el cólera**, "cholera". Such changes of meaning will be found in the dictionary. However there are a very few words which are either masculine or feminine with no change in meaning whatever. Two examples are **mar** and **azúcar**; one may say **el mar está agitado** or **la mar está agitada**. Words of this type are marked *nm & nf* in the dictionary.

Formation of the plural

Nouns whose plural is formed by adding *-s* are:

> — those ending in an unstressed vowel: **pluma, plumas.**
> — those ending in a stressed *-é*: **bebé, bebés**.

Nouns whose plural is formed by adding *-es* are:

> — the names of vowels: **a, aes; i, íes; o, oes; u, úes.**
> — nouns ending in a consonant or stressed *-i*: *color* → *colores; anís* → *anises*.

When a compound noun is written as separate elements only the first element indicates the plural: *ojos de buey, patas de gallo*.

All irregular plurals are indicated at the appropriate entries in the dictionary.

The adjective

The adjective usually goes after the noun, and agrees with it in gender and number: **un coche rojo; las chicas guapas.**

However, indefinite, interrogative and exclamative adjectives are placed before the noun, as are adjectives expressing cardinal numbers: *¡qué vergüenza!; ¿cuántos leones hay?; hay treinta leones.*

Formation of the masculine and feminine

Most adjectives have a double ending, one for the feminine and one for the masculine. The common ones are those ending in *-o/-a, -or/-ora* and those ending in or *-és/-esa* formed from place names: *guapo,-a, trabajador,-ra, barcelonés,-esa*.

Some, however, have a single ending: those which end in *-a, -e, -i, -í, -n, -l, -r, -s, -z* and *-ista*: *alegre, marroquí, común, fiel, familiar, cortés, capaz.*

Formation of the plural

The adjective follows the same rules as are given for the noun above.

Comparative and superlative

The comparative is formed with *más ... que* or *menos ... que*: *Pedro es más alto que Alberto, los perros corren menos que los tigres.*

When *que* in a comparative expression is followed by a verb, it is replaced by *de lo que*: *esto es más complicado de lo que parece.*

The English comparative phrases "as ... as" and "so ... as" are rendered by *tan ... como*: *mi patio es tan grande como el tuyo.*

The superlative is formed with *el más ... de* or *el menos ... de*: *el chico más listo de la clase.*

The absolute superlative is formed by placing *muy* before the adjective or by adding the suffix *-ísimo/-ísima*: *muy preocupado, preocupadísimo.*

Observations

A few adjectives have special forms for the comparative and superlative:

	comparative	superlative
bueno,-a	*mejor*	*el/la mejor*
malo,-a	*peor*	*el/la peor*
grande	*mayor*	*el/la mayor*

Comparative and superlative forms ending in *-or* do not change when forming the feminine singular: *la mejor solución.*

Demonstrative adjectives

		near me	near you	away from both
masculine	singular	*este*	*ese*	*aquel*
	plural	*estos*	*esos*	*aquellos*
femenine	singular	*esta*	*esa*	*aquella*
	plural	*estas*	*esas*	*aquellas*

Possessive adjectives

one possessor		yo		tú		él, ella, usted	
masculine	singular	*mi*	*mío*	*tu*	*tuyo*	*su*	*suyo*
possession	plural	*mis*	*míos*	*tus*	*tuyos*	*sus*	*suyos*
femenine	singular	*mi*	*mía*	*tu*	*tuya*	*su*	*suya*
possession	plural	*mis*	*mías*	*tus*	*tuyas*	*sus*	*suyas*

Note that the forms on the left are those which precede the noun; those on the right follow it: *es mi pariente* → *es pariente mía*,   *son sus problemas* → *son problemas suyos*.

several possessors		nosotros,-as	vosotros,-as	ellos,-as, ustedes	
masculine possession	singular	*nuestro*	*vuestro*	*su*	*suyo*
	plural	*nuestros*	*vuestros*	*sus*	*suyos*
femenine possession	singular	*nuestra*	*vuestra*	*su*	*suya*
	plural	*nuestras*	*vuestras*	*sus*	*suyas*

The pronoun

Demonstrative pronouns

		near me	near you	away from both
masculine	singular	*éste, este*	*ése, ese*	*aquél, aquel*
	plural	*éstos, estos*	*ésos, esos*	*aquéllos, aquellos*
femenine	singular	*ésta, esta*	*ésa, esa*	*aquélla, aquella*
	plural	*éstas, estas*	*ésas, esas*	*aquéllas, aquellas*
neuter	singular	*esto*	*eso*	*aquello*

These are used to convey the distance between the person or thing they represent and the speaker or speakers: *no viajaré en este coche, viajaré en aquél*.

Possessive pronouns

one possessor		yo	tú	él, ella, usted
masculine possession	singular	*mío*	*tuyo*	*suyo*
	plural	*míos*	*tuyos*	*suyos*
femenine possession	singular	*mía*	*tuya*	*suya*
	plural	*mías*	*tuyas*	*suyas*

Like the adjective, the possessive pronoun agrees with the noun denoting the thing possessed: *esta camisa es mía, la tuya está en el armario*.

several possessors		nosotros,-as	vosotros,-as	ellos,-as, ustedes
masculine possession	singular plural	*nuestro* *nuestros*	*vuestro* *vuestros*	*suyo* *suyos*
femenine possession	singular plural	*nuestra* *nuestras*	*vuestra* *vuestras*	*suya* *suyas*

Personal pronouns

The following table shows recommended use, although in colloquial Spanish variations will be encountered.

subject	strong object	weak object	
		direct	**indirect**
yo	*mí*	*me*	*me*
tú	*ti*	*te*	*te*
él	*él*	*lo*	*le*
ella	*ella*	*la*	*le*
usted m	*usted*	*lo*	*le*
usted f	*usted*	*la*	*le*
nosotros,-as	*nosotros,-as*	*nos*	*nos*
vosotros,-as	*vosotros,-as*	*os*	*os*
ellos	*ellos*	*los*	*les*
ellas	*ellas*	*las*	*les*
ustedes m pl	*ustedes*	*las*	*les*
ustedes f pl	*ustedes*	*las*	*les*

Use

The Spanish subject pronoun is used only for emphasis or to prevent ambiguity as the person of the subject is already conveyed by the verb. When neither of these reasons for its use exists, its presence in the sentence renders the style heavy and is to be avoided.

The strong object pronouns are always used as complements or objects preceded by a preposition: *esta carta es para ti, aquélla es para mí, ¿son de ustedes estos papeles?*

Weak object pronouns precede a verb or are suffixed to an infinitive, imperative or gerund: *lo tienes que hacer; tienes que hacerlo; haciéndolo así se gana tiempo; ¡hazlo ya!*

When several weak pronouns accompany the verb, whether preceding or following it, the second and first person pronouns come before the third: *póntelo; se lo ha dicho*. The pronoun se always precedes the others: *pónselo*.

Note that while it is considered acceptable to use *le* as a weak object pronoun instead of *lo* when a man is being referred to, this is incorrect when referring to women or to objects of either gender, the same is true of *les* instead of *los*.

Se may also be an impersonal subject equivalent to the English "one", "you", "they", "people" or the passive voice: *hay tantos accidentes porque se conduce demasiado rápido.*

When *le* and *les* precede another third person pronoun they are replaced by *se* as in *se lo mandaron*. It is incorrect to say *le lo mandaron*.

Usted and *ustedes* are the second person pronouns used for courtesy. The accompanying verb is in the third person.

Vos is used in several Latin American countries instead of *tú*.

The preposition

General

The most usual Spanish prepositions are: *a, ante, bajo, cabe, con, contra, de, desde, en, entre, hacia, hasta, para, por, según, sin, so, sobre, tras*. Consult the dictionary for their use.

Uses of *por* and *para*

The basic difference between these prepositions is that *por* looks back to the roots, origins or causes of a thing, while *para* looks forwards to the result, aim, goal or destination.

por is used to express:

— cause, reason, motive (usually to say why something has happened): *lo hizo por amor*.
— the period in which the action takes place: *vendrán por la mañana*.
— the place where the action takes place: *pasean por la calle*.
— the means: *lo enviaron por avión*.
— the agent of the passive voice: *el incendio fue provocado por el portero.*
— substitution, equivalence: *aquí puedes comer por mil pesetas*.
— distribution, proportion: *cinco por ciento; trescientas pesetas por persona*.
— multiplication and measurements: *cinco por dos son diez*.
— "in search of" with verbs of movement (*ir, venir* ...): *voy por pan*.
— *estar + por +* infinitive expresses:
   – an action still to be performed: *la cena está por hacer*.
   – an action on the point of being performed: *estaba por llamarte*.
— *tener/dar + por* expresses opinion: *lo dieron por perdido*.

para is used to express:

— purpose: *esto sirve para limpiar los cristales*
— finality, destiny (often in the future): *es para tu padre, compra pescado para la cena*.
— direction of movement, i.e. "towards": *salen para Valencia*.
— deadlines: *lo quiero para mañana*.
— comparison: *es muy alta para la edad que tiene*.
— *estar + para +* infinitive expresses imminence: *está para llegar*.

The adverb

Position of the adverb

As a rule, when the word to be qualified is an adjective or an adverb, the adverb is placed immediately before it: *un plato bien cocinado*.

When the word to be qualified is a verb, the adverb may be placed before or after it: *hoy iré al mercado; iré al mercado hoy.*

Negative adverbs are always placed before the verb: *no lo he visto; nunca volverás a verme.*

Very rarely, adverbs may be placed between the auxiliary verb and the principal verb: *ha llegado felizmente a su destino.*

The verb

Moods

Spanish verbs have three moods, the *indicative*, *subjunctive* and *imperative*.

The indicative is generally used to indicate real actions. It is mainly used in independent statements: *los coches circulan por la calzada.*

The subjunctive is mainly used in subordinate statements where the actions are considered to be potential or doubtful, but not real: *es posible que venga*; or else necessary or desired: *¡ojalá venga!*

The imperative is used to express orders: *¡Ven!; ¡Venid pronto!*

In negative imperatives the subjunctive is used: *¡No vengas!*

Person

The endings of verbs vary according to whether the subject is the first, second or third person, singular or plural (see *Personal pronouns*). While in English it is not possible to omit the subject, this is quite common in Spanish since the ending of the verb indicates the subject.

Formation of tenses

For the formation of all tenses of both regular and irregular verbs see the Spanish verb conjugation tables at the end of this section.

Pronominal or reflexive verbs

Pronominal or reflexive verbs are those which are conjugated with a personal pronoun functioning as a complement, coinciding in person with the subject: for example the verb *cambiar* has a pronominal form which is *cambiarse: cambia moneda; se cambia de ropa*.

The personal pronouns (*me, te, se, nos, os, se*) are placed before the verb in all tenses and persons of the indicative and subjunctive moods, but are suffixed onto the infinitive, gerund and imperative.

In compound tenses the pronoun is placed immediately before the auxiliary verb.

Passive voice

The passive voice in Spanish is formed with the auxiliary verb *ser* and the past participle of the conjugating verb: *el cazador hirió al jabalí* → *el jabalí fue herido por el cazador.*

The use of this form of passive statement is less frequent than in English. However, another construction the reflexive (or impersonal) passive is quite common: *se vende leña; se alquilan apartamentos; se habla inglés.*

Uses of ser and estar

The English verb "to be" may be rendered in Spanish by two verbs: *ser* and *estar*.

When followed by a noun:

— *ser* is used without a preposition to indicate occupation or profession: *Jaime es el director de ventas* (*Jaime is the sales manager*), *Eduardo es médico* (*Eduardo is a doctor*).

— *ser* with the preposition *de* indicates origin or possession: *soy de Salamanca* (*I am from Salamanca*), *es de Alberto* (*it is Alberto's*).

— *ser* with *para* indicates destination: *el disco es para Pilar* (*the record is for Pilar*).

— *estar* cannot be followed directly by a noun, it always takes a preposition and the meaning is dictated by the preposition. It is worth noting, however, its special use with *de* to indicate that someone is performing a function which do not usually perform: *Andrés está de secretario* (*Andrés is acting as secretary*).

Where the verb is followed by an adjective:

— *ser* expresses a permanent or inherent quality: *Jorge es rubio; sus ojos son grandes.*

— *estar* expresses a quality which is neither permanent nor inherent: *Mariano está resfriado; el cielo está nublado.*

Sometimes both verbs may be used with the same adjective, but there is a change of meaning. For example, *Lorenzo es bueno* means that Lorenzo is a good man but *Lorenzo está bueno* means either that he is no longer ill or, colloquially, that he is good-looking.

Finally, *estar* is used to indicate position and geographical location: *tu cena está en el microondas; Tafalla está en Navarra.*

Models for the conjugation of regular verbs

Simple tenses

1st conjugation – AMAR

Present indicative	amo, amas, ama, amamos, amáis, aman.
Past simple	amé, amaste, amó, amamos, amasteis, amaron.
Past continuous indicative	amaba, amabas, amaba, amábamos, amabais, amaban.
Future indicative	amaré, amarás, amará, amaremos, amaréis, amarán.
Conditional	amaría, amarías, amaría, amaríamos, amaríais, amarían.
Present subjunctive	ame, ames, ame, amemos, améis, amen.
Past subjunctive	amara, amaras, amara, amáramos, amarais, amaran; amase, amases, amase, amásemos, amaseis, amasen.
Future subjunctive	amare, amares, amare, amáremos, amareis, amaren.
Imperative	ama (tú), ame (él/Vd.), amemos (nos.) amad (vos.) amen (ellos/Vds.).
Gerund	amando.
Past participle	amado,-a.

2nd conjugation – TEMER

Present indicative	temo, temes, teme, tememos, teméis, temen.
Past simple	temí, temiste, temió, temimos, temisteis, temieron.
Past continuous indicative	temía, temías, temía, temíamos, temíais, temían.
Future indicative	temeré, temerás, temerá, temeremos, temeréis, temerán.
Conditional	temería, temerías, temería, temeríamos, temeríais, temerían.
Present subjunctive	tema, temas, tema, temamos, temáis, teman.
Past subjunctive	temiera, temieras, temiera, temiéramos, temierais, temieran; temiese, temieses, temiese, temiésemos, temieseis, temiesen.
Future subjunctive	temiere, temieres, temiere, temiéremos, temiereis, temieren.
Imperative	teme (tú), tema (él/Vd.), temamos (nos.) temed (vos.) teman (ellos/Vds.).
Gerund	temiendo.
Past participle	temido,-a.

3rd conjugation – PARTIR

Present indicative	parto, partes, parte, partimos, partís, parten.
Past simple	partí, partiste, partió, partimos, partisteis, partieron.
Past continuous indicative	partía, partías, partía, partíamos, partíais, partían.
Future indicative	partiré, partirás, partirá, partiremos, partiréis, partirán.

Conditional	partiría, partirías, partiría, partiríamos, partiríais, partirían.
Present subjunctive	parta, partas, parta, partamos, partáis, partan.
Past subjunctive	partiera, partieras, partiera, partiéramos, partierais, partieran; partiese, partieses, partiese, partiésemos, partieseis, partiesen.
Future subjunctive	partiere, partieres, partiere, partiéremos, partiereis, partieren.
Imperative	parte (tú), parta (él/Vd.), partamos (nos.) partid (vos.) partan (ellos/Vds.).
Gerund	partiendo.
Past participle	partido,-a.

Note that the imperative proper has forms for the second person (*tú* and *vosotros*) only; all other forms are taken from the present subjunctive.

Compound tenses

Present Perfect	he, has, ha, hemos, habeis, han	amado / temido / partido
Pluperfect	había, habías, había, habíamos, habíais, habían	amado / temido / partido
Future Perfect	habré, habrás, habrá, habremos, habreis, habrán	amado / temido / partido
Perfect Conditional	habría, habrías, habría, habríamos, habríais, habrían	amado / temido / partido
Past Anterior	hube, hubiste, hubo, hubimos, hubisteis, hubieron	amado / temido / partido
Present Perfect subjunctive	haya, hayas, haya, hayamos, hayáis, hayan	amado / temido / partido
Pluperfect subjunctive	hubiera, hubieras, hubiera, hubiéramos, hubierais, hubieran hubiese, hubieses, hubiese, hubiésemos, hubieseis, hubiesen	amado / temido / partido

A

a *prep* **1** *(dirección)* to: *girar a la derecha*, to turn (to the) right; *irse a casa*, to go home; *subir al autobús*, to get on the bus. **2** *(destino)* to, towards. **3** *(distancia)* away: *a cien kilómetros de casa*, a hundred kilometres away from home. **4** *(lugar)* at, on: *a la entrada*, at the entrance; *a la izquierda*, on the left. **5** *(tiempo)* at: *a las once*, at eleven; *a los tres días*, three days later; *a tiempo*, in time; *estamos a 30 de mayo*, it's the thirtieth of May. **6** *(modo, manera)*: *a ciegas*, blindly; *a oscuras*, in the dark; *a pie*, on foot. **7** *(instrumento)*: *a lápiz*, in pencil; *escrito a mano*, handwritten; *escrito a máquina*, typewritten. **8** *(precio)* a: *a 3 euros el kilo*, three euros a kilo. **9** *(medida)* at: *a 90 kilómetros por hora*, at 90 kilometres an hour. **10** *(finalidad)* to: *vino a vernos*, he came to see us. **11** *(complemento directo, no se traduce)*: *vi a Juana*, I saw Juana. **12** *(complemento indirecto)* to: *te lo di a ti*, I gave it to you. **13** *verbo* **a** + *inf*: *aprender a nadar*, to learn (how) to swim. **14** *(como imperativo)*: *¡a dormir!*, bedtime!; *¡a ver!*, let's see! **15** *(para)* for: *les compré unos caramelos a los niños*, I bought some sweets for the children. **16** *(de)* from: *se lo compré a mi vecino*, I bought it from my neighbour.

abadía *nf (edificio)* abbey.

abajo *adv* **1** *(situación)* below, down: *ahí abajo*, down there. **2** *(en una casa)* downstairs. **3** *(dirección)* down, downward: *calle abajo*, down the street.

▶ *interj* ¡abajo ...! down with ...!

abalanzarse *vpr* **1** *(tirarse)* to leap [*pt & pp* **leaped** o **leapt**], pounce: *el tigre se aba-* lanzó sobre su presa, the tiger pounced on its prey. **2** *(precipitarse)* to rush: *todos se abalanzaron hacia la salida*, everybody rushed towards the exit.

abandonado,-a *adj* **1** *(desamparado, desierto)* abandoned. **2** *(descuidado)* neglected. **3** *(desaseado)* unkempt.

abandonar *vt* **1** *(desamparar)* to abandon. **2** *(lugar)* to leave [*pt & pp* **left**]. **3** *(actividad)* to give up.

▶ *vpr* **abandonarse 1** *(descuidarse)* to let oneself go. **2** *(entregarse)* to take to: *se abandonó al juego*, he took to gambling.

abandono *nm* neglect.

abanicar *vt* to fan.

abanico *nm* **1** *(para dar aire)* fan. **2** *(gama)* range.

abaratar *vt* to make cheaper, reduce the price of.

▶ *vpr* **abaratarse** to become cheaper.

abarcar *vt* **1** *(englobar)* to cover, embrace. **2** *(abrazar)* to embrace.

abarrotado,-a *adj* packed.

abarrotar *vt* to pack.

abastecer *vt* to supply.

▶ *vpr* **abastecerse** to stock up.

abastecimiento *nm* supply.

abasto *nm*.

● **dar abasto** to cope: *es que no doy abasto*, I just can't cope.

abatido,-a *adj* dejected, depressed.

abatir *vt* **1** *(derribar)* to bring down [*pt & pp* **brought**]; *(árbol)* to cut down [*pt & pp* **cut**]. **2** *(bajar)* to lower. **3** *(matar)* to shoot [*pt & pp* **shot**]. **4** *(desanimar)* to depress.

▶ *vpr* **abatirse 1** *(ave)* to swoop. **2** *(avión)* to dive. **3** *(desanimarse)* to lose heart [*pt & pp* **lost**].

abdicar *vt-vi* to abdicate.

abdomen *nm* abdomen.

abdominal *adj* abdominal.

▶ *nf pl* **abdominales** *(ejercicios)* sit-ups.

abecedario *nm* alphabet.

abedul *nm* birch tree.

abeja *nf* bee.

■ **abeja reina** queen bee.

abertura *nf* opening, gap.

abeto *nm* fir tree.

abierto,-a *adj* **1** *(puerta, boca, ojos)* open.
2 *(grifo)* on, running. **3** *(sincero)* frank. **4** *(tolerante)* open-minded.

● **con los brazos abiertos** with open arms.

abismo *nm* abyss.

ablandar *vt* **1** *(poner blando)* to soften. **2** *(conmover)* to move.

▶ *vpr* **ablandarse** to soften, go soft.

abnegación *nf* abnegation, self-denial.

abochornar *vt* to embarrass.

▶ *vpr* **abochornarse** to be embarrassed.

abofetear *vt* to slap.

abogacía *nf* legal profession.

abogado,-a *nm,f* lawyer.

■ **abogado defensor** counsel for the defense.

■ **abogado laboralista** labour lawyer.

abolición *nf* abolition.

abolir *vt* to abolish.

abolladura *nf* dent.

abollar *vt* to dent.

abominable *adj* abominable, loathsome.

abonado,-a *adj* **1** *(pagado)* paid. **2** *(tierra)* fertilized.

▶ *nm,f (a teléfono, revista)* subscriber; *(a teatro etc)* season-ticket holder.

abonar *vt* **1** *(pagar)* to pay [*pt & pp* **paid**]. **2** *(tierra)* to fertilize. **3** *(subscribir)* to subscribe.

▶ *vpr* **abonarse** *(a revista)* to subscribe; *(a teatro etc)* to buy a season ticket [*pt & pp* **bought**].

abono *nm* **1** *(pago)* payment. **2** *(para tierra)* fertilizer. **3** *(a revista)* subscription; *(a teatro, tren, etc)* season-ticket.

abordaje *nm* boarding.

abordar *vt* **1** *(barco - acercarse)* to come alongside; *(- embestir)* to ram into; *(- atacar)* to board. **2** *(persona)* to approach. **3** *(tema)* to deal with [*pt & pp* **dealt**], tackle.

aborigen *adj* aboriginal.

▶ *nm* aborigine.

aborrecer *vt* to abhor, hate.

abortar *vi* **1** *(voluntariamente)* to abort; *(involuntariamente)* to miscarry. **2** *(fracasar)* to fail.

aborto *nm* **1** *(voluntario)* abortion; *(espontáneo)* miscarriage. **2** *fam (persona)* ugly person.

abotonar *vt* to button, button up.

▶ *vpr* **abotonarse** to button, button up.

abrasador,-ra *adj* burning, scorching.

abrasar *vt* *(quemar)* to burn [*pt & pp* **burnt**].

▶ *vi (comida, etc)* to be boiling hot.

▶ *vpr* **abrasarse** **1** *(bosque, edificio)* to burn down [*pt & pp* **burnt** o **burned**]. **2** *(persona)* to burn oneself.

● **abrasarse de calor** to be sweltering.

abrazar *vt* **1** *(persona)* to embrace. **2** *(doctrina, fe)* to embrace.

▶ *vpr* **abrazarse** to embrace, hug.

abrazo *nm* hug, embrace.

abrebotellas *nm* bottle opener.

abrecartas *nm* letter-opener, paper-knife [*pl* **-ves**].

abrelatas *nm* GB tin-opener; US can-opener.

abrevadero *nm* drinking trough.

abreviar *vt (acortar)* to shorten; *(texto)* to abridge; *(palabra)* to abbreviate.

abreviatura *nf* abbreviation.

abridor *nm* opener.

abrigar *vt* **1** *(contra el frío)* to wrap up, keep warm. **2** *(proteger)* to shelter, protect. **3** *(sospechas)* to harbour. **4** *(esperanzas)* to cherish.

▶ *vi (ropa)* to be warm.

▶ *vpr* **abrigarse 1** *(contra el frío)* to wrap oneself up. **2** *(protegerse)* to take shelter.

abrigo *nm* **1** *(prenda)* coat, overcoat. **2** *(refugio)* shelter.

■ **ropa de abrigo** warm clothing.

abril *nm* April.

abrillantador *nm* polish.

abrillantar *vt* to polish, shine [*pt & pp* **shined**].

abrir *vt* **1** *(gen)* to open. **2** *(cremallera)* to undo [*pt* **undid**; *pp* **undone**]. **3** *(túnel)* to dig [*pt & pp* **dug**]. **4** *(luz)* to switch on, turn on. **5** *(grifo, gas)* to turn on. **6** *(encabezar)* to head, lead [*pt & pp* **led**].

▶ *vpr* **abrirse 1** *(gen)* to open; *(flores)* to

bloom. **2** *(sincerarse)* to open out. **3** *arg (largarse)* to clear off.
- **abrir el apetito** to whet one's appetite.
- **abrir paso** to make way.
- **en un abrir y cerrar de ojos** in the twinkling of an eye.

abrochar *vt-vpr* to do up, fasten: ***abróchense los cinturones***, please fasten your seat-belts.

abrupto,-a *adj* **1** *(terreno)* rugged. **2** *(persona)* abrupt.

ábside *nm* apse.

absolución *nf* absolution.

absolutamente *adv* absolutely.

absoluto,-a *adj* absolute.
- **en absoluto** not at all.

absolver *vt (de pecado)* to absolve; *(de cargo)* to acquit.

absorbente *adj* **1** *(algodón, papel)* absorbent. **2** *(trabajo)* absorbing, engrossing.
▶ *nm* absorbent.

absorber *vt* to absorb.

absorto,-a *adj* **1** *(pasmado)* amazed. **2** *(ensimismado)* absorbed, engrossed.

abstemio,-a *adj* abstemious, teetotal.
▶ *nm,f* teetotaller.

abstención *nf* abstention.

abstenerse *vpr* **1** *(en votación)* to abstain. **2** *(de hacer algo)* to refrain *(de,* from).

abstinencia *nf* abstinence.

abstracto,-a *adj* abstract.

absurdo,-a *adj* absurd.

abuchear *vt* to boo.

abuela *nf* **1** *(pariente)* grandmother. Familiarmente, **grandma** o **granny**. **2** *(vieja)* old woman [*pl* **women**].
- **no tener abuela** to be very full of oneself.

abuelo *nm* **1** *(pariente)* grandfather. Familiarmente, **grandad** o **grandpa**. **2** *(viejo)* old man [*pl* **men**].
▶ *nm pl* **abuelos** grandparents.

abultado,-a *adj* bulky, big.

abultar *vt* **1** *(aumentar)* to enlarge, increase. **2** *(exagerar)* to exaggerate.
▶ *vi* to be bulky.

abundancia *nf* abundance, plenty.

abundante *adj* abundant, plentiful.

abundar *vi* to abound, be plentiful.

aburrido,-a *adj* **1** *(con ser)* boring, tedious: **es un libro muy aburrido**, it's a very boring book. **2** *(con estar)* bored: **estoy aburrido**, I'm bored.

aburrimiento *nm* boredom.

aburrir *vt* to bore.
▶ *vpr* **aburrirse** to get bored.

abusar *vi* **abusar de 1** *(persona)* to take advantage of; *(autoridad, paciencia, hospitalidad)* to abuse. **2** *(sexualmente)* to sexually abuse.
- **abusar de la bebida** to drink too much [*pt* **drank**; *pp* **drunk**].
- **abusar de la situación** to take unfair advantage of the situation.

abusivo,-a *adj* excessive.

abuso *nm* **1** *(uso excesivo)* abuse, misuse. **2** *(injusticia)* injustice.
- **abuso de confianza** betrayal of trust.
- **abuso de poder** abuse of power.
- **abuso sexual** sexual abuse.
- **abusos deshonestos** indecent assault *sing*.

abusón,-ona *nm,f* **1** *fam (gorrón)* sponger. **2** *(egoísta)* selfish.

acá *adv* **1** *(lugar)* here, over here: *de acá para allá*, to and fro, up and down. **2** *(tiempo)*: *de entonces acá*, since then.

acabado,-a *adj* **1** *(completo)* finished. **2** *(agotado)* worn-out: **una persona acabada**, a has-been.
▶ *nm* **acabado** finish.

acabar *vt* **1** *(gen)* to finish; *(completar)* to complete: **he acabado el trabajo**, I've finished the work. **2** *(consumir)* to use up, run out of [*pt* **ran**; *pp* **run**]: **hemos acabado el agua mineral**, we've run out of mineral water.
▶ *vi* **1** *(gen)* to finish, end; *(pareja)* to split up [*pt & pp* **split**]: **ya he acabado**, I've finished; **acabar en punta**, to have a pointed end. **2 acabar por + *inf* acabar + *ger*** to end up: **acabarás comprando el vestido**, you'll end up buying the dress.
▶ *vpr* **acabarse** *(terminarse)* to end, finish; *(no quedar)* to run out [*pt* **ran**; *pp* **run**].
- **acabar bien** to have a happy ending.
- **acabar con** to destroy, put an end to.
- **acabar de** to have just: **acabo de pintarlo**, I've just painted it.
- **acabar mal 1** *(cosa)* to end badly. **2** *(persona)* to come to a bad end.
- **¡acabáramos!** at last!
- **¡se acabó!** that's it!

acacia *nf* acacia.
academia *nf* **1** *(institución)* academy. **2** *(escuela)* school.
 ■ **academia de idiomas** language school.
 ■ **academia militar** military academy.
académico,-a *adj* academic: *estudios académicos*, academic qualifications.
 ► *nm,f* academician.
acallar *vt* **1** *(silenciar)* to silence. **2** *(apaciguar)* to pacify.
acalorado,-a *adj* **1** *(con calor)* heated. **2** *(exaltado)* excited; *(debate, conciencia)* heated, angry.
acampada *nf* camping.
 ● **ir de acampada** to go camping.
acampar *vi* to camp.
acantilado *nm* cliff.
acaparar *vt* **1** *(alimentos, mercancías)* to hoard; *(mercado)* to corner, buy up [*pt & pp* **bought**]. **2** *(monopolizar)* to monopolize: *acaparó la atención de todos*, she commanded everyone's attention.
acariciar *vt* **1** *(persona)* to caress, fondle; *(animal)* to stroke. **2** *(esperanzas, idea)* to cherish.
 ► *vpr* **acariciarse** to caress each other.
acarrear *vt* **1** *(causar)* to cause, bring [*pt & pp* **brought**]. **2** *(transportar)* to carry, transport.
acaso *adv* **1** *(en preguntas)*: *¿acaso no me crees?*, don't you believe me?; *¿acaso no lo sabías?*, are you saying you didn't know? **2** *fml (quizá)* perhaps, maybe: *acaso necesite tu ayuda*, I might need your help.
 ● **por si acaso** just in case.
acatar *vt* *(leyes, orden)* to obey, comply with.
acatarrarse *vpr* to catch a cold [*pt and pp* **caught**].
acaudalado,-a *adj* rich, wealthy.
acceder *vi* **1** *(consentir)* to consent, agree. **2** *(tener entrada)* to enter: *por aquí se accede al jardín*, this leads to the garden. **3** *(alcanzar)* to accede: *acceder al poder*, to come to power; *acceder al trono*, to succeed to the throne. **4** INFORM to access.
accesible *adj* accessible.
acceso *nm* **1** *(entrada)* access, entry. **2** *(carretera)* approach road. **3** *(ataque)* fit.
 ■ **acceso aleatorio** INFORM random access.

 ■ **acceso al trono** accession.
 ■ **acceso directo** direct access.
accesorio,-a *adj* accessory.
 ► *nm* **accesorio** accessory.
accidentado,-a *adj* **1** *(turbado)* agitated: *una vida accidentada*, a stormy life, a troubled life. **2** *(terreno)* uneven, rough.
 ► *nm,f (persona herida)* casualty, accident victim.
accidental *adj* accidental.
accidentarse *vpr* to have an accident.
accidente *nm* **1** *(percance)* accident. **2** *(geográfico)* feature.
 ● **por accidente** by chance.
 ■ **accidente aéreo** plane crash.
 ■ **accidente de circulación** traffic accident, road accident.
 ■ **accidente de coche** car crash.
 ■ **accidente laboral** industrial accident.
acción *nf* **1** *(actividad)* action: *una película de acción*, an action film. **2** *(acto)* act, deed: *una buena acción*, a good deed. **3** *(efecto)* effect: *la acción del agua sobre la piel*, the effect of water on the skin. **4** *(en bolsa)* share. **5** *(en cine, teatro)* action, plot. **6** *(bélica)* action.
 ■ **acción de gracias** thanksgiving.
accionar *vt* **1** *(manivela)* to pull. **2** *(pieza mecánica)* to operate; *(alarma etc)* to set off [*pt & pp* **set**].
accionista *nmf* shareholder, stockholder.
acebo *nm* holly.
acechar *vt* to lie in wait for [*pt* **lay**; *pp* **lain**]: *un gran peligro nos acecha*, great danger looms ahead.
acecho.
 ● **al acecho** in wait.
aceite *nm* oil.
 ● **perder aceite** to leak oil.
 ■ **aceite de girasol** sunflower oil.
 ■ **aceite de oliva** olive oil.
aceitera *nf* **1** *(de mesa)* oil bottle. **2** *(de mecánico)* oilcan.
aceitoso,-a *adj* oily.
aceituna *nf* olive.
 ■ **aceituna rellena** stuffed olive.
aceleración *nf* acceleration.
acelerador *nm* accelerator.
acelerar *vt* **1** to accelerate. **2** *(apresurar)* to speed up.
 ► *vpr* **acelerarse** *(ponerse nervioso)* to get overexcited.
acelga *nf* chard.

acento *nm* **1** *(gráfico)* accent, written accent; *(tónico)* stress. **2** *(regional, etc)* accent. **3** *(énfasis)* emphasis, stress.
■ **acento agudo** acute accent.
■ **acento circunflejo** circumflex accent.
■ **acento grave** grave accent.
acentuado,-a *adj* **1** *(palabra, letra)* accented. **2** *(resaltado)* strong, marked.
acentuar *vt* **1** *(palabra, letra)* to accent. **2** *(resaltar)* to emphasize, stress.
► *vpr* **acentuarse** to stand out [*pt & pp* **stood**].
acepción *nf* meaning, sense.
aceptable *adj* acceptable.
aceptación *nf* **1** *(acto)* acceptance. **2** *(éxito)*: **ha tenido mucha aceptación**, it has been very successful; **tiene poca aceptación**, it's not very popular.
aceptar *vt* **1** *(admitir)* to accept, receive. **2** *(aprobar)* to approve of.
acequia *nf* irrigation ditch.
acera *nf* GB pavement; US sidewalk.
● **ser de la acera de enfrente** to be gay.
acerca de *prep* about, concerning.
acercamiento *nm* coming together.
acercar *vt* to bring closer [*pt & pp* **brought**]: **acerca un poco la mesa**, bring the table a little closer; **¿me acercas el agua?**, can you pass the water?
► *vpr* **acercarse** come closer: **acércate**, come closer; **se acerca el verano**, summer is coming.
acero *nm* steel.
■ **acero inoxidable** stainless steel.
acertado,-a *adj* **1** *(opinión etc)* right, correct. **2** *(conveniente)* suitable.
acertante *nmf* winner.
acertar *vt* **1** *(repuesta)* to get right. **2** *(adivinanza)* to guess: **acertar la quiniela**, to win the pools.
► *vi* **1** *(dar con)* to succeed: **acertó con la casa**, he found the right house; **acertó con la respuesta**, he got the answer right; **no acertó a decírselo**, she didn't manage to tell him. **2 acertar a +** *inf* to happen, chance: **yo acertaba a estar allí**, I happened to be there.
acertijo *nm* riddle.
achacar.
● **achacar algo a** ALGN to attribute STH to SB.
achaque *nm* ailment.
achatar *vt* to flatten.

achicharrar *vt* *(planta)* to scorch; *(comida)* to burn [*pt & pp* **burnt**]: **hace un sol que achicharra**, it's boiling hot.
► *vpr* **achicharrarse** *(pasar calor)* to roast: **¡me estoy achicharrando aquí dentro!**, I'm roasting in here!
achuchar *vt* **1** *fam (empujar)* to shove. **2** *(abrazar)* to hug. **3** *(meter prisa a)* to hurry.
achuchón *nm* **1** *fam (empujón)* shove. **2** *fam (indisposición)*: **le dio un achuchón**, he had a funny turn. **3** *fam (abrazo)* hug, squeeze.
acicalarse *vpr* to dress up.
acidez *nf (de fruta, vinagre)* sourness; *(en química)* acidity.
■ **acidez de estómago** heartburn.
ácido,-a *adj* **1** *(sabor)* sharp, tart. **2** acidic.
► *nm* **ácido 1** acid. **2** *arg (droga)* acid, LSD.
acierto *nm* **1** *(solución correcta)* right answer. **2** *(decisión adecuada)* wise decision. **3** *(éxito)* success. **4** *(habilidad)* skill.
● **con acierto** wisely.
aclamar *vt* to acclaim.
aclaración *nf* explanation.
aclarar *vt* **1** *(cabello, color)* to lighten. **2** *(líquido)* to thin. **3** *(enjuagar)* to rinse. **4** *(explicar)* to explain.
► *vpr* **aclararse 1** *(entender)* to understand [*pt & pp* **understood**]. **2** *(tiempo)* to clear up.
● **aclararse la voz** to clear one's throat.
aclimatarse *vpr* to become acclimatized.
acné *nf* acne.
acobardar *vt* to frighten.
► *vpr* **acobardarse** to become frightened.
acogedor,-ra *adj* **1** *(persona)* welcoming. **2** *(lugar)* cosy, warm.
acoger *vt* **1** *(recibir)* to receive; *(invitado)* to welcome: **sus padres me acogieron muy bien**, her parents welcomed me warmly. **2** *(dar refugio a)* to take in: **acogieron a una niña sudanesa**, they took in a little Sudanese girl. **3** *(ideas etc)* to accept, take to.
► *vpr* **acogerse 1** *(refugiarse)* to take refuge. **2** *(a una ley)* to have recourse to.
acogida *nf* **1** *(de persona)* welcome. **2** *(de noticia, libro)* reception.

acometer *vt* **1** *(embestir)* to attack. **2** *(emprender)* to undertake.

acomodado,-a *adj (rico)* well-to-do.

acomodador,-ra *nm,f (hombre)* usher; *(mujer)* usherette.

acomodar *vt* **1** *(adaptar)* to adapt. **2** *(alojar)* to accommodate.
- ► *vpr* **acomodarse 1** *(instalarse)* to make oneself comfortable: *se acomodó en el sillón*, she settled down in the armchair. **2** *(adaptarse)* to adapt oneself.

acompañamiento *nm* **1** *(música)* accompaniment. **2** *(comitiva)* retinue.

acompañante *adj* accompanying.
- ► *nmf* **1** *(gen)* companion. **2** *(músico)* accompanist.

acompañar *vt* **1** *(ir con)* to go with, come with: *me acompañó hasta la parada de autobús*, he came to the bus stop with me; *¿la acompañas a la puerta?*, will you see her to the door? **2** *(adjuntar)* to enclose. **3** *(a cantante)* to accompany.
- ● **le acompaño en el sentimiento** please accept my condolences.

acondicionar *vt* to convert, adapt [*pt & pp* **set**].

aconsejar *vt* to advise: *te aconsejo que estudies*, I advise you to study; *necesito que me aconsejes*, I need your advice.

acontecer *vi* to happen.

acontecimiento *nm* event, happening.

acoplar *vt* **1** *(pieza)* to attach. **2** to couple *(vagones)*, connect.
- ► *vpr* **acoplarse 1** *(piezas)* to fit together. **2** *(persona)* to adjust. **3** *(animales)* to pair, mate.

acorazado,-a *adj* armoured.
- ► *nm* **acorazado** battleship.

acordar *vt* to agree: *acordamos vernos luego*, we agreed to see each other later.
- ► *vpr* **acordarse** to remember: *¿te acuerdas de mí?*, do you remember me?

acorde *adj* in agreement.
- ► *nm* chord.

acordeón *nm* accordion.

acorralar *vt* to corner.

acortar *vt* to shorten.
- ► *vpr* **acortarse** to get shorter.

acosar *vt* **1** *(perseguir)* to hound. **2** *(hostigar)* to harass.

acoso *nm* **1** *(persecución)* hounding. **2** *(hostigamiento)* harassment.

acostar *vt* to put to bed.
- ► *vpr* **acostarse 1** *(irse a la cama)* to go to bed. **2** *(tumbarse)* to lie down [*pt* **lay**; *pp* **lain**].
- ● **acostarse con ALGN** to sleep with SB [*pt & pp* **slept**].

acostumbrado,-a *adj* **1** *(persona)* accustomed, used to. **2** *(hecho)* usual, customary.

acostumbrar *vi-vt-vpr* **acostumbrar(se)** to get used to: *tuve que acostumbrarme a conducir por la izquierda*, I had to get used to driving on the left.
- ● **acostumbrar a ALGN a algo** to get SB used to STH.
- ● **acostumbrar a hacer algo** to be in the habit of doing STH: *no acostumbro a fumar por la mañana*, I don't usually smoke in the morning.

acre¹ *adj* **1** *(olor)* acrid. **2** *(sabor)* bitter.

acre² *nm (medida)* acre.

acreditado,-a *adj* reputable, well-known.

acreditar *vt* **1** *(demostrar, probar)* to prove. **2** *(cuenta bancaria)* to credit. **3** *(embajador, periodista)* to accredit.
- ► *vpr* **acreditarse** to gain a reputation.

acreedor,-ra *adj* deserving.
- ► *nm,f* creditor.

acribillar *vt* **1** *(llenar de agujeros)*: *acribillar a ALGN a balazos*, to riddle SB with bullets. **2** *(molestar)*: *acribillar a ALGN a preguntas*, to bombard SB with questions.

acrílico,-a *adj* acrylic.

acrobacia *nf* acrobatics.

acróbata *nmf* acrobat.

acta *nf* **1** *(de reunión)* minutes *pl*. **2** *(certificado)* certificate.
- ► *nf pl* **actas** minutes.
- ● **constar en acta** to be recorded in the minutes.
- ● **levantar acta** to take the minutes.
- ■ **acta notarial** notarial deed.

actitud *nf* attitude.

activar *vt (poner en funcionamiento)* to activate; *(acelerar)* to expedite.
- ► *vpr* **activarse** to become activated.

actividad *nf* activity.

activista *adj* - *nmf* activist.

activo,-a *adj* active.
- ► *nm* **activo** assets *pl*.
- ■ **activo disponible** liquid assets *pl*.

acto *nm* **1** *(acción)* act. **2** *(ceremonia)* ceremony. **3** *(de obra)* act.

- **acto seguido** immediately afterwards.
- **en el acto** at once.
- **hacer acto de presencia** to put in an appearance.
- **acto de clausura** closing ceremony.
■ **acto inaugural** opening ceremony.
■ **acto reflejo** reflex action.
■ **acto sexual** sexual act.

actor *nm* actor.

actriz *nf* actress.

actuación *nf* **1** *(interpretación)* performance. **2** *(acción)* action: *su rápida actuación le salvó la vida*, his quick action saved her life. **3** *(comportamiento)* behaviour.

actual *adj* **1** *(de este momento)* present, current. **2** *(moderno)* up-to-date.

actualidad *nf* **1** *(momento presente)* present time, present. **2** *(hechos)* current affairs *pl*.
- **en la actualidad** at present, at the present time.
■ **temas de actualidad** current affairs.

actualizar *vt* **1** *(poner al día)* to bring up to date *[pt & pp* **brought]**. **2** *(programa)* to upgrade; *(página de Internet)* to refresh.

actualmente *adv* *(hoy en día)* nowadays; *(ahora)* at present.

actuar *vi* **1** *(obrar)* to act. **2** *(actor)* to act; *(cantante, bailarín)* to perform.

acuarela *nf* watercolour.

acuario *nm* aquarium.

acuático,-a *adj* aquatic, water.

acudir *vi* (*ir*) to go; *(venir)* to come.
- **acudir a ALGN** to turn to SB.
- **acudir en ayuda de ALGN** to come to SB's aid.

acueducto *nm* aqueduct.

acuerdo *nm* agreement.
- **¡de acuerdo!** all right!, O.K.!
- **de acuerdo con** in accordance with.
- **de común acuerdo** by mutual agreement.
- **estar de acuerdo** to agree.
- **llegar a un acuerdo** to reach (an) agreement.
- **ponerse de acuerdo** to come to an agreement.

acumular *vt* to accumulate.

acunar *vt* to rock.

acuñar *vt* **1** *(moneda)* to mint. **2** *(palabra)* to coin.

acupuntura *nf* acupuncture.

acurrucarse *vpr* to curl up.

acusación *nf* *(inculpación)* accusation; *(en derecho)* charge.

acusado,-a *adj - nm,f* accused.

acusar *vt* **1** *(culpar)* to accuse; *(en derecho)* to charge. **2** *(manifestar)* to show signs of *[pt* **showed**; *pp* **shown]**.
▶ *vpr* **acusarse 1** *(confesarse)* to confess. **2** *(acentuarse)* to become more pronounced.
- **acusar recibo de** to acknowledge receipt of.

acusica *adj - nmf fam* telltale.

acústica *nf* acoustics.

acústico,-a *adj* acoustic.

adaptable *adj* adaptable.

adaptación *nf* adaptation.

adaptar *vt* **1** *(modificar)* to adapt. **2** *(ajustar)* to adjust.
▶ *vpr* **adaptarse** to adapt.

adecuado,-a *adj* adequate, suitable.

adecuar *vt* to adapt, make suitable.

adefesio *nm* **1** *(persona)* freak. **2** *(cosa)* monstrosity.
- **estar hecho un adefesio** to look a sight.

adelantado,-a *adj* **1** *(precoz)* precocious. **2** *(aventajado)* advanced. **3** *(desarrollado)* developed. **4** *(reloj)* fast.
- **por adelantado** in advance.

adelantamiento *nm* overtaking.
- **hacer un adelantamiento** to overtake.

adelantar *vt* **1** *(mover adelante)* to move forward. **2** *(reloj)* to put forward. **3** *(pasar adelante)* to pass; *(vehículo)* to overtake. **4** *(dinero)* to pay in advance *[pt & pp* **paid]**.
▶ *vi* **1** *(progresar)* to make progress. **2** *(reloj)* to be fast.
▶ *vpr* **adelantarse 1** *(ir delante)* to go ahead. **2** *(llegar temprano)* to be early. **3** *(anticiparse)* to get ahead. **4** *(reloj)* to gain, be fast.

adelante *adv* forward: *dio un paso adelante*, he took a step forward.
▶ *interj* come in!
- **en adelante** from now on.
- **hacia adelante** forwards.
- **más adelante** later on.

adelanto *nm* **1** *(avance)* advance: *los adelantos de la ciencia*, the progress of science. **2** advance.

adelgazamiento *nm* slimming.
adelgazar *vt* to make slim.
▶ *vi (perder peso)* to lose weight [*pt & pp* **lost**]; *(con régimen)* to slim.
ademán *nm* gesture.
▶ *nm pl* **ademanes** manners.
además *adv* **1** *(por añadidura)* besides. **2** *(también)* also.
● **además de** besides.
● **y además ...** and what's more ....
adentrarse *vpr* .
● **adentrarse en** to go into.
adentro *adv* inside.
▶ *nm pl* **adentros**: *dijo para sus adentros*, she said to herself.
adepto,-a *nm,f* follower, supporter.
aderezar *vt (condimentar)* to season; *(ensalada)* to dress.
adeudar *vt* **1** *(deber)* to owe. **2** *(cuenta)* to debit.
▶ *vpr* **adeudarse** to get into debt.
adherir *vt* to stick [*pt & pp* **stuck**].
▶ *vpr* **adherirse 1** *(pegarse)* to stick [*pt & pp* **stuck**]. **2 adherirse a** *(unirse)* to join, become a member of; *(seguir)* to follow.
adhesivo,-a *adj* adhesive, sticky.
▶ *nm* **adhesivo** adhesive.
adicción *nf* addiction.
adición *nf* addition.
adicto,-a *adj* addicted.
▶ *nm,f* **1** *(a droga)* addict. **2** *(partidario)* supporter.
● **adicto a algo** addicted to STH.
adiestrar *vt* to train.
▶ *vpr* **adiestrarse** to train oneself.
adinerado,-a *adj* wealthy.
adiós *nm* goodbye.
▶ *interj (despidiéndose)* goodbye!; *(al cruzarse)* hello!
adivinanza *nf* riddle.
adivinar *vt* **1** *(respuesta, nombre)* to guess: *¿a que no adivinas qué te he comprado?*, you'll never guess what I've bought for you. **2** *(futuro)* to forecast. **3** *(enigma)* to solve.
adivino,-a *nm,f* fortune-teller.
adjetivo,-a *adj* adjective, adjectival.
▶ *nm* **adjetivo** adjective.
adjudicar *vt* to award: *¡adjudicado!*, sold!
▶ *vpr* **adjudicarse** to appropriate.
adjunto,-a *adj* **1** *(en carta)* enclosed. **2** *(asistente)* assistant.
▶ *nm,f* assistant.

administración *nf* **1** *(de empresa)* administration, management. **2** *(de medicamento)* administering. **3 la Administración** GB the Government; US the Administration.
■ **administración de empresas** business studies.
■ **administración de Hacienda** tax office.
■ **administración de lotería** lottery office.
■ **administración pública** public administration.
administrador,-ra *nm,f* administrator: *es muy buena administradora*, she knows how to stretch money.
administrar *vt* **1** *(organizar)* to manage. **2** *(proporcionar)* to give: *le administró un antibiótico*, he gave him an antibiotic.
▶ *vpr* **administrarse** to manage one's own money.
administrativo,-a *adj* administrative.
▶ *nm,f (funcionario)* official; *(de empresa, banco)* office worker.
admirable *adj* admirable.
admiración *nf* **1** *(estima)* admiration. **2** *(sorpresa)* amazement. **3** *(signo)* exclamation mark.
admirador,-ra *nm,f* admirer.
admirar *vt* **1** *(estimar)* to admire. **2** *(sorprender)* to amaze, surprise.
▶ *vpr* **admirarse** to be astonished.
admisión *nf* admission.
● **"reservado el derecho de admisión"** the management reserves the right to refuse admission.
admitir *vt* **1** *(dar entrada a, reconocer)* to admit: *admito que he sido yo*, I admit that it was me; *me han admitido en el club*, I've been admitted to the club. **2** *(aceptar)* to accept: *no se admiten talones*, we don't accept cheques. **3** *(permitir)* to allow.
ADN *abr (ácido desoxirribonucleico)* deoxyribonucleic acid, DNA.
adobar *vt* to marinate.
adolescencia *nf* adolescence.
adolescente *adj* - *nmf* adolescent.
adonde *adv* where.
adónde *adv* where.
adopción *nf* adoption.
adoptar *vt* to adopt.

adoptivo,-a *adj* adoptive.

adoquín *nm (piedra redonda)* cobble; *(piedra cuadrada)* paving stone.

adorable *adj* adorable.

adoración *nf* adoration, worship.

adorar *vt* to adore, worship.

adormecer *vt* **1** *(dar sueño a)* to send to sleep [*pt & pp* **sent**]. **2** *(calmar)* to calm.
▶ *vpr* **adormecerse 1** *(dormirse)* to fall asleep [*pt* **fell**; *pp* **fallen**]. **2** *(entumecerse)* to go to sleep, go numb.

adormilarse *vpr* to doze, drowse.

adornar *vt* to decorate.

adorno *nm* decoration: *los adornos navideños*, the Christmas decorations.
● **de adorno** decorative.

adosado,-a *adj*: *casas adosadas*, semi-detached houses.

adquirir *vt (conseguir)* to acquire; *(comprar)* to buy [*pt & pp* **bought**], get: *ha adquirido una gran experiencia en dos años*, she has acquired a lot of experience in two years; *no pude adquirir las entradas para el partido*, I couldn't get the tickets for the match.

adquisición *nf* **1** *(acción, cosa comprada)* acquisition, purchase. **2** *(de idioma, hábito)* acquisition.

adrede *adv* on purpose.

aduana *nf* customs *pl*.
● **pasar por la aduana** to go through customs.

aduanero,-a *adj* customs.
▶ *nm,f* customs officer.

adueñarse *vpr* **adueñarse de** to seize.

adulación *nf* adulation, flattery.

adular *vt* to adulate, flatter.

adulterar *vt* to adulterate.

adulterio *nm* adultery.

adulto,-a *adj* - *nm,f* adult.

adverbio *nm* adverb.

adversario,-a *adj* opposing.
▶ *nm,f* adversary, opponent.

adversidad *nf* adversity.

adverso,-a *adj* adverse.

advertencia *nf* **1** *(aviso)* warning: *que te sirva de advertencia*, let this be a warning to you. **2** *(consejo)* advice.

advertir *vt* **1** *(avisar)* to warn: *me advirtieron de que no saliese*, they warned me not to go out. **2** *(aconsejar)* to advise. **3** *(darse cuenta de)* to notice.

adviento *nm* advent.

aéreo,-a *adj* **1** *(vista, fotografía)* aerial. **2** *(tráfico)* air.

aerodinámico,-a *adj* aerodynamic.

aeródromo *nm* GB aerodrome; US airfield.

aeromodelismo *nm* aeroplane modelling.

aeronáutica *nf* aeronautics *sing*.

aeronave *nf* airship.

aeroplano *nm* GB aeroplane; US airplane.

aeropuerto *nm* airport.

aerosol *nm* aerosol, spray.

afable *adj* affable.

afán *nm* **1** *(anhelo)* eagerness: *con afán*, keenly. **2** *(esfuerzo)* hard work.
■ **afán de lucro**: *una organización sin afán de lucro*, a non-profitmaking organization.

afanar *vt fam* to nick, pinch.
● **afanarse en/por hacer algo** to take great pains to do STH.

afear *vt* **1** *(persona)* to make ugly. **2** *(conducta)* to condemn.

afección *nf* *(enfermedad)* complaint, illness.

afectado,-a *adj* **1** *(poco natural)* affected. **2** *(fingido)* pretended.

afectar *vt* **1** *(concernir)* to affect. **2** *(impresionar)* to move.
▶ *vpr* **afectarse** *(impresionarse)* to be affected, be moved.

afecto *nm* affection: *con todo mi afecto*, with all my love.
● **tenerle afecto a** ALGN to be fond of SB.

afectuoso,-a *adj* affectionate.

afeitado *nm* shave, shaving.

afeitar *vt-vpr* **afeitar(se)** to shave.

afeminado,-a *adj* effeminate.

Afganistán *nm* Afghanistan.

afgano,-a *adj* Afghan.
▶ *nm,f (persona)* Afghan.
▶ *nm* **afgano** *(idioma)* Afghan.

afianzar *vt* **1** *(asegurar)* to strengthen. **2** *(consolidar)* to consolidate: *afianzar un régimen*, to consolidate a regime.
▶ *vpr* **afianzarse** to steady oneself.

afición *nf* **1** *(inclinación)* liking: *tiene afición por la música*, he's fond of music. **2** *(pasatiempo)* hobby.
● **la afición** fans *pl*, supporters *pl*.

aficionado,-a *adj* **1** *(entusiasta)* keen, fond. **2** *(no profesional)* amateur.
▶ *nm,f* **1** *(entusiasta)*, fan, enthusiast. **2** *(no profesional)* amateur.

aficionar vt to make fond.
▶ vpr **aficionarse** to become fond.
afilado,-a adj sharp.
afilar vt to sharpen.
afín adj **1** *(semejante)* similar. **2** *(relacionado)* related. **3** *(próximo)* adjacent, next.
afinar vt **1** *(piano, etc)* to tune. **2** *(perfeccionar)* to perfect, polish. **3** *(puntería)* to sharpen.
afirmación nf statement, assertion.
afirmar vt **1** *(aseverar)* to state, say [pt & pp **said**]. **2** *(afianzar)* to strenghten.
▶ vpr **afirmarse** *(ratificarse)* to steady oneself.
afirmativo,-a adj affirmative.
afligir vt **1** *(aquejar)* to afflict. **2** *(apenar)* to grieve.
▶ vpr **afligirse** to grieve, be distressed.
aflojar vt **1** *(soltar)* to loosen. **2** fam *(dinero)* to pay up [pt & pp **paid**].
▶ vi *(disminuir)* to weaken.
▶ vpr **aflojarse** to come loose.
● **aflojar el paso** to slow down.
● **aflojar la mosca** to fork out, cough up.
afluente nm tributary.
afonía nf loss of voice.
afónico,-a adj hoarse.
● **estar afónico,-a** to have lost one's voice.
afortunado,-a adj **1** *(con suerte)* lucky, fortunate. **2** *(feliz)* happy.
Africa nf Africa.
africano,-a adj - nm,f African.
afrontar vt to face up to.
afuera adv outside: **vengo de afuera**, I've just been outside.
▶ interj out of the way!
▶ nf pl **afueras** outskirts.
agachar vt *(cabeza)* to lower.
▶ vpr **agacharse 1** *(acuclillarse)* to crouch down; *(inclinarse)* to bend down [pt & pp **bent**]. **2** *(encogerse)* to cower. **3** *(protegerse)* to duck down: *¡agáchate!*, duck!
agallas nf **1** *(de pez)* gills. **2** fam courage sing, guts.
agarrado,-a adj stingy.
● **bailar agarrado** to dance cheek to cheek.
agarrar vt **1** *(coger fuerte)* to grab; *(sujetar)* to hold [pt & pp **held**]: *un hombre la agarró del brazo*, a man grabbed her arm; *agárralo fuerte*, hold it tight. **2** *(pillar)* to

catch [pt & pp **caught**]: *agarró un resfriado*, she caught a cold.
▶ vpr **agarrarse** to hold on [pt & pp **held**], cling [pt & pp **clung**].
● **agarrarse a un clavo ardiendo** to clutch at straws.
agencia nf agency.
■ **agencia de viajes** travel agency.
■ **agencia inmobiliaria** estate agent's.
agenda nf **1** *(libro)* diary. **2** *(orden del día)* agenda.
■ **agenda de direcciones** address book.
agente nmf agent.
■ **agente de cambio y bolsa** stockbroker.
■ **agente de policía** police officer.
ágil adj agile.
agilidad nf agility.
agilizar vt to speed up.
agitar vt **1** *(líquido, botella)* to shake [pt **shook**; pp **shaken**]; *(pañuelo, mano)* to wave. **2** *(inquietar)* to agitate.
▶ vpr **agitarse 1** *(inquietarse)* to become agitated. **2** *(mar)* to become rough.
aglomeración nf *(acumulación)* agglomeration; *(de gente)* crowd.
agobiado,-a adj: *está agobiado de trabajo*, he's up to his eyes in work; *está agobiada de deudas*, she's burdened with debts.
agobiar vt **1** *(abrumar)* to overwhelm: *los exámenes me agobian*, exams get on top of me. **2** *(deprimir)* to get down: *le agobiaba la idea de mudarse*, the idea of moving house was getting her down.
▶ vpr **agobiarse** get worked up.
agobio nm **1** *(ahogo)* suffocation: *es un agobio el calor que hace en agosto*, it's so hot in August it's unbearable. **2** *(preocupación)* worry: *agobios económicos*, financial worries. **3** *(presión)* pressure: *los agobios de la vida moderna*, the pressures of modern life.
agolparse vpr to crowd, throng.
agonía nf *(sufrimiento)* agony, grief; *(de moribundo)* death throes: *murió después de una larga agonía*, death was slow in coming to her.
agonizar vi to be dying.
agosto nm August.
● **hacer su agosto** to make a packet, make a pile.

agotado,-a *adj* **1** *(cansado)* exhausted. **2** *(libro)* out of print; *(mercancía)* sold out.

agotador,-ra *adj* exhausting.

agotamiento *nm* exhaustion.

agotar *vt* to exhaust.

▶ *vpr* **agotarse 1** *(cansarse)* to become exhausted. **2** *(acabarse)* to run out [*pt* **ran**; *pp* **run**]; *(existencias)* to be sold out.

agraciado,-a *adj* **1** *(atractivo)* attractive. **2** *(ganador)* winning.

agradable *adj* nice, pleasant.

agradar *vi* to please: *esto me agrada*, I like this.

agradecer *vt* **1** *(dar las gracias a)* to thank: *gracias por venir*, thank you for coming. **2** *(estar agradecido por)* to be grateful for: *te estaría muy agradecido si vinieras*, I would be very grateful if you came.

▶ *vpr* **agradecerse** *(venir bien)* to be welcome: *siempre se agradece un descanso*, a rest is always welcome.

agradecido,-a *adj* grateful, thankful: *le quedaría muy agradecido si ...*, I would be very grateful if ....

agradecimiento *nm* gratitude, thankfulness.

agrado *nm* pleasure: *no es de su agrado*, it isn't to his liking.

agrandar *vt* **1** *(aumentar)* to enlarge. **2** *(exagerar)* to exaggerate.

▶ *vpr* **agrandarse** to enlarge, become larger.

agrario,-a *adj* agrarian.

agravante *nm & nf* **1** *(gen)* added difficulty. **2** JUR aggravating circumstance.

agravar *vt* to aggravate.

▶ *vpr* **agravarse** to get worse.

agredir *vt* to attack.

agregar *vt* to add.

▶ *vpr* **agregarse** to join.

agresión *nf* aggression.

agresivo,-a *adj* aggressive.

agresor,-ra *nm,f* aggressor.

agrícola *adj* agricultural.

agricultor,-ra *nm,f* farmer.

agricultura *nf* agriculture, farming.

agridulce *adj* **1** *(gen)* bittersweet. **2** *(salsa)* sweet and sour.

agrietar *vt-vpr* **agrietar(se)** to crack.

agrio,-a *adj* sour.

▶ *nm pl* **agrios** citrus fruits.

agrónomo,-a *nm,f* agronomist.

agrupación *nf* **1** *(acción)* grouping together. **2** *(asociación)* association.

agrupar *vt* to group, group together.

▶ *vpr* **agruparse 1** *(congregarse)* to group together. **2** *(asociarse)* to associate.

agua *nf* water.

● **estar con el agua en el cuello** to be up to one's neck in it.

● **estar más claro que el agua** to be as clear as day.

● **hacérsele la boca agua a uno** to make one's mouth water.

● **nunca digas de esta agua no beberé** never say never.

● **romper aguas**: *ha roto aguas*, her waters have broken.

■ **agua bendita** holy water.

■ **agua con gas** sparkling water.

■ **agua corriente** running water.

■ **agua de colonia** cologne, eau de cologne.

■ **agua del grifo** tap water.

■ **agua dulce** fresh water.

■ **agua mineral** mineral water.

■ **agua oxigenada** hydrogen peroxide.

■ **agua potable** drinking water.

■ **agua salada** salt water.

■ **agua sin gas** still water.

■ **aguas residuales** sewage *sing*.

■ **aguas termales** thermal waters.

aguacate *nm* avocado [*pl* **-s**], avocado pear.

aguacero *nm* heavy shower, downpour.

aguado,-a *adj* watered down.

aguafiestas *nmf* killjoy.

aguantar *vt* **1** *(sostener)* to hold [*pt & pp* **held**]; *(peso)* to support, bear [*pt* **bore**; *pp* **borne**]: *¿me aguantas la carpeta un momento?*, can you hold my folder for a minute?; *las vigas aguantan el techo*, the beams support the ceiling. **2** *(sufrir - frases afirmativas)* to put up with; *(- frases negativas)* to stand [*pt & pp* **stood**]: *no sé cómo aguanta a su marido*, I don't know how she puts up with her husband; *no aguanto a gente como él*, I can't stand people like him. **3** *(contener - respiración)* to hold; *(- risa, lágrimas)* to hold back [*pt & pp* **held**]. **4** *(durar)* to last: *el coche tendrá que aguantar un año más*, the car will have to last another year.

▶ *vpr* **aguantarse 1** *(contenerse)* to restrain

oneself. **2** *(resignarse)*: **tendrás que aguantarte**, you'll have to put up with it; **si te duele, te aguantas**, if it hurts, tough!

aguante *nm* **1** *(paciencia)* patience. **2** *(resistencia)* stamina.

aguar *vt* to water down.

• **aguarle la fiesta a ALGN** to spoil SB's fun [*pt & pp* **spoilt**].

aguardar *vt-vi* to wait *(for)*, await: **aguarda un momento**, wait a minute; **nos aguardan tiempos mejores**, better times are ahead; **no sé lo que me aguarda el futuro**, I don't know what the future has in store for me.

aguardiente *nm* liquor, brandy.

aguarrás *nm* turpentine.

agudeza *nf* **1** *(de dolor, sentidos)* sharpness. **2** *(viveza)* wit. **3** *(comentario)* witticism.

agudo,-a *adj* **1** *(afilado)* sharp. **2** *(dolor, acento, ángulo)* acute. **3** *(ingenioso)* witty. **4** *(voz)* high-pitched. **5** *(palabra)* oxytone.

aguijón *nm* **1** *(de animal)* sting. **2** *(de planta)* thorn, prickle. **3** *(estímulo)* sting, spur.

águila *nf* eagle.

aguileño,-a *adj* aquiline.

aguilucho *nm* eaglet.

aguinaldo *nm* Christmas bonus.

aguja *nf* **1** *(de coser, jeringuilla)* needle. **2** *(de reloj)* hand. **3** *(de tocadiscos)* stylus. **4** *(de torre, iglesia)* spire, steeple. **5** *(de tren)* GB point; US switch.

• **buscar una aguja en un pajar** to look for a needle in a haystack.

agujerear *vt* to makes holes in.

agujero *nm* hole.

▪ **agujero negro** black hole.

agujetas *nf pl* stiffness *sing*.

• **tener agujetas** to feel stiff [*pt & pp* **felt**].

aguzar *vt* **1** *(afilar)* to sharpen. **2** *(estimular)* to spur on.

• **aguzar el oído** to prick up one's ears.

ahí *adv* there: **¿estás ahí?**, are you there?

• **ahí abajo** down there.

• **ahí arriba** up there.

• **ahí fuera** out there.

• **ahí mismo** right here.

• **de ahí que** hence, therefore.

• **por ahí 1** *(lugar)* round there. **2** *(aproximadamente)* more or less.

ahijado,-a *nm,f* godchild [*pl* -**children**]; *(chico)* godson; *(chica)* goddaughter.

ahínco *nm* enthusiasm: **con ahínco**, enthusiastically.

ahogado,-a *adj* **1** *(persona)* drowned. **2** *(voz, llanto)* stifled.

ahogar *vt* **1** *(en agua -personas)* to drown; *(-plantas)* to soak. **2** *(reprimir)* to stifle: **ahogar las lágrimas**, to hold back one's tears.

▶ *vpr* **ahogarse 1** *(en agua)* to be drowned. **2** *(asfixiarse -gen)* to choke; *(-por el calor)* to suffocate. **3** *(motor)* to be flooded.

• **ahogarse en un vaso de agua** to make a mountain out of a molehill.

ahondar *vt* to deepen.

▶ *vt-vi* to go deep: **ahondar en un problema**, to examine a problem in depth.

ahora *adv* **1** *(en este momento)* now. **2** *(hace un momento)* a moment ago. **3** *(dentro de un momento)* in a minute, shortly: **ahora vuelvo**, I'll be back in a minute, I'll be right back.

• **ahora bien** however.

• **ahora mismo 1** (en este momento) right now. **2** (enseguida) right away.

• **ahora o nunca** now or never.

• **de ahora en adelante** from now on.

• **hasta ahora** until now, so far.

• **por ahora** for the time being.

ahorcar *vt* to hang.

▶ *vpr* **ahorcarse** to hang oneself.

ahorrador,-ra *adj* thrifty.

ahorrar *vt* *(tiempo, dinero, energía)* to save.

▶ *vpr* **ahorrarse** *(esfuerzo, problema)* to save oneself.

ahorros *nm pl* savings.

ahuecar *vt* **1** *(vaciar)* to hollow out. **2** *(descompactar)* to fluff out. **3** *(voz)* to deepen.

• **ahuecar el ala** to clear off.

ahumado,-a *adj* *(gen)* smoked; *(bacon)* smoky.

▶ *nm* **ahumado** *(proceso)* smoking.

ahumar *vt-vi* to smoke.

ahuyentar *vt* *(espantar)* to scare away; *(alejar)* to drive away.

aire *nm* **1** *(fluido)* air. **2** *(viento)* wind: **hace aire**, it's windy. **3** *(aspecto)* air, appearance. **4** *(estilo)* style. **5** *(música)* air, melody.

• **a mi aire** my way.

• **al aire libre** in the open air, outdoors.

● **cambiar de aires** to have a change of scene.

● **darse aires** to put on airs.

● **estar en el aire** to be in the air.

● **saltar por los aires** to blow up [*pt* **blew**; *pp* **blown**].

● **tomar el aire** to get some fresh air.

■ **aire acondicionado** air conditioning.

airear *vt* **1** *(ventilar)* to air. **2** *(asunto)* to publicize.

▶ *vpr* **airearse** to get some fresh air.

airoso,-a *adj* graceful.

● **salir airoso,-a** to be successful.

aislado,-a *adj* **1** *(apartado)* isolated. **2** *(eléctricamente)* insulated.

aislamiento *nm* **1** *(acción, estado)* isolation. **2** *(eléctrica)* insulation.

aislante *adj* insulating.

▶ *nm* insulator.

aislar *vt* **1** *(apartar)* to isolate. **2** *(eléctricamente)* to insulate.

▶ *vpr* **aislarse** to isolate oneself.

ajá *interj* aha!

ajedrez *nm* *(juego)* chess; *(tablero y piezas)* chess set.

ajeno,-a *adj* **1** *(de otro)* another's: *no me importan las opiniones ajenas*, I don't care about other people's opinions; *jugar en campo ajeno*, to play away from home. **2** *(indiferente)* not involved: *ajeno a la conversación*, not involved in the conversation. **3** *(ignorante)* unaware of, oblivious to: *estaba ajeno al peligro*, he was oblivious to the danger.

ajetreado,-a *adj* busy, hectic.

ajetreo *nm* bustle.

ajillo *loc* **al ajillo** with garlic.

ajo *nm* garlic.

● **estar en el ajo** to be in on it.

ajuar *nm* **1** *(de novia)* trousseau. **2** *(de bebé)* layette. **3** *(de casa)* furnishings.

ajustado,-a *adj* **1** *(ropa)* tight, close-fitting. **2** *(presupuesto)* tight. **3** *(resultado, victoria)* close.

ajustar *vt* **1** *(adaptar)* to adjust; *(uso técnico)* to fit: *se puede ajustar la temperatura*, the temperature can be adjusted. **2** *(apretar)* to tighten: *hay que ajustar los tornillos*, you must tighten the screws. **3** *(acordar)* to arrange.

▶ *vpr* **ajustarse 1** *(ceñirse)* to fit. **2** *(ponerse de acuerdo)* to come to an agreement.

● **ajustar cuentas 1** (dinero) to settle up. **2** (asunto pendiente) to settle an old score.

ajusticiar *vt* to execute.

al *contr* → a.

ala *nf* **1** *(de ave)* wing. **2** *(de sombrero)* brim. **3** *(de hélice)* blade. **4** *(futbolista)* winger.

● **cortarle las alas a ALGN** to clip SB's wings.

● **dar alas a ALGN** to encourage SB.

■ **ala delta** hang glider.

alabanza *nf* praise.

alabar *vt* to praise.

▶ *vpr* **alabarse** to boast.

alabastro *nm* alabaster.

alacena *nf* wall cupboard.

alacrán *nm* scorpion.

alado,-a *adj* winged.

alambre *nm* wire.

alameda *nf* **1** *(bosque)* poplar grove. **2** *(paseo)* avenue.

álamo *nm* poplar.

alarde *nm* display.

● **hacer alarde de** to flaunt, show off [*pt* **showed**; *pp* **shown**].

alargado,-a *adj* long, elongated.

alargar *vt* **1** *(prenda)* to lengthen; *(cuerda)* to stretch: *he alargado la falda*, I've lengthened my skirt. **2** *(prolongar)* to prolong, extend: *decidimos alargar las vacaciones*, we decided to prolong our holiday; *quieren alargar el permiso de maternidad*, they want to extend maternity leave. **3** *(brazo, mano)* to stretch out: *alargó la mano para coger un trozo de pan*, he stretched his hand out to get a piece of bread. **4** *(dar)* to pass: *¿me alargas un plato?*, can you pass me a plate?

▶ *vpr* **alargarse** to go on for a long time.

alarido *nm* screech, yell.

alarma *nf* alarm.

● **dar la alarma** to raise the alarm.

■ **alarma antirrobo 1** *(para casa)* burglar alarm. **2** *(para coche)* car alarm.

■ **alarma contra incendios** fire alarm.

alarmante *adj* alarming.

alarmar *vt* to alarm.

▶ *vpr* **alarmarse** to be alarmed.

alba *nf* dawn, daybreak.

● **al alba** at dawn, at daybreak.

albañil *nm* bricklayer.

albaricoque *nm* apricot.

alberca *nf* water tank.
albergar *vt* **1** *(alojar)* to put up, accommodate. **2** *(esperanzas)* to cherish. **3** *(duda, rencor)* to harbour.
▶ *vpr* **albergarse** to stay.
albergue *nm* **1** *(hostal)* hostel. **2** *(refugio)* shelter.
■ **albergue juvenil** youth hostel.
albino,-a *adj - nm,f* albino.
albóndiga *nf* meatball.
albornoz *nm* bathrobe.
alborotado,-a *adj* **1** *(agitado)* agitated, excited. **2** *(desordenado)* untidy. **3** *(irreflexivo)* reckless.
alborotador,-ra *adj* rowdy.
▶ *nm,f* troublemaker.
alborotar *vt* **1** *(agitar)* to agitate, excite. **2** *(desordenar)* to make untidy. **3** *(sublevar)* to incite to rebel.
▶ *vi* to make a racket.
▶ *vpr* **alborotarse** to get excited.
alboroto *nm* **1** *(griterío)* din, racket. **2** *(desorden)* uproar, commotion.
albufera *nf* lagoon.
álbum *nm* album.
alcachofa *nf* artichoke.
alcalde *nm* mayor.
alcaldesa *nf* mayoress.
alcaldía *nf* **1** *(cargo)* mayorship. **2** *(oficina)* mayor's office.
alcance *nm* **1** *(de persona)* reach: *fuera del alcance de los niños*, out of children's reach. **2** *(de arma, emisora)* range. **3** *(trascendencia)* scope, importance. **4** *(inteligencia)*: *persona de pocos alcances*, person of low intelligence.
● **al alcance de la mano** within arm's reach, at hand.
● **al alcance de la vista** within sight.
alcantarilla *nf* *(cloaca)* sewer; *(boca)* drain.
alcantarillado *nm* sewer system.
alcanzar *vt* **1** *(lugar, edad, temperatura)* to reach; *(persona)* to catch up with [*pt & pp* **caught**]: *ya alcanza la estantería*, she can reach the shelf now. **2** *(pasar)* to pass, hand over: *alcánzame el pan*, pass me the bread. **3** *(conseguir)* to attain, achieve.
▶ *vi* *(ser suficiente)* to be sufficient, be enough: *el pan no alcanza para todos*, there's not enough bread for everyone.
● **alcanzar a + inf** to manage to + inf: *no*

alcancé a oírlo, I didn't manage to hear it.
alcaparra *nf* caper.
alcázar *nm* **1** *(fortaleza)* fortress. **2** *(palacio)* palace.
alcoba *nf* bedroom.
alcohol *nm* alcohol.
● **sin alcohol** non-alcoholic.
alcohólico,-a *adj - nm,f* alcoholic.
alcoholismo *nm* alcoholism.
alcornoque *nm* **1** *(árbol)* cork oak. **2** *(persona)* blockhead.
aldaba *nf* **1** *(llamador)* knocker. **2** *(pestillo)* latch.
aldea *nf* hamlet, small village.
aldeano,-a *nm,f* villager.
aleación *nf* alloy.
alegar *vt* to allege, plead.
● **alegar que** to claim that.
alegrar *vt* **1** *(poner contento)* to make happy: *me alegra saberlo*, I'm pleased to hear it. **2** *(animar -persona)* to cheer up; *(-habitación)* to brighten up.
▶ *vpr* **alegrarse 1** *(ponerse contento)* to be happy, be pleased: *se alegró mucho de vernos*, she was very pleased to see us. **2** *fam (emborracharse)* to get tipsy.
alegre *adj* **1** *(persona - contenta)* happy; *(- borracha)* tipsy. **2** *(color)* bright. **3** *(música)* lively. **4** *(espacio)* cheerful.
alegría *nf* happiness.
● **¡qué alegría!**: *¡qué alegría volverte a ver!*, how wonderful to see you again!
alejamiento *nm* **1** *(separación)* distance, separation. **2** *(entre personas)* estrangement.
alejar *vt* **1** *(llevar lejos)* to move away. **2** *(separar)* to separate, estrange.
▶ *vpr* **alejarse** to go away, move away.
aleluya *interj* hallelujah.
alemán,-ana *adj* German.
▶ *nm,f (persona)* German.
▶ *nm* **alemán** *(idioma)* German.
Alemania *nf* Germany.
alentar *vt* to encourage.
alergia *nf* allergy.
● **tener alergia a** to be allergic to.
alérgico,-a *adj* allergic.
alero *nm* **1** *(del tejado)* eaves *pl*. **2** *(futbolista)* winger.
alerta *adv* on the alert: *estuvimos alerta toda la noche*, we were on the alert the whole night.

▶ *nf* alert.

▶ *interj* look out!

● **dar la voz de alerta** to give the alert.

aleta *nf* **1** *(de pescado)* fin. **2** *(de la nariz)* wing.

aletargar *vt* to make drowsy.

▶ *vpr* **aletargarse** to get drowsy.

aletear *vi* to flutter.

alevosía *nf* treachery.

● **con alevosía** with malice aforethought.

alfabético,-a *adj* alphabetical.

alfabeto *nm* alphabet.

alfalfa *nf* alfalfa, lucerne.

alfarería *nf* pottery.

alfarero,-a *nm,f* potter.

alféizar *nm* windowsill.

alférez *nm* second lieutenant.

alfil *nm* bishop.

alfiler *nm* **1** *(en costura)* pin. **2** *(joya)* brooch.

● **no caber ni un alfiler** to be crammed full.

■ **alfiler de corbata** tiepin.

alfombra *nf (grande)* carpet; *(pequeña)* rug.

alfombrar *vt* to carpet.

alga *nf* alga; *(marina)* seaweed; *(de agua dulce)* weed.

algarabía *nf* hubbub.

algarroba *nf* **1** *(fruto)* carob bean. **2** *(planta)* vetch.

álgebra *nf* algebra.

algo *pron (en frases afirmativas)* something; *(en frases interrogativas)* anything: **vamos a tomar algo**, let's have something to drink; *¿hay algo que no entiendas?*, is there anything you don't understand?

▶ *adv (un poco)* a bit, a little: **te queda algo grande**, it's a bit too big for you.

● **algo así** something like that.

● **algo es algo** something is better than nothing.

● **por algo será** there must be a reason for it.

algodón *nm* cotton.

■ **algodón hidrófilo** cotton wool.

algodonero,-a *adj* cotton.

alguacil *nm* bailiff.

alguien *pron (en frases afirmativas)* somebody, someone; *(en frases interrogativas y negativas)* anybody, anyone: **alguien se lo habrá olvidado**, somebody must have left it behind; *¿conoces alguien que*

hable japonés?, do you know anyone who speaks Japanese?

algún *adj* → alguno,-a.

alguno,-a *adj (en frases afirmativas)* some; *(en frases interrogativas)* any; *(en frases negativas)* no, not ... any: **me he comprado algunos libros**, I've bought some books; *¿tienes alguna idea mejor?*, do you have any better idea?; **sin éxito alguno**, with no success at all; **no vino persona alguna**, nobody came.

▶ *pron (en frases afirmativas)* someone, somebody; *(en frases interrogativas)* anybody: **hubo alguno que se quejó**, there was somebody who complained; **puedes quedarte con alguna de estas fotos**, you can keep some of those pictures; *¿alguno sabe la respuesta?*, does anyone know the answer?

● **alguno,-a que otro,-a** some, a few.

alhaja *nf* **1** *(joya)* jewel. **2** *(objeto valioso)* valuable thing.

alhelí *nm* wallflower.

aliado,-a *adj* allied.

▶ *nm,f* ally.

alianza *nf* **1** *(pacto)* alliance. **2** *(anillo)* wedding ring.

aliar *vt* to ally.

▶ *vpr* **aliarse** to form an alliance.

alias *adv* alias.

▶ *nm* alias.

alicates *nm pl* pliers.

aliciente *nm* incentive, inducement.

aliento *nm* **1** *(respiración)* breath: **le huele el aliento**, his breath smells. **2** *(ánimo)* spirit, courage.

● **contener el aliento** to hold one's breath [*pt & pp* **held**].

● **dar aliento a** ALGN to encourage SB.

● **sin aliento** breathless.

aligerar *vt* **1** *(descargar)* to lighten. **2** *(aliviar)* to alleviate. **3** *(acelerar)* to speed up.

alijo *nm* consignment: **un alijo de drogas**, a consignment of drugs.

alimaña *nf* vermin.

alimentación *nf* **1** *(acción)* feeding. **2** *(comida)* food; *(dieta)* diet: **trabaja en el ramo de la alimentación**, she works in the food industry; **una alimentación sana**, a healthy diet.

■ **alimentación manual** INFORM manual feed.

alimentar *vt* **1** *(dar alimento a)* to feed [*pt*

& pp **fed**]: *la leona alimenta a sus crías*, the lioness feeds her cubs. **2** *(pasiones etc)* to encourage. **3** INFORM to feed [*pt & pp* **fed**].

▶ *vi (servir de alimento)* to be nutritious, be nourishing: *el pescado alimenta mucho*, fish is very nutritious.

▶ *vpr* **alimentarse** to feed oneself [*pt & pp* **fed**].

● **alimentarse de algo** tto live on STH.

alimenticio,-a *adj* nutritious.

alimento *nm* food.

alinear *vt-vpr* **alinear(se)** to align, line up.

aliñar *vt (ensalada)* to dress; *(guiso)* to season.

aliño *nm (de ensalada)* dressing; *(de guiso)* seasoning.

alisar *vt* to smooth.

alistarse *vpr* to enlist.

aliviar *vt* **1** *(enfermedad, dolor)* to relieve. **2** *(carga, peso)* to lighten. **3** *(consolar)* to comfort.

▶ *vpr* **aliviarse** to get better.

alivio *nm* relief: *¡qué alivio!*, what a relief!

● **de alivio** *fam* dreadful.

allá *adv* **1** *(lugar)* there: *allá va tu madre*, there goes your mother. **2** *(tiempo)* back: *allá por los años sesenta*, back in the sixties.

● **allá abajo** down there.

● **allá arriba** up there.

● **allá tú/vosotros** that's your problem.

● **el más allá** the beyond.

● **más allá** further, further on.

allanar *vt* **1** *(terreno)* to level, flatten. **2** *(dificultad etc)* to overcome [*pt* **overcame**; *pp* **overcome**].

allegado,-a *adj* close.

▶ *nm,f* relative.

allí *adv* **1** *(lugar)* there. **2** *(tiempo)* then, at that moment: *hasta allí*, up until then.

● **allí está** there it is.

● **allí arriba** up there.

● **por allí** that way.

alma *nf* soul.

● **en el alma**: *te lo agradezco en el alma*, I thank you from the bottom of my heart; *lo siento en el alma*, I'm truly sorry.

● **no había ni un alma** there was not a soul.

● **no puedo con mi alma** I'm shattered.

● **se me cayó el alma a los pies** my heart sank.

● **ser el alma de la fiesta** to be the life and soul of the party.

almacén *nm* **1** *(depósito)* warehouse. **2** *(habitación)* storeroom.

▶ *nm pl* **almacenes** department store *sing*.

almacenamiento *nm* storage.

almacenar *vt* **1** *(gen)* to store. **2** *(acumular)* to store up.

almanaque *nm* almanac.

almeja *nf* clam.

almendra *nf* almond.

■ **almendra garapiñada** sugared almond.

almendro *nm* almond tree.

almíbar *nm* syrup.

almidón *nm* starch.

almirante *nm* admiral.

almohada *nf* pillow.

● **consultar algo con la almohada** to sleep on STH [*pt & pp* **slept**].

almohadilla *nf* **1** *(cojín)* small cushion. **2** *(para alfileres)* pin cushion. **3** *(tampón)* inkpad.

almohadón *nm* cushion.

almorzar *vi* to have lunch.

▶ *vt* to have for lunch.

almuerzo *nm* lunch.

alocado,-a *adj* wild, reckless.

alojamiento *nm* lodging, accommodation.

alojar *vt* **1** *(hospedar)* to put up: *alojaron a los refugiados en varios albergues*, they put the refugees up in different hostels. **2** *(tener espacio para)* to accommodate, house: *la Villa Olímpica puede alojar a 12.000 atletas*, the Olympic Village can accommodate 12,000 athletes.

▶ *vpr* **alojarse** *(persona)* to stay; *(bala)* to lodge.

alondra *nf* lark.

alpargata *nf* rope-soled sandal, espadrille.

alpinismo *nm* mountaineering.

alpinista *nmf* mountaineer, mountain climber.

alpiste *nm* birdseed.

alquilar *vt* **1** *(dar en alquiler - casa)* to rent out, GB let [*pt & pp* **let**]; *(- coche, bicicleta)* to hire, rent; *(- aparato)* to rent. **2** *(tomar en alquiler - casa)* to rent; *(- coche, bicicleta)* to hire, rent.

● **se alquila piso** GB flat to let; US apartment for rent.

alquiler *nm* **1** *(cesión - de casa)* renting, GB letting; *(- de coche etc)* hire, rental; *(- de aparato)* rental. **2** *(cuota - de casa)* rent; *(- de coche etc)* hire charge; *(- de aparato)* rental.

alquitrán *nm* tar.

alrededor *adv* **1** *(en torno)* around: *mira alrededor*, look around. **2** *(al rededor de, en torno a)* around; *(aproximadamente)* around, about: *estabn sentados alrededor de la mesa*, they sat around the table; *volveré alrededor de las nueve*, I'll be back around nine o'clock; *alrededor de veinte*, about twenty.

► *nm pl* **alrededores** surrounding area *sing.*

alta *nf* **1** *(a un enfermo)* discharge: *dar de alta*, to discharge from hospital. **2** *(ingreso)* membership: *darse de alta en un club*, to join a club.

altar *nm* altar.

altavoz *nm* loudspeaker.

alteración *nf* **1** *(cambio)* alteration. **2** *(excitación)* agitation. **3** *(alboroto)* disturbance.

● **alteración del orden público** breach of the peace.

alterar *vt* **1** *(cambiar)* to alter, change. **2** *(enfadar)* to annoy. **3** *(preocupar)* to disturb, upset *[pt & pp upset]*.

► *vpr* **alterarse** **1** *(cambiar)* to change. **2** *(deteriorarse)* to go bad, go off. **3** *(enfadarse)* to lose one's temper *[pt & pp lost]*.

altercado *nm* **1** *(discusión)* argument. **2** *(disturbio)* disturbance: *después del partido hubo algún altercado*, there were diturbances after the match.

● **tener un altercado con** ALGN to have an argument with SB.

alternar *vt-vi (sucederse)* to alternate.

► *vi (relacionarse)* to socialize, mix.

alternativa *nf* alternative.

● **no tener alternativa** to have no alternative, have no choice.

alternativo,-a *adj* alternative.

alteza *nf* Highness.

● **su alteza real** *(hombre)* His Royal Highness; *(mujer)* Her Royal Highness.

altibajos *nm pl* ups and downs: *los alti-*

bajos de la vida, the ups and downs of life.

altillo *nm (armario)* cupboard.

altitud *nf* height, altitude.

altivez *nf* haughtiness, arrogance.

altivo,-a *adj* haughty, arrogant.

alto *nm (parada)* halt, stop: *dar el alto*, to call to a halt, stop.

► *interj* ¡**alto**! halt!, stop!

■ **alto el fuego** ceasefire.

alto,-a *adj* **1** *(gen)* high: *tacón alto*, high heel; *la marea está alta*, it's high tide; *una puntuación muy alta*, a very high score. **2** *(persona, edificio, árbol)* tall: *un hombre alto*, a tall man. **3** *(sonido, voz)* loud: *la música está muy alta*, the music is very loud; *dilo en voy alta*, say it loud. **4** *(ejecutivo, funcionario)* high, top.

► *nm* **alto 1** *(altura)*: *Pepe mide dos metros de alto*, Pepe's two metres tall. **2** *(elevación)* height, hillock.

► *adv* **1** *(volar, subir)* high: *los aviones vuelan muy alto*, aeroplanes fly very high. **2** *(hablar)* loud, loudly: *habla más alto*, speak more loudly.

● **a altas horas de la noche** late at night.

● **en lo alto de** on top of.

● **pasar por alto** to pass over.

● **por todo lo alto** in a grand way.

● **tirando alto** at the most.

■ **alta costura** haute couture.

■ **alta fidelidad** high fidelity.

■ **alta mar** high seas.

altruismo *nm* altruism.

altruista *nmf* altruist.

altura *nf* **1** *(gen)* height: *las alturas me dan vértigo*, heights make me dizzy. **2** *(persona)* tall: *mide dos metros de altura*, he's two metres tall. **3** *(cosa)* high: *mide dos metros de altura*, it's two metres high. **4** *(altitud)* altitude. **5** *(nivel)* level: *no te pongas a su altura*, don't sink to his level. **6** *(valía)* worth; *(categoría)* standing.

● **a estas alturas** at this stage: *a estas alturas del curso*, at this stage of the course; *a estas alturas de la noche*, at this time of night.

● **a la altura de** next to: *a la altura de la catedral*, next to the cathedral.

● **estar a la altura de** ALGN to measure up to SB.

- **estar a la altura de las circunstancias** to be worthy of the occasion.

alubia *nf* bean.

alucinación *nf* hallucination.

alucinante *adj* **1** *(substancia)* hallucinatory. **2** *fam (increíble)* mind-blowing.

alucinar *vi* **1** *(tener alucinaciones)* to hallucinate. **2** *fam (asombrarse)* to be amazed: **me alucina lo bien que canta**, I'm amazed how well she sings.

alud *nm* avalanche.

aludir *vi* to allude.

alumbrado *nm* lighting.

■ **alumbrado público** street lighting.

alumbrar *vt* **1** *(iluminar -calles, habitación)* to light [*pt & pp* **lighted** o **lit**]; *(monumento, estadio)* to light up, illuminate. **2** *(enseñar)* to enlighten.
▶ *vi* **1** *(gen)* to give light. **2** *(parir)* to give birth.

aluminio *nm* aluminium, US aluminum.

alumno,-a *nm,f (de colegio)* pupil; *(de universidad)* student.

alunizar *vi* to land on the moon.

alusión *nf* allusion, reference.

- **hacer alusión a** to allude to.

aluvión *nm* flood.

alza *nf* **1** *(de precios)* rise, increase. **2** *(de zapato)* raised insole.

- **en alza** rising, growing.

alzamiento *nm* **1** *(elevación)* raising, lifting. **2** *(rebelión)* uprising, insurrection.

alzar *vt* **1** *(levantar -mano, cabeza)* to raise, lift; *(voz)* to raise; *(cosa, persona)* to lift up. **2** *(construir)* to build [*pt & pp* **built**].
▶ *vpr* **alzarse 1** *(levantarse)* to rise [*pt* **rose**; *pp* **risen**], get up. **2** *(sublevarse)* to rise [*pt* **rose**; *pp* **risen**], rebel.

- **alzarse con** *(premio)* to win; *(botín)* to carry off [*pt* **ran**; *pp* **run**].

ama *nf*.

■ **ama de casa** housewife [*pl* **-ves**].

■ **ama de llaves** housekeeper.

amabilidad *nf* kindness: **¿tendría la amabilidad de acompañarme?**, would you be so kind as to come with me?; **tenga la amabilidad de comunicarle la noticia**, please be so kind as to tell him the news.

- **con amabilidad** kindly.

amable *adj* kind, nice: **muy amable por su parte**, that's very kind of you.

amaestrar *vt* to train.

amainar *vi (viento, temporal)* to die down.

amamantar *vt* to breast-feed, suckle.

amanecer *vi* **1** *(hacerse de día)* to dawn. **2** *(clarear)* to get light: **en verano amanece pronto**, it gets light early in summer. **3** *(despertar)* to wake up [*pt* **woke**; *pp* **woken**]: **amanecimos en Praga**, we woke up in Prague; **la ciudad amaneció nevada**, in the morning the city was white with snow.
▶ *nm* dawn, daybreak: **al amanecer**, at dawn, at daybreak.

amanerado,-a *adj* affected.

amansar *vt* to tame.

amante *adj* loving, fond.
▶ *nmf* lover.

amapola *nf* poppy.

amar *vt* to love.

amargado,-a *adj* embittered, resentful.
▶ *nm,f* misery guts.

amargar *vt* **1** *(persona)* to make bitter. **2** *(ocasión)* to spoil [*pt & pp* **spoilt**].
▶ *vi (sabor)* to taste bitter.
▶ *vpr* **amargarse** to become bitter.

- **amargarle la existencia a** ALGN to make SB's life a misery.

amargo,-a *adj* bitter.

amargura *nf* bitterness.

- **con amargura** bitterly.

amarillento,-a *adj* yellowish.

amarillo,-a *adj* yellow.
▶ *nm* **amarillo** yellow.

amarra *nf* mooring cable.

- **soltar amarras** to cast off [*pt & pp* **cast**].

amarrar *vt* **1** *(atar)* to tie, fasten. **2** to moor *(embarcación)*.

amasar *vt* **1** *(masa)* to knead; *(cemento)* to mix. **2** *(dinero)* to amass.

amateur *adj - nmf* amateur.

amazona *nf* horsewoman [*pl* **-women**].

ámbar *nm* amber.

ambición *nf* ambition.

- **tener ambición** to be ambitious.

ambicionar *vt* to want, aspire to: **siempre ambicionó ser rico**, it was always his ambition to be rich.

ambicioso,-a *adj* ambitious.

ambiental *adj* **1** *(contaminación, impacto)* environmental. **2** *(música)* background.

ambiente *nm* **1** *(aire)* air, atmosphere: **el ambiente está muy cargado**, the air's very stuffy in here. **2** *(entorno)* environment; *(de casa, ciudad, época)* atmosphere: *un ambiente de trabajo agradable*, a pleasant working environment; *un ambiente familiar feliz*, a happy home environment; *hay muy buen ambiente entre los jugadores*, there is a very good atmosphere among the players; *los colores cálidos crean un ambiente íntimo*, warm colours create an intimate atmosphere. **3** *(animación)* life, atmosphere: *en esta ciudad no hay ambiente*, this town's dead.

● **el ambiente (gay)** the gay scene.
ambigüedad *nf* ambiguity.
ambiguo,-a *adj* ambiguous.
ámbito *nm* **1** *(espacio)* sphere: *en el ámbito nacional*, nationwide. **2** *(campo)* field: *en el ámbito de la informática*, in the computer science field.
ambos,-as *adj-pron* both: *os felicito a ambos*, I congratulate both of you.
ambulancia *nf* ambulance.
ambulante *adj* itinerant, travelling.
ambulatorio *nm* surgery, clinic.
amén *nm* amen.
amenaza *nf* threat.
■ **amenaza de bomba** bomb scare.
■ **amenaza de muerte** death threat.
amenazar *vt-vi* to threaten: *el edificio amenaza ruina*, the building is on the verge of collapse.
● **amenazar con hacer algo** to threaten to do STH.
ameno,-a *adj (agradable)* pleasant; *(entretenido)* entertaining.
América *nf* America.
■ **América Central** Central America.
■ **América del Norte** North America.
■ **América del Sur** South America.
■ **América Latina** Latin America.
americana *nf* jacket.
americanismo *nm* Americanism.
americano,-a *adj - nm,f* American.
ametralladora *nf* machine gun.
amianto *nm* asbestos.
amígdala *nf* tonsil.
amigo,-a *adj* **1** *(gen)* friendly: *son muy amigos*, they're good friends. **2** *(aficionado)* fond: *no es amiga de la lectura*, she's not fond of reading.
▶ *nm,f* **1** *(gen)* friend. **2** *(novio)* boyfriend; *(novia)* girlfriend.

● **hacerse amigo,-a de** to make friends with.
■ **amigo,-a íntimo,-a** very close friend.
amistad *nf* friendship.
▶ *nf pl* **amistades** friends.
● **hacer amistad con ALGN** to make friends with SB.
amistoso,-a *adj* friendly.
amnesia *nf* amnesia.
amnistía *nf* amnesty.
amo *nm* **1** *(señor)* master. **2** *(dueño)* owner.
amodorrarse *vpr* to become drowsy.
amoldar *vt* to adapt, adjust.
▶ *vpr* **amoldarse** to adapt oneself.
amonestar *vt* **1** *(reprender)* to reprove. **2** *(advertir)* to warn.
amoniaco *nm* ammonia.
amontonar *vt (cosas)* to pile up.
▶ *vpr* **amontonarse** **1** *(problemas, trabajo)* to pile up. **2** *(gente)* to crowd together.
amor *nm* love.
● **amor a primera vista** love at first sight.
● **hacer el amor** to make love.
● **por amor al arte** for the love of it.
■ **amor propio** self-esteem.
amoratado,-a *adj* **1** *(de frío)* blue. **2** *(de un golpe)* black and blue.
amordazar *vt* **1** *(persona)* to gag. **2** *(perro)* to muzzle.
amorío *nm* love affair.
amoroso,-a *adj* loving, affectionate.
amortiguador *nm* shock absorber.
amortiguar *vt* **1** *(golpe etc)* to deaden, cushion. **2** *(sonido)* to muffle.
amotinarse *vpr* to rebel, mutiny.
amparar *vt* to protect, shelter.
▶ *vpr* **ampararse** **1** *(protegerse)* to take shelter, protect oneself. **2** **ampararse en** *(una ley)* to seek protection in [*pt & pp* **sought**].
amparo *nm* **1** *(protección)* protection. **2** *(refugio)* shelter.
ampliación *nf* **1** *(de edificio, plazo)* extension. **2** *(de negocio, mercado)* expansion. **3** *(de fotografía)* enlargement.
ampliar *vt* **1** *(edificio, plazo)* to extend. **2** *(negocio, mercado)* to expand. **3** *(estudios)* to further. **4** *(fotografía)* to enlarge, blow up [*pt* **blew**; *pp* **blown**].
amplio,-a *adj* **1** *(espacioso)* roomy, spacious: *una vivienda amplia*, a spacious

house. **2** *(prenda)* loose, loose-fitting: *una camisa amplia*, a loose shirt. **3** *(margen, gama)* wide; *(mayoría)* large.

ampolla *nf* **1** *(en la piel)* blister. **2** *(burbuja)* bubble. **3** *(para líquidos)* ampoule.

amueblar *vt* to furnish.

amuleto *nm* charm, amulet.

■ **amuleto de la suerte** lucky charm.

anal *adj* anal.

analfabeto,-a *adj - nm,f* illiterate.

analgésico,-a *adj* analgesic.

▶ *nm* **analgésico** analgesic.

análisis *nm* analysis [*pl* **-ses**].

● **hacer un análisis de algo** to analyse STH.

■ **análisis de sangre** blood test.

analizar *vt* to analyse.

anaranjado,-a *adj* orange.

▶ *nm* **anaranjado** orange.

anarquía *nf* anarchy.

anarquista *adj - nmf* anarchist.

anatomía *nf* anatomy.

anca *nf* haunch.

■ **ancas de rana** frogs' legs.

ancho,-a *adj* **1** *(calle, cama, habitación)* wide; *(espalda, cara)* broad. **2** *(prenda)* loose, loose-fitting: *esos pantalones le quedan muy anchos*, those trousers are too big for you.

▶ *nm* **ancho** breadth, width.

● **a sus anchas 1** comfortable. **2** at one's ease.

● **estar muy ancho** to have plenty of space.

● **de ancho**: *tres metros de ancho*, three metres wide.

● **quedarse tan ancho,-a** to behave as if nothing had happened.

anchoa *nf* anchovy.

anchura *nf* breadth, width.

anciano,-a *adj* elderly.

▶ *nm,f (hombre)* elderly man [*pl* **men**]; *(mujer)* elderly woman [*pl* **women**].

ancla *nf* anchor.

anclar *vi* to anchor.

andadas.

● **volver a las andadas** to go back to one's old tricks.

andaluz,-za *adj* Andalusian.

▶ *nm,f (persona)* Andalusian.

▶ *nm* **andaluz** *(dialecto)* Andalusian.

andamio *nm* scaffolding.

andar *vi* **1** *(caminar)* to walk: *andaba por la calle principal*, I was walking along the main street; *se fue a casa andando*, she walked home. **2** *(moverse)* to go: *este coche anda despacio*, this car goes very slowly. **3** *(funcionar)* to work, go: *este reloj no anda*, this watch doesn't work; *el coche nuevo anda muy bien*, the new car goes very well. **4** *(estar)* to be: *¿cómo andas?*, how are you?, how's it going?; *¿quién anda por ahí?*, who's there?; *anda por los cincuenta*, he's around fifty years old.

▶ *nm* walk, pace.

● **¡anda ya!** come off it!

● **andar de puntillas** to tiptoe.

● **andar con cuidado, andarse con cuidado** to be careful.

● **andarse por las ramas** to beat about the bush [*pt* **beat**; *pp* **beaten**].

● **todo se andará** all in good time.

andén *nm* platform.

Andes *nm pl* **los Andes** the Andes.

Andorra *nm* Andorra.

andorrano,-a *adj - nm,f* Andorran.

andrajo *nm* rag, tatter.

andrajoso,-a *adj (persona)* ragged; *(ropa)* ragged, in tatters.

anécdota *nf* anecdote.

anemia *nf* anaemia.

anestesia *nf* anaesthesia.

anestesiar *vt* to anaesthetize.

anestésico *nm* anaesthetic.

anexo,-a *adj* attached, joined: *el documento anexo*, the attached document.

▶ *nm* **anexo** annex.

anfibio,-a *adj* amphibious.

▶ *nm* **anfibio** amphibian.

anfiteatro *nm* amphitheatre.

anfitrión,-ona *nm,f (hombre)* host; *(mujer)* hostess.

ángel *nm* angel.

■ **ángel de la guarda** guardian angel.

angina *nf* angina.

● **tener anginas** to have a sore throat.

■ **angina de pecho** angina pectoris.

anglosajón,-na *adj* Anglosaxon.

▶ *nm,f (persona)* Anglosaxon.

▶ *nm* **anglosajón** *(idioma)* Anglosaxon.

angosto,-a *adj* narrow.

anguila *nf* eel.

angula *nf* elver.

ángulo *nm* **1** *(geometría)* angle. **2** *(rincón)* corner.

- **ángulo agudo** acute angle.
- **ángulo muerto** blind spot.
- **ángulo recto** right angle.

angustia *nf* anguish, distress.

angustiar *vt* **1** *(afligir)* to distress. **2** *(preocupar)* to worry.

▶ *vpr* **angustiarse 1** *(afligirse)* to become distressed. **2** *(preocuparse)* to worry.

angustioso,-a *adj* distressing.

anhelar *vt* to long for, yearn for.

anidar *vi* to nest.

anilla *nf* ring.

anillo *nm* ring.

- **venir como anillo al dedo** to be opportune.
- **anillo de boda** wedding ring.
- **anillo de compromiso** engagement ring.

animación *nf* **1** *(actividad)* activity. **2** *(viveza)* liveliness. **3** *(película)* animation.

animado,-a *adj* **1** *(persona)* cheerful. **2** *(situación)* animated, lively. **3** *(calle)* full of people.

animal *adj* **1** *(reino, instinto)* animal. **2** *(persona)* stupid.

▶ *nm* **1** *(ser vivo)* animal. **2** *(persona bruta)* blockhead.

- **animal de carga** beast of burden.
- **animal doméstico 1** *(de granja)* domestic animal. **2** *(de compañía)* pet.

animar *vt* **1** *(alentar)* to encourage. **2** *(alegrar - persona)* to cheer up; *(- habitación, calle)* to brighten up; *(- fiesta, reunión)* to liven up.

▶ *vpr* **animarse 1** *(alegrarse - persona)* to cheer up; *(- fiesta, reunión)* to liven up. **2** *(decidirse)* to make up one's mind.

ánimo *nm* **1** *(estado emocional)* spirits: *su ánimo no decayó ni un momento*, she never once lost her spirits. **2** *(aliento)* encouragement: *gritos de ánimo*, cries of encouragement. **3** *(intención)* intention, purpose: *no tiene ánimo de irse*, she has no intention of going. **4** *(valor)* courage.

▶ *interj* cheer up!

- **dar ánimos a ALGN** to encourage SB.

animoso,-a *adj* brave, courageous.

aniquilar *vt* to annihilate, destroy.

anís *nm* **1** *(planta)* anise; *(semilla)* aniseed. **2** *(bebida)* anisette.

aniversario *nm* anniversary.

- **aniversario de boda** wedding anniversary.

ano *nm* anus.

anoche *adv* last night.

anochecer *vi* **1** *(hacerse de noche)* to get dark. **2** *(persona)* to be at nightfall, reach at nightfall: *anochecimos en Burgos*, we were in Burgos at nightfall.

▶ *nm* nightfall, dusk.

- **al anochecer** at nightfall, at dusk.

anomalía *nf* anomaly.

anónimo,-a *adj* anonymous.

▶ *nm* **anónimo** *(carta)* anonymous letter.

anorak *nm* anorak.

anorexia *nf* anorexia.

anormal *adj* abnormal.

anotación *nf* note, annotation.

anotar *vt* **1** *(apuntar)* to make a note of, take down: *he anotado la matrícula*, I've made a note of the registration number. **2** *(acotar)* to annotate. **3** *(tanto)* score.

ansia *nf* **1** *(deseo)* longing: *tener ansia de algo*, to have a longing for STH; *tener ansias de hacer algo*, to long to do STH. **2** *(sufrimiento)* anguish.

ansiar *vt* to long for, yearn for.

ansiedad *nf* anxiety.

ansioso,-a *adj* **1** *(deseoso)* eager. **2** *(preocupado)* anxious.

- **estar ansioso,-a por hacer algo** to be eager to do STH.

antagonista *adj* antagonistic.

▶ *nmf* antagonist.

ante¹ *prep* **1** *(delante de)* before: *testificar ante el juez*, to give evidence before the judge. **2** *(frente a)* in the face of: *ante estas circunstancias*, under the circumstances; *no se desanima ante las dificultades*, she doesn't lose heart in the face of difficulties.

- **ante todo 1** *(primero)* first of all. **2** *(por encima de)* above all.

ante² *nm* **1** *(animal)* elk, moose. **2** *(piel)* suede.

anteanoche *adv* the night before last.

anteayer *adv* the day before yesterday.

antebrazo *nm* forearm.

antecedente *adj - nm* antecedent.

▶ *nm pl* **antecedentes** *(de una persona)* record *sing*; *(de una situación)* background *sing*.

- **antecedentes penales** criminal record *sing*.

anteceder *vt* to antecede, precede.

antecesor,-ra *nm,f* **1** *(en un cargo)* predecessor. **2** *(antepasado)* ancestor.

antelación.

● **con antelación** in advance.

antemano *adv* .

● **de antemano** beforehand, in advance.

antena *nf* **1** *(de aparato)* aerial, antenna. **2** *(de animal)* antenna [*pl* **antennae**].

● **estar en antena** to be on the air.

■ **antena parabólica** satellite dish.

anteojos *nm pl* glasses.

antepasado *nm* ancestor.

antepenúltimo,-a *adj* antepenultimate.

anteponer *vt* to put before: *antepuso su carrera profesional a su vida personal*, he put his career before his private life.

anterior *adj* previous: *en la página anterior*, on the previous page; *el día anterior*, the day before, the previous day.

anterioridad.

● **con anterioridad** previously, beforehand.

● **con anterioridad a** prior to, before.

anteriormente *adv* previously, before.

antes *adv* **1** *(en el tiempo -previamente)* before; *(-más temprano)* earlier: *unas horas antes*, some hours before; *te lo he dicho antes*, I told you earlier. **2** *(en el espacio)* before: *la piscina está antes del cruce*, the swimming pool is before the crossroads.

● **antes de** before: *antes de leer el periódico*, before reading the paper.

● **antes de nada** first of all.

● **antes de que** before: *antes de que yo naciera*, before I was born.

● **cuanto antes** as soon as possible.

● **lo antes posible** as soon as possible.

antesala *nf* anteroom, antechamber.

antiadherente *adj* nonstick.

antiaéreo,-a *adj* anti-aircraft.

antibiótico,-a *adj* antibiotic.

▶ *nm* **antibiótico** antibiotic.

anticiclón *nm* anticyclone, high pressure area.

anticipación *nf* .

● **con anticipación** in advance.

anticipar *vt* **1** *(fecha)* to bring forward [*pt & pp* **brought**]: *anticiparon la reunión*, they brought the meeting forward. **2** *(dinero)* to advance, pay in advance [*pt & pp* **paid**]: *le anticiparon parte del sueldo*, they paid her part of her salary in advance.

▶ *vpr* **anticiparse 1** *(suceder antes)* to be

early. **2** *(adelantarse)* to beat to it [*pt* **beat**; *pp* **beaten**]: *él se me anticipó*, he beat me to it.

anticipo *nm* advance.

● **ser un anticipo de algo** to be a foretaste of STH.

anticonceptivo,-a *adj* contraceptive.

▶ *nm* **anticonceptivo** contraceptive.

anticongelante *adj* - *nm* antifreeze.

anticuado,-a *adj* old-fashioned, antiquated.

anticuario *nm* antiquary, antiques dealer.

antídoto *nm* antidote.

antifaz *nm* mask.

antigualla *nf* old thing.

antiguamente *adv* in the past.

antigüedad *nf* **1** *(período)* antiquity. **2** *(edad)*: *una ciudad de tres mil años de antigüedad*, a city which is three thousand years old. **3** *(en empleo)* seniority.

▶ *nf pl* **antigüedades** *(monumentos)* antiquities; *(objetos)* antiques.

● **en la antigüedad** in ancient times.

antiguo,-a *adj* **1** *(muy viejo)* ancient: *la antigua Grecia*, ancient Greece. **2** *(viejo)* old: *un piso en un bloque antiguo*, a flat in an old building. **3** *(anterior)* old, former: *mi antiguo jefe*, my former boss. **4** *(pasado)* old-fashioned: *llevaba un vestido antiguo*, she was wearing an old-fashioned dress.

antílope *nm* antelope.

antipatía *nf* antipathy, dislike.

antipático,-a *adj* unpleasant: *ese hombre me cae antipático*, I find this man unpleasant.

antirrobo *adj* antitheft.

▶ *nm* antitheft device.

antítesis *nf* antithesis.

antivirus *nm* antivirus system.

antojarse *vpr* **1** *(encapricharse)* to fancy, feel like [*pt & pp* **felt**]: *se le antojaron unas olivas*, she fancied some olives. **2** *(suponer)* to think [*pt & pp* **thought**], imagine: *se me antoja que ...*, I have a feeling that ....

antojo *nm* **1** *(capricho)* whim; *(de embarazada)* craving. **2** *(en la piel)* birthmark.

antología *nf* anthology.

antónimo,-a *adj* antonymous.

▶ *nm* **antónimo** antonym.

antorcha *nf* torch.

antro *nm fam* dump, hole.

antropología *nf* anthropology.

anual *adj* annual, yearly.

anudar *vt* to knot, tie.

anular[1] *adj* ring-shaped.

▶ *nm* ring finger.

anular[2] *vt* (*gen*) to annul, cancel; (*matrimonio*) to annul; (*gol*) to disallow; (*ley*) to repeal.

anunciar *vt* **1** (*notificar*) to announce. **2** (*hacer publicidad de*) to advertise.

▶ *vpr* **anunciarse** to advertise oneself.

anuncio *nm* **1** (*en periódico*) advertisement, advert, ad; (*en televisión, radio*) advertisement, advert, commercial. **2** (*notificación*) announcement. **3** (*presagio*) sign, omen. **4** (*cartel*) poster.

anverso *nm* obverse.

anzuelo *nm* **1** (*para pescar*) hook. **2** (*aliciente*) lure.

● **morder el anzuelo** to take the bait.

añadidura *nf* .

● **por añadidura** besides, in addition.

añadir *vt* to add.

añejo,-a *adj* (*vino*) mature; (*costumbre*) age-old; (*noticia*) old.

añicos *nm pl*.

● **hacer añicos** to smash.

● **hacerse añicos** to be smashed to pieces.

año *nm* year: *mi hermano se marchó hace un año*, my brother left a year ago.

● **tener ... años** to be ... years old: *tengo 20 años*, I'm 20 years old; *¿cuántos años tienes?*, how old are you?

■ **año bisiesto** leap year.

■ **Año Nuevo** New Year: *¡feliz Año Nuevo!*, happy New Year!

■ **años luz** light years.

añorar *vt* to long for, miss.

▶ *vi* to pine.

aorta *nf* aorta.

apacentar *vt* (*ganado*) to pasture.

▶ *vpr* **apacentarse** (*pacer*) to graze.

apacible *adj* (*persona*) gentle; (*tiempo*) mild; (*vida*) peaceful.

apaciguar *vt* to pacify, calm down.

▶ *vpr* **apaciguarse** to calm down.

apadrinar *vt* **1** (*en bautizo*) to act as godfather to. **2** (*artista*) to sponsor.

apagado,-a *adj* **1** (*luz*) off; (*fuego*) out. **2** (*persona*) subdued. **3** (*color*) dull.

apagar *vt* **1** (*fuego*) to extinguish, put out. **2** (*luz*) to turn off. **3** (*aparato*) to turn off, switch off. **4** (*color*) to soften.

▶ *vpr* **apagarse** (*luz*) to go out.

apagón *nm* power cut, blackout.

apalabrar *vt* to agree to.

apalear *vt* to beat [*pt* **beat**; *pp* **beaten**], thrash.

apañarse *vpr* to manage: *ya se apañará sola*, she'll manage on her own.

● **apañárselas** to get by, manage.

aparador *nm* **1** (*escaparate*) shop window. **2** (*mueble*) sideboard.

aparato *nm* **1** (*máquina*) machine; (*dispositivo*) device. **2** (*electrodoméstico*) appliance; (*televisor, radio*) set. **3** (*de gimnasio*) piece of apparatus. **4** (*para los dientes*) brace; (*audífono*) hearing aid. **5** (*conjunto de órganos*) system. **6** (*ostentación*) pomp. **7** POL machine: *el aparato del partido*, the party machine, the party apparatus.

■ **aparato de radio** radio set.

■ **aparato de televisión** television set.

■ **aparato digestivo** digestive system.

aparcamiento *nm* **1** (*acción*) parking. **2** (*lugar*) GB car park; US parking lot; (*en la calle*) place to park.

aparcar *vt-vi* to park.

aparecer *vi* **1** (*gen*) to appear; (*objeto perdido*) to turn up: *apareció un delfín muerto en la playa*, a dead dolphin appeared on the beach; *¿ha aparecido tu cartera?*, has your wallet turned up? **2** (*dejarse ver*) to show up [*pt* **showed**; *pp* **shown**], turn up: *apareció en casa dos días después*, she showed up a home two days later.

aparejador,-ra *nm,f* (*de obras*) clerk of works; (*perito*) quantity surveyor.

aparentar *vt* **1** (*simular*) to feign, pretend. **2** (*edad*) to look: *no aparenta su edad*, he doesn't look his age.

▶ *vi* to show off [*pt* **showed**; *pp* **shown**].

aparente *adj* apparent.

aparentemente *adv* apparently.

aparición *nf* **1** (*acción*) appearance. **2** (*espectro*) apparition.

apariencia *nf* appearance.

● **guardar las apariencias** to keep up appearances.

apartado,-a *adj* **1** (*lejano*) distant. **2** (*aislado*) isolated, remote.

▶ *nm* **apartado** section.

■ **apartado de correos** post office box.

apartamento *nm* **1** *(piso pequeño)* small flat, small apartment. **2** *(de vacaciones)* apartment.

apartar *vt* **1** *(alejar)* to move away: *aparta la silla de la ventana*, move the chair away from the window. **2** *(poner a un lado)* to set aside [*pt & pp* **set**]: *he apartado los tomates maduros*, I've set aside the ripe tomatoes.
▶ *vpr* **apartarse** *(de un lugar)* to move away: *apártate de la ventana*, come away from the window; *¡apártate!*, stand aside!, move out of the way!
● **apartar la mirada, apartar la vista** to look away.

aparte *adv* **1** *(a un lado)* aside, to one side; *(por separado)* apart, separately: *puso el pescado aparte*, he put the fish to one side; *eso se paga aparte*, you have to pay for that separately. **2** *(además)* besides: *aparte de ser un profesional, es muy modesto*, besides being a professional, he's very modest.
▶ *adj (distinto)* special: *eso es un caso aparte*, that's completely different.
▶ *nm* **1** *(comentario)* aside. **2** paragraph: *punto y aparte*, full stop, new paragraph.

apasionado,-a *adj* passionate.

apasionante *adj* exciting, fascinating.

apasionar *vt* to excite, fascinate.
▶ *vpr* **apasionarse** to get excited, become enthusiastic.

apatía *nf* apathy.

apático,-a *adj* apathetic.

apeadero *nm (de trenes)* halt.

apearse *vpr (de caballo)* to dismount; *(de vehículo)* to get off.

apechugar *vi fam* to grin and bear it.

apedrear *vt* to throw stones at [*pt* **threw**; *pp* **thrown**].

apego *nm* attachment, fondness.
● **tener apego a** to be attached to, be fond of.

apelación *nf* appeal.

apelar *vi* to appeal.

apellidarse *vpr* to be called: *¿cómo se apellida usted?*, what's your surname?

apellido *nm* surname, family name.
■ **apellido de soltera** maiden name.

apenar *vt* to sadden, make sad.
▶ *vpr* **apenarse** to be saddened.

apenas *adv* **1** *(casi no)* hardly, scarcely: *apenas daba crédito a mis oídos*, I could hardly believe my ears; *apenas llevaba equipaje*, she had hardly any luggage. **2** *(casi nunca)* hardly ever: *apenas sale con los amigos*, he hardly ever goes out with his friends. **3** *(sólo)* only, just: *apenas hace cinco minutos que se ha ido*, he left just five minutes ago. **4** *(tan pronto como)* as soon as, no sooner: *apenas se acostó, se quedó dormido*, as soon as he got into bed, he fell asleep.
● **apenas si** hardly.

apéndice *nm* **1** *(órgano)* appendix [*pl* **appendixes**]. **2** *(de libro)* appendix [*pl* **appendices**].

apendicitis *nf* appendicitis.

apercibirse *vpr* to notice.

aperitivo *nm* **1** *(bebida)* aperitif [*pl* **-s**]. **2** *(comida)* appetizer.

apertura *nf* **1** *(gen)* opening; *(de temporada, curso académico)* start, beginning. **2** POL liberalization.

apestar *vi* to stink [*pt* **stank**; *pp* **stunk**].

apetecer *vi*: *me apetece un café*, I feel like a coffee, I fancy a coffee; *¿te apetece ir al cine?*, do you fancy going to the cinema?

apetecible *adj* **1** *(plan, oferta)* desirable, tempting. **2** *(comida)* appetizing.

apetito *nm* appetite.
● **abrir el apetito** to whet one's appetite.
● **tener apetito** to be hungry.

apetitoso,-a *adj* appetizing.

apiadarse *vpr* to take pity.

apicultura *nf* beekeeping.

apilar *vt* to pile up, put in a pile.
▶ *vpr* **apilarse** to pile up.

apiñarse *vpr* to crowd together.

apio *nm* celery.

apisonadora *nf* steamroller.

aplacar *vt* to placate, soothe.
▶ *vpr* **aplacarse** to become appeased.

aplanar *vt* **1** *(igualar)* to level, make even. **2** *(deprimir)* to depress.
▶ *vpr* **aplanarse** to be depressed.

aplastante *adj* crushing, overwhelming: *una victoria aplastante*, a landslide victory.

aplastar *vt* **1** *(chafar)* to squash, flatten. **2** *(vencer)* to crush, destroy.

aplaudir *vt* **1** *(palmotear)* to clap, applaud. **2** *(aprobar)* to approve, praise.

aplauso *nm* **1** *(palmadas)* applause: ***fuertes aplausos***, loud applause. **2** *(aprobación)* approval, praise.

aplazar *vt (reunión, acto)* to postpone, put off; *(pago)* to defer.

aplicación *nf* application.

aplicado,-a *adj* **1** *(ciencia)* applied. **2** *(estudiante)* studious, diligent.

aplicar *vt* **1** *(extender)* to apply: ***aplicó la pomada sobre la picadura***, she applied some cream to the bite, she put some cream on the bite. **2** *(poner en práctica)* to put into practice: ***aplica todo lo que has aprendido***, put everything you've learnt into practice.

▶ *vpr* **aplicarse 1** *(ponerse)* to apply. **2** *(esforzarse)* to apply oneself.

aplomo *nm* assurance, self-possession.

apocado,-a *adj* spiritless.

apoderar *vt* to authorize.

▶ *vpr* **apoderarse** to take possession.

● **apoderarse de** to take possession of.

apodo *nm* nickname.

apogeo *nm (punto culminante)* summit, height: ***está en pleno apogeo de su carrera***, she's at the height of her career.

apología *nf* apologia, defence.

aporrear *vt (persona)* to beat [*pt* **beat**; *pp* **beaten**]; *(puerta)* to bang on, hammer on; *(piano)* to hammer at.

aportación *nf* contribution.

aportar *vt* to contribute.

● **aportar su granito de arena** to chip in one's small contribution.

aposento *nm* **1** *(cuarto)* room. **2** *(hospedaje)* lodgings *pl*.

aposta *adv* on purpose.

apostar *vt-vi-vpr* **apostar(se)** to bet [*pt & pp* **bet**]: *¿qué te apuestas?*, how much do you bet?

apóstol *nm* apostle.

apoteosis *nf* apotheosis.

apoyar *vt* **1** *(reclinar)* to rest, lean [*pt & pp* **leant**]: ***apoyó la cabeza en mi hombro***, she rested her head on my shoulder; ***apoya la escalera contra la pared***, lean the ladder against the wall. **2** *(basar)* to base, found. **3** *(defender)* to back, support.

▶ *vpr* **apoyarse 1** *(reclinarse)* to lean [*pt & pp* **leant**]: ***apóyate en mi brazo***, lean on my arm. **2** *(basarse)* to be based.

apoyo *nm* support.

apreciable *adj* **1** *(perceptible)* appreciable, noticeable. **2** *(estimable)* valuable.

apreciar *vt* **1** *(sentir aprecio por)* to regard highly. **2** *(valorar)* to appreciate. **3** *(detectar)* to notice, detect.

▶ *vpr* **apreciarse** to be noticeable.

aprecio *nm* esteem, regard.

● **sentir aprecio por** ALGN to be fond of SB.

apremiar *vt (meter prisa a)* to urge, press.

▶ *vi (ser urgente)* to be urgent.

● **el tiempo apremia** time is short.

aprender *vt-vi* to learn [*pt & pp* **learnt**].

● **aprenderse algo de memoria** to learn STH by heart.

aprendizaje *nm* learning.

aprendiz,-za *nm,f* apprentice, trainee.

aprensión *nf* apprehension.

aprensivo,-a *adj* apprehensive.

apresar *vt* to catch [*pt & pp* **caught**], capture.

apresuradamente *adv* hurriedly, in great haste.

apresurar *vt-vpr* **apresurar(se)** to hurry.

apretado,-a *adj* **1** *(ajustado)* tight: ***estos pantalones me quedan muy apretados***, these trousers are very tight on me. **2** *(ocupado)* busy: ***un día muy apretado***, a very busy day. **3** *(apretujado)* cramped: ***íbamos un poco apretados en el coche***, we were a bit cramped in the car. **4** *(reñido)* close: ***un resultado muy apretado***, a very close result.

apretar *vt* **1** *(estrechar)* to squeeze: ***me apretó la mano***, he squeezed my hand. **2** *(tornillo, nudo)* to tighten. **3** *(pulsar - botón)* to press; *(- gatillo)* to pull. **4** *(exigir)* to put pressure on push hard: ***la maestra nos aprieta mucho***, the teacher puts a lot of pressure on us.

▶ *vi* **1** *(prendas)* to be too tight: ***esta falda me aprieta***, this skirt is too tight on me. **2** *(esforzarse)* to work harder: ***tendrás que apretar más si quieres aprobar***, you'll have to work harder if you want to pass.

▶ *vpr* **apretarse** *(agolparse)* to crowd together.

● **apretar el paso** to quicken one's pace.

● **apretarse el cinturón** to tighten one's belt.

apretón *nm* squeeze.

■ **apretón de manos** handshake.

apretujar *vt* to squeeze.

▶ *vpr* **apretujarse** to squeeze together.

aprieto *nm* fix, awkward situation.

● **poner a** ALGN **en un aprieto** to put SB in an awkward situation.

● **salir del aprieto** to get out of trouble.

aprisa *adv* quickly.

aprisionar *vt* to trap.

aprobación *nf (gen)* approval; *(de ley)* passing.

aprobado,-a *adj* approved, passed.

▶ *nm* **aprobado** pass.

aprobar *vt* **1** *(decisión, plan, préstamo)* to approve. **2** *(comportamiento)* to approve of. **3** *(examen, ley)* to pass.

apropiado,-a *adj* appropriate, suitable.

apropiarse *vpr* to appropriate.

● **apropiarse de algo** to appropriate STH.

aprovechado,-a *adj* **1** *(bien empleado)* well used, well spent. **2** *(diligente)* diligent. **3** *(sinvergüenza)* opportunistic.

▶ *nm,f* opportunist.

aprovechar *vt* **1** *(sacar provecho de)* to make good use of: *aprovecha bien el tiempo*, she makes good use of her time; *¡aprovecha!*, make the most of it! **2** *(emplear)* to use: *aproveché la tarde para estudiar*, I used the afternoon to study.

▶ *vi* to be useful.

▶ *vpr* **aprovecharse** to take advantage.

● **aprovechar la oportunidad** to seize the opportunity.

● **aprovecharse de la situación** to take advantage of the situation.

● **¡que aproveche!** enjoy your meal!

aprovisionar *vt* to supply, provide.

aproximación *nf* approximation.

aproximadamente *adv* approximately, roughly.

aproximado,-a *adj* approximate.

aproximar *vt* to bring near [*pt & pp* brought].

▶ *vpr* **aproximarse** to approach, draw near [*pt* drew; *pp* drawn]: *se aproxima el invierno*, winter is approaching.

aptitud *nf* aptitude, ability.

apto,-a *adj* **1** *(apropiado)* suitable. **2** *(capaz)* capable, able.

● **apta para todos los públicos** GB U-certificate; US rated G.

● **no apta** for adults only.

apuesta *nf* bet.

apuesto,-a *adj* good-looking.

apuntador,-ra *nm,f* prompter.

apuntar *vt* **1** *(señalar)* to point at. **2** *(arma)* to aim. **3** *(anotar)* to note down, make a note of. **4** *(en teatro)* to prompt.

▶ *vi (con arma)* to aim.

▶ *vt-vpr* **apuntar(se)** *(inscribir - en curso)* GB to enrol; US to enroll; *(- en lista)* to put down: *¿te has apuntado para la excursión?*, have you put your name down for the trip?

● **apuntarse un tanto** to score a point.

apunte *nm* **1** *(nota)* note. **2** *(dibujo)* sketch.

▶ *nm pl* **apuntes** *(de clase)* notes.

apuñalar *vt* to stab.

apurar *vt* **1** *(terminar)* to finish up: *apurar una copa*, to drain a glass. **2** *(apremiar)* to urge. **3** *(avergonzar)* to embarrass.

▶ *vpr* **apurarse** *(preocuparse)* to worry.

● **si me apuras ...** if you press me...

apuro *nm* **1** *(dificultad)* predicament, tight spot; *(de dinero)* hardship: *está en un verdadero apuro*, she's in a real predicament. **2** *(vergüenza)* embarrassment.

● **dar apuro** to embarrass: *me da apuro pedírselo*, it embarrasses me to ask him.

● **pasar apuros** to be hard up.

● **¡qué apuro!** how embarrassing!

aquel,-lla *adj* that [*pl* those]: *aquel libro*, that book; *aquella casa*, that house.

aquél,-lla *pron* that one [*pl* those]: *no quiero éste, quiero aquél*, I don't want this one, I want that one.

aquello *pron*: *aquello fue lo que más me gustó*, that was what I liked the most; *¿te acuerdas de aquello que me dijiste?*, do you remember what you told me?

aquí *adv* **1** *(lugar)* here: *estoy aquí*, I'm here. **2** *(tiempo)* now: *de aquí a 2037*, from now until 2037.

● **aquí abajo** down here.

● **aquí arriba** up here.

● **de aquí en adelante** from now on.

● **de aquí para allá** up and down, to and fro.

● **de aquí que** hence, therefore.

● **hasta aquí podíamos llegar** that's the end of it.

● **por aquí por favor** this way please.

árabe *adj (gen)* Arab; *(de Arabia)* Arabian; *(alfabeto, número)* Arabic.

▶ *nmf (persona)* Arab; *(de Arabia)* Arabian.

▶ *nm (idioma)* Arabic.

arado *nm* plough.

arandela *nf* washer.

araña *nf* **1** *(animal)* spider. **2** *(lámpara)* chandelier.

arañar *vt-vpr* **arañar(se)** to scratch.

arañazo *nm* scratch.

arar *vt* to plough.

arbitrar *vt* **1** *(fútbol, rugby, boxeo)* to referee; *(tenis)* to umpire. **2** *(conflicto)* to arbitrate.

arbitrario,-a *adj* arbitrary.

árbitro *nm* **1** *(en fútbol, rugby, boxeo)* referee; *(en tenis)* umpire. **2** *(en conflicto)* arbiter, arbitrator.

árbol *nm* tree.

■ **árbol de Navidad** Christmas tree.

■ **árbol genealógico** family tree.

arbolado,-a *adj* wooded.

▶ *nm* **arbolado** woodland.

arboleda *nf* small wood.

arbusto *nm* shrub, bush.

arca *nf* chest.

■ **arca de Noé** Noah's ark.

■ **arcas públicas** Treasury.

arcada *nf* **1** *(de puente)* arcade. **2** *(al vomitar)*: **me dieron arcadas**, I retched.

arcaico,-a *adj* archaic.

arce *nm* maple tree.

archipiélago *nm* archipelago [*pl* **-os** o **-oes**].

archivador,-ra *nm,f* archivist.

▶ *nm* **archivador** filing cabinet.

archivar *vt* **1** *(ordenar)* to file. **2** INFORM to save.

archivo *nm* **1** *(documento)* file. **2** *(lugar)* archive. **3** *(mueble)* filing cabinet.

■ **archivo adjunto** INFORM attachment.

arcilla *nf* clay.

arco *nm* **1** ARQ arch. **2** MAT arc. **3** *(de violín, flecha)* bow.

■ **arco iris** rainbow.

arder *vi* **1** *(quemarse)* to burn [*pt & pp* **burnt**]; *(sin llama)* to smoulder; US to smolder. **2** *(estar muy caliente)* to be boiling hot: **la sopa está ardiendo**, the soup is boiling hot.

● **la cosa está que arde** things are getting pretty hot.

ardiente *adj* **1** *(encendido)* burning, hot. **2** *(apasionado)* passionate, ardent.

ardilla *nf* squirrel.

ardor *nm* **1** *(calor)* burning, heat. **2** *(fervor)* GB ardour; US ardor.

■ **ardor de estómago** heartburn.

arduo,-a *adj* arduous.

área *nf* **1** *(zona, medida)* area: **área de servicio**, service area. **2** *(en fútbol)* penalty area.

arena *nf* **1** *(de playa, desierto)* sand. **2** *(para combates)* arena. **3** *(para torear)* bullring.

■ **arenas movedizas** quicksand *sing*.

arenal *nm* sands *pl*, sandy area.

arenoso,-a *adj* sandy.

arenque *nm* herring.

■ **arenque ahumado** kipper.

Argel *nm* **1** *(ciudad)* Algiers. **2** *(país)* Algeria.

argelino,-a *adj - nm,f* Algerian.

Argentina *nf* Argentina, the Argentine.

argentino,-a *adj - nm,f* Argentinian.

argolla *nf* ring.

argot *nm* **1** *(popular)* slang. **2** *(técnico)* jargon.

argumentación *nf* arguments *pl*.

argumentar *vt-vi* to argue.

argumento *nm* **1** *(razón)* argument. **2** *(de novela, obra, etc)* plot.

árido,-a *adj* **1** *(tierra)* arid, dry. **2** *(texto, tema)* dry.

Aries *nm* Aries.

arisco,-a *adj* unsociable, unfriendly.

arista *nf* edge.

aristocracia *nf* aristocracy.

aristócrata *nmf* aristocrat.

aritmética *nf* arithmetic.

arma *nf* weapon.

▶ *nf pl* **armas 1** *(profesión)* armed services. **2** *(heráldica)* arms, armorial bearings.

■ **arma blanca** knife [*pl* **-ves**].

■ **arma de fuego** firearm.

■ **arma homicida** murder weapon.

■ **arma nuclar** nuclear weapon.

armada *nf* navy.

armadura *nf* **1** *(defensa)* armour. **2** *(armazón)* framework.

armamento *nm* armament.

armar *vt* **1** *(proveer de armas)* to arm. **2**

(montar -mueble) to assemble, put together; *(-tienda)* to put up. **3** *(ruido, alboroto)* to make.
▶ *vpr* **armarse** to arm oneself.
● **armar jaleo** to make a racket.
● **armarse de paciencia** to summon up one's patience.
● **armarse de valor** to pluck up courage.
● **va a armarse la gorda** there's going to be real trouble.

armario *nm (de cocina)* cupboard; *(de ropa)* GB wardrobe; US closet.

armatoste *nm* **1** *(cosa)* monstrosity. **2** *(persona)* useless great oaf [*pl* -**s**].

armazón *nm* frame.

armiño *nm* ermine.

armisticio *nm* armistice.

armonía *nf* harmony.

armónica *nf* harmonica, mouth organ.

armónico,-a *adj* harmonic.
▶ *nm* **armónico** harmonic.

armonioso,-a *adj* harmonious.

aro *nm* **1** *(gen)* hoop, ring. **2** *(juego)* hoop. **3** *(servilletero)* napkin ring.
● **pasar por el aro** to knuckle under.

aroma *nm* aroma; *(del vino)* bouquet.

aromático,-a *adj* aromatic.

arpa *nf* harp.

arpón *nm* harpoon.

arqueología *nf* archaeology.

arqueólogo,-a *nm,f* archaeologist.

arquero *nm* archer.

arquitecto,-a *nm,f* architect.

arquitectura *nf* architecture.

arraigado,-a *adj* deeply rooted.

arraigar *vt* to establish, strengthen.
▶ *vi-vpr* **arraigar(se)** to take root.

arrancar *vt* **1** *(planta)* to uproot, pull up. **2** *(clavo, muela)* to pull out. **3** *(pluma)* to pluck. **4** *(página)* to tear out. **5** *(arrebatar)* to snatch: *me arrancó el libro de las manos*, she snatched the book out of my hands.
▶ *vi* **1** *(coche)* to start. **2** *(ordenador)* to boot. **3** *(provenir)* to stem from.
● **arrancar a correr** to break into a run [*pt* **broke**; *pp* **broken**].

arranque *nm* **1** *(de motor)* starting mechanism: *el motor de arranque*, the starter motor. **2** *(energía)* go. **3** *(arrebato)* fit: *un arranque de ira*, a fit of rage.

arrasar *vt* **1** *(destruir)* to raze, demolish. **2** *(aplanar)* to level.

▶ *vi* to sweep the board: *arrasó en las elecciones*, she swept the board in the elections.

arrastrar *vt* **1** *(llevar por el suelo)* to drag (along), pull *(along)*: *¡no arrastres la silla!*, don't drag the chair! **2** *(soportar)* to have: *arrastra la enfermedad desde hace años*, he's had the illness for years.
▶ *vi* to trail on the ground: *le arrastran los pantalones*, his trousers trail on the ground.
▶ *vpr* **arrastrarse 1** *(reptar)* to crawl. **2** *(humillarse)* to creep [*pt & pp* **crept**], crawl.

arrear *vt* **1** *(animales)* to drive [*pt* **drove**; *pp* **driven**]. **2** *(pegar)* to hit [*pt & pp* **hit**]: *arrearle una bofetada a ALGN*, to slap SB in the face.
▶ *vi* to move fast.
● **¡arreando!** get moving!

arrebatar *vt* **1** *(quitar)* to snatch. **2** *(atraer)* to captivate.
▶ *vpr* **arrebatarse** *(enfurecerse)* to become furious.

arrebato *nm* fit, outburst.

arreciar *vi* *(viento)* to get stronger; *(tormenta)* to get worse.

arrecife *nm* reef.

arreglar *vt* **1** *(resolver - conflicto)* to settle; *(- asunto)* to sort out: *el tiempo lo arregla todo*, time heals all wounds. **2** *(ordenar)* to tidy, tidy up. **3** *(reparar)* to mend, fix up.
▶ *vpr* **arreglarse 1** *(componerse)* to get ready, dress up; *(cabello)* to do. **2** *fam (apañarse)* to manage: *arréglatelas como puedas*, do as best you can.
● **¡ya te arreglaré!** I'll teach you!

arreglo *nm* **1** *(reparación)* repair. **2** *(acuerdo)* agreement.
● **con arreglo a** according to.
● **no tiene arreglo 1** (cosa) it can't be mended. **2** (situación) nothing can be done about it.

arremeter *vi* to attack.

arremolinarse *vpr* **1** *(polvo, hojas)* to whirl. **2** *(gente)* to mill around.

arrendar *vt* to rent, lease.

arrendatario,-a *nm,f* tenant.

arrepentido,-a *adj* sorry.

arrepentimiento *nm* regret, repentance.

arrepentirse *vpr* to regret, be sorry: *se*

arrepiente de haberlo hecho, he regrets doing it, he's sorry he did it.

arrestar *vt* to arrest.

arresto *nm* arrest.

■ **arresto domiciliario** house arrest.

arriar *vt* **1** *(velas)* to lower. **2** *(bandera)* to strike [*pt & pp* **struck**].

arriba *adv* **1** *(dirección)* up; *(encima)* on (the) top: *mirad hacia arriba*, look up. **2** *(situación)* above: *desde arriba*, from above; *véase más arriba*, see above; *arriba del todo*, right at the top. **3** *(piso)* upstairs: *vive arriba*, she lives upstairs.
▶ *interj* up!: *¡arriba el Atlético!*, up (with) Atlético!; *¡arriba la República!*, long live the Republic!
● **cuesta arriba** uphill.
● **de arriba abajo** from top to bottom.
● **hacia arriba** upwards.
● **patas arriba** *fam* upside down.

arriesgado,-a *adj* **1** *(peligroso)* risky, dangerous. **2** *(atrevido)* bold, rash.

arriesgar *vt-vpr* **arriesgar(se)** to risk.
● **arriesgar el pellejo** to risk one's neck.

arrimar *vt* to move closer, bring closer: *arrima la mesa a la pared*, move the table closer to the wall.
▶ *vpr* **arrimarse** to come closer, come nearer: *arrímate a la ventana*, come closer to the window.
● **arrimarse a** ALGN to seek SB's protection [*pt & pp* **sought**].
● **arrimarse al sol que más calienta** to get on the winning side.

arrinconar *vt* **1** *(apartar)* to put in a corner. **2** *(acorralar)* to corner. **3** *(desestimar)* to ignore. **4** *(abandonar)* to lay aside [*pt & pp* **laid**].
▶ *vpr* **arrinconarse** *(aislarse)* to isolate oneself.

arrodillado,-a *adj* on one's knees.

arrodillarse *vpr* to kneel down [*pt & pp* **knelt**].

arrogancia *nf* arrogance.

arrogante *adj* arrogant.

arrojar *vt* **1** *(tirar)* to throw [*pt* **threw**; *pp* **thrown**]; *(con fuerza)* to hurl, fling [*pt & pp* **flung**]. **2** *(echar)* to throw out [*pt* **threw**; *pp* **thrown**]. **3** *(resultado)* to show [*pt* **showed**; *pp* **shown**].
▶ *vi* to vomit.
▶ *vpr* **arrojarse** to throw oneself [*pt* threw; *pp* **thrown**]: *se arrojó sobre él*, he jumped on him.
● **"prohibido arrojar basuras"** "no dumping".

arrollar *vt* **1** *(enrollar)* to roll, roll up. **2** *(viento, agua)* to sweep away [*pt & pp* **swept**]. **3** *(derrotar)* to rout. **4** *(atropellar)* to run over [*pt* **ran**; *pp* **run**].

arropar *vt* *(abrigar)* to wrap up; *(en la cama)* to tuck in: *arropa a sus hijos cada noche*, she tucks her children in every night.

arroyo *nm* **1** *(río)* stream. **2** *(en la calle)* gutter.

arroz *nm* rice.
■ **arroz con leche** rice pudding.
■ **arroz integral** brown rice.

arrozal *nm* rice field.

arruga *nf* *(en la piel)* wrinkle; *(en la ropa)* crease.

arrugar *vt-vpr* **arrugar(se)** **1** *(piel)* to wrinkle. **2** *(ropa)* to crease. **3** *(papel)* to crumple.
● **arrugar el ceño** to frown.

arruinar *vt* **1** *(empobrecer)* to bankrupt, ruin. **2** *(estropear)* to ruin.
▶ *vpr* **arruinarse** to be bankrupt, be ruined.

arrullar *vt* **1** *(pájaro)* to coo. **2** *(adormecer)* to lull, sleep [*pt & pp* **slept**].

arrullo *nm* **1** *(de pájaro)* cooing. **2** *(nana)* lullaby.

arsenal *nm* **1** *(de armas)* arsenal. **2** *(astillero)* shipyard.

arsénico *nm* arsenic.

arte *nm* **1** *(gen)* art: *bellas artes*, fine arts. **2** *(habilidad)* craft, skill: *tiene arte para dibujar*, she's good at drawing. **3** *(astucia)* cunning.
● **como por arte de magia** as if by magic.
● **con malas artes** by evil means.
■ **arte dramático** drama.
■ **artes de pesca** fishing tackle *sing*.
■ **artes marciales** martial arts.
■ **artes plásticas** plastic arts.

artefacto *nm* device.
■ **artefacto explosivo** explosive device, bomb.

arteria *nf* artery.

artesanía *nf* **1** *(actividad)* craftsmanship. **2** *(productos)* handicrafts: *feria de artesanía*, craft fair.

artesano,-a *nm,f* craftsman [*pl* **-men**], artisan.

ártico,-a *adj* Arctic.
▶ *nm* **el Ártico** the Arctic.
articulación *nf* joint.
articulado,-a *adj* articulated.
articular *vt-vpr* **articular(se)** to articulate.
artículo *nm* article.
■ **artículos de consumo** consumer goods.
artificial *adj* artificial.
artillería *nf* artillery.
■ **artillería pesada** heavy artillery.
artillero *nm* artilleryman [*pl* -**men**].
artimaña *nf* trick.
artista *nmf* artist.
■ **artista de cine** film star.
■ **artista invitado** guest star.
artístico,-a *adj* artistic.
artritis *nf* arthritis.
arzobispo *nm* archbishop.
as *nm* ace.
asa *nf* handle.
asado,-a *adj (carne)* roast; *(pescado, patata)* baked: *pollo asado,* roast chicken.
▶ *nm* **asado** roast.
asalariado,-a *adj* salaried, wage-earning.
▶ *nm,f* wage earner.
asaltante *adj* attacking, assaulting.
▶ *nmf* attacker.
asaltar *vt* **1** *(atacar)* to assault, attack. **2** *(robar -banco)* to rob, raid; *(-persona)* to mug.
asalto *nm* **1** *(ataque)* assault, attack. **2** *(robo -de banco)* raid, robbery; *(-a persona)* mugging. **3** *(en boxeo)* round.
● **tomar por asalto** to take by storm.
asamblea *nf* **1** *(en parlamento)* assembly. **2** *(reunión)* meeting.
asar *vt (carne)* to roast; *(pescado, patata)* to bake.
▶ *vpr* **asarse** to roast: *¡aquí nos estamos asando!,* we're roasting in here!
ascendente *adj* ascending, ascendant.
▶ *nm* ascendant.
ascender *vi* **1** *(subir)* to climb. **2** *(de categoría)* to be promoted: *ascendió a director,* he was promoted to manager. **3** *(sumar)* to amount: *la cuenta asciende a 30 euros,* the bill amounts to 30 euros.
▶ *vt* to promote.
ascendiente *nmf* ancestor.

ascenso *nm* **1** *(subida -de temperatura, precio)* rise; *(-de montaña)* ascent. **2** *(-de empleado, equipo)* promotion.
ascensor *nm* GB lift; US elevator.
asco *nm* disgust.
● **dar asco** to be disgusting.
● **estar hecho un asco** to be filthy.
● **¡qué asco!** how disgusting!, how revolting!
ascua *nf* ember, red hot coal.
● **estar en ascuas** to be on tenterhooks.
aseado,-a *adj (limpio)* clean; *(arreglado)* neat, tidy.
asear *vt (limpiar)* to clean; *(arreglar)* to tidy.
▶ *vpr* **asearse** *(lavarse)* to wash; *(arreglarse)* to clean oneself up, tidy oneself up.
asediar *vt* **1** to besiege. **2** *(molestar)* to importunate.
asegurado,-a *adj* insured.
▶ *nm,f* policy holder.
aseguradora *nf* insurance company.
asegurar *vt* **1** *(fijar)* to secure. **2** *(coche, casa)* to insure. **3** *(garantizar)* to ensure, guarantee: *sus notas le aseguraban una plaza en la universidad,* her grades ensured her of a place at university. **4** *(afirmar)* to assure: *te aseguro que es verdad,* I assure you that it's true.
▶ *vpr* **asegurarse 1** *(cerciorarse)* to make sure. **2** *(tomar un seguro)* to insure oneself.
asemejarse *vpr* to look alike.
● **asemejarse a** ALGN to look like SB, resemble SB.
asentimiento *nm* assent, consent.
asentir *vi* to assent, agree; *(con la cabeza)* to nod.
aseo *nm* **1** *(limpieza)* cleanliness, tidying up. **2** *(cuarto)* bathroom, toilet.
■ **aseo personal** personal hygiene.
asequible *adj* accessible: *a un precio asequible,* at a reasonable price.
aserrar *vt* to saw [*pt* **sawed**; *pp* **sawn**].
asesinar *vt* *(gen)* to kill, murder; *(rey, presidente)* to assassinate.
asesinato *nm* *(gen)* killing, murder; *(de rey, presidente)* assassination.
asesino,-a *adj* murderous.
▶ *nm,f (gen)* killer; *(de rey, presidente)* assassin.
asesorar *vt* to advise, give advice.
▶ *vpr* **asesorarse** to seek advice.

asesor,-ra *nm,f* adviser, consultant.
■ **asesor fiscal** tax consultant.
asfaltar *vt* to asphalt.
asfalto *nm* asphalt.
asfixia *nf* asphyxia, suffocation.
asfixiar *vt* to asphyxiate, suffocate.
▶ *vpr* **asfixiarse** to suffocate.
así *adv* **1** *(de esta manera)* like that, like this, in this way: *hazlo así*, do it like this. **2** *(de esa manera)* that way: *¡no me hables así!*, don't talk to me like that! **3** *(tanto)* as: *así usted como yo*, both you and I.
▶ *adj* such: *un hombre así*, a man like that, such a man.
● **así así** so-so.
● **así de...** this: *era así de grande*, it was this big.
● **así que 1** (de manera que) so, therefore. **2** (tan pronto como) as soon as: *llovía, así que cogimos los paraguas*, it was raining, so we took our umbrellas; *así que lo sepa, te lo diré*, as soon as I know, I'll tell you.
● **así sea** so be it.
● **aun así 1** even so. **2** (por así decirlo) so to speak.
● **y así sucesivamente** and so on.
Asia *nf* Asia.
asiático,-a *adj - nm,f* Asian.
asiduo,-a *adj* assiduous, frequent.
asiento *nm* **1** *(silla etc)* seat; *(de bicicleta)* saddle. **2** *(emplazamiento)* site.
asignar *vt* **1** *(adjudicar)* to assign, allot. **2** *(nombrar)* to appoint.
asignatura *nf* subject.
■ **asignatura pendiente 1** *(suspenso)* failed subject. **2** *(asunto pendiente)* unresolved matter.
asilo *nm* *(amparo)* asylum; *(residencia)* home.
■ **asilo de ancianos** old people's home.
■ **asilo político** political asylum.
asimilar *vt* to assimilate.
▶ *vpr* **asimilarse** to be assimilated.
asimismo *adv* **1** *(también)* also. **2** *(de esta manera)* likewise.
asir *vt* to seize, grasp.
▶ *vpr* **asirse** to hold on [*pt & pp* **held**].
asistencia *nf* **1** *(presencia)* attendance: *la asistencia es obligatoria*, attendance is compulsory. **2** *(público)* audience, public. **3** *(ayuda)* assistance.

■ **asistencia médica** medical care.
■ **asistencia social** social work.
■ **asistencia técnica** technical assistance.
asistenta *nf* cleaning lady.
asistente *adj* attending.
▶ *nmf* assistant.
■ **asistente social** social worker.
asistir *vi* to attend, be present: *asistir a la escuela*, to attend school.
▶ *vt* **1** *(ayudar)* to assist, help: *la enfermera asistió al médico*, the nurse helped the doctor. **2** *(cuidar)* to treat: *en un hospital estarás mejor asistido*, you'll be treated better in a hospital.
asma *nf* asthma.
asmático,-a *adj - nm,f* asthmatic.
asno *nm* ass, donkey.
asociación *nf* association.
■ **asociación de vecinos** residents' association.
asociado,-a *adj* associated.
▶ *nm,f* associate, partner.
asociar *vt* to associate.
▶ *vpr* **asociarse** to form a partnership.
● **asociarse a algo** to join STH, become a member of STH.
● **asociarse con ALGN** to go into partnership with SB.
asolar *vt* to devastate.
asomar *vi* *(aparecer)* to appear, show [*pt* **showed**; *pp* **shown**].
▶ *vt* *(sacar)* to stick out [*pt & pp* **stuck**]: *asomó la cabeza*, he stuck his head out.
▶ *vpr* **asomarse** *(a ventana)* to lean out; *(a balcón)* to come out.
● **prohibido asomarse por la ventanilla** do not lean out of the window.
asombrado,-a *adj* amazed, astonished.
asombrar *vt* to amaze, astonish.
▶ *vpr* **asombrarse** to be amazed, be astonished.
asombro *nm* amazement, astonishment.
● **no salgo de mi asombro** I can't get over it.
asombroso,-a *adj* amazing, astonishing.
asomo *nm* sign, indication.
● **ni por asomo** by no means.
aspa *nf* **1** *(cruz)* X-shaped cross. **2** *(de molino)* arm; *(de ventilador)* blade.
aspaviento *nm* .
● **hacer aspavientos** to make a big fuss.

aspecto nm **1** *(apariencia)* look, appearance. **2** *(faceta)* aspect.
● **tener buen aspecto** to look good.
● **tener mal aspecto** to look awful.

aspereza nf roughness, coarseness.

áspero,-a adj rough, coarse.

aspiración nf **1** *(al respirar)* inhalation. **2** *(ambición)* aspiration, ambition.

aspiradora nf vacuum cleaner, GB hoover.
● **pasar la aspiradora** to vacuum, GB hoover.

aspirante adj aspiring.
▶ nmf candidate.

aspirar vt **1** *(al respirar)* to inhale, breathe in. **2** *(absorber)* to suck in, draw in [pt **drew**; pp **drawn**].
▶ vi to aspire to.

aspirina® nf aspirin®.

asqueroso,-a adj **1** *(sucio)* dirty, filthy. **2** *(desagradable)* disgusting.

asta nf **1** *(de bandera)* flagpole. **2** *(de lanza)* shaft. **3** *(cuerno)* horn.
● **a media asta** at half-mast.

asterisco nm asterisk.

asteroide nm asteroid.

astilla nf splinter.

astillero nm shipyard, dockyard.

astro nm star.

astrología nf astrology.

astrólogo,-a nm,f astrologer.

astronauta nmf astronaut.

astronomía nf astronomy.

astrónomo,-a nm,f astronomer.

astucia nf **1** *(sagacidad)* astuteness, shrewdness; *(malicia)* cunning. **2** *(treta)* trick.

astuto,-a adj *(sagaz)* astute, shrewd; *(malicioso)* cunning.

asumir vt **1** *(gen)* to assume, take part on. **2** *(aceptar)* to come to term with, accept: *lo tengo asumido*, I've come to terms with it.

asunto nm **1** *(cuestión)* matter, subject: *un asunto internacional*, an international matter. **2** *(ocupación)* affair, business: *no quiero que nadie se meta en mis asuntos*, I don't want anybody interfering in my affairs.
● **no es asunto tuyo** it's none of your business.
■ **asuntos exteriores** Foreign Affairs.

asustadizo,-a adj easily frightened.

asustar vt to frighten.
▶ vpr **asustarse** to be frightened.

atacar vt to attack.

atajar vi to take a shortcut.
▶ vt **1** *(interrumpir)* to interrupt. **2** *(interceptar)* to intercept, head off.

atajo nm short cut.

atalaya nf watchtower.

ataque nm **1** *(gen)* attack. **2** *(acceso)* fit: *ataque de tos*, fit of coughing.
■ **ataque aéreo** air raid.
■ **ataque cardíaco** heart attack.
■ **ataque de nervios** nervous breakdown.

atar vt to tie, fasten.
▶ vpr **atarse** to tie up, do up: *átate los zapatos*, tie your shoelaces up.
● **atar cabos** to put two and two together.

atardecer vi to get dark, grow dark [pt **grew**; pp **grown**].
▶ nm evening, dusk: *al atardecer*, at dusk.

atareado,-a adj busy.

atascar vt to block, obstruct.
▶ vpr **atascarse** **1** *(obstruirse)* to get blocked: *el fregadero se ha atascado*, the sink has got blocked. **2** *(quedarse detenido)* to get stuck: *el coche se atascó en el barro*, the car got stuckin the mud. **3** *(mecanismo)* to jam: *la llave se ha atascado en la cerradura*, the key's jammed in the lock.

atasco nm **1** *(obstrucción)* obstruction. **2** *(de tráfico)* traffic jam.

ataúd nm coffin.

ateísmo nm atheism.

atemorizar vt to frighten.
▶ vpr **atemorizarse** to become frightened.

atención nf **1** *(interés)* attention. **2** *(cortesía)* courtesy.
● **con atención** attentively, carefully.
● **llamar la atención** to attract attention.
● **llamarle la atención a** ALGN to tell SB off: *el profesor le llamó la atención*, the teacher told him off.
● **prestar atención** to pay attention [pt & pp **paid**].
■ **atención al cliente** customer service.

■ **atención personalizada** personalized service.

atender *vt* **1** *(cliente)* to attend to; *(bar, tienda)* to serve: *¿ya la atienden?*, are you being served? **2** *(enfermo)* to take care of, look after. **3** *(asunto, protesta)* to deal with [*pt & pp* **dealt**]: *atienden las quejas de los clientes*, they deal with customers' complaints. **4** *(consejo, aviso)* to need. **5** *(llamada)* to answer: *¿puedes atender el teléfono?*, can you answer the phone?

► *vi* to pay attention [*pt & pp* **paid**]: *atendió a la explicación*, she paid attention to the explanation.

atenerse *vpr* .

● **atenerse a algo** to abide by STH: *tienes que atenerte a las consecuencias*, you have to abide by the consequences.

atentado *nm* attack, assault: *un atentado contra el ministro*, an attempt on the minister's life.

■ **atentado terrorista** terrorist attack.

atentamente *adv* **1** *(con atención)* attentively. **2** *(amablemente)* politely; *(en carta)* sincerely, faithfully: *le saluda atentamente*, yours sincerely, yours faithfully.

atentar *vi* .

● **atentar contra** ALGN to make an attempt on SB's life.

● **atentar contra algo** to offend against STH: *un programa que atenta contra el buen gusto*, a programme which offends against good taste.

atento,-a *adj* **1** *(pendiente)* attentive. **2** *(amable)* polite, courteous.

● **estar atento,-a a 1** *(escuchar)* to pay attention to [*pt & pp* **paid**]. **2** *(vigilar)* to keep an eye out for.

ateo,-a *adj - nm,f* atheist.

aterrador,-ra *adj* terrifying.

aterrar *vt* to terrify.

► *vpr* **aterrarse** to be terrified.

aterrizaje *nm* landing.

aterrizar *vi* to land.

aterrorizar *vt* **1** *(causar miedo a)* to terrify: *las serpientes me aterrorizan*, snakes terrify me. **2** *(intimidar)* to terrorize: *el secuestrador aterrorizaba a los pasajeros*, the hijacker terrorized the passengers.

► *vpr* **aterrorizarse** to be terrified.

atesorar *vt* to hoard.

atiborrarse *vpr* to stuff oneself.

ático *nm* *(buhardilla)* attic; *(piso -último)* top floor; *(-lujoso)* penthouse.

atinar *vi* to be right: *no sé si atiné al decir eso*, I don't know if I was right to say that.

● **atinar con**: *atiné con la calle enseguida*, I managed to find the street straightaway.

● **atinar en** to hit [*pt & pp* **hit**]: *atinó en el blanco*, he hit the target.

atizar *vt* **1** *(fuego)* to poke, stir. **2** *(pasiones)* to rouse. **3** *(golpe, patada)* to deal [*pt & pp* **dealt**].

atlántico,-a *adj* Atlantic.

● **el (océano) Atlántico** the Atlantic *(Ocean)*.

atlas *nm* atlas.

atleta *nmf* athlete.

atlético,-a *adj* athletic.

atletismo *nm* athletics.

atmósfera *nf* atmosphere.

atmosférico,-a *adj* atmospheric.

atolladero *nm* fix, jam.

atolondrado,-a *adj* **1** *(aturullado)* scatterbrained. **2** *(aturdido)* confused, stunned.

atómico,-a *adj* atomic.

átomo *nm* atom.

atónito,-a *adj* astonished, amazed.

átono,-a *adj* atonic, unstressed.

atontado,-a *adj* **1** *(aturdido)* stunned, confused. **2** *(tonto)* stupid, silly.

atontar *vt* **1** *(atundir)* to stun, bewilder. **2** *(volver tonto)*: *la televisión la atonta*, television dulls her mind.

atormentar *vt* to torment.

► *vpr* **atormentarse** to torment oneself.

atornillar *vt* to screw.

atracador,-ra *nm,f* *(de banco)* bank robber; *(en la calle)* mugger.

atracar *vt* *(robar - banco)* to hold up [*pt & pp* **held**], rob; *(- persona)* to mug.

► *vi* *(barco - acercarse)* to come alongside; *(- amarrar)* to tie up.

► *vpr* **atracarse** *(de comida)* to gorge oneself.

atracción *nf* attraction.

● **sentir atracción por** ALGN to be attracted to SB.

atraco *nm* *(de banco)* hold-up, robbery; *(de persona)* mugging.

atracón *nm fam* binge.
● **darse un atracón de algo** to stuff oneself with STH.

atractivo,-a *adj* attractive.
► *nm* **atractivo** *(de persona)* attractiveness, charm; *(de cosa)* attraction.

atraer *vt* to attract.

atragantarse *vpr* to choke: *se atragantó con una espina*, he choked on a fish bone; *se le ha atragantado su vecina*, she can't stand her neighbour.

atrancar *vt* **1** *(puerta)* to bar, bolt. **2** *(tubería)* to block.
► *vpr* **atrancarse 1** *(tubería)* to get blocked. **2** *(puerta)* to jam.

atrapar *vt* to capture, catch [*pt & pp* **caught**].

atrás *adv* **1** *(posición)* back: *dio un salto atrás*, she jumped back; *vamos a sentarnos atrás*, let's sit at the back; *la puerta de atrás*, the back door. **2** *(tiempo)* ago: *días atrás*, several days ago.
► *interj* stand back!, move back!
● **dejar atrás** to leave behind.
● **echarse atrás** to go back on one's word.
● **ir hacia atrás** to go backwards.
● **quedarse atrás** to fall behind.
● **volverse atrás** to change one's mind, back out.

atrasado,-a *adj* **1** *(reloj)* slow. **2** *(pago)* overdue. **3** *(país)* backward, underdeveloped. **4** *(ideas)* old-fashioned.

atrasar *vt* **1** *(salida)* to delay. **2** *(reloj)* to put back.
► *vi (reloj)* to be slow.
► *vpr* **atrasarse 1** *(tren etc)* to be late. **2** *(quedarse atrás)* to stay behind.

atraso *nm* **1** *(retraso)* delay. **2** *(de reloj)* slowness. **3** *(de país)* backwardness.
► *nm pl* **atrasos** arrears.

atravesar *vt* **1** *(cruzar)* to cross. **2** *(poner oblicuamente)* to put across, lay across [*pt & pp* **laid**]. **3** *(bala etc)* to pierce, run through [*pt* **ran**; *pp* **run**]. **4** *(crisis, situación)* to go through.
► *vpr* **atravesarse** to be in the way.
● **atravesársele ALGN a uno** not to be able to bear SB.

atrayente *adj* attractive.

atreverse *vpr* to dare: *¡atrévete!*, I dare you!, you just dare!; *¿a que no te atreves?*, I bet you wouldn't dare!; *no me atreví a contestar*, I didn't dare answer.

atrevido,-a *adj* **1** *(osado)* daring, bold. **2** *(insolente)* cheeky. **3** *(indecoroso)* risqué.

atrevimiento *nm* **1** *(osadía)* daring, boldness. **2** *(insolencia)* cheek, insolence.

atribuir *vt* to attribute, ascribe.
► *vpr* **atribuirse** *(crimen)* to admit to having committed; *(acto terrorista)* to claim responsibility for.

atributo *nm* attribute, quality.

atril *nm* lectern.

atrio *nm* **1** *(patio)* atrium. **2** *(vestíbulo)* vestibule.

atrocidad *nf* **1** *(crueldad)* atrocity. **2** *(disparate)* silly remark.
● **cometer una atrocidad** to commit an atrocity.

atropellar *vt* to knock down, run over [*pt* **ran**; *pp* **run**]: *lo atropelló un autobús*, he was knocked down by a bus.

atropello *nm* **1**: *ha habido muchos atropellos aquí*, a lot of people have been run over here. **2** *(abuso)* outrage, abuse.

atroz *adj* **1** *(bárbaro)* atrocious, appalling. **2** *(enorme)* enormous, huge. **3** *(horrible)* awful, atrocious.

ATS *abr* **(ayudante técnico sanitario)** medical auxiliary.

atuendo *nm* attire.

atún *nm* tuna.

aturdir *vt* **1** *(pasmar)* to stun. **2** *(confundir)* to confuse.
► *vpr* **aturdirse** to be confused.

audacia *nf* audacity, boldness.

audaz *adj* audacious, bold.

audición *nf* **1** *(acción)* hearing. **2** *(para obra etc)* audition. **3** *(concierto)* concert.

audiencia *nf* **1** *(recepción, público)* audience. **2** *(tribunal)* court.

audífono *nm* hearing aid.

audiovisual *adj* audio-visual.

auditorio *nm* **1** *(público)* audience. **2** *(lugar)* auditorium.

auge *nm* **1** *(buen momento)* boom. **2** *(subida)* rise. **3** *(crecimiento)* growth.
● **en auge** *(prosperando)* booming; *(subiendo)* on the rise.

augurar *vt* *(persona)* to predict; *(suceso)* to augur.

augurio *nm* omen.

aula *nf (en escuela)* classroom; *(en universidad)* lecture hall.

aullar *vi* to howl.

aullido *nm* howl.

aumentar *vt* **1** *(incrementar)* to increase, raise. **2** *(en óptica)* to magnify. **3** *(fotos)* to enlarge.
► *vi* to increase, rise [*pt* **rose**; *pp* **risen**].

aumento *nm* **1** *(incremento)* rise, increase: *un aumento de sueldo*, a pay rise. **2** *(en óptica)* magnification. **3** *(de foto)* enlargement.
● **ir en aumento** to be on the increase.
aun *adv* even.
● **aun así** even so.
● **aun cuando** although, even though.
aún *adv* **1** *(en afirmativas, interrogativas)* still: *aún la estoy esperando*, I'm still waiting for her; *¿aún está allí?*, is he still there? **2** *(en negativas)* yet: *aún no ha llegado*, he hasn't arrived yet; *¿aún no sabes montar en bici?*, don't you know how to ride a bike yet? **3** *(en comparaciones)* even: *dicen que aún hará más frío*, they say it's going to get even colder.
aunque *conj* **1** *(a pesar de que)* although, even though: *aunque no quería, tuve que ir*, although I didn't want to, I had to go. **2** *(incluso)* even if: *pásate por casa aunque sea tarde*, drop by my house even if it's late. **3** *(pero)* although, though: *me gusta Barcelona, aunque prefiero Sevilla*, I like Barcelona, although I prefer Seville.
aureola *nf* aureole, halo [*pl* -**os** o -**oes**].
auricular *nm* *(de teléfono)* receiver, earpiece.
▶ *nm pl* **auriculares** headphones, earphones.
aurora *nf* dawn.
auscultar *vt* to sound, auscultate.
ausencia *nf* absence.
● **brillar por su ausencia** to be conspicuous by one's absence.
ausentarse *vpr* to go away, leave [*pt & pp* **left**].
ausente *adj* **1** *(no presente)* absent. **2** *(distraído)* absentminded.
▶ *nmf* absentee.
austeridad *nf* austerity.
austero,-a *adj* austere.
Australia *nf* Australia.
australiano,-a *adj* - *nm,f* Australian.
Austria *nf* Austria.
austríaco,-a *adj* - *nm,f* Austrian.
auténtico,-a *adj* *(cuadro)* authentic, genuine; *(persona, afecto)* genuine; *(piel, joya)* real.
auto[1] *nm* *(coche)* car.
auto[2] *nm* *(orden)* decree, writ.

autobús *nm* bus.
autocar *nm* coach.
autodidacta *adj* self-taught.
▶ *nmf*: *es un autodidacta*, he's self-taught.
autoedición *nf* desktop publishing.
autoescuela *nf* driving school.
autógrafo *nm* autograph.
autómata *nm* automaton.
automático,-a *adj* automatic.
automóvil *nm* GB car; US automobile.
automovilismo *nm* motoring.
■ **automovilismo deportivo** motor racing.
automovilista *nmf* motorist.
autonomía *nf* **1** *(independencia)* autonomy. **2** *(comunidad)* autonomous region. **3** *(de coche)* range.
autónomo,-a *adj* **1** POL autonomous, self-governing. **2** *(trabajador)* self-employed; *(traductor etc)* freelance.
▶ *nm,f* *(trabajador)* self-employed person; *(traductor, etc)* freelancer.
autopista *nf* GB motorway; US expressway; US freeway.
■ **autopista de la información** information superhighway.
autopsia *nf* autopsy.
autor, -ra *nm,f* **1** *(de libro)* author, writer. **2** *(de canción)* writer. **3** *(de crimen)* perpetrator.
autoridad *nf* authority.
autoritario,-a *adj* authoritarian.
autorización *nf* authorization.
autorizar *vt* to authorize.
autorretrato *nm* self-portrait.
autoservicio *nm* **1** *(restaurante)* self-service restaurant. **2** *(gasolinera)* self-service petrol station. **3** *(supermercado)* supermarket.
autostop *nm* hitch-hiking.
● **hacer autostop** to hitch-hike.
autovía *nf* GB dual-carriageway; US highway.
auxiliar *vt* to help, assist.
▶ *adj* auxiliary.
▶ *nmf* assistant.
■ **auxiliar administrativo** administrative assistant.
■ **auxiliar de vuelo** flight attendant.
auxilio *nm* help, assistance.
▶ *interj*: *¡auxilio!*, help!
● **pedir auxilio** to ask for help.

avalancha *nf* avalanche.

avance *nm* **1** *(progreso, movimiento)* advance. **2** *(pago)* advance payment.

■ **avance informativo** news preview.

avanzar *vt* **1** *(adelantar)* to advance, move forward: *avanzó la ficha*, she moved the counter forward. **2** *(anticipar)* to tell in advance [*pt & pp* told].

▶ *vi* **1** *(ir hacia adelante)* to advance, to move forward. **2** *(progresar)* to make progress.

avaricia *nf* avarice, greed.

avaricioso,-a *adj* avaricious, greedy.

avaro,-a *adj* miserly.

▶ *nm,f* miser.

avasallar *vt* to subjugate, subdue.

ave *nf* bird.

■ **ave de rapiña** bird of prey.

■ **ave rapaz** bird of prey.

AVE *abr* (**Alta Velocidad Española**) *Spanish high-speed train*.

avecinarse *vpr* to be on the way.

avellana *nf* hazelnut.

avemaría *nf* Hail Mary.

avena *nf* oats *pl*.

avenida *nf* **1** *(calle)* avenue. **2** *(de río)* flood.

avenirse *vpr* to agree.

● **avenirse a algo** to agree to STH.

● **avenirse con ALGN** to get on well with SB.

aventajado,-a *adj* outstanding.

aventajar *vt* **1** *(ir por delante de)* to lead [*pt & pp* led], be ahead of: *el Celta aventaja al Betis en un punto*, Celta leads Betis by one point. **2** *(superar)* to surpass.

aventura *nf* **1** *(suceso)* adventure. **2** *(riesgo)* venture. **3** *(relación amorosa)* affair, love affair.

aventurero,-a *adj* adventurous.

▶ *nm,f* *(hombre)* adventurer; *(mujer)* adventuress.

avergonzado,-a *adj* **1** *(por mala acción)* ashamed. **2** *(por situación bochornosa)* embarrassed.

avergonzar *vt* **1** *(por mala acción)* to shame. **2** *(por situación bochornosa)* to embarrass.

▶ *vpr* **avergonzarse 1** *(por mala acción)* to be ashamed. **2** *(por situación bochornosa)* to be embarrassed.

avería *nf* **1** *(en coche)* breakdown. **2** *(en máquina)* fault.

tener una avería to break down [*pt* broke; *pp* broken].

averiado,-a *adj* **1** *(aparato)* faulty, not working. **2** *(coche)* broken down.

● **"Averiado"** "Out of order".

averiarse *vpr* **1** *(coche)* to break down [*pt* broke; *pp* broken]. **2** *(máquina)* to malfunction.

averiguar *vt* to find out [*pt & pp* found].

aversión *nf* aversion.

● **sentir aversión por** to loathe.

avestruz *nm* ostrich.

aviación *nf* **1** *(civil)* aviation. **2** *(militar)* air force.

aviador,-ra *nm,f* aviator; *(hombre)* airman [*pl* -men]; *(mujer)* airwoman [*pl* -women].

avidez *nf* eagerness.

ávido,-a *adj* avid, eager.

avión *nm* plane, GB aeroplane; US airplane.

● **por avión** by airmail.

■ **avión a reacción** jet plane.

■ **avión de combate** fighter plane.

■ **avión de papel** paper dart.

avioneta *nf* light aircraft.

avisar *vt* **1** *(informar)* to tell [*pt & pp* told]: *avísame cuando llegues*, let me know when you arrive, tell me when you arrive. **2** *(advertir)* to warn. **3** *(mandar llamar)* to call for: *avisar al médico*, to send for the doctor.

aviso *nm* **1** *(información)* notice. **2** *(advertencia)* warning.

● **estar sobre aviso** to be on the alert.

● **hasta nuevo aviso** until further notice.

● **poner a ALGN sobre aviso** to warn SB about STH.

● **sin previo aviso** without prior warning.

avispa *nf* wasp.

avispero *nm* *(nido)* wasps' nest.

avivar *vt* **1** *(fuego)* to stoke up. **2** *(pasiones)* to arouse; *(dolor)* to intensify. **3** *(paso)* to quicken. **4** *(colores)* to brighten.

▶ *vpr* **avivarse** to become brighter, become livelier.

axila *nf* armpit.

ay *interj* **1** *(dolor)* ouch!, ow! **2** *(pena)* alas!

ayer *adv* **1** *(el día anterior)* yesterday: *llegaron ayer*, they arrived yesterday. **2** *(en el pasado)* in the past.

▶ *nm* past.

- **antes de ayer** the day before yesterday.
- **ayer por la mañana** yesterday morning.
- **ayer por la noche** last night.

ayuda *nf* help, assistance.

■ **ayuda humanitaria** humanitarian aid.

ayudante *nmf* assistant.

ayudar *vt* to help, aid, assist.

▶ *vpr* **ayudarse 1** *(apoyarse)* to make use of. **2** *(unos a otros)* to help one another.

ayunar *vi* to fast.

ayunas *nm pl* .

- **en ayunas** without having eaten breakfast.
- **tomar en ayunas** take on an empty stomach.

ayuno *nm* fast, fasting.

ayuntamiento *nm* **1** *(corporación)* town council. **2** *(edificio)* town hall.

azabache *nm* jet.

azada *nf* hoe.

azafata *nf* **1** *(de avión)* flight attendant. **2** *(de congresos)* hostess.

azafrán *nm* saffron.

azahar *nm (de naranjo)* orange blossom; *(de limonero)* lemon blossom.

azar *nm* chance.

- **al azar** at random.
- **por azar** by chance.

azotaina *nf fam* spanking.

azotar *vt* **1** *(con látigo)* to whip. **2** *(golpear)* to beat [*pt* **beat**; *pp* **beaten**].

azote *nm* **1** *(látigo)* whip. **2** *(latigazo)* lash. **3** *(manotada)* smack. **4** *(calamidad)* scourge.

azotea *nf* flat roof.

- **estar mal de la azotea** *fam* to have a screw loose.

azteca *adj* - *nmf* Aztec.

azúcar *nm & nf* sugar.

azucarar *vt* **1** *(endulzar)* to sugar, sweeten. **2** *(bañar)* to coat with sugar, ice with sugar.

azucarero,-a *adj* sugar.

▶ *nm* **azucarero** sugar bowl.

azucena *nf* white lily.

azufre *nm* sulphur.

azul *adj* - *nm* blue.

■ **azul celeste** sky blue.

■ **azul marino** navy blue.

azulado,-a *adj* blue, bluish.

azulejo *nm* tile.

B

baba *nf* **1** *(de adulto)* spittle. **2** *(de perro)* slobber. **3** *(de niño)* dribble.
● **se le cae la baba con ella** *fam* he's besotted with her.

babear *vi* **1** *(adulto)* to drool. **2** *(perro)* to slobber. **3** *(niño)* to dribble.

babero *nm* **1** *(de bebé)* bib. **2** *(para colegio)* overall.

babi *nm* child's overall.

babor *nm* port, port side.

babosa *nf* slug.

baboso,-a *adj* **1** *(perro)* slobbering. **2** *(niño)* dribbling. **3** *(pegajoso)* slimy.
► *nm,f fam (persona pegajosa)* creep.

baca *nf (de coche)* roof rack.

bacalao *nm* cod.
● **cortar el bacalao** to have the final say.

bache *nm* **1** *(en carretera)* pothole. **2** *(en el aire)* air pocket. **3** *fig (mal momento)* bad patch.

bachillerato *nm (in Spain)* secondary school course.

bacilo *nm* bacillus [*pl* **bacilli**].

bacon *nm* bacon.

bacteria *nf* bacterium [*pl* **bacteria**].

bafle *nm* loudspeaker.

bahía *nf* bay.

bailar *vt-vi* **1** *(danzar)* to dance. **2** *(quedar grande)* to be too big: *le bailaba la falda*, her skirt was too big for her. **3** *(mesa)* to be wobbly. **4** *(pieza, tornillo)* to be loose.
● **sacar a ALGN a bailar** to ask SB to dance.

bailarín,-ina *adj* dancing.
► *nm,f* dancer.
■ **bailarina de ballet** ballerina, ballet dancer.

baile *nm* **1** *(danza, fiesta)* dance: *el baile típico de Andalucía*, Andalucía's typical dance. **2** *(de etiqueta)* ball.
■ **baile de disfraces** masked ball.

baja *nf* **1** *(descenso)* fall, drop. **2** *(en guerra)* casualty. **3** *(por enfermedad)* sick leave: *está de baja*, he's off sick. **4** injury: *fue baja en el partido*, he didn't play because he was injured.
● **darse de baja 1** *(de un club)* to resign. **2** *(en una suscripción)* to cancel. **3** *(por enfermedad)* to take sick leave.
■ **baja maternal** maternity leave.

bajada *nf* **1** *(acción)* descent. **2** *(en carretera etc)* slope. **3** *(de temperatura)* fall, drop.

bajamar *nf* low tide.

bajar *vt* **1** *(de un lugar alto)* to bring down [*pt & pp* **brought**], take down: *bajó un libro de la estantería*, he took a book down from the shelf. **2** *(mover abajo)* to lower: *¿has bajado las persianas?*, have you lowered the blinds?; *bájame la cremallera*, can you undo my zip? **3** *(recorrer de arriba abajo)* to come down, go down: *bajamos la escalera*, we went down the stairs. **4** *(brazos)* to lower; *(cabeza)* to bow. **5** *(voz, radio, volumen)* to lower, to turn down. **6** *(precios)* to reduce. **7** *(fiebre)* to bring down. **8** INFORM *(de la red)* to download.
► *vi* **1** *(ir abajo -acercándose)* to come down; *(- alejándose)* to go down: *¡baja de ahí!*, come down from there!; *¿bajas en ascensor?*, are you going down in the lift?; *me ha bajado la regla*, my period has started. **2** *(apearse - de coche)* to get out; *(- de bicicleta, caballo, avión, tren)* to

get off. **3** *(reducirse)* to fall [*pt* **fell**; *pp* **fallen**], drop, come down: *el euro sigue bajando*, the euro continues to fall; *los precios han bajado*, prices have come down. **4** to go down, be relegated: *mi equipo ha bajado a segunda*, my team has been relegated to the 2nd division.
▶ *vpr* **bajarse 1** *(ir abajo — acercándose)* to come down; *(- alejándose)* to go down. **2** *(apearse - de coche)* to get out; *(- de bicicleta, caballo, avión, tren)* to get off. **3** *(agacharse)* to bend down [*pt & pp* **bent**]. **4** *(pantalones, falda)* to pull down.

bajo,-a *adj* **1** *(de poca altura)* low: *una casa baja*, a low house; *precios bajos*, low prices; *con la cabeza baja*, with his head bowed. **2** *(persona)* short. **3** *(tosco)* vulgar. **4** *(territorio, río)* lower. **5** *(inferior)* poor, low: *la clase baja*, the lower classes; *los bajos fondos*, the underworld.
▶ *adv* **bajo 1** *(volar)* low. **2** *(hablar)* softly, quietly.
▶ *prep (gen)* under; *(con temperaturas)* below: *bajo las estrellas*, under the stars; *10 grados bajo cero*, 10 degrees below zero; *bajo tierra*, underground.
▶ *nm* **bajo 1** *(piso)* GB ground floor; US first floor. **2** *(instrumento)* bass.
▶ *nm pl* **bajos** GB ground floor; US first floor.
• **bajo ningún concepto** under no circumstances.
• **por lo bajo 1** (disimuladamente) on the sly. **2** (en voz baja) in a low voice.
■ **la Baja Edad Media** the late Middle Ages.

bajón *nm* **1** *fig (descenso)* fall. **2** *(de salud)* relapse.

bala *nf* bullet: *un disparo de bala*, a gunshot; *un cristal a prueba de balas*, a bullet-proof glass.
• **como una bala** *fam* like a shot.
■ **bala de fogueo** blank cartridge.
■ **bala de cañón** cannon ball.
■ **bala perdida 1** *(proyectil)* stray bullet. **2** *(persona)* good-for-nothing.

balance *nm* **1** balance, balance sheet. **2** *(resultado)* result: *¿cuál es el balance de estos dos años?*, what have we achieved over these two years?
• **hacer balance de algo** to evaluate STH.

balancear *vi-vpr* **balancear(se)** *(mecerse)* to rock; *(en columpio)* to swing; *(barco)* to roll.
▶ *vt* to balance.

balanceo *nm* swinging, rocking, rolling.

balancín *nm* **1** *(mecedora)* rocking chair. **2** *(de niños)* seesaw.

balanza *nf* **1** *(para pesar)* scales *pl*. **2** balance.
■ **balanza comercial** balance of trade.
■ **balanza de pagos** balance of payments.

balar *vi* to bleat.

balazo *nm* **1** *(disparo)* shot: *lo mató de un balazo*, he shot him dead. **2** *(herida)* bullet wound.

balbucear *vi* **1** *(al hablar)* to stutter. **2** *(niño)* to babble.

balcón *nm* balcony.

balda *nf* shelf [*pl* -**ves**].

baldado,-a *adj* **1** *(inválido)* crippled. **2** *fam (cansado)* shattered.

balde *nm* *(cubo)* bucket, pail.
• **de balde** free, for nothing.
• **en balde** in vain.

baldosa *nf* floor tile.

balear *adj* Balearic.
■ **Islas Baleares** Balearic Islands.

balido *nm* bleat.

baliza *nf* **1** *(en el mar)* buoy. **2** *(en tierra)* beacon.

ballena *nf* whale.

ballesta *nf* **1** *(arma)* crossbow. **2** *(muelle)* spring.

ballet *nm* ballet.

balneario *nm* spa, health resort.

balón *nm* ball.

baloncesto *nm* basketball.

balonmano *nm* handball.

balonvolea *nf* volleyball.

balsa *nf* **1** *(charca)* pool, pond. **2** *(barca)* raft.
• **como una balsa de aceite 1** (mar) like a millpond. **2** (situación) very peaceful.

bálsamo *nm* balsam, balm.

báltico,-a *adj* Baltic.
■ **el mar Báltico** the Baltic Sea.

bambú *nm* bamboo [*pl* -**s**].

banana *nf* banana.

banca *nf* **1** *(sector)* banking; *(los bancos)* the banks: *trabaja en la banca*, he's in banking. **2** *(asiento)* bench.
■ **banca telefónica** telephone banking.

bancario,-a *adj* banking.
bancarrota *nf* bankruptcy.
● **declararse en bancarrota** to go bankrupt.
banco *nm* **1** *(institución financiera)* bank. **2** *(asiento)* bench; *(de iglesia)* pew. **3** *(mesa)* bench.
■ **banco de arena** sandbank.
■ **banco de carpintero** workbench.
■ **banco de datos** data bank.
■ **banco de esperma** sperm bank.
■ **banco de niebla** tog bank.
■ **banco de órganos** organ bank.
■ **banco mundial** World Bank.
■ **banco de peces** shoal of fish.
■ **banco de sangre** blood bank.
banda[1] *nf* **1** *(de gala)* sash. **2** *(lado)* side.
● **cerrarse en banda** to dig [*pt & pp* **dug**] one's heels in.
■ **banda de frecuencia** radio band.
■ **banda magnética** magnetic srip.
■ **banda sonora** sound track.
■ **banda transportadora** conveyor belt.
banda[2] *nf* **1** *(de ladrones)* gang. **2** *(musical)* band.
bandada *nf* flock.
bandazo *nm:* **el coche iba dando bandazos,** the car was swerving from side to side; **iba dando bandazos, sin trabajo fijo,** he was constantly moving from one job to another.
bandeja *nf* tray.
● **poner o servir algo en bandeja a ALGN** to hand STH to SB on a plate.
bandera *nf* flag.
banderín *nm* pennant, small flag.
bandido,-a *nm,f* bandit.
bando[1] *nm* *(facción)* faction, party.
bando[2] *nm* *(edicto)* edict, proclamation.
bandolero *nm* bandit.
banquero,-a *nm,f* banker.
banqueta *nf* **1** *(taburete)* stool, footstool. **2** *(banco)* little bench.
banquete *nm* banquet, feast.
■ **banquete de boda** wedding reception.
banquillo *nm* **1** *(de acusados)* dock. **2** *(en deporte)* bench.
bañador *nm* *(de mujer)* bathing costume, swimming costume; *(de hombre)* swimming trunks *pl*.
bañar *vt* **1** *(en bañera)* to bath. **2** *(con oro,*

plata) to plate. **3** *(con salsa)* to coat. **4** *(con licor)* to soak.
▶ *vpr* **bañarse** *(en bañera)* to have a bath, take a bath; *(en el mar, piscina)* to swim [*pt* **swam**; *pp* **swum**]: **¿te has bañado ya?,** have you been in the water?; **prohibido bañarse,** no swimming.
bañera *nf* bath, bathtub.
bañista *nmf* bather, swimmer.
baño *nm* **1** *(acción)* bath. **2** *(bañera)* bath, bathtub. **3** *(capa)* coat, coating. **4** *(sala de baño)* bathroom. **5** *(wáter)* toilet.
▶ *nm pl* **baños** *(balneario)* spa *sing*.
● **tomar baños de sol** to sunbathe.
■ **baño María** bain-marie.
■ **baño turco** Turkish bath.
bar *nm* *(cafetería)* café, snack bar; *(de bebidas alcohólicas)* bar.
baraja *nf* pack, deck.
barajar *vt* **1** *(naipes)* to shuffle. **2** *(posibilidades)* to consider.
baranda *nf* handrail, banister.
barandilla *nf* handrail, banister.
baratija *nf* trinket, knick-knack.
barato,-a *adj* cheap.
▶ *adv* **barato** cheaply, cheap.
barba *nf* beard: **barba de un día,** one day's growth of stubble.
● **afeitarse la barba** to shave one's beard.
● **dejarse la barba** to grow a beard [*pt* **grew**; *pp* **grown**].
● **por barba** each, a head: **tocan a 10 euros por barba,** it's 10 euros a head.
barbaridad *nf* **1** *(crueldad)* cruelty. **2** *(disparate)* piece of nonsense: **¡qué barbaridad!,** how awful!; **cuesta una barbaridad,** it costs a fortune.
bárbaro,-a *adj* **1** HIST barbarian. **2** *(cruel)* cruel. **3** *(temerario)* daring. **4** *fam (grande)* enormous: **fue un éxito bárbaro,** it was a smashing success. **5** *fam (espléndido)* tremendous, terrific: **¡qué bárbaro! bueno,** great!; **¡qué bárbaro! malo,** how awful!
▶ *nm,f* HIST barbarian.
barbecho *nm* fallow land.
barbería *nf* barber's.
barbero *nm* barber.
barbilla *nf* chin.
barbudo,-a *adj* bearded.
▶ *nm* bearded man.
barca *nf* boat.
barcaza *nf* **1** *(de desembarco)* lighter. **2** *(para cruzar rías)* barge.

barco *nm* boat, ship.
■ **barco cisterna** tanker.
■ **barco de guerra** warship.
■ **barco de pesca** fishing boat.
■ **barco de vapor** steamer.
■ **barco de vela** sailing boat, yacht.
barniz *nm* varnish.
barnizar *vt* to varnish.
barómetro *nm* barometer.
barón *nm* baron.
barquero,-a *nm,f (hombre)* boatman [*pl* -men]; *(mujer)* boatwoman [*pl* -women].
barquillo *nm* wafer.
barra *nf* **1** *(de hierro)* bar. **2** *(en armario)* rail. **3** *(de cortina)* rod. **4** *(de bicicleta)* crossbar. **5** *(de hielo)* block. **6** *(de pan)* loaf [*pl* -ves]. **7** *(de bar, cafetería)* bar. **8** *(de arena)* sandbank.
■ **barra de labios** lipstick.
■ **barra fija** horizontal bar.
■ **barra libre** free bar.
■ **barras asimétricas** asymmetric bars.
■ **barras paralelas** parallel bars.
barraca *nf* **1** *(cabaña)* hut; *(chabola)* shanty. **2** *(de feria)* stall.
barranco *nm* **1** *(precipicio)* precipice. **2** *(entre montañas)* gully.
barrendero,-a *nm,f* street sweeper.
barreño *nm* large bowl.
barrer *vt* **1** *(con escoba)* to sweep [*pt & pp* swept]. **2** *(rival)* to sweep aside [*pt & pp* swept].
● **barrer para adentro** to look after number one.
barrera *nf* barrier.
● **traspasar una barrera** to pass a mark.
■ **barrera aduanera** customs barrier.
■ **barrera de coral** coral reef.
■ **barrera del sonido** sound barrier.
■ **barrera generacional** generation gap.
■ **barrera psicológica** psychological barrier.
barriada *nf* neighbourhood.
barricada *nf* barricade.
barriga *nf* belly: *me duele la barriga*, I have stomachache.
● **tener barriga** to have a belly.
barril *nm* barrel, keg.
barrio *nm* GB district, area; US neighborhood: *es de mi barrio*, he lives near where I live; *vivo en un barrio de las*

afueras, I live in the suburb; *cine de barrio*, local cinema.
● **irse al otro barrio** *fam* to kick the bucket.
■ **barrio bajo** seedy area.
■ **barrio histórico** old town.
■ **barrio residencial** residential area.
barrizal *nm* mire.
barro *nm* **1** *(lodo)* mud: *estás lleno de barro*, you are covered in mud. **2** *(arcilla)* clay: *objetos de barro*, earthenware.
barroco,-a *adj* baroque.
▶ *nm* **barroco** baroque.
barrote *nm* **1** *(de celda)* bar. **2** *(de escalera, silla)* rung.
bártulos *nm pl* things, stuff *sing*.
● **liar los bártulos** to pack up.
barullo *nm* .
● **armar barullo** to make a racket.
basar *vt* to base.
▶ *vpr* **basarse** to be based: *¿en qué te basas para decir eso?*, what basis do you have to say that?; *una teoría basada en la investigación*, a theory based on research.
báscula *nf* scales *pl*.
■ **báscula de baño** bathroom scales *pl*.
base *nf* **1** *(superficie)* base. **2** *(fundamento)* basis. **3** *(fondo)* background. **4** *(componente principal)*: *la base de su dieta es la carne*, his diet is meat-based; *la base del éxito*, the key to success; *carecer de base*, to lack foundation; *partiendo de esta base*, on this assumption.
▶ *adj* **1** *(texto)* draft. **2** *(alimento, idea)* basic.
● **a base de**: *un postre hecho a base de leche y huevos*, a pudding made of milk and eggs; *a base de mucho trabajo*, by working hard; *comimos a base de bien*, we had a lot to eat.
■ **base aérea** air base.
■ **base de datos** database.
■ **base espacial** space station.
básico,-a *adj* basic.
basílica *nf* basilica.
bastante *adj-pron* **1** *(suficiente)* enough, sufficient. **2** *(abundante)* quite a lot: *creo que hay bastante alcohol*, I think there's enough alcohol; *¿fue mucha gente?- Sí, había bastante público*, were there many people?- Yes, there were quite a lot of people in the audience.

► *adv* **1** enough: *no hay bastante*, there isn't enough. **2** *(un poco)* fairly, quite.

bastar *vi* to be sufficient, be enough: *con eso no basta*, that's not enough.

● **¡basta ya!** that's enough!

● **bastarse a sí mismo** to be self-sufficient.

● **con la intención basta** it's the thought that counts.

bastardo,-a *adj* **1** *(ilegítimo)* bastard. **2** *(despreciable)* base, mean.

bastidor *nm* **1** *(de puerta, cuadro)* frame. **2** *(de coche)* chassis.

● **entre bastidores** behind the scenes.

basto *nm pl* **bastos** *(baraja española)* clubs.

basto,-a *adj* **1** *(grosero)* coarse, rough. **2** *(sin pulimentar)* rough, unpolished.

bastón *nm* **1** *(para andar)* stick, walking stick. **2** *(de militar)* baton.

basura *nf* GB rubbish; US garbage.

● **tirar algo a la basura** to throw STH away, throw STH in the bin [*pt* **threw**; *pp* **thrown**].

● **sacar la basura** to take out the rubbish.

basurero *nm* **1** *(vertedero)* rubbish dump. **2** *(persona)* GB dustman [*pl* -**men**]; US garbage man.

bata *nf* **1** *(de casa)* dressing gown. **2** *(de trabajo)* overall; *(de médicos etc)* white coat. **3** *(de colegial)* child's overall.

batacazo.

● **darse un batacazo** to fall over [*pt* **fell**; *pp* **fallen**].

batalla *nf* battle.

● **de batalla** *fam* ordinary, everyday: *zapatos de batalla*, everyday shoes.

■ **batalla campal** pitched battle.

■ **batalla naval 1** naval battle. **2** *(juego)* battleships.

batallón *nm* battalion.

bate *nm* bat.

batería *nf* **1** *(de coche)* battery: *me quedé sin batería*, my battery went dead. **2** *(cañones)* battery. **3** *(de conjunto)* drums: *toco la batería*, I play the drums.

► *nmf* drummer.

● **en batería** *(coches)* at an angle to the curb.

■ **batería de cocina** cookware set.

batido,-a *adj* **1** *(camino)* beaten. **2** *(huevos)* beaten.

► *nm* **batido** milk shake.

batidora *nf* *(manual)* whisk; *(eléctrica)* blender.

batín *nm* dressing gown.

batir *vt* **1** *(huevos)* to beat [*pt* **beat**; *pp* **beaten**]; *(nata, claras)* to whip. **2** *(palmas)* to clap. **3** *(metales)* to hammer. **4** *(alas)* to flap. **5** *(vencer)* to beat [*pt* **beat**; *pp* **beaten**], defeat. **6** to break [*pt* **broke**; *pp* **broken**]: *batió el récord del mundo*, she broke the world record. **7** *(terreno)* to reconnoitre.

► *vi* **1** *(viento, olas)* to beat. **2** *(persiana)* to rattle.

► *vpr* **batirse** to fight [*pt* & *pp* **fought**].

● **batirse en duelo** to fight a duel.

batuta *nf* baton.

● **llevar la batuta** to call the shots [*pt* & *pp* **led**].

● **tomar la batuta** to take charge.

baúl *nm* trunk.

bautismo *nm* baptism, christening.

bautizar *vt* **1** to baptize, christen. **2** *(poner nombre a)* to name: *la han bautizado con el nombre de su abuela*, she's been named after her grandmother. **3** *(apodar)* to nickname.

bautizo *nm* **1** *(sacramento)* baptism, christening. **2** *(fiesta)* christening party. **3** *(de un barco)* christening, naming.

baya *nf* berry.

bayeta *nf* cloth.

bayoneta *nf* bayonet.

baza *nf* **1** *(en naipes)* trick. **2** *(ocasión)* chance: *es mi mejor baza*, it's my best weapon; *jugar la última baza*, to play one's best card.

● **meter baza** to butt in.

bazar *nm* bazaar.

bazo *nm* spleen.

bebé *nm* baby.

bebedor,-ra *adj* drinking.

► *nm,f* hard drinker.

beber *vt* to drink [*pt* **drank**; *pp* **drunk**]: *si bebes, no conduzcas*, don't drink and drive; *no bebo alcohol*, I don't drink.

● **beber a la salud de** ALGN to toast SB.

● **beber los vientos por** ALGN (fam) to be crazy about SB.

bebida *nf* drink, beverage.

● **darse a la bebida** to take to drink.

● **dejar la bebida** to stop drinking.

■ **bebida alcohólica** alcoholic drink.

bebido,-a *adj* drunk.

beca *nf* **1** *(ayuda)* grant. **2** *(por méritos)* scholarship.

■ **beca de investigación** research grant.

becerro *nm* calf [*pl* **-ves**].

bechamel *nf* béchamel sauce, white sauce.

bedel *nm* beadle, head porter.

beige *adj* - *nm* beige.

béisbol *nm* baseball.

belén *nm* nativity scene, crib.

belga *adj* - *nmf* Belgian.

Bélgica *nf* Belgium.

bélico *adj*: **conflicto bélico**, war; **juguete bélico**, war toy.

belleza *nf* **1** *(cualidad)* beauty. **2** *(persona)* beauty: **es una belleza**, she's a beauty, she's a beautiful woman.

bello,-a *adj* beautiful.

● **bellas artes** fine arts.

bellota *nf* acorn.

bemol *nm* flat.

bendecir *vt* to bless: **¡que Dios te bendiga!**, God bless you!

bendición *nf* blessing.

► *nf pl* **bendiciones** wedding ceremony.

bendito,-a *adj* **1** blessed. **2** *(maldito)* blessed, blasted.

► *nm,f*: **es un bendito**, he's a simple soul.

● **dormir como un bendito** to sleep like a baby.

beneficencia *nf* beneficence, charity.

beneficiar *vt* to benefit, favour: **eres el más beneficiado**, you have benefited most; **esta lluvia no beneficia a nadie**, this rain is no benefit.

► *vpr* **beneficiarse** to benefit from.

beneficio *nm* profit: **margen de beneficios**, profit margin; **no sacó grandes beneficios**, he didn't benefit much; **en beneficio de todos**, in the interest of everyone; **en mi propio beneficio**, to my own advantage.

■ **beneficio bruto** gross profit.

■ **beneficio neto** clear profit.

beneficioso,-a *adj* beneficial, useful.

benéfico,-a *adj* charitable: **función benéfica**, charity performance.

bengala *nf* flare.

benigno,-a *adj* **1** *(tumor)* benign. **2** *(clima)* mild.

benjamín,-ina *nm,f* youngest child [*pl* **children**].

berberecho *nm* cockle.

berenjena *nf* GB aubergine; US eggplant.

bermudas *nf pl* Bermuda shorts.

berrear *vi* **1** *(becerro)* to bellow. **2** *(niño)* to howl, bawl.

berrido *nm* **1** *(de becerro)* bellow. **2** *(de niño)* howl, shriek.

berrinche *nm* tantrum: **se llevó un berrinche**, she flew into a temper.

berro *nm* watercress, cress.

berza *nf* cabbage.

besamel *nf* bechamel sauce, white sauce.

besar *vt* to kiss.

► *vpr* **besarse** to kiss.

beso *nm* kiss.

● **dar un beso a ALGN** to kiss SB, give SB a kiss.

■ **beso de tornillo** French kiss.

bestia *nf* *(animal)* beast.

► *nmf* *(persona)* brute: **conduce a lo bestia**, he drives like a brute.

► *adj* brutish: **¡no seas bestia!**, don't be so brutish!; **¡qué bestia, cómo come!**, the way she eats is amazing.

■ **bestia de carga** beast of burden.

■ **bestia negra** bête noire.

bestial *adj* **1** *(brutal)* beastly, bestial. **2** *fam (enorme)* enormous. **3** *fam (extraordinario)* great, fantastic.

bestialidad *nf* **1** *(brutalidad)* bestiality, brutality. **2** *(tontería)* stupidity. **3** *fam (gran cantidad)* tons *pl*: **una bestialidad de comida**, tons of food.

besugo *nm* **1** *(pez)* sea bream. **2** *(persona)* idiot.

● **sostener un diálogo para besugos** to talk at cross purposes.

betún *nm* *(para zapatos)* shoe polish: **deberías darle betún a tus zapatos**, you should polish your shoes.

biberón *nm* baby bottle.

● **dar el biberón al niño** to give the baby his bottle.

Biblia *nf* Bible.

bíblico,-a *adj* biblical.

bibliografía *nf* **1** *(en libro)* bibliography. **2** *(de curso)* reading list.

biblioteca *nf* **1** *(edificio)* library. **2** *(mueble)* bookcase, bookshelf [*pl* **-ves**].

■ **biblioteca universitaria** university library.

bibliotecario,-a *nm,f* librarian.
bicarbonato *nm* bicarbonate.
bíceps *nm* biceps.
bicho *nm* **1** *(insecto)* bug. **2** *(mala persona)* nasty character: **es un mal bicho**, she's a nasty piece of work; **es un bicho raro**, he's a weirdo.
● **todo bicho viviente** every Tom, Dick or Harry.
● **bicho malo nunca muere** the devil looks after his own.
bici *nf fam* bike: **ir en bici**, to cycle.
bicicleta *nf* bicycle: **ir en bicicleta a algún sitio**, to cycle somewhere.
■ **bicicleta de carreras** racing bicycle.
■ **bicicleta de montaña** mountain bike.
■ **bicicleta estática** exercise bike.
bidé *nm* bidet.
bidón *nm* **1** *(pequeño)* can. **2** *(grnade)* drum.
bien *adv* **1** *(de manera satisfactoria)* well: **canta bien**, he sings well; **no veo muy bien**, I can't see very well. **2** *(correctamente)* right, correctly: **contestó bien**, he answered correctly; **lo sé muy bien**, I know perfectly well. **3** *(debidamente)* properly: **siéntate bien**, sit properly; **¡pórtate bien!**, behave yourself! **4** happily: **yo bien iría**, I would gladly go. **5** *(de acuerdo)*: **¡muy bien!**, O.K., all right. **6** *(de buena gana)* willingly. **7** *(mucho)* very; *(bastante)* quite: **es bien sencillo**, it's very simple; **bien tarde**, pretty late; **un chocolate bien caliente**, a nice and hot chocolate. **8** *(fácilmente)* easily: **bien se ve que ...**, it is easy to see that ...; **¡bien podía haber venido antes!**, he could have come earlier.
▶ *nm* good: **el bien y el mal**, good and evil; **hombre de bien**, honest man; **hacer el bien**, to do good; **lo hice por su bien**, I did it for his own good.
▶ *adj* well-to-do: **gente bien**, the upper classes.
▶ *nm pl* **bienes** property *sing*, possessions.
● **ahora bien** however.
● **bien que** although.
● **en bien de** for the sake of.
● **estar bien 1** (de gusto, olor, aspecto) to be good, be nice. **2** (de salud) to be well: **¿estás bien?**, are you O.K.?; **esa peli está muy bien**, that film is really good.

● **más bien** rather.
● **si bien** although.
● **bien...bien...** either...or....
● **¡ya está bien!** that's enough!
■ **bienes de consumo** consumer goods.
■ **bienes gananciales** shared possessions.
■ **bienes inmuebles** real estate *sing*.
bienestar *nm* well-being, comfort.
● **estado de bienestar** welfare state.
bienhechor,-ra *adj* beneficial.
▶ *nm,f (hombre)* benefactor; *(mujer)* benefactress.
bienio *nm* two-year period: **cada bienio**, every two years.
bienvenida *nf* welcome.
● **dar la bienvenida a** ALGN to welcome SB.
● **fiesta de bienvenida** welcome party.
bienvenido,-a *adj* welcome.
bifurcarse *vpr* **1** *(camino)* to fork, branch off: **nuestros caminos se bifurcaron**, our lifes took separate ways. **2** *(vía de tren)* to diverge.
bigote *nm* **1** *(de persona)* moustache. **2** *(de gato)* whiskers *pl*.
bikini *nm* bikini: **estaba sin la parte de arriba del bikini**, she was doing topless.
bilingüe *adj* bilingual.
bilingüismo *nm* bilingualism.
bilis *nf* **1** *(hiel)* bile. **2** *(mal humor)* spleen.
billar *nm* **1** *(juego)* billiards. **2** *(mesa)* billiard table.
▶ *nm pl* **billares** billiard hall.
billete *nm* **1** *(de banco)* note: **un billete de diez euros**, a ten-euro note. **2** *(de tren, autobús, sorteo, etc)* ticket: **sacar un billete**, to buy a ticket.
■ **billete de ida** one-way ticket.
■ **billete de ida y vuelta** GB return ticket; US round-trip ticket.
billetero *nm* wallet.
billón *nm* trillion; GB *(antiguamente)* billion.
bimensual *adj* two-monthly.
bimestral *adj* two-monthly.
bingo *nm* **1** *(juego)* bingo. **2** *(sala)* bingo hall.
biodegradable *adj* biodegradable.
biografía *nf* biography.

biología *nf* biology.
biológico,-a *adj* **1** *(ciclo, madre)* biological. **2** *(alimento)* organic.
biólogo,-a *nm,f* biologist.
biombo *nm* folding screen.
biquini *nm* bikini.
birlar *vt fam* to pinch, nick.
birria *nf fam* load of junk: **este libro es una birria**, this book is rubbish; **ese vestido es una birria**, that dress is really horrible.
bis *adv* **1** *(dos veces)* twice. **2** *(en calle)* A: **viven en el 23 bis**, they live at 23A.
▸ *nm (en concierto)* encore: **hacer un bis**, to play one encore.
bisabuelo,-a *nm,f (hombre)* great-grandfather; *(mujer)* great-grandmother: **mis bisabuelos**, my great-grandparents.
bisagra *nf* hinge.
bisexual *adj* - *nmf* bisexual.
bisiesto *adj:* **año bisiesto**, leap year.
bisnieto,-a *nm,f (chico)* great-grandson; *(chica)* great-granddaughter: **mis bisnietos**, my great-grandchildren.
bisonte *nm* bison.
bisté *nm* steak.
bistec *nm* steak.
bisturí *nm* scalpel.
bisutería *nf* imitation jewellery.
bit *nm* bit.
bizco,-a *adj* cross-eyed.
bizcocho *nm* sponge cake.
blanco,-a *adj* **1** *(color, pelo, vino)* white: **lo pintó de blanco**, he painted it white. **2** *(tez)* fair: **es muy blanco**, his skin is really fair; **estás muy blanco**, you look really pale.
▸ *nm* **blanco 1** *(color)* white. **2** *(objetivo físico)* target. **3** *(hueco)* blank, gap; *(en escrito)* blank space: **un cheque en blanco**, a blank cheque; **votar en blanco**, to return a blank ballot paper.
▸ *nm,f* white man/ woman.
● **dar en el blanco 1** (acertar diana) to hit the mark [*pt & pp* **hit**]. **2** (dar en el blanco) to hit the nail on the head [*pt & pp* **hit**].
● **quedarse en blanco 1** (no entender) not to understand [*pt & pp* **understood**]. **2** (olvidar) to forget everything [*pt* **forgot**; *pp* **forgotten**]: **me quedé en blanco**, my mind went blank.
■ **blanco del ojo** white of the eye.
blancura *nf* whiteness.

blando,-a *adj* **1** *(superficie, madera, queso)* soft; *(carne)* tender. **2** *(persona)* soft.
blandura *nf* **1** *(de superficie, madera, queso)* softness; *(de carne)* tenderness. **2** *fig (dulzura)* gentleness, sweetness.
blanquear *vt* **1** *(poner blanco)* to whiten. **2** *(con cal)* to whitewash. **3** *fam (dinero)* to launder.
blasfemar *vi* **1** *(decir palabrotas)* to swear [*pt* **swore**; *pp* **sworn**], curse. **2** *(contra Dios)* to blaspheme.
blasfemia *nf* **1** *(palabrota)* curse. **2** *(contra Dios)* blasphemy.
bledo *nm* .
● **me importa un bledo** *fam* I couldn't care less.
blindado,-a *adj (coche)* armoured, armour-plated; *(puerta)* reinforced.
blindar *vt* to armour.
bloc *nm* pad, notepad.
bloque *nm* **1** *(de piedra)* block. **2** *(de papel)* pad, notepad. **3** POL bloc.
● **en bloque** en bloc, en masse.
■ **bloque de pisos** block of flats.
bloquear *vt* **1** *(camino, entrada)* to block. **2** *(precios, cuentas)* to freeze [*pt* **froze**; *pp* **frozen**]. **3** *(puerto, país)* to blockade. **4** *(mecanismo)* to jam. **5** *(volante)* to lock.
▸ *vpr* **bloquearse 1** *(quedarse paralizado)* to freeze [*pt* **froze**; *pp* **frozen**]. **2** *(quedarse en blanco)* to have a blank. **3** *(mecanismo)* to jam. **4** *(volante)* to lock.
blusa *nf* blouse.
blusón *nm* loose blouse.
boa *nf* boa.
bobada *nf* stupid thing.
● **decir bobadas** to talk nonsense.
bobina *nf* **1** *(carrete)* reel, bobbin. **2** *(eléctrica)* coil.
bobo,-a *adj* silly, foolish.
▸ *nm,f* fool, dunce.
boca *nf* **1** mouth. **2** *(abertura)* entrance, opening. **3** *(de río)* mouth.
● **andar en boca de todos** to be the talk of the town.
● **boca abajo** face down.
● **boca arriba** face up.
● **no abrir la boca** not to say a word [*pt & pp* **said**].
● **no decir esta boca es mía** not to say a word [*pt & pp* **said**].
● **se me hace la boca agua** it makes my mouth water.

- **meterse en la boca del lobo** to put one's head in the lion's mouth.
- **hacer a** ALGN **el boca a boca** to give SB the kiss of life.
■ **boca a boca 1** mouth to mouth resuscitation. **2** word of mouth: *nos enteramos por el boca a boca*, we found out by word of mouth.
■ **boca de mar** crab stick.
■ **boca de metro** GB underground entrance; US subway entrance.
■ **boca del estómago** pit of the stomach.
■ **boca de riego** hydrant.
bocacalle *nf* side street: *la primera bocacalle a la izquierda*, the first turn to the left.
bocadillo *nm* **1** *(de pan de molde)* sandwich. **2** *(en barra)* roll. **3** *(en cómics)* speech balloon.
bocado *nm* **1** *(mordisco)* bite. **2** *(de comida)* mouthful. **3** *(piscolabis)* snack.
bocanada *nf* **1** *(de humo)* puff. **2** *(de viento)* gust.
bocata *nm* **1** *fam (de pan de molde)* sandwich. **2** *(en barra)* roll.
bocazas *nmf fam* bigmouth.
boceto *nm* *(dibujo)* sketch; *(proyecto)* outline.
bochorno *nm* **1** *(calor)* sultry weather, close weather, stifling heat: *hace mucho bochorno*, it's really close; *¡qué bochorno!*, how embarrassing! **2** *(vergüenza)* embarrassment, shame.
bochornoso,-a *adj* **1** *(tiempo)* hot, sultry. **2** *(vergonzoso)* shameful.
bocina *nf* horn.
- **tocar la bocina** to blow one's horn [*pt* **blew**; *pp* **blown**], sound one's horn.
boda *nf* **1** *(ceremonia)* marriage, wedding. **2** *(fiesta)* reception.
■ **bodas de oro** golden wedding *sing.*
■ **bodas de plata** silver wedding *sing.*
bodega *nf* **1** *(de vinos)* cellar, wine cellar. **2** *(tienda)* wine shop. **3** *(almacén)* pantry. **4** *(de barco, avión)* hold.
bodegón *nm* still-life painting.
bodrio *nm* *fam* load of trash: *¡menudo bodrio!*, what a load of rubbish!; *¡vaya bodrio de película!*, what a useless film!
bofetada *nf* slap in the face: *dar una bofetada a* ALGN, to slap SB in the face.

bofetón *nm* slap.
boga *nf* .
- **estar en boga** to be in fashion.
bohemio,-a *adj - nm,f* bohemian.
boicot *nm* boycott.
boicotear *vt* to boycott.
boina *nf* beret.
bol *nm* bowl.
bola *nf* **1** *(cuerpo esférico)* ball. **2** *(de helado)* scoop. **3** *fam (mentira)* fib, lie: *¡nos metió una bola!*, he told us such a fib!
► *nf pl* **bolas** *fam (testículos)* balls: *estar en bolas, ir en bolas*, to be (stark) naked.
- **ir a su bola** to do one's own thing.
■ **bola de nieve** snowball.
■ **bola del mundo** globe.
■ **bola de partido** match ball.
bolera *nf* bowling alley.
bolero *nm* *(baile)* bolero [*pl* -**s**].
boletín *nm* bulletin.
■ **boletín de inscripción** registration form.
■ **boletín de suscripción** suscription form.
■ **boletín informativo** news bulletin.
boleto *nm* **1** *(de lotería)* ticket. **2** *(de quiniela)* coupon.
boli *nm* *fam* ballpen, Biro®.
bólido *nm* **1** racing car. **2.** fireball.
bolígrafo *nm* ballpoint pen, Biro®.
Bolivia *nf* Bolivia.
boliviano,-a *adj - nm,f* Bolivian.
bollo *nm* **1** *(dulce)* bun. **2** *(de pan)* roll. **3** *(abolladura)* dent. **4** *(chichón)* bump. **5** *(lío)*: *armar un bollo*, to make a fuss.
bolo *nm* skittle, ninepin: *jugar a los bolos*, to go bowling.
bolsa¹ *nf* **1** *(gen)* bag: *bolsa de papel*, paper bag; *bolsa de plástico*, plastic bag. **2** *(en los ojos)* bag.
■ **bolsa de basura** bin liner.
■ **bolsa de viaje** travel bag.
bolsa² *nf* stock exchange: *jugar a la bolsa*, to play the market.
■ **bolsa de trabajo 1** *(en periódico)* job section. **2** *(en empresa)* employment exchange.
bolsillo *nm* pocket: *lo pagó de su propio bolsillo*, she paid for it out of her own pocket.

bolso *nm* **1** *(de hombro)* GB handbag; US purse. **2** *(monedero)* purse.

bomba[1] *nf* **1** *(explosivo)* bomb: ***poner una bomba***, to plant a bomb. **2** *(gran noticia)* bombshell. **3** *(éxito)* smash hit.
● **a prueba de bomba** bomb-proof.
● **pasarlo bomba** to have a ball.
■ **bomba atómica** atomic bomb.
■ **bomba de hidrógeno** hydrogen bomb.
■ **bomba de humo** smoke bomb.
■ **bomba fétida** stink bomb.
■ **bomba lacrimógena** tear gas canister.

bomba[2] *nf (para bombear)* pump.

bombacho *nm* **(pantalón) bombacho** baggy trousers *pl.*

bombardear *vt* **1** *(desde tierra)* to bombard. **2** *(desde el aire)* to bomb.

bombardeo *nm* **1** *(desde tierra)* bombardment. **2** *(desde el aire)* bombing.

bombear *vt (agua)* to pump.

bombero,-a *nm,f (hombre)* firefighter, fireman [*pl* **-men**]; *(mujer)* firefighter, firewoman [*pl* **-women**].

bombilla *nf* light bulb, bulb.

bombo *nm* **1** bass drum. **2** *(para sorteo)* drum.
● **dar bombo** to hype.
● **darse bombo** to blow one's own trumpet [*pt* **blew**; *pp* **blown**].

bombón *nm* **1** *(de chocolate)* chocolate. **2** *fam (persona)* knock-out.

bombona *nf* cylinder, bottle.
■ **bombona de butano** butane cylinder.

bonachón,-ona *adj* kind, good-natured.
▶ *nm,f* kind soul.

bondad *nf* **1** *(cualidad)* goodness. **2** *(afabilidad)* kindness: ***tenga la bondad de contestar***, be so good as to reply.

bondadoso,-a *adj* kind, good-natured.

boniato *nm* sweet potato [*pl* **-es**].

bonito,-a *adj* **1** nice,: ***ese color quedará bonito***, that color will look very nice; ***han ganado una bonita cifra***, they have won a nice little sum. **2** pretty, lovely.
▶ *nm* **bonito** *(pez)* tuna, bonito.

bono *nm* **1** bond. **2** *(vale)* voucher. **3** *(para transporte)* pass.
■ **bono del Tesoro** Treasury bond.

bonobús *nm* multiple-journey bus ticket.

boquerón *nm* fresh, anchovy.

boquete *nm* opening: ***hacer un boquete***, to make a hole.

boquiabierto,-a *adj* .
● **quedarse boquiabierto** to be left speechless: ***me has dejado boquiabierto***, I am flabbergasted.

boquilla *nf* **1** *(de pipa, instrumento)* mouthpiece. **2** *(sujeta cigarrillos)* cigarette holder. **3** *(filtro de cigarrillo)* tip.
● **tabaco con boquilla** tipped cigarttes.

borda *nf* gunwale.
● **arrojar por la borda** to throw overboard [*pt* **threw**; *pp* **thrown**].

bordado,-a *adj* embroidered.
▶ *nm* **bordado** embroidering, embroidery.

bordar *vt* **1** *(mantel, sábana)* to embroider. **2** *(hacer muy bien)* to perform exquisitely: ***un discurso bordado***, an excellent speech.

borde[1] *adj fam* nasty: ***ser borde con alguien***, to be nasty to SB.
▶ *nm,f*: ***¡eres un borde!***, you're a nasty piece of work!

borde[2] *nm (extremo)* edge; *(de prenda)* hem; *(de camino)* side; *(de vaso, taza)* rim: ***al borde de un ataque de nervios***, on the brink of a nervous breakdown; ***al borde del mar***, beside the sea; ***al borde de la muerte***, at death's door.

bordear *vt* **1** *(rodear caminando o en vehículo)* to skirt. **2** *(haber alrededor)* to border: ***el camino que bordeaba el lago***, the path bordering the lake; ***un paseo bordeado de fuentes***, a way lined with fountains. **3** *(aproximarse a)* to border, verge: ***bordea los cincuenta***, he's close to fifty.

bordillo *nm* kerb.

bordo *nm* board.
● **a bordo** on board.

borrachera *nf*.
● **pillar una borrachera** to get drunk.

borracho,-a *nm,f* drunk.
▶ *nm,f* drunkard.
● **estar borracho,-a como una cuba** to be blind drunk.

borrador *nm* **1** *(de texto)* rough copy, first draft. **2** *(de pizarra)* duster. **3** *(goma)* GB rubber; US eraser.

borrar *vt* **1** *(con goma etc)* to erase, rub out. **2** *(tachar)* to cross out; *(de una lista)* cross off. **3** INFORM to delete.

borrasca *nf* **1** area of low pressure. **2** *(tormenta)* storm.

borrego,-a *nm,f* **1** *(animal)* lamb. **2** *fam (persona)* sheep.

borrico,-a *nm,f* **1** *(animal)* donkey. **2** *fam (persona)* ass, dimwit.

borrón *nm* **1** *(de tinta)* ink blot. **2** *(deshonra)* blemish.

● **hacer borrón y cuenta nueva** to wipe the slate clean.

borroso,-a *adj* blurred: *veo borroso*, I see everything blurred.

bosque *nm* wood; *(grande)* forest.

bosquejar *vt* to sketch, outline.

bostezar *vi* to yawn.

bostezo *nm* yawn.

bota[1] *nf (calzado)* boot.

● **ponerse las botas 1** (al comer) to stuff oneself. **2** (al ganar dinero) to rake it.

■ **botas de esquí** ski boots.

■ **botas de fútbol** football boots.

bota[2] *nf (de vino)* wineskin.

botánica *nf* botany.

botánico,-a *adj* botanical.

▶ *nm,f* botanist.

botar *vt* **1** *(pelota)* to bounce. **2** *(barco)* to launch.

▶ *vi (saltar)* to jump.

bote[1] *nm* small boat.

■ **bote salvavidas** lifeboat.

bote[2] *nm (salto)* bounce.

bote[3] *nm* **1** *(recipiente)* tin, can; *(para propinas)* jar for tips, box for tips: *2 euros para el bote*, 2 euros for the tip box. **2** *(de lotería)* jackpot.

● **tener algo en el bote** to have STH in the bag.

bote[4].

● **estar de bote en bote** to be jam-packed.

botella *nf* bottle.

botellín *nm* small bottle.

boticario,-a *nm,f* GB chemist; US druggist.

botijo *nm* drinking jug.

botín[1] *nm (calzado)* ankle boot.

botín[2] *nm* **1** *(de guerra)* booty. **2** *(de ladrones)* loot.

botiquín *nm* **1** *(de medicinas)* first-aid kit. **2** *(enfermería)* sick bag.

botón *nm* **1** *(de camisa)* button. **2** *(tecla)* button: *pulsar un botón*, to press a button.

■ **botón de arranque** starter.

■ **botón de muestra** sample.

botones *nm (de hotel)* GB bellboy; US bellhop.

bóveda *nf* vault.

■ **bóveda celeste** firmament.

■ **bóveda de cañón** barrel vault.

bovino,-a *adj* bovine: *ganado bovino*, cattle.

boxeador,-a *nm* boxer.

boxear *vi* to box.

boxeo *nm* boxing.

boya *nf* **1** buoy. **2** *(corcho de pesca)* float.

bragas *nf pl* panties, knickers: *me pilló en bragas*, he caught me with my pants down.

bragueta *nf* fly, flies: *llevas la bragueta abierta*, your flies are open.

bramar *vi* to bellow, roar.

bramido *nm* bellow, roar.

brasa *nf* live coal.

● **a la brasa** barbecued.

brasero *nm* **1** *(de carbón)* brazier. **2** *(eléctrico)* electric, heater.

Brasil *nm* Brazil.

brasileño,-a *adj - nm,f* Brazilian.

bravío,-a *adj (feroz)* ferocious; *(salvaje)* wild.

bravo,-a *adj* **1** *(valiente)* brave, courageous. **2** *(fiero)* fierce, ferocious: *toro bravo*, fighting bull. **3** *(mar)* rough.

▶ *interj* well done!, bravo!

bravura *nf* **1** *(valentía)* bravery, courage. **2** *(fiereza)* fierceness, ferocity.

braza *nf* **1** *(medida)* fathom. **2** *(en natación)* breast stroke.

● **nadar a braza** to swim breaststroke [*pt* **swam**; *pp* **swum**].

brazada *nf* stroke: *en dos brazadas*, with two strokes.

brazalete *nm* bracelet.

brazo *nm* **1** *(de persona, sillón)* arm: *llevaba un niño en brazos*, she carried a baby in her arm; *es su brazo derecho*, he's his right-hand man. **2** *(de animal)* foreleg. **3** *(de río, candelabro, árbol)* branch.

▶ *nm pl* **brazos** *(trabajadores)* hands, workers.

● **a brazo partido 1** (sin armas) hand to hand. **2** (con empeño) tooth and nail.

● **cruzarse de brazos 1** (literalmente)

to fold one's arms. **2** (no actuar) to remain idle.

● **iban cogidos del brazo** they went arm in arm.

■ **brazo armado** military wing.

■ **brazo de mar** inlet.

brea nf tar, pitch.

brecha nf **1** (abertura) break, opening. **2** MIL breach. **3** (herida) gash.

● **seguir en la brecha**: *sigue en la brecha*, he's still in the thick of things.

Bretaña nf (en Francia) Brittany.

■ **Gran Bretaña** Great Britain.

breva nf early fig.

● **¡no caerá esa breva!** not much chance of that happening!

breve adj short, brief.

► nf (nota musical) breve.

● **dentro de breves momentos** shortly.

● **en breve** soon, shortly.

brevedad nf brevity, briefness.

● **con la mayor brevedad** as soon as possible.

bribón,-ona adj roguish.

► nm,f rogue.

bricolaje nm do-it-yourself, DIY.

brida nf bridle.

brigada nf **1** (unidad militar) brigade. **2** (de policía) squad.

■ **brigada antidisturbios** riot squad.

brillante adj **1** (luz, color) bright; (pelo, calzado) shiny: *el pelo te quedará brillante*, your hair will look nice and shiny. **2** (destacado) brilliant: *un alumno brillante*, a brilliant student.

► nm (diamante) diamond.

brillar vi **1** (sol, luz, ojos, oro) to shine [pt & pp shone]. **2** (algo mojado) to glisten. **3** (centellear) to sparkle. **4** (sobresalir) to shine [pt & pp shone], to be outstanding.

brillo nm **1** (resplandor) shine. **2** (de estrella) brightness, brilliance. **3** (esplendor) splendour, brilliance. **4** (de papel) glossiness.

● **sacar brillo 1** (a suelo, zapatos) to shine [pt & pp shone]. **2** (a madera) to polish.

brincar vi to jump, leap: *brincaba de alegría*, he jumped for joy.

brinco nm jump, leap.

● **dar brincos** to jump, hop: *daba brincos de alegría*, he jumped for joy.

brindar vi to toast.

► vt (proporcionar) to offer: *brindar a ALGN algo*, to offer STH to SB; *me brindó su apoyo*, she gave me her support; *me brindaban todo lo que necesitaba*, they provided me with everything I needed; *ahora que me brindan la oportunidad*, now they give me the chance.

► vpr **brindarse** to offer, volunteer.

brindis nm toast: *un brindis por los novios*, a toast to the bride and groom.

brío nm **1** (pujanza) strength. **2** (resolución) determination. **3** (valentía) courage.

brisa nf breeze: *brisa del mar*, sea breeze.

británico,-a adj British.

► nm,f (hombre) British man [pl men], Briton; (mujer) woman [pl women], Briton: *los británicos*, the British, British people.

broca nf drill bit.

brocha nf paintbrush: *pintor de brocha gorda*, house painter.

■ **brocha de afeitar** shaving brush.

broche nm **1** (cierre) fastener. **2** (joya) brooch.

● **el broche de oro** the perfect finish.

broma nf joke: *lo he dicho en broma*, it was a joke; *se lo tomó en broma*, he took it as a joke; *¡no estoy para bromas!*, I'm not in the mood for jokes!

● **gastar una broma a ALGN** to play a joke on SB.

■ **broma pesada** practical joke.

bromear vi to joke.

bromista adj fond of joking.

► nmf joker.

bronca nf row, quarrel.

● **armar una bronca** to kick up a fuss.

● **buscar bronca** to be looking for a fight.

● **echar una bronca a ALGN** to come down on SB.

bronce nm bronze.

bronceado,-a adj tanned.

► nm **bronceado** tan, suntan.

bronceador nm suntan lotion.

broncearse vpr to tan, get a tan.

bronquios nm pl bronchial tubes: *padece de los bronquios*, he has a bad chest.

bronquitis nf bronchitis.

brotar vi **1** (planta) to sprout, bud. **2** (hoja) to sprout, come out. **3** (agua) to spring [pt sprang; pp sprung]. **4** (conflicto, *protesta)* to spring up [*pt* **sprang**; *pp* **sprung**]. **5** *(epidemia)* to break out [*pt* **broke**; *pp* **broken**].

brote *nm* **1** *(de planta)* bud, sprout. **2** *(de conflicto, epidemia)* outbreak.

bruces *adv*: **me di de bruces con tu padre**, I bumped into your father; **se cayó de bruces**, she fell flat on her face.

bruja *nf* **1** *(hechicera)* witch. **2** *fam (harpía)* old hag.

brujería *nf* witchcraft, sorcery.

brujo *nm* wizard, sorcerer.

brújula *nf* compass.

bruma *nf* mist, fog.

brusco,-a *adj* **1** *(persona)* brusque, abrupt. **2** *(movimiento)* sudden.

brusquedad *nf* **1** *(de carácter)* brusqueness, abruptness. **2** *(de movimiento)* suddenness.

brutal *adj* **1** *(salvaje)* brutal, beastly, savage. **2** *(enorme)* colossal. **3** *(genial)* great, terrific.

brutalidad *nf* **1** *(crueldad)* brutality. **2** *(necedad)* stupidity.

bruto,-a *adj* **1** *(necio)* stupid, ignorant. **2** *(tosco)* rough, coarse. **3** *(montante, peso)* gross. **4** *(piedra)* rough. **5** *(petróleo)* crude.
► *nm,f* brute, beast.

bucal *adj* oral.

buceador,-ra *nm,f* diver.

bucear *vi* to swim under water [*pt* **swam**; *pp* **swum**].

buceo *nm* diving.

bucle *nm* curl, ringlet.

budismo *nm* Buddhism.

budista *adj - nmf* Buddhist.

buen *adj* → **bueno,-a**.

buenaventura *nf* good luck, fortune.
● **decirle a** ALGN **la buenaventura** to tell SB's fortune.

bueno,-a *adj* **1** *(gen)* good [*comp* **better**; *superl* **best**]: **una película muy buena**, a very good film; **tiene buen gusto**, he has good taste; **lo bueno es que...**, the good thing is that.... **2** *(persona - amable)* kind; *(- agradable)* nice, polite. **3** *(apropiado)* right, suitable: **no es bueno para los pequeños**, it's not suitable for small children. **4** *(grande)* big; *(considerable)* considerable: **un buen número de participantes**, quite a few participants. **5** *(tiempo)* good [*comp* **better**; *superl* **best**], nice.

► *interj* **¡bueno!** *(sorpresa)* hey!; *(de acuerdo)* OK!, all right!

► *adv* **1**: **bueno, pues...**, well.... **2**: **pero, bueno...**, but anyway.

► *nm,f*: **la buena de su madre**, his poor old mother.
● **buenas noches (antes de dormir)** good evening, good night.
● **buenas tardes** good afternoon.
● **buenos días** good morning.
● **estar bueno,-a 1** *(de salud)* to be in good health. **2** *(guapo)* to be good-looking.
● **de buenas a primeras** *fam* from the very start.
● **¡ésta sí que es buena!** *fam* that's a good one!
● **por las buenas** willingly.

buey *nm* ox.

búfalo *nm* buffalo.

bufanda *nf* scarf [*pl* **-s** o **-ves**].

bufé *nm* buffet.
■ **bufé libre** self-service buffet.

bufete *nm* **1** *(mesa)* writing desk. **2** *(de abogado)* lawyer's office: **abrir bufete**, to set up as a lawyer.

bufido *nm* snort.

bufón,-ona *nm,f* **1** HIST jester. **2** *(gracioso)* clown.

buhardilla *nf* **1** *(desván)* attic. **2** *(ventana)* dormer window.

búho *nm* owl.

buitre *nm* vulture.

bujía *nf* spark plug.

bulbo *nm* bulb.

bulevar *nm* boulevard.

Bulgaria *nf* Bulgaria.

búlgaro,-a *adj* Bulgarian.
► *nm,f (persona)* Bulgarian.
► *nm* **búlgaro** *(idioma)* Bulgarian.

bulla *nf* **1** *(ruido)* din, uproar, racket: **metió mucha bulla**, he made a real racket. **2** *(multitud)* crowd. **3** *(prisa)* rush: **tengo bulla**, I am in a hurry; **no le metas bulla**, don't hurry her up.

bullicio *nm* **1** *(ruido)* hubbub. **2** *(actividad)* hustle and bustle.

bullicioso,-a *adj* **1** *(ruidoso)* noisy. **2** *(animado)* busy.

bulto *nm* **1** *(tamaño)* size, bulk. **2** *(forma)* shape, form. **3** *(hinchazón)* swelling, lump. **4** *(equipaje)* item of luggage: **voy cargado de bultos**, I have a lot of luggage; **¿cuán-**

tos bultos lleva?, how many pieces of luggage do you have?; *no ocupa bulto*, it doesn't take up any space; *vinieron para hacer bulto*, they came to swell the numbers.

- **calcular algo a bulto** to make a rough estimate of STH.
- **escurrir el bulto** to dodge the question.

buñuelo *nm* **1** *(dulce)* doughnut. **2** *(de bacalao etc)* fritter.

buque *nm* ship.

- **buque cisterna** tanker.
- **buque de guerra** warship.
- **buque escuela** training ship.
- **buque mercante** merchant ship.
- **buque nodriza** mother ship.

burbuja *nf* bubble.

- **hacer burbujas** to blow bubbles [*pt* blew; *pp* blown].

burbujear *vi* to bubble.

burgués,-esa *adj* bourgeois, middle-class.

▶ *nm,f (hombre)* middle class man; *(mujer)* middle class woman: *los burgueses*, the middle class.

burguesía *nf* bourgeoisie, middle class.

burla *nf* mockery, gibe.

- **hacer burla a ALGN** to mock SB.

burlar *vt* **1** *(engañar)* to deceive, trick. **2** *(eludir)* to dodge, evade.

▶ *vpr* **burlarse** to mock.

- **burlarse de ALGN** to make fun of SB, laugh at SB.

burlón,-ona *adj* mocking.

▶ *nm,f* mocker, joker.

burocracia *nf* bureaucracy.

burrada *nf* **1** *fam (tontería)* stupid thing: *decir burradas*, to talk nonsense; *hacer burradas*, to do stupid things. **2** *fam (gran cantidad)*: *una burrada*, loads, tons; *una burrada de gente*, loads of people; *cuesta una burrada*, it costs a hell of a lot.

burro,-a *nm,f* **1** *(asno)* donkey. **2** *(ignorante)* idiot. **3** *(bruto)* brute.

▶ *adj* **1** *(tonto)* stupid, thick. **2** *(bruto)* brute.

- **no ver tres en un burro** to be as blind as a bat.

bursátil *adj*: *mercado bursátil*, stock exchange; *actividad bursátil*, activity on the stock exchange.

busca *nf* search: *fueron en busca de los desaparecidos*, they went to search for the disappeared; *ir en busca de fortuna*, to seek one's fortune; *estar en busca y captura*, to be wanted.

buscador,-ra *nm,f* searcher, seeker.

▶ *nm* **buscador** INFORM search engine.

buscar *vt (gen)* to look for, search for; *(en diccionario)* to look up: *busco piso*, I'm looking for a flat; *búscalo en el diccionario*, look it up in the dictionary; *"chico busca chica"*, boy wants to meet girl; *ir a buscar algo*, to go and get STH; *vinieron a buscarme a la estación*, they came to pick me up from the station.

- **buscársela** *fam* to be looking for trouble.
- **buscarse la vida 1** *(ganar dinero)* to try and earn a living. **2** *(arreglárselas)* to manage on one's own.

búsqueda *nf* **1** *(de objeto, persona)* search, quest. **2** INFORM search.

- **hacer una búsqueda** to do a search.

busto *nm* **1** *(escultura)* bust. **2** *(pecho - de mujer)* bust; *(- de hombre)* chest.

butaca *nf* **1** *(sillón)* armchair. **2** *(en teatro)* seat.

butano *nm* butane.

butifarra *nf* pork sausage.

buzo *nm* diver.

buzón *nm* **1** *(en casa)* GB letter-box; US mailbox. **2** *(en calle)* GB post box; US mailbox. **3** INFORM mailbox.

- **echar una carta al buzón** to post a letter.
- **buzón de sugerencias** suggestions box.
- **buzón de voz** voicemail.

byte *nm* byte.

C

cabal *adj* exact, precise.
► *nm pl* cabales.
● **estar en sus cabales** to be in one's right mind.

cabalgar *vi* to ride [*pt* **rode**; *pp* **ridden**].

cabalgata *nf* cavalcade.

caballa *nf* mackerel.

caballar *adj* equine, horse.

caballería *nf* **1** *(tropa montada)* cavalry. **2** *(montura)* mount.

caballero *nm* **1** *(señor)* gentleman [*pl* **-men**]. **2** HIST knight.

caballete *nm* **1** *(de pintor)* easel. **2** *(de tejado)* ridge. **3** *(de mesa)* trestle. **4** *(de nariz)* bridge.

caballitos *nm pl (tiovivo)* GB merry-go-round *sing*; US carousel *sing*.

caballo *nm* **1** horse. **2** *(en ajedrez)* knight. **3** *(en naipes)* queen. **4** *arg (heroína)* smack, horse.
► *mpl* **caballos** *(potencia)* horsepower.
● **a caballo** on horseback.
● **montar a caballo** to ride [*pt* **rode**; *pp* **ridden**].
● **a caballo entre ...** halfway between ....

cabaña *nf* **1** *(choza)* cabin, hut. **2** *(ganado)* livestock.

cabecear *vi* **1** *(negar)* to shake one's head [*pt* **shook**; *pp* **shaken**]. **2** *(dormirse)* to nod. **3** *(animal)* to move its head.
► *vt (balón)* to head.

cabecera *nf* **1** *(de página)* top, head. **2** *(de periódico)* headline. **3** *(de cama)* bedhead.

cabecilla *nmf* leader.

cabellera *nf* **1** *(pelo)* hair, head of hair. **2** *(de cometa)* tail.

cabello *nm* hair.

■ **cabello de ángel** sweet pumpkin preserve.

caber *vi* **1** *(encajar)* to fit: *no me caben estos pantalones*, these trousers don't fit; *en esta lata caben diez litros*, this can holds ten litres; *no caben más*, there is no room for any more. **2** *(pasar)* to fit, go: *el sofá no cabe por la puerta*, the sofa doesn't go through the door. **3** *(ser posible)* to be possible: *cabe decir que ...*, it's possible to say that ..., it can be said that .... **4** to go: *ocho entre dos caben a cuatro*, two into eight goes four times.
● **dentro de lo que cabe** all things considered.
● **no cabe duda** there is no doubt.
● **no me cabe en la cabeza** I can't believe it.

cabestrillo *nm* sling.
● **en cabestrillo** in a sling.

cabeza *nf* **1** head: *se ha dado un golpe en la cabeza*, she's bumped her head; *¡usa la cabeza!*, use your head!; *la cabeza me daba vueltas*, my head was spinning; *ha ganado por una cabeza*, she won by a head. **2** *(de ganado)* head.
► *nmf* head, leader.
● **a la cabeza de** at the front, at the top of.
● **cabeza abajo** upside down.
● **cabeza arriba** the right way up.
● **por cabeza** a head, per person.
● **sentar la cabeza** to settle down.
● **volver la cabeza** to look round.
● **estar mal de la cabeza** to be mad.
● **írsele de la cabeza a** ALGN: *se me ha ido de la cabeza*, it's gone right out of my head.

- **lavarse la cabeza** to wash one's hair.
- **no tener ni pies ni cabeza** to be absurd.
- **tener cabeza para algo** to have a good head: *tiene cabeza para los negocios*, she has a good head for business.
- **cabeza de ajo** head of garlic.
- **cabeza de familia** head of the family.
- **cabeza de turco** scapegoat.
- **cabeza rapada** skinhead.

cabezada *nf* **1** *(golpe recibido)* crack on the head; *(golpe dado)* butt. **2** *(saludo)* nod.
- **echar una cabezada** to have a snooze.

cabezazo *nm* **1** *(golpe dado)* butt; *(golpe recibido)* bump on the head. **2** *(en fútbol)* header.

cabezonada *nf fam* pigheaded action.

cabezón,-ona *adj* **1** *(de cabeza grande)* bigheaded. **2** *(terco)* pigheaded.

cabezota *adj* pigheaded.
- ▶ *nm,f* pigheaded person.

cabezudo,-a *adj* **1** *(de cabeza grande)* bigheaded. **2** *(terco)* pigheaded.
- ▶ *nm* **cabezudo** bigheaded dwarf.

cabida *nf* capacity, room.
- **tener cabida para** to hold [*pt & pp* **held**].

cabina *nf* cabin, booth.
- **cabina telefónica** phone box.

cabizbajo,-a *adj* crestfallen.

cable *nm* cable.
- **echarle un cable a ALGN** to give SB a hand.

cabo *nm* **1** *(extremo)* end. **2** *(final)* end: *al cabo de un mes*, in a month. **3** *(cuerda)* strand. **4** GEOG cape. **5** *(militar)* corporal.
- **de cabo a rabo** from head to tail.
- **llevar a cabo** to carry out.

cabra *nf* goat.
- **estar loco,-a como una cabra** to be as mad as a hatter.

cabrear *vt fam* to make angry.
- ▶ *vpr* **cabrearse** *fam* to get worked up.

cabreo.
- **pillar un cabreo** to get mad.

cabrero *nm* goatherd.

cabriola *nf*.
- **hacer cabriolas 1** *(persona)* to carpet about. **2** *(caballo)* to prance, prance about.

cabrito *nm* kid.

cabrón,-ona *nm,f vulg (hombre)* bastard; *(mujer)* bitch.

- ▶ *nm* **cabrón** *(animal)* billy goat.

caca *nf* **1** *fam* poo, US poop. **2** *fam (cosa sucia)* dirty thing. **3** *fam (basura)* load of rubbish.
- **hacer caca** to do a poo.

cacahuete *nm* peanut.

cacao *nm* **1** *(planta)* cacao. **2** *(polvo, bebida)* cocoa. **3** *fam (jaleo)* mess, chaos.

cacarear *vi* **1** *(gallina)* to cluck. **2** *(gallo)* to crow.
- ▶ *vt* to boast about.

cacatúa *nf* cockatoo [*pl* **-s**].

cacería *nf* hunt, hunting party.

cacerola *nf* saucepan.

cachalote *nm* cachalot, sperm whale.

cacharro *nm* **1** *(de cocina)* pot: *fregar los cacharros*, to do the dishes. **2** *fam (cosa)* thing, piece of junk. **3** *fam (coche)* banger.

caché *nm* cache memory.

cachear *vt* to search, frisk.

cachete *nm* *(bofetada)* slap: *le dio un cachete*, she slapped him.

cachivache *nm* thingummy.
- ▶ *nm pl* **cachivaches** junk *sing*.

cacho *nm fam* bit, piece.

cachondearse *vpr* to poke fun (de, at).

cachondeo *nm* **1** *fam (diversión)* laugh: *¡vaya cachondeo!*, what a laugh! **2** *(cosa poco seria)* joke, farce: *esta competición es un cachondeo*, this competition is a joke.

cachondo,-a *adj* **12** *fam (divertido)* funny. **2** *(excitado)* horny ; GB randy.

cachorro,-a *nm,f (de perro)* puppy; *(de león, tigre)* cub.

cacique *nm* **1** *(indio)* cacique. **2** *(déspota)* tyrant.

caco *nm fam* thief [*pl* **-ves**].

cacto *nm* cactus.

cactus *nm* cactus.

cada *adj* **1** *(para individualizar)* each: *tres caramelos para cada uno*, three sweets for each; *cada cual, cada uno*, each one, every one. **2** *(con números, tiempo)* every: *cada cuatro años hay un año bisiesto*, there's a leap year every four years; *nos vemos cada viernes*, we meet every Friday; *ocho de cada diez*, eight out of (every) ten. **3** *(uso enfático)*: *¡dice cada tontería!*, he says such stupid things!; *¡sale con cada excusa!*, the excuses she comes out with!
- **¿cada cuánto?** how often?

- **cada vez más** more and more.
- **cada vez que** whenever, every time that.

cadáver *nm* corpse, body.

cadena *nf* **1** *(de eslabones, establecimientos)* chain. **2** *(industrial)* line. **3** *(montañosa)* range. **4** *(musical)* music centre. **5** *(de televisión)* channel. **6** *(de radio)* station.
► *nf pl* **cadenas** *(de nieve)* tyre chains.
- **tirar de la cadena del wáter** to flush the toilet.
■ **cadena alimenticia** food chain.
■ **cadena de fabricación** production line.
■ **cadena de montaje** assembly line.
■ **cadena perpetua** life imprisonment.

cadera *nf* hip.

caducar *vi* to expire: *¿cuándo caduca tu pasaporte?*, when does your passport expire?; *¿cuándo caduca la leche?*, what's the sell-by date on the milk?

caducidad *nf* **1** *(de documento)* expiration, loss of validity. **2** *(de alimento)* best before date.

caduco,-a *adj* **1** *(pasado)* expired, out-of-date. **2** *(viejo)* decrepit. **3** *(árbol)* deciduous.

caer *vi* **1** *(gen)* to fall [*pt* **fell**; *pp* **fallen**]: *cayó por la escalera*, she fell down the stairs. **2** *(derrumbarse)* to fall down [*pt* **fell**; *pp* **fallen**]. **3** *(hallarse)* to be located: *el camino cae a la derecha*, the road is on the right. **4** *(coincidir fechas)* to be: *el día cuatro cae en jueves*, the fourth is a Thursday. **5** *(el sol)* to go down. **6** *(entender)*: *no caigo*, I don't get it.
► *vpr* **caerse 1** *(gen)* to fall [*pt* **fell**; *pp* **fallen**]: *se cayó del caballo*, she fell off her horse. **2** *(soltarse- hojas, botón)* to fall off; *(diente)* to fall out.
- **caer bien 1** *(comida)* to agree with. **2** *(prenda)* to suit. **3** *(persona)*: *me cae bien*, I like her.
- **caer de cabeza** to fall on one's head.
- **caer de rodillas** to fall on one's knees.
- **caer mal 1** *(comida)* not to agree with. **2** *(prenda)* not to suit. **3** *(persona)*: *me cae mal*, I don't like him.
- **caer en la cuenta de** to realize.
- **caer enfermo,-a** to fall ill [*pt* **fell**; *pp* **fallen**].
- **dejar caer** to drop.
- **estar al caer** to be about to arrive.

café *nm* **1** *(bebida)* coffee: *me encanta el café*, I love coffee. **2** *(cafetería)* café.
- **café con leche** white coffee.
■ **café descafeinado** decaffeinated coffee.
■ **café exprés** expresso [*pl* **-s**].
■ **café solo** black coffee.

cafeína *nf* caffeine.

cafetera *nf* coffeepot.

cafetería *nf* cafeteria, café.

cagada *nf* **1** *vulg (mierda)* shit. **2** *vulg (error)* cockup.

cagar *vi vulg* to shit.
► *vpr* **cagarse** *vulg* to shit oneself.
- **cagarse de miedo** *vulg* to be shit-scared.

caída *nf* **1** *(gen)* fall: *tuvo una mala caída*, he had a bad fall. **2** *(pérdida)* loss: *la caída del cabello*, hair loss. **3** *(de precios)* fall, drop. **4** *(de tejidos)* body, hang. **5** INFORM *(de red)* crash.
- **a la caída del sol** at sunset.
- **caída de ojos** look.

caído,-a *adj* **1** *(gen)* fallen. **2** *(desanimado)* downhearted.
- **caído,-a de hombros** round-shouldered.
- **caído,-a del cielo** out of the blue.

caimán *nm* alligator.

caja *nf* **1** *(gen)* box; *(de madera)* chest; *(grande)* crate. **2** *(de bebidas)* case. **3** *(en tienda, bar)* cash desk; *(en supermercado)* checkout; *(en banco)* cashier's desk. **4** *(tipografía)* case.
- **hacer caja** to cash up.
■ **caja de ahorros** savings bank.
■ **caja de cambios** gearbox.
■ **caja fuerte** safe.
■ **caja negra** black box.
■ **caja registradora** cash register.

cajero,-a *nm,f* cashier.
■ **cajero automático** cash dispenser.

cajetilla *nf* packet *(of cigarettes)*.

cajón *nm* **1** *(en mueble)* drawer. **2** *(caja grande)* crate.
- **cajón de sastre** jumble.

cal *nf* lime.

cala *nf* cove.

calabacín *nm* GB courgette; US zucchini.

calabaza *nf* pumpkin.
- **darle calabazas *(a estudiante)* 1** to fail. **2** *(a pretendiente)* to turn down.

calabozo *nm* **1** *(prisión)* jail. **2** *(celda)* cell.

calado,-a *adj fam (empapado)* soaked.
▶ *nm* **calado** *(del agua)* depth.
● **calado,-a hasta los huesos** soaked to the skin.

calamar *nm* squid.
■ **calamares a la romana** squid fried in batter.

calambre *nm* **1** *(muscular)* cramp. **2** *(eléctrico)* shock, electric shock.

calamidad *nf* **1** *(desastre)* calamity, disaster. **2** *(persona)* disaster.

calar *vt* **1** *(mojar)* to soak, drench. **2** *(agujerear)* to go through, pierce. **3** *fam (intención)* to rumble: *les han calado*, they've been rumbled; *¡te tengo calado!*, I've got your number!
▶ *vpr* **calarse 1** *(con agua)* to get soaked. **2** *(sombrero)* to pull down. **3** *(motor)* to stop, stall.
● **calarse hasta los huesos** to get soaked to the skin.

calavera *nf* skull.
▶ *nm* tearaway.

calcar *vt* **1** *(dibujo)* to trace. **2** *(imitar)* to copy.

calcetín *nm* sock.

calcinar *vt* *(carbonizar)* to burn [*pt & pp* **burnt**].

calcio *nm* calcium.

calco *nm* **1** *(de dibujo)* tracing. **2** *(imitación)* copy.

calcomanía *nf* transfer.

calculadora *nf* calculator.

calculador,-ra *adj* calculating.

calcular *vt* **1** *(gen)* to calculate, work out. **2** *(suponer)* to reckon: *¿cuántos años le calculas?*, how old do you reckon he is?

cálculo *nm* **1** *(de cantidad, presupuesto)* calculation: *si no me fallan los cálculos*, if my calculations are correct. **2** *(conjetura)* conjecture, guess. **3** *(del riñón, etc)* stone.

caldear *vt* **1** *(calentar)* to warm, liven. **2** *(excitar)* to heat up, warm up: *sus declaraciones caldearon los ánimos*, his statements provoked an angry response.

caldera *nf* boiler.

calderilla *nf* small change.

caldero *nm* cauldron.

caldo *nm* **1** *(sopa)* broth. **2** *(para cocinar)* stock.
■ **caldo de cultivo** culture medium.

calefacción *nf* heating.
■ **calefacción central** central heating.

calendario *nm* calendar.

calentador *nm* heater.

calentamiento *nm* warming: *ejercicios de calentamiento*, warming-up exercises.
■ **calentamiento del planeta** global warming.

calentar *vt-vi* **1** *(comida, cuerpo)* to warm up; *(agua, horno, etc)* to heat, heat up: *¿me puedes calentar la leche?*, can you heat the milk up for me? **2** *(deportista)* to warm up.
▶ *vpr* **calentarse 1** *(gen)* to get hot, get warm. **2** *(enfadarse)* to become angry. **3** *(excitarse sexualmente)* to get horny [*pt* **got**; *pp* **got** (US **gotten**)].
● **calentar los sesos** to get hot under the collar.

calentura *nf* fever, temperature.

calibre *nm* **1** *(de arma)* calibre. **2** *(importancia)* importance.

calidad *nf* **1** *(de producto)* quality: *vino de calidad*, good-quality wine. **2** *(cualidad)* kind, quality, type: *distintas calidades de papel*, different types of paper.
● **en calidad de** as: *en calidad de amigo*, as a friend.
■ **calidad de vida** quality of life.

cálido,-a *adj* warm.

caliente *adj* **1** *(ardiendo)* hot; *(templado)* warm. **2** *(acalorado)* heated, spirited. **3** *fam (excitado)* horny ; GB randy.
● **en caliente** in the heat of the moment.

calificación *nf* *(nota)* mark, grade.

calificar *vt* **1** *(etiquetar)* to describe. **2** *(dar nota)* to mark, grade.

calificativo,-a *adj* qualifying.
▶ *nm* **calificativo** qualifier, epithet.

caligrafía *nf* **1** *(arte)* calligraphy: *caligrafía gótica*, Gothic calligraphy. **2** *(rasgos)* handwriting: *ejercicios de caligrafía*, handwriting exercises.

callado,-a *adj* silent, quiet.

callar *vi-vpr* **callar(se)** *(dejar de hablar)* to stop talking; *(no hablar)* to say nothing [*pt & pp* **said**], remain silent: *¡cállate!*, shut up!
▶ *vt (no decir)* to keep to oneself: *calló su opinión*, he kept his opinion to himself.

calle *nf* **1** street, road: *¿en qué calle vi*

ves?, which street do you live in?; *vigila al cruzar la calle*, be careful when you cross the road. **2** *(en atletismo)* lane.

● **poner a** ALGN **de patitas en la calle** to throw SB out [*pt* **threw**; *pp* **thrown**].

■ **calle mayor** high street, main street.

■ **calle peatonal** pedestrian street.

callejear *vi* to wander the streets.

callejero,-a *adj (persona)* fond of going out.

▶ *nm* **callejero** street directory.

callejón *nm* alley.

■ **callejón sin salida** cul-de-sac, dead end.

callista *nmf* chiropodist.

callo *nm (en mano, planta del pie)* callus; *(en dedo del pie)* corn.

▶ *nm pl* **callos** tripe *sing*.

calma *nf* **1** *(tranquilidad)* calm. **2** *fam (cachaza)* slowness, phlegm.

● **mantener la calma** to keep calm.

● **perder la calma** to lose one's patience [*pt & pp* **lost**].

calmante *adj* soothing.

▶ *nm* painkiller.

calmar *vt* **1** *(nervios)* to calm; *(persona)* to calm down. **2** *(dolor)* to relieve, soothe.

▶ *vt-vpr* **calmar(se)** *(persona)* to calm down.

▶ *vpr* **calmarse** *(dolor, etc)* to abate.

calor *nm* **1** *(sensación)* heat: *hace calor*, it is hot; *tengo calor*, I feel warm, I feel hot. **2** *(pasión)* enthusiasm, ardour.

caloría *nf* calorie.

calumnia *nf* calumny, slander.

calumniar *vt* to calumniate, slander.

caluroso,-a *adj* **1** *(tiempo)* warm, hot. **2** *(entusiasta)* warm, enthusiastic.

calva *nf* bald patch.

calvario *nm fig* heavy burden, cross.

calvicie *nf* baldness.

calvo,-a *adj* **1** *(persona)* bald: *se está quedando calvo*, he's going bald. **2** *(terreno)* bare, barren.

▶ *nm,f* bald person: *algunas mujeres encuentran atractivos a los calvos*, some women find bald men attractive.

calzada *nf* road, roadway.

calzado *nm* footwear, shoes *pl*.

calzador *nm* shoehorn.

calzar *vt* **1** to put shoes on: *calza al niño*, put the baby's shoes on. **2** *(llevar)* to wear [*pt* **wore**; *pp* **worn**]: *calza sandalias*, she wears sandals.

▶ *vpr* **calzarse** to put one's shoes on.

● **¿qué número calzas?** what size shoes do you take?

calzón *nm (de deporte)* shorts *pl*.

calzoncillos *nm pl* underpants, pants.

cama *nf* bed.

● **irse a la cama** to go to bed.

● **guardar cama** to stay in bed.

● **hacer la cama** to make the bed.

■ **cama de matrimonio** double bed.

■ **cama individual** single bed.

camaleón *nm* chameleon.

cámara *nf* **1** *(fotográfica)* camera. **2** *(sala)* chamber, room. **3** *(institución)* chamber. **4** *(del parlamento)* house. **5** *(de rueda)* inner tube.

● **a cámara lenta** in slow motion.

■ **cámara alta** POL upper house.

■ **cámara baja** POL lower house.

■ **cámara de aire** air chamber.

camarada *nmf* **1** *(colega)* colleague; *(de colegio)* schoolmate. **2** POL comrade.

camaradería *nf* **1** companionship. **2** camaraderie.

camarero,-a *nm,f* **1** *(en bar - hombre)* waiter; *(- mujer)* waitress. **2** *(en barco, - hombre)* steward; *(- mujer)* stewardess.

camarón *nm* shrimp.

camarote *nm* cabin.

cambiar *vt* **1** *(modificar)* to change: *han cambiado el horario*, they've changed the timetable; *¿puede cambiarme las patatas por arroz?*, could I have rice instead of the chips? **2** *(de sitio)* to shift; *(de casa)* to move. **3** *(intercambiar)* to exchange, swap: *cambiar impresiones*, to exchange views; *te cambio el libro por estas tarjetas*, I'll swap you the book for these cards. **4** *(moneda extranjera)* to change, exchange.

▶ *vi* **1** *(gen)* to change: *has cambiado mucho*, you've changed a lot. **2** *(viento)* to veer.

▶ *vpr* **cambiarse** to change: *cambiarse de ropa*, to get changed.

● **cambiar de** to change: *cambiar de idea*, to change one's mind; *cambiar de color*, to change colour; *cambiar de trabajo*, to change jobs.

cambio *nm* **1** *(gen)* change: *va a haber cambios en la empresa*, there are going to be changes in the company; *no me*

has devuelto el cambio, you haven't given me back my change. **2** *(canje)* exchange. **3** *(de divisas)* exchange, rate; *(de acciones)* price. **4** *(de tren)* switch. **5** *(de marchas)* gear change.
● **a cambio de** in exchange for.
● **en cambio 1** *(por otro lado)* on the other hand. **2** *(en lugar de)* instead.
■ **cambio automático** *(de coche)* automatic transmission.
■ **cambio de marchas** gearshift.
camello *nm* **1** camel. **2** *arg (de drogas)* drugpusher, pusher.
camerino *nm* dressing room.
camilla *nf* stretcher.
camillero *nm* stretcher-bearer.
caminante *nmf* traveller, walker.
caminar *vt-vi* to walk: *me encanta caminar por el monte*, I love walking in the mountains.
caminata *nf* long walk, trek.
camino *nm* **1** *(sendero)* path, track: *no te alejes del camino*, don't satray from the path. **2** *(ruta)* way: *iremos por otro camino*, we'll go a different way. **3** *(viaje)* journey. **4** *(medio)* way.
● **abrirse camino** to make a way for oneself, start out.
● **ir por buen camino** to be on the right track.
● **ir por mal camino** to be on the wrong track.
● **ponerse en camino** to set off [*pt & pp* **set**].
camión *nm* GB lorry ; US truck.
■ **camión cisterna** tanker.
■ **camión de mudanzas** removal van.
■ **camión frigorífico** refrigerated truck.
camionero,-a *nm,f* GB lorry driver; US truck driver.
camioneta *nf* van.
camisa *nf* shirt.
● **en mangas de camisa** in one's shirtsleeves.
● **cambiar de camisa** to change sides.
● **meterse en camisa de once varas** to meddle in other people's business.
■ **camisa de fuerza** straitjacket.
camisería *nf* shirt shop.
camiseta *nf* **1** *(interior)* vest. **2** *(exterior)* T-shirt. **3** *(de deportes)* shirt.
camisón *nm* nightdress, nightgown, nightie.

campamento *nm* camp.
■ **campamento de refugiados** refuge camp.
■ **campamento de verano** summer camp.
campana *nf* bell.
■ **campana extractora** cooker hood.
campanada *nf* stroke.
campanario *nm* belfry, bell tower.
campanilla *nf* **1** *(de mesa)* small bell. **2** *(úvula)* uvula. **3** *(flor)* campanula, bellflower.
campante *adj*: *se quedó tan campante*, she didn't bat an eyelid.
campaña *nf* campaign.
■ **campaña electoral** electoral campaign.
campechano,-a *adj (franco)* frank, open; *(jovial)* good-natured, good-humoured.
campeonato *nm* championship.
● **de campeonato 1** *(enorme)* huge, enormous. **2** *(fantástico)* fantastic, amazing. **3** *(malo)* terrible, awful. **4** *(tremendo)* terrific.
campeón,-ona *nm,f* champion.
campesino,-a *adj* country, rural.
▶ *nm,f (que vive en el campo)* country person [*pl* **people**]; *(que trabaja en el campo)* farm worker; *(pobre)* peasant.
campestre *adj* country, rural.
camping *nm* camping site.
● **ir de camping** to go camping.
campiña *nf* countryside.
campo *nm* **1** *(extensión de terreno)* country, countryside; *(paisaje)* countryside: *vivir en el campo*, to live in the country. **2** *(terreno cultivado)* field: *campos de maíz*, cornfields. **3** *(de deportes, batalla)* field. **4** *(ámbito)* space; *(área)* field, scope: *en el campo de la medicina*, in the field of medicine.
● **dejarle a ALGN el campo libre** to leave the field open for SB [*pt & pp* **left**].
● **ir campo a través** to cut across the fields [*pt & pp* **cut**].
■ **campo de batalla** battlefield.
■ **campo de concentración** concentration camp.
■ **campo de fútbol** football pitch, football ground.
■ **campo de golf** golf course.
■ **campo de trabajo** work camp.
■ **campo magnético** magnetic field.
■ **campo visual** visual field.

camuflaje *nm* camouflage.

camuflar *vt* to camouflage.

can *nm* dog.

cana *nf* grey hair.

● **echar una cana al aire** to let one's hair down [*pt & pp* **let**].

Canadá *nm* Canada.

canadiense *adj – nmf* Canadian.

canal *nm* **1** (*artificial*) canal. **2** (*natural*) channel. **3** (*de televisión*) channel.

▶ *nm & nf* (*de tejado*) gutter.

■ **canal de la Mancha** English Channel.

■ **canal de Panamá** Panama Canal.

canalizar *vt* **1** (*río, área*) to canalize. **2** (*riego*) to channel. **3** (*recursos, energía*) to channel, direct.

canalla *nm* (*persona ruin*) swine.

▶ *nf* (*gente despreciable*) riffraff.

canalón *nm* (*en tejado*) gutter; (*en pared*) drainpipe.

canapé *nm* **1** (*sofá*) couch, sofa. **2** (*comida*) canapé.

Canarias *nf pl* **islas Canarias** Canary Islands.

canario,-a *adj* (*de las Canarias*) from the Canary Islands.

▶ *nm,f* (*habitante*) Canary Islander.

▶ *nm* **canario** (*pájaro*) canary.

canasta *nf* basket.

canastilla *nf* **1** (*cestita*) small basket. **2** (*de bebé*) layette.

canasto *nm* large basket.

cancelar *vt* **1** (*anular*) to cancel. **2** (*deuda*) to pay off [*pt & pp* **paid**], settle.

cáncer *nm* **1** (*tumor*) cancer. **2** (*signo*) Cancer.

cancha *nf* court.

canción *nf* song.

■ **canción de cuna** lullaby.

cancionero *nm* **1** (*de canciones*) songbook. **2** (*de poemas*) collection of poems.

candado *nm* padlock.

candelabro *nm* candelabra.

candidato,-a *nm,f* candidate.

candidatura *nf* **1** (*propuesta*) candidacy. **2** (*lista*) list of candidates.

cándido,-a *adj* innocent, ingenuous.

candil *nm* oil lamp.

candor *nm* ingenuousness, innocence.

canela *nf* cinnamon.

■ **canela en rama** stick cinnamon.

canelones *nm pl* cannelloni.

cangrejo *nm* crab.

■ **cangrejo (de río)** crayfish.

canguro *nm* kangaroo [*pl* **-s**].

▶ *nmf* baby-sitter.

● **hacer de canguro** to babysit [*pt & pp* **babysat**].

caníbal *adj* cannibalistic.

▶ *nmf* cannibal.

canica *nf* marble: *jugar a las canicas*, to play marbles.

canijo,-a *adj* weak, sickly.

canilla *nf* **1** (*espinilla*) shinbone. **2** (*carrete*) bobbin.

canino,-a *adj* canine.

▶ *nm* **canino** canine tooth [*pl* **teeth**].

canjear *vt* to exchange.

canoa *nf* canoe.

cano,-a *adj* grey, grey-haired.

canonizar *vt* to canonize.

canoso,-a *adj* gress, grey-haired.

cansado,-a *adj* **1** (*fatigado*) tired. **2** (*harto*): *cansado de algo*, tired of STH; *estoy cansada de tus excusas*, I'm tired of your excuses. **3** (*trabajo, viaje*) tiring, boring.

cansancio *nm* tiredness.

cansar *vt* **1** (*fatigar*) to tire, tire out: *me cansa bailar toda la noche*, dancing all night tires me out. **2** (*molestar*) to annoy: *me cansan sus discursos*, I'm fed up with his speeches.

▶ *vi* to be tiring: *subir escaleras cansa mucho*, going up stairs is very tiring.

▶ *vpr* **cansarse** to get tired.

cantante *adj* singing.

▶ *nmf* singer.

cantar *vt-vi* **1** (*gen*) to sing [*pt* **sang**; *pp* **sung**]; (*insecto*) to chirp; (*gallo*) to crow. **2** *fam* (*confesar*) to squeal.

▶ *vi* **1** *fam* (*oler mal*) to stink [*pt* **stank**; *pp* **stunk**]. **2** *fam* (*llamar la atención*) to stick out like a sore thumb [*pt & pp* **stuck**].

cántaro *nm* **1** (*recipiente*) pitcher. **2** (*contenido*) pitcherful.

● **llover a cántaros** to pour down.

cante *nm* singing.

● **dar el cante** *fam* to look ridiculous.

■ **cante hondo** flamenco.

cantera *nf* **1** (*de piedra*) quarry. **2** (*fútbol*) young players *pl*.

cántico *nm* canticle.

cantidad *nf* **1** (*volumen*) quantity, amount: *mucha cantidad y poca cali-*

dad, a large quantity and not much quality. **2** *(de dinero)* sum, amount.

▶ *adv* **1** *fam (mucho)* a lot: ***me gusta cantidad***, I love it. **2** *fam (un montón)* cantidad de, lots of: ***había cantidad de comida***, there was lots of food.

cantimplora *nf* water bottle.

cantina *nf* **1** *(en fábrica, colegio)* canteen. **2** *(en estación)* buffet, cafeteria.

canto[1] *nm* **1** *(arte)* singing. **2** *(canción)* song.

■ **canto del cisne** swan song.

canto[2] *nm* **1** *(borde)* edge: ***de cuchillo***, blunt edge. **2** *(piedra)* stone.

● **de canto** sideways.

■ **canto rodado** boulder.

cantor,-ra *adj* singing: ***pájaro cantor***, songbird.

▶ *nm,f* singer.

canturrear *vi* to hum.

canutas *nf pl fam* .

● **pasarlas canutas** to have a hard time.

caña *nf* **1** *(planta)* reed. **2** *(tallo)* cane. **3** *(de pescar)* fishing rod. **4** *(de cerveza)* beer, glass of beer.

● **meter caña 1** *fam* (en coche) to go at full speed. **2** (a persona) to have a go at.

■ **caña de azúcar** sugar cane.

cañaveral *nm* cane plantation.

cañería *nf (tubo)* pipe.

▶ *nf pl* **cañerías** pipes, piping.

caño *nm* **1** *(tubo)* pipe, tube. **2** *(de fuente)* spout.

cañón *nm* **1** *(de artillería)* cannon. **2** *(de arma)* barrel. **3** *(tubo)* tube, pipe. **4** *(de chimenea)* flue. **5** GEOG canyon. **6** *(de pluma)* quill.

● **estar al pie del cañón** to be hard at work.

caoba *nf* mahogany.

caos *nm* chaos.

capa *nf* **1** *(prenda)* cloak, cape. **2** *(baño)* coat: ***una capa de pintura***, a coat of paint. **3** layer: ***la capa de ozono***, the ozone layer. **4** *(estrato social)* stratum.

● **andar de capa caída** to be on the decline.

capacidad *nf* **1** *(cabida)* capacity: ***el barco tiene capacidad para 800 pasajeros***, the ship has a capacity of 800 passengers. **2** *(habilidad)* capability, ability: ***capacidad mental***, mental ability; ***tiene***

capacidad para la música, she has a talent for music.

capar *vt* to geld, castrate.

caparazón *nm* shell.

capataz *nmf (hombre)* foreman [pl -**men**]; *(mujer)* forewoman [pl -**women**].

capaz *adj* capable, able: ***una persona muy capaz***, a very capable person.

● **ser capaz de algo** to be capable of STH: ***es capaz de todo***, she's capable of anyting.

capellán *nm* chaplain.

caperuza *nf* **1** *(prenda)* hood. **2** *(tapa)* cap.

capicúa *adj* palindromic.

▶ *nm* palindromic number.

capilla *nf (de iglesia)* chapel.

■ **capilla ardiente** funeral chapel.

capital *adj (principal)* capital.

▶ *nm (dinero)* capital.

▶ *nf (ciudad)* capital.

■ **capital de provincia** provincial capital.

capitalismo *nm* capitalism.

capitalista *adj - nmf* capitalist.

capitán,-ana *nm,f* captain.

capitel *nm* capital.

capítulo *nm (de libro)* chapter; *(de serie televisiva)* episode.

capó *nm* GB bonnet; US hood.

capota *nf* folding top.

capote *nm* **1** *(prenda)* cloak with sleeves. **2** *(de torero)* cape.

capricho *nm* whim, caprice.

● **darse un capricho** to treat oneself.

caprichoso,-a *adj* capricious, whimsical.

capricornio *nm* Capricorn.

cápsula *nf* capsule.

captar *vt* **1** *(atraer interés, atención)* to capture; *(adeptos)* to attract. **2** *(ondas, emisora)* to pick up. **3** *(agua)* to collect. **4** *(comprender)* to understand [pt & pp **understood**].

captura *nf (de persona, animal)* capture; *(de alijo)* seizure.

capturar *vt (persona animal)* to capture; *(alijo)* to seize.

capucha *nf* hood.

capullo *nm* **1** *(de insectos)* cocoon. **2** *(de flor)* bud. **3** *vulg (estúpido)* silly bugger.

caqui[1] *nm (fruta)* persimmon.

caqui[2] *adj* khaki.

▶ *nm (color)* khaki.

cara *nf* **1** face: *lávate la cara*, wash your face. **2** *(lado)* side; *(de moneda)* side: *un cubo tiene seis caras*, a cube has six sides. **3** *(descaro)* cheek, nerve: *tuvo la cara de pedirme un favor*, he had the cheek to ask me a favor; *¡vaya cara!*, what a cheek!
● **cara a cara** face to face.
● **cara o cruz** heads or tails.
● **dar la cara** to take responsibility.
● **de cara a** opposite, facing.
● **echar en cara** to reproach for.
● **tener buena cara** to look well.
● **tener cara de + adj** to look + adj: *tiene cara de cansado*, he looks tired.
● **tener mala cara** to look ill.
● **verse las caras** to come face to face.
● **tener cara de pocos amigos** to look unfriendly.

carabela *nf* caravel.

carabina *nf* **1** *(arma)* carbine, rifle. **2** *fam (acompañante)* chaperone.

caracol *nm* **1** *(de tierra)* snail; *(de mar)* winkle. **2** *(del oído)* cochlea.

caracola *nf* conch.

carácter *nm* **1** *(personalidad, genio)* character: *tiene un carácter muy agradable*, she's got a very pleasant character; *tiene mucho carácter*, he's got a strong personality. **2** *(condición)* nature: *el proyecto tiene carácter científico*, this project is of a scientific nature. **3** *(de imprenta)* character.
● **tener buen carácter** to be good-natured.
● **tener mal carácter** to be bad-tempered.

característica *nf* characteristic.

característico,-a *adj* characteristic.

caracterizar *vt (distinguir)* to characterize.
► *vpr* **caracterizarse** *(distinguirse)* to be characterized, be known: *se caracteriza por su humildad*, he's known for his humility.

carambola *nf (billar)* GB cannon; US carom.

caramelo *nm* **1** *(golosina)* GB sweet; US candy. **2** *(azúcar quemado)* caramel.
● **a punto de caramelo** caramelized.

caravana *nf* **1** *(vehículo)* caravan. **2** *(atasco)* GB tailback; US backup.

carbón *nm* **1** *(mineral)* coal. **2** *(lápiz)* charcoal.
■ **carbón vegetal** charcoal.

carboncillo *nm* charcoal.

carbonero,-a *adj* coal.
► *nm,f* coal dealer.

carbonizar *vt-vpr* **carbonizar(se)** to carbonize, burn [*pt & pp* **burnt**].

carbono *nm* carbon.

carburador *nm* GB carburettor; US carburetor.

carburante *nm* fuel.

carcajada *nf* burst of laughter, guffaw.
● **reírse a carcajadas** to laugh one's head off.

cárcel *nf* prison, jail: *en la cárcel*, in prison, in jail.

carcelero *nm* jailer, warder.

carcoma *nf* woodworm.

cardenal[1] *nm (de la iglesia)* cardinal.

cardenal[2] *nm (hematoma)* bruise.

cardíaco,-a *adj* cardiac, heart.

cardinal *adj* cardinal.

cardo *nm* **1** *(planta)* thistle. **2** *fam (persona - arisco)* prickly customer; *(- fea)* ugly person.

carecer *vi*: *carecer de algo*, to lack STH; *carecen de lo necesario para vivir*, they lack the basic necessities to live; *carece de dinero propio*, she doesn't have her own money.

carencia *nf* lack.

carestía *nf* **1** *(precio alto)* high cost. **2** *(falta)* scarcity.

careta *nf* mask.

carga *nf* **1** *(mercancías)* load. **2** *(peso)* burden. **3** *(flete)* cargo, freight. **4** *(tributo)* tax. **5** *(obligación)* duty. **6** *(explosiva, eléctrica, militar)* charge. **7** *(de pluma, bolígrafo)* refill.
■ **carga eléctrica** electric charge.

cargado,-a *adj* **1** *(con mercancías)* loaded. **2** *(habitación)* stuffy. **3** *(día, tiempo)* sultry, cloudy. **4** *(bebida)* strong. **5** *(persona)* burdened: *estoy cargado de responsabilidades*, I'm loaded with responsibility.
● **cargado,-a de espaldas** round-shouldered.

cargador *nm* **1** *(de mercancías)* loader. **2** *(instrumento)* charger.

cargamento *nm (de tren, camión)* load; *(de avión, barco)* cargo.

cargante *adj* annoying.

cargar *vt* **1** *(vehículo, arma, mercancías)* to load. **2** *(pluma, encendedor)* to fill. **3** *(pila)* to charge. **4** *(precio)* to charge. **5** *(de trabajo, responsabilidad)* to burden. **6** *fam (molestar)* to bother, annoy.

▶ *vi (atacar)* to charge.

▶ *vpr* **cargarse** **1** *fam (destrozar)* to smash, ruin. **2** *(cielo)* to get cloudy, get overcast. **3** *fam (suspender)* to fail. **4** *fam (matar)* to knock off.

● **cargar con 1** (peso) to carry. **2** (responsabilidad) to take: *carga tú con la maleta, que eres más fuerte*, you carry the suitcase, you're stronger; *yo cargo con toda la responsabilidad*, I take full responsibility.

● **cargar algo en cuenta de** ALGN to debit SB's account with STH.

● **cargar las tintas** to exaggerate.

● **cargar con el muerto 1** *fam* (con la responsabilidad) to be left holding the baby. **2** (con la culpa) to get the blame.

cargo *nm* **1** *(puesto)* post, position: *un cargo directivo*, a management post. **2** *(gobierno, custodia)* charge, responsibility: *tiene dos empleados a su cargo*, he has two employees. **3** *(en cuenta)* charge, debit. **4** charge, accusation: *han retirado los cargos contra el acusado*, they've dropped the charges against the accused.

● **correr a cargo de** ALGN **1** *(responsabilidad)* to be the responsibility of SB. **2** *(gasto)* to be paid for by SB [*pt & pp* **paid**].

● **estar al cargo de** to be in charge.

● **hacerse cargo de 1** (responsabilizarse de) to take charge of. **2** (entender) to take into consideration, realize.

Caribe *nm* **el Caribe** the Caribbean.

caricatura *nf* caricature.

caricia *nf* **1** *(a persona)* caress, stroke. **2** *(a animal)* stroke.

● **hacerle caricias a** ALGN to caress SB, stroke SB.

caridad *nf* charity.

caries *nf* **1** *(enfermedad)* tooth decay, caries *inv*. **2** *(agujero)* cavity.

cariño *nm* **1** *(afecto)* love, affection, fondness. **2** *(apelativo)* darling.

● **coger cariño a** to grow fond of.

cariñoso,-a *adj* loving, affectionate.

caritativo,-a *adj* charitable.

carmesí *adj - nm* crimson.

carmín *adj - nm* carmine.

carnal *adj* **1** *(deseo, placer)* carnal: *pecado carnal*, carnal sin. **2** *(pariente)* first: *primo carnal*, first cousin.

carnaval *nm* carnival.

carne *nf* **1** *(de persona, fruta)* meat: *no come carne*, she doesn't eat meat. **2** *(de persona, fruta)* flesh.

● **en carne viva** raw.

● **ser de carne y hueso** to be only human.

● **ser uña y carne** to be as thick as thieves.

■ **carne asada** roasted meat.

■ **carne de buey** beef.

■ **carne de gallina** goose flesh, goose bumps: *se me pone la carne de gallina*, it gives me goose bumps.

■ **carne picada** mincemeat.

carné *nm* card.

■ **carné de conducir** driving licence.

■ **carné de identidad** identity card.

carnero *nm* ram.

carnet *nm* → carné.

carnicería *nf* **1** *(tienda)* butcher's. **2** *(matanza)* carnage, slaughter.

carnicero,-a *adj* **1** *(carnívoro)* carnivorous. **2** *fig (sangriento)* bloodthirsty, sanguinary.

▶ *nm,f* butcher.

carnívoro,-a *adj* carnivorous.

carnoso,-a *adj* fleshy.

caro,-a *adj* expensive, dear.

▶ *adv* **caro** at a high price.

carpa¹ *nf (pez)* carp.

carpa² *nf (toldo)* marquee; (de circo) big top.

carpeta *nf* folder, file.

carpintería *nf* **1** *(labor)* carpentry. **2** *(taller)* carpenter's shop.

carpintero *nm* carpenter.

carraspera *nf* hoarseness.

carrera *nf* **1** *(acción de correr)* run, running. **2** race: *una carrera de caballos*, a horse race. **3** *(estudios)* university education: *quiero hacer la carrera de medicina*, I want to study medicine. **4** *(profesión)* career. **5** *(trayecto)* route. **6** *(camino)* road. **7** *(en las medias)* ladder.

● **hacer la carrera** to walk the streets.

■ **carrera armamentística** arms race.

■ **carrera ciclista** cycle race.

■ **carrera de coches** motor race.

■ **carrera de obstáculos** obstacle race.

■ **carrera de relevos** relay race.

carrerilla *nf* .

- **saber algo de carrerilla** to know STH parrot fashion [*pt* **knew**; *pp* **known**].
- **tomar carrerilla** to take a run-up.

carreta *nf* cart.

carrete *nm* **1** *(de película)* roll of film, film. **2** *(de hilo, pesca)* reel.

carretera *nf* road.
- **carretera comarcal** local road; country road.
- **carretera de acceso** access road.
- **carretera de circunvalación** GB ring road; US beltway.
- **carretera nacional** GB A road, main road; US state highway.

carretilla *nf* wheelbarrow.
- **saber algo de carretilla** to know STH parrot fashion [*pt* **knew**; *pp* **known**].

carril *nm* **1** *(de carretera)* lane. **2** *(ferrocarril)* rail.
- **carril bici** GB cycle lane; US bikeway.

carrillo *nm* cheek.

carro *nm* **1** *(carreta)* cart. **2** *(militar)* tank. **3** *(en supermercado, aeropuerto)* trolley. **4** *(de máquina de escribir)* carriage.
- **¡para el carro!** *fam* hold your horses!

carrocería *nf* bodywork.

carromato *nm* wagon.

carroña *nf* carrion.

carroza *nf* **1** *(de caballos)* coach, carriage. **2** *(de carnaval)* float.
- ► *adj fam (anticuado)* out-of-date.
- ► *nmf fam (persona anticuada)* old fogey.

carruaje *nm* carriage, coach.

carta *nf* **1** *(documento)* letter. **2** *(naipe)* card. **3** *(en restaurante)* menu.
- **echar una carta** to post a letter.
- **echarle las cartas a** ALGN to tell SB's fortune [*pt & pp* **told**].
- **poner las cartas sobre la mesa** to put one's cards on the table.
- **tomar cartas en algo** to intervene in STH, step in.
- **carta blanca** carte blanche.
- **carta certificada** registered letter.
- **carta de recomendación** letter of introduction.

cartabón *nm* set square.

cartearse *vpr* to correspond, write to each other.

cartel *nm* poster.

cartelera *nf* **1** *(para carteles)* GB hoarding; US billboard. **2** *(en periódicos)* entertainment guide.

cartera *nf* **1** *(monedero)* wallet. **2** *(de colegial)* satchel, schoolbag. **3** *(de ejecutivo)* briefcase. **4** portfolio [*pl* -**s**]: *ministro sin cartera*, minister without portfolio.

carterista *nmf* pickpocket.

cartero,-a *nm,f (hombre)* GB postman [*pl* -**men**]; US mailman; *(mujer)* GB postwoman [*pl* -**women**]; US mailwoman.

cartilla *nf* **1** *(para leer)* first reader. **2** *(cuaderno)* book.
- **cartilla de ahorros** savings book.
- **cartilla del seguro** social security card.

cartón *nm* **1** *(material)* cardboard: *una caja de cartón*, a cardboard box. **2** *(de cigarrillos, leche)* carton.
- **cartón piedra** papier mâché.

cartuchera *nf* cartridge belt.

cartucho *nm* **1** *(con explosivo, tinta)* cartridge. **2** *(de monedas)* roll *(of coins)*.

cartulina *nf* card.

casa *nf* **1** *(edificio)* house. **2** *(hogar)* home: *vete a casa*, go home. **3** *(linaje)* house: *la casa de los Borbón*, the House of Bourbon. **4** *(empresa)* firm, company.
- **como Pedro por su casa** as if he owned the place.
- **jugar en casa** to play at home.
- **llevar la casa** to run the house [*pt* **ran**; *pp* **run**].
- **tirar la casa por la ventana** to go all out.
- **casa adosada** terraced house.
- **casa consistorial** town hall.
- **casa de campo** country house.
- **casa de citas** brothel.
- **casa de empeños** pawn-shop.
- **casa de huéspedes** guesthouse, boarding house.
- **casa de socorro** first aid post.
- **casa pareada** semi-detached house.

casaca *nf* long coat.

casado,-a *adj* married: *está casado con Ana*, he's married to Ana.
- ► *nm,f* married person: *los recién casados*, the newlyweds.

casamiento *nm* **1** *(matrimonio)* marriage. **2** *(ceremonia)* wedding.

casar *vt (personas)* to marry.
- ► *vi* **1** *(colores)* to go well together. **2** *(cuentas)* to match.
- ► *vpr* **casarse** to get married.

● **casarse de penalti** *fam* to have a shotgun wedding.
cascabel *nm* bell.
cascada *nf* waterfall, cascade.
cascado,-a *adj* **1** *(voz)* harsh, hoarse. **2** *fam (persona)* worn-out. **3** *(casa)* broken-down.
cascanueces *nm* nutcracker.
cascar *vt* **1** *(romper)* to crack: *cascar nue-ces*, to crack nuts. **2** *fam (pegar)* to beat [*pt* **beat**; *pp* **beaten**], thrash.
▶ *vi* **1** *fam (morir)* to peg out. **2** *fam (charlar)* to chat away.
▶ *vpr* **cascarse** *(romperse)* to crack.
cáscara *nf* **1** *(de huevo, nuez)* shell. **2** *(de plátano)* skin. **3** *(de naranja, limón)* peel, rind. **4** *(de grano)* husk.
cascarón *nm* eggshell.
cascarrabias *nmf fam* grouch.
casco *nm* **1** *(protector)* helmet. **2** *(envase)* empty bottle. **3** *(de barco)* hull. **4** *(de caballo)* hoof [*pl* **-ves**].
▶ *nm pl* **cascos** *(auriculares)* headphones.
● **ser ligero,-a de cascos** to be scatter-brained.
■ **casco antiguo** old town.
■ **casco azul** blue beret.
■ **casco urbano** city centre; US downtown area.
cascote *nm* piece of rubble, piece of debris.
caserío *nm* **1** *(casa)* country house. **2** *(pueblo)* hamlet.
casero,-a *adj* **1** *(persona)* home-loving. **2** *(productos)* home-made.
▶ *nm,f (dueño - hombre)* landlord; *(- mujer)* landlady.
caseta *nf* **1** *(de feria)* stall. **2** *(de bañistas)* GB bathing hut; US bath house. **3** *(de perro)* kennel.
casete *nm (aparato)* cassette player, cassette recorder.
▶ *nf (cinta)* cassette *(tape)*.
casi *adv* **1** *(gen)* almost, nearly: *casi he terminado*, I've nearly finished; *tiene casi diez años*, she's almost ten; *casi se cae al río*, he almost fell in the river. **2** *(en frases negativas)* hardly: *casi nunca*, hardly ever; *casi no crece*, it hardly grows; *no queda casi nada de leche*, there's hardly any milk left.
● **¡casi nada!** *fam irón* is that all?

casilla *nf* **1** *(de casillero)* pigeonhole. **2** *(cuadrícula)* square. **3** *(de formulario)* box.
● **sacar a ALGN de sus casillas** to drive SB mad.
casillero *nm* pigeonholes *pl.*
casino *nm* casino [*pl* **-s**].
caso *nm* case: *un caso difícil de resolver*, a case difficult to solve; *nunca había oído un caso igual*, I had never heard of a case like it.
● **el caso es que ...** the thing is that ....
● **en caso de que** if.
● **en ese caso** in that case.
● **en todo caso** anyhow, at any rate.
● **hacer caso a** to pay attention to [*pt & pp* **paid**].
● **venir al caso** to be relevant.
caspa *nf* dandruff.
casta *nf* **1** *(grupo social)* caste. **2** *(linaje)* lineage, descent. **3** *(de cosa)* quality.
castaña *nf* **1** *(fruto)* chestnut. **2** *(de pelo)* bun. **3** *fam (bofetada)* slap.
● **darse una castaña** to come a cropper.
● **sacarle las castañas del fuego a ALGN** to save SB's bacon.
castañetear *vi* to chatter: *le castañetean los dientes*, his teeth are chattering.
castaño,-a *adj* chestnut-coloured; *(pelo)* brown.
▶ *nm* **castaño** *(árbol)* chestnut tree.
castañuela *nf* castanet.
castellano,-a *adj* Castilian.
▶ *nm,f (persona)* Castilian.
▶ *nm* **castellano** *(idioma)* Castilian, Spanish.
castidad *nf* chastity.
castigar *vt* **1** *(niño, condenado)* to punish. **2** *(deportista)* to penalize. **3** *(dañar)* to harm.
castigo *nm* *(de niño, condenado)* punishment.
Castilla *nf* Castile.
■ **Castilla la Nueva** New Castile.
■ **Castilla la Vieja** Old Castile.
castillo *nm* castle.
● **hacer castillos en el aire** to build castles in the air.
■ **castillo de arena** sandcastle.
■ **castillo de fuegos artificiales** firework display.
■ **castillo de naipes** house of cards.
casto,-a *adj* chaste.

castor *nm* beaver.

castrar *vt* **1** *(capar toro, hombre)* to castrate. **2** *(caballo)* to geld.

casual *adj* accidental, chance.

● **por un casual** just by chance.

casualidad *nf* chance, coincidence.

● **por casualidad** by chance.

● **¡qué casualidad!** what a coincidence!

cataclismo *nm* cataclysm.

catacumbas *nf pl* catacombs.

catalán,-ana *adj* Catalan, Catalonian.
► *nm,f (persona)* Catalan, Catalonian.
► *nm* **catalán** *(idioma)* Catalan.

catalejo *nm* spyglass.

catálogo *nm* catalogue.

Cataluña *nf* Catalonia.

catar *vt* to taste.

catarata *nf* **1** *(de agua)* waterfall. **2** *(en ojo)* cataract.

catarro *nm* cold.

catástrofe *nf* catastrophe.

cate *nm fam* fail.

catear *vt fam* GB to fail; US to flunk.

catecismo *nm* catechism.

catedral *nf* cathedral.

catedrático,-a *nm,f (de universidad)* professor; *(de instituto)* head of department.

categoría *nf* **1** *(rango)* category: **hay tres categorías de votantes**, there are three categories of voters. **2** *(calidad)* quality: **un producto de categoría**, a quality product. **3** *(nivel)* level: **en categoría juvenil**, at junior level.

● **de primera categoría** first-class.

cateto *nm (de triángulo)* cathetus.

cateto,-a *nm,f (palurdo)* dimwit.

catolicismo *nm* Catholicism.

católico,-a *adj - nm,f* Catholic.

catorce *num* fourteen; *(en fechas)* fourteenth.

cauce *nm* **1** *(de río)* river bed. **2** *(canal)* channel: **hay que seguir los cauces reglamentarios**, you have to follow the official channels.

caucho *nm* rubber.

caudal *nm* **1** *(de río)* volume of water. **2** *(riqueza)* fortune, wealth.

caudaloso,-a *adj* with a large flow.

caudillo *nm* chief, leader.

causa *nf* **1** *(motivo, ideal)* cause: **por causas naturales**, from natural causes; **una buena causa**, a good cause. **2** *(proceso)* lawsuit.

● **a causa de** because of, on account of.

causar *vt* **1** *(provocar)* to cause, bring about *[pt & pp* **brought**]. **2** *(proporcionar)* to give: **me causa un gran placer ...**, it's a pleasure for me to ...; **me causó buena impresión**, she made a good impression on me.

cautela *nf* caution.

cauteloso,-a *adj* cautious.

cautivar *vt* **1** *(hacer cautivo)* to take prisoner, capture. **2** *(atraer)* to captivate, charm.

cautiverio *nm* captivity.

cautividad *nf* captivity.

cautivo,-a *adj - nm,f* captive.

cauto,-a *adj* cautious.

cava *nm (bebida)* cava.
► *nf (bodega)* wine cellar.

cavar *vt* to dig *[pt & pp* **dug**].

caverna *nf* cavern, cave.

caviar *nm* caviar.

cavidad *nf* cavity.

cavilar *vi* to ponder.

cayado *nm* **1** *(de pastor)* crook. **2** *(de obispo)* crozier.

caza *nf* **1** *(acción)* hunting. **2** *(con escopeta)* shooting: **le gusta ir de caza**, he enjoys going hunting. **3** *(animales)* game.
► *nm (avión)* fighter.
■ **caza mayor** big game.
■ **caza menor** small game.

cazadora *nf (chaqueta)* jacket.

cazador,-ra *adj* hunting.
► *nm,f* hunter.
■ **cazador furtivo** poacher.

cazar *vt* **1** *(animal)* to hunt. **2** *(con escopeta)* to shoot. **3** *fam (coger)* to catch *[pt & pp* **caught**].

cazo *nm* **1** *(cucharón)* ladle. **2** *(cacerola)* saucepan.

cazuela *nf* casserole.

CD-ROM *nm* CD-ROM.

cebada *nf* barley.

cebar *vt* to fatten *(up)*.

● **cebarse en/con** ALGN to take it out on SB, vent one's anger on SB.

cebo *nm* **1** *(para animales)* food. **2** *(para pescar)* bait.

cebolla *nf* onion.

cebolleta *nf* **1** *(hierba)* chive. **2** *(cebolla)* spring onion.

cebra *nf* zebra.

ceder *vt (dar)* to give.

▶ *vi* **1** *(rendirse)* to give yield: ***cedió a mis peticiones***, she gave in to my requests. **2** *(caerse)* to fall [*pt* **fell**; *pp* **fallen**], give way: ***las paredes cedieron***, the walls caved in.

● **ceder el paso** GB to give way ; US to yield.

cedro *nm* cedar.

cegar *vt* **1** *(persona)* to blind: ***cegado por la ira***, blind with rage. **2** *(puerta, ventana)* to wall up.

▶ *vpr* **cegarse** *fig (obstinarse)* to become blinded.

ceguera *nf* blindness.

ceja *nf* eyebrow.

● **tener algo entre ceja y ceja** to have STH in one's head.

celda *nf* cell.

celebración *nf* **1** *(fiesta)* celebration. **2** *(de reunión, congreso, etc)* holding.

celebrar *vt* **1** *(festejar)* to celebrate. **2** *(reunión, congreso, etc)* to hold [*pt & pp* **held**]. **3** *(alabar)* to praise. **4** *(alegrarse de)* to be happy about: ***celebro lo de tu ascenso***, I congratulate you on your promotion. **5** *(misa)* to say [*pt & pp* **said**].

▶ *vpr* **celebrarse** to take place, be held.

célebre *adj* well-known, famous.

celebridad *nf* celebrity.

celeste *adj* **1** *(del cielo)* celestial. **2** *(azul)* light.

celo[1] *nm* **1** *(entusiasmo)* zeal. **2** *(cuidado)* care.

▶ *nm pl* **celos** jealousy *sing*.

● **estar en celo** to be on heat, be in season.

● **tener celos** to be jealous.

celo®[2] *nm* GB Sellotape®; US Scotch tape®.

celofán *nm* Cellophane®.

celoso,-a *adj* **1** *(envidioso)* jealous. **2** *(entusiasta, cuidadoso)* zealous.

celta *adj* Celtic.

▶ *nmf (persona)* Celt.

▶ *nm (idioma)* Celtic.

célula *nf* cell.

celulitis *nf* cellulite.

cementerio *nm* cemetery, graveyard.

■ **cementerio de coches** scrapyard.

cemento *nm* cement.

■ **cemento armado** reinforced concrete.

cena *nf (comida por la noche)* dinner, supper; *(formal)* dinner.

■ **la Santa Cena** the Last Supper.

cenar *vi* to have dinner, have supper.

▶ *vt* to have for dinner, have for supper: ***¿qué has cenado?***, what did you have for dinner?

cencerro *nm* cowbell.

● **estar como un cencerro** to be nuts.

cenicero *nm* ashtray.

ceniza *nf* ash.

▶ *nf pl* **cenizas** *(restos)* ashes.

censo *nm* census.

■ **censo electoral** electoral roll.

censura *nf* **1** *(de prensa, cine, etc)* censorship: ***pasar por la censura***, to be censured. **2** *(crítica)* censure.

censurar *vt* **1** *(prensa, cine, etc)* to censor. **2** *(criticar)* to censure, criticize.

centavo,-a *adj* hundredth.

▶ *nm* **centavo** *(parte)* hundredth.

centella *nf* **1** *(rayo)* flash of lightning. **2** *(chispa)* spark.

centellear *vi* to sparkle; *(estrella)* to twinkle.

centena *nf* hundred.

centenar *nm* hundred.

centenario,-a *adj* centennial.

▶ *nm,f (persona)* centenarian.

▶ *nm* **centenario** *(aniversario)* centenary.

centeno *nm* rye.

centésimo,-a *num* hundredth: ***una centésima de segundo***, a hundredth of a second.

centígrado,-a *adj* centigrade.

centilitro *nm* centiliter.

centímetro *nm* centimetre.

céntimo *nm* cent, centime.

● **estar sin un céntimo** to be penniless.

centinela *nm & nf* sentry.

centolla *nf* spider crab.

centollo *nm* spider crab.

central *adj* central.

▶ *nf* **1** *(oficina principal)* head office, headquarters *pl*. **2** power station.

■ **central nuclear** nuclear power station.

■ **central telefónica** telephone exchange.

centralita *nf* switchboard.

centrar *vt* to centre.

▶ *vpr* **centrarse 1** *(basarse)* to be centred. **2** *(concentrarse)* to concentrate.

céntrico,-a *adj* central: ***una calle céntrica***, a street in the centre of town.

centro *nm* **1** *(gen)* GB centre; US center. **2** *(de la ciudad)* town centre; US downtown.

■ **centro ciudad** GB town centre, city centre; US downtown.

■ **centro comercial** GB shopping centre; US mall.

■ **centro de mesa** centrepiece.

■ **centro docente** school.

■ **centro hospitalario** hospital.

■ **centro recreativo** leisure centre.

ceñido,-a *adj* close-fitting.

ceñir *vt* **1** *(apretar)* to cling to [*pt & pp* **clung**], fit tight. **2** *(rodear)* to hug around the waist.

▶ *vpr* **ceñirse** to limit oneself: *ceñirse al tema*, to keep to the subject.

ceño *nm* frown.

● **fruncir el ceño** to frown.

cepa *nf* **1** *(de vid)* vine. **2** *(tronco)* stump.

● **de pura cepa** true: *es un galés de pura cepa*, he's a true Welshman, he's every inch a Welshman.

cepillar *vt* **1** *(pelo, zapato, etc)* to brush. **2** *(madera)* to plane.

▶ *vpr* **cepillarse 1** *(pelo, zapatos, etc)* to brush. **2** *fam (matar)* to do in. **3** *fam (acabarse)* to finish: *se cepilló todo el pastel*, she gobbled up the whole cake. **4** *vulg (copular)* to lay [*pt & pp* **laid**].

cepillo *nm* **1** *(para pelo, zapatos, etc)* brush. **2** *(de carpintero)* plane. **3** *(para limosnas)* alms box.

■ **cepillo de dientes** toothbrush.

■ **cepillo de ropa** clothes brush.

cepo *nm* **1** *(trampa)* trap. **2** *(para coche)* wheel clamp.

cera *nf* **1** *(vela)* wax; *(de abeja)* beeswax. **2** *(de oreja)* earwax. **3** *(para muebles, suelo)* polish.

cerámica *nf* ceramics, pottery: *una cerámica*, a piece of pottery.

cerca¹ *nf (valla)* fence.

cerca² *adv* near, close: *aquí cerca*, near here.

● **cerca de 1** *(cercano a)* near. **2** *(casi)* nearly: *¿vives cerca del parque?*, do you live near the park?; *cerca de un año*, nearly a year.

● **de cerca** close up: *lo vi de cerca*, I saw it close up.

cercado,-a *adj* fenced in.

▶ *nm* **cercado** enclosure.

cercanía *nf* proximity, nearness.

cercano,-a *adj* **1** *(lugar)* nearby: *un pueblo cercano*, a nearby village; *cercano a la estación*, near the station. **2** *(tiempo)* near: *en un futuro cercano*, in the near future. **3** *(pariente, amigo)* close.

cercar *vt* **1** *(vallar)* to fence in. **2** *(rodear)* to surround. **3** *(asediar)* to besiege.

cerciorarse *vpr* to make sure of.

cerco *nm* **1** *(marco)* frame. **2** *(asedio)* siege.

cerda *nf* **1** *(pelo - de caballo)* horsehair; *(- de cerdo)* bristle. **2** *(animal)* sow.

cerdo *nm* **1** *(animal)* pig. **2** *(carne)* pork.

cereal *adj - nm* cereal.

cerebral *adj* **1** *(del cerebro)* cerebral, brain. **2** *(frío)* calculating.

cerebro *nm* **1** brain. **2** *(persona, inteligencia)* brains *pl*.

ceremonia *nf* ceremony.

ceremonioso,-a *adj* ceremonious, formal.

cereza *nf* cherry.

cerezo *nm* cherry tree.

cerilla *nf* match.

cero *nm* **1** zero [*pl* **-os** o **-oes**]: *cero coma seis*, zero point six. **2** nought, zero: *saqué un cero en física*, I got a nought in physics. **3** nil: *ganamos tres a cero*, we won three-nil.

● **bajo cero** below zero.

● **ser un cero a la izquierda** to be useless.

cerrado,-a *adj* **1** *(gen)* shut, closed. **2** *(con llave)* locked. **3** *(persona)* uncommunicative, reserved. **4** *(acento)* broad. **5** *(curva)* sharp.

cerradura *nf* lock.

cerrajero *nm* locksmith.

cerrar *vt* **1** to close, shut [*pt & pp* **shut**]. **2** *(con llave)* to lock. **3** *(grifo, gas)* to turn off. **4** *(luz)* to switch off. **5** *(cremallera)* to zip *(up)*. **6** *(un negocio definitivamente)* to close down. **7** *(carta)* to seal.

▶ *vi* to shut [*pt & pp* **shut**].

▶ *vpr* **cerrarse 1** *(gen)* to close, shut [*pt & pp* **shut**]: *la puerta se cerró*, the door closed. **2** *(obstinarse)* to stand fast [*pt & pp* **stood**]. **3** *(terminar)* to finish: *el plazo se cierra el día 15 de este mes*, the closing date is the 15th of this month.

● **cerrar la boca** to shut up [*pt & pp* **shut**].

cerro *nm* hill.

● **irse por los cerros de Úbeda** to go off at a tangent.

cerrojo *nm* bolt.

● **echar el cerrojo** to bolt the door.

certamen *nm* competition, contest.

■ **certamen literario** literary contest.

certero,-a *adj* **1** *(disparo)* accurate. **2** *(seguro)* certain, sure.

certeza *nf* certainty.

certidumbre *nf* certainty.

certificado,-a *adj* **1** *(documento)* certified. **2** *(envío)* registered.

► *nm* **certificado** *(documento)* certificate.

■ **certificado médico** medical certificate.

certificar *vt* **1** *(gen)* to certify. **2** *(carta, paquete)* to register.

cerveza *nf* beer: *le gusta la cerveza*, he likes beer.

■ **cerveza de barril** GB draught beer; US draft beer.

■ **cerveza rubia** lager.

cesar *vi* **1** *(parar)* to cease, stop. **2** *(en un empleo)* to leave [*pt & pp* **left**].

● **sin cesar** nonstop.

cese *nm* **1** *(fin)* cessation. **2** *(despido)* dismissal.

césped *nm* lawn, grass: *cortar el césped*, to mow the lawn.

● **prohibido pisar el césped** keep off the grass.

cesta *nf* basket.

■ **cesta de la compra** shopping basket.

cesto *nm* basket.

cetáceo *nm* cetacean.

cetro *nm* sceptre.

chabacanería *nf* coarseness, vulgarity.

chabacano,-a *adj* coarse, vulgar.

chabola *nf* shack.

chacal *nm* jackal.

chacha *nf fam* maid, housemaid.

cháchara *nf fam* prattle, idle talk.

● **estar de cháchara** to chatter, GB have a natter.

chachi *adj arg* great, terrific.

chafar *vt* **1** *(aplastar)* to flatten. **2** *(arrugar)* to crumple. **3** *fam (estropear)* to spoil, ruin: *me han chafado el plan*, they've spoiled my plan. **4** *(desanimar)* to depress.

chal *nm* shawl.

chalado,-a *adj* mad, crazy.

● **estar chalado,-a por** to be mad about.

chalé *nm* **1** *(gen)* house. **2** *(en campo, playa)* villa.

chaleco *nm* GB waistcoat; US vest.

■ **chaleco salvavidas** life jacket.

chalet *nm* chalé.

champán *nm* champagne.

champiñón *nm* mushroom.

champú *nm* shampoo [*pl* **-s**].

chamuscar *vt* to singe, scorch.

► *vpr* **chamuscarse** to be singed.

chanchullo *nm fam* fiddle, wangle.

chancla *nf* **1** *(de playa)* GB flip-flop; US thong. **2** *(zapato viejo)* old shoe.

chancleta *nf* GB flip-flop; US thong.

chándal *nm* track suit, jogging suit.

chantaje *nm* blackmail.

● **hacer chantaje** to blackmail.

chantajear *vt* to blackmail.

chantajista *nmf* blackmailer.

chapa *nf* **1** *(de metal)* sheet. **2** *(de madera)* panel. **3** *(tapón)* bottle top. **4** *(insignia)* badge. **5** *(de coche)* bodywork.

■ **chapa de identificación** identity disc.

chapado,-a *adj* plated: *chapado en plata*, silver-plated.

● **chapado,-a a la antigua** old-fashioned.

chaparrón *nm* downpour, heavy shower.

chapotear *vi* to splash.

chapoteo *nm* splashing.

chapucero,-a *adj (trabajo)* botched; *(persona)* bungling.

► *nm,f* bungler.

chapurrear *vt* to speak badly [*pt* **spoke**; *pp* **spoken**]: *chapurrear el francés*, to have a smattering of French.

chapuza *nf* **1** *(trabajo mal hecho)* botch, botched job. **2** *(trabajo ocasional)* odd job.

● **hacer una chapuza** to do a botched job.

chapuzón *nm* dip.

● **darse un chapuzón** to have a dip.

chaqué *nm* morning coat.

chaqueta *nf* jacket.

● **cambiar de chaqueta** *fam* to change sides.

chaquetón *nm* short coat, three-quarter coat.

charanga *nf* brass band.

charca *nf* pool, pond.

charco *nm (de lluvia)* puddle; *(de sangre, etc)* pool.

charcutería *nf* pork butcher's shop, delicatessen.

charla *nf* **1** *(conversación)* chat, talk. **2** *(conferencia)* talk, lecture.

charlar *vi* to chat, talk.

charlatán,-ana *adj* **1** *(parlanchín)* talkative. **2** *(chismoso)* gossipy.
▶ *nm,f* **1** *(parlanchín)* chatterbox. **2** *(embaucador)* charlatan.

charol *nm* **1** *(barniz)* varnish. **2** *(cuero)* patent leather.

chárter *adj* - *nm* charter.

chasco *nm* **1** *(broma)* trick. **2** *(decepción)* disappointment.
● **llevarse un chasco** to be disappointed.

chasis *nm* chassis.

chasquido *nm* **1** *(de látigo, madera)* crack. **2** *(de lengua)* click.

chatarra *nf* **1** *(metal)* scrap metal. **2** *fam (monedas)* small change.

chatarrero,-a *nm,f* scrap dealer.

chatear *vi* to chat.

chato,-a *adj* **1** *(nariz)* snub. **2** *(persona)* snub-nosed. **3** *(objeto)* flat.
▶ *nm,f* **1** *(persona)* snub-nosed person. **2** *fam (apelativo)* love, dear.
▶ *nm* **chato** *(vaso)* small glass.

chaval,-la *nm,f* kid, youngster; *(chico)* lad; *(chica)* lass.

checo,-a *adj* Czech.
▶ *nm,f (persona)* Czech.
▶ *nm* **checo** *(idioma)* Czech.
■ **República Checa** Czech Republic.

chepa *nf fam* hump.

cheque *nm* GB cheque; US check.
● **extender un cheque** to issue a cheque.
■ **cheque abierto** open cheque.
■ **cheque al portador** cheque payable to bearer.
■ **cheque cruzado** crossed cheque.
■ **cheque de viaje** traveller's cheque.
■ **cheque en blanco** blank cheque.
■ **cheque sin fondos** dud cheque.

chequeo *nm* checkup.

chicha *nf* meat.

chichón *nm* bump, lump.

chicle *nm* chewing gum.

chico,-a *adj* small, little.
▶ *nm,f* **1** *(niño)* kid; *(niña)* girl. **2** *(muchacho)* boy, guy; *(muchacha)* girl.
▶ *nm* **chico** *(aprendiz)* office boy.

chiflado,-a *adj* mad, crazy.

chifladura *nf* craziness, madness.

Chile *nm* Chile.

chileno,-a *adj* - *nm,f* Chilean.

chillar *vi* **1** *(persona)* to scream, yell; *(gritar)* to shout. **2** *(ave)* to screech. **3** *(cerdo)* to squeal. **4** *(ratón)* to squeak.

chillido *nm* **1** *(de persona)* scream, yell. **2** *(de ave)* screech. **3** *(de cerdo)* squeal. **4** *(de ratón)* squeak.

chillón,-ona *adj* **1** *(persona)* screaming. **2** *(color)* loud, garish.

chimenea *nf* **1** *(exterior)* chimney. **2** *(hogar)* fireplace. **3** *(de barco)* funnel.

chimpancé *nm* chimpanzee.

china[1] *nf* **1** *(piedra)* pebble. **2** *arg (droga)* piece, deal.

china[2] *nf (porcelana)* china.

China *nf* China.

chinchar *vt fam* to annoy, pester.
▶ *vpr* **chincharse** *fam* to grin and bear it.
● **¡chínchate!** so there!

chinche *nm & nf* **1** *(bicho)* bedbug. **2** *(pesado)* bore, nuisance.

chincheta *nf* GB drawing pin; US thumbtack.

chinchilla *nf* chinchilla.

chino,-a *adj* Chinese.
▶ *nm,f (persona)* Chinese person; *(hombre)* Chinese man; *(mujer)* Chinese woman: **los chinos**, the Chinese.
▶ *nm* **chino** *(idioma)* Chinese.

chip *nm* INFORM chip.
▶ *nm pl* **chips** crisps.

chipirón *nm* baby squid.

chiquillada *nf* childish prank.

chiquillo,-a *nm,f* kid, youngster.

chiquito,-a *adj* tiny, very small.
▶ *nm* **chiquito** small glass of wine.
● **no andarse con chiquitas** not to mess about.

chiringuito *nm fam (en playa)* bar, restaurant; *(en carretera)* roadside snack bar.

chiripa *nf fam* fluke, stroke of luck.
● **por chiripa** by sheer luck.

chirriar *vi* **1** *(rueda, frenos)* to screech. **2** *(puerta)* to creak. **3** *(aves)* to squawk. **4** *(persona)* to sing out of tune [*pt* **sang**; *pp* **sung**].

chirrido *nm* **1** *(de rueda, frenos)* screech. **2** *(de puerta)* creaking. **3** *(de aves)* squawk.

chisme *nm* **1** *(cotilleo)* piece of gossip. **2** *(trasto)* knick-knack; *(de cocina etc)* gadget: *¿cómo funciona este chisme?*, how does this thing work?

chismorrear *vi* to gossip.

chismorreo *nm* gossip.

chismoso,-a *adj* gossipy.

▶ *nm,f* gossip.

chispa *nf* 1 *(de fuego)* spark. 2 *(poco)* bit, scrap: *no queda ni una chispa de azúcar*, there isn't a bit of sugar left. 3 *fig (ingenio)* wit.

● **echar chispas** to be raging.

● **tener chispa** to be witty, be funny.

chispazo *nm* spark, flash.

chispear *vi* 1 *(leña)* to spark. 2 *(lloviznar)* to drizzle slightly. 3 *(relucir)* to sparkle.

chisporrotear *vi (leña)* to crackle; *(aceite)* to spit; *(carne)* to sizzle.

chisporroteo *nm (de leña)* crackling; *(de aceite)* spitting; *(de carne)* sizzling.

chistar *vi* .

● **no chistar** not to say a word.

● **sin chistar** without a word.

chiste *nm* joke.

● **contar un chiste** to tell a joke [*pt & pp* **told**].

■ **chiste verde** blue joke, dirty joke.

chistera *nf* top hat.

chistoso,-a *adj* witty, funny.

chivarse *vpr* 1 *(niño)* to tell: *se chivó al profe*, he told the teacher. 2 *(delincuente)* to squeal, GB grass.

chivato,-a *nm,f fam (delator)* informer, GB grass; *(acusica)* GB telltale; US tattletale.

▶ *nm* **chivato** *(piloto)* warning light.

chivo,-a *nm,f* kid.

■ **chivo expiatorio** scapegoat.

chocante *adj (raro)* odd, strange; *(sorprendente)* startling; *(escandaloso)* shocking.

chocar *vi* 1 *(colisionar)* to collide, crash: *los dos coches chocaron en la esquina*, the two cars collided on the corner; *la moto chocó contra una farola*, the motorbike crashed into a lamppost. 2 *(enfrentarse)* to clash. 3 *fig (sorprender)* to surprise: *esto me choca*, I am surprised at this. 4 *(escandalizar)* to shock.

▶ *vt* 1 *(manos)* to shake [*pt* **shook**; *pp* **shaken**]. 2 *(copas)* to clink.

● **¡chócala!** put it there!

● **¡choca esos cinco!** put it there!

chochear *vi* 1 *(anciano)* to be senile. 2 *(de cariño)*: *chochear por ALGN*, to dote on SB.

chocolate *nm* 1 *(de cacao)* chocolate. 2 *arg (hachís)* dope, hash.

● **las cosas claras y el chocolate espeso** let's get things clear.

■ **chocolate a la taza** drinking chocolate.

■ **chocolate con leche** milk chocolate.

chocolatina *nf* chocolate bar.

chófer *nm (particular)* chauffeur; *(de autocar etc)* driver.

chollo *nm* 1 *fam (ganga)* bargain, snip. 2 *(trabajo)* cushy number.

chopo *nm* poplar.

choque *nm* 1 *(colisión)* collision, crash. 2 *(enfrentamiento)* clash. 3 *(discusión)* dispute, quarrel. 4 MED shock.

chorizar *vt fam* to pinch, nick.

chorizo *nm* 1 *(embutido)* spicy sausage. 2 *fam (ratero)* thief [*pl* **-ves**].

chorlito *nm* plover.

chorrada *nf* 1 *fam (necedad)* piece of nonsense: *eso son chorradas*, that is nonsense; *decir chorradas*, to talk rubbish. 2 *(regalito)* little something.

chorrear *vi* 1 *(a chorros)* to spout, gush. 2 *(gotear)* to drip: *estoy chorreando de sudor*, I'm dripping with sweat.

chorro *nm* 1 *(de líquido)* stream, jet. 2 *(de vapor)* jet.

● **a chorros** in abundance: *hablar a chorros*, to talk nineteen to the dozen.

■ **chorro de vapor** steam jet.

choza *nf* hut.

christmas *nm* Christmas card.

chubasco *nm* heavy shower.

chubasquero *nm* raincoat.

chuchería *nf* 1 *(golosina)* GB sweet; US candy. 2 *(trasto)* trinket, knick-knack. 3 *(bocado)* tidbit, delicacy.

chucho *nm fam* dog.

chufa *nf* tiger nut.

chuleta *nf (de carne)* chop.

chulo,-a *adj* 1 *(engreído)* cocky. 2 *fam (bonito)* nice: *¡qué vestido tan chulo!*, what a nice dress!

▶ *nm,f (presuntuoso)* show-off.

▶ *nm* **chulo** *(proxeneta)* pimp.

chumbera *nf* prickly pear.

chungo,-a *adj arg (malo)* rotten, nasty, lousy; *(roto)* knackered: *el tiempo está chungo*, the weather's lousy; *lo tenemos chungo*, we've got problems.

chupado,-a *adj* 1 *(delgado)* skinny, emaciated. 2 *fam (fácil)* dead easy.

chupar *vt* 1 *(succionar)* to suck. 2 *(lamer)* to lick. 3 *(absorber)* to absorb, soak up.

▶ *vpr* **chuparse** *(adelgazar)* to get thin.

- **chuparse el dedo** to suck one's thumb.
- **chuparse los dedos** to lick one's fingers.
- **chupar del bote** *fam* to scrounge.
- **¡chúpate ésa!** *fam* stick that in your pipe and smoke it!

chupete *nm* GB dummy ; US pacifier.

chupetear *vt* to lick.

churrería *nf* fritter shop.

churro *nm* **1** *(comida)* fritter. **2** *fam (chapuza)* botch.

chusma *nf* riffraff.

chut *nm* shot, kick.

chutar *vi* to shoot [*pt & pp* **shot**].
  ▶ *vpr* **chutarse** *arg (con droga)* to shoot up [*pt & pp* **shot**].
- **... y va que chuta** ... and no problem.

cibercafé *nm* Internet café, cybercafé.

ciberespacio *nm* cyberspace.

cibernética *nf* cybernetics *(sing)*.

cicatriz *nf* scar.

cicatrizar *vt-vpr* **cicatrizar(se)** to heal.

ciclismo *nm* cycling.

ciclista *adj* cycle, cycling.
  ▶ *nmf* cyclist.

ciclo *nm* **1** *(gen)* cycle. **2** *(de conferencias)* series. **3** *(de películas)* season.

ciclón *nm* cyclone.

ciego,-a *adj* **1** *(persona)* blind. **2** *(conducto)* blocked up.
  ▶ *nm,f (persona)* blind person: *los ciegos*, the blind.
- **a ciegas** blindly.

cielo *nm* **1** *(gen)* sky. **2** REL heaven. **3** *(apelativo)* darling.
- **a cielo raso** in the open *(air)*.
- **como caído del cielo** out of the blue.
- **despejarse el cielo** to clear up.
- **poner a algo/ALGN por los cielos** to praise STH/SB to the skies.
- **poner el grito en el cielo** to hit the ceiling [*pt & pp* **hit**].
- **cielo raso** ceiling.

ciempiés *nm* centipede.

cien *num* a hundred, one hundred: *cien libras*, one hundred pounds.
- **cien por cien** a hundred per cent.
- **ponerse a cien** *fam* to blow one's top.

ciénaga *nf* marsh, bog.

ciencia *nf* science.
- **a ciencia cierta** with certainty.
- **ciencia ficción** science fiction.

- **ciencias aplicadas** applied sciences.
- **ciencias empresariales** business studies.
- **ciencias exactas** exact sciences.

científico,-a *adj* scientific.
  ▶ *nm,f* scientist.

ciento *num* a hundred, one hundred: *ciento diez euros*, one hundred and ten euros; *había cientos de personas*, there were hundreds of people.
- **por ciento** per cent.
- **ciento por ciento** a hundred per cent.
- **ciento y la madre** *fam* the world and his wife.

cierre *nm* **1** *(acción)* closing, shutting. **2** *(de prenda)* fastener. **3** *(de collar, pulsera)* clasp. **4** *(mecanismo)* catch. **5** *(de fábrica)* closure; *(de tienda)* close-down.
- **cierre centralizado** central locking.
- **cierre patronal** lockout.

cierto,-a *adj* **1** *(seguro)* certain, sure. **2** *(verdadero)* true: *eso no es cierto*, that's not true. **3** *(algún)* (a) certain, some: *cierto día*, one day.
  ▶ *adv* **cierto** certainly.
- **estar en lo cierto** to be right.
- **por cierto** by the way.

ciervo *nm* deer.

cifra *nf* **1** *(número)* figure, number, digit: *un número de cuatro cifras*, a four-figure number. **2** *(cantidad)* amount, figure: *una cifra récord*, a record number; *la cifra total*, the total amount. **3** *(código)* cipher, code.

cigala *nf* Dublin Bay prawn.

cigarra *nf* cicada.

cigarrillo *nm* cigarette.

cigarro *nm* **1** *(cigarrillo)* cigarette. **2** *(puro)* cigar.

cigüeña *nf (ave)* stork.

cilíndrico,-a *adj* cylindrical.

cilindro *nm* cylinder.

cima *nf* summit, peak: *la cima del Everest*, Everest's summit; *está en la cima de su carrera*, he's at the peak of his career.

cimiento *nf* **1** *(de edificio)* foundation. **2** *(base)* basis.

cinc *nm* zinc.

cinco *num* five; *(en fechas)* fifth.

cincuenta *num* fifty.

cine *nm* **1** *(lugar)* GB cinema; US movie theater. **2** *(arte)* cinema.
- **ir al cine** GB to go to the cinema; US to go to the movies.

■ **cine mudo** silent films *(pl)*.
■ **cine negro** film noir.
cinematografía *nf* film making, cinematography.
cinematográfico,-a *adj* film.
cínico,-a *adj* cynical.
► *nm,f* cynic.
cinismo *nm* cynicism.
cinta *nf* **1** *(casete, vídeo)* tape. **2** *(tira)* tape, band; *(decorativa)* ribbon.
■ **cinta adhesiva** sticky tape.
■ **cinta aislante** insulating tape.
■ **cinta magnética** magnetic tape.
■ **cinta métrica** tape measure.
■ **cinta transportadora** conveyor belt.
■ **cinta virgen** blank tape.
cintura *nf* waist.
cinturón *nm* belt.
● **apretarse el cinturón** to tighten one's belt.
■ **cinturón de seguridad** seat belt, safety belt.
ciprés *nm* cypress.
circo *nm (espectáculo)* circus.
circuito *nm* circuit.
circulación *nf* **1** *(de sangre, dinero)* circulation. **2** *(de vehículos)* traffic.
● **poner en circulación** to put into circulation.
● **retirar de la circulación** to withdraw from circulation *[pt withdrew; pp withdrawn]*.
circular *adj* circular.
► *nf (carta)* circular.
► *vi* **1** *(sangre)* to circulate. **2** *(trenes, autobuses)* to run *[pt ran; pp run]; (coches)* to drive *[pt drove; pp driven]; (peatones)* to walk. **3** *(rumor, noticia)* to go round, circulate.
circulatorio,-a *adj (de la sangre)* circulatory; *(del tráfico)* traffic.
círculo *nm* **1** *(forma)* circle. **2** *(asociación)* club.
■ **círculo vicioso** vicious circle.
circunferencia *nf* circumference.
circunstancia *nf* circumstance.
● **poner cara de circunstancias** *fam* to look grave.
circunstancial *adj* circumstantial.
circunvalación *nf* → carretera.
cirio *nm* candle.
● **armar un cirio** *fam* to kick up a rumpus.

ciruela *nf* plum.
■ **ciruela claudia** greengage.
■ **ciruela pasa** prune.
ciruelo *nm* plum tree.
cirugía *nf* surgery.
■ **cirugía estética** cosmetic surgery.
■ **cirugía plástica** plastic surgery.
cirujano,-a *nm,f* surgeon.
cisne *nm* swan.
cisterna *nf* cistern, tank.
cita *nf* **1** *(para negocios, médico, etc)* appointment. **2** *(con novio, novia)* date. **3** *(mención)* quotation.
● **darse cita** to meet *[pt & pp met]*.
● **tener una cita** to have an appointment.
citar *vt* **1** *(convocar)* to arrange to meet: *nos ha citado a las doce*, he's arranged to meet us at twelve o'clock. **2** *(mencionar)* to quote. **3** *(ante tribunal)* to summon.
● **estar citado,-a con** ALGN to have an appointment with SB.
cítrico,-a *adj* citric.
► *nm pl* **cítricos** citrus fruits.
ciudad *nf (grande)* city; *(más pequeña)* town.
■ **ciudad dormitorio** dormitory town.
■ **ciudad universitaria** university campus.
ciudadano,-a *adj* civic.
► *nm,f* citizen.
cívico,-a *adj* **1** *(derechos)* civic. **2** *(persona)* public spirited.
civil *adj* civil.
civilización *nf* civilization.
civilizado,-a *adj* civilized.
civilizar *vt* to civilize.
► *vpr* **civilizarse** to become civilized.
civismo *nm* community spirit.
cizaña.
● **meter cizaña** to sow discord *[pt sowed; pp sown]*.
clamar *vi (clamar por algo)* GB to clamour for STH; US to clamor for STH.
► *vt* to cry out for: *clamar venganza*, to cry out for revenge.
clamor *nm* GB clamour; US clamor.
clan *nm* clan.
clandestino,-a *adj* **1** *(actividad, reunión)* clandestine, secret. **2** *(periódico, asociación)* underground.
clara *nf* **1** *(de huevo)* egg white. **2** *(bebida)* shandy.

claraboya *nf* skylight.
clarear *vi* **1** *(amanecer)* to get light, dawn. **2** *(tiempo)* to clear up.
► *vpr* **clarearse** to be transparent.
claridad *nf* **1** *(inteligibilidad)* clarity, clearness. **2** *(luz)* light. **3** *(de sonido)* clarity. **4** *(de imagen)* sharpness, clarity.
● **con claridad** clearly.
clarificar *vt* to clarify.
clarín *nm* bugle.
► *nmf* bugler.
clarinete *nm* clarinet.
► *nmf* clarinettist.
claro,-a *adj* **1** *(gen)* clear: *una respuesta clara*, a clear answer; *un día claro*, a clear day. **2** *(color)* light. **3** *(salsa)* thin. **4** *(evidente)* clear.
► *adv* **claro** clearly.
► *nm* *(hueco)* gap, space; *(de bosque)* clearing.
► *interj* **¡claro!** of course!
● **claro que no** of course not.
● **claro que sí** of course.
● **estar claro** to be clear.
● **poner en claro** to make plain, clear up.
● **más claro que el agua** *fam* as clear as day.
clase *nf* **1** *(alumnos)* class: *una clase de 25 alumnos*, a class of 25 pupils. **2** *(lección)* lesson, class: *tengo clase de inglés*, I've got an English lesson. **3** *(aula)* classroom. **4** *(tipo)* type, sort: *hay muchas clases de flores*, there are many kinds of flowers.
● **asistir a clase** to attend class.
● **dar clase** to teach.
● **toda clase de** all sorts of.
■ **clase alta** upper class.
■ **clase baja** lower class.
■ **clase media** middle class.
■ **clase de conducir** driving lesson.
■ **clase obrera** working class.
■ **clase particular** private class.
clásico,-a *adj* classical; *(prototípico)* classic.
► *nm* **clásico** classic.
clasificación *nf* **1** *(ordenación)* classification, sorting. **2** *(deportiva)* league, table.
clasificar *vt* **1** *(ordenar)* to class, classify. **2** *(documentos, cartas)* to sort.
► *vpr* **clasificarse** *(deportista)* to qualify.
claustro *nm* **1** *(de iglesia)* cloister. **2** *(profesores)* staff; *(junta)* staff meeting.

claustrofobia *nf* claustrophobia.
cláusula *nf* clause.
clausura *nf* *(cierre)* closure.
clausurar *vt* **1** *(terminar)* to close, bring [*pt & pp* **brought**] to a close. **2** *(cerrar)* to close, close down: *clausurar un local*, to close down a bar.
clavar *vt* **1** *(sujetar)* to nail. **2** *(a golpes)* to hammer: *clávalo a la puerta*, nail it to the door; *clavó el clavo en la pared*, she hammered the nail into the wall. **3** *(aguja, cuchillo)* to stick [*pt & pp* **stuck**]: *me clavó una aguja en el brazo*, she stuck a needle in my arm. **4** *fam (cobrar caro)* to rip off.
► *vpr* **clavarse** to get: *me clavé una astilla en el dedo*, I got a splinter in my finger.
● **clavar los ojos en** to rivet one's eyes on.
clave *nf* **1** *(de enigma etc)* key: *palabra clave*, keyword; *hombre clave*, key man. **2** *(de signos)* code. **3** key: *en clave de sol*, in the key of G.
► *nm* *(instrumento)* harpsichord.
clavel *nm* carnation.
clavícula *nf* collarbone, clavicle.
clavija *nf* **1** peg, pin. **2** *(enchufe macho)* plug; *(pata de enchufe)* pin.
clavo *nm* **1** *(de metal)* nail. **2** *(especia)* clove.
● **dar en el clavo** to hit the nail on the head [*pt & pp* **hit**].
claxon *nm* horn, hooter.
● **tocar el claxon** to blow one's horn [*pt* **blew**; *pp* **blown**].
clemencia *nf* mercy, clemency.
clérigo *nm* clergyman [*pl* -**men**], priest.
clero *nm* clergy.
cliente *nmf* **1** *(de empresa)* client. **2** *(de tienda)* customer.
clientela *nf* **1** *(de empresa)* clients. **2** *(de tienda)* customers. **3** *(de restaurante)* clientele.
clima *nm* **1** *(de país, ciudad)* climate. **2** *(de reunión)* atmosphere.
climatizado,-a *adj* air-conditioned.
clímax *nm* climax.
clínica *nf* clinic, private hospital.
clínico,-a *adj* clinical.
clip *nm* **1** *(para papel)* paper clip. **2** *(para pelo)* GB hair-grip; US bobby pin.

● **de clip** clip-on: *pendientes de clip*, clip-on earrings.
clítoris nm clitoris.
cloaca nf sewer.
clon nm clone.
clonar vt to clone.
cloro nm chlorine.
clorofila nf chlorophyll.
club nm club.
■ **club nocturno** nightclub.
coartada nf alibi.
coba nf fam soft soap.
● **dar coba a** ALGN to soft-soap SB.
cobarde adj cowardly.
▶ nmf coward.
cobardía nf cowardice.
cobertizo nm shed.
cobertura nf cover.
cobijar vt **1** (cubrir) to cover. **2** (proteger) to shelter.
▶ vpr **cobijarse** to take shelter.
cobra nf cobra.
cobrador,-ra nm,f **1** (de deudas) collector. **2** (de autobús - hombre) conductor; (- mujer) conductress.
cobrar vt **1** (fijar precio por) to charge; (cheques) to cash; (salario) to earn: *me cobró cien euros*, he charged me a hundred euros. **2** (caza) to retrieve. **3** (adquirir) to gain, get: *cobrar cariño*, to take a liking; *cobrar fuerzas*, to gather strength.
▶ vi to be paid: *aún no he cobrado*, I haven't been paid yet.
● **¡vas a cobrar!** you're in for it!
cobre nm copper.
cobro nm cashing, collection.
■ **cobro revertido** reverse charge.
coca nf arg (droga) cocaine.
cocaína nf cocaine.
cocción nf (acción de guisar) cooking; (en agua) boiling; (en horno) baking.
cocear vi to kick.
cocer vt-vpr **cocer(se)** (guisar) to cook; (hervir) to boil; (hornear) to bake.
coche nm **1** (automóvil) GB car; US car, automobile. **2** (de tren, de caballos) carriage, coach.
■ **coche blindado** bullet-proof car.
■ **coche bomba** car bomb.
■ **coche cama** sleeping car.
■ **coche de alquiler** hire car.
■ **coche de bomberos** fire engine.

■ **coche de carreras** racing car.
■ **coche de época** vintage car.
■ **coche fúnebre** hearse.
■ **coche restaurante** dining car.
cochera nf **1** (garaje) garage. **2** (para autobús) depot.
cochero nm coachman [pl -**men**].
cochinillo nm sucking pig.
cochino,-a adj **1** (sucio) filthy. **2** (miserable) bloody: *¡cochino trabajo!*, damn work!
▶ nm,f **1** (animal) pig; (- macho) boar; (- hembra) sow. **2** fam (persona) dirty person.
cocido,-a adj cooked; (en agua) boiled.
▶ nm **cocido** (plato) stew.
cociente nm quotient.
cocina nf **1** (lugar) kitchen. **2** (gastronomía) cooking, cuisine: *cocina española*, Spanish cooking. **3** (aparato) GB cooker; US stove.
■ **cocina casera** home cooking.
■ **cocina de mercado** food in season.
■ **cocina económica** cooking range.
cocinar vt to cook.
cocinero,-a nm,f cook.
coco¹ nm **1** (árbol) coconut palm. **2** (fruta) coconut.
coco² nm **1** fam (fantasma) bogeyman [pl -**men**]. **2** fam (cabeza) head, nut.
● **comer el coco a** ALGN fam to brainwash SB.
● **comerse el coco** fam to get worked up.
cocodrilo nm crocodile.
cocotero nm coconut palm.
cóctel nm **1** (bebida) cocktail. **2** (fiesta) cocktail party.
codazo nm nudge; (violento) jab (with the elbow).
● **darle un codazo a** ALGN to nudge SB.
● **abrirse paso a codazos** to elbow one's way through.
codearse vpr (codearse con alguien) to rub shoulders with SB.
codicia nf greed.
codiciar vt to covet, long for.
codicioso,-a adj covetous, greedy.
código nm code.
■ **código de barras** bar code.
■ **código de circulación** highway code.
■ **código genético** genetic code.
■ **código postal** GB postcode; US zipcode.

codo *nm* elbow.
- **codo con codo** side by side.
- **empinar el codo** to knock them back.
- **hablar por los codos** to talk nineteen to the dozen.

codorniz *nf* quail.

coeficiente *nm* coefficient.
- **coeficiente de inteligencia** intelligence quotient.

cofre *nm* trunk, chest.

coger *vt* **1** *(tomar)* to take: *coge un trozo más grande*, take a bigger piece; *¿quién me ha cogido el libro?*, who's taken my book? **2** *(apresar)* to catch: *¿a que no me coges?*, I bet you can't catch me. **3** *(aceptar)* to take: *coger un empleo*, to take a job. **4** *(tren etc)* to catch [*pt & pp* **caught**]. **5** *(tomar prestado)* to borrow: *te he cogido el lápiz*, I've borrowed your pencil. **6** *(fruta, flor)* to pick. **7** *(enfermedad)* to catch [*pt & pp* **caught**]. **8** *(entender)* to get: *no he cogido el chiste*, I didn't get the joke.
- **coger a ALGN por sorpresa** to catch SB by surprise [*pt & pp* **caught**].

cogollo *nm* **1** *(de lechuga etc)* heart. **2** *(brote)* shoot.

cogote *nm* back of the neck, nape.

coherencia *nf* coherence.

coherente *adj* coherent.
- **coherente con algo** in line with something.

cohete *nm* rocket.

cohibir *vt* to inhibit.
► *vpr* **cohibirse** to feel embarrassed [*pt & pp* **felt**].

COI *abr* (**Comité Olímpico Internacional**) International Olympic Committee, IOC.

coincidencia *nf* coincidence.

coincidir *vi* **1** *(fechas, resultados)* to coincide. **2** *(estar de acuerdo)* to agree: *todos coincidimos en que...*, we all agree that.... **3** *(encontrarse)* to meet: *coincidieron en la panadería*, they met at the baker's.

cojear *vi* **1** *(persona)* to limp, hobble. **2** *(mueble)* to wobble.

cojera *nf* **1** *(acción)* limp. **2** *(estado)* lameness.

cojín *nm* cushion.

cojo,-a *adj* **1** *(persona)* lame. **2** *(mueble)* wobbly.

cojón *nm vulg* ball, bollock.

► *interj* **¡cojones!** *vulg* fuck it!
- **por cojones** *vulg* like it or not.
- **tener cojones** *vulg* to have guts, have balls.

col *nf* cabbage.
■ **col de Bruselas** Brussels sprout.

cola¹ *nf* **1** *(de animal)* tail. **2** *(de vestido)* train. **3** *(fila)* GB queue; US line.
- **hacer cola** GB to queue up; US to stand in line [*pt & pp* **stood**].
- **traer cola** to have serious consequences.
- **cola de caballo 1** *(planta)* horsetail. **2** *(peinado)* ponytail.

cola² *nf* *(pegamento)* glue.

colaboración *nf* **1** *(en tarea)* collaboration. **2** *(en prensa)* contribution.

colaborador,-ra *nm,f* **1** *(en tarea)* collaborator. **2** *(en prensa)* contributor.

colaborar *vi* **1** *(en tarea)* to collaborate. **2** *(en prensa)* to contribute. **3** *(dar dinero)* to contribute.

colada *nf* washing.
- **tender la colada** to hang out the washing.

colador *nm* **1** *(de té, café)* strainer. **2** *(de alimentos)* colander.

colar *vt* *(filtrar)* to strain, filter.
► *vpr* **colarse 1** *(en un lugar)* to sneak in: *se coló en el concierto*, he sneaked into the concert. **2** *(en una cola)* to push in: *un chico intentó colarse*, a boy tried to push in. **3** *(equivocarse)* to be wrong, slip up: *te has colado*, you're wrong. **4** *(enamorarse)* to fall [*pt* **fell**; *pp* **fallen**].

colcha *nf* bedspread.

colchón *nm* mattress.

colchoneta *nf* **1** *(de gimnasio)* mat. **2** *(de playa)* air bed.

colección *nf* collection.

coleccionar *vt* to collect.

coleccionista *nmf* collector.

colecta *nf* collection.

colectivo,-a *adj* collective.

colega *nmf* **1** *(de trabajo)* colleague. **2** *fam (amigo)* GB mate; US buddy.

colegial,-la *nm,f* *(chico)* schoolboy; *(chica)* schoolgirl.

colegio *nm* **1** *(escuela)* school. **2** *(asociación)* college, body, association.
■ **colegio de pago** fee-paying school.
■ **colegio electoral** polling station.
■ **colegio estatal** state school.

■ **colegio mayor** hall of residence.

■ **colegio privado** private school.

■ **colegio público** state school.

cólera¹ *nf (furia)* anger, rage.

● **montar en cólera** to fly into a temper [*pt* **flew**; *pp* **flown**].

cólera² *nm (enfermedad)* cholera.

coleta *nf* pigtail.

colgador *nm* hanger, coat hanger.

colgante *adj* hanging.

colgar *vt* **1** *(cuadro)* to hang [*pt & pp* **hung**], put up; *(colada)* to hang out; *(abrigo)* to hang up. **2** *(ahorcar)* to hang [*pt & pp* **hanged**]. **3** *(teléfono)* to put down: *¡me colgó el teléfono!*, he hung up on me! **4** *(abandonar)* to give up: *colgar los libros*, to give up studying.

▶ *vi* **1** *(estar suspendido)* to hang. **2** *(teléfono)* to put down, hang up: *¡no cuelgue!*, hold the line, please!

▶ *vpr* **colgarse** *(ahorcarse)* to hang oneself.

colibrí *nm* humming bird.

cólico *nm* colic.

coliflor *nf* cauliflower.

colilla *nf* cigarette end, cigarette butt.

colina *nf* hill.

colirio *nm* eyewash.

colisión *nf* collision, clash.

collar *nm* **1** *(joya)* necklace. **2** *(de animal)* collar.

colmado *nm* grocer's.

colmar *vt* **1** *(vaso, copa)* to fill to the brim. **2** *(ambiciones, etc)* to fulfil.

● **colmar de** to heap on: *le colmaron de elogios*, they heaped praise on him.

colmena *nf* beehive.

colmillo *nm* **1** *(de persona)* eye tooth [*pl* **teeth**], canine tooth. **2** ZOOL fang; *(de elefante, jabalí)* tusk.

colmo *nm* height, limit.

● **¡esto es el colmo!** this is too much!

● **para colmo** to top it all, to make matters worse.

colocación *nf* **1** *(acto)* placing. **2** *(situación)* situation. **3** *(empleo)* employment.

colocar *vt* **1** *(situar)* to place, put: *colocó la bolsa en el suelo*, he placed the bag on the ground; *coloca la ropa en el armario*, put your clothes in the wardrobe. **2** *(emplear)* to give a job to. **3** *(acciones)* to place. **4** *(dinero)* to place, invest. **5** *(mercancías)* to sell well.

▶ *vpr* **colocarse** **1** *(situarse)* to place oneself. **2** *(trabajar)* to get a job. **3** *arg (con alcohol)* to get sozzled; *(con drogas)* to get stoned.

Colombia *nf* Colombia.

colombiano,-a *adj - nm,f* Colombian.

colon *nm* colon.

colonia¹ *nf (grupo, territorio)* colony.

▶ *nf pl* **(colonias)** summer camp.

colonia² *nf (perfume)* cologne.

colonial *adj* colonial.

colonización *nf* colonization.

colonizar *vt* to colonize.

colono *nm (inmigrante)* colonist, settler.

coloquial *adj* colloquial.

coloquio *nm* talk, discussion.

color *nm* GB colour; US color: *una alfombra de color verde*, a green carpet.

● **verlo todo de color de rosa** to see life through rose-coloured spectacles [*pt* **saw**; *pp* **seen**].

colorado,-a *adj (rojo)* red; *(rojizo)* reddish.

● **ponerse colorado,-a** to blush.

colorante *adj* GB colouring; US coloring.

▶ *nm* GB colouring; US dye.

● **sin colorantes** with no artificial colourings.

colorear *vt* GB to colour; US to color.

colorete *nm* rouge.

colorido *nm* GB colour; US color.

colorín *nm* .

● **... y colorín colorado este cuento se ha acabado** ... and that's the end of the story.

colosal *adj* colossal, huge.

columna *nf* column.

■ **columna vertebral** spine, spinal column.

columpiar *vt* to push on a swing.

▶ *vpr* **columpiarse** to swing [*pt & pp* **swung**].

columpio *nm* swing.

coma¹ *nf* **1** *(signo)* comma. **2** *(en matemáticas)* point.

coma² *nm* coma.

● **entrar en coma** to go into a coma.

comadreja *nf* weasel.

comadrona *nf* midwife [*pl* **-ves**].

comandante *nm* **1** *(oficial)* commander, commanding officer. **2** *(graduación)* major.

comando *nm* **1** *(de combate)* commando [*pl* **-os** o **-oes**]. **2** INFORM command.

comarca nf area, region.
comarcal adj local.
comba nf **1** (curvatura) bend; (en madera) warp. **2** (cuerda) skipping rope.
● **saltar a la comba** GB to skip; US jump rope.
combate nm **1** (lucha) combat, battle: **zona de combate**, combat zone. **2** (en boxeo) fight.
combatiente adj fighting.
▶ nmf fighter.
combatir vi to fight [pt & pp **fought**].
▶ vt to fight [pt & pp **fought**], combat: **combatir el cáncer**, to fight cancer.
combinación nf **1** (de elementos, números) combination. **2** (prenda) slip.
combinar vt **1** (ingredientes, esfuerzos) to combine. **2** (colores) to match.
▶ vi to match, go with: **ese color combina muy bien con los muebles**, that colour matches the furniture really well.
combustible adj combustible.
▶ nm fuel.
combustión nf combustion.
comedia nf **1** (obra) comedy. **2** (farsa) farce, pretence.
● **hacer comedia** to put on an act.
comediante,-a nm,f **1** (hombre) actor; (mujer) actress. **2** (falso) hypocrite.
comedor,-ra adj: **ser muy comedor**, to eat a lot.
▶ nm **comedor 1** (de casa) dining room. **2** (de fábrica) canteen. **3** (de colegio) dining hall. **4** (muebles) dining-room suite.
comentar vt **1** (por escrito) to comment on; (oralmente) to talk about, discuss. **2** (decir) to tell [pt & pp **told**]: **Juan me comentó que...**, Juan told me that....
comentario nm remark, comment.
▶ nm pl **comentarios** gossip sing.
● **sin comentarios** no comment.
comentarista nmf commentator.
comenzar vt-vi to begin, start.
comer vt **1** (ingerir) to eat [pt **ate**; pp **eaten**]. **2** (color) to fade. **3** (corroer) to corrode. **4** (gastos, celos) to eat up [pt **ate**; pp **eaten**].
▶ vi **1** (alimentarse) to eat [pt **ate**; pp **eaten**]. **2** (al mediodía) to have lunch: **me ha invitado a comer**, she's invited me to lunch.
▶ vpr **comerse** (saltarse) to omit; (párrafo) to skip; (palabra) to swallow: **se come las palabras**, he slurs.

● **comerse las uñas** to bite one's nails [pt **bit**; pp **bitten**].
● **dar de comer** to feed [pt & pp **fed**].
● **comerse algo con los ojos** fam to devour STH with one's eyes.
comercial adj commercial.
comercializar vt to commercialize, market.
comerciante nmf **1** (tendero) GB shopkeeper; US storekeeper. **2** (negociante) trader, dealer. **3** (exportador) merchant. **4** (interesado) moneymaker.
comerciar vi **1** (comprar y vender) to trade, deal [pt & pp **dealt**]. **2** (hacer negocios) to do business.
comercio nm **1** (ocupación) commerce, trade. **2** (tienda) GB shop; US store.
■ **comercio electrónico** e-commerce.
comestible adj edible.
▶ nm pl **comestibles** groceries, food sing.
cometa nm (astro) comet.
▶ nf (juguete) kite.
cometer vt (crimen) to commit; (falta, error) to make.
cometido nm **1** (encargo) task. **2** (deber) duty.
cómic nm comic.
comicios nm pl elections.
cómico,-a adj comic.
▶ nmf comedian, comic.
comida nf **1** (comestibles) food: **necesitan comida y medicinas**, they need food and medicine. **2** (a cualquier hora) meal: **la primera comida del día es el desayuno**, the first meal of the day is breakfast. **3** (a mediodía) lunch: **voy a hacer la comida**, I'm going to make lunch.
■ **comida basura** junk food.
comienzo nm start, beginning.
comillas nf pl inverted commas.
comilona nf blowout, feast.
comilón,-ona adj - nm,f big eater, glutton.
comino nm cumin.
● **me importa un comino** fam I couldn't care less.
comisaría nf (de policía) police station.
comisario nm (de policía) GB superintendent; US captain.
comisión nf **1** (retribución) commission. **2** (comité) committee. **3** (encargo) assignment.
comité nm committee.
comitiva nf suite, retinue.

como *adv* **1** *(lo mismo que)* as: *negro como el tizón*, as dark as night. **2** *(de tal modo)* like: *hablas como un político*, you talk like a politician. **3** *(según)* as: *como dice tu amigo*, as your friend says. **4** *(en calidad de)* as: *como invitado*, as a guest. **5** *(aproximadamente)* about, around: *tengo como cien novelas*, I've got about a hundred novels.
► *conj* **1** *(así que)* as soon as. **2** *(si)* if: *como lo vuelvas a hacer ...*, if you do it again .... **3** *(porque)* as, since: *como llegamos tarde no pudimos entrar*, since we arrived late we couldn't get in.
● **como quiera que** since, as.
● **como no sea** unless it is.
● **como sea** whatever happens, no matter what.
● **como si nada** as if nothing had happened.
● **hacer como si** to pretend to: *hace como si no viese nada*, he's pretending not to see anything.

cómo *adv* **1** *(de qué modo)* how: *¿cómo se hace?*, how do you do it? **2** *(por qué)* why: *¿cómo no viniste?*, why didn't you come? **3** *(exclamación)* how: *¡cómo corre el tiempo!*, how time flies!
● **¿a cómo va ...?** how much is ...?
● **¿cómo es ...?** **1** (físicamente) what does he look like? **2** (de carácter) what is he like?
● **¿cómo es eso?** how come?
● **¿cómo es que ...?** how is it that ...?
● **¿cómo está usted?** **1** (al conocerse) how do you do? **2** (de salud) how are you?
● **¡cómo no!** but of course!, certainly!

cómoda *nf* chest of drawers.
comodidad *nf* **1** *(confort)* comfort. **2** *(facilidad)* convenience: *para su comodidad*, for your convenience.
comodín *nm* joker.
cómodo,-a *adj* **1** *(confortable)* comfortable, cosy. **2** *(útil)* convenient: *el metro me resulta más cómodo*, the underground is more convenient for me.
comodón,-ona *adj* comfort loving.
► *nm,f* comfort lover.
compact disc *nm* compact disc.
compacto,-a *adj* compact.
compadecer *vt* to pity, feel sorry for [*pt & pp* **felt**].

► *vpr* **compadecerse** to have pity.
compaginar *vt* to combine.
► *vpr* **compaginarse** to go together.
compañerismo *nm* comradeship.
compañero,-a *nm,f* **1** *(de tarea)* fellow, mate. **2** *(de trabajo)* colleague. **3** *(pareja)* partner.
■ **compañero,-a de clase** classmate.
■ **compañero,-a de piso** flatmate.
compañía *nf* company.
● **hacer compañía a ALGN** to keep SB company.
■ **compañía de seguros** insurance company.
■ **compañía de teatro** theatre company.
comparable *adj* comparable.
comparación *nf* comparison.
comparar *vt* to compare.
comparativo,-a *adj* comparative.
comparecer *vi* to appear.
compartimento *nm* compartment.
compartimiento *nm* compartment.
compartir *vt* to share: *comparten piso*, they share a flat.
compás *nm* **1** *(instrumento)* compass, a pair of compasses. **2** *(ritmo)* time.
● **llevar el compás** to keep time, beat time [*pt* **beat**; *pp* **beaten**].
compasión *nf* compassion, pity.
● **tener compasión (de ALGN)** to feel sorry (for SB) [*pt & pp* **felt**].
compasivo,-a *adj* compassionate.
compatible *adj* compatible.
compatriota *nmf* compatriot,; *(hombre)* fellow countryman [*pl* **-men**]; *(mujer)* fellow countrywoman.
compenetrarse *vpr* to understand each other [*pt & pp* **understood**].
compensar *vt* **1** *(indemnizar)* to compensate. **2** *(resarcir)* to make up for.
► *vi* to be worthwhile: *este trabajo no me compensa*, this job's not worth my while.
competencia *nf* **1** *(rivalidad)* competition. **2** *(competidores)* competitors *pl*. **3** *(habilidad)* competence, ability. **4** *(incumbencia)*: *no tengo competencia en el asunto*, I have no authority in the matter; *no es competencia del tribunal*, it's beyond the competence of the court.
competente *adj* competent, capable.

competición *nf* competition.
competidor,-ra *adj* competing.
▶ *nm,f* competitor.
competir *vi* to compete.
competitivo,-a *adj* competitive.
compinche *nmf fam* chum, pal.
complacer *vt* to please: *me complace anunciar...*, I am pleased to announce.
complaciente *adj* obliging.
complejidad *nf* complexity.
complejo,-a *adj* complex.
▶ *nm* **complejo** complex.
complemento *nm* complement.
▶ *nm pl* **complementos** accessories.
■ **complemento directo** direct object.
■ **complemento indirecto** indirect object.
completar *vt* to complete, finish.
completo,-a *adj* **1** *(entero, total)* complete: *la obra completa*, the complete works; *un completo fracaso*, a complete failure. **2** *(lleno)* full: *el teatro está completo*, the theatre is full.
● **al completo 1** (lleno) full up, filled to capacity. **2** (la totalidad de) the whole, all of.
● **por completo** completely.
complexión *nf* constitution, build.
complicación *nf* complication.
● **buscarse complicaciones** to make life difficult for oneself.
complicado,-a *adj* complicated, complex.
complicar *vt* **1** *(situación)* to complicate: *este problema ha complicado las cosas*, this problem has complicated matters. **2** *(implicar)* to involve.
▶ *vpr* **complicarse** *(involucrarse)* to become complicated, become involved.
● **complicarse la vida** to make life difficult for oneself.
cómplice *nmf* accomplice.
complot *nm* plot, conspiracy.
componente *adj - nm* component.
componer *vt* **1** *(formar)* to make up: *los jugadores que componen el equipo*, the players that make up the team. **2** *(música)* to compose; *(poema)* to write, compose. **3** *(reparar)* to mend, repair.
▶ *vpr* **componerse**: *componerse de algo*, to consist of STH.
● **componérselas** *fam* to manage, make do.

comportamiento *nm* GB behaviour; US behavior.
comportar *vt* to involve.
▶ *vpr* **comportarse** to behave, act.
● **comportarse mal** to behave badly, misbehave.
● **saber comportarse** to know how to behave [*pt* **knew**; *pp* **known**].
composición *nf* composition.
● **hacerse una composición de lugar** to weigh up the pros and cons.
compositor,-ra *nm,f* composer.
compota *nf* compote.
compra *nf* purchase, buy.
● **hacer la compra** to do the shopping.
● **ir de compras** to go shopping.
■ **compra a plazos** hire purchase.
comprador,-ra *nm,f* buyer.
comprar *vt* **1** *(adquirir)* to buy [*pt & pp* **bought**]. **2** *(sobornar)* to bribe, buy off [*pt & pp* **bought**].
comprender *vt* **1** *(entender)* to understand [*pt & pp* **understood**]: *no me comprende*, he doesn't understand me. **2** *(contener)* to comprise, include.
comprensible *adj* understandable.
comprensión *nf* understanding.
comprensivo,-a *adj* **1** *(que entiende)* understanding. **2** *(que contiene)* comprehensive.
compresa *nf* **1** *(higiénica)* sanitary towel. **2** *(venda)* compress.
comprimido,-a *adj* compressed.
▶ *nm* **comprimido** tablet.
comprimir *vt* **1** *(apretar)* to compress. **2** *(reprimir)* to restrain.
comprobación *nf* verification, check.
comprobante *nm* proof.
comprobar *vt* **1** *(verificar)* to check: *comprueba los frenos*, check the brakes. **2** *(demostrar)* to prove: *comprobar una hipótesis*, to prove a hypothesis.
comprometer *vt* **1** *(exponer a riesgo)* to compromise. **2** *(obligar)* to commit.
▶ *vpr* **comprometerse 1** *(prometer)* to commit oneself. **2** *(novios)* to get engaged.
● **comprometerse a hacer algo** to undertake to do STH.
● **comprometerse con ALGN** to get engaged to SB.
compromiso *nm* **1** *(obligación)* commitment. **2** *(acuerdo)* agreement. **3** *(dificultad)*

difficult situation, bind. **4** *(cita)* engagement.

● **poner a** ALGN **en un compromiso** to put SB in a tight spot.

compuesto,-a *adj* compound: *una palabra compuesta*, a compound word.

► *nm* **compuesto** compound.

computadora *nf* computer.

cómputo *nm* computation, calculation.

comulgar *vi* to receive Holy Communion.

● **comulgar con algo** to agree with STH.

común *adj* common: *una característica común a todos los pájaros*, a characteristic common to all birds; *un nombre muy común*, a very common name.

● **por lo común** generally.

● **tener en común** to have in common.

comunicación *nf* **1** *(relación)* communication: *problemas de comunicación*, communication problems. **2** *(comunicado) (oficial)* communication. **3** *(telefónica)* connection. **4** *(contacto)* contact: *estar en comunicación con* ALGN, to be in contact with SB, be in touch with SB.

► *nf pl* **comunicaciones** communications.

comunicado *nm* communiqué.

■ **comunicado de prensa** press release.

comunicar *vi* **1** *(teléfono)* GB to be engaged; US to be busy. **2** *(ponerse en contacto)* to get in touch, get in contact.

► *vt* **1** *(hacer saber)* to inform: *ha comunicado la noticia a la prensa*, he has informed the press. **2** *(transmitir)* to communicate: *comunica su alegría a todos*, she communicates her happiness to everyone. **3** *(unir)* to connect, link: *un pasillo comunica los edificios*, the buildings are connected by a walkway.

► *vpr* **comunicarse 1** *(relacionarse)* to communicate. **2** *(unirse)* to be connected.

● **comunicarse con** ALGN to get in touch with SB.

comunidad *nf* community.

■ **comunidad de propietarios** owners' association.

■ **Comunidad Europea** European Community.

comunión *nf* communion: *la Sagrada comunión*, Holy Communion.

comunismo *nm* communism.

comunista *adj* - *nmf* communist.

con *prep* **1** *(compañía, instrumento, medio)* with: *¿con quién vives?*, who do you live with?; *hay que comerlo con una cuchara*, you have to eat it with a spoon. **2** *(modo, circunstancia)* in, with: *¿vas a salir con ese frío?*, are you going out in this cold?; *con una sonrisa*, with a smile. **3** *(a pesar de)* in spite of: *con ser tan fuerte ...*, in spite of his being so strong .... **4** *(relación)* to: *sé amable con ella*, be kind to her.

● **con que** as long as, if.

● **con tal (de) que** provided that.

● **con todo** nevertheless.

cóncavo,-a *adj* concave.

concebir *vt-vi* to conceive.

conceder *vt* **1** *(dar préstamo, deseo)* to grant; *(premio)* to award. **2** *(admitir)* to concede, admit.

concejal,-la *nm,f* town councillor.

concentración *nf* **1** *(atención)* concentration. **2** *(de gente)* rally.

concentrar *vt* **1** *(gen)* to concentrate. **2** *(reunir)* to bring [*pt & pp* **brought**] together.

► *vpr* **concentrarse 1** *(gen)* to concentrate: *no puedo concentrarme*, I can't concentrate. **2** *(reunirse)* to gather: *la gente se concentraba en la plaza*, people gathered in the square.

concepto *nm* **1** *(idea)* concept. **2** *(opinión)* opinion, view.

● **bajo ningún concepto** under no circumstances.

● **en concepto de** by way of.

concertar *vt* **1** *(entrevista, cita)* to arrange. **2** *(precio)* to agree on.

► *vi (concordar)* to agree.

► *vpr* **concertarse** *(acordar)* to reach an agreement.

concesión *nf* **1** *(en negociación)* concession. **2** *(de premio)* awarding.

concesionario *nm* dealer.

concha *nf* shell.

conciencia *nf* **1** *(moral)* conscience. **2** *(conocimiento)* awareness.

● **a conciencia** conscientiously.

● **con la conciencia tranquila** with a clear conscience.

● **remorderle a** ALGN **la conciencia** to have a guilty conscience.

concierto *nm* **1** *(espectáculo)* concert; *(obra)* concerto [*pl* **-s**]. **2** *(acuerdo)* agreement.

• **sin orden ni concierto** any old how.
concilio *nm* council.

■ **Concilio Vaticano** Vatican Council.
conciso,-a *adj* concise, brief.
concluir *vt (deducir)* to conclude, infer.
▶ *vt-vi-vpr* **concluir(se)** *(terminar)* to finish.
conclusión *nf* conclusion.

• **llegar a una conclusión** to come to a conclusion.
concordancia *nf* concordance, agreement.
concordar *vt* to make agree, reconcile.
▶ *vi* to agree, tally: **las dos declaraciones no concuerdan**, the two statements don't agree.
concretar *vt* **1** *(precisar)* to specify: **concretar una hora**, to fix a time, set a time. **2** *(resumir)* to summarize.
▶ *vpr* **concretarse** to become a reality.
concreto,-a *adj* **1** *(real)* concrete. **2** *(particular)* specific, definite.

• **en concreto 1** (en particular) in particular. **2** (para ser exacto) to be precise.
concurrido,-a *adj* busy, crowded.
concursante *nmf* **1** *(de concurso)* contestant, participant. **2** *(a empleo)* candidate.
concursar *vi* **1** *(en concurso)* to compete. **2** *(para empleo)* to be a candidate.
concurso *nm* **1** *(competición - gen)* competition; *(- de belleza, deportivo)* contest; *(- en televisión)* quiz show. **2** *(concurrencia)* gathering.
condado *nm* county.
conde *nm* count.
condecoración *nf* decoration, medal.
condecorar *vt* to decorate.
condena *nf* sentence.

• **cumplir una condena** to serve a sentence.
condenado,-a *adj* convicted.
▶ *nm,f* convict.

• **trabajar como un condenado** to slog one's guts out.
condenar *vt* **1** *(declarar culpable)* to convict. **2** *(sentenciar)* to sentence. **3** *(a muerte)* to condemn, sentence: **el juez lo condenó por el robo**, the judge convicted him of the robbery; **lo han condenado a dos años de cárcel**, he has been sentenced to two years in prison. **4** *(desaprobar)* to condemn: **todos los partidos**

condenaron el atentado, all the parties condemned the attack.
condensar *vt-vpr* **condensar(se)** to condense.
condesa *nf* countess.
condescendiente *adj* **1** obliging. **2** *pey* condescending, patronizing.
condición *nf* **1** *(gen)* condition: **me puso una condición**, she set one condition; **la casa está en buenas condiciones**, the house is in good condition. **2** *(naturaleza)* nature: **de condición apacible**, of an easy-going nature. **3** *(estado social)* status, position: **de condición humilde**, of humble origen.

• **a condición de que** on condition that, provided *(that)*.
■ **condiciones de trabajo** working conditions.
condicional *adj - nm* conditional.
condicionar *vt* to condition.
condimentar *vt* to season, GB flavour; US flavor.
condimento *nm* seasoning, GB flavouring; US flavoring.
condón *nm* condom.
cóndor *nm* condor.
conducción *nf* **1** *(de coche)* driving. **2** *(de calor)* conduction. **3** *(por tubería)* piping; *(eléctrica)* wiring.
conducir *vt* **1** *(guiar)* to lead [*pt & pp* led]; *(coche, animales)* to drive [*pt* drove; *pp* driven]. **2** *(moto)* to ride [*pt* rode; *pp* ridden]. **3** *(negocio)* to manage. **4** *(transportar)* to transport; *(líquidos)* to convey.
▶ *vi* **1** *(dirigir un vehículo)* to drive: **¿sabes conducir?**, can you drive? **2** *(llegar)* to lead [*pt & pp* led]: **esta carretera conduce a Teruel**, this road leads to Teruel; **esto no conduce a nada**, this leads nowhere.
▶ *vpr* **conducirse** *(comportarse)* to behave, act.
conducta *nf* conduct, behaviour.
conducto *nm* **1** *(tubería)* pipe, conduit. **2** *(del cuerpo)* duct. **3** *(medio)* channel: **por conductos oficiales**, through official channels.

• **por conducto de** through.
conductor,-ra *adj* conductive.
▶ *nm,f* driver.
▶ *nm* **conductor** conductor.
■ **conductor en prácticas** learner driver.
conectar *vt* **1** *(unir)* to connect: **conecta la impresora al ordenador**, connect the

printer to the computer. **2** *(aparato, luz, etc)* to switch on, turn on.

conejillo *nm* **conejillo de Indias** guinea pig.

conejo *nm* rabbit.

conexión *nf* connection.

■ **conexión en directo** live link-up.

confección *nf* **1** *(de prendas)* dressmaking. **2** *(elaboración)* making.

confeccionar *vt* **1** *(prenda)* to make *(up)*. **2** *(plato)* to prepare. **3** *(lista)* to draw up [*pt* **drew**; *pp* **drawn**].

conferencia *nf* **1** *(charla)* talk, lecture. **2** *(congreso)* conference. **3** *(llamada telefónica)* long-distance call.

■ **conferencia de prensa** press conference.

conferenciante *nmf* lecturer.

confesar *vt-vpr* **confesar(se)** to confess.

confesión *nf* confession.

confesonario *nm* confessional.

confesor *nm* confessor.

confeti *nm* confetti *inv*.

confiado,-a *adj* **1** *(crédulo)* confiding, unsuspecting. **2** *(de uno mismo)* self-confident.

confianza *nf* **1** *(seguridad)* confidence: *tiene mucha confianza en sí mismo*, he's got a lot of self-confidence. **2** *(fe)* trust: *tengo confianza en ti*, I have trust in you. **3** *(familiaridad)* familiarity. **4** *(ánimo)* encouragement.

● **de confianza** reliable.

● **en confianza** confidentially.

● **tomarse demasiadas confianzas** to take liberties.

confiar *vi* **1** *(tener fe)*: *confiar en ALGN/algo*, to trust SB/STH; *confío en ti*, I trust you. **2** *(estar seguro)* confiar en + infinitivo, to be confident that, be sure that: *confío en aprobar el examen*, I'm confident that I'll pass the exam.

▶ *vt* **1** *(secreto)* to confide. **2** *(misión, trabajo)* to entrust.

▶ *vpr* **confiarse 1** *(despreocuparse)* to be too confident. **2** *(confesarse)* to make confessions.

confidencial *adj* confidential.

confidente,-a *nm,f* **1** *(hombre)* confidant; *(mujer)* confidante. **2** *(de la policía)* informer.

configuración *nf* **1** *(forma)* configuration, shape. **2** INFORM configuration.

■ **configuración por defecto** default settings *pl*.

configurar *vt* **1** *(formar)* to configure, shape. **2** INFORM to configure.

confirmación *nf* confirmation.

confirmar *vt* to confirm.

● **la excepción confirma la regla** the exception proves the rule.

confite *nm* GB sweet; US candy.

confitería *nf (bombonería)* GB sweet shop; US candy shop; *(pastelería)* cake shop.

confitura *nf* preserve.

conflictivo,-a *adj (tema)* controversial; *(persona)* difficult.

conflicto *nm* conflict.

■ **conflicto bélico** armed conflict.

■ **conflicto laboral** labour dispute.

conformar *vt* **1** *(dar forma a)* to shape. **2** *(constituir)* to make up.

▶ *vpr* **conformarse** *(contentarse)* to resign oneself, be content.

conforme *adj* **1** *(de acuerdo)*: *estar conforme*, to agree. **2** *(satisfecho)* satisfied, happy: *está conforme con lo que le pagan*, he's satisfied with what he's paid.

▶ *adv (según)* as: *conforme lo veo yo*, as I see it.

▶ *nm* approval.

● **conforme a** in accordance with: *conforme a las reglas*, in accordance with the rules.

conformidad *nf* **1** *(acuerdo)* agreement. **2** *(aprobación)* consent, approval.

● **en conformidad con** in accordance with.

confort *nm* comfort.

● **"todo confort"** *(en anuncio)* "all mod. cons.".

confortable *adj* comfortable.

confortar *vt* to comfort.

confrontar *vt* **1** *(carear)* to bring face to face [*pt & pp* **brought**]. **2** *(cotejar)* to compare.

▶ *vi (lindar)* to border.

▶ *vpr* **confrontarse** *(enfrentarse)* to face.

confundir *vt* **1** *(mezclar)* to mix up: *has confundido los cuadernos*, you've got the exercise books mixed up. **2** *(desconcertar)* to confuse: *sus palabras me confundieron*, his words confused me. **3** *(no reconocer)* to mistake [*pt* **mistake**; *pp* **mistaken**]: *la confundí con su hermana*, I mistook her for her sister. **4** *(turbar)* to confound.

▶ *vpr* **confundirse 1** *(mezclarse)* to mingle. **2** *(equivocarse)* to be mistaken, make a mistake. **3** *(turbarse)* to be confounded.

confusión *nf* **1** *(desorden)* confusion. **2** *(equivocación)* mistake. **3** *(turbación)* confusion, embarrassment.

confuso,-a *adj* **1** *(persona)* confused. **2** *(instrucciones, explicación)* confused, confusing. **3** *(imagen)* blurred.

congelación *nf* **1** *(de agua, comida)* freezing. **2** *(de dedos, nariz)* frostbite.

congelado,-a *adj* **1** *(agua, comida)* frozen. **2** *(dedos, nariz)* frostbitten.

▶ *nm pl* **congelados** frozen food *sing.*

congelador *nm* freezer.

congelar *vt-vpr* **congelar(se)** to freeze [*pt* **froze**; *pp* **frozen**].

● **congelar precios** to freeze prices [*pt* **froze**; *pp* **frozen**].

congeniar *vi* to get along well.

congénito,-a *adj* congenital.

congestión *nf* congestion.

congoja *nf* **1** *(angustia)* anguish. **2** *(pena)* grief.

congregar *vt-vpr* **congregar(se)** to congregate.

congreso *nm* conference, congress.

■ **congreso de los Diputados** lower house of Spanish Parliament.

congrio *nm* conger eel.

cónico,-a *adj* conical.

conífera *nf* conifer.

conífero,-a *adj* coniferous.

conjugación *nf* conjugation.

conjugar *vt* to conjugate.

conjunción *nf* conjunction.

conjuntamente *adv* jointly.

conjuntivitis *nf* conjunctivitis.

conjunto,-a *adj* joint.

▶ *nm* **conjunto 1** *(grupo)* group, collection. **2** *(todo)* whole. **3** *(de música - pop)* band, group; *(- clásica)* ensemble. **4** *(prenda)* outfit. **5** *(en matemáticas)* set.

● **en conjunto** as a whole, altogether.

conjuro *nm* exorcism.

conmemoración *nf* commemoration.

conmemorar *vt* to commemorate.

conmigo *pron* with me, to me: *conmigo mismo*, with myself, to myself; *hablaba conmigo*, he was talking to me.

conmoción *nf* **1** *(agitación)* commotion.

2 *(cerebral)* concussion. **3** *(levantamiento)* riot.

conmovedor,-ra *adj* moving, touching.

conmover *vt* **1** *(persona)* to move, touch. **2** *(cosa)* to shake [*pt* **shook**; *pp* **shaken**].

▶ *vpr* **conmoverse** to be moved, be touched.

conmutador *nm* switch.

cono *nm* cone.

conocedor,-ra *adj - nm,f* expert.

conocer *vt* **1** *(persona - gen)* to know [*pt* **knew**; *pp* **known**]; *(- por primera vez)* to meet [*pt & pp* **met**]: *¿conoces a Juan?*, do you know Juan?; *la conocí ayer*, I met her for the first time yesterday. **2** *(resultado, tema)* to know [*pt* **knew**; *pp* **known**]; *(noticia)* to hear [*pt & pp* **heard**]. **3** *(país, lugar)* to have been to: *no conozco Francia*, I've never been to France.

▶ *vpr* **conocerse** *(a uno mismo)* to know oneself [*pt* **knew**; *pp* **known**]; *(dos personas)* to know each other, be acquainted with each other; *(- por primera vez)* to meet [*pt & pp* **met**]: *nos conocemos desde hace años*, we've known each other for years; *¿cuándo os conocisteis?*, when did you meet?

● **conocer de vista** to know by sight [*pt* **knew**; *pp* **known**].

● **dar a conocer** to make known.

● **darse a conocer** to make oneself known.

conocido,-a *adj* **1** *(reconocible)* familiar. **2** *(famoso)* well-known.

▶ *nm,f* acquaintance.

conocimiento *nm* **1** *(saber)* knowledge. **2** *(sensatez)* good sense. **3** *(conciencia)* consciousness.

● **perder el conocimiento** to lose consciousness [*pt & pp* **lost**].

● **recobrar el conocimiento** to regain consciousness.

● **tener conocimiento de** to know about [*pt* **knew**; *pp* **known**].

conque *conj* so.

conquista *nf* conquest.

conquistador,-ra *adj* conquering.

▶ *nm,f* conqueror.

▶ *nm* **conquistador** *(ligón)* lady-killer.

conquistar *vt* **1** *(con armas)* to conquer. **2** *(victoria, título)* to win [*pt & pp* **won**]. **3** *(ligar con)* to win over [*pt & pp* **won**].

consagrar *vt* **1** *(hostia, iglesia)* to consecrate. **2** *(esfuerzo, tiempo)* to devote, dedicate. **3** *(artista, costumbre)* to establish.

▶ *vpr* **consagrarse** *(dedicarse, consagrarse a)* to devote oneself to.

consciente *adj* conscious.

consecuencia *nf* consequence, result.

● **a consecuencia de** as a result of, due to.

● **en consecuencia** consequently, therefore.

consecutivo,-a *adj* consecutive.

conseguir *vt (cosa)* to obtain, get; *(objetivo)* to attain, achieve.

● **conseguir + inf** to manage to + *inf*: *conseguí abrirlo*, I managed to open it.

● **¡lo conseguí!** I did it!

consejero,-a *nm,f* **1** *(asesor)* adviser. **2** POL counsellor.

consejo *nm* **1** *(recomendación)* advice: *te daré un consejo*, I'll give you a piece of advice. **2** *(junta)* council, board.

■ **consejo de administración** board of directors.

■ **consejo de guerra** court-martial.

■ **consejo de ministros** cabinet.

consenso *nm* consensus.

consentido,-a *adj* spoilt.

▶ *nm,f* spoiled child *[pl* **children***]*.

consentimiento *nm* consent.

consentir *vt* **1** *(permitir)* to allow, permit, tolerate. **2** *(a un niño)* to spoil *[pt & pp* **spoilt***]*.

▶ *vi (acceder a)* to consent, give way.

conserje *nmf* **1** *(de hotel, oficina)* porter. **2** *(de escuela)* caretaker.

conserjería *nf* porter's lodge.

conservas *nf pl* tinned food, canned food.

conservación *nf* **1** *(de naturaleza, especie)* conservation. **2** *(de alimentos)* preservation. **3** *(mantenimiento)* maintenance.

conservador,-ra *adj* conservative.

▶ *nm,f* **1** POL conservative. **2** *(de museos)* curator.

conservante *nm* preservative.

conservar *vt* **1** *(alimentos)* to preserve. **2** *(calor)* retain. **3** *(guardar)* to keep: *todavía conserva el vestido de novia*, she still keeps her wedding dress.

conservatorio *nm* conservatory, conservatoire.

considerable *adj* considerable.

consideración *nf* **1** *(deliberación, atención)* consideration. **2** *(respeto)* regard.

● **de consideración** important: *herido de consideración*, seriously injured.

● **tomar en consideración** to take into consideration.

considerado,-a *adj* **1** *(atento)* considerate. **2** *(apreciado)* respected.

● **estar bien considerado** to be well thought of.

● **estar mal considerado** to be badly thought of.

considerar *vt* **1** *(reflexionar)* to consider, think over *[pt & pp* **thought***]*: *tengo que considerar su propuesta*, I have to consider their proposal. **2** *(respetar)* to treat with consideration. **3** *(juzgar)* to consider: *lo considero imposible*, I consider it (to be) impossible.

consigna *nf* **1** *(en estación etc)* GB left-luggage office; US check-room. **2** *(eslogan)* slogan. **3** *(orden)* orders *pl*.

consigo *pron (con él)* with him; *(con ella)* with her; *(con usted, ustedes, vosotros,-as)* with you; *(con ellos,-as)* with them; *(con uno mismo)* with oneself: *lo trajo consigo*, she brought it with her; *llevaban las maletas consigo*, they carried their suitcases with them.

consiguiente *adj* consequent.

● **por consiguiente** therefore, consequently.

consistencia *nf* **1** *(densidad)* consistency. **2** *(coherencia)* coherence.

consistente *adj* **1** *(denso)* thick. **2** *(coherente)* sound.

consistir *vi* to consist (**en**, of).

consistorio *nm* town council.

consola *nf* **1** *(mueble)* console table. **2** INFORM console.

consolador,-ra *adj* consoling, comforting.

consolar *vt* to console, comfort.

▶ *vpr* **consolarse** to take comfort.

consomé *nm* consommé, clear soup.

consonante *adj* - *nf* consonant.

consorte *nmf* spouse: *príncipe consorte*, prince consort.

conspiración *nf* conspiracy, plot.

conspirar *vi* to conspire, plot.

constancia *nf* **1** *(perseverancia)* perseverance. **2** *(prueba)* evidence.

constante *adj* **1** *(invariable)* constant. **2** *(persona)* persevering.

► *nf* **1** *(matemática)* constant. **2** *(característica)* constant feature.

■ **constantes vitales** vital signs.

constar *vi* **1** *(consistir en)* to consist (**de**, of). **2** *(ser cierto)*: **me consta que ha llegado**, I am absolutely certain that he has arrived, I know for a fact that he has arrived. **3** *(figurar)* to appear: **en el contrato consta que la casa es suya**, the house appears as his in the contract.

constatar *vt* to verify, confirm.

constelación *nf* constellation.

constipado,-a *adj* suffering from a cold.

► *nm* **constipado** cold.

constiparse *vpr* to catch a cold [*pt & pp* **caught**].

constitución *nf* constitution.

constitucional *adj* constitutional.

constituir *vt* to constitute.

► *vpr* **constituirse** to set oneself up [*pt & pp* **set**].

construcción *nf* **1** *(acción)* construction, building. **2** *(edificio)* building.

● **en construcción** under construction.

constructivo,-a *adj* constructive.

constructor,-ra *adj* construction, building.

► *nm,f* constructor, builder.

construir *vt* to build [*pt & pp* **built**], construct.

consuelo *nm* consolation, comfort.

cónsul *nmf* consul.

consulado *nm* **1** *(oficina)* consulate. **2** *(cargo)* consulship.

consulta *nf* **1** *(pregunta)* consultation. **2** *(de médico)* GB surgery ; US office: **horas de consulta**, surgery hours.

consultar *vt* *(persona)* to consult; *(libro)* to look it up in.

consultorio *nm* **1** *(de médico)* GB surgery ; US office. **2** *(en periódicos)* problem page, advice column; *(en radio)* phone-in.

consumición *nf* **1** *(acción)* consumption. **2** *(bebida)* drink.

consumidor,-ra *adj* consuming.

► *nm,f* consumer.

consumir *vt* **1** *(gastar, usar)* to consume, use: **este coche consume mucha gasolina**, this car uses a lot of petrol. **2** *(comer)* to eat [*pt* **ate**; *pp* **eaten**]. **3** *(beber)* to drink [*pt* **drank**; *pp* **drunk**], consume: **ha consumido mucho alcohol**, he has consumed a large amount of alcohol. **4** *(fuego)* to consume. **5** *(celos, envidia)* to consume.

► *vpr* **consumirse** **1** *(gastarse)* to be consumed. **2** *(destruirse)* to be destroyed. **3** *(quemarse)* to burn down [*pt & pp* **burnt**].

consumo *nm* consumption.

contabilidad *nf* **1** *(profesión)* accountancy. **2** *(ciencia)* accountancy, bookkeeping.

● **llevar la contabilidad** to keep the books, do the accounts.

contable *adj* countable.

► *nmf* accountant.

contactar *vt* *(contactar con* ALGN*)* to contact SB, get in touch with SB.

contacto *nm* **1** *(entre personas, cosas)* contact. **2** *(de coche)* ignition.

● **mantenerse en contacto con** to keep in touch with.

contado,-a *adj* few: **en contadas ocasiones**, on very few occasions.

● **pagar al contado** to pay cash [*pt & pp* **paid**].

contador,-ra *adj* counting.

► *nm,f* *(contable)* accountant.

► *nm* **contador** meter.

contagiar *vt* **1** *(enfermedad)* to transmit, pass on. **2** *(persona)* to infect.

► *vpr* **contagiarse** *(enfermedad)* to be infectious; *(persona)* to become infected.

contagio *nm* contagion, infection.

contagioso,-a *adj* *(enfermedad)* contagious; *(risa)* infectious.

contaminación *nf* *(de agua, radiactiva)* contamination; *(atmosférica)* pollution.

contaminar *vt* *(agua, con radiactividad)* to contaminate; *(aire)* to pollute.

► *vpr* **contaminarse** **1** *(agua, con radioactividad)* to become contaminated. **2** *(aire)* to become polluted.

contar *vt* **1** *(calcular)* to count. **2** *(explicar)* to tell [*pt & pp* **told**].

► *vi* to count.

● **a contar desde** starting from.

● **contar con** ALGN **1** *(confiar)* to count on SB, rely on SB. **2** *(incluir)* to count SB in: **cuento contigo**, I'm counting on you.

● **contar con algo 1** (esperar) to expect STH. **2** (tener) to have STH: **la casa cuenta con un pequeño jardín**, the house has a small garden.

contemplar *vt-vi* to contemplate.

contemporáneo,-a *adj - nm,f* contemporary.

contenedor *nm* container.

■ **contenedor de basura** rubbish bin.

■ **contenedor de escombros** skip.

■ **contenedor de vidrio** bottle bank.

contener *vt* **1** *(tener dentro)* to contain, hold [*pt & pp* **held**]: *el libro contiene muchas ilustraciones*, the book contains a lot of illustrations. **2** *(reprimir)* to contain, hold back [*pt & pp* **held**]: *no pudo contener las lágrimas*, she couldn't contain her tears.

contenido,-a *adj* restrained, self-controlled.

▶ *nm* **contenido** content, contents *pl*.

contentar *vt* to please.

▶ *vpr* **contentarse** to be pleased.

contento,-a *adj* happy.

▶ *nm* **contento** happiness.

contestación *nf (respuesta)* answer, reply.

contestador *nm* **contestador automático** answering machine.

contestar *vt (pregunta, teléfono)* to answer.

▶ *vi (replicar)* to answer back: *¡no contestes a tu padre!*, don't answer your father back!

contexto *nm* context.

● **sacar algo de contexto** to take STH out of context.

contienda *nf* contest, dispute.

contigo *pron* with you.

contiguo,-a *adj* contiguous, adjoining.

continental *adj* continental.

continente *nm* **1** continent. **2** *(recipiente)* container.

continuación *nf* continuation.

● **a continuación** next.

continuamente *adv* **1** *(repetidamente)* continually, constantly. **2** *(sin interrupción)* continuously.

continuar *vt-vi* to continue, carry on: *continuaremos el debate después de comer*, we'll continue the discussion after lunch, we'll carry on with the discussion after lunch; *Pablo continúa en Francia*, Pablo is still in France.

continuidad *nf* continuity.

continuo,-a *adj* **1** *(ininterrumpido)* continuous. **2** *(repetido)* continual: *sus continuas quejas*, her continual complaints.

▶ *nm* **continuo** continuum.

contorno *nm* **1** *(silueta)* outline. **2** *(perímetro)* perimeter.

▶ *nm pl* **contornos** *(afueras)* surroundings *pl*.

contorsión *nf* contortion.

contra *prep* against: *tres contra uno*, three against one.

▶ *nm fam* drawback.

● **los pros y los contras** the pros and cons.

● **llevar la contra** to contradict.

● **en contra** against.

● **en contra de ...** contrary to ...: *en contra de lo que decían*, contrary to what they said.

contraataque *nm* counterattack.

contrabajo *nm* **1** *(instrumento)* double bass. **2** *(voz)* basso profundo.

contrabandista *nmf* smuggler.

contrabando *nm* **1** *(actividad)* smuggling. **2** *(mercancía)* contraband.

contracción *nf* contraction.

contracepción *nf* contraception.

contradecir *vt* to contradict.

▶ *vpr* **contradecirse** to contradict oneself.

contradicción *nf* contradiction.

contraer *vt* **1** *(encoger)* to contract. **2** *(enfermedad)* to catch [*pt & pp* **caught**]. **3** *(deuda, compromiso)* to contract.

● **contraer matrimonio** to get married.

contrapeso *nm* **1** *(de balanza)* counterweight. **2** *(compensación)* counterbalance.

contraportada *nf* **1** *(de periódico, revista)* back page. **2** *(de libro)* inside cover.

contrariar *vt* **1** *(oponer)* to oppose. **2** *(disgustar)* to annoy. **3** *(dificultar)* to obstruct.

contrariedad *nf* **1** *(disgusto)* annoyance. **2** *(dificultad)* setback.

contrario,-a *adj* **1** *(opuesto dirección, sentido)* contrary, opposite. **2** *(opinión)* contrary. **3** *(rival)* opposing. **4** *(perjudicial)* harmful.

▶ *nm,f* opponent.

● **al contrario** on the contrary.

● **llevar la contraria** to oppose.

contrarreloj *adj* against the clock.

▶ *nf* time trial.

contraseña *nf* password.

contrastar *vt* **1** *(comparar)* to contrast. **2** *(pesos, medidas)* to check. **3** *(oro, plata)* to hallmark.

▶ *vi* to contrast.

contraste *nm* **1** *(oposición)* contrast. **2** *(pesos, medidas)* verification. **3** *(oro, plata)* hallmark.

contratar *vt* **1** *(servicio etc)* to sign a contract for. **2** *(empleado)* to hire, take.

contratiempo *nm* **1** *(inconveniente)* setback. **2** *(accidente)* mishap.

contrato *nm* contract.

■ **contrato de alquiler** lease, leasing agreement.

contraventana *nf* shutter.

contribución *nf* **1** *(aportación)* contribution. **2** *(impuesto)* tax.

■ **contribución urbana** local property tax.

contribuir *vt-vi* to contribute.

contribuyente *adj* taxpaying.

▶ *nmf* taxpayer.

contrincante *nm* opponent, rival.

control *nm* **1** *(dominio)* control. **2** *(verificación)* examination, inspection.

■ **control remoto** remote control.

■ **control de natalidad** birth control.

■ **control de pasaportes** passport control.

■ **control de policía** police checkpoint.

controlador,-ra *nm,f* **controlador,-ra aéreo,-a** air traffic controller.

controlar *vt* to control.

▶ *vpr* **controlarse** to control oneself.

controversia *nf* controversy.

controvertido,-a *adj* controversial.

contusión *nf* contusion, bruise.

convalecer *vi* to convalesce.

convalidar *vt* to validate.

convencer *vt* to convince: *eso no me convence*, that doesn't convince me; *la convencí para que se quedara*, I persuaded her to stay.

▶ *vpr* **convencerse** to become convinced.

convencimiento *nm* conviction.

● **tener el convencimiento de que** to be convinced that.

convención *nf* convention.

convencional *adj* conventional.

conveniencia *nf* **1** *(comodidad)* convenience. **2** *(ventaja)* advantage. **3** *(idoneidad)* advisability.

conveniente *adj* **1** *(cómodo)* convenient. **2** *(ventajoso)* advantageous. **3** *(aconsejable)* advisable.

convenio *nm* agreement.

■ **convenio colectivo** collective bargaining.

convenir *vi* **1** *(ser oportuno)* to suit: *cada cual hace lo que le conviene*, everybody does what suits them best. **2** *(ser aconsejable)*: *te conviene descansar*, you should get some rest; *conviene que te presentes*, you'd better be there. **3** *(acordar, convenir en)* to agree (on): *convinieron en que se repartirían el trabajo*, they agreed to share the work.

● **a convenir** negotiable.

convento *nm* *(de monjas)* convent; *(de monjes)* monastery.

convergencia *nf* convergence.

conversación *nf* conversation.

● **dar conversación a ALGN** to talk to SB.

conversar *vi* to talk.

conversión *nf* conversion.

convertir *vt* **1** *(transformar)*: *convertir algo en algo*, to turn STH into STH; *convirtieron la tienda en restaurante*, the shop was turned into a restaurant. **2** *(a religión)* to convert.

▶ *vpr* **convertirse 1** *(transformarse, convertirse en algo)* to turn into STH, become STH. **2** *(a religión)* to convert.

convexo,-a *adj* convex.

convicción *nf* conviction: *tengo la convicción de que ...*, I firmly believe that ....

convidado,-a *nm,f* guest.

convidar *vt* **1** *(invitar)* to invite; *(ofrecer)* to offer. **2** *(incitar)* to inspire, prompt: *este tiempo convida a quedarse en casa*, this weather makes you want to stay at home.

convincente *adj* convincing.

convite *nm* **1** *(invitación)* invitation. **2** *(comida)* banquet.

convivencia *nf* **1** *(de personas)* living together. **2** *(simultaneidad)* coexistence.

convivir *vi* to live together.

convocar *vt* to call: *convocar una reunión*, to call a meeting.

convocatoria *nf* **1** *(llamamiento)* call: *una convocatoria de huelga*, a strike call. **2** *(examen)* examination, sitting.

cónyuge *nmf* spouse.

▶ *nm pl* **cónyuges** husband and wife, married couple.

coñac *nm* cognac, brandy.

coño *nm vulg* cunt.
► *interj* **¡coño!** *vulg (sorpresa)* fuck me!;
(disgusto) for fuck's sake!
cooperación *nf* cooperation.
cooperar *vi* to cooperate.
cooperativa *nf* cooperative *(society)*.
coordinación *nf* coordination.
coordinador,-ra *adj* coordinating.
► *nm,f* coordinator.
coordinar *vt* to coordinate.
copa *nf* **1** *(recipiente)* glass. **2** *(bebida)*
drink. **3** *(de árbol)* top. **4** *(trofeo)* cup.
● **ir de copas** to go (out) drinking.
● **tomar una copa** to have a drink.
copia *nf* copy.
■ **copia de seguridad** backup: *¿has hecho una copia de seguridad de ese
archivo?*, have you backed that file up?
copiar *vt* **1** *(reproducir)* to copy. **2** *(escribir)*
to take down.
► *vi (en examen)* to copy.
copiloto *nm* **1** *(de avión)* copilot. **2** *(de coche)* co-driver.
copión,-ona *nm,f* **1** *fam (en examen)* cheat.
2 *fam (imitador)* copycat.
copla *nf (verso)* verse.
► *nf pl* **coplas** folk songs.
copo *nm (de cereal)* flake; *(de nieve)* snowflake; *(de algodón)* ball *(of cotton)*.
cópula *nf* **1** *(en gramática)* copula. **2** *(coito)*
copulation.
copulativo,-a *adj* copulative.
coquetear *vi* to flirt.
coqueto,-a *adj* flirtatious.
coraje *nm* **1** *(valor)* courage. **2** *(ira)* anger.
coral[1] *adj* choral.
► *nf* choir.
coral[2] *nm* coral.
coraza *nf* **1** *(armadura)* armour. **2** *(caparazón)* shell.
corazón *nm* **1** *(gen)* heart. **2** *(de fruta)*
core.
● **de (todo) corazón** sincerely.
● **me dice el corazón que ...** I have a
feeling that ....
● **partirle el corazón a ALGN** to break [*pt*
broke; *pp* **broken**] SB's heart.
● **tener buen corazón** to be kind-hearted.
corazonada *nf* **1** *(impresión)* hunch, feeling. **2** *(impulso)* impulse.
corbata *nf* tie.
corcel *nm* steed, charger.

corchete *nm* **1** *(cierre)* hook and eye. **2**
(paréntesis) square bracket.
corcho *nm* **1** *(material, tapón)* cork. **2** *(panel)* cork mat.
cordel *nm* string, cord.
cordero,-a *nm,f* lamb.
cordial *adj* cordial, friendly.
cordillera *nf* mountain range.
cordón *nm* **1** *(cuerda)* cord, string; *(de zapatos)* lace, shoelace. **2** *(cadena humana)*
cordon.
■ **cordón policial** police cordon.
■ **cordón umbilical** umbilical cord.
Corea *nf* Korea.
■ **Corea del Norte** North Korea.
■ **Corea del Sur** South Korea.
coreano,-a *adj* Korean.
► *nm,f (persona)* Korean.
► *nm* **coreano** *(idioma)* Korean.
corear *vt* to chorus.
coreografía *nf* choreography.
cornada *nf* thrust with a horn.
● **sufrir una cornada** to be gored.
cornamenta *nf* **1** *(de toro)* horns *pl*; *(de
ciervo)* antlers *pl*. **2** *fam (de marido)* cuckold's horns *pl*.
córnea *nf* cornea.
córner *nm* corner.
● **sacar un córner** to take a corner.
corneta *nf* bugle.
► *nmf* bugler.
cornisa *nf* cornice.
coro *nm* **1** *(grupo)* choir. **2** *(composición)*
chorus.
● **a coro** all together.
corola *nf* corolla.
corona *nf* **1** *(de rey)* crown. **2** *(de flores etc)*
wreath.
coronación *nf* coronation.
coronar *vt* to crown.
coronel *nm* colonel.
coronilla *nf (en la cabeza)* crown of the
head.
● **estar hasta la coronilla** *fam* to be fed
up.
corporación *nf* corporation.
corporal *adj* corporal, body.
corpulento,-a *adj* heavily-built, corpu-
lent.
corral *nm* **1** *(de aves)* yard. **2** *(de cerdos,
ovejas)* pen. **3** *(de caballos, ganado)* corral.
correa *nf* **1** *(de piel)* strap. **2** *(cinturón)* belt.
3 *(de perro)* lead. **4** *(de máquina)* belt.

corrección *nf* **1** *(arreglo)* correction. **2** *(educación)* courtesy. **3** *(reprimenda)* rebuke.

correcto,-a *adj* **1** *(exacto, adecuado)* correct. **2** *(educado)* polite, courteous.

corredor,-ra *adj* running.
▶ *nm,f* **1** *(atleta)* runner. **2** *(ciclista)* cyclist. **3** *(agente)* broker.
▶ *nm* **corredor** corridor.
■ **corredor de bolsa** stockbroker.

corregir *vt* **1** *(enmendar)* to correct. **2** *(reprender)* to reprimand.
▶ *vpr* **corregirse** to mend one's ways.

correo *nm* **1** *(servicio, correspondencia)* GB post; US mail. **2** *(persona)* courier. **3** *(tren)* mail train.
▶ *nm pl* **correos** *(oficina)* post office *sing*.
● **echar al correo** GB to post; US to mail.
● **mandar por correo** GB to post; US to mail.
■ **correo aéreo** airmail.
■ **correo certificado** GB registered post; US registered mail.
■ **correo electrónico** e-mail, electronic mail: *envíamelo por correo electrónico*, e-mail it to me.
■ **correo urgente** express mail.

correr *vi* **1** *(persona, animal)* to run [*pt* **ran**; *pp* **run**]. **2** *(viento)* to blow [*pt* **blew**; *pp* **blown**]. **3** *(agua)* to flow. **4** *(tiempo)* to pass. **5** *(noticias)* to spread [*pt & pp* **spread**]. **6** *(darse prisa)* to hurry.
▶ *vt* **1** *(recorrer)* to travel through. **2** *(carrera)* to run [*pt* **ran**; *pp* **run**]. **3** *(deslizar)* to close; *(cortina)* to draw [*pt* **drew**; *pp* **drawn**].
▶ *vpr* **correrse 1** *(desplazarse - persona)* to move over; *(objeto)* to shift. **2** *vulg (tener orgasmo)* to come.
● **correr con los gastos de** to pay for [*pt & pp* **paid**].
● **correr el pestillo** to bolt the door.
● **correr la voz** to pass it on.
● **correr prisa** to be urgent.
● **correr un riesgo** to run a risk [*pt* **ran**; *pp* **run**].
● **dejar correr algo** to let STH pass.

correspondencia *nf* **1** *(relación)* correspondence. **2** *(cartas)* GB post; US mail. **3** *(de trenes etc)* connection.

corresponder *vi* **1** *(equivaler)* to correspond. **2** *(pertenecer)* to belong, pertain. **3** *(devolver)* to return.
▶ *vpr* **corresponderse 1** *(ajustarse)* to correspond. **2** *(cartearse)* to correspond. **3** *(amarse)* to love each other.

correspondiente *adj* **1** *(perteneciente)* corresponding. **2** *(apropiado)* suitable, appropriate. **3** *(respectivo)* respective.

corresponsal *nmf* correspondent.

corretear *vi* to run about [*pt* **ran**; *pp* **run**].

correveidile *nmf* telltale.

corrida *nf*: *dar una corrida*, to make a desh.
■ **corrida de toros** bullfight.

corriente *adj* **1** *(frecuente)* common. **2** *(no especial)* ordinary. **3** *(agua)* running. **4** *(fecha)* current, present: *el cinco del corriente*, the fifth of the present month.
▶ *nf* **1** *(masa de agua)* current, stream. **2** *(de aire)* GB draught; US draft. **3** *(eléctrica)* current. **4** *(de arte etc)* current, trend.
● **al corriente** up to date.
● **estar al corriente de algo** to know about STH.
● **seguirle la corriente a ALGN** to humour SB.
● **salirse de lo corriente** to be out of the ordinary.
■ **Corriente del Golfo** Gulf Stream.

corro *nm* **1** *(círculo)* circle, ring. **2** *(juego)* ring-a-ring-a-roses.

corrosivo,-a *adj* **1** *(sustancia)* corrosive. **2** *(comentario)* caustic.

corrupción *nf* **1** *(perversión)* corruption. **2** *(putrefacción)* rot, decay.
■ **corrupción de menores** corruption of minors, child abuse.

corsario *nm* corsair, pirate.

corsé *nm* corset.

cortacésped *nm & nf* lawnmower.

cortado,-a *adj* **1** *(partido)* cut; *(en lonchas)* sliced. **2** *(estilo)* concise, clipped. **3** *(tímido)* shy.
▶ *nm* **cortado** coffee with a dash of milk.

cortante *adj* **1** *(objeto)* cutting, sharp. **2** *(aire)* biting.

cortar *vt* **1** *(partir)* to cut [*pt & pp* **cut**]; *(trinchar)* to carve; *(árbol)* to cut down [*pt & pp* **cut**]: *cortó un trozo de queso*, she cut a piece of cheese. **2** *(en costura)* to cut out [*pt & pp* **cut**]. **3** *(interrumpir)* to cut off [*pt & pp* **cut**], interrupt: *nos han cortado el teléfono*, our telephone has been disconnected. **4** *(calle, carretera)* to close.
▶ *vi* to cut: *este cuchillo no corta*, this knife doesn't cut.

▶ *vpr* **cortarse 1** *(herirse)* to cut [*pt & pp* cut]: **me he cortado el dedo**, I've cut my finger. **2** *(pelo - por otro)* to have one's hair cut; *(- uno mismo)* to cut one's hair [*pt & pp* cut]. **3** *(leche)* to sour, curdle. **4** *(sentir vergüenza)* to get embarrassed.

● **cortar por lo sano** *fam* to take drastic measures.

cortaúñas *nm* nail clippers *pl*.

corte[1] *nf* court.

▶ *nf pl* **las Cortes** Spanish parliament *(sing)*.

corte[2] *nm* **1** *(herida, interrupción)* cut: **tiene un corte en la ceja**, he's got a cut on his eyebrow; **se ha hecho un corte**, she's cut herself; **un corte del suministro eléctrico**, a power cut. **2** *(filo)* edge. **3** *fam (vergüenza)* embarrassment: **me da corte pedírselo de nuevo**, I'm embarrassed to ask him again. **4** *fam (respuesta brusca)* rebuff.

● **darle un corte a ALGN** to put SB down.

■ **corte de luz** powercut.

■ **corte de pelo** haircut.

■ **corte y confección** dressmaking.

cortejo *nm* **1** *(acompañantes)* entourage. **2** *(galanteo)* courting.

cortés *adj* courteous, polite.

cortesía *nf* courtesy, politeness.

corteza *nf* **1** *(de árbol)* bark. **2** *(de pan)* crust. **3** *(de fruta)* peel, skin. **4** *(de queso)* rind.

■ **corteza terrestre** earth's crust.

cortijo *nm* farm, farmhouse.

cortina *nf* curtain.

● **cortina de humo** smoke screen.

corto,-a *adj* **1** *(calle, cuerda, etc.)* short: **lleva el pelo corto**, he's got short hair. **2** *(tonto)* thick.

● **corto de vista** short-sighted.

● **quedarse corto** *fam* to underestimate.

cortocircuito *nm* short circuit.

cortometraje *nm* short film, short.

cosa *nf* **1** *(objeto)* thing: **pon tus cosas aquí dentro**, put your things in here. **2** *(asunto)* thing, matter: **casarse es una cosa seria**, getting married is a big thing.

▶ *nf pl* **cosas** *fam (manías)* hang-ups.

● **¿alguna cosa más?** anything else?

● **entre una cosa y otra** with one thing and another.

● **como si tal cosa** as if nothing had happened.

● **cosa de** about.

● **ser poquita cosa** *fam* to be not much to look at.

coscorrón *nm* bump on the head.

cosecha *nf* **1** *(acción)* harvest. **2** *(producto)* crop. **3** *(tiempo)* harvest time. **4** *(año del vino)* vintage.

● **de su propia cosecha** of one's own invention.

cosechadora *nf* combine harvester.

cosechar *vt (recoger - cosecha)* to harvest, gather; *(- éxitos etc)* to reap.

coser *vt* **1** *(ropa)* to sew [*pt* sewed; *pp* sewn]. **2** *(botón)* to sew [*pt* sewed; *pp* sewed o sewn] on. **3** *(herida)* to stitch up. **4** *(atravesar)* to pierce: **coser a balazos**, to riddle with bullets.

● **ser coser y cantar** to be plain sailing.

cosmético,-a *adj* cosmetic.

▶ *nm* **cosmético** cosmetic.

cosmonauta *nmf* cosmonaut.

cosmos *nm* cosmos.

cosquillas *nf pl*.

● **hacer cosquillas a ALGN** to tickle SB.

● **tener cosquillas** to be ticklish.

cosquilleo *nm* tickling.

costa[1] *nf* coast.

costa[2].

● **a costa de** at the expense of.

● **a toda costa** at all costs.

costado *nm* side.

● **por los cuatro costados** through and through: **inglés por los cuatro costados**, English through and through.

costar *vt* **1** *(valer)* to cost [*pt & pp* cost]: **¿cuánto te ha costado el billete?**, how much did your ticket cost? **2** *(esfuerzo, tiempo)* to take: **le ha costado mucho trabajo**, it has taken her a lot of hard work; **me ha costado dos horas**, it has taken me two hours.

▶ *vi* **1** *(al comprar)* to cost [*pt & pp* cost]. **2** *(ser difícil)* to be difficult: **me cuesta el italiano**, I find Italian difficult; **me cuesta creerlo**, I find it difficult to believe.

● **cueste lo que cueste** at any cost.

● **costar un ojo de la cara** *fam* to cost an arm and a leg [*pt & pp* cost].

costarricense *adj - nmf* Costa Rican.

coste *nm* cost.

■ **coste de (la) vida** cost of living.

costero,-a *adj* coastal, seaside.

costilla *nf* **1** *(de persona, animal)* rib. **2** *(como comida)* cutlet.

costo[1] *nm (precio)* cost.

costo[2] *nm arg (hachís)* dope.

costoso,-a *adj* **1** *(caro)* costly, expensive. **2** *(difícil)* hard.

costra *nf* **1** *(de pan)* crust. **2** *(de herida)* scab.

costumbre *nf* **1** *(hábito)* habit: **tengo la costumbre de comer temprano**, it is my habit to have lunch early. **2** *(tradición)* custom: **es una costumbre rusa**, it's a Russian custom.

costura *nf* **1** *(cosido)* sewing. **2** *(línea de puntadas)* seam.

costurera *nf* seamstress.

costurero *nm* sewing basket.

cotidiano,-a *adj* daily, everyday.

cotilla *nmf fam* busybody.

cotillear *vi fam* to gossip.

cotilleo *nm fam* gossip, gossiping.

cotizar *vI (en bolsa)* to be quoted.

▶ *vpr* **cotizarse** to sell at [*pt & pp* **sold**].

coto *nm* reserve.

● **poner coto a algo** to put a stop to STH.

■ **coto de caza** game preserve.

cotorra *nf* **1** *(animal)* parrot. **2** *fam (persona)* chatterbox.

coyote *nm* coyote.

coz *nf* kick.

● **dar una coz** to kick.

cráneo *nm* skull, cranium.

cráter *nm* crater.

creación *nf* creation.

creador,-ra *adj* creative.

▶ *nm,f* creator.

crear *vt* **1** *(producir)* to create. **2** *(fundar)* to found, establish. **3** *(inventar)* to invent.

creativo,-a *adj* creative.

crecer *vi* **1** *(persona, planta)* to grow [*pt* **grew**; *pp* **grown**]. **2** *(aumentar)* to grow [*pt* **grew**; *pp* **grown**], increase: **crece la influencia de la televisión**, the influence of television is increasing. **3** *(corriente, marea)* to rise [*pt* **rose**; *pp* **risen**].

▶ *vpr* **crecerse** *(engreírse)* to become conceited.

crecida *nf* spate.

creciente *adj (capital, interés)* growing; *(luna)* crescent.

crecimiento *nm* growth, increase.

crédito *nm* **1** *(al comprar)* credit. **2** *(préstamo)* loan. **3** *(fama)* reputation.

● **dar crédito a** to believe.

credo *nm* **1** creed. **2** *(creencias)* credo [*pl* -s].

crédulo,-a *adj* credulous, gullible.

creencia *nf* belief.

creer *vi* **1** *(tener fe; creer en algo/ALGN)* to believe in STH/SB: **¿crees en Dios?**, do you believe in God? **2** *(pensar)* to think [*pt & pp* **thought**]: **no creo**, I don't think so.

▶ *vt* **1** *(gen)* to believe: **no me creyó**, he didn't believe me. **2** *(pensar)* to think [*pt & pp* **thought**], suppose: **creo que vamos a ganar**, I think we've going to win.

▶ *vpr* **creerse** *(considerarse)* to think [*pt & pp* **thought**]: **¿quién te has creído que eres?**, who do you think you are?

● **creo que sí** I think so.

● **creo que no** I don't think so.

creíble *adj* credible, believable.

creído,-a *adj* arrogant: **ser un creído**, to be full of oneself.

crema *nf* **1** *(nata)* cream. **2** *(natillas)* custard. **3** *(de cara)* face cream.

▶ *adj* cream, cream-coloured.

cremallera *nf* **1** *(de vestido)* zipper, zip (fastener). **2** *(de máquina)* rack.

cremoso,-a *adj* creamy.

crepúsculo *nm* twilight.

cresta *nf* **1** *(de ola)* crest. **2** *(de gallo)* comb.

● **estar en la cresta de la ola** to be on the crest of a wave.

creyente *adj* believing.

▶ *nmf* believer.

cría *nf* **1** *(de plantas)* growing; *(de animales)* breeding. **2** *(cachorro)* baby: **una cría de oso**, a baby bear. **3** *(camada)* litter. **4** *(nidada)* brood.

criadero *nm* **1** *(de plantas)* nursery. **2** *(de animales)* farm; *(de perros)* kennels. **3** *(de ratas)* breeding ground.

criado,-a *adj (animal)* reared; *(persona)* bred.

▶ *nm,f* servant.

● **bien criado,-a** well-bred.

● **mal criado,-a** ill-bred.

criar *vt* **1** *(educar)* to bring up [*pt & pp* **brought**]. **2** *(dar el pecho)* to nurse. **3** *(plantas)* to grow [*pt* **grew**; *pp* **grown**]; *(animales)* to breed [*pt & pp* **bred**].

criatura *nf* **1** *(ser)* creature. **2** *(niño)* baby, child [*pl* **children**].

crimen *nm* **1** *(delito)* crime. **2** *(asesinato)* murder.

cross *nm* cross-country race.
cruce *nm* **1** *(acción)* crossing. **2** *(de calles)* crossroads. **3** *(de carreteras)* junction. **4** *(para peatones)* crossing. **5** *(de razas)* crossbreeding. **6** *(interferencia telefónica)* crossed line: **hay un cruce en las líneas**, the lines are crossed.
crucero *nm* **1** *(buque)* cruiser. **2** *(viaje)* cruise. **3** *(de templo)* transept.
crucificar *vt* to crucify.
crucifijo *nm* crucifix.
crucigrama *nm* crossword.
crudo,-a *adj* **1** *(sin cocer)* raw; *(poco hecho)* underdone. **2** *(imagen)* harsh. **3** *(clima)* harsh. **4** *(color)* off-white.
  ► *nm* **crudo** *(petróleo)* oil, crude.
cruel *adj* cruel.
crueldad *nf* cruelty.
crujido *nm* **1** *(de puerta)* creak. **2** *(de seda, papel)* rustle. **3** *(de dientes)* grinding.
crujiente *adj* crunchy.
crujir *vi* **1** *(puerta)* to creak. **2** *(seda, hojas)* to rustle. **3** *(dientes)* to grind [*pt & pp* **ground**].
crustáceo *nm* crustacean.
cruz *nf* **1** *(figura)* cross. **2** *(de moneda)* tails *pl*. **3** *(carga)* cross.
  ● **¿cara o cruz?** heads or tails?
  ■ **Cruz Roja** Red Cross.
cruzada *nf* HIST crusade.
cruzado,-a *adj* **1** *(brazos, piernas, cheque)* crossed. **2** *(animal)* crossbred. **3** *(prenda)* double-breasted.
  ► *nm* **cruzado** crusader.
cruzar *vt* **1** *(río, piernas, animales)* to cross: **cruzamos la calle**, we crossed the street. **2** *(miradas, palabras)* to exchange.
  ► *vpr* **cruzarse** to pass each other.
  ● **cruzarse de brazos** to stand [*pt & pp* **stood**] by and do nothing.
cuaderno *nm* **1** *(de notas)* notebook. **2** *(escolar)* exercise book.
cuadra *nf* stable.
cuadrado,-a *adj* square: **diez metros cuadrados**, ten square metres.
  ► *nm* **cuadrado** square.
  ● **elevar un número al cuadrado** to square a number.
cuadrar *vi* **1** *(cuentas)* to add up. **2** *(versiones)* to tally [*pt & pp* **-ied**].
  ► *vpr* **cuadrarse** *(persona)* to stand firm [*pt & pp* **stood**]; *(militar)* to stand to attention.

criminal *adj* - *nmf* criminal.
crin *nf* mane.
crío,-a *nm,f fam* kid.
crisis *nf* **1** *(mal momento)* crisis. **2** *(ataque)* fit, attack: **crisis de asma**, asthma attack.
crisma *nf fam* head.
  ● **romperse la crisma** *fam* to split one's head open.
cristal *nm* **1** *(gen)* glass: **un cristal**, a piece of glass. **2** *(fino, mineral)* crystal. **3** *(de ventana)* (window) pane.
  ■ **cristal de aumento** magnifying glass.
cristalería *nf* **1** *(fábrica)* glassworks. **2** *(tienda)* glassware shop. **3** *(vasos, copas)* glassware.
cristalino,-a *adj* transparent, clear.
  ► *nm* **cristalino** crystalline lens.
cristiandad *nf* Christendom.
cristianismo *nm* Christianity.
cristiano,-a *adj* - *nm,f* Christian.
Cristo *nm* Christ.
criterio *nm* **1** *(norma)* criterion. **2** *(juicio)* judgement. **3** *(opinión)* opinion.
crítica *nf* **1** *(juicio, censura)* criticism. **2** *(reseña)* review: **escribir una crítica**, to write a review. **3** *(conjunto de críticos)* critics *pl*.
criticar *vt* *(actuación, postura)* to criticize.
  ► *vi (murmurar)* to gossip.
crítico,-a *adj* critical.
  ► *nm,f* critic.
criticón,-ona *adj fam* faultfinding.
  ► *nm,f fam* faultfinder.
croar *vi* to croak.
croata *adj* Croatian, Croat.
  ► *nmf (persona)* Croat, Croatian.
  ► *nm (idioma)* Croat, Croatian.
croissant *nm* croissant.
crol *nm* crawl.
cromo *nm* **1** *(metal)* chromium. **2** *(estampa)* picture card.
  ● **ir hecho,-a un cromo** *fam* to look a real sight.
cromosoma *nm* chromosome.
crónica *nf* **1** *(texto histórico)* chronicle. **2** *(en periódico)* article.
crónico,-a *adj* chronic.
cronológico,-a *adj* chronological.
cronometrar *vt* to time.
cronómetro *nm* stopwatch.
croqueta *nf* croquette.
croquis *nm* sketch.

cuadrícula *nf* grid.

cuadriculado,-a *adj* squared: *papel cuadriculado*, squared paper.

cuadricular *vt* to divide into squares.

cuadrilátero *nm* ring.

cuadrilla *nf* **1** *(de trabajadores)* team. **2** *(de bandidos)* gang.

cuadro *nm* **1** *(pintura)* painting. **2** *(cuadrado)* square. **3** *(descripción)* description. **4** *(escena, paisaje)* sketch. **5** *(diagrama)* chart. **6** *(bancal)* bed, patch.

● **a cuadros 1** *(estampado)* checkered. **2** *(camisa)* checked, check.

■ **cuadro de mandos** control panel.

■ **cuadro facultativo** medical staff.

■ **cuadro sinóptico** diagram.

cuadrúpedo,-a *adj* quadruped.

▶ *nm* **cuadrúpedo** quadruped.

cuádruple *adj* quadruple, fourfold.

cuajar *vt* **1** *(leche)* to curdle; *(yogur, flan)* to set [*pt & pp* **set**]; *(sangre)* to clot. **2** *(adornar)* to fill with.

▶ *vi* – *vpr* **cuajarse 1** *(leche)* to curdle; *(yogur, flan)* to set [*pt & pp* **set**]; *(sangre)* to clot. **2** *(nieve)* to settle. **3** *(lograrse)* to be a success: *la cosa no cuajó*, it didn't come off.

cual *pron (precedido de artículo - persona)* who, whom; *(- cosa)* which: *los trabajadores, los cuales estaban en huelga ...*, the workers, who were on strike ...; *la gente a la cual preguntamos dijo que ...*, the people whom we asked said that ...; *ésta es la revista para la cual trabajo*, this is the magazine which I work for; *la ciudad en la cual nací*, the city I was born in.

● **cada cual** everyone, everybody.

● **con lo cual** with the result that.

● **lo cual** which.

cuál *pron* which one, what: *¿cuál es el más alto?*, which one is the tallest?; *no sé cuáles son tus maletas*, I don't know which suitcases are yours.

cualidad *nf* quality.

cualificado,-a *adj* qualified, skilled.

cualquier *adj* → cualquiera.

cualquiera *adj* any: *una dificultad cualquiera*, any difficulty; *cualquier cuchillo sirve,* any knife will do.

▶ *pron* **1** *(persona indeterminada)* anybody, anyone; *(cosa indeterminada)* any, any one: *cualquiera te lo puede decir*, any-

body can tell you; *coge cualquiera de ellos*, take any of them. **2** *(nadie)* nobody: *¡cualquiera lo coge!*, nobody would take it!

▶ *nmf* nobody: *ser un cualquiera*, to be a nobody.

● **cualquier cosa** anything.

● **cualquier día de éstos** one of these days.

● **cualquier otro** anyone else.

● **cualquiera que** whatever, whichever.

● **en cualquier sitio** anywhere.

cuando *adv* when: *fue entonces cuando se lo dije*, that was when I told her.

▶ *conj* **1** *(temporal)* when: *cuando era pequeño*, when I was little; *cuando deje de llover*, when it stops raining. **2** *(condicional)* if: *cuando ella lo dice...*, if she says so....

● **aun cuando** even though.

● **de (vez en) cuando** now and then.

cuándo *adv* when: *¿cuándo vendrás a verme?*, when will you come to see me?

cuantía *nf* amount.

cuantioso,-a *adj* large.

cuanto *nm* quantum.

cuanto,-a *adj (singular)* as much as; *(plural)* as many as: *puedes beber cuanta agua quieras*, you can drink as much water as you want; *coge cuantos libros desees*, take as many books as you want.

▶ *pron (singular)* everything, all; *(plural)* all who, everybody who: *vendió cuanto tenía*, he sold everything he had; *gasta cuanto gana*, she spends every penny she earns; *cuantos entraron se asustaron*, everybody who came in was frightened.

▶ *adv* **cuanto**: *cuanto antes*, as soon as possible; *cuanto más ..., más ...*, the more ..., the more; *cuanto menos ..., menos ...*, the less ..., the less ...; *en cuanto*, as soon as; *en cuanto a*, as far as; *por cuanto*, insofar as.

● **unos,-as cuantos,-as** some, a few.

cuánto,-a *adj* **1** *(interrogativo - singular)* how much; *(- plural)* how many: *¿cuánto dinero cuesta?*, how much money does it cost?; *¿cuántos coches hay?*, how many cars are there? **2** *(exclamativo)* what a lot of: *¡cuánta gente!*, what a lot of people!

▶ *pron (singular)* how much; *(plural)* how many: *¿cuánto pesas?*, how much do

you weigh?; **¿cuántos erais?**, how many
of you were there?
▶ *adv* how, how much: **dime cuánto me
has echado de menos**, tell me how you
have missed me; **¡cuánto me alegro!**,
I'm so glad!

cuarenta *num* forty.
● **cantarle las cuarenta a** ALGN to give
SB a piece of one's mind.

cuarentena *nf* **1** *(de edad)* forty. **2** *(aislamiento)* quarantine.

cuaresma *nf* Lent.

cuartel *nm* barracks.
● **no dar cuartel** to show no mercy [*pt*
showed; *pp* **shown**].
■ **cuartel general** headquarters *inv*.

cuartilla *nf* sheet of paper.

cuarto,-a *num* fourth.
▶ *nm* **cuarto 1** *(parte)* quarter: **un cuarto
de hora**, a quarter of an hour. **2** *(habitación)* room.
▶ *nm pl* **cuartos** *fam (dinero)* money.
■ **cuarto creciente** first quarter.
■ **cuarto menguante** last quarter.
■ **cuarto de aseo** bathroom.
■ **cuarto de baño** bathroom.
■ **cuarto de estar** living room.
■ **cuartos de final** quarter finals.

cuarzo *nm* quartz.

cuatro *num* four; *(en fechas)* fourth.
● **decir cuatro cosas a** ALGN to say a
few things to SB.
■ **cuatro por cuatro** four-wheel drive.

cuatrocientos,-as *num* four hundred.

cuba *nf* cask, barrel.
● **estar como una cuba** *fam* to be blind
drunk.

Cuba *nf* Cuba.

cubalibre *nm (de ron)* rum and coke; *(de
ginebra)* gin and coke.

cubano,-a *adj - nm,f* Cuban.

cubertería *nf* cutlery.

cúbico,-a *adj* cubic.

cubierta *nf* **1** *(tapa)* covering. **2** *(de libro)*
jacket. **3** *(techo)* roof. **4** *(de neumático)* GB
tyre; US tire. **5** *(de barco)* deck.

cubierto,-a *adj* **1** covered. **2** *(cielo)* overcast.
▶ *nm* **cubierto 1** *(techumbre)* cover. **2** *(en
la mesa)* place setting. **3** *(menú)* set menu.
▶ *nm pl* **cubiertos** *(para comer)* cutlery.
● **estar a cubierto** to be under cover.
● **ponerse a cubierto** to take cover.

cubilete *nm* **1** *(de dados)* dice cup. **2** *(molde)* mould.

cubito *nm* **cubito (de hielo)** ice cube.

cubo¹ *nm* **1** *(recipiente)* bucket. **2** *(contenido)* bucketful. **3** *(de rueda)* hub.
■ **cubo de la basura** GB dustbin; US garbage can.

cubo² *nm (figura)* cube.

cubrir *vt* **1** *(tapar)* to cover. **2** *(esconder)* to
hide [*pt* **hid**; *pp* **hidden**]. **3** *(poner techo a)* to
put a roof on. **4** *(puesto, vacante)* to fill.
▶ *vpr* **cubrirse 1** *(abrigarse)* to cover oneself. **2** *(protegerse)* to protect oneself. **3**
(cielo) to become overcast.

cucaracha *nf* cockroach.

cuchara *nf* spoon.

cucharada *nf* spoonful.
■ **cucharada (sopera)** tablespoonful.

cucharilla *nf* teaspoon.
■ **cucharilla de café** coffee spoon.

cucharón *nm* ladle.

cuchichear *vi* to whisper.

cuchicheo *nm* whispering.

cuchilla *nf* blade.
■ **cuchilla de afeitar** razor blade.

cuchillo *nm* knife [*pl* **-ves**].
■ **cuchillo del pan** breadknife [*pl* **-ves**].

cuchitril *nm* hovel.

cuclillas *adv* **en cuclillas** crouching,
squatting.

cuclillo *nm* cuckoo.

cuco,-a *adj* **1** *fam (bonito)* cute. **2** *fam (taimado)* shrewd.

cucurucho *nm* **1** *(de papel)* cone. **2** *(helado)* cornet, cone.

cuello *nm* **1** *(de persona, animal)* neck. **2**
(de prenda) collar. **3** *(de botella)* bottleneck.
● **estar metido,-a hasta el cuello** *fam*
to be up to one's neck in it.
■ **cuello alto** GB polo neck; US turtleneck.
■ **cuello de pico** V-neck.

cuenca *nf* basin.

cuenco *nm* bowl.

cuenta *nf* **1** *(bancaria)* account. **2** *(factura)*
bill. **3** *(operación)* calculation, sum. **4**
(cómputo) count. **5** *(de collar)* bead.
● **ajustarle las cuentas a** ALGN to give
SB a piece of one's mind.
● **caer en la cuenta de algo** to realize
STH; *(ver, oler, oír)* to notice STH.

- **darse cuenta de algo** to realize STH.
- **en resumidas cuentas** in short.
- **más de la cuenta** too much.
- **perder la cuenta** to lose [*pt & pp* **lost**] count.
- **por cuenta de** by.
- **tener en cuenta** to take into account.
- **trabajar por cuenta propia** to be self-employed.
- ■ **cuenta atrás** countdown.
- ■ **cuenta corriente** current account.

cuentagotas *nm* dropper.

cuentakilómetros *nm* speedometer.

cuentista *nmf (mentiroso)* fibber.

cuento *nm (narración corta)* short story, story, tale: *cuéntame un cuento*, tell me a story.

- **no me vengas con cuentos** don't come to me telling tales.
- **ser el cuento de la lechera** counting one's chickens before they are hatched.
- **venir a cuento** to be relevant.
- **vivir del cuento** *fam* to live by one's wits.
- ■ **cuento chino** tall story.
- ■ **cuento de hadas** fairy tale.

cuerda *nf* **1** *(soga)* rope; *(cordel)* string. **2** *(de guitarra, violín)* string. **3** *(de reloj)* spring.

- **dar cuerda a un reloj** to wind up a watch.
- ■ **cuerda floja** tightrope.
- ■ **cuerdas vocales** vocal chords.

cuerdo,-a *adj* - *nm,f* sane *(person)*.

cuerno *nm (de toro)* horn; *(de ciervo)* antler.

- **ponerle los cuernos a ALGN** *fam* to cuckold SB.
- **romperse los cuernos** *fam* to break one's back [*pt* **broke**; *pp* **broken**].

cuero *nm* **1** *(de animal)* skin, hide. **2** *(curtido)* leather.

- **en cueros** *fam* starkers.
- ■ **cuero cabelludo** scalp.

cuerpo *nm* **1** *(de persona, animal)* body: *el cuerpo humano*, the human body. **2** *(objeto)* body, object. **3** *(tronco)* trunk. **4** *(grupo)* body, corps. **5** *(cadáver)* body, corpse. **6** *(parte principal)* main part: *el cuerpo del libro*, the main body of the book.

- **a cuerpo** without a coat.
- **a cuerpo de rey** like a king.
- **de cuerpo entero** full-length.

- **en cuerpo y alma** wholeheartedly.
- **estar de cuerpo presente** to lie in state [*pt* **lay**; *pp* **lain**].
- **tomar cuerpo** to take shape.
- ■ **cuerpo de bomberos** fire brigade.
- ■ **cuerpo diplomático** diplomatic corps.
- ■ **cuerpo extraño** foreign body.

cuervo *nm* raven.

cuesta *nf* slope.

- **a cuestas** on one's back, on one's shoulders.
- **cuesta abajo** downhill.
- **cuesta arriba** uphill.
- **la cuesta de enero** the January squeeze.

cuestión *nf* **1** *(pregunta)* question. **2** *(asunto)* matter, question. **3** *(discusión)* dispute, quarrel.

- **en cuestión** in question.
- **ser cuestión de vida o muerte** to be a matter of life or death.

cuestionar *vt* to question.

cuestionario *nm* questionnaire.

cueva *nf* cave.

cuidado *nm* **1** *(atención)* care: *me lo hizo con sumo cuidado*, she did it with great care. **2** *(recelo)* worry.

- ► *interj* ¡**cuidado**! look out!, watch out!
- **al cuidado de** in the care of.
- **"Cuidado con el perro"** "Beware of the dog."
- **tener cuidado** to be careful.
- ■ **cuidados intensivos** intensive care *sing*.

cuidadoso,-a *adj* careful.

cuidar *vt-vi* to look after, take care of: *cuidó de su hermana*, he looked after his sister.

- ► *vpr* **cuidarse** to take care of oneself.

culata *nf* **1** *(de arma)* butt. **2** *(de motor)* cylinder head.

culebra *nf* snake.

culebrón *nm fam* soap opera.

culinario,-a *adj* culinary, cooking.

culo *nm* **1** *(trasero)* bottom, backside, GB bum; US butt. **2** *(de recipiente)* bottom.

- **caer de culo** *fam* to fall flat on one's bottom [*pt* **fell**; *pp* **fallen**].
- **ir de culo** *fam* to be rushed off one's feet.

- **¡vete a tomar por el culo!** *vulg* fuck off!

culpa *nf* **1** *(culpabilidad)* guilt, blame. **2** *(falta)* fault: *esto es culpa mía*, it's my fault.

- **echar la culpa a** to blame.
- **por culpa de algo** because of STH.
- **tener la culpa de** to be to blame for.

culpabilidad *nf* guilt, culpabilility.

culpable *adj* guilty.
▶ *nmf* offender, culprit.

culpar *vt* to blame.
▶ *vpr* **culparse** to blame oneself.

cultivar *vt* **1** *(terreno)* to cultivate, farm. **2** *(plantas)* to grow [*pt* **grew**; *pp* **grown**].

cultivo *nm* **1** *(de terreno)* cultivation, farming. **2** *(en laboratorio)* culture.

culto,-a *adj* **1** *(con cultura)* cultured, educated. **2** *(estilo)* refined. **3** *(palabra)* learned.
▶ *nm* **culto** worship.

- **rendir culto a** to pay homage to, worship.

cultura *nf* culture.

cultural *adj* cultural.

cumbre *nf* **1** *(de montaña)* summit, top. **2** *(culminación)* pinnacle, height. **3** *(reunión)* summit.

cumpleaños *nm* birthday.

cumplido,-a *adj* **1** *(terminado)* completed. **2** *(abundante)* large, ample. **3** *(educado)* polite.
▶ *nm* **cumplido** compliment.

cumplidor,-ra *adj* dependable.

cumplir *vt* **1** *(orden)* to carry out. **2** *(compromiso, obligación)* to fulfil. **3** *(promesa)* to keep. **4** *(condena)* to serve. **5** *(años)*: *mañana cumplo veinte años*, I'll be twenty tomorrow.
▶ *vi* to do one's duty.
▶ *vpr* **cumplirse** *(realizarse)* to be fulfilled.

cuna *nf* **1** *(de bebé)* GB cot; US crib, cradle. **2** *(linaje)* birth, lineage. **3** *(origen)* cradle, beginning.

cundir *vi* **1** *(extenderse)* to spread [*pt* & *pp* **spread**]: *cundió el pánico*, panic spread. **2** *(dar de sí)*: *el arroz cunde mucho*, rice goes a long way; *hoy no me ha cundido el día*, I didn't get much done today.

cuneta *nf* ditch.

cuña *nf* wedge.

cuñado,-a *nm,f (hombre)* brother-in-law; *(mujer)* sister-in-law.

cuota *nf* **1** *(pago)* membership fee, dues *pl*. **2** *(porción)* quota, share.

cupón *nm* **1** *(vale)* coupon. **2** *(de lotería)* ticket.

cúpula *nf* **1** *(pago)* cupola, dome. **2** *(dirigentes)* leadership.

cura *nm (párroco)* priest.
▶ *nf (curación)* cure.

curación *nf* cure, healing.

curandero,-a *nm,f* quack.

curar *vt* **1** *(sanar)* to cure: *es posible curar muchos tipos de cáncer*, many types of cancer can be cured. **2** *(herida)* to dress; *(enfermedad)* to treat. **3** *(carne, pescado)* to cure; *(piel)* to tan; *(madera)* to season.
▶ *vpr* **curarse 1** *(recuperarse)* to recover, get well. **2** *(herida)* to heal up.

curiosear *vi* to have a look.

curiosidad *nf* curiosity.

- **tener curiosidad por algo** to be curious about STH.

curioso,-a *adj* **1** *(interesado)* curious, inquisitive. **2** *(indiscreto)* nosy. **3** *(extraño)* strange: *¡qué curioso*, how strange!
▶ *nm,f (cotilla)* busybody.

currante *nmf arg* worker.

currar *vi arg* to work, grind [*pt* & *pp* **ground**].

currículum *nm* curriculum *(vitae)*.

curro *nm arg* work, job.

cursar *vt* **1** *(estudiar)* to study. **2** *(enviar)* to send [*pt* & *pp* **sent**], dispatch. **3** *(tramitar)* to submit.

cursi *adj* affected.

cursillo *nm* short course.

curso *nm* **1** course: *un curso de informática*, a computer course. **2** year: *¿en qué curso estás?*, what year are you in? **3** *(dirección, de río)* course.

- **estar en curso** to be under way.
- **dejar que las cosas sigan su curso** to let things take their course [*pt* & *pp* **let**].
- **en curso** current: *el año en curso*, the current year.
- **curso académico** academic year, school year.
- **curso intensivo** intensive course.

cursor *nm* cursor.

curtir *vt* **1** *(piel)* to tan. **2** *(acostumbrar)* to harden.

▶ *vpr* **curtirse 1** *(por el sol)* to get tanned. **2** *(acostumbrarse)* to become hardened.
curva *nf* **1** curve. **2** *(de carretera)* bend.
curvo,-a *adj* curved, bent.
cúspide *nf* **1** *(cumbre)* summit. **2** *(apogeo)* pinnacle, height.

custodiar *vt* to keep, take care of.
cutis *nm* skin, complexion.
cuyo,-a *pron* whose, of which.
● **en cuyo caso** in which case.

D

dado *nm* die.

dado,-a *adj* given.

● **dadas las circunstancias** in view of the circumstances.

● **dado que** given that.

daltonismo *nm* colour blindness.

dama *nf* **1** *(señora)* lady. **2** *(en ajedrez)* queen; *(en damas)* king.

▶ *nf pl* **damas** GB draughts; US checkers.

■ **dama de honor** bridesmaid.

damnificado,-a *nm,f* victim.

danés,-esa *adj* Danish.

▶ *nm,f (persona)* Dane.

▶ *nm* **danés** *(idioma)* Danish.

danza *nf* dance.

danzar *vt-vi* to dance.

dañar *vt (cosa)* to damage; *(persona)* to harm.

▶ *vpr* **dañarse 1** *(cosa)* to get damaged; *(persona)* to get hurt. **2** *(pudrirse)* to go bad.

dañino,-a *adj* harmful.

daño *nm* **1** *(en cosas)* damage. **2** *(en personas)* harm.

● **hacer daño 1** (doler) to hurt [*pt & pp* **hurt**]: *me estás haciendo daño*, you're hurting me. **2** *(perjudicar)* to do harm: *un poco de trabajo no hace daño*, a bit of work doesn't do any harm.

● **hacerse daño** to hurt oneself [*pt & pp* **hurt**].

■ **daños y perjuicios** damages.

dar *vt* **1** *(gen)* to give. **2** *(luz, gas)* to turn on. **3** *(fruto, flores)* to bear [*pt* **bore**; *pp* **borne**]. **4** *(las horas)* to strike [*pt & pp* **struck**]. **5** *(película)* to show [*pt* **showed**; *pp* **shown**]; *(obra de teatro)* to perform. **6** *(golpear)* to hit [*pt & pp* **hit**]. **7** *(fiesta)* to have.

▶ *vi* **1** *(caer)* to fall [*pt* **fell**; *pp* **fallen**]. **2** *(mirar a)* to look out: *mi cuarto da al jardín*, my room looks out onto the garden.

▶ *vpr* **darse 1** *(entregarse)* to devote oneself. **2** *(chocar)* to crash.

● **da lo mismo** it's all the same.

● **dar algo por bueno** to accept STH.

● **dar con** to find [*pt & pp* **found**].

● **dar de comer** to feed [*pt & pp* **fed**].

● **dar de sí** to give, stretch.

● **dar por** to consider, assume: *lo daban por muerto*, they assumed he was dead; *dalo por hecho*, consider it done.

● **dar un paseo** to take a walk.

● **darse a la bebida** to take to drink.

● **darse por vencido,-a** to give up.

dardo *nm* dart.

datar *vt - vi* to date.

dátil *nm* date.

dato *nm* piece of information.

▶ *nm pl* **datos** *(información)* information *sing*; *(informáticos)* data.

■ **datos personales** personal details.

de *prep* **1** *(posesión)* 's, s': *el coche de María*, María's car; *el libro del chico*, the boy's book; *los libros de los chicos*, the boys' books. **2** of: *una foto de mi madre*, a photo of my mother; *la ciudad de Roma*, the city of Rome; *el mes de noviembre*, the month of November; *la puerta del colegio*, the school gate; *los árboles del jardín*, the trees in the garden. **3** *(materia, tema)*: *una profesora de inglés*, an English teacher; *un curso de alemán*, a German course; *una novela de aventuras*, an adventure story; *una película de terror*, a horror film. **4** *(composición)*: *un balón de cuero*, a leather ball; **muebles de madera**, wooden furniture; **un vaso de plástico**, a plastic cup. **5** (contenido) of: **una botella de agua**, a bottle of water; **un paquete de arroz**, a packet of rice. **6** (origen, procedencia) from: **es de Navarra**, he's from Navarre; **esta carretera va de Soria a Burgos**, this road goes from Soria to Burgos. **7** (descripción) with, in: **la chica del pelo largo**, the girl with long hair; **el hombre de negro**, the man in black; **una mujer de treinta años**, a woman of thirty. **8** (agente) by: **un libro de Dickens**, a book by Dickens. **9** (expresiones de tiempo): **es la una de la tarde**, it's one o'clock in the afternoon; **el tren de las diez**, the ten o'clock train; **abren de nueve a siete**, they open from nine until seven; **nunca viajamos de noche**, we never travel at night; **de niño era rubio**, I was blond when I was a child; **de día**, by day; **de noche**, at night. **10 de + inf** if: **de seguir así, acabarás en la cárcel**, if you continue like this, you'll end up in prison.

debajo adv underneath, below.

● **debajo de** under.

debate nm debate.

debatir vt (moción) to debate; (tema) to discuss.

▶ vpr **debatirse** to struggle.

deber nm (obligación) duty.

▶ vt (dinero) to owe.

▶ aux **1 deber + inf** (obligación) must, to have to; (recomendación) should: **debo irme**, I must go; **deberías ir al médico**, you should see the doctor. **2 deber de** (conjetura) must: **deben de ser las seis**, it must be six o'clock; **no deben de haber llegado**, they can't have arrived.

▶ vpr **deberse a** to be caused by: **muchos accidentes se deben a la imprudencia**, many accidents are caused by carelessness; **¿a qué se debe la caída del cabello?**, what causes hair loss?

▶ nm pl **deberes** (de escuela) homework sing.

debidamente adv duly.

debido,-a adj **1** (dinero) owed. **2** (apropiado) due, proper: **con el debido respeto**, with all due respect.

● **como es debido** properly.

● **debido,-a a** due to, owing to.

débil adj **1** (persona) weak. **2** (ruido) faint. **3** (luz) dim.

debilidad nf weakness.

● **tener debilidad por** to have a weakness for.

debilitar vt to weaken.

▶ vpr **debilitar(se)** to weaken.

debutar vi to make one's debut.

década nf decade.

decadencia nf decadence.

● **caer en decadencia** to fall into decline [pt fell; pp fallen].

decaer vi to decline.

decaído,-a adj **1** (débil) weak. **2** (triste) sad.

decapitar vt (en ejecución) to behead; (en accidente) to decapitate.

decena nf group of ten: **dos decenas de personas**, about twenty people; **decenas de miles**, tens of thousands.

decenio nm decade.

decente adj **1** (decoroso) decent. **2** (honesto) honest. **3** (limpio) tidy.

decepción nf disappointment.

decepcionante adj disappointing.

decepcionar vt to disappoint.

decidido,-a adj (audaz) determined.

decidir vt - vi to decide.

▶ vt (convencer) to persuade.

▶ vpr **decidirse** to decide, make up one's mind.

decilitro nm GB decilitre; US deciliter.

décima nf tenth.

decimal adj - nm decimal.

decímetro nm GB decimetre; US decimeter.

décimo,-a num tenth.

▶ nm **décimo** lottery ticket.

decimoctavo,-a num eighteenth.

decimocuarto,-a num fourteenth.

decimonoveno,-a num nineteenth.

decimoquinto,-a num fifteenth.

decimoséptimo,-a num seventeenth.

decimosexto,-a num sixteenth.

decimotercero,-a num thirteenth.

decir vt **1** (gen) to say [pt & pp said]: **¿qué dijo?**, what did he say?; **dijo que vendría mañana**, he said he'd come tomorrow. **2** (a alguien) to tell [pt & pp told]: **dime lo que piensas**, tell me what you think; **no se lo digas a nadie**, don't tell anybody. **3** (órdenes) to tell [pt & pp told]: **dijo que nos fuéramos**, she told us to leave; **le dijeron que no fumara**, they told him not to smoke.

▶ *vpr* **decirse** to say to oneself [*pt & pp* **said**].

● **como quien dice** so to speak.

● **como si dijéramos** so to speak.

● **decir para sí** to say to oneself [*pt & pp* **said**].

● **es decir** that is to say.

● **querer decir** to mean [*pt & pp* **meant**].

● **se dice ...** they say ..., it is said ....

decisión *nf* **1** (*resolución*) decision. **2** (*firmeza*) determination.

decisivo,-a *adj* decisive.

declaración *nf* **1** (*afirmación pública*) statement. **2** (*de guerra, amor*) declaration. **3** (*escrito formal*) statement.

● **prestar declaración** (en juicio) to give evidence.

■ **declaración de la renta** income tax return.

declarar *vt* **1** (*gen*) to declare: *¿no tiene nada que declarar?*, do you have anything to declare? **2** (*considerar*) to find [*pt & pp* **found**]: *lo declararon inocente*, he was found not guilty.

▶ *vi* **1** (*afirmar*) to state. **2** (*dar testimonio*) to testify.

▶ *vpr* **declararse 1** (*considerarse*) to declare oneself. **2** (*fuego, guerra*) to start, break out [*pt* **broke**; *pp* **broken**].

● **declararse a** ALGN (confesar su amor) to declare one's love to SB.

declinar *vi* (*salud, negocio, ventas*) to decline.

▶ *vt* (*rechazar*) to decline.

decoración *nf* **1** (*de casa, pastel*) decoration. **2** (*de teatro*) scenery, set.

decorado *nm* scenery, set.

decorador,-ra *nm,f* decorator.

decorar *vt* to decorate.

decorativo,-a *adj* decorative.

decretar *vt* to decree.

decreto *nm* decree.

dedal *nm* thimble.

dedicar *vt* to dedicate.

▶ *vpr* **dedicarse** to devote oneself: *se dedicó a los pobres*, he devoted himself to the poor; *¿a qué te dedicas?*, what do you do?

dedicatoria *nf* dedication.

dedillo *nm* .

● **conocer un lugar al dedillo** to know a place like the back of one's hand [*pt* **knew**; *pp* **known**].

● **saber algo al dedillo** to know STH inside out.

dedo *nm* (*de la mano*) finger; (*del pie*) toe.

● **cualquiera con dos dedos de frente sabe que...** anyone with half a brain knows that....

● **hacer dedo** to hitchhike.

■ **dedo anular** ring finger.

■ **dedo del corazón** middle finger.

■ **dedo gordo** thumb.

■ **dedo índice** forefinger, index finger.

■ **dedo meñique** little finger.

deducción *nf* deduction.

deducir *vt* **1** (*inferir*) to deduce. **2** (*descontar*) to deduct.

defecto *nm* defect, fault.

defectuoso,-a *adj* defective, faulty.

defender *vt* **1** (*país, acusado, intereses*) to defend. **2** (*opinión*) to maintain.

▶ *vpr* **defenderse** (*arreglárselas*) to manage: *en francés me defiendo*, I can get by in French.

defensa *nf* GB defence; US defense.

▶ *nmf* (*jugador*) defender.

▶ *nf pl* **defensas** (*del organismo*) defences.

● **en defensa propia** in self-defence.

defensivo,-a *adj* defensive.

● **estar a la defensiva** to be on the defensive.

defensor,-ra *adj* defending.

▶ *nm,f* defender.

■ **defensor del pueblo** ombudsman.

deferencia *nf* deference.

deficiencia *nf* deficiency.

deficiente *adj* deficient, inadequate: *deficiente en calcio*, deficient in calcium.

■ **deficiente mental** person with a mental handicap: *los deficientes mentales*, the mentally handicapped.

déficit *nm* **1** (*comercial, presupuestario*) deficit. **2** (*falta*) shortage.

definición *nf* definition.

definir *vt* to define.

▶ *vpr* **definirse** to state one's position.

definitivo,-a *adj* definitive, final.

deformar *vt* to deform.

▶ *vpr* **deformarse** to be deformed.

deforme *adj* deformed, misshapen.

defraudar *vt* **1** (*decepcionar*) to disappoint. **2** (*estafar*) to defraud; (*robar*) to steal.

degenerar *vi* to degenerate.

degollar *vt* to slit the throat of: *los piratas les degollaron*, the pirates slit their throats.

dehesa *nf* pasture.

dejado,-a *adj* **1** *(descuidado)* negligent. **2** *(perezoso)* lazy.

dejar *vt* **1** *(gen)* to leave [*pt & pp* **left**]. **2** *(permitir)* to let [*pt & pp* **let**]: *déjame entrar*, let me in. **3** *(prestar)* to lend [*pt & pp* **lent**]: *¿me dejas tu bici?*, will you lend me your bike?, can I borrow your bike?
▶ *aux* **1 dejar de** + *inf* to stop: *deja de gritar*, stop shouting. **2 no dejar de** + *inf*: *no dejaron de bailar*, they went on dancing; *no deja de sorprender que ...*, it always surprises me how ...; *no dejes de incluir tu dirección*, don't forget to include your address.
▶ *vpr* **dejarse 1** *(abandonarse)* to let oneself go. **2** *(olvidar)* to forget [*pt* **forgot**; *pp* **forgotten**]: *no te dejes el libro*, don't forget your book; *me he dejado las llaves en casa*, I've left my keys at home. **3** *(cesar)* to stop: *déjate de llorar*, stop crying; *déjaos de tonterías*, forget that non-sense.
● **¡déjalo!** don't worry about it.
● **dejar a un lado** to leave aside [*pt & pp* **left**].
● **dejar atrás** to leave behind [*pt & pp* **left**].
● **dejar caer** to drop.
● **dejar en paz** to leave alone [*pt & pp* **left**].
● **dejar mal** to let down [*pt & pp* **let**].
● **dejar plantado,-a** to stand up [*pt & pp* **stood**].
● **dejarse llevar (por algo)** to get carried away (with STH).

delantal *nm* apron.

delante *adv (enfrente)* in front: *ve tú delante*, you go in front.
▶ *prep* **delante de** *(enfrente de)* in front of: *delante de nuestra casa*, in front of our house.
● **de delante** front: *la rueda de delante*, the front wheel.
● **hacia delante** forward.
● **por delante** ahead.

delantera *nf* **1** *(frente)* front. **2** *(en deporte)* forward line. **3** *(ventaja)* lead, advantage.
● **tomar la delantera** to take the lead, go into the lead.

delantero,-a *adj (rueda)* front; *(pata)* fore.

▶ *nm* **delantero** *(deportista)* forward.
■ **delantero centro** centre forward.

delatar *vt* **1** *(denunciar)* to inform on. **2** *(revelar)* to reveal.

delegación *nf* **1** *(personas)* delegation. **2** *(sucursal)* branch.

delegado,-a *adj* delegated.
▶ *nm,f* delegate.

delegar *vt* to delegate.

deletrear *vt* to spell [*pt & pp* **spelt**].

delfín[1] *nm (animal)* dolphin.

delfín[2] *nm (heredero)* dauphin.

delgadez *nf* thinness.

delgado,-a *adj* thin.

deliberado,-a *adj* deliberate, intentional.

deliberar *vt (decidir)* to deliberate.
▶ *vi* to deliberate.

delicadeza *nf* **1** *(cuidado)* care; *(suavidad)* gentleness. **2** *(finura)* delicacy. **3** *(tacto)* tact.

delicado,-a *adj* **1** *(en general)* delicate. **2** *(persona – discreto)* tactful; *(- sensible)* sensitive; *(- tiquismiquis)* hard to please.

delicia *nf* delight.

delicioso,-a *adj* delicious.

delimitar *vt* to mark off.

delincuencia *nf* crime.

delincuente *adj - nmf* criminal.

delineante *nmf (hombre)* draughtsman [*pl* **-men**]; *(mujer)* draughtswoman [*pl* **-women**].

delirar *vi* **1** *(por fiebre)* to be delirious. **2** *(decir tonterías)* to talk nonsense.

delito *nm* offence, crime.

delta *nm* delta.

demanda *nf* **1** *(solicitud)* request. **2** *(de producto)* demand. **3** *(legal)* lawsuit.
● **presentar una demanda contra** ALGN to sue SB.

demandar *vt* **1** JUR to sue. **2** *(pedir)* to demand.

demás *adj* other: *los demás libros*, the other books.
▶ *pron* the others, the rest: *yo me fui, los demás se quedaron*, I left, the rest stayed.
● **lo demás** the rest.
● **por lo demás** otherwise.
● **y demás** and so on.

demasiado,-a *adj (singular)* too much; *(plural)* too many: *demasiado ruido*, too much noise; *demasiados coches*, too many cars.

► *adv* **demasiado** *(después de verbo)* too much; *(delante de adjetivo)* too: ***comes demasiado***, you eat too much; ***es demasiado caro***, it's too expensive.

demente *adj* mad, insane.

► *nmf* lunatic.

democracia *nf* democracy.

demócrata *adj* democratic.

► *nmf* democrat.

democrático,-a *adj* democratic.

demoler *vt* to demolish.

demonio *nm* demon, devil.

● **de mil demonios** *fam* horrific.

● **oler a demonios** to smell awful.

● **¡qué demonios!** *fam* what the devil!, what the hell!

● **ser un demonio** to be a devil.

demora *nf* delay.

demorar *vt* to delay.

► *vpr* **demorarse** to be delayed.

demostración *nf* **1** *(muestra)* demonstration. **2** *(ostentación)* show. **3** *(prueba)* proof.

demostrar *vt* **1** *(mostrar)* to demonstrate. **2** *(ostentar)* to show [*pt* **showed**; *pp* **shown**]. **3** *(probar)* to prove.

demostrativo,-a *adj* demonstrative.

► *nm* **demostrativo** demonstrative.

denegar *vt* to refuse.

denominación *nf* denomination.

denominador *nm* denominator.

■ **denominador común** common denominator.

denominar *vt* to denominate, name.

densidad *nf* density.

denso,-a *adj* dense.

dentadura *nf* teeth *pl*.

■ **dentadura postiza** false teeth.

dental *adj* dental.

dentellada *nf* **1** *(mordisco)* bite. **2** *(señal)* toothmark.

dentera.

● **dar dentera a** ALGN to set SB's teeth on edge [*pt & pp* **set**].

dentífrico *nm* toothpaste.

dentista *nmf* dentist.

dentro *adv* *(gen)* inside; *(de edificio)* indoors.

► *prep* **dentro de** in: *lo tengo dentro del bolso*, I've got it in my bag; *dentro de dos días*, in two days' time.

● **dentro de lo posible** as far as possible.

● **dentro de lo que cabe** under the circumstances.

● **dentro de poco** shortly.

● **por dentro** inside.

denuncia *nf* report, complaint.

● **presentar una denuncia** to lodge a complaint.

denunciar *vt* *(situación)* to condemn; *(delito)* to report.

departamento *nm* **1** *(sección)* department. **2** *(de tren)* compartment.

dependencia *nf* **1** *(de persona, drogas)* dependence, dependency. **2** *(en edificio)* outbuilding.

depender *vi* to depend: *depende de ti*, it depends on you.

dependiente,-a *nm,f* sales assistant.

depilar *vt* *(con cera)* to wax; *(con pinzas)* to pluck.

deportar *vt* to deport.

deporte *nm* sport.

● **por deporte** as a hobby.

■ **deporte acuático** water sport.

■ **deporte de aventura** adventure sport.

■ **deporte de riesgo** high-risk sport.

deportista *nmf* *(hombre)* sportsman [*pl* -**men**]; *(mujer)* sportswoman [*pl* -**women**].

deportividad *nf* sportsmanship.

deportivo,-a *adj* **1** *(centro, club)* sports. **2** *(conducta)* sporting. **3** *(imparcial)* sportsmanlike.

depositar *vt* to deposit.

► *vpr* **depositarse** *(poso)* to settle.

depósito *nm* **1** *(en un banco)* deposit. **2** *(poso)* deposit. **3** *(almacén)* store. **4** *(receptáculo)* tank.

■ **depósito de cadáveres** mortuary.

■ **depósito de gasolina** petrol tank.

depre *nf fam* depression.

● **estar depre** to be feeling down.

depresión *nf* depression.

■ **depresión nerviosa** nervous depression.

deprimente *adj* depressing.

deprimido,-a *adj* depressed.

deprimir *vt* to depress.

► *vpr* **deprimirse** to get depressed.

deprisa *adv* quickly.

● **vivir deprisa** to live fast.

■ **¡deprisa!** quick!

derecha *nf* **1** *(dirección)* right. **2** *(mano)* right hand; *(pierna)* right leg. **3** POL right wing.

- **a la derecha** to the right: *girar a la derecha*, to turn right.
- **de derechas** right-wing.

derecho,-a *adj* **1** *(diestro)* right. **2** *(recto)* straight: *¡ponte derecho!*, stand up straight! **3** *(de pie)* standing.
▶ *nm* **derecho 1** *(poder, oportunidad)* right. **2** *(ley)* law.
▶ *nm pl* **derechos** rigths.
- **al derecho** the right way.
- **¡no hay derecho!** it's not fair!
- **derecho civil** civil law.
- **derechos de autor** copyright.
- **derechos humanos** human rights.

deriva *nf* drift.
- **ir a la deriva** to be adrift.

derivado,-a *adj* derived.
▶ *nm* **derivado** derivative.

derivar *vt* to direct.
▶ *vi-vpr* **derivar(se) 1** *(proceder)* to derive. **2** *(ir a la deriva)* to drift.

derramar *vt* **1** *(leche, vino)* to spill [*pt & pp* **spilt**]. **2** *(sangre, lágrimas)* to shed [*pt & pp* **shed**].
▶ *vpr* **derramarse** to spill [*pt & pp* **spilt**].

derrapar *vi* to skid.

derretir *vt-vpr* **derretirse** to melt.

derribar *vt* **1** *(edificio)* to demolish. **2** *(persona)* to knock down. **3** *(avión)* to shoot down [*pt & pp* **shot**]. **4** *(gobierno)* to bring down [*pt & pp* **brought**].

derribo *nm* demolition.
- **materiales de derribo** debris.

derrochar *vt* **1** *(dinero)* to squander. **2** *(simpatía, talento)* to be full of.

derroche *nm* **1** *(de dinero)* waste. **2** *(de simpatía, talento)* display.

derrota¹ *nf* *(de rival, enemigo)* defeat.

derrota² *nf* *(de barco)* route.

derrotar *vt* to defeat.

derruir *vt* to demolish.

derrumbamiento *nm* *(de edificio, techo)* collapse.
- **derrumbamiento de tierras** landslide.

derrumbar *vt* to demolish.
▶ *vpr* **derrumbarse** *(edificio, techo)* to collapse.

desabrochar *vt* to undo [*pt* **undid**; *pp* **undone**], unfasten.
▶ *vpr* **desabrochar(se)** to come undone.

desacierto *nm* mistake.

desaconsejar *vt* to advise against.

desacuerdo *nm* disagreement.

desafiar *vt* to defy.

desafinar *vi* to be out of tune.
▶ *vpr* **desafinarse** to get out of tune.

desafío *nm* **1** *(reto)* challenge. **2** *(duelo)* duel.

desafortunado,-a *adj* unfortunate.

desagradable *adj* unpleasant.

desagradar *vt*: *me desagrada la situación*, I don't like the situation; *no me desagrada el olor*, I don't dislike the smell.

desagradecido,-a *adj* ungrateful.

desagrado *nm* displeasure, discontent.
- **con desagrado** reluctantly.

desagüe *nm* drain.

desahogarse *vpr* to off steam [*pt & pp* **let**]: *¡desahógate!*, let yourself go!

desahogo *nm* **1** *(alivio)* relief. **2** *(comodidad)* comfort.

desahuciar *vt* **1** *(inquilino)* to evict. **2** *(paciente)* to pronounce incurable: *los médicos lo desahuciaron*, the doctors pronounced him incurable.

desalentador,-ra *adj* discouraging.

desalentar *vt* to discourage.
▶ *vpr* **desalentarse** to lose heart [*pt & pp* **lost**].

desaliento *nm* discouragement.

desaliñado,-a *adj* scruffy.

desalojar *vt* **1** *(persona)* to remove. **2** *(inquilino)* to evict. **3** *(ciudad)* to evacuate. **4** *(edificio)* to clear.

desamparado,-a *adj* **1** *(sin defensas)* helpless. **2** *(abandonado)* abandoned.

desandar *vt* to go back over.
- **desandar lo andado** to retrace one's steps.

desangrarse *vpr* to bleed to death [*pt & pp* **bled**].

desanimado,-a *adj* despondent.
- **estar desanimado** to be in low spirits.

desanimar *vt* to dishearten.
▶ *vpr* **desanimarse** to be discouraged, be disheartened.

desánimo *nm* despondency.

desapacible *adj* unpleasant.

desaparecer *vi* to disappear, vanish.

desaparición *nf* disappearance.

desapercibido,-a *adj* unprepared.

● **pasar desapercibido** to go unnoticed.

desaprovechar *vt* to waste.

desarmar *vt* **1** *(quitar armas)* to disarm. **2** *(desmontar)* to dismantle.

desarme *nm* disarmament.

■ **desarme nuclear** nuclear disarmament.

desarrollar *vt* **1** *(gen)* to develop. **2** *(realizar)* to carry out.

▶ *vpr* **desarrollarse 1** *(crecer)* to develop. **2** *(ocurrir)* to take place.

desarrollo *nm* development.

● **en vías de desarrollo** developing.

desarticular *vt* **1** *(organización)* to dismantle. **2** *(huesos)* to dislocate.

desastre *nm* disaster.

desastroso,-a *adj* disastrous.

desatar *vt* **1** *(nudo)* to untie. **2** *(perro)* to set loose [*pt & pp* **set**]. **3** *(conflicto, debate)* to spark.

▶ *vpr* **desatarse 1** *(soltarse)* to come untied, come undone. **2** *(desmadrarse)* to lose all restraint [*pt & pp* **lost**]. **3** *(tormenta)* to break [*pt* **broke**; *pp* **broken**].

desatascar *vt* to unblock.

desatornillar *vt* to unscrew.

desatrancar *vt* **1** *(tubería)* to unblock. **2** *(puerta)* to force open.

desayunar *vt* to have for breakfast: *desayuné cereales*, I had cereals for breakfast.

▶ *vi* to have breakfast.

desayuno *nm* breakfast.

desbarajuste *nm* disarray.

desbaratar *vt* **1** *(plan)* to ruin. **2** *(fortuna)* to squander.

desbordamiento *nm* overflowing.

desbordante *adj* boundless.

desbordar *vt* *(sobrepasar)* to surpass.

▶ *vpr* **desbordarse 1** *(río)* to overflow. **2** *(persona)* to lose one's self-control [*pt & pp* **lost**].

descabellado,-a *adj* wild, crazy.

descafeinado,-a *adj* **1** *(café)* decaffeinated. **2** *fam (sin fuerza)* GB anaemic; US anemic.

descalificar *vt* **1** *(de un concurso)* to disqualify. **2** *(desprestigiar)* to dismiss.

descalzar *vt* to take off SB's shoes.

▶ *vpr* **descalzarse** to take off one's shoes.

descalzo,-a *adj* barefoot.

descampado,-a *adj* open.

▶ *nm* **descampado** area of open ground.

descansar *vi* **1** *(reposar)* to have a rest; *(en el trabajo)* to take a break. **2** *(dormir)* to sleep [*pt & pp* **slept**]. **3** *(apoyarse)* to rest.

▶ *vt* to rest.

● **descansar en paz** to rest in peace.

● **¡descansen armas!** order arms!

● **que descanses** sleep well.

descansillo *nm* landing.

descanso *nm* **1** *(reposo)* rest; *(en el trabajo)* break. **2** *(alivio)* relief. **3** *(en obra de teatro)* interval; *(en encuentro deportivo)* half time.

descapotable *adj* - *nm* convertible.

descarado,-a *adj* brazen.

▶ *nm,f* cheeky devil.

descarga *nf* **1** *(de mercancías)* unloading. **2** *(de electricidad)* discharge. **3** *(de fuego)* discharge, volley. **4** *(en ordenador)* download.

descargar *vt* **1** *(mercancías)* to unload. **2** *(conciencia)* to ease. **3** *(de obligaciones)* to discharge. **4** *(golpe)* to strike [*pt & pp* **struck**]. **5** *(enfado)* to vent. **6** *(arma)* to fire, discharge. **7** *(en ordenador)* to download.

▶ *vpr* **descargarse 1** *(persona)* to unburden oneself. **2** *(batería)* to go flat.

descaro *nm* cheek, nerve: *¡qué descaro!*, what a nerve!

descarrilamiento *nm* derailment.

descarrilar *vi* to be derailed.

descartar *vt* to rule out.

descendencia *nf* offspring, children.

descender *vi* **1** *(persona)* to go down, come down: *el gato descendió del árbol*, the cat came down from the tree; *el camino desciende*, the path goes down. **2** *(temperatura, índice)* to drop, fall [*pt* **fell**; *pp* **fallen**]. **3** *(derivar)* to derive.

descendiente *adj* decreasing.

▶ *nmf* descendant.

descenso *nm* **1** *(de escalera, cumbre)* descent. **2** *(de temperatura, índice)* fall.

descifrar *vt* to decipher.

descojonarse *vpr* vulg to piss oneself laughing.

descolgar *vt* **1** *(cuadro, cortina)* to take down. **2** *(teléfono)* to pick up.

▶ *vpr* **descolgarse 1** *(aparecer)* to show up unexpectedly [*pt* **showed**; *pp* **shown**]. **2** *(desvincularse)* to dissociate oneself.

descolorido,-a *adj* faded.

descomponer *vt* **1** *(sustancia)* to break down [*pt* **broke**; *pp* **broken**]. **2** *(pudrir)* to decompose. **3** *(desordenar)* to mess up, upset [*pt & pp* **upset**].

▶ *vpr* **descomponerse 1** *(pudrirse)* to decompose. **2** *(enfadarse)* to lose one's temper [*pt & pp* **lost**].

descomposición *nf* **1** *(putrefacción)* decomposition, decay. **2** *(diarrea)* GB diarrhoea; US diarrhea.

descompuesto,-a *adj* **1** *(podrido)* decomposed. **2** *(alterado)* upset.

● **estar descompuesto,-a** GB to have diarrhhoea; US to have diarrhea.

descomunal *adj* huge, enormous.

desconcertar *vt* to disconcert.

▶ *vpr* **desconcertarse** to be disconcerted, be confused.

desconectar *vt* to disconnect.

▶ *vpr* **desconectarse** *fam* to stop listening, switch off.

desconfiado,-a *adj* distrustful.

desconfianza *nf* mistrust.

desconfiar *vi* to be distrustful.

descongelar *vt* **1** *(comida)* to thaw. **2** *(nevera)* to defrost.

desconocer *vt* not to know [*pt* **knew**; *pp* **known**]: *desconozco los detalles*, I don't know the details.

desconocido,-a *adj* **1** *(no conocido)* unknown. **2** *(extraño)* strange, unfamiliar.

▶ *nm,f* stranger.

● **estar desconocido,-a** to be unrecognizable.

■ **lo desconocido** the unknown.

desconocimiento *nm* ignorance.

desconsuelo *nm* distress.

descontado,-a *adj* **1** *(rebajado)* discounted. **2** *(excluido)* left out.

● **dar por descontado** to take for granted.

● **por descontado** needless to say.

descontar *vt* **1** *(rebajar)* to deduct. **2** *(excluir)* to leave out [*pt & pp* **left**].

descontento,-a *adj* dissatisfied.

▶ *nm* **descontento** dissatisfaction.

descontrol *nm* lack of control.

descontrolarse *vpr* to run out of control [*pt* **ran**; *pp* **run**].

descorchar *vt* to uncork.

descortés *adj* rude.

descoser *vt* to unpick.

▶ *vpr* **descoserse** to come unstitched.

descosido,-a *adj* unstitched.

▶ *nm* **descosido** split seam.

● **como un descosido** *fam* like mad.

descremado,-a *adj* skimmed.

describir *vt* to describe.

descripción *nf* description.

descuartizar *vt* **1** *(res)* to quarter. **2** *(víctima)* to cut into pieces [*pt & pp* **cut**].

descubierto,-a *adj* **1** *(sin cubrir)* uncovered; *(sin sombrero)* bareheaded. **2** *(piscina)* outdoor.

▶ *nm* **descubierto** *(en cuenta)* overdraft.

● **al descubierto** in the open.

● **en descubierto** overdrawn.

descubridor,-ra *nm,f* discoverer.

descubrimiento *nm* discovery.

descubrir *vt* **1** *(encontrar)* to discover. **2** *(revelar)* to make known. **3** *(averiguar)* to find out [*pt & pp* **found**].

▶ *vpr* **descubrirse** to take off one's hat.

descuento *nm* discount.

descuidado,-a *adj* **1** *(negligente)* careless. **2** *(desaseado)* slovenly.

descuidar *vt* **1** *(no atender)* to neglect. **2** *(no preocuparse)* not to worry: *descuida, ya lo hago yo*, don't worry, I'll do it.

▶ *vpr* **descuidarse** not to be careful: *como te descuides, te roban la cartera*, if you're not careful, they'll steal your wallet.

descuido *nm* **1** *(negligencia)* carelessness: *en un descuido*, in a moment of carelessness. **2** *(desaliño)* slovenliness. **3** *(desliz)* slip, error.

desde *prep* **1** *(lugar)* from: *desde aquí no se ve*, you can't see it from here. **2** *(tiempo)* since: *salen juntos desde junio*, they've been going out together since June.

● **desde ... hasta** from ... to.

● **desde ahora** from now on.

● **desde entonces** since then.

● **desde hace** for: *vivo aquí desde hace cinco años*, I've lived here for five years.

● **desde luego** of course.

● **desde que 1** ever since: *desde que nos conocemos, nunca me ha mentido*, ever since I've known him, he's never lied to me. **2** as soon as: *desde que la vi, supe que nos llevaríamos bien*, as soon as I saw her, I knew we'd get on well.

desdecirse *vpr* to go back on one's word.

desdén *nm* disdain.

desdentado,-a *adj* toothless.

desdeñar *vt* to disdain.

desdicha *nf* misfortune.

desdichado,-a *adj* hapless.

desdoblar *vt* to unfold.

deseable *adj* desirable.

desear *vt* to want.

desechable *adj* disposable.

desechar *vt* to reject.

desecho *nm* waste: *materiales de desecho*, waste material.

► *nm pl* **desechos 1** *(basura)* waste *sing.*
2 *(sobras)* leftovers.

desembarazarse *vpr*: *desembarazarse de*, to get rid of.

desembarcar *vi* to land.

desembarco *nm* landing.

desembocadura *nf* **1** *(de río)* mouth. **2** *(de calle)* end.

desembocar *vi* **1** *(río)* to flow. **2** *(calle, acontecimiento)* to lead [*pt & pp* **led**].

desembolsar *vt* to pay [*pt & pp* **paid**].

desempatar *vt (partido)* to decide.

► *vi* to break a tie [*pt* **broke**; *pp* **broken**]:
los empatados seguirán jugando hasta desempatar, the tied players will continue until one wins.

desempate *nm* breakthrough: *forzaron el desempate en el último minuto*, they made a breakthrough in the last minute.

desempeñar *vt* **1** *(objeto empeñado)* to redeem. **2** *(obligación)* to discharge. **3** *(cargo)* to hold [*pt & pp* **held**]. **4** *(papel)* to play.

desempleado,-a *adj* unemployed.

► *nm,f* unemployed person: *los desempleados*, the unemployed.

desempleo *nm* unemployment.

● **cobrar el desempleo** to be on the dole.

desempolvar *vt* **1** *(muebles etc)* to dust. **2** *(algo escondido)* to dig out [*pt & pp* **dug**].

desencadenar *vt* **1** *(crisis, debate)* to spark. **2** *(quitar cadenas a)* to unchain.

► *vpr* **desencadenarse 1** *(tormenta, guerra)* to break out [*pt* **broke**; *pp* **broken**]. **2** *(acontecimientos)* to start.

desenchufar *vt* to unplug.

desenfadado,-a *adj* light-hearted.

desenfocado,-a *adj* out of focus.

desenfundar *vt-vi* to draw [*pt* **drew**; *pp* **drawn**].

desenganchar *vt* **1** *(soltar)* to unhook. **2** *(caballerías)* to unhitch.

desengañar *vt* **1** *(anunciar la verdad a)* to put right. **2** *(desilusionar)* to disappoint.

► *vpr* **desengañarse** to be disappointed.

● **¡desengáñate!** face it!

desengaño *nm* disappointment.

desenlace *nm* **1** *(de aventura)* outcome. **2** *(de libro, película)* ending.

desenmascarar *vt* to unmask.

desenredar *vt* to untangle.

► *vpr* **desenredarse** to disentangle oneself.

desenrollar *vt* **1** *(papel)* to unroll. **2** *(cable)* to unwind [*pt & pp* **unwound**].

desenroscar *vt* to unscrew.

desentenderse *vpr* **1** *(desentenderse de (responsabilidad))* to wash one's hand of. **2** *(necesidad)* to ignore. **3** *(tarea)* to forget about [*pt* **forgot**; *pp* **forgotten**].

desenterrar *vt* **1** *(objeto escondido)* to unearth. **2** *(cadáver)* to dig up [*pt & pp* **dug**]. **3** *(recuerdos)* to recall.

desentonar *vi* **1** *(al cantar)* to be out of tune. **2** *(no casar, desentonar con)* not to match.

desenvolver *vt* to unwrap.

► *vpr* **desenvolverse 1** *(transcurrir)* to develop. **2** *(espabilarse)* to manage: *se desenvuelve como fotógrafo*, he earns his living as a photographer; *el ambiente en el que se desenvuelve*, the circles he moves in.

deseo *nm* **1** *(anhelo)* wish. **2** *(apetito sexual)* desire.

deseoso,-a *adj* eager.

desequilibrio *nm* imbalance.

■ **desequilibrio mental** mental disorder.

desertar *vi (soldado)* to desert.

desértico,-a *adj (clima, zona)* desert.

desertor,-ra *nm,f* deserter.

desesperación *nf* **1** *(irritación)* exasperation. **2** *(angustia)* desperation.

desesperado,-a *adj* **1** *(irritado)* exasperated. **2** *(angustiado)* desperate.

desesperar *vt* **1** *(irritar)* to exasperate. **2** *(angustiar)* to drive to despair.

► *vi-vpr* **desesperar(se) 1** *(irritarse)* to be exasperated. **2** *(angustiarse)* to despair.

desfachatez *nf* cheek.

desfallecer *vi* **1** *(desmayarse)* to faint. **2** *(decaer)* to lose heart [*pt & pp* **lost**].

desfasado,-a adj (teoría, objeto, etc) outdated; (persona) old-fashioned.

desfavorable adj unfavourable.

desfiladero nm **1** (barranco) gorge. **2** (paso) narrow pass.

desfilar vi **1** (marchar en fila) to march past. **2** (irse) to file out.

desfile nm parade.

desgana nf **1** (inapetencia) lack of appetite. **2** (indiferencia) indifference.

• **con desgana** reluctantly.

desgarbado,-a adj ungainly.

desgarrar vt **1** (romper) to tear [pt **tore**; pp **torn**]. **2** (corazón) to break [pt **broke**; pp **broken**].

desgarrón nm tear, rip.

desgastar vt **1** (ropa, neumático) to wear [pt **wore**; pp **worn**]. **2** (debilitar) to wear down [pt **wore**; pp **worn**].

▶ vpr **desgastarse 1** (ropa, neumático) to get worn; (pintura, esmalte) to get worn away. **2** (persona) to wear oneself out [pt **wore**; pp **worn**].

desgaste nm **1** (de ropa) wear. **2** (debilitamiento) weakening.

desgracia nf **1** (mala suerte) misfortune. **2** (pérdida de favor) disfavour. **3** (accidente) mishap.

• **caer en desgracia** GB to lose favour; US to lose favor [pt & pp **lost**].

• **por desgracia** unfortunately.

• **¡qué desgracia!** how awful!

desgraciado,-a adj **1** (desafortunado) unlucky. **2** (infeliz) unhappy.

▶ nm,f wretch.

desgravar vt to deduct.

▶ vi to be tax-deductible.

deshabitado,-a adj uninhabited.

deshacer vt **1** (labor, tarea) to undo [pt **undid**; pp **undone**]. **2** (nudo) to undo. **3** (destruir) to destroy. **4** (planes) to upset [pt & pp **upset**]. **5** (disolver) to dissolve; (fundir) to melt. **6** (maleta) to unpack.

▶ vpr **deshacerse 1** (costura, nudo) to come undone. **2** (disolverse) to dissolve; (fundirse) to melt. **3** (librarse): **deshacerse de**, to get rid of.

• **deshacerse en elogios** to be full of praise.

deshecho,-a adj **1** (destruido) destroyed. **2** (disuelto) dissolved; (fundido) melted. **3** (cansado) shattered.

deshidratar vt to dehydrate.

▶ vpr **deshidratarse** to get dehydrated.

deshielo nm (de río, glaciar) thaw; (de congelador) defrosting.

deshinchar vt to deflate, let down.

▶ vpr **deshincharse** (neumático) to go flat; (globo, hinchazón) to go down.

deshojar vt (flor) to strip the petals off; (planta) to strip the leaves off.

• **deshojar la margarita** to play she loves me, she loves me not.

deshollinador nm chimney sweep.

deshonesto,-a adj **1** (no honrado) dishonest. **2** (inmoral) indecent.

deshonra nf GB dishonour; US dishonor.

deshora.

• **a deshora** inopportunely, at the wrong time: **come a deshora**, he eats at odd hours.

deshuesar vt to bone.

desierto,-a adj (deshabitado) uninhabited; (vacío) deserted.

▶ nm **desierto** desert.

designar vt **1** (nombrar) to appoint. **2** (fijar) to designate.

desigual adj **1** (diferente) unequal. **2** (irregular) uneven. **3** (variable) changeable.

desigualdad nf **1** (diferencia) inequality. **2** (irregularidad) unevenness. **3** (inconstancia) changeability.

desilusión nf disappointment.

desilusionado,-a adj disappointed.

desilusionar vt to disappoint.

desinfectante adj - nm disinfectant.

desinfectar vt to disinfect.

desinflar vt to deflate.

▶ vpr **desinflarse 1** (perder el aire) to deflate. **2** fam (perder el ánimo) to come back down to earth.

desintegrarse vpr to disintegrate.

desinterés nm lack of interest.

desinteresado,-a adj unselfish.

desinteresarse vpr to lose interest [pt & pp **lost**].

desistir vi to desist.

desleal adj disloyal.

deslizar vt-vi to slide.

▶ vpr **deslizarse 1** (resbalar) to slip; (sobre agua) to glide. **2** (escabullirse) to slip. **3** (río) to flow.

deslumbrante adj dazzling.

deslumbrar vt to dazzle.

desmadre nm fam chaos.

desmayarse vpr to faint.

desmayo *nm* **1** *(ataque)s* fainting fit. **2** *(desánimo)* discouragement.

desmejorado,-a *adj* deteriorated.

desmejorar *vt* to make worse.
▶ *vi-vpr* **desmejorar(se)** to get worse.

desmemoriado,-a *adj* forgetful.

desmentir *vt* **1** *(negar)* to deny. **2** *(contradecir)* to contradict.

desmenuzar *vt* **1** *(pan, galletas)* to crumble. **2** *(idea, proyecto)* to scrutinize.

desmesurado,-a *adj* excessive.

desmontable *adj* detachable.

desmontar *vt* **1** *(mueble)* to dismantle. **2** *(edificio)* to knock down. **3** *(arma)* to uncock.
▶ *vi (del caballo)* to dismount.

desnatado,-a *adj (leche)* skimmed; *(yogur)* low-fat.

desnivel *nm* **1** *(desigualdad)* unevenness. **2** *(cuesta)* slope. **3** *(distancia vertical)* drop.

desnudar *vt* to undress.
▶ *vpr* **desnudarse** to get undressed.

desnudo,-a *adj* **1** *(persona)* naked. **2** *(habitación, paisaje)* bare.
▶ *nm* **desnudo** *(en arte)* nude.

desobedecer *vt* to disobey.

desobediencia *nf* disobedience.

desobediente *adj* disobedient.

desocupado,-a *adj* **1** *(libre)* free. **2** *(ocioso)* unoccupied. **3** *(desempleado)* unemployed.

desocupar *vt* to vacate.

desodorante *adj - nm* deodorant.

desolación *nf* **1** *(abandono)* desolation. **2** *(tristeza)* grief.

desorden *nm* **1** *(falta de orden)* disorder: *en desorden*, in disarray. **2** *(alteración)* disorder.

desordenado,-a *adj* **1** *(sin orden)* untidy, messy. **2** *(desaseado)* slovenly. **3** *(vida)* disorderly.

desordenar *vt (liar)* to mess up; *(alterar)* to disturb.

desorganización *nf* disorganization.

desorganizado,-a *adj* disorganized.

desorganizar *vt* to disrupt.

desorientar *vt* to disorientate.
▶ *vpr* **desorientarse** to lose one's bearings [*pt & pp* lost].

despabilado,-a *adj* **1** *(despierto)* wide awake. **2** *(listo)* smart.

despabilarse *vpr* **1** *(despertarse)* to wake up [*pt* woke; *pp* woken]. **2** *(animarse)* to liven up.

despachar *vt* **1** *(terminar)* to finish. **2** *(resolver)* to resolve. **3** *(enviar)* to dispatch. **4** *(despedir)* to sack. **5** *(en tienda)* to serve; *(vender)* to sell [*pt & pp* sold]. **6** *(asunto)* to deal with [*pt & pp* dealt].
● **despacharse a gusto** to get a load off one's mind.

despacho *nm* **1** *(en oficina)* office; *(en casa)* study. **2** *(envío)* dispatch. **3** *(venta)* sale. **4** *(tienda)* shop. **5** *(comunicación)* message.
■ **despacho de localidades** box-office.

despacio *adv* slowly.

despampanante *adj* stunning.

desparpajo *nm* **1** *(desenvoltura)* self-assurance. **2** *(descaro)* nerve.

despectivo,-a *adj* **1** *(gesto, tono)* contemptuous. **2** *(palabra)* pejorative.

despedazar *vt* to cut into pieces [*pt & pp* cut].

despedida *nf* goodbye: *fiesta de despedida*, farewell party.
■ **despedida de soltero** stag night.
■ **despedida de soltera** hen night.

despedir *vt* **1** *(lanzar)* to throw [*pt* threw; *pp* thrown]. **2** *(emitir)* to give off. **3** *(del trabajo)* to dismiss. **4** *(decir adiós a)* to say goodbye to [*pt & pp* said].
▶ *vpr* **despedirse 1** *(decirse adiós)* to say goodbye [*pt & pp* said]. **2** *(dar por perdido)* to forget [*pt* forgot; *pp* forgotten].
● **despedirse a la francesa** to take French leave.
● **salir despedido,-a** to be thrown out.

despegar *vt (desenganchar)* to detach.
▶ *vi (avión)* to take off.
▶ *vpr* **despegarse** to detach oneself.

despegue *nm* takeoff.

despeinado,-a *adj* unkempt: *ir despeinado*, to have untidy hair.

despeinar *vt*: *despeinar a ALGN*, to mess up SB's hair.
▶ *vpr* **despeinarse** to get one's hair messed up: *odio el viento porque me despeino*, I hate wind because I get my hair messed up.

despejado,-a *adj* clear.

despejar *vt* **1** *(habitación, calle)* to clear. **2** *(despertar)* to wake up [*pt* woke; *pp* woken].
▶ *vi* to clear up.
▶ *vpr* **despejarse 1** *(tiempo, cielo)* to clear up. **2** *(persona)* to clear one's head.

despellejar *vt* to skin.

▶ *vpr* **despellejarse** to peel.

despensa *nf* pantry.

despeñar *vt* to throw over a cliff [*pt* **threw**; *pp* **thrown**].

▶ *vpr* **despeñarse** *(accidentalmente)* to plunge; *(adrede)* to throw oneself off [*pt* **threw**; *pp* **thrown**]: *el coche se salió de la carretera y se despeñó al mar*, the car came off the road and plunged into the sea.

desperdiciar *vt* to waste.

desperdicio *nm* waste.

▶ *nm pl* **desperdicios** scraps.

desperezarse *vpr* to stretch.

desperfecto *nm (daño)* slight damage.

despertador *nm* alarm clock.

despertar *vt* **1** *(persona, animal)* to wake [*pt* **woke**; *pp* **woken**]. **2** *(apetito)* to rouse.

▶ *vi-vpr* **despertar(se)** *(persona, animal)* to wake up [*pt* **woke**; *pp* **woken**].

despiadado,-a *adj* ruthless.

despido *nm* dismissal.

despierto,-a *adj* **1** *(no dormido)* awake. **2** *(espabilado)* lively.

despilfarrar *vt* to squander.

despilfarro *nm* waste.

despistado,-a *adj* absent-minded.

▶ *nm,f:* **ser un despistado**, to be absent-minded.

● **hacerse el despistado** to pretend not to have noticed/understood etc.

despistar *vt (desorientar)* to confuse.

▶ *vpr* **despistarse 1** *(perderse)* to get lost. **2** *(distraerse)* to get distracted.

despiste *nm* **1** *(error)* mistake. **2** *(falta de atención)* absent-mindedness.

desplazar *vt (trasladar)* to move.

▶ *vpr* **desplazarse** to travel: *se desplaza en moto*, he travels around by motorbike; *me desplazo con frecuencia a Madrid*, I frequently visit Madrid.

desplegar *vt* **1** *(mapa)* to unfold. **2** *(alas)* to spread [*pt & pp* **spread**]. **3** *(actividad, cualidad)* to display. **4** *(tropas, armas)* to deploy.

desplomarse *vpr* to collapse.

desplumar *vt* **1** *(quitar plumas a)* to pluck. **2** *fam (estafar)* to fleece.

despoblar *vt* to depopulate.

▶ *vpr* **despoblarse** to become depopulated.

despojar *vt* **1** *(quitar)* to strip. **2** *(privar)* to despoil.

▶ *vpr* **despojarse de 1** *(ropa)* to take off. **2** *(prejuicios)* to free oneself from.

desposar *vt fml* to marry.

▶ *vpr* **desposarse** *fml* to get married.

despreciar *vt* **1** *(menospreciar)* to despise. **2** *(rechazar)* to reject.

desprecio *nm* contempt.

desprender *vt (soltar)* to detach.

▶ *vpr* **desprenderse 1** *(deshacerse)*: **desprenderse de**, to part with. **2** *(soltarse)* to come off. **3** *(deducirse)*: *eso es lo que se desprende de un estudio reciente*, that is what emerges from a recent study.

desprendimiento *nm* **1** *(generosidad)* generosity. **2** *(de tierra)* landslide.

despreocuparse *vpr* not to worry: *despreocúpate*, don't worry.

desprevenido,-a *adj* unprepared.

● **coger a** ALGN **desprevenido,-a** to take SB by surprise.

desprovisto,-a *adj* lacking.

después *adv* **1** *(más tarde)* afterwards, later: *iremos después*, we'll go later. **2** *(entonces)* then: *y después dijo que sí*, and then he said yes.

▶ *prep* **después de** *(tras)* after: *después de cenar*, after supper.

● **después de Cristo** AD.

● **después de todo** after all.

● **poco después** soon after.

despuntar *vt* to blunt.

▶ *vi* **1** *(planta)* to sprout. **2** *(destacar)* to excel.

destacado,-a *adj* outstanding.

destacar *vt* **1** *(tropas)* to detach. **2** *(resaltar)* to emphasize.

▶ *vpr* **destacarse** to stand out [*pt & pp* **stood**].

destapar *vt* **1** *(olla, caja)* to take the lid off. **2** *(botella)* to open. **3** *(cama)* to take the covers off. **4** *(secreto)* to uncover.

▶ *vpr* **destaparse** *(en la cama)* to push the covers off.

destartalado,-a *adj* shabby.

destellar *vi* to sparkle.

destello *nm* **1** *(en luz)* sparkle. **2** *(de ingenio)* flash.

destemplado,-a *adj* **1** *(sonido, voz)* harsh. **2** *(tiempo)* unpleasant.

● **sentirse destemplado,-a** not to feel well [*pt & pp* **felt**].

desteñir *vt* to fade.

▶ *vi-vpr* **desteñir(se) 1** *(perder intensidad)* to fade. **2** *(soltar tinte)* to run [*pt* **ran**; *pp* **run**].

desternillarse *vpr fam* .

● **desternillarse de risa** to split one's sides laughing [*pt & pp* **split**].

desterrado,-a *adj* exiled.

▶ *nm,f* exile.

desterrar *vt* to exile.

destiempo *adv* **a destiempo** at the wrong time: *una pregunta a destiempo*, an untimely proposal.

destierro *nm* exile.

destinar *vt* **1** *(asignar)* to allocate: *el Gobierno destina una parte del presupuesto para colegios*, the government allocates a part of the budget to schools. **2** *(a un puesto)* to post: *me destinaron a Cáceres*, I was posted to Cáceres.

destinatario,-a *nm,f* **1** *(de carta)* addressee. **2** *(de mercancías)* consignee.

destino *nm* **1** *(sino)* destiny, fate. **2** *(lugar)* destination. **3** *(empleo)* post.

● **con destino a** bound for: *el tren con destino a Bilbao*, the train to Bilbao.

destitución *nf* dismissal.

destituir *vt* to dismiss.

destornillador *nm* screwdriver.

destornillar *vt* to unscrew.

destreza *nf* skill.

destripar *vt* **1** *(animal)* to gut. **2** *(cosa)* to tear open [*pt* **tore**; *pp* **torn**]. **3** *fam (chiste, relato)* to spoil.

destronar *vt* to dethrone.

destrozado,-a *adj* **1** *(zapatos)* ruined; *(coche)* wrecked; *(cristal)* shattered; *(mueble)* falling to pieces. **2** *(persona - físicamente)* shattered; *(- anímicamente)* devastated.

destrozar [4] *vt* **1** *(zapatos, mueble)* to ruin; *(coche)* to wreck; *(cristal)* to shatter; *(edificio, ciudad)* to destroy. **2** *(persona - físicamente)* to shatter *(- anímicamente)* to devastate.

destrozo *nm* destruction.

● **destrozos** damage (sing.).

destrucción *nf* destruction.

destructivo,-a *adj* destructive.

destructor,-ra *adj* destructive.

▶ *nm* **destructor** destroyer.

destruir *vt* to destroy.

desunir *vt* to divide.

desuso *nm* disuse.

● **caer en desuso** to become obsolete.

desvalido,-a *adj* GB defenceless; US defenseless.

▶ *nm,f* indigent.

desvalijar *vt (local)* to ransack; *(persona)* to rob.

desván *nm* loft, attic.

desvanecer *vt (nubes, sospechas)* to dispel.

▶ *vpr* **desvanecerse 1** *(desaparecer)* to disappear. **2** *(desmayarse)* to faint.

desvelar *vt* **1** *(quitar el sueño a)* to keep awake. **2** *(dar a conocer)* to reveal.

▶ *vpr* **desvelarse 1** *(estar en vela)* to be unable to sleep: *me desvelé*, I couldn't get to sleep. **2** *(dedicarse)* to do everything one can.

desventaja *nf* disadvantage.

desvergonzado,-a *adj* shameless.

desvestir *vt-vpr* **desvestir(se)** to undress.

desviación *nf* **1** *(de trayectoria)* deviation. **2** *(de carretera)* diversion.

desviar *vt* **1** *(trayectoria)* to deviate. **2** *(golpe)* to deflect. **3** *(carretera)* to divert. **4** *(tema)* to change.

▶ *vpr* **desviarse** *(de un camino)* to go off course; *(coche)* to take a detour.

desvío *nm* diversion.

desvivirse *vpr* **1** *(hacer lo posible)* to do one's utmost. **2** *(desear)* to long for.

detallado,-a *adj* detailed.

detallar *vt* **1** *(tratar con detalle)* to detail. **2** *(especificar)* to specify.

detalle *nm* **1** *(pormenor)* detail. **2** *(delicadeza)* gesture.

● **¡qué detalle!** how nice!

● **tener un detalle** to be considerate.

● **vender al detalle** to retail.

detectar *vt* to detect.

detective *nmf* detective.

detención *nf* **1** *(parada)* stop. **2** *(arresto)* arrest.

detener *vt* **1** *(parar)* to stop. **2** *(arrestar)* to arrest.

▶ *vpr* **detenerse** to stop.

detenido,-a *adj* **1** *(minucioso)* careful. **2** *(arrestado)* under arrest.

▶ *nm,f* prisoner.

detenimiento *nm* care: *con detenimiento*, carefully.

detergente *adj - nm* detergent.

deteriorar *vt* to damage.

▶ *vpr* **deteriorarse** to deteriorate.

deterioro *nm* deterioration.
determinación *nf* **1** *(valor)* determination. **2** *(decisión)* decision. **3** *(firmeza)* firmness.
determinado,-a *adj* **1** *(alguno)* certain. **2** *(concreto)* particular, specific. **3** *(decidido)* determined. **4** GRAM definite.
determinante *adj* decisive.
▶ *nm* GRAM determiner.
determinar *vt* **1** *(decidir)* to decide. **2** *(fijar)* to determine. **3** *(causar)* to bring about [*pt & pp* **brought**].
detestar *vt* to detest.
detrás *adv (gen)* behind: *el jardín está detrás*, the garden is at the back.
▶ *prep* **detrás de** behind: *detrás de la puerta*, behind the door.
● **ir detrás de** to be after.
deuda *nf* debt.
■ **deuda externa** foreing debt.
devastar *vt* to devastate.
devoción *nf* devotion.
devolución *nf* **1** *(de dinero pagado)* refund. **2** *(de artículo comprado)* return.
devolver *vt* **1** to give back. **2** *(vomitar)* to vomit.
devorador,-ra *adj* devouring.
▶ *nm,f* devourer.
■ **devoradora de hombres** man-eater.
devorar *vt* to devour.
devoto,-a *adj* **1** *(religioso)* devout. **2** *(dedicado)* devoted.
día *nm* **1** *(gen)* day. **2** *(horas de luz)* daylight.
● **¡buenos días!** good morning!
● **cada día** every day.
● **del día** fresh.
● **día a día** day by day: *el día a día de un veterinario*, the day-to-day life of a veterinarian.
● **días alternos** every other day.
● **hoy en día** today, now, nowadays.
● **poner al día** to bring up to date [*pt & pp* **brought**].
● **ponerse al día** to get up to date.
● **todos los días** every day.
● **vivir al día** to live for today.
● **día de año nuevo** New Year's Day.
■ **día de fiesta** holiday.
■ **día de Reyes** Epiphany.
■ **día festivo** holiday.
■ **día hábil** working day.
■ **día laborable** working day.
■ **día libre** day off.
■ **día útil** working day.
■ **Día de los difuntos** All Souls' Day.
diabetes *nf* diabetes.
diabético,-a *adj - nm,f* diabetic.
diablo *nm* devil.
● **¡al diablo con ...!** to hell with ...!
● **¿qué diablos ...?** what the hell ...?: *¿qué diablos es eso?*, what the hell is that?
diablura *nf* mischief.
diadema *nf* diadem.
diagnosticar *vt* to diagnose.
diagnóstico *nm* diagnosis.
diagonal *adj - nf* diagonal.
diagrama *nm* diagram.
■ **diagrama de flujo** flowchart.
dialecto *nm* dialect.
dialogar *vi* to talk.
diálogo *nm* dialogue.
diamante *nm* diamond.
diámetro *nm* diameter.
diana *nf* **1** *(toque de corneta)* reveille. **2** *(blanco de tiro)* target; *(para dardos)* dartboard. **3** *(centro)* bull's eye.
diapositiva *nf* slide.
diariamente *adv* daily.
diario,-a *adj* daily.
▶ *nm* **diario 1** *(prensa)* newspaper. **2** *(íntimo)* diary, journal.
● **a diario** every day.
diarrea *nf* GB diarrhoea; US diarrhea.
dibujante *nmf* **1** *(artista)* artist. **2** *(delineante - hombre)* GB draughtsman [*pl* **-men**]; US draftsman [*pl* **-men**]; *(- mujer)* GB draughtswoman [*pl* **-women**]; US draftswoman [*pl* **-women**].
dibujar *vt* **1** to draw [*pt* **drew**; *pp* **drawn**]. **2** *(describir)* to describe.
dibujo *nm* **1** *(gen)* drawing. **2** *(estampado)* pattern.
■ **dibujos animados** cartoons.
diccionario *nm* dictionary.
dicha *nf* **1** *(felicidad)* happiness. **2** *(suerte)* good luck.
dicho,-a *adj* said.
▶ *nm* **dicho** saying.
● **dicho de otra manera** in other words.
● **dicho y hecho** no sooner said thandone.
● **mejor dicho** or rather.
● **propiamente dicho** strictly speaking.
dichoso,-a *adj* **1** *(feliz)* happy. **2** *(con suerte)* lucky. **3** *fam (maldito)* damn: *¡este dichoso, calor!*, this damn heat!

diciembre *nm* December.
dictado *nm* dictation.
dictador *nm* dictator.
dictadura *nf* dictatorship.
dictar *vt* **1** *(carta)* to dictate. **2** *(inspirar)* to inspire. **3** *(leyes)* to make.
didáctico,-a *adj* teaching.
diecinueve *num* nineteen; *(en fechas)* nineteenth.
dieciocho *num* eighteen; *(en fechas)* eighteenth.
dieciséis *num* sixteen; *(en fechas)* sixteenth.
diecisiete *num* seventeen; *(en fechas)* seventeenth.
diente *nm* **1** *(de la boca)* tooth [*pl* **teeth**]. **2** *(de ajo)* clove.
• **apretar los dientes** to grit one's teeth [*pt & pp* **set**].
■ **diente de leche** milk tooth [*pl* **teeth**].
■ **diente picado** decayed tooth [*pl* **teeth**].
diéresis *nf* diaeresis.
diestro,-a *adj* **1** *(mano)* right; *(persona)* right-handed. **2** *(hábil)* skilful.
▶ *nm* **diestro** bullfighter.
• **a diestro y siniestro** right, left and centre.
dieta[1] *nf* *(régimen)* diet.
dieta[2] *nf* *(asamblea)* assembly.
▶ *nf pl* **dietas** expenses allowance *sing*.
diez *num* ten; *(en fechas)* tenth.
difamar *vt* *(en declaración)* to slander; *(en escrito)* to libel.
diferencia *nf* difference: *diferencia de edad*, age difference.
• **a diferencia de** unlike.
diferenciar *vt* to differentiate.
▶ *vpr* **diferenciarse** to differ.
diferente *adj* different.
diferido,-a *adj* recorded.
difícil *adj* **1** *(costoso)* difficult. **2** *(improbable)* unlikely.
difícilmente *adv*: *difícilmente será suficiente*, it's unlikely to be enough.
dificultad *nf* difficulty.
dificultar *vt* to hamper, hinder.
dificultoso,-a *adj* difficult.
difundir *vt* **1** *(luz)* to diffuse. **2** *(noticia)* to spread [*pt & pp* **spread**]. **3** *(por radio, televisión)* to broadcast [*pt & pp* **broadcast**].
▶ *vpr* **difundirse 1** *(luz)* to be diffused. **2** *(noticia)* to spread [*pt & pp* **spread**].

difunto,-a *adj* late.
▶ *nm,f* deceased.
difusión *nf* **1** *(de luz)* diffusion. **2** *(de noticia)* spreading. **3** *(por radio, televisión)* broadcast.
digerir *vt* to digest.
digestión *nf* digestion.
digestivo,-a *adj* digestive.
▶ *nm* **digestivo** digestive drink.
digital *adj* digital.
dignarse *vpr* to deign.
dignidad *nf* **1** *(cualidad)* dignity. **2** *(cargo)* rank. **3** *(persona)* dignitary.
digno,-a *adj* **1** *(merecedor)* worthy: *digno de confianza*, trustworthy. **2** *(adecuado)* fitting. **3** *(respetable)* respectable.
dilatación *nf* dilatation.
dilatar *vt* **1** *(abrir)* to dilate. **2** *(propagar)* to spread [*pt & pp* **spread**]. **3** *(diferir)* to put off.
▶ *vpr* **dilatarse** to dilate.
dilema *nm* dilemma.
diligencia *nf* **1** *(cualidad)* diligence. **2** *(trámite)* procedure. **3** *(carreta)* stagecoach.
diligente *adj* **1** *(eficaz)* diligent. **2** *(rápido)* quick.
diluir *vt* to dilute.
diluviar *vi* to pour with rain.
diluvio *nm* flood.
dimensión *nf* **1** *(magnitud física)* dimension. **2** *(tamaño)* size: *vehículos de grandes dimensiones*, large vehicles.
diminutivo,-a *adj* diminutive.
▶ *nm* **diminutivo** diminutive.
diminuto,-a *adj* tiny.
dimisión *nf* resignation.
dimitir *vt* to resign.
Dinamarca *nf* Denmark.
dinámico,-a *adj* dynamic.
dinamita *nf* dynamite.
dinastía *nf* dynasty.
dineral *nm* fortune.
dinero *nm* **1** *(capital)* money. **2** *(fortuna)* wealth.
■ **dinero al contado** cash.
■ **dinero contante y sonante** cash.
■ **dinero en efectivo** cash.
■ **dinero negro** undeclared money.
■ **dinero suelto** loose change.
dinosaurio *nm* dinosaur.
dintel *nm* lintel.

diócesis *nf* diocese.
dioptría *nf* dioptre.
dios *nm* god.
● **a la buena de Dios** at random.
● **Dios mediante** God willing.
● **¡Dios mío!** my God!
● **ni Dios** *fam* not a soul.
● **¡por Dios!** for God's sake!
● **todo Dios** *fam* everybody.
diosa *nf* goddess.
dióxido *nm* dioxide.
■ **dióxido de carbono** carbon dioxide.
diploma *nm* diploma.
diplomacia *nf* diplomacy.
diplomático,-a *adj* diplomatic.
▶ *nm,f* diplomat.
diptongo *nm* diphthong.
diputado,-a *nm,f* deputy.
dique *nm* **1** (*en río*) dyke; (*en puerto*) dock. **2** (*rompeolas*) breakwater.
■ **dique de contención** dam.
■ **dique seco** dry dock.
dirección *nf* **1** (*rumbo*) direction; (*sentido*) way. **2** (*directores de empresa*) management. **3** (*domicilio*) address. **4** (*oficina*) manager's office. **5** (*de coche*) steering.
■ **dirección asistida** power steering.
■ **dirección electrónica** e-mail address.
directiva *nf* management.
directivo,-a *adj* managerial.
▶ *nm,f* executive.
directo,-a *adj* direct.
● **en directo** (*transmisión*) live.
director,-ra *adj* guiding.
▶ *nm,f* **1** (*gerente*) manager. **2** (*de colegio*) GB headteacher; US principal. **3** (*de orquesta*) conductor.
dirigente *adj* (*clase, elite*) ruling.
▶ *nm,f* leader.
dirigir *vt* **1** (*orientar*) to direct. **2** (*negocio*) to manage. **3** (*orquesta*) to conduct. **4** (*carta, mensaje*) to address: **no me dirigió la palabra**, he didn't even speak to me.
▶ *vpr* **dirigirse 1** (*ir*) to go. **2** (*hablar*) to address, speak to [*pt* **spoke**; *pp* **spoken**].
discapacitado,-a *adj* disabled.
▶ *nm,f* disabled person: **los discapacitados**, the disabled.
discernir *vt* to discern, distinguish.
disciplina *nf* discipline.
disciplinado,-a *adj* disciplined.
discípulo,-a *nm,f* **1** disciple. **2** (*alumno*) pupil.

disco *nm* **1** (*de música*) record. **2** (*en deporte*) discus. **3** (*de ordenador*) disk.
■ **disco compacto** compact disc.
■ **disco duro** hard disk.
■ **disco flexible** floppy disk.
discordia *nf* discord.
discoteca *nf* discotheque.
discreción *nf* discretion.
● **a discreción** at will.
discreto,-a *adj* **1** (*callado*) discreet. **2** (*sobrio*) sober. **3** (*moderado*) modest.
discriminación *nf* discrimination.
discriminar *vt* to discriminate.
disculpa *nf* apology.
● **pedir disculpas a ALGN** to apologize to SB.
disculpar *vt* to excuse.
▶ *vpr* **disculparse** to apologize.
discurrir *vi* **1** (*río*) to flow. **2** (*tiempo*) to pass. **3** (*reflexionar*) to reason.
discurso *nm* **1** (*conferencia*) speech. **2** (*del tiempo*) course.
discusión *nf* **1** (*disputa*) argument. **2** (*debate*) discussion.
discutir *vt-vi* **1** (*debatir*) to discuss. **2** (*disputar*) to argue.
disecar *vt* **1** (*animales*) to stuff. **2** (*en laboratorio*) to dissect.
diseñador,-ra *nm,f* designer.
diseñar *vt* to design.
diseño *nm* design.
● **de diseño** designer: **ropa de diseño**, designer clothes.
■ **diseño gráfico** graphic design.
disfraz *nm* **1** (*para engañar*) disguise. **2** (*para fiesta*) costume.
disfrazar *vt* **1** (*para engañar*) to disguise. **2** (*para fiesta*) to dress up (**de,** as).
▶ *vpr* **1** (*para engañar*) to disguise oneself. **2** (*para fiesta*) to dress up (**de,** as).
disfrutar *vt* to enjoy.
disgustado,-a *adj* upset.
disgustar *vt* (*molestar*) to upset [*pt & pp* **upset**].
▶ *vpr* **disgustarse 1** (*molestarse*) to be displeased, be upset. **2** (*pelearse*) to quarrel.
disgusto *nm* **1** (*contratiempo*) upset. **2** (*pelea*) quarrel.
● **a disgusto** against one's will.
● **dar un disgusto a ALGN** to upset SB [*pt & pp* **upset**].
● **llevarse un disgusto** to be upset.

disimular vt *(ocultar)* to hide [pt **hid**; pp **hidden**]: *no pudo disimular su sorpresa*, she couldn't hide her surprise.

▶ vi *(fingir)* to pretend: *no disimules, sé que me has oído*, don't bother pretending, I know you heard me.

disimulo nm: *con disimulo*, surreptitiously; *sin disimulo*, quite openly.

disminución nf decrease.

disminuido,-a adj handicapped.

▶ nm,f handicapped person: *los disminuidos*, the handicapped.

disminuir vt to reduce.

▶ vi to decrease, fall [pt **fell**; pp **fallen**].

disolver vt-vpr **disolver(se)** to dissolve.

disparar vt **1** *(arma)* to fire: *disparar un tiro*, to fire a shot. **2** *(balón)* to drive [pt **drove**, pp **driven**].

▶ vi *(con arma)* to shoot [pt & pp **shot**].

▶ vpr **dispararse 1** *(precio)* to shoot up [pt & pp **shot**]. **2** *(correr)* to dash off. **3** *(arma)* to go off.

● **disparar contra** ALGN to shoot at SB [pt & pp **shot**].

● **salir disparado,-a** to shoot off [pt & pp **shot**].

disparatado,-a adj *(aventura, situación)* crazy; *(creencia, cantidad)* absurd.

disparate nm **1** *(tontería)* absurdity: *sería un disparate creer que...*, it would be absurd to think that.... **2** *(enormidad)*: *le costó un disparate*, it cost her a packet; *un disparate de dinero*, a ridiculous amount of money.

● **decir disparates** to talk nonsense.

disparo nm shot.

dispensar vt **1** *(conceder)* to dispense, give. **2** *(eximir)* to exempt. **3** *(perdonar)* to forgive [pt **forgave**; pp **forgiven**].

● **¡dispense!** pardon me!

dispensario nm dispensary.

dispersar vt-vpr **dispersar(se)** to disperse.

disponer vt-vi *(colocar)* to arrange.

▶ vt **1** *(preparar)* to prepare. **2** *(ordenar)* to order.

▶ vi *(poseer)* to have.

▶ vpr **disponerse** *(prepararse)* to be set to.

disponible adj **1** *(preparado)* available. **2** *(sobrante)* spare. **3** *(a mano)* on hand.

disposición nf **1** *(actitud)* disposition. **2** *(talento)* talent. **3** *(colocación)* arrangement. **4** *(estado de ánimo)* frame of mind.

● **a su disposición** at your disposal.

● **estar en disposición de** to be ready to.

dispositivo nm device.

■ **dispositivo de seguridad 1** *(medidas)* security measures pl. **2** *(mecanismo)* safety device.

dispuesto,-a adj **1** *(colocado)* arranged. **2** *(preparado)* ready. **3** *(despabilado)* bright.

disputa nf dispute.

disputar vt **1** *(discutir)* to dispute. **2** *(partido)* to play.

▶ vpr **disputarse** *(partido)* to be played.

disquete nm diskette.

disquetera nf disk drive.

distancia nf **1** *(separación)* distance. **2** fig *(diferencia)* difference.

● **guardar las distancias** to keep one's distance.

distante adj distant.

distar vi to be distant: *dista unos 3 km del pueblo*, it is about 3 km from the village.

● **distar mucho de** to be far from.

distinción nf distinction.

distinguido,-a adj distinguished.

distinguir vt **1** *(diferenciar)* to distinguish. **2** *(ver)* to see [pt **saw**; pp **seen**].

▶ vpr **distinguirse 1** *(destacar)* to be distinguished. **2** *(ser visible)* to be visible.

distintivo,-a adj distinctive.

▶ nm **distintivo** *(insignia)* badge; *(marca)* mark.

distinto,-a adj different.

distracción nf **1** *(divertimiento)* amusement. **2** *(despiste)* distraction.

distraer vt **1** *(divertir)* to keep amused. **2** *(atención)* to distract. **3** *(fondos)* to embezzle.

▶ vpr **distraerse 1** *(divertirse)* to keep oneself amused. **2** *(despistarse)* to get distracted.

distraído,-a adj: *estar distraído*, to not be paying attention.

distribución nf **1** *(reparto)* distribution. **2** *(colocación)* arrangement.

distribuir vt **1** *(repartir)* to distribute. **2** *(colocar)* to arrange.

distrito nm district.

disturbio nm riot.

disuadir vt *(por persuasión)* to dissuade; *(por intimidación)* to deter.

diurno,-a adj **1** *(curso, autobús)* daytime. **2** *(animal)* diurnal.

diversidad *nf* diversity.

diversión *nf* (*gozo*) fun; (*pasatiempo*) pastime: *no hay que desaprovechar tanta diversión*, it is too much fun to miss; *una diversión sana*, a healthy pastime.

diversos,-as *adj pl* several, various.

divertido,-a *adj* (*que hace reír*) funny; (*que entretiene*) fun.

divertir *vt* to amuse.
▶ *vpr* **divertirse** to enjoy oneself.

dividir *vt* to divide.

divino,-a *adj* **1** divine. **2** *fam* gorgeous, divine.

divisa *nf* **1** (*insignia*) badge. **2** (*de escudo*) device. **3** (*moneda*) foreign currency.

divisar *vt* make out.

división *nf* division.

divorciado,-a *adj* divorced.
▶ *nm,f* (*hombre*) divorcé; (*mujer*) divorcée.

divorciarse *vpr* to get divorced.

divorcio *nm* divorce.

divulgar *vt* **1** (*dar a conocer*) to make public. **2** (*propagar*) to spread [*pt & pp* **spread**].

DNI *abr* (**Documento Nacional de Identidad**) identity card.

dobladillo *nm* hem.

doblaje *nm* dubbing.

doblar *vt* **1** (*duplicar*) to double. **2** (*plegar*) to fold. **3** (*esquina*) to turn. **4** (*película*) to dub.
▶ *vi* **1** (*girar*) to turn: *doblar a la derecha*, to turn right. **2** (*campana*) to toll.
▶ *vpr* **doblarse 1** (*plegarse*) to fold. **2** (*torcerse*) to bend [*pt & pp* **bent**]. **3** (*rendirse*) to give in.

doble *adj* (*dos veces*) double.
▶ *nm* double: *gana el doble que yo*, she earns twice as much as I do.
▶ *nmf* (*sosia*) double; (*especialista - hombre*) stunt man [*pl* **men**]; (- *mujer*) stunt woman [*pl* **women**].
▶ *adv* double.
● **ver doble** to see double.
■ **doble fondo** false bottom.
■ **doble personalidad** split personality.

doblez *nm* (*pliegue*) fold.

doce *num* twelve; (*en fechas*) twelfth.

docena *nf* dozen.

docente *adj* teaching.

dócil *adj* docile.

doctorado *nm* doctorate.

doctor,-ra *nm,f* doctor.

doctrina *nf* doctrine.

documentación *nf* documentation: *le pidió su documentación*, she asked him for his ID.

documental *adj* - *nm* documentary.

documento *nm* document.

dólar *nm* dollar.

doler *vi* **1** (*físicamente*) to hurt [*pt & pp* **hurt**]: *me duele la pierna*, my leg hurts; *me duele la cabeza*, I've got a headache. **2** (*apenar*) to hurt [*pt & pp* **hurt**]: *me duele verte así*, it hurts me to see you like this.
▶ *vpr* **dolerse 1** (*arrepentirse*) to feel sorry [*pt & pp* **felt**]. **2** (*lamentarse*) to complain.

dolor *nm* **1** (*físico*) pain; (*sordo*) ache. **2** (*moral*) pain.
■ **dolor de cabeza** headache.
■ **dolor de estómago** stomachache.
■ **dolor de garganta** sore throat.
■ **dolor de muelas** toothache.

dolorido,-a *adj* **1** (*físicamente*) sore. **2** (*apenado*) hurt.

doloroso,-a *adj* painful.

domador,-ra *nm,f* (*de leones*) tamer; (*de caballos*) horse-breaker.

domar *vt* (*leones*) to tame; (*caballos*) to break in [*pt* **broke**; *pp* **broken**].

domesticar *vt* to domesticate.

doméstico,-a *adj* domestic.
▶ *nm,f* servant.

domicilio *nm* address.

dominante *adj* **1** (*mayoritario*) dominant. **2** (*avasallador*) domineering.

dominar *vt* **1** (*gen*) to dominate. **2** (*avasallar*) to domineer. **3** (*controlar*) to control. **4** (*tema*) to master. **5** (*paisaje*) to overlook.

domingo *nm* Sunday.
■ **domingo de Ramos** Palm Sunday.
■ **domingo de Resurrección** Easter Sunday.

dominical *adj* Sunday.
▶ *nm* Sunday newspaper.

dominicano,-a *adj* - *nm,f* Dominican.
■ **República Dominicana** Dominican Republic.

dominio *nm* **1** (*territorio*) dominion. **2** (*poder*) control. **3** (*de tema*) mastery. **4** INFORM domain.

dominó *nm* (*ficha*) domino; (*juego*) dominoes *pl*.

don[1] *nm* (*regalo, talento*) gift.

don[2] *nm* (*título*) don.

donación nf donation.

donante nmf donor.

donar vt to donate.

donativo nm donation.

doncella nf **1** (virgen) maiden. **2** (criada) maidservant.

donde conj where.

● **de donde** from where.

● **hasta donde la vista alcanza** as far as the eye can see.

dónde pron where: ¿**dónde está?**, where is it?

dondequiera adv wherever.

dorado,-a adj (gen) gold; (color) golden.

dorar vt to gild.

dormilón,-ona nm,f fam sleepyhead.

dormir vi to sleep [pt & pp **slept**].

▶ vpr **dormirse** to go to sleep.

● **dormir a pierna suelta** to sleep like a log [pt & pp **slept**].

● **dormir la mona** to sleep it off [pt & pp **slept**].

● **dormir la siesta** to have a nap.

dormitar vi to doze.

dormitorio nm **1** (en casa) bedroom. **2** (colectivo) dormitory. **3** (muebles) bedroom suite.

dorso nm back.

dos num two; (en fechas) second.

● **cada dos por tres** every five minutes.

● **de dos en dos** in twos.

● **dos puntos** colon.

doscientos,-as num two hundred.

dosis nf dose.

dote nm & nf (ajuar) dowry.

▶ nf (talento) talent.

dragón nm dragon.

drama nm drama.

dramático,-a adj dramatic.

droga nf drug.

■ **droga blanda** soft drug.

■ **droga dura** hard drug.

drogadicción nf drug addiction.

drogadicto,-a nm,f drug addict.

drogar vt to drug.

▶ vpr **drogarse** to take drugs.

droguería nf hardware and household goods shop.

dromedario nm dromedary.

ducha nf shower.

● **darse una ducha** to have a shower.

duchar vt to shower.

▶ vpr **ducharse** to have a shower.

duda nf doubt: **si tienes dudas, pregúntame**, if you have any queries, ask me.

● **en caso de duda** if in doubt.

● **sin duda** undoubtedly.

● **sin lugar a dudas** without doubt.

dudar vi **1** (estar inseguro) to be unsure. **2** (vacilar) to hesitate.

▶ vt to doubt: **lo dudo**, I doubt it.

● **dudar de** ALGN to suspect SB.

dudoso,-a adj **1** (inseguro) doubtful. **2** (vacilante) hesitant. **3** (sospechoso) dubious.

duelo nm duel.

● **batirse en duelo** to fight a duel [pt & pp **fought**].

duende nm **1** (elfo) elf [pl -**ves**]. **2** (encanto) charm: **es una chica con duende**, she's got charm.

dueño,-a nm,f **1** (propietario) owner. **2** (de casa alquilada - hombre) landlord; (- mujer) landlady.

dulce adj **1** (comida, bebida) sweet. **2** (persona, voz) soft, gentle.

▶ nm **1** (caramelo) sweet. **2** (pastel) cake.

■ **dulce de membrillo** quince jelly.

dulzura nf **1** (de postre, vino) sweetness. **2** (de persona, voz) gentleness.

duna nf dune.

dúo nm **1** (pareja) duo. **2** (composición) duet.

duodécimo,-a num twelfth.

dúplex adj - nm duplex.

duplicado,-a adj duplicate.

▶ nm **duplicado** duplicate.

duplicar vt **1** (documento, llave) to duplicate. **2** (cantidad) to double.

▶ vpr **duplicarse** to double.

duque nm duke.

duquesa nf duchess.

duración nf duration: **tiempo de duración**, duration; **una llamada de 15 minutos de duración**, a 15-minute call.

duradero,-a adj lasting.

durante adv **1** (a lo largo de un periodo) for: **llovió durante tres días**, it rained for three days; **tendremos el problema durante años**, we'll have this problem for years; **durante todo el día**, all day long. **2** (dentro de un periodo) during, in: **durante octubre**, during October, in October; **durante la noche**, during the night, in the night.

durar *vi* to last: ***la reunión duró una hora***, the meeting lasted an hour; ***la película dura tres horas***, the film is three hours long.

dureza *nf* **1** *(de material)* hardness. **2** *(de carácter)* toughness. **3** *(en el pie)* corn.

duro,-a *adj* **1** *(gen)* hard; *(carne)* tough. **2** *(difícil)* hard, difficult. **3** *(cruel)* tough. **4** *(resistente)* strong.
▶ *nm* **duro** *fam* tough guy.
▶ *adv* hard: ***trabaja duro***, he works hard.
● **no tener un duro** to be broke.
● **no valer un duro** to be worth nothing.

E

ebanista *nmf* cabinet-maker.
ébano *nm* ebony.
ebrio,-a *adj* drunk.
ebullición *nf*.
● **en ebullición** boiling: *entrar en ebullición*, to come to the boil.
eccema *nm* eczema.
echar *vt* **1** *(lanzar)* to throw [*pt* **threw**; *pp* **thrown**]. **2** *(del trabajo)* to sack. **3** *(expulsar)* to throw out [*pt* **threw**; *pp* **thrown**]. **4** *(correo)* GB to post; US to mail. **5** *(brotar)* to sprout. **6** *(poner)* to put. **7** *(emanar)* to give off. **8** *fam (en el cine, teatro)* to show [*pt* **showed**; *pp* **shown**].
► *vi-vpr* **echar(se) a** + *inf* to begin to [*pt* **began**; *pp* **begun**]: *echar a correr*, to run off.
► *vpr* **echarse 1** *(lanzarse)* to throw oneself [*pt* **threw**; *pp* **thrown**]. **2** *(tenderse)* to lie down [*pt* **lay**; *pp* **lain**].
● **echar algo a perder** to spoil STH [*pt & pp* **spoilt**].
● **echar cuentas** to take stock.
● **echar de menos** to miss.
● **echar la llave** to lock the door.
● **echar en cara** to reproach for: *les echó en cara su pereza*, he reproached them for their laziness.
● **echar por tierra 1** (edificio) to demolish. **2** (planes) to ruin.
● **echar una mano** to lend a hand [*pt & pp* **lent**].
● **echarse a perder** (comida) to go off.
● **echarse atrás 1** (inclinarse) to lean back [*pt & pp* **leant**]. **2** (desdecirse) to back out.
eclesiástico,-a *adj* ecclesiastical.
► *nm* **eclesiástico** ecclesiastic.
eclipse *nm* eclipse.

eco *nm* echo [*pl* -**es**].
● **tener eco** to arouse interest.
ecología *nf* ecology.
ecológico,-a *adj* **1** *(gen)* ecological. **2** *(cultivo)* organic.
ecologista *adj* environmental.
► *nmf* environmentalist.
economato *nm* company store.
economía *nf* **1** *(de un país)* economy. **2** *(ciencia)* economics.
► *nf pl* **economías** savings: *hacer economías*, to make savings.
■ **economía de mercado** market economy.
■ **economía sumergida** black economy.
económico,-a *adj* **1** *(de la economía)* economic. **2** *(barato)* economical.
economista *nmf* economist.
economizar *vt* to economize on.
► *vi* to economize.
ecosistema *nm* ecosystem.
ecuación *nf* equation.
ecuador *nm* equator.
Ecuador *nm* Ecuador.
ecuatorial *adj* equatorial.
ecuatoriano,-a *adj - nm,f* Ecuadorian.
edad *nf* age: *a la edad de tres años*, at the age of three; *¿qué edad tiene usted?*, how old are you?
■ **edad media** Middle Ages *pl*.
■ **la tercera edad 1** *(etapa de la vida)* old age. **2** *(gente mayor)* senior citizens *pl*.
■ **edad del pavo** awkward age.
edición *nf* **1** *(tirada)* edition. **2** *(publicación)* publication.
■ **edición electrónica** electronic publishing.
edificar *vt* to build [*pt & pp* **built**].

edificio *nm* building.

editar *vt* **1** *(publicar - novela etc)* to publish; *(- disco)* to release. **2** *(texto, película, informática)* to edit.

editor,-ra *adj* publishing.
▶ *nm,f* **1** *(que publica)* publisher. **2** *(que prepara)* editor.
■ **editor de texto** text editor.

editorial *adj* publishing.
▶ *nm (artículo)* editorial, leading article.
▶ *nf* publishing house.

edredón *nm* quilt.
■ **edredón nórdico** duvet.

educación *nf* **1** *(enseñanza)* education. **2** *(crianza)* upbringing. **3** *(cortesía)* manners *pl.*
■ **educación física** physical education.

educado,-a *adj* polite.

educar *vt* **1** *(enseñar)* to educate. **2** *(criar)* to bring up [*pt & pp* **brought**].

educativo,-a *adj* educational.

efectivamente *adv* **1** *(realmente)* actually. **2** *(en confirmación)* indeed: *¿así que usted fue engañado?- Efectivamente,* so, you were misled?- That's right.

efectivo,-a *adj* **1** *(eficaz)* effective. **2** *(verdadero)* real.
▶ *nm* **efectivo** *(dinero)* cash.
▶ *nm pl* **efectivos** forces.
● **hacerse efectivo,-a 1** (pago) to be made. **2** (medida) to come into effect.

efecto *nm* **1** *(gen)* effect. **2** *(impresión)* impression. **3** *(fin)* purpose. **4** *(pelota)* spin: *dar efecto a la pelota,* to put some spin on the ball.
● **a tal efecto** to this end.
● **en efecto** indeed.
● **hacer efecto** to take effect.
■ **efecto invernadero** greenhouse effect.
■ **efectos especiales** special effects.
■ **efectos personales** personal belongings.

efectuar *vt* **1** *(maniobra, investigación, etc)* to carry out. **2** *(pago, viaje, etc)* to make.
▶ *vpr* **efectuarse** *(realizarse)* to be carried out; *(acto etc)* to take place.

efervescente *adj* **1** *(pastilla)* effervescent. **2** *(bebida)* fizzy. **3** *(persona)* high-spirited.

eficacia *nf* **1** *(efectividad)* effectiveness. **2** *(eficiencia)* efficacy.

eficaz *adj* **1** *(que surte efecto)* effective. **2** *(eficiente)* efficient.

eficiencia *nf* efficiency.

eficiente *adj* efficient.

efímero,-a *adj* ephemeral.

egipcio,-a *adj - nm,f* Egyptian.

Egipto *nm* Egypt.

egoísmo *nm* selfishness, egoism.

egoísta *adj* selfish, egoistic.
▶ *nmf* egoist.

eje *nm* **1** *(en geometría, astronomía)* axis. **2** *(de motor)* shaft. **3** *(de ruedas)* axle.

ejecución *nf* **1** *(de orden)* execution. **2** *(de pieza musical)* performance. **3** *(ajusticiamiento)* execution.

ejecutar *vt* **1** *(orden)* to carry out. **2** *(pieza musical)* to perform. **3** *(programa informático)* to run [*pt* **ran**; *pp* **run**]. **4** *(ajusticiar)* to execute.

ejecutivo,-a *adj - nm,f* executive.

ejemplar *adj (modélico)* exemplary.
▶ *nm (obra)* copy: *ejemplar gratuito,* free copy. **2** *(espécimen)* specimen.

ejemplo *nm* example.
● **dar ejemplo** to set an example [*pt & pp* **set**].
● **por ejemplo** for example, for instance.
● **predicar con el ejemplo** to practice what one preaches.

ejercer *vt* **1** *(profesión etc)* to practise. **2** *(derecho, poder)* to exercise. **3** *(influencia)* to exert.
▶ *vi (trabajar)* to practise: *ejerce de abogado,* he practises law.

ejercicio *nm* **1** *(gen)* exercise. **2** *(de derecho, autoridad)* exercice. **3** *(financiero)* year.
● **hacer ejercicio** to exercise.
■ **ejercicio fiscal** tax year.
■ **ejercicio físico** physical exercise.

ejercitar *vt* **1** *(músculo, derecho, etc)* to exercise. **2** *(profesión)* to practise. **3** *(enseñar)* to train.
▶ *vpr* **ejercitarse** *(aprender)* to train.

ejército *nm* army.

el *det* **1** the: *el coche,* the car. **2 el +** *de* the one: *el de tu amigo,-a,* your friend's; *el de Valencia,* the one from Valencia. **3 el +** *que* the one: *el que vino ayer,* the one who came yesterday; *el que me diste,* the one you gave me.

él *pron* **1** *(sujeto - persona)* he; *(- cosa, animal)* it: *él vive aquí,* he lives here. **2** *(des-*

pués de preposición - persona) him; (- cosa, animal) it: **vino con él**, she came with him.
● **de él** (posesivo) his: **es de él**, it's his.
● **él mismo** himself.
elaboración nf **1** (de producto) manufacture, production. **2** (de lista, presupuesto) drawing up. **3** (de informe) writing.
elaborar vt **1** (producto) to make, manufacture. **2** (lista, presupuesto) to draw up [pt **drew**; pp **drawn**]. **3** (informe) to write [pt **wrote**; pp **written**].
elástico,-a adj elastic.
▶ nm **elástico** elastic.
▶ nm pl **elásticos** braces.
elección nf **1** (nombramiento) election. **2** (opción) choice.
▶ nf pl **elecciones** elections.
■ **elecciones generales** general election sing.
elector,-ra nm,f elector.
electorado nm electorate.
electoral adj electoral.
electricidad nf electricity.
■ **electricidad estática** static electricity.
electricista nmf electrician.
eléctrico,-a adj electric.
electrocutar vt to electrocute.
▶ vpr **electrocutarse** to be electrocuted.
electrodoméstico nm home electrical appliance.
electrónica nf electronics.
electrónico,-a adj electronic.
elefante nm elephant.
elegancia nf elegance.
elegante adj elegant.
elegir vt **1** (escoger) to chose [pt **chose**; pp **chosen**]. **2** (por votación) to elect.
elemental adj **1** (obvio) elementary. **2** (primordial) essential.
elemento nm **1** (gen) element. **2** (individuo) type: **elementos indeseables**, undesirables.
▶ nm pl **elementos 1** (atmosféricos) elements. **2** (fundamentos) rudiments.
● **estar uno en su elemento** to be in one's element.
elevación nf **1** (de terreno) elevation. **2** (de precios, temperatura) rise.
elevado,-a adj **1** (edificio) tall; (montaña, número) high. **2** (ideales, pensamientos) lofty.
elevar vt to raise.

▶ vpr **elevarse 1** (aumentar) to rise [pt **rose**; pp **risen**]. **2** (ascender - avión) to climb; (- globo) to rise [pt **rose**; pp **risen**].
eliminación nf elimination.
eliminar vt **1** (gen) to eliminate. **2** (obstáculo, mancha) to remove.
eliminatoria nf **1** (en torneo, competición) qualifying competition; (vuelta) qualifying round. **2** (para carrera) heat.
eliminatorio,-a adj qualifying.
ella pron **1** (sujeto - persona) she; (- cosa, animal) it: **ella vive aquí**, she lives here. **2** (después de preposición - persona) her; (- cosa, animal) it: **vino con ella**, he came with her.
● **de ella** hers: **es de ella**, it's hers.
ello pron it.
● **estoy en ello** I'm working on it.
● **por ello** for that reason.
ellos,-as pron **1** (sujeto) they. **2** (complemento) them.
● **de ellos** theirs: **es de ellas**, it's theirs.
elogiar vt to praise.
elogio nm praise.
embajada nf embassy.
embajador,-ra nm,f ambassador.
embalaje nm packing.
embalar vt to pack.
▶ vpr **embalarse** fam to go too fast.
embalsamar vt to embalm.
embalse nm reservoir.
embarazada adj pregnant.
▶ nf pregnant woman [pl **women**].
embarazo nm **1** (preñez) pregnancy. **2** (turbación) embarrassment. **3** (obstáculo) obstruction.
embarazoso,-a adj embarrassing.
embarcación nf boat.
■ **embarcaciones de recreo** leisure craft.
embarcadero nm jetty.
embarcar vt-vpr **embarcar(se)** to embark.
embargo nm **1** (incautación de bienes) seizure. **2** (prohibición de comercio) embargo.
● **sin embargo** however.
embarque nm **1** (de personas) boarding; (de mercancías) loading.
embarrado,-a adj muddy.
embarullar vt to muddle.
▶ vpr **embarullarse** fam to get into a muddle.
embellecer vt to embellish.

embestir *vt (acometer)* to attack; *(toro)* to charge.

emblema *nm* emblem.

embolsarse *vpr* to pocket.

emborrachar *vt* to make drunk.
▶ *vpr* **emborracharse** to get drunk.

emboscada *nf* ambush.
● **tender una emboscada** to lay an ambush [*pt & pp* **laid**].

embotellamiento *nm* **1** *(de tráfico)* traffic jam. **2** *(de bebida)* bottling.

embotellar *vt* to bottle.

embrague *nm* clutch.

embrión *nm* embryo [*pl* **-s**].

embrollo *nm* **1** *(confusión)* muddle. **2** *(mentira)* lie.

embrujo *nm* **1** *(hechizo)* spell. **2** *(fascinación)* magic.

embudo *nm* funnel.

embuste *nm* lie.

embustero,-a *adj* lying.
▶ *nm,f* liar.

embutido *nm* cold meat.

emergencia *nf (imprevisto)* emergency.

emerger *vi* **1** *(aparecer)* to emerge. **2** *(submarino)* to surface.

emigración *nf* emigration.

emigrante *adj* - *nmf* emigrant.

emigrar *vi (persona)* to emigrate; *(ave)* to migrate.

emilio *nm fam (mensaje electrónico)* e-mail.

eminente *adj* eminent.

emisario,-a *nm,f* emissary.

emisión *nf* **1** *(de energía, gas)* emission. **2** *(de bonos, acciones)* issue. **3** *(en radio, TV)* broadcast.

emisor,-ra *adj* **1** *(banco)* issuing. **2** *(centro)* broadcasting.
▶ *nm* **emisor** radio transmitter.

emisora *nf* radio station.

emitir *vt* **1** *(sonido, luz, calor)* to emit. **2** *(bonos, acciones)* to issue. **3** *(programa de radio, TV)* to broadcast [*pt & pp* **broadcast**].

emoción *nf* **1** *(sentimiento)* emotion. **2** *(excitación)* excitement.
● **¡qué emoción!** how exciting!

emocionante *adj* **1** *(conmovedor)* moving. **2** *(excitante)* exciting.

emocionar *vt* **1** *(conmover)* to move. **2** *(excitar)* to excite.
▶ *vpr* **emocionarse 1** *(conmoverse)* to be moved. **2** *(excitarse)* to get excited.

emotivo,-a *adj* emotional.

empachar *vt* to give indigestion: *la mantequilla me empacha*, butter gives me indigestion.
▶ *vpr* **empacharse** to get indigestion.

empacho *nm* indigestion.

empalagar *vt (dulces)*: *la nata me empalaga*, I find cream sickly.

empalagoso,-a *adj* **1** *(dulces)* sickly. **2** *(persona)* smarmy.

empalmar *vt* **1** *(tuberías, cables)* to join. **2** *(planes etc)* to combine.
▶ *vi (enlazar)* to connect.

empalme *nm* **1** *(de tuberías, cables)* connection. **2** *(de carreteras, vías)* junction.

empanada *nf* pasty.
● **tener una empanada mental** not to be able to think straight.

empanadilla *nf* pasty.

empañar *vt* **1** *(cristal)* to steam up. **2** *(reputación)* to tarnish.
▶ *vpr* **empañarse 1** *(cristal)* to steam up. **2** *(reputación)* to become tarnished.

empapar *vt* to soak.
▶ *vpr* **empaparse** to get soaked.

empapelar *vt* **1** *(pared)* to paper. **2** *fam (persona)* to book.

empaquetar *vt* to pack.

emparedado,-a *nm* **emparedado** sandwich.

emparejar *vt (cosas)* to match; *(personas)* to pair off.
▶ *vpr* **emparejarse** to pair off.

empastar *vt* to fill.

empaste *nm* filling.

empatar *vi* **1** *(acabar igualados)* to draw [*pt* **drew**; *pp* **drawn**]; *(igualar)* to equalize: *estamos empatados*, we're equal; *empataron a cero*, they drew nil-nil. **2** *(en votación etc)* to tie.
▶ *vt (partido)* to draw [*pt* **drew**; *pp* **drawn**].

empate *nm* tie, draw.

empedrado,-a *adj* paved.
▶ *nm* **empedrado** paving.

empedrar *vt* to pave.

empeine *nm* instep.

empeñar *vt* **1** *(objeto)* to pawn. **2** *(palabra)* to pledge.
▶ *vpr* **empeñarse 1** *(endeudarse)* to get into debt. **2** *(insistir)* to insist.

empeño *nm* **1** *(insistencia)* determination; *(esfuerzo)* effort; *(intento)* attempt.
● **con empeño** eagerly.
● **tener empeño en** to be eager to.

empeorar *vi* to worsen.
▶ *vt* to make worse.
▶ *vpr* **empeorarse** to get worse.
empequeñecer *vt* to diminish.
emperador *nm* emperor.
emperatriz *nf* empress.
empezar *vt-vi* to begin [*pt* **began**; *pp* **begun**], start: *el profesor empezó la clase*, the teacher began the lesson; *he empezado la botella*, I've started the bottle; *empezó a llover*, it began to rain.
● **al empezar** at the beginning.
● **para empezar** to begin with.
empinado,-a *adj* steep.
empinar *vt* to raise, lift.
▶ *vpr* **empinarse** *(persona)* to stand on tiptoe [*pt & pp* **stood**]; *(animal)* to rear.
● **empinar el codo** (fam) to drink heavily [*pt* **drank**; *pp* **drunk**].
empleado,-a *nm,f (gen)* employee; *(oficinista)* clerk.
■ **empleado,-a de hogar** domestic servant.
emplear *vt* 1 *(usar)* to employ. 2 *(dinero, tiempo)* to spend [*pt & pp* **spent**].
● **le está bien empleado** it serves him right.
empleo *nm* 1 *(puesto)* job. 2 *(trabajo)* employment. 3 *(uso)* use.
empobrecer *vt* to impoverish.
▶ *vpr* **empobrecerse** to become impoverished.
empollar *vt* 1 *(huevo)* to hatch. 2 fam *(lección)* to swot upon.
empollón,-ona *adj* fam swotty.
▶ *nm,f* fam swot.
empotrado,-a *adj* built-in.
empotrar *vt (mueble)* to build in [*pt & pp* **built**]; *(cable)* to embed.
▶ *vpr* **empotrarse** to crash into: *el coche se empotró en el escaparate*, the car crashed into the shop window.
emprender *vt* to undertake.
● **emprender la marcha** to start out.
empresa *nf* 1 *(compañía)* firm, company: *el mundo de la empresa*, the world of business. 2 *(acción)* enterprise, venture.
■ **empresa de trabajo temporal** temp recruitment agency.
empresarial *adj* managerial: *estudios empresariales*, business studies.
empresario,-a *nm,f* 1 *(hombre)* businessman [*pl* **-men**]; *(mujer)* businesswoman [*pl* **-women**]. 2 *(patrón)* employer.

empujar *vt* to push.
● **empujar a** ALGN **a hacer algo** to drive SB to do STH.
empuje *nm* 1 *(fuerza)* push. 2 *(presión)* pressure. 3 *(energía)* drive.
empujón *nm* push, shove.
● **a empujones** by fits and starts.
empuñar *vt* to grasp.
en *prep* 1 *(lugar - gen)* in, at; *(- en el interior)* in, inside; *(- sobre)* on: *en casa*, at home; *en Valencia*, in Valencia; *en el cajón*, in the drawer; *en la mesa*, on the table. 2 *(tiempo - año, mes, estación)* in; *(- día)* on: *en 2004*, in 2004; *en un viernes*, on a Friday. 3 *(dirección)* into: *entró en su casa*, he went into his house. 4 *(transporte)* by, in: *ir en coche*, to go by car; *ir en avión*, to fly. 5 *(tema, materia)* at, in: *es experto en política*, he's an expert in politics. 6 *(modo)* in: *en voz baja*, in a low voice; *en inglés*, in English.
● **en seguida** at once, straight away.
enamorado,-a *adj* in love.
▶ *nm,f* lover.
enamorar *vt* to win the heart of [*pt & pp* **won**].
▶ *vpr* **enamorarse** to fall in love [*pt* **fell**; *pp* **fallen**].
enano,-a *adj - nm,f* dwarf [*pl* **-s** o **-ves**].
● **disfrutar como un enano** to have a whale of a time.
encabezamiento *nm* 1 *(de carta, documento)* heading. 2 *(de periódico)* headline.
encabezar *vt* 1 *(en escrito)* to head. 2 *(ser líder)* to lead [*pt & pp* **led**].
encabritarse *vpr* 1 *(caballo)* to rear up. 2 *(barco)* to rise [*pt* **rose**; *pp* **risen**]; *(coche, avión)* to stall. 3 *(enojarse)* to get cross.
encadenar *vt* 1 *(poner cadenas a)* to chain. 2 *(enlazar)* to link. 3 *fig (atar)* to tie down.
encajar *vt* 1 *(acoplar)* to fit. 2 *(comentario, broma, golpe)* to take.
▶ *vi (coincidir)* to fit.
encaje *nm (tejido)* lace.
encallar *vi* 1 *(barco)* to run aground [*pt* **ran**; *pp* **run**]. 2 *(plan, proyecto)* to founder.
encaminar *vt (guiar, orientar)* to direct.
▶ *vpr* **encaminarse** *(dirigirse)* to head.
encantado,-a *adj* 1 *(contento)* delighted: *está encantada con el coche nuevo*, she's delighted with the new car. 2 *(embrujado)* enchanted. 3 *(distraído)* absent-minded.

• **encantado,-a de conocerle** *fml* pleased to meet you.

encantador,-ra *nm,f (hechicero)* enchanter; *(hechicera)* enchantress.
▶ *adj (agradable)* charming.

encantamiento *nm* enchantment.

encantar *vt* to cast a spell on [*pt & pp* **cast**].
▶ *vi:* **me encanta la natación**, I love swimming.

encanto *nm* **1** *(hechizo)* spell. **2** *(atractivo)* charm. **3** *fam (apelativo)* darling: **lo que tú digas, encanto**, whatever you say, darling.

• **como por encanto** as if by magic.

• **ser un encanto** to be a darling.

encapricharse *vpr* to take a fancy.

encapuchado,-a *adj* hooded.

encarcelar *vt* to imprison.

encargado,-a *adj* in charge.
▶ *nm,f (responsable)* person in charge; *(de negocio - hombre)* manager; *(- mujer)* manageress: **el encargado del departamento de estadística**, the head of the statistics department.

encargar *vt* **1** *(encomendar)* to entrust. **2** *(solicitar)* to order.
▶ *vpr* **encargarse** to take charge: **yo me encargo de lo demás**, I'll take care of the rest.

• **encargar a ALGN que haga algo** to ask SB to do STH.

encargo *nm* **1** *(recado)* errand; *(tarea)* job. **2** *(de productos)* order.

• **por encargo** to order.

encariñarse *vpr* to become fond.

encarrilar *vt* to get back on track: **la prioridad es encarrilar la economía**, the priority is to get the economy back on track.

encauzar *vt* **1** *(corriente, río)* to channel. **2** *(discusión, persona)* to guide.

encendedor *nm* lighter.

encender *vt* **1** *(fuego, vela, cigarro)* to light [*pt & pp* **lit**]; *(cerilla)* to strike [*pt & pp* **struck**]. **2** *(luz, radio, tele)* to turn on, switch on. **3** *(pasión)* to inflame; *(entusiasmo)* to arouse.
▶ *vpr* **encenderse** **1** *(luz, radio, tele)* to come on. **2** *(persona - excitarse)* to flare up; *(- ruborizarse)* to blush.

encendido,-a *adj (mejillas, color)* glowing; *(rostro)* red.
▶ *nm* **encendido** ignition.

encerado,-a *adj* waxed.
▶ *nm* **encerado** black board.

encerar *vt* to polish.

encerrar *vt* **1** *(persona- en habitación)* to shut in [*pt & pp* **shut**]; *(- en cárcel)* to lock up; *(ganado)* to pen. **2** *fig (contener)* to contain.
▶ *vpr* **encerrarse** to shut oneself in [*pt & pp* **shut**]; *(con llave)* to lock oneself in.

encestar *vi* to score, score a basket.

encharcado,-a *adj* flooded, swamped.

encharcar *vt (suelo)* to flood.
▶ *vpr* **encharcarse** *(suelo)* to get flooded.

enchufado,-a *nm,f fam* wirepuller.

• **ser un enchufado 1** *(gen)* to have good contacts. **2** *(en la escuela)* to be teacher's pet.

enchufar *vt* **1** *(aparato)* to plug in. **2** *fam (persona)* to pull strings for: **enchufó a su hija en la empresa**, he got his daughter a job in the company.

enchufe *nm* **1** *(de aparato- hembra)* socket; *(macho)* plug. **2** *fam (cargo)* easy job; *(influencias)* connections *pl*.

encía *nf* gum.

enciclopedia *nf* GB encyclopaedia; US encyclopedia.

encierro *nm* **1** *(protesta)* sit-in. **2** *(de toros)* running of the bulls.

encima *adv* **1** *(más arriba)* above; *(sobre)* on top: **está allí encima**, it's there on top. **2** *(consigo)* on me/you/him *etc*: **¿llevas cambio encima?**, do you have any change on you? **3** *(además)* in addition.

• **encima de** on.

• **estar encima de ALGN** to be on SB's back.

• **por encima 1** *(a más altura)* above. **2** *(de pasada)* superficially.

• **por encima de** above.

• **por encima de todo** above all.

• **quitarse a ALGN de encima** to get rid of SB.

• **quitarse algo de encima** to get rid of STH.

encina *nf* evergreen oak.

encinta *adj* pregnant.

enclenque *adj (flaco)* skinny; *(enfermizo)* sickly.

encoger *vt* to shrink [*pt* **shrank**; *pp* **shrunk**].

▶ *vi-vpr* **encoger(se)** to shrink.
● **encogerse de hombros** to shrug one's shoulders.
encolar *vt* to glue.
encontrar *vt* **1** *(hallar)* to find [*pt & pp* found]. **2** *(persona)* to come across. **3** *(creer)* to think [*pt & pp* thought]: **no lo encuentro justo**, I don't think it's fair.
▶ *vpr* **encontrarse 1** *(hallarse)* to be. **2** *(personas)* to meet [*pt & pp* met]. **3** *(sentirse)* to feel [*pt & pp* felt]: **ayer me encontraba bien, pero hoy me encuentro mal**, yesterday I felt fine, but today I feel ill.
● **encontrarse con 1** (persona) to meet [*pt & pp* met]. **2** (objeto, situación) to find [*pt & pp* found].
encorvar *vt* to bend [*pt & pp* bent].
▶ *vpr* **encorvarse** to bend over [*pt & pp* bent].
encrucijada *nf* crossroads *pl*.
● **estar en una encrucijada** to be at a crossroads.
encuadernación *nf* **1** *(proceso)* bookbinding. **2** *(cubierta)* binding.
encuadernador,-ra *nm,f* bookbinder.
encuadernar *vt* to bind [*pt & pp* bound].
encubrir *vt* *(ocultar)* to conceal; *(delito)* to cover up; *(criminal)* to shelter.
encuentro *nm* **1** *(coincidencia)* encounter. **2** *(reunión)* meeting. **3** *(en deporte)* match. **4** *(choque)* collision.
● **salir al encuentro de** ALGN to go to meet SB.
encuesta *nf* **1** *(sondeo)* survey. **2** *(pesquisa)* inquiry.
enderezar *vt* **1** *(poner derecho)* to straighten out. **2** *(poner vertical)* to set upright [*pt & pp* set]. **3** *(guiar)* to direct.
▶ *vpr* **enderezarse** to straighten up.
endeudarse *vpr* to get into debt.
endibia *nf* endive.
endulzar *vt* **1** *(hacer dulce)* to sweeten. **2** *(suavizar)* to alleviate.
endurecer *vt-vpr* **endurecer(se)** to harden.
enemigo,-a *adj* enemy.
▶ *nm,f* enemy.
● **pasarse al enemigo** to go over to the enemy.
enemistar *vt* to make enemies of.
▶ *vpr* **enemistarse** to become enemies.
● **enemistarse con** ALGN to fall out with SB [*pt* fell; *pp* fallen].

energía *nf* energy.
■ **energía atómica** atomic power.
■ **energía eléctrica** electric power.
■ **energía nuclear** nuclear power.
■ **energía solar** solar power, solar energy.
enérgico,-a *adj* **1** *(persona, ejercicio)* energetic. **2** *(ataque, protesta)* vigorous.
enero *nm* January.
enésimo,-a *adj* **1** *(en matemáticas)* nth. **2** *fam* umpteenth: **te lo digo por enésima vez**, this is the umpteenth time I've told you.
enfadado,-a *adj* angry.
enfadar *vt* to make angry.
▶ *vpr* **enfadarse** to get angry.
enfado *nm* anger: **tiene que controlar sus enfados**, she must control her temper.
énfasis *nm & nf* emphasis.
● **poner énfasis en algo** to emphasize STH.
enfermar *vi* to fall ill [*pt* fell; *pp* fallen].
enfermedad *nf* *(estado de enfermo)* illness; *(patología específica)* disease.
■ **enfermedad contagiosa** contagious disease.
■ **enfermedad hereditaria** hereditary disease.
■ **enfermedad terminal** terminal illness.
■ **enfermedad venérea** venereal disease.
enfermería *nf* **1** *(profesión)* nursing. **2** *(lugar)* infirmary.
enfermero,-a *nm,f* *(hombre)* nurse, male nurse; *(mujer)* nurse.
enfermo,-a *adj* ill [*comp* worse; *superl* worst], sick.
▶ *nm,f* sick person: **los enfermos**, the ill, the sick.
■ **enfermo terminal** terminal patient.
enfocar *vt* **1** *(con cámara)* to focus on. **2** *(con luz, faro)* to shine a light on [*pt & pp* shone]. **3** *(problema etc)* to approach.
enfoque *nm* **1** *(de imagen)* focus. **2** *(de asunto)* approach.
enfrentamiento *nm* confrontation.
enfrentar *vt* **1** *(afrontar)* to face. **2** *(encarar)* to bring face to face [*pt & pp* brought].
▶ *vpr* **enfrentarse 1** *(encararse)* to face up. **2** *(pelearse)* to have a confrontation.

enfrente *adv* opposite: *la casa de enfrente*, the house opposite.
● **enfrente de** opposite.

enfriamiento *nm* **1** *(acción)* cooling. **2** *(catarro)* cold.

enfriar *vt* to cool down.
▶ *vpr* **enfriarse 1** *(algo caliente)* to cool down. **2** *(tener frío)* to get cold. **3** *(acatarrarse)* catch a cold [*pt & pp* **caught**]. **4** *(pasión, entusiasmo)* to cool off.

enfundar *vt* to put in its case; *(espada)* to sheathe; *(pistola)* to put in its holster.

enfurecer *vt* to infuriate.
▶ *vpr* **enfurecerse** *(persona)* to get furious.

enfurruñarse *vpr fam* to sulk.

engalanar *vt* to adorn.
▶ *vpr* **engalanarse** to dress up.

enganchar *vt* **1** *(gen)* to hook; *(animales)* to hitch; *(vagones)* to couple. **2** *(atraer)* to attract.
▶ *vpr* **engancharse 1** *(prenderse)* to get caught. **2** *(en ejército)* to enlist. **3** *arg (a drogas)* to get hooked.

enganche *nm (de vagones)* coupling.

engañar *vt* **1** *(gen)* to deceive. **2** *(estafar)* to cheat. **3** *(mentir)* to lie to. **4** *(a la pareja)* to be unfaithful to.
▶ *vi (llevar a error)* to be deceptive: *las apariencias engañan*, appearances can be deceptive.
▶ *vpr* **engañarse 1** *(ilusionarse)* to deceive oneself. **2** *(equivocarse)* to be mistaken.
● **engañar el hambre** to stave off hunger.

engaño *nm* **1** *(gen)* deceit. **2** *(estafa)* trick.

engatusar *vt fam* to sweet-talk.
● **engatusar a** ALGN **para que haga algo** to sweet-talk SB into doing STH.

engendrar *vt* to engender.

englobar *vt* to include.

engordar *vt (animal)* to fatten.
▶ *vi* **1** *(persona)* to put on weight: *he engordado cinco kilos*, I've put on five kilos. **2** *(alimento)* to be fattening.

engorro *nm* nuisance.

engrasar *vt* **1** *(gen)* to lubricate; *(con grasa)* to grease; *(con aceite)* to oil. **2** *(sobornar)* to bribe.

engreído,-a *adj* vain, conceited.

engullir *vt* to gobble up.

enhebrar *vt* to thread.

enhorabuena *nf* congratulations *pl*.
● **dar la enhorabuena a** ALGN to congratulate SB.

enigma *nm* enigma, puzzle.

enjabonar *vt* **1** *(lavar)* to soap. **2** *(adular)* to soft-soap.

enjambre *nm* swarm.

enjaular *vt* **1** *(en jaula)* to cage. **2** *fam (en cárcel)* to put inside.

enjuagar *vt-vpr* **enjuagar(se)** to rinse.

enjuague *nm* **1** *(proceso)* rinse. **2** *(líquido)* mouthwash.

enjuto,-a *adj* lean.

enlace *nm* **1** *(conexión)* link. **2** *(boda)* marriage. **3** *(intermediario)* liaison. **4** *(en internet)* link.
■ **enlace sindical** GB shop steward; US union delegate.

enlatar *vt* to can, tin.

enlazar *vt (unir)* to link.
▶ *vi (trenes etc)* to connect.

enloquecer *vi* **1** *(volverse loco)* to go mad. **2** *fam (gustar mucho)* to be mad about: *le enloquecen las motos*, she's mad about motorbikes.
▶ *vt (volver loco)* to drive mad [*pt* **drove**; *pp* **driven**].
▶ *vpr* **enloquecerse** to go mad.

enmarañar *vt* **1** *(entrelazar)* to tangle. **2** *(asunto, situación)* to muddle.
▶ *vpr* **enmarañarse 1** *(cabellos, hilos, etc)* to get tangled. **2** *(persona)* to get caught up.

enmendar *vt* **1** *(error)* to correct; *(daño)* to repair. **2** *(texto, ley)* to amend.
▶ *vpr* **enmendarse** to mend one's ways.

enmienda *nf* **1** *(de error)* correction; *(de daño)* repair. **2** *(de texto, ley)* amendment.

enmudecer *vi* **1** *(quedar mudo)* to be struck dumb. **2** *(callarse)* to fall silent [*pt* **fell**; *pp* **fallen**].

ennegrecer *vt* **1** *(poner negro)* to blacken. **2** *(oscurecer)* to darken.
▶ *vpr* **ennegrecerse 1** *(ponerse negro)* to turn black. **2** *(oscurecerse)* to darken.

enojado,-a *adj (enfadado)* angry; *(molesto)* annoyed.

enojar *vt (enfadar)* to anger; *(molestar)* to annoy.
▶ *vpr* **enojarse** *(enfadarse)* to get angry; *(molestarse)* to get annoyed.

enojo *nm (enfado)* anger; *(molestia)* annoyance.

enorgullecer vt to fill with pride.
▶ vpr **enorgullecerse** to be proud, feel proud [pt & pp **felt**].
● **enorgullecerse de algo** to pride oneself on STH.

enorme adj enormous, huge.

enraizar vi-vpr **enraizar(se)** to take root.

enredadera nf creeper, climbing plant.

enredar vt 1 (enmarañar) to tangle. 2 (dificultar) to complicate. 3 (involucrar): **enredar a ALGN en algo**, to get SB involved in STH.
▶ vi (hacer travesuras) to get up to mischief.
▶ vpr **enredarse** 1 (cuerda, pelo) to get tangled. 2 (complicarse) to get complicated; (en discusión) to get caught up. 3 (tener una aventura) to have an affair.

enredo nm 1 (maraña) tangle. 2 (confusión) mix-up, mess. 3 (amoroso) love affair.
▶ nm pl **enredos** (trastos) bits and pieces.

enrejado nm 1 (de verja, balcón) railings pl. 2 (celosía) trellis.

enrevesado,-a adj complicated, difficult.

enriquecer vt 1 (hacer rico) to make rich. 2 (mejorar) to enrich.
▶ vpr **enriquecerse** to get rich.

enrojecer vt 1 (volver rojo) to redden. 2 (ruborizar) to make blush.
▶ vpr **enrojecerse** 1 (ruborizarse) to go red, blush. 2 (volverse rojo) to turn red.

enrollado,-a adj 1 (papel, alfombra) rolled up. 2 fam (persona) cool: **una tía enrollada**, a cool babe.
● **estar enrollado,-a con ALGN 1** (en conversación) to be deep in conversation with SB. **2** (en relación sentimental) to be going out with SB.

enrollar vt to roll up.
▶ vpr **enrollarse** fam (hablar) to go on and on.
● **enrollarse con ALGN** to get off with SB.

enroscar vt 1 (cable) to twist. 2 (tornillo) to screw; (tapa) to screw on.
▶ vpr **enroscarse** (cable) to roll up; (serpiente) to coil up.

ensalada nf salad.

ensaladera nf salad bowl.

ensaladilla nf salad.
■ **ensaladilla rusa** Russian salad.

ensanchamiento nm widening, broadening.

ensanchar vt (agrandar) to widen; (prenda) to let out [pt & pp **let**].
▶ vpr **ensancharse** (envanecerse) to become conceited.

ensanche nm 1 (de carretera) widening. 2 (de ciudad) new development.

ensangrentado,-a adj bloodstained, bloody.

ensangrentar vt to stain with blood.
▶ vpr **ensangrentarse** to get covered with blood.

ensayar vt 1 (obra de teatro) to rehearse; (música) to practise. 2 (probar) to try out.

ensayo nm 1 (de obra de teatro) rehearsal; (de música) practice. 2 (prueba) test, trial. 3 (literario) essay.
■ **ensayo general** dress rehearsal.

enseguida adv at once, straight away.

ensenada nf cove.

enseñanza nf 1 (educación) education. 2 (docencia) teaching.
● **enseñanzas** teachings.
■ **enseñanza primaria** primary education.
■ **enseñanza secundaria** secondary education.
■ **enseñanza superior** higher education.

enseñar vt 1 (en escuela etc) to teach [pt & pp **taught**]. 2 (mostrar) to show [pt **showed**; pp **shown**].
● **enseñar a ALGN a hacer algo** to teach SB to do STH [pt & pp **taught**].
● **enseñar los dientes** to bare one's teeth.

enseres nm pl (de casa) household, belongings; (de profesión) equipment.

ensillar vt to saddle.

ensimismarse vpr 1 (absorberse) to become engrossed. 2 (abstraerse) to become lost in thought.

ensombrecer vt to cast a shadow over [pt & pp **cast**].
▶ vpr **ensombrecerse** to darken.

ensordecedor,-ra adj deafening.

ensordecer vt to deafen.
▶ vi to go deaf.

ensuciar vt 1 (manchar) to get dirty: **lo ensucian todo**, they get everything dirty. 2 (reputación, nombre) to sully.

▶ *vpr* **ensuciarse** to get dirty.

ensueño *nm* daydream, fantasy.

● **de ensueño** fantastic: *playas de ensueño*, fantastic beaches.

entablar *vt (conversación)* to start; *(amistad)* to strike up [*pt & pp* **struck**].

entender *nm* opinion: *a mi entender*, in my opinion.

▶ *vt* **1** *(comprender)* to understand [*pt & pp* **understood**]. **2** *(opinar)* to consider.

▶ *vi* to know: *¿tú entiendes de motores?*, do you know anything about engines?

▶ *vpr* **entenderse 1** *(conocerse)* to know what one is doing [*pt* **knew**; *pp* **known**]: *yo me entiendo*, I know what I am doing. **2** *fam (llevarse bien)* to get along well together.

● **dar a entender que ...** to imply that ....

● **entenderse con** ALGN to have an affair with SB.

● **hacerse entender** to make oneself understood.

● **no entender ni jota** *fam* not to understand a word [*pt & pp* **understood**].

entendido,-a *nm,f* expert.

entendimiento *nm* understanding.

enterado,-a *adj* knowledgeable.

▶ *nm,f fam* expert.

enterarse *vpr* **1** *(averiguar)* to find out [*pt & pp* **found**]. **2** *(darse cuenta)* to notice: *ni se enteró de que me había ido*, he didn't even notice I had gone. **3** *(comprender)* to understand [*pt & pp* **understood**]: *no se entera de nada*, she doesn't understand a thing.

● **¡te vas a enterar!** you'll be sorry!

entereza *nf* **1** *(integridad)* integrity. **2** *(firmeza)* firmness. **3** *(fortaleza)* fortitude.

enternecedor,-ra *adj* touching.

entero,-a *adj* **1** *(completo)* whole. **2** *(persona - íntegro)* upright; *(- sereno)* composed. **3** *(robusto)* robust.

▶ *nm* **entero** point: *la inflación ha subido dos enteros*, inflation has risen two points.

enterrador,-ra *nm,f* gravedigger.

enterrar *vt* to bury.

● **enterrarse en vida** to cut oneself off from the world [*pt & pp* **cut**].

entidad *nf* **1** *(organismo)* body. **2** *(ente, ser)* entity.

● **de entidad** important.

■ **entidad bancaria** bank.

■ **entidad financiera** finance company.

■ **entidad pública 1** *(organismo estatal)* public authority. **2** *(empresa estatal)* public enterprise.

entierro *nm* **1** *(acto)* burial. **2** *(ceremonia)* funeral.

entonación *nf* intonation.

entonar *vt* **1** *(nota)* to pitch; *(canción)* to sing [*pt* **sang**; *pp* **sung**]. **2** *(organismo)* to tone up. **3** *(colores)* to match.

▶ *vi (al cantar)* to sing in tune [*pt* **sang**; *pp* **sung**].

entonces *adv* then.

● **desde entonces** since then.

● **por aquel entonces** at that time.

entornar *vt* **1** *(ojos)* to half-close. **2** *(puerta)* to leave ajar [*pt & pp* **left**].

entorno *nm* environment.

entorpecer *vt (dificultar)* to obstruct, hinder.

entrada *nf* **1** *(acción)* entrance, entry. **2** *(lugar)* entrance: *entrada principal*, main entrance. **3** *(en espectáculo - billete)* ticket; *(admisión)* admission: *hay que sacar las entradas*, we have to buy the tickets. **4** *(pago inicial)* down payment. **5** *(en libro)* entry. **6** INFORM input.

▶ *nf pl* **entradas** *(en la cabeza)* receding hairline *sing*: *tiene entradas*, he has a receding hairline.

● **de entrada** from the start.

● **"Prohibida la entrada"** "No admittance".

entrañable *adj* beloved.

entrañas *nf pl* **1** *(vísceras)* entrails. **2** *(sentimientos)* heart *sing*.

entrar *vi* **1** *(ir adentro)* to come in, go in. **2** *(en una sociedad etc)* to join. **3** *(encajar)* to fit: *este tornillo no entra*, this screw doesn't fit. **4** *(empezar año, estación)* to begin [*pt* **began**; *pp* **begun**]. **5** *(en fase, etapa)* to enter: *entramos en una nueva era*, we are entering a new era. **6** *(venir)*: *me entró dolor de cabeza*, I got a headache; *me entraron ganas de llorar*, I felt like crying.

▶ *vt* **1** *(traer desde fuera)* to bring in. **2** *(datos)* to enter.

● **entrado,-a en años** *fam* well on in years.

● **no me entra en la cabeza** *fam* I can't believe it.

entre *prep* **1** *(dos términos)* between; *(más de dos términos)* among. **2** *(sumando)* counting: ***entre niños y adultos somos doce***, counting children and adults, there are twelve of us.
• **de entre** among.
• **entre una cosa y otra** what with one thing and another.
• **entre tanto** meanwhile.

entreabierto,-a *adj* **1** *(ojos, boca, ventana)* half-open. **2** *(puerta)* ajar.

entreabrir *vt* **1** *(ojos, boca, ventana)* to half open. **2** *(puerta)* to leave ajar [*pt & pp* **left**].

entreacto *nm* interval.

entrecejo *nm* .
• **fruncir el entrecejo** to frown.

entrecot *nm* entrecôte.

entrega *nf* **1** *(acción)* handing over; *(de mercancía)* delivery. **2** *(de posesiones)* surrender. **3** *(fascículo)* instalment. **4** *(devoción)* dedication.
■ **entrega contra reembolso** cash on delivery.

entregar *vt* **1** *(dar)* to hand over; *(deberes, solicitud)* to hand in. **2** *(mercancía)* to deliver. **3** *(posesiones, armas)* to surrender. **4** *(premio, trofeo)* to present. **5** *(rehén)* to hand over.
▶ *vpr* **entregarse 1** *(rendirse)* to give in, surrender. **2** *(dedicarse)* to devote oneself.

entremés *nm* *(plato)* hors d'oeuvre.

entrenador,-ra *nm,f* trainer, coach.

entrenamiento *nm* *(acción)* training; *(sesión)* training session.

entrenar *vt-vpr* **entrenar(se)** to train.

entresuelo *nm* mezzanine.

entretanto *adv* meanwhile.

entretener *vt* **1** *(retrasar)* to delay, detain. **2** *(divertir)* to entertain. **3** *(distraer)* to distract.
▶ *vpr* **entretenerse 1** *(retrasarse)* to be late; *(detenerse)* to hang around [*pt & pp* **hung**]. **2** *(divertirse)* keep oneself amused.

entretenido,-a *adj* **1** *(divertido)* entertaining. **2** *(complicado)* time-consuming.

entretenimiento *nm* entertainment.

entrever *vt* **1** *(vislumbrar)* to glimpse. **2** *(conjeturar)* to guess.

entrevista *nf* **1** *(de prensa, trabajo)* interview. **2** *(reunión)* meeting.

entrevistar *vt* to interview.
▶ *vpr* **entrevistarse** to have a meeting.

entristecer *vt* to sadden.

▶ *vpr* **entristecerse** to be saddened.

entrometerse *vpr* to meddle, interfere.

entrometido,-a *adj* meddling, interfering.
▶ *nm,f* meddler, busybody.

enturbiar *vt* to cloud.
▶ *vpr* **enturbiarse 1** *(líquido)* to get cloudy. **2** *(relación, entusiasmo)* to be clouded.

entusiasmado,-a *adj* excited, enthusiastic.

entusiasmar *vt* to excite: ***me entusiasma la ópera***, I love opera; ***el pavo no me entusiasma***, I am not very keen on turkey.
▶ *vpr* **entusiasmarse** to get enthusiastic.

entusiasmo *nm* enthusiasm.
• **con entusiasmo** enthusiastically.

entusiasta *adj* enthusiastic.
▶ *nmf* enthusiast.

enumerar *vt* to enumerate.

enunciado *nm* statement.

enunciar *vt* to state.

envasar *vt* *(en paquete)* to pack; *(en botella)* to bottle; *(en lata)* to can, tin.
• **envasado,-a al vacío** vacuum-packed.

envase *nm* *(recipiente)* container; *(botella)* bottle.

envejecer *vt* *(hacer viejo)* to age; *(dar aspecto viejo)* to make look older.
▶ *vi* *(hacerse viejo)* to grow old [*pt* **grew**; *pp* **grown**]; *(tomar aspecto viejo)* to age.

envejecido,-a *adj* aged, old-looking.

envejecimiento *nm* ageing.

envenenamiento *nm* poisoning.

envenenar *vt* to poison.
▶ *vpr* **envenenarse** to poison oneself.

envergadura *nf* **1** *(relevancia)* importance. **2** *(de pájaro)* spread. **3** *(de avión)* span.

enviado,-a *nm,f* correspondent, envoy.
■ **enviado,-a especial** special correspondent.

enviar *vt* **1** *(mandar)* to send [*pt & pp* **sent**]. **2** *(mercancías)* to ship.

envidia *nf* envy.
• **dar envidia** to make envious.
• **tener envidia de** to envy.

envidiar *vt* to envy.

envidioso,-a *adj* envious.

envío nm **1** *(acción)* sending. **2** *(remesa)* consignment; *(de mercancía)* dispatch, shipment. **3** *(paquete)* parcel.

■ **envío contra reembolso** cash on delivery.

enviudar vi *(hombre)* to become a widower ; be widowed; *(mujer)* to become a widew, be widowed.

envoltorio nm **1** *(de caramelo etc)* wrapper. **2** *(lío)* bundle.

envoltura nf wrapping.

envolver vt **1** *(cubrir)* to wrap. **2** *(rodear)* to surround. **3** *(implicar)* to involve.

▶ vpr **envolverse 1** *(con ropa)* to wrap oneself up. **2** *(implicarse)* to get involved.

enyesar vt **1** *(pared)* to plaster. **2** *(pierna, brazo)* to put in plaster.

épico,-a adj epic.

epidemia nf epidemic.

epílogo nm GB epilogue; US epilog.

episodio nm **1** *(de narración, serie)* episode. **2** *(suceso)* incident, episode.

época nf **1** *(período)* time, period: *una época de cambios*, a time of change; *en la época romana*, in Roman times. **2** *(del año)* season.

● **por aquella época** about that time.

equilibrado,-a adj balanced.

equilibrar vt-vpr **equilibrar(se)** to balance.

equilibrio nm balance.

● **hacer equilibrios** to do a balancing act.

● **mantener el equilibrio** to keep one's balance.

● **perder el equilibrio** to lose one's balance [pt & pp **lost**].

■ **equilibrio ecológico** ecological balance.

equilibrista nmf tightrope walker.

equipaje nm luggage, baggage.

● **hacer el equipaje** to pack, do the packing.

■ **equipaje de mano** hand luggage.

equipar vt to equip.

▶ vpr **equiparse** to kit oneself out.

equipo nm **1** *(de personas, jugadores)* team. **2** *(equipamiento)* equipment. **3** *(de soldado)* kit; *(de deportista)* gear. **4** *(ordenador)* machine.

● **trabajar en equipo** to work as a team.

● **trabajo en equipo** teamwork.

■ **equipo de alta fidelidad** hi-fi stereo system.

■ **equipo de salvamento** rescue team.

equitación nf **1** *(acto)* horse riding. **2** *(arte)* horsemanship.

equivalente adj - nm equivalent.

equivaler vi **1** *(ser igual)* to be equivalent. **2** *(significar)* to be tantamount.

equivocación nf mistake, error.

● **por equivocación** by mistake.

equivocado,-a adj mistaken, wrong.

equivocarse vpr **1** *(no tener razón)* to be mistaken, be wrong. **2** *(cometer un error)* to make a mistake: *equivocarse de número*, to get the wrong number; *equivocarse de tren*, to catch the wrong train.

equívoco,-a adj equivocal, ambiguous.

▶ nm **equívoco** misunderstanding.

era nf *(período)* era, age.

erección nf erection.

erguir vt to raise.

▶ vpr **erguirse 1** *(ponerse derecho)* to straighten up. **2** *(engreírse)* to swell with pride [pt **swelled**; pp **swollen**].

erigir vt to erect.

▶ vpr **erigirse** to set oneself up.

erizar vt to make stand on end.

▶ vpr **erizarse** to stand on end [pt & pp **stood**].

erizo nm hedgehog.

■ **erizo de mar** sea urchin.

ermita nf hermitage.

ermitaño,-a nm,f hermit.

▶ nm **ermitaño** *(cangrejo)* hermit crab.

erosión nf erosion.

erótico,-a adj erotic.

erotismo nm eroticism.

erradicar vt *(gen)* to eradicate; *(enfermedad)* to stamp out.

errante adj wandering.

errar vt *(objetivo, disparo)* to miss; *(pronóstico)* to get wrong: *erró su camino*, he took the wrong path.

▶ vi **1** *(vagar)* to wander, rove. **2** *(divagar)* to be mistaken.

errata nf misprint, erratum [pl **errata**].

erróneo,-a adj wrong.

error nm **1** *(equivocación)* mistake, error. **2** INFORM error: *un mensaje de error*, an error message.

● **caer en un error** to make a mistake.

● **estar en un error** to be mistaken.

● **por error** by mistake.

■ **error de cálculo** miscalculation.

■ **error de imprenta** misprint.

eructar *vi* to belch.

eructo *nm* belch.

erupción *nf* **1** *(volcánica)* eruption. **2** *(cutánea)* rash.

esbelto,-a *adj* slim, slender.

esbozar *vt* **1** *(dibujar)* to sketch. **2** *(explicar resumidamente)* to outline.

● **esbozar una sonrisa** to give a hint of a smile.

esbozo *nm* **1** *(dibujo)* sketch. **2** *(explicación resumida)* outline.

escabeche *nm* pickle.

escabullirse *vpr* **1** *(zafarse)* to worm one's way out. **2** *(escaparse)* to slip away.

escafandra *nf* diving suit.

escala *nf* **1** *(gen)* scale. **2** *(escalera)* ladder.

● **a escala** scale: *un modelo a escala*, a scale model.

● **a gran escala** on a large scale.

● **a pequeña escala** on a small scale.

● **hacer escala 1** (avión) to stop over. **2** (barco) to put in.

■ **escala musical** musical scale.

escalada *nf* climbing.

● **la escalada del terrorismo** the rise of terrorism.

■ **escalada libre** free climbing.

escalador,-ra *nm,f* climber.

escalar *vt* to climb.

escalera *nf* **1** *(de edificio)* stairs *pl*. **2** *(portátil)* ladder. **3** *(naipes)* run.

■ **escalera de caracol** spiral staircase.

■ **escalera mecánica** escalator.

escalerilla *nf* *(de barco)* gangway; *(de avión)* steps *pl*.

escalinata *nf* staircase.

escalofriante *adj* spine-chilling.

escalofrío *nm* shiver: *me entraron escalofríos*, I started shivering.

escalón *nm* *(peldaño)* step.

escalope *nm* escalope.

escama *nf* **1** *(de pez, reptil)* scale. **2** *(de jabón)* flake.

escampar *vi* to stop raining.

escándalo *nm* **1** *(acto inmoral)* scandal. **2** *(alboroto)* racket.

● **armar un escándalo** to kick up a fuss.

escandaloso,-a *adj* **1** *(inmoral)* scandalous. **2** *(ruidoso)* noisy.

Escandinavia *nf* Scandinavia.

escandinavo,-a *adj* - *nm,f* Scandinavian.

escanear *vt* to scan.

escáner *nm* scanner.

escaño *nm* **1** *(banco)* bench. **2** *(en parlamento)* seat.

escapada *nf* **1** *(huida)* escape. **2** *fam (viaje)* quick trip. **3** *(en ciclismo)* breakaway.

escapar *vi-vpr* **escapar(se)** *(lograr salir)* to escape; *(irse corriendo)* to run away [*pt* ran; *pp* run].

▶ *vpr* **escaparse 1** *(gas etc)* to leak out. **2** *(autobús etc)* to miss: *se me escapó*, I missed it.

● **escaparse de las manos** to slip out of one's hands.

● **escaparse por los pelos** *fam* to have a narrow escape.

● **escapársele la risa a ALGN** to burst out laughing [*pt & pp* burst].

● **no se le escapa (ni) una** he doesn't miss a thing.

escaparate *nm* shop window.

escape *nm* **1** *(huida)* escape. **2** *(de gas etc)* leak. **3** *(de coche)* exhaust.

escarabajo *nm* beetle.

escarbar *vt* *(suelo)* to scratch; *(fuego)* to poke.

▶ *vpr* **escarbarse** *(dientes, nariz)* to pick.

escarcha *nf* frost.

escarlata *adj* - *nm* scarlet.

escarlatina *nf* scarlet fever.

escarmentar *vt* to punish.

▶ *vi-vpr* **escarmentar(se)** to learn one's lesson [*pt & pp* learnt]: *para que escarmientes*, that'll teach you a lesson.

escarmiento *nm* lesson, punishment.

● **servir de escarmiento** to serve as a lesson.

escarola *nf* GB curly endive; US escarole.

escarpado,-a *adj* **1** *(inclinado)* steep. **2** *(abrupto)* rugged.

escasear *vi* to be scarce.

escasez *nf* shortage.

escaso,-a *adj* scarce, scant: *de escaso interés*, of little interest.

● **andar escaso de algo** to be short of STH.

escayola *nf* plaster.

escayolar *vt* to put in plaster.

escena *nf* **1** *(gen)* scene. **2** *(escenario)* stage.

● **montar una escena** to make a scene.

● **poner en escena** to stage.

escenario nm **1** *(en teatro)* stage. **2** *(de suceso)* scene. **3** *(ambientación)* setting.

escenografía nm **1** *(en cine)* set design. **2** *(en teatro)* stage design.

escéptico,-a adj GB sceptical; US skeptical.
▶ nm,f GB sceptic; US skeptic.

esclavitud nf slavery.

esclavizar vt to enslave.

esclavo,-a nm,f slave.
● **ser esclavo,-a de algo** to be a slave to STH.

esclusa nf *(de canal)* lock; *(compuerta)* sluice gate.

escoba nf broom.

escobilla nf **1** *(gen)* brush. **2** *(de coche)* windscreen wiper blade.

escocer vi **1** *(herida)* to smart. **2** *(ánimo)* to hurt [pt & pp **hurt**].
▶ vpr **escocerse** *(irritarse)* to get sore.

escocés,-a adj Scottish.
▶ nm,f *(persona)* Scot; *(hombre)* Scotsman [pl **-men**]; *(mujer)* Scotswoman [pl **-women**].
▶ nm **escocés** *(dialecto)* Scots.

Escocia nf Scotland.

escoger vt to choose [pt **chose**; pp **chosen**].
● **tener donde escoger** to have plenty of choice.

escolar adj school.
▶ nmf *(chico)* schoolboy; *(chica)* schoolgirl.
■ **escolares** schoolchildren.

escollo nm **1** *(en el mar)* reef, rock. **2** *(obstáculo)* difficulty.

escolta nmf escort.
▶ nf escort.

escoltar vt to escort.

escombros nm pl rubble sing.

esconder vt to hide [pt **hid**; pp **hidden**], conceal.
▶ vpr **esconderse** to hide [pt **hid**; pp **hidden**].

escondidas loc a escondidas in secret.
● **hacer algo a escondidas de** ALGN to do STH behind SB's back.

escondido,-a adj hidden.

escondite nm hiding place.
● **jugar al escondite** to play hide-and-seek.

escondrijo nm hiding place.

escopeta nf shotgun.

■ **escopeta de aire comprimido** airgun.

escorpión nm scorpion.

escote[1] nm *(de vestido)* neckline.

escote[2].
● **pagar a escote** to share the expenses.

escotilla nf hatchway.

escozor nm **1** *(picor)* irritation, smarting. **2** *(resentimiento)* resentment.

escribir vt-vi to write [pt **wrote**; pp **written**].
▶ vpr **escribirse 1** *(dos personas)* to write to each other. **2** *(palabra)* to spell [pt & pp **spelt**]: *se escribe con "j"*, it's spelt with a "j".

escrito,-a adj written.
▶ nm **escrito** piece of writing, document.
● **por escrito** in writing.

escritor,-ra nm,f writer.

escritorio nm **1** *(mueble)* writing desk. **2** *(oficina)* office. **3** INFORM desktop.

escritura nf writing.
■ **escritura de propiedad** title deed.
■ **Sagradas Escrituras** Holy Scriptures.

escrúpulo nm **1** *(recelo)* scruple. **2** *(aprensión)* fussiness.

escrupuloso,-a adj **1** *(cuidadoso)* scrupulous. **2** *(aprensivo)* finicky, fussy.

escrutinio nm **1** *(examen)* scrutiny. **2** *(recuento de votos)* count.

escuadra nf **1** *(instrumento)* square. **2** *(de soldados)* squad.

escuadrón nm squadron.

escucha nf *(acción)* listening.
■ **escuchas telefónicas** phone tapping sing.

escuchar vt **1** *(atender)* to listen to. **2** *(oír)* to hear [pt & pp **heard**].

escudo nm shield.

escuela nf school.
■ **escuela privada** private school.
■ **escuela pública** state school.

escueto,-a adj *(estilo, lenguaje)* plain; *(explicación)* succint.

esculpir vt *(piedra)* to sculpt; *(madera)* to carve.

escultor,-ra nm,f *(hombre)* sculptor; *(mujer)* sculptress.

escultura nf sculpture.

escupir vi to spit [pt & pp **spat**].
▶ vt *(comida, palabras)* to spit out [pt & pp **spat**].
● **escupirle a** ALGN to spit at SB [pt & pp **spat**].

escurreplatos *nm* dish rack.

escurridizo,-a *adj* slippery.

escurridor *nm* **1** *(colador)* colander. **2** *(de platos)* dish rack.

escurrir *vt (platos)* to drain; *(ropa)* to wring out [*pt & pp* **wrung**]; *(comida)* to strain.
▶ *vi* to drip.
▶ *vpr* **escurrirse 1** *fam (escapar)* to slip away. **2** *(resbalarse)* to slip.

ese,-a *adj* that: *ese coche*, that car.

ése,-a *pron* that one: *toma ésa*, take that one.
● **ni por ésas** even so.

esencia *nf* essence.

esencial *adj* essential.

esfera *nf* **1** *(figura)* sphere. **2** *(de reloj)* face.
● **las altas esferas** the upper echelons.

esférico,-a *adj* spherical.

esfinge *nf* sphinx.

esforzarse *vpr* to try hard.
● **esforzarse por hacer algo** to try hard to do STH.

esfuerzo *nm* effort.
● **hacer un esfuerzo** to make an effort.

esfumarse *vpr* **1** *(desvanecerse)* to fade away. **2** *fam (largarse)* to disappear.

esgrima *nf* fencing.

esguince *nm* sprain.

eslabón *nm* link.
■ **eslabón perdido** missing link.

eslip *nm* briefs *pl*, underpants *pl*.

eslogan *nm* slogan.

esmaltar *vt* to enamel.

esmalte *nm* enamel.
■ **esmalte de uñas** nail polish, nail varnish.

esmeralda *nf* emerald.

esmerarse *vpr* to do one's best.

esmero *nm* great care.

esmoquin *nf* GB dinner jacket; US tuxedo.

eso *pron* that.
● **a eso de las ...** *(hora)* around ....
● **¡eso es!** that's it!
● **nada de eso** not at all: *¿exageraciones? nada de eso*, exaggerations? not at all; *no fumo ni nada de eso*, I don't smoke or anything like that.
● **¿y cómo es eso?** how come?

esófago *nm* GB oesophagus; US esophagus.

espabilado,-a *adj* **1** *(listo)* quick-witted. **2** *(despierto)* awake.

espabilar *vt* **1** *(despertar)* to wake up [*pt* **woke**; *pp* **woken**]. **2** *(hacer más avispado)*: *espabilar a ALGN*, to sharpen SB's wits.
▶ *vi (darse prisa)* to get a move on.
▶ *vpr* **espabilarse 1** *(despertarse)* to wake up [*pt* **woke**; *pp* **woken**]. **2** *(avisparse)* to buck one's ideas up. **3** *(darse prisa)* to get a move on.

espacial *adj (cohete etc)* space; *(en física)* spatial.

espacio *nm* **1** *(sitio)* space: *necesitamos más espacio*, we need more room. **2** *(de tiempo)* period. **3** *(en radio, televisión)* programme.
■ **espacio aéreo** air space.
■ **espacio radiofónico** radio programme.
■ **espacio televisivo** TV programme.

espacioso,-a *adj* spacious, roomy.

espada *nf* sword.
▶ *nf pl* **espadas** *(naipe - baraja francesa)* spades; *(- baraja española)* swords.
● **entre la espada y la pared** with one's back to the wall.

espaguetis *nm pl* spaghetti *sing*.

espalda *nf* **1** *(parte del cuerpo)* back. **2** *(en natación)* backstroke.
● **a espaldas de ALGN** behind SB's back.
● **dar la espalda a** to turn one's back on.
● **de espaldas** backwards.

espantapájaros *nm* scarecrow.

espantar *vt* **1** *(asustar)* to frighten, scare. **2** *(ahuyentar)* to frighten away.
▶ *vpr* **espantarse** to get frightened.

espanto *nm* fright, dread.
● **estar curado de espantos** to have seen it all before.
● **¡qué espanto!** how awful!

espantoso,-a *adj* **1** *(terrible)* frightful, dreadful. **2** *(muy feo)* hideous, frightful.

español,-la *adj* Spanish.
▶ *nm,f (persona)* Spaniard.
▶ *nm* **español** *(idioma)* Spanish, Castilian.

esparadrapo *nm* GB sticking plaster; US Band-Aid.

esparcir *vt* **1** *(desparramar)* to scatter. **2** *(divulgar)* to spread [*pt & pp* **spread**].
▶ *vpr* **esparcirse** to amuse oneself.

espárrago *nm pl* asparagus *sing*: **un espárrago** an asparagus tip.

● **mandar a ALGN a freír espárragos** *fam* to tell SB to get lost [*pt & pp* **told**].

esparto *nm* esparto grass.

espátula *nf* **1** *(para cocinar, etc.)* spatula. **2** *(de pintor)* palette knife [*pl* -**ves**]. **3** *(para rascar)* scraper.

especia *nf* spice.

especial *adj* special.

● **en especial** especially.

especialidad *nf* GB speciality ; US specialty.

especialista *adj* - *nmf* specialist.

especializarse *vpr* to specialize.

especie *nf* **1** *(de animales, plantas)* species. **2** *(tipo)* kind, sort.

especificar *vt* to specify.

específico,-a *adj* specific.

▶ *nm* **específico** specific.

espécimen *nm* specimen.

espectacular *adj* spectacular.

espectáculo *nm* **1** *(escena)* spectacle, sight: **un triste espectáculo**, a sad spectacle. **2** *(de TV, radio etc)* show.

● **montar un espectáculo** to make a scene.

espectador,-ra *nm,f* **1** *(en un estadio)* spectator. **2** *(en teatro, cine)* member of the audience; *(de televisión)* viewer.

espectro *nm* **1** spectrum. **2** *(fantasma)* spectre.

especular *vi* to speculate.

espejismo *nm* **1** *(fenómeno óptico)* mirage. **2** *(ilusión)* illusion.

espejo *nm* mirror: **deja de mirarte al espejo**, stop looking at yourself in the mirror.

■ **espejo retrovisor** rear-view mirror.

espeleología *nf* potholing, caving.

espeluznante *adj* hair-raising, terrifying.

espera *nf* wait.

● **en espera de ...** waiting for ....

esperanza *nf* hope.

● **con la esperanza de que ...** in the hope that ....

● **darle esperanzas a ALGN** to give SB hope.

● **perder la esperanza** to lose hope [*pt & pp* **lost**].

■ **esperanza de vida** life expectancy.

esperar *vt* **1** *(aguardar)* to wait for, await:

espera un momento, wait a moment. **2** *(confiar)* to hope for, expect: **espero que sí**, I hope so; **espero ganar la carrera**, I hope to win the race. **3** *(bebé)* to expect.

▶ *vi* to wait: **esperaré hasta que lleguen**, I'll wait until they get here.

● **hacer esperar a ALGN** to keep SB waiting.

● **puedes esperar sentado,-a** *fam* you'll be waiting till the cows come home.

esperma *nm* sperm.

espesar *vt-vpr* **espesar(se)** to thicken.

espeso,-a *adj* *(gen)* thick; *(niebla, bosque)* dense, thick; *(nieve)* deep.

espesor *nm* *(grosor)* thickness; *(densidad)* density.

espía *nmf* spy.

espiar *vt* to spy on.

espiga *nf* **1** *(de trigo)* ear; *(de flor)* spike. **2** *(clavija)* peg.

espina *nf* **1** *(de planta)* thorn. **2** *(de pez)* fishbone. **3** *(duda)* suspicion.

● **dar mala espina** to arouse one's suspicion.

■ **espina dorsal** spine, backbone.

espinacas *nf pl* spinach *sing*.

espinilla *nf* **1** *(tibia)* shinbone. **2** *(grano)* blackhead.

espinoso,-a *adj* **1** *(planta)* thorny. **2** *(pez)* bony. **3** *(problema etc)* thorny, awkward.

espionaje *nm* spying, espionage.

espiral *adj* - *nf* spiral.

espirar *vt-vi* to exhale, breathe out.

espíritu *nm* spirit.

■ **Espíritu Santo** Holy Ghost.

espiritual *adj* spiritual.

espléndido,-a *adj* **1** *(magnífico)* splendid, magnificent. **2** *(generoso)* lavish.

esplendor *nm* **1** *(magnificencia)* GB splendour; US splendor. **2** *(resplandor)* radiance.

espolvorear *vt* to sprinkle, dust.

esponja *nf* sponge.

esponjoso,-a *adj* spongy.

espontaneidad *nf* spontaneity.

espontáneo,-a *adj* spontaneous.

esporádico,-a *adj* sporadic.

esposar *vt* to handcuff.

esposas *nf pl* handcuffs.

esposo,-a *nm,f* spouse; *(hombre)* husband; *(mujer)* wife [*pl* -**ves**].

▶ *nm pl* **esposos** husband and wife.

espuela *nf* spur.

espuma *nf* **1** *(de mar)* foam; *(de olas)* surf; *(de jabón)* lather; *(de cerveza)* froth. **2** *(impurezas)* scum.

● **crecer como la espuma** to mushroom.

■ **espuma de afeitar** shaving foam.

espumadera *nf* skimmer.

espumoso,-a *adj (jabón)* foamy; *(cerveza)* frothy; *(vino)* sparkling.

esquela *nf (carta)* short letter.

■ **esquela mortuoria** death notice.

esquelético,-a *adj* **1** *(en biología)* skeletal. **2** *fam (flaco)* skinny.

esqueleto *nm* **1** *(de cuerpo)* skeleton. **2** *(de edificio)* framework.

● **mover el esqueleto** *fam* to get down.

esquema *nm (plan)* outline; *(gráfica)* diagram.

esquí *nm* **1** *(tabla)* ski. **2** *(deporte)* skiing.

■ **esquí acuático** water-skiing.

esquiador,-ra *nm,f* skier.

esquiar *vi* to ski.

esquilar *vt* to shear.

esquimal *adj - nmf* Eskimo.

esquina *nf* corner.

● **a la vuelta de la esquina** just around the corner.

● **doblar la esquina** to turn the corner.

esquivar *vt* **1** *(persona)* to avoid. **2** *(golpe)* to dodge.

estabilidad *nf* stability.

estabilizar *vt* to stabilize.

▶ *vpr* **estabilizarse** to stabilize, become stable.

estable *adj* stable, steady.

establecer *vt (gen)* to establish.

▶ *vpr* **establecerse** *(instalarse)* to settle; *(abrir un negocio)* to set up in business [*pt & pp* **set**].

establecimiento *nm* **1** *(acto)* establishment. **2** *(local)* establishment; *(tienda)* shop; *(almacén)* store.

establo *nm* stable.

estaca *nf* **1** *(palo con punta)* stake. **2** *(garrote)* stick, club.

estación *nf* **1** *(del año)* season. **2** *(de tren)* station.

■ **estación de esquí** ski resort.

■ **estación de servicio** service station.

■ **estación espacial** space station.

estacionar *vt* to park.

▶ *vpr* **estacionarse 1** *(estancarse)* to be stationary. **2** *(vehículo)* to park.

estadio *nm* **1** *(deportivo)* stadium. **2** *(fase)* stage, phase.

estadística *nf* **1** *(ciencia)* statistics. **2** *(dato)* statistic.

estado *nm* **1** *(situación)* state. **2** *(médico)* condition: *su estado es grave*, his condition is serious. **3** *(país)* state. **4** *(resumen)* return, summary.

● **estar en buen estado** to be in good condition.

● **estar en mal estado 1** (alimento) to be off. **2** (carretera) to be in poor condition.

● **estar en estado** to be pregnant.

■ **estado civil** marital status.

■ **estado de ánimo** state of mind.

■ **estado de cuentas** statement of account.

■ **estado de excepción** state of emergency.

■ **estado del bienestar** welfare state.

■ **estado mayor** staff.

estadounidense *adj* American: *un ciudadano estadounidense*, a US citizen.

▶ *nmf* American.

estafa *nf* **1** *(timo)* swindle. **2** *(fraude)* fraud.

estafador,-ra *nm,f (timador)* swindler.

estafar *vt* **1** *(timar)* to swindle. **2** *(defraudar)* to defraud.

estalactita *nf* stalactite.

estalagmita *nf* stalagmite.

estallar *vi* **1** *(bomba)* to explode. **2** *(neumático, globo)* to burst [*pt & pp* **burst**]. **3** *(rebelión, guerra)* to break out [*pt* **broke**; *pp* **broken**].

estallido *nm* **1** *(de bomba)* explosion. **2** *(de neumático, globo)* bursting. **3** *(de rebelión, guerra)* outbreak.

estambre *nm* **1** *(tejido)* worsted. **2** *(de planta)* stamen.

estampa *nf* **1** *(imagen)* picture. **2** *(aspecto)* appearance.

estampado,-a *adj* printed.

▶ *nm* **estampado** *(tela)* print.

estampido *nm* bang.

estancarse *vpr* **1** *(líquido)* to stagnate. **2** *(proceso)* to come to a standstill.

estancia *nf* **1** *(permanencia)* stay. **2** *(aposento)* room.

estanco *nm* tobacconist's.

estándar *adj - nm* standard.

estandarte *nm* standard, banner.

estanque *nm* pool, pond.
estanquero,-a *nm,f* tobacconist.
estante *nm* (gen) shelf [*pl* -**ves**]; (para libros) bookcase.
estantería *nf* shelves *pl*.
estaño *nm* tin.
estar *vi* **1** (en lugar, posición) to be: **estaba sobre la mesa**, it was on the table; **allí está**, there it is; **estamos a dos de noviembre**, it's the second of November. **2** (permanecer) to be, stay: **estuvimos allí diez días**, we were there for ten days.
▸ *aux* **estar** + *gerundio* to be: **estar comiendo**, to be eating.
▸ *vpr* **estarse** (permanecer) to spend [*pt & pp* **spent**]: **se estuvo todo el día leyendo**, he spent all day reading.
● **está bien** it's all right.
● **estar al caer**: **la nueva versión está al caer**, the new version will be here any day now.
● **estar de 1** (gen) to be: **están de vacaciones**, they're on holiday. **2** (trabajar) to be working as: **está de profesor**, he is working as a teacher.
● **estar de más** not to be needed.
● **¡ya le está bien!** it serves him right!
estatal *adj* state.
estático,-a *adj* static.
estatua *nf* statue.
estatura *nf* height.
● **de mediana estatura** of medium height.
estatuto *nm* statute.
este *adj* - *nm* east.
este,-a *adj* this: **este libro**, this book.
éste,-a *pron* this one.
● **éste... aquél...** the former... the latter....
estela *nf* **1** (de barco) wake; (de avión) GB vapour trail; US vapor trail. **2** *fig* (huella) trail.
estelar *adj* **1** (sideral) stellar. **2** (actuación, elenco) star.
estepa *nf* steppe.
estéreo *adj* stereo.
▸ *nm* stereo [*pl* -**s**].
estéril *adj* sterile.
esterilizar *vt* to sterilize.
esternón *nm* sternum.
estética *nf* GB aesthetics; US esthetics.
esteticista *nmf* beautician.

estético,-a *adj* GB aesthetic; US esthetic.
estetoscopio *nm* stethoscope.
estiércol *nm* **1** (excremento) dung. **2** (abono) manure.
estilo *nm* **1** (gen) style. **2** (en natación) stroke.
● **algo por el estilo** something like that.
■ **estilo braza** breast stroke.
■ **estilo crol** crawl stroke.
■ **estilo de vida** way of life, lifestyle.
■ **estilo espalda** back stroke.
■ **estilo mariposa** butterfly stroke.
estilográfica *nf* fountain pen.
estima *nf* esteem.
estimado,-a *adj* **1** (apreciado) esteemed. **2** (valorado) valued.
● **estimada señora** (en carta) Dear Madam.
● **estimado señor** (en carta) Dear Sir.
estimar *vt* **1** (apreciar) to esteem; (objeto) to value. **2** (juzgar) to consider.
estimular *vt* **1** (avivar) to stimulate. **2** (animar) to encourage.
estímulo *nm* **1** stimulus. **2** (aliciente) encouragement.
estirar *vt* to stretch.
▸ *vi* (crecer) to shoot up [*pt & pp* **shot**].
▸ *vpr* **estirarse** (desperezarse) to stretch.
● **estirar las piernas** *fam* to stretch one's legs.
● **estirar la pata** *fam* to kick the bucket.
estirón *nm* pull, tug.
● **pegar un estirón** to shoot up [*pt & pp* **shot**].
estival *adj* summer.
esto *pron* this.
● **esto de...** the business about...: **me gusta esto de la informática**, I like this computer thing.
estofado,-a *adj* stewed.
▸ *nm* **estofado** stew.
estómago *nm* stomach: **le duele el estómago**, he has a stomachache.
● **revolverle el estómago a ALGN** to turn SB's stomach.
Estonia *nf* Estonia.
estonio,-a *adj* - *nm,f* Estonian.
estoque *nm* sword.
estorbar *vt* **1** (dificultar) to hinder. **2** (molestar) to annoy.
▸ *vi* to get in the way.
estorbo *nm* **1** (obstáculo) obstruction. **2** (molestia) hindrance; (persona) nuisance.

estornudar *vi* to sneeze.

estornudo *nm* sneeze.

estos,-as *adj pl* these.

éstos,-as *pron* these.

● **en éstas** *fam* just then.

estrafalario,-a *adj fam* eccentric.

estragón *nm* tarragon.

estrangular *vt* to strangle.

estratagema *nf* stratagem.

estrategia *nf* strategy.

estratégico,-a *adj* strategic.

estrechar *vt* **1** *(calle)* to narrow; *(vestido)* to take in. **2** *(abrazar)* to embrace.

▶ *vpr* **estrecharse 1** *(calle)* to narrow, get narrower. **2** *(relaciones)* to strengthen, tighten.

● **estrechar la mano** to shake hands [*pt* **shook;** *pp* **shaken**].

estrechez *nf (gen)* narrowness.

▶ *nf pl* **estrecheces** *(dificultades)* financial straits, hardship.

■ **estrechez de miras** narrow-mindedness.

estrecho,-a *adj* **1** *(gen)* narrow; *(vestido, zapatos)* tight. **2** *(amistad etc)* close.

▶ *nm* **estrecho** straits *pl*: *estrecho de Gibraltar*, Straits of Gibraltar.

● **ser estrecho de miras** to be narrow-minded.

estrella *nf* star.

● **tener buena estrella** to be lucky.

● **tener mala estrella** to be unlucky.

● **ver las estrellas** to see stars [*pt* **saw;** *pp* **seen**].

■ **estrella de cine** film star.

■ **estrella de mar** starfish.

■ **estrella fugaz** shooting star.

■ **estrella polar** pole star.

estrellar *vt fam (hacer pedazos)* to smash to pieces, shatter.

▶ *vpr* **estrellarse** *(chocar)* to crash, smash.

estremecer *vt* to shake [*pt* **shook;** *pp* **shaken**].

▶ *vpr* **estremecerse** *(de miedo)* to shudder; *(de frío)* to shiver.

estrenar *vt* **1** *(gen)* to use for the first time; *(ropa)* to wear for the first time [*pt* **wore;** *pp* **worn**]. **2** *(obra de teatro)* to open; *(película)* to release.

▶ *vpr* **estrenarse 1** *(persona)* to make one's debut. **2** *(obra de teatro)* to open; *(película)* to be released.

estreno *nm* **1** *(de cosa)* first use. **2** *(de artista)* debut. **3** *(de obra de teatro)* first night, opening night; *(de película)* premiere.

estreñido,-a *adj* constipated.

estreñimiento *nm* constipation.

estreñir *vt* to constipate.

▶ *vpr* **estreñirse** to become constipated.

estrépito *nm* din, noise.

estrepitoso,-a *adj* **1** *(ruidoso)* noisy. **2** *(fracaso)* resounding.

estrés *nm* stress.

estribillo *nm* **1** *(de poesía)* refrain. **2** *(de canción)* chorus. **3** *(muletilla)* pet phrase.

estribo *nm (de montura)* stirrup.

● **perder los estribos** to lose one's head [*pt & pp* **lost**].

estribor *nm* starboard.

estricto,-a *adj* strict.

estridente *adj* **1** *(ruido)* strident, shrill. **2** *(color)* loud, garish.

estrofa *nf* stanza.

estropajo *nm* scourer.

estropeado,-a *adj (roto)* broken; *(dañado)* damaged.

estropear *vt* **1** *(máquina)* to damage, break [*pt* **broke;** *pp* **broken**]. **2** *(plan etc)* to spoil [*pt & pp* **spoilt**], ruin.

▶ *vpr* **estropearse 1** *(máquina)* to break down [*pt* **broke;** *pp* **broken**]. **2** *(plan, etc)* to go wrong. **3** *(comida)* to go off.

estructura *nf* structure.

estruendo *nm* **1** *(ruido)* great noise, din. **2** *(confusión)* uproar.

estrujar *vt* **1** *(gen)* to crush. **2** *(papel)* to crumple. **3** *(persona)* to bleed dry [*pt & pp* **bled**].

estuario *nm* estuary.

estuche *nm* case, box.

estudiante *nmf* student.

estudiar *vt-vi* to study.

estudio *nm* **1** *(gen)* study. **2** *(apartamento, oficina)* studio [*pl* **-s**].

▶ *nm pl* **estudios 1** *(conocimientos)* studies, education *sing*: *¿cómo te van los estudios?*, how are you getting on at school/university? **2** *(de cine, televisión)* studio [*pl* **-s**].

■ **estudios primarios** primary education *sing*.

■ **estudios secundarios** secondary education *sing*.

■ **estudios superiores** higher education *sing*.

estudioso,-a *adj* studious.
estufa *nf* heater.
■ **estufa de gas** gas heater, gas fire.
■ **estufa eléctrica** electric heater.
estupefacto,-a *adj* astounded.
estupendo,-a *adj* wonderful.
► *interj* ¡**estupendo!** great!
estupidez *nf* stupidity.
estúpido,-a *adj* stupid.
► *nm,f* idiot.
etapa *nf* **1** *(gen)* stage. **2** *(en competición)*
leg, stage.
etarra *adj* ETA.
► *nmf* member of ETA.
etcétera *nf* etcetera, and so on.
eternidad *nf* eternity: **tardaste una
eternidad**, you took ages.
eterno,-a *adj* eternal, everlasting.
ética *nf* ethics.
ético,-a *adj* ethical.
etiqueta *nf* **1** *(rótulo)* label. **2** *(formalidad)*
etiquette.
etiquetar *vt* to label.
● **etiquetar a ALGN de algo** to label SB
(as) STH.
etnia *nf* ethnic group.
étnico,-a *adj* ethnic.
eucalipto *nm* eucalyptus.
eucaristía *nf* Eucharist.
eufemismo *nm* euphemism.
euforia *nf* euphoria, elation.
eufórico,-a *adj* euphoric.
euro *nm* euro [*pl* -**s**].
Europa *nf* Europe.
europeo,-a *adj - nm,f* European.
eutanasia *nf* euthanasia.
evacuación *nf* evacuation.
evacuar *vt* to evacuate.
evadir *vt* **1** *(peligro etc)* to avoid. **2** *(capital)*
to evade.
► *vpr* **evadirse** *(escaparse)* to escape.
evaluación *nf* **1** *(gen)* evaluation. **2** *(examen)* exam; *(acción)* assessment.
■ **evaluación continua** continuous assessment.
evaluar *vt* to evaluate, assess.
evangelio *nm* gospel.
evaporación *nf* evaporation.
evaporar *vt-vpr* **evaporar(se)** to evaporate.
evasión *nf* **1** *(fuga)* escape. **2** *(rechazo)*
avoidance.

evasiva *nf* evasive answer: **contestó con
evasivas**, she would not to give a
straight answer.
eventual *adj* **1** *(posible)* possible. **2** *(trabajo)* casual, temporary.
► *nmf* casual worker, temporary worker.
eventualmente *adv* *(posiblemente)* possibly; *(por casualidad)* by chance.
evidencia *nf* obviousness.
● **poner a ALGN en evidencia** to show
SB up.
evidente *adj* evident, obvious.
evitar *vt* to avoid.
evocar *vt* **1** *(recuerdo)* to evoke. **2** *(espíritu)*
to invoke.
evolución *nf* *(gen)* evolution; *(de enfermedad)* development; *(de enfermo)* progress: **la
evolución de los precios**, the price trend.
evolucionar *vi* *(gen)* to evolve; *(enfermedad)* to develop; *(enfermo)* progress.
exactitud *nf* accuracy.
exacto,-a *adj* exact, accurate.
► *interj* ¡**exacto!** *(expresando acuerdo)*
precisely!, exactly!; *(diciendo que sí)* yes!
exageración *nf* exaggeration.
exagerado,-a *adj* **1** *(gen)* exaggerated:
¡no seas exagerado!, don't exaggerate!
2 *pey (excesivo)* excessive.
exagerar *vt-vi* to exaggerate.
exaltado,-a *adj* **1** *(acalorado - persona)*
exalted; *(- discusión)* heated. **2** *(apasionado)* hot-headed.
exaltar *vt* **1** *(acalorar)* to work up. **2** *(alabar)* to exalt.
► *vpr* **exaltarse** *(excitarse)* to get worked
up.
examen *nm* **1** *(prueba)* exam, examination. **2** *(estudio)* examination.
● **presentarse a un examen** to take an
exam.
■ **examen de conciencia** soul search-
ing.
■ **examen de conducir** driving test.
■ **examen médico** check-up, medical.
examinador,-ra *adj* examining.
► *nm,f* examiner.
examinar *vt* **1** *(estudiante)* to examine. **2**
(considerar) to look into, consider.
► *vpr* **examinarse** to take an exam: **me
examiné de instructor**, I took the instructor's exam.
excavación *nf* **1** *(acción)* excavation, dig-
ging. **2** *(lugar)* dig.

excavar *vt (gen)* to dig *[pt & pp* **dug***]; (en arqueología)* to excavate.

exceder *vt* to exceed.

▶ *vpr* **excederse** to go too far: *excederse en sus funciones,* to exceed one's duty.

excelente *adj* excellent.

excéntrico,-a *adj* eccentric.

excepción *nf* exception.

● **a excepción de** except for.

● **de excepción** exceptional.

excepcional *adj* exceptional.

excepto *adv* except, apart from.

exceptuar *vt* to except, leave out *[pt & pp* **left***]*.

excesivo,-a *adj* excessive.

exceso *nm (demasía)* excess; *(de mercancía)* surplus.

● **con exceso** too much: *trabajar con exceso,* to work too hard.

● **en exceso** in excess, excessively.

■ **tener exceso de peso** to be overweight.

■ **exceso de equipaje** excess baggage.

■ **exceso de velocidad** speeding: *la multaron por exceso de velocidad,* she was fined for speeding.

excitación *nf* **1** *(acción)* excitation. **2** *(sentimiento)* excitement.

excitante *adj* **1** *(emocionante)* exciting. **2** *(efecto)* stimulating.

▶ *nm* stimulant.

excitar *vt* **1** *(gen)* to excite. **2** *(emociones)* to stir up.

▶ *vpr* **excitarse** to get excited.

exclamación *nf* exclamation.

exclamar *vt-vi* to exclaim.

exclamativo,-a *adj* exclamatory.

excluir *vt* to exclude.

exclusivamente *adv* exclusively.

exclusivo,-a *adj* exclusive.

excremento *nf* excrement: *excrementos de perro,* dog mess.

excursión *nf* excursion, outing.

● **ir de excursión** to go on an excursion, go on an outing.

excursionismo *nm* hiking.

excursionista *nmf (turista)* tripper; *(a pie)* hiker.

excusa *nf* excuse.

● **¡no hay excusa que valga!** there's no excuse for it!

excusar *vt* **1** *(disculpar)* to excuse. **2** *(eximir)* to exempt.

▶ *vpr* **excusarse** to apologize.

exento,-a *adj* exempt.

exhaustivo,-a *adj* exhaustive, thorough.

exhausto,-a *adj* exhausted.

exhibición *nf* **1** *(exposición)* exhibition. **2** *(de película)* showing.

exhibir *vt (mostrar)* to exhibit, put on, show *[pt* **showed***; pp* **shown***]*.

▶ *vpr* **exhibirse** *(hacer ostentación)* to show off *[pt* **showed***; pp* **shown***]*.

exigencia *nf* **1** *(petición)* demand: *no me vengas con exigencias,* don't come to me demanding things. **2** *(requisito)* requirement.

exigente *adj* demanding.

exigir *vt (pedir)* to demand; *(necesitar)* to require, demand: *este trabajo exige mucho esfuerzo,* this job requires a lot of effort.

exiliado,-a *adj* exiled.

▶ *nm,f* exile.

exiliar *vt* to exile.

▶ *vpr* **exiliarse** to go into exile.

exilio *nm* exile: *en el exilio,* in exile.

existencia *nf* existence.

▶ *nf pl* **existencias** inventory *sing,* stocks.

● **en existencia** in stock.

existir *vi* **1** *(ser real)* to exist: *los fantasmas no existen,* ghosts don't exist. **2** *(haber)* to be: *existen muchos problemas,* there are many problems.

éxito *nm* success.

● **con éxito** successfully.

● **tener éxito** to be successful.

exótico,-a *adj* exotic.

expansión *nf* **1** *(dilatación)* expansion. **2** *(difusión)* spreading. **3** *(recreo)* relaxation.

expectación *nf* expectation.

expectativa *nf* **1** *(esperanza)* expectation. **2** *(posibilidad)* prospect.

● **estar a la expectativa** to be on the lookout.

■ **expectativa de vida** life expectancy.

expedición *nf* **1** *(viaje, grupo)* expedition. **2** *(envío)* shipping.

expediente *nm* **1** *(investigación)* inquiry. **2** *(informe)* dossier, record. **3** *(recurso)* expedient: *abrirle expediente a ALGN,* to start proceedings against SB.

● **cubrir el expediente** *fam* to go through the motions.

■ **expediente académico** academic record.

■ **expediente médico** medical record.

expedir vt **1** *(documento)* to issue. **2** *(carta, paquete)* to dispatch.

expensas nf pl expenses.

● **a expensas de** at the expense of.

experiencia nf **1** *(gen)* experience. **2** *(experimento)* experiment.

● **por experiencia** from experience.

experimentado,-a adj **1** *(persona)* experienced. **2** *(método)* tested.

experimental adj experimental.

experimentar vt **1** *(probar)* to test. **2** *(sentir)* to experience; *(cambio)* to undergo [pt **underwent**; pp **undergone**]: *experimentar una mejoría*, to improve.

experimento nm experiment.

experto,-a adj - nm,f expert.

expirar vi to expire.

explicación nf explanation.

explicar vt to explain.

▶ vpr **explicarse 1** *(comprender)* to understand [pt & pp **understood**]: *no me lo explico*, I can't understand it. **2** *(hacerse entender)* to make oneself understood: *¿me explico?*, is that clear?

explícito,-a adj explicit.

exploración nf exploration.

explorador,-ra adj exploring.

▶ nm,f explorer.

explorar vt to explore.

explosión nf explosion.

● **hacer explosión** to explode.

explosionar vt-vi to explode.

explosivo,-a adj explosive.

▶ nm **explosivo** explosive.

explotación nf exploitation.

■ **explotación agrícola** farm.

■ **explotación forestal** forestry.

explotar vt *(sacar provecho de)* to exploit; *(mina)* to work; *(tierra)* to cultivate.

▶ vi *(explosionar)* to explode.

exponer vt **1** *(explicar)* to explain. **2** *(mostrar)* to show [pt **showed**; pp **shown**]. **3** *(arriesgar)* to expose.

▶ vpr **exponerse** *(arriesgarse)* to expose oneself.

exportación nf export.

exportador,-ra adj exporting.

▶ nm,f exporter.

exportar vt to export.

exposición nf **1** *(de arte)* exhibition. **2** *(de fotografía)* exposure. **3** *(explicación)* explanation. **4** *(riesgo)* exposure.

exprés adj express.

expresamente adv **1** *(específicamente)* specifically. **2** *(adrede)* on purpose.

expresar vt to express.

▶ vpr **expresarse** to express oneself.

expresión nf expression.

■ **expresión corporal** free expression.

expresivo,-a adj **1** *(elocuente)* expressive. **2** *(afectuoso)* affectionate.

expreso,-a adj express.

▶ nm **expreso** *(tren)* express train, express.

exprimidor nm squeezer.

exprimir vt to squeeze.

expropiar vt to expropriate.

expuesto,-a adj **1** *(al descubierto)* exposed: *el vino expuesto al aire se deteriora*, wine deteriorates when exposed to the air. **2** *(peligroso)* dangerous.

expulsar vt **1** *(gen)* to expel. **2** *(jugador)* to send off [pt & pp **sent**].

expulsión nf **1** *(gen)* expulsion. **2** *(de jugador)* sending off.

exquisito,-a adj **1** *(belleza, modales)* exquisite. **2** *(comida)* delicious.

éxtasis nm **1** *(estado)* ecstasy. **2** *(droga)* ecstasy.

extender vt **1** *(gen)* to extend. **2** *(mapa, papel)* to spread out [pt & pp **spread**]. **3** *(brazo etc)* to stretch out. **4** *(documento)* to draw up [pt **drew**; pp **drawn**]; *(cheque)* to make out; *(pasaporte, certificado)* to issue. **5** *(mantequilla, pintura)* to spread [pt & pp **spread**].

▶ vpr **extenderse 1** *(propagarse)* to extend. **2** *(durar)* to extend, last. **3** *(terreno)* to stretch out.

extensión nf **1** *(gen)* extension. **2** *(dimensión)* extent.

extenso,-a adj **1** *(territorio)* extensive. **2** *(documento, película)* long.

exterior adj **1** *(de fuera)* exterior, outer: *la parte exterior*, the outside. **2** *(extranjero)* foreign: *política exterior*, foreign policy.

▶ nm **1** *(parte de fuera)* exterior, outside. **2** *(de una persona)* appearance.

● **en exteriores** on location.

exteriorizar vt to show [pt **showed**; pp **shown**].

exterminar vt to exterminate.

exterminio nm extermination.

externo,-a *adj* external, outward: ***parte externa***, outside.
● **"Para uso externo"** "External use only".
extinción *nf* extinction.
extinguir *vt* **1** *(fuego)* to extinguish, put out. **2** *(especie)* to make extinct.
▶ *vpr* **extinguirse 1** *(fuego)* to go out. **2** *(especie)* to become extinct.
extintor *nm* fire extinguisher.
extirpar *vt* **1** *(tumor, órgano)* to remove. **2** *(destruir)* to eradicate.
extra *adj* **1** *(adicional)* extra. **2** *(superior)* top: ***calidad extra***, top quality.
▶ *nmf (actor)* extra.
▶ *nm* **1** *(gasto)* extra expense. **2** *(plus)* bonus.
extracto *nm* **1** *(substancia)* extract. **2** *(resumen)* summary.
■ **extracto de cuenta** statement of account.
extractor *nm* extractor.
extraer *vt* to extract.
extraescolar *adj* out-of-school.
● **actividades extraescolares** out-of-school activities.
extranjero,-a *adj* foreign.
▶ *nm,f* foreigner.
▶ *nm* **extranjero** foreign countries *pl*.
● **viajar al extranjero** to travel abroad.
● **vivir en el extranjero** to live abroad.
extrañar *vi (sorprender)* to surprise: ***no me extraña***, it doesn't surprise me.
▶ *vpr* **extrañarse** *(sorprenderse)* to be surprised.
extraño,-a *adj* **1** *(raro)* strange. **2** *(desconocido)* alien, foreign.
▶ *nm,f* stranger.

extraordinario,-a *adj* extraordinary.
extrarradio *nm* outskirts *pl*.
extraterrestre *adj* extraterrestrial, alien.
▶ *nmf* alien.
extravagancia *nf* extravagance.
extravagante *adj* extravagant.
extraviado,-a *adj* missing, lost: ***perro extraviado***, stray dog.
extraviar *vt* **1** *(persona)* to lead astray [*pt & pp* **led**]. **2** *(objeto)* to mislay.
▶ *vpr* **extraviarse 1** *(persona)* to get lost. **2** *(objeto)* to get mislaid.
extremado,-a *adj* extreme.
extremar *vt* to carry to extremes: ***extremar las precauciones***, to take extra precautions.
▶ *vpr* **extremarse** to do one's best.
extremidad *nf (parte extrema)* extremity; *(punta)* end, tip.
▶ *nf pl* **extremidades** limbs, extremities.
extremo,-a *adj* **1** *(máximo)* extreme: ***la extrema derecha***, the far right. **2** *(distante)* far: ***la punta extrema de la isla***, the far end of the island.
▶ *nm* **extremo 1** *(límite)* extreme; *(punta)* end. **2** *(en deporte)* wing.
● **en último extremo** as a last resort.
● **hasta tal extremo** to such a point.
extrovertido,-a *adj* - *nm,f* extrovert.
eyaculación *nf* ejaculation.
■ **eyaculación precoz** premature ejaculation.
eyacular *vi* to ejaculate.

F

fa *nf (nota)* F.

fábrica *nf* **1** *(industria)* factory. **2** *(fabricación)* manufacture.

■ **fábrica de cerveza** brewery.

■ **fábrica de conservas** canning plant.

fabricación *nf* manufacture.

● **de fabricación casera** home-made.

● **de fabricación propia**: *venden cerámica de fabricación propia*, they sell their own pottery.

■ **fabricación en serie** mass production.

fabricante *nmf* manufacturer.

fabricar *vt* **1** *(crear)* to make; *(en fábrica)* to manufacture. **2** *(inventar)* to invent.

● **fabricar en serie** to mass-produce.

fábula *nf* fable.

● **de fábula** wonderful.

fabuloso,-a *adj* fabulous, fantastic.

faceta *nf* faceta.

facha[1] *nf* **1** *fam (aspecto)* look. **2** *(mamarracho)*: *estar hecho,-a una facha*, to look a mess.

facha[2] *adj - nmf pey* fascist.

fachada *nf* **1** *(de edificio)* façade, front. **2** *fam (apariencia)* façade, show.

facial *adj* facial.

fácil *adj* **1** *(sencillo)* easy. **2** *(probable)* probable: *es fácil que se haya perdido*, it's quite likely to have got lost. **3** *pey (mujer)* loose.

facilidad *nf* **1** *(sencillez)* easiness. **2** *(talento)* talent, gift.

■ **facilidades de pago** credit terms.

facilitar *vt* **1** *(simplificar)* to make easy: *este método facilita el aprendizaje del inglés*, this method makes it easier to learn English. **2** *(proporcionar)* to provide:

el consulado le facilitará un visado, the consulate will provide you with a visa.

factible *adj* feasible, practicable.

factor *nm* factor.

factoría *nf* factory.

factura *nf* bill: *la factura de la luz*, the electricity bill.

● **pasar factura 1** *(hacer pagar)* to make pay: *pasar factura a ALGN*, to make SB pay. **2** *(traer consecuencias)* to take its toll.

● **presentar factura a ALGN** to invoice SB, send a bill to SB *[pt & pp* **sent***]*.

■ **factura pro forma** pro forma invoice.

facturar *vt* **1** *(cobrar)* to invoice; *(vender)* to have a turnover of. **2** *(equipaje)* to check in.

facultad *nf* **1** *(capacidad)* faculty. **2** *(autoridad)* power. **3** *(de universidad)* faculty.

faena *nf* **1** *(tarea)* job. **2** *fam (mala pasada)* dirty trick.

● **estar metido,-a en faena** *fam* to be hard at work.

■ **faenas de la casa** housework *sing*.

faisán *nm* pheasant.

faja *nf* **1** *(de mujer)* girdle. **2** *(cinturón)* belt. **3** *(banda)* sash. **4** *(correo)* wrapper. **5** *(franja)* strip.

fajo *nm (de billetes)* wad; *(de papeles)* bundle.

falda *nf* **1** *(prenda)* skirt. **2** *(regazo)* lap. **3** *(ladera)* slope.

■ **falda escocesa** kilt.

■ **falda pantalón** culottes *pl*.

fallar[1] *vt (tiro, penalty)* to miss.

▶ *vi* **1** *(no funcionar)* to fail. **2** *(decepcionar, no acudir)* to let down *[pt & pp* **let***]*: *hasta la fecha no me ha fallado nunca*, he's never let me down yet.

• **fallar los cálculos a** ALGN to miscalculate: *le fallaron los cálculos y el avión se estrelló*, he miscalculated and the plane crashed.

fallar² *vt (premio)* to award.

fallecer *vi fml* to die.

fallecimiento *nm* death.

fallo¹ *nm* **1** *(error)* mistake; *(fracaso)* failure. **2** *(defecto)* fault.

fallo² *nm* **1** *(de tribunal)* judgement. **2** *(premio)* awarding.

falsear *vt* **1** *(informe etc)* to falsify; *(hechos)* to distort. **2** *(documento)* to forge.

falsedad *nf* **1** *(hipocresía)* falseness. **2** *(mentira)* falsehood.

falsificación *nf* forgery.

falsificador,-ra *nm,f* forger.

falsificar *vt* to forge.

falso,-a *adj* **1** *(declaración)* false, untrue. **2** *(persona)* false.

■ **falsa alarma** false alarm.

falta *nf* **1** *(carencia)* lack, shortage. **2** *(ausencia)* absence. **3** *(error)* mistake: *falta de ortografía*, spelling mistake. **4** *(defecto)* fault, defect. **5** *(mala acción)* misdeed. **6** *(de menstruación)* missed period. **7** *(delito menor)* misdemeanour. **8** *(en fútbol)* foul; *(en tenis)* fault.

• **a falta de algo** for want of STH, for lack of STH.

• **hacer falta** to be necessary: *no hace falta preguntar*, there is no need to ask; *te hará falta un cuchillo*, you'll need a knife.

• **sin falta** without fail.

■ **falta de educación** bad manners *pl*.

faltar *vi* **1** *(cosa)* to be missing; *(persona)* to be absent. **2** *(haber poco)* to be needed: *me falta azúcar*, I haven't got enough sugar; *no le falta de nada*, she's got everything she needs; *falta luz*, there isn't enough light. **3** *(no acudir)* to miss. **4** *(incumplir)* to break [*pt* **broke**; *pp* **broken**]: *faltar a su palabra*, to break one's word. **5** *(quedar)* to be left: *faltan dos semanas para el examen*, there are two weeks to go till the exam.

• **¡lo que me faltaba!** that's all I needed!

• **¡no faltaba más! 1** (por supuesto) of course! **2** (por supuesto que no) absolutely not!

falto,-a.

• **estar falto de** to be short of: *el centro está falto de personal*, the centre is short of staff.

• **falto,-a de recursos** without resources.

fama *nf* **1** *(renombre)* fame, renown. **2** *(reputación)* reputation.

• **tener buena fama** to have a good name.

• **tener mala fama** to have a bad name.

famélico,-a *adj* starving.

familia *nf* **1** *(parientes)* family. **2** *(prole)* children *pl*.

• **estar en familia** to be among friends.

familiar *adj* **1** *(de la familia)* family. **2** *(conocido)* familiar. **3** *(lenguaje)* informal.

▶ *nmf* relation, relative.

familiaridad *nf* familiarity.

familiarizarse *vpr* to become familiar.

famoso,-a *adj* famous.

fan *nmf* fan.

fanático,-a *adj* - *nm,f* fanatic.

fanfarrón,-ona *nm,f (ostentoso)* show-off, braggart.

▶ *adj* .

• **ser fanfarrón 1** (ostentoso) to be a show-off. **2** (bravucón) to be a braggart.

fanfarronear *vi* **1** *(ostentar)* to show off [*pt* **showed**; *pp* **shown**]. **2** *(bravear)* to brag.

fango *nm (barro)* mud.

fantasía *nf* fantasy.

• **tener mucha fantasía** to be too full of imagination.

fantasma *nm* **1** *(espectro)* ghost. **2** *fam (fanfarrón)* show-off, braggart.

fantástico,-a *adj* fantastic.

fantoche *nm* **1** *(títere)* puppet. **2** *pey (fanfarrón)* braggart. **3** *pey (mamarracho)* nincompoop.

fardar *vi fam* to show off [*pt* **showed**; *pp* **shown**].

fardo *nm (paquete)* bundle.

faringe *nf* pharynx.

farmacéutico,-a *adj* pharmaceutical.

▶ *nm,f* **1** *(licenciado)* pharmacist. **2** *(en una farmacia)* GB chemist; US druggist, pharmacist.

farmacia *nf* **1** *(estudios)* pharmacology. **2** *(tienda)* GB chemist's; US drugstore, pharmacy.

fármaco *nm* drug.

faro *nm* **1** *(torre)* lighthouse. **2** *(en coche)* headlight. **3** *fig (guía)* guiding light.
■ **faros antiniebla** foglamps.

farol *nm* **1** *(de luz)* lantern; *(farola)* streetlamp, streetlight. **2** *fam (fardada)* brag; *(engaño)* bluff.
● **marcarse un farol** *fam* to brag, boast.

farola *nf* streetlight, streetlamp.

farsa *nf* **1** *(obra de teatro)* farce. **2** *(enredo)* sham, farce.

farsante *nmf* fake.

fascículo *nm* part, GB instalment; US installment.

fascinación *nf* fascination.

fascinante *adj* fascinating.

fascinar *vt* to fascinate.

fascismo *nm* fascism.

fascista *adj - nmf* fascist.

fase *nf* **1** *(etapa)* stage. **2** *(en física)* phase.

fastidiar *vt* **1** *(molestar)* to annoy, bother. **2** *(dañar)* to hurt [*pt & pp* **hurt**]. **3** *fam (estropear)* to ruin, spoil [*pt & pp* **spoilt**].
▸ *vpr* **fastidiarse 1** *(aguantarse)* to put up with: *si no le gusta que se fastidie*, if he doesn't like it that's tough. **2** *fam (estropearse)* to get damaged, get broken: *se ha fastidiado el tocadiscos*, the record-player's broken. **3** *(lastimarse)* to hurt oneself [*pt & pp* **hurt**]: *me he fastidiado la mano*, I've hurt my hand.
● **¡no fastidies!** *fam* you're kidding!

fastidio *nm* **1** *(molestia)* bother, nuisance. **2** *(aburrimiento)* boredom.

fatal *adj* **1** *(inexorable)* fateful. **2** *(mortal)* deadly, fatal. **3** *fam (muy malo)* awful, terrible.
▸ *adv fam* badly, terribly: *canta fatal*, he sings really badly; *me siento fatal*, I feel awful.

fatiga *nf (cansancio)* fatigue.
▸ *nf pl* **fatigas** *(molestia)* troubles, difficulties.

fatigar *vt* **1** *(cansar)* to wear out [*pt* **wore**; *pp* **worn**], tire. **2** *(molestar)* to annoy.
▸ *vpr* **fatigarse** to get tired.

fauces *nf pl* jaws.

fauna *nf* fauna.

favor *nm* GB favour; US favor.
● **a favor de** GB in favour of; US in favor of.
● **por favor** please.
● **tener algo a su favor** to have STH in one's GB favour, US favor.

favorable *adj* GB favourable; US favorable; *(condiciones)* suitable.

favorecer *vt* **1** *(ayudar)* GB to favour; US to favor. **2** *(agraciar)* to suit.

favorito,-a *adj* - *nm,f* GB favourite; US favorite.

fax *nm* fax.
● **enviar por fax** to fax.

fe *nf* **1** *(creencia)* faith. **2** *(certificado)* certificate.
● **de buena fe** in good faith.
● **de mala fe** in bad faith.
■ **fe de erratas** errata.

fealdad *nf* ugliness.

febrero *nm* February.

fecha *nf* **1** *(día, mes, etc)* date. **2** *(día)* day.
▸ *nf pl* **fechas** *(época)* time *sing*: *por esas fechas*, at that time.
● **con fecha...** dated....
● **hasta la fecha** to date.
■ **fecha de caducidad** best before date: *"fecha de caducidad..."*, "best before...".
■ **fecha límite** deadline.

fechar *vt* to date.

fechoría *nf (de malhechor)* misdeed; *(de niño)* mischief.

fecundación *nf* fertilization.
■ **fecundación in vitro** in vitro fertilization.

fecundar *vt* to fertilize.

fecundo,-a *adj* fertile.

federación *nf* federation.

felicidad *nf* happiness.
● **¡felicidades!** congratulations!

felicitación *nf (tarjeta)* greetings card.
▸ *nf pl* **felicitaciones** congratulations.

felicitar *vt* to congratulate.
● **felicitar a ALGN las Navidades** to wish SB Merry Christmas.
● **felicitar a ALGN por su santo** to wish SB a happy saint's day.
● **¡te/os felicito!** congratulations!

felino,-a *adj* feline.
▸ *nm* **felino** feline.

feliz *adj* **1** *(contento)* happy. **2** *(acertado)* fortunate.
● **¡feliz Navidad!** Happy Christmas!, Merry Christmas!

felpa *nf* felt.

felpudo,-a *adj (textil)* plushy.
▸ *nm* **felpudo** doormat.

femenino,-a *adj (mujer, vestido)* feminine; *(sexo)* female; *(en gramática)* feminine.

feminista adj - nmf feminist.

fenomenal adj **1** (extraordinario) phenomenal. **2** fam (fantástico) fantastic, terrific. **3** fam (enorme) huge.
▶ adv wonderfully, marvellously.

fenómeno nm **1** (hecho) phenomenon. **2** (prodigio) genius. **3** (monstruo) freak.
▶ adj fam fantastic, terrific.

feo,-a adj **1** (gen) ugly. **2** (malo) nasty. **3** (indigno) rude.
▶ nm **feo** (ofensa) slight, snub.
● **hacerle un feo a ALGN** to slight SB, snub SB.

féretro nm coffin.

feria nf **1** (exhibición) fair. **2** (fiesta) fair, festival.
■ **feria de muestras** trade fair.

fermentar vi to ferment.

ferocidad nf ferocity.

feroz adj fierce, ferocious.

ferretería nf **1** (tienda) hardware store. **2** (género) hardware. **3** (ferrería) forge.

ferrocarril nm GB railway; US railroad.

ferroviario,-a adj GB railway; US railroad.
▶ nm,f (trabajador) GB railway worker; US railroad worker.

fértil adj fertile.

fertilidad nf fertility.

fertilizante adj fertilizing.
▶ nm (abono) fertilizer.

fertilizar vt to fertilize.

festejar vt **1** (celebrar) to celebrate. **2** (agasajar) to fête.

festejo nm (celebración) celebration.
▶ nm pl **festejos** festivities.

festín nm feast, banquet.

festival nm festival.

festividad nf **1** (fiesta) festivity, celebration. **2** (día) feast day.

festivo,-a adj **1** (alegre) festive. **2** (agudo) witty.

feto nm (embrión) fetus, foetus.

fiable adj reliable.

fiambre nm **1** (de carne) cold meat. **2** fam (cadáver) stiff, corpse.

fiambrera nf lunch box.

fianza nf **1** (depósito) deposit, security. **2** (para acusado) bail.
● **bajo fianza** on bail.

fiar vt to sell on credit [pt & pp **sold**].
▶ vpr **fiarse** (confiarse) to trust.

● **de fiar** trustworthy.
● **"No se fía"** "No credit given".

fibra nf **1** (filamento) GB fibre; US fiber. **2** (de madera) grain.

ficción nf fiction.

ficha nf **1** (tarjeta) index card; (datos) file. **2** (de máquina) token. **3** (en juegos) counter; (de ajedrez) piece, man [pl **men**]; (de dominó) domino [pl -**es**].
■ **ficha policial** police record.
■ **ficha técnica 1** (de producto) specifications pl. **2** (de película) credits pl.

fichaje nm signing.

fichar vt **1** (anotar) to put on an index card, put on a file. **2** fam (conocer) to size up: **lo tengo bien fichado**, I've got him sized up. **3** (futbolista etc) to sign up.
▶ vi (al entrar) to clock in; (al salir) to clock out.
● **estar fichado,-a por la policía** to have a police record.

fichero nm **1** (de ordenador) file. **2** (archivo) card index. **3** (mueble) filing cabinet.

ficticio,-a adj fictitious.

fidelidad nf **1** (lealtad) fidelity. **2** (exactitud) accuracy.

fideo nm noodle.
● **estar como un fideo** fam to be as thin as a rake.

fiebre nf **1** (enfermedad) fever. **2** (agitación) fever, excitement.
● **tener fiebre** GB to have a temperature; US to have a fever.

fiel adj **1** (leal) faithful. **2** (exacto) accurate.
▶ nm (de balanza) needle, pointer.
● **ser fiel a** to be faithful to.

fieltro nm felt.

fiero,-a adj **1** (animal salvaje) wild; (feroz) fierce, ferocious. **2** (persona) cruel.
▶ nf **fiera 1** (animal) wild animal. **2** (persona) beast, brute. **3** (genio) wizard. **4** (toro) bull.
● **estar hecho,-a una fiera** fam to be in a rage.
● **ser una fiera para algo** to be brilliant at STH.

fiesta nf **1** (día festivo) holiday. **2** (celebración) party. **3** (festividad) celebration, festivity. **4** feast.
● **estar de fiesta** to be in a festive mood.
● **hacer fiesta un día** to take a day off.
● **¡tengamos la fiesta en paz!** let's have no more arguments!

figura 144

■ **la fiesta nacional** bullfighting.

figura *nf* **1** *(objeto)* figure. **2** *(forma)* shape. **3** *(personaje)* figure.

figurar *vt* **1** *(representar)* to represent. **2** *(simular)* to pretend.

▶ *vi (aparecer)* to figure.

▶ *vpr* **figurarse** *(imaginarse)* to imagine.

● **¡figúrate!** just imagine!

● **ya me lo figuraba** I thought as much.

fijador *nm* **1** *(para cabello - laca)* hairspray, hair gel; *(-gomina)* hair gel. **2** *(para dibujo etc)* fixative. **3** *(para fotografías)* fixer.

fijar *vt* **1** *(sujetar)* to fix, fasten. **2** *(pegar)* to stick [*pt & pp* **stuck**]. **3** *(establecer)* to set [*pt & pp* **set**].

▶ *vpr* **fijarse 1** *(darse cuenta)* to notice. **2** *(poner atención)* to pay attention [*pt & pp* **paid**].

● **¡fíjate!, ¡fíjese!** fancy that!

● **fijar la vista** to stare.

fijo,-a *adj* **1** *(sujeto)* fixed, fastened. **2** *(establecido)* set. **3** *(firme)* steady, firm. **4** *(permanente)* fixed, permanent.

fila *nf* **1** *(línea)* line. **2** *(en cine, clase)* row.

▶ *nf pl* **filas** *(servicio militar)* ranks.

● **en fila india** in single file.

● **en primera fila** in the front row.

● **llamar a ALGN a filas** to call SB up.

● **poner en fila** to line up.

● **¡rompan filas!** fall out!, dismiss!

filatelia *nf* philately, stamp collecting.

filete *nm (de carne, pescado)* fillet; *(solomillo)* sirloin.

■ **filete de lomo** rump steak.

filial *adj* filial.

▶ *adj - nf (empresa)* subsidiary.

filipino,-a *adj - nmf* Filipino.

filmar *vt (gen)* to film; *(escena, película)* to shoot [*pt & pp* **shot**].

filme *nm* GB film; US movie.

filo *nm* edge: **arma de doble filo**, two-edged sword.

● **al filo de la medianoche** on the stroke of midnight.

filosofía *nf* philosophy.

filósofo,-a *nm,f* philosopher.

filtrar *vt-vi (líquido)* to filter.

▶ *vpr* **filtrarse** *(información)* to leak (out).

filtro[1] *nm* filter.

filtro[2] *nm (poción)* love potion.

fin *nm* **1** *(final)* end. **2** *(objetivo)* purpose, aim.

● **a fin de** in order to.

● **a fin de que** so that.

● **al fin y al cabo** when all's said and done.

● **el fin justifica los medios** the end justifies the means.

● **en fin** anyway.

● **no tener fin** to be endless.

● **poner fin a algo** to put a stop to something.

● **¡por fin!** at last!

● **sin fines lucrativos** not-for-profit.

■ **fin de año** New Year's Eve.

■ **fin de fiesta** grand finale.

■ **fin de semana** weekend.

final *adj* final.

▶ *nm (conclusión)* end.

▶ *nf (en competición)* final.

● **al final** in the end.

■ **final de línea** terminus.

finalidad *nf* purpose, aim.

finalista *adj* in the final: *equipo finalista*, team in the final.

▶ *nmf* finalist.

finalizar *vt-vi* to end, finish.

finalmente *adv* finally.

financiación *nf* financing.

financiar *vt* to finance.

financiero,-a *adj* financial.

▶ *nm,f* financier.

finanzas *nm pl* finances.

finca *nf* property, estate.

■ **finca urbana** building.

fingir *vt* to feign: *fingió su secuestro*, he faked his own kidnapping; *fingí no entenderlo*, I pretended no to understand him; *fingió locura*, she feigned madness.

▶ *vpr* **fingirse** to pretend to be.

finlandés,-esa *adj* Finnish.

▶ *nm,f (persona)* Finn.

▶ *nm* **finlandés** *(idioma)* Finnish.

Finlandia *nf* Finland.

fino,-a *adj* **1** *(tela, pelo, etc.)* fine. **2** *(persona, papel, etc.)* thin. **3** *(alimento)* fine, choice. **4** *(sentidos)* sharp, acute. **5** *(educado)* refined, polite. **6** *(sutil)* subtle.

▶ *nm* **fino** *(vino)* dry sherry.

● **ir fino,-a** *fam* to have had a few.

● **no estar fino 1** *(de salud)* not to be feeling well: *hoy no estoy muy fino*, I'm not feeling very well today. **2** *(agudo, centrado)* not to be on the ball: *hoy no* *estás muy fino, ¿verdad?*, you're not on the ball today, are you.

finura nf **1** *(calidad)* fineness. **2** *(agudeza)* sharpness, acuteness. **3** *(refinamiento)* refinement.

firma nf **1** *(autógrafo)* signature. **2** *(acto)* signing. **3** *(empresa)* firm.

firmamento nm firmament.

firmar vt to sign.

firme adj firm, steady.
► nm *(de carretera)* road surface.
► adv hard.
● **¡firmes!** attention!
● **mantenerse firme** to stand one's ground.

firmeza nf firmness.

fiscal adj fiscal.
► nmf GB public prosecutor; US district attorney.

fisgar vt fam to pry, snoop.

fisgón,-ona adj *(espía)* snooper; *(curioso)* busybody.

fisgonear vt to pry, snoop.

física nf physics.

físico,-a adj physical.
► nm,f *(profesión)* physicist.
► nm **físico** *(aspecto)* physique.

fisonomía nf *(de persona)* physiognomy; *(de país, ciudad)* aspect, appearance.

flaco,-a adj **1** *(delgado)* skinny. **2** *(débil)* weak.

flamante adj **1** *(vistoso)* splendid, brilliant. **2** *(nuevo)* brand-new.

flan nm caramel custard, crème caramel.
● **estar hecho,-a un flan** fam to be shaking like a leaf.

flaquear vi **1** *(ceder)* to weaken, give in. **2** *(fallar)* to fail. **3** *(desalentarse)* to lose heart [pt & pp **lost**]. **4** *(disminuir)* to decrease.

flash nm **1** *(en fotografía)* flash. **2** *(noticia breve)* newsflash.

flato nm stitch.

flauta nf flute.
► nmf flautist.
■ **flauta de Pan** panpipes.
■ **flauta dulce** recorder.
■ **flauta travesera** transverse flute.

flautista nmf flautist.

flecha nf arrow.
● **salir como una flecha** to go off like a shot.

flechazo nm **1** *(disparo)* arrow shot. **2** *(herida)* arrow wound. **3** *(enamoramiento)* love at first sight.

fleco nm **1** *(adorno)* fringe. **2** *(deshilachado)* frayed edge.

flemón nm gumboil, abscess.

flequillo nm GB fringe; US bangs pl.

flexible adj flexible.

flexión nf **1** *(doblegamiento)* flexion. **2** *(gramatical)* inflection. **3** *(ejercicio)* GB press-up; US push-up.

flexo nm anglepoise lamp.

flipar vt arg: *le flipan las motos*, he's crazy about motorbikes.
► vi to be amazed: *yo flipaba, te lo juro*, I was absolutely amazed.
► vpr **fliparse** arg *(con drogas)* to get stoned.

flojear vi **1** *(disminuir)* to fall off [pt **fell**; pp **fallen**]. **2** *(debilitarse)* to weaken.

flojo,-a adj **1** *(suelto)* loose. **2** *(débil)* weak: *un viento muy flojo*, a light wind. **3** *(perezoso)* lazy.
● **me la trae floja** vulg I couldn't give a toss.

flor nf flower.
● **a flor de piel** skin-deep.
● **echarle flores a ALGN** to pay compliments to SB [pt & pp **paid**].
● **en flor** in blossom.
● **en la flor de la vida** in the prime of life.
● **la flor y nata** the cream.
● **¡ni flores!** no idea!

flora nf flora.

florecer vi **1** *(plantas)* to flower, bloom; *(árboles)* to blossom. **2** *(prosperar)* to flourish, thrive.
► vpr **florecerse** *(pan etc)* to go mouldy.

floreciente adj flourishing.

florero nm vase.

florido,-a adj **1** *(con flores)* flowery. **2** *(selecto)* choice, select.

florista nmf florist.

floristería nf florist's.

flota nf fleet.

flotador nm **1** *(para pescar)* float. **2** *(de niño)* rubber ring.

flotar vi **1** *(gen)* to float. **2** *(ondear)* to wave, flutter.

flote nm floating.
● **a flote** afloat.
● **salir a flote 1** *(recuperarse)* to get back on one's feet. **2** *(descubrirse)* to emerge.

fluido,-a *adj* **1** *(sustancia)* fluid. **2** *(lenguaje)* fluent.
▶ *nm* **fluido** fluid.
■ **fluido eléctrico** current.
fluir *vi* to flow.
flujo *nm* **1** *(gen)* flow. **2** rising tide: *flujo y reflujo*, ebb and flow. **3** INFORM stream.
flúor *nm* fluorine.
fluorescente *adj* fluorescent.
▶ *nm* fluorescent light.
fluvial *adj* river.
foca *nf* **1** *(animal)* seal. **2** *fam (persona)* fat lump.
foco *nm* **1** *(centro)* centre, focal point. **2** *(en fotografía, física)* focus. **3** *lámpara – en teatro)* spotlight; *(- en estadio)* floodlight.
■ **foco de atención** focus of attention.
fofo,-a *adj* **1** *(material)* soft, spongy. **2** *(persona)* flabby.
fogata *nf* bonfire.
folclore *nm* folklore.
folio *nm* sheet of paper.
follaje *nm* foliage, leaves *pl*.
follar *vi-vpr* **follar(se)** *vulg (copular)* to fuck, screw.
folleto *nm* *(prospecto)* leaflet; *(explicativo)* instruction leaflet; *(turístico)* brochure.
follón *nm* **1** *fam (alboroto)* rumpus, fuss. **2** *fam (enredo, confusión)* mess. **3** *(problemas)* trouble.
● **armar follón** *fam* to kick up a rumpus.
fomentar *vt (industria, turismo)* to promote; *(desarrollo, ahorro)* to encourage; *(crecimiento)* to foster.
fonda *nf* **1** *(para comer)* restaurant. **2** *(para alojarse)* guest house.
fondo *nm* **1** *(parte más baja)* bottom. **2** *(parte más lejana)* end, back. **3** *(segundo término)* background. **4** *(de dinero)* fund. **5** *(de libros etc)* stock.
▶ *nm pl* **fondos** *(dinero)* funds.
● **a fondo** thoroughly.
● **en el fondo** deep down, at heart.
● **tocar fondo** to reach rock bottom.
■ **fondo común** kitty.
■ **fondo del mar** sea bed.
fontanero,-a *nm,f* plumber.
footing *nm* jogging.
● **hacer footing** to jog, go jogging.
forajido,-a *nm,f* outlaw.
forastero,-a *adj* foreign.
▶ *nm,f* stranger.

forcejear *vi* to wrestle.
forense *adj* forensic.
▶ *nmf* forensic surgeon.
forestal *adj* forest.
forjar *vt* **1** *(metales)* to forge. **2** *(plan)* to make.
forma *nf* **1** *(figura)* form, shape. **2** *(manera)* way. **3** *(condiciones físicas)* form.
▶ *nf pl* **formas** **1** *(modales)* manners, social conventions. **2** *fam (de mujer)* curves.
● **de forma que** so that.
● **de todas formas** anyway.
● **estar en baja forma** to be off form.
● **estar en forma 1** *(físicamente)* to be fit. **2** *(mentalmente)* to be on form.
● **ponerse en forma** to get fit.
● **forma de pago** method of payment.
■ **forma física** physical fitness.
formación *nf* **1** *(gen)* formation. **2** *(educación)* training.
formal *adj* **1** *(serio)* serious. **2** *(cumplidor)* reliable, dependable. **3** *(cortés)* polite.
formalidad *nf* **1** *(en actitud)* formality. **2** *(seriedad)* seriousness. **3** *(fiabilidad)* reliability. **4** *(trámite)* formality.
formar *vt* **1** *(dar forma a)* to form. **2** *(integrar, constituir)* to form, constitute. **3** *(educar)* to educate; *(en técnicas)* to train.
▶ *vi (colocarse)* to form up.
▶ *vpr* **formarse** *(desarrollarse)* to grow [*pt* grew; *pp* grown], develop.
● **¡a formar!** fall in!
● **estar formado,-a por** to be made up of.
● **formar parte de algo** to be a part of STH.
formatear *vt* to format.
formato *nm* **1** *(de revista, disco)* format. **2** *(del papel)* size.
formidable *adj* **1** *(tremendo)* tremendous. **2** *(maravilloso)* wonderful.
▶ *interj* **¡formidable!** great!
fórmula *nf* formula.
formular *vt* **1** *(teoría)* to formulate. **2** *(queja, petición)* to make.
● **formular un deseo** to express a wish.
● **formular una pregunta** to ask a question.
formulario,-a *adj* routine: *una visita formularia*, a formal visit.
▶ *nm* **formulario** *(documento)* form: *formulario de solicitud*, application form.
fornido,-a *adj* strapping, hefty.

forofo,-a *nm,f* fan.

forrar *vt* **1** *(por dentro)* to line. **2** *(por fuera)* to cover.

▶ *vpr* **forrarse** *fam (de dinero)* to make a packet.

forro *nm* **1** *(interior)* lining. **2** *(funda)* cover.

● **ni por el forro** *fam* no way.

fortalecer *vt (estructura, organismo)* to fortify, strengthen.

▶ *vpr* **fortalecerse** to become stronger.

fortaleza *nf* **1** *(vigor)* strength. **2** *(de espíritu)* fortitude. **3** *(castillo)* fortress.

fortuna *nf* **1** *(destino)* fortune. **2** *(suerte)* luck. **3** *(capital)* fortune.

● **por fortuna** fortunately.

forzar *vt* **1** *(obligar)* to force. **2** *(reventar - puerta)* to force open, break open [*pt* **broke**; *pp* **broken**]; *(-cerradura)* to force.

forzosamente *adv* inevitably.

forzoso,-a *adj* **1** *(inevitable)* inevitable. **2** *(obligatorio)* obligatory.

forzudo,-a *adj* strong, brawny.

fosa *nf* **1** *(sepultura)* grave. **2** *(hoyo)* pit.

■ **fosas nasales** nostrils.

fósforo *nm* **1** *(elemento)* phosphorus. **2** *(cerilla)* match.

fósil *nm* fossil.

foso *nm (gen)* pit; *(de castillo etc)* moat.

foto *nf fam* photo [*pl* **-s**].

● **hacer una foto** to take a photo.

● **hacerle una foto a ALGN** to take a photo of SB.

fotocopia *nf* photocopy.

fotocopiadora *nf* photocopier.

fotocopiar *vt* to photocopy.

fotografía *nf* **1** *(proceso)* photography. **2** *(retrato)* photograph.

fotografiar *vt* to photograph.

fotográfico,-a *adj* photographic.

fotógrafo,-a *nm,f* photographer.

frac *nm* dress coat.

fracasar *vi* to fail.

fracaso *nm* failure.

fracción *nf* **1** *(parte)* fraction. **2** POL faction.

fraccionar *vt* to split [*pt & pp* **split**].

fractura *nf* fracture.

fracturar *vt-vpr* **fracturar(se)** to fracture, break [*pt* **broke**; *pp* **broken**].

fragancia *nf* fragrance.

fragante *adj* fragrant.

fragata *nf* frigate.

frágil *adj* **1** *(delicado)* fragile. **2** *(débil)* frail.

fragilidad *nf* **1** *(de algo rompible)* fragility. **2** *(debilidad)* frailty.

fragmentarse *vpr* to break up [*pt* **broke**; *pp* **broken**].

fragmento *nm* **1** *(pedazo)* fragment. **2** *(literario)* passage.

fraile *nm* friar.

frambuesa *nf* raspberry.

francés,-esa *adj* French.

▶ *nm,f (persona)* French person; *(hombre)* Frenchman [*pl* **-men**]; *(mujer)* Frenchwoman [*pl* **-women**]: **los franceses**, the French, French people.

▶ *nm* **francés** *(idioma)* French.

Francia *nf* France.

franco *nm (moneda)* franc.

franco,-a *adj (sincero)* frank, open.

● **franco fábrica** ex-works.

franela *nf* flannel.

franja *nf* **1** *(banda)* band, strip. **2** *(de tierra)* strip.

franquear *vt* **1** *(dejar libre)* to free, clear. **2** *(atravesar)* to cross. **3** *(carta)* to frank.

● **a franquear en destino** postage paid.

franqueo *nm* postage.

franqueza *nf* frankness, openness.

● **con toda franqueza** to be honest with you.

frasco *nm* flask.

frase *nf* **1** *(oración)* sentence. **2** *(expresión)* phrase.

■ **frase hecha** set phrase.

fraternal *adj* fraternal, brotherly.

fraternidad *nf* fraternity, brotherhood.

fraterno,-a *adj* fraternal, brotherly.

fraude *nm* fraud.

■ **fraude fiscal** tax evasion.

frecuencia *nf* frequency.

● **con frecuencia** frequently, often.

frecuentar *vt* to frequent.

frecuente *adj* **1** *(repetido)* frequent. **2** *(usual)* common.

frecuentemente *adv* frequently, often.

fregadero *nm* kitchen sink.

fregar *vt* **1** *(lavar)* to wash. **2** *(frotar)* to scrub. **3** *(suelo)* to mop.

● **fregar los platos** to do the washing up.

fregona *nf* **1** *pey (sirvienta)* skivvy. **2** *(utensilio)* mop.

freidora *nf* fryer.

freír *vt* **1** to fry. **2** *fam (molestar)* to annoy.

frenar *vt-vi (vehículo)* to brake.
▶ *vt (proceso)* to check.
frenazo *nm* sudden braking.
● **dar un frenazo** to jam on the brakes.
freno *nm* **1** *(de vehículo)* brake. **2** *(de caballería)* bit.
● **pisar el freno** to put one's foot on the brake.
● **poner freno a algo** to curb STH.
■ **frenos de disco** disc brakes.
frente *nm (gen)* front.
▶ *nf (de la cabeza)* forehead.
▶ *adv* **frente a** in front of, opposite: *frente al supermercado*, opposite the supermarket; *frente al mar*, facing the sea.
● **al frente de** at the head of.
● **frente a frente** face to face.
● **hacer frente a algo** to face STH, stand up to STH [*pt & pp* **stood**].
● **no tener dos dedos de frente** to be as thick as two short planks.
fresa *nf* **1** *(planta)* strawberry plant. **2** *(fruto)* strawberry. **3** *(de dentista)* drill.
▶ *adj* red.
fresco,-a *adj* **1** *(gen)* cool: *una brisa fresca*, a cool breeze; *agua fresca*, cold water. **2** *(tela, vestido)* light, cool. **3** *(aspecto)* fresh. **4** *(comida)* fresh. **5** *(reciente)* fresh, new: *tengo noticias frescas*, I have news. **6** *(impasible)* cool. **7** *(desvergonzado)* cheeky, shameless.
▶ *nm* **fresco 1** *(frescor)* fresh air. **2** *(pintura)* fresco [*pl* **-os** o **-oes**].
● **al fresco** in the cool.
● **hacer fresco** to be chilly.
● **¡qué fresco!** what a nerve!
● **quedarse tan fresco** not to bat an eyelid.
● **tomar el fresco** to get some fresh air.
frescor *nm* coolness, freshness.
frescura *nf* **1** *(frescor)* freshness, coolness. **2** *(desvergüenza)* cheek, nerve. **3** *(calma)* coolness.
● **¡qué frescura!** what a nerve!
fresno *nm* ash tree.
fresón *nm* large strawberry.
frialdad *nf* coldness.
fricción *nf* **1** *(gen)* friction. **2** *(friega)* rubbing.
frigorífico,-a *adj* refrigerating: *cámara frigorífica*, cold store.
▶ *nm* **frigorífico 1** *(doméstico)* refrigerator, fridge. **2** *(cámara)* cold storage room.

frío,-a *adj* cold.
▶ *nm* **frío** cold.
● **hacer frío** to be cold.
● **hace un frío que pela** *fam* it's freezing cold.
● **tener frío, pasar frío** to be cold: *¿tienes frío?*, are you cold?
friolero,-a *adj* sensitive to the cold: *es muy friolero*, he really feels the cold.
▶ *nf* **friolera 1** *(cosa insignificante)* trifle. **2** *fam (gran cantidad)* fortune: *gastó la friolera de 200 euros en unos zapatos*, he spent no less than 200 euros on a pair of shoes.
frito,-a *adj* **1** *(comida)* fried. **2** *fam (harto)* exasperated, fed up.
▶ *nm pl* **fritos** fried food *sing*.
● **quedarse frito,-a 1** *fam (dormido)* to fall asleep [*pt* **fell**; *pp* **fallen**]. **2** *(muerto)* to snuff it.
● **tener a uno frito,-a con algo**: *me tiene frito con eso del coche*, I'm fed up of hearing about that car.
frívolo,-a *adj* frivolous.
frondoso,-a *adj* leafy.
frontal *adj* **1** *(choque)* head-on. **2** *(oposición)* direct.
frontera *nf* **1** *(geográfica)* frontier; *(entre países)* border. **2** *fig (barrera)* limit, frontier.
fronterizo,-a *adj* border.
frontón *nm* **1** *(juego)* pelota; *(cancha)* pelota court. **2** *(de fachada)* pediment.
frotar *vt* to rub.
fructífero,-a *adj* fruitful.
fruncir *vt* **1** *(tela)* to gather. **2** *(labios)* to purse, pucker.
● **fruncir el ceño** to frown.
frustración *nf* frustration.
frustrar *vt* **1** *(plan)* to frustrate, thwart. **2** *(persona)* to frustrate.
▶ *vpr* **frustrarse 1** *(proyectos, planes)* to fail. **2** *(persona)* to get frustrated.
fruta *nf* fruit.
■ **fruta del tiempo** seasonal fruit.
■ **fruta seca** dried fruit.
frutal *adj* fruit.
▶ *nm* fruit tree.
frutería *nf* fruit shop.
frutero,-a *adj* fruit.
▶ *nm,f* fruiterer.
▶ *nm* **frutero** fruit bowl.

fruto *nm* fruit.
- **dar fruto** to bear fruit [*pt* **bore**; *pp* **borne**].
- **sacar fruto de algo** to profit from STH.
■ **frutos secos 1** (*almendras etc*) nuts. **2** (*pasas etc*) dried fruit *sing*.

fuego *nm* **1** (*gen*) fire. **2** (*lumbre*) light. **3** (*fogón de cocina*) burner, ring. **4** (*ardor*) GB ardour; US ardor.
- **a fuego lento 1** (cocinar) on a low flame. **2** (al horno) in a slow oven.
- **¿me da fuego?** have you got a light?
■ **fuegos artificiales** fireworks.
■ **fuegos de artificio** fireworks.

fuelle *nm* bellows *pl*.

fuente *nf* **1** (*manantial*) spring. **2** (*artificial*) fountain. **3** (*recipiente*) serving dish. **4** (*de información*) source: *de fuente desconocida*, from an unknown source.

fuera *adv* **1** (*gen*) out, outside: *por fuera*, on the outside. **2** (*en otro lugar*) away; (*en el extranjero*) abroad: *esta semana está fuera por negocios*, he's away on business this week; *estudió fuera*, she studied abroad. **3** (*excepto*) except for, apart from.
► *interj* **¡fuera!** get out!; (*en tenis etc*) out!
- **estar fuera de sí** to be beside oneself.
- **fuera de combate** knocked out.
- **fuera de duda** beyond doubt.
- **fuera de lo normal** extraordinary.
■ **fuera de juego** offside.

fuerte *adj* **1** (*gen*) strong. **2** (*intenso*) severe. **3** (*sonido*) loud. **4** (*golpe*) heavy.
► *nm* **1** (*fortificación*) fort. **2** (*punto fuerte*) strong point.
► *adv* **1** (*comer*) a lot. **2** (*golpear, nevar*) hard: *¡habla más fuerte!*, speak up!
- **¡abrázame fuerte!** hold me tight!
- **estar fuerte en algo** to be good at STH.

fuerza *nf* (*poder, resistencia*) strength: *emplear la fuerza*, to use force.
► *nf pl* **fuerzas** authorities: *las fuerzas vivas del pueblo*, the most important people in the village.
- **a fuerza de** by dint of, by force of.
- **a la fuerza** by force.
- **por la fuerza** by force.
■ **fuerza de gravedad** force of gravity.
■ **fuerza de voluntad** willpower.
■ **fuerza mayor** force majeure.

■ **fuerza motriz** driving force.
■ **fuerzas aéreas** air force *sing*.
■ **fuerzas del orden público** police force *sing*.

fuga *nf* **1** (*escapada*) escape. **2** (*de gas, líquido*) leak. **3** (*pieza musical*) fugue.
- **darse a la fuga** to take flight.
■ **fuga de divisas** capital flight.

fugarse *vpr* to flee, escape: *se fugó de la cárcel*, she escaped from prison.

fugaz *adj* fleeting, brief.

fugitivo,-a *adj* **1** (*en fuga*) fleeing. **2** (*efímero*) ephemeral, fleeting.
► *nm,f* fugitive, runaway.

fulano,-a *nm,f* (*persona cualquiera*) so-and-so.
► *nm* **fulano** *fam* fellow, guy.
► *nf* **fulana** *pey* whore, tart.
■ **Don Fulano,-a de tal** Mr So-and-so.

fulminante *adj* (*despido*) instant; (*muerte*) sudden; (*enfermedad*) devastating; (*mirada*) withering.

fumador,-ra *adj* smoking.
► *nm,f* smoker.
- **los no fumadores** non-smokers.

fumar *vt-vi-vpr* **fumar(se)** to smoke.
- **"No fumar"** "No smoking".

fumigar *vt* to fumigate.

función *nf* **1** (*gen*) function. **2** (*cargo*) duties *pl*. **3** (*espectáculo*) performance.
- **en función de** according to.
- **en funciones** acting: *el presidente en funciones*, the acting president.
■ **función de noche** late performance.
■ **función de tarde** matinée.

funcionamiento *nm* operation, working.
- **poner en funcionamiento** to put into operation.

funcionar *vi* to work.
- **hacer funcionar algo** to make STH work.
- **"No funciona"** "Out of order".

funcionario,-a *nm,f* civil servant.

funda *nf* **1** (*flexible*) cover. **2** (*rígida*) case. **3** (*de arma blanca*) sheath. **4** (*de diente*) cap.
■ **funda de almohada** pillowcase.

fundación *nf* foundation.

fundador,-ra *nm,f* founder.

fundamental *adj* fundamental.

fundamento *nm* **1** (*base*) basis, grounds *pl*. **2** (*seriedad*) seriousness; (*confianza*) reliability.

► *nm pl* **fundamentos 1** *(de teoría)* basic principles. **2** *(de edificio)* foundations.

● **sin fundamento** unfounded.

fundar *vt* **1** *(crear)* to found; *(erigir)* to raise. **2** *(basar)* to base, found.

► *vpr* **fundarse** *(teoría, afirmación)* to be based; *(persona)* to base oneself.

fundición *nf* **1** *(fusión)* smelting. **2** *(lugar)* foundry, smelting works.

fundir *vt* **1** *(un sólido)* to melt. **2** *(metal)* to cast [*pt & pp* **cast**]; *(hierro)* to smelt. **3** *(bombilla, plomos)* to blow [*pt* **blew**; *pp* **blown**]. **4** *(unir)* to unite, join.

fúnebre *adj* **1** *(mortuorio)* funeral. **2** *(lúgubre)* mournful, lugubrious.

funeral *adj* funeral.

► *nm pl* **funerales 1** *(entierro)* funeral *sing*. **2** *(ceremonia)* memorial service.

funerario,-a *adj* funerary, funeral.

► *nf* **funeraria** *(establecimiento)* undertaker's.

funesto,-a *adj* ill-fated.

funicular *nm* funicular railway.

furgón *nm* **1** *(furgoneta)* van. **2** *(de tren)* GB goods wagon; US boxcar.

furgoneta *nf* van.

furia *nf* fury, rage.

● **ponerse hecho,-a una furia** to fly into a rage [*pt* **flew**; *pp* **flown**].

furibundo,-a *adj* furious.

furioso,-a *adj* furious.

● **ponerse furioso,-a** to get furious.

furor *nm* fury, rage.

● **causar furor, hacer furor** to be all the rage.

furtivo,-a *adj* furtive.

fusible *nm* fuse.

fusil *nm* rifle.

fusilamiento *nm* execution.

fusilar *vt* *(ejecutar)* to shoot [*pt & pp* **shot**].

fusión *nf* **1** *(de metales)* fusion; *(de hielo)* thawing. **2** *(de empresas)* merger.

fusionar *vt-vpr* **fusionar(se) 1** *(metales)* to fuse. **2** *(empresas)* to merge.

fútbol *nm* GB football, soccer; US soccer.

■ **fútbol americano** American football.

futbolín *nm* GB table football, US table soccer.

futbolista *nmf* GB footballer, football player, soccer player; US soccer player.

futuro,-a *adj* future.

► *nm* **futuro** future.

G

gabardina *nf* **1** *(tela)* gabardine. **2** *(impermeable)* raincoat.

gabinete *nm* **1** *(despacho)* study. **2** POL cabinet.

gacela *nf* gazelle.

gafas *nf pl* glasses.
- **gafas de natación** goggles.
- **gafas de sol** sunglasses.

gafe *adj* jinxed.
▶ *nm*: **eres un gafe**, you've got a jinx on you.
• **tener gafe** to be jinxed.

gai *adj* - *nm* gay.

gaita *nf* bagpipes *pl.*
• **¡menuda gaita!** what a drag!

gaitero,-a *nm,f* piper, bagpipe player.

gajo *nm (de naranja)* section.

gala *nm (espectáculo)* show: **cena de gala**, gala dinner; **traje de gala**, evening dress.
• **hacer gala de** to make a show of.

galán *nm* **1** *(pretendiente)* heartthrob. **2** *(actor)* leading man.
- **galán de noche 1** *(mueble)* valet. **2** *(planta)* night jasmine.

galante *adj* courteous, gallant.

galantería *nf* **1** *(elegancia)* gallantry. **2** *(piropo)* compliment.

galápago *nm* sea turtle.

galardón *nm* award.

galardonar *vt* to award a prize to.

galaxia *nf* galaxy.

galería *nf* **1** *(en casa, mina, teatro)* gallery. **2** *(túnel)* underground passage.
- **galería de arte** art gallery.
- **galerías comerciales** GB shopping arcade *sing;* US mall *sing.*

Gales *nm* **(País de) Gales** Wales.

galés,-a *adj* Welsh.

▶ *nm,f (hombre)* Welshman [*pl* -**men**]; *(mujer)* Welshwoman [*pl* -**women**]: **los galeses**, the Welsh.
▶ *nm* **galés** *(idioma)* Welsh.

galgo *nm* greyhound.

Galicia *nf* Galicia.

gallego,-a *adj (de Galicia)* Galician.
▶ *adj* - *nm,f (persona)* Galician.
▶ *nm* **gallego** *(idioma)* Galician.

galleta *nf* **1** GB biscuit; US cookie. **2** *fam (bofetada)* slap.
- **galleta salada** cracker.

gallina *nf (ave)* hen.
▶ *nmf fam (cobarde)* chicken, coward.
• **jugar a la gallinita ciega** to play blind man's bluff.

gallinero *nm* **1** *(corral)* henhouse. **2** *(en teatro)* the gods. **3** *fam (lugar ruidoso)* bedlam, madhouse.

gallo *nm* **1** *(ave)* cock, rooster. **2** *(nota falsa)* false note.
• **en menos que canta un gallo** in a flash.
- **gallo de pelea** fighting cock.

galón[1] *nm (distintivo)* stripe.

galón[2] *nm (medida)* gallon.

galopar *vi* to gallop.

galope *nm* gallop.

gama *nf (variedad)* range: **una amplia gama de posibilidades**, a wide range of possibilities; **toda la gama de azules**, every shade of blue.
• **de gama alta** top of the range.

gamba *nf* prawn: **cóctel de gambas**, prawn cocktail.
• **meter la gamba** *fam* to put one's foot in it.

gamberrada *nf* act of hooliganism.

gamberro,-a *adj* loutish.
▶ *nm,f* hooligan.

gamo *nm* fallow deer.

gamuza *nf* 1 *(animal)* chamois. 2 *(paño)* chamois leather.

gana *nf* wish, desire: *el público se reía con ganas*, the audience laughed loudly; *el equipo jugó sin ganas*, the team played half-heartedly.
● **de buena gana** willingly.
● **de mala gana** reluctantly.
● **dar la gana** to want, like: *no me da la gana*, I don't want to; *haz lo que te dé la gana*, do what you like; *hace lo que le da la (real) gana*, he does as he pleases.
● **quedarse con las ganas**: *me quedé con las ganas de verlo*, I never got to see it.
● **tener ganas de** to want, feel like [*pt & pp* felt]: *no tengo ganas de salir esta noche*, I don't feel like going out tonight; *tenía muchas ganas de verla*, he was really looking forward to seeing her; *he perdido las ganas de comer*, I lost my appetite.

ganadería *nf* 1 *(cría)* livestock farming. 2 *(ganado)* livestock.

ganadero,-a *adj* stock.
▶ *nm,f* farmer.

ganado *nm* livestock.
■ **ganado ovino** sheep.
■ **ganado porcino** pigs.
■ **ganado vacuno** cattle.

ganador,-ra *adj* winning.
▶ *nm,f* winner.

ganancia *nf* gain, profit.

ganar *vt* 1 *(premio, concurso)* to win [*pt & pp* won]: *ganó el premio a la mejor actriz*, she won the award for best actress; *¿quién ganó el torneo?*, who won the tournament? 2 *(dinero)* to earn: *todos ganan la misma cantidad de dinero*, they all earn the same amount of money; *¿cuánto ganas al mes?*, how much do you earn a month? 3 *(a un contrincante)* to beat [*pt* beat; *pp* beaten]: *Bruguera ganó a Costa en tres sets*, Bruguera beat Costa en three sets; *a mí me ganas en deportes*, you're better in sports than I am.
▶ *vi* 1 *(en el trabajo)* to earn. 2 *(en competición)* to win [*pt & pp* won]. 3 *(mejorar)* to improve.
● **ganarse la confianza de ALGN** to win SB's trust [*pt & pp* won].

● **ganarse la vida** to earn one's living.
● **ganar tiempo** to save time.
● **salir ganando** to do well.

ganchillo *nm* 1 *(aguja)* crochet hook. 2 *(labor)* crochet.

gancho *nm* hook.
● **tener gancho** to be popular: *tiene mucho gancho con los tíos*, she's very popular with guys.

gandul,-la *adj* idle, lazy.
▶ *nm,f* lazybones.

ganga *nf* bargain.

gangrena *nf* gangrene.

gángster *nm* gangster.

ganso *nm* goose [*pl* geese]; *(macho)* gander.
▶ *nm,f* **ganso,-a** *fig* dimwit.
● **hacer el ganso** to play the fool.

garabatear *vt-vi* to scribble, scrawl.

garabato *nm* 1 *(al escribir)* scrawl, scribble. 2 *(al dibujar)* doodle.

garaje *nm* 1 *(cochera)* garage. 2 *(taller)* garage.

garantía *nf* 1 *(período)* guarantee. 2 *(documento)* guarantee, warranty.

garantizar *vt* *(gen)* to guarantee.

garbanzo *nm* chickpea.

garbo *nm* gracefulness, jauntiness.
● **hacer algo con garbo** to do STH with style.

garfio *nm* hook.

garganta *nf* 1 throat: *me duele la garganta*, I've got a sore throat. 2 *(desfiladero)* gorge.

gargantilla *nf* necklace.

gárgaras *nm pl* gargle *sing*.
● **hacer gárgaras** to gargle.

garita *nf* sentry box.

garra *nf* 1 *(de león, oso, etc)* claw; *(de águila, halcón, etc)* talon. 2 *fig* force: *este libro tiene garra*, this book's a gripping read.
● **caer en las garras de ALGN** to fall into SB's clutches.

garrafa *nf* container: *una garrafa de cinco litros*, a five-litre container.

garrafal *adj* monumental, enormous: *un error garrafal*, a terrible mistake.

garrapata *nf* tick.

garrotazo *nm* blow with a stick.

garrote *nm* 1 *(palo)* thick stick, cudgel. 2 *(pena capital)* garrotte.

gas *nm* gas: *una estufa de gas*, a gas fire;

agua con gas, a fizzy water; ***agua sin gas***, stil water.

▶ *nm pl* **gases** *(flato)* flatulence *sing*.

● **a todo gas** at full speed.

● **tener gases** to have wind.

■ **gas butano** butane.

■ **gas ciudad** town gas.

■ **gas lacrimógeno** tear-gas.

■ **gas natural** natural gas.

gasa *nf* gauze: ***una gasa***, a piece of gauze.

gaseoso,-a *adj* **1** *(estado)* gaseous. **2** *(bebida)* carbonated, fizzy.

▶ *nf* **gaseosa** fizzy lemonade.

gasoil *nm* diesel, diesel oil.

gasóleo *nm* diesel, diesel oil.

gasolina *nf* GB petrol; US gas, US gasoline.

● **echar gasolina** to put some petrol in.

■ **gasolina normal** two-star petrol.

■ **gasolina sin plomo** lead-free petrol.

■ **gasolina súper** four-star petrol.

gasolinera *nf* GB petrol station; US gas station.

gastado,-a *adj* **1** *(ropa, calzado)* worn out. **2** *(pila)* used up.

gastar *vt* **1** *(dinero)* to spend [*pt & pp* **spent**]: ***gasta mucho dinero en ropa***, she spends a lot of money in clothes. **2** *(usar)* to use: ***hay que gastar menos agua***, we must use less water; ***este coche gasta mucha gasolina***, this car uses a lot of petrol; ***¿qué champú gastas tú?***, what shampoo do you use?; ***¿qué número de zapato gastas?***, what size shoes do you take?

▶ *vpr* **gastarse 1** *(agotarse)* to run out [*pt* ran; *pp* run]: ***se ha gastado todo el café***, the coffee has run out. **2** *(ropa)* to wear out [*pt* wore; *pp* worn]: ***las suelas de los zapatos se han gastado***, the soles of my shoes have worn out.

● **gastar bromas** to play practical jokes.

gasto *nm* **1** *(de dinero)* expenditure, expense: ***haz un esfuerzo por moderar tus gastos***, make an effort to reduce your expenses. **2** *(de agua, luz)* consumption.

● **con todos los gastos pagados** all expenses paid.

● **correr con los gastos** to pay [*pt & pp* **paid**].

● **cubrir gastos** to cover costs.

■ **gastos de envío** postage and packing.

■ **gastos de viaje** travelling expenses.

gastronomía *nf* gastronomy.

gatear *vi* to crawl.

gatillo *nm (de arma)* trigger.

gato,-a *nm,f (animal)* cat.

▶ *nm* **gato** *(de coche)* jack.

● **a gatas** on all fours.

● **aquí hay gato encerrado** there's something fishy going on here.

● **buscarle tres pies al gato** *fam* to complicate things.

● **dar gato por liebre a** ALGN *fam* to take SB in.

gavilán *nm* sparrow hawk.

gaviota *nf* gull.

gazapo[1] *nm (cría de conejo)* young rabbit.

gazapo[2] *nm* **1** *(errata)* misprint. **2** *(error)* blunder, slip.

gazpacho *nm* cold tomato soup.

gel *nm* gel.

■ **gel de ducha** shower gel.

gelatina *nf* **1** *(sustancia)* gelatine. **2** *(de fruta)* jelly.

gemelo,-a *adj* - *nm,f (hermano)* twin: ***somos hermanos gemelos***, we're twin brothers.

▶ *nm* **gemelo** *(músculo)* calf muscle.

▶ *nm pl* **gemelos 1** *(de camisa)* cufflinks. **2** *(prismáticos)* binoculars.

gemido *nm (de persona)* groan; *(de animal)* whine.

Géminis *nm* Gemini: ***soy géminis***, I'm Gemini.

gemir *vi (persona)* to groan; *(animal)* to whine.

gen *nm* gene.

genealógico,-a *adj* genealogical.

generación *nf* generation.

generador *nm* generator.

general *adj* general: ***carretera general***, main road.

▶ *nm (oficial)* general.

● **en general** in general.

● **por lo general** generally.

generalizar *vt* to spread [*pt & pp* **spread**].

▶ *vpr* **generalizarse** to spread, become widespread.

generar *vt* to generate.

género *nm* **1** *(clase)* sort: ***un proyecto de este género***, a project of this sort; ***es único en su género***, it's unique of its kind. **2** *(gramatical)* gender. **3** *(especie)* genus. **4** *(en literatura)* genre. **5** *(tela)* cloth. **6** *(producto)* merchandise.

■ **género humano** mankind, the human race.

■ **géneros de punto** knitwear *sing.*

generosidad *nf* generosity.

generoso,-a *adj* generous.

genético,-a *adj* genetic.

genial *adj* brilliant.

genio *nm* **1** *(carácter)* temper: *tiene el genio de su madre*, she's got her mother's temper; *Paco tiene mal genio*, Paco is bad tempered. **2** *(persona)* genius: *fue un genio*, he was a genius. **3** *(criatura imaginaria)* genie: *el genio de la lámpara*, the genie of the lamp.

● **tener mal genio** to be bad-tempered.

genitales *nm pl* genitals.

gente *nf* **1** *(personas)* people: *hay mucha gente*, there are a lot of people; *la gente venía de todas partes*, people came from all around. **2** *(familia)* family: *mi gente*, my family.

■ **gente bien** posh people.

gentil *adj* *(amable)* kind.

▶ *adj - nmf (pagano)* heathen, pagan; *(no judío)* gentile.

gentileza *nf* **1** *(elegancia)* grace. **2** *(cortesía)* politeness.

● **por gentileza de** by courtesy of.

gentío *nm* crowd.

gentuza *nf pey* riffraff.

genuino,-a *adj* genuine, real.

geografía *nf* geography.

geográfico,-a *adj* geographic.

geología *nf* geology.

geológico,-a *adj* geological.

geometría *nf* geometry.

geométrico,-a *adj* geometric.

geranio *nm* geranium.

gerente *nmf (hombre)* manager; *(mujer)* manager, manageress.

germen *nm* germ.

germinar *vi* to germinate.

gerundio *nm* gerund.

gestación *nf* **1** *(embarazo)* pregnancy. **2** *(de proyecto)* gestation.

gesticular *vi* to gesticulate.

gestión *nf* **1** *(negociación)* negotiation. **2** *(de negocio)* administration, management: *mala gestión*, bad management. **3** *(diligencia)* step: *hacer las gestiones para algo*, to take the steps for STH.

● **tener que hacer unas gestiones** to have some business to do.

gestionar *vt* **1** *(tramitar)* to arrange. **2** *(administrar)* to run [*pt* **ran**; *pp* **run**], manage.

gesto *nm* **1** *(con el cuerpo)* grimace, gesture: *tiene los mismos gestos que su padre*, he makes the same gestures as his father. **2** *(con la cara)* expression: *con el gesto preocupado*, with a worried expression. **3** *(acción)* gesture: *fue un bonito gesto*, it was a nice gesture.

● **hacer un gesto** to signal: *hizo un gesto para que se acercara el camarero*, he signalled to the waiter to come over.

gestor,-ra *nm,f* agent.

■ **gestor administrativo** business agent.

gestoría *nf* business agency.

Gibraltar *nm* Gibraltar.

gigante,-a *adj* giant, gigantic.

▶ *nm,f* giant.

gigantesco,-a *adj* gigantic.

gilipollas *adj vulg* stupid.

▶ *nmf vulg* jerk: *¡es un gilipollas!*, he's a real jerk!

gimnasia *nf* **1** *(deporte)* gymnastics. **2** *(como asignatura)* games, physical education, PE: *es profesor de gimnasia*, he's a games teacher, he's a PE teacher.

● **hacer gimnasia** to exercise, work out: *hace una hora de gimnasia al día*, he exercises for an hour a day.

■ **gimnasia rítmica** rhythmic gymnastics.

gimnasio *nm* gymnasium, gym.

gimnasta *nmf* gymnast.

gimotear *vi* to whine, whimper.

ginebra *nf* gin.

ginecología *nf* gynaecology.

ginecólogo,-a *nm,f* gynaecologist.

gira *nf* **1** *(artística)* tour: *el grupo está de gira*, the group is on tour. **2** *(excursión)* trip, excursion.

girar *vi* **1** *(dar vueltas)* to rotate, revolve; *(rápidamente)* to spin [*pt & pp* **spun**]: *la Tierra gira alrededor del Sol*, the Earth revolves around the Sun. **2** *(torcer)* to turn: *gira a la derecha*, turn right. **3** *(conversación)* to centre around: *la conversación giraba en torno al divorcio*, the conversation centred around divorce.

▶ *vt-vi (llave, volante)* to turn.

girasol *nm* sunflower.

giratorio,-a *adj* **1** *(puerta, eje)* revolving. **2** *(movimiento)* circular.

giro *nm* **1** *(vuelta)* turn: *el conductor hizo un giro brusco*, the driver made a sharp turn; *el nuevo giro de las conversaciones*, the new turn talks have taken. **2** *(de dinero)* money order. **3** *(frase idiomática)* turn of phrase.

■ **giro bancario** banker's draft.

■ **giro de 180 grados** U-turn.

■ **giro postal** money order.

gitano,-a *adj* - *nm,f* gypsy.

glacial *adj* glacial.

glaciar *nm* glacier.

glándula *nf* gland.

global *adj* total.

globo *nm* **1** *(esfera)* globe, sphere. **2** *(de aire)* balloon. **3** *(Tierra)* globe.

■ **globo aerostático** hot air balloon.

■ **globo ocular** eyeball.

■ **globo terráqueo** globe.

glóbulo *nm* **1** globule. **2** *(en sangre)* corpuscle.

gloria *nf* **1** *(triunfo, honor)* glory. **2** *(fama)* fame. **3** *(cielo)* heaven.

● **cubrirse de gloria** to excel oneself.

● **da gloria verla** she looks wonderful.

● **estar en la gloria** to be in seventh heaven.

glorieta *nf* **1** *(rotonda)* roundabout. **2** *(en jardín)* arbour, bower.

glorioso,-a *adj* glorious.

glosario *nm* glossary.

glotón,-ona *adj* gluttonous.

► *nm,f* glutton.

glucosa *nf* glucose.

gobernador,-ra *adj* governing.

► *nm,f* governor.

gobernante *adj* governing, ruling.

► *nmf* ruler, leader.

gobernar *vt* **1** *(país)* to govern. **2** *(barco)* to steer.

gobierno *nm* **1** *(de país)* government. **2** *(dirección)* direction, control. **3** *(timón)* rudder.

● **para su gobierno** for your information.

goce *nm* enjoyment.

gol *nm* goal: *el gol de la victoria*, the winning goal; *el gol del empate*, the equalizer.

● **marcar un gol** to score a goal.

golear *vt* to thrash: *nos golearon por cinco a cero*, they thrashed us five nil.

golf *nm* golf.

golfo *nm* *(bahía)* gulf.

■ **golfo Pérsico** Persian Gulf.

golfo,-a *adj* - *nm,f* *(gamberro)* lout; *(niño malo)* rascal, devil.

golondrina *nf* swallow.

golosinas *nf* GB sweets; US candy *sing*.

goloso,-a *adj* sweet-toothed.

golpe *nm* **1** *(porrazo)* blow, knock. **2** *(ruido)* knock, bang: *dio un golpe fuerte en la puerta*, she banged on the door; *la puerta se cerró con un fuerte golpe*, the door slammed shut. **3** *(en coche)* bump. **4** *(desgracia)* blow: *fue un duro golpe*, it was a terrible blow. **5** *fam (robo)* job.

● **al primer golpe de vista** at first glance.

● **darse un golpe** to bang: *se dio un golpe en la cabeza*, he banged his head.

● **de golpe (y porrazo)** suddenly.

● **de un golpe** all at once.

● **no dar golpe** not to do a thing.

■ **golpe de Estado** coup d'état.

■ **golpe de suerte** stroke of luck.

■ **golpe mortal** death blow.

golpear *vt* **1** *(gen)* to hit [*pt & pp* **hit**]: *le golpeó en la cabeza*, he hit him on the head. **2** *(puerta)* to bang on: *alguien golpeó la puerta*, someone banged on the door.

goma *nf* **1** *(material)* rubber: *suelas de goma*, rubber soles. **2** *(de borrar)* GB rubber; US eraser. **3** *(tira elástica)* elastic band. **4** *arg (condón)* rubber.

■ **goma elástica** rubber band.

gomina *nf* hair gel.

góndola *nf* *(barco)* gondola.

gordo,-a *adj* **1** *(persona, cara)* fat. **2** *(libro, jersey)* thick. **3** *(accidente, problema)* serious.

► *nm,f* *(hombre)* fat man [*pl* **men**]; *(mujer)* fat woman [*pl* **women**].

► *nm (en lotería)* first prize, jackpot.

● **me cae gordo** I can't stand him.

● **se armó la gorda** it was absolute mayhem.

gordura *nf* fatness, obesity.

gorila *nm* gorilla.

gorra *nf* *(con visera)* cap; *(de bebé)* bonnet.

● **de gorra** *fam* free: *comer de gorra*, to scrounge a meal.

gorrión *nm* sparrow.

gorro *nm* **1** *(de lana)* hat. **2** *(de bebé)* bonnet.

● **estar hasta el gorro de algo** *fam* to be fed up to the back teeth with STH.

■ **gorro de baño** swimming cap.

■ **gorro de ducha** shower cap.

gorrón,-ona *adj fam* sponging.

▶ *nm,f* sponger, parasite.

gota *nf* **1** *(de líquido)* drop: *gotas de lluvia*, drops of rain; *la caían gotas de sudor*, he was dripping with sweat. **2** *(enfermedad)* gout.

● **caer cuatro gotas** to be spitting with rain.

● **la gota que colma el vaso** the straw that breaks the camel's back.

● **ser como dos gotas de agua** to be like two peas in a pod.

gotear *vi* to drip.

gotera *nf* leak.

gótico,-a *adj* Gothic.

gozada *nf fam* delight.

● **¡qué gozada!** it's great!

gozar *vi* to enjoy oneself.

● **gozar con** to delight in.

● **gozar de** to enjoy: *goza de buena salud*, he enjoys good health.

gozo *nm* delight, pleasure.

● **no caber en sí de gozo** to be overjoyed.

grabación *nf* recording.

■ **grabación digital** digital recording.

grabado,-a *adj* engraved, stamped.

▶ *nm* **grabado 1** *(técnica)* engraving, print. **2** *(ilustración)* engraving.

grabadora *nf* recorder.

grabar *vt* **1** *(en piedra)* to engrave. **2** *(sonido, imagen)* to record: *van a grabar un tema nuevo*, they're going to record a new song; *quiero grabar la película de esta noche*, I want to record the film that is on tonight. **3** INFORM to save.

● **tener algo grabado en la memoria** engraved memory: *lo tengo grabado en la memoria*, it's engraved on my memory.

gracia *nf* **1** *(donaire)* gracefulness. **2** *(encanto)* charm: *tiene una gracia especial*, she has a special charm. **3** *(elegancia)* elegance. **4** *(chiste)* joke: *está todo el día haciendo gracias*, he makes silly remarks all day long.

● **dar las gracias a** ALGN to thank SB.

● **gracias a** thanks to.

● **hacer gracia** to be funny: *sus chistes me hacen gracia*, his jokes make me laugh; *tus comentarios no le hicieron ninguna gracia*, she didn't find your comments at all funny.

● **¡muchas gracias!** thank you very much!

● **¡qué gracia!** how funny!

● **tener gracia** to be funny: *sus chistes tienen gracia*, his jokes are funny.

gracioso,-a *adj* **1** *(chiste)* funny; *(persona)* funny, amusing: *¡qué gracioso!*, how funny!; *lo gracioso es que...*, the funny thing is that.... **2** *(atractivo)* cute, sweet: *¡qué niño más gracioso!*, what a cute little boy!

▶ *nm,f* joker: *¿quién ha sido el gracioso que ha puesto sal en la azucarera?*, which joker put salt in the sugar bowl?

● **hacerse el gracioso** to try to be funny.

grada *nf* **1** *(peldaño)* step. **2** *(asiento)* row of seats: *las gradas estaban repletas*, the stands were packed.

grado *nm* *(gen)* degree: *estábamos a 21 grados*, it was 21 degrees; *un ángulo de 90 grados*, a 90-degree angle; *quemaduras de tercer grado*, third-degree burns.

● **de buen grado** willingly.

● **en mayor grado** to a greater extent.

● **en menor grado** to a lesser extent.

graduable *adj* adjustable.

graduación *nf* **1** *(acción)* adjustment. **2** *(militar)* rank: *un oficial de alta graduación*, a high-ranking officer. **3** *(de universidad)* graduation.

■ **graduación alcohólica** strength, alcohol content.

■ **graduación de la vista** eye test.

gradual *adj* gradual.

graduar *vt* **1** *(regular)* to adjust: *la temperatura se gradúa con este botón*, you can adjust the temperature with this switch. **2** *(ordenar)* to grade: *han graduado estos ejercicios según su dificultad*, these exercises have been graded according to difficulty.

▶ *vpr* **graduarse** to graduate: *se graduó en medicina*, she got a degree in medicine.

- **graduarse la vista** to have one's eyes tested.

grafía *nf* spelling.

gráfico,-a *adj* graphic.
▶ *nf* **gráfica** graph.
▶ *nm* **gráfico** graph.
■ **gráfico de barras** bar chart.

gragea *nf* pill.

gramática *nf* grammar.

gramatical *adj* grammatical.

gramo *nm* gram, gramme.

gramófono *nm* gramophone.

gran *adj* → grande.

granada *nf* **1** *(fruta)* pomegranate. **2** *(bomba)* grenade.

granate *adj - nm* *(color)* maroon.
▶ *nm* *(piedra)* garnet.

grande *adj* **1** *(de tamaño)* big, large: *una casa grande*, a big house. **2** *(de número, cantidad)* large: *un gran número de participantes*, a large number of participants; *una gran cantidad de dinero*, a large sum of money. **3** *(de importancia)* great: *un gran escritor*, a great writer; *hoy es un gran día*, today is a great day.
▶ *nm* **1** *(eminencia)* big name: *uno de los grandes del teatro español*, one of the big names in the Spanish theatre. **2** *(noble)* grandee, nobleman [*pl* -**men**].
● **celebrar algo a lo grande** to celebrate STH in style.
● **pasarlo en grande** to have a great time.
■ **grandes almacenes** department store.

grandioso,-a *adj* grandiose.

granel *adv* **a granel** *(sólidos)* loose, in bulk; *(líquidos)* in bulk: *compro harina a granel*, I buy flour loose.

granero *nm* granary, barn.

granito *nm* granite.

granizada *nf* hailstorm.

granizado *nm* granita: *un granizado de limón*, a lemon granita.

granizar *vi* to hail: *está granizando*, it's hailing.

granizo *nm* hail.

granja *nf* farm.

granjero,-a *nm,f* farmer.

grano *nm* **1** *(de arroz)* grain; *(de café)* bean. **2** *(en la piel)* spot, pimple: *te ha salido un grano en la nariz*, you've got a spot on your nose.

▶ *nm pl* **granos** cereals.
● **ir al grano** *fam* to come to the point.
● **poner su granito de arena** to do one's bit.

granuja *nm* rascal.

granulado,-a *adj* granulated.

grapa *nf* **1** *(para papel)* staple. **2** *(bebida)* grappa.

grapadora *nf* stapler.

grapar *vt* to staple.

grasa *nf* **1** *(comestible)* fat: *esta carne tiene mucha grasa*, there's a lot of fat in this meat. **2** *(lubricante, suciedad)* grease: *una mancha de grasa*, a grease stain.

grasiento,-a *adj* greasy.

graso,-a *adj* **1** *(pelo, piel)* greasy. **2** *(alimentos)* fatty.

gratamente *adv* pleasantly.

gratinar *vt* to brown under the grill.

gratis *adv* free: *es gratis*, it's free.

gratitud *nf* gratitude.

grato,-a *adj* agreeable, pleasant.

gratuito,-a *adj* **1** *(gratis)* free. **2** *(arbitrario)* gratuitous, arbitrary.

grava *nf* gravel.

grave *adj* **1** *(accidente, enfermedad)* serious: *no creo que sea grave*, I don't think it's serious; *está muy grave*, she's very seriously ill. **2** *(situación)* difficult. **3** *(expresión)* solemn. **4** *(acento)* grave. **5** *(voz)* deep, low.

gravedad *nf* **1** *(de la Tierra)* gravity. **2** *(importancia)* seriousness: *está herida de gravedad*, she's seriously injured. **3** *(de sonido)* depth.

graznar *vi* **1** *(cuervo)* to caw, croak. **2** *(oca)* to cackle, gaggle.

graznido *nm* **1** *(de cuervo)* caw, croak. **2** *(de oca)* cackle, gaggle.

Grecia *nf* Greece.

gremio *nm* *(históricamente)* guild; *(profesión)* profession.

greña *nf* mop of hair.

griego,-a *adj* *(de Grecia)* Greek.
▶ *adj - nm, f* *(persona)* Greek.
▶ *nm* **griego** *(idoma)* Greek.

grieta *nf* **1** *(en la pared)* crack, crevice. **2** *(en la piel)* chap.

grifo *nm* GB tap; US faucet.

grillo *nm* *(insecto)* cricket.
▶ *nm pl* **grillos** *(grilletes)* fetters *pl*.

grima
- **dar grima a** ALGN to set SB's teeth on edge [*pt & pp* **set**].

gripe *nf* flu, influenza: *está con gripe*, she's got flu.

gris *adj - nm* GB grey; US gray.

grisáceo,-a *adj* greyish.

gritar *vi* (*gen*) to shout; (*chillar*) to cry out, scream: *no grites a los niños*, don't shout at the children.

griterío *nm* shouting, uproar.

grito *nm* **1** (*gen*) shout: *se oían gritos de protesta*, you could hear the shouts of protest; *los manifestantes daban gritos*, the demonstrators were shouting. **2** (*de dolor*) cry: *dio un grito de dolor*, she cried out in pain. **3** (*de miedo*) scream.
- **a grito limpio** *fam* at the top of one's voice.
- **a voz en grito** at the top of one's voice.
- **hablar a gritos** to talk to the top of one's voice.
- **poner el grito en el cielo** to hit the roof [*pt & pp* **hit**].
- **ser el último grito** to be the latest fashion.

grosella *nf* redcurrant.
- **grosella silvestre** gooseberry.

grosería *nf* **1** (*vulgaridad*) coarseness, rudeness. **2** (*dicho vulgar*) rude remark.

grosero,-a *adj* **1** (*vulgar*) coarse, rough. **2** (*maleducado*) rude.
- ► *nm,f*: *es un grosero*, he's really rude.

grosor *nm* thickness.

grúa *nf* **1** crane. **2** (*para averías*) breakdown van; (*por mal aparcamiento*) tow truck.
- **"No aparcar, se avisa grúa"** "Any vehicles parked here will be towed away".

grueso,-a *adj* **1** (*objeto*) thick. **2** (*persona*) fat, stout.
- ► *nm* **grueso 1** (*grosor*) thickness. **2** (*parte principal*) main body: *el grueso del grupo*, the main body of the group.

grulla *nf* crane.

grumete *nm* cabin boy.

grumo *nm* **1** (*de salsa*) lump. **2** (*de sangre*) clot.

gruñido *nm* **1** (*de cerdo*) grunt. **2** (*de perro*) growl. **3** (*de persona*) grumble.

gruñir *vi* **1** (*cerdo*) to grunt. **2** (*perro*) to growl. **3** (*persona*) to grumble.

gruñón,-ona *adj* grumpy.
- ► *nm,f* grumbler, moaner.

grupo *nm* group.
- **reunirse en grupos** to gather in groups.
- **grupo de noticias** newsgroup.

gruta *nf* cave.

guadaña *nf* scythe.

guantazo *nm* slap.

guante *nm* glove: *unos guantes de lana*, a pair of woollen gloves.
- **echarle el guante a** ALGN to catch SB.

guantera *nf* glove compartment.

guapo,-a *adj* **1** (*hombre*) good-looking; (*mujer*) pretty, beautiful: *estás muy guapo hoy*, you look really nice today; *ven aquí, guapo*, come here, love. **2** *arg* (*objeto*) cool, smart: *un coche la mar de guapo*, a really smart car.

guarda *nmf* (*vigilante*) guard; (*de zoo*) keeper.
- ► *nf* **1** (*custodia*) custody, care. **2** (*de la ley etc*) observance.
- **guarda de seguridad** security guard.
- **guarda forestal** forest ranger.
- **guarda jurado** armed segurity guard.

guardabarros *nm* mudguard.

guardabosque *nmf* forest ranger.

guardacostas *nm* **1** (*embarcación*) coastguard ship. **2** (*vigilante*) coastguard.

guardaespaldas *nm* bodyguard.

guardameta *nmf* goalkeeper.

guardar *vt* **1** (*en su sitio*) to put away: *guarda tus juguetes*, put your toys away; *guardó el billete en el bolsillo*, he put the note in his pocket. **2** (*mantener*) to keep: *todavía guardo la foto en la cartera*, I still keep the photo in my wallet; *¿podrás guardar un secreto?*, can you keep a secret? **3** (*para otra ocasión*) to save: *guárdame un trozo*, save a piece for me; *lo guardaré para otra ocasión*, I'll save it for another time. **4** (*vigilar*) to guard, watch over: *un perro guarda la casa*, a dog guards the house. **5** INFORM to save. **6** (*leyes*) to observe, obey.
- **guardar las apariencias** to keep up appearances.
- **guardar cama** to stay in bed.
- **guardar rencor a** ALGN to bear SB a grudge [*pt* **bore**; *pp* **borne**].
- **guardar silencio** to remain silent.

● **guardarse de hacer algo** to be careful not to do STH.

● **tenérsela guardada a ALGN** to have it in for SB.

guardarropa *nm* **1** *(en museo, discoteca)* cloakroom. **2** *(armario)* wardrobe.

▶ *nmf (persona)* cloakroom attendant.

guardería *nf* crèche, nursery.

guardia *nmf (vigilante)* guard.

▶ *nf* **1** *(defensa)* defense, protection. **2** *(servicio)* turn of duty. **3** *(tropa)* guard.

● **estar de guardia** to be on duty: *médico de guardia*, doctor on duty.

● **estar en guardia** to be on one's guard.

■ **guardia civil** civil guard.

■ **guardia de tráfico** traffic warden.

■ **guardia urbano** policeman [*pl* -**men**].

■ **guardia urbana 1** *(mujer guardia)* policewoman [*pl* -**women**]. **2** *(cuerpo)* local police.

guardián,-ana *nm,f* guardian, keeper.

guarecer *vt* to shelter, protect.

▶ *vpr* **guarecerse** to take shelter.

guarida *nf* **1** *(de animales)* den. **2** *(de personas)* hideout: *una guarida de ladrones*, a den of thieves.

guarnición *nf* **1**: *filete con guarnición de patatas fritas*, steak with chips. **2** *(militar)* garrison.

guarrada *nf (cosa indecente)* disgusting thing; *(cosa sucia)* dirty thing.

guarrería *nf (cosa indecente)* disgusting thing; *(cosa sucia)* dirty thing: *el suelo estaba lleno de guarrerías*, the floor was covered in crap.

guarro,-a *adj* **1** *(sucio)* dirty, filthy. **2** *(indecente)* disgusting, revolting.

▶ *nm,f* **1** *(persona sucia)* dirty pig. **2** *(persona indecente)* revolting swine.

guasa *nf* joke: *¡no es para tomárselo a guasa!*, it's no joking matter!

● **estar de guasa** to be in a jesting mood.

guasearse *vpr* to make fun.

guasón,-ona *adj* joking.

▶ *nm,f* jester, joker.

Guatemala *nf* Guatemala.

guatemalteco,-a *adj* - *nm,f* Guatemalan.

guateque *nm* party.

guay *adj fam* great: *¡qué guay!*, great!; *lo pasamos guay*, we had a great time.

gubernamental *adj* government.

guerra *nf* war: *estamos en guerra*, we're at war.

● **dar guerra a ALGN** to give SB trouble.

■ **guerra civil** civil war.

■ **guerra mundial** world war.

■ **guerra santa** holy war.

guerrear *vi* to war.

guerrero,-a *adj* warlike.

▶ *nm,f* warrior, soldier.

guerrilla *nf* **1** *(lucha armada)* guerrilla warfare. **2** *(banda)* guerrilla band.

guerrillero,-a *nm,f* guerrilla.

guía *nmf (persona)* guide: *un guía turístico*, a tourist guide.

▶ *nf (libro)* guidebook: *una guía de campings*, a campsite guide; *una guía de Madrid*, a guide to Madrid.

■ **guía telefónica** telephone directory.

guiar *vt* **1** *(instruir, orientar)* to guide, lead [*pt & pp* **led**]: *me guió hacia la salida*, he guided me to the exit; *nos guió por la ciudad*, he took us round the city; *déjate guiar por tus sentimientos*, let yourself be guided by your feelings. **2** *(coche)* to drive [*pt* **drove**; *pp* **driven**], steer. **3** *(avión)* to pilot.

▶ *vpr* **guiarse** to follow: *me guiaba por su ejemplo*, I followed his example.

guijarro *nm* pebble.

guillotina *nf* guillotine.

guinda *nf* cherry.

● **poner la guinda** to add the finishing touch.

guindilla *nf* red pepper.

guiñar *vt* to wink.

guiño *nm* wink.

guiñol *nm* puppet theatre.

guión *nm* **1** hyphen: *se escribe con guión*, it's spelt with a hyphen. **2** *(de discurso)* notes *pl*. **3** *(de película)* script.

guionista *nmf* scriptwriter.

guiri *nmf arg* foreigner.

guirigay *nm* racket, din.

guirnalda *nf* garland.

guisado,-a *adj* cooked, prepared.

▶ *nm* **guisado** stew.

guisante *nm* pea.

guisar *vt (cocinar)* to cook; *(carne, pescado)* to stew.

guiso *nm* stew.

güisqui *nm* whisky.

guitarra *nf* guitar.

■ **guitarra eléctrica** electric guitar.

guitarrista *nmf* guitarist.

gula *nf* gluttony.

gusano *nm* **1** *(de tierra)* worm; *(de mariposa)* caterpillar. **2** *(persona)* miserable wretch, worm.

■ **gusano de seda** silkworm.

gustar *vi*: **me gusta**, I like it; **le gusta leer**, she likes reading; **no me gustó la película**, I didn't like the film; **le gusta mi prima**, he likes my cousin, he fancies my cousin.

● **gustar más** to prefer: *¿cuál te gusta más?*, which one do you prefer?; *me gusta más el otro*, I prefer the other one.

● **cuando guste** *fml* whenever you want.

gusto *nm* **1** *(sentido)* taste: *tiene un gusto dulce*, it has a sweet taste; *tenemos gustos muy diferentes*, we've got very different tastes. **2** *(sabor)* flavour: *no le noto el gusto*, I can't taste the flavour. **3** *(placer)* pleasure: *tenemos el gusto de invitarles a la boda*, we are pleased to invite you to the wedding; *el gusto por la lectura*, the love of reading. **4** *(capricho)* whim, fancy.

● **con mucho gusto** with pleasure.

● **dar gusto** to be nice: *da gusto no tener que ir a trabajar*, it's nice not to have to go to work; *da gusto verte tan alegre*, it's lovely to see you so happy.

● **de buen gusto** in good taste.

● **una broma de mal gusto** a joke in very bad taste.

● **estar a gusto, sentirse a gusto** to feel comfortable [*pt & pp* **felt**].

● **por gusto** out of choice.

● **tanto gusto** pleased to meet you.

gustosamente *adv* gladly, willingly.

gustoso,-a *adj* **1** *(sabroso)* tasty. **2** *(con gusto)* gladly, willingly: *lo haré gustoso*, I'll do it gladly.

H

haba *nf* broad bean.

haber *aux* to have: *no ha llamado*, he hasn't phoned.

▶ *nm* **1** *(cuenta corriente)* credit. **2** *(posesiones)* property. **3** *(sueldo)* salary.

● **haber de** to have to, must: *he de salir*, I have to go out; *no hemos de olvidar*, we must not forget.

● **hay** there is/there are: *hay una respuesta*, there is an answer; *hay dos habitaciones*, there are two bedrooms; *hubo un accidente*, there was an accident; *había miles de personas*, there were thousands of people.

● **hay que** you have to: *hay que tener mucho cuidado*, you have to be very careful; *hay que cerrar siempre esta puerta*, this door must always be closed.

● **¿qué hay?** how is it going?, how are things?

hábil *adj* **1** *(diestro)* skilful. **2** *(despabilado)* clever.

● **ser hábil en algo** to be good at STH.

habilidad *nf* **1** *(maestría)* skill. **2** *(astucia)* cleverness.

● **tener habilidad para algo** to be good at STH.

habilidoso,-a *adj* skilful.

habilitar *vt* **1** *(espacio)* to fit out. **2** *(capacitar)* to authorize. **3** INFORM to enable.

hábilmente *adv* skilfully.

habitación *nf* **1** *(cuarto)* room. **2** *(dormitorio)* bedroom.

habitante *nmf* inhabitant.

habitar *vt* to live in.

hábitat *nm* habitat.

hábito *nm* **1** *(costumbre)* habit. **2** *(vestido)* habit.

habitual *adj* **1** *(normal)* usual. **2** *(cliente, visitante)* regular.

habituar *vt* to accustom.

▶ *vpr* **habituarse** to become accustomed.

habla *nf* **1** *(facultad)* speech. **2** *(idioma)* language: *países de habla hispana*, Spanish-speaking countries.

● **¡al habla!** speaking!

hablador,-ra *adj* **1** *(parlanchín)* talkative. **2** *(chismoso)* gossipy.

▶ *nm,f* **1** *(parlanchín)* chatterbox [*pl* -**es**]. **2** *(chismoso)* gossip.

hablante *nmf* speaker.

hablar *vi* **1** *(gen)* to talk: *¿de qué hablas?*, what are you talking about?; *hablas demasiado*, you talk too much. **2** *(en situaciones formales)* to speak [*pt* **spoke**; *pp* **spoken**]: *el ministro habló de la crisis*, the minister spoke about the crisis. **3** *(dirigir la palabra)* to speak [*pt* **spoke**; *pp* **spoken**]: *no se hablan*, they don't speak to each other.

▶ *vt* *(idioma)* to speak [*pt* **spoke**; *pp* **spoken**].

● **hablar con** ALGN to speak to SB [*pt* **spoke**; *pp* **spoken**]: *hablaré con tu padre*, I'll speak to your father about it.

● **¡ni hablar!** certainly not!

hacer *vt* **1** *(crear, producir, causar)* to make: *hacer la comida*, to make lunch; *hacer ruido*, to make a noise; *hacer un dibujo*, to draw a picture; *hacer planes*, to make plans. **2** *(actividad, estudios, trayecto)* to do: *¿qué haces?*, what are you doing?; *hacer los deberes*, to do one's homework; *hago medicina*, I'm doing Medicine; *hi-*

cimos 250 km, we did 250 km. **3** *(inducir, obligar)* to make: *la peli me hizo llorar*, the film made me cry; *me hizo esperar*, she made me wait. **4** *(transformar)* to make: *ese corte de pelo la hace mayor*, that haircut makes her look older. **5** *(aparentar)* to act: *hacer el imbécil*, to act the fool.

▸ *vi* **1** *(representar)* to play: *hice de Julio César*, I played Julius Caesar. **2** *(tiempo meteorológico)* to be: *hace calor*, it's hot; *hace sol*, it's sunny; *hace buen día*, it's a fine day.

▸ *vpr* **hacerse 1** *(pretender ser)* to pretend to be: *no te hagas el inocente*, don't pretend to be innocent; *se hizo el importante*, he acted important. **2** *(convertirse en)* to become, turn, get: *me haré socio del club*, I'll become a member of the club; *te estás haciendo viejo*, you're getting old.

● **hace 1** (tiempo pasado) ago. **2** (tiempo que dura) for: *compré la moto hace tres años*, I bought the bike three years ago; *tengo la moto desde hace tres años*, I've had the bike for three years; *hace una semana que no lo veo*, I have not seen him for a week.

● **hacer bien** to do the right thing.

● **hacer mal** to do the wrong thing.

● **hacerse a un lado** to step aside.

● **hacerse con** to get hold of.

hacha *nf* axe.

hachís *nm* hashish.

hacia *prep* **1** *(dirección)* towards: *se dirigía hacia el castillo*, he was going towards the castle. **2** *(tiempo)* about, around: *estaré en casa hacia las diez*, I'll be home around ten.

● **hacia abajo** downwards.

● **hacia adelante** forwards.

● **hacia arriba** upwards.

● **hacia atrás** backwards.

hacienda *nf* **1** *(finca)* estate. **2 Hacienda** *(ministerio - en Reino Unido)* the Treasury; *(- en Estado Unidos)* the Treasury Department; *(sucursal)* tax office.

■ **hacienda pública** public funds *pl*, public finances *pl*.

hada *nf* fairy.

■ **hada madrina** fairy godmother.

halagar *vt* to flatter: *me halaga*, I'm flattered.

halago *nm* compliment.

halcón *nm* falcon.

hallar *vt* to find: *lo hallaron muerto*, he was found dead.

▸ *vpr* **hallarse** *(estar)* to be.

hallazgo *nm* **1** *(descubrimiento)* finding, discovery. **2** *(cosa descubierta)* find.

halterofilia *nf* weight-lifting.

hamaca *nf* hammock.

hambre *nf* **1** *(apetito)* hunger. **2** *(escasez de alimentos)* famine.

● **tener hambre** to be hungry.

● **ser un muerto de hambre** to be a good-for-nothing.

hambriento,-a *adj* hungry.

hamburguesa *nf* hamburger.

hámster *nm* hamster.

hangar *nm* hangar.

harapiento,-a *adj* ragged, tattered.

harapo *nm* rag, tatter.

harina *nf* flour.

● **eso es harina de otro costal** that's another kettle of fish.

hartar *vt* *(hartar a ALGN)* to make SB fed up: *me estás hartando con tus mentiras*, I'm getting fed up with your lies.

▸ *vpr* **hartarse 1** *(atiborrarse)* to eat one's fill [*pt* ate; *pp* eaten]. **2** *(cansarse)* to get fed up: *me estoy hartando de esperar*, I'm getting fed up with waiting.

harto,-a *adj* **1** *(repleto)* full. **2** *fam (cansado)* fed up.

hasta *prep* **1** *(tiempo)* until, till: *no supe nada de la fiesta hasta ayer*, I knew nothing about the party until yesterday; *hasta ahora*, until now. **2** *(lugar)* as far as: *te acompañaré hasta la iglesia*, I'll go with you as far as the church. **3** *(cantidad)* up to: *lee hasta dos libros por semana*, she reads up to two books a week.

▸ *conj* even: *hasta mi hermano pequeño podría hacerlo*, even my little brother could do it.

● **hasta cierto punto** to a certain extent.

● **¡hasta luego!** see you later!

● **hasta que** until: *quédate aquí hasta que venga a recogerte*, stay here until I come to pick you up.

haya *nf* *(árbol)* beech.

haz *nm* **1** *(de leña)* bundle; *(de cereales)* sheaf [*pl* -ves]. **2** *(de luz)* beam.

hazaña *nf* deed, exploit.

hazmerreír *nm* laughing stock.

hebilla *nf* buckle.

hebra *nf (de hilo)* thread.

hebreo,-a *adj - nm,f* Hebrew.

hechicero,-a *nm,f (hombre)* sorcerer, wizard; *(mujer)* sorceress, witch.

hechizar *vt* **1** *(embrujar)* to bewitch. **2** *(cautivar)* to charm.

hechizo *nm* spell, charm.

hecho,-a *adj* **1** *(manufacturado)* made: **está hecho de plástico**, it's made of plastic; **está muy bien hecho**, it's very well made. **2** *(persona)* mature.
- ► *nm* **hecho 1** *(realidad)* fact. **2** *(suceso)* event.
- ► *interj* **¡hecho!** done!
- ● **bien hecho** (bistec) well done.
- ● **¡bien hecho!** (para dar ánimos) well done!
- ● **de hecho** in fact.
- ● **dicho y hecho** no sooner said than done.
- ● **estar hecho,-a a algo** to be used to STH.
- ● **hecho,-a a mano** hand-made.
- ● **hecho,-a a máquina** machine-made.
- ■ **hecho consumado** fait accompli.

hectárea *nf* hectare.

hectolitro *nm* GB hectolitre; US hectoliter.

hectómetro *nm* GB hectometre; US hectometer.

hedor *nm* stink, stench.

helada *nf* frost.

heladería *nf* GB ice-cream parlour; US ice-cream parlor.

heladero,-a *nm,f* ice-cream seller.

helado,-a *adj* frozen.
- ► *nm* **helado** ice cream.
- ● **quedarse helado,-a** *fam* to be flabbergasted.

helar *vi* to freeze *[pt* **froze**; *pp* **frozen**]: **anoche heló**, there was a frost last night.
- ► *vpr* **helarse** to freeze *[pt* **froze**; *pp* **frozen**]: **me estoy helando**, I'm freezing.

helecho *nm* fern.

hélice *nf* propeller.

helicóptero *nm* helicopter.

hembra *nf* female.

hemisferio *nm* hemisphere.

hemorragia *nf* GB haemorrhage; US hemorrhage.

hender *vt-vpr* **hender(se)** to split *[pt & pp* **split**], crack.

heno *nm* hay.

heptágono *nm* heptagon.

herbívoro,-a *adj* herbivorous.
- ► *nm,f* herbivore.

heredar *vt* to inherit.

heredero,-a *nm,f (hombre)* heir; *(mujer)* heiress: **el heredero del trono**, the heir to hte throne.

hereditario,-a *adj* hereditary.

herejía *nf* heresy.

herencia *nf* **1** *(bienes)* inheritance. **2** *(genética)* heredity.

herida *nf (con arma)* wound; *(en accidente)* injury.

herido,-a *adj (con arma)* wounded; *(en accidente)* injured: **resultó herida**, she was injured.
- ► *nm,f (con arma)* wounded person; *(en accidente)* injured person.

herir *vt (con arma)* to wound; *(en accidente)* to injure; *(emocionalmente)* to hurt *[pt & pp* **hurt**].

hermanastro,-a *nm,f (hombre)* stepbrother; *(mujer)* stepsister.

hermandad *nf* **1** *(congregación - de hombres)* brotherhood; *(- de mujeres)* sisterhood. **2** *(parentesco)* brotherhood.

hermano,-a *nm,f (hombre)* brother; *(mujer)* sister.
- ► *nm pl* **hermanos** *(sólo hombres)* brothers; *(hombres y mujeres)* brothers and sisters: **somos ocho hermanos**, there are eight of us.
- ■ **hermana política** sister-in-law.
- ■ **hermano político** brother-in-law.

hermético,-a *adj* **1** *(al vacío)* hermetic, airtight. **2** *(inaccesible)* impenetrable.

hermoso,-a *adj* beautiful, lovely.

hermosura *nf* beauty.

hernia *nf* hernia, rupture.

héroe *nm* hero *[pl* **-es**].

heroico,-a *adj* heroic.

heroína *nf* **1** *(mujer)* heroine. **2** *(droga)* heroin.

heroísmo *nm* heroism.

herradura *nf* horseshoe.

herramienta *nf* tool.

herrar *vt* **1** *(caballo)* to shoe. **2** *(ganado)* to brand.

herrería *nf* **1** *(taller)* forge. **2** *(tienda)* blacksmith's shop.

herrero *nm* blacksmith.
hervir *vt-vi* to boil.
heterosexual *adj* - *nmf* heterosexual.
hexágono *nm* hexagon.
hez *nf* scum, dregs *pl*.
► *nf pl* heces GB faeces; US feces.
hibernación *nf* hibernation.
hibernar *vi* to hibernate.
hidratante *adj* moisturizing.
hidratar *vt* 1 to hydrate. 2 *(piel)* to moisturize.
hidráulico,-a *adj* hydraulic.
hidroavión *nm* seaplane.
hidrógeno *nm* hydrogen.
hiedra *nf* ivy.
hielo *nm* ice.
● romper el hielo to break the ice [*pt* broke; *pp* broken].
hiena *nf* hyaena, hyena.
hierba *nf* 1 *(césped, pasto)* grass. 2 *(para cocinar)* herb. 3 *arg (marihuana)* grass.
■ hierba mate maté.
hierbabuena *nf* mint.
hierro *nm* iron.
■ hierro colado cast iron.
■ hierro de fundición cast iron.
■ hierro forjado wrought iron.
■ hierro fundido cast iron.
hígado *nm* liver.
higiene *nf* hygiene.
higiénico,-a *adj* hygienic.
higo *nm* fig.
■ higo chumbo prickly pear.
higuera *nf* fig tree.
hijastro,-a *nm,f (chico)* stepson; *(chica)* stepdaughter; *(sin especificar)* stepchild [*pl* -children].
hijo,-a *nm,f (chico)* son; *(chica)* daughter; *(sin especificar)* child [*pl* children].
■ hija política daughter-in-law.
■ hijo político son-in-law.
■ hijo,-a único,-a only child [*pl* children]: es hija única, she's an only child.
hilar *vt* to spin [*pt & pp* spun].
hilera *nf* row.
hilo *nm* 1 *(de coser)* thread. 2 *(lino)* linen: camisa de hilo, linen shirt. 3 *(telefónico)* wire.
● con un hilo de voz in a thin voice.
● perder el hilo to lose the thread [*pt & pp* lost].
● seguir el hilo de una conversación to follow a conversation.

■ hilo musical piped music.
himno *nm* hymn.
■ himno nacional national anthem.
hincapié.
● hacer hincapié en to insist on.
hincar *vt* to drive in [*pt* drove; *pp* driven].
● hincar el diente to bite [*pt* bit; *pp* bitten], to get one's teeth into.
hincha *nmf* fan, supporter.
hinchar *vt* to inflate, blow up [*pt* blew; *pp* blown].
► *vpr* hincharse 1 *(parte del cuerpo)* to swell up [*pt* swelled; *pp* swollen]. 2 *(engreírse)* to get conceited. 3 *fam (comer)* to stuff oneself: me hinché de patatas fritas, I stuffed myself with crisps.
● hincharse de reír to have a good laugh.
hinchazón *nf* swelling.
hipermercado *nm* hypermarket.
hípico,-a *adj* horse: carreras hípicas, horse races; un concurso hípico, a show-jumping competition.
hipnosis *nf* hypnosis.
hipnotizar *vt* to hypnotize.
hipo *nm* hiccups: tengo hipo, I've got hiccups.
hipocresía *nf* hypocrisy.
hipócrita *adj* hypocritical.
► *nmf* hypocrite.
hipódromo *nm* racetrack, racecourse.
hipopótamo *nm* hippopotamus.
hipoteca *nf* mortgage.
hipótesis *nf* hypothesis.
hipotético,-a *adj* hypothetical.
hirviente *adj* boiling.
hispánico,-a *adj* Hispanic, Spanish.
hispanidad *nf* 1 *(cultura)* Spanishness. 2 *(mundo hispánico)* Hispanic world.
hispano,-a *adj* 1 *(de España)* Spanish, Hispanic. 2 *(de América)* Spanish-American.
► *nm,f* 1 *(de España)* Spaniard. 2 *(de América)* Spanish American; US Hispanic.
hispanoamericano,-a *adj* Spanish American.
hispanohablante *adj* Spanish-speaking.
► *nmf* Spanish speaker.
histeria *nf* hysteria.
■ histeria colectiva mass hysteria.
histérico,-a *adj* hysterical.
historia *nf* 1 *(estudio del pasado)* history. 2 *(relato)* story.

- **pasar a la historia** to go down in history.

historiador,-ra *nm,f* historian.

historial *nm* **1** *(médico)* record. **2** *(currículo)* curriculum vitae.

histórico,-a *adj* **1** *(del pasado)* historical. **2** *(trascendente)* historic.

historieta *nf (viñetas)* comic strip.

hobby *nm* hobby.

hocico *nm (de cerdo)* snout; *(de perro)* muzzle.

hockey *nm* hockey.

- **hockey sobre hielo** ice hockey.
- **hockey sobre hierba** hockey.

hogar *nm* **1** *(casa)* home. **2** *(de chimenea)* hearth.

- **sin hogar** homeless.

hoguera *nf* bonfire.

hoja *nf* **1** *(de planta)* leaf [*pl* -**ves**]. **2** *(de flor)* petal. **3** *(de papel)* sheet. **4** *(de libro)* page. **5** *(de metal)* sheet. **6** *(de cuchillo)* blade.

- **de hoja caduca** deciduous.
- **de hoja perenne** evergreen.
- **hoja de afeitar** razor blade.
- **hoja de ruta** waybill.
- **hoja de servicios** record of service.

hojalata *nf* tin: *juguetes de hojalata*, tin toys.

hojaldre *nm & nf* puff pastry.

hojarasca *nf* **1** *(hojas secas)* fallen leaves *pl*, dead leaves *pl*. **2** *(palabras)* verbiage.

hojear *vt* to leaf through, flick through.

hola *interj* hello!, hi!

Holanda *nf* Holland.

holandés,-esa *adj* Dutch.

▶ *nm,f (hombre)* Dutchman [*pl* -**men**]; *(mujer)* Dutchwoman [*pl* -**women**]; *(sin especificar)* Dutch person: *los holandeses*, the Dutch.

▶ *nm* **holandés** *(idioma)* Dutch.

holgado,-a *adj* **1** *(ropa)* loose, baggy. **2** *(de dinero)* comfortable.

holgazán,-ana *adj* idle, lazy.

▶ *nm,f* layabout.

holgazanear *vi* to lounge about.

holgazanería *nf* idleness, laziness.

hollín *nm* soot.

hombre *nm* **1** *(varón)* man [*pl* **men**]. **2** *(especie)* man [*pl* **men**], mankind.

▶ *interj* ¡**hombre!** what a surprise!: *¡hombre, claro!*, well, of course!, you bet!

- **hombre anuncio** sandwich man [*pl* **men**].

- **hombre de estado** statesman [*pl* **men**].
- **hombre de negocios** businessman [*pl* **men**].
- **hombre del saco** *fam* bogey man [*pl* **men**].

hombrera *nf* **1** *(en abrigo)* shoulder pad. **2** *(de uniforme)* epaulette.

hombro *nm* shoulder.

- **arrimar el hombro** to help out.
- **encogerse de hombros** to shrug one's shoulders.

homenaje *nm* tribute, homage.

- **en homenaje a** in tribute to.

homicida *adj* homicidal: *el arma homicida*, the murder weapon.

▶ *nmf* murderer.

homicidio *nm* homicide, murder.

homogéneo,-a *adj* homogeneous.

homologado,-a *adj (producto)* approved.

homólogo,-a *nm,f* opposite number.

homónimo *nm* homonym.

homosexual *adj* - *nmf* homosexual.

homosexualidad *nf* homosexuality.

hondo,-a *adj* deep.

▶ *nm* **hondo** depths *pl*.

Honduras *nm* Honduras.

hondureño,-a *adj* - *nm,f* Honduran.

honestidad *nf* **1** *(honradez)* honesty. **2** *(recato)* modesty.

honesto,-a *adj* **1** *(honrado)* honest. **2** *(recatado)* modest.

hongo *nm (planta)* fungus [*pl* **fungi**]; *(como comida)* mushroom.

honor *nm (honra)* GB honour; US honor.

▶ *nm pl* **honores** GB honours; US honors.

- **en honor a la verdad** to be fair.
- **en honor de** GB in honour of; US in honor of.

honorario,-a *adj* honorary.

▶ *nm pl* **honorarios** fee *sing*.

honra *nf* **1** *(dignidad)* GB honour; US dignity. **2** *(respeto)* respect.

- **¡y a mucha honra!** and proud of it!

honradez *nf* honesty.

honrado,-a *adj (honesto)* honest.

honrar *vt* **1** *(respetar)* GB to honour; US to honor. **2** *(enaltecer)* to do credit to: *eso te honra*, that does you credit.

▶ *vpr* **honrarse** GB to be honoured; US to be honored.

hora *nf* **1** *(60 minutos)* hour: *estará listo en dos horas*, it will be ready in two hours. **2** *(tiempo)* time: *¿qué hora es?*, what time is it?; *¿tiene hora, por favor?*, have you got the time?; *es hora de irse a la cama*, it's time to go bed. **3** *(cita)* appointment: *mañana tengo hora con el dentista*, I have an appointment with the dentist for tomorrow.

● **a altas horas** in the small hours.

● **a primera hora** first thing.

● **a todas horas** all the time.

● **de última hora** last-minute: *cambios de última hora*, last-minute changes; *noticias de última hora*, breaking news.

● **¡ya era hora!** about time too!

■ **hora de cenar** suppertime.

■ **hora de comer** lunchtime.

■ **hora oficial** standard time.

■ **hora punta 1** *(tráfico)* rush hour. **2** *(electricidad, teléfonos)* peak time.

■ **horas de oficina** business hours.

■ **horas extras** overtime.

horario *nm* **1** *(de trenes, clases)* timetable. **2** *(de trabajo, consulta)* hours *pl*: *¿qué horario tienes?*, what hours do you work?; *tengo horario de mañana*, I work mornings.

■ **horario de atención al público** opening hours *pl*.

horca *nf* *(patíbulo)* gallows *pl*.

horizontal *adj* horizontal.

horizonte *nm* horizon.

horma *nf* **1** *(molde)* mould; GB mould; US mold. **2** *(de zapato)* last.

● **encontrar uno la horma de su zapato** to meet one's match [*pt & pp* **met**].

hormiga *nf* ant.

hormigón *nm* concrete.

■ **hormigón armado** reinforced concrete.

hormigonera *nf* cement mixer.

hormigueo *nm* prickling sensation.

hormiguero *nm* anthill.

● **ser un hormiguero** to be crawling with people.

hormona *nf* hormone.

hornada *nf* batch.

horno *nm* **1** *(de cocina)* oven. **2** *(de fábrica)* furnace. **3** *(para cerámica, ladrillos)* kiln.

● **al horno 1** (manzana, patata, pescado) baked. **2** (pollo) roast.

● **no está el horno para bollos** *fam* it's not the right time.

● **ser un horno** to be like an oven.

■ **horno microondas** microwave oven.

horóscopo *nm* horoscope.

horquilla *nf* **1** *(de pelo)* hairgrip, hairpin. **2** *(de bicicleta)* fork. **3** *(instrumento agrícola)* pitchfork.

horrendo,-a *adj* awful, frightful.

horrible *adj* horrible, dreadful.

horror *nm* **1** *(miedo)* horror. **2** *fam (muchísimo)* an awful lot: *me costó un horror*, it cost me an awful lot.

● **¡qué horror!** how awful!

● **tener horror a algo** to hate STH.

horrorizar *vt* to horrify.

▶ *vpr* **horrorizarse** to be horrified.

horroroso,-a *adj* **1** *(atroz)* horrible. **2** *fam (malísimo)* dreadful, awful.

hortalizas *nf pl* vegetables.

hortelano,-a *nm,f* GB market gardener; US truck farmer.

● **ser como el perro del hortelano** to be dog in the manger.

hortensia *nf* hydrangea.

hortera *adj fam* tacky, trashy.

horterada *nf fam* trash: *es una horterada*, it's trash, it's really tacky.

hospedaje *nm* *(alojamiento)* lodging; *(precio)* cost of lodging.

hospedar *vt* to give lodging.

▶ *vpr* **hospedarse** to stay.

hospital *nm* hospital: *estuvo en el hospital varios días*, she was in hospital for several days.

hospitalario,-a *adj* **1** *(acogedor)* hospitable. **2** *(de hospital)* hospital.

hospitalidad *nf* hospitality.

hospitalizar *vt* to hospitalize.

hostal *nm* small hotel.

hostelería *nf* hotel and catering industry.

hostia *nf* **1** *(oblea)* host. **2** *fam (golpe)* thump: *¡que te doy una hostia!*, I'll thump you one!

▶ *interj* **¡hostia!** *fam (enfado)* damn it!, bugger!; *(sorpresa)* bloody hell!

● **pegarse una hostia** *fam*: *me pegué una hostia con la moto*, I came a cropper on my motorbike; *se pegó una hostia contra la mesa*, she bashed into the table.

- **ser la hostia 1** *(fam)* (fantástico) to be bloody amazing. **2** (penoso) to be bloody useless.

hostil *adj* hostile.

hostilidad *nf* hostility.
▶ *nf pl* **hostilidades** hostilities.

hotel *nm* hotel.

hotelero,-a *adj* hotel.
▶ *nm,f* hotel keeper.

hoy *adv* **1** *(día)* today. **2** *(actualmente)* now.
- **de hoy en adelante** from now on.
- **hoy en día** nowadays.
- **hoy por hoy** at the present time.

hoyo *nm* hole.

hoyuelo *nm* dimple.

hoz¹ *nf (instrumento agrícola)* sickle.

hoz² *nf (entre montañas)* ravine.

hucha *nf* money box.

hueco,-a *adj (vacío)* hollow.
▶ *nm* **hueco 1** *(cavidad)* hollow. **2** *(de tiempo)* free time; *(de espacio)* gap. **3** *(vacante)* vacancy.

huelga *nf* strike.
- **declararse en huelga** to go on strike.
- **estar en huelga** to be on strike.
- **huelga de celo** work-to-rule.
- **huelga de hambre** hunger strike.
- **huelga general** general strike.

huelguista *nmf* striker.

huella *nf* **1** *(de pie)* footprint; *(de animal, máquina)* track. **2** *(vestigio)* trace, sign.
- **dejar huella** to leave one's mark [*pt & pp* **left**].
- **huella dactilar** fingerprint.

huérfano,-a *adj - nm,f* orphan.
- **ser huérfano,-a de madre** to have lost one's mother.
- **ser huérfano,-a de padre** to have lost one's father.

huerta *nf* **1** *(negocio agrícola)* GB market garden; US truck garden. **2** *(huerto - de verduras)* vegetable garden; *(- de frutales)* orchard.

huerto *nm (de verduras)* vegetable garden; *(de frutales)* orchard.

hueso *nm* **1** *(del cuerpo)* bone. **2** *(de aceituna, cereza)* stone.
- **estar en los huesos** to be nothing but skin and bone.
- **ser un hueso duro de roer** to be a hard nut to crack.

huésped,-da *nm,f* guest.

huesudo,-a *adj* bony.

huevo *nm* egg.
▶ *nm pl* **huevos** *vulg* balls.
- **costar un huevo** *vulg* to cost an arm and a leg [*pt & pp* **cost**].
- **estar hasta los huevos** *vulg* to be pissed off.
- **huevo duro** hard-boiled egg.
- **huevo escalfado** poached egg.
- **huevo estrellado** fried egg.
- **huevo frito** fried egg.
- **huevo pasado por agua** soft-boiled egg.
- **huevos revueltos** scrambled eggs.

huida *nf* escape, flight.

huir *vi* **1** *(escapar)* to escape, flee. **2** *(evitar)* to avoid STH: **huir de algo**, to avoid STH.

hule *nm* oilcloth.

humanidad *nf* **1** *(cualidad)* humanity. **2** *(género humano)* humanity, mankind.
▶ *nf pl* **humanidades** *(estudios)* humanities.

humanitario,-a *adj* humanitarian.

humano,-a *adj* **1** *(del hombre)* human. **2** *(benigno)* humane.
▶ *nm* **humano** human being.

humareda *nf* cloud of smoke.

humear *vi* **1** *(echar humo)* to smoke. **2** *(echar vaho)* to steam.

humedad *nf* **1** *(en la atmósfera)* humidity: *en la costa la humedad es muy alta*, the humidity is very high on the coast. **2** *(en pared, suelo)* damp: *huele a humedad*, it smells of damp; *hay mucha humedad en esta casa*, this house is very damp.

humedecer *vt* to moisten, dampen.
▶ *vpr* **humedecerse** to become damp.

húmedo,-a *adj* **1** *(tiempo, clima)* humid. **2** *(pelo, tierra)* damp. **3** *(ojos)* moist.

humildad *nf (sumisión)* humility.

humilde *adj* humble.

humillación *nf* humiliation.

humillar *vt* to humiliate, humble.
▶ *vpr* **humillarse** to humble oneself.

humo *nm* **1** *(de cigarro, incendio)* smoke. **2** *(vapor)* steam.
- **bajarle los humos a ALGN** to take SB down a peg or two.
- **subírsele los humos a ALGN** to become conceited.

humor *nm* **1** *(ánimo)* mood: *cambios de humor*, mood swings. **2** *(gracia)* GB humour; US humor: *una película de hu-*

mor, a comedy film. **3** *(líquido)* GB humour; US humor.

● **tener humor para (hacer) algo** to feel like (doing) STH [*pt & pp* **felt**].

● **estar de buen humor** to be in a good mood.

● **estar de mal humor** to be in a bad mood.

■ **humor negro** black comedy.

humorista *nmf* **1** *(cómico - hombre)* comedian; *(- mujer)* comedienne. **2** *(escritor)* humorist.

humorístico,-a *adj* humorous.

hundido,-a *adj* **1** *(barco, ojos)* sunken: *el coche estaba hundido en el fango*, the car was sunk in the mud. **2** *(persona)* crushed: *aquellas palabras la dejaron hundida*, those words left her feeling crushed.

hundimiento *nm* **1** *(de barco)* sinking. **2** *(de tierra)* subsidence. **3** *(de edificio)* collapse.

hundir *vt* **1** *(mano, puñal)* to plunge. **2** *(barco)* to sink [*pt* **sank**; *pp* **sunk**]. **3** *(persona, empresa)* to sink [*pt* **sank**; *pp* **sunk**]: *la sequía hundió al país en una crisis económica*, the drought plunged the country into an economic crisis.

▶ *vpr* **hundirse 1** *(barco)* to sink. **2** *(edificio)* to collapse. **3** *(empresa)* to go under. **4** *(bolsa, precio)* to plummet. **5** *(persona)* to sink [*pt* **sank**; *pp* **sunk**]: *me hundí en la depresión*, I sunk into depression.

húngaro,-a *adj - nm,f* Hungarian.

huracán *nm* hurricane.

huraño,-a *adj* unsociable.

hurgar *vt* *(remover)* to poke around in.

● **hurgarse las narices** to pick one's nose.

hurra *interj* hurray!, hurrah!

hurtadillas *adv* **a hurtadillas** stealthily.

hurtar *vt* *(robar)* to steal [*pt* **stole**; *pp* **stolen**].

husmear *vt* **1** *(oler)* to sniff out, scent. **2** *(fisgonear)* to pry into.

I

iceberg *nm* iceberg.
icono *nm* icon.
ida *nf* **1** *(partida)* going, departure. **2** *(viaje)* outward journey.
▪ **billete de ida** GB single; US one-way ticket.
▪ **billete de ida y vuelta** GB return ticket; US round-trip ticket.
idea *nf* idea: *¡qué buena idea!*, what a good idea!
● **cambiar de idea** to change one's mind.
● **hacerse a la idea** to get used to the idea.
● **hacerse una idea de algo** to get an idea of STH.
● **ni idea** *fam* no idea, not a clue.
▪ **idea fija** obsession.
ideal *adj - nm* ideal.
idealista *adj* idealistic.
▶ *nmf* idealist.
idealizar *vt* to idealize.
idear *vt* **1** *(concebir)* to think up. **2** *(inventar)* to invent.
ídem *pron* ditto.
idéntico,-a *adj* identical.
identidad *nf* identity.
identificación *nf* identification.
identificar *vt* to identify.
▶ *vpr* **identificar(se)** to identify oneself.
● **identificarse con** ALGN to identify oneself with SB.
ideología *nf* ideology.
idioma *nm* language.
idiota *adj* idiotic, stupid.
▶ *nmf* idiot.
idiotez *nf* stupid thing.
● **decir idioteces** to talk nonsense, GB talk rubbish.

ido,-a *adj* **1** *(loco)* mad. **2** *(despistado)* absent-minded.
ídolo *nm* idol.
idóneo,-a *adj* suitable, fit.
iglesia *nf* church.
iglú *nm* igloo [*pl* -s].
ignorancia *nf* ignorance.
ignorante *adj* ignorant.
▶ *nmf* ignoramus.
ignorar *vt* **1** *(no saber)* not to know [*pt* knew; *pp* known], be ignorant of. **2** *(no hacer caso)* to ignore.
igual *adj* **1** *(idéntico)* the same: *tus zapatos son iguales a los míos*, your shoes are the same as mine; *cortó el pastel en ocho trozos iguales*, he cut the cake into eight equal pieces. **2** *(en jerarquía)* equal: *todos somos iguales*, we are all equal.
▶ *nm* **1** *(en categoría)* equal: *sólo habla con sus iguales*, he only speaks to his equals. **2** *(signo)* equals sign.
▶ *adv* **1** *(quizá)* maybe: *igual no vienen*, they may not come. **2** *(de la misma manera)* the same: *piensan igual*, they think the same.
● **dar igual** not to matter: *da igual lo que digas*, it doesn't matter what you say.
● **es igual** it doesn't matter.
● **igual de...** as... as: *soy igual de alto que tú*, I'm as tall as you.
● **por igual** equally.
igualar *vt* **1** *(hacer igual)* to make equal. **2** *(allanar)* to level; *(pulir)* to smooth.
▶ *vi* DEP to equalize.
▶ *vpr* **igualarse** to become equal [*pt* became; *pp* become].
● **igualar el marcador** to equalize.

igualdad *nf* equality.
- **igualdad de derechos** equal rights.
- **igualdad de oportunidades** equal opportunities.

igualmente *adv* **1** *(del mismo modo)* equally. **2** *(también)* also.
- **¡igualmente!** the same to you: *¡felices vacaciones! -Igualmente*, happy holidays! -The same to you.

ilegal *adj* illegal.

ilegible *adj* illegible.

ileso,-a *adj* unharmed, unhurt.

ilimitado,-a *adj* unlimited.

iluminación *nf* lighting, illumination.

iluminar *vt* to light up [*pt & pp* **lit**], illuminate.

ilusión *nf* **1** *(esperanza)* hope. **2** *(imagen falsa)* illusion.
- **hacerle ilusión algo a** ALGN: *me hace mucha ilusión que vengas*, I'm really looking forward to you coming.
- **hacerse ilusiones** to build up one's hopes [*pt & pp* **built**].
- **¡qué ilusión!** how wonderful!

ilusionado,-a *adj* excited.
- **estar ilusionado,-a con** to be excited about.

ilusionarse *vpr* **1** *(esperanzarse)* to build up one's hopes [*pt & pp* **built**]. **2** *(entusiasmarse)* to get excited.

iluso,-a *adj* deluded, deceived.
- ▶ *nm,f* dupe.

ilustración *nf* illustration.

ilustrar *vt* to illustrate.

ilustre *adj* illustrious, distinguished.

imagen *nf* **1** *(gen)* image. **2** *(en televisión)* picture.
- **ser la viva imagen de** ALGN to be the spitting image of SB.

imaginación *nf* imagination: *han sido imaginaciones mías*, it was just my imagination.

imaginar *vt-vpr* **imaginar(se)** to imagine: *me imagino que sí*, I imagine so.
- **¡imagínate!** just imagine!

imaginario,-a *adj* imaginary.

imán *nm* magnet.

imbécil *adj* stupid.
- ▶ *nmf* idiot, imbecile.

imitación *nf* **1** *(copia)* imitation. **2** *(parodia)* impression: *hizo una imitación muy buena del director*, he did a great impression of the headmaster.

- **de imitación** imitation: *joyas de imitación*, imitation jewellery.

imitador,-ra *nm,f* **1** *(gen)* imitator. **2** *(humorista)* impressionist, impersonator.

imitar *vt* **1** *(copiar)* to imitate, copy: *el niño imita a su abuelo*, the boy copies his grandfather. **2** *(gestos)* to mimic; *(como diversión)* to do an impression of, GB take off: *imita bien al profesor*, he's good at taking off the teacher.

impaciencia *nf* impatience.

impacientar *vt* to make ... lose patience, exasperate.
- ▶ *vpr* **impacientarse** to get impatient.

impaciente *adj* impatient.
- **estar impaciente por hacer algo** to be impatient to do STH.

impacto *nm* impact.
- **impacto de bala** *(señal)* bullet hole; *(tiro)* bullet wound: *murió por impacto de bala*, he was shot dead.

impar *adj* odd.
- ▶ *nm* odd number.

imparcial *adj* impartial.

impasible *adj* impassive.

impecable *adj* impeccable, faultless.

impedido,-a *adj* disabled.
- ▶ *nm,f* disabled person: *los impedidos*, the disabled.

impedimento *nm* impediment, obstacle.

impedir *vt* **1** *(imposibilitar)* to prevent: *intentaron impedir que entrara en el país*, they tried to prevent him from entering the country. **2** *(dificultar)* to impede, hinder.
- **impedir el paso** to block the way.

impenetrable *adj* impenetrable.

impensable *adj* unthinkable.

imperativo,-a *adj* imperative.
- ▶ *nm* **imperativo** imperative.

imperceptible *adj* imperceptible.

imperdible *nm* safety pin.

imperdonable *adj* unforgivable, inexcusable.

imperfección *nf* **1** *(cualidad)* imperfection. **2** *(defecto)* defect, fault.

imperfecto,-a *adj* **1** *(defectuoso)* flawed, imperfect. **2** *(acción, tiempo verbal)* imperfect.
- ▶ *nm* **imperfecto** imperfect, imperfect tense.

imperialismo *nm* imperialism.

imperio *nm* empire.

imperioso,-a *adj* **1** *(dominante)* imperious. **2** *(necesario)* urgent, pressing.
impermeable *adj* waterproof.
▶ *nm* raincoat.
impersonal *adj* impersonal.
impertinente *adj* impertinent.
▶ *nmf* impertinent person.
ímpetu *nm* **1** *(impulso)* impetus. **2** *(energía)* energy. **3** *(violencia)* violence.
impetuoso,-a *adj* impetuous.
implantar *vt* **1** *(corazón, cabello)* to implant. **2** *(reforma)* to introduce.
implicar *vt* **1** *(involucrar)* to involve, implicate. **2** *(conllevar)* to imply.
implorar *vt* to implore, beg.
imponente *adj* **1** *(impresionante)* impressive. **2** *fam (estupendo)* terrific.
imponer *vt* **1** *(castigo, tarea)* to impose: *impone sus ideales a los demás*, he imposes his ideas on others. **2** *(respeto, miedo)* to inspire. **3** *(dinero)* to deposit.
▶ *vpr* **imponerse 1** *(hacerse obedecer)* to impose one's authority. **2** *(vencer)* to win [*pt & pp* won]: *el español se impuso en el último set*, the Spaniard won the final set.
importación *nf* import.
● **de importación** imported.
importador,-ra *adj* importing.
▶ *nm,f* importer.
importancia *nf* importance.
● **darle importancia a algo** to attach importance to STH.
● **darse importancia** to give oneself airs.
● **quitarle importancia a algo** to make light of STH, play STH down.
● **tener importancia** to be important, matter.
importante *adj* **1** *(gen)* important: *una persona importante*, an important person. **2** *(considerable)* considerable: *una suma importante*, a considerable sum.
importar *vi* **1** *(tener importancia)* to matter: *me importa mucho tu opinión*, your opinion matters a lot to me; *no me importa*, I don't care. **2** *(molestar)* to mind: *¿te importaría cerrar la ventana?*, would you mind closing the window?
▶ *vt (traer de fuera)* to import.
● **¡a ti qué te importa!** mind your own business.
● **lo que importa es que...** the important thing is that....
● **me importa un bledo** *fam* I couldn't care less.

● **no importa** it doesn't matter.
importe *nm* **1** *(coste)* cost: *el importe de las entradas*, the cost of the tickets. **2** *(cantidad)* amount: *el importe total*, the total amount.
imposibilidad *nf* impossibility.
imposible *adj* impossible.
● **hacer lo imposible** to do the impossible, do one's utmost.
impostor,-ra *nm,f* impostor.
impotencia *nf* impotence.
impotente *adj* impotent.
impreciso,-a *adj* vague, imprecise.
impregnar *vt* to impregnate.
imprenta *nf* **1** *(arte)* printing. **2** *(taller)* printer's, printing house. **3** *(máquina)* (printing) press.
imprescindible *adj* essential, indispensable.
impresión *nf* **1** *(sensación)* impression. **2** *(de texto)* printing. **3** *(huella)* impression, imprint.
● **causar buena impresión** to make a good impression.
● **me da la impresión de que...** I have the impression that...
impresionable *adj* impressionable.
impresionante *adj* impressive, striking.
impresionar *vt* **1** *(causar admiración a)* to impress: *me impresionó el paisaje*, the scenery impressed me. **2** *(conmover)* to touch, move. **3** *(disco)* to cut [*pt & pp* cut]. **4** *(fotografía)* to expose.
▶ *vpr* **impresionarse 1** *(estar admirado)* to be impressed. **2** *(conmoverse)* to be touched, be moved.
impreso,-a *adj* printed.
▶ *nm* **impreso** *(formulario)* form.
▶ *nm pl* **impresos** *(en carta etc)* printed matter *sing*.
impresora *nf* printer.
■ **impresora de chorro de tinta** inkjet printer.
■ **impresora láser** laser printer.
impresor,-ra *nm,f* printer.
imprevisible *adj* **1** *(hecho)* unforeseeable. **2** *(persona)* unpredictable.
imprevisto,-a *adj* unforeseen, unexpected.
▶ *nm* **imprevisto** *(incidente)* unforeseen event.
▶ *nm pl* **imprevistos** incidental expenses.

imprimir vt to print.

improbable adj improbable, unlikely.

impropio,-a adj 1 (incorrecto) improper. 2 (inadecuado) unsuitable.

improvisar vt-vi to improvise.

improviso adv **de improviso** unexpectedly; (de repente) suddenly.

imprudencia nf imprudence, rashness.

imprudente adj (irreflexivo) imprudent, rash; (al conducir) careless, reckless.

impuesto nm **impuesto** tax, duty.

• **libre de impuestos** duty-free.

■ **impuesto sobre el valor añadido (IVA)** value added tax (VAT).

■ **impuesto sobre la renta** income tax.

impulsar vt 1 (empujar) to drive forward [pt **drove**; pp **driven**], propel: *la fuerza del motor impulsa al coche*, the power of the engine drives the car forward. 2 (animar) to drive [pt **drove**; pp **driven**]. 3 (promocionar) to boost, promote: *impulsar la creación de empleo*, to boost job creation.

impulsivo,-a adj impulsive.

impulso nm 1 (deseo súbito) impulse, urge: *un impulso me llevó a comprarle flores*, I bought her flowers on an impulse; *sintió el impulso de abrazarlo*, she had the urge to hug him. 2 (fuerza, velocidad) momentum. 3 (estímulo) boost: *um impulso a su carrera*, a boost to her career.

• **coger impulso** to gather momentum.

impureza nf impurity.

impuro,-a adj impure.

inaccesible adj inaccessible.

inaceptable adj unacceptable.

inactivo,-a adj inactive.

inadaptado,-a adj maladjusted.

▶ nm,f misfit.

inadecuado,-a adj 1 (inapropiado) unsuitable, inappropriate. 2 (insuficiente) inadequate.

inadmisible adj unacceptable.

inagotable adj inexhaustible.

inaguantable adj intolerable, unbearable.

inalámbrico,-a adj cordless.

▶ nm **inalámbrico** cordless telephone.

inalterable adj 1 (no alterable) unalterable. 2 (impasible) impassive, imperturbable.

inanimado,-a adj inanimate.

inapreciable adj 1 (incalculable) invaluable, priceless. 2 (insignificante) imperceptible.

inauguración nf opening, inauguration.

inaugural adj opening, inaugural.

inaugurar vt to open, inaugurate.

incalculable adj incalculable.

incansable adj untiring, tireless.

incapacidad nf 1 (falta de capacidad) inability. 2 (incompetencia) incompetence.

■ **incapacidad laboral** industrial disability.

incapaz adj 1 (no capaz) incapable. 2 (incompetente) incompetent.

• **ser incapaz de hacer algo** to be incapable of doing STH.

incendiar vt to set on fire [pt & pp **set**], set fire to.

▶ vpr **incendiarse** to catch fire [pt & pp **caught**].

incendio nm fire.

■ **incendio forestal** forest fire.

■ **incendio provocado** arson.

incentivo nm incentive.

incertidumbre nf uncertainty.

incesante adj incessant, unceasing.

incidente nm incident.

incierto,-a adj 1 (dudoso) uncertain, doubtful. 2 (desconocido) unknown.

incineración nf (de basura) incineration; (de cadáver) cremation.

incinerar vt (basura) to incinerate; (cadáver) to cremate.

incisivo,-a adj 1 (que corta) cutting, sharp. 2 (mordaz) incisive.

▶ nm **incisivo** (diente) incisor.

incitar vt to incite.

• **incitar a ALGN a algo** to incite SB to STH.

inclemencia nf inclemency, harshness.

inclinación nf 1 (pendiente) slope. 2 (tendencia) inclination. 3 (saludo) bow.

■ **inclinación de cabeza** nod.

inclinado,-a adj (plano) inclined; (tejado) sloping.

inclinar vt 1 (ladear) to tilt; (cuerpo) to bow; (cabeza) to nod: *inclina la botella*, tilt the bottle. 2 (persuadir) to dispose, move.

▶ vpr **inclinarse** 1 (ladearse) to lean [pt & pp **leant**]: *se inclinó sobre el pupitre*, he leant over the desk. 2 (propender a) to be inclined, feel inclined [*pt & pp* felt]: *me inclino a creerlo*, I'm inclined to believe him.

incluido,-a *adj* included.

incluir *vt* **1** *(gen)* to include: *el precio incluye el desayuno*, the price includes breakfast. **2** *(en carta etc)* to enclose.

inclusive *adv* inclusive.

incluso *adv-conj-prep* even.

incógnita *nf* **1** unknown quantity. **2** *(misterio)* mystery.

incógnito,-a *adj* unknown.

● **de incógnito** incognito.

incoherencia *nf* incoherence.

incoloro,-a *adj* colourless.

incombustible *adj* fireproof, incombustible.

incomodar *vt* **1** *(causar molestia a)* to inconvenience. **2** *(avergonzar)* to make feel uncomfortable. **3** *(enojar)* to annoy.

► *vpr* **incomodarse 1** *(avergonzarse)* to feel uncomfortable [*pt & pp* felt]. **2** *(enfadarse)* to get annoyed, get angry.

incomodidad *nf* **1** *(falta de comodidad)* discomfort. **2** *(molestia)* inconvenience. **3** *(malestar)* unrest, uneasiness.

incómodo,-a *adj* **1** *(gen)* uncomfortable: *una silla incómoda*, an uncomfortable chair. **2** *(molesto)* awkward: *preguntas incómodas*, awkward questions.

● **sentirse incómodo,-a** to feel uncomfortable [*pt & pp* felt], feel awkward.

incomparable *adj* incomparable.

incompatible *adj* incompatible.

incompetencia *nf* incompetence.

incompetente *adj* incompetent.

incompleto,-a *adj* incomplete.

incomprendido,-a *adj* misunderstood.

incomprensible *adj* incomprehensible.

incomprensión *nf* lack of understanding.

incomunicado,-a *adj* **1** *(aislado)* isolated; *(por la nieve)* cut off. **2** *(preso)* in solitary confinement.

incomunicar *vt* **1** *(aislar)* to isolate, cut off [*pt & pp* cut]. **2** *(preso)* to put in solitary confinement.

inconcebible *adj* inconceivable, unthinkable.

inconfundible *adj* unmistakable.

inconsciente *adj* **1** MED unconscious. **2** *(irreflexivo)* thoughtless.

incontable *adj* countless, uncountable.

inconveniente *adj* **1** *(inoportuno)* inconvenient. **2** *(inapropiado)* inappropiate: *tiene ventajas e inconvenientes*, it has advantages and disadvantages; *no hay inconveniente*, there's no problem.

► *nm (desventaja)* drawback; *(dificultad)* problem.

● **tener inconveniente** to mind: *no tengo inconveniente*, I don't mind.

incordiar *vt* to pester, bother.

incorporar *vt* **1** *(añadir)* to incorporate. **2** *(levantar)* to help to sit up.

► *vpr* **incorporarse 1** *(levantarse)* to sit up [*pt & pp* sat]. **2** *(a puesto, regimiento)* to join.

● **incorporarse a filas** to join up.

incorrección *nf* **1** *(inexactitud)* incorrectness. **2** *(error)* mistake, error. **3** *(descortesía)* discourtesy.

incorrecto,-a *adj* **1** *(inexacto)* incorrect. **2** *(descortés)* impolite.

incorregible *adj* incorrigible.

incrédulo,-a *adj* incredulous.

► *nm,f* GB sceptic; US skeptic.

increíble *adj* incredible, unbelievable.

incrementar *vt* to increase.

incremento *nm* increase, rise.

incrustar *vt* **1** *(introducir)* to embed. **2** *(joyas, nácar)* to inlay [*pt & pp* inlaid].

► *vpr* **incrustarse** to become embedded.

incubadora *nf* incubator.

incubar *vt* to incubate.

inculto,-a *adj* uneducated.

incultura *nf* lack of culture.

incumplir *vt (deber)* not to fulfil; *(promesa)* to break [*pt* broke; *pp* broken]; *(contrato)* to breach.

incurable *adj* incurable.

indagar *vt* to investigate, inquire into.

indecente *adj* indecent, obscene.

indecisión *nf* indecision.

indeciso,-a *adj* **1** *(sin decidir)* undecided. **2** *(dudoso)* indecisive.

indefenso,-a *adj* defenceless.

indefinido,-a *adj* **1** *(impreciso)* undefined, vague. **2** *(ilimitado)* indefinite.

indemnización *nf* **1** *(acción)* indemnification. **2** *(compensación)* compensation.

■ **indemnización por daños y perjuicios** damages *pl*.

■ **indemnización por despido** severance pay.

indemnizar *vt* to compensate.
independencia *nf* independence.
independiente *adj* independent.
independizarse *vpr* to become independent.
indestructible *adj* indestructible.
indeterminado,-a *adj* **1** *(por determinar)* indeterminate. **2** *(indefinido)* indefinite.
India *nf* India.
indicación *nf* **1** *(señal)* sign. **2** *(pista)* hint, indication.
▶ *nf pl* **indicaciones** *(instrucciones)* instructions.
● **hacerle una indicación a** ALGN to signal to SB.
indicador,-ra *adj* indicating.
▶ *nm* **indicador** *(gen)* indicator; *(uso técnico)* gauge.
■ **indicador de dirección** indicator.
■ **indicador de gasolina** petrol gauge.
indicar *vt* **1** *(señalar)* to indicate, show [*pt* showed; *pp* shown]: *¿está indicado en el mapa?*, is it indicated on the map?; *me indicaron el camino para ir a la playa*, they showed me the way to the beach. **2** *(decir)* to tell [*pt & pp* told]: *el médico le indicó que no bebiera alcohol*, the doctor told him not to drink alcohol.
indicativo,-a *adj-nm* indicative.
índice *nm* **1** *(gen)* index. **2** *(dedo)* index finger, forefinger. **3** *(indicio)* sign, indication.
■ **índice alfabético** alphabetical index.
■ **índice de mortalidad** death rate.
■ **índice de natalidad** birth rate.
■ **índice de precios al consumo** retail price index.
indicio *nm* sign, indication.
indiferencia *nf* indifference.
indiferente *adj* indifferent: *me es indiferente*, I don't mind, it makes no difference to me.
● **serle una cosa indiferente a** ALGN not to care about STH: *la política le es indiferente*, he doesn't care about politics.
indígena *adj* indigenous, native.
▶ *nmf* native.
indigente *adj* destitute.
▶ *nmf* destitute person: *los indigentes*, the destitute.

indigestarse *vpr* to get indigestion.
indigestión *nf* indigestion.
indigesto,-a *adj* indigestible.
indignación *nf* indignation.
indignado,-a *adj* indignant.
indignante *adj* outrageous, infuriating.
indignar *vt* to infuriate, make angry: *me indignó su actitud*, his attitude infuriated me.
▶ *vpr* **indignarse** to become annoyed.
indigno,-a *adj* **1** *(impropio)* unworthy. **2** *(vil)* low, undignified.
indio,-a *adj* - *nm,f* Indian.
● **hacer el indio** to play the fool.
indirecta *nf* hint, insinuation.
● **lanzar una indirecta** to drop a hint.
indirecto,-a *adj* indirect.
indiscreción *nf* **1** *(falta de discreción)* indiscretion. **2** *(comentario)* indiscreet remark.
indiscreto,-a *adj* **1** *(falto de discreción)* indiscreet. **2** *(falto de tacto)* tactless.
indiscutible *adj* unquestionable, indisputable.
indispensable *adj* indispensable, essential.
● **lo indispensable** the essentials.
indispuesto,-a *adj* indisposed, unwell.
indistinto,-a *adj* **1** *(poco claro)* indistinct, vague. **2** *(indiferente)*: *me es indistinto*, it makes no difference to me.
individual *adj (gen)* individual; *(habitación, cama)* single.
▶ *nm pl* **individuales** singles.
individuo *nm* **1** *(persona)* person [*pl* people], individual. **2** *pey (tipo)* bloke, guy.
indudable *adj* doubtless, unquestionable.
● **es indudable que...** there is no doubt that....
indudablemente *adv* undoubtedly, unquestionably.
indultar *vt* to pardon.
indulto *nm* pardon.
indumentaria *nf* clothing, clothes *pl*.
industria *nf* industry.
industrial *adj* industrial.
▶ *nmf* industrialist.
industrializar *vt* to industrialize.
▶ *vpr* **industrializarse** to become industrialized.
ineficaz *adj (persona, método)* inefficient; *(medida)* ineffective, ineffectual.

INEM *abr* (**Instituto Nacional de Empleo**) Spanish department of employment.

inepto,-a *adj* inept, incompetent.
► *nm,f*: **es una inepta**, she's totally incompetent.

inercia *nf* inertia.
● **hacer algo por inercia** to do STH out of habit.

inesperado,-a *adj* unexpected.

inestable *adj* **1** (*gen*) unstable, unsteady. **2** (*tiempo*) changeable.

inestimable *adj* inestimable, invaluable.

inevitable *adj* inevitable, unavoidable.

inexacto,-a *adj* inexact, inaccurate.

inexistente *adj* non-existent, inexistent.

inexperiencia *nf* inexperience.

inexperto,-a *adj* inexperienced.

inexplicable *adj* inexplicable.

infalible *adj* infallible.

infancia *nf* childhood.

infante,-a *nm,f* (*hombre*) prince; (*mujer*) princess.

infantería *nf* infantry.
■ **infantería de marina** marines *pl*.

infantil *adj* **1** (*libro, enfermedad*) children's. **2** (*educación, población*) child. **3** (*aniñado*) childlike; (*en sentido peyorativo*) childish.

infarto *nm* heart attack.

infatigable *adj* indefatigable, tireless.

infección *nf* infection.

infeccioso,-a *adj* infectious.

infectar *vt* to infect.
► *vpr* **infectarse** to become infected.

infeliz *adj* unhappy.
► *nmf* poor wretch.

inferior *adj* **1** (*situado debajo*) lower: **labio inferior**, lower lip. **2** (*cantidad*) less, lower: **un número inferior a diez**, a number less than ten. **3** (*en calidad*) inferior.
► *nmf* subordinate.

inferioridad *nf* inferiority.
● **en inferioridad de condiciones** at a disadvantage.

infestar *vt* to infest.
● **infestado,-a de 1** infested with. **2** crawling with.

infiel *adj* **1** (*desleal*) unfaithful. **2** (*inexacto*) inaccurate.
► *nmf* (*unbeliever*) infidel.

infierno *nm* hell.
● **¡vete al infierno!** go to hell.

infinidad *nf* infinity.
● **en infinidad de ocasiones** on countless occasions.
● **una infinidad de** countless, innumerable.

infinitivo *nm* infinitive.

infinito,-a *adj* infinite.
► *nm* **infinito** infinity.
► *adv* (*muchísimo*) infinitely.

inflación *nf* inflation.

inflamable *adj* inflammable.

inflamación *nf* inflammation.

inflamar *vt* to set on fire [*pt & pp* **set**].
► *vpr* **inflamarse** to become inflamed.

inflar *vt* **1** (*globo, neumático*) to inflate, blow up [*pt* **blew**; *pp* **blown**]. **2** (*hechos, noticias*) to exaggerate.
► *vpr* **inflarse 1** (*engreírse*) to get conceited. **2** *fam* (*hartarse*) to stuff oneself.

inflexible *adj* inflexible.

influencia *nf* influence.
● **tener influencias** to be influential.

influir *vi* to influence.

información *nf* **1** (*datos*) information. **2** (*oficina*) information desk. **3** (*noticias*) news: **información nacional**, national news.

informal *adj* **1** (*ambiente, reunión*) informal. **2** (*ropa*) casual. **3** (*irresponsable*) unreliable.

informar *vt* to inform.
► *vi* to report.
► *vpr* **informarse** to find out [*pt & pp* **found**].

informática *nf* computer science, computing.

informático,-a *adj* computer, computing.
► *nm,f* computer expert.

informativo,-a *adj* informative.
► *nm* **informativo** news bulletin.

informatizar *vt* to computerize.

informe *adj* shapeless.
► *nm* report.
► *nm pl* **informes** references.

infracción *nf* (*fiscal, de circulación*) GB offence; US offense; (*de ley*) infringement.
■ **infracción de tráfico** GB driving offence; US traffic violation.

infundado,-a *adj* unfounded, groundless.

infusión *nf* infusion: **infusión de manzanilla**, camomile tea; **infusión de menta**, mint tea.

ingeniar vt to think up [pt & pp **thought**].
▶ vpr **ingeniarse** to manage.
● **ingeniárselas para hacer algo** to manage to do STH.
ingeniería nf engineering.
ingeniero,-a nm,f engineer.
ingenio nm **1** (chispa) wit. **2** (aparato) device.
● **aguzar el ingenio** to sharpen one's wits.
ingenioso,-a adj (inteligente) ingenious, clever; (con chispa) witty.
ingenuidad nf naïveté, ingenuousness.
ingenuo,-a adj naïve, ingenuous.
▶ nm,f: **eres un ingenuo**, you're so naïve.
ingerir vt to consume, ingest.
Inglaterra nf England.
ingle nf groin.
inglés,-esa adj English.
▶ nm,f (persona) English person; (hombre) Englishman [pl -**men**]; (mujer) Englishwoman [pl -**women**]: **los ingleses**, the English.
▶ nm **inglés** (idioma) English.
ingratitud nf ingratitude.
ingrato,-a adj **1** (persona) ungrateful. **2** (tarea) thankless.
ingrediente nm ingredient.
ingresar vt **1** (dinero) to deposit, pay in [pt & pp **paid**]. **2** (paciente) to admit.
▶ vi (en colegio) to enter; (en club etc) to become a member; (ejército) to join up; (en hospital) to be admitted to.
ingreso nm **1** (en organización) entry. **2** (en hospital, club, etc) admission. **3** (en cuenta bancaria) deposit.
▶ nm pl **ingresos** income sing.
inhalar vt to inhale.
inhóspito,-a adj inhospitable.
inhumano,-a adj inhuman, cruel.
iniciación nf initiation, introduction.
inicial adj - nf initial.
iniciar vt **1** (introducir) to initiate. **2** (empezar) to begin [pt **began**; pp **begun**].
▶ vpr **iniciarse** to begin [pt **began**; pp **begun**], start.
● **iniciarse en algo** to start to learn about STH.
iniciativa nf initiative.
inicio nm beginning, start.
injusticia nf injustice, unfairness.
injustificado,-a adj unjustified.

injusto,-a adj unjust, unfair.
inmaduro,-a adj (persona) immature; (fruta) unripe.
inmediato,-a adj (reacción, respuesta) immediate.
● **de inmediato** immediately.
● **inmediato,-a a** next to, near.
inmejorable adj unbeatable, unsurpassable.
inmenso,-a adj immense, vast.
inmigración nf immigration.
inmigrante adj - nmf immigrant.
inmigrar vi to immigrate.
inmobiliaria nf GB estate agency ; US real estate agency.
inmoral adj immoral.
inmortal adj - nmf immortal.
inmortalizar vt to immortalize.
▶ vpr **inmortalizarse** to be immortal.
inmóvil adj still, motionless.
● **permanecer inmóvil** to stand still [pt & pp **stood**].
inmueble nm building.
inmunidad nf immunity.
innecesario,-a adj unnecessary.
innegable adj undeniable.
innovación nf innovation.
innumerable adj innumerable, countless.
inocencia nf **1** (de acusado) innocence. **2** (ingenuidad) innocence, naïveté.
inocente adj **1** (libre de culpa) innocent. **2** (ingenuo) naïve. **3** (no culpable) not guilty, innocent.
▶ nmf (persona - no culpable) innocent person; (- ingenua) naïve person: **para proteger a los inocentes**, to protect the innocent.
● **declarar a ALGN inocente** to find SB not guilty [pt & pp **found**].
inodoro,-a adj odourless.
▶ nm **inodoro** toilet.
inofensivo,-a adj inoffensive, harmless.
inolvidable adj unforgettable.
inoportuno,-a adj inopportune, untimely.
inoxidable adj (gen) rustproof; (acero) stainless.
inquietar vt-vpr **inquietar(se)** to worry.
inquieto,-a adj **1** (agitado) restless. **2** (preocupado) worried, anxious.
inquietud nf **1** (agitación) restlessness. **2** (preocupación) worry, anxiety.

inquilino,-a *nm,f* tenant.
insaciable *adj* insatiable.
insatisfecho,-a *adj* **1** *(persona)* dissatisfied. **2** *(deseo, curiosidad)* unsatisfied.
inscribir *vt* **1** *(grabar)* to inscribe. **2** *(apuntar)* to register.
▶ *vpr* **inscribirse 1** *(en colegio)* to enrol. **2** *(en club, organización)* to join. **3** *(en concurso)* to enter.
inscripción *nf* **1** *(grabado)* inscription. **2** *(registro)* enrolment, registration.
insecticida *adj - nm* insecticide.
insecto *nm* insect.
inseguridad *nf* **1** *(falta de confianza)* insecurity. **2** *(duda)* uncertainty. **3** *(peligro)* lack of safety: **hay inseguridad ciudadana**, the streets are not safe.
inseguro,-a *adj* **1** *(falto de confianza)* insecure. **2** *(falto de estabilidad)* unsteady. **3** *(que duda)* uncertain. **4** *(peligroso)* unsafe.
insensato,-a *adj* foolish.
insensible *adj* **1** *(persona)* insensitive. **2** *(miembro)* numb, insensible.
inseparable *adj* inseparable.
insertar *vt* to insert.
inservible *adj* useless, unusable.
insignia *nf* **1** *(distintivo)* badge. **2** *(bandera)* flag, banner; *(de barco)* pennant.
insignificante *adj* insignificant.
insinuar *vt* to insinuate, hint.
● **insinuarse a** ALGN to make advances to SB.
insípido,-a *adj* insipid.
insistir *vi* to insist.
insolación *nf* sunstroke.
insolente *adj* **1** *(irrespetuoso)* insolent, rude. **2** *(arrogante)* haughty.
▶ *nmf* **1** *(irrespetuoso)* insolent person. **2** *(arrogante)* haughty person.
insólito,-a *adj* unusual.
insomnio *nm* insomnia.
insoportable *adj* unbearable, intolerable.
inspección *nf* inspection.
inspeccionar *vt* to inspect.
inspector,-ra *nm,f* inspector.
■ **inspector de Hacienda** GB tax inspector; US revenue agent.
■ **inspector de policía** police inspector.
inspiración *nf* **1** *(de artista)* inspiration. **2** *(inhalación)* inhalation.
inspirar *vt* **1** *(aspirar)* to inhale, breathe in. **2** *(infundir)* to inspire.
▶ *vpr* **inspirarse** to be inspired.

instalación *nf* **1** *(colocación)* installation. **2** *(equipo)* system: **instalación eléctrica**, electrical system wiring.
▶ *nf pl* **instalaciones** *(recinto)* installations; *(servicios)* facilities.
instalar *vt* **1** *(colocar)* to install. **2** *(equipar)* to fit up.
▶ *vpr* **instalarse** *(establecerse)* to settle.
instancia *nf* *(solicitud)* request; *(escrito)* application form.
● **a instancias de** at the request of.
instantánea *nf* snapshot.
instantáneo,-a *adj* **1** *(repuesta, reacción)* instantaneous. **2** *(éxito, resultado)* instant. **3** *(café)* instant.
instante *nm* moment, instant.
● **a cada instante** all the time.
● **al instante** immediately.
instintivo,-a *adj* instinctive.
instinto *nm* instinct.
● **por instinto** instinctively.
■ **instinto maternal** maternal instinct.
institución *nf* institution, establishment.
■ **institución benéfica** charitable foundation.
instituir *vt* to institute.
instituto *nm* **1** *(organismo)* institute. **2** *(de enseñanza)* GB secondary school; US high school.
■ **instituto de belleza** beauty salon.
instrucción *nf* education.
▶ *nf pl* **instrucciones** instructions.
■ **instrucción militar** military training.
instructivo,-a *adj* **1** *(experiencia, curso)* instructive. **2** *(juguete, película)* educational.
instructor,-ra *nm,f* instructor.
instruir *vt* to instruct.
instrumental *nm* instruments *pl*.
instrumento *nm* instrument.
insuficiencia *nf* lack, shortage.
■ **insuficiencia cardíaca** heart failure.
■ **insuficiencia respiratoria** respiratory failure.
insuficiente *adj* insufficient.
▶ *nm* *(calificación)* fail.
insultar *vt* to insult.
insulto *nm* insult.
insuperable *adj* insuperable, unsurpassable.
intacto,-a *adj* intact.
integración *nf* integration.

integral *adj* **1** *(total)* comprehensive. **2** *(sin refinar - pan, harina)* wholemeal; *(- arroz)* brown.

íntegro,-a *adj* **1** *(completo)* whole, entire. **2** *(honrado)* honest, upright.

intelectual *adj - nmf* intellectual.

inteligencia *nf* **1** *(facultad)* intelligence. **2** *(comprensión)* understanding.

■ **inteligencia artificial** artificial intelligence.

inteligente *adj* intelligent, clever.

intemperie *nf*.

● **a la intemperie** in the open air, outdoors.

intención *nf* intention.

● **tener intención de** to intend.

■ **buena intención** good will.

■ **mala intención** ill will.

intencionado,-a *adj* intentional, deliberate.

intensidad *nf (gen)* intensity; *(de viento)* force.

intensificar *vt* to intensify.

intensivo,-a *adj* intensive.

intenso,-a *adj (gen)* intense; *(dolor)* acute.

intentar *vt* to try, attempt.

intento *nm* attempt, try.

intercalar *vt* to put in, insert.

intercambiar *vt* to exchange, swap.

intercambio *nm* exchange.

interceder *vi* to intercede.

● **interceder por ALGN** to intercede on SB's behalf.

interceptar *vt (mensaje, balón, etc)* to intercept; *(tráfico)* to hold up [*pt & pp* **held**].

interés *nm* interest.

● **poner interés en algo** to take an interest in STH.

● **tener interés en algo** to be interested in STH.

■ **intereses creados** vested interests.

interesado,-a *adj* **1** *(gen)* interested, concerned. **2** *(egoísta)* selfish, self-interested.

▶ *nm,f* **1** *(gen)* interested party: *los interesados en ir a la excursión*, those interested in going on the excursion. **2** *(persona egoísta)* selfish person: *es una interesada*, she's selfish.

interesante *adj* interesting.

interesar *vi* to interest: *esto te interesará*, this will interest you; *¿te interesa venir?*, are you interested in coming?

● **interesarse por algo** to be interested in STH.

● **interesarse por ALGN** to ask about SB.

interferencia *nf* interference.

interferir *vt (interponerse en)* to interfere with.

▶ *vi* to interfere.

interfono *nm* intercom.

interior *adj* **1** *(jardín, patio)* interior. **2** *(estancia, piso)* inner. **3** *(bolsillo)* inside. **4** *(comercio, política)* domestic, internal. **5** *(mar, desierto)* inland.

▶ *nm* **1** *(parte interna)* inside, inner part. **2** *(alma)* soul. **3** *(de país)* interior.

● **en el interior de** inside.

interjección *nf* interjection.

interlocutor,-ra *nm,f* interlocutor.

intermediario,-a *adj* intermediate.

▶ *nm,f* middleman [*pl* -**men**].

intermedio,-a *adj* **1** *(nivel)* intermediate. **2** *(tamaño)* medium.

▶ *nm* **intermedio** intermission, interval.

interminable *adj* interminable, endless.

intermitente *adj* intermittent.

▶ *nm* GB indicator; US turn signal.

internacional *adj* international.

internado *nm* boarding school.

internar *vt* to intern.

▶ *vpr* **internarse** to penetrate deep.

internauta *nmf* Net user.

interno,-a *adj* **1** *(gen)* internal. **2** *(política)* domestic, internal.

▶ *nm,f* boarder.

interpretación *nf* **1** *(explicación)* interpretation. **2** *(actuación)* performance. **3** *(traducción)* interpreting.

interpretar *vt* **1** *(explicar, traducir)* to interpret: *no sé cómo interpretar su silencio*, I don't know how to interpret his silence. **2** *(obra, pieza)* to perform; *(papel)* to play; *(canción)* to sing [*pt* **sang**; *pp* **sung**].

intérprete *nmf* **1** *(traductor)* interpreter. **2** *(actor, músico)* performer.

interrogación *nf* **1** *(interrogatorio)* interrogation, questioning. **2** *(signo)* question mark.

interrogante *nm* question mark.

interrogar *vt* **1** *(testigo)* to question. **2** *(sospechoso, detenido)* to interrogate, question.

interrogativo,-a *adj* interrogative.

interrogatorio *nm (de testigo)* questioning;

(de sospechoso, detenido) interrogation, questioning.

interrumpir *vt* **1** *(persona, emisión)* to interrupt. **2** *(vacaciones)* to cut short [*pt & pp* **cut**].

interrupción *nf* interruption.

interruptor *nm* switch.

interurbano,-a *adj (transporte)* inter-city; *(llamada)* long-distance.

intervalo *nm* **1** *(de tiempo)* interval. **2** *(de espacio)* gap.

intervención *nf* **1** *(gen)* intervention. **2** *(operación)* operation. **3** *(discurso)* speech.

■ **intervención quirúrgica** operation.

intervenir *vi* **1** *(tomar parte)* to take part. **2** *(interferir, mediar)* to intervene: *tuvo que intervenir el profesor*, the teacher had to intervene.

▶ *vt* **1** *(paciente)* to operate on. **2** *(cuentas)* to audit.

interventor,-ra *nm,f* supervisor, inspector.

■ **interventor,-ra de cuentas** auditor.

intestino *nm* intestine.

intimidad *nf* **1** *(amistad)* intimacy. **2** *(vida privada)* private life [*pl* **-ves**].

● **en la intimidad** in private.

íntimo,-a *adj* **1** *(secreto, ambiente)* intimate. **2** *(vida)* private. **3** *(amistad)* close.

intolerable *adj* intolerable, unbearable.

intolerante *adj* intolerant.

intoxicación *nf* poisoning.

■ **intoxicación alimenticia** food poisoning.

intoxicar *vt* to poison.

intranet *nm* intranet.

intranquilidad *nf* restlessness, uneasiness.

intranquilo,-a *adj* **1** *(nervioso)* restless. **2** *(preocupado)* worried, uneasy.

intransitivo,-a *adj* intransitive.

intratable *adj* **1** *(persona)* unsociable. **2** *(asunto)* intractable.

intriga *nf* **1** *(maquinación)* intrigue. **2** *(de película etc)* plot.

intrigar *vt* to intrigue: *me intriga su pasado*, I'm intrigued by her past.

▶ *vi* to plot, scheme.

introducción *nf* introduction.

introducir *vt* **1** *(meter)* to put in, insert: *introduzca la moneda en la ranura*, insert the coin in the slot. **2** *(instaurar)* to bring in [*pt & pp* **brought**]: *han introduci-*

do un nuevo impuesto, they've brought in a new tax.

▶ *vpr* **introducirse** to enter, get in: *se introdujo en el coche*, he got into the car.

intromisión *nf* interference, meddling.

introvertido,-a *adj* introverted.

▶ *nm,f* introvert.

intruso,-a *nm,f* intruder.

intuición *nf* intuition.

● **por intuición** intuitively.

intuir *vt* **1** *(saber)* to know by intuition [*pt* **knew**; *pp* **known**]. **2** *(presentir)* to sense.

intuitivo,-a *adj* intuitive.

inundación *nf* flood.

inundar *vt* to flood.

inútil *adj* useless.

▶ *nmf fam* good-for-nothing: *es una inútil*, she's useless.

inutilizar *vt* **1** *(gen)* to make useless, render useless. **2** *(máquina)* to put out of action.

invadir *vt* **1** *(ejército)* to invade. **2** *(sentimiento)* to overcome [*pt* **overcame**; *pp* **overcome**].

inválido,-a *adj* **1** *(documento, ley)* invalid. **2** *(persona)* disabled, handicapped.

▶ *nm,f* disabled person, handicapped person: *los inválidos*, the disabled, the handicapped.

invariable *adj* invariable.

invasión *nf* invasion.

invasor,-ra *adj* invading.

▶ *nm,f* invader.

invencible *adj (obstáculo)* insurmountable; *(ejército etc)* invincible.

invención *nf* **1** *(invento)* invention. **2** *(mentira)* fabrication.

inventar *vt* **1** *(crear)* to invent. **2** *(mentir)* to make up: *¡te lo estás inventando!*, you're making it up!

inventario *nm* inventory.

● **hacer el inventario** GB to do the stocktaking; US to take inventory.

invento *nm* invention.

inventor,-ra *nm,f* inventor.

invernadero *nm* greenhouse, hothouse.

invernal *adj* wintry, winter.

invernar *vi* **1** *(pasar el invierno)* to winter. **2** *(animales)* to hibernate.

inverosímil *adj* unlikely.

inversión *nf* **1** *(de dinero, tiempo)* investment. **2** *(del orden)* inversion.

inverso,-a *adj* inverse, opposite.

● **a la inversa** the other way round.

inversor,-ra *nm,f* investor.
invertebrado,-a *adj* invertebrate.
▶ *nm* **invertebrado** invertebrate.
invertir *vt* **1** *(orden)* to invert. **2** *(dirección)* to reverse. **3** *(tiempo)* to spend [*pt & pp* **spent**]. **4** *(dinero, tiempo)* to invest.
investigación *nf* **1** *(policial, judicial)* investigation, inquiry. **2** *(científica, académica)* research.
investigador,-ra *adj* investigating.
▶ *nm,f* **1** *(científico)* researcher. **2** *(detective)* investigator.
investigar *vt* **1** *(indagar)* to investigate. **2** *(estudiar)* to do research on.
invierno *nm* winter.
invisible *adj* invisible.
invitación *nf* invitation.
invitado,-a *nm,f* guest.
invitar *vt* to invite: *me ha invitado a comer*, she's invited me to lunch; *déjame que te invite a un café*, let me buy you a coffee.
▶ *vi* to pay [*pt & pp* **paid**]: *invito yo*, I'll get it, I'll pay; *invita la casa*, it's on the house.
● **invitar a** ALGN **a hacer algo** to invite SB to do STH.
involuntario,-a *adj* involuntary.
inyección *nf* injection.
● **poner una inyección** to give an injection.
inyectar *vt* to inject.
▶ *vpr* **inyectarse** to give oneself an injection, inject oneself.
IPC *abr* (**Índice de Precios al Consumo**) Retail Price Index.
ir *vi* **1** *(gen)* to go: *¿adónde vas?*, where are you going?; *fui andando*, I walked, I went on foot. **2** *(camino etc)* to lead: *este camino va a la aldea*, this road leads you to the village. **3** *(funcionar)* to work: *el ascensor no va*, the lift isn't working. **4** *(sentar bien)* to suit; *(gustar)* to like: *el rojo te va*, red suits you; *no me va el pop*, I don't like pop. **5** *(tratar)* to be about: *¿de qué va la película?*, what's the film about?
▶ *aux* **1** *ir + a + infin*: *voy a salir*, I'm going out. **2** *ir + gerundio*: *vas mejorando*, you're getting better; *fuimos corriendo*, we ran.
▶ *vpr* **irse 1** *(marcharse)* to go away, leave

[*pt & pp* **left**]. **2** *(deslizarse)* to slip. **3** *(gastarse)* to go, disappear.
● **¿cómo te va?** how are you?, how it's going?
● **¿cómo van?** what's the score?
● **ir a pie** to go on foot.
● **ir de compras** to go shopping.
● **ir de culo** *fam* to be rushed off one's feet.
● **ir en coche** to go by car.
● **ir en tren** to go by train.
● **ir por** to go and get: *voy por el coche*, I'm going to get the car.
● **ir tirando** to get by, manage.
● **irse a pique 1** *(barco)* to sink [*pt* **sank**; *pp* **sunk**]. **2** *(proyecto)* to fall through [*pt* **fell**; *pp* **fallen**].
● **irse de la lengua** to tell it all [*pt & pp* **told**].
● **¡qué va!** not at all!, no way!
● **¡vete tú a saber!** who knows!
● **¡ya voy!** I'm coming!
ira *nf* anger, rage, wrath.
Irak *nm* Iraq.
Irán *nm* Iran.
iraní *adj - nmf* Iranian.
iraquí *adj - nmf* Iraqi.
iris *nm* iris.
Irlanda *nf* Ireland.
■ **Irlanda del Norte** Northern Ireland.
irlandés,-esa *adj* Irish.
▶ *nm,f* *(hombre)* Irishman [*pl* **-men**]; *(mujer)* Irish woman [*pl* **women**].
▶ *nm* **irlandés** *(idioma)* Irish.
ironía *nf* irony.
irónico,-a *adj* ironic.
IRPF *abr* (**Impuesto sobre la Renta de las Personas Físicas**) income tax.
irracional *adj* irrational.
irreal *adj* unreal.
irregular *adj* irregular.
irremediable *adj* irremediable, hopeless.
irresistible *adj* **1** *(muy atractivo)* irresistible. **2** *(insoportable)* unbearable.
irrespetuoso,-a *adj* disrespectful.
irresponsable *adj* irresponsible.
▶ *nmf*: *es un irresponsable*, he's so irresponsible.
irritación *nf* irritation.
irritar *vt* to irritate, annoy.
▶ *vpr* **irritarse** to get irritated, get annoyed.

irrompible *adj* unbreakable.
irrumpir *vi* to burst [*pt & pp* **burst**].
isla *nf* island.
islamismo *nm* Islam.
islandés,-esa *adj* Icelandic.
▶ *nm,f (persona)* Icelander.
▶ *nm* **islandés** *(idioma)* Icelandic.
Islandia *nf* Iceland.
isleño,-a *nm,f* islander.
islote *nm* small island.
Israel *nm* Israel.
israelí *adj* - *nmf* Israeli.
israelita *adj* - *nmf (en la Biblia)* Israelite;
(hoy día) Israeli.
istmo *nm* isthmus.
Italia *nf* Italy.
italiano,-a *adj* - *nm,f* Italian.

itinerario *nm* itinerary, route.
ITV *abr (**Inspección Técnica de Vehículos**)* MOT test.
IVA *abr (**Impuesto sobre el Valor Añadido**)* Value-Added Tax; *(abreviatura)* VAT.
izar *vt* to hoist: *izar la bandera*, to hoist the flag.
izquierda *nf* **1** *(dirección)* left: *el restaurante está a la izquierda*, the restaurant is on the left; *gira a la izquierda*, turn left. **2** *(mano)* left hand; *(pierna)* left leg. **3** POL left wing.
● **a la izquierda** to the left.
● **de izquierdas** left-wing.
izquierdo,-a *adj* left: *mano izquierda*, left hand.

J

jabalí *nm* wild boar.
jabón *nm* soap.
■ **jabón de afeitar** shaving soap.
■ **jabón de tocador** toilet soap.
jabonar *vt* → enjabonar.
jabonera *nf* soapdish.
jaca *nf* pony.
jacinto *nm* hyacinth.
jactarse *vpr* to boast, brag.
jadear *vi* to pant, gasp.
jalea *nf* jelly.
■ **jalea real** royal jelly.
jaleo *nm* **1** *(alboroto)* racket, din: *¡no ar-méis tanto jaleo!*, stop making such a racket! **2** *(escándalo)* fuss, commotion. **3** *(riña)* row. **4** *(confusión)* muddle.
jamás *adv* never; *(con superlativos)* ever: *jamás he escrito un libro*, I have never written a book; *el mejor libro que ja-más se haya escrito*, the best book ever written.
● **nunca jamás** never ever.
● **por siempre jamás** for ever and ever.
jamón *nm* ham.
■ **jamón de York** boiled ham.
■ **jamón serrano** cured ham.
Japón *nm* Japan.
japonés,-esa *adj* Japanese.
▶ *nmf (hombre)* Japanese man [*pl* **men**]; *(mujer)* Japanese woman [*pl* **women**]: *los japoneses*, the Japanese.
▶ *nm* **japonés** *(idioma)* Japanese.
jaque *nm* check.
■ **jaque mate** checkmate.
jaqueca *nf* migraine, headache.
jarabe *nm* syrup.
■ **jarabe para la tos** cough syrup, cough mixture.

jardín *nm* garden.
■ **jardín botánico** botanical garden.
■ **jardín de infancia** nursery school.
jardinera *nf (para plantas)* plant stand; *(en ventana)* window box.
jardinería *nf* gardening.
jardinero,-a *nm,f* gardener.
jarra *nf* GB jug; US pitcher.
● **con los brazos en jarras** arms akim-bo, hands on hips.
■ **jarra de cerveza** beer mug.
jarro *nm* GB jug, US pitcher.
jarrón *nm* vase.
jaula *nf* **1** *(para animales)* cage. **2** *(de em-balaje)* crate.
jauría *nf* pack of hounds.
jazmín *nm* jasmine.
jefatura *nf* **1** *(cargo, dirección)* leadership. **2** *(sede)* central office; *(militar)* headquarters *inv*.
jefe,-a *nm,f (superior)* boss; *(de departa-mento)* head; *(de partido, asociación)* leader; *(de tribu)* chief.
■ **jefe de estación** station master.
■ **jefe de Estado** Head of State.
■ **jefe de Estado Mayor** Chief of Staff.
■ **jefe de redacción** editor-in-chief.
■ **jefe de taller** foreman [*pl* -**men**].
jerarquía *nf* **1** *(gradación)* hierarchy. **2** *(categoría)* rank.
jerga *nf* **1** *(técnica)* jargon. **2** *(vulgar)* slang.
jergón *nm* straw mattress.
jeringuilla *nf* syringe.
jeroglífico,-a *adj* hieroglyphic.
▶ *nm* **jeroglífico 1** *(texto antiguo)* hie-roglyph. **2** *(juego)* rebus.
jersey *nm* sweater, pullover, GB jumper.
jeta *nf* **1** *fam (cara)* mug, face. **2** *(hocico)* snout. **3** *(descaro)* nerve, cheek.

● **ser un jeta** *fam* to have a nerve, have a cheek.

● **tener jeta** *fam* to have a nerve, have a cheek.

jilguero *nm* goldfinch.

jinete *nm* rider, horseman [*pl* **-men**].

jirafa *nf* giraffe.

jirón *nm* **1** *(tela desgarrada)* shred, strip. **2** *(pedazo suelto)* bit, scrap.

● **hecho,-a jirones** in shreds, in tatters.

JJ.OO. *abr (Juegos Olímpicos)* Olympic Games.

joder *vt* **1** *vulg (copular)* to fuck, screw. **2** *vulg (fastidiar)* GB to piss off; US to piss. **3** *vulg (lastimar)* to hurt [*pt & pp* **hurt**].

▶ *vt-vpr* **joder(se)** *vulg (echar a perder, estropear)* to fuck up.

▶ *vpr* **joderse 1** *vulg (aguantarse)* to put up with it. **2** *vulg (lastimarse)* to knock oneself up. **3** *vulg (estropearse)* to go bust, be buggered.

▶ *interj* **¡joder!** *vulg* bloody hell!, fuck!

● **¡hay que joderse!** *vulg* would you fucking believe it?

● **¡la jodiste!** *vulg* you screwed up!

● **¡no me jodas!** *vulg* come on, don't give me that!

● **¡que se joda!** *vulg* fuck him/her!

jodido,-a *adj* **1** *vulg (maldito)* bloody, fucking. **2** *vulg (molesto)* annoying. **3** *vulg (enfermo)* in a bad way; *(cansado)* knackered, exhausted. **4** *vulg (estropeado, roto)* fucked, kaput, buggered. **5** *vulg (difícil)* complicated.

jolgorio *nm* **1** *fam (juerga)* binge. **2** *(diversión)* revelry.

● **¡qué jolgorio!** what fun!

jolín *interj* **1** *fam (sorpresa)* gosh!, good grief! **2** *(enfado)* blast!, damn!

jornada *nf* day.

▶ *nf pl* **jornadas** conference *sing*, congress *sing*.

■ **jornada completa** full-time.

■ **jornada laboral** working day.

jornal *nm* day's wage.

● **trabajar a jornal** to be paid by the day.

jornalero,-a *nm,f* day labourer.

joroba *nf* **1** *(deformidad)* hump. **2** *fam (fastidio)* nuisance, drag.

jorobado,-a *adj* hunchbacked, humpbacked.

▶ *nm,f* hunchback, humpback.

jorobar *vt* **1** *fam (fastidiar)* to annoy, bother. **2** *fam (romper)* to smash up, break [*pt* **broke**; *pp* **broken**]. **3** *fam (estropear)* to ruin, wreck.

▶ *vpr fam (aguantarse)* to put up with it.

● **me joroba** it really gets up my nose.

● **¡no jorobes! 1** *(indicando fastidio)* stop pestering me! **2** *(indicando incredulidad)* pull the other one!

jota *nf* **1** *(letra)* the letter J. **2** *(cantidad mínima)* jot, scrap.

● **ni jota** not an iota.

joven *adj* young.

▶ *nmf (hombre)* youth, young man [*pl* **men**]; *(mujer)* girl, young woman [*pl* **women**].

jovial *adj* jovial, good-humoured.

joya *nf* **1** *(alhaja)* jewel, piece of jewellery. **2** *(persona)* real treasure, godsend.

joyería *nf* **1** *(tienda)* jewellery shop, jeweller's. **2** *(comercio)* jewellery trade.

joyero,-a *nm,f* jeweller.

▶ *nm* **joyero** jewel case, jewel box.

juanete *nm* bunion.

jubilación *nf* **1** *(acción)* retirement. **2** *(dinero)* pension.

■ **jubilación anticipada** early retirement.

jubilado,-a *adj* retired.

▶ *nm,f* retired person: *los jubilados*, the retired.

jubilar *vt* **1** *(trabajador)* to pension off. **2** *fam (desechar)* to get rid of, ditch.

▶ *vpr* **jubilarse** to retire.

júbilo *nm* jubilation, joy.

judía *nf (planta)* bean.

■ **judía blanca** haricot bean.

■ **judía pinta** kidney bean.

■ **judía verde** French bean, green bean.

judicial *adj* judicial.

judío,-a *adj* **1** *(religión)* Jewish. **2** *fam (tacaño)* mean, stingy.

▶ *nm,f (persona)* Jew.

juego *nm* **1** *(para entretenerse)* game. **2** *(acto)* play. **3** *(en tenis)* game. **4** *(de apuestas)* gambling: *perdió mucho dinero en el juego*, he lost a lot of money gambling. **5** *(conjunto de piezas)* set.

● **a juego** matching.

● **hacer juego** to match.

● **seguir el juego a ALGN** to play along with SB.

■ **juego de café** coffee set, coffee service.

■ **juego de té** tea set, tea service.

■ **juego de manos** sleight of hand.

■ **juego de palabras** play on words, pun.

■ **juegos de azar** games of chance.

■ **juegos malabares** juggling *sing*.

■ **Juegos Olímpicos** Olympic Games.

juerga *nf fam* binge, rave-up.

● **estar de juerga** to be living it up, be having a good time.

● **irse de juerga** to go out on the town.

juerguista *adj* fun-loving.

▶ *nmf:* **es un juerguista**, he's always living it up.

jueves *nm* Thursday.

● **no ser nada del otro jueves** to be nothing special.

juez *nmf* judge.

■ **juez de banda** linesman [*pl* -men].

■ **juez de línea** linesman [*pl* -men].

■ **juez de paz** justice of the peace.

jugada *nf* **1** *(en ajedrez)* move; *(en billar)* shot; *(en dardos)* throw. **2** *fam (trastada)* dirty trick.

● **hacerle una mala jugada a** ALGN to play a dirty trick on SB.

jugador,-ra *nm,f* **1** *(en deportes, juegos)* player. **2** *(apostador)* gambler.

jugar *vt-vi (para divertirse)* to play: **están jugando un partido de fútbol**, they're playing a football match; **¡juegas tú!**, it's your turn!

▶ *vpr* **jugarse 1** *(apostar)* to bet [*pt & pp* **bet**]. **2** *(arriesgar)* to risk: **se jugó la vida**, he risked his life.

● **jugar el todo por el todo** to stake everything one has.

● **jugar limpio** to play fair.

● **jugársela a** ALGN **1** *(engañar)* to trick SB. **2** *(ser infiel)* to two-time SB.

● **jugar sucio** to play dirty.

● **¿quién juega?** whose go, whose turn is it?

jugarreta *nf fam* dirty trick.

jugo *nm* juice.

● **sacar el jugo a algo** to make the most of STH.

● **sacar el jugo a** ALGN to exploit SB, bleed SB dry [*pt & pp* **bled**].

jugoso,-a *adj* **1** *(comida, fruta)* juicy. **2** *(rentable)* profitable.

juguete *nm* toy.

● **ser el juguete de** ALGN to be SB's plaything.

juguetear *vi* to play.

juguetería *nf* **1** *(tienda)* toy shop. **2** *(comercio)* toy business.

juguetón,-ona *adj* playful.

juicio *nm* **1** *(facultad)* judgement. **2** *(sensatez)* reason, common sense. **3** *(proceso)* trial, lawsuit.

● **a mi juicio** in my opinion.

● **dejar algo a juicio de** ALGN to leave STH to SB's discretion [*pt & pp* **left**].

● **emitir un juicio sobre algo** to express an opinion about STH.

● **en su sano juicio** in one's right mind.

● **llevar a** ALGN **a juicio** to take legal action against SB, sue SB.

● **perder el juicio** to go mad.

● **quitar el juicio a** ALGN to drive SB insane [*pt* **drove**; *pp* **driven**].

● **juicio final** last judgement.

juicioso,-a *adj (persona)* judicious, sensible; *(decisión)* wise.

julio *nm* July.

junco *nm* rush, reed.

jungla *nf* jungle.

junio *nm* June.

junta *nf* **1** *(reunión)* meeting. **2** *(conjunto de personas)* board, committee. **3** *(sesión)* session, sitting. **4** *(militar)* junta. **5** *(juntura)* joint.

■ **junta directiva** board of directors.

■ **junta electoral** electoral board.

juntar *vt* **1** *(unir)* to put together; *(piezas)* to assemble: **juntaron las dos camas**, they put the two beds together. **2** *(coleccionar)* to collect. **3** *(reunir -dinero)* to raise; *(-gente)* to gather together.

▶ *vpr* **juntarse 1** *(unirse a)* to join; *(ríos, caminos)* to meet [*pt & pp* **met**]. **2** *(reunirse)* to get together.

junto,-a *adj* together.

▶ *adv* .

● **junto a** near, close to.

● **junto con** together with.

● **todo junto** all together.

jurado,-a *adj* sworn.

▶ *nm* **jurado 1** *(tribunal)* jury. **2** *(en concurso)* panel of judges, jury.

▶ *nmf* juror, member of the jury.

juramento *nm* **1** *(promesa)* oath. **2** *(blasfemia)* swearword.

- **tomar juramento a** ALGN to swear SB in [*pt* **swore**; *pp* **sworn**].
- **juramento falso** perjury.

jurar *vt* to swear [*pt* **swore**; *pp* **sworn**].
▶ *vi (blasfemar)* to swear [*pt* **swore**; *pp* **sworn**], curse.

- **jurar en falso** to commit perjury.
- **jurar fidelidad** to pledge allegiance.
- **tenérsela jurada a** ALGN to have it in for SB.

jurídico,-a *adj* legal, juridical.
justicia *nf* justice.
justificación *nf* justification.
justificante *nm (del médico)* note: *traigo un justificante del médico*, I've brought a note from the doctor.

- **justificante de compra** receipt.
- **justificante de pago** proof of payment.

justificar *vt* to justify.
▶ *vpr* **justificarse** to justify oneself.

- **justificarse con** ALGN **por algo** to justify oneself for STH.

justo,-a *adj* **1** *(con justicia)* fair, just: *¡no es justo!*, it's not fair! **2** *(apretado)* tight: *este pantalón me está justo*, these trousers are tight on me. **3** *(exacto)* exact: *necesito saber las medidas justas*, I need to know the exact measurements; *me dio el dinero justo*, she gave me the right money. **4** *(escaso)*: *me queda el dinero justo*, I've just got enough money left; *vamos muy justos de tiempo*, we've only just got enough time.
▶ *nm pl* **los justos** the just: *siempre acaban pagando justos por pecadores*, the innocent always end up paying for the sins of the guilty.
▶ *adv* **justo** exactly, precisely: *lo has hecho justo al revés*, you've done exactly the opposite.

juvenil *adj* youthful, young.
▶ *adj - nmf (en deporte)* under 18.

juventud *nf* **1** *(edad)* youth. **2** *(aspecto joven)* youthfulness. **3** *(conjunto de jóvenes)* young people, youth.

juzgado *nm* court.

- **ser de juzgado de guardia** to be absolutely scandalous.

juzgar *vi* **1** *(gen)* to judge. **2** *(en tribunal)* to try. **3** *(considerar)* to consider, think [*pt & pp* **thought**].

K

karaoke *nm (aparato, fenómeno)* karaoke; *(local)* karaoke bar.
kárate *nm* karate.
karateca *nmf* karate expert.
kart *nm* go-cart.
katiuskas *nf pl* wellingtons.
ketchup *nm* ketchup.
kilo *nm* kilo.
kilogramo *nm* kilogram, kilogramme.
kilométrico,-a *adj* kilometric.
▶ *nm* **kilométrico** runabout ticket.

kilómetro *nm* kilometre, kilometer.
kilovatio *nm* kilowatt.
kimono *nm* kimono [*pl* -s].
kiosko *nm →* quiosco.
kiwi *nm* kiwi.
Kleenex® *nm* Kleenex®, tissue.
km/h *abr (**kilómetros hora**)* kilometres (US kilometers) per hour, kph.
koala *nm* koala.
Kuwait *nm* Kuwait.
kuwaití *adj-nmf* Kuwaiti.

L

la¹ *det* the: *la casa*, the house.

la² *pron (persona, ella)* her; *(usted)* you; *(cosa, animal)* it: *la miré*, I looked at her; *encantado de conocerla*, pleased to meet you; *la cogí*, I took it.

la³ *nm (nota musical)* la, A.

laberinto *nm* maze, labyrinth.

labia.
• **tener labia** to have the gift of the gab.

labio *nm* lip.

labor *nf* **1** *(trabajo)* task. **2** *(de costura)* needlework; *(de punto)* knitting.

laborable *adj* working: *día laborable*, working day.

laboral *adj* GB labour; US labor.

laboratorio *nm* laboratory.

laborioso,-a *adj* arduous.

labrador,-ra *nm,f (propietario)* farmer; *(trabajador)* farm worker.

labrar *vt (tierra, metal)* to work; *(madera)* to carve; *(piedra)* to cut [*pt & pp* **cut**].

laca *nf* **1** *(barniz)* lacquer. **2** *(para pelo)* hair lacquer, hair spray.
■ **laca de uñas** nail polish; GB nail varnish.

lacayo *nm* **1** *(persona servil)* lackey. **2** *(criado)* footman [*pl* -**men**].

lacio,-a *adj (cabello)* straight.

lacrimógeno,-a *adj* tearful: *una historia lacrimógena*, a tear jerker.

lactancia *nf* lactation.

lácteo,-a *adj* dairy, milk.

ladera *nf* slope, hillside.

lado *nm* side: *al otro lado de la calle*, on the other side of the street; *se sentó a mi lado*, she sat down by my side; *escribe en los dos lados del folio*, write on both sides of the sheet.

• **al lado** close by, near by.
• **al lado de** next to, beside.
• **dar de lado a** ALGN to ignore SB.
• **dejar a un lado** to set aside [*pt & pp* **set**].
• **en algún lado** somewhere.
• **hacerse a un lado** to get out of the way.
• **por un lado... por otro...** on the one hand... on the other hand....
• **por todos lados** everywhere.

ladrar *vi* to bark.

ladrido *nm* bark.
▶ *nm pl* **ladridos** barking.

ladrillo *nm* brick.

ladrón,-ona *nm,f* thief [*pl* -**ves**].

lagartija *nf* lizard, wall lizard.

lagarto *nm* lizard.

lago *nm* lake.

lágrima *nf* tear.

laguna *nf* **1** *(lago)* pool. **2** *(en memoria, conocimientos)* gap.

lamentable *adj (resultado, gestión)* lamentable, deplorable; *(error)* regrettable; *(aspecto, estado)* sorry, deplorable.

lamentar *vt* to regret, be sorry about.
▶ *vpr* **lamentarse** to complain: *lamentarse de algo*, to regret STH.

lamento *nm (de tristeza)* wail; *(de dolor)* moan, cry.

lamer *vt* to lick.

lámina *nf* **1** *(hoja)* sheet. **2** *(ilustración)* plate, illustration.

lámpara *nf* lamp.
■ **lámpara de mesa** table lamp.
■ **lámpara de pie** standard lamp.

lamparón *nm* stain.

lana *nf* wool.

● **de lana** woollen: *guantes de lana*, woollen gloves.

lancha *nf* launch.

■ **lancha motora** motor launch, motor-boat.

langosta *nf* **1** *(crustáceo)* lobster. **2** *(insecto)* locust.

langostino *nm* prawn, king prawn.

lánguido,-a *adj* weak, languid.

lanza *nf* *(en torneo)* lance; *(arrojadiza)* spear.

lanzadera *nf* shuttle.

lanzamiento *nm* **1** *(de objeto)* throwing. **2** *(de cohete, nave, producto)* launch.

■ **lanzamiento de disco** the discus.

■ **lanzamiento de jabalina** the javelin.

lanzar *vt* **1** *(tirar)* to throw [*pt* **threw**; *pp* **thrown**]; *(con violencia)* to fling [*pt & pp* **flung**], hurl. **2** *(cohete, nave, producto)* to launch.

► *vpr* **lanzarse** to throw oneself [*pt* **threw**; *pp* **thrown**].

● **lanzar un grito** to scream.

● **lanzar una mirada** to cast a glance [*pt & pp* **cast**].

● **lanzar un penalti** to take a penalti.

lapa *nf* limpet.

● **pegarse como una lapa** to cling like a leech [*pt & pp* **clung**].

lápida *nf* tombstone.

lápiz *nm* pencil.

■ **lápiz de color** GB crayon, coloured pencil; US crayon, colored pencil.

■ **lápiz de labios** lipstick.

largar *vt* **1** *(cuerda, amarras)* to let out [*pt & pp* **let**]. **2** *fam (golpe, discurso)* to give: *le largó una bofetada*, she slapped him; *me largó un sermón*, he gace me a lecture.

► *vpr* **largarse** *fam* to get out, leave [*pt & pp* **left**].

● **¡lárgate!** get out!

largo,-a *adj* long.

► *adv* **largo** for a long time.

► *nm* length: *tiene dos metros de largo*, it's two metres long.

► *interj* **¡largo!** get out!

● **a la larga** in the long run.

● **a lo largo** lengthwise.

● **a lo largo de** *(recorrido)* along; *(tiempo, espacio)* throughout.

● **pasar de largo** to pass by.

● **tener para largo** to have a long wait ahead.

largometraje *nm* feature film, full-length film.

larguirucho,-a *adj* lanky.

laringe *nf* larynx.

larva *nf* larva.

las *det* the: *las casas*, the houses.

► *pron (ellas)* them; *(ustedes)* you: *las vi*, I saw them; *a ustedes no las conozco*, I don't know you.

láser *nm* laser.

lástima *nf* pity, shame.

● **por lástima** out of pity.

● **¡qué lástima!** what a pity!, what a shame!

● **sentir lástima por** ALGN to feel sorry for SB [*pt & pp* **felt**].

lastimar *vt* to hurt [*pt & pp* **hurt**].

► *vpr* **lastimarse** to get hurt.

lata *nf* **1** *(hojalata)* tinplate. **2** *(envase)* tin, can; *(de bebida)* can. **3** *fam (fastidio)* bore, nuisance.

● **dar la lata** to annoy.

● **en lata** canned, tinned.

lateral *adj* lateral, side.

► *nm* **1** *(calle)* side street. **2** *(lado)* side.

latido *nm* beat.

latifundio *nm* **1** *(terreno)* large estate. **2** *(sistema)* division of land into large estates.

latigazo *nm* **1** *(golpe)* lash. **2** *fam (trago)* swig.

látigo *nm* whip.

latín *nm* Latin.

latino,-a *adj* - *nm,f* Latin.

Latinoamérica *nm* Latin America.

latinoamericano,-a *adj* - *nm,f* Latin American.

latir *vi (corazón)* to beat; *(herida)* to throb.

latitud *nf* latitude.

latón *nm* brass.

latoso,-a *adj fam* annoying, boring.

laúd *nm* lute.

laurel *nm* **1** *(árbol)* bay tree. **2** *(hoja)* bay leaf [*pl* **-ves**].

lava *nf* lava.

lavable *adj* washable.

lavabo *nm* **1** *(pila)* washbasin. **2** *(cuarto de baño)* bathroom. **3** *(público)* toilet.

lavadero *nm* laundry room.

lavado *nm* wash.

lavadora *nf* washing machine.

lavandería *nf* laundry.

■ **lavandería automática** GB launderette; US laundromat.

lavaplatos *nm* → lavavajillas.
lavar *vt* **1** *(manos, ropa)* to wash. **2** *(platos)* to wash up. **3** *(limpiar)* to clean.
▸ *vpr* **lavarse** to have a wash, get washed.
● **lavar a mano** to wash by hand, hand-wash.
● **lavar en seco** to dry-clean.
● **lavar y marcar** to shampoo and set.
lavavajillas *nm* **1** *(máquina)* dishwasher. **2** *(líquido)* washing-up liquid.
laxante *adj* - *nm* laxative.
lazada *nf* **1** *(nudo)* knot. **2** *(lazo)* bow.
lazarillo *nm* guide.
lazo *nm* **1** *(lazada)* bow. **2** *(nudo)* knot. **3** *(vínculo)* tie, bond.
■ **lazo corredizo** slipknot.
le *pron* **1** *(objeto directo)* him; *(usted)* you: *¿Pedro?, no le conozco*, Peter?, I don't know him; *no le conozco a usted*, I don't know you. **2** *(objeto indirecto - a él)* him; *(- a ella)* her; *(a cosa, animal)* it; *(a usted)* you: *le he comprado un libro*, I've bought him/her/you a book.
leal *adj* loyal, faithful.
lealtad *nf* loyalty, faithfulness.
lección *nf* lesson.
● **dar una lección a** ALGN to teach SB a lesson [*pt & pp* **taught**].
leche *nf* **1** *(gen)* milk. **2** *fam (golpe)* bash. **3** *fam (suerte)* luck.
● **tener mala leche** *fam* to have a nasty temper.
■ **leche condensada** condensed milk.
■ **leche descremada** skimmed milk.
■ **leche en polvo** powdered milk.
■ **leche entera** whole milk.
lechería *nf* dairy.
lechero,-a *adj* milk.
▸ *nm,f (hombre)* milkman [*pl* -**men**], dairyman [*pl* -**men**]; *(mujer)* milkmaid, dairymaid.
lecho *nm* bed.
lechón *nm* sucking pig.
lechuga *nf* lettuce.
lechuza *nf* barn owl.
lector,-ra *nm,f* **1** *(de libros)* reader. **2** *(profesor)* language assistant.
▸ *nm* **lector** *(aparato)* reader.
lectura *nf* **1** *(acción)* reading. **2** *(textos)* reading matter. **3** *(interpretación)* interpretation, reading.
leer *vt* to read [*pt & pp* **read**]: *¿te gusta leer?*, do you like reading?

● **leer en voz alta** to read aloud.
legal *adj* **1** *(gen)* legal. **2** *fam (persona)* truthful, honest.
legalidad *nf* legality.
legalizar *vt* to legalize.
legaña *nf* sleep.
legañoso,-a *adj* bleary-eyed.
legendario,-a *adj* legendary.
legible *adj* legible.
legión *nf* legion.
legionario *nm (en Roma)* legionary; *(actual)* legionnaire.
legislación *nf* legislation.
legislar *vt* to legislate.
legislativo,-a *adj* legislative.
legislatura *nf* term of office.
legítimo,-a *adj* **1** *(hijo, heredero, gobierno)* legitimate. **2** *(genuino)* genuine, real.
legua *nf* league.
● **se nota a la legua** you can tell it a mile away.
legumbre *nf* pulse.
lejanía *nf* distance.
lejano,-a *adj* distant.
lejía *nf* bleach.
lejos *adv* far, far away: *¿está lejos tu casa?*, is it far to your house?; *Australia está muy lejos*, Australia is very far away, Australia is a long way away.
● **a lo lejos** in the distance, far away.
● **de lejos** from afar.
lema *nm* **1** *(norma)* motto [*pl* -**os** o -**oes**]. **2** *(eslogan)* slogan.
lencería *nf* **1** *(de mujer)* underwear, lingerie. **2** *(tienda)* lingerie shop. **3** *(ropa blanca)* linen.
lengua *nf* **1** *(en la boca)* tongue. **2** *(idioma)* language. **3** *(de tierra)* strip.
● **morderse la lengua** to hold one's tongue [*pt & pp* **held**].
● **no tener pelos en la lengua** not to mince one's words.
● **irse de la lengua** to let the cat out of the bag [*pt & pp* **let**].
● **sacarle la lengua a** ALGN to stick one's tongue out at SB [*pt & pp* **stuck**].
● **tener algo en la punta de la lengua** to have STH on the tip of one's tongue.
■ **lengua materna** mother tongue.
lenguado *nm* sole.
lenguaje *nm* **1** *(gen)* language. **2** *(habla)* speech.

lengüeta *nf* **1** *(de zapato)* tongue. **2** *(de instrumento)* reed.

lente *nm & nf* lens.

■ **lente de aumento** magnifying glass.

■ **lentes de contacto** contact lenses.

lenteja *nf* lentil.

lentejuela *nf* sequin.

lentilla *nf* contact lens.

lentitud *nf* slowness.

lento,-a *adj* slow.

leña *nf* **1** *(madera)* firewood. **2** *fam (paliza)* thrashing.

● **dar leña a** ALGN to thrash SB.

● **echar leña al fuego** to add fuel to the fire.

leñador,-ra *nm,f* woodcutter.

leño *nm* log.

Leo *nm* Leo.

león,-ona *nm,f (macho)* lion; *(hembra)* lioness.

leonera *nf* lion's den.

● **ser una leonera** to be a tip.

leopardo *nm* leopard.

leotardos *nm pl* thick tights.

lepra *nf* leprosy.

leproso,-a *nm,f* leper.

les *pron* **1** *(objeto indirecto - a ellos)* them; *(- a ustedes)* you: **les he comprado un regalo**, I've bought them/you a present. **2** *(objeto directo - ellos)* them; *(- ustedes)* you: **no les conozco**, I don't know them/you.

lesbiana *nf* lesbian.

lesión *nf* injury.

lesionar *vt* to injure.

▶ *vpr* **lesionarse** to injure oneself, get injured.

letal *adj* lethal, deadly.

letargo *nm* lethargy.

letón,-ona *adj - nm,f* Latvian.

Letonia *nf* Latvia.

letra *nf* **1** *(del alfabeto)* letter. **2** *(de imprenta)* type. **3** *(escritura)* handwriting: **una letra muy clara**, a very clear handwriting. **4** *(de canción)* lyrics *pl*, words *pl*.

▶ *nf pl* **letras** *(humanidades)* arts; *(literatura)* letters.

■ **letra de cambio** bill of exchange, draft.

■ **letra mayúscula** capital letter.

■ **letra minúscula** small letter.

letrero *nm* sign, notice.

levadura *nf* yeast.

levantar *vt* **1** *(alzar)* to raise; *(bulto, trampilla)* to lift: **levantó la mano**, she raised her hand. **2** *(construir)* to erect, build [*pt & pp* **built**]. **3** *(sanción, embargo)* to lift.

▶ *vpr* **levantarse** **1** *(ponerse de pie)* to rise [*pt* **rose**; *pp* **risen**], stand up [*pt & pp* **stood**]. **2** *(de la cama)* to get up, rise [*pt* **rose**; *pp* **risen**]. **3** *(sublevarse)* to rebel.

● **levantar acta** to draw up a statement [*pt* **drew**; *pp* **drawn**].

● **levantar la vista** to look up.

● **levantarse con el pie izquierdo** to get out of bed on the wrong side.

● **se levanta la sesión** the court is adjourned.

levante *nm* **1** *(este)* east. **2** *(viento)* east wind.

leve *adj* **1** *(ligero)* light. **2** *(poco importante)* slight, trifling.

léxico,-a *adj* lexical.

▶ *nm* **léxico** *(vocabulario)* vocabulary.

ley *nf (gen)* law; *(del parlamento)* act, bill.

● **aprobar una ley** to pass a bill.

leyenda *nf* legend.

liar *vt* **1** *(atar)* to tie up; *(envolver)* to wrap up: **lió los libros**, he tied the books up. **2** *(cigarrillo)* to roll. **3** *(confundir)* to confuse: **me habéis liado con tantos consejos**, you've confused me with all your advice. **4** *(implicar)* to involve.

▶ *vpr* **liarse** **1** *(complicarse)* to get mixed up. **2** *fam (con* ALGN*)* to have an affair.

● **liarse a hacer algo** to start doing STH: **se lió a pintar y perdió la noción del tiempo**, he started painting and lost all notion of time.

libanés,-esa *adj - nm,f* Lebanese.

Líbano *nm* Lebanon.

libélula *nf* dragonfly.

liberación *nf (de país)* liberation; *(de preso, rehén)* freeing, release.

liberado,-a *adj* liberated.

liberal *adj - nmf* liberal.

liberar *vt (país)* to liberate; *(preso, rehén)* to free, release.

libertad *nf* freedom, liberty.

● **poner en libertad** to release, set free [*pt & pp* **set**].

■ **libertad bajo fianza** bail.

■ **libertad condicional** probation.

libertador,-ra *nm,f* liberator.

Libia *nf* Libya.

libio,-a *adj - nm,f* Libyan.

libra nf **1** (moneda, peso) pound. **2 Libra** (signo, constelación) Libra.

librar vt (librar a ALGN de algo) to free SB from STH.
▶ vi to have the day off: **libro los martes**, I have Tuesdays off.
▶ vpr **librarse 1** (deshacerse) to get rid: **se libró de él**, she got rid of him. **2** (evitar) to escape: **se libró del castigo**, he escaped punishment.
● **librar una batalla** to fight a battle [pt & pp **fought**].

libre adj free.
● **libre de impuestos** tax-free, duty-free.
■ **libre albedrío** free will.
■ **libre cambio** free trade.
■ **libre comercio** free trade.

librería nf **1** (tienda) bookshop. **2** (estantería) bookcase.

librero,-a nm,f bookseller.

libreta nf notebook.

libro nm book.
■ **libro de bolsillo** paperback.
■ **libro de caja** cash-book.
■ **libro de consulta** reference book.
■ **libro de reclamaciones** complaints book.
■ **libro de texto** textbook.

licencia nf **1** (documento) licence, permit. **2** (permiso) permission. **3** (en el ejército) leave.
■ **licencia de armas** firearms licence.

licenciado,-a nm,f graduate.

licenciarse vpr to graduate.

licenciatura nf degree.

lícito,-a adj licit, lawful.

licor nm liqueur.

licuadora nf juice extractor, juicer.

licuar vt to liquefy.

líder nmf leader.

lidiar vi to fight [pt & pp **fought**], struggle.
▶ vt (toros) to fight [pt & pp **fought**].

liebre nf hare.

lienzo nm **1** (tela) cloth. **2** (para pintar) canvas. **3** (cuadro) painting.

liga nf **1** (para media) garter. **2** (en política, deporte) league.

ligadura nf tie, bond.
■ **ligadura de trompas** tubal ligation.

ligamento nm ligament.

ligar vt **1** (atar) to tie, bind [pt & pp **bound**]. **2** (unir) to bind [pt & pp **bound**]: **nos liga** **una estrecha amistad**, we are bound by a close friendship. **3** (salsa) to thicken.
▶ vi fam (conquistar) to pick up.

ligereza nf **1** (liviandad) lightness. **2** (prontitud) swiftness. **3** (agilidad) agility. **4** (frivolidad) flippancy, frivolity.

ligero,-a adj **1** (liviano) light. **2** (leve) slight. **3** (rápido) swift. **4** (ágil) agile. **5** (frívolo) flippant, thoughtless.
● **a la ligera** lightly.

light adj **1** (comida) low-calorie; (refresco) diet. **2** (tabaco) light.

ligón,-ona nm,f fam flirt.

ligue nm fam pick-up.

lija nf sandpaper.

lijar vt to sand.

lila adj - nf lilac.

lima¹ nf (utensilio) file.
● **comer como una lima** to eat like a horse [pt ate; pp **eaten**].
■ **lima de uñas** nail file.

lima² nf (fruta) lime.

limar vt **1** (uñas, metal) to file. **2** (perfeccionar) to polish up.
● **limar asperezas** to smooth things off.

limitación nf limitation, limit.

limitado,-a adj limited.

limitar vt to limit.
▶ vi to border: **España limita al norte con Francia**, Spain borders on France to the north.
▶ vpr **limitarse** to limit oneself: **límitate a contestar las preguntas**, just answer the questions.

límite nm **1** (tope) limit. **2** (frontera) boundary, border.

limón nm lemon.

limonada nf lemonade.

limonero nm lemon tree.

limosna nf alms.
● **dar limosna** to give money.
● **pedir limosna** to beg.

limpiabotas nm bootblack.

limpiacristales nmf - nm window cleaner.

limpiaparabrisas nm GB windscreen wiper; US windshield wiper.

limpiar vt **1** (gen) to clean. **2** (con paño) to wipe. **3** fam (robar) to clean out.
▶ vpr **limpiarse** to clean oneself.
● **limpiarse la nariz** to wipe one's nose.

limpieza nf **1** (cualidad) cleanness, cleanliness. **2** (acción) cleaning. **3** (honradez) honesty, fairness.

● **hacer limpieza general** to spring-clean.

■ **limpieza en seco** dry-cleaning.

■ **limpieza étnica** ethnic cleansing.

limpio,-a *adj* **1** *(gen)* clean. **2** *(persona)* neat, tidy. **3** *(juego)* fair. **4** *(sin impuestos)* net: **ganó 40.000 limpios**, he made 40,000 clear profit.

● **dejar limpio,-a** to clean out.

● **poner en limpio** to make a fair copy of.

lince *nm* **1** *(animal)* lynx. **2** *(persona)* sharp-eyed person.

linchar *vt* to lynch.

lindar *vi* to border.

lindo,-a *adj* pretty, nice, lovely.

● **de lo lindo** a great deal.

línea *nf* **1** *(gen)* line: **una línea recta**, a straight line. **2** *(tipo)* figure.

● **cuidar la línea** to watch one's weight.

● **en línea** on-line.

● **fuera de línea** off-line.

■ **línea aérea** airline.

■ **línea continua** solid white line.

■ **línea férrea** railway line.

lineal *adj* linear.

lingote *nm* ingot.

lingüística *nf* linguistics.

lino *nm* **1** *(tela)* linen. **2** *(planta)* flax.

linterna *nf* torch.

lío *nm* **1** *(embrollo)* mess, muddle: **tiene la habitación hecha un lío**, his room is in a right mess. **2** *(problema)* trouble: **se ha metido en un buen lío**, she's got herself in big trouble; **no te metas en líos**, don't get into trouble. **3** *(atado)* bundle, parcel.

● **armar un lío** to make a fuss.

● **hacerse un lío** to get muddled up.

● **¡qué lío!** what a mess!

● **tener un lío con ALGN** to be having an affair with SB.

liquen *nm* lichen.

liquidación *nf* **1** *(de deuda)* settlement. **2** *(de mercancías)* clearance sale.

liquidar *vt* **1** *(deuda)* to settle. **2** *(mercancías)* to sell off *[pt & pp* **sold***]*. **3** *fam (matar)* to kill.

líquido,-a *adj* liquid.

▶ *nm* **líquido** liquid.

lira *nf* lira.

lírica *nf* lyric poetry.

lírico,-a *adj* lyrical.

lirio *nm* iris.

lirón *nm* dormouse *[pl* **dormice***]*.

● **dormir como un lirón** to sleep like a log *[pt & pp* **slept***]*.

lisiado,-a *adj* crippled.

▶ *nm,f* cripple.

liso,-a *adj* **1** *(superficie)* smooth, even. **2** *(pelo)* straight. **3** *(color)* plain.

lista *nf* **1** *(relación)* list. **2** *(raya)* stripe.

● **pasar lista** to call the register.

■ **lista de correo** mailing list.

■ **lista de espera 1** *(gen)* waiting list. **2** *(para avión)* standby.

■ **lista de la compra** shopping list.

■ **lista negra** blacklist.

listado,-a *adj* striped.

▶ *nm* **listado 1** *(lista)* list. **2** INFORM listing.

listín *nm* telephone directory.

listo,-a *adj* **1** *(preparado)* ready: **¿estás lista?**, are you ready? **2** *(inteligente)* clever, smart.

listón *nm* **1** *(de madera)* lath. **2** *(en salto de altura)* bar.

● **poner el listón muy alto** to set very high standards.

litera *nf* *(en dormitorio)* bunk bed; *(en barco)* bunk; *(en tren)* couchette.

literal *adj* literal.

literario,-a *adj* literary.

literato,-a *nm,f* **1 literato** writer, man of letters *[pl* **men***]*. **2 literata** writer, woman of letters *[pl* **women***]*.

literatura *nf* literature.

litoral *adj* coastal.

▶ *nm* coast.

litro *nm* GB litre; US liter.

Lituania *nf* Lithuania.

lituano,-a *adj* - *nm,f* Lithuanian.

lívido,-a *adj* livid.

llaga *nf* ulcer, sore.

● **poner el dedo en la llaga** to touch a sore spot.

llama[1] *nf* *(de fuego)* flame.

● **en llamas** ablaze.

llama[2] *nm* *(animal)* llama.

llamada *nf* **1** *(telefónica)* phone call: **hacer una llamada**, to make a (phone) call. **2** *(a la puerta)* knock; *(con timbre)* ring.

■ **llamada a cobro revertido** GB reverse-charge call; US collect call.

llamamiento *nm* call.

llamar *vt* **1** *(gen)* to call: *¿me has llamado?*, did you call me?; *he llamado un taxi*, I've called a taxi. **2** *(dar nombre a)* to name, call: *lo han llamado Abel*, they've called him Abel. **3** *(por teléfono)* to phone, call, ring [*pt* **rang**; *pp* **rung**]: *te llamaré mañana*, I'll call you tomorrow.
▶ *vi* **1** *(a la puerta)* to knock; *(al timbre)* to ring [*pt* **rang**; *pp* **rung**]: *llaman a la puerta*, someone's knocking at the door. **2** *(por teléfono)* to phone, call, ring [*pt* **rang**; *pp* **rung**]: *¿quién llama?*, who's calling?
▶ *vpr* **llamarse** *(tener nombre)* to be called, be named: *¿cómo te llamas?*, what's your name?; *me llamo Juan*, my name is Juan.
● **llamar la atención** to attract attention.
● **llamar la atención a** ALGN to tell SB off [*pt* & *pp* **told**].
llamarada *nf* sudden blaze, sudden flame.
llamativo,-a *adj* showy, flashy.
llano,-a *adj* **1** *(plano)* flat; *(nivelado)* even, level. **2** *(franco)* open, frank. **3** *(sencillo)* simple.
▶ *nm* **llano** *(llanura)* plain.
llanta *nf* rim.
llanto *nm* crying, weeping.
llanura *nf* plain.
llave *nf* **1** *(de puerta etc)* key. **2** *(herramienta)* spanner.
● **bajo llave** under lock and key.
● **cerrar con llave** to lock.
■ **llave de contacto** ignition key.
■ **llave de paso 1** *(del agua)* stopcock. **2** *(del gas)* mains tap.
■ **llave inglesa** adjustable spanner.
■ **llave maestra** master key.
llavero *nm* key ring.
llegada *nf* **1** *(gen)* arrival. **2** *(en deportes)* finishing line.
llegar *vi* **1** *(gen)* to arrive, reach: *llegaré a casa a las dos*, I'll arrive home at two. **2** *(alcanzar)* to reach: *¿llegas al estante?*, can you reach the shelf? **3** *(ser suficiente)* to be enough: *los bocadillos no llegaron para todos*, there weren't enough sandwiches for everyone; *no me llega el dinero*, I haven't got enough money. **4** *(suceder)* to come, arrive: *llegó el momento*, the moment arrived. **5** **llegar + a +** *inf*: *llegó a decir que no la quería*, he even

said he didn't love her; *no llegué a ver al rey*, I didn't manage to see the king.
▶ *vpr* **llegarse** *(ir)* to go, nip: *llégate al estanco*, nip to the tobacconist's.
llenar *vt* **1** *(gen)* to fill (up); *(formulario)* to fill in; *(tiempo)* to fill, occupy. **2** *(satisfacer)* to fulfil, please: *llenó el vaso*, he filled the glass; *llena el depósito de gasolina, por favor*, please fill up the tank with petrol.
▶ *vi* to be filling: *las patatas llenan mucho*, potatoes are very filling.
▶ *vpr* **llenarse 1** *(gen)* to fill (up). **2** *(de gente)* to get crowded.
lleno,-a *adj* **1** *(gen)* full: *la caja está llena de libros*, the box is full of books. **2** *(de gente)* crowded.
▶ *nm* **lleno** *(en teatro)* full house.
● **de lleno** fully.
llevadero,-a *adj* bearable, tolerable.
llevar *vt* **1** *(transportar)* to carry: *el tren llevaba carbón*, the train was carrying coal. **2** *(prenda)* to wear [*pp* **worn**], have on: *llevaba un abrigo verde*, she was wearing a green coat. **3** *(acompañar)* to take; *(conducir, guiar)* to lead [*pt* & *pp* **led**]: *te llevaré al zoo*, I'll take you to the zoo. **4** *(aguantar)* to cope with: *¿qué, cómo lo llevas?*, well, how are you coping? **5** *(libros, cuentas)* to keep: *mi mujer lleva las cuentas*, my wife keeps the accounts. **6** *(dirigir)* to be in charge of, manage, run [*pt* **ran**; *pp* **run**]: *lleva la fábrica ella sola*, she runs the factory all by herself. **7** *(tiempo)* to be: *llevo un mes aquí*, I have been here for a month. **8** *(exceder)* to be ahead: *te llevo tres años*, I'm three years older than you. **9** *(vida)* to lead [*pt* & *pp* **led**]: *lleva una vida muy sana*, he leads a very healthy life. **10 llevar +** *pp* to have: *llevo hechas cuatro cartas*, I've done four letters.
▶ *vpr* **llevarse 1** *(coger)* to take: *los ladrones se lo llevaron todo*, the burglars took everything. **2** *(premio)* to win [*pt* & *pp* **won**]: *se llevó el tercer premio*, he won third prize. **3** *(estar de moda)* to be fashionable: *este color ya no se lleva*, this colour is not fashionable anymore. **4** *(entenderse)* to get on: *se lleva bien con todo el mundo*, he gets on well with everybody. **5** *(en matemáticas)* to carry over.

- **llevar las de perder** to be likely to lose.
- **llevarse un chasco** to be disappointed.
- **llevarse un susto** to get a shock.

llorar vi **1** *(persona)* to cry, weep [pt & pp **wept**]: *no llores*, don't cry. **2** *(ojos)* to water: *te lloran los ojos*, your eyes are watering. **3** *fam (quejarse)* to moan.
▸ vt to mourn.

lloriquear vi to whine.

llorón,-ona nm,f crybaby.

lloroso,-a adj tearful.

llover vi to rain: *¿llueve?*, is it raining?
- **llover a cántaros** to pour down.

llovizna nf drizzle.

lloviznar vi to drizzle.

lluvia nf **1** *(de agua)* rain. **2** *(de regalos)* shower. **3** *(de balas)* hail. **4** *(de preguntas, insultos)* barrage.
- **bajo la lluvia** in the rain.
■ **lluvia ácida** acid rain.

lluvioso,-a adj rainy, wet.

lo det the: *lo bueno*, the good thing.
▸ pron *(él)* him; *(usted)* you; *(cosa, animal)* it: *no lo he visto*, I haven't seen him; *a usted no lo conozco*, I don't know you; *cómpralo*, buy it.
- **lo cual** which.
- **lo que** what.

lobo,-a nm,f *(macho)* wolf [pl -ves]; *(hembra)* she-wolf [pl -ves].
- **oscuro,-a como la boca del lobo** pitch-dark.
■ **lobo de mar** old salt.

lóbulo nm lobe.

local adj local.
▸ nm premises pl.

localidad nf **1** *(pueblo)* village; *(ciudad)* town. **2** *(asiento)* seat. **3** *(entrada)* ticket.
- **"No hay localidades"** "Sold out".

localizar vt **1** *(encontrar)* to locate, find [pt & pp **found**]. **2** *(fuego, dolor)* to localize.

loción nf lotion.

loco,-a adj mad, crazy.
▸ nm,f lunatic.
- **¡ni loco,-a!** no way!
- **volverse loco,-a** to go crazy.
■ **loco,-a de remate** stark mad.

locomotora nf engine, locomotive.

locuaz adj loquacious, talkative.

locución nf phrase.

locura nf madness, insanity.
- **hacer locuras** to do crazy things.

locutor,-ra nm,f announcer.

lodo nm mud, mire.

lógica nf logic.

lógico,-a adj logical.

logotipo nm logo [pl -s].

lograr vt **1** *(trabajo, beca)* to get, obtain. **2** *(objetivo)* to attain, achieve.
- **lograr hacer algo** to manage to do STH: *lograron subir hasta la cima*, they managed to climb up to the top.

logro nm success, achievement.

loma nf hill, hillock.

lombriz nf earthworm.

lomo nm **1** *(de animal)* back. **2** *(de cerdo)* loin. **3** *(de libro)* spine.
- **ir a lomos de** to ride [pt **rode**; pp **ridden**].

lona nf canvas.

loncha nf slice.

londinense adj of London, from London: *el metro londinense*, the London Underground.
▸ nmf Londoner.

Londres nm London.

longaniza nf pork sausage.

longitud nf **1** *(largo)* length: *tiene una longitud de diez metros*, it's ten metres in length, it's ten metres long. **2** *(geográfica)* longitude.

loro nm parrot.

los det the: *los niños*, the boys.
▸ pron *(ellos)* them; *(ustedes)* you: *los vi*, I saw them; *encantado de conocerlos*, pleased to meet you.

losa nf **1** *(de suelo)* flagstone, stone. **2** *(de sepulcro)* gravestone.

lote nm **1** *(de productos)* lot. **2** *(en informática)* batch.
- **darse el lote** GB to neck; US to make out.

lotería nf lottery.
- **tocarle la lotería a ALGN 1** *(ganar dinero)* to win the lottery [pt & pp **won**]. **2** *(tener suerte)* to be very lucky.

loto nf *(juego)* lottery.
▸ nm *(planta)* lotus.

loza nf **1** *(material)* china. **2** *(vajilla)* crockery.

lubina nf bass.

lubricante nm lubricant.

lubricar vt to lubricate.

lucero nm bright star.

lucha *nf* **1** *(pelea)* fight, struggle. **2** *(deporte)* wrestling.

luchador,-ra *nm,f* **1** *(gen)* fighter. **2** *(deportista)* wrestler.

luchar *vi* **1** *(pelear)* to fight [*pt & pp* **fought**]. **2** *(como deporte)* to wrestle.

lúcido,-a *adj* clear, lucid.

luciérnaga *nf* glow-worm.

lucio *nm* pike.

lucir *vi* **1** *(brillar)* to shine [*pt & pp* **shone**]. **2** *(dar luz)* to be bright: *esta bombilla no luce mucho*, this bulb's not very bright. **3** *(quedar bien)* to look good: *ese cuadro no luce nada ahí*, that picture doesn't look very good there.

▶ *vt (presumir)* to show off [*pt* **showed**; *pp* **shown**]: *lucía sus joyas*, she was showing off her jewellery.

▶ *vpr* **lucirse 1** *(presumir)* to show off [*pt* **showed**; *pp* **shown**]. **2** *irón (meter la pata)* to excel oneself.

lucrativo,-a *adj* lucrative, profitable.

lucro *nm* gain, profit.

luego *adv* **1** *(más tarde)* later: *ahora no puedo, luego iré*, I can't just now, I'll go later. **2** *(después de algo)* then: *primero comieron y luego durmieron la siesta*, first they had lunch and then a nap.

▶ *conj* therefore, then.

● **desde luego** of course.

● **hasta luego** see you later, so long.

lugar *nm* **1** *(sitio)* place: *es un lugar muy tranquilo*, it's a very quiet place. **2** *(posición)* position: *ocupa un lugar muy importante en la organización*, she has an important position in the organization. **3** *(espacio)* space, room: *ocupa mucho lugar*, it takes up a lot of space, it takes up a lot of room.

● **dar lugar a** to give rise to.

● **en lugar de** instead of.

● **en primer lugar** firstly.

● **fuera de lugar** out of place.

● **tener lugar** to take place, happen.

lugareño,-a *nm,f* local.

lúgubre *adj* lugubrious, gloomy, dismal.

lujo *nm* luxury.

● **de lujo** luxury: *un artículo de lujo*, a luxury good.

lujoso,-a *adj* luxurious.

lumbre *nf* **1** *(fuego)* fire. **2** *(para cigarrillo)* light.

lumbrera *nf* genius.

luminoso,-a *adj* bright.

luna *nf* **1** *(astro)* moon. **2** *(cristal - de ventana)* window pane; *(- de vehículo)* GB windscreen, US windshield. **3** *(espejo)* mirror.

● **estar en la luna** to be miles away.

■ **luna de miel** honeymoon.

■ **luna llena** full moon.

lunar *adj* lunar.

▶ *nm* **1** *(en la piel)* mole; *(postizo)* beauty spot. **2** *(en tejido)* spot, polka-dot.

● **de lunares** spotted.

lunático,-a *adj* **1** *(loco)* mad, crazy. **2** *(temperamental)* changeable, moody.

▶ *nm,f* lunatic.

lunes *nm* Monday.

lupa *nf* magnifying glass.

lustrar *vt* to polish, shine [*pt & pp* **shined**].

lustre *nm* **1** *(brillo)* polish, shine, lustre. **2** *(prestigio)* glory.

lustro *nm* period of five years, five-year period.

luto *nm* mourning.

● **estar de luto** to be in mourning.

● **ir de luto** to wear mourning [*pt* **wore**; *pp* **worn**].

■ **luto riguroso** deep morning.

Luxemburgo *nm* Luxembourg.

luz *nf* **1** *(gen)* light. **2** *fam (electricidad)* electricity.

● **a todas luces** evidently.

● **apagar la luz** to turn off the light, switch off the light.

● **dar a luz** to give birth to.

● **encender la luz** to turn on the light, switch on the light.

● **sacar a la luz** to bring to light [*pt & pp* **brought**].

■ **luces de carretera** full-beam headlights.

■ **luces de cruce** dipped headlights.

■ **luces de posición** sidelights.

■ **luz del día** daylight

M

macabro,-a *adj* macabre.

macarra *nm* **1** *fam (de prostituta)* pimp. **2** *(hortera)* flash Harry. **3** *(rufián)* lout.

macarrones *nm pl* macaroni.

macedonia *nf* fruit salad.

maceta *nf* plant pot, flowerpot.
● **regar las macetas** to water the plants.

macetero *nm* flowerpot stand.

machacar *vt* **1** *(ajo, piedra)* to crush; *(patata)* to mash. **2** *fam (estudiar)* to swot.
▶ *vi fam (insistir en)* to harp on.
● **machacársela** *vulg* to wank.

machacón,-ona *adj* tiresome.

machete *nm (arma)* machete.

machismo *nm* male chauvinism.

machista *nmf* male chauvinist.

macho *adj* **1** *(hombre)* male. **2** *(viril)* manly, virile.
▶ *nm* **1** *(animal)* male. **2** *(pieza)* male piece, male part.
■ **macho cabrío** he-goat.

macizo,-a *adj* **1** *(sólido)* solid; *(fuerte)* well-built. **2** *(atractivo)* gorgeous.
▶ *nm* **macizo 1** *(de flores)* bed. **2** *(montañoso)* massif [*pl* **-s**].

macro *nf* INFORM macro [*pl* **-s**].

macuto *nm* knapsack.

madeja *nf* skein, hank.

madera *nf* **1** *(gen)* wood; *(para la construcción)* timber: *una mesa de madera*, a wooden table. **2** *fig (talento)* talent.
● **¡toca madera!** touch wood!
● **tener madera de...** to have the makings of...: *tiene madera de policía*, he's got the makings of a policeman.

madero *nm* **1** *(tabla)* piece of timber. **2** *arg (policía)* cop.

madrastra *nf* stepmother.

madre *nf* mother.
● **¡madre mía!** *fam* good heavens!
● **¡la madre que te parió!** *vulg* you bastard!
● **¡tu madre!** *vulg* up yours!
■ **futura madre** mother-to-be.
■ **madre de alquiler** surrogate mother.
■ **madre política** mother-in-law.

madriguera *nf* **1** *(de conejo etc)* hole, burrow. **2** *(de gente)* den, hideout.

madrina *nf* **1** *(de bautizo)* godmother. **2** *(de boda)* matron of honour.

madrugada *nf* **1** *(después de medianoche)* early morning. **2** *(alba)* dawn.
● **de madrugada** in the small hours: *a las 5 de la madrugada*, at 5 a.m..

madrugador,-ra *adj* early rising.
▶ *nm,f* early riser.

madrugar *vi* to get up early.

madrugón *nm* .
● **pegarse un madrugón** to get up at the crack of dawn.

madurar *vt (fruta)* to ripen. **2** *fig (plan)* to think out [*pt & pp* **thought**].
▶ *vi* to mature.

madurez *nf* **1** *(de persona)* maturity. **2** *(de la fruta)* ripeness.

maduro,-a *adj* **1** *(persona)* mature. **2** *(fruta)* ripe.

maestro,-a *nm,f* teacher.
▶ *adj (principal)* main.
▶ *nm* **maestro** *(compositor)* composer; *(director)* conductor; *(ajedrez)* master.

mafia *nf* mafia.

magdalena *nf* sponge cake.

magia *nf* magic.
● **hacer magia** to do magic.
■ **magia negra** black magic.

mágico,-a *adj* **1** *(con magia)* magic. **2** *(maravilloso)* magical.

magisterio *nm* teaching.

magistrado,-a *nm,f* judge.

magnate *nm* magnate, tycoon.

magnético,-a *adj* magnetic.

magnetismo *nm* magnetism.

magnetófono *nm* tape recorder.

magnífico,-a *adj* magnificent, splendid.

magnitud *nf* magnitude.

mago,-a *nm,f* magician, wizard.

■ **los Reyes Magos** the Three Kings, the Three Wise Men.

magullar *vt* to bruise.

▶ *vpr* **magullarse** to get bruised.

mahometano,-a *adj - nm,f* Mohammedan.

mahonesa *nf* mayonnaise.

maíz *nm* maize; US corn.

majadería *nf (acción)* stupid thing; *(palabras)* nonsense.

majadero,-a *adj* dim-witted.

▶ *nm,f* dimwit.

majestad *nf* majesty.

majestuoso,-a *adj* majestic, stately.

majo,-a *adj* **1** pretty, lovely. **2** *(simpático)* nice.

▶ *nm,f (tratamiento)* sunshine: **mira, majo, haz lo que te dé la gana**, look, sunshine, just do what you want.

mal *adj* **1** *(desagradable, adverso)* bad [*comp* **worse**; *superl* **worst**]: **he tenido un mal día**, I've had a bad day; **no está mal este color**, this colour isn't bad. **2** *(enfermo)* ill.

▶ *nm* **1** evil, wrong: **el bien y el mal**, good and evil; **es un mal menor**, it's the lesser of two evils. **2** *(daño)* harm. **3** *(enfermedad)* illness, disease.

▶ *adv* badly, wrong: **está mal hecho**, it's badly done; **lo hizo mal**, he did it wrong; **la dirección estaba mal**, the address was wrong.

● **encontrarse mal** to feel ill.

● **menos mal que...** thank goodness....

● **nada mal** not bad: **la peli no está nada mal**, the film's not bad at all; **no canta nada mal**, she's not a bad singer.

● **tomar a mal** to take badly.

■ **mal de amores** lovesickness.

■ **mal de ojo** evil eye: **le han echado mal de ojo**, they gave her the evil eye.

malabarista *nmf* juggler.

malcriado,-a *adj* spoilt.

malcriar *vt* to spoil [*pt & pp* **spoilt**].

maldad *nf* **1** *(cualidad)* evil. **2** *(acto)* evil deed.

maldecir *vt-vi* to curse.

maldición *nf* curse.

maldito,-a *adj* **1** *(condenado)* cursed, damned. **2** *fam (puñetero)* damned, bloody.

● **¡maldita sea!** damn!

maleducado,-a *adj* rude, bad-mannered.

maleficio *nm* curse, spell.

malentendido *nm* misunderstanding.

malestar *nm* **1** *(incomodidad)* discomfort. **2** *fig (inquietud)* uneasiness.

maleta *nf* suitcase, case.

● **hacer la maleta** to pack.

maletero *nm* **1** *(de coche)* GB boot; US trunk. **2** *(persona)* porter.

maletín *nm* briefcase.

maleza *nf (malas hierbas)* weeds *pl*.

malgastar *vt (tiempo)* to waste; *(dinero)* squander.

malhablado,-a *adj* foul-mouthed.

malhechor,-ra *nm,f* criminal.

malherido,-a *adj* seriously injured.

malhumor *nm* bad temper.

● **estar de malhumor** to be in a bad mood.

● **tener malhumor** to be bad-tempered.

malhumorado,-a *adj* bad-tempered.

malicia *nf* **1** *(mala intención)* malice. **2** *(picardía)* mischief.

malicioso,-a *adj* malicious.

maligno,-a *adj* malignant.

malintencionado,-a *adj* ill-intentioned.

malla *nf* **1** *(red)* mesh. **2** *(prenda)* leotard.

Mallorca *nf* Majorca.

malo,-a *adj* **1** *(perjudicial, imperfecto)* bad [*comp* **worse**; *superl* **worst**]. **2** *(malvado)* wicked. **3** *(travieso)* naughty. **4** *(nocivo)* harmful. **5** *(enfermo)* ill [*comp* **worse**; *superl* **worst**], sick. **6** *(difícil)* difficult.

● **estar de malas** to be out of luck.

● **estar malo,-a** to be ill.

● **lo malo es que...** the trouble is that....

● **por las malas** by force.

■ **mala hierba** weed.

maloliente *adj* foul-smelling.

malpensado,-a *adj* suspicious.

malsonante *adj* offensive.
maltratar *vt* to ill-treat
maltrecho,-a *adj* battered, injured.
malva *adj - nm (color)* mauve.
● **estar criando malvas** to be pushing up daisies.
malvado,-a *adj* wicked, evil.
▶ *nm,f* villain.
Malvinas *nf pl* **Islas Malvinas** the Falkland Islands, the Falklands.
mama *nf* **1** *(de mujer)* breast; *(de animal)* udder. **2** *fam (madre)* mum, mummy.
mamá *nf fam* mum, mummy.
mamar *vi (niño)* to suck.
▶ *vt* **1** *(leche)* to suck. **2** *(aprender de pequeño)* to grow up with [*pt* **grew**; *pp* **grown**].
▶ *vpr* **mamarse** *fam* to get drunk.
● **dar de mamar a ALGN** to breastfeed SB.
mamarracho *nm* **1** *fam (ridículo)* sight. **2** *(tonto)* idiot.
mamífero,-a *adj* mammalian, mammal.
▶ *nm* **mamífero** mammal.
mampara *nf* screen.
manada *nf (de vacas, elefantes)* herd; *(de ovejas)* flock; *(de lobos, perros)* pack.
manantial *nm* spring.
manar *vi* **1** *(salir)* to flow, run [*pt* **ran**; *pp* **run**]. **2** *fig (abundar)* to abound.
manazas *nmf fam* clumsy person: *¡eres un manazas!*, you're so clumsy!
mancha *nf (de sangre, aceite, comida)* stain; *(de bolígrafo)* mark; *(en la piel)* spot.
■ **mancha solar** sunspot.
manchado,-a *adj* stained.
manchar *vt-vi* to stain.
▶ *vpr* **mancharse** to get dirty: *ten cuidado de no mancharte*, be careful not to get dirty; *se me ha manchado la camisa de tinta*, I got ink over my shirt.
manco,-a *adj* one-handed.
▶ *nm,f* person with one hand.
mandamiento *nm* commandment.
■ **los Diez Mandamientos** the Ten Commandments.
mandar *vt* **1** *(ordenar)* to order: *no me gusta mandar*, I don't like to give orders; *no hace lo que le mandan*, he doesn't do as he is told. **2** *(enviar)* to send [*pt & pp* **sent**].
● **mandar recuerdos** to send regards [*pt & pp* **sent**].

● **mandar a ALGN a hacer algo** to send SB to do STH.
● **mandar a ALGN a paseo** *fam* to send SB packing [*pt & pp* **sent**].
● **mandar algo por correo** to post STH.
● **¿mande?** *fam* pardon?
mandarina *nf* mandarin, tangerine.
mandato *nm* **1** *(orden)* order, command. **2** *(judicial)* writ, warrant. **3** POL mandate, term of office: *durante su mandato*, during his mandate.
mandíbula *nf* jaw.
mando *nm* **1** *(autoridad)* command. **2** *(para mecanismos)* control.
▶ *nm pl* **mandos** *(militares)* high-ranking officers; *(políticos)* high-ranking members.
● **estar al mando de** to be in charge of.
● **tomar el mando** **1** *(militar)* to take command. **2** *(en deporte)* to take the lead.
■ **mando a distancia** remote control.
mandón,-ona *adj* bossy.
▶ *nm,f* bossy person: *es un mandón*, he is very bossy, he likes to boss people about.
manecilla *nf (de reloj)* hand.
manejable *adj* manageable, easy-to-handle.
manejar *vt* **1** *(manipular)* to handle, operate. **2** *(dirigir)* to run [*pt* **ran**; *pp* **run**].
▶ *vpr* **manejarse** to manage.
manejo *nm* **1** *(uso)* use: *es de fácil manejo*, it's easy to use. **2** *(de negocio)* running. **3** *(de dinero)* handling.
manera *nf* way, manner: *lo hizo a su manera*, he did it his way.
▶ *nf pl* **maneras** *(educación)* manners: *de muy buenas maneras pidió que me fuera*, he very politely asked me to leave.
● **de manera que** so that.
● **de ninguna manera** by no means.
● **de todas maneras** anyway, in any case.
● **de mala manera** **1** *fam (contestar)* rudely. **2** *(pegar)* hard.
● **de una manera u otra** one way or another.
■ **manera de ser** character, the way SB is.
manga *nf* sleeve: *en mangas de camisa*,

in shirtsleeves; *una camisa de manga corta*, a short-sleeved shirt.
- **sacarse algo de la manga** to pull STH out of one's hat.
- **tener manga ancha** to be too easy-going.
- ■ **manga de incendios** fire horse.
- ■ **manga pastelera** piping bag.

mangar *vt arg* to knock off, pinch.

mango¹ *nm (asa)* handle.

mango² *nm (fruta)* mango [*pl* -**os** o -**oes**].

manguera *nf* **1** *(de jardín)* hose, hose-pipe. **2** *(de bombero)* fire hose.

manía *nf* **1** *(ojeriza)* dislike. **2** *(afición)* habit: *tiene la manía de venir sin avisar*, he has the annoying habit of turning up without phoning first. **3** *(obsesión)* mania: *tiene la manía de coleccionar chapas*, he is obsessed with collecting badges.
- **cogerle manía a** ALGN *fam* to take a dislike to SB: *la maestra le tiene manía*, the teacher's got it in for him.

maniático,-a *adj* fussy, cranky.
▶ *nm,f* fussy person, cranky person: *es un maniático de los detalles*, he's obsessed with details; *es una maniática de la ropa*, she's crazy about clothes.

manicomio *nm* mental hospital.

manifestación *nf* **1** *(de protesta etc)* demonstration. **2** *(expresión)* manifestation. **3** *(declaración)* statement, declaration.

manifestante *nmf* demonstrator.

manifestar *vt (opinión)* to express, state; *(sentimiento)* to show [*pt* **showed**; *pp* **shown**].
▶ *vpr* **manifestarse** **1** *(en la calle)* to demonstrate. **2** *(declarar)* to declare oneself: *se manifiesta contrario al aborto*, he's against abortion. **3** *(hacerse evidente)* to become apparent.

manilla *nf (de reloj)* hand.

manillar *nm* handlebars *pl*.

maniobra *nf* manoeuvre.

maniobrar *vi* to manoeuvre.

manipular *vt* **1** *(persona)* to manipulate. **2** *(mercancías)* to handle.

maniquí *nm (muñeco)* dummy.
▶ *nmf (modelo)* model.

manitas *nmf* handy person: *es un manitas*, he's very handy.

manivela *nf* crank.

manjar *nm* delicacy.

mano *nf* **1** *(de persona)* hand. **2** *(de animal)* forefoot, forepaw. **3** *(de reloj)* hand. **4** *(de pintura etc)* coat. **5** *fig (habilidad)* skill.
- **cogidos,-as de la mano** hand in hand.
- **dar la mano** **1** *(saludar)* to shake hands [*pt* **shook**; *pp* **shaken**]. **2** *(para ayudar)* to offer one's hand.
- **de segunda mano** second-hand.
- **echar una mano** to lend a hand [*pt & pp* **lent**].
- **en un mano a mano** between the two of them.
- **estar en buenas manos** to be in good hands.
- **hecho,-a a mano** handmade.
- **tener mano izquierda** to be tactful.
- **pillar a** ALGN **con las manos en la masa** *fam* to catch SB red-handed [*pt & pp* **caught**].
- ■ **mano de obra** labour.

manojo *nm* bunch.

manopla *nf* **1** *(guante)* mitten. **2** *(para lavarse)* flannel.

manosear *vt (objeto)* to paw; *(persona)* to touch up.

manotazo *nm* cuff, slap.
- **dar un manotazo a** ALGN to slap SB.

mansedumbre *nf* **1** *(de personas)* meekness, gentleness. **2** *(de animales)* tameness.

mansión *nf* mansion.

manso,-a *adj* **1** *(animal)* tame, docile. **2** *(persona)* meek, gentle.

manta *nf* **1** *(para abrigarse)* blanket. **2** *(pez)* manta ray.
▶ *nmf fam (perezoso)* lazybones *inv*.
- **a manta** *fam* loads of: *había turistas a manta*, there were loads of tourists.
- ■ **manta de viaje** travelling rug.

manteca *nf* **1** *(grasa)* fat. **2** *(mantequilla)* butter.
- ■ **manteca de cacao** cocoa butter.
- ■ **manteca de cerdo** lard.

mantecado *nm* Christmas cake.

mantecoso,-a *adj* greasy, buttery.

mantel *nm* tablecloth.

mantelería *nf* table linen.

mantener *vt* **1** *(conservar)* to keep: *esto lo mantiene vivo*, this keeps him alive. **2** *(almacenar)* to store: *mantener en un lugar seco*, store in a dry place. **3** *(sostener)* to support, hold up [*pt & pp* **held**]. **4** *(ideas)* to defend. **5** *(sustentar)* to support.

► *vpr* **mantenerse 1** *(alimentarse)* to support oneself. **2** *(continuar)* to keep; *(mantenerse en contacto)* to keep in touch.

● **mantener algo en secreto** to keep STH a secret.

● **mantener el equilibrio** to keep one's balance.

● **mantenerse en contacto con ALGN** to keep in touch with SB.

mantenimiento *nm* maintenance.

● **clase de mantenimiento** keep-fit class.

● **servicio de mantenimiento** maintenance service.

mantequilla *nf* butter.

manto *nm* cloak.

mantón *nm* shawl.

■ **mantón de Manila** embroidered silk shawl.

manual *adj - nm* manual.

manufactura *nf (obra)* manufacture.

manufacturar *vt* to manufacture.

manuscrito,-a *adj* handwritten.

► *nm* **manuscrito** manuscript.

manzana *nf* **1** *(fruta)* apple. **2** *(de casas)* block.

manzanilla *nf* **1** *(flor)* camomile. **2** *(infusión)* camomile tea. **3** *(vino)* manzanilla sherry.

manzano *nm* apple tree.

maña *nf* skill.

mañana *nf (parte del día)* morning: *a la mañana siguiente*, next morning; *por la mañana*, in the morning.

► *nm (porvenir)* tomorrow, the future: *hay que pensar en el mañana*, you have to think of the future.

► *adv* tomorrow: *lo haré mañana*, I'll do it tomorrow.

● **de la noche a la mañana** overnight.

● **hasta mañana** see you tomorrow.

● **pasado mañana** the day after tomorrow.

mañoso,-a *adj* good with one's hands.

mapa *nm* map.

● **borrar del mapa** *fam* to get rid of.

■ **mapa de carreteras** road map.

mapamundi *nm* map of the world.

maqueta *nf* **1** *(de edificio)* scale model. **2** *(de libro)* dummy. **3** *(de disco)* demo.

maquillaje *nm* make-up.

maquillar *vt* to make up.

► *vpr* **maquillarse** to put one's make-up on.

máquina *nf* machine.

■ **máquina de afeitar** razor, shaver.

■ **máquina de coser** sewing machine.

■ **máquina de escribir** typewriter.

■ **máquina de fotos** camera.

■ **máquina de tabaco** cigarette machine.

■ **máquina fotográfica** camera.

■ **máquina quitanieves** snowplough.

■ **máquina tragaperras** slot machine.

maquinaria *nf* machinery.

maquinilla *nf* **maquinilla de afeitar** razor.

maquinista *nmf (de tren)* engine driver.

mar *nm & nf* **1** *(gen)* sea. **2** *(marea)* tide. **3** *fam* very, a lot: *la mar de dificultades*, a lot of difficulties; *llovía a mares*, it was pouring down; *lo pasamos la mar de bien*, we had a great time.

● **en alta mar** on the high seas.

● **hacerse a la mar** to put out to sea.

● **mar adentro** out to sea.

● **¡pelillos a la mar!** *fam* let bygones be bygones!

■ **mar de fondo** groundswell.

■ **mar gruesa** heavy sea.

■ **mar Cantábrico** Cantabrian Sea, Bay of Biscay.

maraca *nf* maraca.

maratón *nm* marathon.

maravilla *nf* wonder, marvel.

● **a las mil maravillas** wonderfully well.

● **de maravilla** great.

maravillar *vt* to astonish, dazzle.

► *vpr* **maravillarse** to wonder, marvel at.

maravilloso,-a *adj* wonderful, marvellous.

marca *nf* **1** *(señal)* mark, sign. **2** *(de comestibles, productos del hogar)* brand; *(de otros productos)* make: *productos de su propia marca*, products of their own; *¿de qué marca es tu coche?*, what make is your car? **3** *(récord)* record.

● **de marca** top-quality: *ropa de marca*, designer clothes.

■ **marca de fábrica** trademark.

■ **marca personal** personal best.

■ **marca registrada** registered trademark.

marcador *nm* scoreboard.
marcar *vt* **1** *(señalar)* to mark: **quedó marcado para siempre**, he was marked for life. **2** *(hacer un tanto)* to score. **3** *(a otro jugador)* to mark. **4** *(pelo)* to set [*pt & pp* set]. **5** *(al teléfono)* to dial. **6** *(acentuar)* to accentuate.
▶ *vi* **1** *(hacer un tanto)* to score. **2** *(al teléfono)* to dial.
● **marcar el compás** to keep time.
● **marcar el paso** to mark time.
marcha *nf* **1** *(al caminar)* march. **2** *(progreso)* course, progress. **3** *(partida)* departure. **4** *(velocidad)* speed. **5** *(música)* march. **6** *fam (energía)* go, energy: **tiene mucha marcha**, she's full of energy.
● **acelerar la marcha** to speed up.
● **a marchas forzadas** against the clock.
● **a toda marcha** at full speed.
● **salir de marcha** to go out.
■ **marcha atlética** walking race.
■ **marcha atrás** reverse gear.
marchar *vi* **1** *(ir)* to go, walk. **2** *(funcionar)* to work, go well.
▶ *vpr* **marcharse** to leave [*pt & pp* left].
● **¡marchando!** coming up!
marchitar *vt-vpr* **marchitar(se)** to wither.
marchito,-a *adj* withered.
marchoso,-a *adj* lively, wild.
▶ *nm,f* raver, fun-lover: **es una marchosa**, she loves going out.
marciano,-a *adj - nm,f* Martian.
marco *nm* **1** *(de cuadro, ventana)* frame. **2** *fig* framework, setting. **3** *(moneda)* mark.
■ **marco legal** legal framework.
marea *nf* tide.
■ **marea alta** high tide.
■ **marea baja** low tide.
■ **marea negra** oil slick.
mareado,-a *adj* **1** *(con náuseas)* sick. **2** *(aturdido)* dizzy, giddy. **3** *(borracho)* tipsy.
marear *vt-vi (molestar)* to annoy, bother; *(hacer sentir mal)* to make feel sick.
▶ *vpr* **marearse** *(sentir náuseas)* to get sick; *(sentirse aturdido)* to feel dizzy.
marejada *nf* swell.
maremoto *nm* seaquake.
mareo *nm* **1** *(con náuseas)* sickness. **2** *(aturdimiento)* dizziness.
marfil *nm* ivory.
margarina *nf* margarine.

margarita *nf* daisy.
margen *nm* **1** *(de papel)* margin. **2** *(extremidad)* border, edge. **3** COM margin.
▶ *nf (de río)* bank.
● **dar margen para** to give scope for.
● **quedarse al margen** to keep out.
■ **margen de error** margin of error.
marginado,-a *adj* excluded.
▶ *nm,f* social misfit.
marginar *vt* to leave out [*pt & pp* left], exclude.
marica *nm fam* GB poof [*pl* -s]; US fag.
maricón *nm vulg* GB poof [*pl* -s]; US fag.
mariconada *nf vulg* dirty trick: **estoy harto de sus mariconadas**, I'm sick of him pissing about.
marido *nm* husband.
marihuana *nf* marijuana.
marimorena.
● **se armó la marimorena** there was a terrible row.
marina *nf* **1** *(pintura)* seascape. **2** *(barcos)* seamanship.
■ **marina de guerra** navy.
marinero,-a *adj* sea.
▶ *nm* **marinero** sailor.
marino,-a *adj* marine.
▶ *nm* **marino** seaman [*pl* -men].
marioneta *nf* puppet, marionette.
mariposa *nf* **1** butterfly. **2** *(marica)* GB poof [*pl* -s]; US fag.
● **nadar al estilo mariposa** to do the butterfly.
mariquita *nf (insecto)* ladybird.
▶ *nm fam (marica)* GB poof [*pl* -s]; US fag.
marisco *nm* shellfish, seafood.
marisma *nf* salt marsh.
marisquería *nf* seafood restaurant.
marítimo,-a *adj* maritime, sea.
mármol *nm (material)* marble; *(de cocina)* worktop.
marqués,-esa *nm,f (hombre)* marquis; *(mujer)* marchioness.
marranada *nf (porquería)* filthy thing; *(vileza)* dirty trick.
marrano,-a *adj (sucio)* dirty.
▶ *nm* **marrano** **1** *(animal)* pig. **2** *fam (sucio)* dirty pig.
marrón *adj - nm* brown.
■ **marrón glacé** marron glacé.
marroquí *adj - nm,f* Moroccan.
Marruecos *nm* Morocco.
Marte *nm* Mars.

martes *nm* Tuesday.
■ **martes de carnaval** Shrove Tuesday.
■ **martes y trece** Friday the thirteenth.
martillazo *nm* hammer blow: **se dio un martillazo en el dedo**, he hit his finger with a hammer; **lo destrozó a martillazos**, he smashed it with a hammer.
martillear *vt* to hammer.
martillo *nm* hammer.
mártir *nmf* martyr.
martirio *nm* **1** *(muerte)* martyrdom. **2** *(sufrimiento)* torment.
martirizar *vt* **1** *(matar)* to martyr. **2** *(hacer sufrir)* to torment.
maruja *nf fam* typical housewife [*pl* **-ves**].
marxismo *nm* Marxism.
marxista *adj - nmf* Marxist.
marzo *nm* March.
mas *conj* but.
más *adv* **1** *(comparativo)* more: **más pequeño**, smaller; **más caro**, more expensive, dearer. **2** *(con números o cantidades)* more: **más de tres**, more than three; **¿no quieres más?**, don't you want more?; **son más de las dos**, it's past two o'clock. **3** *(superlativo)* most: **el más caro**, the most expensive; **el más pequeño**, the smallest. **4** *(de nuevo)* anymore: **no voy más a ese sitio**, I'm not going there anymore. **5** *(con pronombre)* else: **¿algo más?**, anything else?; **¿hay alguien más?**, is there anybody else?; **no quiero nada más**, I don't want anything else.
▶ *pron* more: **¿quieres más?**, do you want any more?
▶ *nm (signo)* plus.
● **a lo más** at the most.
● **como el que más** as well as anyone.
● **de más** spare, extra: **una cama de más**, an extra bed.
● **estar de más** to be unwanted.
● **es más** what's more.
● **más bien** rather.
● **más o menos** more or less.
● **ni más ni menos** no less.
● **por más (que)** however much.
● **sin más ni más** just like that.
● **tener sus más y sus menos** to have good and bad things.
■ **el más allá** the beyond.
masa *nf* **1** *(de volumen)* mass. **2** *(de pan)* dough. **3** *(multitud)* crowd: **las masas**, the masses.
● **en masa** en masse.

masacre *nf* massacre.
masaje *nm* massage.
masajista *nmf (hombre)* masseur; *(mujer)* masseuse.
mascar *vt-vi* to chew.
máscara *nf* mask.
mascarilla *nf* **1** *(máscara)* mask. **2** *(cosmética)* face pack. **3** *(de médico)* face mask.
mascota *nf* **1** *(de club)* mascot. **2** *(animal doméstico)* pet.
masculino,-a *adj* **1** *(no femenino)* male. **2** *(para hombres)* men's. **3** *(sustantivo)* masculine.
▶ *nm* **masculino** masculine.
masivo,-a *adj* massive.
masoquismo *nm* masochism.
masoquista *adj* masochistic.
▶ *nmf* masochist.
masticar *vt-vi* to masticate, chew.
mástil *nm* **1** mast. **2** *(de bandera)* flagpole.
masturbación *nf* masturbation.
masturbar *vt-vpr* **masturbar(se)** to masturbate.
mata *nf* **1** *(arbusto)* bush. **2** *(ramita)* sprig.
■ **mata de pelo** mop of hair.
matadero *nm* slaughterhouse, abattoir.
matamoscas *nm (insecticida)* flykiller; *(pala)* flyswatter.
matanza *nf* slaughter.
matar *vt-vi* to kill.
▶ *vpr* **matarse** to kill oneself.
● **llevarse a matar con** to be at daggers drawn with.
● **matarlas callando** to be a wolf in a sheep's clothing.
● **que me maten si...** I'll be damned if....
matasellos *nm* postmark.
matasuegras *nm* party blower.
mate¹ *adj (sin brillo)* matt.
mate² *nm (ajedrez)* checkmate.
matemáticas *nf pl* mathematics *sing*.
matemático,-a *adj* mathematical.
▶ *nm,f* mathematician.
materia *nf* **1** *(sustancia)* matter. **2** *(asignatura)* subject.
● **entrar en materia** to get down to business.
■ **materia grasa** fat.
■ **materia prima** raw material.
material *adj* material.
▶ *nm* material, equipment.

■ **material de oficina** office equipment.

■ **material escolar** school materials *pl*.

materialista *adj* materialistic.

▶ *nmf* materialist.

maternal *adj (instinto)* maternal; *(amor)* motherly.

■ **baja maternal** maternity leave.

maternidad *nf* maternity, motherhood.

materno,-a *adj* maternal: *leche materna*, mother's milk; *idioma materno*, mother tongue.

matinal *adj* morning.

▶ *nf* morning showing.

matiz *nm* **1** *(color)* shade, tint. **2** *fig (variación)* nuance.

matón,-ona *nm,f fam (en la escuela)* bully; *(asesino)* thug.

matorral *nm* bushes *pl*, thicket.

matrícula *nf* **1** *(en curso)* registration: *el plazo de matrícula empieza...*, the first day for registration is...; *ha ido a hacer la matrícula*, he's gone to matriculate. **2** *(número)* registration number; *(placa)* GB number plate; US licence plate.

■ **matrícula de honor** honours.

matricular *vt-vpr* **matricular(se)** to register, enrol.

matrimonio *nm* **1** *(ceremonia, institución)* marriage. **2** *(pareja)* married couple.

● **contraer matrimonio con ALGN** to marry SB.

matutino,-a *adj* morning.

maullar *vi* to mew, miaow.

maullido *nm* miaow.

▶ *nm pl* **maullidos** mewing.

maxilar *adj* maxillary.

▶ *nm* jaw.

máxima *nf* **1** *(principio)* maxim. **2** *(temperatura)* maximum temperature.

máximo,-a *adj* maximum: *a la máxima velocidad*, at maximum speed; *hice lo máximo posible*, I did as much as I could.

▶ *nm* **máximo** maximum.

mayo *nm* May.

mayonesa *nf* mayonnaise.

mayor *adj* **1** *(comparativo)* bigger, greater, larger; *(persona)* older; *(hermanos, hijos)* elder. **2** *(superlativo)* biggest, greatest, largest; *(persona)* oldest; *(hermanos, hijos)* eldest. **3** *(adulto)* grown-up: *son muy mayores*, they are very old.

▶ *adj - nm (adulto)* grown-up, adult: *los mayores*, the grown-ups.

● **al por mayor** wholesale: *comprar al por mayor*, to buy wholesale.

● **ser mayor de edad** to be of full age.

mayordomo *nm* butler.

mayoría *nf* majority, most: *la mayoría de la gente*, the majority of the people, most of the people.

■ **mayoría absoluta** absolute majority.

■ **mayoría de edad** adulthood: *ha llegado a la mayoría de edad*, he's come of age.

mayorista *nmf* wholesaler.

mayormente *adv* chiefly, principally.

mayúscula *nf* capital letter.

mayúsculo,-a *adj* **1** *(enorme)* huge. **2** *(letra)* capital.

maza *nf* mace.

mazapán *nm* marzipan.

mazmorra *nf* dungeon.

mazo *nm* mallet.

mazorca *nf* cob.

me *pron* **1** *(como objeto)* me: *no me lo digas*, don't tell me. **2** *(reflexivo)* myself: *me veo en el espejo*, I can see myself in the mirror. **3** *(con partes del cuerpo)* my: *me rompí la pierna*, I broke my leg. **4** *(uso reflexivo)*: *me fui*, I went; *me lo comí*, I ate it.

meada *nf vulg* piss, slash.

● **echar una meada** *vulg* to have a slash.

mear *vi fam* to piss, have a piss.

▶ *vpr* **mearse** *fam* to wet oneself.

mecánica *nf* **1** *(ciencia)* mechanics. **2** *(mecanismo)* mechanism.

mecánico,-a *adj* mechanical.

▶ *nm,f* mechanic.

mecanismo *nm* mechanism.

mecanografía *vt* typing.

mecanografiar *vt* to type.

mecanógrafo,-a *nm,f* typist.

mecedora *nf* rocking chair.

mecer *vt-vpr* **mecer(se)** to rock.

mecha *nf* **1** *(de vela)* wick. **2** *(de bomba)* fuse.

▶ *nf pl* **mechas** *(en el pelo)* highlights.

mechero *nm* lighter.

mechón *nm (de pelo)* lock.

medalla *nf (condecoración)* medal; *(religiosa)* medallion.

medallón *nm* medallion.

media *nf (promedio)* average: *una media de 10 al año*, an average of 10 a year.

▶ *fpl* **medias** *(hasta la cintura)* tights; *(hasta la pierna)* stockings.
● **hacer media** to knit.
Véase también **medio,-a**.
mediados *nm pl* .
● **a mediados de** in the middle of.
mediano,-a *adj* **1** *(de tamaño)* middle-sized. **2** *(de calidad)* average, medium.
medianoche *nf* midnight.
mediante *adj* by means of.
● **Dios mediante** God willing.
medicamento *nm* medicine.
medicina *nf* medicine.
medicinal *adj* medicinal.
médico,-a *adj* medical.
▶ *nm,f* doctor, physician.
■ **médico,-a de cabecera** general practitioner.
■ **médico,-a de guardia** doctor on duty.
■ **médico,-a forense** forensic surgeon.
medida *nf* **1** *(acción)* measurement. **2** *(unidad)* measure: *una medida de azúcar*, one measure of sugar. **3** *(prudencia)* moderation. **4** *(disposición)* measure, step.
● **a la medida de** according to.
● **a medida que** as: *a medida que bajas*, as you go down; *a medida que pasa el tiempo*, as time goes by.
● **hecho a la medida** made-to-measure.
● **tomar medidas** to take steps.
medieval *adj* medieval.
medio,-a *adj* **1** *(mitad)* half: *media clase está enferma*, half the class is ill; *medio kilo*, half a kilo. **2** *(intermedio)* middle: *a media tarde*, in the middle of the afternoon. **3** *(promedio)* average: *velocidad media*, average speed.
▶ *nm* **medio 1** *(mitad)* half [*pl* **-ves**]. **2** *(centro)* middle: *en medio de algo*, in the middle of something. **3** *(contexto)* environment.
▶ *adv* half: *medio terminado,-a*, half-finished.
▶ *nm pl* **medios** *(recursos)* means.
● **a medias 1** *(sin terminar)* half done, half finished. **2** *(entre dos)* between the two: *has dejado el trabajo a medias*, you've left the job half done; *el libro lo escribimos a medias*, we wrote the book between the two of us; *lo pagamos a medias*, we went halves on it.

● **por medio de algo** by means of STH.
● **por todos los medios** by all means.
● **quitar de en medio** to get out of the way.
● **trabajar media jornada** to work part-time.
■ **media pensión** half board.
■ **medio ambiente** environment.
■ **medio centro** centre half [*pl* **-ves**].
■ **medio de transporte** means of transport.
■ **medios de comunicación** the mass media.
mediocre *adj* mediocre.
mediodía *nm* **1** *(las doce)* noon, midday. **2** *(hora del almuerzo)* lunchtime.
medir *vt* **1** *(tomarr medidas)* to measure. **2** *(calcular)* to gauge: *mide muy bien sus actos*, he considers the consequences of his actions. **3** *(moderar)* to weigh: *mide tus palabras*, weigh your words.
meditación *nf* meditation.
meditar *vt-vi* to meditate, think [*pt & pp* **thought**].
mediterráneo,-a *adj* - *nm,f* Mediterranean.
■ **el mar Mediterráneo** the Mediterranean Sea.
médula *nf* marrow.
■ **médula espinal** spinal cord.
medusa *nf* jellyfish.
megáfono *nm* megaphone, loudspeaker.
mejicano,-a *adj* - *nm,f* Mexican.
Méjico *nm* Mexico.
mejilla *nf* cheek.
mejillón *nm* mussel.
mejor *adj-adv* **1** *(comparativo)* better: *es mejor no hablar de esto*, it's better not to talk about this. **2** *(superlativo)* best: *mi mejor amigo*, my best friend.
● **a lo mejor** perhaps, maybe.
● **mejor dicho** rather.
● **tanto mejor** so much the better.
mejora *nf* improvement.
mejorar *vt* to improve.
▶ *vi-vpr* **mejorar(se) 1** *(reponerse)* to recover, get better. **2** *(el tiempo)* to clear up.
mejoría *nf* improvement.
melancolía *nf* melancholy.
melancólico,-a *adj* melancholic.
melena *nf* **1** *(de persona)* long hair. **2** *(de león, caballo)* mane.

melenudo,-a *adj* long-haired.
▶ *nm,f (hombre)* long-haired man [*pl* **men**]; *(mujer)* long-haired woman [*pl* **women**].
mellizo,-a *adj - nm,f* twin.
melocotón *nm* peach.
melocotonero *nm* peach tree.
melodía *nf* melody.
melodioso,-a *adj* melodious.
melón *nm* melon.
membrana *nf* membrane.
membrete *nm* letterhead.
membrillo *nm* **1** *(árbol)* quince tree. **2** *(fruta)* quince. **3** *(dulce)* quince jelly.
memo,-a *adj fam* silly, foolish.
▶ *nm,f* fool, simpleton.
memoria *nf* **1** *(gen)* memory. **2** *(informe)* report.
▶ *nf pl* **memorias** *(biografía)* memoirs.
● **de memoria** by heart.
● **en memoria de** ALGN in memory of SB.
● **hacer memoria** to try to remember.
■ **memoria caché** cache memory.
memorizar *vt* to memorize.
menaje *nm* household equipment.
mención *nf* mention.
mencionar *vt* to mention.
mendigar *vi* to beg.
mendigo,-a *nm,f* beggar.
mendrugo *nm* hard crust of bread.
menear *vt* **1** *(agitar)* to shake [*pt* **shook**; *pp* **shaken**]; *(cola)* to wag. **2** *fam (el cuerpo)* to wiggle.
▶ *vpr* **menearse** to sway, swing [*pt & pp* **swung**].
menestra *nf* vegetable stew.
mengano,-a *nm,f* so-and-so.
menisco *nm* meniscus.
menopausia *nf* menopause.
menor *adj* **1** *(comparativo)* smaller, lesser; *(persona)* younger. **2** *(superlativo)* smallest, least; *(persona)* youngest.
▶ *nmf* **menor (de edad)** minor.
● **al por menor** retail.
Menorca *nf* Minorca.
menos *adj* **1** *(comparativo - con incontables)* less; *(- con contables)* fewer: **lleva menos tiempo**, it takes less time. **2** *(superlativo - con incontables)* the least; *(con contables)* the fewest: **el que lleva menos tiempo**, the one that takes the least time.
▶ *adv* **1** *(comparativo - con incontables)* less; *(- con contables)* fewer. **2** *(superlativo - con incontables)* the least; *(con contables)* the fewest. **3** *(para hora)* to: **las tres menos cuarto**, a quarter to three.
▶ *prep (excepto)* except, but.
▶ *nm* minus.
● **a menos que** unless.
● **al menos** at least.
● **por lo menos** at least.
● **¡menos mal!** thank God!
menospreciar *vt* **1** *(no valorar)* to undervalue, underrate. **2** *(despreciar)* to despise.
mensaje *nm* message.
mensajero,-a *nm,f* messenger.
menstruación *nf* menstruation.
mensual *adj* monthly.
mensualidad *nf (sueldo)* monthly salary; *(de un pago)* instalment: **pagar en mensualidades**, to pay in monthly instalments.
menta *nf* mint.
mental *adj* mental.
mentalidad *nf* mentality.
mentalizar *vt* to make aware.
▶ *vpr* **mentalizarse** *(prepararse)* to prepare oneself.
mente *nf* mind.
● **tener en mente hacer algo** to intend to do STH.
mentir *vi* to lie, tell lies [*pt & pp* **told**].
mentira *nf* lie: **decir mentiras**, to tell lies.
● **parece mentira** it's unbelievable.
■ **mentira piadosa** white lie.
mentiroso,-a *nm,f* liar.
mentón *nm* chin.
menú *nm* menu.
menudo,-a *adj* **1** *(pequeño)* small, tiny. **2** fine: **¡menudo lío!**, what a fine mess!
● **a menudo** often, frequently.
meñique *nm* little finger.
mercadillo *nf* market, street market.
mercado *nm* market.
■ **mercado de divisas** foreign exchange market.
■ **mercado de valores** stock-market.
■ **mercado negro** black market.
■ **Mercado Común** Common Market.
mercancía *nf* goods *pl*.
mercante *adj* merchant.
▶ *nm* merchant ship.
mercantil *adj* mercantile, commercial.

mercería *nf (tienda)* GB haberdasher's; US notions store.

mercurio *nm* mercury.

merecer *vt-vi* **merecer(se)** to deserve.

merecido,-a *adj* deserved.

▶ *nm* **merecido** just deserts *pl*: *se llevó su merecido*, he got his just deserts.

merendar *vi* to have an afternoon snack, have tea.

merendero *nm* picnic spot.

merengue *nm* meringue.

meridiano,-a *adj* **1** *(de mediodía)* meridian. **2** *fig (claro)* obvious.

▶ *nm* **meridiano** meridian.

meridional *adj* southern.

merienda *nf* afternoon snack, tea.

mérito *nm* merit, worth: *él tiene mucho mérito*, he is admirable.

● **hacer méritos** to prove oneself.

merluza *nf (pescado)* hake.

● **coger una merluza** to get drunk, get pissed.

mermar *vi* **1** *(bajar)* to decrease, drop. **2** *(perder volumen)* to shrink [*pt* **shrank**; *pp* **shrunk**].

▶ *vt* to reduce.

mermelada *nf (de cítricos)* marmalade; *(de otras frutas)* jam.

mero¹ *nm (pez)* grouper.

mero,-a² *adj* mere, pure.

mes *nm* month.

mesa *nf (de salón, comedor)* table; *(de despacho)* desk.

● **poner la mesa** to set the table [*pt & pp* **set**].

● **quitar la mesa** to clear the table.

■ **mesa camilla** table with a heater underneath.

■ **mesa de centro** coffee table.

■ **mesa de despacho** desk.

■ **mesa de operaciones** operating table.

■ **mesa de trabajo** desk.

■ **mesa redonda** round table.

meseta *nf* tableland, plateau.

mesilla *nf* small table.

■ **mesilla de noche** bedside table.

mesón *nm (venta)* inn, tavern.

mestizo,-a *adj* of mixed race, half-breed.

meta *nf* **1** *(portería)* goal; *(de carreras)* finishing line. **2** *fig (objetivo)* aim, goal.

metabolismo *nm* metabolism.

metáfora *nf* metaphor.

metal *nm (gen)* metal.

metálico,-a *adj* metallic.

▶ *nm* **metálico** cash.

● **pagar en metálico** to pay cash [*pt & pp* **paid**].

metalúrgico,-a *adj* metallurgical.

▶ *nm,f* metalworker.

metamorfosis *nf* metamorphosis.

meteorito *nm* meteorite.

meteorología *nf* meteorology.

meter *vt* **1** *(introducir)* to put: *mete el pie en el agua*, put your foot in the water; *mete la ropa para que no se moje*, bring the clothes in so that they don't get wet. **2** *(punto)* to score: *nos metieron tres goles*, they scored three goals against us. **3** *fam (dar)* to give: *me metieron una multa*, I got fined. **4** *(ropa)* to take in.

▶ *vpr* **meterse** **1** *(entrar)* to get in: *se metió en la cama*, she got into bed; *se metió por una rendija*, it went through a crack. **2** *(introducir)* to put: *métetelo en el bolsillo*, put it in your pocket. **3** *(entrometerse)* to interfere, meddle: *no te metas en lo que no te importa*, mind your own business. **4** *(dedicarse)* to go into: *se metió en política*, he went into politics.

● **meter miedo a** ALGN to frighten SB.

● **meterse a hacer algo** to start doing STH.

● **meterse con** ALGN **1** *(burlarse)* to tease SB. **2** *(atacar)* to pick on SB.

meticuloso,-a *adj* meticulous.

metódico,-a *adj* methodical.

método *nm (sistema)* method; *(libro)* manual.

metomentodo *nmf fam* busybody.

metralleta *nf* submachine gun.

métrico,-a *adj* metric.

metro¹ *nm (medida)* metre.

■ **metro cuadrado** square metre.

metro² *nm (transporte)* GB underground, tube; US subway.

metropolitano,-a *adj* metropolitan.

▶ *nm* **metropolitano** *fml* GB underground, tube; US subway.

mexicano,-a *adj - nm,f* Mexican.

México *nm* Mexico.

mezcla *nf* **1** *(acción - de razas, colores)* mixing; *(- de cafés, tabacos)* blending: *es una mezcla de estilos*, it's a combination of styles. **2** *(producto - de razas, colores)* mixture; *(- de cafés, tabacos)* blend.

mezclar *vt* **1** *(razas, colores)* to mix; *(cafés, tabacos)* blend. **2** *(desordenar)* to mix up.
▶ *vpr* **mezclarse** *(cosas)* to get mixed up; *(personas)* to get involved.
mezquino,-a *adj* **1** *(avaro)* stingy, niggardly. **2** *(mentalidad)* petty, small-minded. **3** *(escaso)* miserable, paltry.
mezquita *nf* mosque.
mi[1] *adj* my.
mi[2] *nm (nota)* E.
mí *pron* **1** me. **2** *(mí mismo,-a)* myself.
miau *nm* miaow, mew.
michelín *nm fam* spare tyre.
microbio *nm* microbe.
microchip *nm* microchip.
micrófono *nm* microphone.
microondas *nm* microwave.
microscopio *nm* microscope.
miedo *nm* fear.
● **dar miedo** to be scary.
● **dar miedo a ALGN** to frighten SB.
● **tener miedo** to be afraid.
● **de miedo** *fam* great, terrific.
miedoso,-a *adj* fearful.
miel *nf* honey.
miembro *nm* **1** *(socio)* member: **país miembro**, member state. **2** *(extremidad)* limb. **3** *(pene)* penis.
mientras *conj* **1** while: **mientras esperaba, leía un libro**, while I waited, I read a book. **2** *(condición)* as long as, while: **mientras pueda**, as long as I can.
▶ *adv* meanwhile: **Juan abría la caja. Mientras, Pedro vigilaba**, Juan was opening the safe. Pedro, meanwhile, was on the lookout.
● **mientras no** until.
● **mientras que** while, whereas.
● **mientras tanto** meanwhile, in the meantime.
miércoles *nm* Wednesday.
mierda *nf* **1** *fam* shit. **2** *fam (porquería)* dirt, filth.
● **mandar a ALGN a la mierda** to tell SB to piss off.
● **¡vete a la mierda!** go to hell!
miga *nf* crumb.
● **hacer buenas migas con ALGN** to get along well with SB.
migaja *nf* crumb.
migración *nf* migration.
migraña *nf* migraine.

mil *num* thousand: **dos mil**, two thousand.
milagro *nm* miracle, wonder.
milagroso,-a *adj* **1** *(cura, remedio)* miraculous. **2** *(asombroso)* marvellous.
milenario,-a *adj* ancient.
milenio *nm* millenium.
milésimo,-a *num* thousandth: **una milésima de segundo**, a thousandth of a second.
mili *nf fam* military service.
miligramo *nm* milligramme, milligram.
mililitro *nm* millilitre.
milímetro *nm* millimetre.
militante *adj - nmf* militant.
militar *adj* military.
▶ *nm* military man [*pl* **men**], soldier.
▶ *vi* POL to be a militant.
milla *nf* mile.
millar *nm* thousand.
millón *nm* million: **dos millones**, two million.
millonario,-a *nm,f* **1** *(hombre)* millionaire. **2** *(mujer)* millionairess.
▶ *adj*: **ayudas millonarias**, aid worth millions; **tiene unos ingresos millonarios**, he earns millions.
mimar *vt* to spoil [*vt & pp* **spoilt**].
mimbre *nm* wicker.
mímica *nf* mime.
mimo *nm* **1** *(mímica)* mime. **2** *(cariño)*: **lo hizo con mucho mimo**, he did it very lovingly; **trátalo con mimo**, treat it with care.
mimoso,-a *adj* affectionate.
mina *nf* **1** *(yacimiento)* mine. **2** *(paso subterráneo)* underground passage. **3** *(de lápiz)* lead. **4** *(bomba)* mine: **un campo de minas**, a minefield.
mineral *adj - nm* mineral.
minería *nf* mining.
minero,-a *adj* mining.
▶ *nm,f* miner.
miniatura *nf* miniature.
minifalda *nf* miniskirt.
mínima *nf* minimum temperature.
mínimo,-a *adj (gasto)* minimal; *(cantidad, temperatura)* minimum.
▶ *nm* **mínimo** minimum: **lo redujeron al mínimo**, they reduced it to a minimum.
● **como mínimo** at least.
■ **mínimo común múltiplo** lowest common multiple.

ministerio *nm* ministry ; US department.
■ **Ministerio del Interior** GB Home Office; US Department of the Interior.
ministro,-a *nm,f* minister.
■ **primer,-ra ministro,-a** prime minister.
minoría *nf* minority.
minorista *nmf* retailer.
minucioso,-a *adj* **1** (*trabajo*) minute, detailed. **2** (*persona*) meticulous.
minúscula *nf* small letter.
minúsculo,-a *adj* minute, tiny.
minusválido,-a *adj* handicapped, disabled.
▶ *nm,f* handicapped person, disabled person: **los minusválidos**, the handicapped, the disabled.
minutero *nm* minute hand.
minuto *nm* minute.
mío,-a *adj* my, of mine: **es problema mío**, that's my problem; **un pariente mío**, a relative of mine.
▶ *pron* mine: **este libro es mío**, this book is mine.
miope *adj* short-sighted.
miopía *nf* shortsightedness, myopia.
mirada *nf* look.
● **echar una mirada a** to have a look at.
mirador *nm* viewpoint.
miramiento *nm* consideration.
mirar *vi* **1** (*ver*) to look at: **no me mires así**, don't look at me like that. **2** (*observar*) to watch: **se la quedó mirando**, he stared at her; **lo estaba mirando de arriba abajo**, she looked him up and down. **3** (*dar a*) to overlook: **la habitación mira al mar**, the room overlooks the sea.
▶ *vpr* **mirarse** (*a uno mismo*) to look at oneself.
● **mirar algo con buenos ojos** to approve of STH.
● **mirar algo con malos ojos** to disapprove of STH.
● **mirar por** to look after.
● **¡mira qué listo eres!** do you think you are so clever?
● **¡mira quién habla!** *fam* look who's talking!
mirilla *nf* peephole.
mirlo *nm* blackbird.
mirón,-ona *adj* **1** *pey* peeping. **2** (*espectador*) onlooking.

▶ *nm,f* **1** *pey* voyeur. **2** (*espectador*) onlooker.
misa *nf* mass.
■ **misa del gallo** midnight mass.
miserable *adj* **1** (*desgraciado*) miserable. **2** (*canalla*) wretched.
miseria *nf* **1** (*desgracia*) misery. **2** (*pobreza*) extreme poverty.
misericordia *nf* mercy, pity, compassion.
misil *nm* missile.
misión *nf* mission.
misionero,-a *nm,f* missionary.
mismo,-a *adj* **1** (*igual*) same: **al mismo tiempo**, at the same time. **2** (*enfático - propio*) own; (*- uno mismo*) oneself: **sus mismos amigos no lo entienden**, not even his own friends understand him; **lo haré yo mismo**, I'll do it myself.
▶ *pron* same: **es el mismo que vimos ayer**, it's the same one that we saw yesterday.
▶ *adv* right: **aquí mismo**, right here.
● **uno mismo** oneself, yourself.
misterio *nm* mystery.
misterioso,-a *adj* mysterious.
místico,-a *adj - nm,f* mystic.
mitad *nf* **1** half [*pl* **-ves**]: **la mitad de una botella**, half a bottle. **2** (*en medio*) middle: **en mitad de la carretera**, in the middle of the road.
● **a mitad de** halfway through.
mitin *nm* rally.
mito *nm* myth.
mitología *nf* mythology.
mixto,-a *adj* mixed.
mobiliario *nm* furniture.
mocasín *nm* loafer.
mochila *nf* rucksack, backpack.
mochuelo *nm* little owl.
moco *nm* mucus.
● **limpiarse los mocos** to wipe one's nose.
● **no es moco de pavo** *fam* it's not to be taken lightly.
mocoso,-a *nm,f fam* brat.
moda *nf* fashion.
● **estar de moda** to be in fashion.
● **ir a la moda** to be fashionable.
● **pasado de moda** old-fashioned.
modales *nm pl* manners.
● **con buenos modales** politely.

modalidad *nf* **1** *(tipo)* form. **2** *(de deporte)* category.

modelar *vt* to model, shape.

modelo *adj - nm* model.

▶ *nmf* fashion model.

módem *nm* modem.

■ **módem fax** fax modem.

moderado,-a *adj - nm,f* moderate.

moderador,-ra *adj* moderating.

▶ *nm,f* chairperson; *(hombre)* chairman [*pl* -**men**]; *(mujer)* chairwoman [*pl* -**women**].

moderar *vt* to moderate.

▶ *vpr* **moderarse** to restrain oneself, control oneself.

modernizar *vt* to modernize.

▶ *vpr* **modernizar(se)** to get up to date.

moderno,-a *adj* **1** *(gen)* modern. **2** *(ropa, persona)* trendy.

modestia *nf* modesty.

modesto,-a *adj* modest.

modificación *nf* modification, change.

modificar *vt* to modify, change.

▶ *vpr* **modificar(se)** to change, alter.

modismo *nm* idiom.

modista *nmf (que confecciona)* dressmaker; *(que diseña)* fashion designer.

modisto *nm (sastre)* tailor; *(diseñador)* fashion designer.

modo *nm (manera)* manner, way.

▶ *nm pl* **modos** manners.

● **de cualquier modo** anyway.

● **de ningún modo** by no means.

● **de todos modos** anyhow, in any case.

● **en cierto modo** to a certain extent.

modorra *nf* drowsiness: *me está entrando la modorra*, I'm beginning to feel sleepy.

módulo *nm* module.

mofarse *vpr* to scoff: *se mofa de todos*, he scoffs at everyone.

moflete *nm fam* chubby cheek.

mogollón *nm fam* loads, heaps: *un mogollón de gente*, loads of people.

▶ *adv fam* a lot: *me gusta mogollón*, I just love it.

moho *nm* mould.

mohoso,-a *adj* mouldy.

mojado,-a *adj* wet.

mojar *vt (empapar)* to wet; *(humedecer)* to dampen.

▶ *vpr* **mojarse 1** *(con líquido)* to get wet. **2** *fam (comprometerse)* to commit oneself.

molar *vi arg (gustar)*: *me mola cantidad*, it's cool, I'm really into it; *¿te mola esa tía?*, do you fancy that girl?

molde *nm* mould.

molécula *nf* molecule.

moler *vt* **1** *(café)* to grind [*pt & pp* **ground**]; *(trigo)* to mill. **2** *(cansar)* to wear out [*pt* **wore**; *pp* **worn**]: *me deja molido*, it wears me out.

molestar *vt-vi* to disturb, bother: *perdona que te moleste, pero...*, sorry to bother you, but...; *que nadie me moleste*, I don't want to be disturbed.

▶ *vpr* **molestarse 1** *(tomarse el trabajo)* to bother: *no te molestes en llamarme*, don't bother to phone me. **2** *(ofenderse)* to get upset: *espero que no te molestes*, I hope you don't get upset.

molestia *nf* **1** *(incomodidad)* nuisance, bother. **2** *(dolor)* slight pain, discomfort.

● **"Rogamos disculpen las molestias"** "We apologize for any inconvenience".

● **tomarse la molestia** to take the trouble.

molesto,-a *adj* **1** *(que incomoda)* annoying, troublesome. **2** *(enfadado)* annoyed. **3** *(incómodo)* uncomfortable.

molido,-a *adj* **1** *(café)* ground; *(trigo)* milled. **2** *fam (cansado)* worn-out.

molinero,-a *nm,f* miller.

molinillo *nm* grinder, mill.

■ **molinillo de café** coffee grinder.

molino *nm* mill.

■ **molino de viento** windmill.

molusco *nm* mollusc.

momentáneo,-a *adj* momentary.

momento *nm* **1** *(gen)* moment, instant. **2** *(época)* time: *en el momento presente*, at the present time.

● **al momento** at once.

● **de momento** for the time being.

● **en el momento** straight away.

● **por el momento** for the time being.

momia *nf* mummy.

mona *nf fam (borrachera)* .

● **coger una mona** to get drunk.

● **dormir la mona** to sleep it off [*pt & pp* **slept**].

Mónaco *nm* Monaco.

monada *loc* **ser una monada 1** *(persona)* to be gorgeous, be cute. **2** *(cosa)* to be lovely.

monaguillo *nm* altar boy.
monarca *nm* monarch.
monarquía *nf* monarchy.
monasterio *nm* monastery.
monda *nf (piel)* peel, skin.
● **ser la monda 1** *fam* (divertido) to be a scream. **2** (el colmo) to be the limit.
mondadientes *nm* toothpick.
mondar *vt (pelar)* to peel.
● **mondarse de risa** to laugh one's head off.
moneda *nf* **1** *(unidad monetaria)* currency, money. **2** *(pieza)* coin.
■ **moneda falsa** counterfeit money.
■ **moneda suelta** small change.
■ **moneda única** single currency.
monedero *nm* purse.
monigote *nm* **1** *(muñeco)* rag doll, paper doll. **2** *(pintado)* doodle. **3** *(tonto)* fool.
monitor,-ra *nm,f (profesor)* instructor.
▶ *nm* **monitor** *(pantalla)* monitor.
monja *nf* nun.
monje *nm* monk.
mono,-a *adj (bonito)* pretty, cute.
▶ *nm* **mono 1** *(animal)* monkey. **2** *(prenda - de trabajo)* overalls *pl*; *(- de vestir)* cat-suit. **3** *arg (de drogas)* cold turkey.
monólogo *nm* monologue.
monopatín *nm* skateboard.
monopolio *nm* monopoly.
monosílabo,-a *adj* monosyllabic.
▶ *nm* **monosílabo** monosyllable.
monotonía *nf* monotony.
monótono,-a *adj* monotonous.
monstruo *nm* monster.
● **ser un monstruo** to be a phenomenon.
monstruoso,-a *adj* **1** *(atroz)* monstrous. **2** *(grande)* outrageous, huge.
montacargas *nm* GB goods lift; US freight elevator.
montaje *nm* **1** *(de aparato, mueble)* assembly. **2** *(de película)* cutting, editing. **3** *(de obra teatral)* staging. **4** *(de exposición)* setting up.
■ **montaje fotográfico** photomontage.
montaña *nf* mountain.
■ **montaña rusa** big dipper.
montañero,-a *nm,f* mountain climber, mountaineer.
montañismo *nm* mountain climbing, mountaineering.
montañoso,-a *adj* mountainous.
montar *vi* **1** *(a vehículo)* to mount, get on.

2 *(caballo, bicicleta)* to ride [*pt* **rode**; *pp* **ridden**].
▶ *vt* **1** *(cabalgar)* to ride [*pt* **rode**; *pp* **ridden**]. **2** *(nata)* to whip; *(claras)* whisk. **3** *(máquinas)* to assemble. **4** *(joyas)* to set [*pt & pp* **set**]. **5** *(negocio, exposición)* to set up [*pt & pp* **set**]. **6** *(película)* to edit, mount. **7** *(obra de teatro)* to stage.
▶ *vpr* **montarse** *(subirse - a autobús, tren)* to get on; *(-a coche)* to get into.
● **montárselo** *fam* to have things nicely worked out: *se lo monta muy bien*, he really has it made!
monte *nm* **1** *(montaña)* mountain, mount; *(más baja)* hill. **2** *(bosque)* woodland. **3** *(terreno)* scrubland.
■ **monte de piedad** pawnshop.
montículo *nm* mound, hillock.
montón *nm* **1** *(pila)* heap, pile. **2** *fam (gran cantidad)* loads *pl*, great quantity: *un montón de gente*, loads of people; *tiene un montón de dinero*, he is loaded.
● **ser del montón** to be nothing special.
montura *nf* **1** *(animal)* mount. **2** *(silla)* saddle. **3** *(de gafas)* frame.
monumental *adj* **1** *(de monumento)* of monuments. **2** *(enorme)* huge, massive.
monumento *nm* monument.
moño *nm (de pelo)* bun.
● **estar hasta el moño** to be fed up to the back teeth.
moqueta *nf* fitted carpet.
mora *nf* **1** *(de moral)* mulberry. **2** *(zarzamora)* blackberry.
morada *nf fml* abode, dwelling.
morado,-a *adj* dark purple.
▶ *nm* **morado 1** *(color)* dark purple. **2** *(golpe)* bruise.
● **pasarlas moradas** *fam* to have a tough time.
● **tener un ojo morado** to have a black eye.
moral *adj* moral.
▶ *nf* **1** *(reglas)* morality, morals *pl*. **2** *(ánimo)* morale, spirits *pl*: *nos levantó la moral*, it raised our spirits.
■ **doble moral** double standards.
moraleja *nf* moral.
moratón *nm* bruise.
morbo *nm fam* morbidity: *me da morbo esa historia*, I'm really curious about that stuff; *esa tía tiene mucho morbo*, that girl is really sexy.

morboso,-a *adj* **1** *(malsano)* morbid. **2** *(atractivo)* sexy.

morcilla *nf* black pudding.

● **que le den morcilla** *fam* he can drop dead for all I care.

mordaza *nf* gag.

mordedura *nf* bite.

morder *vt-vi* to bite.

mordisco *nm* bite.

mordisquear *vt* to nibble.

moreno,-a *adj* **1** *(pelo)* dark. **2** *(persona - de pelo)* dark-haired. **3** *(de piel)* dark-skinned. **4** *(bronceado)* tanned.

► *nm* **moreno** suntan.

● **ponerse moreno** to tan.

morera *nf* white mulberry tree.

morfema *nm* morpheme.

moribundo,-a *adj* dying.

morir *vi-vpr* **morir(se)** to die.

● **morirse de hambre 1** *(literalmente)* to starve. **2** *(estar hambriento)* to be starving.

● **morirse de miedo** to be scared stiff.

● **morirse de risa** to kill oneself laughing.

● **morirse de sed** to be dying of thirst.

moro,-a *adj* **1** *(norteafricano)* Moorish. **2** *(musulmán)* Moslim.

► *nm,f* **1** *(norteafricano)* Moor. **2** *(musulmán)* Moslim.

moroso,-a *adj* in arrears.

► *nm,f* defaulter.

morriña *nf fam* homesickness.

morro *nm* **1** *fam (de persona)* mouth, lips. **2** *(de animal)* snout, nose.

● **estar de morros** to be in a huff.

● **¡vaya morro!** *fam* what a cheek!

morsa *nf* walrus.

mortadela *nf* mortadella.

mortal *adj* **1** *(persona)* mortal. **2** *(mortífero)* lethal.

► *nmf* mortal.

mortalidad *nf* mortality.

mortero *nm* mortar.

mortífero,-a *adj* deadly, fatal, lethal.

mosaico *nm* mosaic.

mosca *nf* fly.

● **estar mosca 1** *(sospechar)* to smell a rat. **2** *(estar enfadado)* to be annoyed.

● **por si las moscas** just in case.

● **¿qué mosca te ha picado?** what's biting you?

● **tener la mosca detrás de la oreja** *fam* to smell a rat.

moscardón *nm* blowfly.

mosquearse *vpr* **1** *fam (enfadarse)* to get cross. **2** *(sospechar)* to smell a rat.

mosquito *nm* mosquito [*pl* -os o -oes].

mostaza *nf* mustard.

mosto *nm* grape juice.

mostrador *nm* counter.

■ **mostrador de facturación** check-in desk.

mostrar *vt* **1** *(enseñar)* to show [*pt* showed; *pp* shown]: **nos mostró el camino**, he showed us the way. **2** *(exponer)* to exhibit, display. **3** *(señalar)* to point out.

► *vpr* **mostrarse** to be: **se mostró muy interesado**, he was very interested; **muéstrate atento con ellos**, look after them; **se han mostrado partidarios del cambio**, they are in favour of the change.

mota *nf* speck.

mote *nm* nickname.

motín *nm* riot.

motivar *vt* **1** *(causar)* to cause, give rise to. **2** *(estimular)* to motivate.

motivo *nm* **1** *(causa)* motive, reason. **2** *(de dibujo, música)* motif [*pl* -s].

● **con motivo de 1** *(debido a)* owing to. **2** *(con ocasión de)* on the occasion of.

moto *nf fam* motorbike.

● **ir como una moto** *fam* to be in a rush.

motocicleta *nf* motorbike.

motociclismo *nm* motorcycling.

motociclista *nmf* motorcyclist.

motor,-ra *adj* motor.

► *nm* **motor** *(no eléctrico)* engine; *(eléctrico)* motor.

■ **motor de búsqueda** search engine.

■ **motor de explosión** internal combustion engine.

■ **motor de reacción** jet engine.

motora *nf* small motorboat.

motorista *nmf* motorcyclist.

mover *vt* **1** *(gen)* to move: **no muevas la cabeza**, don't move your head. **2** *(suscitar)* to incite: **movido por el afán de riquezas**, motivated by the greed of riches.

► *vpr* **moverse 1** *(gen)* to move: **no te muevas**, don't move. **2** *fam (hacer gestiones)* to take steps, get moving.

móvil *adj* movable, mobile.

▶ *nm* **1** *(teléfono)* mobile (phone), cellular phone. **2** *(motivo)* motive, inducement.
movilizar *vt* to mobilize.
movimiento *nm (gen)* movement, motion.
● **ponerse en movimiento 1** *(coche)* to get going. **2** *(negocio)* to start up.
■ **movimiento de caja** turnover.
■ **movimiento sísmico** earth tremor.
mozo,-a *adj* young.
▶ *nm,f (chico)* boy, lad; *(chica)* girl, lass.
▶ *nm* **mozo 1** *(de hotel)* buttons. **2** *(de estación)* porter.
muchacho,-a *nm,f (chico)* boy, lad; *(chica)* girl, lass.
muchedumbre *nf* multitude, crowd.
mucho,-a *adj* **1** *(frases afirmativas - singular)* a lot of, much; *(- plural)* a lot of, many: *bebe mucho vino*, he drinks a lot of wine; *tenemos muchos problemas*, we have a lot of problems. **2** *(frases negativas e interrogativas - singular)* much; *(- plural)* many: *no tenemos mucho tiempo*, we don't have much time; *¿marcaste muchos goles?*, did you score many goals?
▶ *pron (singular - frases afirmativas)* a lot, much; *(- frases negativas e interrogativas)* much; *(plural)* many: *aún me queda mucho por hacer*, I've still got a lot left to do; *no es mucho lo que pido*, I'm not asking for much; *muchos no acabaron el examen*, many didn't finish the exam.
▶ *adv* **mucho 1** *(gen)* a lot: *hoy he comido mucho*, I've eaten a lot today; *lo siento mucho*, I'm very sorry. **2** *(comparaciones)* much: *es mucho más caro de lo que pensaba*, it's much more expensive than I thought. **3** *(mucho tiempo)* a long time: *hace mucho que no la veo*, I haven't seen her for a long time. **4** *(frecuentemente)* often, much: *no la veo mucho*, I don't see her much.
● **como mucho** at the most.
● **por mucho que** however much.
muda *nf* **1** *(de ropa)* change of clothes. **2** *(de animal)* moulting.
mudanza *nf* removal: *estoy de mudanza*, I'm moving house.
mudar *vt* **1** *(cambiar)* to change. **2** *(trasladar)* to change, move. **3** *(plumas)* to moult. **4** *(voz)* to break [*pt* broke, *pp* broken]. **5** *(piel)* to shed [*pt & pp* shed].

▶ *vpr* **mudarse 1** to change: *mudarse de ropa*, to change one's clothes. **2** *(de residencia)* to move.
mudo,-a *adj* dumb: *me quedé mudo de asombro*, I was left speechless.
▶ *nm,f*: *los mudos*, the dumb.
mueble *nm* piece of furniture: *un mueble antiguo*, a piece of antique furniture.
▶ *nm pl* **muebles** furniture: *los muebles buenos son muy caros*, good furniture is very expensive.
■ **mueble bar** drinks cabinet.
■ **mueble de cocina** kitchen unit.
mueca *nf* grimace.
● **hacer muecas** to pull faces.
muela *nf* tooth [*pl* teeth].
● **dolor de muelas** toothache.
■ **muela del juicio** wisdom tooth [*pl* teeth].
muelle[1] *nm (en puerto)* dock.
muelle[2] *nm (resorte)* spring.
muerte *nf* death.
● **dar muerte** to kill.
● **de mala muerte** miserable, wretched.
● **estar de muerte** *fam* to be out of this world.
muerto,-a *adj* **1** *(sin vida)* dead. **2** *fam (cansado)* dead beat.
▶ *nm,f* dead person: *los muertos*, the dead.
● **estar muerto de hambre** to be starving.
● **estar muerto de miedo** to be scared to death.
● **estar muerto de risa** to laugh one's head off.
● **hacer el muerto** to float on one's back.
muestra *nf* **1** *(ejemplar)* sample. **2** *(señal)* proof, sign.
● **dar muestras de** to show signs of [*pt* showed; *pp* shown].
muestrario *nm* collection of samples.
mugido *nm* **1** *(de vaca)* moo [*pl* -s]. **2** *(de toro)* bellow.
mugir *vi* **1** *(vaca)* to moo. **2** *(toro)* to bellow.
mugre *nf* filth.
mujer *nf* **1** woman [*pl* women]. **2** *(esposa)* wife [*pl* -ves].
■ **mujer de la limpieza** cleaning lady.
mulato,-a *adj - nm,f* mulatto.
muleta *nf* crutch.
muletilla *nf (frase repetida)* tag.
mullir *vt* **1** *(esponjar)* to soften. **2** *(la tierra)* to break up [*pt* broke; *pp* broken].

mulo,-a *nm,f (macho)* mule; *(hembra)* she-mule.

multa *nf* fine: *me han puesto una multa*, I got fined.

multar *vt* to fine.

multicolor *adj* multicoloured.

multinacional *adj - nf* multinational.

múltiple *adj* **1** *(numeroso)* multiple: *un enchufe múltiple*, a multiple socket. **2** *(muchos)* many, a number of: *tiene múltiples inconvenientes*, it has a number of disadvantages.

multiplicación *nf* multiplication.

multiplicar *vt-vpr* **multiplicar(se)** to multiply.

múltiplo,-a *adj - nm,f* multiple.

multitud *nf* multitude, crowd.

mundial *adj* worldwide, world.

▸ *nm* world championship.

mundo *nm* world.

● **haber corrido mundo** to have been around.

■ **todo el mundo** everybody.

munición *nf* ammunition.

municipal *adj* municipal.

▸ *nmf (hombre)* policeman [*pl* -**men**]; *(mujer)* policewoman [*pl* -**women**].

municipio *nm* **1** *(ciudad)* municipality. **2** *(ayuntamiento)* town council.

muñeca *nf* **1** *(del brazo)* wrist. **2** *(juguete)* doll.

muñeco *nm* **1** *(monigote)* dummy. **2** *(juguete)* doll.

■ **muñeco de nieve** snowman.

■ **muñeco de peluche** soft toy.

muñequera *nf* wristband.

mural *adj - nm* mural.

muralla *nf* wall.

murciélago *nm* bat.

murmullo *nm* **1** *(de voces)* mutter, murmuring. **2** *(de hojas)* rustle.

murmurar *vt* to mutter.

▸ *vi* to gossip.

muro *nm* wall.

musa *nf* muse.

musaraña *nf* shrew.

● **estar pensando en las musarañas** to be daydreaming.

muscular *adj* muscular.

músculo *nm* muscle.

musculoso,-a *adj* muscular.

museo *nm* museum.

musgo *nm* moss.

música *nf* music.

■ **música de cámara** chamber music.

■ **música de fondo** background music.

musical *adj - nm* musical.

músico,-a *adj* musical.

▸ *nm,f* musician.

musitar *vi* to mumble.

muslo *nm* thigh.

mustio,-a *adj* **1** *(plantas)* withered, faded. **2** *(persona)* sad, depressed.

musulmán,-ana *adj - nm,f* Muslim, Moslem.

mutilar *vt* to mutilate.

mutuo,-a *adj* mutual, reciprocal.

muy *adv* **1** *(con adjetivo)* very: *muy bonito*, very nice. **2** *fam (con nombre)* real: *es muy hombre*, he's a real man; *es muy mujer*, she's a real woman.

● **Muy Señor mío** *(en carta)* Dear Sir.

N

nabo *nm* turnip.

nácar *nm* mother-of-pearl.

nacer *vi* **1** *(persona, animal)* to be born: *nací en Madrid*, I was born in Madrid. **2** *(río)* to rise [*pt* **rose**; *pp* **risen**]. **3** *(tener su origen)* to originate, start.

naciente *adj* **1** *(nuevo)* new. **2** *(creciente)* growing.

nacimiento *nm* **1** *(de persona, animal)* birth. **2** *(de río)* source. **3** *(de proyecto, estado)* birth.

nación *nf* nation.

nacional *adj* **1** *(bandera, equipo, seguridad)* national. **2** *(productos, mercados, vuelos)* domestic.

nacionalidad *nf* nationality.

nacionalismo *nm* nationalism.

nacionalista *adj* - *nmf* nationalist.

nacionalizar *vt* to nationalize.

nada *pron* nothing, not... anything: *¿qué compraste? - nada*, what did you buy? - nothing; *no quiero nada*, I don't want anything.
▶ *adv* not at all: *no me gusta nada*, I don't like it at all; *no es nada fácil*, it isn't at all easy.
▶ *nf* nothingness.
● **como si nada** as if nothing had happened.
● **-de nada** -don't mention it.

nadador,-ra *nm,f* swimmer.

nadar *vi* to swim [*pt* **swam**; *pp* **swum**].

nadie *pron* nobody, not... anybody: *allí no había nadie*, there was nobody there, there wasn't anybody there.

naipe *nm* card.

nalga *nf* buttock.

nana *nf* lullaby.

naranja *adj* - *nm (color)* orange.

▶ *nf (fruta)* orange.

naranjada *nf* orangeade.

naranjo *nm* orange tree.

narciso *nm (flor blanca)* narcissus; *(flor amarilla)* daffodil.

narcótico,-a *adj* narcotic.
▶ *nm* **narcótico** narcotic.

narcotraficante *nmf* drug trafficker.

narcotráfico *nm* drug trafficking.

nariz *nf* nose.
▶ *interj* **¡narices!** *fam* darn it!
● **estar hasta las narices de** *fam* to be fed up to the back teeth with.

narración *nf* **1** *(acción)* narration, account. **2** *(relato)* story.

narrador,-ra *nm,f* narrator.

narrar *vt* to tell [*pt & pp* **told**], narrate.

nasal *adj* nasal.

nata *nf* **1** *(para montar)* cream. **2** *(de leche hervida)* skin.
■ **nata montada** whipped cream.

natación *nf* swimming.

natal *adj* of birth.
■ **ciudad natal** home town.
■ **país natal** native country.

natalidad *nf* birth-rate.

natillas *nf pl* custard.

nativo,-a *adj* - *nm,f* native.

natural *adj* **1** *(color, estado, gesto)* natural. **2** *(fruta, flor)* fresh. **3** *(yogur)* plain.
● **como es natural** of course.
● **ser natural de** to come from.

naturaleza *nf* nature.
● **en plena naturaleza** in the wild.
● **por naturaleza** naturally.
■ **naturaleza muerta** still life.

naturalidad *nf* naturalness.
● **con naturalidad** naturally.

naufragar *vi* **1** *(barco)* to be wrecked. **2** *(persona)* to be shipwrecked. **3** *(proyecto, plan)* to fail.

naufragio *nm* **1** *(de barco)* shipwreck. **2** *(de proyecto, plan)* failure.

náufrago,-a *adj* shipwrecked.

▶ *nm,f* castaway, shipwrecked person.

náusea *nf* nausea, sickness: *me da náuseas*, it makes me sick.

● **sentir náuseas/tener náuseas** to feel sick.

náutica *nf* boating and sailing.

náutico,-a *adj* nautical.

navaja *nf* **1** *(cuchillo)* penknife [*pl* -ves], pocketknife [*pl* -ves]. **2** *(molusco)* razor-shell.

■ **navaja de afeitar** razor.

navajazo *nm* stab.

naval *adj* naval.

Navarra *nf* Navarre.

navarro,-a *adj* - *nm,f* Navarrese.

nave *nf* **1** *(barco)* ship. **2** *(de iglesia)* nave.

■ **nave espacial** spaceship.

■ **nave industrial** industrial building.

■ **nave lateral** aisle.

navegable *adj* navigable.

navegación *nf* navigation.

navegador *nm* *(en Internet)* browser.

navegante *adj* sailing.

▶ *nmf* navigator.

navegar *vi* to navigate, sail.

● **navegar por Internet** to surf the Net.

Navidad *nf* Christmas: *¡Feliz Navidad!*, Merry Christmas!

navideño,-a *adj* Christmas: *regalos navideños*, Christmas presents.

navío *nm* ship.

neblina *nf* mist.

necesariamente *adv* necessarily.

necesario,-a *adj* necessary: *es necesario cambiar la ley*, the law needs to be changed; *es necesario que te esfuerces*, you need to make an effort.

● **hacerse necesario,-a 1** *(algo)* to be required. **2** *(persona)* to become essential.

● **más de lo necesario** more than necessary.

● **si fuera necesario** if need be.

neceser *nm* **1** *(de aseo)* GB toilet bag; US toilet kit. **2** *(de maquillaje)* make-up bag.

necesidad *nf* **1** *(falta)* need: *la necesidad de un cambio*, the need for a change; *la necesidad de comer*, the need to eat. **2** *(cosa esencial)* necessity. **3** *(pobreza)* poverty, want.

● **de necesidad** essential.

● **hacer sus necesidades** to relieve oneself.

● **tener necesidad de algo** to need STH.

necesitado,-a *adj* needy, poor.

necesitar *vt* to need: *necesito que me ayudes*, I need you to help me.

● **"Se necesita camarero"** "Waiter required".

necio,-a *adj* foolish.

▶ *nm,f* fool.

neerlandés,-esa *adj* Dutch.

▶ *nm,f (hombre)* Dutchman [*pl* -men]; *(mujer)* Dutch woman [*pl* women].

▶ *nm* **neerlandés** *(idioma)* Dutch.

nefasto,-a *adj* **1** *(desastroso)* disastrous. **2** *(perjudicial)* harmful. **3** *(pésimo)* awful, dreadful.

negación *nf* **1** *(de un ideal)* negation. **2** *(de una acusación)* denial. **3** *(negativa)* refusal. **4** *(en gramática)* negative.

negado,-a *adj* useless.

▶ *nm,f* nohoper.

● **ser negado,-a para algo** to be useless at STH.

negar *vt* **1** *(acusación, afirmación)* to deny. **2** *(permiso, solicitud)* to refuse.

▶ *vpr* **negarse** to refuse: *me niego a creerlo*, I refuse to believe it.

● **negar con la cabeza** to shake one's head [*pt* **shook**; *pp* **shaken**].

negativa *nf* refusal.

negativo,-a *adj* negative.

▶ *nm* **negativo** negative.

negligencia *nf* negligence.

negligente *adj* negligent.

negociación *nf* negotiation.

■ **negociación colectiva** collective bargaining.

negociante *nmf* dealer.

negociar *vi* **1** *(comerciar)* to trade, deal [*pt & pp* **dealt**]. **2** *(hablar)* to negotiate.

▶ *vt (hablar)* to negotiate.

negocio *nm* **1** *(comercio, actividad)* business. **2** *(transacción)* deal, transaction.

● **hacer un buen negocio 1** *(trato comercial)* to do a good deal. **2** *(gen)* to do well.

● **hacer negocio 1** *(comerciar)* to do business. **2** *(lucrarse)* to make money.

negro,-a *adj* **1** *(color, raza, pelo)* black. **2** *(tono, ojos, piel)* dark. **3** *(bronceado)* suntanned.
► *nm,f (hombre)* black man [*pl* **men**]; *(mujer)* black woman [*pl* **women**].
► *nm* **negro 1** *(color)* black. **2** *(escritor)* ghostwriter.
● **pasarlas negras** to have a rough time of it.
● **poner negro a** ALGN to get SB's goat: *me pone negro tanta jerga*, all this jargon gets me goat.
● **verlo todo negro** to be very pessimistic.
nene,-a *nm,f* baby.
nervio *nm* **1** nerve. **2** *(de la carne)* tendon, sinew.
● **pasar nervios/tener nervios** to be nervous.
nerviosismo *nm* nervousness.
nervioso,-a *adj* nervous.
● **estar nervioso,-a** to be nervous.
● **poner nervioso,-a a** ALGN to get on SB's nerves.
● **ponerse nervioso,-a** to get all excited.
neto,-a *adj* **1** *(peso, cantidad)* net. **2** *(claro)* neat, clear.
neumático,-a *adj* pneumatic.
► *nm* **neumático** GB tyre; US tire.
neura *nf fam* hang-up, pet obsession: *cada uno tiene sus neuras*, we all have our hang-ups.
► *adj - nmf fam* neurotic.
neurótico,-a *adj - nm,f* neurotic.
neutral *adj - nmf* neutral.
neutro,-a *adj* **1** *(neutral)* neutral. **2** *(género)* neuter.
nevada *nf* snowfall.
nevado,-a *adj (ciudad, prado)* snow-covered; *(montaña, pico)* snow-covered, snow-capped: *todo estaba nevado*, everything was covered in snow.
nevar *vi* to snow: *nieva*, it's snowing.
nevera *nf* fridge, refrigerator.
nexo *nm* link.
ni *conj* **1** *(en doble negación)* neither... nor: *no tengo tiempo ni dinero*, I have got neither time nor money. **2** *(ni siquiera)* not even: *ni por dinero*, not even for money.
● **¡ni hablar!** no way!
Nicaragua *nf* Nicaragua.

nicho *nm* niche.
nicotina *nf* nicotine.
nido *nm* nest.
niebla *nf* fog.
nieto,-a *nm,f (gen)* grandchild [*pl* **-children**]; *(niño)* grandson; *(niña)* granddaughter.
nieve *nf* snow.
ningún *adj →* ninguno,-a.
● **de ningún modo** no way.
● **en ningún momento** never.
ninguno,-a *adj* no, not... any: *no veo ninguna diferencia*, I see no difference, I don't see any difference.
► *pron* **1** *(hablando de varias personas o cosas)* none: *ninguno de nosotros vio nada*, none of us saw anything; *no ha venido ninguno de los invitados*, none of the guests has come; *tengo tres relojes, pero ninguno funciona*, I've got three watches, but none of them works. **2** *(hablando de dos personas o cosas)* neither: *ninguno de los dos funciona*, neither of them works. **3** *(nadie)* nobody, no one: *ninguno lo vio*, nobody saw it, no one saw it.
● **ninguna parte/ningún sitio** nowhere, not ... anywhere: *no lo encuentro por ninguna parte*, I can't find it anywhere.
niñera *nf* nursemaid, nanny.
niñez *nf* childhood.
niño,-a *nm,f (gen)* child [*pl* **children**]; *(chico)* boy; *(chica)* girl; *(bebé)* baby.
● **de niño,-a** as a child.
● **desde niño,-a** from childhood.
níspero *nm* **1** *(fruto)* medlar. **2** *(árbol)* medlar, medlar tree.
nítido,-a *adj* **1** *(imagen, enfoque)* sharp. **2** *(recuerdo, lenguaje)* clear.
nitrógeno *nm* nitrogen.
nivel *nm* **1** *(en una escala, jerarquía)* level: *1.000 metros sobre el nivel del mar*, 1,000 metres above sea level; *nivel de colesterol*, cholesterol level. **2** *(calidad)* standard: *un buen nivel de juego*, a good standard of play; *un equipo de mucho nivel*, a high calibre team. **3** *(instrumento)* level.
● **a nivel del mar** at sea level.
■ **nivel de vida** standard of living.
nivelar *vt* to level.
no *adv* **1** no, not: *no, no quiero agua*, no,

I don't want any water; *ino al racismo!*, no more racism!; *no lejos de aquí*, not far from here; *¿vendrás? - hoy no*, will you be coming? - not today. **2** *(prefijo)* non: *la no violencia*, nonviolence.

▶ *nm* no: *un no rotundo*, a definite no.

● **¡a que no!** I bet you don't.

● **el no va más** the ultimate.

● **..., ¿no?** tag question: *eres Virgo, ¿no?*, you're a Virgo, aren't you?; *lo viste, ¿no?*, you saw it, didn't you?

noble *adj* noble.

▶ *nmf (hombre)* nobleman [*pl* -**men**]; *(mujer)* noblewoman [*pl* -**women**].

nobleza *nf* nobility.

noche *nf* night: *a las nueve de la noche*, at nine p.m..

● **buenas noches 1** (saludo) good evening. **2** (despedida) good night.

● **de la noche a la mañana** overnight.

● **esta noche** tonight.

● **hacerse de noche** to get dark.

● **por la noche** at night.

nochebuena *nf* Christmas Eve.

nochevieja *nf* New Year's Eve.

noción *nf* notion.

▶ *nf pl* **nociones** basic knowledge *sing*: *si tienes nociones de alemán*, if you have a basic knowledge of German.

nocivo,-a *adj* harmful.

nocturno,-a *adj* **1** *(gen)* night. **2** *(animal)* nocturnal.

nogal *nm* walnut tree.

nómada *nmf* nomad.

▶ *adj* nomadic.

nombrar *vt (para un cargo)* to appoint.

nombre *nm* **1** *(gen)* name. **2** *(sustantivo)* noun.

● **a nombre de 1** (carta) addressed to. **2** (cuenta bancaria) in the name of.

● **en nombre de** on behalf of.

■ **nombre artístico** stage name.

■ **nombre de dominio** domain name.

■ **nombre de pila** first name, Christian name.

■ **nombre propio** proper noun.

■ **nombre y apellidos** full name.

nómina *nf* **1** *(lista de empleados)* payroll. **2** *(sueldo)* pay.

● **estar en nómina** to be on the staff.

nórdico,-a *adj* **1** *(del norte)* northern. **2** *(escandinavo)* Nordic.

noreste *nm* northeast.

noria *nf* **1** *(para agua)* water-wheel. **2** *(de feria)* big wheel.

norma *nf* rule.

normal *adj* **1** *(común, usual)* normal. **2** *(nada especial)* ordinary.

normalmente *adv* normally.

noroeste *nm* northwest.

norte *adj - nm (punto cardinal)* north.

● **perder el norte** to lose one's direction.

norteamericano,-a *adj - nm,f* North American, US: *el gobierno norteamericano*, the US government.

Noruega *nf* Norway.

noruego,-a *adj - nm,f* Norwegian.

nos *pron* **1** *(complemento)* us: *nos ha visto*, he has seen us. **2** *(reflexivo)* ourselves: *nos lavamos*, we wash ourselves. **3** *(recíproco)* each other: *nos queremos mucho*, we love each other very much.

nosotros,-as *pron* **1** *(sujeto)* we: *nosotros lo vimos*, we saw it. **2** *(complemento, con preposiciones)* us: *con nosotros,-as*, with us.

nostalgia *nf* nostalgia.

nostálgico,-a *adj* nostalgic.

nota *nf* **1** *(anotación)* note. **2** *(calificación)* GB mark; US grade. **3** *(cuenta)* bill. **4** *fig (detalle)* touch. **5** *(musical)* note.

● **sacar buenas notas** to get good marks.

● **tomar nota de algo 1** (apuntar) to note STH down. **2** (fijarse) to take note of STH.

notable *adj* notable.

▶ *nm* very good: *saqué un notable*, I got a B.

notar *vt* **1** *(percibir)* to notice. **2** *(sentir)* to feel [*pt & pp* **felt**].

▶ *vpr* **notarse 1** *(percibirse)* to show [*pt* **showed**; *pp* **shown**]: *no se nota nada*, it doesn't show. **2** *(sentirse)* to feel [*pt & pp* **felt**].

● **hacerse notar** to draw attention to oneself [*pt* **drew**; *pp* **drawn**].

● **se nota que...** you can see that....

notario,-a *nm,f* notary.

noticia *nf* news *pl*: *una noticia*, a piece of news.

● **dar la noticia** to break the news [*pt* **broke**; *pp* **broken**].

● **las noticias** (en televisión) the news.

● **ser una buena noticia** to be good news.

● **tener noticias de ALGN** to hear from SB.

noticiario *nm* news *sing*.
notificar *vt* to notify.
notorio,-a *adj* well-known.
novatada *nf (broma)* practical joke; *(error)* beginner's mistake.
novato,-a *adj (persona)* inexperienced.
▶ *nm,f* novice, beginner.
novecientos,-as *num* nine hundred.
novedad *nf* **1** *(cualidad)* newness. **2** *(cosa nueva)* novelty. **3** *(cambio)* change. **4** *(noticia)* news *pl*.
novela *nf* novel.
■ **novela corta** short story.
■ **novela negra** hard-boiled novel.
■ **novela policíaca** detective story.
■ **novela rosa** romance.
novelista *nmf* novelist.
noveno,-a *num* ninth.
noventa *num* ninety.
noviazgo *nm* engagement.
noviembre *nm* November.
novillo *nm* young bull.
● **hacer novillos** GB to play truant; US to play hooky.
novio,-a *nm,f* **1** *(chico)* boyfriend; *(chica)* girlfriend. **2** *(prometido - chico)* fiancé; *(- chica)* fiancée. **3** *(en boda - hombre)* bridegroom; *(- mujer)* bride.
nubarrón *nm* storm cloud.
nube *nf* **1** cloud. **2** *(multitud)* swarm, crowd.
● **poner a** ALGN **por las nubes** to praise SB to the skies.
nublado,-a *adj* cloudy, overcast.
nublarse *vpr* to cloud over.
nuboso,-a *adj* cloudy.
nuca *nf* nape of the neck.
nuclear *adj* nuclear.
núcleo *nm* **1** nucleus. **2** *(parte central)* core. **3** *(grupo de gente)* circle, group.
nudillo *nm* knuckle.
nudo *nm* **1** *(atadura)* knot. **2** *(vínculo)* link, tie. **3** *(punto principal)* crux, core. **4** *(de comunicaciones)* GB centre; US center; *(de ferrocarril)* junction.
● **hacer un nudo** to tie a knot.
● **hacérsele a uno un nudo en la garganta** to get a lump in one's throat.
■ **nudo corredizo** slipknot.
nuera *nf* daughter-in-law.
nuestro,-a *adj* our, of ours: *nuestro*

amigo Carlos, our friend Carlos; *es amigo nuestro*, he's a friend of ours.
▶ *pron* ours: *este libro es nuestro*, this book is ours.
■ **los nuestros** *fam* our side, our people.
nuevamente *adv* again.
nueve *num* nine; *(en fechas)* ninth.
nuevo,-a *adj* **1** *(reciente)* new. **2** *(adicional)* further.
▶ *nm,f (recién llegado)* newcomer; *(principiante)* beginner.
● **de nuevo** again.
● **estar como nuevo,-a 1** (objeto) to be as good as new. **2** (persona) to feel like a new man/woman [*pt & pp* **felt**].
● **¿qué hay de nuevo?** *fam* what's new?
nuez *nf* walnut.
■ **nuez de Adán** Adam's apple.
■ **nuez moscada** nutmeg.
nulo,-a *adj* **1** *(inepto)* useless. **2** *(sin valor)* invalid.
numeración *nf* numeration.
■ **numeración arábiga** Arabic numerals *pl*.
■ **numeración romana** Roman numerals *pl*.
numerador *nm* numerator.
numeral *nm* numeral.
numerar *vt* to number.
numérico,-a *adj* numerical.
número *nm* **1** number. **2** *(ejemplar)* number, issue. **3** *(de zapatos)* size. **4** *(en espectáculo)* act, number.
● **en números redondos** in round figures.
● **montar un número** *fam* to make a scene.
numeroso,-a *adj* numerous; *(grupo)* large.
nunca *adv* **1** *(en negativa)* never. **2** *(en interrogativa)* ever: *¿has visto nunca cosa igual?*, have you ever seen anything like it?
● **casi nunca** hardly ever.
● **más que nunca** more than ever.
● **nunca jamás** never ever.
● **nunca más** never again.
nutria *nf* otter.
nutrición *nf* nutrition.
nutrir *vt* to feed [*pt & pp* **fed**].
▶ *vpr* **nutrirse** to feed [*pt & pp* **fed**].
nutritivo,-a *adj* nutritious, nourishing.

Ñ

ñoñería *nf* **1** *(cosa)* insipidness. **2** *(persona)* fussiness.

ñoñez *nf* **1** *(cosa)* insipidness. **2** *(persona)* fussiness.

ñoño,-a *adj* **1** *(cosa)* insipid. **2** *(persona)* fussy.

ñoqui *nm* gnocchi *pl*.

ñu *nm* gnu [*pl* -**s**].

O

o *conj* or.
● **o... o...** either... or....
● **o sea** that is to say.
oasis *nm* oasis.
obedecer *vt (a persona, norma)* to obey.
▶ *vi (a causa)* to be due.
obediencia *nf* obedience.
obediente *adj* obedient.
obesidad *nf* obesity.
obeso,-a *adj* obese.
obispo *nm* bishop.
objeción *nf* objection.
■ **objeción de conciencia** conscientious objection.
objetar *vt* to object.
objetivo,-a *adj* objective.
▶ *nm* **objetivo 1** *(fin)* aim, goal. **2** *(de ataque)* target. **3** *(lente)* lens.
objeto *nm* **1** *(cosa)* object. **2** *(fin)* purpose. **3** *(tema)* object.
● **con objeto de** in order to.
■ **objetos de escritorio** stationery.
■ **objetos perdidos** lost property *sing*.
objetor,-ra *adj* objecting, dissenting.
▶ *nm,f* objector.
● **objetor de conciencia** conscientious objector.
oblicuo,-a *adj* oblique.
obligación *nf (deber)* obligation.
obligar *vt* to oblige, force.
● **obligar a ALGN a hacer algo** to force SB to do STH.
obligatorio,-a *adj* compulsory, obligatory.
oboe *nm* oboe.
obra *nf* **1** *(de arte, ingeniería)* work; *(de literatura)* book; *(de teatro)* play. **2** *(acto)* deed. **3** *(institución)* foundation. **4** *(edificio en construcción)* building site.

▶ *nf pl* **obras** *(en casa)* building work; *(en la calle)* roadworks.
● **"En obras"** "Building works": *página en obras*, site under constructions.
■ **obra benéfica** act of charity.
■ **obra de arte** work of art.
■ **obra de caridad** charitable deed.
■ **obra maestra** masterpiece.
obrar *vi (proceder)* to act.
▶ *vt (trabajar)* to work.
obrero,-a *adj* working.
▶ *nm,f* worker.
obscurecer *vt (ensombrecer)* to darken.
▶ *vi (anochecer)* to get dark.
▶ *vpr* **obscurecerse** *(nublarse)* to get darker.
obscuridad *nf* **1** *(de lugar, color, pelo)* darkness. **2** *(de texto, explicación)* obscurity.
obscuro,-a *adj* **1** *(lugar, color, pelo)* dark. **2** *(origen, texto, explicación)* obscure; *(futuro)* uncertain; *(asunto)* shady.
● **a obscuras** in the dark.
obsequiar *vt* **1** *(dar)* to give. **2** *(agasajar)* to entertain.
● **obsequiar a ALGN con algo** to give SB STH.
obsequio *nm* gift.
observación *nf* observation.
observador,-ra *adj* observant.
▶ *nm,f* observer.
observar *vt* **1** *(mirar)* to observe. **2** *(notar)* to notice. **3** *(cumplir)* to obey.
observatorio *nm* observatory.
■ **observatorio meteorológico** weather station.
obsesión *nf* obsession.

obsesionar *vt* to obsess.

▶ *vpr* **obsesionarse** to become obsessed.

obstáculo *nm* obstacle, hindrance.

obstante.

● **no obstante** however, nevertheless.

obstinado,-a *adj* obstinate, stubborn.

obstinarse *vpr* to persist: *se obstinó en desoír las advertencias*, she persistently ignored the warnings.

obstruir *vt* **1** *(tubería, vena)* to block. **2** *(investigación, justicia)* obstruct.

▶ *vpr* **obstruirse** to get blocked up.

obtención *nf* obtaining: *los documentos necesarios para la obtención del visado*, the documents required for obtaining the visa.

obtener *vt* *(alcanzar)* to obtain.

▶ *vpr* **obtenerse** *(provenir)* to come.

obtuso,-a *adj* obtuse.

obús *nm* shell.

obvio,-a *adj* obvious.

oca *nf* goose [*pl* **geese**].

ocasión *nf* **1** *(momento)* occasion. **2** *(oportunidad)* opportunity, chance. **3** *(ganga)* bargain.

● **dar ocasión a algo** to give rise to STH.

● **de ocasión 1** (segunda mano) second-hand. **2** (barato) bargain.

● **en cierta ocasión** once.

ocasionar *vt (causar)* to cause.

ocaso *nm* **1** *(anochecer)* sunset. **2** *(occidente)* west. **3** *fig (declive)* fall, decline.

occidental *adj* western.

▶ *nmf (persona)* westerner.

occidente *nm* the West.

oceánico,-a *adj* oceanic.

océano *nm* ocean.

ochenta *num* eighty.

ocho *num* eight; *(en fechas)* eighth.

ochocientos,-as *num* eight hundred.

ocio *nm (tiempo libre)* leisure.

ocioso,-a *adj* **1** *(inactivo)* idle. **2** *(inútil)* pointless.

▶ *nm,f* idler.

ocre *adj - nm* ochre.

octavo,-a *num* eighth.

octógono *nm* octagon.

octubre *nm* October.

ocular *adj* eye: *infección ocular*, eye infection.

▶ *nm* eyepiece.

oculista *nmf* oculist.

ocultar *vt* to hide [*pt* **hid**; *pp* **hidden**].

oculto,-a *adj* concealed, hidden.

ocupación *nf* occupation.

ocupado,-a *adj* **1** *(persona)* busy. **2** *(asiento)* taken; *(aseos, teléfono)* engaged. **3** *(territorio)* occupied.

ocupante *nmf* occupant.

ocupar *vt* **1** *(conquistar)* to occupy. **2** *(llenar)* to take up: *ocupa demasiado espacio*, it takes up too much space. **3** *(llevar un tiempo)* to take. **4** *(desempeñar)* to hold [*pt & pp* **held**]: *ocupa el puesto de gerente*, she holds the post of manageress. **5** *(trabajadores)* to employ. **6** *(habitar)* to live in.

▶ *vpr* **ocuparse 1** *(emplearse)* to occupy oneself. **2** *(vigilar)* to look after. **3** *(reflexionar)* to look into.

ocurrencia *nf* **1** *(agudeza)* witty remark. **2** *(idea)* idea.

ocurrente *adj* witty.

ocurrir *vi* to happen, occur.

▶ *vpr* **ocurrirse** : *se me ocurre una idea*, I've had a thought; *no se le ocurrió preguntar*, it didn't occur to her to ask.

● **¿qué te ocurre?** what's the matter?, what's up?

odiar *vt* to hate.

odio *nm* hatred.

odioso,-a *adj* hateful.

odontólogo,-a *nm,f* dental surgeon, odontologist.

oeste *nm* west.

ofender *vt* to offend.

▶ *vpr* **ofenderse** to be offended: *se ofende por nada*, he is easily offended.

ofendido,-a *adj* offended.

ofensa *nf* insult.

ofensiva *nf* offensive.

ofensivo,-a *adj* offensive.

oferta *nf* **1** *(propuesta, ganga)* offer. **2** *(en concurso)* bid, tender. **3** *(suministro)* supply.

● **de oferta** on offer.

■ **oferta y demanda** supply and demand.

oficial *adj* official.

▶ *nm* **1** *(militar)* officer. **2** *(empleado)* clerk. **3** *(obrero)* journeyman: *oficial planchista*, journeyman panel-beater.

oficina *nf* office.

■ **oficina de empleo** GB job centre; US job office.

■ **oficina de prensa** press office.
■ **oficina de turismo** tourist office.
■ **oficina pública** government office.
oficinista *nmf* office worker.
oficio *nm* **1** *(trabajo manual especializado)* trade; *(profesión)* profession: *de oficio soy yesero*, I'm a plasterer by trade. **2** *(misa)* service.
ofimática *nf* office automation.
ofrecer *vt* **1** *(dar - premio, trabajo)* to offer; *(- banquete, fiesta)* to hold [*pt & pp* **held**]; *(- regalo)* to give. **2** *(presentar - posibilidad)* to give; *(- dificultad)* to present.
▶ *vpr* **ofrecerse** *(prestarse)* to offer.
ofrecimiento *nm* offer.
ogro *nm* ogre.
oh *interj* oh!
oídas *loc* **de oídas** by hearsay: *testimonio de oídas*, hearsay evidence; *la conozco de oídas*, I've heard of her.
oído *nm* **1** *(sentido)* hearing. **2** *(órgano)* ear.
● **de oído** by ear.
oír *vt* to hear [*pt & pp* **heard**].
● **¡oye!** hey!
● **como lo oyes** *fam* believe it or not.
ojal *nm* buttonhole.
ojalá *interj* if only, I wish: *¡ojalá fuera rico!*, I wish I were rich!
ojeada *nf* glance, quick look.
● **echar una ojeada 1** (mirar) to have a quick look. **2** (vigilar) to keep an eye on.
ojear *vt* *(mirar)* to have a quick look at.
ojeras *nm pl* bags under the eyes: *tienes ojeras*, you've got bags under your eyes.
ojo *nm* **1** *(órgano)* eye. **2** *(agujero)* hole.
▶ *interj* **¡ojo!** be careful!
● **a ojo** at a rough guess.
● **mirar con buenos ojos** to look favourably on.
● **no pegar ojo** not to sleep a wink.
● **tener ojo clínico** to have a good eye.
■ **ojo de buey** porthole.
■ **ojo de la cerradura** keyhole.
■ **ojo morado** black eye.
ola *nf* wave.
olé *interj* bravo!
oleada *nf* wave: *una oleada de gente*, a surge of people.
oleaje *nm* swell.
óleo *nm* *(material)* oil paint; *(cuadro)* oil painting.
oler *vt-vi* to smell: *huele a gas*, I can smell gas.

● **oler a chamusquina** to smell fishy.
● **olerse algo** to suspect STH.
olfatear *vt* *(oler)* to sniff, smell.
olfato *nm* **1** *(sentido)* sense of smell. **2** *fig* *(intuición)* good nose.
olimpiada *nf* Olympiad.
■ **las Olimpiadas** the Olympic Games.
olímpico,-a *adj* Olympic.
oliva *adj - nm* *(color)* olive.
▶ *nf* *(aceituna)* olive.
■ **olivas rellenas** stuffed olives.
olivar *nm* olive grove.
olivo *nm* olive tree.
olla *nf* pot.
■ **olla a presión** pressure cooker.
■ **olla exprés** pressure cooker.
olmo *nm* elm.
olor *nm* smell: *tiene olor a pescado*, it smells of fish.
■ **olor corporal** body odour.
oloroso,-a *adj* fragrant, sweet-smelling.
olvidadizo,-a *adj* forgetful.
olvidar *vt* **1** *(gen)* to forget [*pt* **forgot**; *pp* **forgotten**]. **2** *(dejar)* to leave [*pt & pp* **left**]: *olvidé la bufanda en el tren*, I left my scarf on the train.
▶ *vpr* **olvidarse** to forget [*pt* **forgot**; *pp* **forgotten**].
olvido *nm* **1** *(falta de memoria)* oblivion. **2** *(lapsus)* oversight.
ombligo *nm* navel.
omisión *nf* omission.
omitir *vt* to omit.
once *num* eleven; *(en fechas)* eleventh.
onceavo,-a *num* eleventh.
onda *nf* **1** *(del pelo)* wave. **2** *(del agua)* ripple.
■ **onda corta** short wave.
■ **onda expansiva** shock wave.
■ **onda larga** long wave.
■ **onda media** medium wave.
ondear *vi* **1** *(bandera)* to flutter. **2** *(agua)* to ripple.
● **ondear a media asta** to be flying at half mast.
ondulación *nf* **1** *(de movimiento)* undulation. **2** *(de pelo)* wave. **3** *(de agua)* ripple.
ondulado,-a *adj* wavy.
ondulante *adj* undulating.
ondular *vt* *(pelo)* to wave.
▶ *vi* *(moverse)* to undulate.
ONG *abr* non-governmental organization, NGO.

ONU *abr* UNO.

opaco,-a *adj* opaque.

opción *nf* option.

ópera *nf* opera.

operación *nf* **1** *(gen)* operation. **2** *(financiera)* transaction, deal.

operador,-ra *nm, f* operator.

■ **operador de mercado** trader.

■ **operador turístico** tour operator.

operar *vt* **1** *(quirúrgicamente)* to operate: *me operaron de la próstata*, I had an operation on my prostate; *la operaron de inmediato*, she was operated on immediately. **2** *(producir)* to bring about [*pt & pp* **brought**].

► *vi (hacer efecto)* to operate.

► *vpr* **operarse** *(quirúrgicamente)* to have an operation: *se ha operado de la nariz*, he's had a nose operation.

operario,-a *nm, f* operator, worker.

opinar *vt* to think [*pt & pp* **thought**].

► *vi* to express an opinion.

opinión *nf (juicio)* opinion.

● **cambiar de opinión** to change one's mind.

■ **opinión pública** public opinion.

oponente *adj* opposing.

► *nmf* opponent.

oponer *vt* **1** *(argumento)* to put forward. **2** *(resistencia)* to offer.

► *vpr* **oponerse** *(estar en contra)* to oppose. **2** *(ser contrario)* to be opposed.

oportunidad *nf* **1** *(ocasión)* opportunity. **2** *(ganga)* bargain. **3** *(conveniencia)* advisability.

oportunista *adj - nmf* opportunist.

oportuno,-a *adj* **1** *(a tiempo)* opportune, timely. **2** *(conveniente)* appropriate.

oposición *nf* **1** *(enfrentamiento)* opposition. **2** *(examen)* competitive examination.

opresión *nf* oppression.

oprimir *vt* **1** *(tecla, botón)* to press. **2** *(persona, pueblo)* to oppress.

optar *vi* **1** *(elegir)* to choose [*pt* **chose**; *pp* **chosen**]: *optó por dimitir*, she chose to resign; *opté por el periodismo*, I chose journalism, I opted for journalism. **2** *(aspirar)* to apply.

optativo,-a *adj* optional, elective.

óptica *nf* **1** *(tienda)* optician's. **2** *(ciencia)* optics.

óptico,-a *adj* optical.

► *nm, f* optician.

optimismo *nm* optimism.

optimista *adj* optimistic.

► *nmf* optimist.

óptimo,-a *adj* optimum.

opuesto,-a *adj* opposite.

oración *nf* **1** *(rezo)* prayer. **2** *(frase)* clause, sentence.

■ **oración principal** main clause.

■ **oración subordinada** subordinate clause.

orador,-ra *nm, f* speaker.

oral *adj* oral.

● **por vía oral** to be taken orally.

orangután *nm* orang-utan.

orar *vi* to pray.

órbita *nf* **1** *(de satélite)* orbit. **2** *(de ojo)* socket.

orca *nf* killer whale.

orden *nm* **1** *(disposición)* order: *en orden alfabético*, in alphabetical order. **2** *fig (clase, tipo)* nature: *consideraciones de orden filosófico*, considerations of a philosophical nature. **3** *(ámbito)* sphere: *la continuidad en el orden político*, continuity in the political sphere.

► *nf* **1** *(mandato, asociación)* order. **2** *(judicial)* warrant.

● **del orden de** GB in the order of; US on the order of.

● **de primer orden** first-rate.

● **poner algo en orden** to sort STH out.

● **por orden de** by order of.

■ **orden de arresto** arrest warrant.

■ **orden de pago** money order.

■ **orden del día** agenda.

■ **orden judicial** court order.

■ **orden público** law and order.

ordenado,-a *adj* tidy.

● **de manera ordenada** in an orderly fashion.

ordenador,-ra *adj* ordering.

► *nm* **ordenador** computer.

● **de ordenador** computer: *juego de ordenador*, computer game.

■ **ordenador personal** personal computer.

■ **ordenador portátil** laptop.

ordenanza *nm* **1** *(en oficina)* messenger. **2** *(soldado)* orderly.

► *nf (código)* order, ordinance.

ordenar *vt* **1** *(arreglar)* to put in order; *(habitación)* to tidy up. **2** *(mandar)* to order: *nos ordenaron bajar del coche*, they ordered us to get out of the car. **3** *(de sacerdote)* to ordain.

● **ordenar las ideas** to collect one's thoughts.
ordeñar *vt* to milk.
ordinal *adj - nm* ordinal.
ordinario,-a *adj* **1** *(corriente)* ordinary. **2** *(grosero)* vulgar, common.

● **de ordinario** usually.
orégano *nm* oregano.
oreja *nf* ear.
orfanato *nm* orphanage.
orgánico,-a *adj* organic.
organigrama *nm* *(de empresa)* organization chart; *(de procedimiento, sistema)* flow chart.
organismo *nm* **1** *(ser viviente)* organism. **2** *(entidad pública)* organization, body.

■ **organismo no gubernamental** non-governmental organization.
organización *nf* organization.
organizado,-a *adj* organized.
organizador,-ra *adj* organizing.
► *nm,f* organizer.
organizar *vt* to organize.
► *vpr* **organizarse 1** *(suceso)* to be: *se organizó un escándalo tremendo*, there was a terrible scandal. **2** *(persona)* to organize oneself.
órgano *nm* organ.
orgasmo *nm* orgasm.
orgía *nf* orgy.
orgullo *nm* pride.

● **tener el orgullo de hacer algo** to be proud to do STH.
orgulloso,-a *adj* proud.
orientación *nf* **1** *(dirección)* orientation. **2** *(enfoque)* approach. **3** *(guía)* guidance.

● **curso de orientación** introductory course.
■ **orientación profesional** vocational guidance.
oriental *adj* eastern.
► *nmf* Oriental.
orientar *vt* **1** *(dirigir)* to orientate. **2** *(guiar)* to guide.
► *vpr* **orientarse** *(encontrar el camino)* to find one's way about [*pt & pp* **found**].
oriente *nm* east.

■ **Oriente Medio** Middle East.
■ **Oriente Próximo** Near East.

orificio *nm* orifice.
origen *nm* origin: *de origen español*, of Spanish extraction.
original *adj - nm* original.
originar *vt* to give rise to.
► *vpr* **originarse** to originate.
originario,-a *adj* original.

● **ser originario,-a de 1** *(persona)* to come from. **2** *(costumbre)* to originate in.
orilla *nf* **1** *(borde)* edge. **2** *(del río)* bank; *(del mar)* shore.

● **a la orilla del mar** by the sea.
orina *nf* urine.
orinal *nm* *(de adulto)* chamber pot; *(de niño)* potty.
orinar *vi* to urinate.
► *vpr* **orinarse** to wet oneself.
oro *nm* gold.

● **de oro** gold: *un reloj de oro*, a gold watch.
orquesta *nf* **1** *(clásica, sinfónica)* orchestra. **2** *(banda)* dance band.
orquídea *nf* orchid.
ortiga *nf* nettle.
ortografía *nf* spelling.
ortográfico,-a *adj* spelling.
ortopédico,-a *adj* *(cirugía)* GB orthopaedic; US orthopedic; *(pierna)* artificial.
oruga *nf* caterpillar.
os *pron* **1** *(complemento directo)* you: *os veo mañana*, I'll see you tomorrow. **2** *(complemento indirecto)* to you: *os lo mandaré*, I'll send it to you. **3** *(reflexivo)* yourselves: *os haréis daño*, you'll hurt yourselves. **4** *(recíproco)* each other: *os queréis mucho*, you love each other very much.
osadía *nf* daring.
osado,-a *adj* daring.
osar *vi* to dare.
oscilar *vi* **1** *(variar)* to fluctuate. **2** *(balancearse)* to oscillate.
oscurecer(se) *vt-vpr* **oscurecer(se)** → obscurecer.
oscuridad *nf* → obscuridad.
oscuro,-a *adj* → obscuro.
oso *nm* bear.

■ **oso de peluche** teddy bear.
■ **oso hormiguero** anteater.
■ **oso panda** panda.
■ **oso pardo** brown bear.
■ **oso polar** polar bear.
ostentación *nf* ostentation.

ostentar *vt* **1** *(exhibir)* to flaunt. **2** *(poseer)* to hold [*pt & pp* **held**].
● **ostentar el cargo de** to hold the position of [*pt & pp* **held**].
ostra *nf* oyster.
▶ *interj* **¡ostras!** GB crikey!; US gee!
● **aburrirse como una ostra** to be bored stiff.
OTAN *abr* NATO.
otoño *nm* GB autumn; US fall.
otorgar *vt* **1** *(conceder)* to grant; *(premio)* to award. **2** *(contrato)* to execute.
otro,-a *adj* **1** *(con sustantivo en singular)* another; *(precedido de determinante o adjetivo posesivo)* other: *vino otra persona en su lugar*, another person came in his place; *la otra silla era más cómoda*, the other chair was more confortable; *mi otro coche es un Porsche*, my other car's a Porsche. **2** *(con sustantivo en plural)* other: *entre otras cosas*, amongst other things.
▶ *pron* **1** *(singular)* another, another one: *¿quieres otro?*, would you like another one? **2** **el otro, la otra** *(cosa, persona)* the other one: *este libro no está mal, pero me gustó más el otro*, this book is all right, but I liked the other one better. **3** **los otros, las otras** *(cosa)* the other ones, the others; *(personas)* the others: *¿quieres estos guantes o los otros?*, do you want these gloves or the other ones?; *los otros también quieren venir*, the others want to come too.
● **entre otras cosas** among other things.
● **otra cosa** something else.
● **otro día** another day.
● **otro tanto** as much.
● **un día sí y otro no** every other day.
ovación *nf* ovation.
oval *adj* oval.
ovalado,-a *adj* oval.
óvalo *nm* oval.
ovario *nm* ovary.
oveja *nf* sheep [*pl* **sheep**].
● **ser la oveja negra de la familia** to be the black sheep of the family.
ovillo *nm* ball of wool.
ovino,-a *adj* sheep.
OVNI *abr* UFO.
óvulo *nm* ovule.
oxidado,-a *adj* rusty.
oxidarse *vpr* to rust, go rusty.
óxido *nm* **1** *(compuesto)* oxide. **2** *(herrumbre)* rust.
oxígeno *nm* oxygen.
oyente *nmf* **1** *(de la radio)* listener. **2** *(estudiante)* GB occasional student; US auditor.
▶ *nm pl* **oyentes** audience *sing*.
ozono *nm* ozone.
■ **capa de ozono** ozone layer.

P

pabellón *nm* **1** *(edificio - aislado)* block, section; *(- anexo en feria)* pavilion. **2** *(bandera)* flag. **3** *(de la oreja)* outer, ear.
■ **pabellón deportivo** sports hall.

pacer *vi* to graze.

pachucho,-a *adj* **1** *(fruta)* overripe. **2** *(persona)* under the weather, off-colour.

paciencia *nf* patience.
● **perder la paciencia** to lose one's patience [*pt & pp* **lost**].
● **tener paciencia** to be patient.

paciente *adj - nmf* patient.

pacificar *vt* to pacify.

pacífico,-a *adj* **1** *(tranquilo)* peaceful. **2** *(del Pacífico)* Pacific.
■ **el océano Pacífico** the Pacific Ocean.

pacifista *adj - nmf* pacifist.

pactar *vt-vi* to agree to: *la cantidad que pactamos*, the amount that we agreed to.

pacto *nm* pact, agreement: *hicieron un pacto*, they made an agreement; *rompimos el pacto*, we broke the agreement.
■ **pacto de no agresión** non-aggression pact.
■ **pacto social** wage settlement.

padecer *vt-vi* to suffer: *padece dolores de cabeza*, he suffers from headaches.
► *vi* to suffer: *padezco del pecho*, I have a bad chest.

padrastro *nm* stepfather.

padre *nm* father.
► *adj fam* terrible: *un disgusto padre*, a terrible disappointment; *un lío padre*, a tremendous row; *pegarse la vida padre*, to live the life of Riley.
► *nmpl* **padres** *(padre y madre)* parents.
■ **padre de familia** family man [*pl* **men**].
■ **padre político** father-in-law.

padrenuestro *nm* Lord's Prayer.

padrino *nm* **1** *(de bautizo)* godfather. **2** *(de boda - padre)* bride's father; *(- amigo)* best friend. **3** *(patrocinador)* sponsor.

paella *nf* paella.

paga *nf* *(sueldo)* pay; *(de niños)* pocket money: *cobro 12 pagas al año*, I get yearly payments.
■ **paga de Navidad** Christmas bonus.
■ **paga extra** bonus.

pagano,-a *adj - nm,f* pagan.

pagar *vt* *(compra, entrada)* to pay for [*pt & pp* **paid**]; *(sueldo, alquiler, cuenta)* to pay [*pt & pp* **paid**]; *(deuda)* to pay off [*pt & pp* **paid**]; *(favor)* to repay [*pt & pp* **repaid**]: *las cervezas ya están pagadas*, the beers have been paid for; *los niños no pagan*, children get in free.
● **pagar al contado** to pay cash [*pt & pp* **paid**].
● **pagar a plazos** to pay in installments [*pt & pp* **paid**].
● **¡me las pagarás!** *fam* you'll pay for this!

página *nf* page.
■ **página personal** home page.
■ **página web** web page.
■ **páginas amarillas** yellow pages.

pago *nm* **1** *(gen)* payment: *un único pago de mil euros*, a single payment of a thousand euros. **2** *(recompensa)* reward.
● **en pago por** in payment for, in return for.
■ **pago al contado** cash payment.
■ **pago anticipado** advance payment.
■ **pago inicial** down payment.
■ **pago por visión** pay per view.

pagoda *nf* pagoda.

país *nm* country.

- **país natal** native country.
- **País Vasco** Basque Country.

paisaje *nm* **1** *(terreno)* landscape. **2** *(vista)* scenery.

paisano,-a *nm,f (compatriota - hombre)* fellow countryman [*pl* **-men**]; *(- mujer)* fellow countrywoman [*pl* **-women**].

► *nm* **paisano** civilian.

- **de paisano** in plain clothes.

paja *nf* **1** *(tallo seco)* straw. **2** *(en escrito, discurso)* padding, waffle. **3** *vulg (masturbación)* wank.

- **hacerse una paja** to wank.

pajarería *nf* pet shop.

pajarita *nf* **1** *(lazo)* bow tie. **2** *(de papel)* paper bird.

pájaro *nm* bird.

- **más vale pájaro en mano que ciento volando** a bird in the hand is worth two in the bush.
- **matar dos pájaros de un tiro** to kill two birds with one stone.
- **pájaro carpintero** woodpecker.

paje *nm* page.

pala *nf* **1** *(para cavar)* spade. **2** *(de cocina)* slice. **3** *(de pelota)* bat. **4** *(de hélice, remo)* blade.

palabra *nf* word: *palabra por palabra*, word for word; *dijo unas palabras*, he said a few words; *es de pocas palabras*, he's not very chatty.

- **dar uno su palabra** to give one's word.
- **dejar a uno con la palabra en la boca** to cut SB off in mid-sentence [*pt & pp* **cut**].
- **en una palabra** in a word, to sum up.
- **tener la palabra** to have the floor.
- **tener la última palabra** to have the final say.
- **¡eso son palabras mayores!** that's quite something!
- **palabra clave** keyword.
- **palabra de honor** word of honour.

palabrota *nf* swearword.

- **decir palabrotas** to swear [*pt* **swore**; *pp* **sworn**].

palacio *nm* palace.

- **palacio de congresos** conference centre.
- **palacio de deportes** sports centre.

- **palacio de justicia** courthouse.
- **palacio real** royal palace.

paladar *nm* palate.

- **tener buen paladar** to have a good palate.

paladear *vt* to savour, relish.

palanca *nf* lever.

- **palanca de cambio** gear lever, gearstick.

palangana *nf* washbasin.

palco *nm* box.

- **palco de autoridades** royal box.

Palestina *nf* Palestine.

palestino,-a *adj - nm,f* Palestinian.

paleta *nf* **1** *(de pintor)* palette. **2** *(de albañil)* trowel. **3** *(de cocina)* slice. **4** *(de hélice etc)* blade.

paleto,-a *nm,f pey* country bumpkin.

palidecer *vi* to turn pale.

palidez *nf* paleness, pallor.

pálido,-a *adj* pale.

palillo *nm* **1** *(mondadientes)* toothpick. **2** *(de tambor)* drumstick.

- **palillos chinos** chopsticks.

paliza *nf* **1** *(zurra)* beating, thrashing. **2** *(derrota)* defeat. **3** *fam (pesadez)* bore.

- **darle una paliza a ALGN 1** *(pegarle)* to beat SB up [*pt* **beat**; *pp* **beaten**]. **2** *(aburrirle)* to bore SB.

palma *nf* **1** *(planta)* palm tree. **2** *(de la mano)* palm.

► *nf pl* **palmas** *(aplausos)* clapping *sing*, applause *sing*.

- **conocer algo como la palma de la mano** to know STH like the back of one's hand [*pt* **knew**; *pp* **known**].
- **llevarse la palma 1** (gen) to be the best. **2** (uso irónico) to take the biscuit.
- **tocar las palmas** to clap.

palmada *nf (golpe)* slap, pat: *le dio una palmada en la espalda*, he patted him on the back.

► *nf pl* **palmadas** *(aplausos)* clapping *sing*.

- **dar palmadas** to clap.

palmera *nf* palm tree.

palmo *nm* span, handspan.

- **palmo a palmo** inch by inch.
- **dejar a ALGN con un palmo de narices** *fam* to take the wind out of SB's sails.

palo *nm* **1** *(vara)* stick: *una pata de palo*, a wooden leg; *el palo de la escoba*, the

broom handle. **2** *(mástil)* mast. **3** *(golpe)* blow: *dar de palos a* ALGN, to beat SB; *¡qué palo si no viene!*, it'll be a real bummer if he doesn't come; *me dio palo que me viera*, I didn't like it when he saw me. **4** *(de naipes)* suit.
- **a palo seco** on its own.
- **dar palos** to hit [*pt & pp* **hit**], strike [*pt & pp* **struck**].
- **dar palos de ciego** to grope about in the dark.
- **de tal palo tal astilla** like father like son.
■ **palo de golf** golf club.

paloma *nf* dove, pigeon.
■ **paloma de la paz** dove of peace.
■ **paloma mensajera** carrier pigeon.

palomar *nm (grande)* pigeon loft; *(pequeño)* dovecote.

palomitas *nf pl* popcorn *sing.*

palomo *nm* pigeon.

palpar *vt* to touch, feel [*pt & pp* **felt**]: *se palpaba la ansiedad*, you could feel the anxiety.

palpitación *nf* palpitation.

palpitar *vi* to palpitate, throb.

pamela *nf* sun hat.

pampa *nf* pampas *pl.*

pamplina *nf* nonsense: *¡muchas pamplinas!*, that's all rubbish!, that's all nonsense!

pan *nm (alimento)* bread; *(hogaza)* round loaf [*pl* **-ves**]; *(barra)* French loaf [*pl* **-ves**]: *no pruebo el pan*, I don't eat bread; *pan con mantequilla*, bread and butter.
- **ganarse el pan** to earn one's living.
- **llamar al pan, pan y al vino, vino** to call a spade a spade.
- **ser más bueno que el pan** to be as good as gold.
- **ser pan comido** to be a piece of cake.
■ **pan de molde** sliced bread.
■ **pan integral** wholemeal bread.
■ **pan rallado** breadcrumbs *pl.*

pana *nf* corduroy.

panadería *nf* bakery, baker's.

panadero,-a *nm,f* baker.

panal *nm* honeycomb.

Panamá *nm* Panama.

panameño,-ña *adj - nm,f* Panamanian.

pancarta *nf* placard.

páncreas *nm* pancreas.

panda *nm* panda.

pandereta *nf* small tambourine.

pandero *nm* tambourine.

pandilla *nf* **1** *(de amigos)* group of friends: *tengo una pandilla guay*, I have very nice friends; *no es de mi pandilla*, he's not in my group of friends. **2** *(de criminales)* gang, band.

panecillo *nm* roll.

panel *nm* panel.
■ **panel solar** solar panel.

panera *nf (de mesa)* bread basket; *(de cocina)* GB bread bin; US bread box.

pánfilo,-a *adj* **1** *(lento)* slow. **2** *(tonto)* stupid.
► *nm,f* fool.

panfleto *nm* pamphlet.

pánico *nm* panic: *un ataque de pánico*, a panic attack.

panorama *nm* **1** *(vista)* panorama, view. **2** *(perspectiva)* outlook.

pantalla *nf* **1** *(gen)* screen. **2** *(de lámpara)* shade.
- **la pequeña pantalla** the small screen, the TV.
■ **pantalla de cristal líquido** liquid crystal display.
■ **pantalla de plasma** plasma screen.
■ **pantalla plana** flat screen.

pantalón *nm* trousers *pl.*
- **bajarse los pantalones** to give in.
- **llevar los pantalones** to wear the trousers [*pt* **wore**; *pp* **worn**].
■ **pantalón corto** shorts *pl*, short trousers *pl.*
■ **pantalón vaquero** jeans *pl.*

pantano *nm (de fango)* marsh; *(embalse)* reservoir.

pantanoso,-a *adj* marshy.

pantera *nf* panther.

pantorrilla *nf* calf [*pl* **-ves**].

pantufla *nf* slipper.

panza *nf fam* paunch, belly.

panzada *nf fam* : *me he dado una panzada de comer*, I have stuffed myself; *¡menuda panzada de dormir!*, I had a really good sleep.

pañal *nm* GB nappy ; US diaper.

paño *nm* **1** *(tela)* cloth, material. **2** *(trapo para polvo)* duster. **3** *(de pared)* panel, stretch.
► *nm pl* **paños** *(prendas)* clothes.
- **en paños menores** in one's underwear.
■ **paño de cocina** tea cloth, tea towel.

pañuelo *nm* **1** *(para sonarse)* handkerchief [*pl* -**s** o -**ves**]. **2** *(para la cabeza)* headscarf [*pl* -**s**], scarf [*pl* -**s**]. **3** *(para el cuello)* scarf [*pl* -**s**].

■ **pañuelo de papel** tissue.

papa¹ *nm (pontífice)* pope.

papa² *nf (patata)* potato [*pl* -**es**].

● **no entender ni papa** not to understand a word.

● **no saber ni papa** not to have the faintest idea.

papá *nm fam* dad, daddy.

■ **Papá Noel** Father Christmas.

papada *nf* double chin.

papagayo *nm* parrot.

papel *nm* **1** *(material)* paper. **2** *(hoja)* piece of paper, sheet of paper. **3** *(en obra, película)* role, part.

● **desempeñar el papel de** to play the part of.

● **hacer un buen papel** to do well.

● **hacer un mal papel** to do badly.

● **perder los papeles** to lose one's temper.

■ **papel carbón** carbon paper.

■ **papel de aluminio** aluminium foil.

■ **papel de calcar** tracing-paper.

■ **papel de fumar** cigarette paper.

■ **papel de lija** sandpaper.

■ **papel de plata** silver paper, tinfoil.

■ **papel higiénico** toilet paper.

■ **papel moneda** paper money.

■ **papel pintado** wallpaper.

■ **papel reciclado** recycled paper.

papeleo *nm fam* red tape.

papelera *nf* **1** *(en oficina)* wastepaper basket. **2** *(en la calle)* GB litter bin; US litter basket.

papelería *nf* stationer's.

papeleta *nf* **1** *(para votar)* ballot paper. **2** *(de examen)* report. **3** *(de sorteo)* ticket. **4** *fam (problema)* : **¡vaya papeleta!**, what an awful situation!

paperas *nf pl* mumps.

papilla *nf* **1** *(para enfermo)* pap. **2** *(para bebé)* baby food.

● **hacer papilla a** ALGN to make mincemeat of SB.

papiro *nm* papyrus.

paquete *nm* **1** *(de libros, ropa)* package, parcel; *(de tabaco, folios, galletas)* packet; *(de azúcar, harina)* bag. **2** *(conjunto)* package: **un paquete de reformas**, a package of reforms. **3** *fam (torpón)* wally, useless tool. **4** *fam (genitales)* package, bulge: **siempre va marcando paquete**, he always wears very tight trousers.

● **ir de paquete** to ride pillion [*pt* **rode**; *pp* **ridden**].

● **meterle un paquete a** ALGN to throw the book at SB [*pt* **threw**; *pp* **thrown**].

■ **paquete bomba** parcel bomb.

■ **paquete de acciones** share package.

■ **paquete de software** software package.

■ **paquete postal** parcel.

Paquistán *nm* Pakistan.

paquistaní *adj* - *nmf* Pakistani.

par *adj* **1** *(igual)* equal. **2** even: **¿pares o nones?**, odd or even?

▶ *nm (pareja)* pair: **tengo un par de dudas**, I have a couple of cuestions; **un par de veces**, a couple of times, twice.

● **a la par 1** (al mismo tiempo) at the same time. **2** (juntos) together.

● **de par en par** wide open.

● **sin par** matchless.

para *prep* **1** *(finalidad)* for, to, in order to: **es para Pepe**, it's for Pepe; **para ahorrar dinero**, (in order) to save money. **2** *(dirección)* for, to: **salimos para Lugo el domingo**, we leave for Lugo on Sunday; **el tren para Toledo**, the train to Toledo; **¿para dónde vas?**, where are you going?; **para adelante**, forwards; **para atrás**, backwards. **3** *(tiempo, fechas límites)* by: **lo necesito para esta tarde**, I need it by this afternoon; **déjalo para luego**, leave for later.

● **dar para** to be sufficient for.

● **hay para rato** it will be some time before it's over.

● **para con** towards, to.

● **para entonces** by then.

● **para que** in order that, so that.

● **¿para qué?** what for?: **¿para qué ha venido?**, why did he come?

parábola *nf* **1** parable. **2** *(curva)* parabola.

parabólico,-a *adj* parabolic: **una antena parabólica**, a satellite dish.

parabrisas *nm* GB windscreen; US windshield.

paracaídas *nm* parachute.

● **tirarse en paracaídas** to parachute.

paracaidista *nmf* **1** *(deportista)* parachutist. **2** *(militar)* paratrooper.

parachoques *nm* **1** *(de coche)* GB bumper; US fender. **2** *(de tren)* buffer.

parada *nf* **1** *(acción)* stop, halt. **2** *(de autobús, tren)* stop. **3** *(pausa)* pause. **4** DEP *(en portería)* save.

■ **parada de taxis** GB taxi stand; US cab stand.

paradero *nm* whereabouts *pl*: **está en paradero desconocido**, his whereabouts are unknown.

parado,-a *adj* **1** *(quieto)* still, motionless: **me quedé un momento parado**, I stopped for a moment; **había un coche parado delante de la iglesia**, there was a car standing in front of the church. **2** *(lento)* slow, awkward. **3** *fam (desempleado)* unemployed.
▶ *nm,f* unemployed person: **los parados**, the unemployed, the jobless; **ha aumentado el número de parados**, the number of unemployed has gone up.
● **quedarse parado** to be made redundant.
● **salir bien parado de algo** to come off well out of STH.
● **salir mal parado de algo** to come off badly out of STH.

parador *nm* hotel.

paraguas *nm* umbrella.

Paraguay *nm* Paraguay.

paraguayo,-a *adj* - *nm,f* Paraguayan.

paragüero *nm* umbrella stand.

paraíso *nm* paradise.

■ **paraíso fiscal** tax haven.

■ **paraíso terrenal** Garden of Eden.

paraje *nm* spot, place.

paralelas *nf pl* parallel bars.

paralelo,-a *adj* parallel.
▶ *nm* **paralelo** parallel.
● **en paralelo** (ELEC) paralell.

parálisis *nf* paralysis [*pl* -**es**].

■ **parálisis cerebral** cerebral palsy.

paralítico,-a *adj* - *nm,f* paralytic.

paralizar *vt* **1** to paralyse. **2** *(tráfico)* to bring to a standstill [*pt & pp* **brought**].
▶ *vpr* **paralizarse** **1** *(miembro)* to be paralysed. **2** *(actividad)* to come to a standstill.

parapente *nm* *(deporte)* paragliding; *(paracaídas)* paraglider.

parar *vt* *(detener)* to stop.

▶ *vi* **1** *(detenerse)* to stop: **¡no para!**, she never stops; **no para de hablar**, he doesn't stop talking. **2** *(acabar)* to end: **fue a parar a la cárcel**, he ended up in prison. **3** *(estar)* to be: **nunca paro en casa**, I'm never at home. **4** *(alojarse)* to stay.
▶ *vpr* **pararse** *(detenerse)* to stop: **se me ha parado el reloj**, my watch has stopped; **no se para en detalles**, he pays no attention to detail.
● **¿dónde vamos a parar?** where's it all going to end?
● **ir a parar** to end up: **el coche fue a parar al río**, the car ended up in the river.
● **pararse en seco** to stop dead.
● **sin parar** nonstop, without stopping: **fuma sin parar**, he smokes nonstop.
● **parar los pies a** ALGN to put SB in his/her place.
● **¡y para de contar!** and that's it!

pararrayos *nm* lightning conductor.

parásito,-a *adj* parasitic.
▶ *nm* **parásito** **1** parasite. **2** *fam (persona)* hanger-on.

parcela *nf* plot.

parche *nm* **1** *(remiendo)* patch. **2** *(de ojo)* eye patch. **3** *(chapuza)* botch.

■ **parche de nicotina** nicotine patch.

parchís *nm* GB ludo; US Parcheesi®.

parcial *adj* **1** *(incompleto)* partial: **eclipse parcial**, partial eclipse; **trabaja a tiempo parcial**, he works part-time. **2** *(subjetivo)* biased, partial.
▶ *nm* *(examen)* mid-term exam.

pardo,-a *adj* drab, dark grey.
▶ *nm* **pardo** drab, dark grey.

parecer *vi* **1** *(por cómo se percibe)* to seem; *(por su aspecto externo)* to look: **parece fácil**, it seems easy, it looks easy; **parece un mono**, it looks like a monkey. **2** *(opinar)* to think [*pt & pp* **thought**]: **me parece que sí**, I think so; **me parece que no**, I don't think so; **no me parece bien**, I don't think it's a good idea; **si te parece bien...**, if it's all right with you...; **¿qué te parece que vayamos al cine?**, what about going to the cinema?; **¿qué te parece?**, what do you think? **3** *(aparentar)* to look as if: **parece que va a llover**, it looks as if it's going to rain.
▶ *vpr* **parecerse** **1** to look alike, be alike: **Hugo y su hermano se parecen**, Hugo

and his brother look alike; *¿en qué nos parecemos?*, in what way are we alike? **2** to look like: *Hugo se parece a su padre*, Hugo looks like his father.

▶ *nm (opinión)* opinion: *a mi parecer*, in my opinion; *cambiar de parecer*, to change one's mind.

● **al parecer** apparently.

● **me parece mal** I think it's wrong.

● **¡parece mentira!** I can't believe it!

● **según parece** apparently.

parecido,-a *adj* similar.

▶ *nm* **parecido** resemblance, likeness.

● **bien parecido,-a** good-looking.

pared *nf* wall.

● **estar entre cuatro paredes** to be cooped up.

● **las paredes oyen** walls have ears.

● **subirse por las paredes** to hit the roof [*pt & pp* **hit**], go up the wall.

■ **pared maestra** main wall.

pareja *nf* **1** *(gen)* pair: *el ejercicio se hace por parejas*, you have to do the exercise in pairs; *he perdido la pareja de este calcetín*, I can't find the other sock. **2** *(de personas)* couple. **3** *(de baile)* partner. **4** *(compañero)* partner: *María es su pareja*, María is his partner; *viven en pareja*, they live as a couple.

● **hacer buena pareja** to be two of a kind.

■ **pareja de hecho** unmarried couple.

parentela *nf* relatives *pl*, relations *pl*.

parentesco *nm* kinship, relationship.

paréntesis *nm* **1** *(signo)* parenthesis, bracket. **2** *(pausa)* break, interruption.

● **hacer un paréntesis** to take a break.

● **entre paréntesis** in brackets.

pariente,-a *nm,f* relative.

parir *vi* to give birth to.

▶ *vt* to give birth to.

parking *nm* *(público)* GB carpark; US parking lot; *(particular)* garage: *una plaza de parking*, a parking space.

parlamentario,-a *adj* parliamentary.

▶ *nm,f* member of parliament.

parlamento *nm* parliament.

■ **Parlamento Europeo** European Parliament.

parlanchín,-ina *adj* talkative.

▶ *nm,f* chatterbox.

paro *nm* **1** *(desempleo)* unemployment. **2** *(interrupción)* stoppage. **3** *(dinero)* unem-

ployment benefit: *estoy cobrando el paro*, I'm getting unemployment benefit.

● **estar en el paro** to be out of work, be unemployed.

■ **paro cardiaco** cardiac arrest.

parodia *nf* parody.

parpadear *vi* **1** *(ojos)* to blink. **2** *(luz)* to flicker; *(estrella)* to twinkle.

párpado *nm* eyelid.

parque *nm* park.

■ **parque de atracciones** funfair.

■ **parque infantil** children's playground.

■ **parque nacional** national park.

■ **parque natural** nature reserve.

■ **parque tecnológico** techonology park.

■ **parque temático** theme park.

■ **parque zoológico** zoo [*pl* -**s**].

parqué *nm* parquet.

parra *nf* grapevine.

● **subirse a la parra** *fam* to hit the roof [*pt & pp* **hit**].

párrafo *nm* paragraph.

parrilla *nf* grill.

● **a la parrilla** grilled.

■ **parrilla de salida** starting grid.

parrillada *nf* mixed grill.

párroco *nm* parish priest.

parroquia *nf* **1** *(zona)* parish; *(iglesia)* parish church. **2** *fam (clientela)* customers *pl*, clientele.

parte *nf* **1** *(gen)* part: *lo han dividido en tres partes*, they've divided it into three parts. **2** *(en negocio)* share, interest. **3** *(en contrato)* party. **4** half: *en la primera parte no hubo goles*, there were no goals in the first half.

▶ *nm (comunicado)* report.

● **a partes iguales** in equal shares.

● **dar parte** to report: *he ido a dar parte del accidente*, I went to report the accident.

● **de parte a parte** from one side to the other.

● **de parte de** on behalf of, from.

● **¿de parte de quién?** who's calling?

● **en ninguna parte** nowhere.

● **en parte** partly.

● **estar de parte de** to support.

● **formar parte de algo** to be part of STH.

● **llevar la mejor parte** to have the best of it.

- **llevar la peor parte** to have the worst of it.
- **por todas partes** everywhere.
- **por una parte..., por otra** on the one hand..., on the other hand....
■ **parte de baja** doctor's note.
■ **parte facultativo** medical report.
■ **parte meteorológico** weather report.

participación *nf* **1** *(colaboración)* participation. **2** *(de lotería)* share. **3** *(comunicado)* announcement.

participante *adj* participating.
▶ *nmf* participant.

participar *vi (tomar parte)* to take part, participate.
▶ *vt (notificar)* to notify, inform.

participio *nm* participle.

partícula *nf* particle.

particular *adj* **1** *(específico)* particular. **2** *(especial)* special: *¿alguna novedad? - Nada de particular*, any news? -Nothing special. **3** *(privado)* private.
▶ *nmf (persona)* private.
▶ *nm (detalle)* particular.
- **en particular** particularly, in particular.
- **sin otro particular** yours faithfully.

partida *nf* **1** *(salida)* departure. **2** *(documento)* certificate. **3** *(remesa)* lot, shipment. **4** *(de juego)* game. **5** *(de soldados)* squad, gang.
- **hacer algo por partida doble** to do STH twice.
■ **partida de nacimiento** birth certificate.

partidario,-a *adj* supporting: *no soy partidario de la huelga*, I don't support the strike.
▶ *nm,f* supporter.

partido *nm* **1** *(grupo)* party, group: *partido político*, political party. **2** *(provecho)* profit, advantage. **3** *(equipo)* team; *(partida)* game, match.
- **sacar partido de** to profit from.
- **ser un buen partido** to be a good catch.
- **tomar partido** to take sides.
■ **partido amistoso** friendly match.
■ **partido de desempate** replay.

partir *vt* **1** *(separar)* to divide, split *[pt & pp* **split***]*. **2** *(romper)* to break *[pt* **broke***; pp* **broken***]*, crack: *pártelo por la mitad*, break it in half. **3** *(repartir)* to share, distribute.

▶ *vi (irse)* to leave *[pt & pp* **left***]*, set out *[pt & pp* **set***]*, set off: *partió con rumbo desconocido*, he set off with an unknown destination: *¿a qué hora partieron?*, what time did they live?

▶ *vpr* **partirse** to split up *[pt & pp* **split***]*, break up *[pt* **broke***; pp* **broken***]*: *se ha partido una pierna*, she's broken her leg.
- **a partir de hoy** from today onwards.
- **partirle la cara a ALGN** to smash SB's face in.
- **partirse de risa** to split one's sides laughing *[pt & pp* **split***]*.

partitura *nf* score.

parto *nm* childbirth, delivery.
- **estar de parto** to be in labour.
■ **parto múltiple** multiple birth.
■ **parto natural** natural birth.
■ **parto prematuro** premature birth.
■ **parto provocado** induced labour.
■ **parto sin dolor** painless childbirth.

párvulo,-a *nm,f* little child *[pl* **children***]*.

pasa *nf* raisin.
■ **pasa de Corinto** currant.

pasable *adj* passable.

pasada *nf (de pintura)* coat; *(con bayeta)* wipe.
- **de pasada 1** *(de paso)* in passing. **2** *(rápidamente)* hastily.
- **jugarle una mala pasada a ALGN** to play a dirty trick on SB.
- **¡qué pasada! 1** *fam (abuso)* what a rip off! **2** *(divertido)* that's something else! **3** *(increíble)* that's amazing: *la fiesta fue una pasada*, the party was amazing; *me compré una pasada de discos*, I bought tons of CD's.

pasadizo *nm* passage.

pasado,-a *adj* **1** *(anterior)* past, gone by: *el lunes pasado*, last Monday. **2** *(último)* last. **3** *(carne)* overdone.
▶ *nm* **pasado** *(momento anterior)* past; *(de un verbo)* past tense.
- **pasadas las... después...:** *llegó pasadas las once*, he arrived after eleven.
- **las... pasadas** gone...: *son las cuatro pasadas*, it's gone four.
- **pasado,-a de moda** out of date, out of fashion.
- **pasado mañana** the day after tomorrow.
- **pasado por agua 1** (huevo) soft-boiled.

2 (con lluvia) very wet: *estas Navidades han estado pasadas por agua*, these Christmas have been very wet.

pasador nm **1** (de puerta etc) bolt, fastener. **2** (de pelo) hair-pin.

pasaje nm **1** (billete) ticket, fare. **2** (pasajeros) passengers pl. **3** (calle) passage, alley. **4** (de texto) passage.

pasajero,-a adj passing.

▶ nm,f passenger.

pasamanos nm handrail.

pasamontañas nm balaclava.

pasaporte nm passport.

pasar vi **1** (ir) to go past, walk past, pass: *pasaba por ahí cuando sucedió*, I was just passing by when it happened. **2** (tiempo) to pass, go by. **3** (entrar) to come in, go in. **4** (cesar) to come to an end. **5** (límite) to exceed: *pasa de la edad que piden*, he is over the age they are asking for. **6** (ocurrir) to happen: *no ha pasado nada*, nothing has happened. **7** fam (mostrar poco interés) not to be bothered: *yo paso de todo*, I'm not bothered.

▶ vt **1** (entregar) to pass: *pásame la sal, por favor*, pass me the salt, please. **2** (trasladar) to carry across. **3** (mensaje) to give. **4** (página) to turn. **5** (calle etc) to cross. **6** (límite) to go beyond. **7** (aventajar) to surpass, beat [pt **beat**; pp **beaten**]. **8** (adelantar) to overtake [pt **overtook**; pp **overtaken**]. **9** (deslizar) to run [pt **ran**; pp **run**]: *pasó el dedo por el estante*, he ran his finger along the shelf. **10** (tolerar) to tolerate, overlook. **11** (examen) to pass. **12** (tiempo) to spend [pt & pp **spent**]: *pasaremos el verano en Roma*, we're spending the summer in Rome. **13** (película) to show [pt **showed**; pp **shown**].

▶ vpr **pasarse 1** (desertar) to pass over. **2** (excederse) to go too far, exaggerate. **3** (pudrirse) to go off. **4** (olvidarse) to forget [pt **forgot**; pp **forgotten**]: *se me pasó la cita completamente*, I completely forgot about the meeting. **5** (ir) to go by, walk past.

● **pasar a** to go on to.

● **pasar por** to be considered.

● **pasar por alto algo** to ignore STH.

● **pasarlo bien** to have a good time.

● **pasarlo mal** to have a bad time.

● **pasar sin** to do without.

● **¿qué pasa?** what's the matter?, what's wrong?

pasarela nf (de barco) walkway; (de modelos) catwalk.

pasatiempo nm pastime, hobby.

Pascua nf (cristiana) Easter; (judía) Passover.

▶ nf pl **Pascuas** Christmas sing.

● **de Pascuas a Ramos** once in a blue moon.

● **estar alegre como unas pascuas** to be as happy as a sandboy.

● **felices Pascuas** merry Christmas.

● **...y santas pascuas** ...and that's that.

■ **Pascua de Resurrección** Easter.

pase nm **1** (permiso) pass, permit. **2** (de película) showing. **3** (del balón) pass.

■ **pase de prensa** press pass.

pasear vt to walk: *sacar a pasear el perro*, to take the dog for a walk.

▶ vi-vpr **pasear(se)** to go for a walk.

paseo nm **1** (a pie) walk, stroll; (en coche) drive; (en bici, a caballo) ride. **2** (calle) avenue, promenade.

● **dar un paseo** to go for a walk.

● **mandar a ALGN a paseo** fam to send SB packing.

■ **paseo marítimo** sea front, promenade.

pasillo nm (de casa) corridor; (de avión) aisle.

pasión nf passion.

pasivo,-a adj passive: *en voz pasiva*, in the passive.

▶ nm **pasivo** (de empresa) liabilities pl.

pasmado,-a adj **1** (asombrado) astonished, amazed. **2** (atontado) stunned.

pasmar vt **1** (asombrar) to astonish, amaze. **2** (atontar) to stun.

▶ vpr **pasmarse** to be astonished, be amazed.

paso nm **1** (al caminar) step, footstep: *¡no des un paso más!*, don't move another step!; *he oído pasos*, I heard footsteps. **2** (ritmo) pace. **3** (camino) way: *me cerró el paso*, he blocked my way. **4** (avance) advance. **5** (trámite) step, move.

● **a dos pasos** just round the corner.

● **abrirse paso** to force one's way through.

● **"Ceda el paso"** "give way".

● **dar el primer paso** to make the first move.

● **dar un paso en falso** to make a wrong move.

● **de paso 1** by the way: *me pilla de paso al trabajo*, it's on my way to work. **2** in passing: *lo dijo de paso*, he mentioned it in passing.

● **estar de paso** to be passing through.

● **marcar el paso** to mark time.

● **paso a paso** step by step.

● **"Prohibido el paso"** "No entry".

■ **paso a nivel** level crossing.

■ **paso de cebra** zebra crossing.

■ **paso de peatones** pedestrian crossing.

■ **paso elevado** flyover.

■ **paso subterráneo** subway.

pasota *adj fam* couldn't-care-less.

▶ *nmf*: *es un pasota*, he couldn't care less about anything.

pasta *nf* **1** *(masa)* paste; *(de pan)* dough. **2** *(fideos, macarrones, etc)* pasta. **3** *(pastelito)* cake. **4** *fam (dinero)* dough, money.

● **ser de buena pasta** to be good-natured.

■ **pasta dentífrica** toothpaste.

■ **pastas de té** biscuits.

pastar *vt-vi* to pasture, graze.

pastel *nm* **1** *(tipo bizcocho)* cake; *(de fruta)* pie, tart: *pastel de manzana*, apple pie. **2** *(colores, etc)* pastel.

● **descubrir el pastel** to let the cat out of the bag [*pt & pp* **let**].

pastelería *nf* cake shop.

pastelero,-a *nm,f* pastrycook.

pastilla *nf* **1** *(medicamento)* tablet, pill. **2** *(de chocolate)* bar. **3** *(de jabón)* cake, bar.

● **a toda pastilla** *fam* at full tilt.

pasto *nm (lugar)* pasture.

● **ser pasto de las llamas** to go up in flames.

pastor,-ra *nm,f (hombre)* shepherd; *(mujer)* shepherdess.

pata¹ *nf* **1** *(gen)* leg. **2** *(garra)* paw. **3** *(pezuña)* hoof [*pl* **-s** o **-ves**].

● **a cuatro patas** on all fours.

● **a la pata coja** hopping.

● **a pata** *fam* on foot.

● **estirar la pata** *fam* to kick the bucket.

● **meter la pata** *fam* to put one's foot in it.

● **patas arriba** upside down.

● **tener mala pata** *fam* to have bad luck.

■ **patas de gallo** crow's feet.

pata² *nf (ave)* female duck.

patada *nf* kick: *abrieron la puerta a patadas*, they kicked the door open.

● **sentar como una patada en el estómago** *fam* to be like a kick in the teeth.

patalear *vi* to stamp one's feet.

pataleo *nm* stamping.

pataleta *nf fam* tantrum.

patata *nf* potato [*pl* **-es**].

■ **patatas fritas 1** *(de bolsa)* GB crisps; US potato chips. **2** *(de sartén)* GB chips; US French fries.

■ **patata caliente** hot potato [*pl* **-es**].

patatús *nm fam* fit: *parece que le va a dar un patatús*, she looks as if she is going to have a fit.

paté *nm* paté.

patear *vt* to kick.

▶ *vi* to stamp one's feet.

▶ *vpr* **patearse** to tramp round.

patentar *vt* to patent.

patente *adj* patent, evident.

▶ *nf* patent.

paternal *adj* paternal.

paternidad *nf* **1** paternity, fatherhood. **2** *(autoría)* authorship.

paterno,-a *adj* paternal.

patético,-a *adj* pathetic.

patín *nm* **1** skate. **2** *(de agua)* pedalo.

■ **patines de ruedas** roller skates.

■ **patines en línea** rollerblades.

patinador,-ra *nm,f* skater.

patinaje *nm* skating.

■ **patinaje artístico** figure skating.

■ **patinaje sobre hielo** ice skating.

patinar *vi* **1** *(con patines)* to skate. **2** *(vehículo)* to skid. **3** *(equivocarse)* to slip up.

patinazo *nm* **1** *(con el coche)* skid. **2** *fam (error)* blunder.

patinete *nm* scooter.

patio *nm* **1** *(de casa)* patio. **2** *(de escuela)* playground.

● **¡cómo está el patio!** what a state things are in!

■ **patio de butacas** GB stalls *pl*; US orchestra.

■ **patio de luces** well.

pato *nm* duck.

● **pagar el pato** *fam* to carry the can.

patoso,-a *adj fam* clumsy.

patria *nf* homeland.

■ **patria chica** home town.

patrimonio *nm* heritage, patrimony.
■ **patrimonio de la humanidad** world heritage.
■ **patrimonio nacional** national heritage.
patriota *nmf* patriot.
patriótico,-a *adj* patriotic.
patriotismo *nm* patriotism.
patrocinar *vt* to sponsor.
patrón,-ona *nm,f* **1** *(santo)* patron saint. **2** *(jefe)* employer, boss; *(de criados - hombre)* master; *(- mujer)* mistress. **3** *(de barco)* skipper.
▶ *nm* **patrón 1** *(de modista)* pattern. **2** *(modelo)* standard.
patrulla *nf* patrol.
■ **coche patrulla** petrol car.
patrullar *vi* to patrol.
pausa *nf* pause.
pausado,-a *adj* slow, deliberate.
pavimentar *vt* **1** *(calle)* to pave. **2** *(suelo)* to tile.
pavimento *nm* **1** *(calle)* roadway. **2** *(suelo)* flooring.
pavo *nm* turkey.
■ **estar en la edad del pavo** to be at an awkward age.
■ **pavo real** peacock.
payasada *nf* piece of clowning.
payaso *nm* clown.
paz *nf* peace.
● **dejar en paz** to leave alone *[pt & pp* left].
● **hacer las paces** to make up, make it up.
● **estar en paz** to be even, be quits.
● **mantener la paz** to keep the peace.
P.D. *abr* **(posdata)** PS, postscript.
peaje *nm* toll.
peatón *nm* pedestrian.
● **paso de peatones** pedestrian crossing.
peatonal *adj* pedestrian.
peca *nf* freckle.
pecado *nm* sin.
■ **pecado capital** deadly sin.
■ **pecado mortal** mortal sin.
■ **pecado original** original sin.
pecador,-ra *adj* sinful.
▶ *nm,f* sinner.
pecar *vi* to sin: *peca de inocente*, he's very naïve.
pecera *nf (redonda)* fishbowl; *(rectangular)* aquarium, fish tank.

pecho *nm* **1** *(tórax)* chest. **2** *(de mujer - busto)* bust; *(- seno)* breast.
● **dar el pecho** to breast-feed.
● **tomarse algo a pecho 1** *(ofenderse)* to take STH to heart. **2** *(interesarse)* to take STH seriously.
pechuga *nf* breast.
■ **pechuga de pollo** chicken breast.
pecoso,-a *adj* freckled.
peculiar *adj* peculiar.
pedagogía *nf* pedagogy.
pedal *nm* pedal.
pedalear *vi* to pedal.
pedante *adj* pedantic.
▶ *nmf* pedant.
pedazo *nm* piece, bit.
● **estar hecho pedazos** to be shattered.
● **hacer pedazos** to break to pieces *[pt* broke; *pp* broken].
● **un pedazo de ...** a really big ..., a huge ....
pedestal *nm* pedestal.
pediatra *nmf* pediatrician.
pedido *nm* **1** order. **2** *(petición)* request, petition.
● **hacer un pedido** to place an order.
pedir *vt* **1** *(gen)* to ask for: *me pidió el teléfono*, he asked me for my phone number. **2** *(mendigar)* to beg. **3** *(mercancías, en restaurante)* to order: *¿qué has pedido de postre?*, what did you order for dessert?
● **a pedir de boca** just as desired.
● **estar pidiendo algo a gritos** to be crying out for something.
● **pedir perdón** to apologise.
● **pedir prestado,-a** to borrow.
pedo *nm fam (ventosidad)* fart.
● **coger un pedo** *fam* to get drunk, get pissed.
● **estar pedo** *fam* to be drunk.
● **tirarse un pedo** *fam* to fart.
pedrada *nf*: *recibió una pedrada en la cara*, he was hit in the face by a stone; *lo rompió de una pedrada*, he thew a stone at it and broke it.
pedregal *nm* stony ground.
pedrusco *nm* rough stone.
pega *nf fam (dificultad)* snag.
● **de pega** fake, false.
● **poner pegas a todo** to find fault with everything *[pt & pp* found].
pegadizo,-a *adj* catchy.
pegajoso,-a *adj* **1** *(sustancia, manos, tiempo)* sticky: *hacía un calor pegajoso*, it was really close. **2** *(persona)* clinging.

pegamento *nm* glue.

pegar[1] *vt* **1** *(adherir - gen)* to stick [*pt & pp* **stuck**]; *(- con pegamento)* to glue. **2** *(arrimar)* to put: *pégalo a la pared*, put it against the wall. **3** *(dos piezas)* to stick together. **4** *(contagiar)* to give: *me has pegado la gripe*, you've given me your flu; *se me ha pegado la costumbre de morder el boli*, I got into the habit of biting the pen.

▶ *vi* **1** *(combinar)* to match: *ese color no pega en el salón*, that colour doesn't look right in the living room; *ese bolso no pega con los zapatos*, that bag doesn't match the shoes. **2** *(adherir)* to stick [*pt & pp* **stuck**].

▶ *vpr* **pegarse** *(adherirse)* to stick [*pt & pp* **stuck**]: *pégate al grupo*, stay close to the group; *se le pegó el acento*, he picked up the accent.

pegar[2] *vt* **1** *(golpear)* to hit [*pt & pp* **hit**]: *ese niño me ha pegado*, that boy has hit me. **2** *(dar)* to give: *me pegó una patada*, he gave me a kick, he kicked me; *deja ya de pegar gritos*, stop shouting.

▶ *vpr* **pegarse** *(golpearse)* to hit each other [*pt & pp* **hit**].

● **pegarle fuego a algo** to set fire to STH [*pt & pp* **set**].

● **pegar un susto a ALGN** to scare SB.

pegatina *nf* sticker.

pegote *nm* **1** *fam (masa)* sticky mess. **2** *fam (chapuza)* botch.

● **tirarse un pegote** to show off [*pt* **showed**; *pp* **shown**]: *le gusta tirarse pegotes*, he likes to show off.

peinado *nm* hair style.

peinar *vt (con peine)* to comb; *(con cepillo)* to brush.

▶ *vpr* **peinarse** to comb one's hair.

● **peinar canas** to be old.

peine *nm* comb.

peineta *nf* ornamental comb.

peladilla *nf* sugared almond.

pelado,-a *adj* **1** *(terreno, árbol)* bald, bare. **2** *(cabeza)* hairless. **3** *fam (sin dinero)* penniless.

▶ *nm* **pelado** *fam (corte de pelo)* haircut.

pelar *vt* **1** *(fruta, verdura)* to peel. **2** *(persona)* to cut SB's hair [*pt & pp* **cut**].

▶ *vpr* **pelarse 1** *(perder piel)* to peel: *se me está pelando la nariz*, my nose is peeling. **2** *(cortarse el pelo)* to get one's hair cut.

● **hacer un frío que pela** it's freezing cold.

peldaño *nm* step.

pelea *nf* fight, quarrel.

pelear *vi-vpr* **pelear(se) 1** *(gen)* to fight [*pt & pp* **fought**], quarrel. **2** *(a golpes)* to come to blows. **3** *(romper una relación)* to fall out [*pt* **fell**; *pp* **fallen**]. **4** *(pareja)* to split up [*pt & pp* **split**].

peletería *nf* fur shop, furrier's.

peliagudo,-a *adj* difficult, tricky.

pelícano *nm* pelican.

película *nf* film.

● **de película** incredible: *fue algo de película*, it was something incredible.

■ **película de acción** adventure film.

■ **película de miedo** horror film.

■ **película de suspense** thriller.

■ **película del oeste** western.

■ **película muda** silent movie.

peligrar *vi* to be in danger.

peligro *nm* danger.

● **estar en peligro** to be in danger.

● **estar fuera de peligro** to be out of danger.

● **poner en peligro** to put at risk, endanger.

peligroso,-a *adj* dangerous.

pelirrojo,-a *adj* red-haired.

▶ *nm,f* redhead.

pellejo *nm (piel)* skin.

● **salvar el pellejo** to save one's skin.

pellizcar *vt* to pinch.

pellizco *nm* pinch: *un pellizco de azúcar*, a pinch of sugar; *le tocó un buen pellizco en la lotería*, he got a tidy sum in the lottery.

pelma *nmf fam* bore, pain.

pelmazo,-a *nm,f fam* bore, pain.

pelo *nm* **1** *(gen)* hair. **2** *(de barba)* whisker. **3** *(de animal)* coat, fur.

● **con pelos y señales** in great detail.

● **no tener pelos en la lengua** to speak one's mind [*pt* **spoke**; *pp* **spoken**]: *no tiene pelos en la lengua*, he doesn't mince his words.

● **no tener un pelo de tonto** to be no fool.

● **no verle el pelo a ALGN** to see neither hide nor hair of SB: *hace mucho que no se te veía el pelo*, I'd seen neither hide nor hair of your for ages.

● **por los pelos** by the skin of one's teeth.

● **tomarle el pelo a** ALGN to pull SB's leg.
● **venir a pelo** to be just what SB needs: *esto me viene a pelo*, this is just what I needed.
pelota *nf* ball.
▶ *nmf fam* crawler.
● **en pelotas** *fam* naked.
● **hacer la pelota a** ALGN *fam* to suck up to SB.
● **tocar las pelotas a** ALGN to bug SB.
■ **pelota vasca** pelota.
pelotazo *nm* **1** *(golpe)* : *recibió un pelotazo en toda la cara*, he got hit in the face with a ball; *rompió el cristal de un pelotazo*, he broke the window with a ball. **2** *(bebida)* drink.
pelotillero,-a *adj fam* crawling.
▶ *nm,f fam* crawler.
pelotón *nm* squad.
peluca *nf* wig.
peluche *nm* plush.
peludo,-a *adj* hairy.
peluquería *nf* hairdresser's.
peluquero,-a *nm,f* hairdresser.
peluquín *nm* hairpiece.
pelusa *nf* fluff.
pelvis *nf* pelvis.
pena *nf* **1** *(tristeza)* grief, sorrow. **2** *(lástima)* pity: *¡qué pena!*, what a pity! **3** *(dificultad)* hardship, trouble. **4** *(castigo)* penalty, punishment.
● **a duras penas** with a great difficulty.
● **ahogar las penas** to drown one's sorrows.
● **dar pena** : *su marido me da mucha pena*, I feel very sorry for her husband; *tengo la casa que da pena*, my house is in a terrible state.
● **valer la pena** to be worth while.
■ **pena capital** capital punishment.
■ **pena de muerte** death penalty.
penalti *nm* penalty.
pendiente *adj* **1** *(por resolver)* pending. **2** *(deuda)* outstanding. **3** *(atento)* : *estaba pendiente de todos los detalles*, none of the details escaped him, he missed nothing; *estáte pendiente del arroz*, keep an eye on the rice.
▶ *nf* slope.
▶ *nm* earring.
● **estar pendiente de** to be waiting for.
● **tener pendiente** to have to resit: *ten-*

go el inglés pendiente, I have to resit English.
péndulo *nm* pendulum.
pene *nm* penis.
penetración *nf* **1** *(acción)* penetration. **2** *(perspicacia)* insight.
penetrante *adj* penetrating.
penetrar *vt* **1** *(atravesar)* to penetrate. **2** *(líquido)* to permeate.
▶ *vi* **1** *(entrar - persona, animal)* to enter; *(- líquido)* to seep; *(- luz)* to filter: *la luz penetraba por las rendijas*, light filtered through the cracks; *el agua penetró por el tejado*, water seeped in through the roof. **2** *fig* to break [*pt* **broke**; *pp* **broken**], pierce: *es difícil penetrar en su mente*, it is difficult to get inside his mind.
penicilina *nf* penicillin.
península *nf* peninsula.
peninsular *adj* peninsular.
penique *nm* penny [*pl* **pence**].
penitencia *nf* penance.
penitente *adj - nmf* penitent.
penoso,-a *adj* **1** *(lamentable)* awful, dreadful. **2** *(trabajoso)* laborious, hard.
pensado,-a *adj* thought-out.
● **bien pensado...** on reflection.
● **el día menos pensado** when you least expect it.
● **tener algo pensado** to have STH in mind.
pensador,-ra *nm,f* thinker.
pensamiento *nm* **1** *(idea, facultad)* thought. **2** *(mente)* mind. **3** *(flor)* pansy.
pensar *vt-vi* *(gen)* to think [*pt & pp* **thought**].
▶ *vt* **1** *(considerar)* to consider. **2** *(imaginar)* to imagine. **3** *(tener la intención de)* to intend.
▶ *vpr* **pensarse** to think about [*pt & pp* **thought**].
● **¡ni pensarlo!** no way!, don't even think about it!
● **pensar bien de** ALGN to think well of SB [*pt & pp* **thought**].
● **pensar hacer algo** to intend to do STH.
● **pensar mal de** ALGN to think badly of SB [*pt & pp* **thought**].
● **sin pensar** without thinking.
pensativo,-a *adj* pensive, thoughtful.
pensión *nf* **1** *(dinero)* pension. **2** *(residencia)* boarding house.

- **cobrar la pensión** to receive one's pension.
- **media pensión** half board.
- **pensión completa** full board.
- **pensión de jubilación** retirement pension.

pensionista *nmf* pensioner.

pentágono *nm* pentagon.

pentagrama *nm* stave, staff [*pl* -s].

penúltimo,-a *adj - nm,f* penultimate.

penumbra *nf* semi-darkness.

peña¹ *nf (roca)* rock.

peña² *nf fam (de amigos)* group of friends: **había mucha peña**, there were loads of people.

- **peña deportiva** supporter's club.

peñasco *nm* crag.

peñón *nm* rock.

peón *nm* **1** *(trabajador)* unskilled labourer. **2** *(en damas)* man [*pl* **men**]. **3** *(en ajedrez)* pawn.

- **peón caminero** roadmender.
- **peón de albañil** bricklayer's labourer.

peonza *nf* top, spinning top.

peor *adj-adv* **1** *(comparativo)* worse: **tu coche es peor que el mío**, your car is worse than mine. **2** *(superlativo)* worst: **su peor enemigo**, his worst enemy.

- **en el peor de los casos** at worst.
- **lo peor es que...** the worst thing is that....
- **peor es nada** it's better than nothing.

pepinillo *nm* gherkin.

pepino *nm* cucumber.

- **me importa un pepino** *fam* I don't give a damn.

pepita *nf* **1** *(de fruta)* seed, pip. **2** *(de metal)* nugget.

pequeñez *nf* **1** *(de tamaño)* smallness. **2** *(insignificancia)* trifle.

pequeño,-a *adj* **1** *(de tamaño)* little, small. **2** *(de edad)* young, small: **tengo dos hermanos pequeños**, I have to younger brothers.

- ▶ *nm,f* child [*pl* **children**].
- **de pequeño,-a** as a child.
- **ser el pequeño** to be the youngest: **soy el más pequeño**, I am the youngest.

pera *nf* pear.

- **pedirle peras al olmo** to ask for the impossible.
- **ser la pera** *fam* to be the limit.

peral *nm* pear tree.

percance *nm* mishap: **ha tenido un percance**, he had suffered a mishap.

percatarse *vpr* to notice.

percebe *nm* goose barnacle.

percha *nf (individual)* hanger; *(de gancho)* coat hook; *(de pie)* coat stand.

perchero *nm (en la pared)* clothes rack; *(de pie)* coat stand.

percibir *vt* **1** *(notar)* to perceive, notice. **2** *(cobrar)* to receive.

percusión *nf* percussion.

perdedor,-ra *adj* losing.

- ▶ *nm,f* loser.

perder *vt* **1** *(gen)* to lose [*pt & pp* lost]. **2** *(malgastar)* to waste: **no perdió ni un segundo**, he didn't waste a moment; **el coche pierde agua**, the car is leaking water. **3** *(tren, avión etc)* to miss. **4** *(arruinar)* to be the ruin of: **le perdió su afición al juego**, gambling was his downfall.

- ▶ *vi* **1** *(salir derrotado)* to lose [*pt & pp* lost]. **2** *(empeorar)* to go downhill: **esta ciudad ha perdido mucho**, this city has gone downhill. **3** *(desteñirse)* to fade.
- ▶ *vpr* **perderse 1** *(extraviarse)* to go astray, get lost: **se me ha perdido el número**, I've lost the number. **2** *(fruta etc)* to be spoiled. **3** *(arruinarse)* to become ruined. **4** *(acontecimiento)* to miss.
- **echar a perder** to spoil [*pt & pp* spoilt].
- **perder de vista** to lose sight of [*pt & pp* lost].
- **salir perdiendo** to come off worse, lose out [*pt & pp* lost].

pérdida *nf* **1** *(extravío)* loss. **2** *(de tiempo, dinero)* waste. **3** *(escape)* leak: **hay una pérdida de aceite**, there's an oil leak.

- **no tener pérdida** to be easy to find: **no tiene pérdida**, you can't miss it.
- **pérdidas y ganancias** profit and loss.

perdido,-a *adj* **1** *(extraviado)* lost: **objetos perdidos**, lost property. **2** *(desorientado)* lost: **en esta ciudad me encuentro perdido**, I feel lost in this city. **3** *(desperdiciado)* wasted. **4** *(bala, perro)* stray.

- **dar algo por perdido** to give STH up for lost.
- **estar loco,-a perdido,-a por** to be madly in love with.

perdigón *nm* pellet.

perdiz *nf* partridge.

perdón *nm* **1** *(indulto)* pardon. **2** *(de pecado)* forgiveness.

● **con perdón** if you'll pardon the expression.

● **pedir perdón** to apologize: *pidió perdón al público*, he apologized to the audience.

● **¡perdón!** sorry!

● **¿perdón?** (al no entender algo) pardon?, sorry?

perdonar *vt* **1** *(error, ofensa)* to forgive [*pt* **forgave**; *pp* **forgiven**]: *nunca lo perdonó*, she never forgave him. **2** *(deuda)* to let off [*pt & pp* **let**]. **3** *(excusar)* to excuse: *perdona que te interrumpa*, sorry to interrupt.

● **¡perdone!** sorry!

● **¿perdone?** (al no entender algo) pardon?, sorry?

● **perdonarle algo a ALGN** to forgive SB for STH [*pt* **forgave**; *pp* **forgiven**].

perdurar *vt* to last, endure.

peregrinar *vi* to go on a pilgrimage.

peregrino,-a *adj* **1** *(ave)* migratory. **2** *(disparatado)* strange, outlandish.

▶ *nm,f* pilgrim.

perejil *nm* parsley.

perenne *adj* perennial, perpetual: *árbol de hoja perenne*, evergreen tree.

pereza *nf* laziness, idleness.

● **¡qué pereza!** what a drag!

● **tener pereza** to feel lazy [*pt & pp* **felt**].

perezoso,-a *adj* lazy, idle.

▶ *nm,f* lazybones.

perfección *nf* perfection.

● **a la perfección** perfectly.

perfeccionar *vt* **1** *(mejorar)* to improve. **2** *(hacer perfecto)* to perfect.

perfecto,-a *adj* **1** *(ideal)* perfect. **2** *(rematado)* complete: *un perfecto desconocido*, a complete stranger.

perfil *nm* **1** *(gen)* profile: *el perfil psicológico*, the psychological profile. **2** *(silueta)* outline.

● **de perfil** in profile.

perfilar *vt* to outline.

▶ *vpr* **perfilarse 1** *(destacarse)* to stand out [*pt & pp* **stood**]. **2** *(concretarse)* to shape up.

perforación *nf* **1** *(acción, orificio)* perforation. **2** *(uso técnico)* drilling, boring.

perforar *vt* **1** *(gen)* to perforate. **2** *(uso técnico)* to drill, bore.

perfumar *vt* to perfume, scent.

perfume *nm* perfume, scent.

perfumería *nf* perfumery, perfume shop.

pergamino *nm* parchment.

periferia *nf* **1** *(gen)* periphery. **2** *(afueras)* outskirts *pl*.

perilla *nf* goatee.

● **venir de perilla** *fam* to be just right.

perímetro *nm* perimeter.

periódico,-a *adj* periodic.

▶ *nm* **periódico** newspaper.

periodismo *nm* journalism.

periodista *nmf* journalist.

periodo *nm* period.

período *nm* period.

peripecia *nf* vicissitude, incident: *pasamos muchas peripecias*, we had to go through a lot; *con tantas peripecias, no sé cómo hemos llegado a tiempo*, with so many incidents, I don't know how we made it on time.

periquito *nm* parakeet.

periscopio *nm* periscope.

perito,-a *adj* expert.

▶ *nm* **perito** expert.

perjudicar *vt* to damage, harm.

perjudicial *adj* damaging, harmful.

perjuicio *nm* *(moral)* injury; *(material)* damage.

● **en perjuicio de** to the detriment of.

perla *nf* **1** *(joya)* pearl. **2** *(maravilla)* gem.

● **de perlas** just right: *me vino de perlas*, it came just right.

■ **perla cultivada** cultured pearl.

permanecer *vi* to remain, stay: *todos permanecieron en silencio*, they all remained silent.

permanente *adj* permanent, lasting.

▶ *nf (del pelo)* perm.

● **hacerse la permanente** to have one's hair permed.

permiso *nm* **1** *(autorización)* permission. **2** *(documento)* permit. **3** leave: *estaba de permiso*, he was on leave.

● **con su permiso** if you'll excuse me.

● **dar permiso** to give permission.

● **pedir permiso** to ask for permission.

● **tener permiso para hacer algo** to have permission to do STH.

■ **permiso de conducir** driving licence.

■ **permiso de residencia** residence permit.

■ **permiso de trabajo** work permit.

permitir *vt* to permit, allow, let [*pt & pp* let]: *no me permitieron entrar*, I wasn't allowed in.

▶ *vpr* **permitirse** to take the liberty of: *se permitió una copa*, he allowed himself a drink; *me permito recordarle que...*, may I remind you that....

● **poder permitirse** to be able to afford: *no puedo permitírmelo*, I can't afford it.

pero *conj* but: *está bien, pero algo lejos*, it's fine, but a bit far; *pero ¿qué pasa?*, but what's wrong?

▶ *nm* objection, fault.

● **ponerle peros a algo** to find fault with STH [*pt & pp* found].

peroné *nm* fibula.

perpendicular *adj - nf* perpendicular.

perpetuo,-a *adj* perpetual, everlasting.

perplejo,-a *adj* perplexed.

perra *nf* bitch.

perrera *nf* (*guardería de perros*) kennel; (*para perros callejeros*) dog pound.

perro,-a *adj* wretched, rotten: *¡que vida tan perra!*, what a wretched life!; *¡qué perra suerte!*, what rotten luck!

▶ *nm,f* **1** dog. **2** *fam* (*persona*) rotter.

● **"Cuidado con el perro"** "Beware of the dog".

● **de perros** foul: *hacía un tiempo de perros*, the weather was foul.

● **llevarse como el perro y el gato** to fight [*pt & pp* fought] like cat and dog.

■ **perro callejero** stray dog.

■ **perro guardián** guard dog.

■ **perro lazarillo** guide dog.

■ **perro policía** police dog.

persa *adj - nmf* Persian.

persecución *nf* **1** (*seguimiento*) pursuit. **2** (*represión*) persecution.

perseguir *vt* **1** (*delincuente, presa*) to pursue, chase. **2** (*pretender*) to be after.

perseverar *vi* to persevere, persist.

persiana *nf* (*gen*) blind; (*enrollable*) roller blind; (*de tablas*) shutter.

● **enrollarse como una persiana** *fam* to go on and on.

persistente *adj* persistent.

persistir *vi* to persist, persevere.

persona *nf* person [*pl* people]: *una persona, dos personas*, one person, two people.

● **en persona** in person.

● **por persona** per person, per head.

■ **persona mayor** adult, grown-up.

personaje *nm* **1** (*en libro, etc*) character. **2** (*persona famosa*) celebrity.

personal *adj* personal.

▶ *nm* personnel, staff.

personalidad *nf* **1** (*carácter*) personality. **2** (*persona famosa*) public figure.

personarse *vpr* to go in person: *la policía se personó enseguida*, the police appeared inmediately.

perspectiva *nf* **1** (*gen*) perspective. **2** (*posibilidad*) prospect. **3** (*vista*) view.

● **en perspectiva** in prospect.

persuadir *vi* to persuade, convince.

▶ *vpr* **persuadirse** to be convinced.

persuasivo,-a *adj* persuasive.

pertenecer *vi* to belong: *pertenecen a una secta*, they belong to a sect.

pertenencia *nf* **1** (*posesión*) ownership. **2** (*afiliación*) membership.

▶ *nf pl* **pertenencias** (*enseres*) belongings.

pértiga *nf* pole.

Perú *nm* Peru.

peruano,-a *adj - nm,f* Peruvian.

perversión *nf* perversion.

perverso,-a *adj* perverse.

pervertir *vt* to pervert.

▶ *vpr* **pervertirse** to become perverted.

pesa *nf* weight: *hacer pesas*, to do weight training.

pesadez *nf* **1** (*molestia*) heaviness: *tengo pesadez de estómago*, I have a heavy feeling in my stomach. **2** (*aburrimiento*) tiresomeness. **3** (*torpeza*) clumsiness.

pesadilla *nf* nightmare.

pesado,-a *adj* **1** (*gen*) heavy. **2** (*aburrido*) dull, tiresome, boring: *¡qué pesado eres!*, you're such a pain! **3** (*torpe*) clumsy. **4** (*sueño*) deep.

● **ponerse pesado,-a** to be a nuisance.

● **sentirse pesado,-a** to feel really full.

pésame *nm* condolences, expression of sympathy.

● **dar el pésame** to offer one's condolences.

pesar *vt-vi* (*gen*) to weigh: *¿cuánto pesas?*, how much do you weigh?

▶ *vi* **1** (*tener mucho peso*) to be heavy: *no pesa mucho*, it's not too heavy. **2** (*sentir*) to be sorry, regret: *me pesa haberlo dicho*, I regret having said it; *le pesan los años*, she's feeling her age.

▶ *nm* **1** *(pena)* sorrow, grief. **2** *(arrepentimiento)* regret.

● **a pesar de** in spite of, despite.

● **a pesar de que** despite the fact that.

pesca *nf* fishing.

■ **pesca de arrastre** trawling.

■ **pesca submarina** underwater fishing.

pescadería *nf* fishmonger's, fish shop.

pescadero,-a *nm,f* fishmonger.

pescadilla *nf* small hake.

pescado *nm* fish.

■ **pescado azul** blue fish.

pescador,-ra *adj* fishing.

▶ *nm* **pescador** fisherman [*pl* -**men**].

pescar *vt* to catch [*pt & pp* **caught**].

▶ *vi* to fish.

● **ir a pescar** to go fishing.

pescuezo *nm* neck.

pesebre *nm* **1** *(para animales)* manger, stall. **2** *(de Navidad)* crib.

pesimismo *nm* pessimism.

pesimista *adj* pessimistic.

▶ *nmf* pessimist.

pésimo,-a *adj* abominable, very bad.

peso *nm* **1** *(gen)* weight. **2** *(balanza)* scales *pl*, balance. **3** *(carga)* weight, burden: *el peso de los años*, the burden of old age. **4** shot: *lanzamiento de peso*, shot put; *levantamiento de peso*, weight-lifting.

● **coger peso** to gain weight.

● **perder peso** to lose [*pt & pp* **lost**] weight.

● **quitarse un peso de encima** to take a load off one's mind.

● **valer su peso en oro** to be worth its weight in gold.

■ **peso neto** net weight.

pesquero,-a *adj* fishing.

▶ *nm* **pesquero** fishing boat.

pestaña *nf* **1** *(del ojo)* eyelash. **2** *(de cartón)* flap.

pestañear *vi* to blink.

● **sin pestañear** without batting an eyelash.

pestañeo *nm* winking, blinking.

peste *nf* **1** *(epidemia)* plague. **2** *(mal olor)* stink, stench: *¡qué peste!*, it really stinks here!

● **echar pestes de** ALGN to slag SB off.

pestillo *nm* bolt.

petaca *nf* **1** *(de cigarrillos)* cigarette case. **2** *(de tabaco)* tobacco pouch.

pétalo *nm* petal.

petanca *nf* petanque.

petardo *nm* **1** *(cohete)* banger. **2** *fam (persona)* : *¡menudo petardo está hecho!*, he's a real pain in the neck. **3** *fam (de hachís)* joint.

petición *nf* *(ruego)* request; *(documento escrito)* petition: *las peticiones del público*, the audience's requests; *por petición popular*, by popular request.

● **a petición de** at the request of.

■ **petición de indulto** appeal for a reprieve.

petirrojo *nm* robin.

peto *nm* **1** *(de armadura)* breastplate. **2** *(de pantalón)* bib.

● **pantalón de peto** dungarees *pl*.

petróleo *nm* oil, petroleum.

petrolero *nm* oil tanker.

petrolífero,-a *adj* oil: *empresa petrolífera*, oil company.

pez *nm* fish.

● **estar como pez en el agua** to be in one's element.

● **estar pez en algo** *fam* to have no idea about STH.

■ **pez de colores** goldfish.

■ **pez espada** swordfish.

■ **pez gordo** *fam* big shot.

pezón *nm* nipple.

pezuña *nf* hoof [*pl* -**s** o -**ves**].

piadoso,-a *adj* **1** *(devoto)* pious, devout. **2** *(compasivo)* compassionate.

pianista *nmf* pianist.

piano *nm* piano [*pl* -**s**]: *yo toco el piano*, I can play the piano.

■ **piano de cola** grand piano.

■ **piano vertical** upright piano.

piar *vi* to chirp.

piara *nf* herd of pigs.

pica *nf* **1** *(lanza)* pike. **2** *(de toros)* goad. **3** *(en naipes)* spade.

picado,-a *adj* **1** *(agujereado)* perforated. **2** *(ajo, cebolla)* chopped; *(carne)* minced. **3** *(mar)* choppy. **4** *(vino)* sour. **5** *(diente)* decayed. **6** *fam (ofendido)* offended. **7** *(cara)* pockmarked.

▶ *nm* **picado** *(de avión)* dive.

● **caer en picado** to plummet.

● **estar picado con algo** to go for STH in a big way.

picador *nm* picador.

picadora *nf* mincer.

picadura *nf* **1** *(de mosquito, serpiente)* bite; *(de abeja, avispa)* sting. **2** *(tabaco)* cut tobacco.

picante *adj* **1** *(sabor)* hot, spicy. **2** *(pícaro)* spicy, naughty.

▸ *nm (especia)* spice; *(comida)* spicy food.

picaporte *nm* **1** *(llamador)* door knocker. **2** *(pomo)* door handle.

picar *vt* **1** *(agujerear)* to prick, pierce. **2** *(toro)* to goad. **3** *(mosquito, serpiente)* to bite [*pt* **bit**; *pp* **bitten**]; *(abeja, avispa)* to sting [*pt & pp* **stung**]. **4** *(algo de comer)* to nibble. **5** *(cebolla, patata, etc)* to chop; *(carne)* to mince; *(hielo)* to crush.

▸ *vi* **1** *(sentir escozor)* to itch: *me pica la nariz*, my nose itches; *una lana que pica*, an itchy wool. **2** *(tomar algo de comer)* to nibble. **3** *(mosquito, serpiente)* to bite [*pt* **bit**; *pp* **bitten**]; *(abeja, avispa)* to sting [*pt & pp* **stung**]; *(pez)* to bite [*pt* **bit**; *pp* **bitten**]. **4** *(estar picante)* to be spicy: *esta sopa pica mucho*, this soup is really spicy.

▸ *vpr* **picarse 1** *(fruta)* to begin to rot [*pt* **began**; *pp* **begun**]. **2** *(diente)* to begin to decay [*pt* **began**; *pp* **begun**]; *(hierro)* to rust; *(fruta)* to go rotten. **3** *(mar)* to get choppy. **4** *(enfadarse)* to take offense.

● **picar alto** to aim high.

● **picarse con algo** to go hooked on sth.

picardía *nf* **1** *(maldad)* slyness; *(astucia)* craftiness. **2** *(palabrota)* swearword.

pícaro,-a *adj* **1** *(malicioso)* mischievous. **2** *(astuto)* sly, crafty.

▸ *nm,f* rogue, scoundrel.

picha *nf vulg* prick.

pichón *nm* young pigeon.

picnic *nm* picnic.

pico *nm* **1** *(de ave)* beak. **2** *(de montaña)* peak. **3** *fam (boca)* mouth. **4** *(punta)* corner. **5** *(herramienta)* pick, pickaxe. **6** *(cantidad)* small amount: *tres mil y pico*, three thousand odd.

● **cerrar el pico** *fam* to keep one's mouth shut.

● **a las dos y pico** after two o'clock.

picor *nm* itch.

picotazo *nm* **1** *(de pájaro)* peck. **2** *(de mosquito, serpiente)* bite; *(de abeja, avispa)* sting.

picotear *vt* **1** *(ave)* to peck at. **2** *(persona)* to nibble.

picudo,-a *adj* pointed.

pie *nm* **1** foot [*pl* **feet**]: *fuimos a pie*, we went on foot; *con los pies descalzos*, barefoot. **2** *(de página)* bottom. **3** *(de columna, lámpara)* base, stand.

● **al pie de la letra** literally.

● **dar pie a** to give occasion for.

● **de los pies a la cabeza** from head to foot.

● **en pie** standing.

● **ponerse de pie** to stand up [*pt & pp* **stood**].

● **ni pies ni cabeza** neither head nor tail.

● **no dar pie con bola** *fam* to get everything wrong.

● **pararle los pies a ALGN** to put SB in his/her place.

● **salir por pies** *fam* to take to one's heels.

● **poner a alguien en pie de guerra** to get SB up in arms.

■ **pie de atleta** athlete's foot.

■ **pie plano** flat foot.

piedad *nf* **1** *(devoción)* piety. **2** *(compasión)* pity, mercy.

● **¡por piedad!** for pity's sake!

● **¡ten piedad de mí!** have mercy on me!

piedra *nf* **1** *(gen)* stone: *un edificio de piedra*, a stone building. **2** *(granizo)* hail. **3** *(de mechero)* flint.

● **colocar la primera piedra** to lay the foundation stone.

● **dejar a ALGN de piedra** to stun SB.

● **menos da una piedra** it's better than nothing.

● **no ser de piedra** not to be made of stone.

■ **piedra angular** cornerstone.

■ **piedra filosofal** philosopher's stone.

■ **piedra pómez** pumice stone.

■ **piedra preciosa** precious stone.

piel *nf* **1** *(de persona)* skin. **2** *(de animal - gen)* skin; *(- de vaca, elefante)* hide; *(- de foca, zorro, visón)* fur. **3** *(cuero - tratado)* leather; *(- sin tratar)* pelt. **4** *(de fruta - gen)* skin; *(- de naranja, manzana, patata)* peel.

● **dejarse la piel** to give one's all.

● **un abrigo de pieles** a fur coat.

■ **piel de gallina** goose pimples: *se me pone la piel de gallina*, it gives me goose pimples.

pienso *nm* fodder.

pierna *nf* leg.

● **dormir a pierna suelta** *fam* to sleep like a log [*pt & pp* **slept**].

● **estirar las piernas** to stretch one's legs.

● **salir por piernas** to take to one's heels.

pieza *nf* **1** *(parte)* piece: *me quedé de una pieza*, I was dumbstruck; *vender algo por piezas*, to sell STH by the piece. **2** *(obra de teatro)* play. **3** *(de ajedrez, damas)* piece, man [*pl* **men**]. **4** part: *las piezas del motor*, the engine parts. **5** *(de exposición)* exhibit. **6** *(remiendo)* patch.

■ **buena pieza** *fam* rogue.

■ **pieza clave** key element.

■ **pieza de recambio** spare part.

■ **pieza literaria** literary work.

pifia *nf fam* blunder.

pigmento *nm* pigment.

pijama *nm* pyjamas *pl*.

pijo,-a *adj fam* posh.

► *nm,f fam* rich kid.

pila *nf* **1** *(eléctrica)* battery. **2** *(de bautismo)* font. **3** *fam (montón)* pile, heap.

pilar *nm* pillar.

píldora *nf* pill.

■ **píldora abortiva** abortion pill.

■ **píldora (anticonceptiva)** (contraceptive) pill.

pillar *vt (atrapar)* to catch [*pt & pp* **caught**]; *(atropellar)* to run [*pt* **ran**; *pp* **run**] over: *lo pilló el tranvía*, he was run over by the train; *a ver si pillo el tren*, let's see if I can catch the train; *te pillé*, I got you; *la pillé robando*, I caught her stealing.

► *vpr* **pillarse** to catch [*pt & pp* **caught**]: *me he pillado el dedo con la puerta*, I caught my finger in the door.

pillo,-a *nm,f* rogue, rascal.

pilotar *vt (avión)* to pilot; *(coche)* to drive [*pt* **drove**; *pp* **driven**]; *(barco)* to steer.

piloto *nmf (de avión, barco)* pilot; *(de coche)* driver.

► *nm (luz - de coche)* tail light, rear light; *(- de aparato)* pilot light.

► *adj* pilot: *piso piloto*, show flat; *programa piloto*, pilot programme.

■ **piloto automático** automatic pilot.

pimentón *nm* paprika.

■ **pimentón picante** hot paprika.

pimienta *nf* pepper.

■ **pimienta molida** ground pepper.

pimiento *nm* pepper.

● **me importa un pimiento** I don't care.

■ **pimiento morrón** sweet red pepper.

pinar *nm* pine grove.

pincel *nm* brush, paintbrush.

pincelada *nf* brush stroke.

● **dar la última pincelada** to give the finishing touch.

pinchadiscos *nmf fam* DJ, disc jockey.

pinchar *vt* **1** *(con objeto punzante)* to prick: *me pinché con una aguja*, I pricked my finger with a needle. **2** *(rueda)* to puncture. **3** *(globo, pelota)* to burst [*pt & pp* **burst**]. **4** *fam (poner una inyección a)* to give a shot to. **5** *fam (provocar)* to needle, wind up [*pt & pp* **wound**]. **6** *fam (teléfono)* to tap.

► *vi (aguja, planta)* to be prickly: *le pinchaba la barba*, his beard was very prickly.

► *vpr* **pincharse 1** *(persona)* to prick oneself. **2** *(rueda)* to puncture. **3** *(globo, pelota)* to burst [*pt & pp* **burst**]. **4** *fam (con droga)* to shoot up [*pt & pp* **shot**].

● **ni pincha ni corta** he counts for nothing.

pinchazo *nm* **1** *(punzada)* prick. **2** *(de rueda)* puncture, flat: *hemos tenido un pinchazo en el camino*, we got a puncture on the way. **3** *(de medicina)* jab. **4** *(de droga)* shot: *tenía pinchazos en el brazo*, he had needle marks on his arm.

pincho *nm* **1** *(espina)* thorn, prickle. **2** *(aperitivo)* tapa, bar snack.

■ **pincho moruno** kebab.

ping-pong® *nm* ping-pong®.

pingüino *nm* penguin.

pino *nm* pine tree: *vive en el quinto pino*, she lives miles away.

pinta *nf* **1** *fam (aspecto)* look: *tiene buena pinta*, it looks good; *¡vaya pinta que tienes!*, what a sight you are!; *¿qué pinta tiene la herida?*, what does the injury look like? **2** *(medida)* pint.

pintada *nf* piece of graffiti: *hay que limpiar estas pintadas*, this graffiti needs cleaning off.

pintado,-a *adj* **1** *(maquillado)* made-up. **2** *(moteado)* spotted.

● **el más pintado** anyone.
● **"recién pintado"** wet paint.
● **ser pintado a** ALGN to be identical to SB.
● **venirle a** ALGN **que ni pintado** to suit SB down to the ground.

pintalabios nm lipstick.

pintar vt **1** (cuadro, pared) to paint. **2** (dar color) GB to colour, US to color; (dibujar) to draw [pt **drew**; pp **drawn**]: *el boli no pinta*, the pen doesn't work. **3** (describir) to paint, describe: *lo pintó todo muy negro*, she painted it all very black. **4** fam (hacer) to do: *¿qué pinta ése aquí?*, what's he doing here?; *¿qué pintas tú en este asunto?*, what business is this of yours?, what has this got to do with you?; *yo aquí no pinto nada*, there's no place for me here.
► vpr **pintarse** to make up one's face.
● **pintarse los labios** to put lipstick on.
● **pintarse los ojos** to use eye make-up.

pintarrajear vt (con pintura) to daub with paint; (con maquillaje) to daub with make-up.

pintaúñas nm nail varnish.

pintor,-ra nm,f painter.
■ **pintor de brocha gorda** house painter.

pintoresco,-a adj picturesque.

pintura nf **1** (arte) painting. **2** (color, bote) paint. **3** (cuadro) picture.

pinza nf **1** (de cangrejo) claw. **2** (para la ropa) peg.
► nf pl **pinzas** (de cocina) tongs; (de manicura) tweezers.

piña nf **1** (fruta) pineapple. **2** (de pino) pine cone. **3** (de personas) close-knit group: *formaban una buena piña*, they were a very close-knit group.
● **darse una piña** to have a crash.

piñón nm (de pino) pine nut.

piojo nm louse [pl **lice**].

piojoso,-a adj lousy.

pionero,-a adj pioneering.
► nm,f pioneer.

pipa[1] nf (de tabaco) pipe.

pipa[2] nf **1** (de fruta) pip, seed. **2** (de girasol) sunflower seeds.
● **pasarlo pipa** fam to have a whale of a time.

pipí nm fam wee: *me estoy haciendo pipí*, I need to do a wee-wee.

● **hacer pipí** to have a wee.

pique nm pique, resentment: *tienen un pique con la empresa*, they have a grudge against the company.
● **irse a pique 1** (barco) to sink [pt **sank**; pp **sunk**]. **2** (plan) to fail.

pirado,-a adj fam crazy, loony.
► nm,f fam nutter, loony.

piragua nf canoe.

piragüismo nm canoeing.

pirámide nf pyramid.

pirarse vpr fam : *me piro*, I'm clearing out, I'm off.
● **pirarse las clases** to skive off school.

pirata nm pirate.

piratería nf piracy.

Pirineos nm pl the Pyrenees.

pirómano,-a nm,f pyromaniac.

piropo nm compliment, piece of flattery.
● **echar un piropo a** to pay a compliment to [pt & pp **paid**].

pirueta nf pirouette, caper.

piruleta nf lollipop.

pirulí nm lollipop.

pis nm fam wee.
● **hacer pis** to have a wee.

pisada nf **1** (acción) footstep. **2** (huella) footprint.

pisapapeles nm paperweight.

pisar vt **1** (con el pie) to tread on [pt **trod**; pp **trodden**], step on: *no pises en la cocina*, don't walk on the kitchen floor; *hace meses que no piso su casa*, I haven't been in her house for months; *"prohibido pisar el césped"*, "keep off the grass". **2** (humillar) to trample on.
● **pisar fuerte** to make a big impact.

piscina nf swimming-pool.

Piscis nm Pisces.

piso nm **1** (planta, suelo) floor. **2** (vivienda) flat, apartment.
■ **piso piloto** show flat.

pisotear vt to trample on.

pisotón nm .
● **darle un pisotón a** ALGN to tread on SB's foot [pt **trod**; pp **trodden**].

pista nf **1** (rastro) trail, track: *la policía le sigue la pista*, the police are on his trail. **2** (indicio) clue: *no le des pistas*, don't give him clues. **3** (de atletismo) track; (de tenis) court; (de esquí) slope, ski run. **4** (de circo) ring. **5** (de aterrizaje) runway.

■ **pista cubierta** indoor track.

■ **pista de baile** dance floor.

pistacho *nm* pistachio [*pl* **-s**].

pistola *nf* pistol.

pistolero *nm* gunman [*pl* **-men**].

pistón *nm* piston.

pitar *vi* (*con silbato*) to blow a whistle [*pt* **blew**; *pp* **blown**]; (*con claxon*) to hoot.

▶ *vt* (*abuchear*) to boo at.

● **irse pitando** to dash.

● **salir pitando** *fam* to be off like a shot.

pitido *nm* whistle.

pitillera *nf* cigarette case.

pitillo *nm* cigarette.

pito *nm* **1** (*silbato*) whistle: *tiene voz de pito*, he has a squeaky voice. **2** (*claxon*) horn. **3** (*abucheo*) booing. **4** *fam* (*pene*) willy.

● **entre pitos y flautas** *fam* what with one thing and another.

● **me importa un pito** *fam* I don't give a damn.

pitorrearse *vpr fam* to take the mickey.

pizarra *nf* **1** (*roca*) slate. **2** (*de escuela*) blackboard.

pizca *nf* bit, jot: *no tiene ni pizca de gracia*, it's not the slightest bit funny; *una pizca de sal*, a pinch of salt.

pizza *nf* pizza.

placa *nf* **1** (*lámina*) plate. **2** (*inscrita*) plaque. **3** (*de policía*) badge. **4** (*de cocinar*) plate.

■ **placa conmemorativa** commemorative plaque.

■ **placa de matrícula** GB number plate; US license plate.

■ **placa solar** solar panel.

placentero,-a *adj* pleasant.

placer *nm* pleasure: *tengo el placer de presentarles a...*, it's my pleasure to introduce you to....

plaga *nf* plague, pest.

plagiar *vt* to plagiarize.

plan *nm* **1** (*proyecto*) plan, project: *¿tienes planes para esta noche?*, have you made any plans for tonight? **2** (*dibujo*) drawing.

● **en plan de broma** *fam* as a joke.

● **no es plan** *fam* that's not on.

■ **plan de estudios** syllabus [*pl* **-ses**].

■ **plan de jubilación** retirement plan.

■ **plan de pensiones** pension plan.

plana *nf* page.

● **en primera plana** on the front page.

plancha *nf* **1** (*de metal*) plate, sheet. **2** (*para planchar*) iron.

● **hacer una plancha** *fam* to put one's foot in it.

● **carne a la plancha** grilled meat.

■ **plancha a vapor** steam iron.

planchar *vt* (*gen*) to iron; (*traje, pantalón*) to press.

planeador *nm* glider.

planear *vt* to plan.

▶ *vi* (*avión*) to glide.

planeta *nm* planet.

planificar *vt* to plan.

plano,-a *adj* flat, even: *pies planos*, flat feet.

▶ *nm* **plano 1** (*mapa*) plan, map. **2** (*superficie*) plane. **3** (*en filmación*) shot.

● **de plano** openly: *confesó de plano*, he made a full confesion.

■ **primer plano 1** (*foto*) close-up. **2** (*plano de foto*) foreground.

planta *nf* **1** plant. **2** (*del pie*) sole. **3** (*piso*) floor: *en la cuarta planta*, on the fourth floor. **4** (*instalación*) plant.

● **de buena planta** good looking.

■ **planta baja** ground floor.

■ **planta depuradora** water purification plant.

plantación *nf* **1** (*acción*) planting. **2** (*terreno*) plantation.

plantar *vt* **1** (*en tierra*) to plant; (*semilla*) to sow. **2** (*colocar*) to set up [*pt & pp* **set**], place. **3** (*persona*) to stand up [*pt & pp* **stood**].

▶ *vpr* **plantarse 1** (*mantenerse*) to stand firm [*pt & pp* **stood**]. **2** (*llegar*) to arrive, get: *en media hora me planto allí*, I'll get there in half an hour.

● **dejar a** ALGN **plantado** to stand SB up [*pt & pp* **stood**].

● **plantar cara a algo** to face up to STH.

plantear *vt* **1** (*planear*) to plan, outline. **2** (*establecer*) to establish. **3** (*problema*) to set [*pt & pp* **set**] out. **4** (*pregunta*) to pose, raise.

▶ *vpr* **plantearse 1** (*persona*) to think [*pt & pp* **thought**] about. **2** (*cuestión*) to arise [*pt* **arose**; *pp* **arisen**]: *todavía no me lo he planteado*, I haven't thought about it yet; *me estoy planteando dejar este trabajo*, I'm thinking about leaving this job.

plantilla *nf* **1** (*de zapato*) insole. **2** (*patrón*) model, pattern. **3** (*personal*) staff.

● **ser de plantilla** to be on the payroll.

plantón
- **darle un plantón a** ALGN to stand SB up [*pt* & *pp* **stood**].

plasma *nm* plasma.
- **plasma sanguíneo** blood plasma.

plástico,-a *adj* plastic.
- ► *nm* **plástico** plastic.

plastilina *nf* Plasticine®.

plata *nf* (*metal*) silver.
- **hablar en plata** *fam* to speak frankly [*pt* **spoke**; *pp* **spoken**].
- **plata de ley** sterling silver.

plataforma *nf* platform.
- **plataforma de lanzamiento** launch-pad.
- **plataforma espacial** space station.
- **plataforma petrolífera** oil rig.
- **zapatos de plataforma** platform shoes.

plátano *nm* **1** (*fruta*) banana. **2** (*árbol*) plane tree.

platea *nf* stalls *pl*.

plateado,-a *adj* **1** (*bañado en plata*) silver-plated. **2** (*color*) silvery.

platillo *nm* **1** (*plato*) saucer. **2** (*de balanza*) pan. **3** (*instrumento*) cymbal.
- **platillo volante** flying saucer.

platino *nm* platinum.

plato *nm* **1** (*recipiente*) plate, dish. **2** (*de comida*) dish. **3** (*en comida*) course.
- **lavar los platos** to do the washing-up, wash up.
- **pagar los platos rotos** to carry the can.
- **plato fuerte** main course.
- **plato precocinado** pre-cooked meal.

plató *nm* set.

playa *nf* beach: *hemos pasado el verano en la playa*, we spent the summer at the beach or seaside.

playeras *nf pl* gym shoes.

playero,-a *adj* beach.

plaza *nf* **1** (*de pueblo, ciudad*) square. **2** (*mercado*) market-place: *hacer la plaza*, to do the shopping. **3** (*sitio*) space. **4** (*asiento*) seat. **5** (*fortaleza*) fortress. **6** (*empleo*) position, post. **7** (*ciudad*) town, city.
- **cubrir una plaza** to fill a vacancy.
- **plaza de garaje** parking space.
- **plaza de toros** bullring.
- **plaza mayor** main square.

plazo *nm* **1** (*de tiempo*) period: *en un pla-*

zo de una semana, within a week; *dentro del plazo*, within the specified period. **2** (*pago*) instalment.
- **a corto plazo** in the short term.
- **a largo plazo** in the long term.
- **a plazos** by instalments.
- **plazo de inscripción** registration period.

plazoleta *nf* small square.

plegable *adj* folding.

plegar *vt* to fold.
- ► *vpr* **plegarse 1** (*doblarse*) to bend [*pt* & *pp* **bent**]. **2** (*rendirse*) to yield, submit.

pleito *nm* litigation, lawsuit.

pleno,-a *adj* full, complete: *en pleno día*, in broad daylight.
- ► *nm* **pleno** full assembly.

pliego *nm* **1** (*hoja*) sheet of paper. **2** (*documento*) document.

pliegue *nm* **1** (*doblez*) fold. **2** (*en ropa*) pleat.

plomo *nm* **1** (*metal*) lead. **2** fuse: *se fundieron los plomos*, the fuses blew. **3** (*pesado*) bore: *no seas plomo*, don't be such a bore!
- **gasolina sin plomo** unleaded petrol.

pluma *nf* **1** (*de ave*) feather. **2** (*de escribir*) quill pen; (*estilográfica*) fountain pen.
- **tener pluma** to be camp.

plumaje *nm* plumage.

plumero *nm* feather duster.
- **se le ve el plumero** you can see through him.

plumier *nm* pencil case.

plural *adj - nm* plural.

pluriempleo *nm* having more than one job: *el problema del pluriempleo*, the problem of people having more than one job.

PNB *abr* (*Producto Nacional Bruto*) GNP, gross national product.

población *nf* **1** (*habitantes*) population. **2** (*ciudad*) city, town; (*pueblo*) village.
- **población activa** working population.

poblado,-a *adj* **1** (*zona*) populated. **2** (*barba*) thick.
- ► *nm* **poblado** settlement.

poblar *vt* **1** (*de personas*) to populate. **2** (*de árboles*) to plant with.
- ► *vpr* **poblarse** to become peopled.

pobre *adj* poor: *gente pobre*, poor people; *¡pobre Luis!*, poor old Luis.
- ► *nmf*: *los pobres*, the poor.

pobreza *nf* poverty.

pocilga *nf* pigsty.

poco,-a *adj (singular)* little, not much; *(plural)* few, not many: **hago poco ejercicio últimamente**, I do very little exercice these days; **tenemos poco tiempo**, we haven't much time.

▶ *pron (singular)* little; *(plural)* not many: **lo poco que aprendí**, what little I learned; **como ése he visto pocos**, I've not seen many like that one; **necesito un poco de dinero**, I need a little money; **he dormido un poco**, I had a little sleep; **ponle un poco de sal**, add a little bit of salt.

▶ *adv* little, not much: **voy poco por allí**, I go there very little, I rarely go there.

● **a poco de** shortly after.

● **dentro de poco** soon, presently.

● **hace poco** not long ago.

● **poco a poco** little by little.

● **poco más o menos** more or less.

● **por poco** nearly.

● **un poco** a little, a bit.

podar *vt* to prune.

poder *vt* **1** *(tener la facultad de)* can, to be able to: **¿puedes echarme una mano?**, can you lend me a hand?; **no pude abrirlo**, I couldn't open it, I was unable to open it. **2** *(tener permiso para)* can, may: **pueden pagar en efectivo**, you can pay in cash; **¿puedo fumar?**, may I smoke? **3** *(en conjeturas)* may, might: **puede que esté enfermo**, he may be ill, he might be ill. **4** *(en quejas, sugerencias)* can: **¡podrías habérmelo dicho!**, you could have told me!; **podríamos ir a esquiar**, we could go skiing.

▶ *nm* **1** *(capacidad, facultad)* power. **2** *(fuerza)* force, strength.

● **estar en el poder** to be in power.

● **estar en poder de** ALGN to be in SB's hands.

● **no poder con** not to be able to cope with.

● **no poder más** to be unable to do more.

● **¿se puede?** may I come in?

■ **poder ejecutivo** executive power.

■ **poder legislativo** legislative power.

■ **poderes mágicos** magic powers.

poderoso,-a *adj* powerful.

podio *nm* podium.

podrido,-a *adj* **1** *(putrefacto)* rotten. **2** *(corrupto)* corrupt.

● **podrido,-a de dinero** stinking rich.

poema *nm* poem.

poesía *nf* **1** *(género)* poetry. **2** *(poema)* poem.

poeta *nmf* poet.

poético,-a *adj* poetic.

poetisa *nf* poetess.

polaco,-a *adj* Polish.

▶ *nm,f (persona)* Pole.

▶ *nm* **polaco** *(idioma)* Polish.

polar *adj* polar.

polea *nf* pulley.

polémica *nf* controversy: **hubo mucha polémica**, there was a big controversy.

polémico,-a *adj* controversial.

polen *nm* pollen.

poli *nmf fam* cop.

▶ *nf* **la poli** *fam* the cops *pl.*

policía *nf* police.

▶ *nmf (hombre)* policeman [*pl* -**men**]; *(mujer)* policewoman [*pl* -**women**].

■ **policía secreta** secret police.

policíaco,-a *adj* police.

■ **novela policíaca** detective story.

policial *adj* police.

polideportivo *nm* sports centre.

polígono *nm* polygon.

■ **polígono industrial** industrial estate.

polilla *nf* moth.

política *nf* **1** *(ciencia)* politics: **se dedica a la política**, he's into politics. **2** *(método)* policy.

político,-a *adj* **1** *(partido, programa)* politic. **2** *(cortés)* tactful. **3** *(parentesco)* : **mi padre político**, my father-in-law; **mi familia política**, my in-laws.

▶ *nm,f* politician.

póliza *nf* certificate, policy.

■ **póliza de seguros** insurance policy.

polizón *nm* stowaway.

polla *nf* **1** *(ave)* young hen. **2** *vulg (pene)* prick, dick.

pollería *nf* poultry shop.

pollito *nm* chick.

pollo *nm* chicken.

■ **pollo asado** roast chicken.

■ **pollo de corral** free-range chicken.

polo *nm* **1** *(gen)* pole. **2** *(helado)* GB ice lolly ; US Popsicle®. **3** *(jersey)* polo shirt.

● **son polos opuestos** they are poles apart.

Polonia *nf* Poland.
polución *nf* pollution.
polvareda *nf* cloud of dust.
polvo *nm* **1** *(en aire, muebles)* dust. **2** *(en farmacia, cosmética)* powder. **3** *vulg (coito)* screw, fuck.
- **echar un polvo** *vulg* to have a screw.
- **estar hecho polvo** *fam* to be knackered.
- **leche en polvo** powdered milk.
■ **polvos de talco** talcum powder *sing.*
pólvora *nf* gunpowder.
polvoriento,-a *adj* dusty.
polvorín *nm* powder magazine.
polvorón *nm* crumbly shortcake.
pomada *nf* cream.
pomelo *nm* grapefruit.
pomo *nm* knob, handle.
pompa *nf* **1** *(de jabón)* bubble. **2** *(ostentación)* pomp.
■ **pompas fúnebres 1** *(ceremonia)* funeral *sing.* **2** *(empresa)* undertaker's.
pómulo *nm* cheekbone.
ponche *nm* punch.
poner *vt* **1** *(colocar)* to place, put, set [*pt & pp* set]: *¿dónde lo pongo?*, where shall I put it?; *ponle un poco más de sal*, put a bit more of salt in. **2** *(instalar)* to install. **3** *(encender)* to turn on, put on: *puso la radio*, she put the radio on. **4** *(huevos)* to lay [*pt & pp* laid]. **5** *(suponer)* to suppose: *pongamos que es así*, let's suppose that it is so. **6** *(dinero)* to place, pay [*pt & pp* paid]. **7** *(dar nombre a)* to name, call: *le pusieron Alba*, they called her Alba. **8** *(escribir)* to put, write [*pt* wrote; *pp* written]. **9** *(estar escrito)* to say [*pt & pp* said]: *¿qué pone en ese letrero?*, what does that sign say? **10** *(establecer)* to open: *han puesto un bar*, they've opened a bar. **11** *(programa, película)* to show [*pt* showed; *pp* shown]. **12** *(carta etc)* to send [*pt & pp* sent]. **13** *(deber, trabajo)* to give, assign. **14 poner + *adj*** to make: *me pone enfermo*, he makes me sick; *poner triste a ALGN*, to make SB feel sad.
▶ *vpr* **ponerse 1** *(colocarse)* to stand [*pt & pp* stood]: *no te pongas delante*, don't stand there; *póngase cómodo*, make youself at home. **2** *(sombrero, ropa)* to put on: *al ponerse el vestido*, as she was putting on her dress; *no te pongas ese traje*, don't wear that suit. **3** *(sol)* to set [*pt & pp* set]. **4** *(volverse)* to become, get, turn: *se puso triste*, he became sad. **5** *(al teléfono - cogerlo)* to answer the phone; *(- acudir)* to come to the phone: *cuando llamé, se puso la señora de la limpieza*, when I phoned, the cleaning lady answered it; *dígale que se ponga*, tell her to come to the phone; *¿se puede poner Lola?*, can I speak to Lola, please? **6** *(llegar)* to get: *me puse allí en 2 horas*, I got there in 2 hours. **7** *fam (drogarse)* to get high.
- **poner al corriente** to bring up to date.
- **poner al día** to bring up to date [*pt & pp* brought].
- **poner de manifiesto** to make evident.
- **poner de relieve** to emphasize.
- **poner en libertad** to set free [*pt & pp* set].
- **poner en práctica** to carry out.
- **poner por las nubes** to praise to the skies.
- **poner reparos** to make objections.
- **ponerse a + *inf*** to start to + *inf.*
- **ponerse a malas con ALGN** to have a falling out with SB.
- **ponerse con algo** to start on STH.
- **ponerse de acuerdo** to agree.
- **ponerse de rodillas** to kneel [*pt & pp* knelt] down.
- **ponerse en pie** to stand up [*pt & pp* stood].
- **ponerse perdido,-a** to get dirty.
poni *nm* pony.
poniente *nm* *(oeste)* west; *(viento)* west wind.
pontífice *nm* pontiff [*pl* -s], pope.
popa *nf* stern.
popular *adj* popular.
popularidad *nf* popularity.
por *prep* **1** *(causa)* because of: *suspendí por no estudiar*, I failed because I hadn't studied; *llegaron tarde por la nieve*, they were late because of the snow; *eso te pasa por imbécil*, this is what you get for being stupid; *lo hice por ti*, I did it for you; *¡por los novios!*, to the bride and groom!; *lo hace por agradar*, he does it to please. **2** *(tiempo)* at, in; *(duración)* for: *por la noche*, at night; *por la mañana*, in the morning; *vino por poco tiempo*,

he didn't stay for long. **3** *(lugar)* along, in, on, by, up, down: *íbamos por la calle*, we were walking along the street; *iremos por la autopista*, we'll go by motorway; *paseo por el parque*, I walk in the park; *bajaba por la escalera*, I was going down the stairs. **4** *(medio)* by: *enviar por avión*, to send by air. **5** *(agente)* by: *escrito por él*, written by him; *comprado por ella*, bought by her. **6** *(distribución)* per: *cinco por ciento*, five per cent. **7** *(en lugar de)* instead of: *ve tú por mí*, you go instead of me; *1,5 euros por una libra*, 1,5 euros to the pound. **8** *(en multiplicación)* times: *tres por dos seis*, three times two is six. **9** *(medidas)* by: *mide tres metros por dos*, it measures three metres by two.

- **estar loco por algn** to be crazy about SB.
- **estar por** (a punto de) to be on the point of.
- **estar por hacer** to remain to be done, not to have been done.
- **ir por** to go and get, fetch: *voy por el periódico*, I'll go and get the paper; *habrá que ir a por el médico*, we'll have to fetch the doctor.
- **por aquí** around here.
- **por casualidad** by chance.
- **por correo** by post.
- **¡por Dios!** for heaven's sake!
- **por lo visto** apparently.
- **por mí** as far as I am concerned.
- **por mucho que...** however much...: *por mucho que trabaje...*, however much she works.
- **¿por qué?** why?
- **por supuesto** of course.
- **por tanto** therefore.
- **por todas partes** everywhere.

porcelana *nf* **1** *(material)* porcelain. **2** *(vajilla)* china.

porcentaje *nm* percentage.

porche *nm* porch.

porcino,-a *adj* pig.

porción *nf* **1** *(parte)* portion, part. **2** *(cuota)* share.

- **queso en porciones** cheese portions.

pordiosero,-a *nm,f* beggar.

pormenor *nm* detail.

pornografía *nf* pornography.

poro *nm* pore.

poroso,-a *adj* porous.

porque *conj* **1** *(causa)* because: *no voy porque no quiero*, I'm not going because I don't want to. **2** *(finalidad)* in order that, so that.

porqué *nm* cause, reason.

porquería *nf* dirt, filth: *está todo hecho una porquería*, everything is covered in dirt; *no comas tantas porquerías*, stop eating rubbish; *me pagan una porquería*, they pay me a pittance.

porra *nf* cudgel, club.

- **mandar a algn a la porra** *fam* to send SB packing [*pt & pp* **sent**].

porrazo *nm* blow, knock: *me di un porrazo en la cabeza*, I banged my head; *se cayó y se dio un porrazo*, she fell over and hurt herself.

porro *nm* arg joint.

porrón *nm* porrón.

portaaviones *nm* aircraft carrier.

portada *nf* **1** *(de libro)* title page. **2** *(de revista)* cover. **3** *(de periódico)* front page. **4** *(de disco)* sleeve.

portador,-ra *nm,f (de objeto)* bearer, holder; *(de virus)* carrier.

- **páguese al portador** pay the bearer [*pt & pp* **paid**].

portaequipajes *nm* luggage rack.

portal *nm* **1** *(entrada)* doorway; *(vestíbulo)* entrance hall: *te espero en el portal*, I'll wait at the front door. **2** *(porche)* porch. **3** *(de Internet)* portal.

portalámparas *nm* bulbholder.

portarse *vpr* to behave, act.

- **portarse bien** to behave well.
- **portarse mal** to behave badly.

portátil *adj* portable.

▶ *nm (ordenador)* laptop, portable.

portavoz *nmf (gen)* spokesperson; *(hombre)* spokesman [*pl* -**men**]; *(mujer)* spokeswoman [*pl* -**women**].

portazo *nm* bang: *se marchó dando un portazo*, she slammed the door and left; *cerró de un portazo*, he slammed the door.

portento *nm* wonder.

portería *nf* **1** *(de edificio)* porter's lodge. **2** *(en fútbol)* goal.

portero,-a *nm,f* **1** *(de edificio)* doorkeeper, porter. **2** *(guardameta)* goalkeeper.

- **portero automático** entry phone.

portorriqueño,-a *adj* → puertorriqueño,-a.

Portugal *nm* Portugal.

portugués,-esa *adj - nm,f* Portuguese.

▶ *nm* **portugués** *(idioma)* Portuguese.

porvenir *nm* future.

posada *nf* lodging-house, inn.

posar *vi* to pose.

▶ *vpr* **posarse 1** *(pájaro)* to alight, perch, sit *[pt & pp* **sat**]. **2** *(sedimento)* to settle.

posdata *nf* postscript.

poseer *vt* to own, possess.

posesión *nf* possession.

● **estar en posesión de algo** to be in possession of STH.

posesivo,-a *adj* possessive.

posguerra *nf* postwar period.

posibilidad *nf* possibility.

▶ *nf pl* **posibilidades** *(recursos)* means.

posible *adj* possible.

● **hacer algo posible** to make STH possible.

● **hacer todo lo posible** to do one's best.

posición *nf* position.

● **perder posisiciones** to lose *[pt & pp* **lost**] ground.

positivo,-a *adj* positive.

poso *nm* **1** *(de mineral)* sediment. **2** *(de café, vino)* dregs *pl*.

posponer *vt* to postpone, delay, put off.

posta.

● **a posta** on purpose.

postal *adj* postal.

▶ *nf* postcard.

poste *nm* post.

■ **poste de la luz** electricity pylon.

póster *nm* poster.

posterior *adj* **1** *(de atrás)* back, rear. **2** *(más tarde)* later.

posteriormente *adv* later.

postizo,-a *adj* false.

▶ *nm* **postizo** hairpiece.

postre *nm* dessert: *¿qué hay de postre?*, what's for dessert?

● **a la postre** at the end of the day.

● **para postre** to cap it all.

postura *nf* **1** *(posición)* posture, position. **2** *(actitud)* attitude, stance.

potable *adj* drinkable.

potaje *nm* stew.

potencia *nf* power.

● **en potencia** potential: *un asesino en potencia*, a potential killer.

■ **potencia nuclear** nuclear power.

potencial *adj - nm* potential.

potente *adj* powerful.

potingue *nm fam* cream.

potro,-a *nm,f* colt, foal.

▶ *nm* **potro 1** *(de tortura)* rack. **2** *(para gimnasia)* vaulting horse.

pozo *nm* **1** *(de agua)* well. **2** *(en mina)* shaft.

■ **pozo de petróleo** oil well.

■ **pozo de sabiduría** fount of wisdom.

práctica *nf* practice.

▶ *nf pl* **prácticas** training *sing*.

● **en la práctica** in practice.

● **poner en práctica** to put into practice.

prácticamente *adv* practically.

practicante *adj* practising.

▶ *nm,f* nurse.

practicar *vt* **1** *(idioma, profesión)* to practice. **2** *(deporte)* to play, do. **3** *(hacer)* to make.

▶ *vi* to practice.

práctico,-a *adj* practical.

pradera *nf* meadow; *(más grande)* prairie.

prado *nm* meadow.

precaución *nf* precaution.

● **actuar con precaución** to act with caution.

● **tomar precauciones** to take precautions.

● **conducir con precaución** to drive *[pt* **drove**; *pp* **driven**] carefully.

■ **medidas de precaución** preventive measures.

precavido,-a *adj* cautious, wary.

precedente *adj* preceding, prior, foregoing.

▶ *nm* precedent.

● **sentar un precedente** to set *[pt & pp* **set**] a precedent.

● **sin precedentes** unprecedented.

preceder *vt-vi* to precede.

precintar *vt* *(paquete)* to seal; *(zona)* to seal off.

precinto *nm* seal.

precio *nm* **1** *(de producto)* price: *¿qué precio tenía?*, how much was it? **2** *fig (valor)* value, worth.

● **a precio de coste** at cost price.

● **no tener precio** to be priceless.

■ **precio de fábrica** factory price.

■ **precio de venta al público** retail price.

preciosidad *nf* : *¡qué preciosidad de vestido!*, what a beautiful dress!

precioso,-a *adj* **1** *(valioso)* precious. **2** *(bello)* beautiful: *¡es una niña preciosa!*, she's a lovely baby!

precipicio *nm* precipice.

precipitación *nf* **1** *(prisa)* rush, haste, hurry. **2** precipitation: *habrá abundantes precipitaciones*, there will be heavy showers.

precipitado,-a *adj* hasty.

precipitar *vt* **1** to precipitate. **2** *(acelerar)* to precipitate, hasten.
► *vpr* **precipitarse 1** *(apresurarse)* to be hasty. **2** *(obrar sin reflexión)* to act rashly.
● **precipitarse a hacer algo** to rush to do STH.
● **precipitarse sobre ALGN** to throw oneself on SB [*pt* **threw**; *pp* **thrown**].

precisamente *adv* **1** *(exactamente)* precisely, exactly. **2** *(justamente)* just.

precisar *vt* **1** *(especificar)* to specify. **2** *(necesitar)* to need.
● **precisar de algo** to need STH

precisión *nf* precision, accuracy.

preciso,-a *adj* **1** *(exacto)* precise, exact, accurate: *instrucciones precisas*, precise instructions; *en aquel preciso instante*, at that very moment. **2** *(necesario)* necessary: *es preciso*, it is necessary; *no es preciso que me ayudes*, you don't need to help me.

precocinado,-a *adj* pre-cooked.

precoz *adj* **1** *(niño)* precocious. **2** *(envejecimiento, eyacualción)* premature.

predecir *vt* to predict, foretell [*pt & pp* **foretold**].

predicado *nm* predicate.

predicar *vt* to preach.

predicción *nf* prediction.
■ **predicción meteorológica** weather forecast.

predominio *nm* predominance.

preescolar *adj* preschool.

prefabricado,-a *adj* prefabricated.

prefacio *nm* preface.

preferencia *nf* preference.
● **tener preferencia** (al volante) to have right of way.

preferible *adj* preferable.

preferir *vt* to prefer: *prefiero el rojo al verde*, I prefer the red one to the green one; *yo preferiría no ir*, I'd rather not go.

prefijo *nm* **1** prefix. **2** *(telefónico)* code.

pregón *nm* public announcement.

pregonar *vt* to announce.

pregunta *nf* question.
● **contestar a una pregunta** to answer a question.
● **hacerle una pregunta a ALGN** to ask SB a question.

preguntar *vt* to ask: *pregúntale la hora*, ask him the time; *me ha preguntado por ti*, she asked after you.
► *vpr* **preguntarse** to wonder.
● **preguntar por ALGN** to ask after SB.
● **preguntarle algo a ALGN** to ask SB STH.

preguntón,-ona *nm,f fam* nosey parker.

prehistoria *nf* prehistory.

prehistórico,-a *adj* prehistoric.

prejuicio *nm* prejudice.

prematuro,-a *adj* premature.
► *nm* **prematuro** premature baby.

premeditación *nf* premeditation.
● **con premeditación** deliberately.

premiar *vt* **1** *(otorgar premio a)* to award a prize to. **2** *(recompensar)* to reward.

premio *nm* **1** *(en concurso, sorteo)* prize. **2** *(recompensa)* reward.
■ **premio de consolación** consolation prize.
■ **premio gordo** jackpot.

prenda *nf* **1** *(de vestir)* garment. **2** *(garantía)* pledge.
● **no soltar prenda** not to say [*pt & pp* **said**] a word.

prender *vt* **1** *(agarrar)* to seize. **2** *(sujetar)* to attach; *(con agujas)* to pin. **3** *(arrestar)* to arrest.
► *vi* **1** *(planta)* to take root. **2** *(fuego etc)* to catch [*pt & pp* **caught**].
► *vpr* **prenderse** to catch fire [*pt & pp* **caught**].

prensa *nf* press.
■ **prensa amarilla** gutter press.
■ **prensa del corazón** gossip magazines *pl*.

prensar *vt* to press.

preñado,-a *adj* pregnant.

preocupación *nf* worry.

preocupado,-a *adj* worried.

preocupar *vt-vpr* **preocupar(se)** to worry.

preparación *nf* preparation: *la prepa-*

ración me llevó varios días, it took me days to prepare it.

preparado,-a *adj* ready, prepared.

▶ *nm* **preparado** *(medicamento)* preparation.

preparar *vt* to prepare: **estoy preparando el discurso**, I'm preparing the speech; **le preparamos una sorpresa**, we had a surprise form him.

▶ *vpr* **prepararse** to get ready: **prepararse a hacer algo**, to get ready to do STH; **me estoy preparando para la entrevista**, I'm preparing for the interview.

● **preparar la comida** to make lunch, get lunch ready.

preparativos *nm pl* preparations, arrangements.

preposición *nf* preposition.

presa *nf* 1 *(cosa prendida)* prey. 2 *(embalse)* dam.

● **ser presa de** to be a victim of.

presagio *nm* 1 *(señal)* omen. 2 *(adivinación)* premonition.

prescindir *vi* to do without: **no puedo prescindir del coche**, I can't do without the car.

presencia *nf* presence.

● **en presencia de** in the presence of.

■ **buena presencia** smart appearance: **tiene muy buena presencia**, he looks very smart.

presenciar *vt (asistir)* to be present at; *(contemplar)* to witness.

presentación *nf* 1 *(gen)* presentation. 2 *(de personas)* introduction.

presentador,-a *nm,f* presenter, host.

presentar *vt* 1 *(gen)* to present. 2 *(mostrar)* to display, show [*pt* showed; *pp* shown]. 3 *(personas)* to introduce.

▶ *vpr* **presentarse** 1 *(comparecer)* to present oneself; *(candidato)* to stand [*pt & pp* stood]: **no se presentó al examen**, he didn't sit the exam; **el futuro se presenta bien**, the future looks good.

● **presentarse voluntario** to volunteer.

presente *adj - nm* present.

● **hacer presente** to remind of.

● **tener presente** to bear [*pt* bore; *pp* borne] in mind.

presentimiento *nm* presentiment.

presentir *vt* to feel [*pt & pp* felt]: **presentía que iba a pasar algo**, I felt that something was going to happen; **presiento que...**, I have a feeling that....

preservar *vt (proteger)* to protect; *(conservar)* to preserve.

preservativo *nm* condom.

presidencia *nf* 1 *(de nación)* presidency. 2 *(en reunión)* chairmanship.

presidente,-a *nm,f* 1 *(de nación, club, etc)* president. 2 *(en reunión - hombre)* chairman [*pl* -men]; *(- mujer)* chairwoman [*pl* -women].

■ **Presidente del Gobierno** Prime Minister.

presidiario,-a *nm,f* convict, prisoner.

presidio *nm* prison, penitentiary.

presidir *vt* 1 *(nación)* to be president of. 2 *(reunión)* to chair.

presión *nf* pressure.

■ **presión arterial** blood pressure.

presionar *vt* 1 *(apretar)* to press. 2 *(coaccionar)* to put pressure on: **se vio presionado por la familia**, his family put pressure on him.

preso,-a *adj* imprisoned.

▶ *nm,f* prisoner: **se lo llevaron preso**, he was taken prisoner; **estuvo presa**, she was in prison.

prestamista *nmf (de dinero)* moneylender; *(de casa de empeños)* pawnbroker.

préstamo *nm (acción)* lending; *(dinero)* loan: **préstamo hipotecario**, mortgage.

prestar *vt* 1 *(dejar prestado)* to lend [*pt & pp* lent], loan; *(pedir prestado)* to borrow: **¿me prestas 10 euros?**, can you lend me 10 euros? 2 *(servicio)* to do, render. 3 *(ayuda)* to give. 4 *(atención)* to pay [*pt & pp* paid].

▶ *vpr* **prestarse** 1 *(ofrecerse)* to lend oneself [*pt & pp* lent]. 2 *(dar motivo)* to cause.

● **no me prestaré a eso** I won't agree to that.

● **prestar declaración** to make a statement.

● **prestar juramento** to swear [*pt* swore; *pp* sworn].

prestidigitador,-a *nm,f* conjuror, magician.

prestigio *nm* prestige: **un abogado de prestigio**, a prestigious lawyer.

presumido,-a *adj* conceited, vain.

▶ *nm,f* : **eres un presumido**, you're very conceited.

presumir *vt (suponer)* to presume, suppose.

► *vi (vanagloriarse)* to be vain, be conceited: ***Pepe presume de guapo***, Pepe fancies himself; ***no presumas de listo***, you think you're very smart, don't you?; ***lo hace para presumir***, he does it to show off.

presunto,-a *adj* presumed, supposed.

presuntuoso,-a *adj* conceited, vain.

presupuesto *nm* **1** *(cálculo anticipado)* estimate; *(coste)* budget. **2** *(supuesto)* presupposition.

pretender *vt* **1** *(querer)* to want to: ***¿qué pretendes?***, what do you want? **2** *(intentar)* to try to: ***pretendía robarle***, she tried to rob him. **3** *(cortejar)* to court.

pretendiente,-a *nm,f* **1** *(enamorado)* suitor. **2** *(a cargo)* applicant.

pretérito,-a *adj* past.

► *nm* **pretérito** preterite, past simple.

■ **pretérito perfecto** present perfect.

pretexto *nm* pretext, excuse.

● **con el pretexto de que...** on the pretext that....

prevención *nf* **1** *(precaución)* prevention. **2** *(medida)* preventive measure. **3** *(prejuicio)* prejudice.

prevenir *vt* **1** *(prever)* to prevent. **2** *(advertir)* to warn.

prever *vt (adivinar)* to foresee [*pt* **foresaw** *pp* **foreseen**]; *(predecir)* to forecast [*pt* and *pp* **forecast**].

previo,-a *adj (anterior)* previous: ***necesita autorización previa***, you need prior permission; ***previo pago de la cuota***, on payment of the fee.

previsión *nf* **1** *(anticipación)* forecast. **2** *(precaución)* precaution.

previsor,-ra *adj* far-sighted.

previsto,-a *adj* : ***su llegada está prevista para las cinco***, he is expected to arrive at five; ***este caso no estaba previsto***, we had not accounted for this case; ***había previsto absolutamente todo***, she had thought of absolutely everything.

● **a la hora prevista** on time.

● **según lo previsto** according to plan.

prieto,-a *adj* tight.

prima *nf* **1** bonus. **2** → primo,-a.

primario,-a *adj* primary.

primavera *nf* **1** *(estación)* spring. **2** *(flor)* primrose.

primaveral *adj* spring.

primer *num* → primero,-a.

primera *nf* **1** *(clase)* first class: ***viajar en primera***, to travel first class. **2** *(marcha)* first gear.

● **de primera** first-class: ***productos de primera***, first-class products; ***aquí se vive de primera***, life is excellent here.

primero,-a *num* first: ***los dos primeros días***, the first two days; ***en primer lugar***, first of all; ***a primera hora***, first thing; ***de primero tomaré una sopa***, I'll have soup for the first course.

► *adv* **primero** first: ***primero hay que hervir la pasta***, first you must boil the pasta.

● **a primeros de mes** at the beginning of the month.

● **lo primero es lo primero** first things first.

● **ser el primero de clase** to be top of the class.

■ **primeros auxilios** first aid *sing*.

■ **primeras curas** first aid *sing*.

primitivo,-a *adj* **1** primitive. **2** *(tosco)* coarse.

primo,-a *adj* **1** *(materia)* raw. **2** *(número)* prime.

► *nm,f* cousin.

► *nm* **primo** simpleton.

● **hacer el primo** *fam* to be taken for a ride.

■ **primo,-a carnal** first cousin.

primogénito,-a *adj* - *nm,f* first-born.

primordial *adj* essential, fundamental.

princesa *nf* princess.

principado *nm* principality.

principal *adj* main, chief.

► *nm* **1** *(jefe)* chief [*pl* -**s**]. **2** *(piso)* first floor.

príncipe *nm* prince.

■ **príncipe azul** Prince Charming.

principiante,-a *nm,f* beginner.

principio *nm* **1** *(inicio)* beginning, start. **2** *(norma)* principle: ***tengo mis principios***, I have my principles.

► *nm pl* **principios** rudiments.

● **al principio** at first: ***al principio de algo***, at the beginning of STH.

● **en principio** in principle.

pringar *vt* **1** *fam (ensuciar)* to make greasy. **2** *fam (comprometer)* : ***pringar a ALGN en algo***, to move SB in STH; ***a mí no me pringues***, don't get me involved.

► *vi* **1** *fam (morir)* to kick the bucket. **2** *fam (trabajar)* to work hard.

► *vpr* **pringarse** *(ensuciarse)* to get covered.

pringoso,-a *adj* greasy.

pringue *nm* **1** *(grasa)* grease. **2** *(suciedad)* dirt.

prioridad *nf* priority.

prioritario,-a *adj* priority.

prisa *nf* hurry.

● **correr prisa** to be urgent: *corre mucha prisa*, it's very urgent; *no me corre prisa*, I'm not in a hurry.

● **darse prisa** to hurry, hurry up.

● **tener prisa** to be in a hurry.

prisión *nf* *(lugar)* prison, jail; *(encarcelamiento)* imprisonment.

● **en prisión preventiva** remanded in custody.

prisionero,-a *nm,f* prisoner: *lo hicieron prisionero*, they took him prisoner.

prisma *nm* prism.

prismáticos *nm pl* binoculars.

privación *nf* deprivation.

► *nf pl* **privaciones** privations.

privado,-a *adj* private.

● **en privado** in private.

privar *vt* **1** *(despojar)* to deprive. **2** *(prohibir)* to forbid [*pt* **forbade**; *pp* **forbidden**]. **3** *fam (gustar)* : *esa tía me priva*, I'm mad about that girl.

► *vi* **1** *(estar de moda)* to be in fashion. **2** *fam (beber)* to drink [*pt* **drank**; *pp* **drunk**].

► *vpr* **privarse** to do without: *no nos privamos de nada*, we don't want for anything.

privilegiado,-a *adj* privileged.

► *nm,f* : *es un privilegiado*, he's really privileged; *los privilegiados*, the privileged.

privilegio *nm* privilege.

pro *nm & nf* advantage.

► *prep* in favour of.

■ **los pros y los contras** the pros and cons.

proa *nf* *(de barco)* prow, bow; *(de avión)* nose.

probabilidad *nf* probability.

probable *adj* probable, likely.

probador *nm* changing room.

probar *vt* **1** *(demostrar)* to prove: *esto prueba su inocencia*, this proves her innocence. **2** *(comprobar)* to try, test: *pruébalo a ver si funciona*, try it to see if it works. **3** *(vino, comida)* to taste, try: *¿quieres probar la sopa?*, do you want to taste the soup? **4** *(prendas)* to try on: *prueba éste, es más grande*, try this one on, it's bigger.

► *vi (intentar)* to try: *ahora probaré yo*, now I will have a go.

probeta *nf* testtube.

problema *nm* problem.

problemático,-a *adj* problematic.

procedencia *nf* **1** *(de persona, producto)* origin, source. **2** *(de tren)* point of departure.

procedente *adj* coming.

proceder *vi* **1** *(pasar)* to proceed: *procedamos a la votación*, let's proceed to the vote. **2** *(venir de)* to come. **3** *(actuar)* to behave: *su manera de proceder*, his way of behaving. **4** *(ser adecuado)* to be appropriate: *si procede, ...*, if appropiate ....

► *nm* GB behaviour; US behavior.

procedimiento *nm (método)* procedure, method.

procesado,-a *adj - nm,f* JUR accused.

► *nm* **procesado** INFORM processing.

procesamiento *nm* **1** INFORM processing. **2** JUR prosecution.

■ **procesamiento de datos** data processing.

■ **procesamiento de textos** word processing.

procesar *vt* **1** *(dato, texto)* to process. **2** JUR to prosecute.

procesión *nf* procession.

proceso *nm* **1** *(gen)* process. **2** JUR trial.

■ **proceso de datos** data processing.

proclamar *vt* to proclaim.

► *vpr* **proclamarse** : *se proclamó rey*, he proclaimed himself king; *se proclamó campeona*, she won the championship.

procrear *vt* to procreate.

procurar *vt* **1** *(intentar)* to try: *procura llegar pronto*, try to get there early; *procuré que no se enterasen*, I didn't let them find out. **2** *(proporcionar)* to manage to get.

prodigio *nm* **1** *(persona)* prodigy. **2** *(milagro)* miracle; *(maravilla)* wonder.

● **niño prodigio** child prodigy.

prodigioso,-a *adj* **1** *(increíble)* prodigious. **2** *(maravilloso)* marvellous.

producción *nf* production.
- **producción en cadena** mass production.
- **producción en serie** mass production.

producir *vt* **1** *(gen)* to produce. **2** *(causar)* to cause. **3** *(con interés)* to yield.
► *vpr* **producirse** to happen.

productividad *nf* productivity.

productivo,-a *adj* productive.

producto *nm* product.
- **producto derivado** by-product.
- **producto interior bruto** gross domestic product.
- **producto químico** chemical.

productor,-ra *adj* productive.
► *nm,f* producer.

proeza *nf* heroic deed.

profanar *vt* to profane, desecrate.

profano,-a *adj* **1** *(no sagrado)* profane, secular. **2** *(no experto)* lay.
► *nm,f* layman [*pl* **-men**], laywoman [*pl* **women**]: *soy un profano en la materia*, I don't know anything about the subject.

profecía *nf* prophecy.

profesión *nf* profession.

profesional *adj* - *nmf* professional.

profesor,-ra *nm,f* teacher; *(de universidad)* lecturer.
- **profesor,-ra de autoescuela** driving instructor.
- **profesor,-ra particular** private tutor.

profesorado *nm* teaching staff.

profeta *nm* prophet.

profetizar *vt* to prophesy.

profundidad *nf* depth: *un metro de profundidad*, one metre deep.

profundizar *vt* to deepen.
► *vt-vi (discurrir)* to go deeply into.

profundo,-a *adj* **1** *(agujero, piscina)* deep: *¿es muy profundo?*, is it very deep?; *es muy poco profundo*, it's very shallow. **2** *(pensamiento, misterio, etc)* profound: *le tenía un profundo respeto*, I had a great respect for her.

progenitor,-ra *nm,f* progenitor, ancestor.
► *nm pl* **progenitores** parents.

programa *nm* **1** *(gen)* programme; US program. **2** INFORM program.

programación *nf* **1** *(televisiva)* programmes *pl*, programming. **2** *(informática)* programming.

programador,-ra *nm,f* INFORM programmer.

programar *vt* **1** *(organizar)* GB to programme; US to program. **2** INFORM to program.

progresar *vi* to progress.

progresista *adj* - *nmf* progressive.

progresivo,-a *adj* progressive.

progreso *nm* progress.
- **hacer progresos** to make progress.

prohibición *nf* prohibition, ban.

prohibido,-a *adj* forbidden, prohibited: *está terminantemente prohibido*, it's strictly forbidden.
- **"Prohibido aparcar"** "No parking".
- **"Prohibido arrojar escombros"** "No dumping".
- **"Prohibido el paso"** "No entry".
- **"Prohibido fumar"** "No smoking".

prohibir *vt (gen)* to forbid [*pt* **forbade**; *pp* **forbidden**]; *(por ley)* to prohibit, ban: *me han prohibido fumar*, I'm not allowed to smoke.

prójimo *nm* fellow man [*pl* **men**].

proletario,-a *adj* - *nm,f* proletarian.

prólogo *nm* prologue.

prolongar *vt (en el tiempo)* to prolong; *(de longitud)* to extend.
► *vpr* **prolongarse** to go on.

promedio *nm* average.

promesa *nf* promise.
- **cumplir (con) una promesa** to keep a promise.
- **hacer una promesa** to make a promise.

prometedor,-ra *adj* promising.

prometer *vt* to promise.
► *vi* to be promising: *un niño que promete*, a boy that has promise; *este contrato promete*, this is a promising contract.
► *vpr* **prometerse** *(pareja)* to get engaged.
- **prometer el oro y el moro** to promise the moon.

prometido,-a *nm,f (hombre)* fiancé; *(mujer)* fiancée.
- **estar prometidos** to be engaged.

promoción *nf* **1** *(gen)* promotion. **2** *(curso)* class, year.
- **en promoción** on special offer.

promocionar *vt* to promote.

promover *vt* to promote.

pronombre *nm* pronoun.

pronosticar *vt* to forecast [*pt & pp* **forecast**].

pronóstico *nm* **1** (*gen*) forecast. **2** (*médico*) prognosis.

■ **pronóstico del tiempo** weather forecast.

prontitud *nf* quickness, promptness.

pronto,-a *adj* quick, fast.

▶ *adv* **pronto 1** (*inmediatamente*) soon. **2** (*rápidamente*) quickly. **3** (*temprano*) early.

▶ *nm* sudden impulse: *me dio un pronto y lo hice*, I did it on a sudden impulse.

● **de pronto** suddenly.

● **¡hasta pronto!** see you soon!

● **levantarse pronto** to get up early.

● **lo más pronto posible** as soon as possible.

● **por lo pronto** (*por ahora*) for the moment; (*para empezar*) for a start.

● **tan pronto como...** as soon as....

pronunciación *nf* pronunciation.

pronunciar *vt* **1** (*palabra*) to pronounce. **2** (*discurso*) to make.

▶ *vpr* **pronunciarse 1** (*declararse*) to declare oneself: *se pronunciaron a favor del cambio*, they declared themselves in favour of the change. **2** (*rebelarse*) to revolt. **3** (*acentuarse*) to become pronounced.

propaganda *nf* **1** POL propaganda. **2** (*anuncios*) advertising.

● **hacer propaganda de algo** to advertise STH.

propagar *vt-vpr* **propagar(se)** to spread [*pt & pp* **spread**].

propenso,-a *adj* **propenso,-a** prone to.

propiedad *nf* **1** (*derecho*) ownership. **2** (*objeto*) property. **3** (*cualidad*) appropriateness.

● **hablar con propiedad** to speak [*pt* **spoke**; *pp* **spoken**] properly.

● **ser propiedad de ALGN** to belong to SB.

■ **propiedad intelectual** copyright.

■ **propiedad privada** private property.

■ **propiedad pública** public ownership.

propietario,-a *nm,f* owner.

propina *nf* tip: *me han dado 2 euros de propina*, thay gave me a 2-euro tip.

propio,-a *adj* **1** (*perteneciente*) own: *en su propio coche*, in her own car; *en defensa propia*, in self-defence. **2** (*indicado*) proper, appropriate. **3** (*particular*) typical, peculiar: *es muy propio de él*, it's very typical of him. **4** (*mismo - él*) himself; (*- ella*) herself; (*- cosa, animal*) itself: *el propio autor*, the author himself.

proponer *vt* (*idea*) to suggest, propose: *¿qué propones?*, what do you suggest?

▶ *vpr* **proponerse** to intend.

● **proponerse hacer algo** to intend to do STH.

proporción *nf* proportion.

▶ *nf pl* **proporciones** size *sing*.

proporcionado,-a *adj* proportionate.

proporcional *adj* proportional.

● **bien proporcionado** well-proportioned.

proporcionar *vt* **1** (*facilitar*) to supply, give. **2** (*acomodar*) to adapt.

proposición *nf* (*sugerencia*) proposition, proposal.

propósito *nm* **1** (*intención*) intention. **2** (*objetivo*) purpose, aim.

● **a propósito** (*por cierto*) by the way. **2** (adrede) on purpose: *no lo hizo a propósito*, he didn't do it on purpose.

● **tener el propósito de hacer algo** to mean [*pt & pp* **meant**] to do STH.

propuesta *nf* proposal.

prórroga *nf* **1** (*de un plazo*) extension. **2** (*en deporte*) GB extra time; US overtime.

prorrogar *vt* **1** (*decisión*) to postpone. **2** (*plazo, contrato*) to extend.

prosa *nf* prose.

proseguir *vt-vi* to continue, carry on.

prospecto *nm* (*de propaganda*) leaflet; (*de medicina*) directions for use.

prosperar *vi* to prosper, thrive [*pt* **thrived** o **throve**; *pp* **thrived**].

prosperidad *nf* prosperity.

próspero,-a *adj* prosperous.

● **próspero año nuevo** happy New Year.

prostitución *nf* prostitution.

prostituta *nf* prostitute.

protagonista *nm,f* **1** (*de película*) main character. **2** (*en obra de teatro*) lead. **3** (*de suceso*): *los protagonistas del crimen*, those involved in the murder.

protagonizar *vt* **1** (*película*) to play the lead in: *protagonizada por Anthony Hopkins*, starring Anthony Hopkins. **2** (*suceso*) to be involved in.

protección *nf* protection.

protector,-ra *adj* protective: *es demasiado protectora*, she's overprotective.

▶ *nm,f* protector.

■ **protector de pantalla** screen saver.

■ **protector solar** sun protection.

proteger *vt* to protect.

proteína *nf* protein.

protesta *nf* protest.

protestante *adj* - *nmf* Protestant.

protestantismo *nm* Protestantism.

protestar *vi* **1** to protest. **2** *(quejarse)* to complain: *deja de protestar*, stop complaining.

prototipo *nm* prototype.

provecho *nm* profit, benefit.

● **¡buen provecho!** enjoy your meal!

● **en provecho propio** for one's own benefit.

● **sacar provecho de** to benefit from.

provechoso,-a *adj* profitable.

proveedor,-ra *nm,f* supplier, purveyor.

■ **proveedor de servicios a Internet** Internet service provider.

proveer *vt* to supply, provide.

provenir *vi* to come.

proverbio *nm* proverb, saying.

provincia *nf* province.

● **de provincia** provincial.

provinciano,-a *adj* - *nm,f pey* provincial.

provisión *nf* provision.

provisional *adj* provisional, temporary.

provisto,-a *adj* provided.

provocar *vt* **1** *(irritar)* to provoke. **2** *(causar)* to cause. **3** *(excitar)* to arouse.

● **provocar un incendio 1** (persona) to commit arson. **2** (explosión) to cause a fire.

provocativo,-a *adj* provocative.

próximamente *adv* soon, shortly.

proximidad *nf* nearness, proximity.

● **en las proximidades de** in the vicinity of.

próximo,-a *adj* **1** *(cercano)* near, close: *próximo a la cima*, near the summit, close to the summit. **2** *(siguiente)* next: *el mes próximo*, next month.

proyección *nf* **1** *(gen)* projection. **2** *(de película)* screening. **3** *(alcance)* scope: *su labor tiene proyección internacional*, his work is well known all over the world.

proyectar *vt* **1** *(luz)* to project. **2** *(película)* to show [*pt* **showed**; *pp* **shown**]. **3** *(planear)* to plan.

proyectil *nm* projectile.

proyecto *nm* **1** *(plan)* plan. **2** *(estudio, esquema)* project.

● **tener algo en proyecto** to be planning STH.

■ **proyecto de ley** bill.

proyector *nm* **1** *(de película etc)* projector. **2** *(reflector)* searchlight.

prudencia *nf* *(sabiduría)* prudence, discretion; *(cuidado)* care: *conduce con prudencia*, drive carefully.

prudente *adj* *(sabio)* sensible, wise, prudent; *(cuidadoso)* careful.

prueba *nf* **1** *(demostración)* proof. **2** *(examen)* test. **3** *(deportiva)* event. **4** evidence: *faltaban pruebas*, there wasn't enough evidence.

● **a prueba de bomba** bombproof.

● **como prueba de** in proof of.

● **estar a prueba** to be on trial.

● **hacer la prueba** to try: *tú haz la prueba*, just try it.

● **poner a prueba** to put to the test.

■ **prueba de acceso** entrance examination.

■ **prueba de alcoholemia** breath test.

■ **prueba de paternidad** paternity test.

■ **prueba de relevos** relay race.

psicoanálisis *nm* psychoanalysis.

psicología *nf* psychology.

psicológico,-a *adj* psychological.

psicólogo,-a *nm,f* psychologist.

psiquiatra *nmf* psychiatrist.

psiquiatría *nf* psychiatry.

psíquico,-a *adj* psychic.

púa *nf* **1** *(pincho)* sharp point. **2** *(de planta)* thorn. **3** *(de animal)* quill. **4** *(de peine)* tooth [*pl* **teeth**].

pubertad *nf* puberty.

pubis *nm* **1** *(área)* pubes *pl*. **2** *(hueso)* pubis.

publicación *nf* publication.

publicar *vt* *(editar)* to publish; *(hacer público)* to make known.

publicidad *nf* **1** *(difusión)* publicity. **2** *(anuncios)* advertising.

● **hacer publicidad de algo** to advertise STH.

publicitario,-a *adj* advertising.

público,-a *adj* public.

▶ *nm* **público 1** *(ciudadanía)* public. **2** *(espectadores)* audience.

● **hacer algo público** to make STH public.

● **en público** in public.

puchero *nm* **1** *(olla)* cooking pot. **2** *(guiso)* stew.

● **hacer pucheros** to pout.

pudor *nm* **1** *(recato)* shyness. **2** *(modestia)* modesty.

● **sin nigún pudor** without any embarrassment.

pudrir *vt-vpr* **pudrirse 1** *(gen)* to rot. **2** *(comida)* to go bad.

pueblo *nm* **1** *(lugar)* village, small town. **2** *(gente)* people. **3** *(nación)* nation.

puente *nm* **1** bridge. **2** *(fiesta)* long weekend.

● **hacer puente** to have a long weekend.

■ **puente aéreo 1** *(de pasajeros)* shuttle service. **2** *(en emergencias)* airlift.

■ **puente colgante** suspension bridge.

■ **puente de mando** bridge.

■ **puente levadizo** drawbridge.

puerco,-a *adj fam* dirty, filthy.

▶ *nm,f (macho)* pig; *(hembra)* sow.

■ **puerco espín** porcupine.

puericultor,-ra *nm,f* **1** *(médico)* paediatrician. **2** *(en guardería)* nursery nurse.

puericultura *nf* **1** *(pediatría)* paediatrics. **2** *(cuidado de niños)* childcare.

puerro *nm* leek.

puerta *nf* **1** *(de casa, edificio)* door: *había alguien en la puerta*, there was someone at the door; *en la puerta del hotel*, outside the hotel. **2** *(verja)* gate. **3** *(entrada)* doorway. **4** *(gol)* goal.

● **a puerta cerrada** behind closed doors.

● **darle a** ALGN **con la puerta en las narices** to slam the door in SB's face.

● **de puerta en puerta** from door to door.

● **de puertas adentro** in private.

● **por la puerta grande** in a grand manner.

■ **puerta blindada** reinforced door.

■ **puerta corredera** sliding door.

■ **puerta de embarque** boarding gate.

■ **puerta giratoria** revolving door.

■ **puerta trasera** back door.

puerto *nm* **1** *(de mar - pequeño)* harbour; *(- grande)* port; *(ciudad)* port. **2** *(de montaña)* mountain pass. **3** INFORM port.

■ **puerto deportivo** marina.

■ **puerto franco** free port.

■ **puerto pesquero** fishing port.

Puerto Rico *nm* Puerto Rico.

puertorriqueño,-a *adj - nm,f* Puerto Rican.

pues *conj* **1** *(ya que)* since, as: *vete, pues estás cansado*, since you are tired, you can go home. **2** *(por lo tanto)* then, therefore. **3** *(repetitivo)* then: *digo, pues...*, I say then.... **4** *(enfático)* well: *pues bien*, well then; *¡pues claro!*, of course!; *pues no*, certainly not; *pues tú dirás*, well, you decide.

puesta *nf* .

■ **puesta al día** updating.

■ **puesta a punto** tuning.

■ **puesta de sol** sunset.

■ **puesta en escena** staging.

■ **puesta en libertad** release.

■ **puesta en marcha 1** *(de vehículo)* starting. **2** *(de proyecto)* implementation.

puesto,-a *adj* **1** *(ropa)* on: *durmió con el vestido puesto*, she slept with her dress on. **2** *(bien arreglado)* well-dressed: *iba muy bien puesta*, she was very well dressed.

▶ *nm* **puesto 1** *(lugar)* place. **2** *(de mercado)* stall; *(de feria etc)* stand. **3** *(empleo)* position, post. **4** MIL post.

● **estar puesto,-a en un tema** to be well up on a subject.

● **puesto que** since.

■ **puesto de periódicos** newspaper stand.

■ **puesto de socorro** first-aid station.

■ **puesto de trabajo** job.

■ **puesto fronterizo** border post.

púgil *nm* boxer.

pugna *nf* fight, battle.

pulcritud *nf* neatness.

pulcro,-a *adj* neat, tidy.

pulga *nf* flea.

● **tener malas pulgas** *fam* to have a nasty streak.

pulgada *nf* inch.

pulgar *nm* thumb.

pulgón *nm* aphid.

pulir *vt* **1** *(pulimentar)* to polish. **2** *(perfeccionar)* to refine.

pulmón *nm* lung.

● **a pleno pulmón** at the top of one's voice.

pulmonar *adj* lung, pulmonary.

pulmonía *nf* pneumonia.

pulpa *nf* **1** *(gen)* pulp. **2** *(de fruta)* flesh.

púlpito *nm* pulpit.

pulpo *nm* octopus.

pulsación *nf* **1** *(de corazón)* beat, throb. **2** *(en mecanografía)* keystroke.

pulsar *vt (tecla, botón)* to press: *pulse F4 para salir*, press F4 to quit.

pulsera *nf* **1** *(brazalete)* bracelet. **2** *(de reloj)* watch strap.

pulso *nm* **1** *(latidos)* pulse. **2** *(seguridad de mano)* : *me tiembla el pulso*, my hand is shaking; *dibújalo a pulso*, draw it freehand.

• **ganarse algo a pulso** to work hard for STH.

• **echar un pulso** to arm-wrestle.

• **tener buen pulso** to have a steady hand.

• **tener mal pulso** to have an unsteady hand.

• **tomarle el pulso a** ALGN to take SB's pulse.

pulverizador *nm* spray, atomizer.

pulverizar *vt* **1** *(sólidos)* to pulverize. **2** *(líquidos)* to atomize, spray.

puma *nf* puma.

punta *nf* **1** *(extremo - de dedo, lengua)* tip; *(- de aguja, cuchillo, lápiz)* point: *vive en la otra punta de la ciudad*, he lives on the other side of town; *la punta de los dedos*, the fingertips. **2** *(pizca)* bit. **3** *(clavo)* tack.

▶ *nf pl* **puntas** *(del pelo)* ends: *córtame las puntas*, I'd like a trim.

• **a punta de pala** loads of: *turistas a punta de pala*, loads of tourists.

• **a punta de pistola** at gunpoint.

• **de punta en blanco** dressed up to the nines.

• **sacar punta a** *(lápiz)* to sharpen.

puntapié *nm* kick.

puntear *vt* **1** *(dibujar)* to dot. **2** *(guitarra)* to pluck.

puntera *nf* toecap.

puntería *nf* aim.

• **tener buena puntería** to be a good shot.

• **tener mala puntería** to be a bad shot.

puntero *nm* pointer.

puntiagudo,-a *adj* pointed.

puntilla.

• **de puntillas** on tiptoe.

punto *nm* **1** *(gen)* point: *ganó por puntos*, he won on points; *no discutieron ese punto*, they didn't discuss that point.

2 *(lunar)* dot: *una línea de puntos*, a dotted line. **3** *(de puntuación)* GB full stop; US period. **4** *(lugar)* spot. **5** *(en costura, cirugía)* stitch.

• **en punto** sharp, on the dot.

• **estar a punto** to be ready.

• **estar a punto de hacer algo** to be on the point of doing STH.

• **estar en su punto** to be just right.

• **hasta cierto punto** up to a certain point.

• **prendas de punto** knitwear.

• **punto por punto** in detail.

■ **punto cardinal** cardinal point.

■ **punto débil** weak point.

■ **punto de cruz** cross-stitch.

■ **punto de ebullición** boiling point.

■ **punto de encuentro** meeting point.

■ **punto de vista** point of view.

■ **punto final** full stop.

■ **punto fuerte** strong point.

■ **punto muerto 1** *(cambio de marchas)* neutral. **2** *(en negociaciones)* impasse, deadlock.

■ **punto y aparte** full stop, new paragraph.

■ **punto y coma** semicolon.

■ **puntos suspensivos** GB dots; US suspension points.

puntuación *nf* **1** *(en ortografía)* punctuation. **2** *(en competición)* scoring; *(total)* score: *una puntuación alta*, a high score.

puntual *adj* **1** *(persona, tren)* punctual. **2** *(exacto)* exact. **3** *(aislado)* odd.

• **llegar puntual** to be on time.

puntualidad *nf* punctuality.

puntualmente *adv* punctually.

puntuar *vt* **1** *(texto)* to punctuate. **2** *(examen)* to mark.

punzada *nf (dolor)* sharp pain.

punzón *nm* punch.

puñado *nm* handful.

• **a puñados** by the score.

puñal *nm* dagger.

puñalada *nf* stab.

puñeta *nf fam* nuisance.

• **en la quinta puñeta** in the back of beyond.

• **hacerle la puñeta a** ALGN to pester SB.

• **mandar a** ALGN **a hacer puñetas** to tell SB to get lost [*pt & pp* **told**], tell SB to go to hell.

• **¡puñetas!** damn!

puñetazo *nm* punch.

● **dar un puñetazo a** ALGN to punch SB.

puño *nm* **1** *(mano)* fist. **2** *(de prenda)* cuff [*pl* -s].

pupa *nf* **1** *fam (en los labios)* cold sore. **2** *fam (daño)* pain.

● **hacerse pupa** to hurt oneself [*pt & pp* hurt].

pupila *nf* pupil.

pupitre *nm* desk.

puré *nm* purée: *puré de tomate*, tomato purée.

■ **puré de patatas** mashed potatoes.

pureza *nf* purity.

purificar *vt* to purify.

puro,-a *adj* **1** *(sin mezclar)* pure. **2** *(mero)* sheer, mere: *por puro aburrimiento*, out of sheer boredom; *es puro músculo*, he's all muscle.

► *nm* **puro** cigar.

● **por pura casualidad** by sheer chance.

púrpura *adj* - *nm* purple.

purpurina *nf* glitter.

pus *nm* pus.

puta *nf vulg* whore.

putada *nf vulg* : *le hizo una putada*, she played a rotten trick on him; *¡qué putada!*, what a bugger!

putear *vi vulg* to go whoring.

► *vt vulg* to fuck about, piss about.

puto,-a *adj vulg* bloody, fucking: *no tenía ni puta gana*, I didn't feel like it at all; *¡ni puta idea!*, I've no bloody idea.

● **de puta madre** *vulg* great, terrific.

puzzle *nm* puzzle.

PVP *abr (Precio de Venta al Público)* Recommended Retail Price, RRP.

Q

que[1] *pron* **1** *(sujeto - persona)* who, that; *(- cosa)* that, which: **la chica que vino**, the girl who came. **2** *(complemento - persona)* whom, who; *(cosa)* that, which: **el libro que me prestaste**, the book that you lent me. **3** *(complemento - de tiempo)* when; *(- de lugar)* where: **el año en que nació**, the year when he was born; **la casa en que vivimos**, the house where we live.

que[2] *conj* **1** *(después de verbos)* that: **dice que está cansado**, he says that he's tired. **2** *(con comparativos)* than: **es más alto que su padre**, he is taller than his father.
● **¿a que no?** I bet you can't.
● **¡que te diviertas!** enjoy yourself!
● **que yo sepa** as far as I know.
● **¡que te mejores!** get well soon.

qué *pron* what?: **¿qué quieres?**, what do you want?
▶ *adj* **1** *(en exclamativas)* how, what: **¡qué bonito!**, how nice!; **¡qué miedo!**, how scary!; **¡qué flor tan bonita!**, what a nice flower! **2** *(en interrogativas)* which?: **no sé qué libro quiere**, I don't know which book he wants; **¿qué edad tienes?**, how old are you?
● **no hay de qué** don't mention it.
● **¿para qué?** what for?
● **¿por qué?** why?
● **¡qué de ...!** what a lot of ...!
● **¡qué lástima!** what a pity!
● **¿qué tal?** how are things?
● **¡y qué!** so what!

quebradero de cabeza *nm* worry, headache.

quebrado,-a *adj* **1** *(roto)* broken. **2** *(sin fondos)* bankrupt. **3** *(terreno)* rough.
▶ *nm* **quebrado** fraction.

quebrantar *vt* **1** *(incumplir)* to break [*pt* **broke**; *pp* **broken**]. **2** *(debilitar)* to weaken.

quebrar *vi* to go bankrupt.
▶ *vt-vpr* **quebrar(se)** to break [*pt* **broke**; *pp* **broken**].

quedar *vi* **1** *(faltar)* to remain, be left: **queda poco**, there's not much left. **2** *(sentar)* to look: **no queda bien aquí**, it doesn't look right here; **te queda muy bien**, it suits you. **3** *(estar situado)* to be: **¿por dónde queda tu casa?**, whereabouts is your house? **4** *(acordar)* to agree.
▶ *vpr* **quedarse 1** *(permanecer)* to remain, stay, be. **2** *(retener)* to keep.
● **quedar bien** to make a good impression.
● **quedar mal** to make a bad impression.
● **quedarse atónito,-a** to be astonished.
● **quedarse sin algo** to run out of STH [*pt* **ran**; *pp* **run**].
● **todo quedó en nada** it all came to nothing.
● **quedarse con** ALGN *fam* to make a fool of SB.
● **quedarse sin blanca** *fam* to be broke.

quehacer *nm* task, chore.
■ **quehaceres domésticos** housework *sing*.

queja *nf* **1** *(protesta)* complaint. **2** *(de dolor)* moan, groan.
● **presentar una queja** to lodge a complaint.

quejarse *vpr* **1** *(protestar)* to complain. **2** *(gimiendo)* to moan, groan.

quejica *adj fam* complaining.
▶ *nmf fam* grumbler, moaner.

quejido *nm* **1** *(gemido)* groan, moan. **2** *(grito)* cry.

quema *nf* **1** *(acción, efecto)* burning. **2** *(fuego)* fire.

quemado,-a *adj* **1** *(por fuego)* burnt. **2** *(resentido)* embittered. **3** *fam (acabado)* spent, burnt-out.

quemadura *nf* **1** *(de fuego, sol)* burn. **2** *(de agua hirviendo)* scald.

quemar *vt* **1** *(gen)* to burn [*pt & pp* burnt]. **2** *(incendiar)* to set on fire [*pt & pp* set]. **3** *fam (acabar)* to burn out [*pt & pp* burnt]. **4** *(calorías)* to burn up.
► *vi (estar muy caliente)* to be burning hot.
► *vpr* **quemarse 1** *(con fuego)* to burn oneself [*pt & pp* burnt]. **2** *(al sol)* to get burnt.

quemarropa *loc* **a quemarropa** at point-blank range.

querer *vt* **1** *(amar)* to love. **2** *(desear)* to want: *quiero que vengas*, I want you to come; *¿quieres venir?*, would you like to come? **3** *(posibilidad)* may: *parece que quiere llover*, it looks like it might rain.
● **lo hice sin querer** I didn't mean to do it.
● **¡qué más quisiera!** if only I could!
● **querer decir** to mean [*pt & pp* meant].
● **querer es poder** where there's a will there's a way.
● **quieras o no** like it or not.

querido,-a *adj* dear, beloved.
► *nm,f* **1** *(amante)* lover; *(mujer)* mistress. **2** *fam (apelativo)* darling.

quesito *nm* cheese portion.

queso *nm* cheese.
● **dárselas a** ALGN **con queso** *fam* to take SB in.
■ **queso de bola** Edam.
■ **queso en lonchas** cheese slices *pl*.
■ **queso rallado** grated cheese.

quicio *nm* door jamb.
● **estar fuera de quicio** to be beside oneself.
● **sacar a** ALGN **de quicio** to get on SB's nerves.

quiebra *nf* bankruptcy.
● **ir a la quiebra** to go bankrupt.

quien *pron* **1** *(sujeto)* who: *fue el jefe quien me lo dijo*, it was the boss who told me; *no hay quien la soporte*, nobody can stand her. **2** *(complemento)* who, whom: *las personas con quienes trabajo*, the people who I work with. **3** *(indefinido)* whoever, anyone who: *quien quiera venir que venga*, whoever wants to, can come.
● **quien más quien menos** everybody.

quién *pron* **1** *(sujeto)* who: *¿quién sabe?*, who knows? **2** *(complemento)* who, whom: *¿con quién hablas?*, who are you talking to?
● **¿de quién?** whose?: *¿de quién es esto?*, whose is this?

quienquiera *pron* whoever.
● **quienquiera que sea** whoever it may be.

quieto,-a *adj* **1** *(sin moverse)* still: *estarse quieto,-a*, to keep still. **2** *(sosegado)* quiet, calm.

quietud *nf* **1** *(sin movimiento)* stillness. **2** *(sosiego)* calm.

quilla *nf* keel.

quilo *nm* → kilo.

quimera *nf* illusion, chimera.

química *nf* chemistry.

químico,-a *adj* chemical.
► *nm,f* chemist.

quimono *nm* kimono [*pl* -s].

quince *num* fifteen; *(en fechas)* fifteenth.

quinceañero,-a *adj* teenage.
► *nm,f (gen)* teenager; *(de 15 años)* fifteen-year-old.

quincena *nf* fortnight.

quincenal *adj* fortnightly.

quiniela *nf* football pools *pl*.
● **hacer la quiniela** to do the pools.

quinientos,-as *num* five hundred.

quinqué *nm* oil lamp.

quinta *nf* **1** *(villa)* country house, villa. **2** *(de soldados)* GB call-up; US draft.
● **ser de la misma quinta** to be the same age.

quintillizo,-a *nm,f* quintuplet, quin.

quinto,-a *num* fifth.
► *nm* **quinto 1** *(soldado)* conscript, recruit. **2** *(cerveza)* small bottle of beer *(20 cl)*.

quintuplicar *vt* to quintuple, increase five-fold.

quiosco *nm* kiosk.
■ **quiosco de periódicos** newspaper stand.

quirófano *nm* operating theatre.

quirúrgico,-a *adj* surgical.

quisquilloso,-a *adj (delicado)* finicky, fussy; *(susceptible)* touchy.

quiste *nm* cyst.

quitamanchas *nm* stain remover.

quitanieves *nm* snowplough.

quitar *vt* **1** *(sacar)* to remove, take out, take off. **2** *(restar)* to subtract. **3** *(robar)* to steal [*pt* **stole**; *pp* **stolen**], rob of. **4** *(coger)* to take. **5** *(apartar)* to take away. **6** *(ropa, zapatos)* to take off. **7** *(dolor)* to relieve. **8** *(mesa)* to clear.

▶ *vpr* **quitarse 1** *(apartarse)* to move away. **2** *(desaparecer)* to go away, come out: *se me han quitado las ganas*, I don't feel like it any more. **3** *(ropa)* to take off.

● **de quita y pon** detachable.

● **quitar de en medio a ALGN** to get rid of SB.

● **quitar la sed** to quench one's thirst.

● **quitarle importancia a algo** to play STH down.

● **quitarse años** to lie about one's age.

● **quitarse de encima** to get rid of.

quizá *adv* perhaps, maybe.

quizás *adv* perhaps, maybe.

R

rábano *nm* radish.

● **¡me importa un rábano!** I don't give a damn.

rabia *nf* **1** *(enfermedad)* rabies. **2** *(enfado)* rage, fury: *me dio rabia*, it made me furious; *¡qué rabia!*, how annoying!

● **tener rabia a** ALGN to have it in for SB.

rabiar *vi* to rage, be furious.

● **rabiar por algo** to be dying for STH.

rabieta *nf fam* tantrum: *le dio una rabieta*, he threw a tantrum.

rabioso,-a *adj* **1** *(por enfermedad)* rabid. **2** *(airado)* furious, angry. **3** *(dolor)* terrible.

rabo *nm* tail.

● **con el rabo entre las piernas** crestfallen.

racha *nf* **1** *(de viento)* gust. **2** *(período)* : *una buena racha*, a run of good luck; *está atravesando una mala racha*, he's having a run of bad luck, he's going through a bad patch.

racial *adj* racial.

racimo *nm* bunch.

ración *nf* **1** *(porción)* portion: *una ración de pulpo*, a portion of octopus. **2** *(parte que toca)* share. **3** *(cantidad fijada)* ration.

racional *adj* rational.

racionar *vt* to ration.

racismo *nm* racism.

racista *adj - nmf* racist.

radar *nm* radar.

radiación *nf* radiation.

radiactividad *nf* radioactivity.

radiactivo,-a *adj* radioactive.

radiador *nm* radiator.

radiante *adj* radiant.

radiar *vt-vi (irradiar)* to radiate.

▶ *vt (retransmitir)* to broadcast [*pt & pp* **broadcast**].

radical *adj-nmf* radical.

radicar *vi* **1** *(encontrarse)* to lie [*pt* **lay**; *pp* **lain**]: *el problema radica en la economía*, the problem lies in the economy. **2** *(arraigar)* to take root.

radio[1] *nm* **1** *(de círculo)* radius [*pl* **radiuses** o **radii**]. **2** *(de rueda)* spoke. **3** *(campo)* scope.

radio[2] *nf* **1** *(radiodifusión)* radio, broadcasting. **2** *(aparato)* radio [*pl* **-s**].

■ **radio macuto** *fam* bush telegraph, grapevine.

radio[3] *nm* **1** *(hueso)* radius [*pl* **radiuses** o **radii**]. **2** *(elemento químico)* radium.

radiocasete *nm* radio-cassette.

radiodifusión *nf* broadcasting.

radiografía *nf* **1** *(técnica)* radiography. **2** *(imagen)* X-ray.

● **hacerse una radiografía** to have an X-ray taken.

radioyente *nmf* listener.

ráfaga *nf* **1** *(de viento)* gust. **2** *(de disparos)* burst. **3** *(de luz)* flash.

raído,-a *adj* threadbare.

raíl *nm* rail.

raíz *nf* root.

● **a raíz de** as a result of.

● **echar raíces** to take root.

● **eliminar algo de raíz** to eliminate STH completely.

■ **raíz cuadrada** square root.

raja *nf* **1** *(corte)* cut: *me he hecho una raja en el dedo*, I've cut my finger. **2** *(grieta)* crack. **3** *(descosido)* split. **4** *(tajada)* slice.

rajar *vt* **1** *(tela)* to split [*pt & pp* **split**]. **2** *(melón etc)* to slice. **3** *(pared)* to crack.

▶ *vi fam (hablar)* to chatter.

▶ *vpr* **rajarse** 1 *(partirse tela)* to split [*pt & pp* **split**]; *(pared)* crack. **2** *fam (desistir)* to back out, quit.

● **rajar de** ALGN to slag SB off.

rajatabla *adv* **a rajatabla** to the letter, strictly.

rallado,-a *adj* grated.

● **pan rallado** breadcrumbs.

rallador *nm* grater.

rallar *vt* to grate.

rama *nf* branch.

● **andarse por las ramas** to beat about the bush [*pt* **beat**; *pp* **beaten**].

rambla *nf* **1** *(lecho de río)* watercourse. **2** *(paseo)* boulevard, avenue.

ramillete *nm* bouquet.

ramo *nm* **1** *(de flores)* bunch. **2** *(ámbito)* field, section.

rampa *nf* ramp.

rana *nf* frog.

rancho *nm* **1** *(granja)* ranch. **2** *(comida)* food.

rancio,-a *adj* **1** *(mantequilla)* rancid. **2** *(linaje)* old, ancient.

rango *nm* rank, class.

● **de alto rango** of high standing.

ranura *nf* **1** *(canal)* groove. **2** *(para monedas, fichas)* slot.

rapapolvo *nm fam* telling-off: **me echaron un buen rapapolvo**, I was given a good telling-off.

rapar *vt* **1** *(afeitar)* to shave. **2** *(cortar al rape)* to crop.

rapaz[1] *nf (ave)* bird of prey.

rapaz[2] *nmf (chico)* kid.

rape[1] *nm (pez)* angler fish.

rape[2].

● **al rape** close-cropped.

rapidez *nf* speed.

● **con rapidez** quickly.

rápido,-a *adj* quick, fast.

▶ *nm pl* **rápidos** *(del río)* rapids.

raptar *vt* to kidnap.

rapto *nm* **1** *(secuestro)* kidnapping. **2** *(impulso)* outburst.

raqueta *nf* **1** racket. **2** *(para nieve)* snowshoe.

raquítico,-a *adj* **1** MED rachitic. **2** *(exiguo)* meagre. **3** *(débil)* weak.

rareza *nf* **1** *(cosa inusual)* rarity. **2** *(peculiaridad)* oddity. **3** *(extravagancia)* quirk: **tiene sus rarezas**, she has her little quirks.

raro,-a *adj* **1** *(poco común)* rare: **esta moneda es muy rara y muy valiosa**, this coin is very rare and very valuable. **2** *(peculiar)* odd, strange: **¡qué raro!**, how odd!, how strange!

● **raras veces** seldom.

ras *loc* **a ras de** : **volaban a ras de tierra**, they flew very low.

rascacielos *nm* skyscraper.

rascar *vt* to scratch: **ráscame la espalda**, can you scratch my back?

rasgar *vt-vpr* **rasgar(se)** to tear [*pt* **tore**; *pp* **torn**], rip.

● **rasgarse las vestiduras** to tear one's hair out.

rasgo *nm* **1** *(línea)* stroke. **2** *(facción)* feature. **3** *(peculiaridad)* characteristic.

● **a grandes rasgos** in outline.

rasguño *nm* scratch.

raso,-a *adj* *(plano)* flat, level; *(liso)* smooth: **el cielo estaba raso**, the sky was clear; **una cucharadita rasa**, one level teaspoonful.

▶ *nm* **raso** *(tejido)* satin.

● **al raso** in the open air.

raspa *nf* **1** *(de pescado)* bone. **2** *(de cereal)* beard.

raspar *vt* **1** *(rascar)* to scrape; *(quitar rascando)* to scrape off. **2** *(vino, toalla, tela)* to be rough: **este vino raspa**, this wine is rough. **3** *fam (birlar)* to nick.

rastrear *vt* **1** *(persona)* to trail, track. **2** *(río)* to drag. **3** *(zona)* to comb, search.

rastrillo *nm* rake.

rastro *nm* **1** *(pista)* trail. **2** *(señal)* trace; *(mercado)* flea market.

rata *nf* rat.

▶ *nm fam (ratero)* pickpocket.

▶ *nmf (tacaño)* miser.

ratero,-a *nm,f* petty thief.

ratificar *vt* to ratify.

▶ *vpr* **ratificarse** to be ratified.

rato *nm (momento)* while: **hace un rato**, a while ago.

● **al poco rato** shortly afterwards.

● **pasar el rato** to kill time.

● **un buen rato** **1** *(tiempo)* a long time. **2** *(distancia)* a long way. **3** *(diversión)* a pleasant time.

ratón *nm* mouse [*pl* **mice**].

ratonera *nf* **1** *(trampa)* mousetrap. **2** *(agujero)* mousehole.

raudal *nm* torrent, flood.

● **a raudales** in abundance.

raya¹ *nf* **1** *(línea)* line. **2** *(de color)* stripe: *a rayas*, striped. **3** *(del pantalón)* crease. **4** *(del pelo)* parting: *se peina con la raya en medio*, he has his parting down the middle. **5** *arg (de cocaína)* line.
- **pasarse de la raya** to overstep the mark.
- **tener a raya** to keep within bounds.

raya² *nf (pez)* skate.

rayado,-a *adj* **1** *(con rayas)* striped. **2** *(papel)* ruled. **3** *(disco)* scratched.

rayar *vt* **1** *(líneas)* to draw lines on [*pt* **drew**; *pp* **drawn**], line, rule. **2** *(superficie)* to scratch. **3** *(tachar)* to cross out.
▶ *vi* to border.

rayo *nm* **1** *(de luz)* ray, beam. **2** *(en el cielo)* flash of lightning.
- **ir como un rayo** to go like a shot.
- **¡que le parta un rayo!** damn him!
■ **rayo de sol** sunbeam.

rayuela *nf* hopscotch.

raza *nf* **1** *(humana)* race. **2** *(animal)* breed.

razón *nf* reason.
- **a razón de tres al día** at a rate of three a day.
- **dar la razón a** ALGN to agree with SB, admit that SB is right.
- **no tener razón** to be wrong.
- **perder la razón** lo lose one's reason [*pt & pp* **lost**].
- **"Razón aquí"** "Enquire within".
- **tener razón** to be right.

razonable *adj* reasonable.

razonamiento *nm* reasoning.

razonar *vi* **1** *(discurrir)* to reason. **2** *(explicar)* to reason out.

re *nm (nota)* D; *(en solfeo)* re, ray.

reacción *nf* reaction.

reaccionar *vi* to react.

reaccionario,-a *adj - nm,f* reactionary.

reacio,-a *adj* reluctant, unwilling.
- **ser reacio,-a a algo** to resist the idea of STH.

reactor *nm* **1** *(nuclear etc)* reactor. **2** *(avión)* jet plane.

real¹ *adj (auténtico)* real.

real² *adj (regio)* royal.
▶ *nm (de feria)* fairground.

realeza *nf* royalty.

realidad *nf* reality.
- **en realidad** really, in fact.
■ **realidad virtual** virtual reality.

realismo *nm* realism.

realista *adj* realistic.
▶ *nmf* realist.

realización *nf (de tarea)* carrying out; *(de propósito)* achievement; *(de sueño)* fulfilment.

realizar *vt* **1** *(propósito, sueño)* to realize. **2** *(tarea)* to accomplish, carry out, do.
▶ *vpr* **realizarse** *(persona)* to fulfil oneself.

realmente *adv* **1** *(bastante)* really. **2** *(en realidad)* in fact, actually.

realzar *vt* **1** *(rasgo, belleza)* to heighten, enhance. **2** *(pintura)* to highlight.

reanimar *vt-vpr* **reanimar(se)** to revive.

reanudar *vt* to renew, resume.

reaparecer *vi* to reappear.

rebaja *nf* reduction: *me hizo una rebaja*, he gave me a discount.
▶ *nf pl* **rebajas** sales: *las rebajas de enero*, the January sales.

rebajar *vt* **1** *(precio, coste)* to reduce; *(color)* to tone down. **2** *(nivel)* to lower. **3** *(a alguien)* to humiliate.
▶ *vpr* **rebajarse** to humble oneself.
- **rebajarse a hacer algo** to lower oneself to do STH.

rebanada *nf* slice.

rebañar *vt (plato)* to clean.

rebaño *nm (de cabras)* herd; *(de ovejas)* flock.

rebasar *vt* to exceed, go beyond.

rebeca *nf* cardigan.

rebelarse *vpr* to rebel.

rebelde *adj* rebellious.
▶ *nmf* rebel.

rebelión *nf* rebellion, revolt.

rebobinar *vt* to rewind [*pt & pp* **rewound**].

reborde *nm* rim.

rebosar *vi (derramarse)* to overflow.
▶ *vt-vi (abundar)* to overflow (-, with).
- **rebosar de salud** to be brimming with health.

rebotar *vi (balón)* to bounce; *(bala)* to ricochet.
▶ *vt (clavo)* to clinch.
▶ *vpr* **rebotarse** *(enfadarse)* to get angry.

rebote *nm* rebound.
- **de rebote** on the rebound.

rebozar *vt (con pan rallado)* to coat in breadcrumbs; *(con huevo)* to batter.

rebuznar *vi* to bray.

rebuzno *nm* bray.

recadero,-a nm,f messenger.

recado nm 1 (mensaje) message. 2 (encargo) errand.

recaer vi 1 (en enfermedad) to suffer a relapse. 2 (responsabilidad) to fall [pt **fell**; pp **fallen**]; (premio) to go.

recaída nf relapse.

recalcar nf to emphasize, stress.

recalentar vt 1 (volver a calentar) to reheat, warm up. 2 (calentar demasiado) to overheat.

recambio nm (de maquinaria) spare part, spare; (de pluma, bolígrafo) refill.

recapacitar vt to think over [pt & pp **thought**].
▶ vi to reflect.

recargable adj (mechero) refillable; (batería) rechargable.

recargado,-a adj 1 (sobrecargado) overloaded. 2 (exagerado) overelaborate, exaggerated.

recargar vt 1 (arma) to reload; (mechero) to refill; (batería) to recharge. 2 (sobrecargar) to overload. 3 (exagerar) to overelaborate.

recargo nm extra charge.
● **sin recargo** at no extra charge.

recaudación nf 1 (recogida) collection. 2 (cantidad recaudada) takings pl.
■ **recaudación de fondos** fundraising.

recaudar vt (impuestos) to collect; (dinero) to raise.

recepción nf 1 (de personas, señal) reception. 2 (de documento, carta) receipt.

recepcionista nmf receptionist.

receptor,-ra adj receiving.
▶ nm TV receiver.
▶ nm,f (de trasplante) recipient.

receta nf 1 (médica) prescription. 2 (culinaria) recipe.

recetar vt to prescribe.

rechazar vt to reject, turn down.

rechazo nm rejection.

rechinar vi (bisagra) to creak; (dientes) to grind [pt & pp **ground**].

rechistar vi to complain.
● **sin rechistar** fam without complaining.

rechoncho,-a adj chubby.

rechupete loc **de rechupete** fam (delicioso) scrumptious, yummy; (fantástico) great, brill.

recibidor nm entrance hall.

recibimiento nm reception, welcome.

recibir vt 1 (carta, señal, etc) to get, receive: **han recibido dinero**, they have received some money; **recibió un buen golpe**, he was hit hard. 2 (persona) to meet [pt & pp **met**].
● **recibe un abrazo de** (en carta) with best wishes from.

recibo nm 1 (resguardo) receipt. 2 (factura) invoice, bill.
● **acusar recibo de** to acknowledge receipt of.
● **eso no es de recibo** that's unacceptable.

reciclable adj recyclable.

reciclado,-a adj recycled.

reciclaje nm recycling.

reciclar vt 1 (materiales) to recycle. 2 (profesionales) to retrain.

recién adv recently, newly: **pan recién hecho**, freshly baked bread.
● **"Recién pintado"** "Wet paint".
■ **recién casados** newlyweds.
■ **recién nacido** newborn baby.

reciente adj recent.

recientemente adv recently, lately.

recinto nm (gen) premises; (cerrado) enclosure.
■ **recinto ferial** fairground.

recio,-a adj 1 (fuerte) strong, robust. 2 (grueso) thick. 3 (duro) hard.

recipiente nm container.

recíproco,-a adj reciprocal, mutual.

recital nm recital.

recitar vt to recite.

reclamación nf 1 (demanda) claim, demand. 2 (queja) complaint, protest.

reclamar vt (pedir) to demand.
▶ vi (quejarse) to complain.

recluso,-a nm,f prisoner.

recluta nm 1 (voluntario) recruit. 2 (obligado) conscript.

reclutar vt to recruit.

recobrar vt-vpr **recobrar(se)** to recover.
● **recobrar el conocimiento** to regain consciousness.

recodo nm bend.

recogedor nm dustpan.

recoger vt 1 (coger del suelo) to pick up. 2 (juntar) to gather. 3 (ordenar) to clear up. 4 (ir a buscar persona) to fetch, pick up. 5 (dar asilo a) to take in.
▶ vpr **recogerse** 1 (irse a casa) to go

home. **2** *(irse a dormir)* to go to bed. **3** *(para meditar)* to retire.
● **recoger la mesa** to clear the table.
● **recogerse el pelo** to gather one's hair up.

recogida *nf* collection.
■ **recogida de equipajes** baggage reclaim.

recogido,-a *adj* **1** *(apartado)* secluded. **2** *(pelo)* gathered up.

recolección *nf* **1** *(recopilación)* summary. **2** *(cosecha)* harvest.

recolectar *vt (cosecha)* to harvest; *(dinero)* to collet.

recomendable *adj* recommendable.

recomendación *nf* recommendation.

recomendado,-a *adj* recommended.

recomendar *vt* to recommend.

recompensa *nf* reward, recompense.
● **en recompensa por algo** in return for STH.

recompensar *vt* **1** *(compensar)* to compensate. **2** *(remunerar)* to reward, recompense.

reconfortar *vt* **1** *(consolar)* to comfort. **2** *(animar)* to encourage.

reconocer *vt* **1** *(gen)* to recognize: *no te había reconocido*, I didn't recognize you. **2** *(a paciente)* to examine. **3** *(una zona)* to reconnoitre. **4** *(un error)* to admit.
▶ *vpr* **reconocerse** *(admitir)* to admit: *se reconoció como el asesino*, he admitted that he was the murderer.

reconocimiento *nm* **1** *(gen)* recognition. **2** *(de zona)* reconnaissance. **3** *(chequeo médico)* examination, check up.

reconquista *nf* reconquest.

reconstrucción *nf* reconstruction.

reconstruir *vt* to reconstruct.

recopilar *vt* to compile, collect.

récord *adj - nm* record.
● **batir un récord** to break [*pt* **broke**; *pp* **broken**] a record.

recordar *vt (nombre, dato)* to remember: *no lo recuerdo*, I don't remember it; *no recuerdo haberlo dicho*, I don't remember having said that; *¿lo recuerdas?*, do you recall it?
▶ *vi* to remember: *no recuerdo*, I can't remember.
● **recordar algo a ALGN** to remind SB of STH.

recordatorio *nm* **1** *(aviso)* reminder. **2** *(tarjeta)* card.

recorrer *vt (atravesar)* to travel round.
● **recorrer con la mirada** to look around: *recorrió la sala con la mirada*, he looked around the room.

recorrido *nm* **1** *(trayecto)* journey. **2** *(distancia)* distance travelled.

recortar *vt* **1** *(muñecos, telas, etc)* to cut out [*pt & pp* **cut**]. **2** *(lo que sobra)* to cut off [*pt & pp* **cut**]. **3** *(presupuesto)* to cut [*pt & pp* **cut**].

recorte *nm* **1** *(acción)* cutting. **2** *(de periódico)* press clipping. **3** *(de presupuesto)* cut.

recostar *vt* to lean [*pt & pp* **leant**].
▶ *vpr* **recostarse** to lie down [*pt* **lay**; *pp* **lain**].

recrear[1] *vt (entretener)* to amuse, entertain.
▶ *vpr* **recrearse** to amuse oneself.

recrear[2] *vt (reproducir)* to recreate.

recreativo,-a *adj* recreational.

recreo *nm* **1** *(entretenimiento)* recreation, amusement. **2** *(en la escuela)* playtime.

recta *nf* **1** *(línea)* straight line. **2** *(en carretera)* straight, straight piece of road: *el accidente ocurrió en una recta*, the accident happened on a straight piece of road.
■ **recta final** final straight.

rectangular *adj* rectangular.

rectángulo *nm* rectangle.

rectificar *vt* **1** *(corregir)* to rectify. **2** *(enderezar)* to straighten.

rectitud *nf (de comportamiento)* uprightness.

recto,-a *adj* **1** *(derecho)* straight. **2** *(honesto)* just, honest.
▶ *nm* **recto** rectum.
▶ *adv* straight on: *sigues recto por aquí y luego tuerces a la derecha*, you go straight on up here and then you turn right.

rector,-ra *adj* ruling, governing.
▶ *nm,f (de universidad)* GB vice-chancellor; US rector.
▶ *nm* **rector** *(párroco)* vicar.

recuadro *nm* box.

recuento *nm* recount.

recuerdo *nm* **1** *(imagen mental)* memory. **2** *(regalo)* souvenir.
▶ *nm pl* **recuerdos** *(saludos)* regards; *(en carta)* best wishes.

recuperación nf **1** (gen) recovery. **2** (clases etc) : **prueba de recuperación**, resit exam; **clase de recuperación**, remedial lesson.

recuperar vt-vpr **recuperar(se)** to recover.
● **recuperar el conocimiento** to regain consciousness.
● **recuperar el tiempo perdido** to make up for los time.

recurrir vi (acogerse - a algo) to resort to; (- a alguien) to turn to.
▶ vt (una sentencia) to appeal against.

recurso nm **1** (medio) resort. **2** JUR appeal.
▶ nm pl **recursos** resources, means.

red nf **1** (de pesca, Internet) net. **2** (sistema) network. **3** fig (trampa) trap.
■ **red de carreteras** road network.

redacción nf **1** (escrito) composition. **2** (escritura) writing. **3** (estilo) wording. **4** (oficina) editorial office. **5** (redactores) editorial staff.

redactar vt (texto, carta) to write [pt **wrote**; pp **written**]; (acuerdo, contrato) to draw up [pt **drew**; pp **drawn**].

redactor,-ra nm,f editor.

redada nf raid.

redicho,-a adj affected.

redil nm fold, sheepfold.

redoblar vt **1** (aumentar) to redouble. **2** (clavo) to clinch.
▶ vi (tambores) to roll.

redondear vt **1** (objeto, borde) to (make) round. **2** (cantidad) to round off; (por encima) to round up; (por debajo) to round down.
▶ vpr **redondearse** (ponerse redondo) to become round.

redondel nm circle.

redondo,-a adj **1** (circular) round. **2** (rotundo) categorical: **un no redondo**, a flat refusal. **3** (perfecto) perfect, excellent: **un negocio redondo**, an excellent business deal.
▶ nm **redondo** (de carne) topside.
▶ nf **redonda** (nota musical) semibreve.
● **a la redonda** around: **no había nada en varios kilómetros a la redonda**, there was nothing for several kilometres around.
● **negarse en redondo** to refuse point blank.
● **salir redondo** to turn out perfect.

reducción nf reduction.

reducido,-a adj (tamaño) small; (espacio, recursos) limited.

reducir vt **1** (disminuir) to reduce. **2** (vencer) to subdue.
▶ vi (al conducir) to change down.
▶ vpr **reducirse a** to boil down to: **todo se reduce a una cuestión de dinero**, it all boils down to a question of money.
● **reducir algo a la mitad** to cut STH by half.

redundancia nf redundancy.
● **valga la redundancia** if you'll excuse the repetition.

reembolsar vt (pagar) to reimburse; (devolver) to refund.

reembolso nm (pago) reimbursement; (devolución) refund.
● **contra reembolso** cash on delivery.

reemplazar vt to replace.
● **reemplazar algo por algo** to replace STH by STH.

referencia nf (mención) reference.
▶ nf pl **referencias** references.
● **con referencia a** with reference to.
● **hacer referencia a** to refer to.

referéndum nm referendum.

referente adj concerning.

referir vt (expresar) to relate, tell [pt & pp **told**].
▶ vpr **referirse** (aludir) to refer: **no se refirió al problema**, he didn't refer to the problem; **¿a qué te refieres?**, what do yo mean?

refilón loc **de refilón** (rozando) obliquely; (de pasada) briefly.

refinado,-a adj refined.

refinar vt **1** (azúcar, petróleo) to refine. **2** (escrito) to polish.
▶ vpr **refinarse** (pulirse) to polish oneself.

refinería nf refinery.

reflejar vt to reflect.
▶ vpr **reflejarse** to be reflected.

reflejo,-a adj (movimiento) reflex.
▶ nm **reflejo 1** (imagen) reflection. **2** (destello) gleam.
▶ mpl **reflejos 1** (reacción) reflexes. **2** (en el pelo) highlights.
● **perder reflejos** to lose one's touch [pt & pp **lost**].
● **tener buenos reflejos** to have good reflexes.

reflexión *nf* reflection.
reflexionar *vt* to reflect.
reflexivo,-a *adj* **1** *(persona)* reflective. **2** *(verbo etc)* reflexive.
reforma *nf* **1** *(cambio)* reform. **2** *(mejora)* improvement. **3** *(de edificio)* alteration: *"Cerrado por reformas"*, "Closed for alterations".
reformar *vt* **1** *(cambiar)* to reform. **2** *(casa etc)* to renovate.
▶ *vpr* **reformarse** to mend one's ways.
reformatorio *nm* reformatory.
reforzar *vt* **1** *(cosas físicas)* to reinforce. **2** *(medidas)* to strengthen.
refrán *nm* proverb, saying.
● **como dice el refrán** as the saying goes.
refrescante *adj* refreshing.
refrescar *vt* **1** *(bebida)* to cool, chill. **2** *(memoria)* to refresh.
▶ *vi (tiempo)* to turn cool: *por la noche refresca*, the nights are cold; *ya empieza a refrescar*, it's getting cooler.
▶ *vpr* **refrescarse 1** *(tomar el fresco)* to take a breath of fresh air. **2** *(con agua)* to freshen up.
refresco *nm* soft drink.
refrigeración *nf* **1** *(enfriamiento)* refrigeration. **2** *(aire acondicionado)* air conditioning.
refrigerador *nm* fridge.
refuerzo *nm* *(fortalecimiento)* reinforcement, strengthening.
▶ *nm pl* **refuerzos** *(tropas)* reinforcements.
refugiado,-a *adj - nm,f* refugee.
refugiar *vt* to shelter.
▶ *vpr* **refugiarse** to take refuge.
refugio *nm* shelter, refuge.
refunfuñar *vi* to grumble.
regadera *nf* watering can.
● **estar como una regadera** to be as mad as a hatter.
regadío *nm* **1** *(sistema)* irrigation. **2** *(terreno)* irrigated land.
regalar *vt* **1** *(dar)* to give: *me han regalado un reloj para mi cumpleaños*, I got a watch for my birthday; *me lo han regalado*, they gave it to me, it was a present. **2** *(halagar)* to flatter.
▶ *vpr* **regalarse** *(darse un capricho)* to spoil oneself [*pt & pp* **spoilt**].
regaliz *nm* liquorice.

regalo *nm* gift, present: *me hicieron un regalo*, they gave me a present.
● **de regalo** free: *si compras dos, te damos otro de regalo*, if you buy two, you get another one free.
regañadientes *loc* **a regañadientes** reluctantly, grudgingly.
regañar *vt fam* to scold, tell off [*pt & pp* **told**].
▶ *vi* to argue, quarrel.
regañina *nf* scolding, telling-off.
regar *vt* **1** *(plantas)* to water. **2** *(terreno)* to irrigate. **3** *(calle)* to hose down.
regata *nf* regatta.
regate *nm* dribble.
regatear *vt* *(en precio)* to haggle.
▶ *vi (futbolista)* to dribble.
regazo *nm* lap.
regenerar *vt* to regenerate.
régimen *nm* **1** *(de comida)* diet. **2** *(político)* régime. **3** *(condiciones)* rules *pl*.
● **estar a régimen** to be on a diet.
● **ponerse a régimen** to go on a diet.
regimiento *nm* regiment.
región *nf* region.
regional *adj* regional.
regir *vt* **1** *(gobernar)* to govern, rule. **2** *(dirigir)* to manage, direct.
▶ *vi (ley etc)* to be in force; *(costumbre)* to prevail.
● **regirse por** to go by.
● **no regir** to have a screw loose.
registrar *vt* **1** *(inspeccionar)* to search, inspect. **2** *(datos)* to register, record. **3** *(nacimiento, venta)* to register.
▶ *vpr* **registrarse 1** *(matricularse)* to register, enrol. **2** *(detectarse)* to be recorded.
registro *nm* **1** *(inspección)* search, inspection: *tenemos una orden de registro*, we have a search warrant. **2** *(inscripción)* registration. **3** *(oficina)* registry; *(libro)* register. **4** *(en música, lingüística)* register.
regla *nf* **1** *(norma)* rule. **2** *(instrumento)* ruler. **3** *(menstruación)* period: *tengo la regla*, I have my period.
● **en regla** in order.
● **por regla general** as a rule.
■ **regla de tres** rule of three.
reglamentario,-a *adj* statutory.
reglamento *nm* regulations *pl*.
regocijar *vt* to delight.
▶ *vpr* **regocijarse** to be delighted.
regocijo *nm* **1** *(placer)* delight. **2** *(júbilo)* merriment.

regordete,-a *adj* plump, chubby.

regresar *vi (volver)* to return, come back, go back.

regreso *nm* return.

● **estar de regreso** to be back.

● **en el viaje de regreso** on the way back.

reguero *nm* trickle.

● **como un reguero de pólvora** like wildfire.

regular *adj* **1** *(habitual)* regular. **2** *(pasable)* so-so, average.

▶ *vt* to regulate.

regularidad *nf* regularity: *lo hace con regularidad,* he does it regularly.

rehabilitar *vt-vpr* **rehabilitar(se)** to rehabilitate.

rehacer *vt* **1** *(volver a hacer)* to do again, redo *[pt* **redid***; pp* **redone]**. **2** *(reconstruir)* to remake, rebuild *[pt & pp* **rebuilt]**. **3** *(reparar)* to repair, mend.

● **rehacer su vida** to rebuild one's life *[pt & pp* **rebuilt]**.

● **rehacerse de algo** to get over STH, recover from STH.

rehén *nmf* hostage.

rehuir *vt* to avoid, shun.

rehusar *vt* to refuse, decline.

reina *nf* queen.

reinado *nm* reign: *durante el reinado de,* in the reign of.

reinar *vi* **1** *(gobernar)* to reign. **2** *(prevalecer)* to rule, prevail.

reincidir *vi* to relapse.

reino *nm* kingdom.

■ **Reino Unido** United Kingdom.

reintegro *nm* **1** *(de dinero de cuenta)* withdrawal. **2** *(de dinero pagado)* reimbursement.

reír *vi-vpr* **reír(se)** to laugh.

reiterar *vt* to reiterate, repeat.

reivindicación *nf* demand, claim.

reivindicar *vt (derecho)* to demand, claim; *(propiedad)* to claim; *(atentado)* to claim responsability for.

reja *nf (de ventana, puerta)* grille.

● **entre rejas** behind bars.

rejilla *nf* **1** *(de ventilación)* grille. **2** *(de chimenea)* grate. **3** *(de silla)* wickerwork: *una silla de rejilla,* a wicker chair.

rejuvenecer *vt* to rejuvenate.

▶ *vpr* **rejuvenecerse** to become rejuvenated.

relación *nf* **1** *(vínculo)* relation. **2** *(conexión)* link. **3** *(listado)* list. **4** *(relato)* account. **5** *(de pareja)* relationship.

● **tener buenas relaciones** to be well connected.

● **tener relaciones sexuales con** ALGN to have sex with SB.

■ **relaciones públicas** public relations.

relacionar *vt* **1** *(vincular)* to relate, connect. **2** *(relatar)* to tell *[pt & pp* **told]**.

▶ *vpr* **relacionarse** *(tener amistad)* to get acquainted; *(estar conectados)* to be related, be connected.

relajación *nf* relaxation.

relajado,-a *adj* **1** *(tranquilo)* relaxed. **2** *(inmoral)* loose, dissolute.

relajar *vt* **1** *(tranquilizar)* to relax. **2** *(suavizar)* to loosen, slacken.

▶ *vpr* **relajarse** **1** *(descansar)* to relax. **2** *(en las costumbres)* to let oneself go *[pt & pp* **let]**. **3** *(dilatarse)* to slacken.

relamer *vt* to lick.

▶ *vpr* **relamerse** to lick one's lips.

relámpago *nm* flash of lightning.

● **pasó como un relámpago** it went past in a flash.

relampaguear *vi* **1** to lighten: *truena y relampaguea,* it's thundering and lightning. **2** *(brillar)* to flash: *sus ojos relampagueaban,* her eyes flashed.

relatar *vt* to relate, tell *[pt & pp* **told]**.

relativo,-a *adj* relative.

▶ *nm* **relativo** relative.

● **relativo a algo** relating to STH.

relato *nm* story, tale.

relax *nm (relajación)* relaxation.

releer *vt* to reread *[pt & pp* **reread]**.

relevante *adj* **1** *(significativo)* relevant. **2** *(importante)* excellent, outstanding.

relevar *vt* **1** *(sustituir)* to relieve. **2** *(eximir)* to exempt from. **3** *(destituir)* to dismiss.

relevo *nm* **1** *(acto, persona)* relief. **2** relay: *los cien metros relevos,* the hundred metre relay.

● **tomar el relevo** to take over.

relieve *nm* relief.

● **poner de relieve** to emphasize.

religión *nf* religion.

religioso,-a *adj* religious.

▶ *nm,f (hombre)* monk; *(mujer)* nun.

relinchar *vi* to neigh, whinny.

reliquia *nf* relic.

rellano *nm* landing.

rellenar *vt* **1** *(volver a llenar)* to refill. **2** *(completar)* to cram. **3** *(cuestionario)* to fill in. **4** *(ave)* to stuff; *(pastel)* to fill.

relleno,-a *adj* **1** *(lleno)* stuffed. **2** *(gordito)* plump.
▶ *nm* **relleno 1** *(de aves)* stuffing; *(de pasteles)* filling. **2** *(en prenda)* padding.

reloj *nm (de pared, mesa)* clock; *(de pulsera)* watch.
● **contra reloj** against the clock.
■ **reloj de arena** hourglass.
■ **reloj de sol** sundial.
■ **reloj despertador** alarm clock.
■ **reloj digital 1** *(de pulsera)* digital watch. **2** *(de pared, mesa)* digital clock.

relojería *nf* **1** *(arte)* watchmaking. **2** *(tienda)* watchmaker's shop.

relojero,-a *nm,f* watchmaker.

reluciente *adj (luz)* bright, shining; *(joyas)* gleaming.

relucir *vi* **1** *(brillar)* to shine [*pt & pp* **shone**]. **2** *(destacar)* to excel.
● **sacar a relucir** to bring up [*pt & pp* **brought**].

remar *vi* to row.

rematar *vt* **1** *(acabar)* to finish off. **2** DEP *(con cabeza)* to head; *(con pie)* to shoot [*pt & pp* **shot**].

remate *nm* **1** *(final)* end. **2** DEP *(con cabeza)* header; *(con pie)* shot.
● **de remate** totally.

remediar *vt* **1** *(solucionar)* to remedy. **2** *(reparar)* to repair. **3** *(evitar)* to avoid: *no lo puedo remediar*, I can't help it.

remedio *nm* **1** *(medicamento)* remedy, cure. **2** *(solución)* solution: *no tiene remedio*, he's hopeless.
● **no tengo más remedio que...** I have no choice but to....

remendar *vt* **1** *(zurcir)* to mend, repair. **2** *(con parche)* to patch.

remesa *nf* **1** *(de dinero)* remittance. **2** *(de mercancías)* consignment, shipment.

remiendo *nm* **1** *(zurcido)* mend. **2** *(parche)* patch.

remite *nm* sender's name and address.

remitente *nmf* sender.

remitir *vt* **1** *(enviar)* to remit, send [*pt & pp* **sent**]. **2** *(referir)* to refer. **3** *(tormenta)* to abate; *(fiebre)* to go down.
▶ *vpr* **remitirse** *(referirse)* to refer.

remo *nm* **1** *(pala)* oar; *(de canoa)* paddle. **2** *(deporte)* rowing.

remojar *vt* to soak.

remojo *nm* soaking.
● **poner algo en remojo** to leave STH to soak.

remojón *nm (intencionado)* dip; *(fortuito)* soaking.
● **darse un remojón** to have a dip.

remolacha *nf* beetroot.
■ **remolacha azucarera** sugar beet.

remolcador *nm* **1** *(barco)* tug, tugboat. **2** *(camión)* tow truck.

remolcar *vt* to tow.

remolino *nm* **1** *(de humo)* whirl; *(de agua)* whirlpool; *(de aire)* whirlwind. **2** *(de pelo)* GB tuft; US cowlick. **3** *(de gente)* swirling mass.

remolón,-ona *adj* lazy, slack.
● **hacerse el remolón** : *no te hagas el remolón y ayúdame a fregar los platos*, don't try to get out of it, come and help me with the washing up.

remolque *nm* **1** *(acción)* towing. **2** *(vehículo)* trailer.
● **a remolque** in tow.

remontar *vt* **1** *(elevar)* to raise. **2** *(río)* to go up. **3** *(superar)* to overcome [*pt* **overcame**; *pp* **overcome**].
▶ *vpr* **remontarse 1** *(al volar)* to soar. **2** *(datar)* to go back, date back: *se remonta a hace muchos años*, it goes back many years.

remordimiento *nm* remorse.

remoto,-a *adj* remote.

remover *vt* **1** *(líquido, salsa)* to stir. **2** *(ensalada)* to toss. **3** *(objeto)* to move. **4** *(tierra)* to turn over. **5** *(tema)* to bring up again [*pt & pp* **brought**].

renacer *vi* to be reborn.
● **hacer renacer** to revive.

renacimiento *nm* rebirth.
● **el Renacimiento** the Renaissance.

renacuajo *nm* tadpole.

rencor *nm* rancour.
● **no le guardo rencor** I don't bear him malice.

rencoroso,-a *adj* rancorous.

rendido,-a *adj* worn out, exhausted.

rendija *nf* crack.

rendimiento *nm* **1** *(de máquina)* output. **2** *(de persona)* performance.

rendir *vt (producir)* to yield, produce.
▶ *vt-vi (dar fruto)* to pay [*pt & pp* **paid**]: *este*

negocio rinde poco, this business doesn't pay much.
▶ *vpr* **rendirse** *(entregarse)* to surrender.
● **rendir cuentas** to account for one's actions.
● **rendir culto a** to worship.
● **rendir homenaje a** to pay homage to [*pt & pp* **paid**].
● **¡me rindo!** *fam* I give up!
renegar *vi (renunciar)* : **renegó de sus principios**, he renounced his beliefs; **no reniegues de tu familia**, don't disown your family.
▶ *vt (negar)* to deny.
renglón *nm* line.
● **a renglón seguido** right after.
reno *nm* reindeer.
renovación *nf* **1** *(de contrato, actividad)* renewal. **2** *(de casa)* renovation.
renovar *vt* **1** *(contrato, actividad)* to renew. **2** *(casa)* to renovate. **3** *(muebles)* to change.
● **renovarse o morir** adapt or perish.
renta *nf* **1** *(ingresos)* income. **2** *(beneficio)* interest. **3** *(alquiler)* rent.
■ **renta per cápita** per capita income.
rentable *adj* profitable.
renunciar *vt* **1** *(dejar)* to give up; *(abandonar)* to abandon; *(rechazar)* to refuse. **2** *(dimitir)* to resign.
● **renunciar al trono** to reliquish the throne.
reñido,-a *adj* **1** *(enemistado)* on bad terms: **están reñidos**, they are on bad terms, they've fallen out. **2** *(muy disputado)* hard-fought.
reñir *vi (discutir)* to quarrel, argue.
▶ *vt (reprender)* to scold.
reo *nmf* offender, culprit.
reojo *vt* **mirar a «sc»algn«/sc» de reojo** to look out of the corner of one's eye at SB.
reparación *nf* **1** *(arreglo)* repair. **2** *(desagravio)* reparation.
reparar *vt* **1** *(arreglar)* to repair, mend. **2** *(desagraviar)* to make amends for.
▶ *vt-vi* **reparar en** to notice, see [*pt* **saw**; *pp* **seen**]: **no reparó en los fallos**, he didn't notice the faults.
● **sin reparar en** regardless of: **sin reparar en gastos**, regardless of the cost.
reparo *nm* objection.
● **no tener reparos en** not to hesitate to.
● **poner reparos a** to object to.

repartidor,-ra *nm,f (hombre)* delivery man; *(mujer)* delivery woman.
repartir *vt* **1** *(distribuir)* to deliver. **2** *(entregar)* to give out; *(correo)* to deliver.
reparto *nm* **1** *(distribución)* delivery. **2** *(en mano)* handing out. **3** *(de mercancías)* delivery. **4** *(actores)* cast.
repasar *vt* **1** *(lección, texto)* to revise, go over. **2** *(máquina, cuenta)* to check. **3** *(remendar)* to mend. **4** *fam (mirar)* to look over.
repaso *nm* **1** *(revisión)* revision; *(de lección)* review: **le dio un último repaso**, he gave it a final check. **2** *(remiendo)* mending. **3** *(a máquina etc)* check, overhaul.
repatriar *vt* to repatriate.
repelente *adj* repellent, repulsive: **es un niño repelente**, he's a little know-all.
repeler *vt* **1** *(rechazar)* to repel, reject. **2** *(repugnar)* : **me repele**, I find it repellent.
repente *nm* sudden impulse.
● **de repente** suddenly.
repentino,-a *adj* sudden.
repercusión *nf* repercussion.
● **tener repercusión en algo** to have repercussions on STH.
repercutir *vi* **1** *(trascender)* to have repercussions. **2** *(rebotar)* to rebound. **3** *(sonido)* to echo.
repertorio *nm* repertoire.
repetición *nf* repetition.
repetidor *nm* relay, booster station.
repetir *vt-vi* to repeat.
● **repetir curso** to repeat a year.
● **el pepino se me repite** cucumber repeats on me.
repicar *vt (campanas)* to peal, ring out [*pt* **rang**; *pp* **rung**].
repique *nm* pealing, ringing.
repisa *nf* shelf [*pl* **-ves**].
■ **repisa de la chimenea** mantelpiece.
repleto,-a *adj* full up.
réplica *nf* **1** *(respuesta)* answer; *(objeción)* retort. **2** *(copia)* replica.
replicar *vt-vi* to answer back, reply.
repoblación *nf* repopulation.
■ **repoblación forestal** reafforestation.
repoblar *vt (zona)* to repopulate; *(bosque)* to reafforest.
repollo *nm* cabbage.
reponer *vt* **1** *(devolver)* to put back, replace.

2 *(obra teatral)* to revive; *(película)* to rerun [*pt* **reran**; *pp* **rerun**].
▸ *vpr* **reponerse** to recover.

reportaje *nm (en televisión)* report; *(prensa)* feature.

reportero,-a *nm,f* reporter.

reposar *vt-vi* to rest.

reposo *nm (de persona)* rest: **el médico me ha mandado reposo**, the doctor has told me to rest.
● **dejar en reposo** to leave to stand [*pt & pp* **left**].

repostar *vt (provisiones)* to stock up with; *(combustible)* to fill up.
▸ *vi (coche)* to fill up, get some petrol; *(avión)* to refuel.

repostería *nf* **1** *(arte)* confectionery. **2** *(pastas)* confectionary, cakes and pastries *pl*.

reprender *vt* to reprimand, scold.

represalia *nf* reprisal, retaliation.
● **tomar represalias contra** ALGN to retaliate against SB.

representación *nf* **1** *(imagen, sustitución)* representation. **2** *(teatral)* performance. **3** *(delegación)* delegation.

representante *nmf* representative.

representar *vt* **1** *(ilustrar, sustituir)* to represent. **2** *(obra de teatro)* to perform. **3** *(edad)* to look: **no representa esa edad**, she doesn't look that age; **representa menos edad de la que tiene**, he looks younger than he is.
● **representar mucho para** ALGN to mean a lot to SB [*pt & pp* **meant**].

representativo,-a *adj* representative.

represión *nf* repression.

reprimido,-a *adj* repressed.
▸ *nm,f* : **es un reprimido**, he's very repressed.

reprimir *vt* to repress.
▸ *vpr* **reprimirse** to restrain oneself.

reprochar *vt* to reproach: **no tengo nada que reprocharte**, I have nothing to reproach you about.
▸ *vpr* **reprocharse** to reproach oneself.

reproche *nm* reproach: **una mirada de reproche**, a reproachful look; **le hizo varios reproches**, she criticized him on several counts.

reproducción *nf* reproduction.

reproducir *vt-vpr* **reproducir(se)** to reproduce.

reptar *vi* to crawl.

reptil *nm* reptile.

república *nf* republic.

republicano,-a *adj* - *nm,f* republican.

repuesto,-a *adj (recuperado)* recovered.
▸ *nm* **repuesto** *(recambio)* spare part: **la rueda de repuesto**, the spare wheel.

repugnancia *nf* repugnance.

repugnante *adj* repugnant.

repugnar *vi* to disgust, revolt: **esa idea me repugna**, I find that idea disgusting.

reputación *nf* reputation.

requerir *vt* **1** *(necesitar)* to require. **2** *(solicitar)* to request: **se requiere mucha paciencia con los niños**, you need to be very patient with children.

requesón *nm* cottage cheese.

requisito *nm* requisite, requirement.

res *nf* beast, animal.

resaca *nf* hangover: **tengo resaca**, I have a hangover.

resaltar *vi* **1** *(sobresalir)* to project, jut out. **2** *fig* to stand out [*pt & pp* **stood**].
▸ *vt* **destacar** to highlight.
● **hacer resaltar** to emphasize.

resbaladizo,-a *adj* slippery.

resbalar *vi-vpr* **resbalar(se)** **1** *(deslizarse)* to slide. **2** *(sin querer)* to slip. **3** *(coche)* to skid. **4** *(no afectar)* : **lo que tú digas me resbala**, I couldn't care less what you say.

resbalón *nm* slip.
● **pegar un resbalón** to slip.

rescatar *vt* **1** *(salvar)* to rescue. **2** *(recuperar)* to recover.

rescate *nm* **1** *(de persona)* rescue. **2** *(dinero)* ransom. **3** *(de algo robado)* recovery.

resecar *vt-vpr* **resecar(se)** to dry up.

reseco,-a *adj* very dry.

resentimiento *nm* resentment.

resentirse *vpr (sufrir)* to be affected by: **la economía se resintió**, the economy was affected; **todavía me resiento del golpe**, I'm still suffering the effects of the blow; **al final la salud se resiente**, in the end it affects your health.

reserva *nf* **1** *(de plazas)* booking, reservation: **quisiera hacer una reserva**, I'd like to make a booking. **2** *(provisión)* reserve. **3** *(cautela)* reservation. **4** *(discreción)* discretion. **5** *(vino)* vintage. **6** *(de animales)* reserve. **7** *(soldado)* reserve.
▸ *nmf (deportista)* reserve, substitute.

▶ *nf pl* **reservas** *(existencias)* reserves: **reservas de petróleo**, oil reserves.

● **sin reservas** unreservedly, wholeheartedly.

reservado,-a *adj* **1** *(plazas)* booked, reserved. **2** *(persona)* reserved, discreet.

▶ *nm* **reservado** private room.

reservar *vt* **1** *(plazas)* to book, reserve. **2** *(provisiones)* to keep, save. **3** *(ocultar)* to keep secret.

▶ *vpr* **reservarse 1** *(conservarse)* to save oneself. **2** *(cautelarse)* to withold [*pt & pp* **witheld**].

resfriado *nm (con congestión)* cold; *(poco importante)* chill.

● **estar resfriado** to have a cold.

● **pillar un resfriado** to catch [*pt & pp* **caught**] a cold.

resfriarse *vpr* to catch a cold [*pt & pp* **caught**].

resguardar *vt* to protect.

resguardo *nm* **1** *(protección)* protection. **2** *(recibo)* receipt.

residencia *nf* residence.

■ **residencia de ancianos** residential home.

■ **residencia de estudiantes** GB hall of residence; US dormitory.

residente *adj - nmf* resident.

residir *vi* **1** *(habitar)* to reside, live. **2** *(radicar)* to lie [*pt* **lay**; *pp* **lain**]: **es ahí donde reside el problema**, that's where the problem lies.

residuo *nm* residue.

■ **residuos radiactivos** radioactive waste *sing*.

resignación *nf* resignation.

resignarse *vpr* to resign.

resina *nf* resin.

resistencia *nf* **1** *(de material)* resistance. **2** *(de persona)* endurance. **3** *(oposición)* reluctance, opposition.

● **sin ofrecer resistencia** without resistance.

resistente *adj* resistant.

● **resistente al calor** heat-resistant.

● **resistente al frío** resistant to cold.

● **resistente al fuego** fire-resistant.

resistir *vt* **1** *(no ceder, aguantar)* to withstand [*pt & pp* **withstood**]: **resistir el paso del tiempo**, to withstand the passage of time. **2** *(tolerar)* to stand [*pt & pp* **stood**], bear [*pt* **bore**; *pp* **borne**]: **no resisto las os-**tras, I can't stand oysters; **no puedo resistir el calor**, I can't bear the heat. **3** *(peso)* to take, bear [*pt* **bore**; *pp* **borne**]. **4** *(tentación etc)* to resist.

▶ *vpr* **resistirse 1** *(negarse)* to refuse. **2** *(forcejear)* to resist. **3** *(oponerse)* to offer resistance. **4** *fam (resultar difícil)* : **la física se le resiste**, he finds physics hard; **me resisto a creerlo**, I find it hard to believe.

resolución *nf* **1** *(ánimo)* resolution, decision. **2** *(solución)* solution: **no encontraban una resolución**, they couldn't find a solution.

resolver *vt* **1** *(decidir)* to resolve: **resolvió dimitir**, he resolved to resign. **2** *(problema)* to solve.

▶ *vpr* **resolverse** to resolve, make up one's mind.

resonancia *nf* **1** *(gen)* resonance. **2** *(efecto)* importance.

● **tener resonancia** to cause a sensation.

■ **resonancia magnética** magnetic resonance scanning.

resonar *vi* to resound.

respaldar *vt* to support, back.

▶ *vpr* **respaldarse** to lean back [*pt & pp* **leant**].

respaldo *nm* **1** *(de asiento)* back. **2** *(apoyo)* support, backing.

respectivo,-a *adj* respective.

● **en lo respectivo a** with regard to.

respecto *nm* .

● **al respecto** on the matter, about: **no ha hecho nada al respecto**, he has done nothing about it; **¿dijo algo al respecto?**, did he say anything on the matter?

● **con respecto a** with regard to, regarding.

respetable *adj* respectable.

respetar *vt* to respect.

respeto *nm* **1** *(consideración)* respect. **2** *fam (miedo)* fear.

● **faltar al respeto a** ALGN to be disrespectful to SB.

● **presentar sus respetos a** ALGN *fml* to pay one's respects to SB [*pt & pp* **paid**].

respetuoso,-a *adj* respectful.

respingón,-ona *adj* snub, turned-up: **nariz respingona**, snub nose.

respiración *nf* breathing: **me quedé sin respiración**, I was out of breath; **me**

dejó sin respiración, it took my breath away.

■ **respiración boca a boca** mouth-to-mouth resuscitation.

respirar *vi* **1** *(tomar aire)* to breathe. **2** *fig (relajar)* to breathe a sigh of relief.

▶ *vt* to breathe.

● **respira hondo** take a deep breath.

respiratorio,-a *adj* respiratory.

respiro *nm* **1** *(descanso)* breather: *deberías tomarte un respiro*, you should take a breather; *luchó sin respiro*, he fought without respite. **2** *(alivio)* relief: *eso es un respiro*, that's a relief.

resplandecer *vi* to shine [*pt & pp* **shone**].

resplandeciente *adj* resplendent.

resplandor *nm (de luz)* brightness.

responder *vt (contestar)* to answer, reply: *no respondió mi pregunta*, he didn't answer my question; *respondió que sí*, he said yes.

▶ *vi* **1** *(contestar)* to answer, reply. **2** *(corresponder)* to answer: *responder a una descripción*, to fit a description; *no responde a nuestras necesidades*, it doesn't meet our requirements. **3** *(replicar)* to answer back. **4** *(reaccionar)* to respond: *no me respondieron los frenos*, my brakes didn't respond, my brakes failed.

● **responder por** to be responsible for.

responsabilidad *nf* responsibility.

responsabilizar *vt* to make responsible, hold responsible [*pt & pp* **held**].

▶ *vpr* **responsabilizarse** to assume responsibility.

responsable *adj* responsible: *un chico muy responsable*, a very responsible boy.

▶ *nmf* **1** *(jefe)* person in charge. **2** *(persona culpable)* : *tú eres el responsable de todo esto*, you are responsible for all this.

respuesta *nf (contestación)* answer, reply; *(reacción)* response: *una buena respuesta del público*, a good response from the public.

resta *nf* substraction.

restablecer *vt* **1** *(contacto)* to reestablish. **2** *(orden)* to restore.

▶ *vpr* **restablecerse** *(recuperarse)* to recover, get better.

restante *adj* remaining.

restar *vt* to subtract.

▶ *vi (quedar)* to be left, remain: *restaba*

una semana, there was a week to go, there was a week left; *sólo resta firmar*, the only thing that remains to be done is to sign.

● **restar importancia a algo** to play STH down.

restauración *nf* **1** *(de muebles etc)* restoration. **2** *(hostelería)* catering.

restaurador,-ra *nm,f* **1** *(de muebles etc)* restorer. **2** *(hostelero)* restauranteur.

restaurante *nm* restaurant.

restaurar *vt* to restore.

resto *nm* **1** *(lo que queda)* rest. **2** *(en matemáticas)* remainder.

▶ *nm pl* **restos** *(gen)* remains; *(de comida)* leftovers.

■ **restos mortales** mortal remains.

restregar *vt* to rub hard.

restricción *nf* restriction.

restringir *vt* to restrict.

resucitar *vt-vi* **1** *(persona)* to resuscitate. **2** *(recuerdos, fiesta)* to revive.

resuelto,-a *adj (decidido)* resolute, bold.

resultado *nm* result.

● **dar buen resultado** to be successful.

resultar *vi* **1** *(funcionar)* to work. **2** *(ocurrir, ser)* to turn out to be: *resultó ser muy simpático*, he turned out to be very nice. **3** *(salir)* to come out: *resultar bien*, to come out well; *resultar mal*, to come out badly; *resultar herido*, to be wounded.

● **resulta que** it turns out that: *resultó que ella no sabía nada*, it turned out that she didn't know anything; *cuando salimos resulta que se puso a llover*, when we went out it started to rain.

resumen *nm* summary.

● **en resumen** in short, to sum up.

resumir *vt* to summarize.

resurrección *nf* resurrection.

retablo *nm* altarpiece.

retaguardia *nf* rearguard: *estar en la retaguardia*, to bring up the rear.

retal *nm* **1** *(trozo de tela)* oddment. **2** *(recorte)* remnant.

retar *vt* to challenge.

retener *vt* **1** *(conservar)* to retain, keep back. **2** *(en la memoria)* to remember. **3** *(arrestar)* to detain, arrest. **4** *(dinero a cuenta)* to deduct.

retina *nf* retina.

retirada *nf* retreat, withdrawal: ***emprendieron la retirada***, they retreated.

retirado,-a *adj* **1** *(apartado)* remote. **2** *(del trabajo)* retired.

retirar *vt (apartar)* to withdraw [*pt* withdrew, *pp* withdrawn].
▶ *vpr* **retirarse 1** *(tropas)* to retreat. **2** *(apartarse)* to withdraw [*pt* **withdrew**; *pp* **withdrawn**]. **3** *(jubilarse)* to retire.
● **puede retirarse** *fml* you may leave.

retiro *nm* **1** *(jubilación)* retirement. **2** *(pensión)* pension. **3** *(lugar, recogimiento)* retreat.

reto *nm* challenge.

retocar *vt* to touch up.

retoque *nm* finishing touch.

retorcer *vt* **1** *(redoblar)* to twist. **2** *(tergiversar)* to distort.
▶ *vpr* **retorcerse** *(de dolor)* to writhe; *(de risa)* to double up: ***me retorcía de dolor***, I writhed with pain; ***se retorcían de risa***, they doubled up with laughter.

retorcido,-a *adj fig* twisted.

retornar *vt (restituir)* to return, give back.
▶ *vi-vpr* **retornar(se)** *(volver)* to come back, go back.

retorno *nm* return.

retraído,-a *adj* withdrawn.

retransmisión *nf* broadcast.
■ **retransmisión en diferido** recorded transmission.
■ **retransmisión en directo** live broadcast.

retransmitir *vt* to broadcast [*pt & pp* **broadcast**].

retrasado,-a *adj (persona)* behind: ***voy muy retrasado***, I'm really behind. **2** *(reloj)* slow. **3** *(tren)* late. **4** *(país)* backward.
▶ *nm,f* mentally retarded person: ***los retrasados***, the mentally retarded.

retrasar *vt* **1** *(salida, proceso)* to delay, put off. **2** *(reloj)* to put back.
▶ *vi-vpr* **retrasar(se)** *(ir atrás)* to fall [*pt* **fell**; *pp* **fallen**] behind: ***me he retrasado con este trabajo***, I'm behind with this work; ***va retrasado en física***, he's behind in physics. **2** *(llegar tarde)* to be late: ***el avión se retrasó***, the plane was late. **3** *(reloj)* to be slow.

retraso *nm* **1** *(de tiempo)* delay: ***siento el retraso***, I'm sorry for the delay. **2** *(subdesarrollo)* backwardness.

retratar *vt* **1** to paint a portrait of. **2** *(fotografiar)* to photograph. **3** *(describir)* to describe.

retrato *nm* **1** portrait. **2** *(foto)* photograph. **3** *(descripción)* description.
■ **retrato robot** identikit picture, photofit picture.

retrete *nm* toilet, lavatory.

retroceder *vi* to go back.

retroceso *nm* backward movement.

retrovisor *nm* rear-view mirror.

retumbar *vi* to resound.

reuma *nm* rheumatism.

reúma *nm* rheumatism.

reunión *nf* meeting.
● **celebrar una reunión** to hold [*pt & pp* **held**] a meeting.
● **convocar una reunión** tto call a meeting.

reunir *vt-vpr* **reunir(se)** *(personas)* to meet [*pt & pp* **met**]; *(cosas)* to get together.

revancha *nf* revenge.

revelación *nf (descubrimiento)* revelation; *(de secreto)* disclosure.

revelado *nm (de película)* developing.

revelar *vt* **1** *(descubrir)* to reveal. **2** *(fotos)* to develop.

reventar *vt* **1** *(hacer estallar)* to burst [*pt & pp* **burst**]. **2** *fam (molestar)* to annoy: ***suamiga me revienta***, I hate his friend.
▶ *vi (estallar)* to burst [*pt & pp* **burst**]: ***reventó de risa***, he killed himself laughing.
▶ *vpr* **reventarse 1** *(estallar)* to burst [*pt & pp* **burst**]. **2** *fam (cansarse)* to tire oneself out.
● **estar a reventar** to be bursting: ***el cine estaba a reventar***, the cinema was full to bursting.

reventón *nm* **1** *(de tubería)* burst. **2** *(de neumático)* blowout.

reverencia *nf* **1** *(veneración)* reverence. **2** *(saludo - de hombre)* bow; *(- de mujer)* curtsey, curtsy.

reversible *adj* reversible.

reverso *nm* reverse.

revés *nm* **1** *(reverso)* back, reverse. **2** *(bofetada)* slap. **3** *(contrariedad)* misfortune. **4** *(en tenis etc)* backhand.
● **al revés 1** *(todo lo contrario)* on the contrary. **2** *(en orden inverso)* the other way round. **3** *(lo de dentro fuera)* inside out. **4** *(lo delantero detrás)* back to front. **5** *(boca abajo)* upside down, the wrong way up.
● **del revés** inside out.

revisar *vt (teoría, edición)* to revise; *(cuenta)* to check.

revisión *nf (de teoría, edición)* revision; *(de cuenta)* check.

■ **revisión de cuentas** audit.

■ **revisión médica** checkup.

■ **revisión salarial** wage review.

revisor,-ra *nm,f* ticket inspector.

■ **revisor ortográfico** spellchecker.

revista *nf* **1** *(publicación)* magazine, review. **2** *(inspección)* inspection. **3** *(espectáculo)* revue.

revistero *nm* magazine rack.

revivir *vi* to revive.

revolcar *vt* **1** *(derribar)* to knock down, knock over. **2** *(vencer)* to floor.

▶ *vpr* **revolcarse** to roll about.

revolotear *vi* to fly about [*pt* flew; *pp* flown], flutter about.

revoltijo *nm* **1** *(plato)* scrambled eggs *pl.* **2** *(lío)* mess, jumble.

revoltoso,-a *adj* **1** *(rebelde)* rebellious. **2** *(travieso)* mischievous, naughty.

▶ *nm,f (sedicioso)* troublemaker.

revolución *nf* revolution.

revolucionar *vt (cambiar)* to revolutionize; *(país)* to stir up.

revolucionario,-a *adj - nm,f* revolutionary.

revólver *nm* revolver.

revolver *vt* **1** *(remover)* to stir; *(agitar)* to shake [*pt* shook; *pp* shaken]. **2** *(desordenar)* to mess up. **3** *(producir náuseas)* to upset [*pt & pp* upset].

▶ *vpr* **revolverse 1** *(moverse)* to turn round: *me revolvía en la cama*, I tossed and turned in bed. **2** *(tiempo)* to turn stormy.

revuelo *nm* fig commotion.

revuelta *nf* **1** *(revolución)* revolt, riot. **2** *(curva)* bend, turn.

revuelto,-a *adj* **1** *(desordenado)* confused, mixed up. **2** *(intrincado)* intricate. **3** *(revoltoso)* agitated.

rey *nm (monarca, en ajedrez)* king.

● **los Reyes** the King and Queen.

■ **los Reyes Magos** the Three Kings, the Three Wise Men.

rezagarse *vpr* to fall behind [*pt* fell; *pp* fallen].

rezar *vi* **1** *(orar)* to pray. **2** *(documento)* to say [*pt & pp* said], read [*pt & pp* read]: *la carta reza así*, the letter says this.

rezo *nm* prayer.

ria *nf* estuary; *(técnicamente)* ria.

riachuelo *nm* stream.

riada *nf* flood.

ribera *nf* **1** *(de río)* bank. **2** *(de mar)* seashore.

rico,-a *adj* **1** *(adinerado)* rich, wealthy. **2** *(abundante)* rich; *(tierra)* fertile. **3** *(sabroso)* tasty, delicious. **4** *fam (niño)* lovely, sweet.

▶ *nm,f (tratamiento)* sunshine: *mira, rico, haz lo que te dé la gana*, look, sunshine, just do what you want.

ridiculez *nf* **1** *(hecho, acción)* ridiculous thing, ridiculous action. **2** *(nimiedad)* triviality: *¡menuda ridiculez!*, how ridiculous!

ridiculizar *vt* to ridicule.

ridículo,-a *adj* ridiculous, absurd.

▶ *nm* **ridículo** ridicule.

● **hacer el ridículo** to make a fool of oneself.

● **poner a** ALGN **en ridículo** to make a fool of SB.

riego *nm* irrigation, watering.

■ **riego sanguíneo** blood circulation.

riel *nm* rail.

rienda *nf* **1** *(brida)* rein. **2** *(control)* restraint.

● **dar rienda suelta a** to give free rein to.

riesgo *nm* risk, danger.

● **correr riesgos** to run [*pt* ran; *pp* run] risks.

rifa *nf* raffle.

rifar *vt* to raffle.

rifle *nm* rifle.

rígido,-a *adj* **1** *(tieso)* rigid. **2** *(severo)* strict.

rigor *nm* **1** *(precisión)* GB rigour, US rigor. **2** *(severidad)* strictness. **3** *(dureza)* harshness.

● **de rigor** indispensable.

● **en rigor** strictly speaking.

riguroso,-a *adj* **1** *(exacto)* rigorous. **2** *(severo)* strict. **3** *(clima)* harsh.

● **en sentido riguroso** strictly speaking.

rima *nf* rhyme.

▶ *nf pl* **rimas** poems.

rimar *vt-vi* to rhyme.

rímel *nm* mascara.

rincón *nm* corner.

rinoceronte *nm* rhinoceros.

riña *nf* **1** *(pelea)* fight. **2** *(discusión)* quarrel.

riñón *nm* kidney.

● **costar un riñón** *fam* to cost a bomb [*pt & pp* cost].

río *nm* rive.

● **río abajo** downstream.

● **río arriba** upstream.

riqueza *nf* **1** *(cualidad)* richness. **2** *(abundancia)* wealth, riches *pl*.

risa *nf* laugh: *eso nos dio risa*, that made us laugh; *me entró la risa tonta*, I got the giggles.

► *nf pl* **risas** laughter *sing*.

● **morirse de risa** to kill oneself laughing.

● **¡qué risa!** what a laugh!

● **tomar algo a risa** to treat STH as a joke.

risueño,-a *adj* **1** *(sonriente)* smiling. **2** *(animado)* cheerful. **3** *(próspero)* bright.

ritmo *nm* **1** *(compás)* rhythm. **2** *(velocidad)* pace, speed: *trabajar a buen ritmo*, to work at a good pace.

rito *nm* rite.

ritual *adj - nm* ritual.

rival *nmf* rival.

rivalidad *nf* rivalry.

rizado,-a *adj* **1** *(pelo)* curly. **2** *(mar)* choppy.

► *nm* **rizado** curling.

rizar *vt (pelo)* to curl.

► *vt-vpr* **rizar(se)** *(pelo)* to curl.

● **rizar el rizo** to split hairs [*pt & pp* **split**].

rizo *nm* **1** *(de pelo)* curl. **2** *(tejido)* terry towelling.

robar *vt (banco, persona)* to rob; *(objeto)* to steal [*pt* **stole**; *pp* **stolen**]; *(casa)* to burgle, break into [*pt* **broke**; *pp* **broken**].

● **robar algo a ALGN** to steal [*pt* **stole**; *pp* **stolen**] STH from SB.

roble *nm* oak tree.

robo *nm* *(a banco, persona)* robbery; *(de objeto)* theft; *(en casa)* burglary.

robot *nm* robot.

robusto,-a *adj* robust, strong.

roca *nf* rock.

roce *nm* **1** *(señal - en superficie)* scuff mark; *(- en piel)* chafing mark. **2** *(contacto físico)* light touch. **3** *(trato)* contact. **4** *(disensión)* friction.

rociar *vt* **1** *(regar)* to spray. **2** *(dispersar)* to scatter.

► *vi* : *hoy ha rociado*, there's a dew this morning.

rocío *nm* dew.

rocoso,-a *adj* rocky.

rodaja *nf* slice.

● **cortado en rodajas** sliced.

rodaje *nm* **1** *(de película)* filming, shooting. **2** *(de vehículo)* running-in.

rodar *vi* **1** *(dar vueltas)* to roll, turn. **2** *(caer)* to roll down. **3** *(rondar)* to wander about, roam. **4** *(vehículos)* to travel, go.

► *vt* **1** *(película)* to shoot [*pt & pp* **shot**]. **2** *(coche)* to run in [*pt* **ran**; *pp* **run**].

rodear *vt* **1** *(cercar)* to surround, encircle: *rodearon el edificio*, they surrounded the building. **2** *(desviarse)* to make a detour: *tuvimos que rodear la montaña*, we had to go round the mountain.

► *vpr* **rodearse** to soround oneself.

rodeo *nm* **1** *(desvío)* detour. **2** *(elusión)* evasiveness: *déjate de rodeos*, stop beating about the bush. **3** *(de ganado)* round-up; *(espectáculo)* rodeo [*pl* -s].

rodilla *nf* knee.

● **ponerse de rodillas** to kneel down [*pt & pp* **knelt**].

rodillera *nf* **1** *(protección)* knee pad; *(venda)* knee bandage. **2** *(en pantalón)* knee patch.

rodillo *nm* **1** *(para pintar)* roller. **2** *(de amasar)* rolling pin.

roedor *nm* rodent.

roer *vt* to gnaw.

rogar *vt* **1** *(suplicar)* to beg. **2** *(pedir)* to ask, request.

● **"Se ruega no fumar"** "No smoking, please".

rojizo,-a *adj* reddish.

rojo,-a *adj* red.

► *nm* **rojo** red.

rol *nm* role: *juegos de rol*, role playing game.

rollizo,-a *adj* plump, chubby.

rollo *nm* **1** *(de tela, papel)* roll: *un rollo de papel higiénico*, a roll of toilet paper. **2** *fam (aburrimiento)* drag, bore, pain: *¡qué rollo!*, what a pain! **3** *fam (asunto)* : *¿de qué va el rollo?*, what is it all about?; *¡qué mal rollo!*, what a downer! **4** *fam (amorío)* affair.

romance *nm* **1** *(poesía)* romance, ballad. **2** *(amorío)* romance.

románico,-a *adj-nm* Romanesque.

romano,-a *adj - nm,f* Roman.

romántico,-a *adj - nm,f* romantic.

rombo *nm* rhombus.

romería *nf* pilgrimage.

romero *nm (hierba)* rosemary.

romero,-a *nm,f (peregrino)* pilgrim.

rompecabezas *nm* **1** *(juego)* puzzle. **2** *(problema)* riddle.

rompeolas *nm* breakwater.

romper *vt-vpr* **romper(se)** *(gen)* to break [*pt* **broke**; *pp* **broken**]; *(papel, tela)* to tear [*pt* **tore**; *pp* **torn**]; *(cristal)* to smash: *se ha roto el televisor*, the television is broken; *se me ha roto la camisa*, I've torn my shirt.
▶ *vt (relaciones)* to break off [*pt* **broke**; *pp* **broken**].
▶ *vt-vpr (gastar)* to wear out [*pt* **wore**; *pp* **worn**].
● **de rompe y rasga** resolute, determined.
● **romper a llorar** to start to cry.
● **romper con ALGN** to split up with SB [*pt & pp* **split**].
● **romperse la cabeza** to rack one's brains.

ron *nm* rum.

roncar *vi* to snore.

ronco,-a *adj (persona)* hoarse; *(voz)* husky.
● **quedarse ronco,-a** to lose one's voice [*pt & pp* **lost**].

ronda *nf* **1** *(patrulla)* patrol. **2** *(de policía)* beat. **3** *(de médico)* round. **4** *(de bebidas, cartas)* round: *¡otra ronda!*, another round! **5** *(músicos)* group of strolling minstrels. **6** *(carretera)* ring road.

rondar *vt-vi* **1** *(vigilar)* to patrol. **2** *(merodear)* to prowl around. **3** *(cifra)* to be about: *el precio rondaba los 10.000 euros*, the price was about 10,000 euros; *creo que ronda los sesenta*, I think she's about sixty.
● **rondar por la cabeza** : *me ronda por la cabeza que ...*, I seem to think that ...; *eso siempre me había rondado por la cabeza*, I'd always had that idea in my head.

ronquera *nf* hoarseness.

ronquido *nm* snore.

ronronear *vi* to purr.

roña *nf (suciedad)* filth, dirt.
▶ *nmf (tacaño)* skinflint.

roñoso,-a *adj* **1** *(sucio)* filthy, dirty. **2** *(oxidado)* rusty. **3** *(tacaño)* mean, tight.

ropa *nf* clothes *pl*.
● **cambiarse de ropa** to change one's clothes.

● **tender la ropa** to hang [*pt & pp* **hung**] out the washing.
■ **ropa interior** underwear.
■ **ropa sucia** dirty washing.

ropero *nm* wardrobe.

rosa *adj - nm (color)* pink.
▶ *nf (flor)* rose.
● **fresco,-a como una rosa** as fresh as a daisy.

rosado,-a *adj (color)* rosy, pink.
▶ *adj - nm* **rosado** *(vino)* rosé.

rosal *nm* rosebush.

rosaleda *nf* rose garden.

rosario *nm* **1** *(para rezar)* rosary. **2** *(infinidad)* string.
● **acabar como el rosario de la aurora** to come to a bad end.

rosca *nf* **1** *(de tuerca)* thread. **2** *(anilla)* ring. **3** *(de pan)* ring-shaped bread roll.
● **hacer la rosca a ALGN** *fam* to butter SB up.
● **no comerse una rosca** *fam* not to get one's oats.
● **pasarse de rosca** *fam* to go too far.

roscón *nm* ring-shaped roll or cake.

rosquilla *nf* doughnut.

rostro *nm fml* face.

rotación *nf* rotation.

roto,-a *adj (gen)* broken; *(tela, papel)* torn.
▶ *nm* **roto** hole, tear.

rotonda *nf* roundabout.

rótula *nf* knee-cap.

rotulador *nm* felt-tip pen.

rotular *vt* to label, letter.

rótulo *nm* **1** *(etiqueta)* label. **2** *(letrero)* sign. **3** *(anuncio)* poster, placard.

rotundo,-a *adj* categorical.

rotura *nf* **1** *(de objeto)* breakage: *rotura de cristales del coche*, window breakage. **2** *(de hueso)* fracture: *sufrió una rotura de caderas*, she fractured her hip, she broke her hip.

roulotte *nf* caravan.

rozadura *nf* scratch.

rozar *vt-vi (tocar ligeramente)* to touch, brush.
▶ *vt (raer)* to rub against: *el zapato me rozaba*, my shoe was rubbing.

rubéola *nf* German measles, rubella.

rubí *nm* ruby.

rubio,-a *adj (hombre)* blond; *(mujer)* blonde.

ruborizarse *vpr* to blush, go red.

rúbrica *nf* **1** *(firma)* flourish. **2** *(título)* title.

rudimentario,-a *adj* rudimentary.
rudo,-a *adj* rough, coarse.
rueda *nf* **1** *(de vehículo)* wheel. **2** *(círculo)* circle, ring.
- **ir sobre ruedas** *fam* to go like clockwork.
■ **rueda de recambio** spare wheel.
ruedo *nm* bullring.
ruego *nm* request.
rufián *nm* **1** *(proxeneta)* pimp. **2** *(canalla)* scoundrel.
rugby *nm* rugby.
rugido *nm (de león)* roar; *(del viento)* howl.
rugir *vi (león)* to roar; *(viento)* to howl.
ruido *nm* **1** *(sonido)* noise. **2** *(jaleo)* din, row.
- **hacer ruido** to make a noise.
- **mucho ruido y pocas nueces** much ado about nothing.
ruidoso,-a *adj* noisy, loud.
ruin *adj* **1** *pey (mezquino)* mean, base. **2** *(pequeño)* petty, insignificant. **3** *(tacaño)* stingy.
ruina *nf* ruin: *al borde de la ruina*, on the brink of ruin; *el edificio amenazaba ruina*, the building was about to collapse.
► *nf pl* **ruinas** ruins.
- **en ruinas** in ruins.
ruinoso,-a *adj* ruinous, disastrous.
ruiseñor *nm* nightingale.
rulo *nm (para pelo)* curler.

Rumanía *nf* Romania.
rumano,-a *adj - nm,f* Romanian, Rumanian.
rumba *nf* rumba.
rumbo *nm* course, direction.
- **con rumbo a** bound for.
- **sin rumbo** aimlessly.
rumiante *adj - nm* ruminant.
rumiar *vi* **1** *(alimentos)* to ruminate. **2** *(decisión)* to meditate.
rumor *nm* **1** *(noticia, voz)* GB rumour; US rumor: *corría el rumor de que...*, there was a rumour going round that.... **2** *(murmullo)* murmur.
rumorearse *vi* GB to be rumoured; US to be rumored: *se rumorea que...*, it is rumoured that....
rupestre *adj (planta)* rock; *(pintura)* cave.
ruptura *nf* **1** *(de acuerdo)* breaking. **2** *(de relación)* breaking-off; *(de matrimonio)* break-up.
rural *adj* rural, country.
Rusia *nf* Russia.
ruso,-a *adj* Russian.
► *nm,f (persona)* Russian.
► *nm* **ruso** *(idioma)* Russian.
rústico,-a *adj* rustic.
- **en rústica** paper-backed.
ruta *nf* route.
- **en ruta** en route.
rutina *nf* routine.
rutinario,-a *adj* monotonous.

S

sábado *nm* Saturday: *el sábado pasado*, last Saturday.

sabana *nf* savannah.

sábana *nf* sheet.

sabelotodo *nmf pey* know-all.

saber *nm* knowledge.

▶ *vt-vi (conocer)* to know [*pt* **knew**; *pp* **knew**]: *sabe mucho de política*, he knows a lot about politics; *¿alguien sabe lo que ha pasado?*, does anyone know what happened; *sé llegar al parque*, I know how to get to the park; *no sé dónde está el coche*, I don't know where the car is.

▶ *vt* **1** *(poder)* can [*pt* **could**]: *¿sabes francés?*, can you speak French?; *sabe tocar el piano*, she can play the piano. **2** *(tener noticias de)* to hear [*pt & pp* **heard**]: *hace mucho que no sé nada de ellos*, I haven't heard anything from them for ages. **3** *(enterarse)* to find out [*pt & pp* **found**]: *cuando supe que era su cumpleaños...*, when I found out it was her birthday....

▶ *vi (tener sabor a)* to taste: *este helado sabe a avellana*, this ice-cream tastes of hazelnuts; *este potaje no sabe a nada*, this stew has no taste.

● **a saber** *fml* namely.

● **hacer saber** to inform.

● **saber mal a** ALGN : *le supo mal que se fueran sin ella*, she was upset that they went without her; *me sabe mal no acompañarte hasta tu casa*, I don't like not walking you home.

● **que yo sepa** as far as I know.

● **¡vete a saber!** *fam* it's anyone's guess.

● **¡y yo qué sé!** *fam* how should I know!

■ **saber hacer** savoir-faire.

sabiduría *nf* **1** *(conocimiento)* knowledge. **2** *(prudencia)* wisdom.

sabiendas *adv* **a sabiendas** knowingly: *lo hizo a sabiendas*, he did it on purpose.

sabio,-a *adj* learned, wise.

▶ *nm,f* wise person: *los sabios*, the wise.

sablazo *nm* **1** *(golpe)* blow with a sabre. **2** *fam (de dinero)* : *le pegaron un buen sablazo en el restaurante*, they ripped him off at the restaurant; *su hijo le pega buenos sablazos*, her son scrounges loads of money off her.

sable *nm* sabre.

sabor *nm* **1** *(gusto)* taste: *esas naranjas no tienen sabor*, those oranges have no taste. **2** *(gusto añadido)* GB flavour, US flavor: *¿de qué sabor lo quieres?*, which flavour would you like?

● **dejar mal sabor de boca** to leave a bad taste in one's mouth [*pt & pp* **left**].

● **tener sabor** to taste: *tiene sabor a limón*, it tastes of lemon.

saborear *vt* GB to savour; US to savor.

sabotaje *nm* sabotage.

sabotear *vt* to sabotage.

sabroso,-a *adj* tasty.

sacacorchos *nm* corkscrew.

sacapuntas *nm* pencil sharpener.

sacar *vt* **1** *(poner fuera)* to take out: *sacó el dinero de la cartera*, he took the money out of his wallet; *saca al perro a pasear*, take the dog out for a walk; *no me saques la lengua*, don't stick your tongue out at me. **2** *(obtener)* to get: *ha sacado buenas notas en los exámenes*, she got good marks in the exams. **3** *(sonsa-*

car) to get out: *le he sacado la información*, I got information out of him. **4** (*mancha*) to remove. **5** (*extraer*) to extract, pull out: *fui al dentista a sacarme una muela*, I went to the dentist to have a tooth out. **6** (*restar*) to subtract. **7** (*premio*) to win [*pt & pp* **won**], get. **8** (*moda*) to introduce, bring out [*pt & pp* **brought**]: *han sacado un nuevo disco*, they have brought out a new record. **9** (*entrada, pasaporte*) to get: *he sacado las entradas para el concierto*, I've bought the tickets for the concert. **10** (*tenis*) to serve; (*fútbol -al principio*) to kick off; (*durante el partido*) to take the kick.

● **sacar a bailar** to ask to dance.

● **sacar a la luz 1** (noticia) to bring to light [*pt & pp* **brought**]. **2** (libro) to publish.

● **sacar a relucir** to mention.

● **sacar adelante 1** (proyecto) to carry out. **2** (hijos) to bring up [*pt & pp* **brought**].

● **sacar algo de algo** to extract STH from STH: *el vino se saca de la uva*, wine is made from grapes; *no hemos sacado nada de todo este jaleo*, we didn't get anything much out of all this mess.

● **sacar brillo a algo** to polish STH.

● **sacar de quicio** to infuriate.

● **sacar de un apuro a ALGN** to get SB out of a mess.

● **sacar algo en limpio** to make sense of STH.

● **sacar la lengua** to stick one's tongue out [*pt & pp* **stuck**]: *sacar punta a un lápiz*, to sharpen a pencil.

● **sacar una foto** to take a photo: *¿me puedes sacar una foto?*, can you take a picture of me, please?

● **sacarse sangre** to have a blood test done.

sacarina *nf* saccharine.

sacerdote *nm* priest.

saciar *vt* **1** (hambre) to satiate; (sed) to quench. **2** (curiosidad, deseo) to satisfy; (ambición) to fulfil.

▶ *vpr* **saciarse** to satiate oneself, be satiated.

saco *nm* **1** (bolsa) sack, bag. **2** (contenido) sackful, bagful.

● **¡que te den por saco!** *vulg* get stuffed!

● **entrar a saco en algo** *fam* to take STH by storm.

■ **saco de dormir** sleeping bag.

sacramento *nm* sacrament.

sacrificar *vt* **1** (gen) to sacrifice: *sacrifican animales en honor a los dioses*, they sacrifice animals in honour of the gods. **2** (animal enfermo) to put down: *tuvimos que sacrificar al perro*, we had to have the dog put down.

▶ *vpr* **sacrificarse** to make sacrifices.

sacrificio *nm* sacrifice.

sacudida *nf* shake, jolt.

sacudir *vt* **1** (agitar) to shake [*pt* **shook**; *pp* **shaken**]. **2** (para quitar el polvo) to shake off [*pt* **shook**; *pp* **shaken**]. **3** (golpear) to beat [*pt* **beat**; *pp* **beaten**]: *sacudía la alfombra con un palo*, she was beating the carpet with a stick.

▶ *vpr* **sacudirse** (quitarse) to shake off [*pt* **shook**; *pp* **shaken**]: *no sé cómo sacudírmelo de encima*, I don't know how to shake him off; *se sacudía las moscas con el rabo*, it flicked the flies off with its tail.

sádico,-a *adj* sadistic.

▶ *nm,f* sadist.

safari *nm* safari.

sagaz *adj* clever, shrewd.

Sagitario *nm* Sagittarius: *yo soy sagitario*, I'm Sagittarius.

sagrado,-a *adj* **1** (religioso) holy: *la iglesia es un lugar sagrado*, the church is a holy place. **2** (que merece respeto) sacred: *para él, la familia es sagrada*, the family is sacred for him.

sajón,-ona *adj - nm,f* Saxon.

sal *nf* **1** (condimento) salt. **2** (gracia) wit.

■ **sal de cocina** cooking salt.

■ **sal de mesa** table salt.

■ **sales de baño** bath salts.

sala *nf* **1** (habitación) room. **2** (sala de estar) living room. **3** (de hospital) ward: *está en la sala de al lado*, he's in the next ward. **4** (de tribunal) courtroom. **5** (cine) cinema.

■ **sala de conciertos** concert hall.

■ **sala de espera** waiting room.

■ **sala de estar** living room.

■ **sala de exposiciones** art gallery.

■ **sala de fiestas** nightclub, discotheque.

- **sala de lectura** reading room.
- **sala X** adult cinema.

salado,-a *adj* **1** *(con sal)* salted: *agua salada*, salt water. **2** *(con demasiada sal)* salty: *el bacalao estaba muy salado*, the cod was very salty. **3** *(no dulce)* savoury: *prefiero picar algo salado*, I prefer to nibble something savoury. **4** *fam* witty.

salamandra *nf* salamander.

salar *vt* to salt.

salario *nm* salary, wages *pl*: *cobran su salario a final de mes*, they get paid at the end of the month.

salchicha *nf* sausage.

salchichón *nm* salami.

saldo *nm* **1** *(de una cuenta)* balance. **2** *(liquidación)* sale: *precios de saldo*, bargain prices; *saldos de fin de temporada*, end of season sale. **3** *(resultado)*: *la manifestación acabó con un saldo de 20 heridos*, the demonstration resulted in 20 people being injured.

salero *nm* **1** *(recipiente)* saltcellar. **2** *(gracia)* charm, wit: *tiene mucho salero*, she's really witty.

saleroso,-a *adj* charming, witty.

salida *nf* **1** *(acto)* departure: *anunciaron la salida del tren*, they announced the departure of the train; *nos encontramos a la salida*, we met on the way out. **2** *(de personas)* exit, way out; *(de aire, gas)* vent; *(de agua)* outlet: *estoy buscando la salida*, I'm trying to find the exit; *puerta de salida*, exit door. **3** *(de autopista)* exit. **4** start: *los atletas estaban en la línea de salida*, the athletes were on the starting line. **5** *(excursión)* trip, outing: *hace dos meses que no hacemos ninguna salida*, we haven't been on an outing for two months; *una salida al extranjero*, a trip abroad. **6** *(solución)* solution: *una salida a mi problema*, a solution to my problem. **7** *(oportunidad)* opening, job opportunity: *estudiar derecho tiene muchas salidas*, there are a lot of job opportunities if you study law. **8** *(ocurrencia)* witty remark.

- **salida de emergencia** emergency exit.
- **salida de tono** improper remark.
- **salida del sol** sunrise.
- **salida nula** false start.

- **salidas internacionales** international departures.
- **salidas nacionales** domestic departures.

salir *vi* **1** *(ir de dentro para afuera)* to go out: *Rafa ha salido*, Rafa has gone out; *salí con mis amigos*, I went out with my friends; *Ana sale con Miguel*, Ana is going out with Miguel. **2** *(venir de dentro para fuera)* to come out: *ven, sal al jardín*, come out here into the garden. **3** *(partir)* to leave [*pt & pp* left]: *el autobús sale a las tres*, the bus leaves at three; *salgo de casa a las siete*, I leave home at seven o'clock; *salieron para Bilbao*, they left for Bilbao. **4** *(aparecer)* to appear: *me gustaría salir por la tele*, I'd like to be on TV; *¿por qué no sales tú en la foto?*, why aren't you in the photo?; *salir en los periódicos*, to be in the newspapers. **5** *(resultar)* to (turn out) to be: *al final todo resultó bien*, everything turned out all right in the end; *la tortilla te ha salido perfecta*, the omelette has turned out perfect; *si me sale este trabajo...*, if I get this job...; *ya le ha salido un diente*, she's got one tooth; *salir vencedor*, to be the winner. **6** *(del trabajo, colegio)* to leave [*pt & pp* left], come out. **7** *(producto)* to come out, be released: *¿cuándo sale esa revista?*, when does that magazine come out? **8** *(sol)* to rise: *¿a qué hora sale el sol?*, what time does the sun rise?; *al cabo de un rato salió el sol*, the sun came out after a while.

▶ *vpr* **salirse 1** *(soltarse, desviarse)* to come off: *el coche se salió de la calzada*, the car came off the road. **2** *(líquido - escaparse)* to leak, leak out; *(- al hervir)* to boil over: *el agua está saliendo de la cisterna*, water is leaking from the cistern; *vigila la leche para que no se salga*, watch the milk so it doesn't boil over.

- **salir a** ALGN to take after SB: *ha salido a su madre*, she takes after her mother.
- **salir adelante** to be successful.
- **salir bien** to turn out well.
- **salir con** ALGN to go out with SB.
- **salir con algo** to come out with STH: *¡ahora me sales con ésa!*, now you come out with this!

- **salir de dudas** to make sure.
- **salir mal** to turn out badly.
- **salir ganando con algo** to do well out of STH.
- **salir perdiendo** to lose out.
- **salir pitando** *fam* to rush out.
- **salirse con la suya** *fam* to get one's own way.

saliva *nf* saliva.

salmo *nm* psalm.

salmón *nm* salmon.

salmonete *nm* red mullet.

salón *nm* **1** *(en casa)* living room, lounge: **estaban viendo la televisión en el salón**, they were watching television in the lounge. **2** *(público)* hall: **el baile se celebró en un gran salón**, the dance was held in a large hall. **3** *(exposición)* show, exhibition.

  - **salón de actos** assembly hall.
  - **salón de baile** ballroom.
  - **salón de belleza** beauty salon, beauty parlour.
  - **salón recreativo** amusement arcade.

salpicadero *nm* dashboard.

salpicadura *nf* splash.

salpicar *vt* **1** *(líquido)* to splash: **me salpicó aceite en la camisa**, I splashed oil on my shirt. **2** *(barro)* to spatter: **un coche me ha salpicado de barro**, a car spattered me with mud. **3** *(charla, discurso)* to sprinkle.

salpicón *nm* : **salpicón de marisco**, seafood salad.

salsa *nf* **1** sauce. **2** *(baile)* salsa.

  - **salsa besamel** white sauce, béchamel sauce.

salsera *nf* gravy boat.

saltador,-ra *nm,f* jumper.

saltamontes *nm* grasshopper.

saltar *vi* **1** *(botar)* to jump: **salto muy alto**, I can jump very high. **2** *(al agua)* to dive: **saltó desde el trampolín**, she dived off the springboard. **3** *(desprenderse)* to come off: **saltó el tapón de la botella**, the top came off the bottle. **4** *(enfadarse)* to blow up [*pt* **blew**; *pp* **blown**]: **salta por nada**, he loses his temper for no reason. ▶ *vt (valla etc)* to jump (over): **el caballo saltó la valla**, the horse jumped over the fence. ▶ *vpr* **saltarse 1** *(ley etc)* to ignore: **se saltó una señal de stop**, he ignored a

stop sign. **2** *(omitir)* to skip, miss out: **me salté ese ejercicio porque era difícil**, I missed that exercise out because it was hard.

- **saltar a la cuerda** to skip.
- **saltar a la vista** to be obvious.
- **saltar en mil pedazos** to break into pieces [*pt* **broke**; *pp* **broken**].
- **saltar en paracaídas** to parachute.
- **saltarse un semáforo** to go through a red light.

saltimbanqui *nmf* acrobat.

salto *nm* **1** *(gen)* jump: **ganó con un salto de 8,95 metros**, he won with a jump of 8.95 metres. **2** *(en natación)* dive: **los saltos eran espectaculares**, the dives were spectacular. **3** *(avance)* leap: **un gran salto hacia adelante**, a great leap forwards.

  - **a salto de mata 1** (al día) : **vivir a salto de mata**, to live from hand to mouth. **2** (de cualquier manera) to live haphazardly.
  - **dar un salto** to jump: **daba saltos de alegría**, he was jumping for joy.
  - **de un salto** : **se levantó de la cama de un salto**, she jumped out of bed; **bajó de un salto**, he jumped down.
  - **salto con pértiga** pole vault.
  - **salto de agua** waterfall, falls *pl*.
  - **salto de altura** high jump.
  - **salto de cama** negligée.
  - **salto de esquí** ski-jump.
  - **salto de longitud** long jump.
  - **salto del ángel** swallow dive.
  - **salto en paracaídas** parachute jump.
  - **salto mortal** somersault.

salud *nf* health: **un problema de salud**, a health problem; **está bien de salud**, he's in good health. ▶ *interj* **¡salud!** *(al brindar)* cheers!; *(al estornudar)* bless you!

- **curarse en salud** to take precautions.

saludable *adj* healthy.

saludar *vt* to say hello to [*pt & pp* **said**]: **quiero saludar a todos mis amigos**, I'd like to say hello to all my friends; **saluda a tus padres de mi parte**, say hello to your parents for me. ▶ *vi* **1** to say hello [*pt & pp* **said**]. **2** to salute: **saludó al oficial**, he saluted the officer.

- **le saluda atentamente 1** (si no conocemos el nombre) yours faithfully. **2** (si conocemos el nombre) yours sincerely.

saludo nm **1** (gen) greeting. **2** (entre militares) salute: **le hice el saludo**, I saluted him.

▶ nm pl **saludos** best wishes: **mis padres te envían saludos**, my parents send you their best wishes.

● **"un (cordial) saludo de ..."** "best wishes from ...".

salvación nf salvation.

Salvador nm **El Salvador** (país) El Salvador.

salvador,-ra nm,f saviour.

salvadoreño,-a adj - nm,f Salvadorian, Salvadoran.

salvajada nf atrocity.

salvaje adj **1** (gen) wild; (pueblo) savage, uncivilized: **animales salvajes**, wild animals; **estudia una tribu salvaje**, he's studying a savage tribe. **2** (brutal) brutal: **un salvaje crimen**, a brutal murder.

▶ nmf savage.

salvamanteles nm table mat.

salvamento nm rescue.

salvar vt **1** (gen) to save, rescue: **el médico le salvó la vida**, the doctor saved his life. **2** (obstáculo) to clear. **3** (dificultad) to overcome [pt **overcame**; pp **overcome**]. **4** (distancia) to cover. **5** (exceptuar) to exclude: **salvando a los presentes**, present company excepted.

▶ vpr **salvarse** (sobrevivir) to survive: **se salvaron todos los ocupantes del coche**, all the occupants in the car survived; **sólo dos cuadros se salvaron del fuego**, only two paintings were saved from the fire.

● **¡sálvese quien pueda!** every man for himself!

salvavidas nm (flotador) life belt; (chaleco) life jacket.

salvo,-a adj safe.

▶ prep **salvo** except, except for: **vendrán todos salvo mi hermana**, everyone's coming except my sister.

● **estar a salvo** to be safe and sound.

● **ponerse a salvo** to reach safety.

● **salvo que** unless: **mañana iremos de excursión, salvo que llueva**, tomorrow we are going on an outing, unless it rains.

san adj → santo,-a.

sanar vt-vi (herida) to heal, cure: **el yodo me ha sanado el corte**, the iodine has healed my cut.

▶ vi (enfermo) to recover, get better: **se tendrá que quedar en el hospital hasta que sane**, he'll have to stay in hospital until he gets better.

sanatorio nm sanatorium.

sanción nf **1** (aprobación) sanction. **2** (multa) fine: **le han puesto una sanción por exceso de velocidad**, he's been fined for breaking the speed limit. **3** (castigo) sanction: **sanciones económicas**, economic sanctions; **una sanción de cuatro partidos**, a four-game suspension.

sancionar vt **1** (aprobar) to sanction. **2** (castigar) to penalize.

sandalia nf sandal.

sandía nf watermelon.

sándwich nm sandwich.

sangrar vt-vi (persona, animal) to bleed: **sangra por la nariz**, his nose is bleeding.

▶ vt (texto) to indent.

sangre nf blood: **me está saliendo sangre**, I'm bleeding.

● **a sangre fría** in cool blood.

● **de sangre fría** cold-blooded.

● **de sangre caliente** warm-blooded.

● **hacerse sangre** to bleed.

■ **sangre fría** sangfroid, calmness.

sangría nf **1** (bebida) sangria. **2** (pérdida de sangre) bleeding. **3** (masacre) bloodbath. **4** (texto) indentation.

sangriento,-a adj bloody.

sanidad nf (servicios) public health.

sanitario,-a adj health.

▶ nm pl **sanitarios** bathroom fittings.

sano,-a adj **1** healthy. **2** (entero) undamaged, intact.

● **sano y salvo** safe and sound.

santiamén adv **en un santiamén** in the twinkling of an eye.

santidad nf saintliness, holiness.

santiguarse vpr to cross oneself.

santo,-a adj **1** (lugar, vida, misa) holy. **2** (con nombre) Saint: **Santo Tomás**, Saint Thomas. **3** (para enfatizar) blessed: **todo el santo día**, the whole day long.

▶ nm,f saint: **su madre es una santa**, his mother is a saint.

▶ nm **santo** (onomástica) saint's day: **hoy es mi santo**, today is my saint's day.

● **¿a santo de qué...?** why on earth...?

● **írsele a** ALGN **el santo al cielo** *fam* : **se me fue el santo al cielo**, it slipped my mind.

■ **Santa Claus** Santa Claus, Father Christmas.

■ **santo y seña** password.

santuario *nm* sanctuary.

sapo *nm* toad.

saque *nm* **1** *(tenis)* service. **2** *(fútbol)* kick-off. **3** *fam (apetito)* appetite: **tiene buen saque**, he has a hearty appetite.

■ **saque de banda** throw-in.

■ **saque de esquina** corner.

saquear *vt (ciudad)* to sack, plunder; *(casa, comercio)* to loot.

sarampión *nm* measles.

sarcasmo *nm* sarcasm.

sarcástico,-a *adj* sarcastic.

sarcófago *nm* sarcophagus.

sardina *nf* sardine.

sargento *nm* sergeant.

sarpullido *nm* rash.

sarta *nf* string: **una sarta de mentiras**, a pack of lies.

sartén *nf* GB frying pan; US skillet.

● **tener la sartén por el mango** to have the upper hand.

sastre,-a *nm,f (hombre)* tailor; *(mujer)* dressmaker.

sastrería *nf* **1** *(tienda)* tailor's. **2** *(oficio)* tailoring.

satélite *nm* satellite.

satén *nm* satin.

satírico,-a *adj* satyrical.

satisfacción *nf* satisfaction: **a mi entera satisfacción**, to my complete satisfaction; **es para mí una satisfacción...**, it's a pleasure for me....

satisfacer *vt* **1** *(complacer)* to satisfy: **un ordenador que satisface todas tus necesidades**, a computer that satisfies all your needs; **me satisface ver tanta gente reunida hoy aquí**, I'm pleased to see so many people gathered here today. **2** *(deuda)* to pay [*pt & pp* **paid**].

▶ *vpr* **satisfacerse** to be satisfied.

satisfactorio,-a *adj* satisfactory.

satisfecho,-a *adj* **1** *(contento)* satisfied, pleased: **está satisfecho de su trabajo**, he is satisfied with his work. **2** *(lleno)* full: **no quiero postre, me he quedado satisfecha**, I don't want any dessert, I'm full.

sauce *nm* willow.

■ **sauce llorón** weeping willow.

saudí *adj - nmf* Saudi.

saudita *adj - nmf* Saudi.

sauna *nf* sauna.

savia *nf* sap.

saxofón *nm* saxophone.

sazonar *vt* to season.

se¹ *pron* **1** *(reflexivo - a él mismo)* himself; *(- a ella misma)* herself; *(- a usted mismo)* yourself; *(- a ellos mismos)* themselves; *(- a ustedes mismos)* yourselves: **el niño se ha cortado**, the boy has cut himself; **se compró una falda**, she bought herself a skirt; **el gato se lame**, the cat licks itself; **¿se divierte usted?**, are you enjoying yourself?; **los niños se portaron bien**, the children behaved themselves; **¿se han divertido ustedes?**, have you enjoyed yourselves? **2** *(recíproco)* one another, each other: **se quieren**, they love each other; **se felicitaron**, they congratulated one another. **3** *(enfático)* : **¿se ha lavado las manos?**, has he washed his hands?; **se muerde las uñas**, she bites her nails. **4** *(en pasivas e impersonales)* : **se dice que...**, it is said that...; **se suspendió el partido**, the match was postponed; **se han abierto las puertas**, the doors have been opened; **aquí se come bien**, the food is good here; **se habla español**, Spanish spoken; **véase la página 35**, see page 35; **se hacen arreglos**, we do repairs; **¿cómo se escribe?**, how do you spell it?

se² *pron (objeto indirecto - a él)* him; *(- a ella)* her; *(cosa)* it; *(- a usted/ustedes)* you; *(- a ellos/ellas)* them: **dáselo a él**, give it to him; **pídeselo a tu madre**, ask your mother for it; **ya se lo he contado**, I've already told you; **a ellos no se lo he dicho**, I haven't told them.

secador *nm* dryer.

■ **secador de pelo** hair-dryer.

secadora *nf* clothes-dryer, tumble-dryer.

secano *nm* dry land.

secante *adj →* papel.

secar *vt (pelo, ropa, piel)* to dry; *(lágrimas, vajilla)* to wipe.

▶ *vpr* **secarse 1** *(con toalla)* to dry: **se está secando el pelo**, she's drying her hair. **2** *(resecarse - planta)* to die; *(- río)* to

dry up: *se ha secado el cactus*, the cactus has died; *el río se seca en verano*,
the river dries up in the summer. **3** *(herida)* to heal.

sección *nf* **1** *(división)* section. **2** *(en tienda, oficina)* department.

seco,-a *adj* **1** *(no mojado)* dry: *recoge la
ropa cuando esté seca*, bring the wash-
ing in when it's dry; *limpiar en seco*, dry
clean only. **2** *(frutos, flores)* dried: *higos
secos*, dried figs. **3** *(golpe, ruido)* sharp. **4**
(persona) unfriendly.

● **a secas** simply, just.

● **en seco** sharply, suddenly: *frenar en
seco*, to stop dead.

secretaría *nf* secretary's office.

secretario,-a *nm,f* secretary: *secretario,-a de dirección*, executive secretary.

secreto,-a *adj* secret.

▶ *nm* **secreto** secret.

● **en secreto** in secret.

secta *nf* sect.

sector *nm* **1** *(de personas)* section: *un sector de la opinión pública*, a section of
the public. **2** *(zona)* area: *vivo en el sector oeste*, I live in the west. **3** *(de la industria)* sector: *el sector privado*, the private
sector; *el sector de la construcción*, the
building industry.

secuela *nf* consequence, effect.

secuencia *nf* sequence.

secuestrador,-ra *nm,f* **1** *(de persona)*
kidnapper. **2** *(de avión)* highjacker.

secuestrar *vt* **1** *(persona)* to kidnap. **2**
(avión) to highjack.

secuestro *nm* **1** *(de persona)* kidnapping.
2 *(de avión)* highjacking.

secundario,-a *adj* secondary: *problema
secundario*, secondary problem; *actriz
secundaria*, supporting actress; *efectos
secundarios*, side effects.

sed *nf* thirst.

● **tener sed** to be thirsty.

seda *nf* silk.

● **ir como una seda** to go smoothly.

■ **seda dental** dental floss.

sedal *nm* fishing line.

sedante *adj - nm* sedative.

sede *nf* **1** *(de organización)* headquarters;
(de empresa) head office: *la sede de la
Unión Europea*, the headquarters of the
European Union; *la empresa tiene su
sede en Madrid*, the company's head of-

fice is in Madrid. **2** *(del gobierno)* seat. **3**
(de acontecimiento) venue: *Francia fue la
sede del Mundial de 1998*, France hos-
ted the 1998 World Cup.

■ **Santa Sede** Holy See.

sediento,-a *adj* thirsty.

sedoso,-a *adj* silky.

seducción *nf* seduction.

seducir *vt* to seduce.

seductor,-ra *adj* **1** *(sexualmente)* seduc-
tive. **2** *(atractivo)* attractive, tempting.

▶ *nm,f* seducer.

segador,-ra *nm,f* reaper.

segadora *nf* harvester.

segar *vt* **1** AGR to reap. **2** *(cortar)* to cut off.

segmento *nm* segment.

segregar *vt* to segregate.

seguido,-a *adj* **1** *(acompañado)* followed:
*entró el presidente, seguido por el al-
calde*, the president entered, followed
by the mayor. **2** *(consecutivo)* consecutive:
dos días seguidos, two days running;
trabaja seis horas seguidas, he works
six hours without a break.

▶ *adv* straight on.

● **en seguida** at once, immediately.

seguidor,-ra *nm,f* follower.

seguir *vt* **1** *(gen)* to follow: *ese perro me
sigue a todas partes*, that dog follows
me everywhere; *el martes sigue al lunes*, Tuesday follows Monday. **2** *(continuar)* to continue. **3** *(hacer)* to do: *sigue
un curso de informática*, he's doing a
computing course.

▶ *vi* **1** *(proseguir)* to go on: *siga todo recto hasta la plaza*, go straight on until
you get to the square; *¡sigue! no te pares*, go on! don't stop! **2** *(permanecer)* to
remain: *siguió de pie*, he remained standing. **3** *(estar todavía)* to be still: *sigue enfermo*, he's still sick; *sigo viviendo en el
mismo piso*, I'm still living in the same
place. **4** *(continuar)* to follow: *lo que sigue*, what follows.

según *prep* *(de acuerdo con)* according to:
según lo que dice María, according to
what María says; *según lo previsto*, according to plan.

▶ *adv* **1** *(depende de)* depending on: *según qué día sea*, depending on what
day it is; *según lo que digan*, depending
on what they say. **2** *(depende)* it depends:
no sé si salir o quedarme aquí, según, I

don't know if I'll go out or I'll stay here, it depends. **3** *(como)* just as: **todo quedó según estaba**, everything stayed just as it was. **4** *(a medida que)* as: **según iban entrando se les daba una copa**, as they came in they were given a drink.

segundero *nm* second hand.

segundo,-a *num* second.

▶ *nf* **segunda** second gear.

▶ *nm* **segundo** second.

● **decir algo con segundas** to say STH with a double meaning [*pt & pp* **said**].

seguramente *adv* **1** *(probablemente)* most likely, probably: **seguramente vendrá hoy**, he'll probably come today. **2** *(ciertamente)* surely.

seguridad *nf* **1** *(contra accidentes)* safety. **2** *(contra robos, ataques)* security: **medidas de seguridad**, security measures. **3** *(certeza)* certainty: **tengo la seguridad de que vendrá**, I'm certain that he will come. **4** *(confianza)* confidence: **es bueno tener seguridad en sí mismo**, it's good to have self-confidence.

● **con toda seguridad** definitely.

■ **seguridad ciudadana** public safety.

■ **Seguridad Social** National Health Service.

seguro,-a *adj* **1** *(físicamente)* safe: **las medicinas deben guardarse en un lugar seguro**, medicines must be kept in a safe place; **ese puente no parece muy seguro**, that bridge doesn't look very safe. **2** *(estable)* secure: **tiene un trabajo seguro**, he's got a secure job. **3** *(fiable)* reliable: **un método muy seguro**, a very reliable method. **4** *(cierto)* definite: **aún no es seguro que venga**, it's not definite that he's coming yet. **5** *(convencido)* confident, sure, certain: **estoy seguro de que no va a defraudarnos**, I'm sure he won't let us down.

▶ *nm* **seguro 1** *(contrato, póliza)* insurance: **me he hecho un seguro de vida**, I've taken out life insurance. **2** *(mecanismo)* safety catch, safety device: **echó el seguro de las puertas del coche**, he put the safety catch on the car doors.

▶ *adv (sin duda)* for sure, definitely: **lo sé seguro**, I know for sure.

● **seguro que...** I bet...: **seguro que se ha olvidado**, I bet he's forgotten.

● **sobre seguro** without risk.

seis *num* six; *(en fechas)* sixth.

● **son las seis** it's six o'clock.

seiscientos,-as *num* six hundred.

seismo *nm* earthquake.

selección *nf* selection.

■ **selección nacional** national team.

seleccionar *vt* to select.

selectividad *nf* university entrance examination.

selecto,-a *adj* : **un club selecto**, an exclusive club; **comida selecta**, fine food; **vinos selectos**, fine wines, choice wines; **una selecta bibliografía**, a select bibliography; **ante un público selecto**, before a selected audience.

sellar *vt* to seal: **han sellado las ventanas con silicona**, they have sealed the windows with silicone; **hay que sellar el documento**, the document must be stamped.

sello *nm* **1** *(de correos)* stamp. **2** *(de estampar, precinto)* seal. **3** *(distintivo)* hallmark.

■ **sello discográfico** record label.

selva *nf* jungle.

semáforo *nm* traffic lights *pl*.

semana *nf* week.

■ **Semana Santa 1** *(gen)* Easter. **2** *(desde el punto de vista religioso)* Holy Week.

semanal *adj* weekly.

semanario *nm* weekly magazine.

semblante *nm* **1** *(cara)* face. **2** *(expresión)* countenance.

sembrado,-a *nm* field.

sembrar *vt* **1** *(con semillas)* to sow [*pt* **sowed**; *pp* **sown**]; *(con plantas)* to plant. **2** *(esparcir)* to scatter, spread [*pt & pp* **spread**].

semejante *adj* **1** *(parecido)* similar: **escribió un libro semejante al mío**, he wrote a book similar to mine. **2** *(tal)* such: **semejante insolencia**, such insolence; **nunca he oído nada semejante**, I've never heard of such a thing.

▶ *nm* fellow being.

semejarse *vpr* **1** to look alike. **2** **semejarse a** to look like, to resemble.

semen *nm* semen.

semestral *adj* six-monthly, half-yearly.

semestre *nm* six-month period, semester.

semicírculo *nm* semicircle.

semifinal *nf* semifinal.

semilla *nf* seed.

seminario *nm* **1** *(clase)* seminar. **2** *(centro religioso)* seminary.

senado *nm* senate.

senador,-ra *nm,f* senator.

sencillez *nf* simplicity.

sencillo,-a *adj* **1** *(fácil)* simple: *el examen es muy sencillo*, the exam is very simple. **2** *(persona)* natural, unaffected.

senda *nf* path.

sendero *nm* path.

sendos,-as *adj* : *recibieron sendos cheques*, each one of them received a cheque.

seno *nm* **1** *(pecho)* breast. **2** *fig* bosom: *en el seno de su familia*, in the bosom of his family. **3** *(matriz)* womb. **4** MAT sine.

sensación *nf* **1** *(percepción)* feeling: *tengo la sensación de que me siguen*, I've got a feeling I'm being followed. **2** *(efecto)* sensation: *es la sensación del año*, it's the sensation of the year; *causar sensación*, to cause a sensation.

sensacional *adj* sensational.

sensatez *nf* good sense.

sensato,-a *adj* sensible.

sensibilidad *nf* sensitivity.

● **perder la sensibilidad en las piernas** to lose all feeling in one's legs.

sensible *adj* **1** *(perceptivo)* sensitive: *es una chica muy sensible*, she's a very sensitive girl; *soy muy sensible al frío*, I'm very sensitive to the cold. **2** *(manifiesto)* perceptible, noticeable: *ha habido un aumento sensible de la temperatura*, there's been a noticeable rise in temperature.

sensual *adj* sensual.

sentado,-a *adj* seated, sitting: *estaba sentada junto a la estufa*, she was sitting next to the heater.

● **dar algo por sentado,-a** to take STH for granted.

sentar *vt* to sit [*pt & pp* sat]: *sienta a la niña en el cochecito*, sit the baby in the pram.

▶ *vi* **1** *(comida)* to agree: *el chocolate no me sienta bien*, chocolate doesn't agree with me. **2** *(ropa)* to suit: *esa corbata te sienta bien*, that tie suits you. **3** *(hacer efecto)* to do: *un poco de aire fresco te sentará bien*, a bit of fresh air will do you good; *le sentó fatal que no la llamaras*, she was really upset that you didn't phone her.

▶ *vpr* **sentarse** to sit down [*pt & pp* sat]: *me senté en un banco*, I sat down on a bench.

● **sentar las bases de algo** to lay the foundations for STH.

sentencia *nf* **1** *(condena)* sentence. **2** *(máxima)* proverb, maxim.

● **dictar sentencia** to pass sentence.

sentenciar *vt* to sentence.

sentido,-a *adj* **1** *(sensible)* heartfelt, deep: *mi más sentido pésame*, my deepest sympathy. **2** *(dolido)* hurt.

▶ *nm* **sentido** **1** *(vista, oído, etc)* sense: *los cinco sentidos*, the five senses. **2** *(dirección)* direction: *tenemos que cambiar de sentido*, we have to change direction; *una calle de sentido único*, a one-way street. **3** *(juicio)* consciousness: *se quedó sin sentido durante unos minutos*, he was unconscious for a few minutes. **4** *(significado)* meaning: *no entiendo el sentido de esa palabra*, I don't understand the meaning of this word. **5** *(lógica)* point: *no le veo el sentido*, I don't see the point in it; *no tiene sentido que hagas eso*, there's no point doing that.

● **perder el sentido** to faint.

● **recobrar el sentido** to regain consciousness.

● **tener sentido** to make sense.

■ **sentido común** common sense.

■ **sentido del humor** sense of humour.

sentimental *adj* sentimental.

sentimiento *nm* feeling.

sentir *nm* **1** *(sentimiento)* feeling. **2** *(opinión)* opinion.

▶ *vt* **1** *(lamentar)* to regret. **2** *(oír)* to hear [*pt & pp* heard]: *sintió pasos a lo lejos*, he heard footsteps in the distance; *no te sentí llegar*, I didn't hear you come.

▶ *vt-vpr* **sentir(se)** to feel [*pt & pp* felt]: *sintió frío*, he felt cold; *con la anestesia no sentirás nada*, you won't feel a thing with the anaesthetic; *hoy me siento feliz*, I feel happy today.

● **¡lo siento!** I'm sorry!

● **sentir miedo** to be afraid.

● **sentirse mal** to feel ill [*pt & pp* felt].

seña *nf* *(indicio, gesto)* sign.

▶ *nf pl* **señas** address *sing*.

● **dar señas de algo** to show signs of STH [*pt* showed; *pp* shown].

● **hacer señas** to signal, gesture: *me hizo una seña para que me acercara*, he gestured to me to come closer.
■ **señas personales** particulars.

señal *nf* **1** *(indicio)* sign: *las nubes son señal de lluvia*, clouds are a sign of rain. **2** *(marca)* mark: *pon una señal en la página*, put a mark on the page. **3** *(vestigio)* trace. **4** *(signo)* signal: *dio la señal y empezó la carrera*, he gave the signal and the race began. **5** *(por teléfono)* tone: *no había señal*, there was no dialling tone. **6** *(de pago)* deposit.
● **dar la señal de salida** to give the starting signal.
● **en señal de** as a sign of, as a token of.
● **hacer señales** to signal, gesture.
■ **señal de comunicar** GB engaged tone; US busy signal.
■ **señal de tráfico** road sign.

señalar *vt* **1** *(indicar)* to show [*pt* **showed**; *pp* **shown**]: *el termómetro señalaba treinta grados*, the thermometer showed thirty degrees. **2** *(marcar)* to mark: *señálalo en rojo*, mark it in red. **3** *(hacer notar)* to point to. **4** *(con el dedo)* to point at: *es de mala educación señalar con el dedo a las personas*, it's rude to point at people; *el niño señalaba los juguetes que le gustaban*, the boy pointed out the toys he liked. **5** *(designar - a persona)* to appoint; *(- fecha, lugar)* to set [*pt & pp* **set**], determine: *la profesora ya ha señalado el día del examen*, the teacher has already set the day of the exam.

señalización *nf* road signs *pl*.
señalizar *vt* to signpost.
señor,-ra *adj fam* fine: *es un señor coche*, it's quite a car.
▶ *nm* **señor 1** *(hombre)* man [*pl* **men**]; *(caballero)* gentleman [*pl* **-men**]: *¿quién es este señor?*, who's this man? **2** *(amo)* master. **3** *(en tratamientos)* sir; *(delante de apellido)* Mr: *el señor Pérez*, Mr Pérez; *sí, señor*, yes, sir.
■ **Nuestro Señor** Our Lord.
señora *nf* **1** *(mujer)* woman [*pl* **women**]; *(dama)* lady: *¿quién es esta señora?*, who's this lady? **2** *(ama)* mistress. **3** *(esposa)* wife [*pl* **-ves**]: *nos presentó a su señora*, he introduced us to his wife. **4** *(en tratamientos)* madam; *(delante de apellido)* Mrs: *la señora Gómez*, Mrs Gómez; *sí,*

señora, yes, madam; *señoras y señores*, ladies and gentlemen.
■ **Nuestra Señora** Our Lady.
señorial *adj* stately.
señorita *nf* **1** *(mujer joven)* young lady. **2** *(delante de apellido)* Miss: *la señorita López*, Miss López. **3** *(profesora)* teacher; *(para dirigirse a ella)* Miss: *la señorita nos ha mandado deberes*, the teacher has set us homework.
señorito *nm* **1** *(tratamiento)* master. **2** *pey* daddy's boy.
separación *nf* **1** *(acción)* separation: *tras la separación de sus padres*, after his parents separated. **2** *(espacio)* gap: *una separación de 15 milímetros*, a gap of 15 millimetres.
separado,-a *adj* **1** *(distanciado)* separate. **2** *(divorciado)* separated.
● **por separado** separately.
separar *vt* **1** *(dividir)* to separate: *los Pirineos separan España de Francia*, the Pyrenees separate Spain from France; *sepáralas en sílabas*, divide them into syllables; *la distancia que nos separa*, the distance between us. **2** *(apartar)* to move: *separó la silla de la pared*, she moved the chair away from the wall. **3** *(guardar)* to set aside [*pt & pp* **set**].
▶ *vpr* **separarse 1** *(de una persona)* to separate, split up [*pt & pp* **split**]: *se han separado*, they have split up. **2** *(ir a otro sitio)* : *nos separamos después de la fiesta*, we went our separate ways after the party. **3** *(apartarse)* to move away: *sepárate de la vía*, move away from the track.
separatismo *nm* separatism.
sepia *nf* cuttlefish.
▶ *adj - nm (color)* sepia.
septentrional *adj* northern.
septiembre *nm* September.
séptimo,-a *num* seventh.
sepulcro *nm* tomb.
sepultar *vt* to bury.
sepultura *nf* grave.
● **dar sepultura a** to bury.
sequedad *nf* **1** *(de terreno, piel)* dryness. **2** *(de carácter)* curtness.
sequía *nf* drought.
séquito *nm* entourage, retinue.
ser *vi* **1** *(gen)* to be: *mi amigo es alemán*, my friend is German; *es médico*, he's a

doctor; **cinco más cinco son diez**, five plus five are ten; **son quince euros**, that'll be fifteen euros; **somos cinco**, there are five of us; **la fiesta es el sábado**, the party is on Saturday. **2** *(pertenecer)* to belong: **el libro es de María**, this book belongs to María; **el cuadro es de Picasso**, the painting is by Picasso. **3** *(material)* to be made of: **la mesa es de madera**, the table is made of wood. **4** *(proceder)* to come from.
▶ *aux* to be: **fue encontrado por Juan**, it was found by Juan; **es de esperar que...**, it is to be expected that....
▶ *nm* **1** *(ente)* being. **2** *(vida)* existence, life [*pl* **-ves**].
● **a no ser que** unless.
● **a poder ser** if possible.
● **de no ser por ...** had it not been for ....
● **érase una vez** once upon a time.
● **es más** furthermore.
● **sea como sea** in any case.
● **ser muy suyo,-a** to be an eccentric.
■ **ser humano** human being.
■ **Ser Supremo** Supreme Being.
■ **ser vivo** living creature.
serenar *vt* to calm, soothe.
▶ *vpr* **serenarse 1** *(persona)* to become calm. **2** *(tiempo)* to clear up.
serenidad *nf* serenity.
● **mantener la serenidad** to keep calm.
sereno,-a *adj* *(sosegado)* calm.
▶ *nm* **sereno** night watchman [*pl* **-men**].
serial *nm* serial.
serie *nf* series *inv*.
seriedad *nf* **1** *(de persona, enfermedad)* seriousness, gravity. **2** *(formalidad)* reliability.
serio,-a *adj* **1** *(persona, enfermedad)* serious: **estás muy serio**, you're very serious; **no era nada serio**, it wasn't anything serious. **2** *(formal)* reliable.
● **en serio** seriously: **decir algo en serio**, to be serious about STH; **tomar algo en serio**, to take STH seriously.
sermón *nm* sermon.
serpentina *nf* streamer.
serpiente *nf* snake.
■ **serpiente de cascabel** rattlesnake.
serrar *vt* to saw [*pt* **sawed**; *pp* **sawn**].
serrín *nm* sawdust.
serrucho *nm* handsaw.
servicial *adj* obliging.

servicio *nm* **1** *(atención)* service: **los servicios de emergencia**, the emergency services. **2** *(criados)* servants *pl*. **3** *(juego)* set: **servicio de té**, tea set. **4** *(tenis)* serve, service. **5** *(retrete)* toilet *sing*: **los servicios están al fondo**, the toilets are down there.
● **estar de servicio** to be on duty.
■ **servicio a domicilio** home delivery service.
■ **servicio militar** military service.
■ **servicio postal** postal service.
servidor,-ra *nm,f* **1** *(servant)* servant. **2** *(eufemismo)* me: **¿Francisco Reyes?, —Servidor**, Francisco Reyes?, —Present.
▶ *nm* **servidor** INFORM server.
servidumbre *nf* **1** *(servilismo)* servitude. **2** *(criados)* servants *pl*.
servilleta *nf* napkin, serviette.
servilletero *nm* napkin ring, serviette ring.
servir *vt* **1** *(comida)* to serve: **¿ya le ven?**, are you being served? **2** *(bebida)* to pour: **¿te sirvo yo?**, shall I pour?
▶ *vi* **1** *(ser útil)* to be useful: **el inglés te servirá mucho para viajar**, English will be very useful for travelling; **creo que esta caja servirá**, I think this box will do. **2** *(trabajar)* to serve: **se puso a servir en una familia rica**, she began working for a rich family; **sirve en el ejército**, he's in the army.
▶ *vpr* **servirse 1** *(comida)* to help oneself: **sírvase usted mismo**, help yourself; **sírvete más pan**, help yourself to more bread. **2** *(utilizar)* to use: **se sirvió de todas sus influencias**, he used all his contacts.
● **servir de** to be used as.
● **servir para** to be used for: **esta máquina sirve para picar carne**, this machine is used for mincing meat; **¿para qué sirve esto?**, what's this for?; **es evidente que sirves para los negocios**, it's obvious that you are good at business; **no sirvo para ser actor**, I'm not good at acting.
● **servirse de** to make use of.
● **sírvase** *fml* please.
sesenta *num* sixty: **los años sesenta**, the sixties.
sesión *nf* **1** *(reunión)* session, meeting: **el presidente inauguró la sesión**, the pres-

ident opened the session. **2** *(de película)* showing: **fuimos a la sesión de las 8**, we went to the 8 o´clock showing.

■ **sesión continua** continuous performance.

seso *nm* brain, brains *pl*: **tiene poco seso**, he hasn't got much of a brain.

seta *nf* mushroom; *(no comestible)* toadstool.

setecientos,-as *num* seven hundred.

setenta *num* seventy: **los años setenta**, the seventies.

setiembre *nm* September.

seto *nm* hedge.

seudónimo *nm* pseudonym; *(de escritores)* pen name.

severo,-a *adj* **1** *(castigo)* severe: **le puso un castigo muy severo**, he gave him a severe punishment. **2** *(persona)* strict: **es un maestro severo**, he's a strict teacher. **3** *(clima, invierno)* harsh.

sexista *adj* sexist.

sexo *nm* **1** *(gen)* sex. **2** *(órganos)* genitals *pl*.

sexto,-a *num* sixth.

sexual *adj* sexual.

sexualidad *nf* sexuality.

short *nm* shorts *pl*.

si[1] *conj* **1** *(condicional)* if: **si deja de llover, saldremos**, if it stops raining, we'll go out; **si lo hubiera sabido, no habría venido**, if I had known, I wouldn't have come. **2** *(para enfatizar)* but: **¡si yo no quería!**, but I didn't want it! **3** *(petición, deseo)* if only: **si pudieras ayudarme**, if only you could help me; **¡si me dejaran ir!**, iif only they would let me go! **4** *(duda)* if, whether: **pregúntale si quiere ir al cine**, ask her if she wants to go to the cinema; **no sé si está o no**, I don't know whether he's in or not.

● **como si** as if.

● **si bien** although.

● **si no** otherwise.

● **¿y si no viene?** what if he doesn't come?

si[2] *nm (nota musical)* ti, si, B.

sí[1] *pron (él)* himself; *(ella)* herself; *(cosa)* itself; *(uno mismo)* oneself; *(plural)* themselves: **hablaba para sí mismo**, he was talking to himself; **siempre habla de sí misma**, she always talks about herself; **el problema es en sí complicado**, the problem is complicated in itself.

● **estar fuera de sí** to be beside oneself.

● **volver en sí** to regain consciousness.

sí[2] *adv* **1** *(en respuestas)* yes: **¿quieres ir?** —**Sí**, do you want to go? —Yes; **creo que sí**, I think so; **espero que sí**, I hope so. **2** *(enfático)* : **sí que me gusta**, I do like it, of course I like it. **3** *(sustituye al verbo)* : **ella no irá, pero yo sí**, she won't go, but I will; **tú no puedes, pero él sí**, you can't, but he can.

▶ *nm* yes.

● **un día sí y otro no** every other day.

Sicilia *nf* Sicily.

sida *nm* AIDS.

siderurgia *nf* iron and steel industry.

sidra *nf* cider.

siega *nf* **1** *(época)* harvest. **2** *(acción)* reaping.

siembra *nf* **1** *(época)* sowing time. **2** *(acción)* sowing.

siempre *adv* always: **siempre dices lo mismo**, you always say the same thing.

● **de siempre** usual: **me dio la excusa de siempre**, he gave me the usual excuse.

● **para siempre** forever, for good.

● **siempre que** whenever: **siempre que viene, me trae un regalo**, whenever he comes, he brings me a present; **...siempre que estés de acuerdo**, ...provided you agree.

● **siempre y cuando** provided, as long as.

sien *nf* temple.

sierra *nf* **1** *(herramienta)* saw. **2** *(cordillera)* mountain range. **3** *(campo)* mountains *pl*: **tienen una casa en la sierra**, they have a house in the mountains.

siervo,-a *nm,f* slave, serf [*pl* **-s**].

siesta *nf* siesta, afternoon nap.

● **echarse una siesta** to have a siesta.

siete *num* seven; *(en fechas)* seventh.

▶ *nm (rasgón)* tear.

sifón *nm* **1** *(tubo acodado)* U-bend. **2** *(tubo encorvado)* siphon. **3** *(bebida)* soda water.

sigla *nf* acronym.

siglo *nm* **1** *(cien años)* century: **el siglo XX**, the 20th century. **2** *(mucho tiempo)* : **hacía un siglo que no te veía**, I hadn't seen you for ages; **llevo siglos esperando**, I've been waiting for ages.

■ **Siglo de Oro** Golden Age.

significado *nm* meaning.

significar *vt* to mean [*pt & pp* **meant**]: *¿eso qué significa?*, what does that mean?

significativo,-a *adj* significant.

signo *nm* (*señal*) sign.
- **signo de admiración** exclamation mark.
- **signo de interrogación** question mark.
- **signo de puntuación** punctuation mark.
- **signo de sumar** plus sign.

siguiente *adj* following, next: *al día siguiente*, the next day; *haz pasar al siguiente*, show the next person in, please.

sílaba *nf* syllable.

silbar *vi* **1** (*con los labios, viento*) to whistle. **2** (*abuchear*) to hiss.

silbato *nm* whistle: *el árbitro tocó el silbato*, the referee blew the whistle.

silbido *nm* whistle: *llamó al perro dando un silbido*, he called the dog with a whistle.

silenciar *vt* **1** (*sonido*) to muffle; (*persona*) to silence. **2** (*noticia*) to hush up.

silencio *nm* silence.
- **guardar silencio** to keep quiet: *guardaron un minuto de silencio*, there was a minute's silence.
- **¡silencio!** be quiet!

silencioso,-a *adj* **1** (*persona*) quiet: *es un chico muy silencioso*, he's a very quiet boy. **2** (*máquina*) silent: *una lavadora silenciosa*, a silent washing machine.

silicona *nf* silicone.

silla *nf* chair.
- **silla de montar** saddle.
- **silla de ruedas** wheelchair.
- **silla eléctrica** electric chair.
- **silla giratoria** swivel chair.
- **silla plegable** folding chair.

sillín *nm* saddle.

sillón *nm* armchair.

silueta *nf* **1** (*contorno*) silhouette: *vi la silueta de la torre*, I saw the silhouette of the tower. **2** (*figura*) figure: *te realza la silueta*, it shows off your figure.

silvestre *adj* wild.

simbólico,-a *adj* symbolic.

simbolizar *vt* to symbolize.

símbolo *nm* symbol.

simetría *nf* symmetry.

simétrico,-a *adj* symmetric.

simiente *nf* seed.

similar *adj* similar.

similitud *nf* similarity.

simio *nm* ape.

simpatía *nf* **1** (*sentimiento*) affection. **2** (*amabilidad*) pleasant manner, friendliness: *cae bien a todo el mundo por su simpatía*, everyone likes her because she's so friendly. **3** (*afinidad*) affinity.

simpático,-a *adj* nice: *es muy simpático*, he's really nice; *no me pareció muy simpática*, I didn't really like her.
- **hacerse el/la simpático,-a** to ingratiate oneself.

simpatizante *nmf* supporter.

simpatizar *vi* **1** (*dos personas*) to get on: *no simpatizo con ella*, I don't get on with her. **2** (*con una idea*) to be sympathetic to.

simple *adj* **1** (*sencillo*) simple: *era un problema muy simple*, it was a very simple problem. **2** (*puro*) mere: *es un simple resfriado*, it's just a cold; *con una simple llamada*, with just a phone call.

simplemente *adv* simply, just.

simplicidad *nf* simplicity.

simplificar *vt* to simplify.

simular *vt* to simulate, feign.

simultáneo,-a *adj* simultaneous.

sin *prep* **1** (*gen*) without: *no conduzcas la moto sin casco*, don't ride the bike without a crash helmet; *me he pasado toda la noche sin dormir*, I didn't sleep a wink all night. **2** (*por hacer*) : *está sin planchar*, it has not been ironed; *el edificio está sin terminar*, the building is unfinished; *un diamante sin tallar*, an uncut diamond.
- **sin embargo** however.
- **sin IVA** exclusive of VAT.

sinagoga *nf* synagogue.

sinceridad *nf* sincerity.
- **con sinceridad** honestly.

sincero,-a *adj* sincere.
- **ser sincero con ALGN** to be honest with SB.

sindicato *nm* trade union.

síndrome *nm* syndrome.
- **síndrome de abstinencia** withdrawal symptoms *pl*.
- **síndrome de Down** Down's syndrome.

sinfín *nm* : **tuvimos un sinfín de problemas**, we had no end of problems; **un sinfín de actuaciones**, hundreds of shows.

sinfonía *nf* symphony.

Singapur *nm* Singapore.

singular *adj* **1** *(único)* singular, single. **2** *(excepcional)* extraordinary. **3** *(raro)* peculiar.

▶ *nm* singular: **el verbo va en singular**, the verb goes in the singular.

siniestro,-a *adj* **1** *(izquierdo)* left, left-hand. **2** *(malvado)* sinister.

▶ *nm* **siniestro** *(accidente)* accident.

● **fue declarado siniestro total** it was declared a write-off.

sino *conj* but: **el partido no es hoy, sino mañana**, the match isn't today, but tomorrow; **no sólo es inteligente, sino también muy simpático**, he's not only clever, but really nice as well.

sinónimo,-a *adj* synonymous.

▶ *nm* **sinónimo** synonym.

sintaxis *nf* syntax.

síntesis *nf* synthesis.

sintético,-a *adj* synthetic.

síntoma *nm* symptom.

sintonizar *vt (emisora)* to tune in to.

▶ *vi (dos personas)* to get on well.

sinvergüenza *nmf* cheeky devil.

siquiera *conj* even if: **ven, siquiera por ella**, do come, even if it's only for her.

▶ *adv* at least: **siquiera dímelo**, tell me about it at least.

● **ni siquiera** not even: **ni siquiera se despidió**, he didn't even say goodbye.

sirena *nf* **1** *(alarma)* siren. **2** *(ninfa)* mermaid.

sirviente,-a *nm,f* servant.

sísmico,-a *adj* seismic.

sistema *nm* system.

sitiar *vt* to besiege.

sitio *nm* **1** *(lugar)* place: **un sitio bonito para hacer un picnic**, a pretty place to have a picnic; **deja el abrigo en cualquier sitio**, leave your coat anywhere. **2** *(espacio)* space, room: **no había sitio en el coche**, there wasn't room in the car; **no encontré sitio para aparcar**, I couldn't find anywhere to park. **3** *(asedio)* siege.

● **hacer sitio a ALGN** to make room for SB.

■ **sitio web** website.

situación *nf* **1** *(coyuntura)* situation. **2** *(posición)* position.

situar *vt (colocar)* to place, locate: **esto lo sitúa entre los mejores**, this puts him among the best; **sitúa Guadalajara en el mapa**, find Guadalajara on the map.

▶ *vpr* **situarse** to position oneself: **se sitúa entre los mejores del mundo**, he is among the best in the world.

sobaco *nm* armpit.

sobar *vt (manosear)* to fondle.

▶ *vi fam (dormir)* to kip.

soberano,-a *adj - nm,f* sovereign: **los soberanos**, the royal couple.

soberbia *nf* **1** *(arrogancia)* arrogance. **2** *(magnificiencia)* sumptuousness.

soberbio,-a *adj* **1** *(arrogante)* arrogant. **2** *(magnífico)* superb.

sobornar *vt* to bribe.

soborno *nm* **1** *(acción)* bribery. **2** *(regalo)* bribe.

● **un intento de soborno** an attempted bribe.

sobra *nf* excess, surplus.

▶ *nf pl* **sobras** leftovers: **dale las sobras al perro**, give the leftovers to the dog.

● **de sobra 1** *(no necesario)* superfluous: **hay comida de sobra para todos**, there is plenty of food for everyone. **2** *(excesivo)* more than enough: **sabes de sobra que no fumo**, you know very well that I don't smoke.

sobrar *vi* **1** *(quedar)* to be left over: **sobran estos pasteles de la fiesta**, these cakes are left from the party. **2** *(sin aprovechar)* to be more than enough: **parece que sobrará comida**, it looks as if there will be more than enough food. **3** *(estar de más)* to be superfluous: **vete a casa, que aquí sobras**, go home, you're not needed here.

sobre *prep* **1** *(encima)* on, upon: **el jarrón está sobre la mesa**, the vase is on the table. **2** *(por encima)* over, above: **el helicóptero volaba sobre la ciudad**, the helicopter flew over the city. **3** *(acerca de)* on, about: **un libro sobre Quevedo**, a book about Quevedo; **hablar sobre algo**, to talk about STH. **4** *(alrededor de)* around, about: **llegaré sobre las once**, I'll get there at about eleven o'clock. **5** *(proporción)* out of: **cuatro sobre cinco**, four out of five.

► *nm* **1** *(de carta)* envelope. **2** *(envoltorio)* packet: *sopa de sobre*, packet soup. **3** *(paquete pequeño)* sachet: *pásame otro sobre de azúcar*, pass me another sachet of sugar.

● **sobre el nivel del mar** above sea level.

● **sobre todo** above all, especially.

sobrecarga *nf* overload.

sobrecargar *vt* to overload.

sobrecogedor,-ra *adj* **1** *(impresionante)* overwhelming. **2** *(que da miedo)* frightening.

sobredosis *nf* overdose.

sobremesa *nf (charla)* after-lunch chat; *(hora)* afternoon.

sobrenatural *adj* supernatural.

sobrentender *vt* to deduce, infer.

► *vpr* **sobrentenderse** to be understood: *se sobreentiende que...*, it goes without saying that....

sobrepasar *vt* **1** *(cantidad)* to exceed. **2** *(récord)* to beat [*pt* **beat**; *pp* **beaten**].

sobresaliente *adj* outstanding.

► *nm (calificación)* A, first: *le pusieron un sobresaliente*, he got an A.

sobresalir *vi* **1** *(destacarse)* to stand out [*pt & pp* **stood**], excel: *sobresalía entre los demás niños*, he stood out among the other children; *sobresale por su inteligencia*, his intelligence is exceptional. **2** *(ser más alto)* to rise [*pt* **rose**; *pp* **risen**] above: *los rascacielos sobresalen entre los demás edificios*, skyscrapers rise above the other buildings. **3** *(estar saliente)* to stick [*pt & pp* **stuck**] out: *el balcón sobresale de la fachada*, the balcony sticks out from the facade. **4** *(abultar)* to protrude.

sobresaltar *vt* to startle.

► *vpr* **sobresaltarse** to be startled.

sobresalto *nm (de sorpresa)* start; *(de temor)* fright.

sobrevivir *vi* to survive.

sobrino,-a *nm,f (chico)* nephew; *(chica)* niece.

sobrio,-a *adj* sober, temperate.

socavón *nm (bache)* pothole.

sociable *adj* sociable, friendly.

social *adj* social.

socialismo *nm* socialism.

socialista *adj - nmf* socialist.

sociedad *nf* **1** *(gen)* society: *la sociedad del siglo XXI*, the 21st century society. **2** *(asociación)* society, association; *(empresa)* company: *los dos hermanos fundaron una sociedad*, the two brothers set up a company.

● **alta sociedad** high society.

■ **sociedad anónima** GB limited company ; US incorporated company.

■ **sociedad de consumo** consumer society.

■ **sociedad limitada** private limited company.

■ **sociedad protectora de animales** society for the protection of animals.

socio,-a *nm,f* **1** *(de un grupo)* member: *son socios del club de tenis*, they're members of the tennis club; *me he hecho socio de la piscina*, I've become a member of the pool. **2** *(de empresa)* partner.

sociología *nf* sociology.

sociólogo,-a *nm,f* sociologist.

socorrer *vt* to help, aid.

socorrismo *nm* life-saving.

socorrista *nmf* life-saver, lifeguard.

socorro *nm* help, aid, assistance.

► *interj* **¡socorro!** help!

● **pedir socorro** to ask for help.

soda *nf* soda water.

sofá *nm* sofa, settee.

sofisticado,-a *adj* sophisticated.

sofocante *adj* suffocating, stifling.

sofocar *vt* **1** *(ahogar)* to suffocate: *me sofocan los lugares con mucha gente*, I can't breathe in crowded places. **2** *(incendio)* to put out, extinguish.

► *vpr* **sofocarse** **1** *(avergonzarse)* to get embarrassed. **2** *(enfadarse)* to get angry.

software *nm* software.

soga *nf* rope.

soja *nf* soya bean.

sol¹ *nm* **1** *(astro)* sun. **2** *(luz)* sunlight, sunshine: *entra mucho sol en esta habitación*, this room gets a lot of sun; *sentémonos al sol*, let's sit in the sun; *hace sol*, it's sunny.

● **tomar el sol** to sunbathe.

■ **sol naciente** rising sun.

sol² *nm (nota)* sol, G.

solamente *adv* only.

solapa *nf* **1** *(de chaqueta)* lapel. **2** *(de sobre, libro)* flap.

solar¹ *adj* solar: *el sistema solar*, the solar system.

solar² *nm (terreno)* plot.

soldado *nm* soldier.

■ **soldado raso** private.

soldadura *nf* **1** *(acción)* welding; *(con estaño)* soldering. **2** *(unión)* weld; *(con estaño)* solder.

soldar *vt (unir)* to weld; *(con estaño)* to solder.

soleado,-a *adj* sunny.

soledad *nf* **1** *(estado)* solitude: *necesito un poco de soledad*, I need to be alone for a while. **2** *(sentimiento)* loneliness: *un sentimiento de soledad*, a feeling of loneliness.

solemne *adj* **1** *(formal, serio)* solemn. **2** *pey* downright: *es una solemne estupidez*, it's downright stupid.

soler *vi* **1** *(presente)* be in the habit of doing: *soler hacer*, to usually do; *no suelo acostarme tarde*, I don't usually go to bed late; *no suelo bromear*, I am not in the habit of joking. **2** *(pasado)* : *solía ir a correr*, he used to go running; *mi padre no solía fumar*, my father didn't use to smoke.

solfeo *nm* solfa.

solicitar *vt* **1** *(pedir)* to request: *solicitó una entrevista con el ministro*, he requested an interview with the minister. **2** *(trabajo)* to apply for: *ha solicitado una beca*, she's applied for a grant.

solicitud *nf* **1** *(petición)* request: *la solicitud de ayuda económica*, the request for economic aid. **2** *(de trabajo)* application: *¿has hecho la solicitud?*, have you made the application? **3** *(impreso)* application form: *hay que rellenar la solicitud*, you have to fill in the application form. **4** *(diligencia)* solicitude.

solidaridad *nf* solidarity.

● **por solidaridad con** ALGN out of solidarity with SB.

solidez *nf* solidity.

sólido,-a *adj* solid.

▶ *nm* **sólido** solid.

solista *nmf* soloist.

solitaria *nf* tapeworm.

solitario,-a *adj* **1** *(sin compañía)* solitary: *lleva una vida solitaria*, she leads a solitary existence. **2** *(sentimiento)* lonely: *una persona solitaria*, a lonely person. **3** *(lu-*

gar) deserted: *una calle solitaria*, a deserted street.

▶ *nm* **solitario** solitaire.

● **en solitario** solo: *ha sacado un álbum en solitario*, he's brought out a solo album.

sollozar *vi* to sob.

sollozo *nm* sob.

sólo *adv* only.

solo,-a *adj* **1** *(sin compañía)* alone: *vive sola*, she lives alone; *déjame solo*, leave me alone; *¿lo has hecho tú solo?*, did you do it by yourself? **2** *(solitario)* lonely: *se siente muy solo*, he feels very lonely. **3** *(único)* one, single: *una sola persona*, one single person; *hay un solo problema*, there's just one problem.

▶ *nm* **solo 1** *fam (café)* black coffee. **2** *(canción)* solo *[pl* -s*]*.

● **a solas** alone, in private.

solomillo *nm* sirloin.

soltar *vt* **1** *(dejar suelto)* to let *[pt & pp* let*]* go of: *¡suéltame!*, let go of me!; *no soltaba el monedero*, she didn't let go of her purse. **2** *(poner en libertad)* to set free *[pt & pp* set*]*, release: *han soltado al sospechoso*, the suspect has been released; *¡venga, suelta la pasta!*, come on, pay up! **3** *(desatar)* to undo *[pt* undid; *pp* undone*]*, unfasten: *soltó el nudo de la corbata*, he undid the knot of his tie. **4** *(desenrollar)* to let out *[pt & pp* let*]*: *ve soltando cuerda*, let out the rope. **5** *fam (decir)* to come out with: *suelta muchos tacos*, he swears a lot; *me soltó un rollo increíble*, he went on and on for ages. **6** *fam (producir)* : *suelta un olor insoportable*, it smells awful; *le soltó un buen golpe*, she hit him hard.

▶ *vpr* **soltarse 1** *(desatarse)* to come undone: *el cordel se ha soltado*, the string has come undone; *se soltó de mi mano*, he let go of my hand. **2** *(desprenderse)* to come off.

● **soltarse el pelo** to let one's hair down.

soltero,-a *adj* single.

▶ *nm,f (hombre)* bachelor; *(mujer)* single woman *[pl* women*]*.

soltura *nf* **1** *(de movimientos)* agility. **2** *(al hablar)* fluency.

soluble *adj* soluble.

solución *nf* solution.

solucionar *vt* to solve.

sombra *nf* **1** *(lugar sin sol)* shade: *se sentó a la sombra a descansar*, he sat down in the shade to rest; *a la sombra del árbol*, in the shade of a tree. **2** *(silueta)* shadow: *a medida que el sol se pone, las sombras se alargan*, as the sun sets, the shadows get longer.
■ **sombra de ojos** eye shadow.

sombrero *nm* hat.
■ **sombrero de copa** top hat.
■ **sombrero de paja** straw hat.

sombrilla *nf* parasol, sunshade.

sombrío,-a *adj* **1** *(lugar)* dark. **2** *(persona, panorama)* gloomy.

someter *vt* **1** *(subyugar)* to subdue. **2** *(exponer)* to subject: *el mineral fue sometido a altas temperaturas*, the mineral was subject to high temperatures; *someter algo a prueba*, to put STH to test. **3** *(proponer)* to put: *sometió su idea a la junta*, he put his idea to the board.
▶ *vpr* **someterse 1** *(rendirse)* to surrender: *el país tuvo que someterse al invasor*, the country had to surrender to the invader. **2** *(tratamiento etc)* to undergo [*pt* **underwent**; *pp* **undergone**]: *el atleta se sometió a un duro entrenamiento*, the athlete underwent a tough training session.

somier *nm* *(de muelles)* spring mattress; *(de láminas)* slats *pl*.

somnífero *nm* sleeping pill.

son *nm* sound.
● **sin ton ni son** without rhyme or reason.
● **venir en son de paz** to come in peace.

sonajero *nm* rattle.

sonámbulo,-a *adj - nm,f* sleepwalker.

sonar *vi* **1** *(con timbrazos)* to ring [*pt* **rang**; *pp* **rung**]: *sonaba el teléfono*, the telephone was ringing. **2** *(con campanadas)* to strike [*pt & pp* **struck**]. **3** *(con pitido)* to beep. **4** *(ponerse en marcha)* to go off: *¿ha sonado el despertador?*, has the alarm clock gone off? **5** *(conocer vagamente)* to sound familiar: *su nombre me suena*, his name sounds familiar, his name rings a bell; *su cara me suena*, her face is familiar. **6** *(letra)* to be pronounced: *en español, la "h" no suena*, in Spanish the "h" is not pronounced. **7** *(parecer)* to

sound: *eso suena a falso*, that sounds false; *el argumento suena interesante*, the plot sounds interesting.
▶ *vpr* **sonarse** to blow one's nose [*pt* **blew**; *pp* **blown**]: *tengo que sonarme*, I have to blow my nose.

sonda *nf* probe.
■ **sonda espacial** space probe.

sondear *vt* **1** *(explorar)* to explore, probe. **2** *(encuestar)* to sound out.
● **sondear a la opinión pública** to sound out public opinion.

sondeo *nm* *(encuesta)* poll.
■ **sondeo de opinión** opinion poll.

soneto *nm* sonnet.

sonido *nm* sound.

sonoro,-a *adj* **1** *(golpe)* loud, resounding. **2** *(consonante)* voiced.
● **banda sonora** SEE banda.

sonreír *vi - vpr* **sonreír(se)** to smile: *el niño me sonrió*, the boy smiled at me; *la vida no le sonríe*, his life is not brilliant.

sonriente *adj* smiling.

sonrisa *nf* smile.

sonrojar *vt* to make blush.
▶ *vpr* **sonrojarse** to blush.

sonrosado,-a *adj* rosy, pink.

soñador,-ra *adj* dreamy.
▶ *nm,f* dreamer.

soñar *vt - vi* to dream: *hoy he soñado contigo*, I dreamt about you last night; *soñaba con ser piloto*, he dreamt of becoming a pilot.
● **soñar despierto** to daydream.
● **¡ni lo sueñes!** in your dreams!

sopa *nf* soup.
■ **sopa de tomate** tomato soup.

sopera *nf* soup tureen.

sopetón *nm* .
● **de sopetón** all of a sudden.

soplar *vi* *(persona, viento)* to blow [*pt* **blew**; *pp* **blown**]: *hoy el viento sopla muy fuerte*, there's a strong wind blowing today.
▶ *vt* **1** *(llevarse)* to blow away [*pt* **blew**; *pp* **blown**]. **2** *(apagar)* to blow out [*pt* **blew**; *pp* **blown**]: *el niño sopló las velas*, the little boy blew out the candles. **3** *(delatar)* to grass. **4** *fam* *(robar)* to swipe, pinch.
▶ *vpr* **soplarse** *fam* *(beber)* to down.
● **soplar una respuesta a ALGN** to whisper an answer to SB.

soplete *nm* blowtorch, blowlamp.

soplo *nm* **1** *(soplido)* blow, puff: **apagó las velas de un soplo**, he blew out the candles with one puff. **2** *(de aire)* puff: **un soplo de viento**, a gust of wind. **3** *fam (de secreto etc)* tip-off [*pl* **-s**].

● **dar un soplo** to squeal.

● **en un soplo** in no time.

soplón,-ona *nm,f fam* informer, squealer.

soportar *vt* **1** *(sostener)* to support: **la viga soporta todo el peso del techo**, the beam supports all the weight of the ceiling. **2** *(aguantar)* to put up with: **¿cómo lo soportas?**, how can you put up with him? **3** *(tolerar)* to stand [*pt & pp* **stood**]: **no soporto a esta chica**, I can't stand this girl.

soporte *nm* support.

soprano *nmf* soprano [*pl* **-s**].

sorber *vt* **1** *(líquido)* to sip. **2** *(con pajita)* to drink [*pt* **drank**; *pp* **drunk**]. **3** *(haciendo ruido)* to slurp. **4** *(absorber)* to soak up.

sorbete *nm* sorbet.

sorbo *nm* sip.

● **beber a sorbos** to sip.

sordera *nf* deafness.

sordo,-a *adj* **1** *(persona)* deaf: **se ha quedado sordo**, he's gone deaf. **2** *(sonido, dolor)* dull: **cayó al suelo y se oyó un golpe sordo**, it fell on the floor with a dull thud.

▶ *nm,f*: **los sordos**, the deaf.

● **sordo,-a como una tapia** as deaf as a post.

● **hacerse el sordo** to pretend not to hear.

sordomudo,-a *adj* deaf and dumb.

▶ *nm,f* deaf mute.

sorprendente *adj* surprising.

sorprender *vt* **1** *(asombrar)* to surprise: **me sorprendió que fuera tan joven**, I was surprised that he was so young. **2** *(coger)* to catch [*pt & pp* **caught**]: **le sorprendió copiando el en examen**, she caught him copying in the exam; **me sorprendió la lluvia**, I got caught in the rain.

▶ *vpr* **sorprenderse** to be surprised.

sorpresa *nf* surprise: **¡menuda sorpresa!**, what a nice surprise!

● **llevarse una sorpresa** to get a surprise.

■ **visita sorpresa** surprise visit.

sortear *vt* **1** *(echar a suertes)* to draw lots for [*pt* **drew**; *pp* **drawn**]; *(rifar)* to raffle: **sortearon un viaje a Nueva York**, they held a prize draw for a trip to New York. **2** *(obstáculos)* to get round.

sorteo *nm* *(de lotería)* draw; *(rifa)* raffle: **gané un coche en un sorteo**, I won a car in a prize draw.

sortija *nf* ring.

sosegado,-a *adj* calm, quiet.

sosegar *vt* - *vpr* **sosegar(se)** to calm down.

sosiego *nm* calmness, peace.

soso,-a *adj* **1** *(sin sabor)* tasteless. **2** *(sin sal)* : **está soso**, it needs salt. **3** *(aburrido)* dull.

sospecha *nf* suspicion: **levantó sus sospechas**, it arouse his suspicions.

sospechar *vt* to suspect: **sospechaban de él**, they suspected him.

sospechoso,-a *adj* suspicious.

▶ *nm,f* suspect.

● **ser sospechoso de algo** to be suspected of STH.

sostén *nm* **1** *(apoyo)* support. **2** *(prenda)* bra, brassiere.

sostener *vt* **1** *(aguantar)* to support, hold up [*pt & pp* **held**]: **las vigas sostienen el techo**, the beams support the ceiling. **2** *(sujetar)* to hold [*pt & pp* **held**]: **sostenía un libro en la mano**, he held a book in his hand. **3** *(conversación, reunión)* to have. **4** *(opinión)* to maintain, affirm: **sostiene que vio un fantasma**, she maintains that she saw a ghost. **5** *(familia)* to support.

▶ *vpr* **sostenerse 1** *(mantenerse)* to support oneself. **2** *(permanecer)* to stay.

● **sostenerse en pie** to stand up [*pt & pp* **stood**].

sota *nf* *(cartas)* jack, knave.

sotana *nf* cassock.

sótano *nm* **1** *(usado como almacén)* cellar. **2** *(en casa)* basement.

Sr. *abr* **(señor)** Mr.

Sra. *abr* **(señora)** Mrs.

stop *nm* stop sign.

su *adj* *(de él)* his; *(de ella)* her; *(de usted/ustedes)* your; *(de ellos)* their; *(de animales, cosas)* its: **su mujer**, his wife; **su marido**, her husband; **el loro está en su jaula**, the parrot is in its cage; **abra su maleta, por favor**, open your suitcase, please; **sus hijos**, their children.

suave *adj* **1** *(piel, tela, color, voz)* soft. **2** *(superficie)* smooth. **3** *(brisa, persona)* gentle. **4** *(clima, sabor, detergente)* mild.

suavemente *adv* softly, smoothly.

suavidad *nf* **1** *(blandura)* softness. **2** *(lisura)* smoothness. **3** *(docilidad)* gentleness, mildness.

suavizante *nm* **1** *(para ropa)* fabric softener. **2** *(para pelo)* conditioner.

suavizar *vt* **1** *(ablandar)* to soften. **2** *(alisar)* to smooth.

subasta *nf* auction.
● **poner en subasta** to sell at auction.

subastar *vt* to auction.

subcampeón,-ona *nm,f* runner-up.

subdesarrollado,-a *adj* underdeveloped.

subdirector,-ra *nm,f* **1** *(de organización)* deputy director. **2** *(de empresa)* assistant manager.

súbdito,-a *adj - nm,f* subject.

subida *nf* **1** *(ascenso)* ascent; *(a montaña)* climb: *al ciclista se le hizo muy difícil la subida*, the cyclist found the ascent very difficult. **2** *(pendiente)* slope: *esta subida es muy pronunciada*, this is a very steep hill. **3** *(aumento)* rise: *una subida en el precio de los alimentos*, a rise in the price of food. **4** *arg (drogas)* high.

subir *vi* **1** *(a coche)* to get in; *(a tren, autobús, avión)* to get on: *sube al coche*, get in the car; *subió al tren*, she got on the train. **2** *(aumentar)* to rise [*pt* **rose**; *pp* **risen**], go up: *ha subido el precio*, the price has gone up. **3** *(categoría, puesto)* to be promoted.
▶ *vt* **1** *(escalar)* to climb: *subimos la montaña*, we climbed the mountain; *subí las escaleras*, I went up the stairs; *¡sube! ¡la vista es fantástica!*, come up! the view is fantastic! **2** *(mover arriba)* to carry up, take up: *sube estos trastos al desván*, take these old things up to the loft. **3** *(incrementar)* to put up: *han subido el precio del pan*, they've put the price of the bread up. **4** *(poner más fuerte)* to turn up: *sube el volumen de la radio*, turn the radio up.
▶ *vpr* **subirse 1** *(a coche)* to get in; *(a tren, autobús, avión)* to get on; *(a caballo)* to mount. **2** *(trepar)* to climb: *se subió al árbol*, he climbed the tree. **3** *(pull up)*: *súbete los calcetines*, pull your socks up.

● **subirse por las paredes** to hit the roof [*pt & pp* **hit**].

súbito,-a *adj* sudden.

subjetivo,-a *adj* subjective.

subjuntivo *nm* subjunctive.

sublevación *nf* rising, revolt.

sublevar *vt* **1** *(amotinar)* to incite to rebellion. **2** *(indignar)* to infuriate.
▶ *vpr* **sublevarse** to rebel.

submarinismo *nm* scuba diving.

submarinista *nmf* scuba diver.

submarino,-a *adj* underwater.
▶ *nm* **submarino** submarine.

subnormal *adj* mentally handicapped.
▶ *nmf* **1** mentally handicapped person. **2** *(insulto)* cretin.

subordinado,-a *adj - nm,f* subordinate.

subrayar *vt* **1** *(con una línea)* to underline: *subrayó las palabras más importantes*, she underlined the most important words. **2** *(recalcar)* to emphasize: *subrayó la importancia de la lectura*, he emphasized the importance of reading.

subsidio *nm* subsidy, aid.
■ **subsidio de desempleo** unemployment benefit.

subsistir *vi* to subsist, survive.

subsuelo *nm* subsoil.

subterráneo,-a *adj* subterranean, underground.
▶ *nm* **subterráneo** underground passage.

suburbano,-a *adj* suburban.

suburbio *nm* poor suburb.

subvención *nf* subsidy, grant.

subvencionar *vt* to subsidize.

sucedáneo,-a *adj* substitute.
▶ *nm* **sucedáneo** substitute.

suceder *vi* **1** *(acontecer)* to happen, occur: *ha sucedido algo imprevisto*, something unexpected has happened; *¿qué sucede?*, what's happening? **2** *(seguir)* to follow. **3** *(sustituir)* to succeed: *el príncipe sucederá a su padre en el trono*, the prince will succeed his father to the throne.

sucesión *nf* **1** *(en un puesto)* succession. **2** *(descendientes)* heirs *pl*.

sucesivamente *adv* successively: *y así sucesivamente*, and so on.

sucesivo,-a *adj* consecutive, successive.
● **en lo sucesivo** from now on.

suceso *nm* **1** *(hecho)* event, happening. **2** *(incidente)* incident. **3** *(delito)* crime.

sucesor,-ra *nm,f* **1** *(en un puesto)* successor. **2** *(heredero)* heir; *(heredera)* heiress.

suciedad *nf* dirt.

sucio,-a *adj* dirty.

● **en sucio** in rough: *primero escribe los textos en sucio*, she writes the texts in rough first.

sucumbir *vi* **1** *(ser vencido)* to succumb, yield. **2** *(morir)* to perish.

sucursal *nf* branch office.

sudadera *nf* sweatshirt.

Sudamérica *nf* South America.

sudamericano,-a *adj* South American.

sudar *vi* to sweat.

● **sudar la gota gorda** *fam* to sweat blood.

sudeste *adj - nm* southeast.

sudoeste *adj - nm* southwest.

sudor *nm* sweat.

sudoroso,-a *adj* sweating.

Suecia *nf* Sweden.

sueco,-a *adj* Swedish.

▶ *nm,f (persona)* Swede.

▶ *nm* **sueco** *(idioma)* Swedish.

● **hacerse el sueco** to pretend not to understand.

suegro,-a *nm,f (hombre)* father-in-law; *(mujer)* mother-in-law.

suela *nf* sole.

sueldo *nm* salary, pay.

suelo *nm* **1** *(en la calle)* ground; *(de interior)* floor. **2** *(tierra)* soil. **3** *(terreno)* land: *hay mucho suelo disponible*, there's a lot of land available.

suelto,-a *adj* **1** *(no sujeto)* loose; *(desatado)* undone: *el tornillo está suelto*, the screw is loose; *este perro no debería estar suelto*, this dog shouldn't be loose. **2** *(estilo etc)* easy. **3** *(desparejado)* odd: *quedan algunas tallas sueltas*, there are some odd sizes left; *se venden sueltos*, they are sold separately.

▶ *nm* **suelto** *(cambio)* small change: *lo siento, no llevo suelto*, sorry, I haven't got any change.

sueño *nm* **1** *(acto)* sleep: *necesito ocho horas de sueño*, I need eight hours' sleep. **2** *(ganas de dormir)* sleepiness: *tengo mucho sueño*, I'm very sleepy. **3** *(lo soñado)* dream: *tuve un sueño muy raro*, I had a very strange dream.

● **echarse un sueñecito** to have a nap.

■ **sueño dorado** cherished dream.

suero *nm* **1** *(de la sangre)* serum. **2** *(de la leche)* whey. **3** *(solución salina)* saline solution.

suerte *nf* **1** *(fortuna)* luck: *¡suerte para tu examen!*, good luck with your exam!; *¡qué suerte!*, how lucky!; *es una suerte que hayas venido*, it's lucky you came; *el número de la suerte*, the lucky number. **2** *(azar)* chance: *fur la suerte la que me llevó hasta ti*, it was fate that led me to you.

● **dar suerte** to bring [*pt & pp* **brought**] good luck.

● **echar a suertes** to cast lots for [*pt & pp* **cast**].

● **por suerte** fortunately.

● **tener suerte** to be lucky.

● **tener mala suerte** to be unlucky.

● **traer suerte** to bring [*pt & pp* **brought**] good luck.

suéter *nm* sweater.

suficiente *adj - pron* enough.

▶ *nm* pass: *saqué un suficiente*, I got a pass.

sufijo *nm* suffix.

sufrido,-a *adj* patient, long-suffering.

sufrimiento *nm* suffering.

sufrir *vt* **1** *(padecer)* to suffer: *sufre fuertes dolores de cabeza*, he suffers from bad headaches. **2** *(ser sujeto de)* to have; *(operación)* to undergo [*pt* **underwent**; *pp* **undergone**]: *sufrió un ataque al corazón*, he had a heart attack; *sufrir un accidente*, to have an accident. **3** *(soportar)* to bear [*pt* **bore**; *pp* **borne**]: *sufrir un cambio*, to change.

▶ *vi* to suffer.

● **hacer sufrir a** ALGN to make SB suffer.

sugerencia *nf* suggestion.

sugerir *vt* to suggest: *sugiero que vayamos en tren*, I suggest that we go by train; *me sugirió que ahorrara un poco más*, he suggested that I should save a bit more; *¿qué te sugiere esta foto?*, what does this photo make you think of?

sugestionar *vt* to influence.

▶ *vpr* **sugestionarse** to get ideas into one's head: *sugestionarse con algo*, to talk oneself into STH.

sugestivo,-a *adj* suggestive.

suicida *adj* suicidal.

▶ *nmf* suicide.

suicidarse *vpr* to commit suicide.

suicidio *nm* suicide.

Suiza *nf* Switzerland.

suizo,-a *adj* - *nm,f* Swiss.

sujetador *nm* bra, brassiere.

sujetapapeles *nm inv* paper clip.

sujetar *vt* **1** *(agarrar)* to hold [*pt & pp* held]: *¿me sujetas el bolso?*, can you hold my bag, please? **2** *(fijar)* to fix, secure: *hay que sujetar estos papeles*, you must fasten these papers together; *sujetó la moqueta con unos clavos*, he nailed the carpet down.

▶ *vpr* **sujetarse** to hold on [*pt & pp* held]: *sujétate a la cuerda*, hold on to the rope; *se sujetaba la gorra*, he held his cap on.

sujeto,-a *adj* **1** *(sometido)* subject: *estamos sujetos a la ley*, we're subject to the law. **2** *(fijo)* fastened: *la estantería está sujeta a la pared*, the shelves are fixed to the wall; *el cuadro no está bien sujeto y podría caerse*, the picture isn't secure and it might fall down.

▶ *nm* **sujeto 1** *(de verbo)* subject. **2** *(persona)* fellow.

sultán *nm* sultan.

suma *nf* **1** *(cantidad)* sum, amount. **2** *(operación)* sum, addition.

● **en suma** in short.

sumar *vt* **1** to add up: *suma estas cifras*, add these numbers up. **2** *(total)* to total: *diez y tres suman trece*, ten and three are thirteen.

▶ *vpr* **sumarse** to join: *nos sumamos a la protesta*, we joined the protest.

● **suma y sigue** carried forward.

sumergir *vt* *(meter en líquido)* to put in; *(con fuerza)* to plunge; *(rápidamente)* to dip: *sumerge la mano en agua caliente*, put your hand in hot water.

▶ *vpr* **sumergirse 1** *(submarinista)* to go underwater, dive; *(submarino)* to dive. **2** *fig (en un ambiente)* to immerse oneself: *se sumergía en su trabajo*, she immersed herself in her work.

suministrar *vt* to provide, supply.

suministro *nm* supply.

sumiso,-a *adj* submissive.

sumo,-a *adj* great: *con sumo cuidado*, with great care.

● **a lo sumo** at most.

súper *adj fam* super, great.

▶ *nm* **1** *fam (supermercado)* supermarket. **2** *(gasolina)* four-star petrol: *este coche funciona con súper*, this car runs on four-star petrol.

superar *vt* **1** *(exceder)* to surpass, exceed: *la realidad supera a la ficción*, the reality surpasses the fiction; *el porcentaje de aprobados supera el 50%*, the percentage of passes is over 50%. **2** *(obstáculo etc)* to overcome [*pt* overcame; *pp* overcome], surmount: *la empresa ha superado la crisis*, the company has overcome the crisis. **3** *(récord)* to break [*pt* broke; *pp* broken]. **4** *(prueba)* to pass: *ha superado la primera prueba*, she's passed the first test.

▶ *vpr* **superarse** to excel oneself: *el atleta se superó y batió el récord*, the athlete excelled himself and broke the record.

superávit *nm* surplus.

superficial *adj* superficial.

superficie *nf* **1** *(parte externa)* surface: *el submarino salió a la superficie*, the submarine came to the surface. **2** *(geometría)* area: *la superficie de un rectángulo*, the area of a rectangle.

superfluo,-a *adj* superfluous.

superior *adj* **1** *(de arriba)* upper: *la estantería superior*, the upper shelf; *la parte superior de la hoja*, the top part of the page. **2** *(mayor)* greater. **3** *(mejor)* superior: *un tejido de superior calidad*, a superior quality material.

● **educación superior** higher education.

● **ser superior a algo** to be better than STH.

superioridad *nf* superiority.

superlativo,-a *adj* superlative.

▶ *nm* **superlativo** superlative.

supermercado *nm* supermarket.

supersónico,-a *adj* supersonic.

superstición *nf* superstition.

supersticioso,-a *adj* superstitious.

supervisar *vt* to supervise.

supervivencia *nf* survival.

superviviente *adj* surviving.

▶ *nmf* survivor.

suplemento *nm* supplement.

■ **suplemento dominical** Sunday supplement.

suplente *adj* - *nmf* substitute.

● **maestro suplente** supply teacher.

supletorio *nm (teléfono)* extension.

suplicar *vt* to beg: *te suplico que no te vayas*, I beg you not to go.

suplicio *nm* **1** *(castigo)* torture. **2** *fig (gran carga)* torment.

suponer *vt* **1** *(creer)* to suppose: *supongo que sí*, I suppose so; *supongo que llegará mañana*, I expect he'll arrive tomorrow. **2** *(dar por sentado)* to assume: *suponía que ibas a estar de acuerdo*, I assumed you would agree. **3** *(acarrear)* to entail: *supone demasiados gastos*, it involves too much expense; *supone un riesgo para la salud*, it is bad for your health.

▶ *nm fam* supposition.

● **es de suponer que...** I would imagine that....

● **supongamos que...** supposing....

suposición *nf* supposition, assumption.

supositorio *nm* suppository.

supremo,-a *adj* supreme.

suprimir *vt (noticia)* to suppress; *(ley, impuestos)* to abolish; *(palabras, texto)* to delete: *tenemos que suprimir gastos*, we must cut out expenses.

supuesto,-a *pp* → suponer.

▶ *adj* **1** *(falso)* supposed, assumed: *el supuesto rey*, the supposed king. **2** *(presunto)* alleged: *el supuesto asesino*, the alleged murderer.

▶ *nm* **supuesto** supposition.

● **dar por supuesto algo** to take STH for granted.

● **por supuesto** of course.

sur *adj - nm* south: *el sur de España*, the south of Spain.

surco *nm* **1** *(en tierra)* trench. **2** *(en disco)* groove.

sureste *adj - nm* southeast.

surgir *vi* **1** *(aparecer)* to arise [*pt* arose; *pp* arisen], appear. **2** *(agua)* to spring forth [*pt* sprang; *pp* sprung].

suroeste *adj - nm* southwest.

surtido,-a *adj* assorted: *bombones surtidos*, assorted chocolates.

▶ *nm* **surtido** assortment: *estar bien surtido de algo*, to be well supplied of STH.

surtidor *nm* **1** *(fuente)* fountain. **2** *(chorro)* jet, spout.

■ **surtidor de gasolina** petrol pump.

surtir *vt (suministrar)* to supply, provide.

● **surtir efecto** to work.

susceptible *adj* **1** *(quisquilloso)* susceptible. **2** *(capaz)* capable: *susceptible de mejora*, capable of improvement. **3** *(sensible)* touchy: *es muy susceptible a las críticas*, she's very sensitive to criticism.

suscribir *vt* **1** *(contrato)* to sign. **2** *(opinión)* to subscribe: *suscribo lo que dice*, I subscribe to what he says.

▶ *vpr* **suscribirse** *(a una revista)* to subscribe to.

suscripción *nf* subscription.

suspender *vt* **1** *(colgar)* to hang up [*pt & pp* hung]: *la lámpara estaba suspendida del techo*, the lamp hung from the ceiling. **2** *(aplazar)* to postpone: *se ha suspendido el concierto*, the concert has been postponed. **3** *(fallar)* to fail: *he suspendido las matemáticas*, I´ve failed mathematics. **4** *(cancelar)* to suspend: *el árbitro suspendió el partido*, the referee suspended the match; *fue suspendido por la lluvia*, it was rained off.

▶ *vi* to fail.

suspense *nm* suspense.

suspensión *nf* **1** *(de coche)* suspension. **2** *(aplazamiento)* postponement. **3** *(cancelación)* suspension.

suspenso *nm* fail: *tiene un suspenso*, he's failed one subject.

suspicacia *nf* suspicion, mistrust.

suspicaz *adj* suspicious, distrustful.

suspirar *vi* to sigh.

● **suspirar por** to long for.

suspiro *nm* sigh: *un suspiro de alivio*, a sigh of relief.

sustancia *nf* substance.

sustantivo *nm* noun.

sustitución *nf* **1** *(transitoria)* substitution: *Shaw estaba en el banquillo para una posible sustitución*, Shaw was be on the bench in case of a possible susbtitution. **2** *(permanente)* replacement: *han nombrado a Sevillano en lugar de Aguirre*, Sevillano has been appointed as a replacement for Aguirre.

sustituir *vt* **1** *(transitoriamente)* to substitute: *el ministro sustituyó al presidente*, the minister stood in for the president. **2** *(permanentemente)* to replace: *han sustituido la tele vieja por una nueva*, they have replaced the old telly with a new one.

sustituto,-a *nm,f* **1** *(transitorio)* substitute. **2** *(permanente)* replacement.

susto *nm* fright, scare.
- **dar un susto a** ALGN to give SB a fright.
- **darse un susto** to get a fright.
- **¡qué susto!** what a fright!

sustraer *vt* **1** *(restar)* to substract. **2** *(robar)* to steal [*pt* **stole**; *pp* **stolen**].

susurrar *vi* **1** *(persona)* to whisper. **2** *(agua)* to murmur. **3** *(hojas)* to rustle.
► *vt* to whisper.

susurro *nm* **1** *(de voz)* whisper. **2** *(de agua)* murmur. **3** *(de hojas)* rustle.

sutil *adj* subtle, delicate.

suyo,-a *adj (de él)* of his; *(de ella)* of hers; *(de usted/ustedes)* yours; *(de ellos)* theirs: *¿es amigo suyo?*, is he a friend of his/hers/yours/theirs?; *vino con un hermano suyo*, he came with a friend of his.
► *pron (de él)* his; *(de ella)* hers; *(de usted/ustedes)* yours; *(de ellos,-as)* theirs: *ha cogido mi coche porque el suyo estaba averiado*, he's taken my car because his has broken down; *éste es el suyo*, this one is his/hers/yours/theirs.
- **ir a lo suyo** to go one's own way.
- **salirse con la suya** to get one's way.
- **hacer de las suyas** to be up to one's tricks.

T

tabaco *nm* **1** *(planta, hoja)* tobacco: *una hoja de tabaco*, a tobacco leaf. **2** *(cigarrillos)* cigarettes *pl*: *ha salido a comprar tabaco*, he's gone to buy some cigarettes; *el tabaco es malo para la salud*, smoking damages your health.
■ **tabaco negro** black tobacco.
■ **tabaco rubio** Virginia tobacco.

tábano *nm* horsefly.

tabarra *nf* .
● **dar la tabarra** *fam* to be a pest.

taberna *nf* pub, bar.

tabique *nm* partition wall.
■ **tabique nasal** nasal bone.

tabla *nf* **1** *(de madera pulida)* board: *una tabla del suelo*, a floorboard. **2** *(de madera basta)* plank: *un puente hecho de tablas*, a bridge made of planks. **3** *(índice)* table. **4** table: *las tablas de multiplicar*, multiplication tables; *la tabla del cinco*, the five times table.
▶ *nf pl* **tablas 1** *(ajedrez)* stalemate *sing*, draw *sing*. **2** *(escenario)* stage *sing*.
■ **tabla de planchar** ironing board.
■ **tabla de surf** surfboard.
■ **tabla de windsurf** sailboard.

tablado *nm* **1** *(suelo)* wooden floor. **2** *(plataforma)* wooden platform.

tablero *nm* **1** *(tablón)* panel, board: *tablero de instrumentos*, instrument panel. **2** *(en juegos)* board. **3** *(encerado)* blackboard.
■ **tablero de ajedrez** chessboard.

tableta *nf* **1** *(de chocolate)* bar. **2** *(pastilla)* tablet.

tablón *nm* **1** *(de madera)* plank. **2** *(en construcción)* beam.
■ **tablón de anuncios** notice board.

tabú *adj - nm* taboo.

taburete *nm* stool.

tacaño,-a *adj* mean, stingy.
▶ *nm,f* miser.

tachadura *nf* crossing out.

tachar *vt* **1** *(anular)* to cross out: *tachó la respuesta incorrecta*, he crossed out the wrong answer.
2 *(acusar)* to acuse: *me tacharon de ladrón*, they accused me of being a thief.

tachón *nm* crossing out.

tachuela *nf* **1** *(clavo)* tack. **2** *(en ropa)* stud.

taco *nm* **1** *(para calzar)* wedge: *puse un taco debajo de la mesa*, I put a wedge under the table. **2** *(para tornillo)* Rawlplug R. **3** *(calendario)* tear-off calendar; *(de entradas)* book; *(de billetes)* wad. **4** *(de billar)* cue. **5** *(de jamón, etc)* cube, piece. **6** *(en botas de fútbol)* stud. **7** *fam (palabrota)* swearword: *no le enseñes a decir tacos*, don't teach him to swear. **8** *fam (año)* year: *ya tiene 60 tacos*, she's already 60.
● **armarse un taco** to get all mixed up.

tacón *nm* heel.

taconear *vi* **1** *(pisar)* to tap one's heels. **2** *(golpear)* to stamp one's heels.

táctica *nf* **1** *(estrategia)* tactics *pl*: *el equipo ha cambiado de táctica*, the team have changed their tactics. **2** *(maniobra concreta)* tactic: *es una táctica muy buena*, it's a very good tactic.

táctil *adj* tactile.

tacto *nm* **1** *(sentido)* touch: *tiene muy desarrollado el tacto*, it has a highly developed sense of touch; *reconocía los objetos por el tacto*, he recognized the objects by touch. **2** *(textura)* feel. **3** *(delicadeza)* tact: *lo dijo con mucho tacto*, he said it with great tact.

• **tener tacto** to be tactful.
tailandés,-esa *adj - nm,f* Thai.
Tailandia *nf* Thailand.
Taiwan *nm* Taiwan.
Taiwanés,-esa *adj - nm,f* Taiwanese.
tajada *nf* **1** *(rodaja)* slice. **2** *(corte)* cut; *(cuchillada)* stab.

• **pillar una tajada** *fam* to get smashed.
• **sacar tajada** to take one's share.
tajante *adj* categorical.
tajo *nm* **1** *(corte)* cut, slash. **2** *(en el terreno)* steep cliff *[pl -s]*. **3** *fam (trabajo)* work.
tal *adj* **1** *(semejante)* such: **en tales condiciones**, in such conditions; **hacían tal ruido que me tuve que ir**, they were making such a racket that I had to leave. **2** *(tan grande)* such, so: **es tal su valor que...**, he is so courageous that.... **3** *(sin especificar - cosa)* such and such; *(- persona)* someone called: **tal día**, such and such a day; **te llamó un tal García**, someone called García phoned you.
▶ *pron (cosa)* something; *(persona)* someone, somebody.

• **como si tal cosa** as if nothing had happened.
• **con tal de que** so long as, provided: **iré yo, con tal de que vayáis conmigo**, I'll go, as long as you come with me.
• **de tal manera que** in such a way that.
• **¿qué tal?** how are things?
• **tal como** just as: **ella es tal como me la imaginaba**, she's just as I imagined.
• **tal cual** just as it is: **me gusta tal cual está**, I like it the way it is.
• **son tal para cual** they are two of a kind.
• **tal vez** perhaps, maybe.
• **y tal (y cual)** and so on.
taladradora *nf* drill.
taladrar *vt (pared)* to drill a hole in.
taladro *nm* **1** *(herramienta)* drill; *(barrena)* gimlet. **2** *(agujero)* drill hole.
talar *vt* to fell, cut down *[pt & pp cut]*.
talco *nm* talc.
talego *nm arg (cárcel)* clink.
talento *nm* talent: **tiene talento para el dibujo**, he has a talent for drawing.
talismán *nm* talisman, lucky charm.
talla *nf* **1** *(estatura)* height; *(altura moral etc)* stature. **2** *(de prenda)* size: **¿qué talla**

usas?, what size are you?; **necesito una talla más grande**, I need a bigger size. **3** *(escultura)* carving, sculpture. **4** *(tallado)* cutting, carving; *(de metal)* engraving.

• **dar la talla 1** (ser lo bastante alto) to be tall enough. **2** (ser competente) to measure up.
tallar *vt* **1** *(madera, piedra)* to carve, shape; *(piedras preciosas)* to cut *[pt & pp cut]*; *(metales)* to engrave. **2** *(medir)* to measure the height of. **3** *(valorar)* to value, appraise.
tallarines *nm pl* noodles.
taller *nm* **1** *(de artesano, profesional)* workshop. **2** *(de pintor)* studio *[pl -s]*. **3** *(industrial)* factory.

■ **taller de coches** garage.
■ **taller de teatro** theatre workshop.
tallo *nm* stem, stalk.
talón *nm* **1** *(de pie, calzado)* heel: **las botas me hacen daño en el talón**, the boots hurt my heels. **2** *(cheque)* GB cheque; US check: **pagaré con un talón**, I'll pay by cheque.

• **pisarle los talones a ALGN** to be hot on SB's heels.
■ **talón de Aquiles** Achilles' heel.
talonario *nm* **1** *(de cheques)* GB cheque book; US check book. **2** *(de recibos)* receipt book.
tamaño *nm* size.

• **del tamaño de** the size of, as big as: **granizo del tamaño de huevos de gallina**, hailstones the size of hens' eggs.
• **de tamaño carnet** passport-size.
• **de tamaño natural** life-size.
■ **tamaño bolsillo** pocket-size.
■ **tamaño familiar** family-size.
tambalearse *vpr (persona)* to stagger, totter; *(mueble)* to wobble.
también *adv* **1** also, too, as well: **Pedro también estaba**, Pedro was also there; **yo también me iba**, I was leaving too; **¿lo harás? —Yo también**, so you'll do it? —Me too. **2** *(además)* besides, in addition.
tambor *nm* **1** *(instrumento)* drum. **2** *(persona)* drummer. **3** *(de lavadora)* drum. **4** *(de detergente)* drum, giant size pack.
Támesis *nm* **el Támesis** the Thames.
tamiz *nm* sieve.
tampoco *adv* neither, nor, not ... either: **Juan no vendrá y María tampoco**, Juan

won't come and María won't either, Juan won't come and neither/nor will María; *yo tampoco*, me neither.

tampón *nm* **1** *(de entintar)* inkpad. **2** *(absorbente)* tampon.

tan *adv* **1** so; *(después de sustantivo)* such: *no quiero una moto tan grande*, I don't want such a big motorbike; *¡son unos chicos tan malos!*, they are such naughty boys; *¡qué edificio tan raro!*, what a strange building! **2** *(con adjetivos o adverbios)* so: *no comas tan deprisa*, don't eat so quickly; *no me gusta tan dulce*, I don't like it so sweet. **3** *(comparativo)* as ... as: *es tan alto como tú*, he's as tall as you are; *tú lo sabes tan bien como yo*, you know as well as I do. **4** *(consecutivo)* so: *pasó tan deprisa que no lo vi*, he went by so fast that I didn't see him.

● **tan siquiera** even, just.

● **tan sólo** only.

tanda *nf* **1** *(conjunto)* batch, lot: *recibió una tanda de palos*, he got a good thrashing. **2** *(serie)* series, course. **3** *(turno)* shift.

tanque *nm* **1** *(depósito)* tank, reservoir. **2** *(carro de combate)* tank. **3** *(vehículo cisterna)* tanker.

tantear *vt* **1** *(calcular)* to estimate, guess. **2** *(probar - medidas)* to size up; *(- pesos)* to feel *[pt & pp felt]*. **3** *fig (examinar)* to put to the test.

▶ *vi (marcar un tanto)* to score.

● **tantear a ALGN** to sound SB out.

● **tantear el terreno** to see how things stand *[pt saw; pp seen]*.

tanto,-a *adj* **1** *(con incontables)* so much; *(con contables)* so many: *no tomes tanta leche*, don't drink so much milk; *¡ha pasado tanto tiempo!*, it's been so long!; *no comas tantos caramelos*, don't eat so many sweets. **2** *(en comparaciones - incontables)* as much; *(- contables)* as many: *gana tanto dinero como mi hermano*, she's earning as much money as my brother; *tengo tantos libros como tú*, I've got as many books as you. **3** *(en cantidades aproximadas)* odd: *cincuenta y tantas personas*, fifty odd people; *tiene treinta y tantos años*, he's thirty something.

▶ *pron (incontables)* so much; *(contables)* so many: *¿hace mucho frío hoy?* —*No tanto como ayer*, is it very cold today?

—Not so much as yesterday; *no había tantos*, there weren't so many.

▶ *adv* **1** *(cantidad)* so much: *¡te quiero tanto!*, I love you so much! **2** *(tiempo)* so long: *¡esperamos tanto!*, we waited for so long! **3** *(frecuencia)* so often.

▶ *nm* **1** *(punto)* point. **2** *(cantidad imprecisa)* so much, a certain amount. **3** *(poco)* bit: *es un tanto estrecho*, it's a bit narrow.

● **a las tantas** very late.

● **estar al tanto 1** *(saber)* to be informed. **2** *(estar alerta)* to be on the alert.

● **poner a ALGN al tanto** to put SB in the picture.

● **mientras tanto** meanwhile.

● **no es para tanto** it's not that bad.

● **otro tanto** as much again, the same again.

● **por lo tanto** therefore.

● **ser uno de tantos** to be one of many.

● **tanto mejor** so much the better.

● **tanto peor** so much the worse.

● **¡y tanto!** oh, yes!, certainly!

● **tanto por ciento** percentage.

tapa *nf* **1** *(cubierta -de caja, olla)* lid; *(-de tarro)* top. **2** *(de libro)* cover: *un libro de tapa dura*, a book with a hard cover. **3** *(de zapato)* heelplate. **4** *(de comida)* tapa, snack.

tapadera *nf* **1** *(de recipiente)* cover, lid. **2** *(de fraude, organización)* cover, front: *una tapadera de la mafia*, a front for the mafia.

tapar *vt* **1** *(cubrir)* to cover. **2** *(abrigar)* to wrap up. **3** *(cerrar - olla, tarro)* to put the lid; *(- botella)* to put the top on: *tapa la caja de galletas*, put the lid on the biscuit tin; *tapó la botella*, she put the top on the bottle. **4** *(obstruir)* to obstruct; *(tubería)* to block: *tapó las grietas con yeso*, he filled in the cracks with plaster. **5** *(ocultar)* to hide *[pt hid; pp hidden]*; *(vista)* to block.

aquel edificio nos tapa el sol, that building blocks out the sun.

▶ *vpr* **taparse** *(cubrirse)* to cover oneself; *(abrigarse)* to wrap up: *tápate bien, que hace frío*, wrap up well, it's cold.

● **taparse los oídos** to put one's fingers in one's ears.

tapete *nm* table runner.

• **estar sobre el tapete** to be under discussion.

• **poner algo sobre el tapete** to bring STH up [*pt & pp* **brought**].

tapia *nf* **1** *(cerca)* garden wall. **2** *(muro)* wall.

• **estar más sordo,-a que una tapia** to be as deaf as a post.

tapiar *vt (jardín, zona)* to wall in; *(puerta, ventana)* to brick up.

tapicería *nf* **1** *(de muebles, coche)* upholstery. **2** *(tienda)* upholsterer's workshop.

tapicero,-a *nm,f* upholsterer.

tapiz *nm* **1** *(de pared)* tapestry. **2** *(alfombra)* rug, carpet.

tapizar *vt* **1** *(muebles, coche)* to upholster. **2** *(una pared)* to cover.

tapón *nm* **1** *(de goma, vidrio)* stopper; *(de botella)* cap, cork; *(de lavabo, bañera)* plug. **2** *(para el oído)* earplug. **3** *fam (persona)* shorty. **4** *(baloncesto)* block. **5** *(embotellamiento)* traffic jam.

■ **tapón de corcho** cork.

taponar *vt* **1** *(agujero)* to block. **2** *(herida)* to plug.

▶ *vpr* **taponarse** to get blocked.

taquigrafía *nf* shorthand.

taquígrafo,-a *nm,f* shorthand writer.

taquilla *nf* **1** *(de tren etc)* ticket office, booking office; *(de teatro, cine)* box-office. **2** *(recaudación)* takings *pl*. **3** *(en vestuario, colegio)* locker.

taquillero,-a *nm,f* ticket clerk.

▶ *adj* popular.

tarántula *nf* tarantula.

tararear *vt* to hum.

tardanza *nf* delay.

tardar *vt (emplear tiempo)* to take: **tardé tres años**, it took me three years; **he tardado una hora en llegar**, it's taken me an hour to get here.

▶ *vi (demorar)* to take long: **tarda en contestar, quizá no esté en casa**, she's taking a long time to answer, perhaps she's not in; **se tarda más en tren**, it takes longer by train; **¡no tardes!**, don't be long.

• **a más tardar** at the latest.

• **¿cuánto se tarda?** how long does it take?

tarde *nf* **1** *(hasta las seis)* afternoon: **son las 4 de la tarde**, it is 4 o'clock in the afternoon. **2** *(después de las seis)* evening.

▶ *adv (hora avanzada)* late: **se está haciendo tarde**, it's getting late.

• **de tarde en tarde** very rarely, not very often.

• **llegar tarde** to be late.

• **más tarde** later.

• **más tarde o más temprano** sooner or later.

• **¡buenas tardes!** **1** *(más temprano)* good afternoon. **2** *(hacia la noche)* good evening.

tardío,-a *adj* late.

tarea *nf* **1** *(gen)* task, job: **limpiar la casa es tarea de todos**, everyone has to clean the house. **2** *(deberes)* homework: **ésta es la tarea de mañana**, this is the homework for tomorrow.

■ **tareas de la casa** chores, housework *sing*.

■ **tareas escolares** homework *sing*.

tarifa *nf* **1** *(precio)* tariff, rate; *(en transporte)* fare: **¿cuál es la tarifa de las llamadas internacionales?**, what's the rate for international calls?; **hay una tarifa reducida para menores de 14 años**, there's a reduced fare for children under 14. **2** *(lista de precios)* price list.

■ **tarifa reducida** reduced rate, special deal.

■ **tarifa turística** tourist class rate.

tarima *nf* platform.

tarjeta *nf* card.

• **pagar con tarjeta** to pay by credit card.

■ **tarjeta amarilla** yellow card.

■ **tarjeta de crédito** credit card.

■ **tarjeta de embarque** boarding card.

■ **tarjeta de visita** **1** *(personal)* GB visiting card; US calling card. **2** *(profesional)* business card.

■ **tarjeta roja** red card.

■ **tarjeta telefónica** phone card.

■ **tarjeta postal** postcard.

tarro *nm* **1** *(recipiente)* jar, pot. **2** *fam (cabeza)* bonce.

tarta *nf* *(pastel)* cake; *(de hojaldre)* tart, pie.

■ **tarta de cumpleaños** birthday cake.

■ **tarta de manzana** apple tart.

tartamudear *vi* to stutter, stammer.

tartamudo,-a *adj* stuttering, stammering.

▶ *nm,f* stutterer, stammerer.

● **ser tartamudo** to have a stutter, have a stammer.

tartera *nf* **1** *(fiambrera)* lunch box. **2** *(cazuela)* baking tin.

tarugo *nm* **1** *(de madera)* lump of wood. **2** *(de pan)* chunk of stale bread. **3** *fam (persona)* blockhead.

tasa *nf* **1** *(valoración)* valuation, appraisal. **2** *(precio)* fee, charge: *los alumnos pagan las tasas en secretaría*, students pay their fees at the secretary's office. **3** *(impuesto)* tax: *las tasas municipales*, local taxes. **4** *(índice)* rate.

■ **tasa de aeropuerto** airport tax.

■ **tasa de desempleo** unemployment rate.

■ **tasa de natalidad** birth rate.

tasar *vt* **1** *(valorar)* to value, appraise. **2** *(poner precio)* to set the price of [*pt & pp* **set**]. **3** *(gravar)* to tax.

tasca *nf* bar, pub.

tatarabuelo,-a *nm,f (hombre)* great-great-grandfather; *(mujer)* great-great-grandmother.

tataranieto,-a *nm,f (gen)* great-great-grandchild [*pl* **-children**]; *(chico)* great-great-grandson; *(chica)* great-great-granddaughter.

tatuaje *nm* **1** *(dibujo)* tattoo [*pl* **-s**]. **2** *(técnica)* tattooing.

tatuar *vt* to tattoo.

taurino,-a *adj* bullfighting.

Tauro *nm* Taurus: *soy tauro*, I'm Taurus.

taxi *nm* taxi, cab.

taxímetro *nm* taximeter, clock.

taxista *nmf* taxi driver, cab driver.

taza *nf* **1** *(recipiente)* cup: *¿quieres una taza de té?*, would you like a cup of tea? **2** *(contenido)* cupful. **3** *(de retrete)* bowl.

tazón *nm* bowl.

te *pron* **1** *(complemento directo)* you; *(complemento indirecto)* you, for you: *te quiero*, I love you; *no quiero verte*, I don't want to see you; *te compraré uno*, I'll buy one for you, I'll buy you one. **2** *(reflexivo)* yourself: *sírvete*, help yourself; *lávate*, get washed. **3** *(con partes del cuerpo)* your: *te sangra la nariz*, your nose is bleeding.

té *nm* tea: *té con limón*, lemon tea.

teatral *adj* **1** *(dramático)* theatrical, dramatic. **2** *(exagerado)* stagy, theatrical.

teatro *nm* **1** *(sala)* theatre. **2** *(profesión)* acting, stage: *se dedica al teatro*, he's an actor, she's an actress. **3** *(género)* drama. **4** *(exageración)* theatrics.

● **hacer teatro** to play-act.

● **obra de teatro** play.

● **es puro teatro** it's all an act.

tebeo *nm* comic.

techo *nm* **1** *(interior)* ceiling. **2** *(exterior, de coche)* roof [*pl* **-s**]. **3** *(tope)* limit.

● **los sin techo** the homeless.

tecla *nf* key.

● **dar en la tecla** to get it right.

● **tocar muchas teclas** to try to do too many things at once.

teclado *nm* keyboard.

teclear *vi* **1** *(en máquina de escribir)* to type. **2** *(en piano)* to play.

► *vt (al ordenador)* to key in, type in; *(al cajero automático)* to enter.

teclista *nmf (músico)* keyboard player; *(mecanógrafo)* keyboarder.

técnica *nf* **1** *(tecnología)* technics *pl*, technology. **2** *(habilidad)* technique, method.

técnico,-a *adj* technical: *el progreso técnico*, technical progress.

► *nm,f* technician, technical expert.

tecnología *nf* technology: *nuevas tecnologías*, new technologies.

teja *nf (en tejado)* tile.

● **pagar a toca teja** to pay on the nail [*pt & pp* **paid**].

tejado *nm* roof [*pl* **-s**].

tejanos *nm pl* jeans.

tejer *vt* **1** *(en telar)* to weave [*pt* **wove**; *pp* **woven**]: *tejió una alfombra*, she wove a carpet. **2** *(con agujas)* to knit [*pt & pp* **knitted** o **knit**]: *she tejió un jersey de lana*, she knitted a woolen jumper. **3** *(araña)* to spin [*pt & pp* **spun**]. **4** *(plan)* to weave, plot.

tejido *nm* **1** *(tela)* fabric, material: *un tejido sintético*, a synthetic material. **2** *(en anatomía)* tissue.

■ **tejido adiposo** fatty tissue.

■ **tejido de punto** knitted fabric.

■ **tejido muscular** muscle tissue.

■ **tejido óseo** bone tissue.

tejón *nm* badger.

tela *nf* **1** *(tejido)* material, fabric, cloth; *(retal)* piece of material. **2** *fam (dinero)* dough. **3** *(cuadro)* painting.

● **poner en tela de juicio** to question.

● **tener tela** to be tricky.

■ **tela de araña** spider's web.
■ **tela metálica** wire netting.
telar *nm* loom.
telaraña *nf* cobweb, spider's web.
tele *nf fam* telly, TV.
● **ver la tele** to watch telly.
telecomunicaciones *nf pl* telecommunications.
telediario *nm* news.
teleférico *nm* cable car.
telefonazo *nm fam* buzz, ring.
● **darle un telefonazo a ALGN** to give SB a ring.
telefonear *vt-vi* to telephone, phone.
telefónico,-a *adj* telephone.
● **una llamada telefónica** a phone call.
telefonista *nmf* telephone operator.
teléfono *nm* **1** *(aparato)* telephone, phone. **2** *(número)* phone number: *¿cuál es tu teléfono?*, what's your phone number?
● **contestar al teléfono** to answer the phone.
● **estar hablando por teléfono** to be on the phone.
● **llamar a ALGN por teléfono** to phone SB, ring SB [*pt* rang; *pp* rung].
■ **teléfono inalámbrico** cordless telephone.
■ **teléfono móvil** mobile phone.
■ **teléfono público** public phone.
telegráfico,-a *adj* telegraphic.
telégrafo *nm* telegraph.
telegrama *nm* telegram, cable.
● **ponerle a ALGN un telegrama** to send SB a telegram.
telenovela *nf* soap opera.
telepatía *nf* telepathy.
telescopio *nm* telescope.
telesilla *nf* chair lift.
telespectador,-ra *nm,f* viewer.
telesquí *nm* ski lift.
teletexto *nm* Teletext®.
televidente *nmf* viewer.
televisar *vt* to televise.
televisión *nf* **1** *(sistema)* television. **2** *fam (aparato)* television set.
● **ver la televisión** to watch television.
televisivo,-a *adj* television.
televisor *nm* television set.
télex *nm* telex.
telón *nm* curtain.
■ **telón de fondo 1** *(en teatro)* backdrop. **2** *(uso figurado)* background.

tema *nm* **1** *(asunto)* subject: *no me interesa el tema*, I'm not interested in the subject; *es un tema delicado*, it's a delicate subject. **2** song: *cantó todos sus viejos temas*, he sang all his old songs.
● **atenerse al tema** to keep to the point.
● **salirse del tema** to go off at a tangent.
■ **temas de actualidad** current affairs.
temblar *vi* **1** *(de frío)* to shiver; *(de miedo)* to tremble; *(con sacudidas)* to shake [*pt* shook; *pp* shaken]: *estaba temblando de frío*, she was shivering with cold; *estaba temblando de miedo*, he was shaking with fear. **2** *(voz)* to quiver.
temblor *nm* tremor, shudder.
■ **temblor de tierra** earthquake.
tembloroso,-a *adj* **1** *(de frío)* shivering; *(de miedo)* trembling; *(con sacudidas)* shaking. **2** *(voz)* quivering.
temer *vt* to fear, be afraid of: *temían lo peor*, they feared the worst; *temía su reacción*, I was afraid of his reaction.
► *vi (preocuparse)* to worry: *no temas*, don't worry.
► *vi-vpr* **temer(se)** *(tener miedo)* to be afraid: *me temo que tiene razón*, I'm afraid he's right.
temerario,-a *adj* reckless, rash.
temeroso,-a *adj* fearful.
temible *adj* dreadful, fearful, frightening.
temor *nm* fear.
temperamento *nm* temperament, nature.
● **tener temperamento** to be temperamental, have a strong character.
temperatura *nf* temperature: *un ascenso de las temperaturas*, a rise in temperatures.
■ **temperatura ambiente** room teperature.
tempestad *nf* storm.
■ **tempestad de nieve** snowstorm.
templado,-a *adj* **1** *(agua, comida)* lukewarm; *(clima, temperatura)* mild, temperate. **2** *(no exagerado)* moderate. **3** *(metal)* tempered: *nervios bien templados*, steady nerves.
templar *vt* **1** *(algo frío)* to warm up; *(algo caliente)* to cool down. **2** *(apaciguar)* to calm down. **3** *(metal)* to temper.

temple *nm* **1** *(fortaleza)* boldness, courage. **2** *(estado de ánimo)* frame of mind, mood. **3** *(de metal)* temper. **4** *(pintura)* tempera.

● **al temple** in tempera.

templo *nm* temple.

● **como un templo** huge.

temporada *nf* **1** *(en artes, deportes, moda)* season: *la temporada de baloncesto*, the basketball season; *la temporada turística*, the tourist season. **2** *(período)* period, time: *voy a pasar una temporada en casa de mis abuelos*, I'm going to live with my grandparents for a time.

● **en plena temporada** at the height of the season.

● **ir por temporadas** to be on and off.

■ **temporada alta** high season.

■ **temporada baja** low season.

temporal *adj* temporary.

▶ *nm* storm.

temprano,-a *adj* early.

▶ *adv* **temprano** early.

tenaz *adj* **1** *(persona - terco)* tenacious; *(- perseverante)* persevering. **2** *(mancha)* difficult to remove.

tenazas *nf pl* *(herramienta)* pincers; *(para el fuego)* tongs.

tendedero *nm* *(cuerda)* clothesline; *(lugar)* drying place.

tendencia *nf* tendency, inclination.

● **tener tendencia a hacer algo** to tend to do STH, have a tendency to do STH.

tender *vt* **1** *(red)* to cast [*pt & pp* **cast**]; *(puente)* to build [*pt & pp* **built**]; *(vía, cable)* to lay [*pt & pp* **laid**]. **2** *(ropa, colada)* to hang out [*pt & pp* **hung**]: *he tendido la ropa esta mañana*, I hung the washing out this morning. **3** *(mano)* to stretch out, hold out [*pt & pp* **held**]. **4** *(emboscada, trampa)* to lay [*pt & pp* **laid**], set [*pt & pp* **set**].

▶ *vi* to tend: *los precios tienden a subir en invierno*, prices tend to rise in winter.

▶ *vpr* **tenderse 1** *(tumbarse)* to lie down [*pt* **lay**; *pp* **lain**]. **2** *(estirarse)* to stretch out.

● **tender la mano a ALGN** **1** *(para saludar)* to shake's SB's hand [*pt* **shook**; *pp* **shaken**]. **2** *(para ayudar)* to lend SB a hand [*pt & pp* **lent**].

tendero,-a *nm,f* shopkeeper.

tendón *nm* tendon, sinew.

tenebroso,-a *adj* **1** *(sombrío)* dark, gloomy. **2** *(siniestro)* sinister, shady.

tenedor *nm* fork.

tener *vt* **1** *(posesión)* to have, have got: *tenemos un examen*, we've got an exam; *tiene el pelo largo*, she's got long hair; *tenía dolor de cabeza*, I had a headache. **2** *(sostener)* to hold [*pt & pp* **held**]: *lo tienes en la mano*, you're holding it. **3** *(coger)* to take: *ten esto*, take this. **4** *(sensación, sentimiento)* to be, feel [*pt & pp* **felt**]: *tengo calor*, I'm hot; *tengo frío*, I'm cold; *tengo hambre*, I'm hungry; *tengo sed*, I'm thirsty. **5** *(mantener)* to keep. **6** *(contener)* to hold [*pt & pp* **held**], contain. **7** *(edad, tamaño)* to be: *tiene diez años*, he's ten, he's ten years old; *la habitación tiene 4 metros de largo*, the room is 4 meters long. **8** *(celebrar)* to hold [*pt & pp* **held**]: *tener una reunión*, to hold a meeting. **9** *(considerar)* to consider, think [*pt & pp* **thought**]: *me tienen por estúpido*, they think I'm a fool.

▶ *aux* **tener que 1** *(obligación-a otra persona)* to have to. **2** *(-a uno mismo)* must: *tienes que estudiar más*, you have to study more; *tengo que irme*, I must leave.

▶ *vpr* **tenerse 1** *(sostenerse)* to stand up [*pt & pp* **stood**]: *estaba tan cansada que no se tenía en pie*, she was so tired that she couldn't stand up. **2** *(considerarse)* to consider oneself, think oneself [*pt & pp* **thought**]: *se tiene por guapo*, he thinks he's handsome.

● **tener compasión** to take pity.

● **tener ganas de** to feel like [*pt & pp* **felt**].

● **tener ilusión** to be enthusiastic.

● **tener miedo** to be frightened.

● **tenerla tomada con ALGN** to have it in for SB.

● **tenerle cariño a** to be fond of.

● **no tener nada que ver con** to have nothing to do with.

● **no tenerse en pie** to be tired out.

● **¿qué tienes?** what's wrong with you?

teniente *nm* lieutenant.

■ **teniente de alcalde** deputy mayor.

tenis *nm* tennis.

■ **tenis de mesa** table tennis.

tenista *nmf* tennis player.

tenor *nm* *(cantante)* tenor.

● **a tenor de** according to.

tensar *vt* *(cable, cuerda)* to tauten; *(arco)* to draw [*pt* **drew**; *pp* **drawn**].

tensión *nf* **1** *(de cable, cuerda, músculo)* tension. **2** *(eléctrica)* voltage: *cables de alta tensión*, high-tension cables. **3** *(sanguínea)* pressure. **4** *(de situación)* tension: *la gran tensión entre los dos países*, the severe tension between the two countries. **5** *(estrés)* stress, strain: *está sometido a mucha tensión*, he's under a lot of stress.
- **tener la tensión alta** to have high blood pressure.
- **tomarle la tensión a** ALGN to take SB's blood pressure.
- **tensión arterial** blood pressure.
- **tensión nerviosa** nervous tension.

tenso,-a *adj* **1** *(cable, cuerda)* taut. **2** *(persona, músculo)* tense: *estás muy tenso*, you are very tense. **3** *(relaciones)* strained.

tentación *nf* temptation.

tentáculo *nm* tentacle.

tentador,-ra *adj* tempting.

tentar *vt* **1** *(palpar)* to feel [*pt & pp* felt], touch: *se tentó en los bolsillos*, he felt his pockets. **2** *(incitar)* to tempt: *me tentó con un pastel de chocolate*, she tempted me with a chocolate cake. **3** *(atraer)* to attract, appeal.

tentativa *nf* attempt: *tentativa de asesinato*, attempted murder.

tenue *adj* **1** *(velo)* thin, light. **2** *(luz, sonido)* faint.

teñir *vt* to dye: *se ha teñido el pelo de rubio*, he's dyed his hair blond.

teología *nf* theology.

teoría *nf* theory.
- **en teoría** theoretically.

teórico,-a *adj* theoretic.
- *nm,f* theoretician, theorist.

terapia *nf* therapy.
- **terapia de choque** shock therapy.
- **terapia de grupo** group therapy.

tercer *num* → tercero,-a.

tercermundista *adj* third-world.

tercero,-a *num* third: *la tercera vez*, the third time; *en el tercer piso*, on the third floor.
- *nm* **tercero** *(en contrato)* third party.
- **tercera edad** old age.
- **a la tercera va la vencida** third time lucky.

tercio *nm* one third.

terciopelo *nm* velvet.

terco,-a *adj* obstinate, stubborn.

térmico,-a *adj* thermic.

terminal *adj* terminal.
- *nf* **1** INFORM terminal. **2** *(de autobuses)* terminus. **3** *(en aeropuerto)* terminal.

terminante *adj* **1** *(categórico)* categorical. **2** *(dato, resultado)* conclusive, definitive.

terminar *vt-vi* *(acabar)* to finish: *aún no he acabado el libro*, I haven't finished the book yet; *las clases terminan a las cinco*, classes finish at five o'clock.
- *vi* **1** *(ir a parar)* to end up, end: *todo terminó bien*, everything ended up all right; *terminó por irse de casa*, he ended up leaving home; *terminó diciendo que...*, he ended by saying that.... **2** *(eliminar)* to put an end. **3** *(reñir)* to break up [*pt* broke; *pp* broken].
- *vpr* **terminarse** **1** *(finalizar)* to finish, be over: *se ha terminado la reunión*, the meeting is over. **2** *(agotarse)* to run out [*pt* ran; *pp* run]: *se nos ha terminado el papel*, we've run out of paper.
- **terminar con** ALGN to finish with SB.
- **no termina de convencerme** I'm not totally convinced.

término *nm* **1** end, finish: *al término de su contrato*, at the end of his contract. **2** *(estación)* terminus. **3** *(límite)* limit, boundary. **4** *(plazo)* term, time. **5** *(palabra, argumento)* term: *un término científico*, a scientific term.
- **dar término a** to conclude.
- **en otros términos** in other words.
- **en primer término** in the foreground.
- **en términos generales** generally speaking.
- **llevar algo a buen término** to carry STH through.
- **poner término a algo** to put an end to STH.
- **por término medio** on average.
- **término medio** average.
- **término municipal** municipal area.

termita *nf* termite.

termo *nm* thermos flask, thermos.

termómetro *nm* thermometer.

termostato *nm* thermostat.

ternera *nf* veal.

ternero,-a *nm,f* calf [*pl* -ves].

ternura *nf* tenderness.

terquedad *nf* obstinacy, stubbornness.

terrado *nm* flat roof [*pl* -s].

313

terraplén *nm* embankment.

terraza *nf* **1** *(balcón)* terrace. **2** *(azotea)* roof terrace. **3** *(de un café)* : *en la terraza de un bar*, outside a bar.

terremoto *nm* earthquake.

terreno,-a *adj* worldly, earthly.
► *nm* **terreno 1** *(tierra)* piece of land, ground; *(solar)* plot, site: *se ha comprado un terrenito*, he has bought a piece of land; *van a construir en ese terreno*, they are going to build on that land. **2** terrain: *un terreno accidentado*, uneven terrain. **3** *(de cultivo)* soil; *(campo)* field. **4** *(ámbito)* field, sphere: *en el terreno de la literatura*, in the field of literature.
● **estar en su propio terreno** to be on home ground.
● **ganar terreno** to gain ground.
● **perder terreno** to lose ground [*pt & pp* **lost**].
● **saber** ALGN **el terreno que pisa** to know what SB's doing [*pt* **knew**; *pp* **known**].
● **ser terreno abonado para algo** to be receptive to STH.
● **sobre el terreno** on the ground.
■ **terreno de juego** pitch.

terrestre *adj* **1** *(vida, transporte)* land, terrestrial. **2** *(animal, vegetación)* land. **3** *(de la Tierra)* : *la superficie terrestre*, the surface of the Earth.
● **por vía terrestre** overland, by land.

terrible *adj* terrible, awful.

terrícola *nmf* earthling.

territorial *adj* territorial.

territorio *nm* territory.

terrón *nm* lump.
■ **terrón de azúcar** lump of sugar.

terror *nm* terror.
■ **película de terror** horror film.

terrorífico,-a *adj* terrifying, frightening.

terrorismo *nm* terrorism.

terrorista *adj - nmf* terrorist.

terso,-a *adj* **1** *(piel)* smooth. **2** *(estilo)* polished, fluent.

tertulia *nf* gathering.
■ **tertulia literaria** literary gathering.
■ **tertulia televisiva** talk show.

tesis *nf* thesis.

tesorero,-a *nm,f* treasurer.

tesoro *nm* **1** *(cosas de valor)* treasure. **2** *(del Estado)* treasury, exchequer. **3** *(tratamiento)* darling.

test *nm* test.
● **preguntas tipo test** multiple-choice questions.
■ **test de embarazo** pregnancy test.

testamento *nm* will, testament.
● **hacer testamento** to make one's will.
■ **Antiguo Testamento** Old Testament.
■ **Nuevo Testamento** New Testament.

testarudo,-a *adj* obstinate, stubborn, pigheaded.

testículo *nm* testicle.

testificar *vt-vi* to testify.

testigo *nmf* witness: *el testigo tuvo que declarar ante el juez*, the witness had to give evidence before the judge; *un testigo del accidente*, someone who had witnessed the accident.
► *nm* baton: *se le cayó el testigo al corredor*, the runner dropped the baton.
■ **testigo ocular** eyewitness.

testimonio *nm* **1** testimony. **2** *(prueba)* evidence, proof.
● **dar testimonio** to give evidence.
● **falso testimonio** perjury.

teta *nf* **1** *fam (de mujer)* tit. **2** *(de animal)* teat.

tetera *nf* teapot.

tetilla *nf* **1** *(de biberón)* teat. **2** *(de hombre)* nipple.

tetina *nf* teat.

tetrabrik *nm* carton.

textil *adj* textile.

texto *nm* text.

textual *adj* **1** *(del texto)* textual. **2** *(exacto)* literal: *esas son palabras textuales suyas*, those are his exact words.

textura *nf* texture.

tez *nf* complexion.

ti *pron* you: *he traído un regalo para ti*, I've brought a present for you; *depende de ti*, it depends on you.
● **ti mismo** yourself.

tía *nf* **1** *(pariente)* aunt: *la tía Rosa*, Auntie Rosa. **2** *fam (mujer)* girl, woman [*pl* **women**], bird: *sale con una tía guapísima*, he's going out with a gorgeous girl; *oye, tía, ¿de qué vas?*, hey, who do you think you are?
■ **tía abuela** great aunt.

tibia *nf* tibia, shinbone.

tibio,-a *adj* tepid, lukewarm.
● **poner tibio a** ALGN to tear SB off [*pt* **tore**; *pp* **torn**].

tiburón *nm* shark.

tic *nm* tic, twitch.

tiempo *nm* **1** *(período, momento)* time: *no tengo tiempo para salir de compras*, I haven't got time to go out shopping; *en tiempos de mi abuelo*, in my grandfather's time; *¡cuánto tiempo sin verte!*, it's been ages since I saw you. **2** *(meteorológico)* weather: *hizo buen tiempo*, the weather was good. **3** *(edad)* age: *¿qué tiempo tiene su niño?*, how old is your baby? **4** *(temporada)* season. **5** MÚS *(compás)* tempo [*pl* -s], time; *(de sinfonía)* movement. **6** *(parte de partido)* half [*pl* -ves]: *primer tiempo*, first half; *segundo tiempo*, second half. **7** tense: *un tiempo compuesto*, a compound tense.

● **antes de tiempo** early.
● **a su debido tiempo** in due course.
● **a tiempo** in time.
● **al mismo tiempo** at the same time.
● **al poco tiempo** soon afterwards.
● **con tiempo** in advance.
● **¿cuánto tiempo?** how long?
● **del tiempo 1** *(fruta)* in season. **2** *(bebida)* at room temperature.
● **el tiempo es oro** time is money.
● **hacer tiempo** to make time.
● **perder el tiempo** to waste time.
● **¿qué tiempo hace?** what's the weather like?
■ **tiempo libre** spare time.
■ **tiempo muerto** time out.

tienda *nf* **1** GB shop; US store: *una tienda de ropa*, a clothes shop. **2** *(de campaña)* tent.

■ **tienda de comestibles** grocer's.

tierno,-a *adj* **1** *(blando)* tender, soft. **2** *(reciente)* fresh. **3** *(cariñoso)* affectionate.

tierra *nf* **1** *(La Tierra)* the Earth; *(superficie sólida)* land: *trabajar la tierra*, to work the land; *éstas son mis tierras*, this is my land. **2** *(terreno cultivado)* soil, land. **3** *(sustancia)* earth, soil: *un puñado de tierra*, a handful of earth; *es buena tierra*, it's good soil. **4** *(zona de origen)* : *en mi tierra*, where I come from; *es de la tierra*, it's local. **5** *(suelo)* ground: *la tierra está helada*, the ground is frozen; *tropezó y cayó por tierra*, she tripped and fell over. **6** la Tierra *(planeta)* the Earth.

● **tocar tierra 1** (barco) to reach harbour. **2** (avión) to touch down.
● **echar tierra sobre algo** to hush STH up.
● **echar algo por tierra** to ruin STH.
● **tomar tierra** to land.
■ **tierra adentro** inland.
■ **tierra firme** terra firma.
■ **tierra natal** homeland.
■ **tierra prometida** promised land.

tieso,-a *adj* **1** *(rígido)* stiff, rigid. **2** *(erguido)* upright, erect. **3** *fam (engreído)* stiff, starchy.

● **ponerse tieso** to stand up straight.

tiesto *nm* flowerpot.

tifón *nm* typhoon.

tigre *nm* tiger.

tijeras *nf pl* scissors *pl*.

tila *nf* lime-blossom tea.

tilde *nf (acento)* accent; *(de la ñ)* tilde.

timador,-ra *nm,f* swindler.

timar *vt* to swindle: *me han timado 50 euros*, I've been swindled 50 euros.

timbal *nm* kettledrum.

timbrazo *nm* ring.

timbre *nm* **1** *(de la puerta)* bell. **2** *(sello)* stamp.

● **llamar al timbre** to ring the bell [*pt* rang; *pp* rung].

timidez *nf* shyness.

tímido,-a *adj* shy.

timo *nm* swindle, fiddle.

timón *nm (de barco)* rudder.

● **llevar el timón** to be at the helm.

tímpano *nm* eardrum.

tinaja *nf* large earthenware jar.

tinglado *nm* **1** *(cobertizo)* shed. **2** *(tablado)* platform. **3** *(desorden)* mess. **4** *fig (intriga)* intrigue. **5** *(asunto)* business; *(montaje)* set-up, racket.

tinieblas *nf pl* darkness.

tinta *nf* ink.

● **cargar las tintas** to exaggerate.
● **de medias tintas** milk-and-water, wishy washy.
● **saber algo de buena tinta** to have got STH straight from the horse's mouth.
● **sudar tinta** to sweat blood.
■ **tinta china** Indian ink.

tinte *nm* **1** *(colorante)* dye. **2** *(proceso)* dyeing. **3** *(tintorería)* dry-cleaner's. **4** *fig (matiz)* overtone: *con un tinte de ironía*, with ironic overtones.

tintero *nm* inkwell.

tintinear *vi* **1** *(vidrio)* to clink, chink. **2** *(campanillas)* to jingle, tinkle.

tintineo *nm* **1** *(de vidrio)* clink, chink. **2** *(de campanillas)* jingling, ting-a-ling.

tinto,-a *adj (vino)* red.

▶ *nm* **tinto** red wine.

tintorería *nf* dry-cleaner's.

tío *nm* **1** *(pariente)* uncle: *el tío Paco*, Uncle Paco; *vienen mis tíos a comer*, my aunt and uncle are coming to lunch. **2** *fam* guy, GB bloke: *¡qué tío más simpático!*, what a nice guy!; *¿de qué vas, tío?*, who do you think you are?

■ **tío abuelo** great uncle.

tiovivo *nm* merry-go-round, roundabout.

típico,-a *adj* **1** *(característico)* typical: *es típico de ella*, it's típical of her; *las tapas son típicas de España*, tapas are typical in Spain. **2** *(tradicional)* traditional: *el traje típico*, the traditional costume.

tipo *nm* **1** *(clase)* sort, kind: *¿qué tipo de coche quieres?*, what kind of car do you want?; *me gustan los de este tipo*, I like this type. **2** *(de intereses, etc)* rate. **3** *(de hombre)* build, physique; *(de mujer)* figure. **4** *fam (hombre)* fellow, bloke, guy: *es un buen tipo*, he's a nice guy.

● **tener buen tipo** to have a good figure.

● **jugarse el tipo** to risk one's neck.

● **aguantar el tipo** to keep cool, keep calm.

■ **tipo de interés** interest rate.

tira *nf* strip: *una tira de tela*, a strip of cloth.

● **la tira** *fam* a lot, loads *pl*: *tiene la tira de amigos*, he's got a lot of friends; *hace la tira de años*, ages ago.

tirachinas *nm* GB catapult; US slingshot.

tirada *nf* **1** *(impresión)* print run: *una tirada de 1000 ejemplares*, a print run of 1000 copies. **2** *(distancia)* long way: *de mi casa a la tuya hay una buena tirada*, it's a long way from my house to yours. **3** *(jugada)* throw: *en la segunda tirada le salió un seis*, he got a six on the second throw.

● **de una tirada** in one go.

tirado,-a *adj* **1** *(en el suelo)* lying: *el libro estaba tirado en el suelo*, the book was lying on the floor. **2** *fam (precio)* dirt cheap: *encontré un hotel tirado de precio*, I found a hotel that was dirt cheap. **3** *fam (problema, examen)* dead easy: *el examen estuvo tirado*, the exam was dead easy.

● **dejar tirado a** ALGN to leave SB in the lurch.

tirador,-ra *nm,f (persona)* shooter.

▶ *nm* **tirador** *(de puerta)* knob; *(de cajón)* handle; *(cordón)* bell-pull.

tiranía *nf* tyranny.

tirano,-a *nm,f* tyrant.

tirante *adj* **1** *(cable, cuerda)* taut, tight. **2** *(relación, situación)* tense.

▶ *nm pl* **tirantes 1** *(de vestido)* straps. **2** *(de pantalón)* GB braces; US suspenders.

tirar *vt* **1** *(lanzar)* to throw [*pt* threw; *pp* thrown]; *(tiro)* to fire; *(bomba)* to drop; *(beso)* to blow [*pt* blew; *pp* blown]: *me tiró una piedra*, he threw a stone at me; *tírame la pelota*, throw the ball to me. **2** *(dejar caer)* to drop. **3** *(desechar)* to throw away [*pt* threw; *pp* thrown]: *voy a tirar toda esta ropa vieja*, I´m going to throw all these old clothes away; *lo tiré a la papelera*, I threw it in the bin. **4** *(derribar)* to knock down; *(casa, árbol)* to knock down; *(vaso, botella)* to knock over: *los jóvenes tiraron al suelo la escultura*, the youths knocked the sculpture over; *han tirado aquel edificio*, they've knocked that building down; *el viento tiró el árbol*, the wind blew the tree down. **5** *(derramar)* to spill [*pt* & *pp* spilt]. **6** *(imprimir)* to print. **7** *(hacer - foto)* to take; *(- línea, plano)* to draw [*pt* drew; *pp* drawn].

▶ *vi* **1** *(cuerda, puerta)* to pull: *tira de la cadena*, pull the chain. **2** *(estufa, chimenea)* to draw [*pt* drew; *pp* drawn]. **3** *(en juegos)* : *tira tú*, it's your turn, it's your go. **4** *fam (funcionar)* to work, run [*pt* ran; *pp* run]. **5** *fam (durar)* to last. **6** *(tender)* : *tiraba a verde*, it was greenish. **7** *(parecerse)* to take after: *tira más bien a su padre*, he rather takes after his father. **8** *(ir)* to go, turn. **9** *fam (gustar)* to like: *le tiran mucho las motos*, he really likes motorbikes. **10** *(disparar)* to shoot [*pt* & *pp* shot].

▶ *vpr* **tirarse 1** *(lanzarse)* to throw oneself [*pt* threw; *pp* thrown]: *se tiró a la piscina*, she jumped into the swimming pool; *alguien se ha tirado del tren*, someone's jumped off the train. **2** *(tumbarse)* to lie down [*pt* lay; *pp* lain]: *se tiró en el sofá*, he lay down on the sofa. **3** *fam* *(tiempo)* to spend [*pt & pp* **spent**]: **se tiró dos años estudiando**, she spent two years studying. **4** to attract, interest: **no le tira estudiar**, he isn't interested in studying. **5** *arg (fornicar)* to lay [*pt & pp* **laid**].

● **ir tirando 1** *(arreglárselas)* to manage. **2** *(tener buena salud)* to be okay.

● **tirar el dinero** to squander money.

● **tirar una moneda al aire** to toss a coin.

● **tirarse de cabeza** to dive.

■ **tira y afloja** give and take.

tirita® *nf* GB plaster; US Band-aid®.

tiritar *vi* to shiver, shake [*pt* **shook**; *pp* **shaken**].

tiro *nm* **1** *(lanzamiento)* throw. **2** *(disparo, ruido)* shot. **3** *(herida)* bullet wound: **tiene un tiro en la pierna**, he's got a bullet wound in his leg. **4** *(de caballos)* team: **animal de tiro**, draught animal. **5** *(de chimenea)* draught. **6** *(de escaleras)* flight.

● **a tiro 1** (de arma) within range. **2** (a mano) within reach.

● **dar un tiro** to shoot [*pt & pp* **shot**], fire a shot.

● **de tiros largos** all dressed up.

● **estar a tiro** to be within range.

● **salirle el tiro por la culata a** ALGN to backfire on oneself.

● **sentar como un tiro a** ALGN **1** (comida) to not agree with SB. **2** (comentario) to make SB really upset.

● **ni a tiros** *fam* not for love nor money.

■ **tiro al blanco** target shooting.

■ **tiro con arco** archery.

tirón *nm* **1** *(acción)* tug: **el niño le pegó un tirón a la falda de su madre**, the child tugged at his mother's skirt; **le dio un tirón de pelos**, she pulled his hair; **sufrió un tirón en un músculo**, he pulled a muscle. **2** *(robo)* bag-snatching: **le han robado el bolso por el procedimiento del tirón**, her bag was snatched.

● **de un tirón** *fam* in one go.

tirotear *vt* to shoot [*pt & pp* **shot**], snipe at.

tiroteo *nm* shooting.

títere *nm* puppet, marionette.

titubear *vi* **1** *(vacilar)* to hesitate: **respondió sin titubear**, he answered without hesitation. **2** *(tartamudear)* to stammer.

titular *adj* appointed, official.

▶ *nmf* **1** *(en deporte)* first-team player. **2** *(de cuenta, pasaporte)* holder.

▶ *nm (de prensa)* headline.

▶ *vt* to call.

▶ *vpr* **titularse** *(obra, película)* to be called.

título *nm* **1** *(de película, libro)* title: **¿cuál es el título de la película?**, what's the name of the film? **2** *(de texto legal)* heading. **3** *(académico)* degree; *(diploma)* certificate, diploma: **tiene el título de licenciado en biología**, he's got a degree in biology; **tiene el título colgado en la pared**, his certificate is hanging on the wall. **4** *(banca)* bond, security. **5** *(premio)* title: **consiguieron el título de liga**, they won the league title.

▶ *nm pl* **títulos** *(méritos)* qualifications, qualities.

■ **título de propiedad** title deed.

tiza *nf* chalk: **una tiza**, a piece of chalk.

toalla *nf* towel.

● **tirar la toalla** to throw in the towel [*pt* **threw**; *pp* **thrown**].

toallero *nm* towel rail.

tobillo *nm* ankle.

tobogán *nm* slide.

tocadiscos *nm* record player.

tocador *nm* **1** *(mueble)* dressing table. **2** *(habitación)* dressing room, boudoir.

■ **tocador de señoras** powder room.

tocar *vt* **1** *(gen)* to touch: **me tocó la mejilla**, he touched my cheek. **2** *(palpar)* to feel [*pt & pp* **felt**]: **tócalo, mira qué suave**, feel it and see how smooth it is. **3** *(hacer sonar - instrumento, canción)* to play; *(- timbre)* to ring [*pt* **rang**; *pp* **rung**]; *(- bocina)* to blow [*pt* **blew**; *pp* **blown**], honk; *(- campanas)* to strike [*pt & pp* **struck**]: **toca la guitarra**, he plays the guitar; **¿has tocado el timbre?**, have you rung the bell? **4** *(dar en)* to hit [*pt & pp* **hit**]. **5** *(mencionar)* to touch on: **no tocó el tema**, she didn't touch on the subject.

▶ *vi* **1** *(corresponder)* to be one's turn: **¿a quién le toca ahora?**, whose turn is it now?; **te toca lavar los platos**, it's your turn to do the dishes. **2** *(caer en suerte)* to win [*pt & pp* **won**]: **le tocó la lotería**, he won the lottery. **3** *(afectar)* to concern: **en lo que a mí me toca**, as far as I am concerned. **4** *(ser parientes)* to be a relative of, be related: **no me toca nada**, she's not related to me in any way.

▶ *vpr* **tocarse** to touch: **no te lo toques**,

don't touch it; *los cables se tocaban*, the wires were touching.

● **tocar a su fin** to be coming to an end.
● **tocar tierra** to touch ground.

tocayo,-a *nm,f* namesake.

tocinería *nf* pork butcher's.

tocino *nm* **1** *(grasa)* lard. **2** *(carne)* bacon.

todavía *adv* **1** *(tiempo -en frases afirmativas)* still; *(-en frases negativas)* yet: **todavía la quiere**, he still loves her; **todavía no lo quiere**, he doesn't want it yet. **2** *(para reforzar)* even: **esto todavía te gustará más**, you'll enjoy this even more.

todo,-a *adj* **1** *(gen)* all: **toda la familia**, all the family; **todo el día**, all day. **2** *(por completo)* whole: **participó toda la clase**, the whole class took part. **3** *(cada)* every: **todos los lunes**, every Monday; **todos los veranos**, every summer. **4** *(enfático)* quite: **ese premio fue todo un logro**, that prize was quite an achievement.

▶ *pron* **1** todo *(sin exclusión)* all, everything: *lo perdieron todo*, they lost everything; *se lo bebió todo*, he drank it all. **2** todos,-as *(everybody, everyone:* *vinieron todos*, everyone came.

▶ *adv* all: *soy todo oídos*, I'm all ears.
● **ante todo** first of all.
● **con todo** in spite of everything.
● **del todo** completely.
● **después de todo** after all.
● **estar en todo** to be really with it.
● **a toda velocidad** at top speed.
● **todo el mundo** everybody, everyone.
● **todo lo más** at the most.
● **sobre todo** especially.
● **todos nosotros/vosotros/ellos** all of us/you/them.

todopoderoso,-a *adj* almighty, all-powerful.
■ **el Todopoderoso** the Almighty.

todoterreno *nm* all-terrain vehicle.

toga *nf* robe, gown.

toldo *nm* awning.

tolerancia *nf* tolerance.

tolerar *vt* **1** *(consentir)* to tolerate: *no tolera que se llegue tarde al trabajo*, he won't tolerate people being late for work. **2** *(inconvenientes)* to stand [*pt & pp* **stood**]: *no puedo tolerar esta situación*, I can't stand this situation. **3** *(gente)* to put up with: *la tolera porque es su hermana*, she puts up with her because she's her sister. **4** *(comida, bebida)* to take.

toma *nf* **1** *(acción)* taking. **2** *(dosis)* dose. **3** *(captura)* capture. **4** *(grabación)* recording. **5** take: *han repetido la toma*, they have repeated the take.
■ **toma de contacto** initial contact.
■ **toma de corriente** power point.
■ **toma de posesión** takeover.
■ **toma de tierra** GB earth wire; US ground wire.

tomar *vt* **1** *(gen)* to take: *tomó un pastel de la bandeja*, he took a cake from the tray; *las tropas tomaron la ciudad*, the troops took the city; *tomaron el autobús*, they took the bus; *toma, es tuyo*, here, this is yours. **2** *(autobús, tren)* to catch [*pt & pp* **caught**], take. **3** *(comida)* to have, eat [*pt* **ate**; *pp* **eaten**]; *(bebida)* to have, drink [*pt* **drank**; *pp* **drunk**]; *(medicina)* to take: *tomo café y tostadas para desayunar*, I have toast and coffee for breakfast; *tomamos mucha agua*, we drank a lot of water; *¿quieres tomar algo?*, would you like a drink? **4** *(baño, ducha)* to have.

▶ *vpr* **tomarse 1** *(vacaciones, comentario)* to take: *tómate un par de semanas*, take a couple of weeks off; *no te lo tomes así*, don't take it like that. **2** *(comida)* to have, eat [*pt* **ate**; *pp* **eaten**]; *(bebida)* to have, drink [*pt* **drank**; *pp* **drunk**]; *(medicina)* to take.

● **tomar apuntes** to take notes.
● **tomar la palabra** to speak [*pt* **spoke**; *pp* **spoken**].
● **tomar tierra** to land.
● **tomarla con** ALGN to have it in for SB.
● **tomarle el pelo a** ALGN to pull SB's leg.
● **tomar el sol** to sunbathe.
● **tomar el fresco** to get some fresh air.
● **tomar por** to take for: *¿me tomas por tonta?*, do you take me for a fool?
● **¡toma ya!** look at that!

tomate *nm* **1** *(verdura)* tomato [*pl* **-es**]. **2** *fam (jaleo)* fuss, commotion. **3** *fam (dificultad)* snag, catch.
● **ponerse como un tomate** to go as red as a beetroot.

tómbola *nf* tombola.

tomillo *nm* thyme.

tomo *nm* volume.

ton.
● **sin ton ni son** without rhyme or reason.

tonalidad *nf* tonality.

tonel *nm* barrel, cask.

● **como un tonel** *fam* as fat as a pig.

tonelada *nf* ton.

tónica *nf* **1** *(bebida)* tonic. **2** *(tendencia)* tendency, trend.

tónico,-a *adj* tonic.

▶ *nm* **tónico** tonic.

tono *nm* **1** *(de sonido, voz)* tone: *siempre habla en el mismo tono de voz*, he always speaks in the same tone of voice; *no me gustó el tono de su nota*, I didn't like the tone of her note. **2** MÚS key, pitch. **3** *(de color)* shade: *me gustan los tonos claros*, I like light shades.

● **a tono con** in tune with, in harmony with.

● **bajar el tono** to lower one's voice.

● **subir el tono** to speak louder [*pt* spoke; *pp* spoken].

● **fuera de tono** inappropriate, out of place.

● **ponerse a tono** to perk oneself up.

tontear *vi* **1** *(decir tonterías)* to act the clown, fool about. **2** *(galantear)* to flirt.

tontería *nf* **1** *(dicho, hecho)* silly thing, stupid thing: *¡qué tontería!*, how silly!; *¡vaya tontería de pregunta!*, what a silly question!; *es una tontería que te vayas ahora*, it's silly for you to go now. **2** *(insignificancia)* little thing: *he comprado unas tonterías*, I've bought a couple of little things; *no te enfades por esa tontería*, don't get angry over a little thing like that.

● **decir tonterías** to talk nonsense.

● **dejarse de tonterías** to be serious.

tonto,-a *adj* silly: *¡no seas tonto!*, don't be silly!; *¡qué fallo más tonto!*, what a stupid mistake!

▶ *nm,f* fool, idiot.

● **hacer el/la tonto,-a** to act the fool.

● **hacerse el/la tonto,-a** to play dumb.

toparse *vpr* **1** *(con alguien)* to bump into, run into [*pt* ran; *pp* run]. **2** *(con algo)* to come across.

tope *adj* top, maximum.

▶ *nm* **1** *(límite)* limit, end: *llegó al tope de su paciencia*, he reached the limit of his patience. **2** *(objeto)* stop: *el tope de la puerta*, the doorstop.

▶ *adv fam* incredibly.

● **a tope 1** *fam* (lleno) packed. **2** (al máximo) flat out: *la sala estaba a tope*, the hall was packed; *Roberto trabaja a tope*, Roberto works flat out.

● **estar hasta los topes** *fam* to be bursting at the seams.

tópico,-a *adj* MED external.

▶ *nm* **tópico** commonplace, cliché.

● **de uso tópico** for external use.

topo *nm* mole.

topónimo *nm* place name.

toque *nm* **1** *(detalle)* touch: *le falta el toque final*, it just needs the finishing touch. **2** *(golpe)* tap: *un toque en el hombro*, a tap on the shoulder; *le dieron un toque a su coche*, someone bumped into his car. **3** *(de campanas)* ringing; *(de timbre)* ring: *te daré un toque*, I'll give you a ring. **4** *(advertencia)* warning: *me dio un toque para que no cogiera sus cosas*, he warned me not to touch his things.

■ **toque de queda** curfew.

toquilla *nf* shawl.

tórax *nm* thorax.

torbellino *nm* whirlwind.

torcedura *nf* sprain.

torcer *vt* **1** *(cuerda, brazo)* to twist: *me torció el brazo*, he twisted my arm. **2** *(doblar)* to bend [*pt & pp* bent]: *el viento tuerce las ramas de los árboles*, the wind bends the branches of the trees. **3** *(inclinar)* to slant.

▶ *vi (girar)* to turn: *tuerce a la derecha*, turn right.

▶ *vpr* **torcerse 1** to sprain: *se torció el tobillo*, she sprained her ankle. **2** *(plan)* to fall through [*pt* fell; *pp* fallen].

● **torcer el gesto** to pull a face.

● **torcer la esquina** to turn the corner.

torcido ,-a *adj (línea, nariz)* crooked. **2** *(cuadro, corbata)* not straight: *el cuadro está torcido*, the picture is not straight. **3** *(alambre, tubería)* bent. **4** *(mente)* twisted.

tordo *nm (pájaro)* thrush.

torear *vt-vi (toro)* to fight [*pt & pp* fought].

▶ *vt (persona)* to tease, confuse.

toreo *nm* bullfighting.

torero,-a *nm,f* bullfighter.

tormenta *nf* storm.

■ **tormenta de arena** sandstorm.

■ **tormenta de nieve** snowstorm.

tormento *nm* **1** *(tortura)* torture. **2** *(dolor)* torment, pain.

tormentoso,-a *adj* stormy.

tornado *nm* tornado [*pl* -s].

torneo *nm* tournament.

tornillo *nm* screw: *le falta un tornillo*, he has a screw loose.

torniquete *nm* **1** *(aspa giratoria)* turnstile. **2** MED tourniquet.

torno *nm* *(de carpintero)* lathe; *(de alfarero)* potter's wheel.

● **en torno a 1** (alrededor de) around. **2** (acerca de) about, concerning.

toro *nm* bull.

● **coger el toro por los cuernos** to take the bull by the horns.

● **ir a los toros** to go to a bullfight.

■ **toro bravo** fighting bull.

torpe *adj* **1** *(patoso)* clumsy: *soy muy torpe en la cocina*, I'm very clumsy in the kitchen. **2** *(tonto)* slow: *es torpe en mates*, he's slow at maths.

torpedo *nm* torpedo [*pl* -es].

torpeza *nf* **1** *(falta de habilidad)* clumsiness. **2** *(falta de inteligencia)* slowness.

● **cometer una torpeza** to make a blunder.

torre *nf* **1** *(de edificio)* tower. **2** *(de ajedrez)* rook, castle.

■ **torre de control** control tower.

torrencial *adj* torrential.

torrente *nm* torrent.

torrija *nf* French toast.

torso *nm* torso [*pl* -s].

torta *nf* **1** *(dulce)* cake. **2** *fam (bofetón)* slap: *me dio una torta*, he slapped my face. **3** *fam (golpe)* thump.

● **ni torta** not a thing: *sin gafas no veo ni torta*, I can't see a thing without glasses.

● **pegarse una torta** to give oneself a bump.

tortazo *nm* **1** *(bofetón)* slap. **2** *(golpe)* thump.

tortícolis *nf* stiff neck: *tenía tortícolis*, I had a stiff neck.

tortilla *nf (de huevos)* omelette.

■ **tortilla de patatas** Spanish omelette.

■ **tortilla francesa** plain omelette.

tórtola *nf* dove.

tortuga *nf* **1** *(de tierra)* GB tortoise; US turtle. **2** *(marina)* turtle.

tortura *nf* torture.

torturar *vt* to torture.

► *vpr* **torturarse** to torture oneself.

tos *nf* cough: *tiene tos*, he's got a cough.

■ **tos ferina** whooping cough.

tosco,-a *adj* rough, coarse.

toser *vi* to cough.

tostada *nf* piece of toast: *una tostada*, a piece of toast; *unas tostadas*, some toast.

tostado,-a *adj* **1** *(pan)* toasted; *(café)* roasted. **2** *(moreno)* tanned. **3** *(color)* brown.

tostador *nm* toaster.

tostadora *nf* toaster.

tostar *vt* **1** *(pan)* to toast; *(café)* to roast. **2** *(piel)* to tan.

► *vpr* **tostarse** to get brown, get tanned.

tostón *nm fam* bore, drag: *madrugar es un tostón*, getting up early is a pain.

total *adj - nm* total: *el coste total del proyecto*, the total cost of the project; *un cambio total*, a complete change.

► *adv* so: *total, ¿que no piensas venir?*, so, you're not coming, then?

totalidad *nf* whole, totality.

tóxico,-a *adj* toxic.

► *nm* **tóxico** poison.

toxicómano,-a *adj, nm,f* drug addict.

tozudo,-a *adj* stubborn.

trabajador,-ra *adj* hard-working.

► *nm,f* worker.

trabajar *vi* to work: *trabaja de camarero*, he works as a waiter; *trabaja mucho*, she works hard; *¿de qué trabajas?*, what do you do?

► *vt (tierra, madera, metal)* to work; *(masa)* to knead.

► *vpr* **trabajarse** *(persona, asunto)* to work on.

trabajo *nm* **1** *(gen)* work: *me gusta el trabajo de oficina*, I like office work; *va al trabajo en coche*, she goes to work by car; *me costó mucho trabajo repararlo*, it was hard work mending it. **2** *(tarea)* task, job. **3** *(empleo)* job: *encontró un trabajo de secretaria*, she found a job as a secretary. **4** essay, project: *hice un trabajo sobre la Guerra Civil*, I did a project on the Civil War.

● **estar sin trabajo** to be unemployed.

■ **trabajo a destajo** piecework.

■ **trabajos forzados** hard labour *sing*.

■ **trabajos manuales** handicrafts.

trabajoso,-a *adj* laborious.

trabalenguas *nm* tongue twister.

trabar *vt* **1** *(unir)* to join. **2** *(amistad, con-*

versación) to strike up [pt & pp **struck**]. **3** (líquido, salsa) to thicken.

▶ vpr **trabarse** (mecanismo) to jam.

● **trabársele la lengua a** ALGN to get tongue-tied.

tracción nf traction.

■ **tracción delantera** front-wheel drive.

■ **tracción trasera** rear-wheel drive.

tractor nm tractor.

tradición nf tradition.

tradicional adj traditional.

traducción nf translation.

■ **traducción automática** machine translation.

■ **traducción simultánea** simultaneous translation.

traducir vt to translate: **lo tradujo al inglés**, she translated it into English.

traductor,-ra nm,f translator.

traer vt **1** (trasladar) to bring [pt & pp **brought**]: ¿**me traes ese libro?**, can you bring me that book?; **mi tío me trajo un regalo de Francia**, my uncle brought me a present from France; **te traerá buena suerte**, it will bring you good luck. **2** (contener) to have: **el periódico trae un reportaje muy interesante**, there's a very interesting article in the newspaper. **3** (causar) to bring about [pt & pp **brought**]: **las lluvias torrenciales traen inundaciones**, torrential rain causes flooding. **4** (vestir) to wear [pt **wore**; pp **worn**]: **traía unas botas nuevas**, she was wearing new boots.

▶ vpr **traerse** to bring [pt & pp **brought**]: **tráete el bañador**, bring your swimming costume.

● **traerse algo entre manos** to be busy with STH.

● **me trae sin cuidado** I couldn't care less.

● **traérselas** fam to be really difficult: **el problema parece fácil, pero se las trae**, the problem looks easy, but it's difficult.

traficante nmf dealer, trafficker.

■ **traficante de armas** arm dealer.

■ **traficante de drogas** drug dealer, drug trafficker.

traficar vi to deal [pt & pp **dealt**], traffic .

tráfico nm traffic.

■ **tráfico aéreo** air traffic.

■ **tráfico de drogas** drug trafficking, drug dealing.

tragaperras nf (**máquina**) **tragaperras** slot machine.

tragar vt-vpr **tragar(se)** **1** (comida, medicina) to swallow. **2** (creer) to fall for it [pt **fell**; pp **fallen**]: **le dije que me iba a China y se lo tragó**, I told her I was going to China and she fell for it.

▶ vt fam (situación, persona) to put up with.

● **tragarse una película** to sit through a film.

tragedia nf tragedy.

trágico,-a adj tragic.

trago nm **1** (sorbo) swig. **2** (bebida) drink.

● **echar un trago** to have a drink.

● **pasar un mal trago** to have a bad time of it.

tragón,-ona adj greedy.

▶ nm,f glutton.

traición nf **1** (deslealtad) betrayal. **2** (delito) treason.

traicionar vt to betray.

traicionero,-a adj treacherous.

traidor,-ra adj treacherous.

▶ nm,f traitor.

tráiler nm **1** (película) trailer. **2** (vehículo) GB articulated lorry ; US trailer truck.

traje nm **1** (de hombre) suit. **2** (de mujer) dress.

■ **traje de baño** bathing suit, bathing costume.

■ **traje de etiqueta** evening dress.

■ **traje de luces** bullfighter's costume.

■ **traje espacial** spacesuit.

trajín nm fam comings and goings pl: **con tanto trajín**, with all the comings and goings.

trajinar vi fam (moverse) bustle about.

trama nf **1** (textil) weft, woof. **2** (argumento) plot.

tramar vt **1** (tejidos) to weave [pt **wove**; pp **woven**]. **2** (preparar) to plot: **estarán tramando algo**, they must be up to something.

tramitar vt (pasaporte, permiso) to process; (crédito) to negotiate.

trámite nm **1** (paso) step. **2** (negociación) procedures pl. **3** (formalismo) formality: **es puro trámite**, it's purely a formality.

tramo nm **1** (de carretera) stretch, section. **2** (de escalera) flight.

trampa nf **1** (para cazar) trap. **2** (trampilla) trapdoor. **3** (engaño) trap, trick.

- **caer en la trampa** to fall into the trap [*pt* **fell**; *pp* **fallen**].
- **hacer trampas** to cheat.
- **tenderle una trampa a** ALGN to set a trap for SB [*pt & pp* **set**].

trampolín *nm* **1** (*de piscina*) springboard, diving board. **2** (*de esquí*) ski jump.

tramposo,-a *adj* tricky.
► *nm,f* cheat.

tranca *nf* **1** (*palo*) club, truncheon. **2** (*para puerta, ventana*) bar.
- **a trancas y barrancas** with great difficulty.

tranquilidad *nf* **1** (*paz*) quiet, piece: *me gusta el campo por la tranquilidad*, I like the countryside because of the peace. **2** (*calma*) calm: *solucionó el problema con mucha tranquilidad*, she solved the problem very calmly; *léelo con tranquilidad*, read it at your leisure.

tranquilizante *nm* tranquillizer.

tranquilizar *vt-vpr* **tranquilizar(se)** (*alguien nervioso*) to calm down; (*alguien preocupado*) to set one's mind at rest [*pt & pp* **set**]: *la música lo tranquiliza*, music calms him down; *llama a tu madre para que se tranquilice*, phone your mother to set her mind at rest.

tranquilo,-a *adj* **1** (*persona, voz, mar*) calm. **2** (*lugar, momento*) quiet, peaceful.
- **dejar a** ALGN **tranquilo** to leave SB alone [*pt & pp* **left**].
- **¡tranquilo!** **1** (*cálmate*) take it easy! **2** (*no te preocupes*) don't worry!

transatlántico,-a *adj* transatlantic.
► *nm* **transatlántico** liner.

transbordador *nm* ferry.
■ **transbordador espacial** space shuttle.

transbordo *nm* (*de pasajeros*) change; (*de equipajes*) transfer.
- **hacer transbordo** to change.

transcurrir *vi* to pass, elapse.

transeúnte *nmf* passer-by [*pl* **passers-by**].

transferencia *nf* transfer.

transferir *vt* to transfer.

transformación *nf* transformation.

transformador *nm* transformer.

transformar *vt* to transform, change: *el mago transformó el bastón en una paloma*, the magician changed the cane into a dove; *la enfermedad transformó su forma de vida*, the illness changed his way of life.

► *vpr* **transformarse** to change.
- **transformar un penalti** to convert a penalty.

transfusión *nf* transfusion.

transición *nf* transition.

transistor *nm* transistor.

transitar *vi* to go, walk.

transitivo,-a *adj* transitive.

tránsito *nm* **1** (*tráfico*) traffic. **2** (*acción*) passage, transit.

transmisión *nf* **1** (*gen*) transmission. **2** (*de radio etc*) broadcast.

transmisor,-ra *adj* transmitting.
► *nm,f* transmitter.

transmitir *vt* **1** (*gen*) to transmit: *las ratas transmiten enfermedades*, rats transmit diseases. **2** to broadcast [*pt & pp* **broadcast**]: *veré el partido que transmiten por la tele*, I'm watching the match on TV.

transparencia *nf* **1** (*de agua, cristal, información*) transparency. **2** (*diapositiva*) slide.

transparentarse *vpr* **1** (*blusa, etc*) to be see-through. **2** (*ropa interior*) to show through [*pt* **showed**; *pp* **shown**].

transparente *adj* **1** (*gen*) transparent. **2** (*blusa, vestido*) see-through.

transpiración *nf* perspiration.

transpirar *vi* to perspire.

transportar *vt* (*gen*) to transport; (*en barco*) to ship: *el camión que transportaba la mercancía*, the lorry transporting the goods; *los autobuses que transportaban a todos los pasajeros*, the buses carrying all the passengers.

transporte *nm* transport.
■ **transporte público** GB public transport; US public transportation.

transportista *nmf* haulier.

tranvía *nm* GB tram; US streetcar.

trapecio *nm* **1** (*de circo, gimnasia*) trapeze. **2** (*en geometría*) trapezium.

trapecista *nmf* trapeze artist.

trapero *nm* rag-and-bone man.

trapo *nm* **1** (*tela vieja*) rag. **2** (*paño*) cloth.
► *nm pl* **trapos** clothes.
- **a todo trapo 1** (*barco*) at full sail. **2** (*persona*) flat out. **3** (*música*) full blast: *iba a todo trapo*, he was going flat out.
■ **trapo de cocina** tea towel.
■ **trapo del polvo** duster.

tráquea *nf* trachea.

tras *prep* **1** *(después de)* after: **tras una larga espera**, after a long wait; **día tras día**, day after day. **2** *(detrás de)* behind: **se escondió tras la puerta**, she hid behind the door.

trascendencia *nf* **1** *(importancia)* significance. **2** *(en filosofía)* transcendence.

trascendental *adj* **1** *(importante)* significant. **2** *(filosofía)* transcendent.

trasero,-a *adj* back, rear.
▶ *nm* **trasero** *fam* bottom, bum: **te voy a dar un azote en el trasero**, I´m going to smack your bottom.

trasladar *vt* **1** *(desplazar)* to move: **su familia se trasladó a Burgos**, his family moved to Burgos. **2** *(de cargo etc)* to transfer: **lo han trasladado a otra sucursal**, he's been transferred to another branch. **3** *(aplazar)* to postpone, adjourn.
▶ *vpr* **trasladarse 1** *(persona)* to go: **nos trasladamos a la habitación**, we went to the room. **2** *(mudarse)* to move.

traslado *nm* **1** *(mudanza)* move: **¿me ayudas con el traslado de los muebles?**, can you help me move the furniture? **2** *(de cargo)* transfer: **ha pedido el traslado**, he's asked for a transfer.

trasluz *nm* diffused light.
● **mirar algo al trasluz** to hold STH against the light [*pt & pp* **held**].

trasnochador,-ra *nm,f* night bird.

trasnochar *vi* to stay up late.

traspasar *vt* **1** *(atravesar)* to go through, pierce. **2** *(cruzar - calle)* to cross over; *(- puerta)* to pass through. **3** *(negocio, jugador)* to transfer.
● **"Se traspasa"** "For sale".

traspaso *nm* **1** *(de negocio)* sale. **2** *(de jugador, competencias)* transfer. **3** *(precio)* take-over fee.

trasplantar *vt* to transplant.

trasplante *nm* transplant.

trastada *nf* dirty trick.
● **hacerle una trastada a** ALGN to play a dirty trick on SB.

trastero *nm* lumber room.

trasto *nm* **1** *(cosa)* piece of junk. **2** *(persona)* useless idiot.
▶ *nm pl* **trastos** *(utensilios)* tackle *sing*.
● **tirarse los trastos a la cabeza** to have a flaming row.

trastornar *vt* **1** *(revolver)* to upset [*pt & pp* **upset**], turn upside down: **la huelga de trenes ha trastornado mis planes**, the train strike has upset my plans. **2** *(enloquecer)* to drive crazy [*pt* **drove**; *pp* **driven**]: **tantos problemas la han trastornado**, so many problems have driven her mad.
▶ *vpr* **trastornarse** to go mad.

trastorno *nm* **1** disruption; *(molestia)* inconvenience. **2** disorder: **trastorno de personalidad**, personality disorder.

tratado *nm* **1** *(pacto)* treaty. **2** *(estudio)* treatise.

tratamiento *nm* **1** *(gen)* treatment: **un tratamiento a base de vitaminas**, a course of vitamins. **2** *(título)* title, form of address.
■ **tratamiento de textos** word processing.

tratar *vt* **1** *(gen)* to treat: **me trataron muy bien**, they treated me very well; **la trataron con antibióticos**, she was treated with antibiotics. **2** *(asunto)* to discuss, deal with [*pt & pp* **dealt**]: **se reunieron para tratar el problema**, they met to discuss the problem. **3** *(tener relación)* to deal with [*pt & pp* **dealt**]: **trata con muchos artistas**, he deals with a lot of artists. **4** INFORM to process.
▶ *vi* **1** *(relacionarse)* to be acquainted: **he tratado más con la hermana**, I'm more acquainted with her sister. **2** *(tener tratos)* to deal [*pt & pp* **dealt**].
▶ *vpr* **tratarse 1** *(ser cuestión)* to be about: **se trata de una prima mía**, it's about a cousin of mine; **tengo un problema —¿de qué se trata?**, I have a problem -what is it?; **sólo se trata de hablar con él**, it's just a matter of talking to him; **tratándose de ti...**, seeing as it's you.... **2** *(tener relación)* to be friendly with: **no se trata con sus vecinos**, he doesn't have any dealings with his neighbours.
● **tratar de 1** *(intentar)* to try to: **trataré de ser puntual**, I´ll try to be punctual. **2** *(dirigirse a)* to address as: **nos tratamos de usted**, we address each other as "usted". **3** *(versar)* to be about: **la película trata de vampiros**, the film is about vampires.

trato *nm* **1** *(de personas)* manner, treatment: **le da muy buen trato al perro**, he treats the dog very well; **tener un trato agradable**, to have a pleasant manner. **2** *(contacto)* contact: **no tengo mucho trato con él**, I haven't got much contact with him. **3** *(acuerdo)* agreement: **han llegado a un trato**, they've reached an agreement. **4** *(comercial)* deal.

● **cerrar un trato** to close a deal.
● **¡trato hecho!** it's a deal!
■ **malos tratos** ill-treatment *sing.*
■ **trato diario** daily contact.

trauma *nm* trauma.

través *nm* .

● **a través de 1** (mediante) through: **a través de la multitud**, through the crowd; **conseguí el trabajo a través de un amigo**, I got the job through a friend. **2** (de un lado a otro) across: **colocaron un tronco a través del arroyo**, they put a log across the stream.

travesía *nf* **1** *(viaje)* voyage, crossing. **2** *(calle)* street. **3** *(distancia)* distance.

travesti *nmf* transvestite.

travesura *nf* mischief, prank.

● **hacer travesuras** to get into mischief.

travieso,-a *adj* mischievous, naughty.

trayecto *nm* **1** *(distancia)* distance, way. **2** *(recorrido)* route: **¿qué trayecto hace el número 4?**, which route does the number 4 take?; **el autobús cubría el trayecto Madrid-Burgos**, the bus was doing the Madrid-Burgos run. **3** *(viaje)* journey: **el trayecto entre Barcelona y Mallorca**, the journey between Barcelona and Majorca.

trayectoria *nf* **1** *(recorrido)* trajectory. **2** *(evolución)* line, course.

■ **trayectoria profesional** career.

trazar *vi* **1** *(línea)* to draw [*pt* **drew**; *pp* **drawn**], trace. **2** *(edificio)* to plan, design. **3** *(frontera)* to mark out.

trazo *nm* **1** *(línea)* line. **2** *(de letra)* stroke.

trébol *nm* **1** *(hierba)* clover. **2** *(naipes)* club.

trece *num* thirteen; *(en fechas)* thirteenth.

trecho *nm* **1** *(distancia)* distance, way: **desde aquí hasta el pueblo hay un buen trecho**, it's a long way from here to the village. **2** *(tramo)* stretch.

tregua *nf* **1** MIL truce. **2** *(descanso)* respite, rest.

treinta *num* thirty; *(en fechas)* thirtieth.

tremendo,-a *adj* **1** *(terrible)* terrible, dreadful: **un crimen tremendo**, a terrible murder. **2** *(muy grande)* tremendous: **una cantidad tremenda**, a tremendous quantity; **tengo unas ganas tremendas de irme**, I'm really looking forward to leaving; **hace un frío tremendo**, it's absolutely freezing.

tren *nm* **1** *(ferrocarril)* train: **fuimos en tren**, we went by train; **perdimos el tren**, we missed the train. **2** *(ritmo)* speed, pace: **a este tren no llegaremos**, we won't get there at this speed.

● **vivir a todo tren** to lead a grand life [*pt & pp* **led**].
● **estar como un tren** to be gorgeous.
■ **tren correo** mail train.
■ **tren de alta velocidad** high-speed train.
■ **tren de cercanías** suburban train.
■ **tren de aterrizaje** undercarriage.
■ **tren de lavado** car wash.
■ **tren directo** through train.

trenza *nf* *(de pelo)* GB plait; US braid.

trenzar *vt* *(pelo)* GB to plait; US to braid.

trepador,-ra *adj* *(planta)* climbing.
► *nm,f fam* go-getter, social climber.

trepar *vt-vi* to climb.

tres *num* three; *(en fechas)* third.

● **no ver tres en un burro** to be as blind as a bat.
■ **tres en raya** noughts and crosses.

trescientos,-as *num* three hundred.

tresillo *nm* three-piece suite.

treta *nf* ruse.

triangular *adj* triangular.

triángulo *nm* triangle.

tribu *nf* tribe.

tribuna *nf* **1** *(plataforma)* platform, rostrum. **2** stand: **dos entradas de tribuna**, two tickets in the stand.

■ **tribuna de prensa** press box.

tribunal *nm* **1** *(gen)* court. **2** *(de examen)* board of examiners.

■ **Tribunal Supremo** Supreme Court.

triciclo *nm* tricycle.

trigal *nm* wheat field.

trigésimo,-a *num* thirtieth.

trigo *nm* wheat.

trillar *vt* to thresh.

trillizo,-a *nm,f* triplet.

trimestral *adj* quarterly, three-monthly.

trimestre *nm* **1** *(académico)* term. **2** *(tres meses)* quarter.

trinar *vi* to warble.

● **está que trina** *fam* she's hopping mad, she's fuming.

trinchar *vt* to carve.

trinchera *nf* trench.

trineo *nm (de perros)* sleigh; *(para jugar)* sledge.

trino *nm* trill.

trío *nm* trio [*pl* **-s**].

tripa *nf* **1** *(intestino)* gut, intestine. **2** *(estómago)* stomach. **3** *(panza)* belly.

triple *adj - nm* triple.

● **el triple** three times: **gano el triple que él**, I earn three times as much as him.

● **triple salto** triple jump.

triplicado *nm* triplicate.

● **por triplicado** in triplicate.

triplicar *vt* to triple, treble.

trípode *nm* tripod.

tripulación *nf* crew.

tripulante *nmf* crew member.

tripular *vt* to man.

triste *adj* **1** *(infeliz-persona, noticia, momento)* sad, unhappy; *(-futuro)* bleak. **2** *(sin vida)* gloomy, dismal: **una casa triste y oscura**, a dark, gloomy house. **3** *(insignificante)* poor, humble.

● **hacer un triste papel** to cut a sorry figure [*pt & pp* **cut**].

tristeza *nf* sadness.

▶ *nf pl* **tristezas** problems, sufferings.

triturar *vt* **1** *(moler-ajo, verdura)* to crush; *(-mineral)* to grind [*pt & pp* **ground**]; *(-papel)* to shred. **2** *(persona-físicamente)* to beat [*pt* **beat**; *pp* **beaten**]; *(-moralmente)* to tear apart [*pt* **tore**; *pp* **torn**].

triunfador,-ra *adj* winning.

▶ *nm,f* winner.

triunfal *adj* triumphant.

triunfar *vi* **1** *(tener éxito)* to succeed: **ha triunfado como escritor**, he's succeeded as a writer; **el jugador espera triunfar en su nuevo club**, the player hopes to do well at his new club. **2** *(ganar)* to win [*pt & pp* **won**]: **los atletas españoles han triunfado en varias pruebas**, the Spanish athletes have won several events. **3** *(prevalecer)* to triumph: **el bien siempre triunfa sobre el mal**, good always triumphs over evil.

● **triunfar en la vida** to succeed in life.

triunfo *nm* **1** *(victoria)* triumph, victory; *(en deportes)* win. **2** *(éxito)* success. **3** *(naipes)* trump.

trivial *adj* trivial, petty.

trocear *vt* to cut up [*pt & pp* **cut**].

trofeo *nm* trophy.

trola *nf fam* lie, fib.

tromba *nf* waterspout.

■ **tromba de agua** violent downpour.

trombón *nm (instrumento)* trombone.

▶ *nmf (músico)* trombonist.

trompa *nf* **1** *(instrumento)* horn. **2** *(de elefante)* trunk. **3** *(de insecto)* proboscis.

● **agarrar una trompa** to get plastered.

trompazo *nm fam* bump.

● **darse un trompazo contra algo** to bang into STH.

trompeta *nf (instrumento)* trumpet.

▶ *nmf (músico)* trumpet player.

trompetista *nmf* trumpet player.

trompicón *nm* **1** *(tropezón)* trip, stumble. **2** *(golpe)* blow, hit.

● **a trompicones** in fits and starts.

tronar *vi* to thunder.

tronchar *vt* to snap.

● **troncharse de risa** to split one's sides laughing [*pt & pp* **split**].

tronco *nm* **1** *(torso)* trunk, torso [*pl* **-s**]. **2** *(tallo de árbol)* trunk; *(leño)* log. **3** *(linaje)* family stock. **4** *arg (compañero)* mate, pal, chum.

● **dormir como un tronco** to sleep like a log [*pt & pp* **slept**].

trono *nm* throne.

tropa *nf* troops *pl*, soldiers *pl*.

tropezar *vi* **1** *(tropicar)* to trip: **tropecé y me caí**, I tripped over; **he tropezado con el bordillo**, I've tripped over the kerb. **2** *(reñir)* to disagree.

▶ *vpr* **tropezarse** to bump into: **me tropecé con tu hermano**, I bumped into your brother.

● **tropezar con 1** *(persona)* to bump into. **2** *(cosa)* to come across. **3** *(dificultad)* to come up against: **el proyecto tropezó con dificultades**, the project ran into difficulties.

tropezón *nm* **1** *(traspié)* trip, stumble. **2** *(error)* slip-up [*pl* **slip-ups**]. **3** *fam (de comida)* piece of food.

● **dar un tropezón** to trip.

tropical *adj* tropical.

trópico *nm* tropic.

tropiezo *nm* **1** *(obstáculo)* trip. **2** *(revés)* setback, mishap.

trotar *vi* to trot.

trote *nm* **1** *(de caballo)* trot. **2** *fam (actividad)* chasing about, hustle and bustle.

● **no estar para esos trotes** not to be up to it.

trozo *nm* piece, chunk.

trucha *nf* trout.

truco *nm* *(ardid)* trick.

● **coger el truco** to get the knack.

■ **truco de magia** magic trick.

■ **truco publicitario** gimmick.

trueno *nm* thunderclap, clap of thunder: *se oían truenos*, you could hear thunder; *rayos y truenos*, thunder and lightning.

trufa *nf* truffle.

tu *adj* your: *tu libro*, your book; *tus libros*, your books.

tú *pron* you: *es más bajo que tú*, he's shorter than you; *¡tú, no te vayas!*, you, stay here!

● **de tú a tú** on equal terms.

tuberculosis *nf* tuberculosis.

tubería *nf* **1** *(de agua-una sola)* pipe; *(-conjunto)* piping, pipes *pl*, plumbing. **2** *(de gas, petróleo)* pipeline.

tubo *nm* **1** *(gen)* tube: *un tubo de pegamento*, a tube of glue; *un tubo de vidrio*, a glass tube. **2** *(tubería)* pipe.

■ **tubo de ensayo** test tube.

■ **tubo de escape** exhaust pipe.

■ **tubo digestivo** alimentary canal.

tuerca *nf* nut.

tuerto,-a *adj* one-eyed, blind in one eye.

▶ *nm,f* one-eyed person.

tufo *nm* stink.

tulipán *nm* tulip.

tumba *nf* **1** *(mausoleo)* tomb: *la tumba de Tutankamon*, Tutankhamen's tomb. **2** *(fosa)* grave: *colocó flores en la tumba*, she placed some flowers on the grave.

● **ser como una tumba** to keep one's mouth shut.

tumbar *vt* to knock down, knock over.

▶ *vi (caer al suelo)* to fall down [*pt* **fell**; *pp* **fallen**].

▶ *vpr* **tumbarse** *(acostarse)* to lie down [*pt* **lay**; *pp* **lain**]: *está tumbado en el sofá*, he's lying down on the sofa.

tumbona *nf (de playa)* deckchair; *(para tumbarse)* lounger.

tumor *nm* tumour.

tumulto *nm* tumult, commotion.

tunecino,-a *adj - nm,f* Tunisian.

túnel *nm* tunnel.

■ **túnel de lavado** car wash.

Túnez *nm* **1** *(ciudad)* Tunis. **2** *(país)* Tunisia.

túnica *nf* tunic.

tupé *nm* quiff [*pl* **-s**].

tupido,-a *adj* dense, thick.

turbante *nm* turban.

turbar *vt* **1** *(alterar)* to unsettle, disturb. **2** *(preocupar)* to upset [*pt & pp* **upset**], worry. **3** *(desconcertar)* to baffle, put off.

▶ *vpr* **turbarse 1** *(preocuparse)* to become upset. **2** *(desconcertarse)* to become confused.

turbina *nf* turbine.

turbio,-a *adj* **1** *(agua)* cloudy. **2** *(asunto, negocio)* shady, dubious.

turbulento,-a *adj* turbulent, troubled.

turco,-a *adj* Turkish.

▶ *nm,f (persona)* Turk.

▶ *nm* **turco** *(idioma)* Turkish.

turismo *nm* **1** *(actividad)* tourism. **2** *(industria)* tourist trade, tourist industry. **3** *(coche)* car.

● **hacer turismo 1** (viajar) to go touring. **2** (visitar monumentos) to go sightseeing.

■ **turismo rural** rural tourism.

turista *nmf* tourist.

turístico,-a *adj* tourist.

turnar *vi* to alternate.

▶ *vpr* **turnarse** to take turns: *nos turnamos para fregar los platos*, we took turns to do the washing-up.

turno *nm* **1** *(en cola, lista)* turn: *cuando me llegó el turno*, when my turn came. **2** *(de trabajo)* shift.

● **de turno** on duty: *el médico de turno*, the doctor on duty.

■ **turno de día** day shift.

■ **turno de noche** night shift.

turquesa *adj - nf* turquoise.

Turquía *nf* Turkey.

turrón *nm* nougat.

tutear *vt* to be on familiar terms with: *nos tuteamos*, we're on familiar terms.

tutor,-ra *nm,f* **1** JUR guardian: *su tío se convirtió en su tutor*, his uncle became his guardian. **2** *(profesor)* tutor.

tuyo,-a *adj* of yours: *es amigo tuyo?*, is he a friend of yours?
▶ *pron* yours: *éste es tuyo*, this one is yours.

▶ *nm pl* **los tuyos** *(familiares)* your family *sing*; *(amigos)* your friends.
TV *abr (televisión)* TV.

U

u *conj* or.

ubicar *vt* to locate.

▶ *vpr* **ubicarse** to be, be situated.

ubre *nf* udder.

UCI *abr* (**Unidad de Cuidados Intensivos**) Intensive Care Unit, ICU.

UE *abr* (**Unión Europea**) EU.

úlcera *nf* ulcer.

últimamente *adv* lately, recently.

ultimar *vt* to finish, complete.

ultimátum *nm* ultimatum.

último,-a *adj* **1** (*gen*) last: *el último día del mes*, the last day of the month. **2** (*más reciente*) latest: *las últimas noticias*, the latest news; *noticias de última hora*, breaking news. **3** (*más alejado*) furthest; (*de más abajo*) bottom, lowest; (*de más arriba*) top; (*de más atrás*) back: *está en el último cajón*, it's in the bottom drawer; *vive en el último piso*, he lives on the top floor; *se suele sentar en la última fila*, she usually sits in the back row. **4** (*definitivo*) final: *mi última oferta*, my final offer.

● **a la última** up to date.

● **en los últimos años** in recent years.

● **en último caso** as a last resort.

● **estar en las últimas 1** (*moribundo*) to be at death's door. **2** (*arruinado*) to be down and out.

● **por último** finally.

ultrajar *vt* to outrage, insult.

ultramarino,-a *adj* overseas.

▶ *nm pl* **ultramarinos** (*tienda*) grocer's; (*comestibles*) groceries.

ultravioleta *adj* ultraviolet.

umbilical *adj* umbilical.

umbral *nm* threshold.

■ **umbral de la pobreza** poverty line.

un,-a *det* a, an: *un coche*, a car; *un huevo*, an egg.

▶ *adj* one: *un hombre de cada tres*, one man in five.

unánime *adj* unanimous.

unanimidad *nf* unanimity.

● **por unanimidad** unanimously.

undécimo,-a *num* eleventh.

único,-a *adj* **1** (*solo*) only: *la única vez*, the only time. **2** (*extraordinario*) unique.

● **es hijo único** he's an only child.

● **moneda única** single currency.

● **talla única** one size only.

● **¡es lo único que nos faltaba!** that's all we needed!

unidad *nf* **1** unit: *una unidad de peso*, a unit of weight; *cuestan a 15 céntimos la unidad*, they cost 15 cents each. **2** (*cohesión*) unity.

unido,-a *adj* (*gen*) united; (*amigos*) close.

unificar *vt* to unify.

uniformar *vt* **1** (*igualar*) to make uniform, standardize. **2** (*vestir de uniforme*) to put into uniform.

uniforme *adj* (*velocidad, ritmo*) uniform; (*temperatura, superficie*) even.

▶ *nm* uniform: *el uniforme de mi colegio*, my school uniform.

unión *nf* **1** (*gen*) union. **2** (*acoplamiento*) joining; (*junta*) joint.

● **la unión hace la fuerza** united we stand.

■ **Unión Europea** European Union.

unir *vt* **1** (*juntar*) to join: *he unido todas las piezas*, I've joined together all the pieces. **2** (*enlazar*) to link: *la línea férrea une las dos ciudades*, the railway line links the two cities. **3** *(relacionar)* to unite: *los une su afición por la música*, they are united by their love of music.

▶ *vpr* **unirse** *(personas)* to join together; *(empresas)* to merge: *unirse a ALGN*, to join SB.

● **estar muy unidos** to be very close.

● **unir fuerzas** to join forces.

unisex *adj* unisex.

unísono.

● **al unísono** in unison.

universal *adj* universal.

universidad *nf* university: *quiere ir a la universidad*, he wants to go to university; *estudia en la universidad*, she's at university.

■ **universidad politécnica** polytechnic.

universitario,-a *adj* university.

▶ *nm,f (en curso)* university student; *(con título)* university graduate.

universo *nm* universe.

uno,-a *adj (número)* one.

▶ *pron* **1** one: *aquí hay uno*, here's one; *es uno de ellos*, he's one of them. **2** *(impersonal)* one, you: *en estos casos, uno no sabe qué hacer*, you don't know what to do in these situations. **3** *fam (persona)* someone, somebody.

▶ *nm (número)* one; *(en fechas)* first.

▶ *adj pl* **unos,-as 1** some: *unas flores*, some flowers; *unos dicen que sí, otros que no*, some say yes, others say no. **2** *(aproximado)* about, around: *seremos unos veinte*, there will be around twenty of us.

● **de uno en uno** one by one.

● **es la una** it's one o´clock.

● **hacerle una a ALGN** to play a dirty trick on SB.

untar *vt (crema, pomada)* to smear; *(mantequilla, queso)* to spread: *untar pan con mantequilla*, to spread butter on bread.

▶ *vpr* **untarse** *(mancharse)* to get stained.

uña *nf* **1** *(de la mano)* nail, fingernail; *(del pie)* nail, toenail. **2** *(de gato)* claw; *(de caballo)* hoof [*pl* -**s** o -**ves**].

● **comerse las uñas** to bite one's nails.

● **ser uña y carne** to be inseparable.

uranio *nm* uranium.

urbanidad *nf* urbanity, politeness.

urbanización *nf* **1** *(proceso)* urbanization. **2** *(conjunto residencial)* housing development, housing estate.

urbanizar *vt* to urbanize, develop.

urbano,-a *adj* urban.

▶ *nm,f fam (policía - hombre)* policeman [*pl* -**men**]; *(- mujer)* policewoman [*pl* -**women**].

urbe *nf* metropolis.

urgencia *nf* **1** *(prisa)* urgency: *la urgencia del caso*, the urgency of the case. **2** *(asunto)* emergency: *ha salido a atender una urgencia*, he's been called out on an emergency.

▶ *nf pl* **urgencias** casualty: *lo llevaron a urgencias*, he was taken to casualty.

● **en caso de urgencia** in case of emergency.

urgente *adj* **1** *(llamada, asunto)* urgent. **2** *(enfermo)* emergency. **3** *(carta)* express.

urgir *vi* to be urgent, be pressing.

urinario,-a *adj* urinary.

▶ *nm* **urinario** urinal.

urna *nf* **1** *(para votar)* ballot box. **2** *(para cenizas)* urn. **3** *(para objetos valiosos)* glass case.

● **acudir a las urnas** to vote.

urólogo,-a *nm,f* urologist.

urraca *nf* magpie.

urticaria *nf* rash.

Uruguay *nm* Uruguay.

uruguayo,-a *adj - nm,f* Uruguayan.

usado,-a *adj* **1** *(gastado)* worn out, old. **2** *(de segunda mano)* secondhand, used.

usar *vt* **1** *(utilizar)* to use. **2** *(prenda)* to wear [*pt* wore; *pp* worn]: *usaba gafas*, she wore glasses.

▶ *vpr* **usarse 1** *(utilizarse)* to be used. **2** *(estar de moda)* to be in fashion.

● **de usar y tirar** disposable.

uso *nm* **1** *(utilización)* use: *el plástico tiene muchos usos*, plastic has a lot of uses; *no se permite el uso de la calculadora en el examen*, the use of calculators is not permitted in the exam. **2** *(ejercicio)* exercise: *el uso de un privilegio*, the exercise of a privilege. **3** *(de prenda)* wearing: *es obligatorio el uso del cinturón de seguridad*, seat belts must be worn. **4** *(costumbre)* usage, custom. **5** *(en farmacia)* application: *uso externo*, external application.

● **al uso**: *al uso europeo*, in the European style; *una comedia al uso*, a comedy of the usual type; *las teorías económicas al uso*, current economic theories.

● **hacer uso de la palabra** to take the floor.

■ **usos y costumbres** ways and customs.

usted *pron fml* you.

usual *adj* usual, customary.

usuario,-a *nm,f* user.

usurero,-a *nm,f* usurer.

utensilio *nm* **1** *(de cocina)* utensil. **2** *(herramienta)* tool.

útero *nm* uterus.

útil *adj* useful.

utilidad *nf* usefulness.

utilización *nf* use.

utilizar *vt* to use, utilize, make use of.

utopía *nf* utopia.

uva *nf* grape: *un racimo de uvas*, a bunch of grapes.

● **estar de mala uva** *fam* to be in a bad mood.

● **de uvas a peras** *fam* once in a blue moon.

● **nos van a dar las uvas** we'll be here all day/night.

UVI *abr (Unidad de Vigilancia Intensiva)* ICU, intensive care unit.

V

vaca *nf* **1** *(animal)* cow. **2** *(carne)* beef.
● **la enfermedad de las vacas locas** mad cow disease.
● **estar como una vaca** to be really fat.
■ **las vacas flacas** the lean years.

vacaciones *nf pl* holiday, holidays, US vacation: *necesitas unas vacaciones*, you need a holiday; *las vacaciones de verano*, the summer holidays.
● **estar de vacaciones** to be on holiday, US on vacation.
● **irse de vacaciones** to go on holiday, US on vacation.

vacante *adj* vacant.
▶ *nf* vacancy.

vaciar *vt* **1** *(recipiente)* to empty. **2** *(contenido)* to pour away, pour out. **3** *(dejar hueco)* to hollow out.

vacilación *nf* **1** *(duda)* hesitation. **2** *(oscilación)* wobbling, unsteadiness.

vacilante *adj* **1** *(dubitativo)* hesitating. **2** *(oscilante)* unsteady.

vacilar *vi* **1** *(dudar)* to hesitate. **2** *(oscilar)* to sway, stagger.

vacío,-a *adj* **1** *(recipiente, lugar)* empty. **2** *(no ocupado)* unoccupied. **3** *(superficial)* vain. **4** *(hueco)* hollow.
▶ *nm* **vacío 1** *(abismo)* void, emptiness: *saltar al vacío*, to jump into the void; *una sensación de vacío*, a feeling of emptiness. **2** *(en física)* vacuum.
● **tener el estómago vacío** to be hungry.
● **envasado al vacío** vacuum-packed.
● **hacerle el vacío a ALGN** to cold-shoulder SB.
■ **vacío de poder** power vacuum.

vacuna *nf* vaccine.

vacunación *nf* vaccination.

vacunar *vt* to vaccinate.
▶ *vpr* **vacunarse** to get vaccinated.

vacuno,-a *adj* bovine.

vadear *vt* **1** *(río)* to ford, wade. **2** *(dificultad)* to overcome [*pt* **overcame**; *pp* **overcome**].

vado *nm* **1** *(de río)* ford. **2** *(en calle)* garage entrance.
■ **"Vado permanente"** "Keep clear".

vagabundo,-a *adj* vagrant.
▶ *nm,f* tramp, vagrant.

vagar *vi* to wander about, roam about.

vagina *nf* vagina.

vago,-a¹ *adj* *(holgazán)* lazy.
▶ *nm,f* idler, loafer.
● **hacer el vago** to laze around.

vago,-a² *adj* *(impreciso)* vague.

vagón *nm* **1** *(para pasajeros)* GB carriage, coach; US car. **2** *(para mercancías)* GB wagon, goods van; US boxcar, freight car.
■ **vagón cama** sleeping-car.
■ **vagón restaurante** restaurant car.

vagoneta *nf* wagon.

vaho *nm* **1** *(vapor)* vapour, steam. **2** *(aliento)* breath.
▶ *nm pl* **vahos** MED inhalation *sing*.

vaina *nf* **1** *(de espada)* sheath, scabbard. **2** *(de guisante, judía)* pod.

vainilla *nf* vanilla.

vaivén *nm* **1** *(de columpio)* swaying, swinging. **2** *(de la gente)* coming and going, bustle. **3** *(cambio)* fluctuation.

vajilla *nf* **1** *(gen)* dishes *pl*, crockery: *pon la vajilla en el lavaplatos*, put the dishes in the dishwasher. **2** *(juego completo)* dinner service: *una vajilla de 24 piezas*, a 24-piece dinner service.

vale *nm* *(de compra)* voucher: *un vale de 5 euros*, a 5-euro voucher.

► *interj* **1** OK, all right: *¡vale! nos veremos a las cinco*, OK! I'll see you at 5 p.m.; *iremos juntos, ¿vale?*, we'll go together, all right? **2** *(pagaré)* IOU, promissory note.

valentía *nf* bravery, courage.

valer *vi* **1** *(tener valor)* to be worth: *un euro vale unas 166 pesetas*, a euro is worth about 166 pesetas; *no vale nada*, it is worthless. **2** *(costar)* to cost [*pt & pp* cost]: *esta mesa vale 2.000 euros*, this table costs 2,000 euros; *¿cuánto vale?*, how much is it? **3** *(ser válido)* to be valid: *mi pasaporte ya no vale*, my passport is no longer valid; *la oferta vale para toda la semana*, the offer is valid for the whole week. **4** *(ganar)* to win [*pt & pp* won], earn: *la protesta le valió la tarjeta roja*, protesting earned him a red card. **5** *(servir)* to be useful, be of use: *esas botas pueden valer para caminar por el campo*, those boots will do for walking in the country; *este lápiz no vale*, this pencil is of no use; *no vale para director*, he's no use as a manager.

► *vpr* **valerse 1** *(usar)* to use, make use: *se valieron de su posición para...*, they used their position to.... **2** *(apañarse)* to manage: *sabe valerse por sí mismo*, he can manage by himself.

● **hacer valer** to assert.

● **no vale** it's no good.

● **vale más...** it's better...: *más vale prevenir que curar*, prevention is better than cure; *más vale tarde que nunca*, better late than never; *más te vale no llegar tarde*, you'd better not arrive late.

● **valer la pena** to be worthwhile: *vale la pena verlo*, it's worth seeing.

● **¡válgame Dios!** Good heavens!

valeroso,-a *adj* courageous, brave.

validez *nf* validity.

válido,-a *adj* valid.

valiente *adj* **1** *(valeroso)* brave. **2** *(excelente)* fine, excellent: *¡valiente tontería!*, that was very stupid!

► *nmf (persona)* brave person: *los valientes*, the brave.

valioso,-a *adj* valuable.

valla *nf* **1** *(cerca)* fence, barrier. **2** *(en atletismo)* hurdle.

■ **valla publicitaria** GB hoarding; US billboard.

vallado *nm* fence, enclosure.

vallar *vt* to fence, enclose.

valle *nm* valley.

valor *nm* **1** *(gen)* value: *no tiene ningún valor*, it's worth nothing. **2** *(precio)* price. **3** *(coraje)* courage, valour. **4** *(desvergüenza)* nerve: *¡hay que tener valor para hablarle así al jefe!*, you have to have a nerve to talk to the boss like that!

► *nm pl* **valores** *(financieros)* securities; *(acciones)* shares.

● **armarse de valor** to pluck up courage.

● **dar valor a** to attach importance to.

● **de valor** valuable.

● **por valor de** worth, to the value of.

● **¡qué valor!** what a nerve!

● **sin ningún valor** worthless, worth nothing.

valoración *nf (de obra de arte)* valuation; *(de pérdidas)* assessment.

valorar *vt* **1** *(tasar)* to value: *valoraron los cuadros antes de la subasta*, they valued the paintings before the auction. **2** *(apreciar)* to value: *valoro mucho tu amistad*, I value your friendship very much; *"se valoran los conocimientos de francés"*, "knowledge of French an advantage".

vals *nm* waltz.

válvula *nf* valve.

vampiro *nm* **1** *(drácula)* vampire. **2** *(aprovechado)* bloodsucker.

vandalismo *nm* vandalism.

vanguardia *nf* **1** *(en arte etc)* avant-garde. **2** MIL vanguard.

vanidad *nf* vanity, conceit.

vanidoso,-a *adj* vain, conceited.

vano,-a *adj* **1** *(inútil)* vain, useless. **2** *(ilusorio)* illusory, futile. **3** *(frívolo)* frivolous. **4** *(arrogante)* vain, conceited.

► *nm* **vano** opening.

● **en vano** in vain.

vapor *nm* **1** *(de agua)* vapour, steam. **2** *(barco)* steamship, steamer.

● **al vapor** steamed: *mejillones al vapor*, steamed mussels.

vaporizador *nm* vaporizer.

vaquería *nf* dairy.

vaquero,-a *adj* **1** *(de vaca)* cow, cattle. **2** *(de tejido)* denim: *una cazadora vaquera*, a denim jacket.

► *nm* **vaquero** GB cowherd; US cowboy.
► *nm pl* **vaqueros** *(pantalones)* jeans: *unos vaqueros*, a pair of jeans.
vara *nf* **1** *(palo)* stick, rod. **2** *(de mando)* staff.
variable *adj* variable, changeable.
variación *nf* variation, change.
variado,-a *adj* varied, mixed.
variante
► *nf* **1** variant. **2** *(carretera)* bypass.
variar *vt-vi* to vary, change: *las temperaturas varían poco en las zonas costeras*, temperatures don't change much in coastal areas.
● **para variar** for a change.
varicela *nf* chickenpox.
variedad *nf* **1** *(pluralidad)* variety, diversity. **2** *(clase)* variety, type.
► *nf pl* **variedades** *(espectáculo)* variety show *sing*.
varilla *nf* **1** *(palito)* stick, rod. **2** *(de paraguas)* rib.
vario,-a *adj* **1** *(distinto)* varied, different. **2** **varios,-as** *(algunos)* some, several: *tiene varios pares de zapatillas*, he's got several pairs of trainers.
variz *nf* varicose vein.
varón *nm* male, man [*pl* **men**].
varonil *adj* manly, virile.
vasco,-a *adj - nm,f* Basque.
vasija *nf* vessel.
vaso *nm* **1** *(de cristal)* glass: *un vaso de agua*, a glass of water. **2** *(de papel, plástico)* cup. **3** *(sanguíneo)* vessel.
vasto,-a *adj* vast, immense.
vaticano,-a *adj* Vatican.
► *nm* **el Vaticano** the Vatican.
■ **la Ciudad del Vaticano** the Vatican City.
vatio *nm* watt.
vaya *interj* ¡**vaya**! **1** *(independiente)* well!: *¡vaya! ¡ya te has vuelto a equivocar!*, oh no! you've done it wrong again! **2** *(con sustantivos)* what a...: *¡vaya casa!*, what a house!; *¡vaya moto más chula!*, what a great motorbike!
vecinal *adj* local.
vecindad *nf* **1** *(barrio)* neighbourhood. **2** *(vecinos)* neighbours *pl*.
vecindario *nm* **1** *(barrio)* neighbourhood. **2** *(vecinos)* neighbours *pl*.
vecino,-a *adj* *(cercano)* neighbouring.

► *nm,f* **1** *(de edificio, calle)* neighbour. **2** *(habitante -de barrio)* resident; *(-de ciudad)* inhabitant.
● **asociación de vecinos** residents' association.
veda *nf* **1** *(gen)* prohibition. **2** *(de caza)* close season.
vega *nf* fertile plain.
vegetación *nf* vegetation.
vegetal *adj - nm* plant.
vegetariano,-a *adj - nm,f* vegetarian.
vehículo *nm* **1** *(gen)* vehicle. **2** *(coche)* car.
veinte *num* twenty; *(en fechas)* twentieth: *el siglo veinte*, the twentieth century.
vejez *nf* old age.
vejiga *nf* bladder.
vela[1] *nf* **1** *(vigilia)* watch, vigil. **2** *(desvelo)* wakefulness. **3** *(de cera)* candle.
● **pasar la noche en vela** to have a sleepless night.
vela[2] *nf* *(de barco)* sail.
● **barco de vela** sailing boat.
velar[1] *vi* **1** *(estar despierto)* to stay awake. **2** *(cuidar)* to watch, look.
► *vt* *(difunto)* to keep vigil over.
velar[2] *vpr* **velarse** *(fotografía)* to get fogged.
velatorio *nm* wake, vigil.
velero *nm* sailing boat.
veleta *nf* *(en tejado)* weathercock.
► *nm,f fig* *(persona)* fickle person.
vello *nm* hair.
velo *nm* veil.
● **correr un tupido velo sobre algo** to draw a veil over STH [*pt* **drew**; *pp* **drawn**].
velocidad *nf* **1** *(rapidez)* speed, velocity. **2** *(marcha)* gear.
■ **velocidad máxima** top speed.
■ **velocidad de transmisión** bit rate.
■ **velocidad operativa** operating speed.
velódromo *nm* cycle track.
veloz *adj* fast, quick, swift.
vena *nf* **1** *(gen)* vein. **2** *(en mina)* vein, seam.
venado *nm* **1** *(animal)* stag, deer. **2** *(carne)* venison.
vencedor,-ra *nm,f* **1** *(gen)* winner. **2** *(en guerra)* conqueror.
► *adj* **1** *(gen)* winning. **2** *(ejército)* conquering, victorious.
vencer *vt* **1** *(derrotar)* to beat [*pt* **beat**; *pp* **beaten**]: *vencimos al otro equipo por 2 a*

1, we beat the other team 2-1; *el español venció en la carrera de 1.500 metros*, the Spaniard won the 1,500 metres race. **2** *(militarmente)* to defeat, conquer. **3** *(problema)* to overcome [*pt* **overcame**; *pp* **overcome**]: *tuvo que vencer el miedo*, he had to overcome his fear; *la venció el sueño*, sleep overcame her.

▶ *vi* **1** *(gen)* to win [*pt & pp* **won**]. **2** *(deuda)* to fall due [*pt* **fell**; *pp* **fallen**]. **3** *(plazo, pasaporte)* to expire.

vencido,-a *adj* **1** *(ejército, persona)* defeated. **2** *(deuda)* due, payable.

venda *nf* **1** *(para heridas)* bandage. **2** *(para los ojos)* blindfold.

vendaje *nm* bandaging.

vendar *vt* to bandage.

● **vendar los ojos a** ALGN to blindfold SB.

vendaval *nm* strong wind, gale.

vendedor,-ra *adj* selling.

▶ *nm,f (hombre)* salesman [*pl* **-men**]; *(mujer)* saleswoman [*pl* **-women**].

vender *vt* **1** *(producto, mercancía)* to sell [*pt & pp* **sold**]. **2** *fig (traicionar)* to betray.

▶ *vpr* **venderse** **1** *(producto, mercancía)* to be sold: *se venden al peso*, they are sold by weight. **2** *(dejarse sobornar)* to sell oneself [*pt & pp* **sold**], accept a bribe.

● **"Se vende"** "For sale".

● **venderse como churros** to sell like hotcakes [*pt & pp* **sold**].

vendimia *nf* grape harvest.

vendimiar *vt* to harvest.

veneno *nm (químico, vegetal)* poison; *(de animal)* venom.

venenoso *adj* poisonous.

venezolano,-a *adj* - *nm,f* Venezuelan.

Venezuela *nf* Venezuela.

venganza *nf* revenge, vengeance.

● **por venganza** out of revenge.

vengar *vt* to avenge.

▶ *vpr* **vengarse** to take revenge: *se vengó del que mató a su padre*, he took revenge on the man who killed his father.

venida *nf* coming, arrival.

venidero,-a *adj* future, forthcoming.

● **en lo venidero** in the future.

venir *vi* **1** *(acercarse)* to come: *¿cuándo vendrás a vernos?*, when will you come to see us?; *¿has venido en tren?*, did you come by train? **2** *(volver)* to be back: *ahora vengo*, I'll be right back. **3** *(llegar)* to

arrive: *¿a qué hora viene el tren?*, what time does the train arrive? **4** *(estar)* to be: *este pantalón me viene grande*, these trousers are too big for me; *mi teléfono viene en la guía*, my phone number is in the book.

▶ *vpr* **venirse** to come back: *nos vinimos a las tres*, we came back at three.

● **el mes que viene** next month.

● **venir a menos** to decline.

● **venir al caso** to be relevant.

● **venir al pelo** to be opportune.

● **venir bien** to be suitable: *¿te viene bien esta tarde?*, does this afternoon suit you?

● **venir de** to come from.

● **venir grande a** ALGN to be too big for SB.

● **venir mal** not to be convenient: *a esa hora me viene mal*, that time isn't convenient.

● **venir motivado,-a por** to be caused by.

● **venir pequeño a** ALGN to be too small for SB.

● **venirse abajo** **1** (edificio) to collapse, fall down [*pt* **fell**; *pp* **fallen**]. **2** (persona) to go to pieces.

● **¡venga!** come on!

● **¡venga ya!** come off it!

venta *nf* **1** *(transacción)* sale, selling. **2** *(hostal)* roadside inn.

● **"En venta"** "For sale".

● **poner a la venta** to put up for sale.

■ **venta al por mayor** wholesale.

■ **venta al por menor** retail.

ventaja *nf* advantage.

ventajoso,-a *adj* advantageous.

ventana *nf* window.

● **doble ventana** double-glazed window.

ventanilla *nf* **1** *(de coche, sobre)* window. **2** *(de cine)* box office.

ventilación *nf* ventilation.

ventilador *nm* fan.

ventilar *vt* **1** *(habitación, ropa)* to air. **2** *fig (tema)* to discuss; *(opinión)* to air; *(problema)* to sort out.

ventisca *nf* snowstorm, blizzard.

ventosa *nf* sucker.

ventoso,-a *adj* windy.

ventrículo *nm* ventricle.

ventrílocuo,-a *nm,f* ventriloquist.

ver *vt* **1** *(percibir, mirar)* to see [*pt* saw; *pp* seen]: **no veo nada**, I can't see a thing; **ya he visto esta película**, I've already seen this film; **voy a ver quién es**, I'll go and see who it is. **2** *(televisión)* to watch. **3** *(parecer)* to look: **te veo preocupado**, you look worried; **lo veo muy feliz**, he looks very happy. **4** *(entender)* to understand [*pt & pp* understood]: **veo difícil que mi equipo gane la liga**, I don't think my team will win the league. **5** *(visitar)* to visit.

▶ *vpr* **verse 1** *(con ALGN)* to meet [*pt & pp* met], see each other [*pt* saw; *pp* seen]: **nos vemos a las ocho, ¿vale?**, I'll meet you at eight o'clock, OK?; **nos vemos bastante a menudo**, we see each other quite often. **2** *(encontrarse)* to find oneself [*pt & pp* found].

● **a ver** let's see.
● **es digno de ver** it is worth seeing.
● **hacer ver algo** to pretend STH.
● **¡hay que ver!** would you believe it!
● **¡cuánto tiempo sin verte!** long time no see!
● **no poder ver** not to be able to stand: **no puede ver a su vecino**, she can't stand her neighbour.
● **no tener nada que ver con** to have nothing to do with.
● **se ve que...** it's clear that...: **se ve que te han cuidado mucho**, they've obviously taken good care of you.
● **verse venir algo** to see STH coming.
● **véase** see.
● **verse obligado,-a a** to be obliged to.
● **ya se ve** of course.
● **vérselas con ALGN** to have it out with SB.

veraneante *nmf* summer resident.
veranear *vi* to spend the summer [*pt & pp* spent].
veraneo *nm* summer holiday.
veraniego,-a *adj* summer.
verano *nm* summer.
veras *adv* .
● **de veras** really, truly: **lo siento de veras**, I'm truly sorry.
veraz *adj* truthful, veracious.
verbal *adj* verbal.
verbena *nf (fiesta)* dance.
verbo *nm* verb.
verdad *nf* **1** truth: **dime la verdad**, tell me the truth. **2** *(confirmación)*: **es bonita, ¿verdad?**, she's pretty, isn't she?; **se compró una casa ¿verdad?**, he bought a house, didn't he?
● **ser verdad** to be true: **¿es verdad que has ganado?**, is it true that you won?; **la historia no es verdad**, it isn't a true story.
● **a decir verdad** to tell you the truth [*pt & pp* told].
● **de verdad 1** (en serio) really: **de verdad, iré mañana**, really, I'll go tomorrow. **2** (como debe ser) real: **Carlos es un amigo de verdad**, Carlos is a real friend.
● **en verdad** really.
verdadero,-a *adj* true, real.
verde *adj* **1** *(color, tela, ojos)* green. **2** *(fruta)* unripe. **3** *fam (chiste)* blue, dirty.
▶ *nm (color)* green.
▶ *nm pl* **los verdes** the Greens.
● **poner verde a ALGN** *fam* to lay into SB.
verdor *nm* greenness.
verdoso,-a *adj* greenish.
verdugo *nm* executioner.
verdulería *nf* greengrocer's.
verdulero,-a *nm,f* greengrocer.
verdura *nf* vegetables *pl*.
veredicto *nm* verdict.
vergonzoso,-a *adj* **1** *(acto)* shameful, shocking. **2** *(persona)* shy, bashful.
vergüenza *nf* **1** *(culpabilidad)* shame: **le debería dar vergüenza**, he should be ashamed of himself; **¡qué vergüenza!**, shame on you! **2** *(bochorno)* embarrassment: **me da vergüenza decirle que me gusta**, I'm embarrassed to tell him that I like him; **¡qué vergüenza!**, how embarrassing! **3** *(escándalo)* disgrace: **es una vergüenza que la playa esté tan sucia**, it's a disgrace that the beach is so dirty.
● **sentir vergüenza** to be ashamed.
verídico,-a *adj* truthful, true: **es verídico**, it is a fact.
verificar *vt* **1** *(confirmar)* to verify, confirm. **2** *(probar)* to prove.
▶ *vpr* **verificarse 1** *(comprobarse)* to come true. **2** *(efectuarse)* to take place.
verja *nf* railing.
vermut *nm* vermouth.
verosímil *adj* likely, probable.
verruga *nf* wart.

versión *nf* version.
● **en versión original** in the original language.
verso *nm* verse.
vértebra *nf* vertebra.
vertebrado,-a *adj - nm,f* vertebrate.
vertebral *adj* vertebral.
vertedero *nm* dump, tip.
verter *vt* 1 *(echar - líquido)* to pour; *(- basura)* to dump. 2 *(derramar)* to spill [*pt & pp* **spilt**]; *(lágrimas)* to shed [*pt & pp* **shed**].
vertical *adj - nf* vertical.
vértice *nm* vertex.
vertiente *nf* 1 *(de monte)* slope. 2 *(aspecto)* aspect.
vértigo *nm* 1 vertigo. 2 *(turbación)* dizziness, giddiness: *las alturas me dan vértigo*, heights make me feel dizzy.
vesícula *nf* vesicle.
vespa® *nf* scooter.
vespertino,-a *adj* evening.
vestíbulo *nm* 1 *(de casa)* hall, entrance. 2 *(de hotel)* hall, lobby.
vestido *nm* dress.
■ **vestido de noche** evening dress.
■ **vestido de novia** wedding dress.
vestimenta *nf* clothes *pl*.
vestir *vt* 1 *(llevar)* to wear [*pt* **wore**; *pp* **worn**]. 2 *(a alguien)* to dress: *¿has vestido ya al niño?*, have you dressed the baby yet? 3 *(cubrir)* to cover.
▶ *vi* 1 to dress: *vestir de negro*, to dress in black. 2 *(ser elegante)* to be elegant, look smart.
▶ *vpr* **vestirse** 1 *(ponerse ropa)* to get dressed: *me visto en un momento y nos vamos*, I'll get dressed quickly and we'll go. 2 *(disfrazarse)* to dress up: *se vistió de marinero*, he dressed up as a sailor.
● **el mismo que viste y calza** the very same.
● **vestirse de punta en blanco** to dress up to the nines.
vestuario *nm* 1 *(ropa)* wardrobe, clothes *pl*. 2 *(uniforme)* uniform. 3 *(camerino)* dressing room; *(en gimnasio etc)* changing room.
veta *nf* 1 *(en mineral)* seam, vein. 2 *(en madera)* grain.
veterano,-a *adj - nm,f* veteran.
veterinaria *nf* veterinary medicine, veterinary science.
veterinario,-a *adj* veterinary.

▶ *nm,f* GB veterinary surgeon, vet; US veterinarian.
veto *nm* veto [*pl* **-es**].
vez *nf* 1 *(ocasión)* time: *la primera vez*, the first time; *tres veces a la semana*, three times a week. 2 *(turno)* turn: *espera a que llegue tu vez*, wait till it's your turn.
● **a la vez** at the same time.
● **a su vez** in turn.
● **a veces** sometimes.
● **alguna vez** 1 *(en afirmación)* sometimes. 2 *(en pregunta)* ever.
● **cada vez** every time.
● **de una vez para siempre** once and for all.
● **¿cuántas veces...?** how many times...?
● **de vez en cuando** from time to time.
● **dos veces** twice.
● **en vez de** instead of.
● **muchas veces** often.
● **otra vez** again.
● **pedir la vez** to ask who's last.
● **rara vez** seldom, rarely.
● **tal vez** perhaps, maybe.
vía *nf* 1 *(camino)* road, way; *(calle)* street. 2 *(de tren - raíl)* track, line; *(-andén)* platform: *la vía férrea*, the railway track; *por la vía dos*, at platform two. 3 *(modo)* way, manner.
● **en vías de** in the process of.
● **por vía aérea** by airmail.
● **por vía oral** to be taken orally.
■ **vía de acceso** slip road.
■ **vía aérea** airway, track.
■ **vía pública** thoroughfare.
■ **Vía Láctea** Milky Way.
■ **vías respiratorias** respiratory tract *sing*.
viable *adj* viable.
viaducto *nm* viaduct.
viajante *nm* commercial traveller.
viajar *vi* to travel: *prefiero viajar en coche*, I prefer travelling by car.
viaje *nm* 1 *(desplazamiento)* journey, trip: *el viaje sólo dura dos horas*, the journey only takes two hours; *hicimos un viaje por toda Europa*, we made a trip round Europe; *un recuerdo de mis viajes al extranjero*, a souvenir from my travels abroad. 2 *(como aventura)* voyage: *el viaje de Colón*, Columbus's voyage. 3 *(carga)* load.

- **¡buen viaje!** have a good journey!
- **estar de viaje** to be away.
- **irse de viaje** to go on a journey, go on a trip.
- **viaje de fin de curso** end-of-year trip.
- **viaje de ida y vuelta** GB return trip; US round trip.
- **viaje de negocios** business trip.
- **viaje de novios** honeymoon.

viajero,-a *adj* travelling.
▶ *nm,f* **1** *(pasajero)* passenger. **2** *(aventurero)* traveller.

víbora *nf* viper.

vibración *nf* vibration.

vibrar *vi* to vibrate.

vicepresidente,-a *nm,f* *(de gobierno)* vice-president; *(de compañía)* vice-chairman.

viceversa *adv* vice versa.

vicio *nm* **1** *(corrupción)* vice, corruption. **2** *(mala costumbre)* bad habit.
- **por vicio** for no reason at all, for the sake of it.

vicioso,-a *adj* depraved.

víctima *nf* victim.

victoria *nf* **1** *(en enfrentamiento, batalla)* victory, triumph. **2** *(en partido)* win: *otra victoria para España*, another win for Spain.
- **cantar victoria** to celebrate.

victorioso,-a *adj* victorious, triumphant.
- **salir victorioso** to win [pt & pp **won**].

vid *nf* vine.

vida *nf* **1** *(de ser vivo)* life [pl **-ves**]: *lleva una vida muy interesante*, she leads a very interesting life; *le falta vida*, it doesn't have much life. **2** *(modo de vivir)* way of life. **3** *(medios)* living: *se gana la vida como escritor*, he earns a living as a writer.
- **de por vida** for life.
- **en mi/tu/su/la vida** never: *en la vida había visto algo así*, I've never seen anything like it.
- **en vida de** during the life of.
- **estar con vida** to be alive.
- **perder la vida** to lose one's life [pt & pp **lost**]: *quitar la vida a ALGN*, to take SB's life.
- **¡vida mía!** my love!
- **vida conyugal** married life [pl **-ves**].

vidente *nmf* clairvoyant.

vídeo *nm* video [pl **-s**].
- **grabar algo en vídeo** to tape STH.

videocámara *nf* camcorder.

videocasete *nm* video cassette.

videoclip *nm* video [pl **-s**].

videoclub *nm* video shop.

videoconsola *nf* game console.

videojuego *nm* video game.

videoteca *nf* video library.

vidriera *nf* **1** *(en casa - ventana)* window; *(- puerta)* glass door. **2** *(obra artística)* stained glass window.

vidrio *nm* glass.

viejo,-a *adj* *(persona)* old, elderly; *(cosa)* old.
▶ *nm,f* *(hombre)* old man [pl **men**]; *(mujer)* old woman [pl **women**].
- **hacerse viejo** to get old.
- **viejo verde** fam dirty old man [pl **men**].

viento *nm* wind: *hace viento*, it's windy.
- **contra viento y marea** at all costs.

vientre *nm* **1** *(barriga)* belly, abdomen. **2** *(vísceras)* bowels *pl*. **3** *(de embarazada)* womb.

viernes *nm* Friday.
- **Viernes Santo** Good Friday.

vietnamita *adj - nm,f* Vietnamese.

viga *nf* **1** *(de madera)* beam, rafter. **2** *(de acero)* girder.

vigente *adj* in use, in force.

vigésimo,-a *num* twentieth.

vigía *nmf* *(persona)* lookout; *(hombre)* watchman [pl **-men**]; *(mujer)* watchwoman [pl **-women**].

vigilancia *nf* **1** *(para controlar)* vigilance: *una vigilancia constante del proceso*, a constant vigilance of the process. **2** *(para evitar daños, robos)* surveillance: *vigilancia por vídeo*, video surveillance.

vigilante *adj* vigilant, watchful.
▶ *nm,f* *(hombre)* watchman [pl **-men**]; *(mujer)* watchwoman [pl **-women**].

vigilar *vt-vi* **1** *(ir con cuidado)* to watch: *vigila el guiso para que no se queme*, watch the stew so that it doesn't burn; *uno vigilaba mientras el otro robaba las joyas*, one kept watch while the other stole the jewels. **2** *(con armas)* to guard: *vigilaba las joyas día y noche*, he guarded the jewels day and night. **3** *(supervisar)* to oversee [pt **oversaw**; pp **overseen**]. **4** *(cuidar)* to look after.

vigor *nm* **1** *(fuerza)* vigour, strength. **2** *(validez)* force, effect.

● **en vigor** in force: *entrar en vigor*, to come into force.

vigoroso,-a *adj* vigorous, strong.

VIH *abr* MED *(Virus de Inmunodeficiencia Humana)* Human Immunodeficiency Virus, HIV.

villa *nf* **1** *(casa)* villa. **2** *(pueblo)* small town.

villancico *nm* Christmas carol.

villano,-a *nm,f* villain.

vinagre *nm* vinegar.

vinagreras *nf pl* cruet stand.

vinagreta *nf* vinaigrette.

vincular *vt* **1** *(unir)* to tie. **2** INFORM to link. **3** *(relacionar)* to relate.

vínculo *nm* **1** *(conexión)* tie, bond. **2** INFORM link.

■ **vínculos familiares** family ties.

vinícola *adj* wine-producing.

vino *nm* wine.

■ **vino blanco** white wine.

■ **vino de Jerez** sherry.

■ **vino de la casa** house wine.

■ **vino rosado** rosé wine.

■ **vino tinto** red wine.

viña *nf* vineyard.

viñedo *nm* vineyard.

viñeta *nf* **1** *(dibujo)* cartoon. **2** *(tira)* comic strip.

viola *nf* viola.

violación *nf* **1** *(transgresión)* violation, infringement. **2** *(sexual)* rape.

violador,-ra *nm,f* rapist.

violar *vt* **1** *(acuerdo, derecho)* to violate. **2** *(persona)* to rape.

violencia *nf* **1** *(brutalidad)* violence. **2** *(vergüenza)* embarrassment.

violento,-a *adj* **1** *(bruto)* violent. **2** *(situación)* embarrassing; *(persona)* awkward: *se sentía violento*, he felt awkward.

violeta *adj - nm (color)* violet.
▶ *nf (flor)* violet.

violín *nm (instrumento)* violin.
▶ *nmf (músico)* violinist.

violinista *nmf* violinist.

violonchelo *nm* cello [*pl* **-s**].

viraje *nm* **1** *(en coche)* swerve. **2** *(de acontecimientos)* change of direction.

virar *vi* to turn.

virgen *adj* **1** *(persona)* virgin. **2** *(cinta)* blank. **3** *(en estado natural)* unspoiled.
▶ *nf* virgin.

Virgo *nm* Virgo: *yo soy virgo*, I'm Virgo.

viril *adj* virile.

virilidad *nf* virility.

virtual *adj* virtual.

virtud *nf* **1** *(cualidad)* virtue. **2** *(eficacia)* property, quality.

● **en virtud de** by virtue of.

virtuoso,-a *adj* virtuous.
▶ *nm,f (artista)* virtuoso [*pl* **-s**].

viruela *nf* smallpox.

virus *nm* virus.

■ **virus informático** computer virus.

viruta *nf* shaving.

visado *nm* visa.

vísceras *nf pl* viscera, entrails.

viscoso,-a *adj* viscous.

visera *nf (de gorra)* peak; *(de casco)* visor.

visibilidad *nf* visibility.

visible *adj* **1** *(que se ve)* visible. **2** *(decente)* decent: *¿estás visible?*, are you decent?

visillo *nm* net curtain.

visión *nf* **1** *(capacidad)* sight, vision. **2** *(perspectiva)* view.

● **ver visiones** to dream, see things [*pt* **saw**; *pp* **seen**].

■ **visión de conjunto** overall view.

visita *nf* **1** *(acción)* visit. **2** *(visitante)* visitor, guest.

● **hacer una visita a** to pay a visit to [*pt & pp* **paid**].

● **"No se admiten visitas"** "No visitors".

visitante *adj* visiting.
▶ *nmf* visitor.

visitar *vt* **1** *(ir a casa de)* to visit, pay a visit [*pt & pp* **paid**], call upon. **2** *(enfermo)* to see [*pt* **saw**; *pp* **seen**].

vislumbrar *vt* **1** *(distinguir)* to discern, make out. **2** *(conjeturar)* to guess, conjecture.

visón *nm* mink.

víspera *nf* **1** *(día anterior)* day before: *la víspera del examen*, the day before the exam. **2** *(de fiesta)* eve: *la víspera de Navidad*, Christmas Eve.

● **en vísperas de** on the eve of.

vista *nf* **1** *(sentido)* sight, vision: *tiene mal la vista*, his eyesight is bad. **2** *(panorama)* view: *una habitación con vistas*, a room with a view. **3** *(perspectiva)* eye: *tiene buena vista para los negocios*, he's got a good eye for business. **4** *(aspecto)* aspect, looks *pl*. **5** *(juicio)* trial, hearing.

- **a la vista** at sight.
- **a simple vista** at first sight.
- **bajar/levantar la vista** to look down/up.
- **con vistas a 1** *(jardín, calle)* overlooking. **2** *(beneficios, resultados)* with a view to.
- **conocer de vista** to know by sight [*pt* knew; *pp* known].
- **en vista de** in view of.
- **estar a la vista** to be evident.
- **hacer la vista gorda** to turn a blind eye.
- **hasta la vista** good-bye, so long.
- **perder de vista** to lose sight of [*pt & pp* lost].
- **salta a la vista que...** it is obvious that....

vistazo *nm* glance, look.
- **de un vistazo** at a glance.
- **echar un vistazo a** to have a look at.

visto,-a *adj* seen.
- **estar bien visto** to be (perfectly) acceptable.
- **estar mal visto** to be frowned upon.
- **por lo visto** as it seems.
- **ser lo nunca visto** to be unheard of.
- **visto para sentencia** for sentencing.
■ **visto bueno** approval.

vistoso,-a *adj* bright, showy, colourful.

visual *adj* visual.

vital *adj* **1** *(de la vida)* vital: **órgano vital**, vital organ. **2** *(esencial)* vital: **su ayuda fue vital**, his help was vital. **3** *(persona)* full of life: **es optimista y vital**, she's optimistic and full of life.

vitalicio,-a *adj* life.

vitalidad *nf* vitality.

vitamina *nf* vitamin.

vitorear *vt* to cheer, acclaim.

vitrina *nf* **1** *(en casa)* glass cabinet, display cabinet. **2** *(de exposición)* glass case, showcase. **3** *(escaparate)* shop window.

viudez *nf* widowhood.

viudo,-a *adj* widowed.
- ► *nm,f (hombre)* widower; *(mujer)* widow.

viva *nm* cheer, shout.
- ► *interj* **¡viva!** hurrah!

víveres *nm pl* food *sing*, provisions.

vivero *nm* **1** *(de plantas)* nursery. **2** *(de peces)* fish farm.

vivienda *nf* **1** *(alojamiento)* housing, accommodation: **problemas de vivienda**, housing problems. **2** *(morada)* home; *(-casa)* house; *(piso)* -flat: **están construyendo nuevas viviendas**, they're building some new homes.

viviente *adj* living, alive.

vivir *vi* **1** *(tener vida)* to live, be alive: **todavía vive**, she's still alive. **2** *(residir)* to live: **vive con sus padres**, he lives with his parents; **¿dónde vives?**, where do you live?
- ► *vt (pasar)* to live through: **los que vivieron la guerra**, those who lived through the war.
- ► *nm* way of life.
- **vivir de** to live on: **vive de su pensión**, she lives on her pension.
- **vivir a lo grande** *fam* to live it up, live in style.
- **¡vivan los novios!** three cheers for the bride and groom!

vivo,-a *adj* **1** *(con vida)* alive, living: **siguen con vida**, they are still alive; **los seres vivos**, living creatures. **2** *(color)* bright, vivid. **3** *(animado)* lively. **4** *(dolor)* acute, sharp. **5** *(listo)* clever: **una niña muy viva**, a very clever girl.
- ► *nm,f* living person: **los vivos**, the living.
- **en vivo** *(programa)* live.

vocablo *nm* word, term.

vocabulario *nm* vocabulary.

vocación *nf* vocation, calling.

vocal *adj* vocal.
- ► *nf (letra, sonido)* vowel.
- ► *nmf (de comité)* member.

vocear *vi (dar voces)* to shout, cry out.
- ► *vt* **1** *(divulgar)* to publish. **2** *(gritar)* to shout, call.

vociferar *vt-vi* to vociferate, shout.

vodka *nm* vodka.

volador,-ra *adj* flying.

volante *adj (volador)* flying.
- ► *nm* **1** *(de vehículo)* steering wheel. **2** *(documento)* note: **pedí un volante para el médico de la piel**, I asked to be referred to the skin specialist.

volar *vi* **1** *(ave, en avión)* to fly [*pt* flew; *pp* flown]. **2** *(desaparecer)* to disappear. **3** *(noticia)* to spread rapidly [*pt & pp* spread].
- ► *vt* **1** *(cometa)* to fly [*pt* flew; *pp* flown]. **2** *(hacer explotar)* to blow up [*pt* blew; *pp* blown].
- **volando** in a rush: **salimos volando**

para coger el tren, we rushed out to catch the train; *tuve que desayunar volando*, I had to eat my breakfast in a hurry.

volcán *nm* volcano [*pl* **-os** o **-oes**].

volcar *vt* **1** *(vaso)* to knock over: *he volcado el azucarero*, I´ve knocked the sugar bowl over. **2** *(vaciar)* to empty: *volcó la caja sobre la mesa*, she emptied the box over the table.

► *vi* **1** *(camión)* to overturn. **2** *(barco)* to capsize.

► *vpr* **volcarse** *(entregarse)* to devote oneself: *su familia se volcó con ella*, her family did everything they could for her.

voleibol *nm* volleyball.

voltaje *nm* voltage.

voltereta *nf* somersault.

voltio *nm* volt.

volumen *nm* volume.

● **bajar el volumen** to turn the volume down.

● **subir el volumen** to turn the volume up.

■ **volumen de negocios** turnover.

voluminoso,-a *adj* voluminous, bulky.

voluntad *nf* **1** *(de decidir)* will. **2** *(propósito)* intention, purpose. **3** *(deseo)* wish: *fue la voluntad de su padre*, it was his father's wish.

● **a voluntad** at will.

● **por propia voluntad** of one's own free will.

■ **buena voluntad** goodwill.

voluntario,-a *adj* voluntary.

► *nm,f* volunteer.

● **ofrecerse voluntario,-a** to volunteer.

volver *vt* **1** *(dar vuelta a)* to turn *(over)*; *(hacia abajo)* to turn upside down; *(de fuera a dentro)* to turn inside out: *volví la hoja*, I turned the page; *volvió el vestido del revés*, she turned the dress inside out. **2** *(convertir)* to turn, make: *me vuelve loco*, he drives me mad.

► *vi* *(regresar)* to come back, go back: *vuelve a casa*, come back home; *volveré dentro de una hora*, I'll be back in an hour; *le gustaría volver a Londres*, he'd like to go back to London.

► *vpr* **volverse 1** *(regresar)* to come back, go back [*pt* **went**; *pp* **gone**]. **2** *(darse la vuelta)* to turn *(round)*: *me volví*, I turned round; *se volvió hacia mí*, he turned to-

wards me. **3** *(convertirse)* to turn, become: *se volvió más simpática*, she became friendlier; *se ha vuelto loco*, he's gone mad.

● **volver a hacer algo** to do STH again: *ha vuelto a salir*, he's gone out again; *volveré a llamar*, I'll ring back.

● **volver en sí** to recover consciousness, come round.

● **volver la cabeza** to look round.

● **volverse atrás** to back out.

vomitar *vi* to vomit, be sick.

► *vt* to bring up [*pt & pp* **brought**].

vómito *nm* **1** *(resultado)* vomit. **2** *(acción)* vomiting.

vosotros,-as *pron* you.

■ **vosotros,-as mismos,-as** yourselves.

votación *nf* *(acto)* vote, voting.

● **someter algo a votación** to put STH to the vote, take a ballot on STH.

votante *nmf* voter.

votar *vi* to vote.

voto *nm* **1** *(papeleta)* vote. **2** *(promesa)* vow. **3** *(deseo)* wish, prayer.

voz *nf* **1** *(gen)* voice: *no me levantes la voz*, don't raise your voice to me. **2** *(grito)* shout: *no me des esas voces*, don't shout! **3** *(en diccionario)* headword. **4** *(rumor)* rumour: *corre la voz de que...*, there's a rumour going round that....

● **a media voz** in a whisper.

● **dar voces** to shout.

● **en voz alta** aloud.

● **en voz baja** in a low voice.

■ **voz activa** active voice.

■ **voz pasiva** passive voice.

vuelco *nm* .

● **dar un vuelco** to overturn.

vuelo *nm* *(de avión, pájaro)* flight: *¿a qué hora sale tu vuelo?*, what time does your flight leave?

● **alzar el vuelo** to take flight.

● **cazarlas al vuelo** to be quick on the uptake.

■ **vuelo sin motor** gliding.

vuelta *nf* **1** *(giro)* turn: *da una vuelta a la llave*, give the key one turn. **2** *(en un circuito)* lap: *faltan dos vueltas*, there are two laps to go. **3** *(paseo a pie)* walk, stroll: *ir a dar una vuelta*, to go for a walk. **4** *(paseo en coche)* drive: *ir a dar una vuelta*, to go for a drive. **5** *(regreso)* return: *un billete de ida y vuelta*, a return ticket; **nos vemos a tu vuelta**, I'll see you when you get back; **la vuelta la haremos en tren**, we'll come back by train. **6** *(dinero de cambio)* change: **quédese con la vuelta**, keep the change. **7** *(reverso)* back, reverse.

● **a la vuelta** on the way back.

● **a la vuelta de la esquina** around the corner.

● **dar la vuelta 1** (alrededor) to go round. **2** (girar) to turn round. **3** (de arriba abajo) to turn upside down. **4** (de dentro a fuera) to turn inside out. **5** (cambiar de lado) to turn over.

● **dar vueltas 1** (caminar mucho) to walk round and round. **2** (girar) to spin [*pt* **spun** o **span**; *pp* **spun**]: **dar vueltas alrededor de algo**, to go around STH.

● **estar de vuelta** to be back.

● **dar vueltas a algo** to turn STH over in one's mind: **he pasado todo el día dándole vueltas al problema**, I've spent all day thinking about the problem.

● **no tiene vuelta de hoja** there are no two ways about it.

● **poner de vuelta y media** to lay into [*pt & pp* **laid**].

■ **vuelta al mundo** round-the-world trip.

■ **vuelta ciclista** cycle race.

vuestro,-a *adj* your, of yours: **vuestra casa**, your house; **un amigo vuestro**, a friend of yours.

▶ *pron* yours: **éstas son las vuestras**, these are yours.

vulgar *adj* **1** *(grosero)* vulgar. **2** *(corriente)* common, ordinary.

vulgaridad *nf* **1** *(grosería)* vulgarity. **2** *(dicho, hecho)* something vulgar: **me parece una vulgaridad**, I think it's vulgar.

vulva *nf* vulva

W

Walkman® *nm* Walkman®.

wáter *nm fam* toilet.

waterpolo *nm* water polo.

W.C. *abr (retrete)* WC, toilet.

web *nf* **1** *(sitio)* website. **2** *(página)* web-page. **3** *(Internet)* Internet.

whisky *nm* whisky; *(irlandés)* whiskey.

windsurf *nm* windsurfing.

windsurfista *nmf* windsurfer.

X

xenofobia *nf* xenophobia.

xilófono *nm* xylophone.

Y

y *conj* **1** *(gen)* and: **señoras y señores**, ladies and gentlemen. **2** *(con hora)* past: **son las tres y cuarto**, it's a quarter past three. **3** *(con números)*: **cuarenta y cuatro**, forty-four. **4** *(en pregunta)* what about: **¿y López?**, what about López?
- **y eso que** although, even though.
- **¿y qué?** so what?
- **¿y si...?** what if...?
- **¡y tanto!** you bet!, and how!

ya *adv* **1** *(con pasado)* already: **ya lo sabía**, I already knew. **2** *(con presente)* now: **es preciso actuar ya**, it is vital that we act now. **3** *(sorpresa)* already: **¿ya te vas?**, are you going already? **4** *(ahora mismo)* immediately, at once. **5** *(luego)* later: **ya lo haré**, I'll do it later; **ya veremos**, we'll see. **6** *(uso enfático)*: **ya lo sé**, I know; **ya entiendo**, I see; **¡ya está!**, that's it!
▶ *interj* **¡ya!** *irón* oh yes!
- **ya era hora** about time too.
- **ya no** not any more, no longer.
- **ya que** since: **ya que te has ofrecido**, since you offered.
- **ya, pero...** yes, but....
- **ya... ya...** whether... or....

yacer *vi* to lie [*pt* **lay**; *pp* **lain**].

yacimiento *nm* bed, deposit.
- **yacimiento arqueológico** archaeological site.

yanqui *adj* - *nmf pey* Yankee.

yate *nm* *(a motor)* pleasure cruiser; *(de vela)* yacht.

yayo,-a *nm,f fam (abuelo)* grandad; *(abuela)* grandma, granny.

yedra *nf* → hiedra.

yegua *nf* mare.

yema *nf* **1** *(de huevo)* yolk. **2** *(del dedo)* fingertip.

yerba *nf* → hierba.

yerno *nm* son-in-law.

yeso *nm* **1** *(mineral)* gypsum. **2** *(en construcción)* plaster.

yo *pron* **1** *(sujeto)* I: **yo me voy**, I'm leaving. **2** *(objeto, con preposición)* me: **ése no soy yo**, that's not me.
▶ *nm* **el yo** the ego, the self.
- **entre tú y yo** between us.
- **yo mismo** myself.

yodo *nm* iodine.

yoga *nm* yoga.

yogur *nm* yoghurt.

yonqui *nmf arg* junkie.

yóquey *nm* jockey.

yoyó *nm* yo-yo [*pl* -**s**].

yudo *nm* judo.

yugo *nm* yoke.

yugular *adj* - *nf* jugular.

yunque *nm* anvil.

yunta *nf* yoke, team of oxen.

Z

zafiro *nm* sapphire.
zaguán *nm* hallway.
zalamería *nf* flattery.
zalamero,-a *adj* flattering.
  ▶ *nm,f* flatterer.
zamarra *nf* sheepskin jacket.
Zambia *nf* Zambia.
zambiano,-a *adj* - *nm,f* Zambian.
zambullida *nf* dive, plunge.
zambullir *vt* (en agua - persona) to duck; (- cosa) plunge.
  ▶ *vpr* **zambullirse 1** (en agua) to dive. **2** (en actividad) to become absorbed.
zampar *vi* to stuff oneself.
  ▶ *vt-vpr* **zampar(se)** to gobble up.
zanahoria *nf* carrot.
zancada *nf* stride.
zancadilla *nf* **1** (para caer) trip. **2** *fam* (engaño) ruse, trick.
  • **ponerle la zancadilla a** ALGN to trip SB up.
zanco *nm* stilt.
zancudas *nf pl* (aves) waders.
zancudo,-a *adj* **1** (ave) wading: *un ave zancuda*, a wader. **2** (persona) longlegged.
zángano,-a *nm,f fam* (persona) idler.
  ▶ *nm* **zángano** (insecto) drone.
zanja *nf* ditch, trench.
zanjar *vt* (asunto) to settle.
zapatear *vt* to stamp.
zapatería *nf* **1** (tienda) shoe shop. **2** (oficio) shoemaking.
zapatero,-a *nm,f* shoemaker.
  ■ **zapatero remendón** cobbler.
zapatilla *nf* slipper.
  ■ **zapatillas de ballet** ballet shoes.
  ■ **zapatillas de deporte** trainers.

zapato *nm* shoe.
  ■ **zapatos de tacón** high-heeled shoes.
zar *nm* tsar, czar.
zarandear *vt* (agitar) to shake [*pt* **shook**; *pp* **shaken**].
  ▶ *vpr* **zarandearse** (contonearse) to swagger, strut.
zarpa *nf* paw; (uña) claw.
zarpar *vi* to set sail [*pt & pp* **set**].
zarpazo *nm* swipe (with a paw): *me dio un zarpazo*, it swiped at me with its paw.
zarza *nf* bramble, blackberry bush.
zarzal *nm* bramble patch.
zarzamora *nf* (planta) blackberry bush; (fruto) blackberry.
zarzuela *nf* Spanish light opera.
zas *interj* crash!, bang!
zigzag *nm* zigzag.
Zimbabwe *nm* Zimbabwe.
zimbabwense *adj* - *nmf* Zimbabwean.
zinc *nm* zinc.
zócalo *nm* **1** (de pared) skirting board. **2** (pedestal) plinth.
zodíaco *nm* zodiac.
zombi *nmf* zombie.
  • **estar zombi** *fam* to be half-asleep.
zona *nf* area, zone.
  ■ **zona azul** pay-and-display parking area.
  ■ **zona urbanizada** built-up area.
  ■ **zona verde** park.
zoo *nm* zoo [*pl* -s].
zoología *nf* zoology.
zoológico,-a *adj* zoological.
  ▶ *nm* **zoológico** zoo [*pl* -s].
zoólogo,-a *nm,f* zoologist.
zoquete *adj fam* (lerdo) stupid.
  ▶ *nmf fam* (lerdo) blockhead.
  ▶ *nm* (de madera) block of wood.